# LITERATURE

## A POCKET ANTHOLOGY

R. S. Gwynn has edited several other books, including *Drama: A Pocket Anthology; Poetry: A Pocket Anthology; Fiction: A Pocket Anthology; Inside Literature: Reading, Responding, Writing* (with Steven Zani); *The Art of the Short Story* (with Dana Gioia); and *Contemporary American Poetry: A Pocket Anthology* (with April Lindner). He has also authored five collections of poetry, including *No Word of Farewell: Selected Poems, 1970–2000.* He has been awarded the Michael Braude Award for verse from the American Academy of Arts and Letters. Gwynn is University Professor of English and Poet-in-Residence at Lamar University in Beaumont, Texas.

# LITERATURE

## A POCKET ANTHOLOGY

**SIXTH EDITION**

*Edited by*

## R. S. Gwynn
Lamar University

**PEARSON**

Boston   Columbus   Indianapolis   New York   San Francisco   Upper Saddle River
Amsterdam   Cape Town   Dubai   London   Madrid   Milan   Munich   Paris   Montréal   Toronto
Delhi   Mexico City   São Paulo   Sydney   Hong Kong   Seoul   Singapore   Taipei   Tokyo

Senior Sponsoring Editor: Katharine Glynn
Assistant Editor: Rebecca Gilpin
Marketing Manager: Aimee Berger
Project Manager: Beth Houston
Project Coordination and Electronic Page Makeup: Integra Software Services Pvt. Ltd.
Associate Director of Design: Andrea Nix
Program Design Lead: Beth Paquin
Cover Image: Martin Ruegner/Getty Images
Procurement Specialist: Roy L. Pickering, Jr.
Printer and Binder: LSC Communications, Inc.
Cover Printer: LSC Communications, Inc.

Acknowledgements of third party content appear on page 1000, which constitutes an extension of this copyright page.

**Library of Congress Cataloging-in-Publication Data**

Literature : a pocket anthology / edited by R.S. Gwynn, Lamar University. —Sixth Edition.
    pages cm
  ISBN 978-0-321-94274-6 (alk. paper)
  ISBN 0-321-94274-4 (alk. paper)
  1. English literature.   2. American literature.   I. Gwynn, R. S.
  PR1109.L57 2015
  808.8—dc23

                                                                    2013037722

**PEARSON**

**www.pearsonhighered.com**

ISBN 10:    0-321-94274-4
ISBN 13: 978-0-321-94274-6

20 2019

# contents

# preface

When the *Pocket Anthology* series first appeared, our chief aim was to offer a clear alternative to the anthologies of fiction, poetry, and drama that were available at the time. *Literature: A Pocket Anthology,* Sixth Edition, incorporates many of the features of three genre-based anthologies: *Fiction: A Pocket Anthology,* Seventh Edition; *Poetry: A Pocket Anthology,* Seventh Edition; and *Drama: A Pocket Anthology,* Sixth Edition.

## What's New in This Edition

As with earlier editions of *Literature,* our goal has been to provide variety and flexibility within the parameters of a brief, affordable anthology. The fiction collection now includes Nathaniel Hawthorne's "Young Goodman Brown," one of the most beloved stories of all time, as well as compelling new selections from masters of the genre, including Guy de Maupassant's "The Necklace," Ernest Hemingway's "Hills Like While Elephants," and John Updike's "A&P." Contemporary short story authors new to this collection include J. G. Ballard, Rick Moody, Etgar Keret, Jill Patterson, and Jonathan Safran Foer. The poetry collection brings new selections from classic and contemporary authors, including John Keats, E. E. Cummings, Langston Hughes, Elizabeth Bishop, and Richard Wilbur, as well as fresh models from poets new to this edition including Denise Duhamel, Kevin Prufer, Rob Griffith, Alexander Long, Chelsea Rathburn, and Caki Wilkinson whose work brings poetry into the 21st century. The drama section includes both Shakespeare's *Twelfth Night* and *Othello* providing Shakespearean classics of comedy and tragedy. Ibsen's *A Doll's House* is also new to this edition. And as always, *Literature: A Pocket Anthology* offers a comprehensive collection of poetry, short fiction, and drama at an affordable price and an appealing length. More than a third of the selections overall represent voices of women, people of color, and writers from cultures outside the United States, and a strong effort has been made to include work that reflects contemporary social questions and will stimulate classroom discussion.

## Goals of This Anthology

*Literature* addresses the four wishes and concerns most commonly expressed by both instructors and students. First, of course, is the variety of selections it contains. Admittedly, a pocket anthology has to be very selective in its contents, so we are especially proud that the stories, poems, and plays in this book represent canonical writers such as Shakespeare, Sidney, and Donne; Poe, Faulkner, and O'Connor; and Sophocles and Henrik Ibsen, as well as newer voices that represent the diversity of gender, ethnic background, and national origin that is essential to any study of contemporary literature. The contents of *Literature* have been shaped both by the advice of experienced instructors, who have cited authors and works that are most often taught and that possess proven appeal to students, and by the editor's own experience as a critic, poet and teacher of literature and creative writing.

Our second goal was flexibility. We wanted a book that could be used as both a primary and a supplemental test in a wide range of courses, from introduction to literature courses, to classes in research methods and application of literary theory, to mixed-genre courses in writing. *Literature* contains, in addition to its generous selection of stories, poems, and plays, biographical headnotes for authors, introductions that cover the techniques and terminology of each of the three major literary genres, and a concise section on writing about literature and research procedures. As an aid to student writing assignments, *Literature* also contains three appendixes that group works from all three genres thematically and provide suggestions for the application of a range of critical approaches.

Third, we wanted an affordable book. Full-size introductory literature. Pearson is committed to keeping the price of the *Pocket Anthology* series reasonable without compromising on design or typeface. We hope that readers will find the attractive layout of *Literature* preferable to the cramped margins and minuscule fonts found in many literature textbooks. Because of its relatively low cost, this volume may be easily supplemented in individual courses with handbooks of grammar and usage, manuals of style, introductions to critical theory, textbooks on research methods, or instructional texts in creative writing. The relatively low price of *Literature* reflects the original claims of the *Pocket Anthology* series—that these books represent "a new standard of value."

Finally, we stressed portability. Many instructors have expressed concern for students who must carry literature books comprising 2,000 or more pages in backpacks already laden with book and materials for other courses. A semester is a short time, and few courses can cover more than a fraction of the material that many full-size collections contain. Although *Literature* may still be a snug fit in most pockets, we trust that sympathetic instructors and their students will appreciate a book that does not add a physical burden to the intellectual one required by college courses.

## Acknowledgments

No book is ever created in a vacuum. A special thanks to Sarah Sjodin, Lamar University, for her assistance in checking facts and proofing during the various stages of the publishing process. We would like to express our gratitude to the instructors who reviewed the current edition of this volume and offered invaluable recommendations for improvement. They are: Gwen S. Argersinger, Mesa Community College; Jonathan Barz, University of Dubuque; Alissa Burger, SUNY Delhi; Sarah V. Clere, Mount Olive College; Loren C. Gruber, Missouri Valley College; Ilyse Kusnetz, Valencia College; Miranda S. Miller, Gillette College; Shamika Mitchell, SUNY Rockland; Dylan Edward Parkhurst, Stephen F. Austin St. University; James Skaggs, Western Kentucky University; and Jeffery White, Bellevue College.

We are also grateful to those who reviewed earlier editions, including Shazia Ali; Eastfield College; Tony Ardizzone, Indiana University, Blooming-ton; Mark G. Aune, California University of Pennsylvania; Lucas Carpenter, Oxford College of Emory University; Michael J. Chappell, Western Connecticut State University; Jo Cochran, Klamath Community College; David Holper, College of the Redwoods; Norman W. Jones, Ohio State University, Mansfield Campus; William E. Matsen, North Hennepin Community College; Elizabeth M. Sloan, Northeast State Community College; Karla Stouse, Indiana University Kokomo; E. Bert Wallace, Campbell University; Royal Ward, Albion College; Portia Weston, Point Park University.

R. S. Gwynn
*Lamar University*

# Introduction to Literature

## Experience, Experiment, Expand:
## Three Reasons to Study Literature

It is a good day in Belton Hall 105. The instructor has assigned a short story by a well-known American writer, and even though spring is making its presence felt among the campus trees and shrubs, no one is gazing wistfully out the open windows. Some interest is stirring in the classroom, hands go up quickly, and, instead of lecturing, all the instructor has to do is field one question and raise another. The days when her teaching technique consisted of a recitation of details for note-taking—the parts of a plot, the structure of a sonnet, the origins of tragedy—seem like memories of gray winter afternoons, and the students' eyes, some of them flashing with anger, focus on one another instead of on the pages of their notebooks. One student complains that the story places women in a subordinate role and turns them into objects of the narrator's lustful eye; another counters that such behavior is exactly what one should expect from the story's protagonist, a teen-age boy working at a dull job in a 1950s supermarket. The instructor is clearly enjoying herself, feeling lucky to be playing the role of referee in the debate, which has grown animated as the members of the class add their opinions and take sides. On occasions like this, discussing and arguing about literature seem as natural as talking about sports, campus gossip, or the movies. It is a good day in Belton Hall 105.

But on the other days—the days of lectures, inscrutable diagrams on the chalkboard, eyes that would rather look at anything other than a piece of lined paper—instructors and students alike ponder the toughest questions of all: What's the point of this? Why do we have to study literature? What value is this study to me? As a way of introducing *Literature: A Pocket Anthology* (6th ed.), I have chosen three words—experience, experiment, expand—to suggest some good reasons why the study of literature is invaluable to any education.

1

## Experience

"We are such stuff / As dreams are made on; and our little life / Is rounded with a sleep," says Shakespeare's great magician Prospero. Our experience of the world is limited by time and place, and even the most resolute traveler can only superficially come to know the complex blends of cultures that make up our world. The act of reading literature provides us with a means of imaginatively entering minds and civilizations that may seem distant to us but actually are only as remote as a turn of the page. To read *Oedipus the King* is to recapture something of the awe with which the Athenians of Sophocles' day witnessed the dramatic reenactments of their ancient history. In reading such a play, we may also realize that the questions the ancient Greeks asked about human destiny are the same ones we still ponder today. True, we may never travel to Africa, but by reading a story by Chinua Achebe we can learn something about customs that in some ways resemble our own but in others seem foreign and strange. A poem by a contemporary American poet such as Ellen Bryant Voigt may bring with it the shock of recognition we reserve for those experiences that touch us most deeply. In literature we are allowed the possibility of inhabiting, for a brief time, lives and minds that are not our own. Men can learn from Adrienne Rich's "Rape" what it feels to be a victim of a sexual assault; women can learn how the protagonist of Raymond Carver's "Cathedral" overcomes both jealousy and prejudice in coming to know an old friend of his wife, a blind man. We can see the world through the eyes of people of genders, races, historical eras, and social classes that may resemble or vastly differ from our own. The perspectives and subjects we experience in literature are as varied and sometimes as troubling as life itself, but in investigating them, we can broaden our understanding of life in ways that other fields of academic study cannot equal. We might eventually agree that the insight that we gain from a literary work is equal or even superior to the experience that we may personally identify with in it. "How frugal is the Chariot / That bears the Human soul," said Emily Dickinson, speaking of the readily available pleasures of reading.

## Experiment

Literature does not write itself, and even the most vivid experience does not automatically translate into a memorable poem, story, or play. To the writer, every event that he or she considers as a likely subject presents a problem in literary form. Which of the genres—drama, fiction, or poetry—can best depict an experience, and which of each genre's innumerable subtypes—comedy or tragedy, short story or novel, open-form poem or sonnet—will work best? To study literature is to learn that every play, story, or poem that has ever been written involves some kind of experiment in literary technique, and much of the study of literature must be given over to questioning why artists make the choices that they do. Edgar Allan Poe once wrote an essay, "The Philosophy of Composition," about how he came to write his famous poem "The Raven," in which he explained in detail the decisions that he made about rhythm, language, setting, and even the sounds of individual words. But many readers have found that "The Raven," or for that matter any successful piece of literature, adds up to more than the sum of its parts; not even the creator has the last word on what the experiment has uncovered. As serious readers, our job is often to go beneath the surface to reveal the underlying structures and meanings. We may never write a short story, poem, or play ourselves, but in being entertained and perhaps instructed by a writer's skill with words, we gain some insight into one of the greatest human mysteries—the motives and methods of those who make art literally out of nothing. To read literature with the goal of learning how it is made is to understand literature not as life itself but as an artful imitation of it. As Richard Wilbur, observing his own daughter's attempts to write a short story, says to her, "It is always a matter, my darling,/Of life or death...." And then he adds, "...as I had forgotten."

## Expand

We expand our understanding by reading, by discussing what we have read, and by writing about it. When talking about a poem in a classroom group, students are often surprised to find that the way one reads a certain passage is not quite the same as a classmate's interpretation and that both differ from the instructor's. Literature is not a science, and many of the meanings we attach to individual works remain largely matters of speculation. This is not to claim that all interpretations, no matter how far-fetched, are equally valid; it is only an observation that complex works of literature offer different channels of interpretation for readers, as any survey of available criticism of a given text will quickly demonstrate. The student's chance to speak his or her piece most often takes the form of the essay answer on an examination, the theme or thesis paper, or the research project. The job of making assertions, backing them up with references to the text, and locating support from outside sources may not be the most exciting aspect of literary study, but it remains the primary way through which students may demonstrate that their initial attempts to understand a story, poem, or play have grown and deepened. In analyzing, researching, and writing about literature, we expand our minds as we realize that none of us has the final word. As in life, the qualifications and adjustments we make as we respond to literary works teach us something about the necessity of not taking things at face value; there is always one more question to ask, one more possibility to weigh and test.

It is no coincidence that the three words that I have chosen all begin with the prefix *ex-*, which means "out of." One of the most common questions from students that I have heard over the years is "What are we supposed to get *out of* this (story, poem, play)?" I may be turning the phrase slightly, but if you have really savored the full experience that good literature offers, then the first thing you should get "out of" will be your own skin—when you do that, you will answer your own question. For a few moments, you may lose your own identity and see through the eyes of an ancient Greek, a modern Nigerian, or a contemporary American woman, and you may just find that in some significant way your own manner of looking at the world will never be quite the same again.

In beginning our study of literature, we must first look at the different literary genres—fiction, poetry, and drama—and discuss their different methods and techniques. Each genre, or type, of literature has its own history and terminology, some of which may be shared with other genres. In the introductory discussions of fiction, poetry, and drama that follow, certain important terms appear in boldface type. An index of critical terms is found at the end of this book.

# FICTION

# Introduction to Fiction

## The Telling of the Tale

The memory begins with a scene like this: the circle contains about thirty boys and girls, all in their preteen years and dressed identically in khaki shorts and t-shirts, who sit on upended sections of logs around a leaping fire. The sun has just dropped beneath the rim of a nearby mountain, and a hint of damp chill steals into the August woods. It is the last night of camp, and they have gathered to sing songs and receive awards. Now one of the counselors, a college student who could pass for an older brother of any of the campers, puts away his guitar and nods to his colleague, a young woman who steps into the ring of firelight and begins to speak. "Many, many years ago," she begins, her solemn voice describing three characters—a brave warrior, a maiden with a beautiful laugh, a wolf cub raised as a pet—"on a night not too different from this...." The surrounding woods seem to grow darker as the campers lean forward toward the rise and fall of her voice and the blaze of the flames. Caught in the spell of her words, they have momentarily left television, Game Boys, and iPod players behind, enacting one of the human race's oldest rituals as they respond to the simple magic of the storyteller's art.

Before we can begin to examine the elements of literary fiction, we must bear in mind that literature in its written form is historically a recent innovation; indeed, its two most common modern forms, the short story and the novel, have been in existence for little more than two centuries. Yet long before the invention of writing, for thousands of years ancient peoples developed complex **oral traditions** of literature; these primitive stories, dealing with the creation of the cosmos and the origins of gods and goddesses, formed a body of **myths,** supernatural narratives widely believed to be true by the people of a given culture, and **legends,** popular stories about characters and events that may contain trace elements of historical truth. Even in modern societies, elements of this primitive folklore survive in regional or ethnic tales passed on through the generations, most often taking the written form of **folk tales** collected by literary scholars; **fairy tales,** like Charles

Perrault's "Beauty and the Beast" or Hans Christian Andersen's "The Little Mermaid"; **beast fables,** stories with animal characters such as those of Aesop (c. 550 B.C.) or Joel Chandler Harris (1848–1908); or **parables,** short realistic tales like those found in the Gospels. Many of these, especially the last two types, are to some degree **didactic,** with the narrative events illustrating a **moral** that is either stated or implied.

Even in modern societies, other ancient forms of oral literature still enjoy a good state of health. These include **anecdotes,** accounts of single incidents usually involving a well-known person, and **riddles** and **jokes** of all types, which often seem to spring into circulation overnight and often unwittingly mirror the basic situations and coarse humor of venerable **fabliaux**—short, realistic tales from the Middle Ages that often turn on a bawdy situation. Recently, much attention has been given to **urban legends,** so named by folklorist Jan Brunvand, which are short narratives involving grotesque incidents that are widely accepted as true. The title of one of Dr. Brunvand's collections, *The Vanishing Hitchhiker,* refers to a ghost tale that virtually every American has heard in one of its many versions.

When myths and legends are assembled around the exploits of a great hero, the result is the **folk epic,** a long narrative in elevated style that is generally considered a starting point for any culture's literary history. Like most types of oral folk literature, epics were originally composed in verse for the sake of memorization, but they otherwise contain the same elements as modern literary forms like the short story and novel. For example, the individual **episodes** of Homer's *Odyssey*—Odysseus's outwitting the Cyclops or his adventures with the sorceress Circe—can stand alone as exciting tales and also can fit into the larger structure of the epic, like chapters in a novel. Later authors, living in societies that had invented writing, consciously imitated the style of folk epics in composing **literary epics.** The *Aeneid* by Virgil (70–19 B.C.) and *The Divine Comedy* by Dante (1265–1321) are two famous examples. In the Middle Ages, **romances,** written in both verse and prose, gained great popularity among all classes. These tales of chivalry— involving a knightly hero and a series of exciting, if improbable, adventures— were ridiculed by Miguel de Cervantes (1547–1616) in *Don Quixote,* a realistic account of an impoverished Spanish gentleman driven mad by reading too many romances. The eventual form that Cervantes gave Don Quixote's adventures was perhaps influenced by **picaresque novels** like the anonymous *Lazarillo of Tormes* (c. 1450), which involved a young orphan (or *picaro,* Spanish for "rascal") in a series of loosely connected adventures. These picaresque tales are rightly considered the ancestors of modern realistic fiction. Many novels, from Henry Fielding's *Tom Jones* to Mark Twain's *The Adventures of Huckleberry Finn* to J. D. Salinger's *The Catcher in the Rye* and Jack Kerouac's *On the Road,* borrow their structure from the picaresque novel, and the modern short story is indebted to their often stark level of realism.

## The Short Story Genre

There is no agreement on the precise origins of the modern short story. One important influence in its development was the Italian **novella** of the late Middle Ages and Renaissance. The most famous collection of these realistic prose narratives is *The Decameron* by Giovanni

Boccaccio (1313–1375). *The Decameron,* in which the individual stories are narrated by young men and women who have taken to the country to escape the Black Death, is an example of a **frame tale,** in which the stories are "framed" by a larger narrative. The famous Arabian collection *A Thousand and One Nights* is one of the earliest examples of this genre (brilliantly resurrected here by Tim Gautreaux in "Died and Gone to Vegas" and likewise the structure of many recent films). In translation, these tales were popular in other countries and widely imitated. In writing his plays, Shakespeare borrowed from Italian writers frequently; his tragedy *Othello* takes its plot from a sensational novella by Giraldi Cinthio. We still use the term novella for short stories that are long enough (usually more than 15,000 words) to be published separately in book form. Count Leo Tolstoy's *The Death of Ivan Ilyich* is a classic Russian example, and Ernest Hemingway's *The Old Man and the Sea* is one of the best-known novellas in English.

The first half of the nineteenth century is the great period of the growth of the short story as a distinct **literary genre,** or type, and its rise takes place in many countries at roughly the same time. Many reasons for this rapid development could be put forth, but perhaps the most important was the literary market established by newspapers and magazines aimed at middle-class audiences. The United States, with its increasingly high rate of literacy and expanding middle class, led the way in this period; Washington Irving's tales such as "Rip Van Winkle" and "The Legend of Sleepy Hollow" were among the first American writings to attain international popularity. Edgar Allan Poe, the first great theorist of the short story and one of its notable practitioners during this period, supported himself primarily (though not very prosperously) as a magazine editor and contributor and thus had a large personal stake in promoting short fiction. Poe's influential review of Nathaniel Hawthorne's *Twice-Told Tales* in 1842 first stated the theory that a short story ought to be a unified artistic creation, as carefully shaped as a sonnet. Poe said:

> A skillful literary artist has constructed a tale. If wise, he has not fashioned his thoughts to accommodate his incidents; but having conceived, with deliberate care, a certain unique or single effect to be wrought out, he then invents such incidents— he then combines such events as may best aid him in establishing this preconceived effect. If his very initial sequence tend not to be the outbringing of this effect, then he has failed in his first step. In the whole composition there should be no word written, of which the tendency, direct or indirect, is not to the one pre-established design. And by such means, with such care and skill, a picture is at length painted which leaves in the mind of him who contemplates it with a kindred art, a sense of the fullest satisfaction.

This idea of the *single effect* is perhaps Poe's most important contribution to the development of the short story as a serious literary genre.

Most of Hawthorne's and Poe's stories are perhaps more properly termed **tales,** if by that term we mean narratives that contain elements that are exotic or supernatural and that to some degree depart from the level of ordinary experience. Poe himself established many of the conventions of the horror, science fiction, and detective tales still being written and read today; **formula fiction,** which rigidly follows the clichés and conventions of a particular genre, is sometimes half-affectionately called **pulp fiction,** a reminder of the low grade of paper once used in inexpensive magazines. Still, the tale remains a lively tradition among serious artists as well. Among the contemporary stories in this book, selections by Faulkner, Oates, and others show their debt to the tradition of the tale.

The short story in its present form, on the other hand, developed somewhat later, and its evolution was part of the larger literary movement of **realism,** which profoundly influenced the arts in the mid-nineteenth century with its "slice of life" approach to subject matter that, in early centuries, would have been deemed inappropriate for serious treatment. It has been rightly noted that realism simply represents the effect of democracy on literary history. Celebrating its appearance as early as 1837, Ralph Waldo Emerson noted, "The literature of the poor, the feelings of the child, the philosophy of the street, the meaning of household life, are the topics of the time." **Naturalism,** an outgrowth of realism that emerged in the second half of the century, also proved influential, for it joined realistic treatments of everyday life with understandings of human behavior drawn from the new sciences of psychology and sociology. Both realism and naturalism remain vital currents in contemporary short fiction, as stories here by Raymond Carver, Alice Walker, and Bobbie Ann Mason will attest.

The twentieth century saw the short story rise to its highest level of popularity and just as rapidly decline in its influence as a literary form. During the first half of the century, when many magazines like *Collier's* and the *Saturday Evening Post* paid large sums for short stories by important authors, the genre flourished. F. Scott Fitzgerald, a frequent contributor to these magazines, kept a meticulous ledger in which he noted, in one six-month period in 1922–1923, that he earned more than $15,000 from magazine sales alone. A decade later, in the depths of the Great Depression, Fitzgerald complained that stories that earlier would have sold for prices in excess of $4,000 now commanded only $2,500. If these amounts seem exorbitant, remember that we are talking about times when a new automobile sold for less than $1,000 and a gallon of gasoline cost a dime! Today, when virtually every college in the country employs one or more writers-in-residence whose primary income comes not from publishing but from teaching, we tend perhaps to underestimate the impact that economic realities have had on the history of literature.

In the second half of the twentieth century, many of the established magazines that regularly ran serious fiction ceased publication. Search a typical magazine rack and you will find only one weekly magazine, *The New Yorker,* and a handful of monthlies containing short stories. Reading tastes have changed, and increased competition from television and other forms of entertainment has made the writing of short stories an expensive pastime for writers. Still, the pages of literary magazines and journals quarterlies continue to provide outlets for publication, and new writers seem undeterred by the prospect of being paid with little more than what one disgruntled writer has called "two free copies of what I've already got." Almost every writer of short fiction who is prominent today first appeared in small-circulation periodicals of this type, and many have continued to publish in magazines that can offer, instead of money, prestige and a discriminating readership numbering in the hundreds. Indeed, the little magazines have traditionally been hospitable to many kinds of **experimental fiction** that editors of commercial magazines would never have considered. Also, recent decades have seen a rise in so-called **short-short** stories or **flash fiction.** If the quantity of contemporary short fiction being published has shrunk from what it was in previous decades, the quality, one might argue, has remained the same or even improved. When we look at lists of recent winners of the Pulitzer or Nobel prizes, we discover many writers who have counted the short story as their first genre.

# Reading and Analyzing Short Fiction

We read for many reasons. In our daily lives, most of our reading is strictly utilitarian—it is part of our jobs or education—or informational, as we scan the headlines of a daily newspaper or drudgereport.com for current events, business trends, or sports scores. We read short stories and other types of fiction for differing reasons. Sometimes our motives are simply to be entertained and to pass the time. Reading matter of this type is usually termed **escapist literature** and includes such popular categories as romance and detective novels, science fiction tales, and westerns. Or we might consciously choose to read "inspirational" fiction that is obviously didactic and contains messages or moral lessons that apply to our own lives. Literary reading, though, occupies a position between the two extremes. Serious literature should certainly entertain us, but on a deeper level than, say, a half-hour episode of a television comedy show does. Similarly, it may also contain an ethical theme with which we can identify, even if it does not try to "preach" its moral message to the reader. A short story that we can treat as a serious work of art will not yield all of its subtlety at first glance; in order to understand and appreciate its author's achievement fully, we may have to examine its components—its plot, characterization, point of view, theme, setting, style, and symbolism—noting how each part contributes to the story's overall effect. With that purpose in mind, let's read a very brief example by a modern American master of the genre, John Cheever's "Reunion" on page 190.

## *Plot*

In his discussion of tragedy in the *Poetics,* Aristotle (384–322 B.C.) gives first importance to **plot** as an element of a play, and most readers would agree that it holds a similar position in a work of fiction. Indeed, if we tell a friend about a short story we have enjoyed, we will probably give a **synopsis** or brief summary of its incidents. In the case of a very brief story like "Reunion," this synopsis is only a few sentences long:

> In "Reunion" the narrator, a teenaged boy, meets his estranged father between trains in New York City. Over the course of an hour and a half, the father's alcoholism and possibly abusive personality are revealed. The story ends with the narrator boarding his train, indicating that this was the last time he saw his father, possibly by choice.

Plot may be defined as a story's sequence of incidents, arranged in dramatic order. One is tempted to insert the word "chronological," but doing so would exclude many stories that depart from this strict ordering of events. Although its use is more characteristic in longer works like novels, many stories employ the **flashback** to narrate incidents in the past. For example, Bobbie Ann Mason's "Shiloh" uses a flashback to describe the death of Leroy and Norma Jean's infant son. Margaret Atwood's "Happy Endings" dispenses with a single plot line entirely, offering numerous possibilities for the fates of her characters. In opposite fashion, writers sometimes use **foreshadowing** to provide hints of future actions in the story; an effective use of foreshadowing prevents a story's outcome from seeming haphazard or contrived. Of course, the manner in which stories handle time is largely illusory. During scenes with dialogue and action, time is slowed down by descriptive and explanatory phrases. In other places, stories cover gaps in chronology or leap over uneventful periods with transitional phrases and passages; the opening sentence of the second paragraph of "Reunion" compresses into a second or two an action that in reality would have taken at least several minutes. Even though "Reunion" does not take serious liberties with chronological time as we experience it, the hour or so of action in the story is compressed into about ten minutes of the reader's time. A plot like this, in which the action is more or less continuous within a single day, is called a **unified plot;** one that stretches over weeks or even longer periods and thus consists of isolated scenes connected by a thin tissue of transitional devices is called an **episodic plot.**

When we speak of the **dramatic structure** of a story, we refer to the exact way in which our emotional involvement in its plot is increased and relaxed. As Janet Burroway observes of the short story in *Writing Fiction, "Only* trouble is interesting." If we are not quickly engaged by the situation of a story and caught up in its plot, we pronounce the cruellest of all critical verdicts on it by closing the book. The first part of this dramatic structure is the **exposition,** which provides the reader with essential information—who, what, when, where—he or she needs to know before continuing. While writers of sophisticated fiction may try to disguise the fact, they often begin their stories with a variation of the "Once upon a time" opening common to fairy tales. A different type of beginning, called the **in medias res** ("in the middle of things") opening after the conventions of the old epic poems, may actually open with a "blind" bit of action before supplying its context. The exposition of "Reunion" is fairly straightforward; in the first paragraph, we learn who (Charlie and his father), what (a lunchtime meeting between trains), when (noon to 1:30 P.M.), and where (in and near Grand Central Station in Manhattan). Cheever might have begun the story with a slightly more "dramatic" sentence ("At twelve o'clock sharp I saw him coming through the crowd"), but he would have to have provided the essential contextual information in short order to avoid unnecessarily confusing the reader.

Exposition in a story usually describes a stable situation, even if it is not an entirely happy one. Charlie tells us that his parents' divorce is three years old and that he has not seen his father in that time. If he had not taken the step of writing the letter arranging the "reunion," that state of affairs might have gone on indefinitely. The appearance of "trouble" constitutes the second part of a plot, the **complication,** the appearance of some circumstance or event that shakes up the stable situation and begins the **rising action** of the story. Complication in a story may be either external and internal, or a combination of the two. A stroke of fortune such as illness or accident that affects a character is a typical example of an external complication, a problem that the characters cannot ignore; an internal complication might not be immediately apparent, the result of a character's deep-seated uncertainties, dissatisfactions, and fears. The external complication in "Reunion" is the father's series of confrontations with waiters; the internal complication is Charlie's growing sense of pity and revulsion. Typically, the complication of a plot is heightened by **conflict** between two characters who have different personalities and goals. Charlie is overjoyed to see his father at the beginning of the story, but despite his knowledge that he will grow up to "be something like him," he is more than eager to escape his company at the end, even if he is unconsciously trying to run away from his own "future and...doom."

The body of a story is called the rising action and usually comprises a number of scenes, containing action and dialogue, which build to **moments of crisis,** points in the story where a resolution of the complication momentarily seems at hand but quickly disappears. Aristotle used the term **peripety** for these moments of reversal, as the hopes of the characters rise and fall. Thus, in "Reunion" all that needs to be resolved, at least on the surface, is for the characters to order lunch, eat, and return in time for the departing train. The father's increasingly obnoxious behavior, however, keeps postponing this resolution until the reunion has turned from a happy occasion to something very different. Unlike most stories, "Reunion" has a rising action as rigidly structured as a joke with its four similar restaurant scenes gradually escalating in absurdity as the father's senseless rage increases.

The central moment of crisis in a plot is the **climax,** or moment of greatest tension, which inaugurates the **falling action** of the story, in which the built-up tension is finally released. Some stories, particularly those involving a heavy use of suspense, have a steep "dramatic curve," and the writer uses all of his or her skills to impel the reader toward the final confrontation. Among the writers included here, Edgar Allan Poe is the master of this kind of plot construction. Often one encounters the **trick ending** (also called the **O. Henry ending,** after the pen name of William Sidney Porter, a popular writer of the nineteenth century). A climax like this depends on a quick reversal of the situation from an unexpected source; its success is always relative to the degree to which the reader is surprised when it occurs. More typically, modern short stories instead rely on climactic devices that are somewhat subtler than unexpected plot twists. Many modern writers have followed James Joyce's lead in building not to a climactic event but to a moment of spiritual insight or revelation, or what Joyce termed an **epiphany.** In the hands of a melodramatic writer insistent on sentimental happy endings, "Reunion" might have concluded with Charlie delivering a "tough love" sermon to his father, who would then fall to his knees and beg his son's forgiveness, having seen the error of his ways. Cheever's more realistic method of climax is, in this case, to avoid the confrontation altogether as Charlie escapes to his train.

The final part of a plot is the **dénouement** (or **resolution**). The French term literally refers to the untying of a knot, and we might compare the emotional release of a story's ending with a piece of cloth that has been twisted tighter and tighter and is then untwisted as the action winds down. The dénouement returns the characters to another stable situation. Just as fairy tales traditionally end with "And they lived happily ever after," many stories conclude with an indication of what the future holds for the characters. In the case of "Reunion," we return to the estrangement between Charlie and his father that existed at the beginning of the story, although this time all indications are that it will be a permanent one. A story's dénouement may be termed either closed or open. A **closed dénouement** ties up everything neatly and explains all unanswered questions the reader might have; a typical example is the "Elementary, my dear Watson" explanation of any remaining loose ends that is provided by the sleuth Sherlock Holmes in the final paragraphs of Arthur Conan Doyle's famous tales. On the other hand, an **open dénouement** leaves us with a few tantalizing questions. The last phrase of "Reunion," which consciously mirrors the story's opening sentence, does not explicitly state *why* Charlie never sees his father again. Was it strictly his own choice? Or did the father die soon after their meeting? Or were other factors involved? We do not know, of course, and such an ending invites us to speculate.

One final word about plots: the fledgling writer attempting to invent a totally original plot is doomed to failure, and it is no exaggeration to say that there is nothing new under the sun where plots of short stories are concerned. These plots often draw on what psychologist Carl Jung called **archetypes,** universal types of characters and situations that all human beings carry in their unconscious minds. Plots deriving from these archetypes may be found in ancient mythologies, fairy tales, and even in contemporary fiction. Among a few of the most familiar are the triangle plot, a love story involving three people; the quest plot, which is unified around a group of characters on a journey; and the transformation plot, in which a weak or physically unattractive character changes radically in the course of the story. "Reunion" is an example of one of the most widely used of all archetypal plots, the **initiation story.** In a plot of this type, the main character, usually a child or adolescent, undergoes an experience (or **rite of passage**) that prepares him or her for adulthood. In this book, such stories as Sarah Orne Jewett's "A White Heron" and Joyce Carol Oates's "Where Are You Going, Where Have You Been?" share the same archetype, although they differ in almost every other respect.

## Characterization

Every story hinges on the actions undertaken by its main character, or **protagonist,** a term drawn from ancient Greek tragedy (literally "first debater") that is more useful in discussions of fiction than such misleading terms as hero or heroine. Additionally, stories may contain an opposing character, or **antagonist,** with whom the protagonist is drawn into conflict. In many modern stories, there is little, in any traditional sense, that is heroic about the protagonists; it may be more accurate to use a negative term, **anti-hero,** to designate one who occupies center stage but otherwise seems incapable of fitting the traditional heroic mold. Indeed, modern writers have often been so reluctant to seem didactic in presenting characters who are "moral beacons" that they go to the opposite extreme in presenting protagonists whom we regard with pity or even disgust instead of with admiration.

A character in a short story may be termed either a **flat character** or a **round character,** depending on the depth of detail the writer supplies. In "Reunion" the father is essentially a flat character, rendered with a few quick strokes of the pen and reduced to a single personality trait, his alcoholic rudeness. Flat minor characters in stories are often **stock characters,** stereotypes who may be necessary to advance the plot but otherwise are not deserving of more than the barest outlines of description. Round characters, on the other hand, are given more than one trait, some of which may even seem contradictory, and are explored in depth as the author delves into the character's past and even into his or her unconscious mind. Characters of this type, usually the protagonists of stories, begin to approach the level of complexity that we associate with real human beings.

**Development** and **motivation** are also important in any consideration of a story's characters. Characters can be termed either **static** or **dynamic,** depending on the degree to which they change in the course of the story. In "Reunion" the father is a static character. His personality was fixed long before the story opens, and Cheever holds out no likelihood that he will ever alter his course. But Charlie does attain some understanding in the course of the story, even if it is at the cost of his own disillusionment with what he wants his father to be. If development in a character is usually clear in a story, then motivation, the reasons the reader is given for a character's actions, may not be so obvious. In many cases, an author will simply tell us what is going on in a character's mind, but in others we are denied access to this level of understanding. Although we can speculate, playing the amateur psychiatrist, about Charlie's father's strange behavior, we are not given any direct insight into his own view of his actions. In some stories, writers may try to plug directly into a character's thoughts by using **interior monologue,** a direct presentation of thought that is somewhat like a soliloquy in drama, or **stream-of-consciousness,** an attempt to duplicate raw sensory data in the same disordered state that the mind receives it. As useful as these devices can be in explaining motivation, they sometimes place excessive demands on readers and are thus comparatively rare.

**Description** of characters also helps us understand the author's intent. In real life, we are told from an early age not to judge people by external appearance, but in fiction the opposite is more often the case: physical description is invariably a sign of what lurks beneath the surface. Given the brevity of most short stories, these physical details may be minimal but revealing in their lack of particulars. Cheever has Charlie describe his father at first as only "a big, good-looking man." Remarkably, the author here uses his protagonist's sense of smell to make the character vivid: Charlie breathes in "a rich compound of whiskey, after-shave lotion, shoe polish, woolens, and the rankness of a mature male." In that burst of imagery, we may momentarily overlook the most important item in the list, the evidence that Charlie's father has been drinking in the morning.

Other elements may add to our understanding of a story's characters. Many writers take particular care in naming their characters in such a way as to draw attention to aspects of their personalities. This device (**characternym** is a coined term that is often employed for it) is sometimes obvious; in her story "Good Country People," Flannery O'Connor calls an unscrupulous seducer Manley Pointer, a name that a moment's thought reveals as an outrageous pun. Similarly, actions in the story, such as speech patterns and mannerisms, may also disclose personality traits. A character's misuse of grammar or stilted vocabulary can *show* us a great deal more about background and self-image than a whole page of background information or analysis. Charlie's father's gestures and loud attempts at ordering in various foreign languages grow more embarrassing until his tongue-tied request for two "Bibson Geefeaters" (a "Beefeater Gibson" is a potent martini made from a well-known brand of gin) comes as the punchline to a grotesque joke on himself.

## Point of View

When we speak of a politician's **point of view** on an issue, we mean his or her attitude toward it, pro or con. In fiction, however, the term point of view is employed in a specialized sense, referring to the question of *authority* in the story. Every story has a **narrator,** a voice or character who provides the reader with information about and insight into characters and incidents; but in some cases the identity of this voice of authority is not immediately apparent. Being too literal minded about the matter of point of view is usually a mistake, and we usually have to accept certain **narrative conventions** without questioning them too seriously if we are to enjoy reading stories. Thus, when we finish reading a detective story narrated by the sleuth, we should not worry ourselves too much about when such a busy character found time to jot down the events of the story. Similarly, we accept as a convention the fact that a narrator may suddenly jump from simply recording a conversation to telling us what one of its participants is thinking. Very early in our lives, we learn how stories are told, just as we have been conditioned to make a mental transition, while watching a movie, when our perspective shifts in the blink of an eye from one character's frightened stare, to the flashing barrel of a gun, to a hand clutching a chest, to another actor's sneer of triumph.

Almost all narrative points of view can be classified as either first person or third person. In **first-person narration,** the narrator is a **participant** in the action. He or she may be either a major character (which is the case with Charlie in "Reunion") or a minor character and may be close to the event in time or distant from it. Although it is never directly stated, the adult Charlie is probably narrating an account of something that happened years before; thus, his repeated phrase about the last time he saw his father has a finality about it that goes far beyond a simple statement like "The last time I saw my father was a week ago in Grand Central Station." In general, first-person stories may seem more immediate than third-person stories, but they are limited by the simple fact that the narrator must be present at all times and must also have some knowledge of what is going on. If, for example, an attempt had been made to tell "Reunion" from the point of view of one of the waiters, the narrator might have to resort to eavesdropping on Charlie and his father in order to report their circumstances. The ability of the narrator to tell the story accurately is also important. An **unreliable narrator,** either through naïvete, ignorance, or impaired mental processes, relates events in such a distorted manner that the reader, who has come to recognize the narrator's unreliability, must literally turn his reporting on its head to make sense. Imagine how we would read "Reunion" if it had been told from the boozy, self-deluding point of view of Charlie's father.

**Third-person narration,** by definition, employs a **nonparticipant** narrator, a voice of authority that never reveals its source and is capable of moving from place to place to describe action and report dialogue. In third-person stories, the question of reliability is rarely an issue, but the matter of **omniscience,** the degree to which the "all-knowing" narrator can reveal the thoughts of characters, is. **Total omniscience** means just that—the narrator knows everything about the characters' lives, their pasts, presents, and futures— and may reveal the thoughts of anyone in the story. An **editorial point of view** goes even further, allowing the god like author to comment directly on the action (also called **authorial intrusion**).

Most contemporary authors avoid total omniscience in short fiction, perhaps sensing that a story's strength is dissipated if more than one perspective is used. Instead, they employ **limited omniscience,** also called **selective omniscience** or the **method of central intelligence,** limiting themselves to the thoughts and perceptions of a single character. This point of view is perhaps the most flexible of all because it allows the writer to compromise between the immediacy of first-person narration and the mobility of third person. A further departure from omniscience is the **dramatic point of view** (also called the **objective point of view**). Here the narrator simply reports dialogue and action with minimal interpretation and no delving into characters' minds. The dramatic point of view, as the name implies, approximates the experience of reading a play; readers are provided only with set descriptions, stage directions and dialogue, and thus must supply motivations that are based solely on this external evidence.

Technically, other points of view are possible, although they are rarely used. Stories have been told in the second person. Note the use of the imperative verbs and an implied "you" in Lorrie Moore's "How to Become a Writer." A plural point of view also may be employed, but such points of view are difficult to sustain and may quickly prove distracting to readers. Also, there is an unwritten rule that point of view should be consistent throughout a story, although occasionally a writer may utilize multiple perspectives to illustrate how the "truth" of any incident is always relative to the way in which it is witnessed.

## Theme

We have already discussed the manner in which fables and other types of didactic literature make their purposes clear by explicitly stating a moral or interpretation at the end of the story. Literary fiction, however, is usually much more subtle in revealing its **theme,** the overall meaning the reader derives from the story. Most of the reading we did as children probably fell into two distinct categories—sheer entertainment or overt didacticism— with very little middle ground. Thus, many readers, coming to serious fiction for the first time, want either to avoid the tedious search for a "message" or to complain: "If the author was trying to say that, then why didn't she just come right out and *say* it?" To further complicate matters, the theoretical manner in which we analyze stories and the preconceptions we bring to bear on them may result in multiple interpretations of meaning. No single statement of theme is likely to be the "correct" one, although it is fair to say that some seem more likely than others.

What, then, is the theme of "Reunion"? A reader insistent on a moral might denounce Charlie's father, inveighing against "demon rum" and its destructive effect on "family values." Another reader, slightly more charitable, might recognize alcoholism as a disease and feel some amount of sympathy for the father. Yet another, perhaps entirely too self-righteous, might fault Charlie for running away from his father, interpreting the older man's actions as a subconscious cry for help. If we investigate Cheever's own troubled biography and note his own serious problems with both parenthood and alcoholism, we may read the story as a psychological confession, with Cheever himself simultaneously playing the roles of father and son. With so many possibilities before us, it is often best to state a story's theme as broadly as possible: "'Reunion,' like most initiation stories, is about growth through loss of innocence. Children have to learn, often through painful experience, that they are not responsible for their parents' well-being, and sometimes they must distance themselves from their parents in order to survive." Such a statement does not encompass every possible nuance of the story's theme, but it does at least provide us with a starting point for arguing about the finer points of Cheever's meaning.

All this is not to say that modern authors are always reticent in revealing their themes. Flannery O'Connor perceives her characters' shortcomings and judges them according to her own Roman Catholic moral standards. Alice Walker has investigated social themes like female genital mutilation in her fiction. Margaret Atwood's feminism is rarely hidden in her stories and poems. Many modern stories are in fact **allegorical tales,** in which the literal events point to a parallel sequence of symbolic ideas. In many stories, the literal setting of the story, a doctor's waiting room or a crowded city bus, is a **microcosm,** a "small world" that reflects the tensions of the larger world outside. Thus, despite their outward sophistication, many of the stories in this anthology reveal their debt to the ancient ethical functions of fables and parables.

## Setting

Novelists can lavish pages of prose on details of setting, just as they can *describe* characters down to such minutiae as the contents of their pockets. But short story writers, hemmed in by limitations of space, rarely have such luxury and must ordinarily limit themselves to very selective descriptions of time and place. When a writer like Edgar Allan Poe goes into great detail in his descriptions, it is likely that **atmosphere,** the emotional aura surrounding a certain setting, is more important to him than the actual physical locale.

**Setting** is simply the time and place of a story, and in most cases the details of description are given to the reader directly by the narrator. A story may employ multiple locations in its different scenes, and its time frame may encompass only a few hours or many years. "Reunion" is a story with relatively few details of setting. Because Cheever wrote his stories almost exclusively for *The New Yorker,* it is not necessary for him to describe the interior of Grand Central Station to an audience doubtless familiar with it, nor do we feel at much of a loss. Similarly, he spends no more than a sentence or two describing each of the restaurants: one has "a lot of horse tack on the walls," one is "Italian," and the other two are not described at all. The time setting is also relatively unimportant here. We know that the action is taking place during the lunch hour on a weekday, probably in the summer, but as far as a more specific time is concerned, we know little or nothing. "Reunion" could be taking place in today or fifty years ago or, for that matter, twenty years from now.

Some stories, however, depend on their **locale** or time setting much more heavily and thus demand fuller exposition of setting. **Historical fiction** usually pays great attention to the altered landscapes and customs of bygone eras. A writer who carelessly lets an electric alarm clock go off in a story set in the early 1800s has committed an anachronism that may be only slightly more obvious than another writer's use of contemporary slang in the same setting. **Local color fiction** depends heavily on the unique characteristics of a particular area, usually a rural one that is off the beaten path. Such places have become increasingly rare in contemporary America, but the deep South and Alaska still provide locales that possess intrinsic interest. Some writers, like William Faulkner or Flannery O'Connor, first established their reputations as practitioners of **regionalism,** setting most of their work in one particular area or country. A contemporary American writer like Bobbie Ann

Mason shows, in virtually every one of the stories in her first collection, her deep roots in her native Kentucky. A South American writer like Gabriel García Márquez continually draws us into the strange world of Colombian villages cut off from the contemporary world, places where past and present, history and folklore, natural and supernatural seamlessly join in what has been labeled **magic realism.**

Stories contain both specific and general settings. The specific setting is the precise time(s) and place(s) where the action takes place. The general setting of a story, its **enveloping action,** is its sense of the "times" and how its characters interact with events and social currents in the larger world. We have already mentioned how the specific setting of a story often is a microcosm that reflects the doings of society at large. It is impossible to read stories by Flannery O'Connor or Alice Walker and not be made aware of the social changes that have transformed the rural South in the past sixty years. Stories sometimes depend on readers' ability to bring their knowledge of history and culture to bear on the events taking place. In reading a story like Ralph Ellison's "A Party Down at the Square," younger readers may be unaware of the widespread horrors of lynchings in an America that older readers can vividly recall.

## Style and Symbol

**Style** in fiction refers equally to the characteristics of language in a particular story and to the same characteristics in a writer's complete works. The more individual a writer's style is, the easier it is to write a **parody,** or satirical imitation, of it, as the well-publicized annual "Faux Faulkner" and "International Imitation Hemingway" contests attest. A detailed analysis of the style in an individual story might include attention to such matters as diction, sentence structure, punctuation (or the lack thereof), and use of figurative language. In English, we usually make a distinction between the differing qualities of words—standard usage versus slang, Latinate versus Germanic vocabulary, abstract versus concrete diction, and so on. While such matters are most meaningful only in the context of an individual story, there is obviously a difference between one character who says, "I have profited to a great degree from the educational benefits of the realm of experience," and another who says, "I graduated from the school of hard knocks." However, in analyzing style, we must be sensitive to the literary fashions of periods other than our own; it is senseless to fault Poe for "flowery diction" when comparing his use of language to that of his contemporaries, who may have similarly lush styles. The prevailing fashion in fiction today is for the unadorned starkness of writers like Bobbie Ann Mason and Raymond Carver—what has been disparagingly called "K-Mart realism" by one critic—but one should not be surprised if, in the present century, fashions shift and writers compete to outdo Faulkner at his most ornate.

The style of "Reunion" is for the most part straightforward, with few flourishes of vocabulary (if we disregard the foreign phrases) or sentence structure. About the only significant departure from this plain style is in the opening paragraph, where Charlie momentarily rises to a slightly elevated rhetorical plateau: " . . . as soon as I saw him I felt that he was my father, my flesh and blood, my future and my doom." The **tone** of the story, or what we can indirectly determine about the author's own feelings about its events from his or her choice of words, is also carefully controlled. Cheever avoids the twin pitfalls of sentimentality on the one hand and cynicism on the other by deftly walking an emotional tightrope. After the opening paragraph, at no point does Charlie tell us how he feels; instead, he lets his father's actions speak for themselves. There are points in "Reunion" where we may laugh, but it is an uncomfortable laugh at which we probably feel a little guilty. The range of possible tones available for use in any given story may run through the whole range of human emotions, from outright comedy or satirical contempt to pathos of the most wrenching sort. It may be possible for an unwary reader to fail to appreciate the keen edge of Flannery O'Connor's irony or the profound philosophical skepticism of Ursula Le Guin but this failure should not be laid at the feet of the writers, who have taken great pains to make their own attitudes clear.

That symbolism in stories is often a troublesome affair for students is indicated by the oft-heard phrase "hidden meanings," as if authors were doing their best to conceal, rather than reveal, the significance of actions and objects in their works. Symbolism may occur in any of the elements discussed earlier: a plot or character or setting may have some symbolic value. There is little heavy symbolism in "Reunion," but if we think about the title, with its suggestions of emotional warmth, and the setting, a busy train station, we can see that Cheever has chosen his title carefully, and it has both ironic and symbolic overtones.

If the details of a plot seem consistently symbolic, with each detail clearly pointing the way to some obvious larger meaning, then we are reading **allegory.** An allegorical reading of Hawthorne's "The Minister's Black Veil" (which he calls a "parable") might focus on the veil as a symbol of human hypocrisy, showing that the story's critique of human behavior is much more important than the intriguing "mystery" of its plot. Many stories do not use symbolism in so schematic a way, however. In a given story, an author may employ a **traditional symbol,** an object that most members of a culture instantly recognize as possessing a shared symbolic meaning. We may recognize a white gown or a red rose symbolizing, on the one hand, innocence, and on the other, romantic love, without having to think very deeply. Familiarity with an individual author's works may also help us recognize a **private symbol,** a symbol that the author has made his or her own by repeated use. To cite one example, Flannery O'Connor's use of bursts of bright light generally herald some kind of dawning spiritual revelation in the mind of one of her characters. Another writer may use certain colors, situations, and actions repeatedly; it is hard to read much of Poe's fiction without becoming aware of the personal horror that small, confined spaces represent for the author or his consistent use of *doppelgänger* characters, "doubles" who mirror each other in significant ways. Finally, we may identify an **incidental symbol** in a story. This may be an object or action that ordinarily would have no deeper meaning but acquires one in a particular story. How can we learn to spot these symbols? Paying close attention to the way an author repeats certain details or otherwise points to their significance is the key. (Repeated words or phrases are called **motifs.**) Deciding what a symbol *means* is often less important than merely realizing that it *exists.* The meaning of incidental symbolism is usually subject to multiple interpretations that do not necessarily contradict one another.

**NATHANIEL HAWTHORNE ▓ (1804–1864)**

*Nathaniel Hawthorne was born in Salem, Massachusetts, and could trace his heritage back to the earliest settlers of New England. He attended Bowdoin College, where his schoolmates included Henry Wadsworth Longfellow and future president Franklin Pierce, for whom Hawthorne later wrote an official campaign biography. For twelve years after his 1825 graduation Hawthorne lived at his parents' home, devoting himself solely to learning the craft of writing. An early novel, Fanshawe (1828), attracted no attention, but a collection of short stories, Twice-Told Tales (1837), was the subject of an enthusiastic review by Edgar Allan Poe (see page 4 in "Introduction"). Hawthorne traveled in Europe in his later years and served as American consul at Liverpool during the Pierce administration. Unlike his friend Ralph Waldo Emerson, whose optimism was a constant in his transcendentalist credo, Hawthorne was a moralist who did not shrink from depicting the dark side of human nature, and his often painful examinations of American history and conscience have set the tone for many subsequent generations of writers. His ambivalent attitude toward his Puritan ancestors' religious beliefs (one of his forebears, John Hathorne, was a magistrate who assisted the prosecution during the infamous Salem witch trials) supplied material for "Young Goodman Brown," which is set shortly before the trials and allegorically reflects the mania for persecution that infected his hometown.*

# Young Goodman Brown

Young Goodman[1] Brown came forth, at sunset, into the street of Salem village,[2] but put his head back, after crossing the threshold, to exchange a parting kiss with his young wife. And Faith, as the wife was aptly named, thrust her own pretty head into the street, letting the wind play with the pink ribbons of her cap, while she called to Goodman Brown.

"Dearest heart," whispered she, softly and rather sadly, when her lips were close to his ear, "pray thee, put off your journey until sunrise, and sleep in your own bed to-night. A lone woman is troubled with such dreams and such thoughts, that she's afraid of herself, sometimes. Pray, tarry with me this night, dear husband, of all nights in the year!"

"My love and my Faith," replied young Goodman Brown, "of all nights in the year, this one night must I tarry away from thee. My journey, as thou callest it, forth and back again, must needs be done 'twixt now and sunrise. What, my sweet, pretty wife, dost thou doubt me already, and we but three months married!"

---

[1] **Goodman** title given by Puritans to a male head of a household; a farmer or other ordinary citizen.
[2] **Salem village** in England's Massachusetts Bay Colony.

"Then, God bless you!" said Faith, with the pink ribbons, "and may you find all well, when you come back."

"Amen!" cried Goodman Brown. "Say thy prayers, dear Faith, and go to bed at dusk, and no harm will come to thee."

So they parted; and the young man pursued his way, until, being about to turn the corner by the meeting-house, he looked back, and saw the head of Faith still peeping after him, with a melancholy air, in spite of her pink ribbons.

"Poor little Faith!" thought he, for his heart smote him. "What a wretch am I, to leave her on such an errand! She talks of dreams, too. Methought, as she spoke, there was trouble in her face, as if a dream had warned her what work is to be done to-night. But, no, no! 'twould kill her to think it. Well; she's a blessed angel on earth; and after this one night, I'll cling to her skirts and follow her to Heaven."

With this excellent resolve for the future, Goodman Brown felt himself justified in making more haste on his present evil purpose. He had taken a dreary road, darkened by all the gloomiest trees of the forest, which barely stood aside to let the narrow path creep through, and closed immediately behind. It was all as lonely as could be; and there is this peculiarity in such a solitude, that the traveller knows not who may be concealed by the innumerable trunks and the thick boughs overhead; so that, with lonely footsteps, he may yet be passing through an unseen multitude.

"There may be a devilish Indian behind every tree," said Goodman Brown, to himself; and he glanced fearfully behind him, as he added, "What if the devil himself should be at my very elbow!"

His head being turned back, he passed a crook of the road, and looking forward again, beheld the figure of a man, in grave and decent attire, seated at the foot of an old tree. He arose, at Goodman Brown's approach, and walked onward, side by side with him.

"You are late, Goodman Brown," said he. "The clock of the Old South was striking as I came through Boston; and that is full fifteen minutes agone."[3]

"Faith kept me back awhile," replied the young man, with a tremor in his voice, caused by the sudden appearance of his companion, though not wholly unexpected.

It was now deep dusk in the forest, and deepest in that part of it where these two were journeying. As nearly as could be discerned, the second traveller was about fifty years old, apparently in the same rank of life as Goodman Brown, and bearing a considerable resemblance to him, though perhaps more in expression than features. Still, they might have been taken for father and son. And yet, though the elder person was as simply clad as the younger, and as simple in manner too, he had

---

[3] **full fifteen minutes agone:** Apparently this mystery man has traveled in a flash from Boston's Old South Church all the way to the woods beyond Salem—as the crow flies, a good sixteen miles.

an indescribable air of one who knew the world, and would not have felt abashed at the governor's dinner-table, or in King William's court,[4] were it possible that his affairs should call him thither. But the only thing about him, that could be fixed upon as remarkable, was his staff, which bore the likeness of a great black snake, so curiously wrought, that it might almost be seen to twist and wriggle itself, like a living serpent. This, of course, must have been an ocular deception, assisted by the uncertain light.

"Come, Goodman Brown!" cried his fellow-traveller, "this is a dull pace for the beginning of a journey. Take my staff, if you are so soon weary."

"Friend," said the other, exchanging his slow pace for a full stop, "having kept covenant by meeting thee here, it is my purpose now to return whence I came. I have scruples, touching the matter thou wot'st[5] of."

"Sayest thou so?" replied he of the serpent, smiling apart. "Let us walk on, nevertheless, reasoning as we go, and if I convince thee not, thou shalt turn back. We are but a little way in the forest, yet."

"Too far, too far!" exclaimed the goodman, unconsciously resuming his walk. "My father never went into the woods on such an errand, nor his father before him. We have been a race of honest men and good Christians, since the days of the martyrs.[6] And shall I be the first of the name of Brown, that ever took this path, and kept—"

"Such company, thou wouldst say," observed the elder person, interpreting his pause. "Well said, Goodman Brown! I have been as well acquainted with your family as with ever a one among the Puritans; and that's no trifle to say. I helped your grandfather, the constable, when he lashed the Quaker woman so smartly through the streets of Salem. And it was I that brought your father a pitch-pine knot, kindled at my own hearth, to set fire to an Indian village, in King Philip's war.[7] They were my good friends, both; and many a pleasant walk have we had along this path, and returned merrily after midnight. I would fain be friends with you, for their sake."

"If it be as thou sayest," replied Goodman Brown, "I marvel they never spoke of these matters. Or, verily, I marvel not, seeing that the least rumor of the sort would have driven them from New England. We are a people of prayer, and good works, to boot, and abide no such wickedness."

"Wickedness or not," said the traveller with the twisted staff, "I have a very general acquaintance here in New England. The deacons of many

[4] **King William's court** back in England, where William III reigned from 1689 to 1702.
[5] **wot'st** know.
[6] **days of the martyrs** a time when many forebears of the New England Puritans had given their lives for religious convictions—when Mary I (Mary Tudor, nicknamed "Bloody Mary"), queen of England from 1553 to 1558, briefly reestablished the Roman Catholic Church in England and launched a campaign of persecution against Protestants.
[7] **King Philip's war** Metacomet, or King Philip (as the English called him), chief of the Wampanoag Indians, had led a bitter, widespread uprising of several New England tribes (1675–78). Metacomet died in the war, as did one out of every ten white male colonists.

a church have drunk the communion wine with me; the selectmen, of divers towns, make me their chairman; and a majority of the Great and General Court are firm supporters of my interest. The governor and I, too—but these are state-secrets."

"Can this be so!" cried Goodman Brown, with a stare of amazement at his undisturbed companion. "Howbeit, I have nothing to do with the governor and council; they have their own ways, and are no rule for a simple husbandman, like me. But, were I to go on with thee, how should I meet the eye of that good old man, our minister, at Salem village? Oh, his voice would make me tremble, both Sabbath-day and lecture-day!"[8]

Thus far, the elder traveller had listened with due gravity, but now burst into a fit of irrepressible mirth, shaking himself so violently, that his snake-like staff actually seemed to wriggle in sympathy.

"Ha! ha! ha!" shouted he, again and again; then composing himself, "Well, go on, Goodman Brown, go on; but pray thee, don't kill me with laughing!"

"Well, then, to end the matter at once," said Goodman Brown, considerably nettled, "there is my wife, Faith. It would break her dear little heart; and I'd rather break my own!"

"Nay, if that be the case," answered the other, "e'en go thy ways, Goodman Brown. I would not, for twenty old women like the one hobbling before us, that Faith should come to any harm."

As he spoke, he pointed his staff at a female figure on the path, in whom Goodman Brown recognized a very pious and exemplary dame, who had taught him his catechism, in youth, and was still his moral and spiritual adviser, jointly with the minister and Deacon Gookin.

"A marvel, truly, that Goody[9] Cloyse should be so far in the wilderness, at night-fall!" said he. "But, with your leave, friend, I shall take a cut through the woods, until we have left this Christian woman behind. Being a stranger to you, she might ask whom I was consorting with, and whither I was going."

"Be it so," said his fellow-traveller. "Betake you to the woods, and let me keep the path."

Accordingly, the young man turned aside, but took care to watch his companion, who advanced softly along the road, until he had come within a staff's length of the old dame. She, meanwhile, was making the best of her way, with singular speed for so aged a woman, and mumbling some indistinct words, a prayer, doubtless, as she went. The traveller put forth his staff, and touched her withered neck with what seemed the serpent's tail.

"The devil!" screamed the pious old lady.

[8]**lecture-day** a weekday when everyone had to go to church to hear a sermon or Bible-reading.
[9] **Goody** short for Goodwife, title for a married woman of ordinary station. In his story, Hawthorne borrows from history the names of two "Goodys"—Goody Cloyse and Goody Cory—and one unmarried woman, Martha Carrier. In 1692 Hawthorne's great-great-grandfather John Hathorne, a judge in the Salem witchcraft trials, had condemned all three to be hanged.

"Then Goody Cloyse knows her old friend?" observed the traveller, confronting her, and leaning on his writhing stick.

"Ah, forsooth, and is it your worship, indeed?" cried the good dame. "Yea, truly is it, and in the very image of my old gossip,[10] Goodman Brown, the grandfather of the silly fellow that now is. But—would your worship believe it?—my broomstick hath strangely disappeared, stolen, as I suspect, by that unhanged witch, Goody Cory, and that, too, when I was all anointed with the juice of smallage and cinquefoil and wolf's bane[11]—"

"Mingled with fine wheat and the fat of a new-born babe," said the shape of old Goodman Brown.

"Ah, your worship knows the receipt," cried the old lady, cackling aloud. "So, as I was saying, being all ready for the meeting, and no horse to ride on, I made up my mind to foot it; for they tell me, there is a nice young man to be taken into communion to-night. But now your good worship will lend me your arm, and we shall be there in a twinkling."

"That can hardly be," answered her friend. "I may not spare you my arm, Goody Cloyse, but here is my staff, if you will."

So saying, he threw it down at her feet, where, perhaps, it assumed life, being one of the rods which its owner had formerly lent to the Egyptian Magi.[12] Of this fact, however, Goodman Brown could not take cognizance. He had cast up his eyes in astonishment, and looking down again, beheld neither Goody Cloyse nor the serpentine staff, but his fellow-traveller alone, who waited for him as calmly as if nothing had happened.

"That old woman taught me my catechism!" said the young man; and there was a world of meaning in this simple comment.

They continued to walk onward, while the elder traveller exhorted his companion to make good speed and persevere in the path, discoursing so aptly, that his arguments seemed rather to spring up in the bosom of his auditor, than to be suggested by himself. As they went, he plucked a branch of maple, to serve for a walking-stick, and began to strip it of the twigs and little boughs, which were wet with evening dew. The moment his fingers touched them, they became strangely withered and dried up, as with a week's sunshine. Thus the pair proceeded, at a good free pace, until suddenly, in a gloomy hollow of the road, Goodman Brown sat himself down on the stump of a tree, and refused to go any farther.

"Friend," said he, stubbornly, "my mind is made up. Not another step will I budge on this errand. What if a wretched old woman do choose to go to the devil, when I thought she was going to Heaven! Is that any reason why I should quit my dear Faith, and go after her?"

---

[10]**gossip** friend or kinsman.
[11]**smallage and cinquefoil and wolf's bane** wild plants—here, ingredients for a witch's brew. receipt: recipe.
[12] **Egyptian Magi** In the Bible, Pharaoh's wise men and sorcerers who by their magical powers changed their rods into live serpents. (This incident, part of the story of Moses and Aaron, is related in Exodus 7:8–12.)

"You will think better of this, by-and-by," said his acquaintance, composedly. "Sit here and rest yourself awhile; and when you feel like moving again, there is my staff to help you along."

Without more words, he threw his companion the maple stick, and was as speedily out of sight, as if he had vanished into the deepening gloom. The young man sat a few moments, by the road-side, applauding himself greatly, and thinking with how clear a conscience he should meet the minister, in his morning-walk, nor shrink from the eye of good old Deacon Gookin. And what calm sleep would be his, that very night, which was to have been spent so wickedly, but purely and sweetly now, in the arms of Faith! Amidst these pleasant and praiseworthy meditations, Goodman Brown heard the tramp of horses along the road, and deemed it advisable to conceal himself within the verge of the forest, conscious of the guilty purpose that had brought him thither, though now so happily turned from it.

On came the hoof-tramps and the voices of the riders, two grave old voices, conversing soberly as they drew near. These mingled sounds appeared to pass along the road, within a few yards of the young man's hiding-place; but owing, doubtless, to the depth of the gloom, at that particular spot, neither the travellers nor their steeds were visible. Though their figures brushed the small boughs by the way-side, it could not be seen that they intercepted, even for a moment, the faint gleam from the strip of bright sky, athwart which they must have passed. Goodman Brown alternately crouched and stood on tip-toe, pulling aside the branches, and thrusting forth his head as far as he durst, without discerning so much as a shadow. It vexed him the more, because he could have sworn, were such a thing possible, that he recognized the voices of the minister and Deacon Gookin, jogging along quietly, as they were wont to do, when bound to some ordination or ecclesiastical council. While yet within hearing, one of the riders stopped to pluck a switch.

"Of the two, reverend Sir," said the voice like the deacon's, "I had rather miss an ordination-dinner than to-night's meeting. They tell me that some of our community are to be here from Falmouth and beyond, and others from Connecticut and Rhode Island; besides several of the Indian powows,[13] who, after their fashion, know almost as much deviltry as the best of us. Moreover, there is a goodly young woman to be taken into communion."

"Mighty well, Deacon Gookin!" replied the solemn old tones of the minister. "Spur up, or we shall be late. Nothing can be done, you know, until I get on the ground."

The hoofs clattered again, and the voices, talking so strangely in the empty air, passed on through the forest, where no church had ever been gathered, nor solitary Christian prayed. Whither, then, could these holy men be journeying, so deep into the heathen wilderness? Young Goodman

[13] **powows:** Indian priests or medicine men.

Brown caught hold of a tree, for support, being ready to sink down on the ground, faint and overburdened with the heavy sickness of his heart. He looked up to the sky, doubting whether there really was a Heaven above him. Yet, there was the blue arch, and the stars brightening in it.

"With Heaven above, and Faith below, I will yet stand firm against the devil!" cried Goodman Brown.

While he still gazed upward, into the deep arch of the firmament, and had lifted his hands to pray, a cloud, though no wind was stirring, hurried across the zenith, and hid the brightening stars. The blue sky was still visible, except directly overhead, where this black mass of cloud was sweeping swiftly northward. Aloft in the air, as if from the depths of the cloud, came a confused and doubtful sound of voices. Once, the listener fancied that he could distinguish the accents of town's-people of his own, men and women, both pious and ungodly, many of whom he had met at the communion-table, and had seen others rioting at the tavern. The next moment, so indistinct were the sounds, he doubted whether he had heard aught but the murmur of the old forest, whispering without a wind. Then came a stronger swell of those familiar tones, heard daily in the sunshine, at Salem village, but never, until now, from a cloud of night. There was one voice, of a young woman, uttering lamentations, yet with an uncertain sorrow, and entreating for some favor, which, perhaps, it would grieve her to obtain. And all the unseen multitude, both saints and sinners, seemed to encourage her onward.

"Faith!" shouted Goodman Brown, in a voice of agony and desperation; and the echoes of the forest mocked him, crying—"Faith! Faith!" as if bewildered wretches were seeking her, all through the wilderness.

The cry of grief, rage, and terror, was yet piercing the night, when the unhappy husband held his breath for a response. There was a scream, drowned immediately in a louder murmur of voices, fading into far-off laughter, as the dark cloud swept away, leaving the clear and silent sky above Goodman Brown. But something fluttered lightly down through the air, and caught on the branch of a tree. The young man seized it, and beheld a pink ribbon.

"My Faith is gone!" cried he, after one stupefied moment. "There is no good on earth; and sin is but a name. Come, devil! for to thee is this world given."

And maddened with despair, so that he laughed loud and long, did Goodman Brown grasp his staff and set forth again, at such a rate, that he seemed to fly along the forest-path, rather than to walk or run. The road grew wilder and drearier, and more faintly traced, and vanished at length, leaving him in the heart of the dark wilderness, still rushing onward, with the instinct that guides mortal man to evil. The whole forest was peopled with frightful sounds; the creaking of the trees, the howling of wild beasts, and the yell of Indians; while, sometimes, the wind tolled like a distant church-bell, and sometimes gave a broad roar around the traveller, as if all

Nature were laughing him to scorn. But he was himself the chief horror of the scene, and shrank not from its other horrors.

"Ha! ha! ha!" roared Goodman Brown, when the wind laughed at him. "Let us hear which will laugh loudest! Think not to frighten me with your deviltry! Come witch, come wizard, come Indian powow, come devil himself! and here comes Goodman Brown. You may as well fear him as he fear you!"

In truth, all through the haunted forest, there could be nothing more frightful than the figure of Goodman Brown. On he flew, among the black pines, brandishing his staff with frenzied gestures, now giving vent to an inspiration of horrid blasphemy, and now shouting forth such laughter, as set all the echoes of the forest laughing like demons around him. The fiend in his own shape is less hideous, than when he rages in the breast of man. Thus sped the demoniac on his course, until, quivering among the trees, he saw a red light before him, as when the felled trunks and branches of a clearing have been set on fire, and throw up their lurid blaze against the sky, at the hour of midnight. He paused, in a lull of the tempest that had driven him onward, and heard the swell of what seemed a hymn, rolling solemnly from a distance, with the weight of many voices. He knew the tune; it was a familiar one in the choir of the village meeting-house. The verse died heavily away, and was lengthened by a chorus, not of human voices, but of all the sounds of the benighted wilderness, pealing in awful harmony together. Goodman Brown cried out; and his cry was lost to his own ear, by its unison with the cry of the desert.

In the interval of silence, he stole forward, until the light glared full upon his eyes. At one extremity of an open space, hemmed in by the dark wall of the forest, arose a rock, bearing some rude, natural resemblance either to an altar or a pulpit, and surrounded by four blazing pines, their tops aflame, their stems untouched, like candles at an evening meeting. The mass of foliage, that had overgrown the summit of the rock, was all on fire, blazing high into the night, and fitfully illuminating the whole field. Each pendent twig and leafy festoon was in a blaze. As the red light arose and fell, a numerous congregation alternately shone forth, then disappeared in shadow, and again grew, as it were, out of the darkness, peopling the heart of the solitary woods at once.

"A grave and dark-clad company!" quoth Goodman Brown.

In truth, they were such. Among them, quivering to-and-fro, between gloom and splendor, appeared faces that would be seen, next day, at the council-board of the province, and others which, Sabbath after Sabbath, looked devoutly heavenward, and benignantly over the crowded pews, from the holiest pulpits in the land. Some affirm that the lady of the governor was there. At least, there were high dames well known to her, and wives of honored husbands, and widows, a great multitude, and ancient maidens, all of excellent repute, and fair young girls, who trembled, lest their mothers should espy them. Either the sudden gleams of light, flashing over the obscure field, bedazzled Goodman Brown, or he recognized a score of the church-members of Salem village, famous for their especial sanctity. Good old Deacon Gookin had arrived, and waited at the skirts of that venerable saint, his revered pastor. But, irreverently consorting with these grave, reputable, and pious people, these elders of the church, these chaste dames and dewy virgins, there were men of dissolute lives and women of spotted fame, wretches given over to all mean and filthy vice, and suspected even of horrid crimes. It was strange to see, that the good shrank not from the wicked, nor were the sinners abashed by the saints. Scattered, also, among their pale-faced enemies, were the Indian priests, or powows, who had often scared their native forest with more hideous incantations than any known to English witchcraft.

"But, where is Faith?" thought Goodman Brown; and, as hope came into his heart, he trembled.

Another verse of the hymn arose, a slow and mournful strain, such as the pious love, but joined to words which expressed all that our nature can conceive of sin, and darkly hinted at far more. Unfathomable to mere mortals is the lore of fiends. Verse after verse was sung, and still the chorus of the desert swelled between, like the deepest tone of a mighty organ. And, with the final peal of that dreadful anthem, there came a sound, as if the roaring wind, the rushing streams, the howling beasts, and every other voice of the unconverted wilderness, were mingling and according with the voice of guilty man, in homage to the prince of all. The four blazing pines threw up a loftier flame, and obscurely discovered shapes and visages of horror on the smoke-wreaths, above the impious assembly. At the same moment, the fire on the rock shot redly forth, and formed a glowing arch above its base, where now appeared a figure. With reverence be it spoken, the figure bore no slight similitude, both in garb and manner, to some grave divine of the New England churches.

"Bring forth the converts!" cried a voice, that echoed through the field and rolled into the forest.

At the word, Goodman Brown stepped forth from the shadow of the trees, and approached the congregation, with whom he felt a loathful brotherhood, by the sympathy of all that was wicked in his heart. He could have well nigh sworn, that the shape of his own dead father beckoned him to advance, looking downward from a smoke-wreath, while a woman, with dim features of despair, threw out her hand to warn him back. Was it his mother? But he had no power to retreat one step, nor to resist, even in thought, when the minister and good old Deacon Gookin seized his arms, and led him to the blazing rock. Thither came also the slender form of a veiled female, led between Goody Cloyse, that pious teacher of the catechism, and Martha Carrier, who had received the devil's promise to be queen of hell. A rampant hag was she! And there stood the proselytes,[14] beneath the canopy of fire.

---

[14]**proselytes** new converts.

"Welcome, my children," said the dark figure, "to the communion of your race! Ye have found, thus young, your nature and your destiny. My children, look behind you!"

They turned; and flashing forth, as it were, in a sheet of flame, the fiend-worshippers were seen; the smile of welcome gleamed darkly on every visage.

"There," resumed the sable form, "are all whom ye have reverenced from youth. Ye deemed them holier than yourselves, and shrank from your own sin, contrasting it with their lives of righteousness, and prayerful aspirations heavenward. Yet, here are they all, in my worshipping assembly! This night it shall be granted you to know their secret deeds; how hoary-bearded elders of the church have whispered wanton words to the young maids of their households; how many a woman, eager for widow's weeds, has given her husband a drink at bedtime, and let him sleep his last sleep in her bosom; how beardless youths have made haste to inherit their fathers' wealth; and how fair damsels—blush not, sweet ones!—have dug little graves in the garden, and bidden me, the sole guest, to an infant's funeral. By the sympathy of your human hearts for sin, ye shall scent out all the places—whether in church, bed-chamber, street, field, or forest—where crime has been committed, and shall exult to behold the whole earth one stain of guilt, one mighty bloodspot. Far more than this! It shall be yours to penetrate, in every bosom, the deep mystery of sin, the fountain of all wicked arts, and which inexhaustibly supplies more evil impulses than human power—than my power, at its utmost!—can make manifest in deeds. And now, my children, look upon each other."

They did so; and, by the blaze of the hell-kindled torches, the wretched man beheld his Faith, and the wife her husband, trembling before that unhallowed altar.

"Lo! there ye stand, my children," said the figure, in a deep and solemn tone, almost sad, with its despairing awfulness, as if his once angelic nature could yet mourn for our miserable race. "Depending upon one another's hearts, ye had still hoped, that virtue were not all a dream. Now are ye undeceived! Evil is the nature of mankind. Evil must be your only happiness. Welcome, again, my children, to the communion of your race!"

"Welcome!" repeated the fiend-worshippers, in one cry of despair and triumph.

And there they stood, the only pair, as it seemed, who were yet hesitating on the verge of wickedness, in this dark world. A basin was hollowed, naturally, in the rock. Did it contain water, reddened by the lurid light? or was it blood? or, perchance, a liquid flame? Herein did the Shape of Evil dip his hand, and prepare to lay the mark of baptism upon their foreheads, that they might be partakers of the mystery of sin, more conscious of the secret guilt of others, both in deed and thought, than they could now be of their own. The husband cast one look at his pale wife, and Faith at him. What polluted wretches would the next glance show them to each other, shuddering alike at what they disclosed and what they saw!

"Faith! Faith!" cried the husband. "Look up to Heaven, and resist the Wicked one!"

Whether Faith obeyed, he knew not. Hardly had he spoken, when he found himself amid calm night and solitude, listening to a roar of the wind, which died heavily away through the forest. He staggered against the rock and felt it chill and damp, while a hanging twig, that had been all on fire, besprinkled his cheek with the coldest dew.

The next morning, young Goodman Brown came slowly into the street of Salem village, staring around him like a bewildered man. The good old minister was taking a walk along the grave-yard, to get an appetite for breakfast and meditate his sermon, and bestowed a blessing, as he passed, on Goodman Brown. He shrank from the venerable saint, as if to avoid an anathema.[15] Old Deacon Goodkin was at domestic worship, and the holy words of his prayer were heard through the open window. "What God doth the wizard pray to?" quoth Goodman Brown. Goody Cloyse, that excellent old Christian, stood in the early sunshine, at her own lattice, catechizing a little girl, who had brought her a pint of morning's milk. Goodman Brown snatched away the child, as from the grasp of the fiend himself. Turning the corner by the meeting-house, he spied the head of Faith, with the pink ribbons, gazing anxiously forth, and bursting into such joy at sight of him, that she skipt along the street, and almost kissed her husband before the whole village. But, Goodman Brown looked sternly and sadly into her face, and passed on without a greeting.

Had Goodman Brown fallen asleep in the forest, and only dreamed a wild dream of a witch-meeting?

Be it so, if you will. But, alas! it was a dream of evil omen for young Goodman Brown. A stern, a sad, a darkly meditative, a distrustful, if not a desperate man, did he become, from the night of that fearful dream. On the Sabbath-day, when the congregation were singing a holy psalm, he could not listen, because an anthem of sin rushed loudly upon his ear, and drowned all the blessed strain. When the minister spoke from the pulpit, with power and fervid eloquence, and, with his hand on the open Bible, of the sacred truths of our religion, and of saint-like lives and triumphant deaths, and of future bliss or misery unutterable, then did Goodman Brown turn pale, dreading, lest the roof should thunder down upon the gray blasphemer and his hearers. Often, awakening suddenly at midnight, he shrank from the bosom of Faith, and at morning or even-tide, when the family knelt down at prayer, he scowled, and muttered to himself, and gazed sternly at his wife, and turned away. And when he had lived long, and was borne to his grave, a hoary corpse, followed by Faith, an aged woman, and children and grandchildren, a goodly procession, besides neighbors, not a few, they carved no hopeful verse upon his tombstone; for his dying hour was gloom.

---

[15]**anathema** an official curse, a decree that casts one out of a church and bans him or her from receiving the sacraments.

---

**EDGAR ALLAN POE** ■ **(1809–1849)**

*Edgar Allan Poe has become so much the captive of his own legend that his name summons up visions of a mad genius who has little in common with the meticulous craftsman of criticism, fiction, and poetry whose influence on world literature has been immense. Born in Boston, Poe was the child of actors and orphaned at age 2. Nevertheless, he lived a privileged childhood as the ward of John Allan, a wealthy Richmond merchant who gave Poe his middle name. After a profligate year at the University of Virginia, successful military service (under an assumed name), and an abortive stay at West Point, Poe broke with his foster father, married his young cousin, and set about a literary career, succeeding as editor of several prominent magazines. However, his irregular habits and a drinking problem, which grew more pronounced following the death of his wife in 1847, led to his mysterious death in Baltimore at the age of 39. Poe's poetry and short fiction have influenced writers as diverse as Charles Baudelaire and Stephen King; genres such as the horror tale and the detective story must list Poe stories such as "The Tell-Tale Heart" or "The Murders in the Rue Morgue" among their earliest important examples. Similarly, Poe's literary criticism has been extremely influential; his theory of the "single effect" is quoted and discussed in the introduction. "The Cask of Amontillado," which begins with its narrator's final confession and ends with his imminent death, is a classic detective tale that is written "in reverse" from the successful murderer's point of view.*

# The Cask of Amontillado[1]

The thousand injuries of Fortunato I had borne as I best could, but when he ventured upon insult, I vowed revenge. You, who so well know the nature of my soul, will not suppose, however, that I gave utterance to a threat. *At length* I would be avenged; this was a point definitively settled—but the very definitiveness with which it was resolved precluded the idea of risk. I must not only punish, but punish with impunity. A wrong is unredressed when retribution overtakes its redresser. It is equally unredressed when the avenger fails to make himself felt as such to him who has done the wrong.

It must be understood that neither by word nor deed had I given Fortunato cause to doubt my good will. I continued as was my wont, to smile in his face, and he did not perceive that my smile *now* was at the thought of his immolation.

---

[1]Amontillado is a much-prized type of sherry.

He had a weak point—this Fortunato—although in other regards he was a man to be respected and even feared. He prided himself on his connoisseurship in wine. Few Italians have the true virtuoso spirit. For the most part their enthusiasm is adopted to suit the time and opportunity to practise imposture upon the British and Austrian *millionaires*. In painting and gemmary, Fortunato, like his countrymen, was a quack, but in the matter of old wines he was sincere. In this respect I did not differ from him materially; I was skilful in the Italian vintages myself, and bought largely whenever I could.

It was about dusk, one evening during the supreme madness of the carnival season[2], that I encountered my friend. He accosted me with excessive warmth, for he had been drinking much. The man wore motley. He had on a tight-fitting parti-striped dress and his head was surmounted by the conical cap and bells. I was so pleased to see him, that I thought I should never have done wringing his hand.

I said to him—"My dear Fortunato, you are luckily met. How remarkably well you are looking to-day! But I have received a pipe of what passes for Amontillado, and I have my doubts."

"How?" said he, "Amontillado? A pipe? Impossible? And in the middle of the carnival?"

"I have my doubts," I replied; "and I was silly enough to pay the full Amontillado price without consulting you in the matter. You were not to be found, and I was fearful of losing a bargain."

"Amontillado!"

"I have my doubts."

"Amontillado!"

"And I must satisfy them."

"Amontillado!"

"As you are engaged, I am on my way to Luchesi. If any one has a critical turn, it is he. He will tell me"—

"Luchesi cannot tell Amontillado from Sherry."

"And yet some fools will have it that his taste is a match for your own."

"Come let us go."

"Whither?"

"To your vaults."

"My friend, no; I will not impose upon your good nature. I perceive you have an engagement Luchesi"—

"I have no engagement; come."

"My friend, no. It is not the engagement, but the severe cold with which I perceive you are afflicted. The vaults are insufferably damp. They are encrusted with nitre."

"Let us go, nevertheless. The cold is merely nothing. Amontillado!

---

[2]The story is presumably set in Rome during the pre-Lent celebrations we know as Mardi Gras.

You have been imposed upon; and as for Luchesi, he cannot distinguish Sherry from Amontillado."

Thus speaking, Fortunato possessed himself of my arm. Putting on a mask of black silk and drawing a *roquelaire*[3] closely about my person, I suffered him to hurry me to my palazzo.

There were no attendants at home; they had absconded to make merry in honour of the time. I had told them that I should not return until the morning and had given them explicit orders not to stir from the house. These orders were sufficient, I well knew, to insure their immediate disappearance, one and all, as soon as my back was turned.

I took from their sconces two flambeaux, and giving one to Fortunato bowed him through several suites of rooms to the archway that led into the vaults. I passed down a long and winding staircase, requesting him to be cautious as he followed. We came at length to the foot of the descent, and stood together on the damp ground of the catacombs of the Montresors.

The gait of my friend was unsteady, and the bells upon his cap jingled as he strode.

"The pipe," said he.

"It is farther on," said I; "but observe the white webwork which gleams from these cavern walls."

He turned toward me and looked into my eyes with two filmy orbs that distilled the rheum of intoxication.

"Nitre?" he asked, at length.

"Nitre," I replied. "How long have you had that cough?"[4]

"Ugh! ugh! ugh!—ugh! ugh! ugh!—ugh! ugh! ugh!—ugh! ugh! ugh!—ugh! ugh! ugh!"

My poor friend found it impossible to reply for many minutes.

"It is nothing," he said, at last.

"Come," I said, with decision, "we will go back; your health is precious. You are rich, respected, admired, beloved; you are happy as once I was. You are a man to be missed. For me it is no matter. We will go back; you will be ill and I cannot be responsible. Besides, there is Luchesi"—

"Enough," he said; "the cough is a mere nothing; it will not kill me. I shall not die of a cough."

"True—true," I replied; "and, indeed, I had no intention of alarming you unnecessarily—but you should use all proper caution. A draught of this Medoc will defend us from the damps."

Here I knocked off the neck of a bottle which I drew from a long row of its fellows that lay upon the mould.

"Drink," I said, presenting him the wine.

He raised it to his lips with a leer. He paused and nodded to me familiarly, while his bells jingled.

[3]cloak
[4]Potassium nitrate, commonly known as saltpeter.

"I drink," he said, "to the buried that repose around us."

"And I to your long life."

He again took my arm and we proceeded.

"These vaults," he said, "are extensive."

"The Montresors," I replied, "were a great numerous family."

"I forget your arms."

"A huge human foot d'or,[5] in a field azure; the foot crushes a serpent rampant[6] whose fangs are imbedded in the heel."

"And the motto?"

*"Nemo me impune lacessit[7]."*

"Good!" he said.

The wine sparkled in his eyes and the bells jingled. My own fancy grew warm with the Medoc. We had passed through walls of piled bones, with casks and puncheons intermingling, into the inmost recesses of the catacombs. I paused again, and this time I made bold to seize Fortunato by an arm above the elbow.

"The nitre!" I said: "see it increases. It hangs like moss upon the vaults. We are below the river's bed. The drops of moisture trickle among the bones. Come, we will go back ere it is too late. Your cough"—

"It is nothing," he said; "let us go on. But first, another draught of the Medoc."

I broke and reached him a flagon of De Grave. He emptied it at a breath. His eyes flashed with a fierce light. He laughed and threw the bottle upwards with a gesticulation I did not understand.

I looked at him in surprise. He repeated the movement—a grotesque one.

"You do not comprehend?" he said.

"Not I," I replied.

"Then you are not of the brotherhood."

"How?"

"You are not of the masons."

"Yes, yes," I said "yes! yes."

"You? Impossible! A mason?"

"A mason," I replied.

"A sign," he said.

"It is this," I answered, producing a trowel from beneath the folds of my *roquelaire.*

"You jest," he exclaimed, recoiling a few paces. "But let us proceed to the Amontillado."

"Be it so," I said, replacing the tool beneath the cloak, and again offering him my arm. He leaned upon it heavily. We continued our route in search of the Amontillado. We passed through a range of low arches, descended,

---

[5]of gold
[6]rearing up
[7]No one attacks me without consequences.

passed on, and descending again, arrived at a deep crypt, in which the foul-ness of the air caused our flambeaux rather to glow than flame.

At the most remote end of the crypt there appeared another less spa-cious. Its walls had been lined with human remains piled to the vault over-head, in the fashion of the great catacombs of Paris. Three sides of this interior crypt were still ornamented in this manner. From the fourth the bones had been thrown down, and lay promiscuously upon the earth, form-ing at one point a mound of some size. Within the wall thus exposed by the displacing of the bones, we perceived a still interior recess, in depth about four feet, in width three, in height six or seven. It seemed to have been constructed for no especial use in itself, but formed merely the interval between two of the colossal supports of the roof of the catacombs, and was backed by one of their circumscribing walls of solid granite.

It was in vain that Fortunato, uplifting his dull torch, endeavoured to pry into the depths of the recess. Its termination the feeble light did not enable us to see.

"Proceed," I said; "herein is the Amontillado. As for Luchesi"—

"He is an ignoramus," interrupted my friend, as he stepped unsteadily forward, while I followed immediately at his heels. In an instant he had reached the extremity of the niche, and finding his progress arrested by the rock, stood stupidly bewildered. A moment more and I had fettered him to the granite. In its surface were two iron staples, distant from each other about two feet, horizontally. From one of these depended a short chain; from the other a padlock. Throwing the links about his waist, it was but the work of a few seconds to secure it. He was too much astounded to resist. Withdrawing the key I stepped back from the recess.

"Pass your hand," I said, "over the wall; you cannot help feeling the nitre. Indeed it is *very* damp. Once more let me *implore* you to return. No? Then I must positively leave you. But I must first render you all the little attentions in my power."

"The Amontillado!" ejaculated my friend, not yet recovered from his astonishment.

"True," I replied; "the Amontillado."

As I said these words I busied myself among the pile of bones of which I have before spoken. Throwing them aside, I soon uncovered a quantity of building stone and mortar. With these materials and with the aid of my trowel, I began vigorously to wall up the entrance of the niche.

I had scarcely laid the first tier of my masonry when I discovered that the intoxication of Fortunato had in a great measure worn off. The earli-est indication I had of this was a low moaning cry from the depth of the recess. It was *not* the cry of a drunken man. There was then a long and obstinate silence. I laid the second tier, and the third, and the fourth; and then I heard the furious vibrations of the chain. The noise lasted for several minutes, during which, that I might hearken to it with the more satisfaction, I ceased my labours and sat down upon the bones. When at last the clanking subsided, I resumed the trowel, and finished without interruption the fifth, the sixth, and the seventh tier. The wall was now nearly upon a level with my breast. I again paused, and holding the flambeaux over the mason-work, threw a few feeble rays upon the figure within.

A succession of loud and shrill screams, bursting suddenly from the throat of the chained form, seemed to thrust me violently back. For a brief moment I hesitated—I trembled. Unsheathing my rapier, I began to grope with it about the recess; but the thought of an instant reassured me. I placed my hand upon the solid fabric of the catacombs, and felt satisfied. I reapproached the wall. I replied to the yells of him who clamoured. I reechoed—I aided—I surpassed them in volume and in strength. I did this, and the clamourer grew still.

It was now midnight, and my task was drawing to a close. I had completed the eighth, the ninth, and the tenth tier. I had finished a portion of the last and the eleventh; there remained but a single stone to be fitted and plastered in. I struggled with its weight; I placed it partially in its destined position. But now there came from out the niche a low laugh that erected the hairs upon my head. It was succeeded by a sad voice, which I had difficulty in recognising as that of the noble Fortunato. The voice said—

"Ha! ha! ha!—he! he!—a very good joke indeed—an excellent jest. We will have many a rich laugh about it at the palazzo—he! he! he!—over our wine—he! he! he!"

"The Amontillado!" I said.

"He! he! he!—he! he! he!—yes, the Amontillado. But is it not getting late? Will not they be awaiting us at the palazzo, the Lady Fortunato and the rest? Let us be gone."

"Yes," I said; "let us be gone."

*"For the love of God, Montresor!"*

"Yes," I said, "for the love of God!"

But to these words I hearkened in vain for a reply. I grew impatient. I called aloud—

"Fortunato!"

No answer. I called again—

"Fortunato!"

No answer still. I thrust a torch through the remaining aperture and let it fall within. There came forth in return only a jingling of the bells. My heart grew sick—on account of the dampness of the catacombs. I hastened to make an end of my labour. I forced the last stone into its position; I plastered it up. Against the new masonry I reerected the old rampart of bones. For the half of a century no mortal has disturbed them.

*In pace requiescat!*[8]

---

[8]Rest in peace.

---

**S A R A H   O R N E   J E W E T T** ■ (1849–1909)

---

*Sarah Orne Jewett was born in the harbor village of South Berwick, Maine, the granddaughter of a sea captain and daughter of a doctor who taught at Bowdoin College and also served as a general practitioner among the local fishermen and farmers. Often ill as a child, Jewett received little formal education and did not attend college, but she was introduced to literature by her well-read father. Jewett's publishing career began early, with children's stories and poems appearing in her teens and acceptances in the* Atlantic Monthly *as she entered her twenties. Jewett's early sketches of Maine people and places owe much to the popular "local color" tradition of the late nineteenth century, but her stories largely avoid the moralizing and sentimentality common to popular fiction of its day. Although she traveled widely in later life, Jewett remained throughout her career a writer inextricably connected with her region. Her realism, common sense, and attention to detail were chiefly brought to bear on a type of American rural life that was quickly disappearing. Sylvia, the "little woods-girl" who is this story's protagonist, is only nine years old, but she receives a remarkable epiphany at the conclusion of this classic tale of initiation.*

# A White Heron

## I

The woods were already filled with shadows one June evening, just before eight o'clock, though a bright sunset still glimmered faintly among the trunks of the trees. A little girl was driving home her cow, a plodding, dilatory, provoking creature in her behavior, but a valued companion for all that. They were going away from whatever light there was, and striking deep into the woods, but their feet were familiar with the path, and it was no matter whether their eyes could see it or not.

There was hardly a night the summer through when the old cow could be found waiting at the pasture bars; on the contrary, it was her greatest pleasure to hide herself away among the huckleberry bushes, and though she wore a loud bell she had made the discovery that if one stood perfectly still it would not ring. So Sylvia had to hunt for her until she found her, and call Co'! Co'! with never an answering Moo, until her childish patience was quite spent. If the creature had not given good milk and plenty of it, the case would have seemed very different to her owners. Besides, Sylvia had all the time there was, and very little use to make of it. Sometimes in pleasant weather it was a consolation to look upon the cow's pranks as an intelligent attempt to play hide and seek, and as the child had no playmates she lent herself to this amusement with a good deal of zest. Though this chase had been so long that the wary animal herself had given an unusual signal of her whereabouts. Sylvia had only laughed when she came upon Mistress Moolly at the swampside, and urged her affectionately homeward with a twig of birch leaves. The old cow was not inclined to wander farther, she even turned in the right direction for once as they left the pasture, and stepped along the road at a good pace. She was quite ready to be milked now, and seldom stopped to browse. Sylvia wondered what her grandmother would say because they were so late. It was a great while since she had left home at half-past five o'clock, but everybody knew the difficulty of making this errand a short one. Mrs. Tilley had chased the horned torment too many summer evenings herself to blame any one else for lingering, and was only thankful as she waited that she had Sylvia, nowadays, to give such valuable assistance. The good woman suspected that Sylvia loitered occasionally on her own account; there never was such a child for straying about out-of-doors since the world was made! Everybody said that it was a good change for a little maid who had tried to grow for eight years in a crowded manufacturing town, but as for Sylvia herself, it seemed as if she never had been alive at all before she came to live at the farm. She thought often with wistful compassion of a wretched geranium that belonged to a town neighbor.

"Afraid of folks," old Mrs. Tilley said to herself, with a smile, after she had made the unlikely choice of Sylvia from her daughter's houseful of children, and was returning to the farm. " 'Afraid of folks,' they said! I guess she won't be troubled no great with 'em up to the old place!" When they reached the door of the lonely house and stopped to unlock it, and the cat came to purr loudly, and rub against them, a deserted pussy, indeed, but fat with young robins, Sylvia whispered that this was a beautiful place to live in, and she never should wish to go home.

The companions followed the shady woodroad, the cow taking slow steps and the child very fast ones. The cow stopped long at the brook to drink, as if the pasture were not half a swamp, and Sylvia stood still and waited, letting her bare feet cool themselves in the shoal water, while the great twilight moths struck softly against her. She waded on through the brook as the cow moved away, and listened to the thrushes with a heart that beat fast with pleasure. There was a stirring in the great boughs overhead. They were full of little birds and beasts that seemed to be wide awake, and going about their world, or else saying goodnight to each other in sleepy twitters. Sylvia herself felt sleepy as she walked along. However, it was not much farther to the house, and the air was soft and sweet. She was not often in the woods so late as this, and it made her feel as if she were a part of the gray shadows and the moving leaves. She was just thinking how long it seemed since she first came to the farm a year ago, and wondering if everything went on in the noisy town just the same as when she was there;

the thought of the great red-faced boy who used to chase and frighten her made her hurry along the path to escape from the shadow of the trees.

Suddenly this little woods-girl is horror-stricken to hear a clear whistle not very far away. Not a bird's-whistle, which would have a sort of friendliness, but a boy's whistle, determined, and somewhat aggressive. Sylvia left the cow to whatever sad fate might await her, and stepped discreetly aside into the brushes, but she was just too late. The enemy had discovered her, and called out in a very cheerful and persuasive tone, "Halloa, little girl, how far is it to the road?" and trembling Sylvia answered almost inaudibly. "A good ways."

She did not dare to look boldly at the tall young man, who carried a gun over his shoulder, but she came out of her bush and again followed the cow, while he walked alongside.

"I have been hunting for some birds," the stranger said kindly, "and I have lost my way, and need a friend very much. Don't be afraid," he added gallantly. "Speak up and tell me what your name is, and whether you think I can spend the night at your house, and go out gunning early in the morning."

Sylvia was more alarmed than before. Would not her grandmother consider her much to blame? But who could have foreseen such an accident as this? It did not seem to be her fault, and she hung her head as if the stem of it were broken, but managed to answer "Sylvy," with much effort when her companion again asked her name.

Mrs. Tilley was standing in the doorway when the trio came into view. The cow gave a loud moo by way of explanation.

"Yes, you'd better speak up for yourself, you old trial! Where'd she tucked herself away this time, Sylvy?" But Sylvia kept an awed silence; she knew by instinct that her grandmother did not comprehend the gravity of the situation. She must be mistaking the stranger for one of the farmer-lads of the region.

The young man stood his gun beside the door, and dropped a lumpy game-bag beside it; then he bade Mrs. Tilley good-evening, and repeated his wayfarer's story, and asked if he could have a night's lodging.

"Put me anywhere you like," he said. "I must be off early in the morning, before day; but I am very hungry, indeed. You can give me some milk at any rate, that's plain."

"Dear sakes, yes," responded the hostess, whose long slumbering hospitality seemed to be easily awakened. "You might fare better if you went out to the main road a mile or so, but you're welcome to what we've got. I'll milk right off, and you make yourself at home. You can sleep on husks or feathers," she proffered graciously. "I raised them all myself. There's good pasturing for geese just below here towards the ma'sh. Now step round and set a plate for the gentleman, Sylvy!" And Sylvia promptly stepped. She was glad to have something to do, and she was hungry herself.

It was a surprise to find so clean and comfortable a little dwelling in this New England wilderness. The young man had known the horrors of its most primitive housekeeping, and the dreary squalor of that level of society which does not rebel at the companionship of hens. This was the best thrift of an old-fashioned farmstead, though on such a small scale that it seemed like a hermitage. He listened eagerly to the old woman's quaint talk, he watched Sylvia's pale face and shining gray eyes with ever growing enthusiasm, and insisted that this was the best supper he had eaten for a month, and afterward the new-made friends sat down in the door-way together while the moon came up.

Soon it would be berry-time, and Sylvia was a great help at picking. The cow was a good milker, though a plaguy thing to keep track of, the hostess gossiped frankly, adding presently that she had buried four children, so Sylvia's mother, and a son (who might be dead) in California were all the children she had left. "Dan, my boy, was a great hand to go gunning," she explained sadly. "I never wanted for pa'tridges or gray squer'ls while he was to home. He's been a great wand'rer, I expect, and he's no hand to write letters. There, I don't blame him, I'd ha' seen the world myself if it had been so I could."

"Sylvy takes after him," the grandmother continued affectionately, after a minute's pause. "There ain't a foot o' ground she don't know her way over, and the wild creatures counts her one o' themselves. Squer'ls she'll tame to come an' feed right out o' her hands, and all sorts o' birds. Last winter she got the jaybirds to bangeing[1] here, and I believe she'd 'a' scanted herself of her own meals to have plenty to throw out amongst 'em, if I hadn't kep' watch. Anything but crows, I tell her, I'm willin' to help support—though Dan he had a tamed one o' them that did seem to have reason same as folks. It was round here a good spell after he went away. Dan an' his father they didn't hitch,— but he never held up his head ag'in after Dan had dared him an' gone off."

The guest did not notice this hint of family sorrows in his eager interest in something else.

"So Sylvy knows all about birds, does she?" he exclaimed, as he looked round at the little girl who sat, very demure but increasingly sleepy, in the moonlight. "I am making a collection of birds myself. I have been at it ever since I was a boy." (Mrs. Tilley smiled.) "There are two or three very rare ones I have been hunting for these five years. I mean to get them on my own grounds if they can be found."

"Do you cage 'em up?" asked Mrs. Tilley doubtfully, in response to this enthusiastic announcement.

"Oh no, they're stuffed and preserved, dozens and dozens of them," said the ornithologist, "and I have shot or snared every one myself. I caught a glimpse of a white heron a few miles from here on Saturday, and I have followed it in this direction. They have never been found in this district at all. The little white heron, it is," and he turned again to look at Sylvia with the hope of discovering that the rare bird was one of her acquaintances.

---

[1] **bangeing** loitering

But Sylvia was watching a hop-toad in the narrow footpath.

"You would know the heron if you saw it," the stranger continued eagerly. "A queer tall white bird with soft feathers and long thin legs. And it would have a nest perhaps in the top of a high tree, made of sticks, something like a hawk's nest."

Sylvia's heart gave a wild beat; she knew that strange white bird, and had once stolen softly near where it stood in some bright green swamp grass, away over at the other side of the woods. There was an open place where the sunshine always seemed strangely yellow and hot, where tall, nodding rushes grew, and her grandmother had warned her that she might sink in the soft black mud underneath and never be heard of more. Not far beyond were the salt marshes just this side the sea itself, which Sylvia wondered and dreamed much about, but never had seen, whose great voice could sometimes be heard above the noise of the woods on stormy nights.

"I can't think of anything I should like so much as to find that heron's nest," the handsome stranger was saying. "I would give ten dollars to anybody who could show it to me," he added desperately, "and I mean to spend my whole vacation hunting for it if need be. Perhaps it was only migrating, or had been chased out of its own region by some bird of prey."

Mrs. Tilley gave amazed attention to all this, but Sylvia still watched the toad, not divining, as she might have done at some calmer time, that the creature wished to get to its hole under the door-step, and was much hindered by the unusual spectators at that hour of the evening. No amount of thought, that night, could decide how many wished-for treasures the ten dollars, so lightly spoken of, would buy.

The next day the young sportsman hovered about the woods, and Sylvia kept him company, having lost her first fear of the friendly lad, who proved to be most kind and sympathetic. He told her many things about the birds and what they knew and where they lived and what they did with themselves. And he gave her a jack-knife, which she thought as great a treasure as if she were a desert-islander. All day long he did not once make her troubled or afraid except when he brought down some unsuspecting singing creature from its bough. Sylvia would have liked him vastly better without his gun; she could not understand why he killed the very birds he seemed to like so much. But as the day waned, Sylvia still watched the young man with loving admiration. She had never seen anybody so charming and delightful; the woman's heart, asleep in the child, was vaguely thrilled by a dream of love. Some premonition of that great power stirred and swayed these young creatures who traversed the solemn woodlands with soft-footed silent care. They stopped to listen to a bird's song; they pressed forward again eagerly, parting the branches—speaking to each other rarely and in whispers; the young man going first and Sylvia following fascinated, a few steps behind, with her gray eyes dark with excitement.

She grieved because the longed-for white heron was elusive, but she did not lead the guest, she only followed, and there was no such thing as speaking first. The sound of her own unquestioned voice would have terrified her—it was hard enough to answer yes or no when there was need of that. At last evening began to fall, and they drove the cow home together, and Sylvia smiled with pleasure when they came to the place where she heard the whistle and was afraid only the night before.

## II

Half a mile from home, at the farther edge of the woods, where the land was highest, a great pine-tree stood, the last of its generation. Whether it was left for a boundary mark, or for what reason, no one could say; the woodchoppers who had felled its mates were dead and gone long ago, and a whole forest of sturdy trees, pines and oaks and maples, had grown again. But the stately head of this old pine towered above them all and made a landmark for sea and shore miles and miles away. Sylvia knew it well. She had always believed that whoever climbed to the top of it could see the ocean; and the little girl had often laid her hand on the great rough trunk and looked up wistfully at those dark boughs that the wind always stirred, no matter how hot and still the air might be below. Now she thought of the tree with a new excitement, for why, if one climbed it at break of day could not one see all the world, and easily discover from whence the white heron flew, and mark the place, and find the hidden nest?

What a spirit of adventure, what wild ambition! What fancied triumph and delight and glory for the later morning when she could make known the secret! It was almost too real and too great for the childish heart to bear.

All night the door of the little house stood open and the whippoorwills came and sang upon the very step. The young sportsman and his old hostess were sound asleep, but Sylvia's great design kept her broad awake and watching. She forgot to think of sleep. The short summer night seemed as long as the winter darkness, and at last when the whippoorwills ceased, and she was afraid the morning would after all come too soon, she stole out of the house and followed the pasture path through the woods, hastening toward the open ground beyond, listening with a sense of comfort and companionship to the drowsy twitter of a half-awakened bird, whose perch she had jarred in passing. Alas, if the great wave of human interest which flooded for the first time this dull little life should sweep away the satisfactions of an existence heart to heart with nature and the dumb life of the forest!

There was the huge tree asleep yet in the paling moonlight, and small and silly Sylvia began with utmost bravery to mount to the top of it, with tingling, eager blood coursing the channels of her whole frame, with her bare feet and fingers, that pinched and held like bird's claws to the monstrous ladder reaching up, up, almost to the sky itself. First she must mount the white oak tree that grew alongside, where she was almost lost among the dark branches and the green leaves heavy and wet with dew; a bird fluttered off its nest, and a red squirrel ran to and fro and scolded pettishly at the harmless housebreaker. Sylvia felt her way easily. She had often climbed there, and knew that higher still one of the oak's upper branches chafed against the pine trunk, just where its lower boughs were set close together. There, when she made the dangerous pass from one tree to the other, the great enterprise would really begin.

She crept out along the swaying oak limb at last, and took the daring step across into the old pine-tree. The way was harder than she thought; she must reach far and hold fast, the sharp dry twigs caught and held her and scratched her like angry talons, the pitch made her thin little fingers clumsy and stiff as she went round and round the tree's great stem, higher and higher upward. The sparrows and robins in the woods below were beginning to wake and twitter to the dawn, yet it seemed much lighter there aloft in the pine-tree, and the child knew she must hurry if her project were to be of any use.

The tree seemed to lengthen itself out as she went up, and to reach farther and farther upward. It was like a great main-mast to the voyaging earth; it must truly have been amazed that morning through all its ponderous frame as it felt this determined spark of human spirit wending its way from higher branch to branch. Who knows how steadily the least twigs held themselves to advantage this light, weak creature on her way! The old pine must have loved his new dependent. More than all the hawks, and bats, and moths, and even the sweet voiced thrushes, was the brave, beating heart of the solitary gray-eyed child. And the tree stood still and frowned away the winds that June morning while the dawn grew bright in the east.

Sylvia's face was like a pale star, if one had seen it from the ground, when the last thorny bough was past, and she stood trembling and tired but wholly triumphant, high in the treetop. Yes, there was the sea with the dawning sun making a golden dazzle over it, and toward that glorious east flew two hawks with slow-moving pinions. How low they looked in the air from that height when one had only seen them before far up, and dark against the blue sky. Their gray feathers were as soft as moths: they seemed only a little way from the tree, and Sylvia felt as if she too could go flying away among the clouds. Westward, the woodlands and farms reached miles and miles into the distance; here and there were church steeples, and white villages, truly it was a vast and awesome world!

The birds sang louder and louder. At last the sun came up bewilderingly bright. Sylvia could see the white sails of ships out at sea, and the clouds that were purple and rose-colored and yellow at first began to fade away. Where was the white heron's nest in the sea of green branches, and was this wonderful sight and pageant of the world the only reward for having climbed to such a giddy height? Now look down again, Sylvia, where the green marsh is set among the shining birches and dark hemlocks; there where you saw the white heron once you will see him again; look, look! a white spot of him like a single floating feather comes up from the dead hemlock and grows larger, and rises, and comes close at last, and goes by the landmark pine with steady sweep of wing and outstretched slender neck and crested head. And wait! wait! do not move a foot or a finger, little girl, do not send an arrow of light and consciousness from your two eager eyes, for the heron has perched on a pine bough not far beyond yours, and cries back to his mate on the nest and plumes his feathers for the new day!

The child gives a long sigh a minute later when a company of shouting cat-birds comes also to the tree, and vexed by their fluttering and lawlessness the solemn heron goes away. She knows his secret now, the wild, light, slender bird that floats and wavers, and goes back like an arrow presently to his home in the green world beneath. Then Sylvia, well satisfied, makes her perilous way down again, not daring to look far below the branch she stands on, ready to cry sometimes because her fingers ache and her lamed feet slip. Wondering over and over again what the stranger would say to her, and what he would think when she told him how to find his way straight to the heron's nest.

"Sylvy, Sylvy!" called the busy old grandmother again and again, but nobody answered, and the small husk bed was empty and Sylvia had disappeared.

The guest waked from a dream, and remembering his day's pleasure hurried to dress himself that might it sooner begin. He was sure from the way the shy little girl looked once or twice yesterday that she had at least seen the white heron, and now she must really be made to tell. Here she comes now, paler than ever, and her worn old frock is torn and tattered, and smeared with pine pitch. The grandmother and the sportsman stand in the door together and question her, and the splendid moment has come to speak of the dead hemlock-tree by the green marsh.

But Sylvia does not speak after all, though the old grandmother fretfully rebukes her, and the young man's kind, appealing eyes are looking straight in her own. He can make them rich with money; he has promised it, and they are poor now. He is so well worth making happy, and he waits to hear the story she can tell.

No, she must keep silence! What is it that suddenly forbids her and makes her dumb? Has she been nine years growing and now, when the great world for the first time puts out a hand to her, must she thrust it aside for a bird's sake? The murmur of the pine's green branches is in her ears, she remembers how the white heron came flying through the golden air and how they watched the sea and the morning together, and Sylvia cannot speak; she cannot tell the heron's secret and give its life away.

Dear loyalty, that suffered a sharp pang as the guest went away disappointed later in the day, that could have served and followed him and loved him as a dog loves! Many a night Sylvia heard the echo of his whistle haunting the pasture path as she came home with the loitering cow. She forgot even her sorrow at the sharp report of his gun and the sight of thrushes and sparrows dropping silent to the ground, their songs hushed and their pretty feathers stained and wet with blood. Were the birds better friends than their hunter might have been—who can tell? Whatever treasures were lost to her, woodlands and summer-time, remember! Bring your gifts and graces and tell your secrets to this lonely country child!

—1886

## GUY DE MAUPASSANT ▪ (1850-1893)

*Born and raised in Normandy, the French novelist and short-story writer Guy de Maupassant (1850–1893) studied law in Paris, then served in the Franco-Prussian War. Afterward he worked for a time as a clerk for the government until, with the support of the novelist Gustave Flaubert (a friend of Maupassant's mother) and later Emile Zola, he decided to pursue a career as a writer. Ironic and pointed, detached yet compassionate, Maupassant explores human folly and its both grim and comic consequences. His first great success came in April 1880, with the publication of the story "Boule de Suif" ("Grease-Ball"), about a prostitute traveling by coach, with a number of bourgeois companions, through Prussian-occupied France during wartime. Maupassant published six novels, including* Bel-Ami *(1885) and* Pierre et Jean *(1888), and a number of collections of stories, before his untimely death from the effects of syphilis, a month short of his forty-third birthday. Like many of his stories, "The Necklace" uses realistic observation and keenly chosen detail to tell its story of a misunderstanding and the years of hard labor that follow from it.*

# The Necklace

### *Translated by Marjorie Laurie*

She was one of those pretty and charming girls who are sometimes, as if by a mistake of destiny, born in a family of clerks. She had no dowry, no expectations, no means of being known, understood, loved, wedded by any rich and distinguished man; and she let herself be married to a little clerk at the Ministry of Public Instruction.

She dressed plainly because she could not dress well, but she was as unhappy as though she had really fallen from her proper station, since with women there is neither caste nor rank: and beauty, grace and charm act instead of family and birth. Natural fineness, instinct for what is elegant, suppleness of wit, are the sole hierarchy, and make from women of the people the equals of the very greatest ladies.

She suffered ceaselessly, feeling herself born for all the delicacies and all the luxuries. She suffered from the poverty of her dwelling, from the wretched look of the walls, from the worn-out chairs, from the ugliness of the curtains. All those things, of which another woman of her rank would never even have been conscious, tortured her and made her angry. The sight of the little Breton peasant who did her humble housework aroused in her regrets which were despairing, and distracted dreams. She thought of the silent antechambers hung with Oriental tapestry, lit by tall bronze candelabra, and of the two great footmen in knee breeches who sleep in the big armchairs, made drowsy by the heavy warmth of the hot-air stove. She thought of the long *salons*[1] fitted up with ancient silk, of the delicate furniture carrying priceless curiosities, and of the coquettish perfumed boudoirs made for talks at five o'clock with intimate friends, with men famous and sought after, whom all women envy and whose attention they all desire.

When she sat down to dinner, before the round table covered with a tablecloth three days old, opposite her husband, who uncovered the soup tureen and declared with an enchanted air, "Ah, the good *pot-au-feu*![2] I don't know anything better than that," she thought of dainty dinners, of shining silverware, of tapestry which peopled the walls with ancient personages and with strange birds flying in the midst of a fairy forest; and she thought of delicious dishes served on marvelous plates, and of the whispered gallantries which you listen to with a sphinxlike smile, while you are eating the pink flesh of a trout or the wings of a quail.

She had no dresses, no jewels, nothing. And she loved nothing but that; she felt made for that. She would so have liked to please, to be envied, to be charming, to be sought after.

She had a friend, a former schoolmate at the convent, who was rich, and whom she did not like to go and see any more, because she suffered so much when she came back.

But one evening, her husband returned home with a triumphant air, and holding a large envelope in his hand.

"There," said he. "Here is something for you."

She tore the paper sharply, and drew out a printed card which bore these words:

"The Minister of Public Instruction and Mme. Georges Ramponneau request the honor of M. and Mme. Loisel's company at the palace of the Ministry on Monday evening, January eighteenth."

[1] **salons** drawing-rooms.
[2] **pot-au-feu** stew.

Instead of being delighted, as her husband hoped, she threw the invitation on the table with disdain, murmuring:

"What do you want me to do with that?"

"But, my dear, I thought you would be glad. You never go out, and this is such a fine opportunity. I had awful trouble to get it. Everyone wants to go; it is very select, and they are not giving many invitations to clerks. The whole official world will be there."

She looked at him with an irritated glance, and said, impatiently:

"And what do you want me to put on my back?"

He had not thought of that; he stammered:

"Why, the dress you go to the theater in. It looks very well, to me."

He stopped, distracted, seeing his wife was crying. Two great tears descended slowly from the corners of her eyes toward the corners of her mouth. He stuttered:

"What's the matter? What's the matter?"

But, by violent effort, she had conquered her grief, and she replied, with a calm voice, while she wiped her wet cheeks:

"Nothing. Only I have no dress and therefore I can't go to this ball. Give your card to some colleague whose wife is better equipped than I."

He was in despair. He resumed:

"Come, let us see, Mathilde. How much would it cost, a suitable dress, which you could use on other occasions, something very simple?"

She reflected several seconds, making her calculations and wondering also what sum she could ask without drawing on herself an immediate refusal and a frightened exclamation from the economical clerk.

Finally, she replied, hesitatingly:

"I don't know exactly, but I think I could manage it with four hundred francs."

He had grown a little pale, because he was laying aside just that amount to buy a gun and treat himself to a little shooting next summer on the plain of Nanterre, with several friends who went to shoot larks down there, of a Sunday.

But he said:

"All right. I will give you four hundred francs. And try to have a pretty dress."

The day of the ball drew near, and Mme. Loisel seemed sad, uneasy, anxious. Her dress was ready, however. Her husband said to her one evening:

"What is the matter? Come, you've been so queer these last three days."

And she answered:

"It annoys me not to have a single jewel, not a single stone, nothing to put on. I shall look like distress. I should almost rather not go at all."

He resumed:

"You might wear natural flowers. It's very stylish at this time of the year. For ten francs you can get two or three magnificent roses."

She was not convinced.

"No; there's nothing more humiliating than to look poor among other women who are rich."

But her husband cried:

"How stupid you are! Go look up your friend Mme. Forestier, and ask her to lend you some jewels. You're quite thick enough with her to do that."

She uttered a cry of joy:

"It's true. I never thought of it."

The next day she went to her friend and told of her distress.

Mme. Forestier went to a wardrobe with a glass door, took out a large jewelbox, brought it back, opened it, and said to Mme. Loisel:

"Choose, my dear."

She saw first of all some bracelets, then a pearl necklace, then a Venetian cross, gold and precious stones of admirable workmanship. She tried on the ornaments before the glass, hesitated, could not make up her mind to part with them, to give them back. She kept asking:

"Haven't you any more?"

"Why, yes. Look. I don't know what you like."

All of a sudden she discovered, in a black satin box, a superb necklace of diamonds, and her heart began to beat with an immoderate desire. Her hands trembled as she took it. She fastened it around her throat, outside her high-necked dress, and remained lost in ecstasy at the sight of herself.

Then she asked, hesitating, filled with anguish:

"Can you lend me that, only that?"

"Why, yes, certainly."

She sprang upon the neck of her friend, kissed her passionately, then fled with her treasure.

The day of the ball arrived. Mme. Loisel made a great success. She was prettier than them all, elegant, gracious, smiling, and crazy with joy. All the men looked at her, asked her name, endeavored to be introduced. All the attachés of the Cabinet wanted to waltz with her. She was remarked by the minister himself.

She danced with intoxication, with passion, made drunk by pleasure, forgetting all, in the triumph of her beauty, in the glory of her success, in a sort of cloud of happiness composed of all this homage, of all this admiration, of all these awakened desires, and of that sense of complete victory which is so sweet to a woman's heart.

She went away about four o'clock in the morning. Her husband had been sleeping since midnight, in a little deserted anteroom, with three other gentlemen whose wives were having a very good time. He threw over her shoulders the wraps which he had brought, modest wraps of common life, whose poverty contrasted with the elegance of the ball dress. She felt this, and wanted to escape so as not to be remarked by the other women, who were enveloping themselves in costly furs.

Loisel held her back.

"Wait a bit. You will catch cold outside. I will go and call a cab."

But she did not listen to him, and rapidly descended the stairs. When they were in the street they did not find a carriage; and they began to look for one, shouting after the cabmen whom they saw passing by at a distance.

They went down toward the Seine, in despair, shivering with cold. At last they found on the quay one of those ancient noctambulant coupés which, exactly as if they were ashamed to show their misery during the day, are never seen round Paris until after nightfall.

It took them to their door in the Rue des Martyrs, and once more, sadly, they climbed up homeward. All was ended, for her. And as to him, he reflected that he must be at the Ministry at ten o'clock.

She removed the wraps which covered her shoulders, before the glass, so as once more to see herself in all her glory. But suddenly she uttered a cry. She no longer had the necklace around her neck!

Her husband, already half undressed, demanded:

"What is the matter with you?"

She turned madly toward him:

"I have—I have—I've lost Mme. Forestier's necklace."

He stood up, distracted.

"What!—how?—impossible!"

And they looked in the folds of her dress, in the folds of her cloak, in her pockets, everywhere. They did not find it.

He asked:

"You're sure you had it on when you left the ball?"

"Yes, I felt it in the vestibule of the palace."

"But if you had lost it in the street we should have heard it fall. It must be in the cab."

"Yes. Probably. Did you take his number?"

"No. And you, didn't you notice it?"

"No."

They looked, thunderstruck, at one another. At last Loisel put on his clothes.

"I shall go back on foot," said he, "over the whole route which we have taken to see if I can find it."

And he went out. She sat waiting on a chair in her ball dress, without strength to go to bed, overwhelmed, without fire, without a thought.

Her husband came back about seven o'clock. He had found nothing.

He went to Police Headquarters, to the newspaper offices, to offer a reward: he went to the cab companies—everywhere, in fact, whither he was urged by the least suspicion of hope.

She waited all day, in the same condition of mad fear before this terrible calamity.

Loisel returned at night with a hollow, pale face; he had discovered nothing.

"You must write to your friend," said he, "that you have broken the clasp of her necklace and that you are having it mended. That will give us time to turn round."

She wrote at his dictation.

At the end of a week they had lost all hope.

And Loisel, who had aged five years, declared:

"We must consider how to replace that ornament."

The next day they took the box which had contained it, and they went to the jeweler whose name was found within. He consulted his books.

"It was not I, madame, who sold that necklace; I must simply have furnished the case."

Then they went from jeweler to jeweler, searching for a necklace like the other, consulting their memories, sick both of them with chagrin and anguish.

They found, in a shop at the Palais Royal, a string of diamonds which seemed to them exactly like the one they looked for. It was worth forty thousand francs. They could have it for thirty-six.

So they begged the jeweler not to sell it for three days yet. And they made a bargain that he should buy it back for thirty-four thousand francs, in case they found the other one before the end of February.

Loisel possessed eighteen thousand francs which his father had left him. He would borrow the rest.

He did borrow, asking a thousand francs of one, five hundred of another, five louis here, three louis[3] there. He gave notes, took up ruinous obligations, dealt with usurers and all the race of lenders. He compromised all the rest of his life, risked his signature without even knowing if he could meet it; and, frightened by the pains yet to come, by the black misery which was about to fall upon him, by the prospect of all the physical privation and of all the moral tortures which he was to suffer, he went to get the new necklace, putting down upon the merchant's counter thirty-six thousand francs.

When Mme. Loisel took back the necklace, Mme. Forestier said to her, with a chilly manner:

"You should have returned it sooner; I might have needed it."

She did not open the case, as her friend had so much feared. If she had detected the substitution, what would she have thought, what would she have said? Would she not have taken Mme. Loisel for a thief?

Mme. Loisel now knew the horrible existence of the needy. She took her part, moreover, all of a sudden, with heroism. That dreadful debt must

[3] **louis** a gold coin worth 20 francs.

be paid. She would pay it. They dismissed their servant; they changed their lodgings; they rented a garret under the roof.

She came to know what heavy housework meant and the odious cares of the kitchen. She washed the dishes, using her rosy nails on the greasy pots and pans. She washed the dirty linen, the shirts, and the dishcloths, which she dried upon a line; she carried the slops down to the street every morning, and carried up the water, stopping for breath at every landing. And, dressed like a woman of the people, she went to the fruiterer, the grocer, the butcher, her basket on her arm, bargaining, insulted, defending her miserable money sou by sou.

Each month they had to meet some notes, renew others, obtain more time.

Her husband worked in the evening making a fair copy of some trades-man's accounts, and late at night he often copied manuscript for five sous a page.

And this life lasted for ten years.

At the end of ten years, they had paid everything, everything, with the rates of usury, and the accumulations of the compound interest.

Mme. Loisel looked old now. She had become the woman of impoverished households—strong and hard and rough. With frowsy hair, skirts askew, and red hands, she talked loud while washing the floor with great swishes of water. But sometimes, when her husband was at the office, she sat down near the window, and she thought of that gay evening of long ago, of the ball where she had been so beautiful and so fêted.

What would have happened if she had not lost that necklace? Who knows? Who knows? How life is strange and changeful! How little a thing is needed for us to be lost or to be saved!

But, one Sunday, having gone to take a walk in the Champs Elysées to refresh herself from the labor of the week, she suddenly perceived a woman who was leading a child. It was Mme. Forestier, still young, still beautiful, still charming.

Mme. Loisel felt moved. Was she going to speak to her? Yes, certainly. And now that she had paid, she was going to tell her all about it. Why not?

She went up.

"Good day, Jeanne."

The other, astonished to be familiarly addressed by this plain goodwife, did not recognize her at all, and stammered:

"But—madam!—I do not know—You must be mistaken."

"No. I am Mathilde Loisel."

Her friend uttered a cry.

"Oh, my poor Mathilde! How you are changed!"

"Yes, I have had days hard enough, since I have seen you, days wretched enough—and that because of you!"

"Of me! How so?"

"Do you remember that diamond necklace which you lent me to wear at the ministerial ball?"

"Yes. Well?"

"Well, I lost it."

"What do you mean? You brought it back."

"I brought you back another just like it. And for this we have been ten years paying. You can understand that it was not easy for us, us who had nothing. At last it is ended, and I am very glad."

Mme. Forestier had stopped.

"You say that you bought a necklace of diamonds to replace mine?"

"Yes. You never noticed it, then! They were very like."

And she smiled with a joy which was proud and naïve at once.

Mme. Forestier, strongly moved, took her two hands.

"Oh, my poor Mathilde! Why, my necklace was paste rhinestone. It was worth at most five hundred francs!"

—1885

---

### KATE CHOPIN ■ (1851–1904)

*Kate Chopin was virtually forgotten for most of the twentieth century. She was rarely mentioned in histories of American literature and was remembered primarily as a chronicler of life among the Louisiana Creoles and Cajuns. Her works had long been out of print, when they were rediscovered in recent decades, initially by feminist critics and subsequently by general readers. Her most important novel,* The Awakening *(1899), today appears frequently on college reading lists and was filmed in 1992 as* Grand Isle. *Born in St. Louis, Chopin spent the 1870s in rural Louisiana, the wife of Oscar Chopin, a cotton broker from New Orleans. Later she lived with her husband on a plantation near Natchitoches, an area that provides the setting of the stories collected in* Bayou Folk *(1894) and* A Night in Arcadie *(1897) and from which she absorbed a rich mixture of French and black cultures. After her husband's death in 1883, Chopin returned to St. Louis with her six children and began her literary career, placing stories and regional pieces in popular magazines. Much of her later work is remarkable for its frank depiction of women's sexuality, a subject rarely broached in the literature of the era, and Chopin became the subject of controversy after the appearance of* The Awakening. *The negative reception of that work caused Chopin to suffer social ostracism and effectively ended her active career as a writer. "The Story of an Hour," as its title indicates, is a brilliant example of compression and unified plot.*

# The Story of an Hour

Knowing that Mrs. Mallard was afflicted with a heart trouble, great care was taken to break to her as gently as possible the news of her husband's death.

It was her sister Josephine who told her, in broken sentences, veiled hints that revealed in half concealing. Her husband's friend Richards was there, too, near her. It was he who had been in the newspaper office when intelligence of the railroad disaster was received, with Brently Mallard's name leading the list of "killed." He had only taken the time to assure himself of its truth by a second telegram, and had hastened to forestall any less careful, less tender friend in bearing the sad message.

She did not hear the story as many women have heard the same, with a paralyzed inability to accept its significance. She wept at once, with sudden, wild abandonment, in her sister's arms. When the storm of grief had spent itself she went away to her room alone. She would have no one follow her.

There stood, facing the open window, a comfortable, roomy armchair. Into this she sank, pressed down by a physical exhaustion that haunted her body and seemed to reach into her soul.

She could see in the open square before her house the tops of trees that were all aquiver with the new spring life. The delicious breath of rain was in the air. In the street below a peddler was crying his wares. The notes of a distant song which some one was singing reached her faintly, and countless sparrows were twittering in the eaves.

There were patches of blue sky showing here and there through the clouds that had met and piled one above the other in the west facing her window.

She sat with her head thrown back upon the cushion of the chair, quite motionless, except when a sob came up into her throat and shook her, as a child who has cried itself to sleep continues to sob in its dreams.

She was young, with a fair, calm face, whose lines bespoke repression and even a certain strength. But now there was a dull stare in her eyes, whose gaze was fixed away off yonder on one of those patches of blue sky. It was not a glance of reflection, but rather indicated a suspension of intelligent thought.

There was something coming to her and she was waiting for it, fearfully. What was it? She did not know; it was too subtle and elusive to name. But she felt it, creeping out of the sky, reaching toward her through the sounds, the scents, the color that filled the air.

Now her bosom rose and fell tumultuously. She was beginning to recognize this thing that was approaching to possess her, and she was striving to beat it back with her will—as powerless as her two white slender hands would have been.

When she abandoned herself a little whispered word escaped her slightly parted lips. She said it over and over under her breath: "Free, free, free!" The vacant stare and the look of terror that had followed it went from her eyes. They stayed keen and bright. Her pulses beat fast, and the coursing blood warmed and relaxed every inch of her body.

She did not stop to ask if it were not a monstrous joy that held her. A clear and exalted perception enabled her to dismiss the suggestion as trivial.

She knew that she would weep again when she saw the kind, tender hands folded in death; the face that had never looked save with love upon her, fixed and gray and dead. But she saw beyond that bitter moment a long procession of years to come that would belong to her absolutely. And she opened and spread her arms out to them in welcome.

There would be no one to live for during those coming years; she would live for herself. There would be no powerful will bending her in that blind persistence with which men and women believe they have a right to impose a private will upon a fellow creature. A kind intention or a cruel intention made the act seem no less a crime as she looked upon it in that brief moment of illumination.

And yet she had loved him—sometimes. Often she had not. What did it matter! What could love, the unsolved mystery, count for in face of this possession of self-assertion which she suddenly recognized as the strongest impulse of her being.

"Free! Body and soul free!" she kept whispering.

Josephine was kneeling before the closed door with her lips to the keyhole, imploring for admission. "Louise, open the door! I beg; open the door—you will make yourself ill. What are you doing, Louise? For heaven's sake open the door."

"Go away. I am not making myself ill." No; she was drinking in a very elixir of life through that open window.

Her fancy was running riot along those days ahead of her. Spring days, and summer days, and all sorts of days that would be her own. She breathed a quick prayer that life might be long. It was only yesterday she had thought with a shudder that life might be long.

She arose at length and opened the door to her sister's importunities. There was a feverish triumph in her eyes, and she carried herself unwittingly like a goddess of Victory. She clasped her sister's waist, and together they descended the stairs. Richards stood waiting for them at the bottom.

Some one was opening the front door with a latchkey. It was Brently Mallard who entered, a little travel-stained, composedly carrying his gripsack and umbrella. He had been far from the scene of the accident, and did not even know there had been one. He stood amazed at Josephine's piercing cry; at Richards' quick motion to screen him from the view of his wife.

But Richards was too late.

When the doctors came they said she had died of heart disease—of joy that kills.

—1894

---

CHARLOTTE PERKINS GILMAN ▉ (1860–1935)

*Charlotte Perkins Gilman was born in Hartford, Connecticut, and, on her father's side, was related to Harriet Beecher Stowe, the author of the great antislavery novel* Uncle Tom's Cabin. *Gilman's father abandoned the family when she was an infant, and her early education was spotty, but she eventually studied at the Rhode Island School of Design. Following marriage and the birth of a daughter, she suffered from severe depression, an experience that she recreates in "The Yellow Wallpaper." In a 1913 essay on the story's autobiographical basis, Gilman relates how, following a "rest cure," her doctor, Weir Mitchell, ordered her "never to touch pen, brush, or pencil again." This advice proved almost catastrophic, and Gilman soon discovered that happiness and emotional stability could be found only in "work, the normal life of every human being; work, in which is joy and growth and service, without which one is a pauper and a parasite." In later life, Gilman became an important public spokesperson for various feminist causes. After she discovered that she had inoperable breast cancer, she chose to end her own life.*

# The Yellow Wallpaper

It is very seldom that mere ordinary people like John and myself secure ancestral halls for the summer.

A colonial mansion, a hereditary estate, I would say a haunted house and reach the height of romantic felicity—but that would be asking too much of fate!

Still I will proudly declare that there is something queer about it.

Else, why should it be let so cheaply? And why have stood so long untenanted?

John laughs at me, of course, but one expects that.

John is practical in the extreme. He has no patience with faith, an intense horror of superstition, and he scoffs openly at any talk of things not to be felt and seen and put down in figures.

John is a physician, and *perhaps*—(I would not say it to a living soul, of course, but this is dead paper and a great relief to my mind)—*perhaps* that is one reason I do not get well faster.

You see, he does not believe I am sick! And what can one do?

If a physician of high standing, and one's own husband, assures friends and relatives that there is really nothing the matter with one but temporary nervous depression—a slight hysterical tendency—what is one to do?

My brother is also a physician, and also of high standing, and he says the same thing.

So I take phosphates or phosphites—whichever it is—and tonics, and air and exercise, and journeys, and am absolutely forbidden to "work" until I am well again.

Personally, I disagree with their ideas.

Personally, I believe that congenial work, with excitement and change, would do me good.

But what is one to do?

I did write for a while in spite of them; but it *does* exhaust me a good deal—having to be so sly about it, or else meet with heavy opposition.

I sometimes fancy that in my condition, if I had less opposition and more society and stimulus—but John says the very worst thing I can do is to think about my condition, and I confess it always makes me feel bad.

So I will let it alone and talk about the house.

The most beautiful place! It is quite alone, standing well back from the road, quite three miles from the village. It makes me think of English places that you read about, for there are hedges and walls and gates that lock, and lots of separate little houses for the gardeners and people.

There is a *delicious* garden! I never saw such a garden—large and shady, full of box-bordered paths, and lined with long grape-covered arbors with seats under them.

There were greenhouses, but they are all broken now.

There was some legal trouble, I believe, something about the heirs and coheirs; anyhow, the place has been empty for years.

That spoils my ghostliness, I am afraid, but I don't care—there is something strange about the house—I can feel it.

I even said so to John one moonlight evening, but he said what I felt was a *draught,* and shut the window.

I get unreasonably angry with John sometimes. I'm sure I never used to be so sensitive. I think it is due to this nervous condition.

But John says if I feel so I shall neglect proper self-control; so I take pains to control myself—before him, at least, and that makes me very tired.

I don't like our room a bit. I wanted one downstairs that opened onto the piazza and had roses all over the window, and such pretty old-fashioned chintz hangings! But John would not hear of it.

He said there was only one window and not room for two beds, and no near room for him if he took another.

He is very careful and loving, and hardly lets me stir without special direction.

I have a schedule prescription for each hour in the day; he takes all care from me, and so I feel basely ungrateful not to value it more.

He said he came here solely on my account, that I was to have perfect rest and all the air I could get. "Your exercise depends on your strength, my dear," said he, "and your food somewhat on your appetite; but air you can absorb all the time." So we took the nursery at the top of the house.

It is a big, airy room, the whole floor nearly, with windows that look all ways, and air and sunshine galore. It was a nursery first, and then playroom and gymnasium, I should judge, for the windows are barred for little children, and there are rings and things in the walls.

The paint and paper look as if a boys' school had used it. It is stripped off—the paper—in great patches all around the head of my bed, about as far as I can reach, and in a great place on the other side of the room low down. I never saw a worse paper in my life. One of those sprawling, flamboyant patterns committing every artistic sin.

It is dull enough to confuse the eye in following, pronounced enough constantly to irritate and provoke study, and when you follow the lame uncertain curves for a little distance they suddenly commit suicide— plunge off at outrageous angles, destroy themselves in unheard-of contradictions.

The color is repellent, almost revolting: a smouldering unclean yellow, strangely faded by the slow-turning sunlight. It is a dull yet lurid orange in some places, a sickly sulphur tint in others.

No wonder the children hated it! I should hate it myself if I had to live in this room long.

There comes John, and I must put this away—he hates to have me write a word.

We have been here two weeks, and I haven't felt like writing before, since that first day.

I am sitting by the window now, up in this atrocious nursery, and there is nothing to hinder my writing as much as I please, save lack of strength.

John is away all day, and even some nights when his cases are serious.

I am glad my case is not serious!

But these nervous troubles are dreadfully depressing.

John does not know how much I really suffer. He knows there is no *reason* to suffer, and that satisfies him.

Of course it is only nervousness. It does weight on me so not to do my duty in any way!

I meant to be such a help to John, such a real rest and comfort, and here I am a comparative burden already!

Nobody would believe what an effort it is to do what little I am able— to dress and entertain, and order things.

It is fortunate Mary is so good with the baby. Such a dear baby!

And yet I *cannot* be with him, it makes me so nervous.

I suppose John never was nervous in his life. He laughs at me so about this wallpaper!

At first he meant to repaper the room, but afterward he said that I was letting it get the better of me, and that nothing was worse for a nervous patient than to give way to such fancies.

He said that after the wallpaper was changed it would be the heavy bedstead, and then the barred windows, and then that gate at the head of the stairs, and so on.

"You know the place is doing you good," he said, "and really, dear, I don't care to renovate the house just for a three months' rental."

"Then do let us go downstairs," I said. "There are such pretty rooms there."

Then he took me in his arms and called me a blessed little goose, and said he would go down to the cellar, if I wished, and have it whitewashed into the bargain.

But he is right enough about the beds and windows and things.

It is as airy and comfortable a room as anyone need wish, and, of course, I would not be so silly as to make him uncomfortable just for a whim.

I'm really getting quite fond of the big room, all but that horrid paper.

Out of one window I can see the garden—those mysterious deep-shaded arbors, the riotous old-fashioned flowers, and bushes and gnarly trees.

Out of another I get a lovely view of the bay and a little private wharf belonging to the estate. There is a beautiful shaded lane that runs down there from the house. I always fancy I see people walking in these numerous paths and arbors, but John has cautioned me not to give way to fancy in the least. He says that with my imaginative power and habit of storymaking, a nervous weakness like mine is sure to lead to all manner of excited fancies, and that I ought to use my will and good sense to check the tendency. So I try.

I think sometimes that if I were only well enough to write a little it would relieve the press of ideas and rest me.

But I find I get pretty tired when I try.

It is so discouraging not to have any advice and companionship about my work. When I get really well, John says we will ask Cousin Henry and Julia down for a long visit; but he says he would as soon put fireworks in my pillow-case as to let me have those stimulating people about now.

I wish I could get well faster.

But I must not think about that. This paper looks to me as if it *knew* what a vicious influence it had!

There is a recurrent spot where the pattern lolls like a broken neck and two bulbous eyes stare at you upside down.

I get positively angry with the impertinence of it and the everlastingness. Up and down and sideways they crawl, and those absurd unblinking eyes are everywhere. There is one place where two breadths didn't match, and the eyes go all up and down the line, one a little higher than the other.

I never saw so much expression in an inanimate thing before, and we all know how much expression they have! I used to lie awake as a child and get more entertainment and terror out of blank walls and plain furniture than most children could find in a toy-store.

I remember what a kindly wink the knobs of our big old bureau used to have, and there was one chair that always seemed like a strong friend.

I used to feel that if any of the other things looked too fierce I could always hop into that chair and be safe.

The furniture in this room is no worse than inharmonious, however, for we had to bring it all from downstairs. I suppose when this was used as a playroom they had to take the nursery things out, and no wonder! I never saw such ravages as the children have made here.

The wallpaper, as I said before, is torn off in spots, and it sticketh closer than a brother—they must have had perseverance as well as hatred.

Then the floor is scratched and gouged and splintered, the plaster itself is dug out here and there, and this great heavy bed, which is all we found in the room, looks as if it had been through the wars.

But I don't mind it a bit—only the paper.

There comes John's sister. Such a dear girl as she is, and so careful of me! I must not let her find me writing.

She is a perfect and enthusiastic housekeeper, and hopes for no better profession. I verily believe she thinks it is the writing which made me sick!

But I can write when she is out, and see her a long way off from these windows.

There is one that commands the road, a lovely shaded winding road, and one that just looks off over the country. A lovely country, too, full of great elms and velvet meadows.

This wallpaper has a kind of subpattern in a different shade, a particularly irritating one, for you can only see it in certain lights, and not clearly then.

But in the places where it isn't faded and where the sun is just so—I can see a strange, provoking, formless sort of figure that seems to skulk about behind that silly and conspicuous front design.

There's sister on the stairs!

Well, the Fourth of July is over! The people are all gone, and I am tired out. John thought it might do me good to see a little company, so we just had Mother and Nellie and the children down for a week.

Of course I didn't do a thing. Jennie sees to everything now.

But it tired me all the same.

John says if I don't pick up faster he shall send me to Weir Mitchell[1] in the fall.

But I don't want to go there at all. I had a friend who was in his hands once, and she says he is just like John and my brother, only more so!

Besides, it is such an undertaking to go so far.

I don't feel as if it was worthwhile to turn my hand over for anything, and I'm getting dreadfully fretful and querulous.

[1] **Weir Mitchell** (1829–1914) famed nerve specialist who actually treated the author, Charlotte Perkins Gilman, for nervous prostration with his well-known "rest cure." (The cure was not successful.) Also the author of Diseases of the Nervous System, Especially of Women (1881).

I cry at nothing, and cry most of the time.

Of course I don't when John is here, or anybody else, but when I am alone.

And I am alone a good deal just now. John is kept in town very often by serious cases, and Jennie is good and lets me alone when I want her to.

So I walk a little in the garden or down that lovely lane, sit on the porch under the roses, and lie down up here a good deal.

I'm getting really fond of the room in spite of the wallpaper. Perhaps *because* of the wallpaper.

It dwells in my mind so!

I lie here on this great immovable bed—it is nailed down, I believe—and follow that pattern about by the hour. It is as good as gymnastics, I assure you. I start, we'll say, at the bottom, down in the corner over there where it has not been touched, and I determine for the thousandth time that I *will* follow that pointless pattern to some sort of a conclusion.

I know a little of the principle of design, and I know this thing was not arranged on any laws of radiation,[2] or alternation, or repetition, or symmetry, or anything else that I ever heard of.

It is repeated, of course, by the breadths, but not otherwise.

Looked at in one way, each breadth stands alone; the bloated curves and flourishes—a kind of "debased Romanesque" with *delirium tremens*—go waddling up and down in isolated columns of fatuity.

But, on the other hand, they connect diagonally, and the sprawling outlines run off in great slanting waves of optic horror, like a lot of wallowing seaweeds in full chase.

The whole thing goes horizontally, too, at least it seems so, and I exhaust myself trying to distinguish the order of its going in that direction.

They have used a horizontal breadth for a frieze, and that adds wonderfully to the confusion.

There is one end of the room where it is almost intact, and there, when the crosslights fade and the low sun shines directly upon it, I can almost fancy radiation after all—the interminable grotesque seems to form around a common center and rush off in headlong plunges of equal distraction.

It makes me tired to follow it. I will take a nap, I guess.

I don't know why I should write this.

I don't want to.

I don't feel able.

And I know John would think it absurd. But I *must* say what I feel and think in some way—it is such a relief!

But the effort is getting to be greater than the relief.

Half the time now I am awfully lazy, and lie down ever so much. John says I mustn't lose my strength, and has me take cod liver oil and lots of tonics and things, to say nothing of ale and wines and rare meat.

[2] **laws of radiation** a principle of design in which all elements are arranged in some circular pattern around a center.

Dear John! He loves me very dearly, and hates to have me sick. I tried to have a real earnest reasonable talk with him the other day, and tell him how I wish he would let me go and make a visit to Cousin Henry and Julia.

But he said I wasn't able to go, nor able to stand it after I got there; and I did not make out a very good case for myself, for I was crying before I had finished.

It is getting to be a great effort for me to think straight. Just this nervous weakness, I suppose.

And dear John gathered me up in his arms, and just carried me upstairs and laid me on the bed, and sat by me and read to me till it tired my head.

He said I was his darling and his comfort and all he had, and that I must take care of myself for his sake, and keep well.

He says no one but myself can help me out of it, that I must use my will and self-control and not let any silly fancies run away with me.

There's one comfort—the baby is well and happy, and does not have to occupy this nursery with the horrid wallpaper.

If we had not used it, that blessed child would have! What a fortunate escape! Why, I wouldn't have a child of mine, an impressionable little thing, live in such a room for worlds.

I never thought of it before, but it is lucky that John kept me here after all; I can stand it so much easier than a baby, you see.

Of course I never mention it to them any more—I am too wise—but I keep watch for it all the same.

There are things in the wallpaper that nobody knows about but me, or ever will.

Behind that outside pattern the dim shapes get clearer every day.

It is always the same shape, only very numerous.

And it is like a woman stooping down and creeping about behind that pattern. I don't like it a bit. I wonder—I begin to think—I wish John would take me away from here!

It is so hard to talk with John about my case, because he is so wise, and because he loves me so.

But I tried it last night.

It was moonlight. The moon shines in all around just as the sun does.

I hate to see it sometimes, it creeps so slowly, and always comes in by one window or another.

John was asleep and I hated to waken him, so I kept still and watched the moonlight on that undulating wallpaper till I felt creepy.

The faint figure behind seemed to shake the pattern, just as if she wanted to get out.

I got up softly and went to feel and see if the paper *did* move, and when I came back John was awake.

"What is it, little girl?" he said. "Don't go walking about like that— you'll get cold."

I thought it was a good time to talk, so I told him that I really was not gaining here, and that I wished he would take me away.

"Why, darling!" said he. "Our lease will be up in three weeks, and I can't see how to leave before."

"The repairs are not done at home, and I cannot possibly leave town just now. Of course, if you were in any danger, I could and would, but you really are better, dear, whether you can see it or not. I am a doctor, dear, and I know. You are gaining flesh and color, your appetite is better, I feel really much easier about you."

"I don't weigh a bit more," said I, "nor as much; and my appetite may be better in the evening when you are here but it is worse in the morning when you are away!"

"Bless her little heart!" said he with a big hug. "She shall be as sick as she pleases! But now let's improve the shining hours by going to sleep, and talk about it in the morning!"

"And you won't go away?" I asked gloomily.

"Why, how can I, dear? It is only three weeks more and then we will take a nice little trip for a few days while Jennie is getting the house ready. Really, dear, you are better!"

"Better in body perhaps—" I began, and stopped short, for he sat up straight and looked at me with such a stern, reproachful look that I could not say another word.

"My darling," said he, "I beg you, for my sake and for our child's sake, as well as for your own, that you will never for one instant let that idea enter your mind! There is nothing so dangerous, so fascinating, to a temperament like yours. It is a false and foolish fancy. Can you trust me as a physician when I tell you so?"

So of course I said no more on that score, and we went to sleep before long. He thought I was asleep first, but I wasn't, and lay there for hours trying to decide whether that front pattern and the back pattern really did move together or separately.

On a pattern like this, by daylight, there is a lack of sequence, a defiance of law, that is a constant irritant to a normal mind.

The color is hideous enough, and unreliable enough, and infuriating enough, but the pattern is torturing.

You think you have mastered it, but just as you get well under way in following, it turns a back-somersault and there you are. It slaps you in the face, knocks you down, and tramples upon you. It is like a bad dream.

The outside pattern is a florid arabesque,[3] reminding one of a fungus. If you can imagine a toadstool in joints, an interminable string of toadstools, budding and sprouting in endless convolutions—why, that is something like it.

---

[3] **arabesque** a type of ornamental style (Arabic in origin) that uses flowers, foliage, fruit, or other figures to create an intricate pattern of interlocking shapes and lines.

That is, sometimes!

There is one marked peculiarity about this paper, a thing nobody seems to notice but myself, and that is that it changes as the light changes.

When the sun shoots in through the east window—I always watch for that first long, straight ray—it changes so quickly that I never can quite believe it.

That is why I watch it always.

By moonlight—the moon shines in all night when there is a moon—I wouldn't know it was the same paper.

At night in any kind of light, in twilight, candlelight, lamplight, and worst of all by moonlight, it becomes bars! The outside pattern, I mean, and the woman behind it is as plain as can be.

I didn't realize for a long time what the thing was that showed behind, that dim subpattern, but now I am quite sure it is a woman.

By daylight she is subdued, quiet. I fancy it is the pattern that keeps her so still. It is so puzzling. It keeps me quiet by the hour.

I lie down ever so much now. John says it is good for me, and to sleep all I can.

Indeed he started the habit by making me lie down for an hour after each meal.

It is a very bad habit, I am convinced, for you see, I don't sleep.

And that cultivates deceit, for I don't tell them I'm awake—oh, no!

The fact is I am getting a little afraid of John.

He seems very queer sometimes, and even Jennie has an inexplicable look.

It strikes me occasionally, just as a scientific hypothesis, that perhaps it is the paper!

I have watched John when he did not know I was looking, and come into the room suddenly on the most innocent excuses, and I've caught him several times *looking at the paper!* And Jennie too. I caught Jennie with her hand on it once.

She didn't know I was in the room, and when I asked her in a quiet, a very quiet voice, with the most restrained manner possible, what she was doing with the paper, she turned around as if she had been caught stealing, and looked quite angry—asked me why I should frighten her so!

Then she said that the paper stained everything it touched, that she had found yellow smooches[4] on all my clothes and John's and she wished we would be more careful!

Did not that sound innocent? But I know she was studying that pattern, and I am determined that nobody shall find it out but myself!

Life is very much more exciting now than it used to be. You see, I have something more to expect, to look forward to, to watch. I really do eat better, and am more quiet than I was.

---

[4] **smooches** smudges or smears.

John is so pleased to see me improve! He laughed a little the other day, and said I seemed to be flourishing in spite of my wallpaper.

I turned it off with a laugh. I had no intention of telling him it was *because* of the wallpaper—he would make fun of me. He might even want to take me away.

I don't want to leave now until I have found it out. There is a week more, and I think that will be enough.

I'm feeling so much better!

I don't sleep much at night, for it is so interesting to watch developments; but I sleep a good deal during the daytime.

In the daytime it is tiresome and perplexing.

There are always new shoots on the fungus, and new shades of yellow all over it. I cannot keep count of them, though I have tried conscientiously.

It is the strangest yellow, that wallpaper! It makes me think of all the yellow things I ever saw—not beautiful ones like buttercups, but old, foul, bad yellow things.

But there is something else about that paper—the smell! I noticed it the moment we came into the room, but with so much air and sun it was not bad. Now we have had a week of fog and rain, and whether the windows are open or not, the smell is here.

It creeps all over the house.

I find it hovering in the dining-room, skulking in the parlor, hiding in the hall, lying in wait for me on the stairs.

It gets into my hair.

Even when I go to ride, if I turn my head suddenly and surprise it—there is that smell!

Such a peculiar odor, too! I have spent hours in trying to analyze it, to find what it smelled like.

It is not bad—at first—and very gentle, but quite the subtlest, most enduring odor I ever met.

In this damp weather it is awful. I wake up in the night and find it hanging over me.

It used to disturb me at first. I thought seriously of burning the house—to reach the smell.

But now I am used to it. The only thing I can think of that it is like is the *color* of the paper! A yellow smell.

There is a very funny mark on this wall, low down, near the mopboard. A streak that runs round the room. It goes behind every piece of furniture, except the bed, a long, straight, even *smooch*, as if it had been rubbed over and over.

I wonder how it was done and who did it, and what they did it for. Round and round and round—round and round and round—it makes me dizzy!

I really have discovered something at last.

Through watching so much at night, when it changes so, I have finally found out.

The front pattern *does* move—and no wonder! The woman behind shakes it!

Sometimes I think there are a great many women behind, and sometimes only one, and she crawls around fast, and her crawling shakes it all over.

Then in the very bright spots she keeps still, and in the very shady spots she just takes hold of the bars and shakes them hard.

And she is all the time trying to climb through. But nobody could climb through that pattern—it strangles so; I think that is why it has so many heads.

They get through and then the pattern strangles them off and turns them upside down, and makes their eyes white!

If those heads were covered or taken off it would not be half so bad.

I think that woman gets out in the daytime!

And I'll tell you why—privately—I've seen her!

I can see her out of every one of my windows!

It is the same woman, I know, for she is always creeping, and most women do not creep by daylight.

I see her in that long shaded lane, creeping up and down. I see her in those dark grape arbors, creeping all round the garden.

I see her on that long road under the trees, creeping along, and when a carriage comes she hides under the blackberry vines.

I don't blame her a bit. It must be very humiliating to be caught creeping by daylight!

I always lock the door when I creep by daylight. I can't do it at night, for I know John would suspect something at once.

And John is so queer now that I don't want to irritate him. I wish he would take another room! Besides, I don't want anybody to get that woman out at night but myself.

I often wonder if I could see her out of all the windows at once.

But, turn as fast as I can, I can only see out of one at one time.

And though I always see her, she *may* be able to creep faster than I can turn! I have watched her sometimes away off in the open country, creeping as fast as a cloud shadow in a wind.

If only that top pattern could be gotten off from the under one! I mean to try it, little by little.

I have found out another funny thing, but I shan't tell it this time! It does not do to trust people too much.

There are only two more days to get this paper off, and I believe John is beginning to notice. I don't like the look in his eyes.

And I heard him ask Jennie a lot of professional questions about me. She had a very good report to give.

She said I slept a good deal in the daytime.

John knows I don't sleep very well at night, for all I'm so quiet!

He asked me all sorts of questions too, and pretended to be very loving and kind.

As if I couldn't see through him!

Still, I don't wonder he acts so, sleeping under this paper for three months.

It only interests me, but I feel sure John and Jennie are affected by it.

Hurrah! This is the last day, but it is enough. John is to stay in town over night, and won't be out until this evening.

Jennie wanted to sleep with me—the sly thing; but I told her I should undoubtedly rest better for a night all alone.

That was clever, for really I wasn't alone a bit! As soon as it was moonlight and that poor thing began to crawl and shake the pattern, I got up and ran to help her.

I pulled and she shook, I shook and she pulled, and before morning we had peeled off yards of that paper.

A strip about as high as my head and half around the room.

And then when the sun came and that awful pattern began to laugh at me, I declared I would finish it today!

We go away tomorrow, and they are moving all my furniture down again to leave things as they were before.

Jennie looked at the wall in amazement, but I told her merrily that I did it out of pure spite at the vicious thing.

She laughed and said she wouldn't mind doing it herself, but I must not get tired.

How she betrayed herself that time!

But I am here, and no person touches this paper but Me—not *alive!*

She tried to get me out of the room—it was too patent! But I said it was so quiet and empty and clean now that I believed I would lie down again and sleep all I could, and not to wake me even for dinner—I would call when I woke.

So now she is gone, and the servants are gone, and the things are gone, and there is nothing left but that great bedstead nailed down, with the canvas mattress we found on it.

We shall sleep downstairs tonight, and take the boat home tomorrow.

I quite enjoy the room, now it is bare again.

How those children did tear about here!

This bedstead is fairly gnawed!

But I must get to work.

I have locked the door and thrown the key down into the front path.

I don't want to go out, and I don't want to have anybody come in, till John comes.

I want to astonish him.

I've got a rope up here that even Jennie did not find. If that woman does get out, and tries to get away, I can tie her!

But I forgot I could not reach far without anything to stand on!

This bed will *not* move!

I tried to lift and push it until I was lame, and then I got so angry I bit off a little piece at one corner—but it hurt my teeth.

Then I peeled off all the paper I could reach standing on the floor. It sticks horribly and the pattern just enjoys it! All those strangled heads and bulbous eyes and waddling fungus growths just shriek with derision!

I am getting angry enough to do something desperate. To jump out of the window would be admirable exercise, but the bars are too strong even to try.

Besides I wouldn't do it. Of course not. I know well enough that a step like that is improper and might be misconstrued.

I don't like to *look* out of the windows even—there are so many of those creeping women, and they creep so fast.

I wonder if they all come out of that wallpaper as I did!

But I am securely fastened now by my well-hidden rope—you don't get *me* out in the road there!

I suppose I shall have to get back behind the pattern when it comes night, and that is hard!

It is so pleasant to be out in this great room and creep around as I please!

I don't want to go outside. I won't, even if Jennie asks me to:

For outside you have to creep on the ground, and everything is green instead of yellow.

But here I can creep smoothly on the floor, and my shoulder just fits in that long smooch around the wall, so I cannot lose my way.

Why, there's John at the door!

It is no use, young man, you can't open it!

How he does call and pound!

Now he's crying to Jennie for an axe.

It would be a shame to break down that beautiful door!

"John, dear!" said I in the gentlest voice. "The key is down by the front steps, under a plantain leaf!"

That silenced him for a few moments.

Then he said, very quietly indeed, "Open the door, my darling!"

"I can't," said I. "The key is down by the front door under a plantain leaf!" And then I said it again, several times, very gently and slowly, and said it so often that he had to go and see, and he got it of course, and came in. He stopped short by the door.

"What is the matter?" he cried. "For God's sake, what are you doing!"

I kept on creeping just the same, but I looked at him over my shoulder.

"I've got out at last," said I, "in spite of you and Jane.[5] And I've pulled off most of the paper, so you can't put me back!"

Now why should that man have fainted? But he did, and right across my path by the wall, so that I had to creep over him every time!

—1892

---

[5] **Jane** presumably the given name of her sister-in-law, Jennie. Some critics have argued that Jane may be the narrator's own name.

---

**WILLA CATHER ▩ (1873–1947)**

*Willa Cather was born in rural Virginia but moved in childhood to the Nebraska farmlands. After graduating from the University of Nebraska, she lived for a time in Pittsburgh (the hometown of the title character in "Paul's Case"), where she moved so that she, like Paul, could attend the theater and concerts. After some years as a drama critic for the Pittsburgh* Daily Leader *and a brief term as a high school English teacher, she moved to New York, where she eventually became managing editor of* McClure's Magazine, *a position she held from 1906 to 1912. Her novels about the settling of the Nebraska farmlands,* O Pioneers! *(1913) and* My Ántonia *(1918), proved successful, and for the rest of her life, Cather devoted her full energies to writing fiction. In her later years, she ranged? further for her subjects—New Mexico for the setting of* Death Comes to the Archbishop *(1927) and Quebec for* Shadows on the Rock *(1931). "Paul's Case," one of the stories that helped her obtain a position with* McClure's, *casts an almost clinical eye on heredity and environment as influences on the protagonist's personality. This deterministic view of character and Paul's desperate attempt to escape the dreary trap of his hometown reflect important themes of naturalism, a literary movement with which Cather would later express dissatisfaction but that dominated much fiction written near the turn of the century.*

# Paul's Case[1]

It was Paul's afternoon to appear before the faculty of the Pittsburgh High School to account for his various misdemeanors. He had been suspended a week ago, and his father had called at the Principal's office and confessed his perplexity about his son. Paul entered the faculty room suave and smiling. His clothes were a trifle outgrown and the tan velvet on the collar of his open overcoat was frayed and worn; but for all that there was something of the dandy about him, and he wore an opal pin in his neatly knotted black four-in-hand, and a red carnation in his buttonhole. This latter adornment the faculty somehow felt was not properly significant of the contrite spirit befitting a boy under the ban of suspension.

---

[1] "A Study in Temperament" (Cather's subtitle).

Paul was tall for his age and very thin, with high, cramped shoulders and a narrow chest. His eyes were remarkable for a certain hysterical brilliancy and he continually used them in a conscious, theatrical sort of way, peculiarly offensive in a boy. The pupils were abnormally large, as though he were addicted to belladonna, but there was a glassy glitter about them which that drug does not produce.

When questioned by the Principal as to why he was there, Paul stated, politely enough, that he wanted to come back to school. This was a lie, but Paul was quite accustomed to lying; found it, indeed, indispensable for overcoming friction. His teachers were asked to state their respective charges against him, which they did with such a rancor and aggrievedness as evinced that this was not a usual case. Disorder and impertinence were among the offenses named, yet each of his instructors felt that it was scarcely possible to put into words the real cause of the trouble, which lay in a sort of hysterically defiant manner of the boy's; in the contempt which they all knew he felt for them, and which he seemingly made not the least effort to conceal. Once, when he had been making a synopsis of a paragraph at the blackboard, his English teacher had stepped to his side and attempted to guide his hand. Paul had started back with a shudder and thrust his hands violently behind him. The astonished woman could scarcely have been more hurt and embarrassed had he struck at her. The insult was so involuntary and definitely personal as to be unforgettable. In one way and another, he had made all his teachers, men and women alike, conscious of the same feeling of physical aversion. In one class he habitually sat with his hand shading his eyes; in another he always looked out of the window during the recitation; in another he made a running commentary on the lecture, with humorous intention.

His teachers felt this afternoon that his whole attitude was symbolized by his shrug and his flippantly red carnation flower, and they fell upon him without mercy, his English teacher leading the pack. He stood through it smiling, his pale lips parted over his white teeth. (His lips were continually twitching, and he had a habit of raising his eyebrows that was contemptuous and irritating to the last degree.) Older boys than Paul had broken down and shed tears under that baptism of fire, but his set smile did not once desert him, and his only sign of discomfort was the nervous trembling of the fingers that toyed with the buttons of his overcoat, and an occasional jerking of the other hand that held his hat. Paul was always smiling, always glancing about him, seeming to feel that people might be watching him and trying to detect something. This conscious expression, since it was as far as possible from boyish mirthfulness, was usually attributed to insolence or "smartness."

As the inquisition proceeded, one of his instructors repeated an impertinent remark of the boy's, and the Principal asked him whether he thought that a courteous speech to have made a woman. Paul shrugged his shoulders slightly and his eyebrows twitched.

"I don't know," he replied. "I didn't mean to be polite or impolite, either. I guess it's a sort of way I have of saying things regardless."

The Principal, who was a sympathetic man, asked him whether he didn't think that a way it would be well to get rid of. Paul grinned and said he guessed so. When he was told that he could go, he bowed gracefully and went out. His bow was but a repetition of the scandalous red carnation.

His teachers were in despair, and his drawing master voiced the feeling of them all when he declared there was something about the boy which none of them understood. He added: "I don't really believe that smile of his comes altogether from insolence; there's something sort of haunted about it. The boy is not strong, for one thing. I happen to know that he was born in Colorado, only a few months before his mother died out there of a long illness. There is something wrong about the fellow."

The drawing master had come to realize that, in looking at Paul, one saw only his white teeth and the forced animation of his eyes. One warm afternoon the boy had gone to sleep at his drawing-board, and his master had noted with amazement what a white, blue-veined face it was; drawn and wrinkled like an old man's about the eyes, the lips twitching even in his sleep, and stiff with a nervous tension that drew them back from his teeth.

His teachers left the building dissatisfied and unhappy; humiliated to have felt so vindictive toward a mere boy, to have uttered this feeling in cutting terms, and to have set each other on, as it were, in the gruesome game of intemperate reproach. Some of them remembered having seen a miserable street cat set at bay by a ring of tormentors.

As for Paul, he ran down the hill whistling the Soldiers' Chorus from *Faust* looking wildly behind him now and then to see whether some of his teachers were not there to writhe under his light-heartedness. As it was now late in the afternoon and Paul was on duty that evening as usher at Carnegie Hall, he decided that he would not go home to supper. When he reached the concert hall the doors were not yet open and, as it was chilly outside, he decided to go up into the picture gallery—always deserted at this hour—where there were some of Raffaelli's gay studies of Paris streets and an airy blue Venetian scene or two that always exhilarated him. He was delighted to find no one in the gallery but the old guard, who sat in one corner, a newspaper on his knee, a black patch over one eye and the other closed. Paul possessed himself of the place and walked confidently up and down, whistling under his breath. After a while he sat down before a blue Rico and lost himself. When he bethought him to look at his watch, it was after seven o'clock, and he rose with a start and ran downstairs, making a face at Augustus, peering out from the cast-room, and an evil gesture at the Venus of Milo as he passed her on the stairway.

When Paul reached the ushers' dressing-room half-a-dozen boys were there already, and he began excitedly to tumble into his uniform. It was one of the few that at all approached fitting, and Paul thought it very becoming—though he knew that the tight, straight coat accentuated his narrow chest, about which he was exceedingly sensitive. He was always considerably excited while he dressed, twanging all over to the tuning of the strings and the preliminary flourishes of the horns in the music-room; but tonight he seemed quite beside himself, and he teased and plagued the boys until, telling him that he was crazy, they put him down on the floor and sat on him.

Somewhat calmed by his suppression, Paul dashed out to the front of the house to seat the early comers. He was a model usher; gracious and smiling he ran up and down the aisles; nothing was too much trouble for him; he carried messages and brought programmes as though it were his greatest pleasure in life, and all the people in his section thought him a charming boy, feeling that he remembered and admired them. As the house filled, he grew more and more vivacious and animated, and the color came to his cheeks and lips. It was very much as though this were a great reception and Paul were the host. Just as the musicians came out to take their places, his English teacher arrived with checks for the seats which a prominent manu-facturer had taken for the season. She betrayed some embarrassment when she handed Paul the tickets, and a *hauteur* which subsequently made her feel very foolish. Paul was startled for a moment, and had the feeling of wanting to put her out; what business had she here among all these fine people and gay colors? He looked her over and decided that she was not appropriately dressed and must be a fool to sit downstairs in such togs. The tickets had probably been sent her out of kindness, he reflected as he put down a seat for her, and she had about as much right to sit there as he had.

When the symphony began Paul sank into one of the rear seats with a long sigh of relief, and lost himself as he had done before the Rico. It was not that symphonies, as such, meant anything in particular to Paul, but the first sigh of the instruments seemed to free some hilarious and potent spirit within him; something that struggled there like the Genius in the bottle found by the Arab fisherman. He felt a sudden zest of life; the lights danced before his eyes and the concert hall blazed into unimaginable splendor. When the soprano soloist came on, Paul forgot even the nastiness of his teacher's being there and gave himself up to the peculiar stimulus such personages always had for him. The soloist chanced to be a German woman, by no means in her first youth, and the mother of many children; but she wore an elaborate gown and a tiara, and above all she had that indefinable air of achievement, that world-shine upon her, which, in Paul's eyes, made her a veritable queen of Romance.

After a concert was over Paul was always irritable and wretched until he got to sleep, and tonight he was even more than usually restless. He had the feeling of not being able to let down, of its being impossible to give up this delicious excitement which was the only thing that could be called

living at all. During the last number he withdrew and, after hastily changing his clothes in the dressing-room, slipped out to the side door where the
soprano's carriage stood. Here he began pacing rapidly up and down the
walk, waiting to see her come out.

Over yonder the Schenley, in its vacant stretch, loomed big and
square through the fine rain, the windows of its twelve stories glowing
like those of a lighted cardboard house under a Christmas tree. All the
actors and singers of the better class stayed there when they were in the
city, and a number of the big manufacturers of the place lived there in
the winter. Paul had often hung about the hotel, watching the people
go in and out, longing to enter and leave school-masters and dull care
behind him forever.

At last the singer came out, accompanied by the conductor, who helped
her into her carriage and closed the door with a cordial *auf wiedersehen*[2]
which set Paul to wondering whether she were not an old sweetheart of
his. Paul followed the carriage over to the hotel, walking so rapidly as not
to be far from the entrance when the singer alighted and disappeared
behind the swinging glass doors that were opened by a negro in a tall hat
and a long coat. In the moment that the door was ajar it seemed to Paul
that he, too, entered. He seemed to feel himself go after her up the steps,
into the warm, lighted building, into an exotic, a tropical world of shiny,
glistening surfaces and basking ease. He reflected upon the mysterious
dishes that were brought into the dining-room, the green bottles in buckets of ice, as he had seen them in the supper party pictures of the *Sunday
World* supplement. A quick gust of wind brought the rain down with sudden vehemence, and Paul was startled to find that he was still outside in
the slush of the gravel driveway; that his boots were letting in the water
and his scanty overcoat was clinging wet about him; that the lights in
front of the concert hall were out, and that the rain was driving in sheets
between him and the orange glow of the windows above him. There it was,
what he wanted—tangibly before him, like the fairy world of a Christmas
pantomime, but mocking spirits stood guard at the doors, and, as the rain
beat in his face, Paul wondered whether he were destined always to shiver
in the black night outside, looking up at it.

He turned and walked reluctantly toward the car tracks. The end had
to come sometime; his father in his night-clothes at the top of the stairs,
explanations that did not explain, hastily improvised fictions that were
forever tripping him up, his upstairs room and its horrible yellow wallpaper, the creaking bureau with the greasy plush collar-box, and over his
painted wooden bed the pictures of George Washington and John Calvin,
and the framed motto, "Feed my Lambs," which had been worked in red
worsted by his mother.

---

[2] **auf wiedersehen** good-bye.

Half an hour later, Paul alighted from his car and went slowly down one of the side streets off the main thoroughfare. It was a highly respectable street, where all the houses were exactly alike, and where businessmen of moderate means begot and reared large families of children, all of whom went to Sabbath-school and learned the shorter catechism, and were interested in arithmetic; all of whom were as exactly alike as their homes, and of a piece with the monotony in which they lived. Paul never went up Cordelia Street without a shudder of loathing. His home was next to the house of the Cumberland[3] minister. He approached it tonight with the nerveless sense of defeat, the hopeless feeling of sinking back forever into ugliness and commonness that he had always had when he came home. The moment he turned into Cordelia Street he felt the waters close above his head. After each of these orgies of living, he experienced all the physical depression which follows a debauch; the loathing of respectable beds, of common food, of a house penetrated by kitchen odors; a shuddering repulsion for the flavorless, colorless mass of everyday existence; a morbid desire for cool things and soft lights and fresh flowers.

The nearer he approached the house, the more absolutely unequal Paul felt to the sight of it all; his ugly sleeping chamber; the cold bathroom with the grimy zinc tub, the cracked mirror, the dripping spigots; his father, at the top of the stairs, his hairy legs sticking out from his night-shirt, his feet thrust into carpet slippers. He was so much later than usual that there would certainly be inquiries and reproaches. Paul stopped short before the door. He felt that he could not be accosted by his father tonight; that he could not toss again on that miserable bed. He would not go in. He would tell his father that he had no car fare, and it was raining so hard he had gone home with one of the boys and stayed all night.

Meanwhile, he was wet and cold. He went around to the back of the house and tried one of the basement windows, found it open, raised it cautiously, and scrambled down the cellar wall to the floor. There he stood, holding his breath, terrified by the noise he had made, but the floor above him was silent, and there was no creak on the stairs. He found a soap-box, and carried it over to the soft ring of light that streamed from the furnace door, and sat down. He was horribly afraid of rats, so he did not try to sleep, but sat looking distrustfully at the dark, still terrified lest he might have awakened his father. In such reactions, after one of the experiences which made days and nights out of the dreary blanks of the calendar, when his senses were deadened, Paul's head was always singularly clear. Suppose his father had heard him getting in at the window and had come down and shot him for a burglar? Then, again, suppose his father had come down, pistol in hand, and he had cried out in time to save himself, and his father had been horrified to think how nearly he had killed him? Then, again,

---

[3] **Cumberland** an offshoot of the Presbyterian Church.

suppose a day should come when his father would remember that night, and wish there had been no warning cry to stay his hand? With this last supposition Paul entertained himself until daybreak.

The following Sunday was fine; the sodden November chill was broken by the last flash of autumnal summer. In the morning Paul had to go to church and Sabbath-school, as always. On seasonable Sunday afternoons the burghers of Cordelia Street always sat out on their front "stoops," and talked to their neighbors on the next stoop, or called to those across the street in neighborly fashion. The men usually sat on gay cushions placed upon the steps that led down to the sidewalk, while the women, in their Sunday "waists,"[4] sat in rockers on the cramped porches, pretending to be greatly at their ease. The children played in the streets; there were so many of them that the place resembled the recreation grounds of a kindergarten. The men on the steps—all in their shirt sleeves, their vests unbuttoned—sat with their legs well apart, their stomachs comfortably protruding, and talked of the prices of things, or told anecdotes of the sagacity of their various chiefs and overlords. They occasionally looked over the multitude of squabbling children, listened affectionately to their high-pitched, nasal voices, smiling to see their own proclivities reproduced in their offspring, and interspersed their legends of the iron kings with remarks about their sons' progress at school, their grades in arithmetic, and the amounts they had saved in their toy banks.

On this last Sunday of November, Paul sat all the afternoon on the lowest step of his "stoop," staring into the street, while his sisters, in their rockers, were talking to the minister's daughters next door about how many shirt-waists they had made in the last week, and how many waffles some one had eaten at the last church supper. When the weather was warm, and his father was in a particularly jovial frame of mind, the girls made lemonade, which was always brought out in a red-glass pitcher, ornamented with forget-me-nots in blue enamel. This the girls thought very fine, and the neighbors always joked about the suspicious color of the pitcher.

Today Paul's father sat on the top step, talking to a young man who shifted a restless baby from knee to knee. He happened to be the young man who was daily held up to Paul as a model, and after whom it was his father's dearest hope that he would pattern. This young man was of a ruddy complexion, with a compressed, red mouth, and faded, near-sighted eyes, over which he wore thick spectacles, with gold bows that curved about his ears. He was clerk to one of the magnates of a great steel corporation, and was looked upon in Cordelia Street as a young man with a future. There was a story that, some five years ago—he was now barely twenty-six—he had been a trifle dissipated but in order to curb his appetites and save the loss of time and strength that a sowing of wild oats might have entailed, he had taken his chief's advice, oft reiterated to his employees, and at

---

[4] **"waists,"** shirtwaist dresses, fashionable at the time.

twenty-one had married the first woman whom he could persuade to share his fortunes. She happened to be an angular schoolmistress, much older than he, who also wore thick glasses, and who had now borne him four children, all near-sighted, like herself.

The young man was relating how his chief, now cruising in the Mediterranean, kept in touch with all the details of the business, arranging his office hours on his yacht just as though he were at home, and "knocking off work enough to keep two stenographers busy." His father told, in turn, the plan his corporation was considering, of putting in an electric railway plant at Cairo. Paul snapped his teeth; he had an awful apprehension that they might spoil it all before he got there. Yet he rather liked to hear these legends of the iron kings, that were told and retold on Sundays and holidays; these stories of palaces in Venice, yachts on the Mediterranean, and high play at Monte Carlo appealed to his fancy, and he was interested in the triumphs of these cash boys who had become famous, though he had no mind for the cash-boy stage.

After supper was over, and he had helped to dry the dishes, Paul nervously asked his father whether he could go to George's to get some help in his geometry, and still more nervously asked for car fare. This latter request he had to repeat, as his father, on principle, did not like to hear requests for money, whether much or little. He asked Paul whether he could not go to some boy who lived nearer, and told him that he ought not to leave his school work until Sunday; but he gave him the dime. He was not a poor man, but he had a worthy ambition to come up in the world. His only reason for allowing Paul to usher was, that he thought a boy ought to be earning a little.

Paul bounded upstairs, scrubbed the greasy odor of the dish-water from his hands with the ill-smelling soap he hated, and then shook over his fingers a few drops of violet water from the bottle he kept hidden in his drawer. He left the house with his geometry conspicuously under his arm, and the moment he got out of Cordelia Street and boarded a downtown car, he shook off the lethargy of two deadening days, and began to live again.

The leading juvenile of the permanent stock company which played at one of the downtown theatres was an acquaintance of Paul's, and the boy had been invited to drop in at the Sunday-night rehearsals whenever he could. For more than a year Paul had spent every available moment loitering about Charley Edwards's dressing-room. He had won a place among Edwards's following not only because the young actor, who could not afford to employ a dresser, often found him useful, but because he recognized in Paul something akin to what churchmen term "vocation."

It was at the theatre and at Carnegie Hall that Paul really lived; the rest was but a sleep and a forgetting. This was Paul's fairy tale, and it had for him all the allurement of a secret love. The moment he inhaled the gassy, painty, dusty odor behind the scenes, he breathed like a prisoner set free, and felt within him the possibility of doing or saying splendid, brilliant, poetic things. The moment the cracked orchestra beat out the overture from *Martha,* or jerked at the serenade from *Rigoletto,* all stupid and ugly things slid from him, and his senses were deliciously, yet delicately fired.

Perhaps it was because, in Paul's world, the natural nearly always wore the guise of ugliness, that a certain element of artificiality seemed to him necessary in beauty. Perhaps it was because his experience of life elsewhere was so full of Sabbath-school picnics, petty economies, wholesome advice as to how to succeed in life, and the unescapable odors of cooking, that he found this existence so alluring, these smartly-clad men and women so attractive, that he was so moved by these starry apple orchards that bloomed perennially under the limelight.

It would be difficult to put it strongly enough how convincingly the stage entrance of that theatre was for Paul the actual portal of Romance. Certainly none of the company ever suspected it, least of all Charley Edwards. It was very like the old stories that used to float about London of fabulously rich Jews, who had subterranean halls there, with palms, and fountains, and soft lamps and richly apparelled women who never saw the disenchanting light of London day. So, in the midst of that smoke-palled city, enamored of figures and grimy toil, Paul had his secret temple, his wishing carpet, his bit of blue-and-white Mediterranean shore bathed in perpetual sunshine.

Several of Paul's teachers had a theory that his imagination had been perverted by garish fiction, but the truth was that he scarcely ever read at all. The books at home were not such as would either tempt or corrupt a youthful mind, and as for reading the novels that some of his friends urged upon him—well, he got what he wanted much more quickly from music; any sort of music, from an orchestra to a barrel organ. He needed only the spark, the indescribable thrill that made his imagination master of his senses, and he could make plots and pictures enough of his own. It was equally true that he was not stage struck—not, at any rate, in the usual acceptation of that expression. He had no desire to become an actor, any more than he had to become a musician. He felt no necessity to do any of these things; what he wanted was to see, to be in the atmosphere, float on the wave of it, to be carried out, blue league after blue league, away from everything.

After a night behind the scenes, Paul found the school room more than ever repulsive; the bare floors and naked walls; the prosy men who never wore frock coats, or violets in their button-holes; the women with their dull gowns, shrill voices, and pitiful seriousness about prepositions that govern the dative. He could not bear to have the other pupils think, for a moment, that he took these people seriously; he must convey to them that he considered it all trivial, and was there only by way of a jest, anyway. He had autographed pictures of all the members of the stock company which he showed his classmates, telling them the most incredible stories of his familiarity with these people, of his acquaintance with the soloists who came to Carnegie Hall, his suppers with them and the flowers he sent them. When these stories lost their effect, and his audience grew listless, he became desperate and would bid all the boys goodbye, announcing that he was going to travel for a while; going to Naples, to Venice, to Egypt. Then, next Monday, he would slip back, conscious and nervously smiling; his sister was ill, and he should have to defer his voyage until spring.

Matters went steadily worse with Paul at school. In the itch to let his instructors know how heartily he despised them and their homilies, and how thoroughly he was appreciated elsewhere, he mentioned once or twice that he had no time to fool with theorems; adding—with a twitch of the eyebrows and a touch of that nervous bravado which so perplexed them— that he was helping the people down at the stock company; they were old friends of his.

The upshot of the matter was that the Principal went to Paul's father, and Paul was taken out of school and put to work. The manager at Carnegie Hall was told to get another usher in his stead; the doorkeeper at the theatre was warned not to admit him to the house; and Charley Edwards remorsefully promised the boy's father not to see him again.

The members of the stock company were vastly amused when some of Paul's stories reached them—especially the women. They were hardworking women, most of them supporting indigent husbands or brothers, and they laughed rather bitterly at having stirred the boy to such fervid and florid inventions. They agreed with the faculty and with his father that Paul's was a bad case.

The east-bound train was ploughing through a January snowstorm; the dull dawn was beginning to show grey when the engine whistled a mile out of Newark. Paul started up from the seat where he had lain curled in uneasy slumber, rubbed the breath-misted window glass with his hand, and peered out. The snow was whirling in curling eddies above the white bottom lands, and the drifts lay already deep in the fields and along the fences, while here and there the long dead grass and dried weed stalks protruded black above it. Lights shone from the scattered houses, and a gang of laborers who stood beside the track waved their lanterns.

Paul had slept very little, and he felt grimy and uncomfortable. He had made the all-night journey in a day coach, partly because he was ashamed, dressed as he was, to go into a Pullman, and partly because he was afraid of being seen there by some Pittsburgh businessman, who might have noticed him in Denny & Carson's office. When the whistle awoke him, he clutched quickly at his breast pocket, glancing about him with an uncertain smile. But the little, clay-bespattered Italians were still sleeping, the slatternly women across the aisle were in open-mouthed oblivion, and even the crumby, crying babies were for the nonce stilled. Paul settled back to struggle with his impatience as best as he could.

When he arrived at the Jersey City station, he hurried through his breakfast manifestly ill at ease and keeping a sharp eye about him. After he reached the Twenty-third Street station, he consulted a cabman, and had himself driven to a men's furnishing establishment that was just opening for the day. He spent upward of two hours there, buying with endless reconsidering and great care. His new street suit he put on in the fitting-room; the frock coat and dress clothes he had bundled into the cab with his linen. Then he drove to a hatter's and a shoe house. His next errand was at Tiffany's, where he selected his silver and a new scarf-pin. He would not wait to have his silver marked, he said. Lastly, he stopped at a trunk shop on Broadway, and had his purchases packed into various traveling bags.

It was a little after one o'clock when he drove up to the Waldorf, and after settling with the cabman, went into the office. He registered from Washington; said his mother and father had been abroad, and that he had come down to await the arrival of their steamer. He told his story plausibly and had no trouble, since he volunteered to pay for them in advance, in engaging his rooms; a sleeping-room, sitting-room and bath.

Not once, but a hundred times Paul had planned this entry into New York. He had gone over every detail of it with Charley Edwards, and in his scrap book at home there were pages of description about New York hotels, cut from the Sunday papers. When he was shown to his sitting-room on the eighth floor, he saw at a glance that everything was as it should be; there was but one detail in his mental picture that the place did not realize, so he rang for the bell boy and sent him down for flowers. He moved about nervously until the boy returned, putting away his new linen and fingering it delightedly as he did so. When the flowers came, he put them hastily into water, and then tumbled into a hot bath. Presently he came out of his white bathroom, resplendent in his new silk underwear, and playing with the tassels of his red robe. The snow was whirling so fiercely outside his windows that he could scarcely see across the street, but within the air was deliciously soft and fragrant. He put the violets and jonquils on the taboret beside the couch, and threw himself down, with a long sigh, covering himself with a Roman blanket. He was thoroughly tired; he had been in such haste, he had stood up to such a strain, covered so much ground in the last twenty-four hours, that he wanted to think how it had all come about. Lulled by the sound of the wind, the warm air, and the cool fragrance of the flowers, he sank into deep, drowsy retrospection.

It had been wonderfully simple; when they had shut him out of the theatre and concert hall, when they had taken away his bone, the whole thing was virtually determined. The rest was a mere matter of opportunity. The only thing that at all surprised him was his own courage—for he realized well enough that he had always been tormented by fear, a sort of apprehensive dread that, of late years, as the meshes of the lies he had told closed about him, had been pulling the muscles of his body tighter and tighter. Until now, he could not remember the time when he had not been dreading something. Even when he was a little boy, it was always there—behind him, or before, or on either side. There had always been the shadowed corner, the dark place into which he dared not look, but from which something seemed always to be watching him—and Paul had done things that were not pretty to watch, he knew.

But now he had a curious sense of relief, as though he had at last thrown down the gauntlet to the thing in the corner.

Yet it was but a day since he had been sulking in the traces; but yesterday afternoon that he had been sent to the bank with Denny & Carson's deposit, as usual—but this time he was instructed to leave the book to be balanced. There was above two thousand dollars in checks, and nearly a thousand in the bank notes which he had taken from the book and quietly transferred to his pocket. At the bank he had made out a new deposit slip. His nerves had been steady enough to permit of his returning to the office, where he had finished his work and asked for a full day's holiday tomorrow, Saturday, giving a perfectly reasonable pretext. The bank book, he knew, would not be returned before Monday or Tuesday, and his father would be out of town for the next week. From the time he slipped the bank notes into his pocket until he boarded the night train for New York, he had not known a moment's hesitation. It was not the first time Paul had steered through treacherous waters.

How astonishingly easy it had all been; here he was, the thing done; and this time there would be no awakening, no figure at the top of the stairs. He watched the snow flakes whirling by his window until he fell asleep.

When he awoke, it was three o'clock in the afternoon. He bounded up with a start; half of one of his precious days gone already! He spent more than an hour in dressing, watching every stage of his toilet carefully in the mirror. Everything was quite perfect; he was exactly the kind of boy he had always wanted to be.

When he went downstairs, Paul took a carriage and drove up Fifth Avenue toward the Park. The snow had somewhat abated; carriages and tradesmen's wagons were hurrying soundlessly to and fro in the winter twilight; boys in woollen mufflers were shovelling off the doorsteps; the avenue stages made fine spots of color against the white street. Here and there on the corners were stands, with whole flower gardens blooming under glass cases, against the sides of which the snow flakes stuck and melted; violets, roses, carnations, lilies of the valley—somehow vastly more lovely and alluring that they blossomed thus unnaturally in the snow. The Park itself was a wonderful stage winter-piece.

When he returned, the pause of the twilight had ceased, and the tune of the streets had changed. The snow was falling faster, lights streamed from the hotels that reared their dozen stories fearlessly up into the storm, defying the raging Atlantic winds. A long, black stream of carriages poured down the avenue, intersected here and there by other streams, tending horizontally. There were a score of cabs about the entrance of his hotel, and his driver had to wait. Boys in livery were running in and out of the awning stretched across the sidewalk, up and down the red velvet carpet laid from the door to the street. Above, about, within it all was the rumble and roar, the hurry and toss of thousands of human beings as hot for plea-sure as himself, and on every side of him towered the glaring affirmation of the omnipotence of wealth.

The boy set his teeth and drew his shoulders together in a spasm of realization: the plot of all dramas, the text of all romances, the nerve-stuff of all sensations was whirling about him like the snow flakes. He burnt like a faggot in a tempest.

When Paul went down to dinner, the music of the orchestra came float-ing up the elevator shaft to greet him. His head whirled as he stepped into the thronged corridor, and he sank back into one of the chairs against the wall to get his breath. The lights, the chatter, the perfumes, the bewilder-ing medley of color—he had, for a moment, the feeling of not being able to stand it. But only for a moment; these were his own people, he told himself. He went slowly about the corridors, through the writing-rooms, smoking-rooms, reception-rooms, as though he were exploring the chambers of an enchanted palace, built and peopled for him alone.

When he reached the dining-room he sat down at a table near a win-dow. The flowers, the white linen, the many-colored wine glasses, the gay toilettes of the women, the low popping of corks, the undulating repe-titions of the *Blue Danube* from the orchestra, all flooded Paul's dream with bewildering radiance. When the roseate tinge of his champagne was added—that cold, precious, bubbling stuff that creamed and foamed in his glass—Paul wondered that there were honest men in the world at all. This was what all the world was fighting for, he reflected; this was what all the struggle was about. He doubted the reality of his past. Had he ever known a place called Cordelia Street, a place where fagged-looking businessmen got on the early car; mere rivets in a machine they seemed to Paul—sickening men, with combings of children's hair always hanging to their coats, and the smell of cooking in their clothes. Cordelia Street—Ah! that belonged to another time and country; had he not always been thus, had he not sat here night after night, from as far back as he could remember, looking pensively over just such shimmering textures, and slowly twirling the stem of a glass like this one between his thumb and middle finger? He rather thought he had.

He was not in the least abashed or lonely. He had no especial desire to meet or to know any of these people; all he demanded was the right to look on and conjecture, to watch the pageant. The mere stage properties were all he contended for. Nor was he lonely later in the evening, in his loge at the Metropolitan. He was now entirely rid of his nervous misgivings, of his forced aggressiveness, of the imperative desire to show himself different from his surroundings. He felt now that his surroundings explained him. Nobody questioned the purple; he had only to wear it passively. He had only to glance down at his attire to reassure himself that here it would be impossible for anyone to humiliate him.

He found it hard to leave his beautiful sitting-room to go to bed that night, and sat long watching the raging storm from his turret window. When he went to sleep it was with the lights turned on in his bedroom; partly because of his old timidity, and partly so that, if he should wake in the night, there would be no wretched moment of doubt, no horrible suspicion of yellow wallpaper, or of Washington and Calvin above his bed.

Sunday morning the city was practically snowbound. Paul breakfasted late, and in the afternoon he fell in with a wild San Francisco boy, a freshman at Yale, who said he had run down for a "little flyer" over Sunday. The young man offered to show Paul the night side of the town, and the two boys went out together after dinner, not returning to the hotel until seven o'clock the next morning. They had started out in the confiding warmth of a champagne friendship, but their parting in the elevator was singularly cool. The freshman pulled himself together to make his train, and Paul went to bed. He awoke at two o'clock in the afternoon, very thirsty and dizzy, and rang for ice-water, coffee, and the Pittsburgh papers.

On the part of the hotel management, Paul excited no suspicion. There was this to be said for him, that he wore his spoils with dignity and in no way made himself conspicuous. Even under the glow of his wine he was never boisterous, though he found the stuff like a magician's wand for wonder-building. His chief greediness lay in his ears and eyes, and his excesses were not offensive ones. His dearest pleasures were the grey winter twilights in his sitting-room; his quiet enjoyment of his flowers, his clothes, his wide divan, his cigarette, and his sense of power. He could not remember a time when he had felt so at peace with himself. The mere release from the necessity of petty lying, lying every day and every day, restored his self-respect. He had never lied for pleasure, even at school; but to be noticed and admired, to assert his difference from other Cordelia Street boys; and he felt a good deal more manly, more honest, even, now that he had no need for boastful pretensions, now that he could, as his actor friends used to say, "dress the part." It was characteristic that remorse did not occur to him. His golden days went by without a shadow, and he made each as perfect as he could.

On the the eighth day after his arrival in New York, he found the whole affair exploited in the Pittsburgh papers, exploited with a wealth of detail which indicated that local news of a sensational nature was at a low ebb. The firm of Denny & Carson announced that the boy's father had refunded the full amount of the theft, and that they had no intention of prosecuting. The Cumberland minister had been interviewed, and expressed his hope of yet reclaiming the motherless lad, and his Sabbath-school teacher declared that she would spare no effort to that end. The rumor had reached Pittsburgh that the boy had been seen in a New York hotel, and his father had gone East to find him and bring him home.

Paul had just come in to dress for dinner; he sank into a chair, weak to the knees, and clasped his head in his hands. It was to be worse than jail, even; the tepid waters of Cordelia Street were to close over him finally and forever. The grey monotony stretched before him in hopeless, unrelieved years; Sabbath-school, Young People's Meeting, the yellow-papered room, the damp dishtowels; it all rushed back upon him with a sickening vividness. He had the old feeling that the orchestra had suddenly stopped, the sinking sensation that the play was over. The sweat broke out on his face, and he sprang to his feet, looked about him with his white, conscious smile, and winked at himself in the mirror. With something of the old childish belief in miracles with which he had so often gone to class, all his lessons unlearned, Paul dressed and dashed whistling down the corridor to the elevator.

He had no sooner entered the dining-room and caught the measure of the music than his remembrance was lightened by his old elastic power of claiming the moment, mounting with it, and finding it all sufficient. The glare and glitter about him, the mere scenic accessories had again, and for the last time, their old potency. He would show himself that he was game, he would finish the thing splendidly. He doubted, more than ever, the existence of Cordelia Street, and for the first time he drank his wine recklessly. Was he not, after all, one of those fortunate beings born to the purple, was he not still himself and in his own place? He drummed a nervous accompaniment to the Pagliacci music and looked about him, telling himself over and over that it had paid.

He reflected drowsily, to the swell of the music and the chill sweetness of his wine, that he might have done it more wisely. He might have caught an outboard steamer and been well out of their clutches before now. But the other side of the world had seemed too far away and too uncertain then; he could not have waited for it; his need had been too sharp. If he had to choose over again, he would do the same thing tomorrow. He looked affectionately about the dining-room, now gilded with a soft mist. Ah, it had paid indeed!

Paul was awakened next morning by a painful throbbing in his head and feet. He had thrown himself across the bed without undressing, and had slept with his shoes on. His limbs and hands were lead heavy, and his tongue and throat were parched and burnt. There came upon him one of those fateful attacks of clearheadedness that never occurred except when he was physically exhausted and his nerves hung loose. He lay still and closed his eyes and let the tide of things wash over him.

His father was in New York; "stopping at some joint or other," he told himself. The memory of successive summers on the front stoop fell upon him like a weight of black water. He had not a hundred dollars left; and he knew now, more than ever, that money was everything, the wall that stood between all he loathed and all he wanted. The thing was winding itself up; he had thought of that on his first glorious day in New York, and had even provided a way to snap the thread. It lay on his dressing-table now; he had got it out last night when he came blindly up from dinner, but the shiny metal hurt his eyes, and he disliked the looks of it.

He rose and moved about with a painful effort, succumbing now and again to attacks of nausea. It was the old depression exaggerated; all the world had become Cordelia Street. Yet somehow he was not afraid of anything, was absolutely calm; perhaps because he had looked into the dark corner at last and knew. It was bad enough, what he saw there, but somehow not so bad as his long fear of it had been. He saw everything clearly now. He had a feeling that he had made the best of it, that he had lived the sort of life he was meant to live, and for half an hour he sat staring at the revolver. But he told himself that was not the way, so he went downstairs and took a cab to the ferry.

When Paul arrived at Newark, he got off the train and took another cab, directing the driver to follow the Pennsylvania tracks out of the town. The snow lay heavy on the roadways and had drifted deep in the open fields. Only here and there the dead grass or dried weed stalks projected, singularly black, above it. Once well into the country, Paul dismissed the carriage and walked, floundering along the tracks, his mind a medley of irrelevant things. He seemed to hold in his brain an actual picture of everything he had seen that morning. He remembered every feature of both his drivers, of the toothless old woman from whom he had bought the red flowers in his coat, the agent from whom he had got his ticket, and all of his fellow-passengers on the ferry. His mind, unable to cope with vital matters near at hand, worked feverishly and deftly at sorting and grouping these images. They made for him a part of the ugliness of the world, of the ache in his head, and the bitter burning on his tongue. He stooped and put a handful of snow into his mouth as he walked, but that, too, seemed hot. When he reached a little hillside, where the tracks ran through a cut some twenty feet below him, he stopped and sat down.

The carnations in his coat were drooping with the cold, he noticed; their red glory all over. It occurred to him that all the flowers he had seen in the glass cases that first night must have gone the same way, long before this. It was only one splendid breath they had, in spite of their brave mockery at the winter outside the glass; and it was a losing game in the end, it seemed, this revolt against the homilies by which the world is run. Paul took one of the blossoms carefully from his coat and scooped a little hole in the snow, where he covered it up. Then he dozed a while, from his weak condition, seemingly insensible to the cold.

The sound of an approaching train awoke him, and he started to his feet, remembering only his resolution, and afraid lest he should be too late. He stood watching the approaching locomotive, his teeth chattering, his lips drawn away from them in a frightened smile; once or twice he glanced nervously sidewise, as though he were being watched. When the right moment came, he jumped. As he fell, the folly of his haste occurred to him with merciless clearness, the vastness of what he had left undone. There flashed through his brain, clearer than ever before, the blue of Adriatic water, the yellow of Algerian sands.

He felt something strike his chest, and that his body was being thrown swiftly through the air, on and on, immeasurably far and fast, while his limbs were gently relaxed. Then, because the picture-making mechanism was crushed, the disturbing visions flashed into black, and Paul dropped back into the immense design of things.

—1904

---

### JAMES JOYCE ■ (1882–1941)

*James Joyce is best known for his masterpiece* Ulysses, *the difficult modernist novel of a single day in the life of Dublin that shortly after its appearance in 1922 became both a classic and the subject of a landmark censorship case, which its publishers eventually won. Joyce's lifelong quarrel with the provincial concerns of Irish religious, cultural, and literary life led him to permanent continental self-exile in Zürich and Paris. Most readers would associate Joyce with his pioneering of experimental techniques such as the fragmentary observations found in his early* Epiphanies *(posthumously published in 1956), his use of interior monologue and stream of consciousness, and the complicated linguistic games of* Finnegans Wake *(1939), forgetting that his earlier works lie squarely in the realm of traditional fiction.* Dubliners

*(1914), his collection of short stories of life in his native city, remains an imposing achievement, as does his autobiographical novel* A Portrait of the Artist as a Young Man *(1916). "Araby" captures the same Dublin that is explored in all of Joyce's works—a place where initiations and disappointments follow one another closely.*

# Araby

North Richmond Street, being blind[1], was a quiet street except at the hour when the Christian Brothers' School set the boys free. An uninhabited house of two stories stood at the blind end, detached from its neighbors in a square ground. The other houses of the street, conscious of decent lives within them, gazed at one another with brown imperturbable faces.

The former tenant of our house, a priest, had died in the back drawing-room. Air, musty from having long been enclosed, hung in all the rooms, and the waste room behind the kitchen was littered with old useless papers. Among these I found a few paper-covered books, the pages of which were curled and damp: *The Abbot,* by Walter Scott, *The Devout Communicant* and *The Memoirs of Vidocq.*[2] I liked the last best because its leaves were yellow. The wild garden behind the house contained a central apple-tree and a few straggling bushes under one of which I found the late tenant's rusty bicycle-pump. He had been a very charitable priest: in his will he had left all his money to institutions and the furniture of his house to his sister.

When the short days of winter came dusk fell before we had well eaten our dinners. When we met in the street the houses had grown somber. The space of sky above us was the color of ever-changing violet and toward it the lamps of the street lifted their feeble lanterns. The cold air stung us and we played till our bodies glowed. Our shouts echoed in the silent street. The career of our play brought us through the dark muddy lanes behind the houses where we ran the gantlet of the rough tribes from the cottages, to the back doors of the dark dripping gardens where odors arose from the ashpits, to the dark odorous stables where a coachman smoothed and combed the horse or shook music from the buckled harness. When we returned to the street light from the kitchen windows had filled the areas. If my uncle was seen turning the corner we hid in the shadow until we had seen him safely housed. Or if Mangan's sister

---

[1] **being blind** dead-end.
[2] **The Abbot ... Vidocq** A historical romance (1820); a book of mediations; and a book by François-Jules Vidocq (1775–1857), a criminal who later turned detective.

came out on the doorstep to call her brother in to his tea we watched her from our shadow peer up and down the street. We waited to see whether she would remain or go in and, if she remained, we left our shadow and walked up to Mangan's steps resignedly. She was waiting for us, her figure defined by the light from the half-opened door. Her brother always teased her before he obeyed and I stood by the railings looking at her. Her dress swung as she moved her body and the soft rope of her hair tossed from side to side.

Every morning I lay on the floor in the front parlor watching her door. The blind was pulled down within an inch of the sash so that I could not be seen. When she came out on the doorstep my heart leaped. I ran to the hall, seized my books and followed her. I kept her brown figure always in my eye and, when we came near the point at which our ways diverged, Iquickened my pace and passed her. This happened morning after morning. I had never spoken to her, except for a few casual words, and yet her name was like a summons to all my foolish blood.

Her image accompanied me even in places the most hostile to romance. On Saturday evenings when my aunt went marketing I had to go to carry some of the parcels. We walked through the flaring streets, jostled by drunken men and bargaining women, amid the curses of laborers, the shrill litanies of shopboys who stood on guard by the barrels of pigs' cheeks, the nasal chanting of street singers, who sang a *come-all-you* about O'Donovan Rossa,[3] or a ballad about the troubles in our native land. These noises converged in a single sensation of life for me: I imagined that I bore my chalice safely through the throng of foes. Her name sprang to my lips at moments in strange prayers and praises which I myself did not understand. My eyes were often full of tears (I could not tell why) and at times a flood from my heart seemed to pour itself out into my bosom. I thought little of the future. I did not know whether I would ever speak to her or not or, if I spoke to her, how I could tell her of my confused adoration. But my body was like a harp and her words and gestures were like fingers running upon the wires.

One evening I went into the back drawing-room in which the priest had died. It was a dark rainy evening and there was no sound in the house. Through one of the broken panes I heard the rain impinge upon the earth, the fine incessant needles of water playing in the sodden beds. Some distant lamp or lighted window gleamed below me. I was thankful that I could see so little. All my senses seemed to desire to veil themselves and, feeling that I was about to slip from them, I pressed the palms of my hands together until they trembled, murmuring: *O love! O love!* many times.

---

[3] **come-all-you about O'Donovan Rossa** a popular ballad.

At last she spoke to me. When she addressed the first words to me I was so confused that I did not know what to answer. She asked me was I going to *Araby*. I forget whether I answered yes or no. It would be a splendid bazaar, she said; she would love to go.

—And why can't you? I asked.

While she spoke she turned a silver bracelet round and round her wrist. She could not go, she said, because there would be a retreat that week in her convent[4]. Her brother and two other boys were fighting for their caps and I was alone at the railings. She held one of the spikes, bowing her head toward me. The light from the lamp opposite our door caught the white curve of her neck, lit up her hair that rested there and, falling, lit up the  hand upon the railing. It fell over one side of her dress and caught the white border of a petticoat, just visible as she stood at ease.

—It's well for you, she said.

—If I go, I said, I will bring you something.

What innumerable follies laid waste my waking and sleeping thoughts after that evening! I wished to annihilate the tedious intervening days. I chafed against the work of school. At night in my bedroom and by day in the classroom her image came between me and the page I strove to read. The syllables of the word *Araby* were called to me through the silence in which my soul luxuriated and cast an Eastern enchantment over me. I asked for leave to go to the bazaar on Saturday night. My aunt was surprised and hoped it was not some Freemason[5] affair. I answered few questions in class. I watched my master's face pass from amiability to sternness; he hoped I was not beginning to idle. I could not call my wandering thoughts together. I had hardly any patience with the serious work of life which, now that it stood between me and my desire, seemed to me child's play, ugly monotonous child's play.

On Saturday morning I reminded my uncle that I wished to go to the bazaar in the evening. He was fussing at the hall-stand, looking for the hat-brush, and answered me curtly:

—Yes, boy, I know.

As he was in the hall I could not go into the front parlor and lie at the window. I left the house in bad humor and walked slowly toward the school. The air was pitilessly raw and already my heart misgave me.

When I came home to dinner my uncle had not yet been home. Still it was early. I sat staring at the clock for some time and, when its ticking began to irritate me, I left the room. I mounted the staircase and gained the upper part of the house. The high cold empty gloomy rooms liberated me and I went from room to room singing. From the front window I saw my

[4] **a retreat ... in her convent** a week of religious services in the convent school.
[5] **Freemason** Catholics were not allowed to become Masons.

companions playing below in the street. Their cries reached me weakened and indistinct and, leaning my forehead against the cool glass, I looked over at the dark house where she lived. I may have stood there for an hour, seeing nothing but the brown-clad figure cast by my imagination, touched discreetly by the lamplight at the curved neck, at the hand upon the railings and at the border below the dress.

When I came downstairs again I found Mrs. Mercer sitting at the fire. She was an old garrulous woman, a pawnbroker's widow, who collected used stamps for some pious purpose. I had to endure the gossip of the tea-table. The meal was prolonged beyond an hour and still my uncle did not come. Mrs. Mercer stood up to go: she was sorry she couldn't wait any longer, but it was after eight o'clock and she did not like to be out late, as the night air was bad for her. When she had gone I began to walk up and down the room, clenching my fists. My aunt said:

—I'm afraid you may put off your bazaar for this night of Our Lord.

At nine o'clock I heard my uncle's latchkey in the halldoor. I heard him talking to himself and heard the hall-stand rocking when it had received the weight of his overcoat. I could interpret these signs. When he was midway through his dinner I asked him to give me the money to go to the bazaar. He had forgotten.

—The people are in bed and after their first sleep now, he said.

I did not smile. My aunt said to him energetically:

—Can't you give him the money and let him go? You've kept him late enough as it is.

My uncle said he was very sorry he had forgotten. He said he believed in the old saying: *All work and no play makes Jack a dull boy*. He asked me where I was going and, when I had told him a second time he asked me did I know *The Arab's Farewell to His Steed*.[6] When I left the kitchen he was about to recite the opening lines of the piece to my aunt.

I held a florin tightly in my hands as I strode down Buckingham Street towards the station. The sight of the streets thronged with buyers and glaring with gas recalled to me the purpose of my journey. I took my seat in a third-class carriage of a deserted train. After an intolerable delay the train moved out of the station slowly. It crept onward among ruinous houses and over the twinkling river. At Westland Row Station a crowd of people pressed to the carriage doors; but the porters moved them back, saying that it was a special train for the bazaar. I remained alone in the bare carriage. In a few minutes the train drew up beside an improvised wooden platform. I passed out on to the road and saw by the lighted dial of a clock that it was ten minutes to ten. In front of me was a large building which displayed the magical name.

---

[6] **The Arab's Farewell to His Steed** a sentimental ballad by a popular poet, Caroline Norton (1808–1877).

I could not find any sixpenny entrance and, fearing that the bazaar would be closed, I passed in quickly through a turnstile, handing a shilling to a weary-looking man. I found myself in a big hall girdled at half its height by a gallery. Nearly all the stalls were closed and the greater part of the hall was in darkness. I recognized a silence like that which pervades a church after a service. I walked into the center of the bazaar timidly. A few people were gathered about the stalls which were still open. Before a curtain, over which the words *Café Chantant*[7] were written in colored lamps, two men were counting money on a salver.[8] I listened to the fall of the coins.

Remembering with difficulty why I had come I went over to one of the stalls and examined porcelain vases and flowered tea-sets. At the door of the stall a young lady was talking and laughing with two young gentlemen. I remarked their English accents and listened vaguely to their conversation.

—O, I never said such a thing!

—O, but you did!

—O, but I didn't!

—Didn't she say that?

—Yes. I heard her.

—O, there's a ... fib!

Observing me the young lady came over and asked me did I wish to buy anything. The tone of her voice was not encouraging; she seemed to have spoken to me out of a sense of duty. I looked humbly at the great jars that stood like eastern guards at either side of the dark entrance to the stall and murmured:

—No, thank you.

The young lady changed the position of one of the vases and went back to the two young men. They began to talk of the same subject. Once or twice the young lady glanced at me over her shoulder.

I lingered before her stall, though I knew my stay was useless, to make my interest in her wares seem the more real. Then I turned away slowly and walked down the middle of the bazaar. I allowed the two pennies to fall against the sixpence in my pocket. I heard a voice call from one end of the gallery that the light was out. The upper part of the hall was now completely dark.

Gazing up into the darkness I saw myself as a creature driven and derided by vanity; and my eyes burned with anguish and anger.

—1914

---

[7] **Café Chantant** a Parisian night club.

[8] **salver** a tray used to serve Holy Communion.

---

**WILLIAM FAULKNER** ▨ (1897–1962)

*William Faulkner came from a family whose name was originally spelled "Falkner," but a misprint in an early book led him to change it. Faulkner spent long periods of his adult life in Hollywood, where he had some success as a screenwriter (a 1991 film,* Barton Fink, *has a character obviously modeled on him), but always returned to Oxford, Mississippi, the site of his fictional Jefferson and Yoknapatawpha County. With Thomas Wolfe and others, he was responsible for the flowering of southern fiction in the early decades of the century, though for Faulkner fame came relatively late in life. Despite the success of* Sanctuary *(1931) and the critical esteem in which other early works such as* The Sound and the Fury *(1929) and* As I Lay Dying *(1930) were held, Faulkner proved too difficult for most readers and failed to attract large audiences for what are now considered his best novels. By the late 1940s, most of his books were out of print. His reputation was revived when Malcolm Cowley's edition of* The Portable Faulkner *appeared in 1946, but despite the success of* Intruder in the Dust *(1948), he was not as well known as many of his contemporaries when he won the Nobel Prize in 1950. A brilliant innovator of unusual narrative techniques in his novels, Faulkner created complex genealogies of characters to inhabit the world of his mythical South. "A Rose for Emily," a modernist experiment in the dislocation of chronological time, invites and challenges the reader to discover the cause–effect relationship between its scenes.*

# A Rose for Emily

## I

When Miss Emily Grierson died, our whole town went to her funeral: the men through a sort of respectful affection for a fallen monument, the women mostly out of curiosity to see the inside of her house, which no one save an old man-servant—a combined gardener and cook—had seen in at least ten years.

It was a big, squarish frame house that had once been white, decorated with cupolas and spires and scrolled balconies in the heavily lightsome style of the seventies, set on what had once been our most select street. But garages and cotton gins had encroached and obliterated even the august names of that neighborhood; only Miss Emily's house was left, lifting its stubborn and coquettish decay above the cotton wagons and the gasoline pumps—an eyesore among eyesores. And now Miss Emily had gone to join the representatives of those august names where they lay in the cedar-bemused cemetery among the ranked and anonymous graves of Union and Confederate soldiers who fell at the battle of Jefferson.

Alive, Miss Emily had been a tradition, a duty, and a care; a sort of hereditary obligation upon the town, dating from that day in 1894 when Colonel Sartoris, the mayor—he who fathered the edict that no Negro woman should appear on the streets without an apron—remitted her taxes, the dispensation dating from the death of her father on into perpetuity. Not that Miss Emily would have accepted charity. Colonel Sartoris invented an involved tale to the effect that Miss Emily's father had loaned money to the town, which the town, as a matter of business, preferred this way of repaying. Only a man of Colonel Sartoris' generation and thought could have invented it, and only a woman could have believed it.

When the next generation, with its more modern ideas, became mayors and aldermen, this arrangement created some little dissatisfaction. On the first of the year they mailed her a tax notice. February came, and there was no reply. They wrote her a formal letter, asking her to call at the sheriff's office at her convenience. A week later the mayor wrote her himself, offering to call or to send his car for her, and received in reply a note on paper of an archaic shape, in a thin, flowing calligraphy in faded ink, to the effect that she no longer went out at all. The tax notice was also enclosed, without comment.

They called a special meeting of the Board of Aldermen. A deputation waited upon her, knocked at the door through which no visitor had passed since she ceased giving china-painting lessons eight or ten years earlier. They were admitted by the old Negro into a dim hall from which a stairway mounted into still more shadow. It smelled of dust and disuse—a close, dank smell. The Negro led them into the parlor. It was furnished in heavy, leather-covered furniture. When the Negro opened the blinds of one window, they could see that the leather was cracked; and when they sat down, a faint dust rose sluggishly about their thighs, spinning with slow motes in the single sunray. On a tarnished gilt easel before the fireplace stood a crayon portrait of Miss Emily's father.

They rose when she entered—a small, fat woman in black, with a thin gold chain descending to her waist and vanishing into her belt, leaning on an ebony cane with a tarnished gold head. Her skeleton was small and spare; perhaps that was why what would have been merely plumpness in another was obesity in her. She looked bloated, like a body long submerged in motionless water, and of that pallid hue. Her eyes, lost in the fatty ridges of her face, looked like two small pieces of coal pressed into a lump of dough as they moved from one face to another while the visitors stated their errand.

She did not ask them to sit. She just stood in the door and listened quietly until the spokesman came to a stumbling halt. Then they could hear the invisible watch ticking at the end of the gold chain.

Her voice was dry and cold. "I have no taxes in Jefferson. Colonel Sartoris explained it to me. Perhaps one of you can gain access to the city records and satisfy yourselves."

"But we have. We are the city authorities, Miss Emily. Didn't you get a notice from the sheriff, signed by him?"

"I received a paper, yes," Miss Emily said. "Perhaps he considers himself the sheriff...I have no taxes in Jefferson."

"But there is nothing on the books to show that, you see. We must go by the—"

"See Colonel Sartoris. I have no taxes in Jefferson."

"But, Miss Emily—"

"See Colonel Sartoris." (Colonel Sartoris had been dead almost ten years.) "I have no taxes in Jefferson. Tobe!" The Negro appeared. "Show these gentlemen out."

## II

So she vanquished them, horse and foot, just as she had vanquished their fathers thirty years before about the smell. That was two years after her father's death and a short time after her sweetheart—the one we believed would marry her—had deserted her. After her father's death she went out very little; after her sweetheart went away, people hardly saw her at all. A few of the ladies had the temerity to call, but were not received, and the only sign of life about the place was the Negro man—a young man then—going in and out with a market basket.

"Just as if a man—any man—could keep a kitchen properly," the ladies said; so they were not surprised when the smell developed. It was another link between the gross, teeming world and the high and mighty Griersons.

A neighbor, a woman, complained to the mayor, Judge Stevens, eighty years old.

"But what will you have me do about it, madam?" he said.

"Why, send her word to stop it," the woman said. "Isn't there a law?"

"I'm sure that won't be necessary," Judge Stevens said. "It's probably just a snake or a rat that nigger of hers killed in the yard. I'll speak to him about it."

The next day he received two more complaints, one from a man who came in diffident deprecation. "We really must do something about it, Judge. I'd be the last one in the world to bother Miss Emily, but we've got to do something." That night the Board of Aldermen met—three graybeards and one younger man, a member of the rising generation.

"It's simple enough," he said. "Send her word to have her place cleaned up. Give her a certain time to do it in, and if she don't..."

"Dammit, sir," Judge Stevens said, "will you accuse a lady to her face of smelling bad?"

So the next night, after midnight, four men crossed Miss Emily's lawn and slunk about the house like burglars, sniffing along the base of the brickwork and at the cellar openings while one of them performed a regular sowing motion with his hand out of a sack slung from his shoulder. They broke open the cellar door and sprinkled lime there, and in all the outbuildings. As they re-crossed the lawn, a window that had been dark was lighted and Miss Emily sat in it, the light behind her, and her upright torso motionless as that of an idol. They crept quietly across the lawn and into the shadow of the locusts that lined the street. After a week or two the smell went away.

That was when people had begun to feel really sorry for her. People in our town, remembering how old lady Wyatt, her great-aunt, had gone completely crazy at last, believed that the Griersons held themselves a little too high for what they really were. None of the young men were quite good enough for Miss Emily and such. We had long thought of them as a tableau, Miss Emily a slender figure in white in the background, her father a spraddled silhouette in the foreground, his back to her and clutching a horsewhip, the two of them framed by the back-flung front door. So when she got to be thirty and was still single, we were not pleased exactly, but vindicated; even with insanity in the family she wouldn't have turned down all of her chances if they had really materialized.

When her father died, it got about that the house was all that was left to her; and in a way, people were glad. At last they could pity Miss Emily. Being left alone, and a pauper, she had become humanized. Now she too would know the old thrill and the old despair of a penny more or less.

The day after his death all the ladies prepared to call at the house and offer condolence and aid, as is our custom. Miss Emily met them at the door, dressed as usual and with no trace of grief on her face. She told them that her father was not dead. She did that for three days, with the ministers calling on her, and the doctors, trying to persuade her to let them dispose of the body. Just as they were about to resort to law and force, she broke down, and they buried her father quickly.

We did not say she was crazy then. We believed she had to do that. We remembered all the young men her father had driven away, and we knew that with nothing left, she would have to cling to that which had robbed her, as people will.

## III

She was sick for a long time. When we saw her again, her hair was cut short, making her look like a girl, with a vague resemblance to those angels in colored church windows—sort of tragic and serene.

The town had just let the contracts for paving the sidewalks, and in the summer after her father's death they began the work. The construction company came with niggers and mules and machinery, and a foreman named Homer Barron, a Yankee—a big, dark, ready man, with a big voice and eyes lighter than his face. The little boys would follow in groups to hear him cuss the niggers, and the niggers singing in time to the rise and fall of picks. Pretty soon he knew everybody in town. Whenever you heard a lot of laughing anywhere about the square, Homer Barron would be in the center of the group. Presently we began to see him and Miss Emily on

Sunday afternoons driving in the yellow-wheeled buggy and the matched team of bays from the livery stable.

At first we were glad that Miss Emily would have an interest, because the ladies all said, "Of course a Grierson would not think seriously of a Northerner, a day laborer." But there were still others, older people, who said that even grief could not cause a real lady to forget *noblesse oblige*[1]— without calling it *noblesse oblige*. They just said, "Poor Emily. Her kinsfolk should come to her." She had some kin in Alabama; but years ago her father had fallen out with them over the estate of old lady Wyatt, the crazy woman, and there was no communication between the two families. They had not even been represented at the funeral.

And as soon as the old people said, "Poor Emily," the whispering began. "Do you suppose it's really so?" they said to one another. "Of course it is. What else could..." This behind their hands; rustling of craned silk and satin behind jalousies closed upon the sun of Sunday afternoon as the thin, swift clop-clop-clop of the matched team passed: "Poor Emily."

She carried her head high enough—even when we believed that she was fallen. It was as if she demanded more than ever the recognition of her dignity as the last Grierson; as if it had wanted that touch of earthiness to reaffirm her imperviousness. Like when she bought the rat poison, the arsenic. That was over a year after they had begun to say "Poor Emily," and while the two female cousins were visiting her.

"I want some poison," she said to the druggist. She was over thirty then, still a slight woman, though thinner than usual, with cold, haughty black eyes in a face the flesh of which was strained across the temples and about the eye-sockets as you imagine a lighthouse-keeper's face ought to look. "I want some poison," she said.

"Yes, Miss Emily. What kind? For rats and such? I'd recom—"

"I want the best you have. I don't care what kind."

The druggist named several. "They'll kill anything up to an elephant. But what you want is—"

"Arsenic," Miss Emily said. "Is that a good one?"

"Is...arsenic? Yes, ma'am. But what you want—"

"I want arsenic."

The druggist looked down at her. She looked back at him, erect, her face like a strained flag. "Why, of course," the druggist said. "If that's what you want. But the law requires you to tell what you are going to use it for."

Miss Emily just stared at him, her head tilted back in order to look him eye for eye, until he looked away and went and got the arsenic and wrapped it up. The Negro delivery boy brought her the package; the druggist didn't come back. When she opened the package at home there was written on the box, under the skull and bones: "For rats."

---

[1] **noblesse oblige** the obligation of members of the nobility to act with dignity.

## IV

So the next day we all said, "She will kill herself"; and we said it would be the best thing. When she had first begun to be seen with Homer Barron, we had said, "She will marry him." Then we said, "She will persuade him yet," because Homer himself had remarked—he liked men, and it was known that he drank with the younger men in the Elks' Club—that he was not a marrying man. Later we said, "Poor Emily," behind the jalousies as they passed on Sunday afternoon in the glittering buggy, Miss Emily with her head high and Homer Barron with his hat cocked and a cigar in his teeth, reins and whip in a yellow glove.

Then some of the ladies began to say that it was a disgrace to the town and a bad example to the young people. The men did not want to interfere, but at last the ladies forced the Baptist minister—Miss Emily's people were Episcopal—to call upon her. He would never divulge what happened during that interview, but he refused to go back again. The next Sunday they again drove about the streets, and the following day the minister's wife wrote to Miss Emily's relations in Alabama.

So she had blood-kin under her roof again and we sat back to watch developments. At first nothing happened. Then we were sure that they were to be married. We learned that Miss Emily had been to the jeweler's and ordered a man's toilet set in silver, with the letters H.B. on each piece. Two days later we learned that she had bought a complete outfit of men's clothing, including a nightshirt, and we said, "They are married." We were really glad. We were glad because the two female cousins were even more Grierson than Miss Emily had ever been.

So we were not surprised when Homer Barron—the streets had been finished some time since—was gone. We were a little disappointed that there was not a public blowing-off, but we believed that he had gone on to prepare for Miss Emily's coming, or to give her a chance to get rid of the cousins. (By that time it was a cabal, and we were all Miss Emily's allies to help circumvent the cousins.) Sure enough, after another week they departed. And, as we had expected all along, within three days Homer Barron was back in town. A neighbor saw the Negro man admit him at the kitchen door at dusk one evening.

And that was the last we saw of Homer Barron. And of Miss Emily for some time. The Negro man went in and out with the market basket, but the front door remained closed. Now and then we would see her at a window for a moment, as the men did that night when they sprinkled the lime, but for almost six months she did not appear on the streets. Then we knew that this was to be expected too; as if that quality of her father which had thwarted her woman's life so many times had been too virulent and too furious to die.

When we next saw Miss Emily, she had grown fat and her hair was turning gray. During the next few years it grew grayer and grayer until it attained an even pepper-and-salt iron-gray, when it ceased turning. Up to the day of her death at seventy-four it was still that vigorous iron-gray, like the hair of an active man.

From that time on her front door remained closed, save for a period of six or seven years, when she was about forty, during which she gave lessons in china-painting. She fitted up a studio in one of the downstairs rooms, where the daughters and granddaughters of Colonel Sartoris' contemporaries were sent to her with the same regularity and in the same spirit that they were sent to church on Sundays with a twenty-five-cent piece for the collection plate. Meanwhile her taxes had been remitted.

Then the newer generation became the backbone and the spirit of the town, and the painting pupils grew up and fell away and did not send their children to her with boxes of color and tedious brushes and pictures cut from the ladies' magazines. The front door closed upon the last one and remained closed for good. When the town got free postal delivery, Miss Emily alone refused to let them fasten the metal numbers above her door and attach a mailbox to it. She would not listen to them.

Daily, monthly, yearly we watched the Negro grow grayer and more stooped, going in and out with the market basket. Each December we sent her a tax notice, which would be returned by the post office a week later, unclaimed. Now and then we would see her in one of the downstairs windows—she had evidently shut up the top floor of the house—like the carven torso of an idol in a niche, looking or not looking at us, we could never tell which. Thus she passed from generation to generation—dear, inescapable, impervious, tranquil, and perverse.

And so she died. Fell ill in the house filled with dust and shadows, with only a doddering Negro man to wait on her. We did not even know she was sick; we had long since given up trying to get any information from the Negro. He talked to no one, probably not even to her, for his voice had grown harsh and rusty, as if from disuse.

She died in one of the downstairs rooms, in a heavy walnut bed with a curtain, her gray head propped on a pillow yellow and moldy with age and lack of sunlight.

## V

The Negro met the first of the ladies at the front door and let them in, with their hushed, sibilant voices and their quick, curious glances, and then he disappeared. He walked right through the house and out the back and was not seen again.

The two female cousins came at once. They held the funeral on the second day, with the town coming to look at Miss Emily beneath a mass of bought flowers, with the crayon face of her father musing profoundly above the bier and the ladies sibilant and macabre; and the very old men—some in their brushed Confederate uniforms—on the porch and the lawn, talking of Miss Emily as if she had been a contemporary of theirs, believing that they had danced with her and courted her perhaps, confusing time with its mathematical progression, as the old do, to whom all the past is not a diminishing road but, instead, a huge meadow which no winter ever quite touches, divided from them now by the narrow bottleneck of the most recent decade of years.

Already we knew that there was one room in that region above stairs which no one had seen in forty years, and which would have to be forced. They waited until Miss Emily was decently in the ground before they opened it.

The violence of breaking down the door seemed to fill this room with pervading dust. A thin, acrid pall as of the tomb seemed to lie everywhere upon this room decked and furnished as for a bridal: upon the valance curtains of faded rose color, upon the rose-shaded lights, upon the dressing table, upon the delicate array of crystal and the man's toilet things backed with tarnished silver, silver so tarnished that the monogram was obscured. Among them lay collar and tie, as if they had just been removed, which, lifted, left upon the surface a pale crescent in the dust. Upon a chair hung the suit, carefully folded; beneath it the two mute shoes and the discarded socks.

The man himself lay in the bed.

For a long while we just stood there, looking down at the profound and fleshless grin. The body had apparently once lain in the attitude of an embrace, but now the long sleep that outlasts love, that conquers even the grimace of love, had cuckolded him. What was left of him, rotted beneath what was left of the nightshirt, had become inextricable from the bed in which he lay; and upon him and upon the pillow beside him lay that even coating of the patient and biding dust.

Then we noticed that in the second pillow was the indentation of a head. One of us lifted something from it, and leaning forward, that faint and invisible dust dry and acrid in the nostrils, we saw a long strand of iron-gray hair.

—1930

---

**ERNEST HEMINGWAY** ■ **(1899–1961)**

*Ernest Hemingway completely embodied the public image of the successful writer for so long that even today, more than five decades after his suicide, it is difficult to separate the celebrity from the serious artist, the sportsman, and carouser from the stylist whose influence on the short story and novel continues to be felt. The complexity of his life and personality still fascinates biographers, even though a half-dozen major studies have already appeared. Born the son of a doctor in a middle-class suburb of Chicago, wounded as a volunteer ambulance driver in Italy during World War I, trained as a reporter on the Kansas City* Star, *Hemingway moved to Paris in the early 1920s, where he was at the center of a brilliant generation of American expatriates that included Gertrude Stein and F. Scott Fitzgerald. His wide travels are reflected in his work. He spent much time in Spain, which provided material for his first novel,* The Sun Also Rises *(1926), and his many later articles on bullfighting. His early stories earned him a reputation for daring subject matter and made him one of the chief spokespersons for the so-called Lost Generation. In the 1930s, he covered the Spanish Civil War, the backdrop for his most popular novel,* For Whom the Bell Tolls *(1940). His African safaris and residence in pre-Castro Cuba were also sources for his fiction. When all else is said, Hemingway's greatest contribution may lie in the terse, stripped-down quality of his early prose, which renders modern alienation with stark concrete details. Hemingway won the Nobel Prize in 1954. The decades since his death have seen the release of much unpublished material—a memoir of his Paris years,* A Moveable Feast *(1964); two novels,* Islands in the Stream *(1970) and* The Garden of Eden *(1986); and a "fictional memoir" of his final African safari,* True at First Light *(1999). "Hills like White Elephants" illustrates Hemingway's "iceberg" approach to short fiction, in which the minimal surface of conversation reveals the deeper subject of the story.*

# Hills like White Elephants

The hills across the valley of the Ebro were long and white. On this side there was no shade and no trees and the station was between two lines of rails in the sun. Close against the side of the station there was the warm shadow of the building and a curtain, made of strings of bamboo beads, hung across the open door into the bar, to keep out flies. The American and the girl with him sat at a table in the shade, outside the building. It was very hot and the express from Barcelona would come in forty minutes. It stopped at this junction for two minutes and went on to Madrid.

"What should we drink?" the girl asked. She had taken off her hat and put it on the table.

"It's pretty hot," the man said.

"Let's drink beer."

"Dos cervezas," the man said into the curtain.                                        5

"Big ones?" a woman asked from the doorway.

"Yes. Two big ones."

The woman brought two glasses of beer and two felt pads. She put the felt pads and the beer glasses on the table and looked at the man and the girl. The girl was looking off at the line of hills. They were white in the sun and the country was brown and dry.

"They look like white elephants," she said.

"I've never seen one," the man drank his beer.                                    10

"No, you wouldn't have."

"I might have," the man said. "Just because you say I wouldn't have doesn't prove anything."

The girl looked at the bead curtain. "They've painted something on it," she said. "What does it say?"

"Anis del Toro. It's a drink."

"Could we try it?"                                                                15

The man called "Listen" through the curtain. The woman came out from the bar.

"Four reales."

"We want two Anis del Toro."

"With water?"

"Do you want it with water?"                                                      20

"I don't know," the girl said. "Is it good with water?"

"It's all right."

"You want them with water?" asked the woman.

"Yes, with water."

"It tastes like licorice," the girl said and put the glass down.                  25

"That's the way with everything."

"Yes," said the girl. "Everything tastes of licorice. Especially all the things you've waited so long for, like absinthe."

"Oh, cut it out."

"You started it," the girl said. "I was being amused. I was having a fine time."

"Well, let's try and have a fine time."                                           30

"All right. I was trying. I said the mountains looked like white elephants. Wasn't that bright?"

"That was bright."

"I wanted to try this new drink. That's all we do, isn't it—look at things and try new drinks?"

"I guess so."

The girl looked across at the hills.                                              35

"They're lovely hills," she said. "They don't really look like white elephants. I just meant the coloring of their skin through the trees."

"Should we have another drink?"

"All right."

The warm wind blew the bead curtain against the table.

"The beer's nice and cool," the man said.                                         40

"It's lovely," the girl said.

"It's really an awfully simple operation, Jig," the man said. "It's not really an operation at all."

The girl looked at the ground the table legs rested on.

"I know you wouldn't mind it, Jig. It's really not anything. It's just to let the air in."

The girl did not say anything.                                                45

"I'll go with you and I'll stay with you all the time. They just let the air in and then it's all perfectly natural."

"Then what will we do afterward?"

"We'll be fine afterward. Just like we were before."

"What makes you think so?"

"That's the only thing that bothers us. It's the only thing that's made us unhappy."                                                              50

The girl looked at the bead curtain, put her hand out and took hold of two of the strings of beads.

"And you think then we'll be all right and be happy."

"I know we will. You don't have to be afraid.

I've known lots of people that have done it."

"So have I," said the girl. "And afterward they were all so happy."

"Well," the man said, "if you don't want to you don't have to. I wouldn't have you do it if you didn't want to. But I know it's perfectly simple."    55

"And you really want to?"

"I think it's the best thing to do. But I don't want you to do it if you don't really want to."

"And if I do it you'll be happy and things will be like they were and you'll love me?"

"I love you now. You know I love you."

"I know. But if I do it, then it will be nice again if I say things are like white elephants, and you'll like it?"                                    60

"I'll love it. I love it now but I just can't think about it. You know how I get when I worry."

"If I do it you won't ever worry?"

"I won't worry about that because it's perfectly simple."

"Then I'll do it. Because I don't care about me."

"What do you mean?"                                                            65

"I don't care about me."

"Well, I care about you."

"Oh, yes. But I don't care about me. And I'll do it and then everything will be fine."

"I don't want you to do it if you feel that way."

The girl stood up and walked to the end of the station. Across, on the  70 other side, were fields of grain and trees along the banks of the Ebro. Far away, beyond the river, were mountains. The shadow of a cloud moved across the field of grain and she saw the river through the trees.

"And we could have all this," she said. "And we could have everything and every day we make it more impossible."

"What did you say?"

"I said we could have everything."

"We can have everything."

"No, we can't."                                                                75

"We can have the whole world."

"No, we can't."

"We can go everywhere."

"No, we can't. It isn't ours any more."

"It's ours."                                                                   80

"No, it isn't. And once they take it away, you never get it back."

"But they haven't taken it away."

"We'll wait and see."

"Come on back in the shade," he said. "You mustn't feel that way."

"I don't feel any way," the girl said. "I just know things."                   85

"I don't want you to do anything that you don't want to do—"

"Nor that isn't good for me," she said. "I know.
Could we have another beer?"

"All right. But you've got to realize—"

"I realize," the girl said. "Can't we maybe stop talking?"

They sat down at the table and the girl looked across at the hills on the  90
dry side of the valley and the man looked at her and at the table.

"You've got to realize," he said, "that I don't want you to do it if you
don't want to. I'm perfectly willing to go through with it if it means anything to you."

"Doesn't it mean anything to you? We could get along."

"Of course it does. But I don't want anybody but you. I don't want any
one else. And I know it's perfectly simple."

"Yes, you know it's perfectly simple."

"It's all right for you to say that, but I do know it."                          95

"Would you do something for me now?"

"I'd do anything for you."

"Would you please please please please please please please stop talking?"

He did not say anything but looked at the bags against the wall of
the station. There were labels on them from all the hotels where they had
spent nights.

"But I don't want you to," he said, "I don't care anything about it."         100

"I'll scream," the girl said.

The woman came out through the curtains with two glasses of beer and
put them down on the damp felt pads. "The train comes in five minutes,"
she said.

"What did she say?" asked the girl.

"That the train is coming in five minutes."

The girl smiled brightly at the woman, to thank her.                          105

"I'd better take the bags over to the other side of the station," the man
said. She smiled at him.

"All right. Then come back and we'll finish the beer."

He picked up the two heavy bags and carried them around the station to the other tracks. He looked up the tracks but could not see the train. Coming back, he walked through the barroom, where people waiting for the train were drinking. He drank an Anis at the bar and looked at the people. They were all waiting reasonably for the train. He went out through the bead curtain. She was sitting at the table and smiled at him.

"Do you feel better?" he asked.

"I feel fine," she said. "There's nothing wrong with me. I feel fine."    110

—1927

---

**ZORA NEALE HURSTON ▪ (1901-1960)**

*Zora Neale Hurston was one of eight children; her father, a carpenter and Baptist preacher, served three terms as mayor of Eatonville, the first all-black town incorporated in the United States. Hurston was took courses at Howard University. She later attended Barnard xollege, where in 1927 she earned a B.A. in anthropology. In early 1925 she moved to New York, where she became part of Harlem Renaissance, a group of young black artists, musicians, and writers (including Langston Hughes, Countee Cullen, Jean Toomer, and Claude McKay) who sought "spiritual emancipation." As a scholar, Hurston made notable contributions to the study of African-American folklore. For twelve years beginning in 1927 she traveled to Haiti, Jamaica, Bermuda, and throughout the South, collecting examples of black myths, fables, and folktales, many of which can be traced back to their African roots, including "Sweat," which employs the "trickster plot" so common to folk literature.*

# Sweat

## I

It was eleven o'clock of a Spring night in Florida. It was Sunday. Any other night, Delia Jones would have been in bed for two hours by this time. But she was a washwoman, and Monday morning meant a great deal to her. So she collected the soiled clothes on Saturday when she returned the clean things. Sunday night after church, she sorted and put the white things to soak. It saved her almost a half-day's start. A great hamper in the bedroom held the clothes that she brought home. It was so much neater than a number of bundles lying around.

She squatted on the kitchen floor beside the great pile of clothes, sorting them into small heaps according to color, and humming a song in a mournful key, but wondering through it all where Sykes, her husband, had gone with her horse and buckboard.[1]

Just then something long, round, limp, and black fell upon her shoulders and slithered to the floor beside her. A great terror took hold of her. It softened her knees and dried her mouth so that it was a full minute before she could cry out or move. Then she saw that it was the big bull whip her husband liked to carry when he drove.

She lifted her eyes to the door and saw him standing there bent over with laughter at her fright. She screamed at him.

"Sykes, what you throw dat whip on me like dat? You know it would skeer me—looks just like a snake, an' you knows how skeered Ah is of snakes."

"Course Ah knowed it! That's how come Ah done it." He slapped his leg with his hand and almost rolled on the ground in his mirth. "If you such a big fool dat you got to have a fit over a earth worm or a string, Ah don't keer how bad Ah skeer you."

"You ain't got no business doing it. Gawd knows it's a sin. Some day Ah'm gointuh drop dead from some of yo' foolishness. 'Nother thing, where you been wid mah rig? Ah feeds dat pony. He ain't fuh you to be drivin' wid no bull whip."

"You sho' is one aggravatin' nigger woman!" he declared and stepped into the room. She resumed her work and did not answer him at once. "Ah done tole you time and again to keep them white folks' clothes outa dis house."

He picked up the whip and glared at her. Delia went on with her work. She went out into the yard and returned with a galvanized tub and set it on the washbench. She saw that Sykes had kicked all of the clothes together again, and now stood in her way truculently, his whole manner hoping, *praying,* for an argument. But she walked calmly around him and commenced to re-sort the things.

"Next time, Ah'm gointer kick 'em outdoors," he threatened as he struck a match along the leg of his corduroy breeches.

Delia never looked up from her work, and her thin, stooped shoulders sagged further.

"Ah ain't for no fuss t'night Sykes. Ah just come from taking sacrament at the church house."

He snorted scornfully. "Yeah, you just come from de church house on a Sunday night, but heah you is gone to work on them clothes. You ain't nothing but a hypocrite. One of them amen-corner Christians—sing, whoop, and shout, then come home and wash white folks' clothes on the Sabbath."

He stepped roughly upon the whitest pile of things, kicking them helter-skelter as he crossed the room. His wife gave a little scream of dismay, and quickly gathered them together again.

---

[1] **buckboard** open wagon with a seat.

"Sykes, you quit grindin' dirt into these clothes! How can Ah git through by Sat'day if Ah don't start on Sunday?"

"Ah don't keer if you never git through. Anyhow, Ah done promised Gawd and a couple of other men, Ah ain't gointer have it in mah house. Don't gimme no lip neither, else Ah'll throw 'em out and put mah fist up side yo' head to boot."

Delia's habitual meekness seemed to slip from her shoulders like a blown scarf. She was on her feet; her poor little body, her bare knuckly hands bravely defying the strapping hulk before her.

"Looka heah, Sykes, you done gone too fur. Ah been married to you fur fifteen years, and Ah been takin' in washin' fur fifteen years. Sweat, sweat, sweat! Work and sweat, cry and sweat, pray and sweat!"

"What's that got to do with me?" he asked brutally.

"What's it got to do with you, Sykes? Mah tub of suds is filled yo' belly with vittles more times than yo' hands is filled it. Mah sweat is done paid for this house and Ah reckon Ah kin keep on sweatin' in it."

She seized the iron skillet from the stove and struck a defensive pose, which act surprised him greatly, coming from her. It cowed him and he did not strike her as he usually did.

"Naw you won't," she panted, "that ole snaggle-toothed black woman you runnin' with ain't comin' heah to pile up on *mah* sweat and blood. You ain't paid for nothin' on this place, and Ah'm gointer stay right heah till Ah'm toted out foot foremost."

"Well, you better quit gittin' me riled up, else they'll be totin' you out sooner than you expect. Ah'm so tired of you Ah don't know whut to do. Gawd! How Ah hates skinny wimmen!"

A little awed by this new Delia, he sidled out of the door and slammed the back gate after him. He did not say where he had gone, but she knew too well. She knew very well that he would not return until nearly daybreak also. Her work over, she went on to bed but not to sleep at once. Things had come to a pretty pass!

She lay awake, gazing upon the debris that cluttered their matrimonial trail. Not an image left standing along the way. Anything like flowers had long ago been drowned in the salty stream that had been pressed from her heart. Her tears, her sweat, her blood. She had brought love to the union and he had brought a longing after the flesh. Two months after the wedding, he had given her the first brutal beating. She had the memory of his numerous trips to Orlando with all of his wages when he had returned to her penniless, even before the first year had passed. She was young and soft then, but now she thought of her knotty, muscled limbs, her harsh knuckly hands, and drew herself up into an unhappy little ball in the middle of the big feather bed. Too late now to hope for love, even if it were not Bertha it would be someone else. This case differed from the others only in that she was bolder than the others. Too late for everything except her little home. She had built it for her old days, and planted one by one the trees and flowers there. It was lovely to her, lovely.

Somehow, before sleep came, she found herself saying aloud: "Oh well, whatever goes over the Devil's back, is got to come under his belly. Sometime or ruther, Sykes, like everybody else, is gointer reap his sowing." After that she was able to build a spiritual earthworks against her husband. His shells could no longer reach her. AMEN. She went to sleep and slept until he announced his presence in bed by kicking her feet and rudely snatching the covers away.

"Gimme some kivah heah, an' git yo' damn foots over on yo' own side! Ah oughter mash you in yo' mouf fuh drawing dat skillet on me."

Delia went clear to the rail without answering him. A triumphant indifference to all that he was or did.

## II

The week was full of work for Delia as all other weeks, and Saturday found her behind her little pony, collecting and delivering clothes.

It was a hot, hot day near the end of July. The village men on Joe Clarke's porch even chewed cane listlessly. They did not hurl the cane-knots as usual. They let them dribble over the edge of the porch. Even conversation had collapsed under the heat.

"Heah come Delia Jones," Jim Merchant said, as the shaggy pony came 'round the bend of the road toward them. The rusty buckboard was heaped with baskets of crisp, clean laundry.

"Yep," Joe Lindsay agreed. "Hot or col', rain or shine, jes' ez reg'lar ez de weeks rool roun' Delia carries 'em an' fetches 'em on Sat'day."

"She better if she wanter eat," said Moss. "Syke Jones ain't wuth de shot an' powder hit would tek tuh kill 'em. Not to *huh* he ain't."

"He sho' ain't," Walter Thomas chimed in. "It's too bad, too, cause she wuz a right pretty li'l trick when he got huh. Ah'd uh mah'ied huh mahself if he hadnter beat me to it."

Delia nodded briefly at the men as she drove past.

"Too much knockin' will ruin *any* oman. He done beat huh 'nough tuh kill three women, let 'lone change they looks," said Elijah Moseley. "How Syke kin stommuck dat big black greasy Mogul he's layin' roun' wid, gits me. Ah swear dat eight-rock couldn't kiss a sardine can Ah done thowed out de back do' 'way las' yeah."

"Aw, she's fat, thass how come. He's allus been crazy 'bout fat women," put in Merchant. "He'd a' been tied up wid one long time ago if he could a' found one tuh have him. Did Ah tell yuh 'bout him come sidlin' roun' *mah* wife—bringin' her a basket uh peecans outa his yard fuh a present? Yessir, mah wife! She tol' him tuh take 'em right straight back home, 'cause Delia works so hard ovah dat washtub she reckon everything on de place taste lak sweat an' soapsuds. Ah jus' wisht Ah'd a' caught 'im 'roun' dere! Ah'd a' made his hips ketch on fiah down dat shell road."

"Ah know he done it, too. Ah sees 'im grinnin' at every 'oman dat passes," Walter Thomas said. "But even so, he useter eat some mighty big hunks uh humble pie tuh git dat li'l 'oman he got. She wuz ez pritty ez a speckled pup! Dat wuz fifteen years ago. He useter be so skeered uh losin' huh, she could make him do some parts of a husband's duty. Dey never wuz de same in de mind."

"There oughter be a law about him," said Lindsay. "He ain't fit tuh carry guts tuh a bear."

Clarke spoke for the first time. "Tain't no law on earth dat kin make a man be decent if it ain't in 'im. There's plenty men dat takes a wife lak dey do a joint uh sugar-cane. It's round, juicy, an' sweet when dey gits it. But dey squeeze an' grind, squeeze an' grind an' wring tell dey wring every drop uh pleasure dat's in 'em out. When dey's satisfied dat dey is wrung dry, dey treats 'em jes' lak dey do a cane-chew. Dey thows 'em away. Dey knows whut dey is doin' while dey is at it, an' hates theirselves fuh it but they keeps on hangin' after huh tell she's empty. Den dey hates huh fuh bein' a cane-chew an' in de way."

"We oughter take Syke an' dat stray 'oman uh his'n down in Lake Howell swamp an' lay on de rawhide till they cain't say Lawd a' mussy. He allus wuz uh ovahbearin niggah, but since dat white 'oman from up north done teached 'im how to run a automobile, he done got too beggety to live—an' we oughter kill 'im," Old Man Anderson advised.

A grunt of approval went around the porch. But the heat was melting their civic virtue and Elijah Moseley began to bait Joe Clarke.

"Come on, Joe, git a melon outa dere an' slice it up for yo' customers. We'se all sufferin' wid de heat. De bear's done got *me*!"

"Thass right, Joe, a watermelon is jes' whut Ah needs tuh cure de eppi-zudicks," Walter Thomas joined forces with Moseley. "Come on dere, Joe. We all is steady customers an' you ain't set us up in a long time. Ah chooses dat long, bowlegged Floridy favorite."

"A god, an' be dough. You all gimme twenty cents and slice away," Clarke retorted. "Ah needs a col' slice m'self. Heah, everybody chip in. Ah'll lend y'all mah meat knife."

The money was all quickly subscribed and the huge melon brought forth. At that moment, Sykes and Bertha arrived. A determined silence fell on the porch and the melon was put away again.

Merchant snapped down the blade of his jackknife and moved toward the store door.

"Come on in, Joe, an' gimme a slab uh sow belly an' uh pound uh coffee—almost fuhgot 'twas Sat'day. Got to git on home." Most of the men left also.

Just then Delia drove past on her way home, as Sykes was ordering magnificently for Bertha. It pleased him for Delia to see.

"Git whutsoever yo' heart desires, Honey. Wait a minute, Joe. Give huh two bottles uh strawberry soda-water, uh quart parched ground-peas, an' a block uh chewin' gum."

With all this they left the store, with Sykes reminding Bertha that this was his town and she could have it if she wanted it.

The men returned soon after they left, and held their watermelon feast.

"Where did Syke Jones git da 'oman from nohow?" Lindsay asked.

"Ovah Apopka. Guess dey musta been cleanin' out de town when she lef'. She don't look lak a thing but a hunk uh liver wid hair on it."

"Well, she sho' kin squall," Dave Carter contributed. "When she gits ready tuh laff, she jes' opens huh mouf an' latches it back tuh de las' notch. No ole granpa alligator down in Lake Bell ain't got nothin' on huh."

## III

Bertha had been in town three months now. Sykes was still paying her room-rent at Della Lewis'—the only house in town that would have taken her in. Sykes took her frequently to Winter Park to "stomps." He still assured her that he was the swellest man in the state.

"Sho' you kin have dat li'l ole house soon's Ah git dat 'oman outadere. Everything b'longs tuh me an' you sho' kin have it. Ah sho' 'bominates uh skinny 'oman. Lawdy, you sho' is got one portly shape on you! You kin git *anything* you wants. Dis is *mah* town an' you sho' kin have it."

Delia's work-worn knees crawled over the earth in Gethsemane[2] and up the rocks of Calvary[3] many, many times during these months. She avoided the villagers and meeting places in her efforts to be blind and deaf. But Bertha nullified this to a degree, by coming to Delia's house to call Sykes out to her at the gate.

Delia and Sykes fought all the time now with no peaceful interludes. They slept and ate in silence. Two or three times Delia had attempted a timid friendliness, but she was repulsed each time. It was plain that the breaches must remain agape.

The sun had burned July to August. The heat streamed down like a million hot arrows, smiting all things living upon the earth. Grass withered, leaves browned, snakes went blind in shedding, and men and dogs went mad. Dog days!

Delia came home one day and found Sykes there before her. She wondered, but started to go on into the house without speaking, even though

---

[2] **Gethsemane** The garden that was the scene of Jesus' arrest (see Matthew 26:36–57); hence, any scene of suffering.

[3] **Calvary** hill outside Jerusalem where Jesus was crucified.

he was standing in the kitchen door and she must either stoop under his arm or ask him to move. He made no room for her. She noticed a soap box beside the steps, but paid no particular attention to it, knowing that he must have brought it there. As she was stooping to pass under his outstretched arm, he suddenly pushed her backward, laughingly.

"Look in de box dere Delia, Ah done brung yuh somethin'!"

She nearly fell upon the box in her stumbling, and when she saw what it held, she all but fainted outright.

"Syke! Syke, mah Gawd! You take dat rattlesnake 'way from heah! You *gottuh*. Oh, Jesus, have mussy!"

"Ah ain't got tuh do nuthin' uh de kin'—fact is Ah ain't got tuh do nothin' but die. Tain't no use uh you puttin' on airs makin' out lak you skeered uh dat snake—he's gointer stay right heah tell he die. He wouldn't bite me cause Ah knows how tuh handle 'im. Nohow he wouldn't risk breakin' out his fangs 'gin *yo* skinny laigs."

"Naw, now Syke, don't keep dat thing 'round tryin' tuh skeer me tuh death. You knows Ah'm even feared uh earth worms. Thass de biggest snake Ah evah did see. Kill 'im Syke, please."

"Doan ast me tuh do nothin' fuh yuh. Goin' 'round tryin' tuh be so damn asterperious.[4] Naw, Ah ain't gonna kill it. Ah think uh damn sight mo' uh him dan you! Dat's a nice snake an' anybody doan lak 'im kin jes' hit de grit."

The village soon heard that Sykes had the snake, and came to see and ask questions.

"How de hen-fire did you ketch dat six-foot rattler, Syke?" Thomas asked.

"He's full uh frogs so he cain't hardly move, thass how Ah eased up on 'm. But Ah'm a snake charmer an' knows how tuh handle 'em. Shux, dat ain't nothin'. Ah could ketch one eve'y day if Ah so wanted tuh."

"Whut he needs is a heavy hick'ry club leaned real heavy on his head. Dat's de bes' way tuh charm a rattlesnake."

"Naw, Walt, y'all jes' don't understand dese diamon' backs lak Ah do," said Sykes in a superior tone of voice.

The village agreed with Walter, but the snake stayed on. His box remained by the kitchen door with its screen wire covering. Two or three days later it had digested its meal of frogs and literally came to life. It rattled at every movement in the kitchen or the yard. One day as Delia came down the kitchen steps she saw his chalky-white fangs curved like scimitars hung in the wire meshes. This time she did not run away with averted eyes as usual. She stood for a long time in the doorway in a red fury that grew bloodier for every second that she regarded the creature that was her torment.

---

[4] **asterperious** haughty.

That night she broached the subject as soon as Sykes sat down to the table.

"Syke, Ah wants you tuh take dat snake 'way fum heah. You done starved me an' Ah put up widcher, you done beat me an Ah took dat, but you done kilt all mah insides bringin' dat varmint heah."

Sykes poured out a saucer full of coffee and drank it deliberately before he answered her.

"A whole lot Ah keer 'bout how you feels inside uh out. Dat snake ain't goin' no damn wheah till Ah gits ready fuh 'im tuh go. So fur as beatin' is concerned, yuh ain't took near all dat you gointer take ef yuh stay 'round *me*."

Delia pushed back her plate and got up from the table. "Ah hates you, Sykes," she said calmly. "Ah hates you tuh de same degree dat Ah useter love yuh. Ah done took an' took till mah belly is full up tuh mah neck. Dat's de reason Ah got mah letter fum de church an' moved mah membership tuh Woodbridge—so Ah don't haftuh take no sacrament wid yuh. Ah don't wantuh see yuh 'round me at all. Lay 'round wid dat 'oman all yuh wants tuh, but gwan 'way fum me an' mah house. Ah hates yuh lak uh suck-egg dog."

Sykes almost let the huge wad of corn bread and collard greens he was chewing fall out of his mouth in amazement. He had a hard time whipping himself up to the proper fury to try to answer Delia.

"Well, Ah'm glad you does hate me. Ah'm sho' tiahed uh you hangin' ontuh me. Ah don't want yuh. Look at yuh stringey ole neck! Yo' rawbony laigs an' arms is enough tuh cut uh man tuh death. You looks jes' lak de devvul's doll-baby tuh *me*. You cain't hate me no worse dan Ah hates you. Ah been hatin' *you* fuh years."

"Yo' ole black hide don't look lak nothin' tuh me, but uh passle uh wrinkled up rubber, wid yo' big ole yeahs flappin' on each side lak uh paih uh buzzard wings. Don't think Ah'm gointuh be run 'way fum mah house neither. Ah'm goin' tuh de white folks 'bout *you*, mah young man, de very nex' time you lay yo' han's on me. Mah cup is done run ovah." Delia said this with no signs of fear and Sykes departed from the house, threatening her, but made not the slightest move to carry out any of them.

That night he did not return at all, and the next day being Sunday, Delia was glad she did not have to quarrel before she hitched up her pony and drove the four miles to Woodbridge.

She stayed to the night service—"love feast"—which was very warm and full of spirit. In the emotional winds her domestic trials were borne far and wide so that she sang as she drove homeward,

Jurden water,[5] black an' col

---

[5] **Jurden water** the River Jordan.

Chills de body, not de soul

An' Ah wantah cross Jurden in uh calm time.

She came from the barn to the kitchen door and stopped.

"Whut's de mattah, ol' Satan, you ain't kickin' up yo' racket?" She addressed the snake's box. Complete silence. She went on into the house with a new hope in its birth struggles. Perhaps her threat to go to the white folks had frightened Sykes! Perhaps he was sorry! Fifteen years of misery and suppression had brought Delia to the place where she would hope *anything* that looked toward a way over or through her wall of inhibitions.

She felt in the match-safe behind the stove at once for a match. There was only one there.

"Dat niggah wouldn't fetch nothin' heah tuh save his rotten neck, but he kin run thew whut Ah brings quick enough. Now he done toted off nigh on tuh haff uh box uh matches. He done had dat 'oman heah in mah house, too."

Nobody but a woman could tell how she knew this even before she struck the match. But she did and it put her into a new fury.

Presently she brought in the tubs to put the white things to soak. This time she decided she need not bring the hamper out of the bedroom; she would go in there and do the sorting. She picked up the pot-bellied lamp and went in. The room was small and the hamper stood hard by the foot of the white iron bed. She could sit and reach through the bedposts—resting as she worked.

"*Ah wantah cross Jurden in uh calm time.*" She was singing again. The mood of the "love feast" had returned. She threw back the lid of the basket almost gaily. Then, moved by both horror and terror, she sprang back toward the door. *There lay the snake in the basket!* He moved sluggishly at first, but even as she turned round and round, jumped up and down in an insanity of fear, he began to stir vigorously. She saw him pouring his awful beauty from the basket upon the bed, then she seized the lamp and ran as fast as she could to the kitchen. The wind from the open door blew out the light and the darkness added to her terror. She sped to the darkness of the yard, slamming the door after her before she thought to set down the lamp. She did not feel safe even on the ground, so she climbed up in the hay barn.

There for an hour or more she lay sprawled upon the hay a gibbering wreck.

Finally she grew quiet, and after that came coherent thought. With this stalked through her a cold, bloody rage. Hours of this. A period of introspection, a space of retrospection, then a mixture of both. Out of this an awful calm.

"Well, Ah done de bes' Ah could. If things ain't right, Gawd knows tain't mah fault."

She went to sleep—a twitch sleep—and woke up to a faint gray sky. There was a loud hollow sound below. She peered out. Sykes was at the wood-pile, demolishing a wire-covered box.

He hurried to the kitchen door, but hung outside there some minutes before he entered, and stood some minutes more inside before he closed it after him.

The gray in the sky was spreading. Delia descended without fear now, and crouched beneath the low bedroom window. The drawn shade shut out the dawn, shut in the night. But the thin walls held back no sound.

"Dat ol' scratch[6] is woke up now!" She mused at the tremendous whirr inside, which every woodsman knows, is one of the sound illusions. The rattler is a ventriloquist. His whirr sounds to the right, to the left, straight ahead, behind, close under foot—everywhere but where it is. Woe to him who guesses wrong unless he is prepared to hold up his end of the argument! Sometimes he strikes without rattling at all.

Inside, Sykes heard nothing until he knocked a pot lid off the stove while trying to reach the match-safe in the dark. He had emptied his pockets at Bertha's.

The snake seemed to wake up under the stove and Sykes made a quick leap into the bedroom. In spite of the gin he had had, his head was clearing now.

"Mah Gawd!" he chattered, "ef Ah could on'y strack uh light!"

The rattling ceased for a moment as he stood paralyzed. He waited. It seemed that the snake waited also.

"Oh, fuh de light! Ah thought he'd be too sick"—Sykes was muttering to himself when the whirr began again, closer, right underfoot this time. Long before this, Sykes' ability to think had been flattened down to primitive instinct and he leaped—onto the bed.

Outside Delia heard a cry that might have come from a maddened chimpanzee, a stricken gorilla. All the terror, all the horror, all the rage that man possibly could express, without a recognizable human sound.

A tremendous stir inside there, another series of animal screams, the intermittent whirr of the reptile. The shade torn violently down from the window, letting in the red dawn, a huge brown hand seizing the window stick, great dull blows upon the wooden floor punctuating the gibberish of sound long after the rattle of the snake had abruptly subsided. All this Delia could see and hear from her place beneath the window, and it made her ill. She crept over to the four o'clocks and stretched herself on the cool earth to recover.

She lay there. "Delia, Delia!" She could hear Sykes calling in a most despairing tone as one who expected no answer. The sun crept on up, and he called. Delia could not move—her legs had gone flabby. She never moved, he called, and the sun kept rising.

"Mah Gawd!" She heard him moan, "Mah Gawd fum Heben!" She heard him stumbling about and got up from her flower-bed. The sun was growing

[6] **scratch** the devil

warm. As she approached the door she heard him call out hopefully, "Delia, is dat you Ah heah?"

She saw him on his hands and knees as soon as she reached the door. He crept an inch or two toward her—all that he was able, and she saw his horribly swollen neck and his one open eye shining with hope. A surge of pity too strong to support bore her away from that eye that must, could not, fail to see the tubs. He would see the lamp. Orlando with its doctors was too far. She could scarcely reach the chinaberry tree, where she waited in the growing heat while inside she knew the cold river was creeping up and up to extinguish that eye which must know by now that she knew.

—1926

---

**RICHARD WRIGHT ■ (1908–1960)**

*Richard Wright was the son of a Mississippi farm worker and mill hand who abandoned the family when the writer was 5 and a mother who was forced by poverty to place her son in orphanages during part of his childhood. As he relates in his autobiography,* Black Boy *(1945), he was largely self-educated through extensive reading; while working for the post office in Memphis, he discovered the essays of H. L. Mencken, whom he credited as the major influence on his decision to become a writer. In Chicago in the 1930s, he became associated with the Federal Writers' Project and, briefly, with the Communist Party. He later lived in New York and, for the last fifteen years of his life, Paris, where he was associated with French existentialist writers such as Jean-Paul Sartre. Wright's first novel,* Native Son *(1940), based on an actual 1938 murder case, describes the chain of circumstances that lead to a black chauffeur's being tried and executed for the accidental slaying of a wealthy white woman. The success of that book established Wright as the leading black novelist of his generation, and while none of his subsequent works attracted the same level of attention, he nevertheless helped define many of the themes that African American writers continue to explore today. "The Man Who Was Almost a Man" was filmed as part of the PBS American Short Story series and, in its association between "manhood" and gun ownership, remains relevant today.*

# The Man who was Almost a Man

Dave struck out across the fields, looking homeward through paling light. Whut's the use talkin wid em niggers in the field? Anyhow, his mother was putting supper on the table. Them niggers can't understan nothing. One of these days he was going to get a gun and practice shooting, then they couldn't talk to him as though he were a little boy. He slowed, looking at the ground.

Shucks, Ah ain scareda them even if they are biggern me! Aw, Ah know what Ahma do. Ahm going by ol Joe's sto n git that Sears Roebuck catlog n look at them guns. Mebbe Ma will lemme buy one when she gits mah pay from ol man Hawkins. Ahma beg her t gimme some money. Ahm ol ernough to hava gun. Ahm seventeen. Almost a man. He strode, feeling his long loose-jointed limbs. Shucks, a man oughta hava little gun aftah he done worked hard all day.

He came in sight of Joe's store. A yellow lantern glowed on the front porch. He mounted steps and went through the screen door, hearing it bang behind him. There was a strong smell of coal oil and mackerel fish. He felt very confident until he saw fat Joe walk in through the rear door, then his courage began to ooze.

"Howdy, Dave! Whutcha want?"

"How yuh, Mistah Joe? Aw, Ah don wanna buy nothing. Ah jus wanted t see ef yuhd lemme look at tha catlog erwhile."

"Sure! You wanna see it here?"

"Nawsuh. Ah wants t take it home wid me. Ah'll bring it back termorrow when Ah come in from the fiels."

"You plannin on buying something?"

"Yessuh."

"Your ma lettin you have your own money now?"

"Shucks. Mistah Joe, Ahm gittin t be a man like anybody else!"

Joe laughed and wiped his greasy white face with a red bandanna.

"Whut you plannin on buyin?"

Dave looked at the floor, scratched his head, scratched his thigh, and smiled. Then he looked up shyly.

"Ah'll tell yuh, Mistah Joe, ef yuh promise yuh won't tell."

"I promise."

"Waal, Ahma buy a gun."

"A gun? What you want with a gun?"

"Ah wanna keep it."

"You ain't nothing but a boy. You don't need a gun."

"Aw, lemme have the catlog, Mistah Joe. Ah'll bring it back."

Joe walked through the rear door. Dave was elated. He looked around at barrels of sugar and flour. He heard Joe coming back. He craned his neck to see if he were bringing the book. Yeah, he's got it. Gawddog, he's got it!

"Here, but be sure you bring it back. It's the only one I got."

"Sho, Mistah Joe."

"Say, if you wanna buy a gun, why don't you buy one from me? I gotta gun to sell."

"Will it shoot?"

"Sure it'll shoot."

"Whut kind is it?"

"Oh, it's kinda old ... a left-hand Wheeler. A pistol. A big one."

"Is it got bullets in it?"

"It's loaded."

"Kin Ah see it?"

"Where's your money?"

"Whut yuh wan fer it?"

"I'll let you have it for two dollars."

"Just two dollahs? Shucks, Ah could buy that when Ah git mah pay."

"I'll have it here when you want it."

"Awright, suh. Ah be in fer it."

He went through the door, hearing it slam again behind him. Ahma git some money from Ma n buy me a gun! Only two dollahs! He tucked the thick catalogue under his arm and hurried.

"Where yuh been, boy?" His mother held a steaming dish of black-eyed peas.

"Aw, Ma, Ah jus stopped down the road t talk wid the boys."

"Yuh know bettah t keep suppah waitin."

He sat down, resting the catalogue on the edge of the table.

"Yuh git up from there and git to the well n wash yosef! Ah ain feedin no hogs in mah house!"

She grabbed his shoulder and pushed him. He stumbled out of the room, then came back to get the catalogue.

"Whut this?"

"Aw, Ma, it's jusa catlog."

"Who yuh git it from?"

"From Joe, down at the sto."

"Waal, thas good. We kin use it in the outhouse."

"Naw, Ma." He grabbed for it. "Gimme ma catlog, Ma."

She held onto it and glared at him.

"Quit hollerin at me! Whut's wrong wid yuh? Yuh crazy?"

"But Ma, please. It ain mine! It's Joe's! He tol me t bring it back t im termorrow."

She gave up the book. He stumbled down the back steps, hugging the thick book under his arm. When he had splashed water on his face and hands, he groped back to the kitchen and fumbled in a corner for the towel. He bumped into a chair; it clattered to the floor. The catalogue sprawled at his feet. When he had dried his eyes he snatched up the book and held it again under his arm. His mother stood watching him.

"Now, ef yuh gonna act a fool over that ol book, Ah'll take it n burn it up."

"Naw, Ma, please."

"Waal, set down n be still!"

He sat down and drew the oil lamp close. He thumbed page after page, unaware of the food his mother set on the table. His father came in. Then his small brother.

"Whutcha got there, Dave?" his father asked.

"Jusa catlog," he answered, not looking up.

"Yeah, here they is!" His eyes glowed at blue-and-black revolvers. He glanced up, feeling sudden guilt. His father was watching him. He eased the book under the table and rested it on his knees. After the blessing was asked, he ate. He scooped up peas and swallowed fat meat without chewing. Buttermilk helped to wash it down. He did not want to mention money before his father. He would do much better by cornering his mother when she was alone. He looked at his father uneasily out of the edge of his eye.

"Boy, how come yuh don quit foolin wid tha book n eat yo suppah?"

"Yessuh."

"How you n ol man Hawkins gitten erlong?"

"Suh?"

"Can't yuh hear? Why don yuh lissen? Ah ast yu how wuz yuh n ol man Hawkins gittin erlong?"

"Oh, swell, Pa. Ah plows mo lan than anybody over there."

"Waal, yuh oughta keep you mind on what yuh doin."

"Yessuh."

He poured his plate full of molasses and sopped it up slowly with a chunk of cornbread. When his father and brother had left the kitchen, he still sat and looked again at the guns in the catalogue, longing to muster courage enough to present his case to his mother. Lawd, ef Ah only had tha pretty one! He could almost feel the slickness of the weapon with his fingers. If he had a gun like that he would polish it and keep it shining so it would never rust! N Ah'd keep it loaded, by Gawd!

"Ma?" His voice was hesitant.

"Hunh?"

"Ol man Hawkins give yuh mah money yit?"

"Yeah, but ain no usa yuh thinking bout throwin nona it erway. Ahm keeping tha money sos yuh kin have cloes t go to school this winter."

He rose and went to her side with the open catalogue in his palms. She was washing dishes, her head bent low over a pan. Shyly he raised the book. When he spoke, his voice was husky, faint.

"Ma, Gawd knows Ah wans one of these."

"One of whut?" she asked, not raising her eyes.

"One of these," he said again, not daring even to point. She glanced up at the page, then at him with wide eyes. "Nigger, is yuh gone plumb crazy?"

"Aw, Ma—"

"Git outta here! Don yuh talk t me bout no gun! Yuh a fool!"

"Ma, Ah kin buy one fer two dollahs."

"Not ef Ah knows it, yuh ain!"

"But yuh promised me one—"

"Ah don care what Ah promised! Yuh ain nothing but a boy yit!"

"Ma, ef yuh lemme buy one Ah'll *never* ast yuh fer nothing no mo."

"Ah tol yuh t git outta here! Yuh ain gonna toucha penny of tha money fer no gun! Thas how come Ah has Mistah Hawkins t pay yo wages t me, cause Ah knows yuh ain got no sense."

"But, Ma, we needa gun. Pa ain got no gun. We needa gun in the house. Yuh kin never tell whut might happen."

"Now don yuh try to maka fool outta me, boy! Ef we did hava gun, yuh wouldn't have it!"

He laid the catalogue down and slipped his arm around her waist.

"Aw, Ma, Ah done worked hard alla summer n ain ast yuh fer nothing, is Ah, now?"

"Thas what yuh spose t do!"

"But Ma, Ah wans a gun. Yuh kin lemme have two dollahs outta mah money. Please, Ma. I kin give it to Pa ... Please, Ma! Ah loves yuh, Ma!"

When she spoke her voice came soft and low.

"What yu wan wida gun, Dave? Yuh don need no gun. Yuh'll git in trouble. N ef yo pa jus thought Ah let yuh have money t buy a gun he'd hava fit."

"Ah'll hide it, Ma. It ain but two dollahs."

"Lawd, chil, whut's wrong wid yuh?"

"Ain nothin wrong, Ma. Ahm almos a man now. Ah wans a gun."

"Who gonna sell yuh a gun?"

"Ol Joe at the sto."

"N it don cos but two dollahs?"

"Thas all, Ma. Jus two dollahs. Please, Ma."

She was stacking the plates away; her hands moved slowly, reflectively. Dave kept an anxious silence. Finally, she turned to him.

"Ah'll let yuh git tha gun if yuh promise me one thing."

"What's tha, Ma?"

"Yuh bring it straight back t me, yuh hear? It be fer Pa."

"Yessum! Lemme go now, Ma."

She stooped, turned slightly to one side, raised the hem of her dress, rolled down the top of her stocking, and came up with a slender wad of bills.

"Here," she said. "Lawd knows yuh don need no gun. But yer pa does. Yuh bring it right back t me, yuh hear? Ahma put it up. Now ef yuh don, Ahma have yuh pa lick yuh so hard yuh won fergit it."

"Yessum."

He took the money, ran down the steps, and across the yard.

"Dave! Yuuuuuh Daaaaave!"

He heard, but he was not going to stop now. "Naw, Lawd!"

The first movement he made the following morning was to reach under the pillow for the gun. In the gray light of dawn he held it loosely, feeling a sense of power. Could kill a man with a gun like this. Kill anybody, black or white. And if he were holding his gun in his hand, nobody could run over him; they would have to respect him. It was a big gun, with a long barrel and a heavy handle. He raised and lowered it in his hand, marveling at its weight.

He had not come straight home with it as his mother had asked; instead he had stayed out in the fields, holding the weapon in his hand, aiming it now and then at some imaginary foe. But he had not fired it; he had been afraid that his father might hear. Also he was not sure he knew how to fire it.

To avoid surrendering the pistol he had not come into the house until he knew that they were all asleep. When his mother had tiptoed to his bedside late that night and demanded the gun, he had first played possum; then he had told her that the gun was hidden outdoors, that he would bring it to her in the morning. Now he lay turning it slowly in his hands. He broke it, took out the cartridges, felt them, and then put them back.

He slid out of bed, got a long strip of old flannel from a trunk, wrapped the gun in it, and tied it to his naked thigh while it was still loaded. He did not go in to breakfast. Even though it was not yet daylight he started for Jim Hawkins' plantation. Just as the sun was rising he reached the barns where the mules and plows were kept.

"Hey! That you, Dave?"

He turned. Jim Hawkins stood eyeing him suspiciously.

"What're yuh doing here so early?"

"Ah didn't know Ah wuz gittin up so early, Mistah Hawkins. Ah was fixin t hitch up ol Jenny n take her t the fiels."

"Good. Since you're so early, how about plowing that stretch down by the woods?"

"Suits me, Mistah Hawkins."

"O.K. Go to it!"

He hitched Jenny to a plow and started across the fields. Hot dog! This was just what he wanted. If he could get down by the woods, he could shoot his gun and nobody would hear. He walked behind the plow, hearing the traces creaking, feeling the gun tied tight to his thigh.

When he reached the woods, he plowed two whole rows before he decided to take out the gun. Finally, he stopped, looked in all directions, then untied the gun and held it in his hand. He turned to the mule and smiled.

"Know whut this is, Jenny? Naw, yuh wouldn know! Yuhs jusa ol mule! Anyhow, this is a gun, n it kin shoot, by Gawd!"

He held the gun at arm's length. Whut t hell, Ahma shoot this thing! He looked at Jenny again.

"Lissen here, Jenny! When Ah pull this ol trigger, Ah don wan yuh t run n acka fool now!"

Jenny stood with head down, her short ears pricked straight. Dave walked off about twenty feet, held the gun far out from him at arm's length, and turned his head. Hell, he told himself, Ah ain afraid. The gun felt loose in his fingers; he waved it wildly for a moment. Then he shut his eyes and tightened his forefinger. Bloom! A report half deafened him and he thought his right hand was torn from his arm. He heard Jenny whinnying and galloping over the field, and he found himself on his knees, squeezing his fingers hard between his legs. His hand was numb; he jammed it into his mouth, trying to warm it, trying to stop the pain. The gun lay at his feet. He did not quite know what had happened. He stood up and stared at the gun as though it were a living thing. He gritted his teeth and kicked the gun. Yuh almos broke mah arm! He turned to look for Jenny; she was far over the fields, tossing her head and kicking wildly.

"Hol on there, ol mule!"

When he caught up with her she stood trembling, walling her big white eyes at him. The plow was far away; the traces had broken. Then Dave stopped short, looking, not believing. Jenny was bleeding. Her left side was red and wet with blood. He went closer. Lawd, have mercy! Wondah did Ah shoot this mule? He grabbed for Jenny's mane. She flinched, snorted, whirled, tossing her head.

"Hol on now! Hol on."

Then he saw the hole in Jenny's side, right between the ribs. It was round, wet, red. A crimson stream streaked down the front leg, flowing fast. Good Gawd! Ah wuzn't shootin at tha mule. He felt panic. He knew he had to stop that blood, or Jenny would bleed to death. He had never seen so much blood in all his life. He chased the mule for half a mile, trying to catch her. Finally she stopped, breathing hard, stumpy tail half arched. He caught her mane and led her back to where the plow and gun lay. Then he stopped and grabbed handfuls of damp black earth and tried to plug the bullet hole. Jenny shuddered, whinnied, and broke from him.

"Hol on! Hol on now!"

He tried to plug it again, but blood came anyhow. His fingers were hot and sticky. He rubbed dirt into his palms, trying to dry them. Then again he attempted to plug the bullet hole, but Jenny shied away, kicking her heels high. He stood helpless. He had to do something. He ran at Jenny; she dodged him. He watched a red stream of blood flow down Jenny's leg and form a bright pool at her feet.

"Jenny ... Jenny," he called weakly.

His lips trembled. She's bleeding t death! He looked in the direction of home, wanting to go back, wanting to get help. But he saw the pistol lying in the damp black clay. He had a queer feeling that if he only did something, this would not be; Jenny would not be there bleeding to death.

When he went to her this time, she did not move. She stood with sleepy, dreamy eyes; and when he touched her she gave a low-pitched whinny and knelt to the ground, her front knees slopping in blood.

"Jenny ... Jenny ..." he whispered.

For a long time she held her neck erect; then her head sank, slowly. Her ribs swelled with a mighty heave and she went over.

Dave's stomach felt empty, very empty. He picked up the gun and held it gingerly between his thumb and forefinger. He buried it at the foot of a tree. He took a stick and tried to cover the pool of blood with dirt—but what was the use? There was Jenny lying with her mouth open and her eyes walled and glassy. He could not tell Jim Hawkins he had shot his mule. But he had to tell something. Yeah, Ah'll tell em Jenny started gittin wil n fell on the joint of the plow ... But that would hardly happen to a mule. He walked across the field slowly, head down.

It was sunset. Two of Jim Hawkins' men were over near the edge of the woods digging a hole in which to bury Jenny. Dave was surrounded by a knot of people, all of whom were looking down at the dead mule.

"I don't see how in the world it happened," said Jim Hawkins for the tenth time.

The crowd parted and Dave's mother, father, and small brother pushed into the center.

"Where Dave?" his mother called.

"There he is," said Jim Hawkins.

His mother grabbed him.

"Whut happened, Dave? Whut yuh done?"

"Nothin."

"C mon, boy, talk," his father said.

Dave took a deep breath and told the story he knew nobody believed.

"Waal," he drawled. "Ah brung ol Jenny down here sos Ah could do mah plowin. Ah plowed bout two rows, just like yuh see." He stopped and pointed at the long rows of upturned earth. "Then somethin musta been wrong wid ol Jenny. She wouldn ack right a-tall. She started snortin n kickin her heels. Ah tried t hol her, but she pulled erway, rearin n goin in. Then when the point of the plow was stickin up in the air, she swung erroun n twisted herself back on it ... She stuck herself n started t bleed. N fo Ah could do anything, she wuz dead."

"Did you ever hear anything like that in all your life?" asked Jim Hawkins.

There were white and black standing in the crowd. They murmured. Dave's mother came close to him and looked hard into his face. "Tell the truth, Dave," she said.

"Looks like a bullet hole to me," said one man.

"Dave, whut yuh do wid the gun?" his mother asked.

The crowd surged in, looking at him. He jammed his hands into his pockets, shook his head slowly from left to right, and backed away. His eyes were wide and painful.

"Did he hava gun?" asked Jim Hawkins.

"By Gawd, Ah tol yuh tha wuz a gun wound," said a man, slapping his thigh.

His father caught his shoulders and shook him till his teeth rattled.

"Tell whut happened, yuh rascal! Tell whut ..."

Dave looked at Jenny's stiff legs and began to cry.

"Whut yuh do wid tha gun?" his mother asked.

"What wuz he doin wida gun?" his father asked.

"Come on and tell the truth," said Hawkins. "Ain't nobody going to hurt ..."

His mother crowded close to him.

"Did yuh shoot tha mule, Dave?"

Dave cried, seeing blurred white and black faces.

"Ahh ddinn gggo tt sshooot hher ... Ah ssswear ffo Gawd Ahh ddin ... Ah wuz a-tryin t sssee ef the old gggun would sshoot—"

"Where yuh git the gun from?" his father asked.

"Ah got it from Joe, at the sto."

"Where yuh git the money?"

"Ma give it t me."

"He kept worryin me, Bob. Ah had t. Ah tol im t bring the gun right back t me ... It was fer yuh, the gun."

"But how yuh happen to shoot that mule?" asked Jim Hawkins.

"Ah wuzn shootin at the mule, Mistah Hawkins. The gun jumped when Ah pulled the trigger ... N fo Ah knowed anythin Jenny was there a-bleedin."

Somebody in the crowd laughed. Jim Hawkins walked close to Dave and looked into his face.

"Well, looks like you have bought you a mule, Dave."

"Ah swear fo Gawd, Ah didn go t kill the mule, Mistah Hawkins!"

"But you killed her!"

All the crowd was laughing now. They stood on tiptoe and poked heads over one another's shoulders.

"Well, boy, looks like yuh done bought a dead mule! Hahaha!"

"Ain tha ershame."

"Hohohohoho."

Dave stood, head down, twisting his feet in the dirt.

"Well, you needn't worry about it, Bob," said Jim Hawkins to Dave's father. "Just let the boy keep on working and pay me two dollars a month."

"Whut yuh wan fer yo mule, Mistah Hawkins?"

Jim Hawkins screwed up his eyes.

"Fifty dollars."

"Whut yuh do wid tha gun?" Dave's father demanded.

Dave said nothing.

"Yuh wan me t take a tree n beat yuh till yuh talk!"

"Nawsuh!"

"Whut yuh do wid it?"

"Ah throwed it erway."

"Where?"

"Ah … Ah throwed it in the creek."

"Waal, c mon home. N firs thing in the mawnin git to tha creek n fin tha gun."

"Yessuh."

"Whut yuh pay fer it?"

"Two dollahs."

"Take tha gun n git yo money back n carry it to Mistah Hawkins, yuh hear? N don fergit Ahma lam you black bottom good fer this! Now march yosef on home, suh!"

Dave turned and walked slowly. He heard people laughing. Dave glared, his eyes welling with tears. Hot anger bubbled in him. Then he swallowed and stumbled on.

That night Dave did not sleep. He was glad that he had gotten out of killing the mule so easily, but he was hurt. Something hot seemed to turn over inside him each time he remembered how they had laughed. He tossed on his bed, feeling his hard pillow. N Pa says he's gonna beat me … He remembered other beatings, and his back quivered. Naw, naw, Ah sho don wan im t beat me tha way no mo. Dam em all! Nobody ever gave him anything. All he did was work. They treat me like a mule, n then they beat me. He gritted his teeth. N Ma had t tell on me.

Well, if he had to, he would take old man Hawkins that two dollars. But that meant selling the gun. And he wanted to keep that gun. Fifty dollars for a dead mule.

He turned over, thinking how he had fired the gun. He had an itch to fire it again. Ef other men kin shoota gun, by Gawd, Ah kin! He was still, listening. Mebbe they all sleepin now. The house was still. He heard the soft breathing of his brother. Yes, now! He would go down and get that gun and see if he could fire it! He eased out of bed and slipped into overalls.

The moon was bright. He ran almost all the way to the edge of the woods. He stumbled over the ground, looking for the spot where he had buried the gun. Yeah, here it is. Like a hungry dog scratching for a bone, he pawed it up. He puffed his black cheeks and blew dirt from the trigger and barrel. He broke it and found four cartridges unshot. He looked around; the fields were filled with silence and moonlight. He clutched the gun stiff and hard in his fingers. But, as soon as he wanted to pull the trigger, he shut his eyes and turned his head. Naw, Ah can't shoot wid mah eyes closed n mah head turned. With effort he held his eyes open; then he squeezed. *Blooooom!* He was stiff, not breathing. The gun was still in his hands. Dammit, he'd done it! He fired again. *Blooooom!* He smiled. *Bloooom! Blooooom! Click, click.* There! It was empty. If anybody could shoot a gun, he could. He put the gun into his hip pocket and started across the fields.

When he reached the top of a ridge he stood straight and proud in the moonlight, looking at Jim Hawkins' big white house, feeling the gun sagging in his pocket. Lawd, ef Ah had just one mo bullet Ah'd taka shot at tha house. Ah'd like t scare ol man Hawkins jusa little...Jusa enough t let im know Dave Saunders is a man.

To his left the road curved, running to the tracks of the Illinois Central. He jerked his head, listening. From far off come a faint *hoooof-hoooof; hoooof-hoooof*... He stood rigid. Two dollahs a mont. Les see now...Tha means it'll take bout two years. Shucks! Ah'll be dam!

He started down the road, toward the tracks. Yeah, here she comes! He stood beside the track and held himself stiffly. Here she comes, erroun the ben...C mon, yuh slow poke! C mon! He had his hand on his gun; something quivered in his stomach. Then the train thundered past, the gray and brown box cars rumbling and clinking. He gripped the gun tightly; then he jerked his hand out of his pocket. Ah betcha Bill wouldn't do it! Ah betcha...The cars slid past, steel grinding upon steel. Ahm ridin yuh ternight, so hep me Gawd! He was hot all over. He hesitated just a moment; then he grabbed, pulled atop of a car, and lay flat. He felt his pocket; the gun was still there. Ahead the long rails were glinting in the moonlight, stretching away, away to somewhere, somewhere where he could be a man....

—1937

## JOHN CHEEVER ▓ (1912–1982)

*John Cheever was associated with* The New Yorker *for most of his creative life. It was the magazine that first published most of his short stories. Cheever's examinations of the tensions of life in white-collar suburbia take many forms—from naturalism to outright fantasy—but virtually all of his fiction is suffused with a melancholy that is often fueled by marital tensions, failed social aspirations, and what one story aptly calls "the sorrows of gin." Born in Quincy, Massachusetts, Cheever was expelled from Thayer Academy at age 17, an event that formed the subject of his first published story, and he worked almost exclusively as a writer of fiction for the rest of his life, with occasional periods spent teaching at universities and writing for television. His most original writing is arguably in his short stories, but novels such as the National Book Award–winning* The Wapshot Chronicle *(1957),* The Wapshot Scandal *(1964),* Bullet Park *(1969), and* Falconer *(1977) brought him to the attention of large audiences.* The Stories of John Cheever *won the Pulitzer Prize in 1979. In recent years, his daughter, Susan Cheever, published a memoir,* Home Before Dark, *and an edition of her father's journals, both of which chronicle Cheever's long struggles with alcoholism and questions of sexual identity. The various aspects of "Reunion" are discussed in detail in the Introduction to Fiction.*

# Reunion

The last time I saw my father was in Grand Central Station. I was going from my grandmother's in the Adirondacks to a cottage on the Cape that my mother had rented, and I wrote my father that I would be in New York between trains for an hour and a half, and asked if we could have lunch together. His secretary wrote to say that he would meet me at the information booth at noon, and at twelve o'clock sharp I saw him coming through the crowd. He was a stranger to me—my mother divorced him three years ago and I hadn't been with him since—but as soon as I saw him I felt that he was my father, my flesh and blood, my future and my doom. I knew that when I was grown I would be something like him; I would have to plan my campaigns within his limitations. He was a big, good-looking man, and I was terribly happy to see him again. He struck me on the back and shook my hand. "Hi, Charlie," he said. "Hi, boy. I'd like to take you up to my club, but it's in the Sixties, and if you have to catch an early train I guess we'd better get something to eat around here." He put his arm around me, and I smelled my father the way my mother sniffs a rose. It was a rich compound of whiskey, after-shave lotion, shoe polish, woolens, and the rankness of a mature male. I hoped that someone would see us together. I wished that we could be photographed. I wanted some record of our having been together.

We went out of the station and up a side street to a restaurant. It was still early, and the place was empty. The bartender was quarreling with a delivery boy, and there was one very old waiter in a red coat down by the kitchen door. We sat down, and my father hailed the waiter in a loud voice. "*Kellner!*" he shouted. "*Garçon! Cameriere! You!*" His boisterousness in the empty restaurant seemed out of place. "Could we have a little service here!" he shouted. "Chop-chop." Then he clapped his hands. This caught the waiter's attention, and he shuffled over to our table.

"Were you clapping your hands at me?" he asked.

"Calm down, calm down, *sommelier*," my father said. "If it isn't too much to ask of you—if it wouldn't be too much above and beyond the call of duty, we would like a couple of Beefeater Gibsons."

"I don't like to be clapped at," the waiter said.

"I should have brought my whistle," my father said. "I have a whistle that is audible only to the ears of old waiters. Now, take out your little pad and your little pencil and see if you can get this straight: two Beefeater Gibsons. Repeat after me: two Beefeater Gibsons."

"I think you'd better go somewhere else," the waiter said quietly.

"That," said my father, "is one of the most brilliant suggestions I have ever heard. Come on, Charlie, let's get the hell out of here!"

I followed my father out of that restaurant into another. He was not so boisterous this time. Our drinks came, and he cross-questioned me about the baseball season. He then struck the edge of his empty glass with his knife and began shouting again. *"Garçon! Kellner! Cameriere! You!* Could we trouble you to bring us two more of the same."

"How old is the boy?" the waiter asked.

"That," my father said, "is none of your God-damned business."

"I'm sorry, sir," the waiter said, "but I won't serve the boy another drink."

"Well, I have some news for you," my father said. "I have some very interesting news for you. This doesn't happen to be the only restaurant in New York. They've opened another on the corner. Come on, Charlie."

He paid the bill, and I followed him out of that restaurant into another. Here the waiters wore pink jackets like hunting coats, and there was a lot of horse tack on the walls. We sat down, and my father began to shout again. "Master of the hounds! Tallyhoo and all that sort of thing. We'd like a little something in the way of a stirrup cup. Namely, two Bibson Geefeaters."

"Two Bibson Geefeaters?" the waiter asked, smiling.

"You know damned well what I want," my father said angrily. "I want two Beefeater Gibsons, and make it snappy. Things have changed in jolly old England. So my friend the duke tells me. Let's see what England can produce in the way of a cocktail."

"This isn't England," the waiter said.

"Don't argue with me," my father said. "Just do as you're told."

"I just thought you might like to know where you are," the waiter said.

"If there is one thing I cannot tolerate," my father said, "it is an impudent domestic. Come on, Charlie."

The fourth place we went to was Italian. *"Buon giorno,"* my father said. *"Per favore, possiamo avere due cocktail americani, forti, forti. Molto gin, poco vermut."*[1]

"I don't understand Italian," the waiter said.

"Oh, come off it," my father said. "You understand Italian, and you know damned well you do. *Vogliamo due cocktail americani. Subito."*

The waiter left us and spoke with the captain, who came over to our table and said, "I'm sorry, sir, but this table is reserved."

"All right," my father said. "Get us another table."

"All the tables are reserved," the captain said.

"I get it," my father said. "You don't desire our patronage. Is that it? Well, the hell with you. *Vada all' inferno.* Let's go, Charlie."

"I have to get my train," I said.

"I'm sorry, sonny," my father said. "I'm terribly sorry." He put his arm around me and pressed me against him. "I'll walk you back to the station. If there had only been time to go up to my club."

"That's all right, Daddy," I said.

[1] The father is ordering drinks in Italian.

"I'll get you a paper," he said. "I'll get you a paper to read on the train."

Then he went up to a newsstand and said, "Kind sir, will you be good enough to favor me with one of your God-damned, no-good, ten-cent afternoon papers?" The clerk turned away from him and stared at a magazine cover. "Is it asking too much, kind sir," my father said, "is it asking too much for you to sell me one of your disgusting specimens of yellow journalism?"

"I have to go, Daddy," I said. "It's late."

"Now, just wait a second, sonny," he said. "Just wait a second. I want to get a rise out of this chap."

"Goodbye, Daddy," I said, and I went down the stairs and got my train, and that was the last time I saw my father.

—1962

---

**RALPH ELLISON ▓ (1914–1995)**

*Ralph Ellison was born in Oklahoma City, where his early interests were primarily musical; he played trumpet and knew many prominent jazz musicians of the great Depression era. In 1933, he attended Tuskegee Institute, intending to study music, but he was drawn to literature through his study of contemporary writers (especially the poet T. S. Eliot). Ellison left school in 1936 for New York City, where he found work for a time with the Federal Writers' Project and began to publish stories and reviews in the later 1930s in progressive magazines such as* New Masses. *Tuskegee and Harlem provided him with material for* Invisible Man *(1952), a brilliant picaresque novel of African American life that established him as a major force in American fiction.* Invisible Man *won the National Book Award in 1953 and in 1965 was voted in a* Book Week *poll the most distinguished novel of the postwar period. Ellison published little subsequently, with two collections of essays,* Shadow and Act *(1964) and* Going to the Territory *(1986); a posthumous volume of collected stories; and an unfinished novel,* Juneteenth *(1999), having to suffice for readers who long anticipated a second novel that might somehow help define the changes four decades had wrought in the experience of black America. "A Party Down at the Square," a brutally direct account of a lynching, is based on true accounts of similar events that appeared primarily in African American newspapers in the 1920s and 1930s. Uncollected and almost forgotten at Ellison's death, it was posthumously reprinted in* Esquire.

# A Party Down at the Square

I don't know what started it. A bunch of men came by my Uncle Ed's place and said there was going to be a party down at the Square, and my uncle hollered for me to come on and I ran with them through the dark and rain and there we were at the Square. When we got there everybody was mad and quiet and standing around looking at the nigger. Some of the men had guns, and one man kept goosing the nigger in his pants with the barrel of a shotgun, saying he ought to pull the trigger, but he never did. It was right in front of the courthouse, and the old clock in the tower was striking twelve. The rain was falling cold and freezing as it fell. Everybody was cold, and the nigger kept wrapping his arms around himself trying to stop the shivers.

Then one of the boys pushed through the circle and snatched off the nigger's shirt, and there he stood, with his black skin all shivering in the light from the fire, and looking at us with a scaired look on his face and putting his hands in his pants pockets. Folks started yelling to hurry up and kill the nigger. Somebody yelled: "Take your hands out of your pockets, nigger; we gonna have plenty heat in a minnit." But the nigger didn't hear him and kept his hands where they were.

I tell you the rain was cold. I had to stick my hands in my pockets they got so cold. The fire was pretty small, and they put some logs around the platform they had the nigger on and then threw on some gasoline, and you could see the flames light up the whole Square. It was late and the streetlights had been off for a long time. It was so bright that the bronze statue of the general standing there in the Square was like something alive. The shadows playing on his moldy green face made him seem to be smiling down at the nigger.

They threw on more gas, and it made the Square bright like it gets when the lights are turned on or when the sun is setting red. All the wagons and cars were standing around the curbs. Not like Saturday though— the niggers weren't there. Not a single nigger was there except this Bacote nigger and they dragged him there tied to the back of Jed Wilson's truck. On Saturday there's as many niggers as white folks.

Everybody was yelling crazy 'cause they were about to set fire to the nigger, and I got to the rear of the circle and looked around the Square to try to count the cars. The shadows of the folks was flickering on the trees in the middle of the Square. I saw some birds that the noise had woke up flying through the trees. I guess maybe they thought it was morning. The ice had started the cobblestones in the street to shine where the rain was falling and freezing. I counted forty cars before I lost count. I knew folks must have been there from Phenix City by all the cars mixed in with the wagons.

God, it was a hell of a night. It was some night all right. When the noise died down I heard the nigger's voice from where I stood in the back, so I pushed my way up front. The nigger was bleeding from his nose and ears, and I could see him all red where the dark blood was running down his black skin. He kept lifting first one foot and then the other, like a chicken on a hot stove. I looked down to the platform they had him on, and they had pushed a ring of fire up close to his feet. It must have been hot to him with the flames almost touching his big black toes. Somebody yelled for the nigger to say his prayers, but the nigger wasn't saying anything now. He just kinda moaned with his eyes shut and kept moving up and down on his feet, first one foot and then the other.

I watched the flames burning the logs up closer and closer to the nigger's feet. They were burning good now, and the rain had stopped and the wind was rising, making the flames flare higher. I looked, and there must have been thirty-five women in the crowd, and I could hear their voices clear and shrill mixed in with those of the men. Then it happened. I heard the noise about the same time everyone else did. It was like the roar of a cyclone blowing up from the gulf, and everyone was looking up into the air to see what it was. Some of the faces looked surprised and scaired, all but the nigger. He didn't even hear the noise. He didn't even look up. Then the roar came closer, right above our heads and the wind was blowing higher and higher and the sound seemed to be going in circles.

Then I saw her. Through the clouds and fog I could see a red and green light on her wings. I could see them just for a second; then she rose up into the low clouds. I looked out for the beacon over the tops of the buildings in the direction of the airfield that's forty miles away, and it wasn't circling around. You usually could see it sweeping around the sky at night, but it wasn't there. Then, there she was again, like a big bird lost in the fog. I looked for the red and green lights, and they weren't there anymore. She was flying even closer to the tops of the buildings than before. The wind was blowing harder, and leaves started flying about, making funny shadows on the ground, and tree limbs were cracking and falling.

It was a storm all right. The pilot must have thought he was over the landing field. Maybe he thought the fire in the Square was put there for him to land by. Gosh, but it scaired the folks. I was scaired too. They started yelling: "He's going to land. He's going to land." And: "He's going to fall." A few started for their cars and wagons. I could hear the wagons creaking and chains jangling and cars spitting and missing as they started the engines up. Off to my right, a horse started pitching and striking his hooves against a car.

I didn't know what to do. I wanted to run, and I wanted to stay and see what was going to happen. The plane was close as hell. The pilot must have been trying to see where he was at, and her motors were drowning out all the sounds. I could even feel the vibration, and my hair felt like it was standing up under my hat. I happened to look over at the statue of the general standing with one leg before the other and leaning back on a sword, and I was fixing to run over and climb between his legs and sit there and watch when the roar stopped some, and I looked up and she was gliding just over the top of the trees in the middle of the Square.

Her motors stopped altogether and I could hear the sound of branches cracking and snapping off below her landing gear. I could see her plain now, all silver and shining in the light of the fire with T.W.A. in black letters under her wings. She was sailing smoothly out of the Square when she hit the high power lines that follow the Birmingham highway through the town. It made a loud crash. It sounded like the wind blowing the door of a tin barn shut. She only hit with her landing gear, but I could see the sparks flying, and the wires knocked loose from the poles were spitting blue sparks and whipping around like a bunch of snakes and leaving circles of blue sparks in the darkness.

The plane had knocked five or six wires loose, and they were dangling and swinging, and every time they touched they threw off more sparks. The wind was making them swing, and when I got over there, there was a crackling and spitting screen of blue haze across the highway. I lost my hat running over, but I didn't stop to look for it. I was among the first and I could hear the others pounding behind me across the grass of the Square. They were yelling to beat all hell, and they came up fast, pushing and shoving, and someone got pushed against a swinging wire. It made a sound like when a blacksmith drops a red hot horseshoe into a barrel of water, and the steam comes up. I could smell the flesh burning. The first time I'd ever smelled it. I got up close and it was a woman. It must have killed her right off. She was lying in a puddle stiff as a board, with pieces of glass insulators that the plane had knocked off the poles lying all around her. Her white dress was torn, and I saw one of her tits hanging out in the water and her thighs. Some woman screamed and fainted and almost fell on a wire, but a man caught her. The sheriff and his men were yelling and driving folks back with guns shining in their hands, and everything was lit up blue by the sparks. The shock had turned the woman almost as black as the nigger. I was trying to see if she wasn't blue too, or if it was just the sparks, and the sheriff drove me away. As I backed off trying to see, I heard the motors of the plane start up again somewhere off to the right in the clouds.

The clouds were moving fast in the wind and the wind was blowing the smell of something burning over to me. I turned around, and the crowd was headed back to the nigger. I could see him standing there in the middle of the flames. The wind was making the flames brighter every minute. The crowd was running. I ran too. I ran back across the grass with the crowd. It wasn't so large now that so many had gone when the plane came. I tripped and fell over the limb of a tree lying in the grass and bit my lip. It ain't well yet I bit it so bad. I could taste the blood in my mouth as I ran over. I guess that's what made me sick. When I got there, the fire had caught the nigger's pants, and the folks were standing around watching, but not too close on account of the wind blowing the flames. Somebody hollered, "Well, nigger, it ain't so cold now, is it? You don't need to put your hands in your pockets now." And the nigger looked up with his great white eyes looking like they was 'bout to pop out of his head, and I had enough. I didn't want to see anymore. I wanted to run somewhere and puke, but I stayed. I stayed right there in the front of the crowd and looked.

The nigger tried to say something I couldn't hear for the roar of the wind in the fire, and I strained my ears. Jed Wilson hollered, "What you say there, nigger?" And it came back through the flames in his nigger voice: "Will one a you gentlemen please cut my throat?" he said. "Will somebody please cut my throat like a Christian?" And Jed hollered back, "Sorry, but ain't no Christians around tonight. Ain't no Jew-boys neither. We're just one hundred percent Americans."

Then the nigger was silent. Folks started laughing at Jed. Jed's right popular with the folks, and next year, my uncle says, they plan to run him for sheriff. The heat was too much for me, and the smoke was making my eyes to smart. I was trying to back away when Jed reached down and brought up a can of gasoline and threw it in the fire on the nigger. I could see the flames catching the gas in a puff as it went in in a silver sheet and some of it reached the nigger, making spurts of blue fire all over his chest.

Well, that nigger was tough. I have to give it to that nigger; he was really tough. He had started to burn like a house afire and was making the smoke smell like burning hides. The fire was up around his head, and the smoke was so thick and black we couldn't see him. And him not moving—we thought he was dead. Then he started out. The fire had burned the ropes they had tied him with, and he started jumping and kicking about like he was blind, and you could smell his skin burning. He kicked so hard that the platform, which was burning too, fell in, and he rolled out of the fire at my feet. I jumped back so he wouldn't get on me. I'll never forget it. Every time I eat barbeque I'll remember that nigger. His back was just like a barbecued hog. I could see the prints of his ribs where they start around from his backbone and curve down and around. It was a sight to see, that nigger's back. He was right at my feet, and somebody behind pushed me and almost made me step on him, and he was still burning.

I didn't step on him though, and Jed and somebody else pushed him back into the burning planks and logs and poured on more gas. I wanted to leave, but the folks were yelling and I couldn't move except to look around and see the statue. A branch the wind had broken was resting on his hat. I tried to push out and get away because my guts were gone, and all I got was spit and hot breath in my face from the woman and two men standing directly behind me. So I had to turn back around. The nigger rolled out of the fire again. He wouldn't stay put. It was on the other side this time. I couldn't see him very well through the flames and smoke. They got some tree limbs and held him there this time and he stayed there till he was ashes. I guess he stayed there. I know he burned to ashes because I saw Jed a week later, and he laughed and showed me some white finger bones still held together with little pieces of the nigger's skin. Anyway, I left when somebody moved around to see the nigger. I pushed my way through the crowd, and a woman in the rear scratched my face as she yelled and fought to get up close.

I ran across the Square to the other side, where the sheriff and his deputies were guarding the wires that were still spitting and making a blue fog. My heart was pounding like I had been running a long ways, and I bent over and let my insides go. Everything came up and spilled in a big gush over the ground. I was sick, and tired, and weak, and cold. The wind was still high, and large drops of rain were beginning to fall. I headed down the street to my uncle's place past a store where the wind had broken a window, and glass lay over the sidewalk. I kicked it as I went by. I remember somebody's fool rooster crowing like it was morning in all that wind.

The next day I was too weak to go out, and my uncle kidded me and called me "the gutless wonder from Cincinnati." I didn't mind. He said you get used to it in time. He couldn't go out himself. There was too much wind and rain. I got up and looked out of the window, and the rain was pouring down and dead sparrows and limbs of trees were scattered all over the yard. There had been a cyclone all right. It swept a path right through the county, and we were lucky we didn't get the full force of it.

It blew for three days steady, and put the town in a hell of a shape. The wind blew sparks and set fire to the white-and-green-rimmed house on Jackson Avenue that had the big concrete lions in the yard and burned it down to the ground. They had to kill another nigger who tried to run out of the county after they burned this Bacote nigger. My Uncle Ed said they always have to kill niggers in pairs to keep the other niggers in place. I don't know though, the folks seem a little skittish of the niggers. They all came back, but they act pretty sullen. They look mean as hell when you pass them down at the store. The other day I was down to Brinkley's store, and a white cropper said it didn't do no good to kill the niggers 'cause things don't get no better. He looked hungry as hell. Most of the croppers look hungry. You'd be surprised how hungry white folks can look. Somebody said that he'd better shut his damn mouth, and he shut up. But from the look on his face he won't stay shut long. He went out of the store muttering to himself and spit a big chew of tobacco right down on Brinkley's floor. Brinkley said he was sore 'cause he wouldn't let him have credit. Anyway, it didn't seem to help things. First it was the nigger and the storm, then the plane, then the woman and the wires, and now I hear the airplane line is investigating to find who set the fire that almost wrecked their plane. All that in one night, and all of it but the storm over one nigger. It was some night all right. It was some party too. I was right there, see. I was right there watching it all. It was my first party and my last. God, but that nigger was tough. That Bacote nigger was some nigger!

—1997

---

**SHIRLEY JACKSON** ■ (1919–1965)

*Shirley Jackson was born in San Francisco and educated at Syracuse University. With her husband, the literary critic Stanley Edgar Hyman, she lived in Bennington, Vermont. There she produced three novels and the popular* Life Among the Savages *(1953), a "disrespectful memoir" of her four children, and a sequel to it,* Raising Demons *(1957). "The Lottery," which created a sensation when it appeared in* The New Yorker *in 1948, remains a fascinating example of an allegory whose ultimate meaning is open to debate. Many readers at the time, for obvious reasons, associated it with the Holocaust, although it should not be approached in such a restrictive manner. "The Lottery" is the only one of Jackson's many short stories that has been widely reprinted (it was also dramatized for television), but she was a versatile writer of humorous articles (for popular magazines) psychological novels, and she authored a popular gotbic horror novel,* The Haunting of Hill House *(1959), which was made into a motion picture called* The Haunting *(1963). Jackson published two collections of short stories,* The Lottery *(1949) and* The Magic of Shirley Jackson *(1966).*

# The Lottery

The morning of June 27th was clear and sunny, with the fresh warmth of a full-summer day; the flowers were blossoming profusely and the grass was richly green. The people of the village began to gather in the square, between the post office and the bank, around ten o'clock; in some towns there were so many people that the lottery took two days and had to be started on June 26th, but in this village, where there were only about three hundred people, the whole lottery took less than two hours, so it could begin at ten o'clock in the morning and still be through in time to allow the villagers to get home for noon dinner.

The children assembled first, of course. School was recently over for the summer, and the feeling of liberty sat uneasily on most of them; they tended to gather together quietly for a while before they broke into boisterous play, and their talk was still of the classroom and the teacher, of books and reprimands. Bobby Martin had already stuffed his pockets full of stones, and the other boys soon followed his example, selecting the smoothest and roundest stones; Bobby and Harry Jones and Dickie Delacroix—the villagers pronounced this name "Dellacroy"—eventually made a great pile of stones in one corner of the square and guarded it against the raids of the other boys. The girls stood aside, talking among themselves, looking over their shoulders at the boys, and the very small children rolled in the dust or clung to the hands of their older brothers or sisters.

Soon the men began to gather, surveying their own children, speaking of planting and rain, tractors and taxes. They stood together, away from the pile of stones in the corner, and their jokes were quiet and they smiled rather than laughed. The women, wearing faded house dresses and sweaters, came shortly after their menfolk. They greeted one another and exchanged bits of gossip as they went to join their husbands. Soon the women, standing by their husbands, began to call to their children, and the children came reluctantly, having to be called four or five times. Bobby Martin ducked under his mother's grasping hand and ran, laughing, back to the pile of stones. His father spoke up sharply, and Bobby came quickly and took his place between his father and his oldest brother.

The lottery was conducted—as were the square dances, the teenage club, the Halloween program—by Mr. Summers, who had time and energy to devote to civic activities. He was a roundfaced, jovial man and he ran the coal business, and people were sorry for him, because he had no children and his wife was a scold. When he arrived in the square, carrying the black wooden box, there was a murmur of conversation among the villagers and he waved and called, "Little late today, folks." The postmaster, Mr. Graves, followed him, carrying a three-legged stool, and the stool was put in the center of the square and Mr. Summers set the black box down on it. The villagers kept their distance, leaving a space between themselves and the stool, and when Mr. Summers said, "Some of you fellows want to give me a hand?" there was a hesitation before two men, Mr. Martin and his oldest son, Baxter, came forward to hold the box steady on the stool while Mr. Summers stirred up the papers inside it.

The original paraphernalia for the lottery had been lost long ago, and the black box now resting on the stool had been put into use even before Old Man Warner, the oldest man in town, was born. Mr. Summers spoke frequently to the villagers about making a new box, but no one liked to upset even as much tradition as was represented by the black box. There was a story that the present box had been made with some pieces of the box that had preceded it, the one that had been constructed when the first people settled down to make a village here. Every year, after the lottery, Mr. Summers began talking again about a new box, but every year the subject was allowed to fade off without anything's being done. The black box grew shabbier each year; by now it was no longer completely black but splintered badly along one side to show the original wood color, and in some places faded or stained.

Mr. Martin and his oldest son, Baxter, held the black box securely on the stool until Mr. Summers had stirred the papers thoroughly with his hand. Because so much of the ritual had been forgotten or discarded, Mr. Summers had been successful in having slips of paper substituted for the chips of wood that had been used for generations. Chips of wood, Mr. Summers had argued, had been all very well when the village was tiny, but now that the population was more than three hundred and likely to keep on growing, it was necessary to use something that would fit more easily into the black box. The night before the lottery, Mr. Summers and Mr. Graves made up the slips of paper and put them in the box, and it was then taken to the safe of Mr. Summers's coal company and locked up until Mr. Summers was ready to take it to the square next morning. The rest of the year, the box was put away, sometimes one place, sometimes another; it had spent one year in Mr. Graves's barn and another year underfoot in the post office, and sometimes it was set on a shelf in the Martin grocery and left there.

There was a great deal of fussing to be done before Mr. Summers declared the lottery open. There were lists to make up—of heads of families, heads of households in each family, members of each household in each family. There was the proper swearing-in of Mr. Summers by the postmaster, as the official of the lottery; at one time, some people remembered, there had been a recital of some sort, performed by the official of the lottery, a perfunctory, tuneless chant that had been rattled off duly each year; some people believed that the official of the lottery used to stand just so when he said or sang it, others believed that he was supposed to walk among the people, but years and years ago this part of the ritual had been allowed to lapse. There had been, also, a ritual salute, which the official of the lottery had had to use in addressing each person who came up to draw from the box, but this also had changed with time, until now it was felt necessary only for the official to speak to each person approaching. Mr. Summers was very good at all this; in his clean white shirt and blue jeans, with one hand resting carelessly on the black box, he seemed very proper and important as he talked interminably to Mr. Graves and the Martins.

Just as Mr. Summers finally left off talking and turned to the assembled villagers, Mrs. Hutchinson came hurriedly along the path to the square, her sweater thrown over her shoulders, and slid into place in the back of the crowd. "Clean forgot what day it was," she said to Mrs. Delacroix, who stood next to her, and they both laughed softly. "Thought my old man was out back stacking wood," Mrs. Hutchinson went on, "and then I looked out the window and the kids were gone, and then I remembered it was the twenty-seventh and came a-running." She dried her hands on her apron, and Mrs. Delacroix said, "You're in time, though. They're still talking away up there."

Mrs. Hutchinson craned her neck to see through the crowd and found her husband and children standing near the front. She tapped Mrs. Delacroix on the arm as a farewell and began to make her way through the crowd. The people separated good-humoredly to let her through; two or three people said, in voices just loud enough to be heard across the crowd, "Here comes your Missus, Hutchinson," and "Bill, she made it after all." Mrs. Hutchinson reached her husband, and Mr. Summers, who had been waiting, said cheerfully, "Thought we were going to have to get on without you, Tessie." Mrs. Hutchinson said, grinning, "Wouldn't have me leave m'dishes in the sink, now would you, Joe?" and soft laughter ran through the crowd as the people stirred back into position after Mrs. Hutchinson's arrival.

"Well, now," Mr. Summers said soberly, "guess we better get started, get this over with, so's we can go back to work. Anybody ain't here?"

"Dunbar," several people said. "Dunbar, Dunbar."

Mr. Summers consulted his list. "Clyde Dunbar," he said. "That's right. He's broke his leg, hasn't he? Who's drawing for him?"

"Me, I guess," a woman said, and Mr. Summers turned to look at her. "Wife draws for her husband," Mr. Summers said. "Don't you have a grown boy to do it for you, Janey?" Although Mr. Summers and everyone else in the village knew the answer perfectly well, it was the business of the official of the lottery to ask such questions formally. Mr. Summers waited with an expression of polite interest while Mrs. Dunbar answered.

"Horace's not but sixteen yet," Mrs. Dunbar said regretfully. "Guess I gotta fill in for the old man this year."

"Right," Mr. Summers said. He made a note on the list he was holding. Then he asked, "Watson boy drawing this year?"

A tall boy in the crowd raised his hand. "Here," he said. "I'm drawing for m'mother and me." He blinked his eyes nervously and ducked his head as several voices in the crowd said things like "Good fellow, Jack," and "Glad to see your mother's got a man to do it."

"Well," Mr. Summers said, "guess that's everyone. Old Man Warner make it?"

"Here," a voice said, and Mr. Summers nodded.

A sudden hush fell on the crowd as Mr. Summers cleared his throat and looked at the list. "All ready?" he called. "Now, I'll read the names—heads of families first—and the men come up and take a paper out of the box. Keep the paper folded in your hand without looking at it until everyone has had a turn. Everything clear?"

The people had done it so many times that they only half listened to the directions; most of them were quiet, wetting their lips, not looking around. Then Mr. Summers raised one hand high and said, "Adams." A man disengaged himself from the crowd and came forward. "Hi, Steve," Mr. Summers said, and Mr. Adams said, "Hi, Joe." They grinned at one another humorlessly and nervously. Then Mr. Adams reached into the black box and took out a folded paper. He held it firmly by one corner as he turned and went hastily back to his place in the crowd, where he stood a little apart from his family, not looking down at his hand.

"Allen," Mr. Summers said. "Anderson...Bentham."

"Seems like there's no time at all between lotteries any more," Mrs. Delacroix said to Mrs. Graves in the back row. "Seems like we got through with the last one only last week."

"Time sure goes fast," Mrs. Graves said.

"Clark . . . Delacroix."

"There goes my old man," Mrs. Delacroix said. She held her breath while her husband went forward.

"Dunbar," Mr. Summers said, and Mrs. Dunbar went steadily to the box while one of the women said, "Go on, Janey," and another said, "There she goes."

"We're next," Mrs. Graves said. She watched while Mr. Graves came around from the side of the box, greeted Mr. Summers gravely, and selected a slip of paper from the box. By now, all through the crowd there were men holding the small folded papers in their large hands, turning them over and over nervously. Mrs. Dunbar and her two sons stood together, Mrs. Dunbar holding the slip of paper.

"Harburt . . . Hutchinson."

"Get up there, Bill," Mrs. Hutchinson said, and the people near her laughed.

"Jones."

"They do say," Mr. Adams said to Old Man Warner, who stood next to him, "that over in the north village they're talking of giving up the lottery."

Old Man Warner snorted. "Pack of crazy fools," he said. "Listening to the young folks, nothing's good enough for *them*. Next thing you know, they'll be wanting to go back to living in caves, nobody work any more, live *that* way for a while. Used to be a saying about 'Lottery in June, corn be heavy soon.' First thing you know, we'd all be eating stewed chickweed and acorns. There's *always* been a lottery," he added petulantly. "Bad enough to see young Joe Summers up there joking with everybody."

"Some places have already quit lotteries," Mrs. Adams said.

"Nothing but trouble in *that*," Old Man Warner said stoutly. "Pack of young fools."

"Martin." And Bobby Martin watched his father go forward. "Overdyke . . . Percy."

"I wish they'd hurry," Mrs. Dunbar said to her older son. "I wish they'd hurry."

"They're almost through," her son said.

"You get ready to run tell Dad," Mrs. Dunbar said.

Mr. Summers called his own name and then stepped forward precisely and selected a slip from the box. Then he called, "Warner."

"Seventy-seventh year I been in the lottery," Old Man Warner said as he went through the crowd. "Seventy-seventh time."

"Watson." The tall boy came awkwardly through the crowd. Someone said, "Don't be nervous, Jack," and Mr. Summers said, "Take your time, son."

"Zanini."

After that, there was a long pause, a breathless pause, until Mr. Summers, holding his slip of paper in the air, said, "All right, fellows." For a minute, no one moved, and then all the slips of paper were opened. Suddenly, all women began to speak at once, saying, "Who is it?" "Who's got it?" "Is it the Dunbars?" "Is it the Watsons?" Then the voices began to say, "It's Hutchinson. It's Bill." "Bill Hutchinson's got it."

"Go tell your father," Mrs. Dunbar said to her older son.

People began to look around to see the Hutchinsons. Bill Hutchinson was standing quiet, staring down at the paper in his hand. Suddenly, Tessie Hutchinson shouted to Mr. Summers, "You didn't give him time enough to take any paper he wanted. I saw you. It wasn't fair!"

"Be a good sport, Tessie," Mrs. Delacroix called, and Mrs. Graves said, "All of us took the same chance."

"Shut up, Tessie," Bill Hutchinson said.

"Well, everyone," Mr. Summers said, "that was done pretty fast, and now we've got to be hurrying a little more to get done in time." He consulted his next list. "Bill," he said, "you draw for the Hutchinson family. You got any other households in the Hutchinsons?"

"There's Don and Eva," Mrs. Hutchinson yelled. "Make *them* take their chance!"

"Daughters draw with their husbands' families, Tessie," Mr. Summers said gently. "You know that as well as anyone else."

"It wasn't fair," Tessie said.

"I guess not, Joe," Bill Hutchinson said regretfully. "My daughter draws with her husband's family, that's only fair. And I've got no other family except the kids."

"Then, as far as drawing for families is concerned, it's you," Mr. Summers said in explanation, "and as far as drawing for households is concerned, that's you, too. Right?"

"Right," Bill Hutchinson said.

"How many kids, Bill?" Mr. Summers asked formally.

"Three," Bill Hutchinson said. "There's Bill, Jr., and Nancy, and little Dave. And Tessie and me."

"All right, then," Mr. Summers said. "Harry, you got their tickets back?"

Mr. Graves nodded and held up the slips of paper. "Put them in the box, then," Mr. Summers directed. "Take Bill's and put it in."

"I think we ought to start over," Mrs. Hutchinson said, as quietly as she could. "I tell you it wasn't *fair*. You didn't give him time enough to choose. *Everybody* saw that."

Mr. Graves had selected the five slips and put them in the box, and he dropped all the papers but those onto the ground, where the breeze caught them and lifted them off.

"Listen, everybody," Mrs. Hutchinson was saying to the people around her.

"Ready, Bill?" Mr. Summers asked, and Bill Hutchinson, with one quick glance around at his wife and children, nodded.

"Remember," Mr. Summers said, "take the slips and keep them folded until each person has taken one. Harry, you help little Dave." Mr. Graves took the hand of the little boy, who came willingly with him up to the box. "Take a paper out of the box, Davy," Mr. Summers said. Davy put his hand into the box and laughed. "Take just *one* paper," Mr. Summers said. "Harry, you hold it for him." Mr. Graves took the child's hand and removed the folded paper from the tight fist and held it while little Dave stood next to him and looked up at him wonderingly.

"Nancy next," Mr. Summers said. Nancy was twelve, and her school friends breathed heavily as she went forward, switching her skirt, and took a slip daintily from the box. "Bill, Jr.," Mr. Summers said, and Billy, his face red and his feet overlarge, nearly knocked the box over as he got a paper out. "Tessie," Mr. Summers said. She hesitated for a minute, looking around defiantly, and then set her lips and went up to the box. She snatched a paper out and held it behind her.

"Bill," Mr. Summers said, and Bill Hutchinson reached into the box and felt around, bringing his hand out at last with the slip of paper in it.

The crowd was quiet. A girl whispered, "I hope it's not Nancy," and the sound of the whisper reached the edges of the crowd.

"It's not the way it used to be," Old Man Warner said clearly. "People ain't the way they used to be."

"All right," Mr. Summers said. "Open the papers. Harry, you open little Dave's."

Mr. Graves opened the slip of paper and there was a general sigh through the crowd as he held it up and everyone could see that it was blank. Nancy and Bill, Jr., opened theirs at the same time, and both beamed and laughed, turning around to the crowd and holding their slips of paper above their heads.

"Tessie," Mr. Summers said. There was a pause, and then Mr. Summers looked at Bill Hutchinson, and Bill unfolded his paper and showed it. It was blank.

"It's Tessie," Mr. Summers said, and his voice was hushed. "Show us her paper, Bill."

Bill Hutchinson went over to his wife and forced the slip of paper out of her hand. It had a black spot on it, the black spot Mr. Summers had made the night before with the heavy pencil in the coal-company office. Bill Hutchinson held it up, and there was a stir in the crowd.

"All right, folks," Mr. Summers said, "let's finish quickly."

Although the villagers had forgotten the ritual and lost the original black box, they still remembered to use stones. The pile of stones the boys had made earlier was ready; there were stones on the ground with the blowing scraps of paper that had come out of the box. Mrs. Delacroix selected a stone so large she had to pick it up with both hands and turned to Mrs. Dunbar. "Come on," she said. "Hurry up."

Mrs. Dunbar had small stones in both hands, and she said, gasping for breath, "I can't run at all. You'll have to go ahead and I'll catch up with you."

The children had stones already, and someone gave little Davy Hutchinson a few pebbles.

Tessie Hutchinson was in the center of a cleared space by now, and she held her hands out desperately as the villagers moved in on her. "It isn't fair," she said. A stone hit her on the side of the head.

Old Man Warner was saying, "Come on, come on, everyone." Steve Adams was in the front of the crowd of villagers, with Mrs. Graves beside him.

"It isn't fair, it isn't right," Mrs. Hutchinson screamed, and then they were upon her.

—1948

---

### HISAYE YAMAMOTO ▨ (1921–2011)

*Yamamoto was born in Redondo Beach, California, the daughter of Japanese immigrants who were strawberry farmers. During World War II, she was held for three years in an Arizona internment camp, where she wrote for the camp newspaper. After the war, she worked for a time as a journalist and began to publish her stories in national magazines and journals. The mother of five, Yamamoto eventually gathered her stories into a collection,* Seventeen Syllables, *which was published in 1987. A Nisei or second-generation Japanese American woman, Yamamoto explores the cultural differences between her peers and the older Issei generation of their mothers. Asked in an interview about writing for an Asian American audience, Yamamoto replied, "I've never thought of writing for anybody. I don't think you can write aiming at a specifically Asian American audience if you want to write freely. No, you just express yourself without thinking of that angle." The "seventeen syllables" of the title refer to the poetic form of the Japanese haiku.*

## Seventeen Syllables

The first Rosie knew that her mother had taken to writing poems was one evening when she finished one and read it aloud for her daughter's approval. It was about cats, and Rosie pretended to understand it thoroughly and appreciate it no end, partly because she hesitated to disillusion her mother about the quantity and quality of Japanese she had learned in all the years now that she had been going to Japanese school every Saturday (and Wednesday, too, in the summer). Even so, her mother must have been skeptical about the depth of Rosie's understanding, because she explained afterwards about the kind of poem she was trying to write.

See, Rosie, she said, it was a *haiku*, a poem in which she must pack all her meaning into seventeen syllables only, which were divided into three lines of five, seven, and five syllables. In the one she had just read, she had tried to capture the charm of a kitten, as well as comment on the superstition that owning a cat of three colors meant good luck.

"Yes, yes, I understand. How utterly lovely,"

Rosie said, and her mother, either satisfied or seeing through the deception and resigned, went back to composing.

The truth was that Rosie was lazy; English lay ready on the tongue but Japanese had to be searched for and examined, and even then put forth tentatively (probably to meet with laughter). It was so much easier to say yes, yes, even when one meant no, no. Besides, this was what was in her mind to say: I was looking through one of your magazines from Japan last night, Mother, and toward the back I found some *haiku* in English that delighted me. There was one that made me giggle off and on until I fell asleep—

It is morning, and lo!
I lie awake, comme il faut,
sighing for some dough.

Now, how to reach her mother, how to communicate the melancholy song? Rosie knew formal Japanese by fits and starts, her mother had even less English, no French. It was much more possible to say yes, yes.

It developed that her mother was writing the *haiku* for a daily newspaper, the *Mainichi Shimbun*, that was published in San Francisco. Los Angeles, to be sure, was closer to the farming community in which the Hayashi family lived and several Japanese vernaculars were printed there, but Rosie's parents said they preferred the tone of the northern paper. Once a week, the *Mainichi* would have a section devoted to *haiku*, and her mother became an extravagant contributor, taking for herself the blossoming pen name, Ume Hanazono.

So Rosie and her father lived for a while with two women, her mother and Ume Hanazono. Her mother (Tome Hayashi by name) kept house, cooked, washed, and, along with her husband and the Carrascos, the Mexican family hired for the harvest, did her ample share of picking tomatoes out in the sweltering fields and boxing them in tidy strata in the cool packing shed. Ume Hanazono, who came to life after the dinner dishes were done, was an earnest, muttering stranger who often neglected speaking when spoken to and stayed busy at the parlor table as late as midnight scribbling with pencil on scratch paper or carefully copying characters on good paper with her fat, pale green Parker.

The new interest had some repercussions on the household routine. Before, Rosie had been accustomed to her parents and herself taking their hot baths early and going to bed almost immediately afterwards, unless her parents challenged each other to a game of flower cards or unless company dropped in. Now if her father wanted to play cards, he had to resort to solitaire (at which he always cheated fearlessly), and if a group of friends came over, it was bound to contain someone who was also writing *haiku,* and the small assemblage would be split in two, her father entertaining the non-literary members and her mother comparing ecstatic notes with the visiting poet.

If they went out, it was more of the same thing. But Ume Hanazono's life span, even for a poet's, was very brief—perhaps three months at most.

One night they went over to see the Hayano family in the neighboring town to the west, an adventure both painful and attractive to Rosie. It was attractive because there were four Hayano girls, all lovely and each one named after a season of the year (Haru, Natsu, Aki, Fuyu), painful because something had been wrong with Mrs. Hayano ever since the birth of her first child. Rosie would sometimes watch Mrs. Hayano, reputed to have been the belle of her native village, making her way about a room, stooped, slowly shuffling, violently trembling (*always* trembling), and she would be reminded that this woman, in this same condition, had carried and given issue to three babies. She would look wonderingly at Mr. Hayano, handsome, tall, and strong, and she would look at her four pretty friends. But it was not a matter she could come to any decision about.

On this visit, however, Mrs. Hayano sat all evening in the rocker, as motionless and unobtrusive as it was possible for her to be, and Rosie found the greater part of the evening practically anaesthetic. Too, Rosie spent most of it in the girls' room, because Haru, the garrulous one, said almost as soon as the bows and other greetings were over, "Oh, you must see my new coat!"

It was a pale plaid of grey, sand, and blue, with an enormous collar, and Rosie, seeing nothing special in it, said, "Gee, how nice."

"Nice?" said Haru, indignantly. "Is that all you can say about it? It's gorgeous! And so cheap, too. Only seventeen-ninety eight, because it was a sale. The saleslady said it was twenty-five dollars regular."

"Gee," said Rosie. Natsu, who never said much and when she said anything said it shyly, fingered the coat covetously and Haru pulled it away.

"Mine," she said, putting it on. She minced in the aisle between the two large beds and smiled happily. "Let's see how your mother likes it."

She broke into the front room and the adult conversation and went to stand in front of Rosie's mother, while the rest watched from the door. Rosie's mother was properly envious. "May I inherit it when you're through with it?"

Haru, pleased, giggled and said yes, she could, but Natsu reminded gravely from the door, "You promised me, Haru."

Everyone laughed but Natsu, who shamefacedly retreated into the bedroom. Haru came in laughing, taking off the coat. "We were only kidding, Natsu," she said. "Here, you try it on now."

After Natsu buttoned herself into the coat, inspected herself solemnly in the bureau mirror, and reluctantly shed it, Rosie, Aki, and Fuyu got their turns, and Fuyu, who was eight, drowned in it while her sisters and Rosie doubled up in amusement. They all went into the front room later, because Haru's mother quaveringly called to her to fix the tea and rice cakes and open a can of sliced peaches for everybody. Rosie noticed that her mother and Mr. Hayano were talking together at the little table—they were discussing a *haiku* that Mr. Hayano was planning to send to the *Mainichi*, while her father was sitting at one end of the sofa looking through a copy of *Life*, the new picture magazine. Occasionally, her father would comment on a photograph, holding it toward Mrs. Hayano and speaking to her as he always did—loudly, as though he thought someone such as she must surely be at least a trifle deaf also.

The five girls had their refreshments at the kitchen table, and it was while Rosie was showing the sisters her trick of swallowing peach slices without chewing (she chased each slippery crescent down with a swig of tea) that her father brought his empty teacup and untouched saucer to the sink and said, "Come on, Rosie, we're going home now."

"Already?" asked Rosie.

"Work tomorrow," he said.

He sounded irritated, and Rosie, puzzled, gulped one last yellow slice and stood up to go, while the sisters began protesting, as was their wont.

"We have to get up at five-thirty," he told them, going into the front room quickly, so that they did not have their usual chance to hang onto his hands and plead for an extension of time.

Rosie, following, saw that her mother and Mr. Hayano were sipping tea and still talking together, while Mrs. Hayano concentrated, quivering, on raising the handleless Japanese cup to her lips with both her hands and lowering it back to her lap. Her father, saying nothing, went out the door, onto the bright porch, and down the steps. Her mother looked up and asked, "Where is he going?"

"Where is he going?" Rosie said. "He said we were going home now."

"Going home?" Her mother looked with embarrassment at Mr. Hayano and his absorbed wife and then forced a smile. "He must be tired," she said.

Haru was not giving up yet. "May Rosie stay overnight?" she asked, and Natsu, Aki, and Fuyu came to reinforce their sister's plea by helping her make a circle around Rosie's mother. Rosie, for once having no desire to stay, was relieved when her mother, apologizing to the perturbed Mr. and Mrs. Hayano for her father's abruptness at the same time, managed to shake her head no at the quartet, kindly but adamant, so that they broke their circle and let her go.

Rosie's father looked ahead into the windshield as the two joined him. "I'm sorry," her mother said. "You must be tired." Her father, stepping on the starter, said nothing. "You know how I get when it's *haiku*," she continued, "I forget what time it is." He only grunted.

As they rode homeward silently, Rosie, sitting between, felt a rush of hate for both—for her mother for begging, for her father for denying her mother. I wish this old Ford would crash, right now, she thought, then immediately, no, no, I wish my father would laugh, but it was too late: already the vision had passed through her mind of the green pick-up crumpled in the dark against one of the mighty eucalyptus trees they were just riding past, of the three contorted, bleeding bodies, one of them hers.

Rosie ran between two patches of tomatoes, her heart working more rambunctiously than she had ever known it to. How lucky it was that Aunt Taka and Uncle Gimpachi had come tonight, though, how very lucky. Otherwise she might not have really kept her half-promise to meet Jesus Carrasco. Jesus was going to be a senior in September at the same school she went to, and his parents were the ones helping with the tomatoes this year. She and Jesus, who hardly remembered seeing each other at Cleveland High where there were so many other people and two whole grades between them, had become great friends this summer—he always had a joke for her when he periodically drove the loaded pick-up up from the fields to the shed where she was usually sorting while her mother and father did the packing, and they laughed a great deal together over infinitesimal repartee during the afternoon break for chilled watermelon or ice cream in the shade of the shed.

What she enjoyed most was racing him to see who could finish picking a double row first. He, who could work faster, would tease her by slowing down until she thought she would surely pass him this time, then speeding up furiously to leave her several sprawling vines behind. Once he had made her screech hideously by crossing over, while her back was turned, to place atop the tomatoes in her green-stained bucket a truly monstrous, pale green worm (it had looked more like an infant snake). And it was when they had finished a contest this morning, after she had pantingly pointed a green finger at the immature tomatoes evident in the lugs at the end of his row and he had returned the accusation (with justice), that he had startlingly brought up the matter of their possibly meeting outside the range of both their parents' dubious eyes.

"What for?" she had asked.

"I've got a secret I want to tell you," he said.

"Tell me now," she demanded.

"It won't be ready till tonight," he said.

She laughed. "Tell me tomorrow then."

"It'll be gone tomorrow," he threatened.

"Well, for seven hakes, what is it?" she had asked, more than twice, and when he had suggested that the packing shed would be an appropriate place to find out, she had cautiously answered maybe. She had not been certain she was going to keep the appointment until the arrival of mother's sister and her husband. Their coming seemed a sort of signal of permission, of grace, and she had definitely made up her mind to lie and leave as she was bowing them welcome.

So as soon as everyone appeared settled back for the evening, she announced loudly that she was going to the privy outside, "I'm going to the *benjo!*" and slipped out the door. And now that she was actually on her way, her heart pumped in such an undisciplined way that she could hear it with her ears. It's because I'm running, she told herself, slowing to a walk. The shed was up ahead, one more patch away, in the middle of the fields. Its bulk, looming in the dimness, took on a sinisterness that was funny when Rosie reminded herself that it was only a wooden frame with a canvas roof and three canvas walls that made a slapping noise on breezy days.

Jesus was sitting on the narrow plank that was the sorting platform and she went around to the other side and jumped backwards to seat herself on the rim of a packing stand. "Well, tell me," she said without greeting, thinking her voice sounded reassuringly familiar.

"I saw you coming out the door," Jesus said. "I heard you running part of the way, too."

"Uh-huh," Rosie said. "Now tell me the secret."

"I was afraid you wouldn't come," he said.

Rosie delved around on the chicken-wire bottom of the stall for number two tomatoes, ripe, which she was sitting beside, and came up with a left-over that felt edible. She bit into it and began sucking out the pulp and seeds. "I'm here," she pointed out.

"Rosie, are you sorry you came?"

"Sorry? What for?" she said. "You said you were going to tell me something."

"I will, I will," Jesus said, but his voice contained disappointment, and Rosie fleetingly felt the older of the two, realizing a brand-new power which vanished without category under her recognition.

"I have to go back in a minute," she said. "My aunt and uncle are here from Wintersburg. I told them I was going to the privy."

Jesus laughed. "You funny thing," he said. "You slay me!"

"Just because you have a bathroom *inside,*" Rosie said. "Come on, tell me."

Chuckling, Jesus came around to lean on the stand facing her. They still could not see each other very clearly, but Rosie noticed that Jesus became very sober again as he took the hollow tomato from her hand and dropped it back into the stall. When he took hold of her empty hand, she could find no words to protest; her vocabulary had become distressingly constricted and she thought desperately that all that remained intact now was yes and no and oh, and even these few sounds would not easily out. Thus, kissed by Jesus, Rosie fell for the first time entirely victim to a helplessness delectable beyond speech. But the terrible, beautiful sensation lasted no more than a second, and the reality of Jesus' lips and tongue and teeth and hands made her pull away with such strength that she nearly tumbled.

Rosie stopped running as she approached the lights from the windows of home. How long since she had left? She could not guess, but gasping yet, she went to the privy in back and locked herself in. Her own breathing deafened her in the dark, close space, and she sat and waited until she could hear at last the nightly calling of the frogs and crickets. Even then, all she could think to say was oh, my, and the pressure of Jesus' face against her face would not leave.

No one had missed her in the parlor, however, and Rosie walked in and through quickly, announcing that she was next going to take a bath. "Your father's in the bathhouse," her mother said, and Rosie, in her room, recalled that she had not seen him when she entered. There had been only Aunt Taka and Uncle Gimpachi with her mother at the table, drinking tea. She got her robe and straw sandals and crossed the parlor again to go outside. Her mother was telling them about the *haiku* competition in the *Mainichi* and the poem she had entered.

Rosie met her father coming out of the bathhouse. "Are you through, Father?" she asked. "I was going to ask you to scrub my back."

"Scrub your own back," he said shortly, going toward the main house.

"What have I done now?" she yelled after him. She suddenly felt like doing a lot of yelling. But he did not answer, and she went into the bathhouse. Turning on the dangling light, she removed her denims and T-shirt and threw them in the big carton for dirty clothes standing next to the washing machine. Her other things she took with her into the bath compartment to wash after her bath. After she had scooped a basin of hot water from the square wooden tub, she sat on the grey cement of the floor and soaped herself at exaggerated leisure, singing "Red Sails in the Sunset" at the top of her voice and using da-da-da where she suspected her words. Then, standing up, still singing, for she was possessed by the notion that any attempt now to analyze would result in spoilage and she believed that the larger her volume the less she would be able to hear herself think, she obtained more hot water and poured it on until she was free of lather. Only then did she allow herself to step into the steaming vat, one leg first, then the remainder of her body inch by inch until the water no longer stung and she could move around at will.

She took a long time soaking, afterwards remembering to go around outside to stoke the embers of the tin-lined fireplace beneath the tub and to throw on a few more sticks so that the water might keep its heat for her mother, and when she finally returned to the parlor, she found her mother still talking *haiku* with her aunt and uncle, the three of them on another round of tea. Her father was nowhere in sight.

At Japanese school the next day (Wednesday, it was), Rosie was grave and giddy by turns. Preoccupied at her desk in the row for students on Book Eight, she made up for it at recess by performing wild mimicry for the benefit of her friend Chizuko. She held her nose and whined a witticism or two in what she considered was the manner of Fred Allen; she assumed intoxication and a British accent to go over the climax of the Rudy Vallee recording of the pub conversation about William Ewart Gladstone; she was the child Shirley Temple piping, "On the Good Ship Lollipop"; she was the gentleman soprano of the Four Inkspots trilling, "If I Didn't Care." And she felt reasonably satisfied when Chizuko wept and gasped, "Oh, Rosie, you ought to be in the movies!"

Her father came after her at noon, bringing her sandwiches of minced ham and two nectarines to eat while she rode, so that she could pitch right into the sorting when they got home. The lugs were piling up, he said, and the ripe tomatoes in them would probably have to be taken to the cannery tomorrow if they were not ready for the produce haulers tonight. "This heat's not doing them any good. And we've got no time for a break today."

It *was* hot, probably the hottest day of the year, and Rosie's blouse stuck damply to her back even under the protection of the canvas. But she worked as efficiently as a flawless machine and kept the stalls heaped, with one part of her mind listening in to the parental murmuring about the heat and the tomatoes and with another part planning the exact words she would say to Jesus when he drove up with the first load of the afternoon. But when at last she saw that the pick-up was coming, her hands went berserk and the tomatoes started falling in the wrong stalls, and her father said, "Hey, hey! Rosie, watch what you're doing!"

"Well, I have to go to the *benjo*," she said, hiding panic.

"Go in the weeds over there," he said, only half-joking.

"Oh, Father!" she protested.

"Oh, go on home," her mother said. "We'll make out for a while."

In the privy Rosie peered through a knothole toward the fields, watching as much as she could of Jesus. Happily she thought she saw him look in the direction of the house from time to time before he finished unloading and went back toward the patch where his mother and father worked. As she was heading for the shed, a very presentable black car purred up the dirt driveway to the house and its driver motioned to her. Was this the Hayashi home, he wanted to know. She nodded. Was she a Hayashi? Yes, she said, thinking that he was a good-looking man. He got out of the car with a huge, flat package and she saw that he warmly wore a business suit. "I have something here for your mother then," he said, in a more elegant Japanese than she was used to.

She told him where her mother was and he came along with her, patting his face with an immaculate white handkerchief and saying something about the coolness of San Francisco. To her surprised mother and father, he bowed and introduced himself as, among other things, the *haiku* editor of the *Mainichi Shimbun*, saying that since he had been coming as far as Los Angeles anyway, he had decided to bring her the first prize she had won in the recent contest.

"First prize?" her mother echoed, believing and not believing, pleased and overwhelmed. Handed the package with a bow, she bobbed her head up and down numerous times to express her utter gratitude.

"It is nothing much," he added, "but I hope it will serve as a token of our great appreciation for your contributions and our great admiration of your considerable talent."

"I am not worthy," she said, falling easily into his style. "It is I who should make some sign of my humble thanks for being permitted to contribute."

"No, no, to the contrary," he said, bowing again.

But Rosie's mother insisted, and then saying that she knew she was being unorthodox, she asked if she might open the package because her curiosity was so great. Certainly she might. In fact, he would like her reaction to it, for personally, it was one of his favorite *Hiroshiges*.

Rosie thought it was a pleasant picture, which looked to have been sketched with delicate quickness. There were pink clouds, containing some graceful calligraphy, and a sea that was a pale blue except at the edges, containing four sampans with indications of people in them. Pines edged the water and on the far-off beach there was a cluster of thatched huts towered over by pine-dotted mountains of grey and blue. The frame was scalloped and gilt.

After Rosie's mother pronounced it without peer and somewhat prodded her father into nodding agreement, she said Mr. Kuroda must at least have a cup of tea after coming all this way, and although Mr. Kuroda did not want to impose, he soon agreed that a cup of tea would be refreshing and went along with her to the house, carrying the picture for her.

"Ha, your mother's crazy!" Rosie's father said, and Rosie laughed uneasily as she resumed judgment on the tomatoes. She had emptied six lugs when he broke into an imaginary conversation with Jesus to tell her to go and remind her mother of the tomatoes, and she went slowly.

Mr. Kuroda was in his shirtsleeves expounding some *haiku* theory as he munched a rice cake, and her mother was rapt. Abashed in the great man's presence, Rosie stood next to her mother's chair until her mother looked up inquiringly, and then she started to whisper the message, but her mother pushed her gently away and reproached, "You are not being very polite to our guest."

"Father says the tomatoes ... ," Rosie said aloud, smiling foolishly.

"Tell him I shall only be a minute," her mother said, speaking the language of Mr. Kuroda.

When Rosie carried the reply to her father, he did not seem to hear and she said again, "Mother says she'll be back in a minute."

"All right, all right," he nodded, and they worked again in silence. But suddenly, her father uttered an incredible noise, exactly like the cork of a bottle popping, and the next Rosie knew, he was stalking angrily toward the house, almost running in fact, and she chased after him crying, "Father! Father! What are you going to do?"

He stopped long enough to order her back to the shed. "Never mind!" he shouted. "Get on with the sorting!"

And from the place in the fields where she stood, frightened and vacillating, Rosie saw her father enter the house. Soon Mr. Kuroda came out alone, putting on his coat. Mr. Kuroda got into his car and backed out down the driveway onto the highway. Next her father emerged, also alone, something in his arms (it was the picture, she realized), and, going over to the bathhouse woodpile, he threw the picture on the ground and picked up the axe. Smashing the picture, glass and all (she heard the explosion faintly), he reached over for the kerosene that was used to encourage the bath fire and poured it over the wreckage. I am dreaming, Rosie said to herself, I am dreaming, but her father, having made sure that his act of cremation was irrevocable, was even then returning to the fields.

Rosie ran past him and toward the house. What had become of her mother? She burst into the parlor and found her mother at the back window watching the dying fire. They watched together until there remained only a feeble smoke under the blazing sun. Her mother was very calm.

"Do you know why I married your father?" she said without turning.

"No," said Rosie. It was the most frightening question she had ever been called upon to answer. Don't tell me now, she wanted to say, tell me tomorrow, tell me next week, don't tell me today. But she knew she would be told now, that the telling would combine with the other violence of the hot afternoon to level her life, her world to the very ground.

It was like a story out of the magazines illustrated in sepia, which she had consumed so greedily for a period until the information had somehow reached her that those wretchedly unhappy autobiographies, offered to her as the testimonials of living men and women, were largely inventions: Her mother, at nineteen, had come to America and married her father as an alternative to suicide.

At eighteen she had been in love with the first son of one of the well-to-do families in her village. The two had met whenever and wherever they could, secretly, because it would not have done for his family to see him favor her—her father had no money; he was a drunkard and a gambler besides. She had learned she was with child; an excellent match had already been arranged for her lover. Despised by her family, she had given premature birth to a stillborn son, who would be seventeen now. Her family did not turn her out, but she could no longer project herself in any direction without refreshing in them the memory of her indiscretion. She wrote to Aunt Taka, her favorite sister in America, threatening to kill herself if Aunt Taka would not send for her. Aunt Taka hastily arranged a marriage with a young man of whom she knew, but lately arrived from Japan, a young man of simple mind, it was said, but of kindly heart. The young man was never told why his unseen betrothed was so eager to hasten the day of meeting.

The story was told perfectly, with neither groping for words nor untoward passion. It was as though her mother had memorized it by heart, reciting it to herself so many times over that its nagging vileness had long since gone.

"I had a brother then?" Rosie asked, for this was what seemed to matter now; she would think about the other later, she assured herself, pushing back the illumination which threatened all that darkness that had hitherto been merely mysterious or even glamorous. "A half-brother?"

"Yes."

"I would have liked a brother," she said.

Suddenly, her mother knelt on the floor and took her by the wrists. "Rosie," she said urgently, "promise me you will never marry!" Shocked more by the request than the revelation, Rosie stared at her mother's face. Jesus, Jesus, she called silently, not certain whether she was invoking the help of the son of the Carrascos or of God, until there returned sweetly the memory of Jesus' hand, how it had touched her and where. Still her mother waited for an answer, holding her wrists so tightly that her hands were going numb. She tried to pull free. Promise, her mother whispered fiercely, promise. Yes, yes, I promise, Rosie said. But for an instant she turned away, and her mother, hearing the familiar glib agreement, released her. Oh, you, you, you, her eyes and twisted mouth said, you fool. Rosie, covering her face, began at last to cry, and the embrace and consoling hand came much later than she expected.

—1988

---

### FLANNERY O'CONNOR ■ (1925–1964)

*Flannery O'Connor was one of the first of many important writers to emerge from the Writers' Workshop of the University of Iowa, where she received an M.F.A. in creative writing. Born in Savannah, Georgia, she attended Georgia State College for Women, graduating in 1945. Plagued by disseminated lupus, the same incurable illness that killed her father in 1941, O'Connor spent most of the last decade of her life living with her mother on a dairy farm near*

*Milledgeville, Georgia, where she wrote and raised peacocks. Unusual among modern American writers in the seriousness of her Christianity (she was a devout Roman Catholic in the largely Protestant South), O'Connor focuses an uncompromising moral eye on the violence and spiritual disorder of the modern world. She is sometimes called a "southern gothic" writer because of her fascination with the grotesque, although today she seems far ahead of her time in depicting a region in which the social and religious certainties of the past are becoming extinct almost overnight. O'Connor's published work includes two short novels,* Wise Blood *(1952) and* The Violent Bear It Away *(1960), and two collections of short stories,* A Good Man Is Hard to Find *(1955) and* Everything That Rises Must Converge, *published posthumously in 1965. A collection of essays and miscellaneous prose,* Mystery and Manners *(1969), and her selected letters,* The Habit of Being *(1979), reveal an engaging social side of her personality that is not always apparent in her fiction. Even the title of the present story displays O'Connor's characteristic irony, for "good" is a word that the story sets on its head in several ways.*

# Good Country People

Besides the neutral expression that she wore when she was alone, Mrs. Freeman had two others, forward and reverse, that she used for all her human dealings. Her forward expression was steady and driving like the advance of a heavy truck. Her eyes never swerved to left or right but turned as the story turned as if they followed a yellow line down the center of it. She seldom used the other expression because it was not often necessary for her to retract a statement, but when she did, her face came to a complete stop, there was an almost imperceptible movement of her black eyes, during which they seemed to be receding, and then the observer would see that Mrs. Freeman, though she might stand there as real as several grain sacks thrown on top of each other, was no longer there in spirit. As for getting anything across to her when this was the case, Mrs. Hopewell had given it up. She might talk her head off. Mrs. Freeman could never be brought to admit herself wrong on any point. She would stand there and if she could be brought to say anything, it was something like, "Well, I wouldn't of said it was and I wouldn't of said it wasn't," or letting her gaze range over the top kitchen shelf where there was an assortment of dusty bottles, she might remark, "I see you ain't ate many of them figs you put up last summer."

They carried on their most important business in the kitchen at breakfast. Every morning Mrs. Hopewell got up at seven o'clock and lit her gas heater and Joy's. Joy was her daughter, a large blonde girl who had an artificial leg. Mrs. Hopewell thought of her as a child though she was thirty-two years old and highly educated. Joy would get up while her mother was eating and lumber into the bathroom and slam the door, and before long,

Mrs. Freeman would arrive at the back door. Joy would hear her mother call, "Come on in," and then they would talk for a while in low voices that were indistinguishable in the bathroom. By the time Joy came in, they had usually finished the weather report and were on one or the other of Mrs. Freeman's daughters, Glynese or Carramae. Joy called them Glycerin and Caramel. Glynese, a redhead, was eighteen and had many admirers; Carramae, a blonde, was only fifteen but already married and pregnant. She could not keep anything on her stomach. Every morning Mrs. Freeman told Mrs. Hopewell how many times she had vomited since the last report.

Mrs. Hopewell liked to tell people that Glynese and Carramae were two of the finest girls she knew and that Mrs. Freeman was a *lady* and that she was never ashamed to take her anywhere or introduce her to anybody they might meet. Then she would tell how she had happened to hire the Freemans in the first place and how they were a godsend to her and how she had had them four years. The reason for her keeping them so long was that they were not trash. They were good country people. She had telephoned the man whose name they had given as reference and he had told her that Mr. Freeman was a good farmer but that his wife was the nosiest woman ever to walk the earth. "She's got to be into everything," the man said. "If she don't get there before the dust settles, you can bet she's dead, that's all. She'll want to know all your business. I can stand him real good," he had said, "but me nor my wife neither could have stood that woman one more minute on this place." That had put Mrs. Hopewell off for a few days.

She had hired them in the end because there were no other applicants but she had made up her mind beforehand exactly how she would handle the woman. Since she was the type who had to be into everything, then, Mrs. Hopewell had decided, she would not only let her be into everything, she would *see to it* that she was into everything—she would give her the responsibility of everything, she would put her in charge. Mrs. Hopewell had no bad qualities of her own but she was able to use other people's in such a constructive way that she never felt the lack. She had hired the Freemans and she had kept them four years.

Nothing is perfect. This was one of Mrs. Hopewell's favorite sayings. 5 Another was: that is life! And still another, the most important, was: well, other people have their opinions too. She would make these statements, usually at the table, in a tone of gentle insistence as if no one held them but her, and the large hulking Joy, whose constant outrage had obliterated every expression from her face, would stare just a little to the side of her, her eyes icy blue, with the look of someone who had achieved blindness by an act of will and means to keep it.

When Mrs. Hopewell said to Mrs. Freeman that life was like that, Mrs. Freeman would say, "I always said so myself." Nothing had been arrived at by anyone that had not first been arrived at by her. She was quicker than Mr. Freeman. When Mrs. Hopewell said to her after they had been on the place for a while, "You know, you're the wheel behind the wheel," and winked, Mrs. Freeman had said, "I know it."

I've always been quick. It's some that are quicker than others."

"Everybody is different," Mrs. Hopewell said.

"Yes, most people is," Mrs. Freeman said.

"It takes all kinds to make the world."

"I always said it did myself."                                           10

The girl was used to this kind of dialogue for breakfast and more of it for dinner; sometimes they had it for supper too. When they had no guest they ate in the kitchen because that was easier. Mrs. Freeman always managed to arrive at some point during the meal and to watch them finish it. She would stand in the doorway if it were summer but in the winter she would stand with one elbow on top of the refrigerator and look down at them, or she would stand by the gas heater, lifting the back of her skirt slightly. Occasionally she would stand against the wall and roll her head from side to side. At no time was she in any hurry to leave. All this was very trying on Mrs. Hopewell but she was a woman of great patience. She realized that nothing is perfect and that in the Freemans she had good country people and that if, in this day and age, you get good country people, you had better hang onto them.

She had had plenty of experience with trash. Before the Freemans she had averaged one tenant family a year. The wives of these farmers were not the kind you would want to be around you for very long. Mrs. Hopewell, who had divorced her husband long ago, needed someone to walk over the fields with her; and when Joy had to be impressed for these services, her remarks were usually so ugly and her face so glum that Mrs. Hopewell would say, "If you can't come pleasantly, I don't want you at all," to which the girl, standing square and rigid-shouldered with her neck thrust slightly forward, would reply, "If you want me, here I am—LIKE I AM."

Mrs. Hopewell excused this attitude because of the leg (which had been shot off in a hunting accident when Joy was ten). It was hard for Mrs. Hopewell to realize that her child was thirty-two now and that for more than twenty years she had had only one leg. She thought of her still as a child because it tore her heart to think instead of the poor stout girl in her thirties who had never danced a step or had any *normal* good times. Her name was really Joy but as soon as she was twenty-one and away from home, she had had it legally changed. Mrs. Hopewell was certain that she had thought and thought until she had hit upon the ugliest name in any language. Then she had gone and had the beautiful name, Joy, changed without telling her mother until after she had done it. Her legal name was Hulga.

When Mrs. Hopewell thought the name, Hulga, she thought of the broad blank hull of a battleship. She would not use it. She continued to call her Joy to which the girl responded but in a purely mechanical way.

Hulga had learned to tolerate Mrs. Freeman who saved her from taking  15
walks with her mother. Even Glynese and Carramae were useful when they

occupied attention that might otherwise have been directed at her. At first she had thought she could not stand Mrs. Freeman for she had found it was not possible to be rude to her. Mrs. Freeman would take on strange resentments and for days together she would be sullen but the source of her displeasure was always obscure; a direct attack, a positive leer, blatant ugliness to her face—these never touched her. And without warning one day, she began calling her Hulga.

She did not call her that in front of Mrs. Hopewell who would have been incensed but when she and the girl happened to be out of the house together, she would say something and add the name Hulga to the end of it, and the big spectacled Joy-Hulga would scowl and redden as if her privacy had been intruded upon. She considered the name her personal affair. She had arrived at it first purely on the basis of its ugly sound and then the full genius of its fitness had struck her. She had a vision of the name working like the ugly sweating Vulcan who stayed in the furnace and to whom, presumably, the goddess had to come when called. She saw it as the name of her highest creative act. One of her major triumphs was that her mother had not been able to turn her dust into Joy, but the greater one was that she had been able to turn it herself into Hulga. However, Mrs. Freeman's relish for using the name only irritated her. It was as if Mrs. Freeman's beady steel-pointed eyes had penetrated far enough behind her face to reach some secret fact. Something about her seemed to fascinate Mrs. Freeman and then one day Hulga real-ized that it was the artificial leg. Mrs. Freeman had a special fondness for the details of secret infections, hidden deformities, assaults upon children. Of dis-eases, she preferred the lingering or incurable. Hulga had heard Mrs. Hopewell give her the details of the hunting accident, how the leg had been literally blasted off, how she had never lost consciousness. Mrs. Freeman could listen to it any time as if it had happened an hour ago.

When Hulga stumped into the kitchen in the morning (she could walk without making the awful noise but she made it—Mrs. Hopewell was cer-tain—because it was ugly-sounding), she glanced at them and did not speak. Mrs. Hopewell would be in her red kimono with her hair tied around her head in rags. She would be sitting at the table, finishing her breakfast and Mrs. Freeman would be hanging by her elbow outward from the refrigerator, look-ing down at the table. Hulga always put her eggs on the stove to boil and then stood over them with her arms folded, and Mrs. Hopewell would look at her—a kind of indirect gaze divided between her and Mrs. Freeman—and would think that if she would only keep herself up a little, she wouldn't be so bad looking. There was nothing wrong with her face that a pleasant expression wouldn't help. Mrs. Hopewell said that people who looked on the bright side of things would be beautiful even if they were not.

Whenever she looked at Joy this way, she could not help but feel that it would have been better if the child had not taken the Ph.D. It had certainly not brought her out any and now that she had it, there was no more excuse for her to go to school again. Mrs. Hopewell thought it was nice for girls to go to school to have a good time but Joy had "gone through." Anyhow, she would not have been strong enough to go again. The doctors had told Mrs. Hopewell that with the best of care, Joy might see forty-five. She had a weak heart. Joy had made it plain that if it had not been for this condition, she would be far from these red hills and good country people. She would be in a university lecturing to people who knew what she was talking about. And Mrs. Hopewell could very well picture her there, looking like a scarecrow and lecturing to more of the same. Here she went about all day in a six-year-old skirt and a yellow sweat shirt with a faded cowboy on a horse embossed on it. She thought this was funny; Mrs. Hopewell thought it was idiotic and showed simply that she was still a child. She was brilliant but she didn't have a grain of sense. It seemed to Mrs. Hopewell that every year she grew less like other people and more like herself—bloated, rude, and squint-eyed. And she said such strange things! To her own mother she had said—without warning, without excuse, standing up in the middle of a meal with her face purple and her mouth half full—"Woman! do you ever look inside? Do you ever look inside and see what you are *not*? God!" she had cried sinking down again and staring at her plate, "Malebranche[1] was right: we are not our own light. We are not our own light!" Mrs. Hopewell had no idea to this day what brought that on. She had only made the remark, hoping Joy would take it in, that a smile never hurt anyone.

The girl had taken the Ph.D. in philosophy and this left Mrs. Hopewell at a complete loss. You could say, "My daughter is a nurse," or "My daughter is a school teacher," or even, "My daughter is a chemical engineer." You could not say, "My daughter is a philosopher." That was something that had ended with the Greeks Nicolas Malebranche (1638–1715), French philosopher, and Romans. All day Joy sat on her neck in a deep chair, reading. Sometimes she went for walks but she didn't like dogs or cats or birds or flowers or nature or nice young men. She looked at nice young men as if she could smell their stupidity.

One day Mrs. Hopewell had picked up one of the books the girl had  20 just put down and opening it at random, she read, "Science, on the other hand, has to assert its soberness and seriousness afresh and declare that it is concerned solely with what-is. Nothing—how can it be for science anything but a horror and a phantasm? If science is right, then one thing stands firm: science wishes to know nothing of nothing. Such is after all the strictly scientific approach to Nothing. We know it by wishing to know nothing of Nothing." These words had been underlined with a blue pencil and they worked on Mrs. Hopewell like some evil incantation in gibberish. She shut the book quickly and went out of the room as if she were having a chill.

---

[1] **Nicolas Malebranche (1638–1715)**, French philosopher.

This morning when the girl came in, Mrs. Freeman was on Carramae. "She thrown up four times after supper," she said, "and was up twict in the night after three o'clock. Yesterday she didn't do nothing but ramble in the bureau drawer. All she did. Stand up there and see what she could run up on."

"She's got to eat," Mrs. Hopewell muttered, sipping her coffee, while she watched Joy's back at the stove. She was wondering what the child had said to the Bible salesman. She could not imagine what kind of a conversation she could possibly have had with him.

He was a tall gaunt hatless youth who had called yesterday to sell them a Bible. He had appeared at the door, carrying a large black suitcase that weighted him so heavily on one side that he had to brace himself against the door facing. He seemed on the point of collapse but he said in a cheerful voice, "Good morning, Mrs. Cedars!" and set the suitcase down on the mat. He was not a bad-looking young man though he had on a bright blue suit and yellow socks that were not pulled up far enough. He had prominent face bones and a streak of sticky-looking brown hair falling across his forehead.

"I'm Mrs. Hopewell," she said.

"Oh!" he said, pretending to look puzzled but with his eyes sparkling, 25 "I saw it said 'The Cedars' on the mailbox so I thought you was Mrs. Cedars!" and he burst out in a pleasant laugh. He picked up the satchel and under cover of a pant, he fell forward into her hall. It was rather as if the suitcase had moved first, jerking him after it. "Mrs. Hopewell!" he said and grabbed her hand. "I hope you are well!" and he laughed again and then all at once his face sobered completely. He paused and gave her a straight earnest look and said, "Lady, I've come to speak of serious things."

"Well, come in," she muttered, none too pleased because her dinner was almost ready. He came into the parlor and sat down on the edge of a straight chair and put the suitcase between his feet and glanced around the room as if he were sizing her up by it. Her silver gleamed on the two sideboards; she decided he had never been in a room as elegant as this.

"Mrs. Hopewell," he began, using her name in a way that sounded almost intimate, "I know you believe in Chrustian service."

"Well, yes," she murmured.

"I know," he said and paused, looking very wise with his head cocked on one side, "that you're a good woman. Friends have told me."

Mrs. Hopewell never liked to be taken for a fool. "What are you sell- 30 ing?" she asked.

"Bibles," the young man said and his eye raced around the room before he added, "I see you have no family Bible in your parlor, I see that is the one lack you got!"

Mrs. Hopewell could not say, "My daughter is an atheist and won't let me keep the Bible in the parlor." She said, stiffening slightly, "I keep my Bible by my bedside." This was not the truth. It was in the attic somewhere.

"Lady," he said, "the word of God ought to be in the parlor."

"Well, I think that's a matter of taste," she began, "I think ..."

"Lady," he said, "for a Chrustian, the word of God ought to be in every  35
room in the house besides in his heart. I know you're a Chrustian because I
can see it in every line of your face."

She stood up and said, "Well, young man, I don't want to buy a Bible
and I smell my dinner burning."

He didn't get up. He began to twist his hands and looking down at them,
he said softly, "Well lady, I'll tell you the truth—not many people want to buy
one nowadays and besides, I know I'm real simple. I don't know how to say a
thing but to say it. I'm just a country boy." He glanced up into her unfriendly
face. "People like you don't like to fool with country people like me!"

"Why!" she cried, "good country people are the salt of the earth!
Besides, we all have different ways of doing, it takes all kinds to make the
world go 'round. That's life!"

"You said a mouthful," he said.

"Why, I think there aren't enough good country people in the world!"  40
she said, stirred. "I think that's what's wrong with it!"

His face had brightened. "I didn't inraduce myself," he said. "I'm Manley
Pointer from out in the country around Willohobie, not even from a place,
just from near a place."

"You wait a minute," she said. "I have to see about my dinner." She
went out to the kitchen and found Joy standing near the door where she
had been listening.

"Get rid of the salt of the earth," she said, "and let's eat."

Mrs. Hopewell gave her a pained look and turned the heat down under
the vegetables. "*I* can't be rude to anybody," she murmured and went back
into the parlor.

He had opened the suitcase and was sitting with a Bible on each knee.  45

"You might as well put those up," she told him. "I don't want one."

"I appreciate your honesty," he said. "You don't see any more real honest people unless you go way out in the country."

"I know," she said, "real genuine folks!" Through the crack in the door
she heard a groan.

"I guess a lot of boys come telling you they're working their way through
college," he said, "but I'm not going to tell you that. Somehow," he said, "I
don't want to go to college. I want to devote my life to Chrustian service.
See," he said, lowering his voice, "I got this heart condition. I may not live
long. When you know it's something wrong with you and you may not live
long, well then, lady...." He paused, with his mouth open, and stared at her.

He and Joy had the same condition! She knew that her eyes were filling  50
with tears but she collected herself quickly and murmured, "Won't you stay
for dinner? We'd love to have you!" and was sorry the instant she heard
herself say it.

"Yes mam," he said in an abashed voice, "I would sher love to do that!"

Joy had given him one look on being introduced to him and then throughout the meal had not glanced at him again. He had addressed several remarks to her, which she had pretended not to hear. Mrs. Hopewell could not understand deliberate rudeness, although she lived with it, and she felt she had always to overflow with hospitality to make up for Joy's lack of courtesy. She urged him to talk about himself and he did. He said he was the seventh child of twelve and that his father had been crushed under a tree when he himself was eight years old. He had been crushed very badly, in fact, almost cut in two and was practically not recognizable. His mother had got along the best she could by hard working and she had always seen that her children went to Sunday School and that they read the Bible every evening. He was now nineteen years old and he had been selling Bibles for four months. In that time he had sold seventy-seven Bibles and had the promise of two more sales. He wanted to become a missionary because he thought that was the way you could do most for people. "He who losest his life shall find it," he said simply and he was so sincere, so genuine and earnest that Mrs. Hopewell would not for the world have smiled. He prevented his peas from sliding onto the table by blocking them with a piece of bread which he later cleaned his plate with. She could see Joy observing sidewise how he handled his knife and fork and she saw too that every few minutes, the boy would dart a keen appraising glance at the girl as if he were trying to attract her attention.

After dinner Joy cleared the dishes off the table and disappeared and Mrs. Hopewell was left to talk with him. He told her again about his childhood and his father's accident and about various things that had happened to him. Every five minutes or so she would stifle a yawn. He sat for two hours until finally she told him she must go because she had an appointment in town. He packed his Bibles and thanked her and prepared to leave, but in the doorway he stopped and wrung her hand and said that not on any of his trips had he met a lady as nice as her and he asked if he could come again. She had said she would always be happy to see him.

Joy had been standing in the road, apparently looking at something in the distance, when he came down the steps toward her, bent to the side with his heavy valise. He stopped where she was standing and confronted her directly. Mrs. Hopewell could not hear what he said but she trembled to think what Joy would say to him. She could see that after a minute Joy said something and that then the boy began to speak again, making an excited gesture with his free hand. After a minute Joy said something else at which the boy began to speak once more. Then to her amazement, Mrs. Hopewell saw the two of them walk off together, toward the gate. Joy had walked all the way to the gate with him and Mrs. Hopewell could not imagine what they had said to each other, and she had not yet dared to ask.

Mrs. Freeman was insisting upon her attention. She had moved from  55
the refrigerator to the heater so that Mrs. Hopewell had to turn and face
her in order to seem to be listening. "Glynese gone out with Harvey Hill
again last night," she said. "She had this sty."

"Hill," Mrs. Hopewell said absently, "is that the one who works in the
garage?"

"Nome, he's the one that goes to chiropracter school," Mrs. Freeman
said. "She had this sty. Been had it two days. So she says when he
brought her in the other night he says, 'Lemme get rid of that sty for
you,' and she says, 'How?' and he says, 'You just lay yourself down acrost
the seat of that car and I'll show you.' So she done it and he popped her
neck. Kept on a-popping it several times until she made him quit. This
morning," Mrs. Freeman said, "she ain't got no sty. She ain't got no traces
of a sty."

"I never heard of that before," Mrs. Hopewell said.

"He ast her to marry him before the Ordinary,"[2] Mrs. Freeman went on,
"and she told him she wasn't going to be married in no *office*."

"Well, Glynese is a fine girl," Mrs. Hopewell said. "Glynese and Carramae  60
are both fine girls."

"Carramae said when her and Lyman was married Lyman said it sure felt
sacred to him. She said he said he wouldn't take five hundred dollars for
being married by a preacher."

"How much would he take?" the girl asked from the stove.

"He said he wouldn't take five hundred dollars," Mrs. Freeman repeated.

"Well we all have work to do," Mrs. Hopewell said.

"Lyman said it just felt more sacred to him," Mrs. Freeman said. "The  65
doctor wants Carramae to eat prunes. Says instead of medicine. Says them
cramps is coming from pressure. You know where I think it is?"

"She'll be better in a few weeks," Mrs. Hopewell said.

"In the tube," Mrs. Freeman said. "Else she wouldn't be as sick as she is."

Hulga had cracked her two eggs into a saucer and was bringing them
to the table along with a cup of coffee that she had filled too full. She sat
down carefully and began to eat, meaning to keep Mrs. Freeman there by
questions if for any reason she showed an inclination to leave. She could
perceive her mother's eye on her. The first round-about question would be
about the Bible salesman and she did not wish to bring it on. "How did he
pop her neck?" she asked.

Mrs. Freeman went into a description of how he had popped her neck.
She said he owned a '55 Mercury but that Glynese said she would rather
marry a man with only a '36 Plymouth who would be married by a preacher.
The girl asked what if he had a '32 Plymouth and Mrs. Freeman said what
Glynese had said was a '36 Plymouth.

---

[2]Judge of probate court.

Mrs. Hopewell said there were not many girls with Glynese's common 70 sense. She said what she admired in those girls was their common sense. She said that reminded her that they had had a nice visitor yesterday, a young man selling Bibles. "Lord," she said, "he bored me to death but he was so sincere and genuine I couldn't be rude to him. He was just good country people, you know," she said, "—just the salt of the earth."

"I seen him walk up," Mrs. Freeman said, "and then later—I seen him walk off," and Hulga could feel the slight shift in her voice, the slight insinuation, that he had not walked off alone, had he? Her face remained expressionless but the color rose into her neck and she seemed to swallow it down with the next spoonful of egg. Mrs. Freeman was looking at her as if they had a secret together.

"Well, it takes all kinds of people to make the world go 'round," Mrs. Hopewell said. "It's very good we aren't all alike."

"Some people are more alike than others," Mrs. Freeman said.

Hulga got up and stumped, with about twice the noise that was necessary, into her room and locked the door. She was to meet the Bible salesman at ten o'clock at the gate. She had thought about it half the night. She had started thinking of it as a great joke and then she had begun to see profound implications in it. She had lain in bed imagining dialogues for them that were insane on the surface but that reached below to depths that no Bible salesman would be aware of. Their conversation yesterday had been of this kind.

He had stopped in front of her and had simply stood there. His face was 75 bony and sweaty and bright, with a little pointed nose in the center of it, and his look was different from what it had been at the dinner table. He was gazing at her with open curiosity, with fascination, like a child watching a new fantastic animal at the zoo, and he was breathing as if he had run a great distance to reach her. His gaze seemed somehow familiar but she could not think where she had been regarded with it before. For almost a minute he didn't say anything. Then on what seemed an insuck of breath, he whispered, "You ever ate a chicken that was two days old?"

The girl looked at him stonily. He might have just put this question up for consideration at the meeting of a philosophical association. "Yes," she presently replied as if she had considered it from all angles.

"It must have been mighty small!" he said triumphantly and shook all over with little nervous giggles, getting very red in the face, and subsiding finally into his gaze of complete admiration, while the girl's expression remained exactly the same.

"How old are you?" he asked softly.

She waited some time before she answered. Then in a flat voice she said, "Seventeen."

His smiles came in succession like waves breaking on the surface of a 80 little lake. "I see you got a wooden leg," he said. "I think you're brave. I think you're real sweet."

The girl stood blank and solid and silent.

"Walk to the gate with me," he said. "You're a brave sweet little thing and I liked you the minute I seen you walk in the door."

Hulga began to move forward.

"What's your name?" he asked, smiling down on the top of her head.

"Hulga," she said.                                                                                    85

"Hulga," he murmured, "Hulga. Hulga. I never heard of anybody name Hulga before. You're shy, aren't you, Hulga?" he asked.

She nodded, watching his large red hand on the handle of the giant valise.

"I like girls that wear glasses," he said. "I think a lot. I'm not like these people that a serious thought don't ever enter their heads. It's because I may die."

"I may die too," she said suddenly and looked up at him. His eyes were very small and brown, glittering feverishly.

"Listen," he said, "don't you think some people was meant to meet   90 on account of what all they got in common and all? Like they both think serious thoughts and all?" He shifted the valise to his other hand so that the hand nearest her was free. He caught hold of her elbow and shook it a little. "I don't work on Saturday," he said. "I like to walk in the woods and see what Mother Nature is wearing. O'er the hills and far away. Picnics and things. Couldn't we go on a picnic tomorrow? Say yes, Hulga," he said and gave her a dying look as if he felt his insides about to drop out of him. He had even seemed to sway slightly toward her.

During the night she had imagined that she seduced him. She imagined that the two of them walked on the place until they came to the storage barn beyond the two back fields and there, she imagined, that things came to such a pass that she very easily seduced him and that then, of course, she had to reckon with his remorse. True genius can get an idea across even to an inferior mind. She imagined that she took his remorse in hand and changed it into a deeper understanding of life. She took all his shame away and turned it into something useful.

She set off for the gate at exactly ten o'clock, escaping without drawing Mrs. Hopewell's attention. She didn't take anything to eat, forgetting that food is usually taken on a picnic. She wore a pair of slacks and a dirty white shirt, and as an afterthought, she had put some Vapex[3] on the collar of it since she did not own any perfume. When she reached the gate no one was there.

She looked up and down the empty highway and had the furious feeling that she had been tricked, that he had only meant to make her walk to the gate after the idea of him. Then suddenly he stood up, very tall, from behind a bush on the opposite embankment. Smiling, he lifted his hat which was new and wide-brimmed. He had not worn it yesterday and

[3]Brand name for nasal spray.

she wondered if he had bought it for the occasion. It was toast-colored with a red and white band around it and was slightly too large for him. He stepped from behind the bush still carrying the black valise. He had on the same suit and the same yellow socks sucked down in his shoes from walking. He crossed the highway and said, "I knew you'd come!"

The girl wondered acidly how he had known this. She pointed to the valise and asked, "Why did you bring your Bibles?"

He took her elbow, smiling down on her as if he could not stop. "You 95 can never tell when you'll need the word of God, Hulga," he said. She had a moment in which she doubted that this was actually happening and then they began to climb the embankment. They went down into the pasture toward the woods. The boy walked lightly by her side, bouncing on his toes. The valise did not seem to be heavy today; he even swung it. They crossed half the pasture without saying anything and then, putting his hand easily on the small of her back, he asked softly, "Where does your wooden leg join on?"

She turned an ugly red and glared at him and for an instant the boy looked abashed. "I didn't mean you no harm," he said. "I only meant you're so brave and all. I guess God takes care of you."

"No," she said, looking forward and walking fast, "I don't even believe in God."

At this he stopped and whistled. "No!" he exclaimed as if he were too astonished to say anything else.

She walked on and in a second he was bouncing at her side, fanning with his hat. "That's very unusual for a girl," he remarked, watching her out of the corner of his eye. When they reached the edge of the wood, he put his hand on her back again and drew her against him without a word and kissed her heavily.

The kiss, which had more pressure than feeling behind it, produced that 100 extra surge of adrenalin in the girl that enables one to carry a packed trunk out of a burning house, but in her, the power went at once to the brain. Even before he released her, her mind, clear and detached and ironic anyway, was regarding him from a great distance, with amusement but with pity. She had never been kissed before and she was pleased to discover that it was an unexceptional experience and all a matter of the mind's control. Some people might enjoy drain water if they were told it was vodka. When the boy, looking expectant but uncertain, pushed her gently away, she turned and walked on, saying nothing as if such business, for her, were common enough.

He came along panting at her side, trying to help her when he saw a root that she might trip over. He caught and held back the long swaying blades of thorn vine until she had passed beyond them. She led the way and he came breathing heavily behind her. Then they came out on a sunlit hillside, sloping softly into another one a little smaller. Beyond, they could see the rusted top of the old barn where the extra hay was stored.

The hill was sprinkled with small pink weeds. "Then you ain't saved?" he asked suddenly, stopping.

The girl smiled. It was the first time she had smiled at him at all. "In my economy," she said, "I'm saved and you are damned but I told you I didn't believe in God."

Nothing seemed to destroy the boy's look of admiration. He gazed at her now as if the fantastic animal at the zoo had put its paw through the bars and given him a loving poke. She thought he looked as if he wanted to kiss her again and she walked on before he had the chance.

"Ain't there somewheres we can sit down sometime?" he murmured, his voice softening toward the end of the sentence. 105

"In that barn," she said.

They made for it rapidly as if it might slide away like a train. It was a large two-story barn, cool and dark inside. The boy pointed up the ladder that led into the loft and said, "It's too bad we can't go up there."

"Why can't we?" she asked.

"Yer leg," he said reverently.

The girl gave him a contemptuous look and putting both hands on the ladder, she climbed it while he stood below, apparently awestruck. She 110 pulled herself expertly through the opening and then looked down at him and said, "Well, come on if you're coming," and he began to climb the ladder, awkwardly bringing the suitcase with him.

"We won't need the Bible," she observed.

"You never can tell," he said, panting. After he had got into the loft, he was a few seconds catching his breath. She had sat down in a pile of straw. A wide sheath of sunlight, filled with dust particles, slanted over her. She lay back against a bale, her face turned away, looking out the front opening of the barn where hay was thrown from a wagon into the loft. The two pink-speckled hillsides lay back against a dark ridge of woods. The sky was cloudless and cold blue. The boy dropped down by her side and put one arm under her and the other over her and began methodically kissing her face, making little noises like a fish. He did not remove his hat but it was pushed far enough back not to interfere. When her glasses got in his way, he took them off of her and slipped them into his pocket.

The girl at first did not return any of the kisses but presently she began to and after she had put several on his cheek, she reached his lips and remained there, kissing him again and again as if she were trying to draw all the breath out of him. His breath was clear and sweet like a child's and the kisses were sticky like a child's. He mumbled about loving her and about knowing when he first seen her that he loved her, but the mumbling was like the sleepy fretting of a child being put to sleep by his mother. Her mind, throughout this, never stopped or lost itself for a second to her feelings. "You ain't said you loved me none," he whispered finally, pulling back from her. "You got to say that."

She looked away from him off into the hollow sky and then down at a black ridge and then down farther into what appeared to be two green swelling lakes. She didn't realize he had taken her glasses but this landscape could not seem exceptional to her for she seldom paid any close attention to her surroundings.

"You got to say it," he repeated. "You got to say you love me."    115

She was always careful how she committed herself. "In a sense," she began, "if you use the word loosely, you might say that. But it's not a word I use. I don't have illusions. I'm one of those people who see *through* to nothing."

The boy was frowning. "You got to say it. I said it and you got to say it," he said.

The girl looked at him almost tenderly. "You poor baby," she murmured. "It's just as well you don't understand," and she pulled him by the neck, face-down, against her. "We are all damned," she said, "but some of us have taken off our blindfolds and see that there's nothing to see. It's a kind of salvation."

The boy's astonished eyes looked blankly through the ends of her hair. "Okay," he almost whined, "but do you love me or don'tcher?"

"Yes," she said and added, "in a sense. But I must tell you something. 120 There mustn't be anything dishonest between us." She lifted his head and looked him in the eye. "I am thirty years old," she said. "I have a number of degrees."

The boy's look was irritated but dogged. "I don't care," he said. "I don't care a thing about what all you done. I just want to know if you love me or don'tcher?" and he caught her to him and wildly planted her face with kisses until she said, "Yes, yes."

"Okay then," he said, letting her go. "Prove it."

She smiled, looking dreamily out on the shifty landscape. She had seduced him without even making up her mind to try. "How?" she asked, feeling that he should be delayed a little.

He leaned over and put his lips to her ear. "Show me where your wooden leg joins on," he whispered.

The girl uttered a sharp little cry and her face instantly drained of 125 color. The obscenity of the suggestion was not what shocked her. As a child she had sometimes been subject to feelings of shame but education had removed the last traces of that as a good surgeon scrapes for cancer; she would no more have felt it over what he was asking than she would have believed in his Bible. But she was as sensitive about the artificial leg as a peacock about his tail. No one ever touched it but her. She took care of it as someone else would his soul, in private and almost with her own eyes turned away. "No," she said.

"I known it," he muttered, sitting up. "You're just playing me for a sucker."

"Oh no no!" she cried. "It joins on at the knee. Only at the knee. Why do you want to see it?"

The boy gave her a long penetrating look. "Because," he said, "it's what makes you different. You ain't like anybody else."

She sat staring at him. There was nothing about her face or her round freezing-blue eyes to indicate that this had moved her; but she felt as if her heart had stopped and left her mind to pump her blood. She decided that for the first time in her life she was face to face with real innocence. This boy, with an instinct that came from beyond wisdom, had touched the truth about her. When after a minute, she said in a hoarse high voice, "All right," it was like surrendering to him completely. It was like losing her own life and finding it again, miraculously, in his.

Very gently, he began to roll the slack leg up. The artificial limb, in a 130 white sock and brown flat shoe, was bound in a heavy material like canvas and ended in an ugly jointure where it was attached to the stump. The boy's face and his voice were entirely reverent as he uncovered it and said, "Now show me how to take it off and on."

She took it off for him and put it back on again and then he took it off himself, handling it as tenderly as if it were a real one. "See!" he said with a delighted child's face. "Now I can do it myself!"

"Put it back on," she said. She was thinking that she would run away with him and that every night he would take the leg off and every morning put it back on again. "Put it back on," she said.

"Not yet," he murmured, setting it on its foot out of her reach. "Leave it off for awhile. You got me instead."

She gave a little cry of alarm but he pushed her down and began to kiss her again. Without the leg she felt entirely dependent on him. Her brain seemed to have stopped thinking altogether and to be about some other function that it was not very good at. Different expressions raced back and forth over her face. Every now and then the boy, his eyes like two steel spikes, would glance behind him where the leg stood. Finally she pushed him off and said, "Put it back on me now."

"Wait," he said. He leaned the other way and pulled the valise toward 135 him and opened it. It had a pale blue spotted lining and there were only two Bibles in it. He took one of these out and opened the cover of it. It was hollow and contained a pocket flask of whiskey, a pack of cards, and a small blue box with printing on it. He laid these out in front of her one at a time in an evenly-spaced row, like one presenting offerings at the shrine of a goddess. He put the blue box in her hand. THIS PRODUCT TO BE USED ONLY FOR THE PREVENTION OF DISEASE, she read, and dropped it. The boy was unscrewing the top of the flask. He stopped and pointed, with a smile, to the deck of cards. It was not an ordinary deck but one with an obscene picture on the back of each card. "Take a swig," he said, offering her the bottle first. He held it in front of her, but like one mesmerized, she did not move.

Her voice when she spoke had an almost pleading sound. "Aren't you," she murmured, "aren't you just good country people?"

The boy cocked his head. He looked as if he were just beginning to understand that she might be trying to insult him. "Yeah," he said, curling his lip slightly, "but it ain't held me back none. I'm as good as you any day in the week."

"Give me my leg," she said.

He pushed it farther away with his foot. "Come on now, let's begin to have us a good time," he said coaxingly. "We ain't got to know one another good yet."

"Give me my leg!" she screamed and tried to lunge for it but he pushed 140 her down easily.

"What's the matter with you all of a sudden?" he asked, frowning as he screwed the top on the flask and put it quickly back inside the Bible. "You just a while ago said you didn't believe in nothing. I thought you was some girl!"

Her face was almost purple. "You're a Christian!" she hissed. "You're a fine Christian! You're just like them all—say one thing and do another. You're a perfect Christian, you're..."

The boy's mouth was set angrily. "I hope you don't think," he said in a lofty indignant tone, "that I believe in that crap! I may sell Bibles but I know which end is up and I wasn't born yesterday and I know where I'm going!"

"Give me my leg!" she screeched. He jumped up so quickly that she barely saw him sweep the cards and the blue box back into the Bible and throw the Bible into the valise. She saw him grab the leg and then she saw it for an instant slanted forlornly across the inside of the suitcase with a Bible at either side of its opposite ends. He slammed the lid shut and snatched up the valise and swung it down the hole and then stepped through himself.

When all of him had passed but his head, he turned and regarded her 145 with a look that no longer had any admiration in it. "I've gotten a lot of interesting things," he said. "One time I got a woman's glass eye this way. And you needn't to think you'll catch me because Pointer ain't really my name. I use a different name at every house I call at and don't stay nowhere long. And I'll tell you another thing, Hulga," he said, using the name as if he didn't think much of it, "you ain't so smart. I been believing in nothing ever since I was born!" and then the toast-colored hat disappeared down the hole and the girl was left, sitting on the straw in the dusty sunlight. When she turned her churning face toward the opening, she saw his blue figure struggling successfully over the green speckled lake.

Mrs. Hopewell and Mrs. Freeman, who were in the back pasture, digging up onions, saw him emerge a little later from the woods and head across the meadow toward the highway. "Why, that looks like that nice dull young man that tried to sell me a Bible yesterday," Mrs. Hopewell said, squinting. "He must have been selling them to the Negroes back in there.

He was so simple," she said, "but I guess the world would be better off if we were all that simple."

Mrs. Freeman's gaze drove forward and just touched him before he disappeared under the hill. Then she returned her attention to the evil-smelling onion shoot she was lifting from the ground. "Some can't be that simple," she said. "I know I never could."

—1955

---

### GABRIEL GARCÍA MÁRQUEZ ■ (b. 1928–2014)

*Gabriel García Márquez was the author of a brilliant seriocomic historical novel,* One Hundred Years of Solitude *(1967). It is one of the landmarks of contemporary fiction and rapidly became an international bestseller. "Magic realism" is the term that is often used to describe the author's unique blend of folklore, historical fact, naturalism, and fantasy, much of it occurring in the fictional village of Macondo. A native of Colombia, García Márquez, the eldest of twelve children, was born in Aracataca, a small town that is the model for the isolated, decaying settlements found in his fiction. García Márquez was trained as a journalist, first coming to public attention in 1955 with his investigative reporting about the government cover-up that followed the sinking of a Colombian navy vessel. After residence in Paris during the late 1950s, he worked for a time as a correspondent for Fidel Castro's official news agency. He has also lived in Mexico and Spain. Other works include the short story collections* No One Writes to the Colonel *(1968),* Leaf Storm and Other Stories *(1972), and* Innocent Eréndira and Other Stories *(1978). His novel* Love in the Time of Cholera *was a major success in 1988. He was ionawarded the Nobel Prize in 1982. In recent years, García Márquez has focused on nonfict.* News of a Kidnapping *(1997) tells the true story of how Colombian drug kingpins took ten citizens hostage to extort favors from their government.*

# A Very Old Man with Enormous Wings

### *Translated by Gregory Rabassa*

On the third day of rain they had killed so many crabs inside the house that Pelayo had to cross his drenched courtyard and throw them into the sea, because the newborn child had a temperature all night and they thought it was due to the stench. The world had been sad since Tuesday. Sea and sky were a single ash-gray thing and the sands of the beach, which on March nights glimmered like powdered light, had become a stew of mud and rotten shellfish. The light was so weak at noon that when Pelayo was coming back to the house after throwing away the crabs, it was hard for him to see what it was that was moving and groaning in the rear of the courtyard. He had to go very close to see that it was an old man, a very old man, lying face down in the mud, who, in spite of his tremendous efforts, couldn't get up, impeded by his enormous wings.

Frightened by that nightmare, Pelayo ran to get Elisenda, his wife, who was putting compresses on the sick child, and he took her to the rear of the courtyard. They both looked at the fallen body with mute stupor. He was dressed like a ragpicker. There were only a few faded hairs left on his bald skull and very few teeth in his mouth, and his pitiful condition of a drenched great-grandfather had taken away any sense of grandeur he might have had. His huge buzzard wings, dirty and half-plucked, were forever entangled in the mud. They looked at him so long and so closely that Pelayo and Elisenda very soon overcame their surprise and in the end found him familiar. Then they dared speak to him, and he answered in an incomprehensible dialect with a strong sailor's voice. That was how they skipped over the inconvenience of the wings and quite intelligently concluded that he was a lonely castaway from some foreign ship wrecked by the storm. And yet, they called in a neighbor woman who knew everything about life and death to see him, and all she needed was one look to show them their mistake.

"He's an angel," she told them. "He must have been coming for the child, but the poor fellow is so old that the rain knocked him down."

On the following day everyone knew that a flesh-and-blood angel was held captive in Pelayo's house. Against the judgment of the wise neighbor woman, for whom angels in those times were the fugitive survivors of a celestial conspiracy, they did not have the heart to club him to death. Pelayo watched over him all afternoon from the kitchen, armed with his bailiff's club, and before going to bed he dragged him out of the mud and locked him up with the hens in the wire chicken coop. In the middle of the night, when the rain stopped, Pelayo and Elisenda were still killing crabs. A short time afterward the child woke up without a fever and with a desire to eat. Then they felt magnanimous and decided to put the angel on a raft with fresh water and provisions for three days and leave him to his fate on the high seas. But when they went out into the courtyard with the first light of dawn, they found the whole neighborhood in front of the chicken coop having fun with the angel, without the slightest reverence, tossing him things to eat through the openings in the wire as if he weren't a supernatural creature but a circus animal.

Father Gonzaga arrived before seven o'clock, alarmed at the strange news. By that time onlookers less frivolous than those at dawn had already arrived and they were making all kinds of conjectures concerning the captive's future. The simplest among them thought that he should be named mayor of the world. Others of sterner mind felt that he should be promoted to the rank of five-star general in order to win all wars. Some visionaries hoped that he could be put to stud in order to implant on earth a race of winged wise men who could take charge of the universe. But Father Gonzaga, before becoming a priest, had been a robust woodcutter. Standing by the wire, he reviewed his catechism in an instant and asked them to open the door so that he could take a close look at that pitiful man who looked more like a huge decrepit hen among the fascinated chickens. He was lying in a corner drying his open wings in the sunlight among the fruit peels and breakfast leftovers that the early risers had thrown him. Alien to the impertinences of the world, he only lifted his antiquarian eyes and murmured something in his dialect when Father Gonzaga went into the chicken coop and said good morning to him in Latin. The parish priest had his first suspicion of an impostor when he saw that he did not understand the language of God or know how to greet His ministers. Then he noticed that seen close up he was much too human: he had an unbearable smell of the outdoors, the back side of his wings was strewn with parasites and his main feathers had been mistreated by terrestrial winds, and nothing about him measured up to the proud dignity of angels. Then he came out of the chicken coop and in a brief sermon warned the curious against the risks of being ingenuous. He reminded them that the devil had the bad habit of making use of carnival tricks in order to confuse the unwary. He argued that if wings were not the essential element in determining the difference between a hawk and an airplane, they were even less so in the recognition of angels. Nevertheless, he promised to write a letter to his bishop so that the latter would write to his primate so that the latter would write to the Supreme Pontiff in order to get the final verdict from the highest courts.

His prudence fell on sterile hearts. The news of the captive angel spread with such rapidity that after a few hours the courtyard had the bustle of a marketplace and they had to call in troops with fixed bayonets to disperse the mob that was about to knock the house down. Elisenda, her spine all twisted from sweeping up so much marketplace trash, then got the idea of fencing in the yard and charging five cents admission to see the angel.

The curious came from far away. A traveling carnival arrived with a flying acrobat who buzzed over the crowd several times, but no one paid any attention to him because his wings were not those of an angel but, rather, those of a sidereal[1] bat. The most unfortunate invalids on earth came in search of health: a poor woman who since childhood had been counting her heartbeats and had run out of numbers, a Portuguese man who couldn't sleep because the noise of the stars disturbed him, a sleepwalker who got up at night to undo the things he had done while awake; and many others with less serious ailments. In the midst of that shipwreck disorder that made the earth tremble, Pelayo and Elisenda were happy with fatigue, for in less than a week they had crammed their rooms with money and the line of pilgrims waiting their turn to enter still reached beyond the horizon.

[1] **sidereal** coming from the stars.

The angel was the only one who took no part in his own act. He spent his time trying to get comfortable in his borrowed nest, befuddled by the hellish heat of the oil lamps and sacramental candles that had been placed along the wire. At first they tried to make him eat some mothballs, which according to the wisdom of the wise neighbor woman, were the food prescribed for angels. But he turned them down, just as he turned down the papal lunches that the penitents brought him, and they never found out whether it was because he was an angel or because he was an old man that in the end he ate nothing but eggplant mush. His only supernatural virtue seemed to be patience. Especially during the first days, when the hens pecked at him, searching for the stellar parasites that proliferated in his wings, and the cripples pulled out feathers to touch their defective parts with, and even the most merciful threw stones at him, trying to get him to rise so they could see him standing. The only time they succeeded in arousing him was when they burned his side with an iron for branding steers, for he had been motionless for so many hours that they thought he was dead. He awoke with a start, ranting in his hermetic language and with tears in his eyes, and he flapped his wings a couple of times, which brought on a whirlwind of chicken dung and lunar dust and a gale of panic that did not seem to be of this world. Although many thought that his reaction had been one not of rage but of pain, from then on they were careful not to annoy him, because the majority understood that his passivity was not that of a hero taking his ease but that of a cataclysm in repose.

Father Gonzaga held back the crowd's frivolity with formulas of maidservant inspiration while awaiting the arrival of a final judgment on the nature of the captive. But the mail from Rome showed no sense of urgency. They spent their time finding out if the prisoner had a navel, if his dialect had any connection with Aramaic, how many times he could fit on the head of a pin, or whether he wasn't just a Norwegian with wings. Those meager letters might have come and gone until the end of time if a providential event had not put an end to the priest's tribulations.

It so happened that during those days, among so many other carnival attractions, there arrived in town the traveling show of the woman who had been changed into a spider for having disobeyed her parents. The admission to see her was not only less than the admission to see the angel, but people were permitted to ask her all manner of questions about her absurd state and to examine her up and down so that no one would ever doubt the truth of her honor. She was a frightful tarantula the size of a ram and with the head of a sad maiden. What was most heart-rending, however, was not her outlandish shape but the sincere affliction with which she recounted the details of her misfortune. While still practically a child she had sneaked out of her parents' house to go to a dance, and while she was coming back through the woods after having danced all night without permission, a fearful thunderclap rent the sky in two and through the crack came the lightning bolt of brimstone that changed her into a spider. Her only nourishment came from the meatballs that charitable souls chose to toss into her mouth. A spectacle like that, full of so much human truth and with such a fearful lesson, was found to defeat without even trying that of a haughty angel who scarcely deigned to look at mortals. Besides, the few miracles attributed to the angel showed a certain mental disorder, like the blind man who didn't recover his sight but grew three new teeth, or the paralytic who didn't get to walk, but almost won the lottery, and the leper whose sores sprouted sunflowers. Those consolation miracles, which were more like mocking fun, had already ruined the angel's reputation when the woman who had been changed into a spider finally crushed him completely. That was how Father Gonzaga was cured forever of his insomnia and Pelayo's courtyard went back to being as empty as during the time it had rained for three days and crabs walked through the bedrooms.

The owners of the house had no reason to lament. With the money they saved they built a two-story mansion with balconies and gardens and high netting so that crabs wouldn't get in during the winter, and with iron bars on the windows so that angels wouldn't get in. Pelayo also set up a rabbit warren close to town and gave up his job as bailiff for good, and Elisenda bought some satin pumps with high heels and many dresses of iridescent silk, the kind worn on Sunday by the most desirable women in those times. The chicken coop was the only thing that didn't receive any attention. If they washed it down with creolin and burned tears of myrrh inside it every so often, it was not in homage to the angel but to drive away the dungheap stench that still hung everywhere like a ghost and was turning the new house into an old one. At first, when the child learned to walk, they were careful that he not get too close to the chicken coop. But then they began to lose their fears and got used to the smell, and before the child got his second teeth he'd gone inside the chicken coop to play, where the wires were falling apart. The angel was no less standoffish with him than with other mortals, but he tolerated the most ingenious infamies with the patience of a dog who had no illusions. They both came down with chicken pox at the same time. The doctor who took care of the child couldn't resist the temptation to listen to the angel's heart, and he found so much whistling in the heart and so many sounds in his kidneys that it seemed impossible for him to be alive. What surprised him most, however, was the logic of his wings. They seemed so natural on that completely human organism that he couldn't understand why other men didn't have them too.

When the child began school it had been some time since the sun and rain had caused the collapse of the chicken coop. The angel went dragging himself about here and there like a stray dying man. They would drive him out of the bedroom with a broom and a moment later find him in the kitchen. He seemed to be in so many places at the same time that they grew to think that he'd been duplicated, that he was reproducing himself all through the house, and the exasperated and unhinged Elisenda shouted that it was awful living in that hell full of angels. He could scarcely eat and his antiquarian eyes had also become so foggy that he went about bumping into posts. All he had left were the bare cannulae[2] of his last feathers. Pelayo threw a blanket over him and extended him the charity of letting him sleep in the shed, and only then did they notice that he had a temperature at night, and was delirious with the tongue twisters of an old Norwegian. That was one of the few times they became alarmed, for they thought he was going to die and not even the wise neighbor woman had been able to tell them what to do with dead angels.

And yet he not only survived his worst winter, but seemed improved with the first sunny days. He remained motionless for several days in the farthest corner of the courtyard, where no one would see him, and at the beginning of December some large, stiff feathers began to grow on his wings, the feathers of a scarecrow, which looked more like another misfortune of decrepitude. But he must have known the reason for those changes, for he was quite careful that no one should notice them, that no one should hear the sea chanteys that he sometimes sang under the stars. One morning Elisenda was cutting some bunches of onions for lunch when a wind that seemed to come from the high seas blew into the kitchen. Then she went to the window and caught the angel in his first attempts at flight. They were so clumsy that his fingernails opened a furrow in the vegetable patch and he was on the point of knocking the shed down with the ungainly flapping that slipped on the light and he couldn't get a grip on the air. But he did manage to gain altitude. Elisenda let out a sigh of relief, for herself and for him, when she saw him pass over the last houses, holding himself up in some way with the risky flapping of a senile vulture. She kept watching him even when she was through cutting the onions and she kept on watching until it was no longer possible for her to see him, because then he was no longer an annoyance in her life but an imaginary dot on the horizon of the sea.

—1968

---

[2] **cannulae** the tubular pieces by which feathers are attached to a body.

---

**CHINUA ACHEBE ■ (1930–2013)**

*Chinua Achebe was born in Ogidi, Nigeria, and, after graduation from University College in Ibadan and study at London University, was employed by the Nigerian Broadcasting Service, where he served for years as a producer. After the appearance of his first novel,* Things Fall Apart, *in 1958 (the title is taken from William Butler Yeats's apocalyptic poem "The Second Coming") he became one of the most widely acclaimed writers to emerge from the former British colonies of Africa. The author of several novels as well as a collection of short stories, Achebe taught in the United States at the University of California–Los Angeles, Stanford University, and the University of Massachusetts–Amherst. One of his chief services to contemporary literature was his editorship of the African Writers Series, which sponsored the first publications of many of his fellow Nigerian writers. Achebe drew heavily on the oral traditions of his native country, but he has been successful in adapting European fictional techniques to deal with subjects like the degradations imposed by colonialism and the relative failure of most post colonial governments to improve on the past for the betterment of the lives of their citizens. "Dead Men's Path" brilliantly illustrates the ongoing conflict between modernization and tribal concerns.*

# Dead Men's Path

Michael Obi's hopes were fulfilled much earlier than he had expected. He was appointed headmaster of Ndume Central School in January 1949. It had always been an unprogressive school, so the Mission authorities decided to send a young and energetic man to run it. Obi accepted this responsibility with enthusiasm. He had many wonderful ideas and this was an opportunity to put them into practice. He had had sound secondary school education which designated him a "pivotal teacher" in the official records and set him apart from the other headmasters in the mission field. He was outspoken in his condemnation of the narrow views of these older and often less-educated ones.

"We shall make a good job of it, shan't we?" he asked his young wife when they first heard the joyful news of his promotion.

"We shall do our best," she replied. "We shall have such beautiful gardens and everything will be just *modern* and delightful. ..." In their two years of married life she had become completely infected by his passion for "modern methods" and his denigration of "these old and superannuated people in the teaching field who would be better employed as traders in the Onitsha market." She began to see herself already as the admired wife of the young headmaster, the queen of the school.

The wives of the other teachers would envy her position. She would set the fashion in everything. ... Then, suddenly, it occurred to her that there might not be other wives. Wavering between hope and fear, she asked her husband, looking anxiously at him.

"All our colleagues are young and unmarried," he said with enthusiasm which for once she did not share. "Which is a good thing," he continued.

"Why?"

"Why? They will give all their time and energy to the school."

Nancy was downcast. For a few minutes she became skeptical about the new school; but it was only for a few minutes. Her little personal misfortune could not blind her to her husband's happy prospects. She looked at him as he sat folded up in a chair. He was stoop-shouldered and looked frail. But he sometimes surprised people with sudden bursts of physical energy. In his present posture, however, all his bodily strength seemed to have retired behind his deep-set eyes, giving them an extraordinary power of penetration. He was only twenty-six, but looked thirty or more. On the whole, he was not unhandsome.

"A penny for your thoughts, Mike," said Nancy after a while, imitating the woman's magazine she read.

"I was thinking what a grand opportunity we've got at last to show these people how a school should be run."

Ndume School was backward in every sense of the word. Mr. Obi put his whole life into the work, and his wife hers too. He had two aims. A high standard of teaching was insisted upon, and the school compound was to be turned into a place of beauty. Nancy's dream-gardens came to life with the coming of the rains, and blossomed. Beautiful hibiscus and allamanda hedges in brilliant red and yellow marked out the carefully tended school compound from the rank neighborhood bushes.

One evening as Obi was admiring his work he was scandalized to see an old woman from the village hobble right across the compound, through a marigold flower-bed and the hedges. On going up there he found faint signs of an almost disused path from the village across the school compound to the bush on the other side.

"It amazes me," said Obi to one of his teachers who had been three years in the school, "that you people allowed the villagers to make use of this footpath. It is simply incredible." He shook his head.

"The path," said the teacher apologetically, "appears to be very important to them. Although it is hardly used, it connects the village shrine with their place of burial."

"And what has that got to do with the school?" asked the headmaster.

"Well, I don't know," replied the other with a shrug of the shoulders. "But I remember there was a big row some time ago when we attempted to close it."

"That was some time ago. But it will not be used now," said Obi as he walked away. "What will the Government Education Officer think of this when he comes to inspect the school next week? The villagers might, for all I know, decide to use the schoolroom for a pagan ritual during the inspection."

Heavy sticks were planted closely across the path at the two places where it entered and left the school premises. These were further strengthened with barbed wire.

Three days later the village priest of *Ani* called on the headmaster. He was an old man and walked with a slight stoop. He carried a stout walking-stick which he usually tapped on the floor, by way of emphasis, each time he made a new point in his argument.

"I have heard," he said after the usual exchange of cordialities, "that our ancestral footpath has recently been closed...."

"Yes," replied Mr. Obi. "We cannot allow people to make a highway of our school compound."

"Look here, my son," said the priest bringing down his walking-stick, "this path was here before you were born and before your father was born. The whole life of this village depends on it. Our dead relatives depart by it and our ancestors visit us by it. But most important, it is the path of children coming in to be born...."

Mr. Obi listened with a satisfied smile on his face.

"The whole purpose of our school," he said finally, "is to eradicate just such beliefs as that. Dead men do not require footpaths. The whole idea is just fantastic. Our duty is to teach your children to laugh at such ideas."

"What you say may be true," replied the priest, "but we follow the practices of our fathers. If you reopen the path we shall have nothing to quarrel about. What I always say is: let the hawk perch and let the eagle perch." He rose to go.

"I am sorry," said the young headmaster. "But the school compound cannot be a thoroughfare. It is against our regulations. I would suggest your constructing another path, skirting our premises. We can even get our boys to help in building it. I don't suppose the ancestors will find the little detour too burdensome."

"I have no more words to say," said the old priest, already outside.

Two days later a young woman in the village died in childbed. A diviner was immediately consulted and he prescribed heavy sacrifices to propitiate ancestors insulted by the fence.

Obi woke up next morning among the ruins of his work. The beautiful hedges were torn up not just near the path but right round the school, the flowers trampled to death and one of the school buildings pulled down .... That day, the white Supervisor came to inspect the school and wrote a nasty report on the state of the premises but more seriously about the "tribal-war situation developing between the school and the village, arising in part from the misguided zeal of the new headmaster."

—1953

**J.G. BALLARD** ▦ **(1930–2009)**

*James Graham Ballad had one of the most unusual upbringings of any English author. He was born and raised in Shanghai, China, where his English father was a prosperous businessman in the large foreign community. With the attack on Pearl Harbor, Ballard and his father and mother were interned in a concentration camp. Ballard eventually recounted his childhood in the best-selling autobiographical novel,* Empire of the Sun *(1984), which also became a 1987 film by Steven Spielberg. Ballard published sixteen volumes of short stories and nine novels. He has most often been considered a science fiction writer, but his work follows few conventions of that genre. Few contemporary writers have explored the imaginative possibilities of dream, fantasy, and nightmare as vividly as Ballard. "The Autobiography of J.G.B." appeared in* The New Yorker *shortly after Ballard's death.*

# The Autobiograpy of J.G.B

On waking one morning, B was surprised to see that Shepperton was deserted. He entered the kitchen at nine o'clock, annoyed to find that neither his post nor the daily newspapers had been delivered, and that a power failure prevented him from preparing his breakfast. He spent an hour staring at the melting ice that dripped from his refrigerator, and then went next door to complain to his neighbor.

Surprisingly, his neighbor's house was empty. His car stood in the drive, but the entire family—husband, wife, children, and dog—had disappeared. Even more odd, the street was filled by an unbroken silence. No traffic moved along the nearby motorway, and not a single aircraft flew overhead toward London Airport. B crossed the road and knocked on several doors. Through the windows, he could see the empty interiors. Nothing in this peaceful suburb was out of place, except for its missing tenants.

Thinking that perhaps some terrible calamity was imminent—a nuclear catastrophe, or a sudden epidemic after a research-laboratory accident— and that by some unfortunate mishap he alone had not been warned, B returned home and switched on his transistor radio. The apparatus worked, but all the stations were silent, the Continental transmitters as well as those of the United Kingdom. Disconcerted, B returned to the street and gazed at the empty sky. It was a calm, sun-filled day, crossed by peaceful clouds that gave no hint of any natural disaster.

B took his car and drove to the center of Shepperton. The town was deserted, and none of the shops were open. A train stood in the station, empty and without any of the passengers who regularly travelled to

London. Leaving Shepperton, B crossed the Thames to the nearby town of Walton. There again he found the streets completely silent. He stopped in front of the house owned by his friend P, whose car was parked in her drive. Using the spare key that he carried, he unlocked the front door and entered the house. But even as he called her name he could see that there was no trace of the young woman. She had not slept in her bed. In the kitchen, the melting ice of the refrigerator had formed a large pool on the floor. There was no electric power, and the telephone was dead.

Resuming his journey, B systematically explored the neighboring towns, circling them all as he approached central London. He was not surprised to find the huge metropolis totally deserted. He drove down an empty Piccadilly, crossed Trafalgar Square in silence, and parked outside the unguarded Buckingham Palace. As dusk fell, he decided to return to Shepperton. He had almost run out of fuel and was forced to break into a filling station. However, no policemen were out on patrol or in their stations. He left behind him an immense city plunged into darkness, where the only lights were the reflections of his headlamps.

B passed a disturbed night, with the radio mute beside his bed. But when he woke to another luminous morning his confidence returned. After an initial doubt, he was relieved to see that Shepperton was still deserted. The food within his refrigerator had begun to rot; he needed fresh provisions and a means of cooking for himself. He drove into Shepperton, broke a window of the supermarket, and collected several cartons of canned meat and vegetables, rice, and sugar. In the hardware store, he found a paraffin stove, and took it home with a tin of fuel. Water no longer flowed in the mains, but he estimated that the contents of the roof cistern would last him a week or more. Further forays to the local stores furnished him with a supply of candles, flashlights, and batteries.

In the following week, B made several expeditions to London. He returned to the houses and flats of his friends, but found them empty. He broke into Scotland Yard and the newspaper offices in Fleet Street, in the hope of finding some explanation for the disappearance of an entire population. Lastly, he entered the Houses of Parliament, and stood in the silent debating *chamber of the Commons*, breathing the stale air. However, there was not the least explanation anywhere of what had taken place. In the streets of the city, he saw not a single cat or dog. It was only when he visited London Zoo that he found that the birds still remained within their cages. They seemed delighted to see B, but flew off with famished cries when he unlocked the bars.

So at least he had a kind of companionship. During the next month, and throughout the summer, B continued his preparations for survival. He drove as far north as Birmingham without seeing a soul, then drove down to the south coast and followed the road from Brighton to Dover. Standing on the cliffs, he gazed at the distant shoreline of France. In the marina, he chose a motorboat with a full tank of fuel and set out across the calm sea, now free of the customary pleasure craft, petroleum tankers, and cross-Channel ferries. At Calais, he wandered for an hour through the deserted streets, and in the silent shops listened in vain to telephones that never rang. Then he retraced his steps to the port and returned to England.

When the summer was followed by a mild autumn, B had established a pleasant and comfortable existence for himself. He had abundant stocks of tinned food, fuel, and water with which to survive the winter. The river was nearby, clear and free of all pollution, and petrol was easy to obtain, in unlimited quantities, from the filling stations and parked cars. At the local police station, he assembled a small armory of pistols and carbines, to deal with any unexpected menace that might appear.

But his only visitors were the birds, and he scattered handfuls of rice and seeds on his lawn and on those of his former neighbors. Already he had begun to forget them, and Shepperton soon became an extraordinary aviary, filled with birds of every species.

Thus the year ended peacefully, and B was ready to begin his true work.

---

### JOHN UPDIKE ▪ (1932–2009)

*Born in the small town of Shillington in rural Pennsylvania, John Updike was the only child of a high school teacher who was the model for the protagonist of* The Centaur *(1963), the novel for which he won the National Book Award. After graduating from Harvard, he studied art abroad and worked for two years on the staff of* The New Yorker, *contributing articles and brilliant light verse. One of the great, versatile talents, Updike excelled at light and serious verse, short fiction, the novel, and criticism. He won the Pulitzer Prize for the novel* Rabbit at Rest *(1990), and throughout his career his books consistently appeared on best-seller lists. One of his novels,* The Witches of Eastwick *(1984), was made into a memorable film starring Jack Nicholson, Susan Sarandon, Michelle Pfeiffer, and Cher. Almost unique among recent writers, Updike moved back and forth successfully among a variety of literary genres, and with his death a large gap appeared in the American literary landscape. "A&P," his most widely anthologized story, invites the contemporary reader to analyze cultural norms that have changed a great deal in the years since it was first published.*

# A&P

In walks three girls in nothing but bathing suits. I'm in the third check-out slot, with my back to the door, so I don't see them until they're over by the bread. The one that caught my eye first was the one in the plaid green two-piece. She was a chunky kid, with a good tan and a sweet broad soft-looking can with those two crescents of white just under it, where the sun never seems to hit, at the top of the backs of her legs. I stood there with my hand on a box of HiHo crackers trying to remember if I rang it up or not. I ring it up again and the customer starts giving me hell. She's one of these cash-register-watchers, a witch about fifty with rouge on her cheekbones and no eyebrows, and I know it made her day to trip me up. She'd been watching cash registers for fifty years and probably never seen a mistake before.

By the time I got her feathers smoothed and her goodies into a bag— she gives me a little snort in passing, if she'd been born at the right time they would have burned her over in Salem—by the time I get her on her way the girls had circled around the bread and were coming back, without a pushcart, back my way along the counters, in the aisle between the check-outs and the Special bins. They didn't even have shoes on. There was this chunky one, with the two-piece—it was bright green and the seams on the bra were still sharp and her belly was still pretty pale so I guessed she just got it (the suit)—there was this one, with one of those chubby berry-faces, the lips all bunched together under her nose, this one, and a tall one, with black hair that hadn't quite frizzed right, and one of these sunburns right across under the eyes, and a chin that was too long—you know, the kind of girl other girls think is very "striking" and "attractive" but never quite makes it, as they very well know, which is why they like her so much—and then the third one, that wasn't quite so tall. She was the queen. She kind of led them, the other two peeking around and making their shoulders round. She didn't look around, not this queen, she just walked straight on slowly, on these long white prima-donna legs. She came down a little hard on her heels, as if she didn't walk in her bare feet that much, putting down her heels and then letting the weight move along to her toes as if she was test-ing the floor with every step, putting a little deliberate extra action into it. You never know for sure how girls' minds work (do you really think it's a mind in there or just a little buzz like a bee in a glass jar?) but you got the idea she had talked the other two into coming in here with her, and now she was showing them how to do it, walk slow and hold yourself straight.

She had on a kind of dirty-pink—beige maybe, I don't know—bathing suit with a little nubble all over it and, what got me, the straps were down. They were off her shoulders looped loose around the cool tops of her arms, and I guess as a result the suit had slipped a little on her, so all around the top of the cloth there was this shining rim. If it hadn't been there you wouldn't have known there could have been anything whiter than those shoulders. With the straps pushed off, there was nothing between the top of the suit and the top of her head except just *her*, this clean bare plane of the top of her chest down from the shoulder bones like a dented sheet of metal tilted in the light. I mean, it was more than pretty.

She had sort of oaky hair that the sun and salt had bleached, done up in a bun that was unraveling, and a kind of prim face. Walking into the A & P with your straps down, I suppose it's the only kind of face you *can* have. She held her head so high her neck, coming up out of those white shoulders, looked kind of stretched, but I didn't mind. The longer her neck was, the more of her there was.

She must have felt in the corner of her eye me and over my shoulder    5
Stokesie in the second slot watching, but she didn't tip. Not this queen. She kept her eyes moving across the racks, and stopped, and turned so slow it made my stomach rub the inside of my apron, and buzzed to the other two, who kind of huddled against her for relief, and they all three of them went up the cat-and-dog-food-breakfast-cereal-macaroni-rice-raisins-seasonings-spreads-spaghetti-soft-drinks-crackers-and-cookies aisle. From the third slot I look straight up this aisle to the meat counter, and I watched them all the way. The fat one with the tan sort of fumbled with the cookies, but on second thought she put the packages back. The sheep pushing their carts down the aisle—the girls were walking against the usual traffic (not that we have one-way signs or anything)—were pretty hilarious. You could see them, when Queenie's white shoulders dawned on them, kind of jerk, or hop, or hiccup, but their eyes snapped back to their own baskets and on they pushed. I bet you could set off dynamite in an A & P and the people would by and large keep reaching and checking oatmeal off their lists and muttering "Let me see, there was a third thing, began with A, asparagus, no, ah, yes, applesauce!" or whatever it is they do mutter. But there was no doubt, this jiggled them. A few houseslaves in pin curlers even looked around after pushing their carts past to make sure what they had seen was correct.

You know, it's one thing to have a girl in a bathing suit down on the beach, where what with the glare nobody can look at each other much anyway, and another thing in the cool of the A & P, under the fluorescent lights, against all those stacked packages, with her feet padding along naked over our checkerboard green-and-cream rubber-tile floor.

"Oh Daddy," Stokesie said beside me. "I feel so faint."

"Darling," I said. "Hold me tight." Stokesie's married, with two babies chalked up on his fuselage already, but as far as I can tell that's the only difference. He's twenty-two, and I was nineteen this April.

"Is it done?" he asks, the responsible married man finding his voice. I forgot to say he thinks he's going to be manager some sunny day, maybe in 1990 when it's called the Great Alexandrov and Petrooshki Tea Company or something.

What he meant was, our town is five miles from a beach, with a big summer    10
colony out on the Point, but we're right in the middle of town, and the women generally put on a shirt or shorts or something before they get out of the car into the street. And anyway these are usually women with six children

and varicose veins mapping their legs and nobody, including them, could care less. As I say, we're right in the middle of town, and if you stand at our front doors you can see two banks and the Congregational church and the newspaper store and three real-estate offices and about twenty-seven old freeloaders tearing up Central Street because the sewer broke again. It's not as if we're on the Cape; we're north of Boston and there's people in this town haven't seen the ocean for twenty years. The girls had reached the meat counter and were asking McMahon something. He pointed, they pointed, and they shuffled out of sight behind a pyramid of Diet Delight peaches. All that was left for us to see was old McMahon patting his mouth and looking after them sizing up their joints. Poor kids, I began to feel sorry for them, they couldn't help it.

Now here comes the sad part of the story, at least my family says it's sad but I don't think it's sad myself. The store's pretty empty, it being Thursday afternoon, so there was nothing much to do except lean on the register and wait for the girls to show up again. The whole store was like a pinball machine and I didn't know which tunnel they'd come out of. After a while they come around out of the far aisle, around the light bulbs, records at discount of the Caribbean Six or Tony Martin Sings or some such gunk you wonder they waste the wax on, six-packs of candy bars, and plastic toys done up in cellophane that fall apart when a kid looks at them anyway. Around they come, Queenie still leading the way, and holding a little gray jar in her hand. Slots Three through Seven are unmanned and I could see her wondering between Stokes and me, but Stokesie with his usual luck draws an old party in baggy gray pants who stumbles up with four giant cans of pineapple juice (what do these bums *do* with all that pineapple juice? I've often asked myself) so the girls come to me. Queenie puts down the jar and I take it into my fingers icy cold. Kingfish Fancy Herring Snacks in Pure Sour Cream: 49¢. Now her hands are empty, not a ring or a bracelet, bare as God made them, and I wonder where the money's coming from. Still with that prim look she lifts a folded dollar bill out of the hollow at the center of her nubbled pink top. The jar went heavy in my hand. Really, I thought that was so cute.

Then everybody's luck begins to run out. Lengel comes in from haggling with a truck full of cabbages on the lot and is about to scuttle into that door marked MANAGER behind which he hides all day when the girls touch his eye. Lengel's pretty dreary, teaches Sunday school and the rest, but he doesn't miss that much. He comes over and says, "Girls, this isn't the beach."

Queenie blushes, though maybe it's just a brush of sunburn I was noticing for the first time, now that she was so close. "My mother asked me to pick up a jar of herring snacks." Her voice kind of startled me, the way voices do when you see the people first, coming out so flat and dumb yet kind of tony, too, the way it ticked over "pick up" and "snacks." All of a sudden I slid right down her voice into her living room. Her father and the other men were standing

around in ice-cream coats and bow ties and the women were in sandals picking up herring snacks on toothpicks off a big plate and they were all holding
drinks the color of water with olives and sprigs of mint in them. When my parents have somebody over they get lemonade and if it's a real racy affair Schlitz
in tall glasses with "They'll Do It Every Time" cartoons stencilled on.

"That's all right," Lengel said. "But this isn't the beach." His repeating
this struck me as funny, as if it had just occurred to him, and he had been
thinking all these years the A & P was a great big dune and he was the head
lifeguard. He didn't like my smiling—as I say he doesn't miss much—but he
concentrates on giving the girls that sad Sunday-school-superintendent stare.

Queenie's blush is no sunburn now, and the plump one in plaid, that  15
I liked better from the back—a really sweet can—pipes up, "We weren't
doing any shopping. We just came in for the one thing."

"That makes no difference," Lengel tells her, and I could see from the
way his eyes went that he hadn't noticed she was wearing a two-piece
before. "We want you decently dressed when you come in here."

"We *are* decent," Queenie says suddenly, her lower lip pushing, getting
sore now that she remembers her place, a place from which the crowd that
runs the A & P must look pretty crummy. Fancy Herring Snacks flashed in
her very blue eyes.

"Girls, I don't want to argue with you. After this come in here with
your shoulders covered. It's our policy." He turns his back. That's policy
for you. Policy is what the kingpins want. What the others want is juvenile
delinquency.

All this while, the customers had been showing up with their carts but,
you know, sheep, seeing a scene, they had all bunched up on Stokesie, who
shook open a paper bag as gently as peeling a peach, not wanting to miss
a word. I could feel in the silence everybody getting nervous, most of all
Lengel, who asks me, "Sammy, have you rung up this purchase?"

I thought and said "No" but it wasn't about that I was thinking. I go  20
through the punches, 4, 9, GROC, TOT—it's more complicated than you think,
and after you do it often enough, it begins to make a little song, that
you hear words to, in my case "Hello (*bing*) there, you (*gung*) hap-py *pee-*
pul (*splat*)!"—the *splat* being the drawer flying out. I uncrease the bill,
tenderly as you may imagine, it just having come from between the two
smoothest scoops of vanilla I had ever known were there, and pass a half
and a penny into her narrow pink palm, and nestle the herrings in a bag
and twist its neck and hand it over, all the time thinking.

The girls, and who'd blame them, are in a hurry to get out, so I say
"I quit" to Lengel quick enough for them to hear, hoping they'll stop and
watch me, their unsuspected hero. They keep right on going, into the
electric eye; the door flies open and they flicker across the lot to their car,
Queenie and Plaid and Big Tall Goony-Goony (not that as raw material she
was so bad), leaving me with Lengel and a kink in his eyebrow.

"Did you say something, Sammy?"

"I said I quit."

"I thought you did."

"You didn't have to embarrass them." 25

"It was they who were embarrassing us."

I started to say something that came out "Fiddle-de-doo." It's a saying of my grandmother's, and I know she would have been pleased.

"I don't think you know what you're saying," Lengel said.

"I know you don't," I said. "But I do." I pull the bow at the back of my apron and start shrugging it off my shoulders. A couple customers that had been heading for my slot begin to knock against each other, like scared pigs in a chute.

Lengel sighs and begins to look very patient and old and gray. He's been 30 a friend of my parents for years. "Sammy, you don't want to do this to your Mom and Dad," he tells me. It's true, I don't. But it seems to me that once you begin a gesture it's fatal not to go through with it. I fold the apron, "Sammy" stitched in red on the pocket, and put it on the counter, and drop the bow tie on top of it. The bow tie is theirs, if you've ever wondered. "You'll feel this for the rest of your life," Lengel says, and I know that's true, too, but remembering how he made that pretty girl blush makes me so scrunchy inside I punch the No Sale tab and the machine whirs "pee-pul" and the drawer splats out. One advantage to this scene taking place in summer, I can follow this up with a clean exit, there's no fumbling around getting your coat and galoshes, I just saunter into the electric eye in my white shirt that my mother ironed the night before, and the door heaves itself open, and outside the sunshine is skating around on the asphalt.

I look around for my girls, but they're gone, of course. There wasn't anybody but some young married screaming with her children about some candy they didn't get by the door of a powder-blue Falcon station wagon. Looking back in the big windows, over the bags of peat moss and aluminum lawn furniture stacked on the pavement, I could see Lengel in my place in the slot, checking the sheep through. His face was dark gray and his back stiff, as if he'd just had an injection of iron, and my stomach kind of fell as I felt how hard the world was going to be to me hereafter.

—1961

---

**RAYMOND CARVER** ▪ **(1938–1988)**

*As a master of the contemporary short story, Raymond Carver built a reputation that was still growing at the end of his life, which came prematurely after a long struggle with cancer. A native of Clatskanie, Oregon, Carver worked at a number of unskilled jobs in his early years. Married and the father of two before he was 20, he knew the working class more intimately than have most American writers. Carver worked his way through Humboldt State College (now the University of California–Humboldt) and, like many major figures in contemporary American writing, was a graduate of the Writers' Workshop of the University of Iowa. Carver's publishing career is bracketed by collections of poetry; his earliest publications were poems, and* A New Path to the Waterfall *appeared posthumously in 1989. The compression of language he learned as a poet may in part account for the lean quality of his prose, which has been called, perhaps unfairly and inaccurately, "minimalist." Carver's last years were spent with his second wife, poet Tess Gallagher, and he taught at a number of universities. His personal victory over alcoholism paralleled the remarkable triumphs of his final years, which included receipt of a prestigious MacArthur Foundation Fellowship.* Where I'm Calling From: New and Selected Stories *was prepared by Carver shortly before his death and appeared in 1988, and* Call If You Need Me, *a volume of his uncollected stories and prose, was published in 2000. Several Carver stories were filmed by Robert Altman in his 1993 movie* Short Cuts. *"Cathedral," one of Carver's late stories, demonstrates the kind of personal "enlightenment" he discovered before his untimely death.*

# Cathedral

This blind man, an old friend of my wife's, he was on his way to spend the night. His wife had died. So he was visiting the dead wife's relatives in Connecticut. He called my wife from his in-laws'. Arrangements were made. He would come by train, a five-hour trip, and my wife would meet him at the station. She hadn't seen him since she worked for him one summer in Seattle ten years ago. But she and the blind man had kept in touch. They made tapes and mailed them back and forth. I wasn't enthusiastic about his visit. He was no one I knew. And his being blind bothered me. My idea of blindness came from the movies. In the movies, the blind moved slowly and never laughed. Sometimes they were led by seeing-eye dogs. A blind man in my house was not something I looked forward to.

That summer in Seattle she had needed a job. She didn't have any money. The man she was going to marry at the end of the summer was in officers' training school. He didn't have any money, either. But she was in love with the guy, and he was in love with her, etc. She'd seen something in the paper: HELP—*Reading to Blind Man,* and a telephone number. She phoned and went over, was hired on the spot. She'd worked with this blind man all summer. She read stuff to him, case studies, reports, that sort of thing. She helped him organize his little office in the county social-service department. They'd become good friends, my wife and the blind man. How do I know these things? She told me. And she told me something else. On her last day in the office, the blind man asked if he could touch her face. She agreed to this. She told me he touched his fingers to every part of her face, her nose—even her neck! She never forgot it. She even tried to write a poem about it. She was always trying to write a poem. She wrote a poem or two every year, usually after something really important had happened to her.

When we first started going out together, she showed me the poem. In the poem, she recalled his fingers and the way they had moved around over her face. In the poem, she talked about what she had felt at the time, about what went through her mind when the blind man touched her nose and lips. I can remember I didn't think much of the poem. Of course, I didn't tell her that. Maybe I just don't understand poetry. I admit it's not the first thing I reach for when I pick up something to read.

Anyway, this man who'd first enjoyed her favors, the officer-to-be, he'd been her childhood sweetheart. So okay. I'm saying that at the end of the summer she let the blind man run his hands over her face, said good-bye to him, married her childhood sweetheart, yes, please add. etc., who was now a commissioned officer, and she moved away from Seattle. But they'd kept in touch, she and the blind man. She made the first contact after a year or so. She called him up one night from an Air Force base in Alabama. She wanted to talk. They talked. He asked her to send a tape and tell him about her life. She did this. She sent the tape. On the tape, she told the blind man about her husband and about their life together in the military. She told the blind man she loved her husband but she didn't like it where they lived and she didn't like it that he was part of the military-industrial thing. She told the blind man she'd written a poem and he was in it. She told him that she was writing a poem about what it was like to be an Air Force officer's wife. The poem wasn't finished yet. She was still writing it. The blind man made a tape. He sent her the tape. She made a tape. This went on for years. My wife's officer was posted to one base and then another. She sent tapes from Moody AFB, McGuire, McConnell, and finally Travis, near Sacramento, where one night she got to feeling lonely and cut off from people she kept losing in that moving-around life. She got to feeling she couldn't go it another step. She went in and swallowed all the pills and capsules in the medicine chest and washed them down with a bottle of gin. Then she got into a hot bath and passed out.

But instead of dying, she got sick. She threw up. Her officer—why should he have a name? he was the childhood sweetheart, and what more does he want?—came home from somewhere, found her, and called the ambulance. In time, she put it all on a tape and sent the tape to the blind man. Over the years, she put all kinds of stuff on tapes and sent the tapes off lickety-split. Next to writing a poem every year, I think it was her chief means of recreation. On one tape, she told the blind man she'd decided to live away from her officer for a time. On another tape, she told him about her divorce. She and I began going out, and of course she told her blind man about it. She told him everything, or so it seemed to me. Once she asked me if I'd like to hear the latest tape from the blind man. This was a year ago. I was on the tape, she said. So I said okay, I'd listen to it. I got us drinks and we settled down in the living room. We made ready to listen. First she inserted the tape into the player and adjusted a couple of dials. Then she pushed a lever. The tape squeaked and someone began to talk in this loud voice. She lowered the volume. After a few minutes of harmless chitchat, I heard my own name in the mouth of this stranger, this blind man I didn't even know! And then this: "From all you've said about him, I can only conclude—" But we were interrupted, a knock at the door, something, and we didn't ever get back to the tape. Maybe it was just as well. I'd heard all I wanted to.

Now this same blind man was coming to sleep in my house.

"Maybe I could take him bowling," I said to my wife. She was at the draining board doing scalloped potatoes. She put down the knife she was using and turned around.

"If you love me," she said, "you can do this for me. If you don't love me, okay. But if you had a friend, any friend, and the friend came to visit, I'd make him feel comfortable." She wiped her hands with the dish towel.

"I don't have any blind friends," I said.

"You don't have *any* friends," she said. "Period. Besides," she said, "goddamn it, his wife's just died! Don't you understand that? The man's lost his wife!"

I didn't answer. She'd told me a little about the blind man's wife. Her name was Beulah. Beulah! That's a name for a colored woman.

"Was his wife a Negro?" I asked.

"Are you crazy?" my wife said. "Have you just flipped or something?" She picked up a potato. I saw it hit the floor, then roll under the stove. "What's wrong with you?" she said. "Are you drunk?"

"I'm just asking," I said.

Right then my wife filled me in with more detail than I cared to know. I made a drink and sat at the kitchen table to listen. Pieces of the story began to fall into place.

Beulah had gone to work for the blind man the summer after my wife had stopped working for him. Pretty soon Beulah and the blind man had themselves a church wedding. It was a little wedding—who'd want to go to such a wedding in the first place?—just the two of them, plus the minister and the minister's wife. But it was a church wedding just the same. It was what Beulah had wanted, he'd said. But even then Beulah must have been carrying the cancer in her glands. After they had been inseparable for eight years—my wife's word, *inseparable*—Beulah's health went into a rapid decline. She died in a Seattle hospital room, the blind man sitting beside the bed and holding on to her hand. They'd married, lived and worked together, slept together—had sex, sure—and then the blind man had to bury her. All this without his having ever seen what the goddamned woman looked like. It was beyond my understanding. Hearing this, I felt sorry for the blind man for a little bit. And then I found myself thinking what a pitiful life this woman must have led. Imagine a woman who could never see herself as she was seen in the eyes of her loved one. A woman who could go on day after day and never receive the smallest compliment from her beloved. A woman whose husband could never read the expression on her face, be it misery or something better. Someone who could wear makeup or not—what difference to him? She could, if she wanted, wear green eye-shadow around one eye, a straight pin in her nostril, yellow slacks, and purple shoes, no matter. And then to slip off into death, the blind man's hand on her hand, his blind eyes streaming tears—I'm imagining now—her last thought maybe this: that he never even knew what she looked like, and she on an express to the grave. Robert was left with a small insurance policy and a half of a twenty-peso Mexican coin. The other half of the coin went into the box with her. Pathetic.

So when the time rolled around, my wife went to the depot to pick him up. With nothing to do but wait—sure, I blamed him for that—I was having a drink and watching the TV when I heard the car pull into the drive. I got up from the sofa with my drink and went to the window to have a look.

I saw my wife laughing as she parked the car. I saw her get out of the car and shut the door. She was still wearing a smile. Just amazing. She went around to the other side of the car to where the blind man was already starting to get out. This blind man, feature this, he was wearing a full beard! A beard on a blind man! Too much, I say. The blind man reached into the backseat and dragged out a suitcase. My wife took his arm, shut the car door, and, talking all the way, moved him down the drive and then up the steps to the front porch. I turned off the TV. I finished my drink, rinsed the glass, dried my hands. Then I went to the door.

My wife said, "I want you to meet Robert. Robert, this is my husband. I've told you all about him." She was beaming. She had this blind man by his coat sleeve.

The blind man let go of his suitcase and up came his hand.

I took it. He squeezed hard, held my hand, and then he let it go.

"I feel like we've already met," he boomed.

"Likewise," I said. I didn't know what else to say. Then I said, "Welcome. I've heard a lot about you." We began to move then, a little group, from the porch into the living room, my wife guiding him by the arm. The blind man was carrying his suitcase in his other hand. My wife said things like, "To your left here, Robert. That's right. Now watch it, there's a chair. That's it. Sit down right here. This is the sofa. We just bought this sofa two weeks ago."

I started to say something about the old sofa. I'd liked that old sofa. But I didn't say anything. Then I wanted to say something else, small-talk, about the scenic ride along the Hudson. How going *to* New York, you should sit on the right-hand side of the train, and coming *from* New York, the left-hand side.

"Did you have a good train ride?" I said. "Which side of the train did you sit on, by the way?"

"What a question, which side!" my wife said. "What's it matter which side?" she said.

"I just asked," I said.

"Right side," the blind man said. "I hadn't been on a train in nearly forty years. Not since I was a kid. With my folks. That's been a long time. I'd nearly forgotten the sensation. I have winter in my beard now," he said. "So I've been told, anyway. Do I look distinguished, my dear?" the blind man said to my wife.

"You look distinguished, Robert," she said. "Robert," she said. "Robert, it's just so good to see you."

My wife finally took her eyes off the blind man and looked at me. I had the feeling she didn't like what she saw. I shrugged.

I've never met, or personally known, anyone who was blind. This blind man was late forties, a heavy-set, balding man with stooped shoulders, as if he carried a great weight there. He wore brown slacks, brown shoes, a light-brown shirt, a tie, a sports coat. Spiffy. He also had this full beard. But he didn't use a cane and he didn't wear dark glasses. I'd always thought dark glasses were a must for the blind. Fact was, I wished he had a pair. At first glance, his eyes looked like anyone else's eyes. But if you looked close, there was something different about them. Too much white in the iris, for one thing, and the pupils seemed to move around in the sockets without his knowing it or being able to stop it. Creepy. As I stared at his face, I saw the left pupil turn in toward his nose while the other made an effort to keep in one place. But it was only an effort, for that eye was on the roam without his knowing it or wanting it to be.

I said, "Let me get you a drink. What's your pleasure? We have a little of everything. It's one of our pastimes."

"Bub, I'm a Scotch man myself," he said fast enough in this big voice.

"Right," I said. Bub! "Sure you are. I knew it."

He let his fingers touch his suitcase, which was sitting alongside the sofa. He was taking his bearings. I didn't blame him for that.

"I'll move that up to your room," my wife said.

"No, that's fine," the blind man said loudly. "It can go up when I go up."

"A little water with the Scotch?" I said.

"Very little," he said.

"I knew it," I said.

He said, "Just a tad. The Irish actor, Barry Fitzgerald? I'm like that fellow. When I drink water, Fitzgerald said, I drink water. When I drink whiskey, I drink whiskey." My wife laughed. The blind man brought his hand up under his beard. He lifted his beard slowly and let it drop.

I did the drinks, three big glasses of Scotch with a splash of water in each. Then we made ourselves comfortable and talked about Robert's travels. First the long flight from the West Coast to Connecticut, we covered that. Then from Connecticut up here by train. We had another drink concerning that leg of the trip.

I remembered having read somewhere that the blind didn't smoke because, as speculation had it, they couldn't see the smoke they exhaled. I thought I knew that much and that much only about blind people. But this blind man smoked his cigarette down to the nubbin and then lit another one. This blind man filled his ashtray and my wife emptied it.

When we sat down at the table for dinner, we had another drink. My wife heaped Robert's plate with cube steak, scalloped potatoes, green beans. I buttered him up two slices of bread. I said, "Here's bread and butter for you." I swallowed some of my drink. "Now let us pray," I said, and the blind man lowered his head. My wife looked at me, her mouth agape. "Pray the phone won't ring and the food doesn't get cold," I said.

We dug in. We ate everything there was to eat on the table. We ate like there was no tomorrow. We didn't talk. We ate. We scarfed. We grazed that table. We were into serious eating. The blind man had right away located his foods, he knew just where everything was on his plate. I watched with admiration as he used his knife and fork on the meat. He'd cut two pieces of meat, fork the meat into his mouth, and then go all out for the scalloped potatoes, the beans next, and then he'd tear off a hunk of buttered bread and eat that. He'd follow this up with a big drink of milk. It didn't seem to bother him to use his fingers once in a while, either.

We finished everything, including half a strawberry pie. For a few moments, we sat as if stunned. Sweat beaded on our faces. Finally, we got up from the table and left the dirty plates. We didn't look back. We took ourselves into the living room and sank into our places again. Robert and my wife sat on the sofa. I took the big chair. We had us two or three more drinks while they talked about the major things that had come to pass for them in the past ten years. For the most part, I just listened. Now and then I joined in. I didn't want him to think I'd left the room, and I didn't want her to think I was feeling left out. They talked of things that had happened to them—to them!—these past ten years. I waited in vain to hear my name on my wife's sweet lips: "And then my dear husband came into my life"—something like that. But I heard nothing of the sort. More talk of Robert. Robert had done a little of everything, it seemed, a regular blind jack-of-all-trades. But most recently he and his wife had had an Amway distributorship, from which, I gathered, they'd earned their living, such as it was. The blind man was also a ham radio operator. He talked in his loud voice about conversations he'd had with fellow operators in Guam, in the Philippines, in Alaska, and even in Tahiti. He said he'd have a lot of friends there if he ever wanted to go visit those places. From time to time, he'd turn his blind face toward me, put his hand under his beard, ask me something. How long had I been in my present position? (Three years.) Did I like my work? (I didn't.) Was I going to stay with it? (What were the options?) Finally, when I thought he was beginning to run down, I got up and turned on the TV.

My wife looked at me with irritation. She was heading toward a boil. Then she looked at the blind man and said, "Robert, do you have a TV?"

The blind man said, "My dear, I have two TVs. I have a color set and a black-and-white thing, an old relic. It's funny, but if I turn the TV on, and I'm always turning it on, I turn on the color set. It's funny, don't you think?"

I didn't know what to say to that. I had absolutely nothing to say to that. No opinion. So I watched the news program and tried to listen to what the announcer was saying.

"This is a color TV," the blind man said. "Don't ask me how, but I can tell."

"We traded up a while ago," I said.

The blind man had another taste of his drink. He lifted his beard, sniffed it, and let it fall. He leaned forward on the sofa. He positioned his ashtray on the coffee table, then put the lighter to his cigarette. He leaned back on the sofa and crossed his legs at the ankles.

My wife covered her mouth, and then she yawned. She stretched. She said, "I think I'll go upstairs and put on my robe. I think I'll change into something else. Robert, you make yourself comfortable," she said.

"I'm comfortable," the blind man said.

"I want you to feel comfortable in this house," she said.

"I am comfortable," the blind man said.

After she'd left the room, he and I listened to the weather report and then to the sports roundup. By that time, she'd been gone so long I didn't know if she was going to come back. I thought she might have gone to bed. I wished she'd come back downstairs. I didn't want to be left alone with a blind man. I asked him if he wanted another drink, and he said sure. Then I asked if he wanted to smoke some dope with me. I said I'd just rolled a number. I hadn't, but I planned to do so in about two shakes.

"I'll try some with you," he said.

"Damn right," I said. "That's the stuff."

I got our drinks and sat down on the sofa with him. Then I rolled us two fat numbers. I lit one and passed it. I brought it to his fingers. He took it and inhaled.

"Hold it as long as you can," I said. I could tell he didn't know the first thing.

My wife came back downstairs wearing her pink robe and her pink slippers.

"What do I smell?" she said.

"We thought we'd have us some cannabis," I said.

My wife gave me a savage look. Then she looked at the blind man and said, "Robert, I didn't know you smoked."

He said, "I do now, my dear. There's a first time for everything. But I don't feel anything yet."

"This stuff is pretty mellow," I said. "This stuff is mild. It's dope you can reason with," I said. "It doesn't mess you up."

"Not much it doesn't, bub," he said, and laughed.

My wife sat on the sofa between the blind man and me. I passed her the number. She took it and toked and then passed it back to me. "Which way is this going?" she said. Then she said, "I shouldn't be smoking this. I can hardly keep my eyes open as it is. That dinner did me in. I shouldn't have eaten so much."

"It was the strawberry pie," the blind man said. "That's what did it," he said, and he laughed his big laugh. Then he shook his head.

"There's more strawberry pie," I said.

"Do you want some more, Robert?" my wife said.

"Maybe in a little while," he said.

We gave our attention to the TV. My wife yawned again. She said, "Your bed is made up when you feel like going to bed, Robert. I know you must have had a long day. When you're ready to go to bed, say so." She pulled his arm. "Robert?"

He came to and said, "I've had a real nice time. This beats tapes, doesn't it?"

I said, "Coming at you," and I put the number between his fingers. He inhaled, held the smoke, and then let it go. It was like he'd been doing it since he was nine years old.

"Thanks, bub," he said. "But I think this is all for me. I think I'm beginning to feel it," he said. He held the burning roach out for my wife.

"Same here," she said. "Ditto. Me, too." She took the roach and passed it to me. "I may just sit here for a while between you two guys with my eyes closed. But don't let me bother you, okay? Either one of you. If it bothers you, say so. Otherwise, I may just sit here with my eyes closed until you're ready to go to bed," she said. "Your bed's made up, Robert, when you're ready. It's right next to our room at the top of the stairs. We'll show you up when you're ready. You wake me up now, you guys, if I fall asleep." She said that and then she closed her eyes and went to sleep.

The news program ended. I got up and changed the channel. I sat back down on the sofa. I wished my wife hadn't pooped out. Her head lay across the back of the sofa, her mouth open. She'd turned so that her robe slipped away from her legs, exposing a juicy thigh. I reached to draw her robe back over her, and it was then that I glanced at the blind man. What the hell! I flipped the robe open again.

"You say when you want some strawberry pie," I said.

"I will," he said.

I said, "Are you tired? Do you want me to take you up to your bed? Are you ready to hit the hay?"

"Not yet," he said. "No, I'll stay up with you, bub. If that's all right. I'll stay up until you're ready to turn in. We haven't had a chance to talk. Know what I mean? I feel like me and her monopolized the evening." He lifted his beard and he let it fall. He picked up his cigarettes and his lighter.

"That's all right," I said. Then I said, "I'm glad for the company."

And I guess I was. Every night I smoked dope and stayed up as long as I could before I fell asleep. My wife and I hardly ever went to bed at the same time. When I did go to sleep, I had these dreams. Sometimes I'd wake up from one of them, my heart going crazy.

Something about the church and the Middle Ages was on the TV. Not your run-of-the-mill TV fare. I wanted to watch something else. I turned to the other channels. But there was nothing on them, either. So I turned back to the first channel and apologized.

"Bub, it's all right," the blind man said. "It's fine with me. Whatever you want to watch is okay, I'm always learning something. Learning never ends. It won't hurt me to learn something tonight. I got ears," he said.

We didn't say anything for a time. He was leaning forward with his head turned at me, his right ear aimed in the direction of the set. Very disconcerting. Now and then his eyelids drooped and then they snapped open again. Now and then he put his fingers into his beard and tugged, like he was thinking about something he was hearing on the television.

On the screen, a group of men wearing cowls was being set upon and tormented by men dressed in skeleton costumes and men dressed as devils. The men dressed as devils wore devil masks, horns, and long tails. This pageant was part of a procession. The Englishman who was narrating the thing said it took place in Spain once a year. I tried to explain to the blind man what was happening.

"Skeletons," he said. "I know about skeletons," he said, and he nodded.

The TV showed this one cathedral. Then there was a long, slow look at another one. Finally, the picture switched to the famous one in Paris, with its flying buttresses and its spires reaching up to the clouds. The camera pulled away to show the whole of the cathedral rising above the skyline.

There were times when the Englishman who was telling the thing would shut up, would simply let the camera move around the cathedrals. Or else the camera would tour the countryside, men in fields walking behind oxen. I waited as long as I could. Then I felt I had to say something. I said, "They're showing the outside of this cathedral now. Gargoyles. Little statues carved to look like monsters. Now I guess they're in Italy. Yeah, they're in Italy. There's paintings on the walls of this one church."

"Are those fresco paintings, bub?" he asked, and he sipped from his drink.

I reached for my glass. But it was empty. I tried to remember what I could remember. "You're asking me are those frescoes?" I said. "That's a good question. I don't know."

The camera moved to a cathedral outside Lisbon. The differences in the Portuguese cathedral compared with the French and Italian were not that great. But they were there. Mostly the interior stuff. Then something occurred to me, and I said, "Something has occurred to me. Do you have any idea what a cathedral is? What they look like, that is? Do you follow me? If somebody says cathedral to you, do you have any notion what they're talking about? Do you know the difference between that and a Baptist church, say?"

He let the smoke dribble from his mouth. "I know they took hundreds of workers fifty or a hundred years to build," he said. "I just heard the man say that, of course. I know generations of the same families worked on a cathedral. I heard him say that, too. The men who began their life's work on them, they never lived to see the completion of their work. In that wise, bub, they're no different from the rest of us, right?" He laughed. Then his eyelids drooped again. His head nodded. He seemed to be snoozing. Maybe he was imagining himself in Portugal. The TV was showing another cathedral now. This one was in Germany. The Englishman's voice droned on. "Cathedrals," the blind man said. He sat up and rolled his head back and forth. "If you want the truth, bub, that's about all I know. What I just said. What I heard him say. But maybe you could describe one to me? I wish you'd do it. I'd like that. If you want to know. I really don't have a good idea."

I stared hard at the shot of the cathedral on the TV. How could I even begin to describe it? But say my life depended on it. Say my life was being threatened by an insane guy who said I had to do it or else.

I stared some more at the cathedral before the picture flipped off into the countryside. There was no use. I turned to the blind man and said, "To begin with, they're very tall." I was looking around the room for clues. "They reach way up. Up and up. Toward the sky. They're so big, some of them, they have to have these supports. To help hold them up, so to speak. These supports are called buttresses. They remind me of viaducts, for some reason. But maybe you don't know viaducts, either? Sometimes the cathedrals have devils and such carved into the front. Sometimes lords and ladies. Don't ask me why this is," I said.

He was nodding. The whole upper part of his body seemed to be moving back and forth.

"I'm not doing so good, am I?" I said.

He stopped nodding and leaned forward on the edge of the sofa. As he listened to me, he was running his fingers through his beard. I wasn't getting through to him, I could see that. But he waited for me to go on just the same. He nodded, like he was trying to encourage me. I tried to think what else to say. "They're really big," I said. "They're massive. They're built of stone. Marble, too, sometimes. In those olden days, when they built cathedrals, men wanted to be close to God. In those olden days, God was an important part of everyone's life. You could tell this from their cathedral-building. I'm sorry," I said, "but it looks like that's the best I can do for you. I'm just no good at it."

"That's all right, bub," the blind man said. "Hey, listen. I hope you don't mind my asking you. Can I ask you something? Let me ask you a simple question, yes or no. I'm just curious and there's no offense. You're my host. But let me ask if you are in any way religious? You don't mind my asking?"

I shook my head. He couldn't see that, though. A wink is the same as a nod to a blind man. "I guess I don't believe in it. In anything. Sometimes it's hard. You know what I'm saying?"

"Sure, I do," he said.

"Right," I said.

The Englishman was still holding forth. My wife sighed in her sleep. She drew a long breath and went on with her sleeping.

"You'll have to forgive me," I said. "But I can't tell you what a cathedral looks like. It just isn't in me to do it. I can't do any more than I've done."

The blind man sat very still, his head down, as he listened to me.

I said, "The truth is, cathedrals don't mean anything special to me. Nothing. Cathedrals. They're something to look at on late-night TV. That's all they are."

It was then that the blind man cleared his throat. He brought something up. He took a handkerchief from his back pocket. Then he said, "I get it, bub. It's okay. It happens. Don't worry about it," he said. "Hey, listen to me. Will you do me a favor? I got an idea. Why don't you find us some heavy paper? And a pen. We'll do something. We'll draw one together. Get us a pen and some heavy paper. Go on, bub, get the stuff," he said.

So I went upstairs. My legs felt like they didn't have any strength in them. They felt like they did after I'd done some running. In my wife's room, I looked around. I found some ballpoints in a little basket on her table. And then I tried to think where to look for the kind of paper he was talking about.

Downstairs, in the kitchen. I found a shopping bag with onion skins in the bottom of the bag. I emptied the bag and shook it. I brought it into the living room and sat down with it near his legs. I moved some things, smoothed the wrinkles from the bag, spread it out on the coffee table.

The blind man got down from the sofa and sat next to me on the carpet.

He ran his fingers over the paper. He went up and down the sides of the paper. The edges, even the edges. He fingered the corners.

"All right," he said. "All right, let's do her."

He found my hand, the hand with the pen. He closed his hand over my hand. "Go ahead, bub, draw," he said. "Draw. You'll see. I'll follow along with you. It'll be okay. Just begin now like I'm telling you. You'll see. Draw," the blind man said.

So I began. First I drew a box that looked like a house. It could have been the house I lived in. Then I put a roof on it. At either end of the roof. I drew spires. Crazy.

"Swell," he said, "Terrific. You're doing fine," he said. "Never thought anything like this could happen in your lifetime, did you, bub? Well, it's a strange life, we all know that. Go on now. Keep it up."

I put in windows with arches. I drew flying buttresses. I hung great doors. I couldn't stop. The TV station went off the air. I put down the pen and closed and opened my fingers. The blind man felt around over the paper. He moved the tips of his fingers over the paper, all over what I had drawn, and he nodded.

"Doing fine," the blind man said.

I took up the pen again, and he found my hand. I kept at it. I'm no artist. But I kept drawing just the same.

My wife opened up her eyes and gazed at us. She sat up on the sofa, her robe hanging open. She said, "What are you doing? Tell me, I want to know."

I didn't answer her.

The blind man said, "We're drawing a cathedral. Me and him are working on it. Press hard," he said to me. "That's right. That's good," he said. "Sure. You got it, bub, I can tell. You didn't think you could. But you can, can't you? You're cooking with gas now. You know what I'm saying? We're going to really have us something here in a minute. How's the old arm?" he said. "Put some people in there now. What's a cathedral without people?"

My wife said, "What's going on? Robert, what are you doing? What's going on?"

"It's all right," he said to her. "Close your eyes now," the blind man said to me.

I did it. I closed them just like he said.

"Are they closed?" he said. "Don't fudge."

"They're closed," I said.

"Keep them that way," he said. He said, "Don't stop now. Draw."

So we kept on with it. His fingers rode my fingers as my hand went over the paper. It was like nothing else in my life up to now.

Then he said, "I think that's it. I think you got it," he said. "Take a look. What do you think?"

But I had my eyes closed. I thought I'd keep them that way for a little longer. I thought it was something I ought to do.

"Well?" he said. "Are you looking?"

My eyes were still closed. I was in my house. I knew that. But I didn't feel like I was inside anything.

"It's really something," I said.

—1983

**JOYCE CAROL OATES** ■ **(b. 1938)**

*Joyce Carol Oates is a prolific writer who has published more than 100 books since her first one appeared in 1963, and she shows few signs of slowing her output. Her new books—whether novels, books of poems, collections of stories, or nonfiction memoirs on subjects like boxing—always draw serious critical attention and more often than not land on the best-seller lists, and she has even written suspense novels pseudonymously as Rosamond Smith. Born in Lockport, New York, she holds degrees from Syracuse and the University of Wisconsin, and she is writer-in-residence at Princeton University, where she also codirected, with her late husband, the* Ontario Review Press. *Oates's work is often violent, a fact for which she has been criticized on numerous occasions. In response, she has remarked that these comments are "always ignorant, always sexist," implying that different standards are often applied to the work of women authors whose realism may be too strong for some tastes. Few readers would argue that her stories and novels exceed the violence of the society they depict.* Them, *a novel of African American life in Detroit, won a National Book Award in 1970, and Oates has since garnered many other honors. "Where Are You Going, Where Have You Been?" is based on a* Life *magazine story about a serial rapist and killer known as "The Pied Piper of Tucson." In 1985, Oates's story was filmed by Joyce Chopra as* Smooth Talk, *starring Laura Dern and Treat Williams. Indicating the long popularity of this story, Oates published a collection of prose pieces in 1999 titled* Where I've Been, and Where I'm Going.

# Where Are You Going, Where Have You Been?

*To Bob Dylan*

Her name was Connie. She was fifteen and she had a quick nervous giggling habit of craning her neck to glance into mirrors or checking other people's faces to make sure her own was all right. Her mother, who noticed everything and knew everything and who hadn't much reason any longer to look at her own face, always scolded Connie about it. "Stop gawking at yourself, who are you? You think you're so pretty?" she would say. Connie would raise her eyebrows at these familiar complaints and look right through her mother, into a shadowy vision of herself as she was right at that moment: she knew she was pretty and that was everything. Her mother had been pretty once too, if you could believe those old snapshots in the album, but now her looks were gone and that was why she was always after Connie.

"Why don't you keep your room clean like your sister? How've you got your hair fixed—what the hell stinks? Hair spray? You don't see your sister using that junk."

Her sister June was twenty-four and still lived at home. She was a secretary in the high school Connie attended, and if that wasn't bad enough—with her in the same building—she was so plain and chunky and steady that Connie had to hear her praised all the time by her mother and her mother's sisters. June did this, June did that, she saved money and helped clean the house and cooked and Connie couldn't do a thing, her mind was all filled with trashy daydreams. Their father was away at work most of the time and when he came home he wanted supper and he read the newspaper at supper and after supper he went to bed. He didn't bother talking much to them, but around his bent head Connie's mother kept picking at her until Connie wished her mother was dead and she herself was dead and it was all over. "She makes me want to throw up sometimes," she complained to her friends. She had a high, breathless, amused voice which made everything she said sound a little forced, whether it was sincere or not.

There was one good thing: June went places with girlfriends of hers, girls who were just as plain and steady as she, and so when Connie wanted to do that her mother had no objections. The father of Connie's best girlfriend drove the girls the three miles to town and left them off at a shopping plaza, so that they could walk through the stores or go to a movie, and when he came to pick them up again at eleven he never bothered to ask what they had done.

They must have been familiar sights, walking around that shopping plaza in their shorts and flat ballerina slippers that always scuffed the sidewalk, with charm bracelets jingling on their thin wrists; they would lean together to whisper and laugh secretly if someone passed by who amused or interested them. Connie had long dark blond hair that drew anyone's eye to it, and she wore part of it pulled up on her head and puffed out and the rest of it she let fall down her back. She wore a pull over jersey blouse that looked one way when she was at home and another way when she was away from home. Everything about her had two sides to it, one for home and one for anywhere that was not home: her walk that could be childlike and bobbing, or languid enough to make anyone think she was hearing music in her head, her mouth which was pale and smirking most of the time, but bright and pink on these evenings out, her laugh which was cynical and drawling at home—"Ha, ha, very funny"—but high-pitched and nervous anywhere else, like the jingling of the charms on her bracelet.

Sometimes they did go shopping or to a movie, but sometimes they went across the highway, ducking fast across the busy road, to a drive-in restaurant where older kids hung out. The restaurant was shaped like a big bottle, though squatter than a real bottle, and on its cap was a revolving figure of a grinning boy who held a hamburger aloft. One night in mid-summer they ran across, breathless with daring, and right away someone leaned out a car window and invited them over, but it was just a boy from high school they didn't like. It made them feel good to be able to ignore him. They went up through the maze of parked and cruising cars to the bright-lit, fly-infested restaurant, their faces pleased and expectant as if they were entering a sacred building that loomed out of the night to give them what haven and what blessing they yearned for. They sat at the counter and crossed their legs at the ankles, their thin shoulders rigid with excitement, and listened to the music that made everything so good: the music was always in the background like music at a church service, it was something to depend upon.

A boy named Eddie came in to talk with them. He sat backward on his stool, turning himself jerkily around in semicircles and then stopping and turning again, and after a while he asked Connie if she would like something to eat. She said she did and so she tapped her friend's arm on her way out—her friend pulled her face up into a brave droll look—and Connie said she would meet her at eleven, across the way. "I just hate to leave her like that," Connie said earnestly, but the boy said that she wouldn't be alone for long. So they went out to his car and on the way Connie couldn't help but let her eyes wander over the windshields and faces all around her, her face gleaming with a joy that had nothing to do with Eddie or even this place; it might have been the music. She drew her shoulders up and sucked in her breath with the pure pleasure of being alive, and just at that moment she happened to glance at a face just a few feet from hers. It was a boy with shaggy black hair, in a convertible jalopy painted gold. He stared at her and then his lips widened into a grin. Connie slit her eyes at him and turned away, but she couldn't help glancing back and there he was still watching her. He wagged a finger and laughed and said, "Gonna get you, baby," and Connie turned away again without Eddie noticing anything.

She spent three hours with him, at the restaurant where they ate hamburgers and drank Cokes in wax cups that were always sweating, and then down an alley a mile or so away, and when he left her off at five to eleven only the movie house was still open at the plaza. Her girlfriend was there, talking with a boy. When Connie came up the two girls smiled at each other and Connie said, "How was the movie?" and the girl said, "You should know." They rode off with the girl's father, sleepy and pleased, and Connie couldn't help but look at the darkened shopping plaza with its big empty parking lot and its signs that were faded and ghostly now, and over at the drive-in restaurant where cars were still circling tirelessly. She couldn't hear the music at this distance.

Next morning June asked her how the movie was and Connie said, "So-so."

She and that girl and occasionally another girl went out several times a week that way, and the rest of the time Connie spent around the house—it was summer vacation—getting in her mother's way and thinking, dreaming, about the boys she met. But all the boys fell back and dissolved into a single face that was not even a face, but an idea, a feeling, mixed up with the urgent insistent pounding of the music and the humid night air of July. Connie's mother kept dragging her back to the daylight by finding things for her to do or saying, suddenly, "What's this about the Pettinger girl?"

And Connie would say nervously, "Oh, her. That dope." She always drew thick clear lines between herself and such girls, and her mother was simple and kindly enough to believe her. Her mother was so simple, Connie thought, that it was maybe cruel to fool her so much. Her mother went scuffling around the house in old bedroom slippers and complained over the telephone to one sister about the other, then the other called up and the two of them complained about the third one. If June's name was mentioned her mother's tone was approving, and if Connie's name was mentioned it was disapproving. This did not really mean she disliked Connie and actually Connie thought that her mother preferred her to June because she was prettier, but the two of them kept up a pretense of exasperation, a sense that they were tugging and struggling over something of little value to either of them. Sometimes, over coffee, they were almost friends, but something would come up—some vexation that was like a fly buzzing suddenly around their heads—and their faces went hard with contempt.

One Sunday Connie got up at eleven—none of them bothered with church—and washed her hair so that it could dry all day long, in the sun. Her parents and sister were going to a barbecue at an aunt's house and Connie said no, she wasn't interested, rolling her eyes to let her mother know just what she thought of it. "Stay home alone then," her mother said sharply. Connie sat out back in a lawn chair and watched them drive away, her father quiet and bald, hunched around so that he could back the car out, her mother with a look that was still angry and not at all softened through the windshield, and in the back seat poor old June all dressed up as if she didn't know what a barbecue was, with all the running yelling kids and the flies. Connie sat with her eyes closed in the sun, dreaming and dazed with the warmth about her as if this were a kind of love, the caresses of love, and her mind slipped over onto thoughts of the boy she had been with the night before and how nice he had been, how sweet it always was, not the way someone like June would suppose but sweet, gentle, the way it was in movies and promised in songs; and when she opened her eyes she hardly knew where she was, the back yard ran off into weeds and a fence line of trees and behind it the sky was perfectly blue and still. The asbestos "ranch house" that was now three years old startled her—it looked small. She shook her head as if to get awake.

It was too hot. She went inside the house and turned on the radio to drown out the quiet. She sat on the edge of her bed, barefoot, and listened for an hour and a half to a program called XYZ Sunday Jamboree, record after record of hard, fast, shrieking songs she sang along with, interspersed by exclamations from "Bobby King": "An' look here you girls at Napoleon's—Son and Charley want you to pay real close attention to this song coming up!"

And Connie paid close attention herself, bathed in a glow of slow-pulsed joy that seemed to rise mysteriously out of the music itself and lay languidly about the airless little room, breathed in and breathed out with each gentle rise and fall of her chest.

After a while she heard a car coming up the drive. She sat up at once, startled, because it couldn't be her father so soon. The gravel kept crunching all the way in from the road—the driveway was long—and Connie ran to the window. It was a car she didn't know. It was an open jalopy, painted a bright gold that caught the sunlight opaquely. Her heart began to pound and her fingers snatched at her hair, checking it, and she whispered "Christ, Christ," wondering how bad she looked. The car came to a stop at the side door and the horn sounded four short taps as if this were a signal Connie knew.

She went into the kitchen and approached the door slowly, then hung out the screen door, her bare toes curling down off the step. There were two boys in the car and now she recognized the driver: he had shaggy, shabby black hair that looked crazy as a wig and he was grinning at her.

"I ain't late, am I?" he said.

"Who the hell do you think you are?" Connie said.

"Toldja I'd be out, didn't I?"

"I don't even know who you are."

She spoke sullenly, careful to show no interest or pleasure, and he spoke in a fast bright monotone. Connie looked past him to the other boy, taking her time. He had fair brown hair, with a lock that fell onto his forehead. His sideburns gave him a fierce, embarrassed look, but so far he hadn't even bothered to glance at her. Both boys wore sunglasses. The driver's glasses were metallic and mirrored everything in miniature.

"You wanta come for a ride?" he said.

Connie smirked and let her hair fall loose over one shoulder.

"Don'tcha like my car? New paint job," he said. "Hey."

"What?"

"You're cute."

She pretended to fidget, chasing flies away from the door.

"Don'tcha believe me, or what?" he said.

"Look, I don't even know who you are," Connie said in disgust.

"Hey, Ellie's got a radio, see. Mine's broke down." He lifted his friend's arm and showed her the little transistor the boy was holding, and now

Connie began to hear the music. It was the same program that was playing inside the house.

"Bobby King?" she said.

"I listen to him all the time. I think he's great."

"He's kind of great," Connie said reluctantly.

"Listen, that guy's *great*. He knows where the action is."

Connie blushed a little, because the glasses made it impossible for her to see just what this boy was looking at. She couldn't decide if she liked him or if he was just a jerk, and so she dawdled in the doorway and wouldn't come down or go back inside. She said, "What's all that stuff painted on your car?"

"Can'tcha read it?" He opened the door very carefully, as if he was afraid it might fall off. He slid out just as carefully, planting his feet firmly on the ground, the tiny metallic world in his glasses slowing down like gelatine hardening and in the midst of it Connie's bright green blouse. "This here is my name, to begin with," he said. ARNOLD FRIEND was written in tarlike black letters on the side, with a drawing of a round grinning face that reminded Connie of a pumpkin, except it wore sunglasses. "I wanta introduce myself, I'm Arnold Friend and that's my real name and I'm gonna be your friend, honey, and inside the car's Ellie Oscar, he's kinda shy." Ellie brought his transistor radio up to his shoulder and balanced it there. "Now these numbers are a secret code, honey," Arnold Friend explained. He read off the numbers 33, 19, 17 and raised his eyebrows at her to see what she thought of that, but she didn't think much of it. The left rear fender had been smashed and around it was written, on the gleaming gold background—DONE BY CRAZY WOMAN DRIVER. Connie had to laugh at that. Arnold Friend was pleased at her laughter and looked up at her. "Around the other side's a lot more—you wanta come and see them?"

"No."

"Why not?"

"Why should I?"

"Don'tcha wanta see what's on the car? Don'tcha wanta go for a ride?"

"I don't know."

"Why not?"

"I got things to do."

"Like what?"

"Things."

He laughed as if she had said something funny. He slapped his thighs. He was standing in a strange way, leaning back against the car as if he were balancing himself. He wasn't tall, only an inch or so taller than she would be if she came down to him. Connie liked the way he was dressed, which was the way all of them dressed: tight faded jeans stuffed into black, scuffed boots, a belt that pulled his waist in and showed how lean he was, and a white pullover shirt that was a little soiled and showed the hard small muscles of his arms and shoulders. He looked as if he probably did hard work, lifting and carrying things. Even his neck looked muscular. And his face was a familiar face, somehow—the jaw and chin and cheeks slightly darkened, because he hadn't shaved for a day or two, and the nose long and hawklike, sniffing as if she were a treat he was going to gobble up and it was all a joke.

"Connie, you ain't telling the truth. This is your day set aside for a ride with me and you know it," he said, still laughing. The way he straightened and recovered from his fit of laughing showed that it had been all fake.

"How do you know what my name is?" she said suspiciously.

"It's Connie."

"Maybe and maybe not."

"I know my Connie," he said, wagging his finger. Now she remembered him even better, back at the restaurant, and her cheeks warmed at the thought of how she sucked in her breath just at the moment she passed him—how she must have looked to him. And he had remembered her. "Ellie and I come out here especially for you," he said. "Ellie can sit in back. How about it?"

"Where?"

"Where what?"

"Where're we going?"

He looked at her. He took off the sunglasses and she saw how pale the skin around his eyes was, like holes that were not in shadow but instead in light. His eyes were like chips of broken glass that catch the light in an amiable way. He smiled. It was as if the idea of going for a ride somewhere, to some place, was a new idea to him.

"Just for a ride, Connie sweetheart."

"I never said my name was Connie," she said.

"But I know what it is. I know your name and all about you, lots of things," Arnold Friend said. He had not moved yet but stood still leaning back against the side of his jalopy. "I took a special interest in you, such a pretty girl, and found out all about you like I know your parents and sister are gone somewheres and I know where and how long they're going to be gone, and I know who you were with last night, and your best girlfriend's name is Betty. Right?"

He spoke in a simple lilting voice, exactly as if he were reciting the words to a song. His smile assured her that everything was fine. In the car Ellie turned up the volume on his radio and did not bother to look around at them.

"Ellie can sit in the back seat," Arnold Friend said. He indicated his friend with a casual jerk of his chin, as if Ellie did not count and she should not bother with him.

"How'd you find out all that stuff?" Connie said.

"Listen: Betty Schultz and Tony Fitch and Jimmy Pettinger and Nancy Pettinger," he said, in a chant. "Raymond Stanley and Bob Hutter—"

"Do you know all those kids?"

"I know everybody."

"Look, you're kidding. You're not from around here."

"Sure."

"But—how come we never saw you before?"

"Sure you saw me before," he said. He looked down at his boots, as if he were a little offended. "You just don't remember."

"I guess I'd remember you," Connie said.

"Yeah?" He looked up at this, beaming. He was pleased. He began to mark time with the music from Ellie's radio, tapping his fists lightly together. Connie looked away from his smile to the car, which was painted so bright it almost hurt her eyes to look at it. She looked at that nane, ARNOLD FRIEND. And up at the front fender was an expression that was familiar—MAN THE FLYING SAUCERS. It was an expression kids had used the year before, but didn't use this year. She looked at it for a while as if the words meant something to her that she did not yet know.

"What're you thinking about? Huh?" Arnold Friend demanded. "Not worried about your hair blowing around in the car, are you?"

"No."

"Think I maybe can't drive good?"

"How do I know?"

"You're a hard girl to handle. How come?" he said. "Don't you know I'm your friend? Didn't you see me put my sign in the air when you walked by?"

"What sign?"

"My sign." And he drew an X in the air, leaning out toward her. They were maybe ten feet apart. After his hand fell back to his side the X was still in the air, almost visible. Connie let the screen door close and stood perfectly still inside it, listening to the music from her radio and the boy's blend together. She stared at Arnold Friend. He stood there so stiffly relaxed, pretending to be relaxed, with one hand idly on the door handle as if he were keeping himself up that way and had no intention of ever moving again. She recognized most things about him, the tight jeans that showed his thighs and buttocks and the greasy leather boots and the tight shirt, and even that slippery friendly smile of his, that sleepy dreamy smile that all the boys used to get across ideas they didn't want to put into words. She recognized all this and also the singsong way he talked, slightly mocking, kidding, but serious and a little melancholy, and she recognized the way he tapped one fist against the other in homage to the perpetual music behind him. But all these things did not come together.

She said suddenly, "Hey, how old are you?"

His smile faded. She could see then that he wasn't a kid, he was much older—thirty, maybe more. At this knowledge her heart began to pound faster.

"That's a crazy thing to ask. Can'tcha see I'm your own age?"

"Like hell you are."

"Or maybe a coupla years older, I'm eighteen."

"Eighteen?" she said doubtfully.

He grinned to reassure her and lines appeared at the corners of his mouth. His teeth were big and white. He grinned so broadly his eyes became slits and she saw how thick the lashes were, thick and black as if painted with a black tarlike material. Then he seemed to become embarrassed, abruptly, and looked over his shoulder at Ellie. "*Him*, he's crazy," he said. "Ain't he a riot, he's a nut, a real character." Ellie was still listening to the music. His sunglasses told nothing about what he was thinking. He wore a bright orange shirt unbuttoned halfway to show his chest, which was a pale, bluish chest and not muscular like Arnold Friend's. His shirt collar was turned up all around and the very tips of the collar pointed out past his chin as if they were protecting him. He was pressing the transistor radio up against his ear and sat there in a kind of daze, right in the sun.

"He's kinda strange," Connie said.

"Hey, she says you're kinda strange! Kinda strange!" Arnold Friend cried. He pounded on the car to get Ellie's attention. Ellie turned for the first time and Connie saw with shock that he wasn't a kid either—he had a fair, hairless face, cheeks reddened slightly as if the veins grew too close to the surface of his skin, the face of a forty-year-old baby. Connie felt a wave of dizziness rise in her at this sight and she stared at him as if waiting for something to change the shock of the moment, make it all right again. Ellie's lips kept shaping words, mumbling along, with the words blasting in his ear.

"Maybe you two better go away," Connie said faintly.

"What? How come?" Arnold Friend cried. "We come out here to take you for a ride. It's Sunday." He had the voice of the man on the radio now. It was the same voice, Connie thought. "Don'tcha know it's Sunday all day and honey, no matter who you were with last night today you're with Arnold Friend and don't you forget it!—Maybe you better step out here," he said, and this last was in a different voice. It was a little flatter, as if the heat was finally getting to him.

"No. I got things to do."

"Hey."

"You two better leave."

"We ain't leaving until you come with us."

"Like hell I am—"

"Connie, don't fool around with me. I mean, I mean, don't fool *around*," he said, shaking his head. He laughed incredulously. He placed his sunglasses on top of his head, carefully, as if he were indeed wearing a wig, and brought the stems down behind his ears. Connie stared at him, another wave of dizziness and fear rising in her so that for a moment he wasn't even in focus but was just a blur, standing there against his gold car, and she had the idea that he had driven up the driveway all right but had come from nowhere before that and belonged nowhere and that everything about him and even about the music that was so familiar to her was only half real.

"If my father comes and sees you—"

"He ain't coming. He's at the barbecue."

"How do you know that?"

"Aunt Tillie's. Right now they're—uh—they're drinking. Sitting around," he said vaguely, squinting as if he were staring all the way to town and over to Aunt Tillie's back yard. Then the vision seemed to get clear and he nodded energetically. "Yeah. Sitting around. There's your sister in a blue dress, huh? And high heels, the poor sad bitch—nothing like you, sweetheart! And your mother's helping some fat woman with the corn, they're cleaning the corn—husking the corn—"

"What fat woman?" Connie cried.

"How do I know what fat woman. I don't know every goddam fat woman in the world!" Arnold Friend laughed.

"Oh, that's Mrs. Hornby ... Who invited her?" Connie said. She felt a little light-headed. Her breath was coming quickly.

"She's too fat. I don't like them fat. I like them the way you are, honey," he said, smiling sleepily at her. They stared at each other for a while, through the screen door. He said softly, "Now what you're going to do is this: you're going to come out that door. You're going to sit up front with me and Ellie's going to sit in the back, the hell with Ellie, right? This isn't Ellie's date. You're my date. I'm your lover, honey."

"What? You're crazy—"

"Yes, I'm your lover. You don't know what that is but you will," he said. "I know that too. I know all about you. But look: it's real nice and you couldn't ask for nobody better than me, or more polite. I always keep my word. I'll tell you how it is, I'm always nice at first, the first time. I'll hold you so tight you won't think you have to try to get away or pretend anything because you'll know you can't. And I'll come inside you where it's all secret and you'll give in to me and you'll love me—"

"Shut up! You're crazy!" Connie said. She backed away from the door. She put her hands against her ears as if she'd heard something terrible, something not meant for her. "People don't talk like that, you're crazy," she muttered. Her heart was almost too big now for her chest and its pumping made sweat break out all over her. She looked out to see Arnold Friend pause and then take a step toward the porch lurching. He almost fell. But, like a clever drunken man, he managed to catch his balance. He wobbled in his high boots and grabbed hold of one of the porch posts.

"Honey?" he said. "You still listening?"

"Get the hell out of here!"

"Be nice, honey. Listen."

"I'm going to call the police—"

He wobbled again and out of the side of his mouth came a fast spat curse, an aside not meant for her to hear. But even this "Christ!" sounded forced. Then he began to smile again. She watched this smile come, awkward as if he were smiling from inside a mask. His whole face was a mask, she thought wildly, tanned down onto his throat but then running out as if he had plastered makeup on his face but had forgotten about his throat.

"Honey—? Listen, here's how it is. I always tell the truth and I promise you this: I ain't coming in that house after you."

"You better not! I'm going to call the police if you—if you don't—"

"Honey," he said, talking right through her voice, "honey, I'm not coming in there but you are coming out here. You know why?"

She was panting. The kitchen looked like a place she had never seen before, some room she had run inside but which wasn't good enough, wasn't going to help her. The kitchen window had never had a curtain, after three years, and there were dishes in the sink for her to do—probably—and if you ran your hand across the table you'd probably feel something sticky there.

"You listening, honey? Hey?"

"—going to call the police—"

"Soon as you touch the phone I don't need to keep my promise and can come inside. You won't want that."

She rushed forward and tried to lock the door. Her fingers were shaking. "But why lock it," Arnold Friend said gently, talking right into her face. "It's just a screen door. It's just nothing." One of his boots was at a strange angle, as if his foot wasn't in it. It pointed out to the left, bent at the ankle. "I mean, anybody can break through a screen door and glass and wood and iron or anything else if he needs to, anybody at all and specially Arnold Friend. If the place got lit up with a fire honey you'd come runnin' out into my arms, right into my arms an' safe at home—like you knew I was your lover and'd stopped fooling around. I don't mind a nice shy girl but I don't like no fooling around." Part of those words were spoken with a slight rhythmic lilt, and Connie somehow recognized them—the echo of a song from last year, about a girl rushing into her boyfriend's arms and coming home again—

Connie stood barefoot on the linoleum floor, staring at him. "What do you want?" she whispered.

"I want you," he said.

"What?"

"Seen you that night and thought, that's the one, yes sir. I never needed to look any more."

"But my father's coming back. He's coming to get me. I had to wash my hair first—" She spoke in a dry, rapid voice, hardly raising it for him to hear.

"No, your Daddy is not coming and yes, you had to wash your hair and you washed it for me. It's nice and shining and all for me, I thank you, sweetheart," he said, with a mock bow, but again he almost lost his balance. He had to bend and adjust his boots. Evidently his feet did not go all the way down; the boots must have been stuffed with something so that he would seem taller. Connie stared out at him and behind him Ellie in the car, who seemed to be looking off toward Connie's right, into nothing. This Ellie said, pulling the words out of the air one after another as if he were just discovering them, "You want me to pull out the phone?"

"Shut your mouth and keep it shut," Arnold Friend said, his face red from bending over or maybe from embarrassment because Connie had seen his boots. "This ain't none of your business."

"What—what are you doing? What do you want?" Connie said. "If I call the police they'll get you, they'll arrest you—"

"Promise was not to come in unless you touch that phone, and I'll keep that promise," he said. He resumed his erect position and tried to force his shoulders back. He sounded like a hero in a movie, declaring something important. He spoke too loudly and it was as if he were speaking to someone behind Connie. "I ain't made plans for coming in that house where I don't belong but just for you to come out to me, the way you should. Don't you know who I am?"

"You're crazy," she whispered. She backed away from the door but did not want to go into another part of the house, as if this would give him permission to come through the door. "What do you ... You're crazy, you ..."

"Huh? What're you saying, honey?"

Her eyes darted everywhere in the kitchen. She could not remember what it was, this room.

"This is how it is, honey: you come out and we'll drive away, have a nice ride. But if you don't come out we're gonna wait till your people come home and then they're all going to get it."

"You want that telephone pulled out?" Ellie said. He held the radio away from his ear and grimaced, as if without the radio the air was too much for him.

"I toldja shut up, Ellie," Arnold Friend said, "you're deaf, get a hearing aid, right? Fix yourself up. This little girl's no trouble and's gonna be nice to me, so Ellie keep to yourself, this ain't your date—right? Don't hem in on me. Don't hog. Don't crush. Don't bird dog. Don't trail me," he said in a rapid meaningless voice, as if he were running through all the expressions he'd learned but was no longer sure which one of them was in style, then rushing on to new ones, making them up with his eyes closed, "Don't crawl under my fence, don't squeeze in my chipmunk hole, don't sniff my glue, suck my popsicle, keep your own greasy fingers on yourself!" He shaded his eyes and peered in at Connie, who was backed against the kitchen table. "Don't mind him honey he's just a creep. He's a dope. Right? I'm the boy for you and like I said you come out here nice like a lady and give me your hand, and nobody else gets hurt, I mean, your nice old bald-headed daddy and your mummy and your sister in her high heels. Because listen: why bring them in this?"

"Leave me alone," Connie whispered.

"Hey, you know that old woman down the road, the one with the chickens and stuff—you know her?"

"She's dead!"

"Dead? What? You know her?" Arnold Friend said.

"She's dead—"

"Don't you like her?"

"She's dead—she's—she isn't here any more—"

"But don't you like her, I mean, you got something against her? Some grudge or something?" Then his voice dipped as if he were conscious of a rudeness. He touched the sunglasses perched on top of his head as if to make sure they were still there. "Now you be a good girl."

"What are you going to do?"

"Just two things, or maybe three," Arnold Friend said. "But I promise it won't last long and you'll like me the way you get to like people you're close to. You will. It's all over for you here, so come on out. You don't want your people in any trouble, do you?"

She turned and bumped against a chair or something, hurting her leg, but she ran into the back room and picked up the telephone. Something roared in her ear, a tiny roaring, and she was so sick with fear that she could do nothing but listen to it—the telephone was clammy and very heavy and her fingers groped down to the dial but were too weak to touch it. She began to scream into the phone, into the roaring. She cried out, she cried for her mother, she felt her breath start jerking back and forth in her lungs as if it were something Arnold Friend were stabbing her with again and again with no tenderness. A noisy sorrowful wailing rose all about her and she was locked inside it the way she was locked inside the house.

After a while she could hear again. She was sitting on the floor with her wet back against the wall.

Arnold Friend was saying from the door, "That's a good girl. Put the phone back."

She kicked the phone away from her.

"No, honey. Pick it up. Put it back right."

She picked it up and put it back. The dial tone stopped.

"That's a good girl. Now, you come outside."

She was hollow with what had been fear, but what was now just an emptiness. All that screaming had blasted it out of her. She sat, one leg cramped under her, and deep inside her brain was something like a pinpoint of light that kept going and would not let her relax. She thought, I'm not going to see my mother again. She thought, I'm not going to sleep in my bed again. Her bright green blouse was all wet.

Arnold Friend said, in a gentle-loud voice that was like a stage voice, "The place where you came from ain't there any more, and where you had in mind to go is canceled out. This place you are now—inside your daddy's house—is nothing but a cardboard box I can knock down any time. You know that and always did know it. You hear me?"

She thought, I have got to think. I have to know what to do.

"We'll go out to a nice field, out in the country here where it smells so nice and it's sunny," Arnold Friend said. "I'll have my arms tight around you so you won't need to try to get away and I'll show you what love is like, what it does. The hell with this house! It looks solid all right," he said. He ran a fingernail down the screen and the noise did not make Connie shiver, as it would have the day before. "Now put your hand on your heart, honey. Feel that? That feels solid too but we know better, be nice to me, be sweet like you can because what else is there for a girl like you but to be sweet and pretty and give in?—and get away before her people come back?"

She felt her pounding heart. Her hand seemed to enclose it. She thought for the first time in her life that it was nothing that was hers, that belonged to her, but just a pounding, living thing inside this body that wasn't really hers either.

"You don't want them to get hurt," Arnold Friend went on. "Now get up, honey. Get up all by yourself."

She stood.

"Now turn this way. That's right. Come over here to me—Ellie, put that away, didn't I tell you? You dope. You miserable creepy dope," Arnold Friend said. His words were not angry but only part of an incantation. The incantation was kindly. "Now come out through the kitchen to me honey, and let's see a smile, try it, you're a brave sweet little girl and now they're eating corn and hot dogs cooked to bursting over an outdoor fire, and they don't know one thing about you and never did and honey you're better than them because not a one of them would have done this for you."

Connie felt the linoleum under her feet; it was cool. She brushed her hair back out of her eyes. Arnold Friend let go of the post tentatively and opened his arms for her, his elbows pointing in toward each other and his wrists limp, to show that this was an embarrassed embrace and a little mocking, he didn't want to make her self-conscious.

She put out her hand against the screen. She watched herself push the door slowly open as if she were safe back somewhere in the other doorway, watching this body and this head of long hair moving out into the sunlight where Arnold Friend waited.

"My sweet little blue-eyed girl," he said, in a half-sung sigh that had nothing to do with her brown eyes but was taken up just the same by the vast sunlit reaches of the land behind him and on all sides of him, so much land that Connie had never seen before and did not recognize except to know that she was going to it.

—1966

---

### MARGARET ATWOOD ▦ (b. 1939)

*Margaret Atwood is a leading figure among Canadian writers, and she is equally skilled as a poet and fiction writer. She is also an internationally known feminist spokesperson in great demand for appearances at symposia on women's issues, and she was named by Ms. magazine as Woman of the Year for 1986. Born in Ottawa, Ontario, she graduated from University of Toronto in 1962, the same year that her first book appeared, and she later did graduate work at Radcliffe and Harvard. She has published two volumes of selected poems, more than a dozen novels and collections of short stories, and a book of literary criticism. In addition, she served as editor of two anthologies of Canadian literature and wrote* Survival: A Thematic Guide to Canadian Literature *(1972), influential work that challenged Canadian writers to explore their own unique cultural heritage. Atwood has served as writer-in-residence at universities in Canada, the United States, and abroad.* The Handmaid's Tale *(1985), a work that presents a future dystopia controlled by a fundamentalist patriarchy, was a best-seller and was filmed in 1990. The ironically titled "Happy Endings" demonstrates Atwood's occasional experimentalism as well as her continuing critiques of male–female relationships.*

# Happy Endings

*John and Mary meet.*
*What happens next?*
*If you want a happy ending, try A.*

## A

John and Mary fall in love and get married. They both have worthwhile and remunerative jobs which they find stimulating and challenging. They buy a charming house. Real estate values go up. Eventually, when they can afford live-in help, they have two children, to whom they are devoted. The children turn out well. John and Mary have a stimulating and challenging sex life and worthwhile friends. They go on fun vacations together. They retire. They both have hobbies which they find stimulating and challenging. Eventually they die. This is the end of the story.

## B

Mary falls in love with John but John doesn't fall in love with Mary. He merely uses her body for selfish pleasure and ego gratification of a tepid kind. He comes to her apartment twice a week and she cooks him dinner, you'll notice that he doesn't even consider her worth the price of a dinner out, and after he's eaten the dinner he fucks her and after that he falls asleep, while she does the dishes so he won't think she's untidy, having all those dirty dishes lying around, and puts on fresh lipstick so she'll look good when he wakes up, but when he wakes up he doesn't even notice, he puts on his socks and his shorts and his pants and his shirt and his tie and his shoes, the reverse order from the one in which he took them off. He doesn't take off Mary's clothes, she takes them off herself, she acts as if she's dying for it every time, not because she likes sex exactly, she doesn't, but she wants John to think she does because if they do it often enough surely he'll get used to her, he'll come to depend on her and they will get married, but John goes out the door with hardly so much as a good-night and three days later he turns up at six o'clock and they do the whole thing over again.

Mary gets run-down. Crying is bad for your face, everyone knows that and so does Mary but she can't stop. People at work notice. Her friends tell her John is a rat, a pig, a dog, he isn't good enough for her, but she can't believe it. Inside John, she thinks, is another John, who is much nicer. This other John will emerge like a butterfly from a cocoon, a Jack from a box, a pit from a prune, if the first John is only squeezed enough.

One evening John complains about the food. He has never complained about the food before. Mary is hurt.

Her friends tell her they've seen him in a restaurant with another woman, whose name is Madge. It's not even Madge that finally gets to Mary: it's the restaurant. John has never taken Mary to a restaurant. Mary collects all the sleeping pills and aspirins she can find, and takes them and a half a bottle of sherry. You can see what kind of a woman she is by the fact that it's not even whiskey. She leaves a note for John. She hopes he'll discover her and get her to the hospital in time and repent and then they can get married, but this fails to happen and she dies.

John marries Madge and everything continues as in A.

## C

John, who is an older man, falls in love with Mary, and Mary, who is only twenty-two, feels sorry for him because he's worried about his hair falling out. She sleeps with him even though she's not in love with him. She met him at work. She's in love with someone called James, who is twenty-two also and not yet ready to settle down.

John on the contrary settled down long ago: this is what is bothering him. John has a steady, respectable job and is getting ahead in his field, but Mary isn't impressed by him, she's impressed by James, who has a motorcycle and a fabulous record collection. But James is often away on his motorcycle, being free. Freedom isn't the same for girls, so in the meantime Mary spends Thursday evenings with John. Thursdays are the only days John can get away.

John is married to a woman called Madge and they have two children, a charming house which they bought just before the real estate values went up, and hobbies which they find stimulating and challenging, when they have the time. John tells Mary how important she is to him, but of course he can't leave his wife because a commitment is a commitment. He goes on about this more than is necessary and Mary finds it boring, but older men can keep it up longer so on the whole she has a fairly good time.

One day James breezes in on his motorcycle with some top-grade California hybrid and James and Mary get higher than you'd believe possible and they climb into bed. Everything becomes very underwater, but along comes John, who has a key to Mary's apartment. He finds them stoned and entwined. He's hardly in any position to be jealous, considering Madge, but nevertheless he's overcome with despair. Finally he's middle-aged, in two years he'll be bald as an egg and he can't stand it. He purchases a handgun, saying he needs it for target practice—this is the thin part of the plot, but it can be dealt with later—and shoots the two of them and himself.

Madge, after a suitable period of mourning, marries an understanding man called Fred and everything continues as in A, but under different names.

## D

Fred and Madge have no problems. They get along exceptionally well and are good at working out any little difficulties that may arise. But their charming house is by the seashore and one day a giant tidal wave approaches. Real estate values go down. The rest of the story is about what caused the tidal wave and how they escape from it. They do, though thousands drown, but Fred and Madge are virtuous and lucky. Finally on high ground they clasp each other, wet and dripping and grateful, and continue as in A.

## E

Yes, but Fred has a bad heart. The rest of the story is about how kind and understanding they both are until Fred dies. Then Madge devotes herself to charity work until the end of A. If you like, it can be "Madge," "cancer," "guilty and confused," and "bird watching."

F

If you think this is all too bourgeois, make John a revolutionary and Mary a counterespionage agent and see how far that gets you. Remember, this is Canada. You'll still end up with A, though in between you may get a lustful brawling saga of passionate involvement, a chronicle of our times, sort of.

You'll have to face it, the endings are the same however you slice it. Don't be deluded by any other endings, they're all fake, either deliberately fake, with malicious intent to deceive, or just motivated by excessive optimism if not by downright sentimentality.

The only authentic ending is the one provided here:

*John and Mary die. John and Mary die. John and Mary die.*

So much for endings. Beginnings are always more fun. True connoisseurs, however, are known to favor the stretch in between, since it's the hardest to do anything with.

That's about all that can be said for plots, which anyway are just one thing after another, a what and a what and a what.

Now try How and Why.

—1983

---

### BOBBIE ANN MASON ▦ (b. 1940)

*Bobbie Ann Mason was born in Mayfield, Kentucky, and grew up on a dairy farm run by her parents. The rural background of her youth figures in many of her best stories, and one of Mason's favorite subjects is the assimilation of the countryside and the South into a larger American culture. Mason's characters may dream of living in log cabins, but they also take adult education courses, watch TV talk shows, and shop in supermarkets and malls. After taking degrees from the University of Kentucky and the University of Connecticut, Mason published her first two books, both works of literary criticism, in the mid-1970s. One of them,* The Girl Sleuth, *was a feminist guide to the exploits of fictional detectives like Nancy Drew that Mason read as a child. After years of attempts, Mason's stories began to appear in prestigious magazines, most prominently* The New Yorker, *and the publication of* Shiloh and Other Stories *(1982) established her as an important new voice in American fiction. She has since published a second collection of short stories and four novels, one of which,* In Country *(1985), was filmed in 1989. "Shiloh," like several of the stories in the collection from which it is taken, gains considerable immediacy from Mason's use of present tense and her sure sense of regional speech patterns. In more recent years, Mason has published a story collection,* Zigzagging Down a Wild Trail *(2001), a biography,*

*Elvis Presley (2003), and a short story collection,* Nancy Culpepper *(2006).* The Girl in the Blue Beret *(2011) is set during the German occupation of France in World War II.*

# Shiloh

Leroy Moffitt's wife, Norma Jean, is working on her pectorals. She lifts three-pound dumbbells to warm up, then progresses to a twenty-pound barbell. Standing with her legs apart, she reminds Leroy of Wonder Woman.

"I'd give anything if I could just get these muscles to where they're real hard," says Norma Jean. "Feel this arm. It's not as hard as the other one."

"That's 'cause you're right-handed," says Leroy, dodging as she swings the barbell in an arc.

"Do you think so?"

"Sure."

Leroy is a truckdriver. He injured his leg in a highway accident four months ago, and his physical therapy, which involves weights and a pulley, prompted Norma Jean to try building herself up. Now she is attending a body-building class. Leroy has been collecting temporary disability since his tractor-trailer jackknifed in Missouri, badly twisting his left leg in its socket. He has a steel pin in his hip. He will probably not be able to drive his rig again. It sits in the backyard, like a gigantic bird that has flown home to roost. Leroy has been home in Kentucky for three months, and his leg is almost healed, but the accident frightened him and he does not want to drive any more long hauls. He is not sure what to do next. In the meantime, he makes things from craft kits. He started by building a miniature log cabin from notched Popsicle sticks. He varnished it and placed it on the TV set, where it remains. It reminds him of a rustic Nativity scene. Then he tried string art (sailing ships on black velvet), a macramé owl kit, a snap-together B-17 Flying Fortress, and a lamp made out of a model truck, with a light fixture screwed in the top of the cab. At first the kits were diversions, something to kill time, but now he is thinking about building a full-scale log house from a kit. It would be considerably cheaper than building a regular house, and besides, Leroy has grown to appreciate how things are put together. He has begun to realize that in all the years he was on the road he never took time to examine anything. He was always flying past scenery.

"They won't let you build a log cabin in any of the new subdivisions," Norma Jean tells him.

"They will if I tell them it's for you," he says, teasing her. Ever since they were married, he has promised Norma Jean he would build her a new home one day. They have always rented, and the house they live in is small and nondescript. It does not even feel like a home, Leroy realizes now.

Norma Jean works at the Rexall drugstore, and she has acquired an amazing amount of information about cosmetics. When she explains to Leroy the three stages of complexion care, involving creams, toners, and moisturizers, he thinks happily of other petroleum products—axle grease, diesel fuel. This is a connection between him and Norma Jean. Since he has been home, he has felt unusually tender about his wife and guilty over his long absences. But he can't tell what she feels about him. Norma Jean has never complained about his traveling; she has never made hurt remarks, like calling his truck a "widow-maker." He is reasonably certain she has been faithful to him, but he wishes she would celebrate his permanent home-coming more happily. Norma Jean is often startled to find Leroy at home, and he thinks she seems a little disappointed about it. Perhaps he reminds her too much of the early days of their marriage, before he went on the road. They had a child who died as an infant, years ago. They never speak about their memories of Randy, which have almost faded, but now that Leroy is home all the time, they sometimes feel awkward around each other, and Leroy wonders if one of them should mention the child. He has the feeling that they are waking up out of a dream together—that they must create a new marriage, start afresh. They are lucky they are still married. Leroy has read that for most people losing a child destroys the marriage—or else he heard this on *Donahue*. He can't always remember where he learns things anymore.

At Christmas, Leroy bought an electric organ for Norma Jean. She used to play the piano when she was in high school. "It don't leave you," she told him once. "It's like riding a bicycle."

The new instrument had so many keys and buttons that she was bewildered by it at first. She touched the keys tentatively, pushed some buttons, then pecked out "Chopsticks." It came out in an amplified fox-trot rhythm, with marimba sounds.

"It's an orchestra!" she cried.

The organ had a pecan-look finish and eighteen preset chords, with optional flute, violin, trumpet, clarinet, and banjo accompaniments. Norma Jean mastered the organ almost immediately. At first she played Christmas songs. Then she bought *The Sixties Songbook* and learned every tune in it, adding variations to each with the rows of brightly colored buttons.

"I didn't like these old songs back then," she said. "But I have this crazy feeling I missed something."

"You didn't miss a thing," said Leroy.

Leroy likes to lie on the couch and smoke a joint and listen to Norma Jean play "Can't Take My Eyes Off You" and "I'll Be Back." He is back again. After fifteen years on the road, he is finally settling down with the woman he loves. She is still pretty. Her skin is flawless. Her frosted curls resemble pencil trimmings.

Now that Leroy has come home to stay, he notices how much the town has changed. Subdivisions are spreading across western Kentucky like an oil slick. The sign at the edge of town says "Pop: 11,500"—only seven hundred more than it said twenty years before. Leroy can't figure out who is living in all the new houses. The farmers who used to gather around the courthouse square on Saturday afternoons to play checkers and spit tobacco juice have gone. It has been years since Leroy has thought about the farmers, and they have disappeared without his noticing.

Leroy meets a kid named Stevie Hamilton in the parking lot at the new shopping center. While they pretend to be strangers meeting over a stalled car, Stevie tosses an ounce of marijuana under the front seat of Leroy's car. Stevie is wearing orange jogging shoes and a T-shirt that says CHATTAHOOCHEE SUPER-RAT. His father is a prominent doctor who lives in one of the expensive subdivisions in a new white-columned brick house that looks like a funeral parlor. In the phone book under his name there is a separate number, with the listing "Teenagers."

"Where do you get this stuff?" asks Leroy. "From your pappy?"

"That's for me to know and you to find out," Stevie says. He is slit-eyed and skinny.

"What else you got?"

"What you interested in?"

"Nothing special. Just wondered."

Leroy used to take speed on the road. Now he has to go slowly. He needs to be mellow. He leans back against the car and says, "I'm aiming to build me a log house, soon as I get time. My wife, though, I don't think she likes the idea."

"Well, let me know when you want me again," Stevie says. He has a cigarette in his cupped palm, as though sheltering it from the wind. He takes a long drag, then stomps it on the asphalt and slouches away.

Stevie's father was two years ahead of Leroy in high school. Leroy is thirty-four. He married Norma Jean when they were both eighteen, and their child Randy was born a few months later, but he died at the age of four months and three days. He would be about Stevie's age now. Norma Jean and Leroy were at the drive-in, watching a double feature (*Dr. Strangelove* and *Lover Come Back*), and the baby was sleeping in the back seat. When the first movie ended, the baby was dead. It was the sudden infant death syndrome. Leroy remembers handing Randy to a nurse at the emergency room, as though he were offering her a large doll as a present. A dead baby feels like a sack of flour. "It just happens sometimes," said the doctor, in what Leroy always recalls as a nonchalant tone. Leroy can hardly remember the child anymore, but he still sees vividly a scene from *Dr. Strangelove* in which the President of the United States was talking in a folksy voice on the hot line to the Soviet premier about the bomber accidentally headed toward Russia. He was in the War Room, and the world map was lit up. Leroy remembers Norma Jean standing catatonically beside him in the hospital and himself thinking: Who is this strange girl? He had forgotten who she was. Now scientists are saying that crib death is caused by a virus. Nobody knows anything, Leroy thinks. The answers are always changing.

When Leroy gets home from the shopping center, Norma Jean's mother, Mabel Beasley, is there. Until this year, Leroy has not realized how much time she spends with Norma Jean. When she visits, she inspects the closets and then the plants, informing Norma Jean when a plant is droopy or yellow. Mabel calls the plants "flowers," although there are never any blooms. She also notices if Norma Jean's laundry is piling up. Mabel is a short, overweight woman whose tight, brown-dyed curls look more like a wig than the actual wig she sometimes wears. Today she has brought Norma Jean an off-white dust ruffle she made for the bed; Mabel works in a custom-upholstery shop.

"This is the tenth one I made this year," Mabel says. "I got started and couldn't stop."

"It's real pretty," says Norma Jean.

"Now we can hide things under the bed," says Leroy, who gets along with his mother-in-law primarily by joking with her. Mabel has never really forgiven him for disgracing her by getting Norma Jean pregnant. When the baby died, she said that fate was mocking her.

"What's that thing?" Mabel says to Leroy in a loud voice, pointing to a tangle of yarn on a piece of canvas.

Leroy holds it up for Mabel to see. "It's my needlepoint," he explains. "This is a *Star Trek* pillow cover."

"That's what a woman would do," says Mabel. "Great day in the morning!"

"All the big football players on TV do it," he says.

"Why, Leroy, you're always trying to fool me. I don't believe you for one minute. You don't know what to do with yourself—that's the whole trouble. Sewing!"

"I'm aiming to build us a log house," says Leroy. "Soon as my plans come."

"Like *heck* you are," says Norma Jean. She takes Leroy's needlepoint and shoves it into a drawer. "You have to find a job first. Nobody can afford to build now anyway."

Mabel straightens her girdle and says, "I still think before you get tied down y'all ought to take a little run to Shiloh."

"One of these days, Mama," Norma Jean says impatiently.

Mabel is talking about Shiloh, Tennessee. For the past few years, she has been urging Leroy and Norma Jean to visit the Civil War battleground there. Mabel went there on her honeymoon—the only real trip she ever took. Her husband died of a perforated ulcer when Norma Jean was ten, but Mabel, who was accepted into the United Daughters of the Confederacy in 1975, is still preoccupied with going back to Shiloh.

"I've been to kingdom come and back in that truck out yonder," Leroy says to Mabel, "but we never yet set foot in that battleground. Ain't that something? How did I miss it?"

"It's not even that far," Mabel says.

After Mabel leaves, Norma Jean reads to Leroy from a list she has made. "Things you could do," she announces. "You could get a job as a guard at Union Carbide, where they'd let you set on a stool. You could get on at the lumberyard. You could do a little carpenter work, if you want to build so bad. You could—"

"I can't do something where I'd have to stand up all day."

"You ought to try standing up all day behind a cosmetics counter. It's amazing that I have strong feet, coming from two parents that never had strong feet at all." At the moment Norma Jean is holding on to the kitchen counter, raising her knees one at a time as she talks. She is wearing two-pound ankle weights.

"Don't worry," says Leroy. "I'll do something."

"You could truck calves to slaughter for somebody. You wouldn't have to drive any big old truck for that."

"I'm going to build you this house," says Leroy. "I want to make you a real home."

"I don't want to live in any log cabin."

"It's not a cabin. It's a house."

"I don't care. It looks like a cabin."

"You and me together could lift those logs. It's just like lifting weights."

Norma Jean doesn't answer. Under her breath, she is counting. Now she is marching through the kitchen. She is doing goose steps.

Before his accident, when Leroy came home he used to stay in the house with Norma Jean, watching TV in bed and playing cards. She would cook fried chicken, picnic ham, chocolate pie—all his favorites. Now he is home alone much of the time. In the mornings, Norma Jean disappears, leaving a cooling place in the bed. She eats a cereal called Body Buddies, and she leaves the bowl on the table, with the soggy tan balls floating in a milk puddle. He sees things about Norma Jean that he never realized before. When she chops onions, she stares off into a corner, as if she can't bear to look. She puts on her house slippers almost precisely at nine o'clock every evening and nudges her jogging shoes under the couch. She saves bread heels for the birds. Leroy watches the birds at the feeder. He notices the peculiar way goldfinches fly past the window. They close their wings, then fall, then spread their wings to catch and lift themselves. He wonders if they close their eyes when they fall. Norma Jean closes her eyes when they are in bed. She wants the lights turned out. Even then, he is sure she closes her eyes.

He goes for long drives around town. He tends to drive a car rather carelessly. Power steering and an automatic shift make a car feel so small and inconsequential that his body is hardly involved in the driving process. His injured leg stretches out comfortably. Once or twice he has almost hit something, but even the prospect of an accident seems minor in a car. He cruises the new subdivisions, feeling like a criminal rehearsing for a robbery. Norma Jean is probably right about a log house being inappropriate here in the new subdivision. All the houses look grand and complicated. They depress him.

One day when Leroy comes home from a drive he finds Norma Jean in tears. She is in the kitchen making a potato and mushroom-soup casserole, with grated-cheese topping. She is crying because her mother caught her smoking.

"I didn't hear her coming. I was standing here puffing away pretty as you please," Norma Jean says, wiping her eyes.

"I knew it would happen sooner or later," says Leroy, putting his arm around her.

"She don't know the meaning of the word 'knock,'" says Norma Jean. "It's a wonder she hadn't caught me years ago."

"Think of it this way," Leroy says. "What if she caught me with a joint?"

"You better not let her!" Norma Jean shrieks. "I'm warning you, Leroy Moffitt!"

"I'm just kidding. Here, play me a tune. That'll help you relax."

Norma Jean puts the casserole in the oven and sets the timer. Then she plays a ragtime tune, with horns and banjo, as Leroy lights up a joint and lies on the couch, laughing to himself about Mabel's catching him at it. He thinks of Stevie Hamilton—a doctor's son pushing grass. Everything is funny. The whole town seems crazy and small. He is reminded of Virgil Mathis, a boastful policeman Leroy used to shoot pool with. Virgil recently led a drug bust in a back room at a bowling alley, where he seized ten thousand dollars' worth of marijuana. The newspaper had a picture of him holding up the bags of grass and grinning widely. Right now, Leroy can imagine Virgil breaking down the door and arresting him with a lungful of smoke. Virgil would probably have been alerted to the scene because of all the racket Norma Jean is making. Now she sounds like a hard-rock band. Norma Jean is terrific. When she switches to a Latin-rhythm version of "Sunshine Superman," Leroy hums along. Norma Jean's foot goes up and down, up and down.

"Well, what do you think?" Leroy says, when Norma Jean pauses to search through her music.

"What do I think about what?"

His mind has gone blank. Then he says, "I'll sell my rig and build us a house." That wasn't what he wanted to say. He wanted to know what she thought—what she *really* thought—about them.

"Don't start in on that again," says Norma Jean. She begins playing "Who'll Be the Next in Line?"

Leroy used to tell hitchhikers his whole life story—about his travels, his hometown, the baby. He would end with a question: "Well, what do you think?" It was just a rhetorical question. In time, he had the feeling that he'd been telling the same story over and over to the same hitchhikers. He quit talking to hitchhikers when he realized how his voice sounded— whining and self-pitying, like some teenage-tragedy song. Now Leroy has the sudden impulse to tell Norma Jean about himself, as if he had just met her. They have known each other so long they have forgotten a lot about each other. They could become reacquainted. But when the oven timer goes off and she runs to the kitchen, he forgets why he wants to do this.

The next day, Mabel drops by. It is Saturday and Norma Jean is cleaning. Leroy is studying the plans of his log house, which have finally come in the mail. He has them spread out on the table—big sheets of stiff blue paper, with diagrams and numbers printed in white. While Norma Jean runs the vacuum, Mabel drinks coffee. She sets her coffee cup on a blueprint.

"I'm just waiting for time to pass," she says to Leroy, drumming her fingers on the table.

As soon as Norma Jean switches off the vacuum, Mabel says in a loud voice, "Did you hear about the datsun dog that killed the baby?"

Norma Jean says, "The word is 'dachshund.'"

"They put the dog on trial. It chewed the baby's legs off. The mother was in the next room all the time." She raises her voice. "They thought it was neglect."

Norma Jean is holding her ears. Leroy manages to open the refrigerator and get some Diet Pepsi to offer Mabel. Mabel still has some coffee and she waves away the Pepsi.

"Datsuns are like that," Mabel says. "They're jealous dogs. They'll tear a place to pieces if you don't keep an eye on them."

"You better watch out what you're saying, Mabel," says Leroy.

"Well, facts is facts."

Leroy looks out the window at his rig. It is like a huge piece of furniture gathering dust in the backyard. Pretty soon it will be an antique. He hears the vacuum cleaner. Norma Jean seems to be cleaning the living room rug again.

Later, she says to Leroy, "She just said that about the baby because she caught me smoking. She's trying to pay me back."

"What are you talking about?" Leroy says, nervously shuffling blueprints.

"You know good and well," Norma Jean says. She is sitting in a kitchen chair with her feet up and her arms wrapped around her knees. She looks small and helpless. She says, "The very idea, her bringing up a subject like that! Saying it was neglect."

"She didn't mean that," Leroy says.

"She might not have *thought* she meant it. She always says things like that. You don't know how she goes on."

"But she didn't really mean it. She was just talking."

Leroy opens a king-sized bottle of beer and pours it into two glasses, dividing it carefully. He hands a glass to Norma Jean and she takes it from him mechanically. For a long time, they sit by the kitchen window watching the birds at the feeder.

Something is happening. Norma Jean is going to night school. She has graduated from her six-week body-building course and now she is taking an adult-education course in composition at Paducah Community College. She spends her evenings outlining paragraphs.

"First, you have a topic sentence," she explains to Leroy. "Then you divide it up. Your secondary topic has to be connected to your primary topic."

To Leroy, this sounds intimidating. "I never was any good in English," he says.

"It makes a lot of sense."

"What are you doing this for, anyhow?"

She shrugs. "It's something to do." She stands up and lifts her dumbbells a few times.

"Driving a rig, nobody cared about my English."

"I'm not criticizing your English."

Norma Jean used to say, "If I lose ten minutes' sleep, I just drag all day." Now she stays up late, writing compositions. She got a B on her first paper—a how-to theme on soup-based casseroles. Recently Norma Jean has been cooking unusual foods—tacos, lasagna, Bombay chicken. She doesn't play the organ anymore, though her second paper was called "Why Music Is Important to Me." She sits at the kitchen table, concentrating on her outlines, while Leroy plays with his log house plans, practicing with a set of Lincoln Logs. The thought of getting a truckload of notched, numbered logs scares him, and he wants to be prepared. As he and Norma Jean work together at the kitchen table, Leroy has the hopeful thought that they are sharing something, but he knows he is a fool to think this. Norma Jean is miles away. He knows he is going to lose her. Like Mabel, he is just waiting for time to pass.

One day, Mabel is there before Norma Jean gets home from work, and Leroy finds himself confiding in her. Mabel, he realizes, must know Norma Jean better than he does.

"I don't know what's got into that girl," Mabel says. "She used to go to bed with the chickens. Now you say she's up all hours. Plus her a-smoking. I like to died."

"I want to make her this beautiful home," Leroy says, indicating the Lincoln Logs. "I don't think she even wants it. Maybe she was happier with me gone."

"She don't know what to make of you, coming home like this."

"Is that it?"

Mabel takes the roof off his Lincoln Log cabin. "You couldn't get me in a log cabin," she says. "I was raised in one. It's no picnic, let me tell you."

"They're different now," says Leroy.

"I tell you what," Mabel says, smiling oddly at Leroy.

"What?"

"Take her on down to Shiloh. Y'all need to get out together, stir a little. Her brain's all balled up over them books."

Leroy can see traces of Norma Jean's features in her mother's face. Mabel's worn face has the texture of crinkled cotton, but suddenly she looks pretty. It occurs to Leroy that Mabel has been hinting all along that she wants them to take her with them to Shiloh.

"Let's all go to Shiloh," he says. "You and me and her. Come Sunday."

Mabel throws up her hand in protest. "Oh, no, not me. Young folks want to be by theirselves."

When Norma Jean comes in with groceries, Leroy says excitedly, "Your mama here's been dying to go to Shiloh for thirty-five years. It's about time we went, don't you think?"

"I'm not going to butt in on anybody's second honeymoon," Mabel says.

"Who's going on a honeymoon, for Christ's sake?" Norma Jean says loudly.

"I never raised no daughter of mine to talk that-a-way," Mabel says.

"You ain't seen nothing yet," says Norma Jean. She starts putting away boxes and cans, slamming cabinet doors.

"There's a log cabin at Shiloh," Mabel says. "It was there during the battle. There's bullet holes in it."

"When are you going to *shut up* about Shiloh, Mama?" asks Norma Jean.

"I always thought Shiloh was the prettiest place, so full of history," Mabel goes on. "I just hoped y'all could see it once before I die, so you could tell me about it." Later, she whispers to Leroy, "You do what I said. A little change is what she needs."

"Your name means 'the king,'" Norma Jean says to Leroy that evening. He is trying to get her to go to Shiloh, and she is reading a book about another century.

"Well, I reckon I ought to be right proud."

"I guess so."

"Am I still king around here?"

Norma Jean flexes her biceps and feels them for hardness. "I'm not fooling around with anybody, if that's what you mean," she says.

"Would you tell me if you were?"

"I don't know."

"What does *your* name mean?"

"It was Marilyn Monroe's real name."

"No kidding!"

"Norma comes from the Normans. They were invaders," she says. She closes her book and looks hard at Leroy. "I'll go to Shiloh with you if you'll stop staring at me."

On Sunday, Norma Jean packs a picnic and they go to Shiloh. To Leroy's relief Mabel says she does not want to come with them. Norma Jean drives, and Leroy, sitting beside her, feels like some boring hitchhiker she has picked up. He tries some conversation, but she answers him in monosyllables. At Shiloh, she drives aimlessly through the park, past bluffs and trails and steep ravines. Shiloh is an immense place, and Leroy cannot see it as a battleground. It is not what he expected. He thought it would look like a golf course. Monuments are everywhere, showing through the thick clusters of trees. Norma Jean passes the log cabin Mabel mentioned. It is surrounded by tourists looking for bullet holes.

"That's not the kind of log house I've got in mind," says Leroy apologetically.

"I know *that*."

"This is a pretty place. Your mama was right."

"It's O.K.," says Norma Jean. "Well, we've seen it. I hope she's satisfied."

They burst out laughing together.

At the park museum, a movie on Shiloh is shown every half hour, but they decide that they don't want to see it. They buy a souvenir Confederate flag for Mabel, and then they find a picnic spot near the cemetery. Norma Jean has brought a picnic cooler, with pimiento sandwiches, soft drinks, and Yodels. Leroy eats a sandwich and then smokes a joint, hiding it behind the picnic cooler. Norma Jean has quit smoking altogether. She is picking cake crumbs from the cellophane wrapper, like a fussy bird.

Leroy says, "So the boys in gray ended up in Corinth. The Union soldiers zapped 'em finally. April 7, 1862."

They both know that he doesn't know any history. He is just talking about some of the historical plaques they have read. He feels awkward, like a boy on a date with an older girl. They are still just making conversation.

"Corinth is where Mama eloped to," says Norma Jean.

They sit in silence and stare at the cemetery for the Union dead and, beyond, at a tall cluster of trees. Campers are parked nearby, bumper to bumper, and small children in bright clothing are cavorting and squealing. Norma Jean wads up the cake wrapper and squeezes it tightly in her hand. Without looking at Leroy, she says, "I want to leave you."

Leroy takes a bottle of Coke out of the cooler and flips off the cap. He holds the bottle poised near his mouth but cannot remember to take a drink. Finally he says, "No, you don't."

"Yes, I do."

"I won't let you."

"You can't stop me."

"Don't do me that way."

Leroy knows Norma Jean will have her own way. "Didn't I promise to be home from now on?" he says.

"In some ways, a woman prefers a man who wanders," says Norma Jean. "That sounds crazy, I know."

"You're not crazy." Leroy remembers to drink from his Coke. Then he says, "Yes, you *are* crazy. You and me could start all over again. Right back at the beginning."

"We *have* started all over again," says Norma Jean. "And this is how it turned out."

"What did I do wrong?"

"Nothing."

"Is this one of those women's lib things?" Leroy asks.

"Don't be funny."

The cemetery, a green slope dotted with white markers, looks like a subdivision site. Leroy is trying to comprehend that his marriage is breaking up, but for some reason he is wondering about white slabs in a graveyard.

"Everything was fine till Mama caught me smoking," says Norma Jean, standing up. "That set something off."

"What are you talking about?"

"She won't leave me alone—*you* won't leave me alone." Norma Jean seems to be crying, but she is looking away from him. "I feel eighteen again. I can't face that all over again." She starts walking away. "No, it *wasn't* fine. I don't know what I'm saying. Forget it."

Leroy takes a lungful of smoke and closes his eyes as Norma Jean's words sink in. He tries to focus on the fact that thirty-five hundred soldiers died on the grounds around him. He can only think of that war as a board game with plastic soldiers. Leroy almost smiles, as he compares the Confederates' daring attack on the Union camps and Virgil Mathis's raid on the bowling alley. General Grant, drunk and furious, shoved the Southerners back to Corinth, where Mabel and Jet Beasley were married years later, when Mabel was still thin and good-looking. The next day, Mabel and Jet visited the battleground, and then Norma Jean was born, and then she married Leroy and they had a baby, which they lost, and now Leroy and Norma Jean are here at the same battleground. Leroy knows he is leaving out a lot. He is leaving out the insides of history. History was always just names and dates to him. It occurs to him that building a house of logs is similarly empty—too simple. And the real inner workings of a marriage, like most of history, have escaped him. Now he sees that building a log house is the dumbest idea he could have had. It was clumsy of him to think Norma Jean would want a log house. It was a crazy idea. He'll have to think of something else, quickly. He will wad the blueprints into tight balls and fling them into the lake. Then he'll get moving again. He opens his eyes. Norma Jean has moved away and is walking through the cemetery, following a serpentine brick path.

Leroy gets up to follow his wife, but his good leg is asleep and his bad leg still hurts him. Norma Jean is far away, walking rapidly toward the bluff by the river, and he tries to hobble toward her. Some children run past him, screaming noisily. Norma Jean has reached the bluff, and she is looking out over the Tennessee River. Now she turns toward Leroy and waves her arms. Is she beckoning to him? She seems to be doing an exercise for her chest muscles. The sky is unusually pale—the color of the dust ruffle Mabel made for their bed.

—1982

---

### ALICE WALKER ▦ (b. 1944)

*Alice Walker wrote the Pulitzer Prize–winning epistolary novel* The Color Purple *(1982). The book and its 1985 film version have made her the most famous living African American woman writer, perhaps the most widely read of any American woman of color. A native of Eatonton, Georgia, Walker was the eighth child of an impoverished farm couple. She attended Spelman College in Atlanta and Sarah Lawrence College on scholarships, graduating in 1965. Walker began her literary career as a poet, eventually publishing six volumes of verse. Walker's short story collections and novels, including* The Temple of My Familiar *(1989) and* Possessing the Secret of Joy *(1992), which takes as its subject the controversial practice of female circumcision among African tribes, have continued to reach large audiences and have solidified her reputation as one of the major figures in contemporary literature. Walker has coined the term "womanist" to stand for the black feminist concerns of much of her fiction. "Everyday Use," a story from the early 1970s, is simultaneously a satisfying piece of realistic social commentary and a subtly satirical variation on the ancient fable of "The City Mouse and the Country Mouse." In more recent years, Walker has published a novel,* Now Is the Time to Open Your Heart *(2004), and* A Poem Traveled Down My Arm *(2003), a collection of poems and drawings. In recent years, Walker has concentrated on activism for a number of causes.*

# Everyday Use

*For your grandmama*

I will wait for her in the yard that Maggie and I made so clean and wavy yesterday afternoon. A yard like this is more comfortable than most people know. It is not just a yard. It is like an extended living room. When the hard clay is swept clean as a floor and the fine sand around the edges lined with tiny, irregular grooves anyone can come and sit and look up into the elm tree and wait for the breezes that never come inside the house.

Maggie will be nervous until after her sister goes: she will stand hopelessly in corners homely and ashamed of the burn scars down her arms and legs, eyeing her sister with a mixture of envy and awe. She thinks her sister has held life always in the palm of one hand, that "no" is a word the world never learned to say to her.

You've no doubt seen those TV shows where the child who has "made it" is confronted, as a surprise, by her own mother and father, tottering in weakly from backstage. (A pleasant surprise, of course: What would they do if parent and child came on the show only to curse out and insult each other?) On TV mother and child embrace and smile into each other's faces. Sometimes the mother and father weep, the child wraps them in her arms and leans across the table to tell how she would not have made it without their help. I have seen these programs.

Sometimes I dream a dream in which Dee and I are suddenly brought together on a TV program of this sort. Out of a dark and soft-seated limousine I am ushered into a bright room filled with many people. There I meet a smiling, gray, sporty man like Johnny Carson who shakes my hand and tells me what a fine girl I have.[*] Then we are on the stage and Dee is embracing me with tears in her eyes. She pins on my dress a large orchid, even though she has told me once that she thinks orchids are tacky flowers.

In real life I am a large, big-boned woman with rough, man-working hands. In the winter I wear flannel nightgowns to bed and overalls during the day. I can kill and clean a hog as mercilessly as a man. My fat keeps me hot in zero weather. I can work outside all day, breaking ice to get water for washing. I can eat pork liver cooked over the open fire minutes after it comes steaming from the hog. One winter I knocked a bull calf straight in the brain between the eyes with a sledge hammer and had the meat hung up to chill before nightfall. But of course all this does not show on television. I am the way my daughter would want me to be: a hundred pounds lighter, my skin like an uncooked barley pancake. My hair glistens in the hot bright lights. Johnny Carson has much to do to keep up with my quick and witty tongue.

[1] **Johnny Carson** late night television host from 1962-1992.

But that is a mistake. I know even before I wake up. Who ever knew a Johnson with a quick tongue? Who can even imagine me looking a strange white man in the eye? It seems to me I have talked to them always with one foot raised in flight, with my head turned in whichever way is farthest from them. Dee, though. She would always look anyone in the eye. Hesitation was no part of her nature.

"How do I look, Mama?" Maggie says, showing just enough of her thin body enveloped in pink skirt and red blouse for me to know she's there, almost hidden by the door.

"Come out into the yard," I say.

Have you ever seen a lame animal, perhaps a dog run over by some careless person rich enough to own a car, sidle up to someone who is ignorant enough to be kind to him? That is the way my Maggie walks. She has been like this, chin on chest, eyes on ground, feet in shuffle, ever since the fire that burned the other house to the ground.

Dee is lighter than Maggie, with nicer hair and a fuller figure. She's a woman now, though sometimes I forget. How long ago was it that the other house burned? Ten, twelve years? Sometimes I can still hear the flames and feel Maggie's arms sticking to me, her hair smoking and her dress falling off her in little black papery flakes. Her eyes seemed stretched open, blazed open by the flames reflected in them. And Dee. I see her standing off under the sweet gum tree she used to dig gum out of; a look of concentration on her face as she watched the last dingy gray board of the house fall in toward the red-hot brick chimney. Why don't you do a dance around the ashes? I'd wanted to ask her. She had hated the house that much.

I used to think she hated Maggie, too. But that was before we raised the money, the church and me, to send her to Augusta to school. She used to read to us without pity; forcing words, lies, other folks' habits, whole lives upon us two, sitting trapped and ignorant underneath her voice. She washed us in a river of make-believe, burned us with a lot of knowledge we didn't necessarily need to know. Pressed us to her with the serious way she read, to shove us away at just the moment, like dimwits, we seemed about to understand.

Dee wanted nice things. A yellow organdy dress to wear to her graduation from high school; black pumps to match a green suit she'd made from an old suit somebody gave me. She was determined to stare down any disaster in her efforts. Her eyelids would not flicker for minutes at a time. Often I fought off the temptation to shake her. At sixteen she had a style of her own: and knew what style was.

I never had an education myself. After second grade the school was closed down. Don't ask me why: in 1927 colored asked fewer questions than they do now. Sometimes Maggie reads to me. She stumbles along good-naturedly but can't see well. She knows she is not bright. Like good looks and money, quickness passed her by. She will marry John Thomas (who has mossy teeth in an earnest face) and then I'll be free to sit here and I guess just sing church songs to myself. Although I never was a good singer. Never could carry a tune. I was always better at a man's job. I used to love to milk till I was hoofed in the side in '49. Cows are soothing and slow and don't bother you, unless you try to milk them the wrong way.

I have deliberately turned my back on the house. It is three rooms, just like the one that burned, except the roof is tin; they don't make shingle roofs any more. There are no real windows, just some holes cut in the sides, like the portholes in a ship, but not round and not square, with rawhide holding the shutters up on the outside. This house is in a pasture, too, like the other one. No doubt when Dee sees it she will want to tear it down. She wrote me once that no matter where we "choose" to live, she will manage to come see us. But she will never bring her friends. Maggie and I thought about this and Maggie asked me, "Mama, when did Dee ever *have* any friends?"

She had a few. Furtive boys in pink shirts hanging about on washday after school. Nervous girls who never laughed. Impressed with her they worshiped the well-turned phrase, the cute shape, the scalding humor that erupted like bubbles in lye. She read to them.

When she was courting Jimmy T she didn't have much time to pay to us, but turned all her faultfinding power on him. He *flew* to marry a cheap gal from a family of ignorant flashy people. She hardly had time to recompose herself.

When she comes I will meet—but there they are!

Maggie attempts to make a dash for the house, in her shuffling way, but I stay her with my hand. "Come back here," I say. And she stops and tries to dig a well in the sand with her toe.

It is hard to see them clearly through the strong sun. But even the first glimpse of leg out of the car tells me it is Dee. Her feet were always neat-looking, as if God himself had shaped them with a certain style. From the other side of the car comes a short, stocky man. Hair is all over his head a foot long and hanging from his chin like a kinky mule tail. I hear Maggie suck in her breath. "Uhnnnh," is what it sounds like. Like when you see the wriggling end of a snake just in front of your foot on the road. "Uhnnnh."

Dee next. A dress down to the ground, in this hot weather. A dress so loud it hurts my eyes. There are yellows and oranges enough to throw back the light of the sun. I feel my whole face warming from the heat waves it throws out. Earrings, too, gold and hanging down to her shoulders. Bracelets dangling and making noises when she moves her arm up to shake the folds of the dress out of her armpits. The dress is loose and flows, and as she walks closer, I like it. I hear Maggie go "Uhnnnh" again. It is her sister's hair. It stands straight up like the wool on a sheep. It is black as night and around the edges are two long pigtails that rope about like small lizards disappearing behind her ears.

"Wa-su-zo-Tean-o!" she says, coming on in that gliding way the dress makes her move. The short stocky fellow with the hair to his navel is all grinning and he follows up with "Asalamalakim, my mother and sister!" He moves to hug Maggie but she falls back, right up against the back of my chair. I feel her trembling there and when I look up I see the perspiration falling off her chin.

"Don't get up," says Dee. Since I am stout it takes something of a push. You can see me trying to move a second or two before I make it. She turns, showing white heels through her sandals, and goes back to the car. Out she peeks next with a Polaroid. She stoops down quickly and lines up picture after picture of me sitting there in front of the house with Maggie cowering behind me. She never takes a shot without making sure the house is included. When a cow comes nibbling around the edge of the yard she snaps it and me and Maggie and the house. Then she puts the Polaroid in the back seat of the car, and comes up and kisses me on the forehead.

Meanwhile Asalamalakim is going through the motions with Maggie's hand. Maggie's hand is as limp as a fish, and probably as cold, despite the sweat, and she keeps trying to pull it back. It looks like Asalamalakim wants to shake hands but wants to do it fancy. Or maybe he don't know how people shake hands. Anyhow, he soon gives up on Maggie.

"Well," I say. "Dee."

"No, Mama," she says. "Not 'Dee,' Wangero Leewanika Kemanjo!"

"What happened to 'Dee'?" I wanted to know.

"She's dead," Wangero said. "I couldn't bear it any longer being named after the people who oppress me."

"You know as well as me you was named after your aunt Dicie," I said. Dicie is my sister. She named Dee. We called her "Big Dee" after Dee was born.

"But who was *she* named after?" asked Wangero.

"I guess after Grandma Dee," I said.

"And who was she named after?" asked Wangero.

"Her mother," I said, and saw Wangero was getting tired. "That's about as far back as I can trace it," I said. Though, in fact, I probably could have carried it back beyond the Civil War through the branches.

"Well," said Asalamalakim, "there you are."

"Uhnnnh," I heard Maggie say.

"There I was not," I said, "before 'Dicie' cropped up in our family, so why should I try to trace it that far back?"

He just stood there grinning, looking down on me like somebody inspecting a Model A car. Every once in a while he and Wangero sent eye signals over my head.

"How do you pronounce this name?" I asked.

"You don't have to call me by it if you don't want to," said Wangero.

"Why shouldn't I?" I asked. "If that's what you want us to call you, we'll call you."

"I know it might sound awkward at first," said Wangero.

"I'll get used to it," I said. "Ream it out again."

Well, soon we got the name out of the way. Asalamalakim had a name twice as long and three times as hard. After I tripped over it two or three times he told me to just call him Hakim-a-barber. I wanted to ask him was he a barber, but I didn't really think he was, so I didn't ask.

"You must belong to those beef-cattle peoples down the road," I said. They said "Asalamalakim" when they met you, too, but they didn't shake hands. Always too busy: feeding the cattle, fixing the fences, putting up salt-lick shelters, throwing down hay. When the white folks poisoned some of the herd the men stayed up all night with rifles in their hands. I walked a mile and a half just to see the sight.

Hakim-a-barber said, "I accept some of their doctrines, but farming and raising cattle is not my style." (They didn't tell me, and I didn't ask, whether Wangero [Dee] had really gone and married him.)

We sat down to eat and right away he said he didn't eat collards and pork was unclean. Wangero, though, went on through the chitlins and corn bread, the greens and everything else. She talked a blue streak over the sweet potatoes. Everything delighted her. Even the fact that we still used the benches her daddy made for the table when we couldn't afford to buy chairs.

"Oh, Mama!" she cried. Then turned to Hakim-a-barber. "I never knew how lovely these benches are. You can feel the rump prints," she said, running her hands underneath her and along the bench. Then she gave a sigh and her hand closed over Grandma Dee's butter dish. "That's it!" she said. "I knew there was something I wanted to ask you if I could have." She jumped up from the table and went over in the corner where the churn stood, the milk in it clabber by now. She looked at the churn and looked at it.

"This churn top is what I need," she said. "Didn't Uncle Buddy whittle it out of a tree you all used to have?"

"Yes," I said.

"Uh huh," she said happily. "And I want the dasher, too."

"Uncle Buddy whittle that, too?" asked the barber.

Dee (Wangero) looked up at me.

"Aunt Dee's first husband whittled the dash," said Maggie so low you almost couldn't hear her. "His name was Henry, but they called him Stash."

"Maggie's brain is like an elephant's," Wangero said, laughing. "I can use the churn top as a centerpiece for the alcove table," she said, sliding a plate over the churn, "and I'll think of something artistic to do with the dasher."

When she finished wrapping the dasher the handle stuck out. I took it for a moment in my hands. You didn't even have to look close to see where hands pushing the dasher up and down to make butter had left a kind of sink in the wood. In fact, there were a lot of small sinks; you could see where thumbs and fingers had sunk into the wood. It was beautiful light yellow wood, from a tree that grew in the yard where Big Dee and Stash had lived.

After dinner Dee (Wangero) went to the trunk at the foot of my bed and started rifling through it. Maggie hung back in the kitchen over the dishpan. Out came Wangero with two quilts. They had been pieced by Grandma Dee and then Big Dee and me had hung them on the quilt frames on the front porch and quilted them. One was in the Lone Star pattern. The other was Walk Around the Mountain. In both of them were scraps of dresses Grandma Dee had worn fifty and more years ago. Bits and pieces of Grandpa Jarrell's paisley shirts. And one teeny faded blue piece, about the size of a penny matchbox, that was from Great Grandpa Ezra's uniform that he wore in the Civil War.

"Mama," Wangero said sweet as a bird. "Can I have these old quilts?"

I heard something fall in the kitchen, and a minute later the kitchen door slammed.

"Why don't you take one or two of the others?" I asked. "These old things was just done by me and Big Dee from some tops your grandma pieced before she died."

"No," said Wangero. "I don't want those. They are stitched around the borders by machine."

"That's make them last better," I said.

"That's not the point," said Wangero. "These are all pieces of dresses Grandma used to wear. She did all this stitching by hand. Imagine!" She held the quilts securely in her arms, stroking them.

"Some of the pieces, like those lavender ones, come from old clothes her mother handed down to her," I said, moving up to touch the quilts. Dee (Wangero) moved back just enough so that I couldn't reach the quilts. They already belonged to her.

"Imagine!" she breathed again, clutching them closely to her bosom.

"The truth is," I said, "I promised to give them quilts to Maggie, for when she marries John Thomas."

She gasped like a bee had stung her.

"Maggie can't appreciate these quilts!" she said. "She'd probably be backward enough to put them to everyday use."

"I reckon she would," I said. "God knows I been saving 'em for long enough with nobody using 'em. I hope she will!" I didn't want to bring up how I had offered Dee (Wangero) a quilt when she went away to college. Then she had told me they were old-fashioned, out of style.

"But they're *priceless*!" she was saying now, furiously; for she has a temper. "Maggie would put them on the bed and in five years they'd be in rags. Less than that!"

"She can always make some more," I said. "Maggie knows how to quilt."

Dee (Wangero) looked at me with hatred. "You just will not understand. The point is these quilts, *these* quilts!"

"Well," I said, stumped. "What would *you* do with them?"

"Hang them," she said. As if that was the only thing you *could* do with quilts.

Maggie by now was standing in the door. I could almost hear the sound her feet made as they scraped over each other.

"She can have them, Mama," she said, like somebody used to never winning anything, or having anything reserved for her. "I can 'member Grandma Dee without the quilts."

I looked at her hard. She had filled her bottom lip with checkerberry snuff and it gave her face a kind of dopey, hangdog look. It was Grandma Dee and Big Dee who taught her how to quilt herself. She stood there with her scarred hands hidden in the folds of her skirt. She looked at her sister with something like fear but she wasn't mad at her. This was Maggie's portion. This was the way she knew God to work.

When I looked at her like that something hit me in the top of my head and ran down to the soles of my feet. Just like when I'm in church and the spirit of God touches me and I get happy and shout. I did something I never had done before: hugged Maggie to me, then dragged her on into the room, snatched the quilts out of Miss Wangero's hands and dumped them into Maggie's lap. Maggie just sat there on my bed with her mouth open.

"Take one or two of the others," I said to Dee.

But she turned without a word and went out to Hakim-a-barber.

"You just don't understand," she said, as Maggie and I came out to the car.

"What don't I understand?" I wanted to know.

"Your heritage," she said. And then she turned to Maggie, kissed her, and said, "You ought to try to make something of yourself, too, Maggie. It's really a new day for us. But from the way you and Mama still live you'd never know it."

She put on some sunglasses that hid everything above the tip of her nose and her chin.

Maggie smiled; maybe at the sunglasses. But a real smile, not scared. After we watched the car dust settle I asked Maggie to bring me a dip of snuff. And then the two of us sat there just enjoying, until it was time to go in the house and go to bed.

—1973

---

**AMY TAN** ▪ **(b. 1952)**

*Amy Tan was born in Oakland, California. Both of her parents were recent Chinese immigrants who had come to America to escape the violence of the civil war between Communists and Nationalists in their homeland. When Tan was a teenager, her mother revealed a secret: as a young woman in China, she had been married to an abusive first husband and had left three daughters there. This situation provided the raw material that became transformed in Tan's story, "A Pair of Tickets." In 1987, Tan and her mother visited China together. Tan's literary career began with her first novel,* The Joy Luck Club *(1989), which consists of sixteen interrelated stories, including "Two Kinds," about a group of Chinese American mothers and their daughters. The book became both a critical success and a best seller, and in 1993, it was made into a movie directed by Wayne Wang. Although Tan explores her Chinese American experience in her fiction, she has reservations about the currently fashionable division of writers into ethnic pigeonholes.*

# Two Kinds

My mother believed you could be anything you wanted to be in America. You could open a restaurant. You could work for the government and get good retirement. You could buy a house with almost no money down. You could become rich. You could become instantly famous.

"Of course, you can be prodigy, too," my mother told me when I was nine. "You can be best anything. What does Auntie Lindo know? Her daughter, she is only best tricky."

America was where all my mother's hopes lay. She had come here in 1949 after losing everything in China: her mother and father, her family home, her first husband, and two daughters, twin baby girls. But she never looked back with regret. There were so many ways for things to get better.

We didn't immediately pick the right kind of prodigy. At first my mother thought I could be a Chinese Shirley Temple. We'd watch Shirley's old movies on TV as though they were training films. My mother would poke my arm and say, *"Ni kan."* —You watch. And I would see Shirley tapping her feet, or singing a sailor song, or pursing her lips into a very round O while saying "Oh, my goodness."

"*Ni kan*," said my mother as Shirley's eyes flooded with tears. "You already know how. Don't need talent for crying!"    5

Soon after my mother got this idea about Shirley Temple, she took me to a beauty training school in the Mission district and put me in the hands of a student who could barely hold the scissors without shaking. Instead of getting big fat curls, I emerged with an uneven mass of crinkly black fuzz. My mother dragged me off to the bathroom and tried to wet down my hair.

"You look like Negro Chinese," she lamented, as if I had done this on purpose.

The instructor of the beauty training school had to lop off these soggy clumps to make my hair even again. "Peter Pan is very popular these days," the instructor assured my mother. I now had hair the length of a boy's, with straight-across bangs that hung at a slant two inches above my eyebrows. I liked the haircut and it made me actually look forward to my future fame.

In fact, in the beginning, I was just as excited as my mother, maybe even more so. I pictured this prodigy part of me as many different images, trying each one on for size. I was a dainty ballerina girl standing by the curtains, waiting to hear the music that would send me floating on my tiptoes. I was like the Christ child lifted out of the straw manger, crying with holy indignity. I was Cinderella stepping from her pumpkin carriage with sparkly cartoon music filling the air.

In all of my imaginings, I was filled with a sense that I would soon   10 become *perfect*. My mother and father would adore me. I would be beyond reproach. I would never feel the need to sulk for anything.

But sometimes the prodigy in me became impatient. "If you don't hurry up and get me out of here, I'm disappearing for good," it warned. "And then you'll always be nothing."

Every night after dinner, my mother and I would sit at the Formica kitchen table. She would present new tests, taking her examples from stories of amazing children she had read in *Ripley's Believe It or Not,* or *Good Housekeeping, Reader's Digest,* and a dozen other magazines she kept in a pile in our bathroom. My mother got these magazines from people whose houses she cleaned. And since she cleaned many houses each week, we had a great assortment. She would look through them all, searching for stories about remarkable children.

The first night she brought out a story about a three-year-old boy who knew the capitals of all the states and even most of the European countries. A teacher was quoted as saying the little boy could also pronounce the names of the foreign cities correctly.

"What's the capital of Finland?" my mother asked me, looking at the magazine story.

All I knew was the capital of California, because Sacramento was the   15 name of the street we lived on in Chinatown. "Nairobi!" I guessed, saying the most foreign word I could think of. She checked to see if that was possibly one way to pronounce "Helsinki" before showing me the answer.

The tests got harder—multiplying numbers in my head, finding the queen of hearts in a deck of cards, trying to stand on my head without using my hands, predicting the daily temperatures in Los Angeles, New York, and London.

One night I had to look at a page from the Bible for three minutes and then report everything I could remember. "Now Jehoshaphat had riches and honor in abundance and ... that's all I remember, Ma," I said.

And after seeing my mother's disappointed face once again, something inside of me began to die. I hated the tests, the raised hopes and failed expectations. Before going to bed that night, I looked in the mirror above the bathroom sink and when I saw only my face staring back—and that it would always be this ordinary face—I began to cry. Such a sad, ugly girl! I made high-pitched noises like a crazed animal, trying to scratch out the face in the mirror.

And then I saw what seemed to be the prodigy side of me—because I had never seen that face before. I looked at my reflection, blinking so I could see more clearly. The girl staring back at me was angry, powerful. This girl and I were the same. I had new thoughts, willful thoughts, or rather thoughts filled with lots of won'ts. I won't let her change me, I promised myself. I won't be what I'm not.

So now on nights when my mother presented her tests, I performed 20 listlessly, my head propped on one arm. I pretended to be bored. And I was. I got so bored I started counting the bellows of the foghorns out on the bay while my mother drilled me in other areas. The sound was comforting and reminded me of the cow jumping over the moon. And the next day, I played a game with myself, seeing if my mother would give up on me before eight bellows. After a while I usually counted only one, maybe two bellows at most. At last she was beginning to give up hope.

Two or three months had gone by without any mention of my being a prodigy again. And then one day my mother was watching *The Ed Sullivan Show*[1] on TV. The TV was old and the sound kept shorting out. Every time my mother got halfway up from the sofa to adjust the set, the sound would go back on and Ed would be talking. As soon as she sat down, Ed would go silent again. She got up, the TV broke into loud piano music. She sat down. Silence. Up and down, back and forth, quiet and loud. It was like a stiff embraceless dance between her and the TV set. Finally she stood by the set with her hand on the sound dial.

She seemed entranced by the music, a little frenzied piano piece with this mesmerizing quality, sort of quick passages and then teasing lilting ones before it returned to the quick playful parts.

"*Ni kan,*" my mother said, calling me over with hurried hand gestures, "Look here."

I could see why my mother was fascinated by the music. It was being pounded out by a little Chinese girl, about nine years old, with a Peter Pan haircut. The girl had the sauciness of a Shirley Temple. She was proudly modest like a proper Chinese child. And she also did this fancy sweep of

[1] **The Ed Sullivan Show** popular television variety show (1948-1971).

a curtsy, so that the fluffy skirt of her white dress cascaded slowly to the floor like the petals of a large carnation.

In spite of these warning signs, I wasn't worried. Our family had no 25 piano and we couldn't afford to buy one, let alone reams of sheet music and piano lessons. So I could be generous in my comments when my mother bad-mouthed the little girl on TV.

"Play note right, but doesn't sound good! No singing sound," my mother complained.

"What are you picking on her for?" I said carelessly. "She's pretty good. Maybe she's not the best, but she's trying hard." I knew almost immediately I would be sorry I said that.

"Just like you," she said. "Not the best. Because you not trying." She gave a little huff as she let go of the sound dial and sat down on the sofa.

The little Chinese girl sat down also to play an encore of "Anitra's Dance,"[2] by Grieg. I remember the song, because later on I had to learn how to play it.

Three days after watching *The Ed Sullivan Show,* my mother told me 30 what my schedule would be for piano lessons and piano practice. She had talked to Mr. Chong, who lived on the first floor of our apartment building. Mr. Chong was a retired piano teacher and my mother had traded housecleaning services for weekly lessons and a piano for me to practice on every day, two hours a day, from four until six.

When my mother told me this, I felt as though I had been sent to hell. I whined and then kicked my foot a little when I couldn't stand it anymore.

"Why don't you like me the way I am? I'm *not* a genius! I can't play the piano. And even if I could, I wouldn't go on TV if you paid me a million dollars!" I cried.

My mother slapped me. "Who ask you be genius?" she shouted. "Only ask you be your best. For you sake. You think I want you be genius? Hnnh! What for! Who ask you!"

"So ungrateful," I heard her mutter in Chinese. "If she had as much talent as she has temper, she would be famous now."

Mr. Chong, whom I secretly nicknamed Old Chong, was very strange, 35 always tapping his fingers to the silent music of an invisible orchestra. He looked ancient in my eyes. He had lost most of the hair on top of his head and he wore thick glasses and had eyes that always looked tired and sleepy. But he must have been younger than I thought, since he lived with his mother and was not yet married.

I met Old Lady Chong once and that was enough. She had this peculiar smell like a baby that had done something in its pants. And her fingers felt like a dead person's, like an old peach I once found in the back of the refrigerator; the skin just slid off the meat when I picked it up.

[2] **"Anitra's Dance"** a section from the incidental music that Edvard Grieg (1843–1907) wrote for *Peer Gynt,* a play by Henrik Ibsen.

I soon found out why Old Chong had retired from teaching piano. He was deaf. "Like Beethoven!" he shouted to me. "We're both listening only in our head!" And he would start to conduct his frantic silent sonatas.

Our lessons went like this. He would open the book and point to different things, explaining their purpose: "Key! Treble! Bass! No sharps or flats! So this is C major! Listen now and play after me!"

And then he would play the C scale a few times, a simple chord, and then, as if inspired by an old, unreachable itch, he gradually added more notes and running trills and a pounding bass until the music was really something quite grand.

I would play after him, the simple scale, the simple chord, and then    40 I just played some nonsense that sounded like a cat running up and down on top of garbage cans. Old Chong smiled and applauded and then said, "Very good! But now you must learn to keep time!"

So that's how I discovered that Old Chong's eyes were too slow to keep up with the wrong notes I was playing. He went through the motions in half-time. To help me keep rhythm, he stood behind me, pushing down on my right shoulder for every beat. He balanced pennies on top of my wrists so I would keep them still as I slowly played scales and arpeggios. He had me curve my hand around an apple and keep that shape when playing chords. He marched stiffly to show me how to make each finger dance up and down, staccato like an obedient little soldier.

He taught me all these things, and that was how I also learned I could be lazy and get away with mistakes, lots of mistakes. If I hit the wrong notes because I hadn't practiced enough, I never corrected myself. I just kept playing in rhythm. And Old Chong kept conducting his own private reverie.

So maybe I never really gave myself a fair chance. I did pick up the basics pretty quickly, and I might have become a good pianist at that young age. But I was so determined not to try, not to be anybody different that I learned to play only the most ear-splitting preludes, the most discordant hymns.

Over the next year I practiced like this, dutifully in my own way. And then one day I heard my mother and her friend Lindo Jong both talking in a loud bragging tone of voice so others could hear. It was after church, and I was leaning against the brick wall wearing a dress with stiff white petticoats. Auntie Lindo's daughter, Waverly, who was about my age, was standing farther down the wall about five feet away. We had grown up together and shared all the closeness of two sisters squabbling over crayons and dolls. In other words, for the most part, we hated each other. I thought she was snotty. Waverly Jong had gained a certain amount of fame as "Chinatown's Littlest Chinese Chess Champion."

"She bring home too many trophy," lamented Auntie Lindo that    45 Sunday. "All day she play chess. All day I have no time do nothing but dust off her winnings." She threw a scolding look at Waverly, who pretended not to see her.

"You lucky you don't have this problem," said Auntie Lindo with a sigh to my mother.

And my mother squared her shoulders and bragged: "Our problem worser than yours. If we ask Jing-mei wash dish, she hear nothing but music. It's like you can't stop this natural talent."

And right then, I was determined to put a stop to her foolish pride.

A few weeks later, Old Chong and my mother conspired to have me play in a talent show which would be held in the church hall. By then, my parents had saved up enough to buy me a secondhand piano, a black Wurlitzer spinet with a scarred bench. It was the showpiece of our living room.

For the talent show, I was to play a piece called "Pleading Child" from 50 Schumann's *Scenes from Childhood.*[3] It was a simple, moody piece that sounded more difficult than it was. I was supposed to memorize the whole thing, playing the repeat parts twice to make the piece sound longer. But I dawdled over it, playing a few bars and then cheating, looking up to see what notes followed. I never really listened to what I was playing. I daydreamed about being somewhere else, about being someone else.

The part I liked to practice best was the fancy curtsy: right foot out, touch the rose on the carpet with a pointed foot, sweep to the side, left leg bends, look up and smile.

My parents invited all the couples from the Joy Luck Club to witness my debut. Auntie Lindo and Uncle Tin were there. Waverly and her two older brothers had also come. The first two rows were filled with children both younger and older than I was. The littlest ones got to go first. They recited simple nursery rhymes, squawked out tunes on miniature violins, twirled Hula Hoops, pranced in pink ballet tutus, and when they bowed or curtsied, the audience would sigh in unison, "Awww," and then clap enthusiastically.

When my turn came, I was very confident. I remember my childish excitement. It was as if I knew, without a doubt, that the prodigy side of me really did exist. I had no fear whatsoever, no nervousness. I remember thinking to myself, This is it! This is it! I looked out over the audience, at my mother's blank face, my father's yawn, Auntie Lindo's stiff-lipped smile, Waverly's sulky expression. I had on a white dress layered with sheets of lace, and a pink bow in my Peter Pan haircut. As I sat down I envisioned people jumping to their feet and Ed Sullivan rushing up to introduce me to everyone on TV.

And I started to play. It was so beautiful. I was so caught up in how lovely I looked that at first I didn't worry how I would sound. So it was a surprise to me when I hit the first wrong note and I realized something

[3] **Scenes from Childhood** a piano work by Robert Shumann (1810–1856) with twelve titled sections and an epilogue.

didn't sound quite right. And then I hit another and another followed that. A chill started at the top of my head and began to trickle down. Yet I couldn't stop playing, as though my hands were bewitched. I kept thinking my fingers would adjust themselves back, like a train switching to the right track. I played this strange jumble through two repeats, the sour notes staying with me all the way to the end.

When I stood up, I discovered my legs were shaking. Maybe I had just 55 been nervous and the audience, like Old Chong, had seen me go through the right motions and had not heard anything wrong at all. I swept my right foot out, went down on my knee, looked up and smiled. The room was quiet, except for Old Chong, who was beaming and shouting, "Bravo! Bravo! Well done!" But then I saw my mother's face, her stricken face. The audience clapped weakly, and as I walked back to my chair, with my whole face quivering as I tried not to cry, I heard a little boy whisper loudly to his mother, "That was awful," and the mother whispered back, "Well, she certainly tried."

And now I realized how many people were in the audience, the whole world it seemed. I was aware of eyes burning into my back. I felt the shame of my mother and father as they sat stiffly throughout the rest of the show.

We could have escaped during intermission. Pride and some strange sense of honor must have anchored my parents to their chairs. And so we watched it all: the eighteen-year-old boy with a fake moustache who did a magic show and juggled flaming hoops while riding a unicycle. The breasted girl with white makeup who sang from *Madame Butterfly* and got honorable mention. And the eleven-year-old boy who won first prize playing a tricky violin song that sounded like a busy bee.

After the show, the Hsus, the Jongs, and the St. Clairs from the Joy Luck Club, came up to my mother and father.

"Lots of talented kids," Auntie Lindo said vaguely, smiling broadly.

"That was somethin' else," said my father, and I wondered if he was 60 referring to me in a humorous way, or whether he even remembered what I had done.

Waverly looked at me and shrugged her shoulders. "You aren't a genius like me," she said matter-of-factly. And if I hadn't felt so bad, I would have pulled her braids and punched her stomach.

But my mother's expression was what devastated me: a quiet, blank look that said she had lost everything. I felt the same way, and it seemed as if everybody were now coming up, like gawkers at the scene of an accident, to see what parts were actually missing. When we got on the bus to go home, my father was humming the busy-bee tune and my mother was silent. I kept thinking she wanted to wait until we got home before shouting at me. But when my father unlocked the door to our apartment, my mother walked in and then went to the back, into the bedroom. No accusations. No blame. And in a way, I felt disappointed. I had been waiting for her to start shouting, so I could shout back and cry and blame her for all my misery.

I assumed my talent-show fiasco meant I never had to play the piano again. But two days later, after school, my mother came out of the kitchen and saw me watching TV.

"Four clock," she reminded me as if it were any other day. I was stunned, as though she were asking me to go through the talent-show torture again. I wedged myself more tightly in front of the TV.

"Turn off TV," she called from the kitchen five minutes later.                    65

I didn't budge. And then I decided. I didn't have to do what my mother said anymore. I wasn't her slave. This wasn't China. I had listened to her before and look what happened. She was the stupid one.

She came out from the kitchen and stood in the arched entryway of the living room. "Four clock," she said once again, louder.

"I'm not going to play anymore," I said nonchalantly. "Why should I? I'm not a genius."

She walked over and stood in front of the TV. I saw her chest was heaving up and down in an angry way.

"No!" I said, and I now felt stronger, as if my true self had finally   70 emerged. So this was what had been inside me all along.

"No! I won't!" I screamed.

She yanked me by the arm, pulled me off the floor, snapped off the TV. She was frighteningly strong, half pulling, half carrying me toward the piano as I kicked the throw rugs under my feet. She lifted me up and onto the hard bench. I was sobbing by now, looking at her bitterly. Her chest was heaving even more and her mouth was open, smiling crazily as if she were pleased I was crying.

"You want me to be someone that I'm not!" I sobbed. "I'll never be the kind of daughter you want me to be!"

"Only two kinds of daughters," she shouted in Chinese. "Those who are obedient and those who follow their own mind! Only one kind of daughter can live in this house. Obedient daughter!"

"Then I wish I wasn't your daughter. I wish you weren't my mother,"   75 I shouted. As I said these things I got scared. It felt like worms and toads and slimy things crawling out of my chest, but it also felt good, as if this awful side of me had surfaced, at last.

"Too late change this," said my mother shrilly.

And I could sense her anger rising to its breaking point. I wanted to see it spill over. And that's when I remembered the babies she had lost in China, the ones we never talked about. "Then I wish I'd never been born!" I shouted. "I wish I were dead! Like them."

It was as if I had said the magic words. Alakazam!—and her face went blank, her mouth closed, her arms went slack, and she backed out of the room, stunned, as if she were blowing away like a small brown leaf, thin, brittle, lifeless.

It was not the only disappointment my mother felt in me. In the years that followed, I failed her so many times, each time asserting my own will, my right to fall short of expectations. I didn't get straight As. I didn't become class president. I didn't get into Stanford. I dropped out of college.

For unlike my mother, I did not believe I could be anything I wanted to    80
be. I could only be me.

And for all those years, we never talked about the disaster at the recital or my terrible accusations afterward at the piano bench. All of that remained unchecked, like a betrayal that was now unspeakable. So I never found a way to ask her why she had hoped for something so large that failure was inevitable.

And even worse, I never asked her what frightened me the most: Why had she given up hope?

For after our struggle at the piano, she never mentioned my playing again. The lessons stopped. The lid to the piano was closed, shutting out the dust, my misery, and her dreams.

So she surprised me. A few years ago, she offered to give me the piano, for my thirtieth birthday. I had not played in all those years. I saw the offer as a sign of forgiveness, a tremendous burden removed.

"Are you sure?" I asked shyly. "I mean, won't you and Dad miss it?"    85

"No, this your piano," she said firmly. "Always your piano. You only one can play."

"Well, I probably can't play anymore," I said. "It's been years."

"You pick up fast," said my mother, as if she knew this was certain. "You have natural talent. You could been genius if you want to."

"No I couldn't."

"You just not trying," said my mother. And she was neither angry nor    90
sad. She said it as if to announce a fact that could never be disproved. "Take it," she said.

But I didn't at first. It was enough that she had offered it to me. And after that, every time I saw it in my parents' living room, standing in front of the bay windows, it made me feel proud, as if it were a shiny trophy I had won back.

Last week I sent a tuner over to my parents' apartment and had the piano reconditioned, for purely sentimental reasons. My mother had died a few months before and I had been getting things in order for my father, a little bit at a time. I put the jewelry in special silk pouches. The sweaters she had knitted in yellow, pink, bright orange—all the colors I hated— I put those in moth-proof boxes. I found some old Chinese silk dresses, the kind with little slits up the sides. I rubbed the old silk against my skin, then wrapped them in tissue and decided to take them home with me.

After I had the piano tuned, I opened the lid and touched the keys. It sounded even richer than I remembered. Really, it was a very good piano. Inside the bench were the same exercise notes with handwritten scales, the same secondhand music books with their covers held together with yellow tape.

I opened up the Schumann book to the dark little piece I had played at the recital. It was on the left-hand side of the page, "Pleading Child." It looked more difficult than I remembered. I played a few bars, surprised at how easily the notes came back to me.

And for the first time, or so it seemed, I noticed the piece on the 95 right-hand side. It was called "Perfectly Contented." I tried to play this one as well. It had a lighter melody but the same flowing rhythm and turned out to be quite easy. "Pleading Child" was shorter but slower; "Perfectly Contented" was longer but faster. And after I played them both a few times, I realized they were two halves of the same song.

—1989

## LOUISE ERDRICH ▪ (b. 1954)

*Louise Erdrich was born in Little Falls, Minnesota, and grew up in North Dakota. Her father was a teacher with the Bureau of Indian Affairs, and both he and her mother encouraged her to write stories from an early age. Erdrich holds degrees from Dartmouth College and Johns Hopkins University, where she studied creative writing. Her novel Love Medicine, from which "The Red Convertible" is taken, is a sequence of fourteen connected stories told by seven narrators. Love Medicine won the National Book Critics Circle Award for 1984. Much of Erdrich's fiction draws on her childhood on the Great Plains and her mixed cultural heritage (her ancestry is German American and Chippewa). In addition to Love Medicine, she has published novels, including The Beet Queen (1986) and Tracks (1988), several prize-winning short stories, and three books of poetry. Erdrich and her late husband Michael Dorris, another Native American writer, appeared in two documentary films shown on PBS and collaborated on a novel, The Crown of Columbus (1991). Along with James Welch and Leslie Marmon Silko, Erdrich has helped to redefine Native American fiction. According to the Columbia Literary History of the United States, "These authors have had to resist the formulaic approaches favored by the publishing industry, which has its own opinions about what constitutes the 'proper' form and content of minority fiction." The Birchbark House, a novel for young readers, and The Antelope Wife, a novel employing the techniques of magic realism, both appeared in 1999. Her most recent novel is The Round House (2012).*

# The Red Convertible

### Lyman Lamartine

I was the first one to drive a convertible on my reservation. And of course it was red, a red Olds. I owned that car along with my brother Henry Junior. We owned it together until his boots filled with water on a windy night and he bought out my share. Now Henry owns the whole car, and his younger brother Lyman (that's myself), Lyman walks everywhere he goes.

How did I earn enough money to buy my share in the first place? My one talent was I could always make money. I had a touch for it, unusual in a Chippewa. From the first I was different that way, and everyone recognized it. I was the only kid they let in the American Legion Hall to shine shoes, for example, and one Christmas I sold spiritual bouquets for the mission door to door. The nuns let me keep a percentage. Once I started, it seemed the more money I made the easier the money came. Everyone encouraged it. When I was fifteen I got a job washing dishes at the Joliet Cafe, and that was where my first big break happened.

It wasn't long before I was promoted to bussing tables, and then the short-order cook quit and I was hired to take her place. No sooner than you know it I was managing the Joliet. The rest is history. I went on managing. I soon became part owner, and of course there was no stopping me then. It wasn't long before the whole thing was mine.

After I'd owned the Joliet for one year, it blew over in the worst tornado ever seen around here. The whole operation was smashed to bits. A total loss. The fryalator was up in a tree, the grill torn in half like it was paper. I was only sixteen. I had it all in my mother's name, and I lost it quick, but before I lost it I had every one of my relatives, and their relatives, to dinner, and I also bought that red Olds I mentioned, along with Henry.

The first time we saw it! I'll tell you when we first saw it. We had gotten a ride up to Winnipeg, and both of us had money. Don't ask me why, because we never mentioned a car or anything, we just had all our money. Mine was cash, a big bankroll from the Joliet's insurance. Henry had two checks—a week's extra pay for being laid off, and his regular check from the Jewel Bearing Plant.

We were walking down Portage anyway, seeing the sights, when we saw it. There it was, parked, large as life. Really as *if* it was alive. I thought of the word *repose*, because the car wasn't simply stopped, parked, or whatever. That car reposed, calm and gleaming, a FOR SALE sign in its left front window. Then, before we had thought it over at all, the car belonged to us and our pockets were empty. We had just enough money for gas back home.

We went places in that car, me and Henry. We took off driving all one whole summer. We started off toward the Little Knife River and Mandaree in Fort Berthold and then we found ourselves down in Wakpala somehow, and then suddenly we were over in Montana on the Rocky Boys, and yet the summer was not even half over. Some people hang on to details when they travel, but we didn't let them bother us and just lived our everyday lives here to there.

I do remember this one place with willows. I remember I laid under those trees and it was comfortable. So comfortable. The branches bent down all around me like a tent or a stable. And quiet, it was quiet, even though there was a powwow close enough so I could see it going on. The air was not too still, not too windy either. When the dust rises up and hangs in the air around the dancers like that, I feel good. Henry was asleep with his arms thrown wide. Later on, he woke up and we started driving again. We were somewhere in Montana, or maybe on the Blood Reserve—it could have been anywhere. Anyway it was where we met the girl.

All her hair was in buns around her ears, that's the first thing I noticed about her. She was posed alongside the road with her arm out, so we stopped. That girl was short, so short her lumber shirt looked comical on her, like a nightgown. She had jeans on and fancy moccasins and she carried a little suitcase.

"Hop on in," says Henry. So she climbs in between us.

"We'll take you home," I says. "Where do you live?"

"Chicken," she says.

"Where the hell's that?" I ask her.

"Alaska."

"Okay," says Henry, and we drive.

We got up there and never wanted to leave. The sun doesn't truly set there in summer, and the night is more a soft dusk. You might doze off, sometimes, but before you know it you're up again, like an animal in nature. You never feel like you have to sleep hard or put away the world. And things would grow up there. One day just dirt or moss, the next day flowers and long grass. The girl's name was Susy. Her family really took to us. They fed us and put us up. We had our own tent to live in by their house, and the kids would be in and out of there all day and night. They couldn't get over me and Henry being brothers, we looked so different. We told them we knew we had the same mother, anyway.

One night Susy came in to visit us. We sat around in the tent talking of this thing and that. The season was changing. It was getting darker by that time, and the cold was even getting just a little mean. I told her it was time for us to go. She stood up on a chair.

"You never seen my hair," Susy said.

That was true. She was standing on a chair, but still, when she unclipped her buns the hair reached all the way to the ground. Our eyes opened. You couldn't tell how much hair she had when it was rolled up so neatly. Then my brother Henry did something funny. He went up to the chair and said, "Jump on my shoulders." So she did that, and her hair reached down past his waist, and he started twirling, this way and that, so her hair was flung out from side to side.

"I always wondered what it was like to have long pretty hair," Henry says. Well we laughed. It was a funny sight, the way he did it. The next morning we got up and took leave of those people.

On to greener pastures, as they say. It was down through Spokane and across Idaho then Montana and very soon we were racing the weather right along under the Canadian border through Columbus, Des Lacs, and then we were in Bottineau County and soon home. We'd made most of the trip, that summer, without putting up the car hood at all. We got home just in time, it turned out, for the army to remember Henry had signed up to join it.

I don't wonder that the army was so glad to get my brother that they turned him into a Marine. He was built like a brick outhouse anyway. We liked to tease him that they really wanted him for his Indian nose. He had a nose big and sharp as a hatchet, like the nose on Red Tomahawk, the Indian who killed Sitting Bull, whose profile is on signs all along the North Dakota highways. Henry went off to training camp, came home once during Christmas, then the next thing you know we got an overseas letter from him. It was 1970, and he said he was stationed up in the northern hill country. Whereabouts I did not know. He wasn't such a hot letter writer, and only got off two before the enemy caught him. I could never keep it straight, which direction those good Vietnam soldiers were from.

I wrote him back several times, even though I didn't know if those letters would get through. I kept him informed all about the car. Most of the time I had it up on blocks in the yard or half taken apart, because that long trip did a hard job on it under the hood.

I always had good luck with numbers, and never worried about the draft myself. I never even had to think about what my number was. But Henry was never lucky in the same way as me. It was at least three years before Henry came home. By then I guess the whole war was solved in the government's mind, but for him it would keep on going. In those years I'd put his car into almost perfect shape. I always thought of it as his car while he was gone, even though when he left he said, "Now it's yours," and threw me his key.

"Thanks for the extra key," I'd said. "I'll put it up in your drawer just in case I need it." He laughed.

When he came home, though, Henry was very different, and I'll say this: the change was no good. You could hardly expect him to change for the better, I know. But he was quiet, so quiet, and never comfortable sitting still anywhere but always up and moving around. I thought back to times we'd sat still for whole afternoons, never moving a muscle, just shifting our weight along the ground, talking to whoever sat with us, watching things. He'd always had a joke, then, too, and now you couldn't get him to laugh, or when he did it was more the sound of a man choking, a sound that stopped up the throats of other people around him. They got to leaving him alone most of the time, and I didn't blame them. It was a fact: Henry was jumpy and mean.

I'd bought a color TV set for my mom and the rest of us while Henry was away. Money still came very easy. I was sorry I'd ever bought it though, because of Henry. I was also sorry I'd bought color, because with black-and-white the pictures seem older and farther away. But what are you going to do? He sat in front of it, watching it, and that was the only time he was completely still. But it was the kind of stillness that you see in a rabbit when it freezes and before it will bolt. He was not easy. He sat in his chair gripping the armrests with all his might, as if the chair itself was moving at a high speed and if he let go at all he would rocket forward and maybe crash right through the set.

Once I was in the room watching TV with Henry and I heard his teeth click at something. I looked over, and he'd bitten through his lip. Blood was going down his chin. I tell you right then I wanted to smash that tube to pieces. I went over to it but Henry must have known what I was up to. He rushed from his chair and shoved me out of the way, against the wall. I told myself he didn't know what he was doing.

My mom came in, turned the set off real quiet, and told us she had made something for supper. So we went and sat down. There was still blood going down Henry's chin, but he didn't notice it and no one said anything, even though every time he took a bite of his bread his blood fell onto it until he was eating his own blood mixed in with the food.

While Henry was not around we talked about what was going to happen to him. There were no Indian doctors on the reservation, and my mom was afraid of trusting Old Man Pillager because he courted her long ago and was jealous of her husbands. He might take revenge through her son. We were afraid that if we brought Henry to a regular hospital they would keep him.

"They don't fix them in those places," Mom said; "they just give them drugs."

"We wouldn't get him there in the first place," I agreed, "so let's just forget about it."

Then I thought about the car.

Henry had not even looked at the car since he'd gotten home, though like I said it was in tip-top condition and ready to drive. I thought the car might bring the old Henry back somehow. So I bided my time and waited for my chance to interest him in the vehicle.

One night Henry was off somewhere. I took myself a hammer. I went out to that car and I did a number on its underside. Whacked it up. Bent the tail pipe double. Ripped the muffler loose. By the time I was done with the car it looked worse than any typical Indian car that has been driven all its life on reservation roads, which they always say are like government promises—full of holes. It just about hurt me, I'll tell you that! I threw dirt in the carburetor and I ripped all the electric tape off the seats. I made it look just as beat up as I could. Then I sat back and waited for Henry to find it.

Still, it took him over a month. That was all right, because it was just getting warm enough, not melting, but warm enough to work outside.

"Lyman," he says, walking in one day, "that red car looks like shit."

"Well it's old," I says. "You got to expect that."

"No way!" says Henry. "That car's a classic! But you went and ran the piss right out of it, Lyman, and you know it don't deserve that. I kept that car in A-one shape. You don't remember. You're too young. But when I left, that car was running like a watch. Now I don't even know if I can get it to start again, let alone get it anywhere near its old condition."

"Well you try," I said, like I was getting mad, "but I say it's a piece of junk."

Then I walked out before he could realize I knew he'd strung together more than six words at once.

After that I thought he'd freeze himself to death working on that car. He was out there all day, and at night he rigged up a little lamp, ran a cord out the window, and had himself some light to see by while he worked. He was better than he had been before, but that's still not saying much. It was easier for him to do the things the rest of us did. He ate more slowly and didn't jump up and down during the meal to get this or that or look out the window. I put my hand in the back of the TV set, I admit, and fiddled around with it good, so that it was almost impossible now to get a clear picture. He didn't look at it very often anyway. He was always out with that car or going off to get parts for it. By the time it was really melting outside, he had it fixed.

I had been feeling down in the dumps about Henry around this time. We had always been together before. Henry and Lyman. But he was such a loner now that I didn't know how to take it. So I jumped at the chance one day when Henry seemed friendly. It's not that he smiled or anything. He just said, "Let's take that old shitbox for a spin." Just the way he said it made me think he could be coming around.

We went out to the car. It was spring. The sun was shining very bright. My only sister, Bonita, who was just eleven years old, came out and made us stand together for a picture. Henry leaned his elbow on the red car's windshield, and he took his other arm and put it over my shoulder, very carefully, as though it was heavy for him to lift and he didn't want to bring the weight down all at once.

"Smile," Bonita said, and he did.

That picture. I never look at it anymore. A few months ago, I don't know why, I got his picture out and tacked it on the wall. I felt good about Henry at the time, close to him. I felt good having his picture on the wall, until one night when I was looking at television. I was a little drunk and stoned. I looked up at the wall and Henry was staring at me. I don't know what it was, but his smile had changed, or maybe it was gone. All I know is I couldn't stay in the same room with that picture. I was shaking. I got up, closed the door, and went into the kitchen. A little later my friend Ray came over and we both went back into that room. We put the picture in a brown bag, folded the bag over and over tightly, then put it way back in a closet.

I still see that picture now, as if it tugs at me, whenever I pass that closet door. The picture is very clear in my mind. It was so sunny that day Henry had to squint against the glare. Or maybe the camera Bonita held flashed like a mirror, blinding him, before she snapped the picture. My face is right out in the sun, big and round. But he might have drawn back, because the shadows on his face are deep as holes. There are two shadows curved like little hooks around the ends of his smile, as if to frame it and try to keep it there—that one, first smile that looked like it might have hurt his face. He has his field jacket on and the worn-in clothes he'd come back in and kept wearing ever since. After Bonita took the picture, she went into the house and we got into the car. There was a full cooler in the trunk. We started off, east, toward Pembina and the Red River because Henry said he wanted to see the high water.

The trip over there was beautiful. When everything starts changing, drying up, clearing off, you feel like your whole life is starting. Henry felt it, too. The top was down and the car hummed like a top. He'd really put it back in shape, even the tape on the seats was very carefully put down and glued back in layers. It's not that he smiled again or even joked, but his face looked to me as if it was clear, more peaceful. It looked as though he wasn't thinking of anything in particular except the bare fields and windbreaks and houses we were passing.

The river was high and full of winter trash when we got there. The sun was still out, but it was colder by the river. There were still little clumps of dirty snow here and there on the banks. The water hadn't gone over the banks yet, but it would, you could tell. It was just at its limit, hard swollen, glossy like an old gray scar. We made ourselves a fire, and we sat down and watched the current go. As I watched it I felt something squeezing inside me and tightening and trying to let go all at the same time. I knew I was not just feeling it myself; I knew I was feeling what Henry was going through at that moment. Except that I couldn't stand it, the closing and opening. I jumped to my feet. I took Henry by the shoulders and I started shaking him. "Wake up," I says, "wake up, wake up, wake up!" I didn't know what had come over me. I sat down beside him again.

His face was totally white and hard. Then it broke, like stones break all of a sudden when water boils up inside them.

"I know it," he says. "I know it. I can't help it. It's no use."

We start talking. He said he knew what I'd done with the car. It was obvious it had been whacked out of shape and not just neglected. He said he wanted to give the car to me for good now, it was no use. He said he'd fixed it just to give it back and I should take it.

"No way," I says, "I don't want it."

"That's okay," he says, "you take it."

"I don't want it, though," I says back to him, and then to emphasize, just to emphasize, you understand, I touch his shoulder. He slaps my hand off.

"Take that car," he says.

"No," I say, "make me," I say, and then he grabs my jacket and rips the arm loose. That jacket is a class act, suede with tags and zippers. I push Henry backwards, off the log. He jumps up and bowls me over. We go down in a clinch and come up swinging hard, for all we're worth, with our fists. He socks my jaw so hard I feel like it swings loose. Then I'm at his ribcage and land a good one under his chin so his head snaps back. He's dazzled. He looks at me and I look at him and then his eyes are full of tears and blood and at first I think he's crying. But no, he's laughing. "Ha! Ha!" he says. "Ha! Ha! Take good care of it."

"Okay," I says, "okay, no problem. Ha! Ha!"

I can't help it, and I start laughing, too. My face feels fat and strange, and after a while I get a beer from the cooler in the trunk, and when I hand it to Henry he takes his shirt and wipes my germs off. "Hoof-and-mouth disease," he says. For some reason this cracks me up, and so we're really laughing for a while, and then we drink all the rest of the beers one by one and throw them in the river and see how far, how fast, the current takes them before they fill up and sink.

"You want to go on back?" I ask after a while. "Maybe we could snag a couple nice Kashpaw girls."

He says nothing. But I can tell his mood is turning again.

"They're all crazy, the girls up here, every damn one of them."

"You're crazy too," I say, to jolly him up. "Crazy Lamartine boys!"

He looks as though he will take this wrong at first. His face twists, then clears, and he jumps up on his feet. "That's right!" he says. "Crazier 'n hell. Crazy Indians!"

I think it's the old Henry again. He throws off his jacket and starts swinging his legs out from the knees like a fancy dancer. He's down doing something between a grouse dance and a bunny hop, no kind of dance I ever saw before, but neither has anyone else on all this green growing earth. He's wild. He wants to pitch whoopee! He's up and at me and all over. All this time I'm laughing so hard, so hard my belly is getting tied up in a knot.

"Got to cool me off!" he shouts all of a sudden. Then he runs over to the river and jumps in.

There's boards and other things in the current. It's so high. No sound comes from the river after the splash he makes, so I run right over. I look around. It's getting dark. I see he's halfway across the water already, and I know he didn't swim there but the current took him. It's far. I hear his voice, though, very clearly across it.

"My boots are filling," he says.

He says this in a normal voice, like he just noticed and he doesn't know what to think of it. Then he's gone. A branch comes by. Another branch. And I go in.

By the time I get out of the river, off the snag I pulled myself onto, the sun is down. I walk back to the car, turn on the high beams, and drive it up the bank. I put it in first gear and then I take my foot off the clutch. I get out, close the door, and watch it plow softly into the water. The headlights reach in as they go down, searching, still lighted even after the water swirls over the back end. I wait. The wires short out. It is all finally dark. And then there is only the water, the sound of it going and running and going and running and running.

—1984

---

## RICK MOODY ▨ (b. 1961)

*One of Rick Moody's nonfiction books,* The Black Veil, *investigates the life of a New England ancestor, a clergyman who accidentally killed a friend and covered his face for the rest of his life. This incident inspired Nathaniel Hawthorne's classic tale "The Minister's Black Veil." Born in New York City, Moody has written a novel,* The Ice Storm, *that was made into an Ang Lee film and a short story that was the basis of another,* Personal Effects. *A musician who has released one solo album and two others with a folk group, Moody wittily describes himself as a "life coach": "My experiences have mainly been at the typewriter or word processor, a place where I am normally very alone. And yet I refuse to allow these things to stop me. Nor will I allow the grim facts of my own life—addiction, mental health problems, childhood in the suburbs—prevent me from realizing my dream." "Boys" illustrates the manner in which contemporary short fiction has found common ground with the personal essay.*

# Boys

*Demonology, 2001*
*Little, Brown*

Boys enter the house, boys enter the house. Boys, and with them the ideas of boys (ideas leaden, reductive, inflexible), enter the house. Boys, two of them, wound into hospital packaging, boys with infant-pattern baldness, slung in the arms of parents, boys dreaming of breasts, enter the house. Twin boys, kettles on the boil, boys in hideous vinyl knapsacks that young couples from Edison, NJ., wear on their shirt fronts, knapsacks coated with baby saliva and staphylococcus and milk vomit, enter the house. Two boys, one striking the other with a rubberized hot dog, enter the house. Two boys, one of them striking the other with a willow switch about the head and shoulders, the other crying, enter the house. Boys enter the house speaking nonsense. Boys enter the house calling for mother. On a Sunday, in May, a day one might nearly describe as perfect, an ice cream truck comes slowly down the lane, chimes inducing salivation, and children run after it, not long after which boys dig a hole in the back yard and bury their younger sister's dolls two feet down, so that she will never find these dolls and these dolls will rot in hell, after which boys enter the house. Boys, trailing after their father like he is the Second Goddamned Coming of Christ Goddamned Almighty, enter the house, repair to the basement to watch baseball. Boys enter the house, site of devastation, and repair immediately to the kitchen, where they mix lighter fluid, vanilla pudding, drain-opening lye, balsamic vinegar, blue food coloring, calamine lotion, cottage cheese, ants, a plastic lizard one of them received in his Christmas stocking, tacks, leftover mashed potatoes, Spam, frozen lima beans, and chocolate syrup in a medium-sized saucepan and heat over a low flame until thick, afterward transferring the contents of this saucepan into a Pyrex lasagna dish, baking the Pyrex lasagna dish in the oven for nineteen minutes before attempting to persuade their sister that she should eat the mixture; later they smash three family heirlooms (the last, a glass egg, intentionally) in a two-and-a-half-hour stretch, whereupon they are sent to their bedroom until freed, in each case thirteen minutes after. Boys enter the house, starchy in pressed shirts and flannel pants that itch so bad, fresh from Sunday school instruction, blond and brown locks (respectively) plastered down but even so with a number of cowlicks protruding at odd angles, disconsolate and humbled, uncertain if boyish things—such as shooting at the neighbor's dog with a pump-action BB gun and gagging the fat boy up the street with a bandanna and showing their shriveled boy-penises to their younger sister—are exempted from the commandment to *Love the Lord thy God with all thy heart and with all thy soul and with all thy mind, and thy neighbor as thyself.* Boys enter the house in baseball gear (only one of the boys can hit): in their spikes, in mismatched tube socks that smell like Stilton cheese. Boys enter the house in soccer gear. Boys enter the house carrying skates. Boys enter the house with lacrosse sticks, and soon after, tossing a lacrosse ball lightly in the living room, they destroy a lamp. One boy enters the house sporting basketball clothes, the other wearing jeans and a sweatshirt. One boy enters the house bleeding profusely and is taken out to get stitches, the other watches. Boys enter the house at the end of term carrying report cards, sneak around the house like spies of foreign nationality, looking for a place to hide the report cards for the time being (under a toaster? in a medicine cabinet?). One boy with a black eye enters the house, one boy without. Boys with acne enter the house and squeeze and prod large skin blemishes in front of their sister. Boys with acne-treatment products hidden about their persons enter the house. Boys, standing just up the street, sneak cigarettes behind a willow in the Elys' yard, wave smoke away from their natural fibers, hack terribly, experience nausea, then enter the house. Boys call each other *Retard, Homo, Geek,* and, later, *Neckless Thug, Theater Fag,* and enter the house exchanging further epithets. Boys enter house with nose-hair clippers, chase sister around house threatening to depilate her eyebrows. She cries. Boys attempt to induce girls to whom they would not have spoken only six or eight months prior to enter the house with them. Boys enter the house with girls efflorescent and homely and attempt to induce girls to sneak into their bedroom, as they still share a single bedroom; girls refuse. Boys enter the house, go to separate bedrooms. Boys, with their father (an arm around each of them), enter the house, but of the monologue preceding and succeeding this entrance, not a syllable is preserved. Boys enter the house having masturbated in a variety of locales. Boys enter the house having masturbated in train-station bathrooms, in forests, in beach houses, in football bleachers at night under the stars, in cars (under a blanket), in the shower, backstage, on a plane, the boys masturbate constantly, identically, three times a day in some cases, desire like a madness upon them, at the mere sound of certain words, words that sound like other words, *interrogative* reminding them of *intercourse, beast* reminding them of *breast, sects* reminding them of *sex,* and so forth, the boys are not very smart yet, and as they enter the house they feel, as always, immense shame at the scale of this self-abusive cogitation, seeing a classmate, seeing a billboard, seeing a fire hydrant, seeing things that should not induce thoughts of masturbation (their sister, e.g.) and then thinking of masturbation anyway. Boys enter the house, go to their rooms, remove sexually explicit magazines from hidden stashes, put on loud music, feel despair. Boys enter the house worried; they argue. The boys are ugly, they are failures, they will never be loved, they enter the house. Boys enter the house and kiss their mother, who feels differently now they have outgrown her. Boys enter the house, kiss their mother, she explains the seriousness of their sister's difficulty, her diagnosis. Boys enter the house, having attempted to locate the spot in their yard where the dolls were buried, eight or nine years prior, without success; they go to their sister's room, sit by her bed. Boys enter the house and tell their completely bald sister jokes about baldness. Boys hold either hand of their sister, laying aside differences, having trudged grimly into the house. Boys skip school, enter house, hold vigil. Boys enter the house after their parents have both gone off to work, sit with their sister and with their sister's nurse. Boys enter the house carrying cases of beer. Boys enter the house, very worried now, didn't know more worry was possible. Boys enter the house carrying con-trolled substances, neither having told the other that he is carrying a controlled substance, though an intoxicated posture seems appropriate under the circumstances. Boys enter the house weeping and hear weeping around them. Boys enter the house embarrassed, silent, anguished, keening, afflicted, angry, woeful, grief-stricken. Boys enter the house on vacation, each clasps the hand of the other with genuine warmth, the one wearing dark colors and having shaved a portion of his head, the other having grown his hair out longish and wearing, uncharacteristically, a tie-dyed shirt. Boys enter the house on vacation and argue bitterly about politics (other subjects are no longer discussed), one boy supporting the Maoist insurgency in a certain Southeast Asian country, one believing that to change the system you need to work inside it; one boy threatens to beat the living shit out of the other, refuses crème brûlée, though it is created by his mother in order to keep the peace. One boy writes home and thereby enters the house only through a mail slot: he argues that the other boy is crypto-fascist, believing that the market can seek its own level on questions of ethics and morals; boys enter the house on vacation and announce future professions; boys enter the house on vacation and change their minds about professions; boys enter the house on vacation, and one boy brings home a sweetheart but throws a tantrum when it is suggested that the sweetheart will have to retire on the folding bed in the basement; the other boy, having no sweetheart, is distant and withdrawn, preferring to talk late into the night about family members gone from this world. Boys enter the house several weeks apart. Boys enter the house on days of heavy rain. Boys enter the house, in different calendar years, and upon entering, the boys seem to do nothing but compose manifestos, for the benefit of parents; they follow their mother around the place, having fashioned these manifestos in celebration of brand-new independence: *Mom, I like to lie in bed late into the morning watching game shows,* or, *I'm never going to date anyone but artists from now on, mad girls, dreamers, practicers of black magic,* or, *A man should eat bologna, sliced meats are important,* or, *An American should bowl at least once a year,* but these manifestos apply only for brief spells, after which they are reversed or discarded. Boys don't enter the house at all, except as ghostly afterimages of younger selves, fleeting images of sneakers dashing up a staircase; soggy towels on the floor of the bathroom; blue jeans coiled like asps in the basin of the washing machine; boys as an absence of boys; blissful at first, you put a thing down on a spot, put this book down, come back later, it's still there; you buy a box of cookies, eat three, later three are missing. Nevertheless, when boys next enter the house, which they ultimately must do, it's a relief, even if it's only in preparation for weddings of acquaintances from boyhood, one boy has a beard, neatly trimmed, the other has rakish sideburns, one boy wears a hat, the other boy thinks hats are ridiculous, one boy wears khakis pleated at the waist, the other wears denim, but each changes into his suit (one suit fits well, one is a little tight), as though suits are the liminary marker of adulthood. Boys enter the house after the wedding and they are slapping each other on the back and yelling at anyone who will listen. *It's a party!* One boy enters the house, carried by friends, having been arrested (after the wedding) for driving while intoxicated, complexion ashen; the other boy tries to keep his mouth shut: the car is on its side in a ditch, the car has the top half of a tree broken over its bonnet, the car has struck another car, which has in turn struck a third, *Everyone will have seen.* One boy misses his brother horribly, misses the past, misses a time worth being nostalgic over, a time that never existed, back when they set their sister's playhouse on fire; the other boy avoids all mention of that time; each of them is once the boy who enters the house alone, missing the other, each is devoted and each callous, and each plays his part on the telephone, over the course of months. Boys enter the house with fishing gear, according to prearranged date and time, arguing about whether to use lures or live bait, in order to meet their father for the fishing adventure, after which boys enter the house again, almost immediately, with live bait, having settled the question; boys boast of having caught fish in the past, though no fish has ever been caught: *Remember when the blues were biting?* Boys enter the house carrying their father, slumped. Happens so fast. Boys rush into the house leading EMTs to the couch in the living room where the body lies, boys enter the house, boys enter the house, boys enter the house. Boys hold open the threshold, awesome threshold that has welcomed them when they haven't even been able to welcome themselves, that threshold which welcomed them when they had to be taken in, here is its tarnished knocker, here is its euphonious bell, here's where the boys had to sand the door down because it never would hang right in the frame, here are the scuff marks from when boys were on the wrong side of the door demanding, here's where there were once milk bottles for the milkman, here's where the newspaper always landed, here's the mail slot, here's the light on the front step, illuminated, here's where the boys are standing, as that beloved man is carried out. Boys, no longer boys, exit.

SHERMAN ALEXIE ■ (b. 1966)

*Sherman Alexie is a Spokane/Coeur d'Alene Indian and grew up on a reservation in Wellpinit, Washington. While at Washington State University as a premed major, Alexie attended a poetry workshop and soon began to publish his work. Two collections of poetry were followed by The Lone Ranger and Tonto Fight in Heaven (1993) and a first novel, Reservation Blues (2005). "This Is What It Means to Say Phoenix, Arizona" was made into a 1998 film, Smoke Signals, and won two awards at the Sundance Film Festival. A prolific author and frequent guest on radio and television talk shows, Alexie has also performed professionally as a stand-up comedian. A young adult novel, The Absolutely True Diary of a Part-Time Indian, appeared in 2007 and received a National Book Award. War Dances, his most recent novel, appeared in 2010.*

# This Is What It Means to Say Phoenix, Arizona

Just after Victor lost his job at the BIA,[1] he also found out that his father had died of a heart attack in Phoenix, Arizona. Victor hadn't seen his father in a few years, only talked to him on the telephone once or twice, but there still was a genetic pain, which was soon to be pain as real and immediate as a broken bone.

Victor didn't have any money. Who does have money on a reservation, except the cigarette and fireworks salespeople? His father had a savings account waiting to be claimed, but Victor needed to find a way to get to Phoenix. Victor's mother was just as poor as he was, and the rest of his family didn't have any use at all for him. So Victor called the Tribal Council.

"Listen," Victor said. "My father just died. I need some money to get to Phoenix to make arrangements."

"Now, Victor," the council said. "You know we're having a difficult time financially."

"But I thought the council had special funds set aside for stuff like this."    5

"Now, Victor, we do have some money available for the proper return of tribal members' bodies. But I don't think we have enough to bring your father all the way back from Phoenix."

"Well," Victor said. "It ain't going to cost all that much. He had to be cremated. Things were kind of ugly. He died of a heart attack in his trailer and nobody found him for a week. It was really hot, too. You get the picture."

---

[1] **BIA** Bureau of Indian Affairs, a federal agency responsible for management of Indian lands and concerns.

"Now, Victor, we're sorry for your loss and the circumstances. But we can really only afford to give you one hundred dollars."

"That's not even enough for a plane ticket."

"Well, you might consider driving down to Phoenix."   10

"I don't have a car. Besides, I was going to drive my father's pickup back up here."

"Now, Victor," the council said. "We're sure there is somebody who could drive you to Phoenix. Or is there somebody who could lend you the rest of the money?"

"You know there ain't nobody around with that kind of money."

"Well, we're sorry, Victor, but that's the best we can do."

Victor accepted the Tribal Council's offer. What else could he do? So   15
he signed the proper papers, picked up his check, and walked over to the Trading Post to cash it.

While Victor stood in line, he watched Thomas Builds-the-Fire standing near the magazine rack, talking to himself. Like he always did. Thomas was a story-teller that nobody wanted to listen to. That's like being a dentist in a town where everybody has false teeth.

Victor and Thomas Builds-the-Fire were the same age, had grown up and played in the dirt together. Ever since Victor could remember, it was Thomas who always had something to say.

Once, when they were seven years old, when Victor's father still lived with the family, Thomas closed his eyes and told Victor this story: "Your father's heart is weak. He is afraid of his own family. He is afraid of you. Late at night he sits in the dark. Watches the television until there's nothing but that white noise. Sometimes he feels like he wants to buy a motorcycle and ride away. He wants to run and hide. He doesn't want to be found."

Thomas Builds-the-Fire had known that Victor's father was going to leave, knew it before anyone. Now Victor stood in the Trading Post with a one-hundred-dollar check in his hand, wondering if Thomas knew that Victor's father was dead, if he knew what was going to happen next.

Just then Thomas looked at Victor, smiled, and walked over to him.   20

"Victor, I'm sorry about your father," Thomas said.

"How did you know about it?" Victor asked.

"I heard it on the wind. I heard it from the birds. I felt it in the sunlight. Also, your mother was just in here crying."

"Oh," Victor said and looked around the Trading Post. All the other Indians stared, surprised that Victor was even talking to Thomas. Nobody talked to Thomas anymore because he told the same damn stories over and over again. Victor was embarrassed, but he thought that Thomas might be able to help him. Victor felt a sudden need for tradition.

"I can lend you the money you need," Thomas said suddenly. "But you   25
have to take me with you."

"I can't take your money," Victor said. "I mean, I haven't hardly talked to you in years. We're not really friends anymore."

"I didn't say we were friends. I said you had to take me with you."

"Let me think about it."

Victor went home with his one hundred dollars and sat at the kitchen table. He held his head in his hands and thought about Thomas Builds-the-Fire, remembered little details, tears and scars, the bicycle they shared for a summer, so many stories.

Thomas Builds-the-Fire sat on the bicycle, waited in Victor's yard. He    30 was ten years old and skinny. His hair was dirty because it was the Fourth of July.

"Victor," Thomas yelled. "Hurry up. We're going to miss the fireworks."

After a few minutes, Victor ran out of his house, jumped the porch railing, and landed gracefully on the sidewalk.

"And the judges award him a 9.95, the highest score of the summer," Thomas said, clapped, laughed.

"That was perfect, cousin," Victor said. "And it's my turn to ride the bike."

Thomas gave up the bike and they headed for the fairgrounds. It was    35 nearly dark and the fireworks were about to start.

"You know," Thomas said. "It's strange how us Indians celebrate the Fourth of July. It ain't like it was *our* independence everybody was fighting for."

"You think about things too much," Victor said. "It's just supposed to be fun. Maybe Junior will be there."

"Which Junior? Everybody on this reservation is named Junior."

And they both laughed.

The fireworks were small, hardly more than a few bottle rockets and a    40 fountain. But it was enough for two Indian boys. Years later, they would need much more.

Afterwards, sitting in the dark, fighting off mosquitoes, Victor turned to Thomas Builds-the-Fire.

"Hey," Victor said. "Tell me a story."

Thomas closed his eyes and told this story: "There were these two Indian boys who wanted to be warriors. But it was too late to be warriors in the old way. All the horses were gone. So the two Indian boys stole a car and drove to the city. They parked the stolen car in front of the police station and then hitchhiked back home to the reservation. When they got back, all their friends cheered and their parents' eyes shone with pride. *You were very brave,* everybody said to the two Indian boys. *Very brave.*"

"Ya-hey," Victor said. "That's a good one. I wish I could be a warrior."

"Me, too," Thomas said.    45

They went home together in the dark, Thomas on the bike now, Victor on foot. They walked through shadows and light from streetlamps.

"We've come a long ways," Thomas said. "We have outdoor lighting."

"All I need is the stars," Victor said. "And besides, you still think about things too much."

They separated then, each headed for home, both laughing all the way.

Victor sat at his kitchen table. He counted his one hundred dollars 50 again and again. He knew he needed more to make it to Phoenix and back. He knew he needed Thomas Builds-the-Fire. So he put his money in his wallet and opened the front door to find Thomas on the porch.

"Ya-hey, Victor," Thomas said. "I knew you'd call me."

Thomas walked into the living room and sat down on Victor's favorite chair.

"I've got some money saved up," Thomas said. "It's enough to get us down there, but you have to get us back."

"I've got this hundred dollars," Victor said. "And my dad had a savings account I'm going to claim."

"How much in your dad's account?"                                          55

"Enough. A few hundred."

"Sounds good. When we leaving?"

When they were fifteen and had long since stopped being friends, Victor and Thomas got into a fistfight. That is, Victor was really drunk and beat Thomas up for no reason at all. All the other Indian boys stood around and watched it happen. Junior was there and so were Lester, Seymour, and a lot of others. The beating might have gone on until Thomas was dead if Norma Many Horses hadn't come along and stopped it.

"Hey, you boys," Norma yelled and jumped out of her car. "Leave him alone."

If it had been someone else, even another man, the Indian boys 60 would've just ignored the warnings. But Norma was a warrior. She was powerful. She could have picked up any two of the boys and smashed their skulls together. But worse than that, she would have dragged them all over to some tipi and made them listen to some elder tell a dusty old story.

The Indian boys scattered, and Norma walked over to Thomas and picked him up.

"Hey, little man, are you okay?" she asked.

Thomas gave her a thumbs up.

"Why they always picking on you?"

Thomas shook his head, closed his eyes, but no stories came to him, no 65 words or music. He just wanted to go home, to lie in his bed and let his dreams tell his stories for him.

Thomas Builds-the-Fire and Victor sat next to each other in the airplane, coach section. A tiny white woman had the window seat. She was busy twisting her body into pretzels. She was flexible.

"I have to ask," Thomas said, and Victor closed his eyes in embarrassment.

"Don't," Victor said.

"Excuse me, miss," Thomas asked. "Are you a gymnast or something?"

"There's no something about it," she said. "I was first alternate on the  70
1980 Olympic team."

"Really?" Thomas asked.

"Really."

"I mean, you used to be a world-class athlete?" Thomas asked.

"My husband still thinks I am."

Thomas Builds-the-Fire smiled. She was a mental gymnast, too. She  75
pulled her leg straight up against her body so that she could've kissed her kneecap.

"I wish I could do that," Thomas said.

Victor was ready to jump out of the plane. Thomas, that crazy Indian storyteller with ratty old braids and broken teeth, was flirting with a beautiful Olympic gymnast. Nobody back home on the reservation would ever believe it.

"Well," the gymnast said. "It's easy. Try it."

Thomas grabbed at his leg and tried to pull it up into the same position as the gymnast. He couldn't even come close, which made Victor and the gymnast laugh.

"Hey," she asked. "You two are Indian, right?"                                    80

"Full-blood," Victor said.

"Not me," Thomas said. "I'm half magician on my mother's side and half clown on my father's."

They all laughed.

"What are your names?" she asked.

"Victor and Thomas."                                                              85

"Mine is Cathy. Pleased to meet you all."

The three of them talked for the duration of the flight. Cathy the gymnast complained about the government, how they screwed the 1980 Olympic team by boycotting.[2]

"Sounds like you all got a lot in common with Indians," Thomas said.

Nobody laughed.

After the plane landed in Phoenix and they had all found their way to  90
the terminal, Cathy the gymnast smiled and waved good-bye.

"She was really nice," Thomas said.

---

[2] **they screwed the 1980 Olympic team by boycotting** in an international movement led by the United States at the direction of President Jimmy Carter, some sixty nations boycotted the 1980 Summer Olympic Games in Moscow as a protest against the Soviet invasion of Afghanistan in December 1979.

"Yeah, but everybody talks to everybody on airplanes," Victor said. "It's too bad we can't always be that way."

"You always used to tell me I think too much," Thomas said. "Now it sounds like you do."

"Maybe I caught it from you."

"Yeah."                                                                                                          95

Thomas and Victor rode in a taxi to the trailer where Victor's father died.

"Listen," Victor said as they stopped in front of the trailer. "I never told you I was sorry for beating you up that time."

"Oh, it was nothing. We were just kids and you were drunk."

"Yeah, but I'm still sorry."

"That's all right."                                                                                             100

Victor paid for the taxi and the two of them stood in the hot Phoenix summer. They could smell the trailer.

"This ain't going to be nice," Victor said. "You don't have to go in."

"You're going to need help."

Victor walked to the front door and opened it. The stink rolled out and made them both gag. Victor's father had lain in that trailer for a week in hundred-degree temperatures before anyone found him. And the only reason anyone found him was because of the smell. They needed dental records to identify him. That's exactly what the coroner said. They needed dental records.

"Oh, man," Victor said. "I don't know if I can do this."                                          105

"Well, then don't."

"But there might be something valuable in there."

"I thought his money was in the bank."

"It is. I was talking about pictures and letters and stuff like that."

"Oh," Thomas said as he held his breath and followed Victor into the   110
trailer.

When Victor was twelve, he stepped into an underground wasp nest. His foot was caught in the hole, and no matter how hard he struggled, Victor couldn't pull free. He might have died there, stung a thousand times, if Thomas Builds-the-Fire had not come by.

"Run," Thomas yelled and pulled Victor's foot from the hole. They ran then, hard as they ever had, faster than Billy Mills, faster than Jim Thorpe,[3] faster than the wasps could fly.

[3] **Billy Mills ... Jim Thorpe** William Mervin "Billy" Mills (born 1938), a member of the Sioux tribe, won a gold medal in the 10,000-meter run at the 1964 Summer Olympic Games in Tokyo, Japan. Jacobus Franciscus "Jim" Thorpe (1888–1953), of the Sac and Fox tribe, is widely regarded as one of the greatest American athletes of the twentieth century; he won gold medals in the pentathlon and decathlon at the 1912 Summer Olympic Games in Stockholm, Sweden. He also played professional football, baseball, and basketball.

Victor and Thomas ran until they couldn't breathe, ran until it was cold and dark outside, ran until they were lost and it took hours to find their way home. All the way back, Victor counted his stings.

"Seven," Victor said. "My lucky number."

Victor didn't find much to keep in the trailer. Only a photo album and 115 a stereo. Everything else had that smell stuck in it or was useless anyway.

"I guess this is all," Victor said. "It ain't much."

"Better than nothing," Thomas said.

"Yeah, and I do have the pickup."

"Yeah," Thomas said. "It's in good shape."

"Dad was good about that stuff."                    120

"Yeah, I remember your dad."

"Really?" Victor asked. "What do you remember?"

Thomas Builds-the-Fire closed his eyes and told this story: "I remember when I had this dream that told me to go to Spokane, to stand by the Falls in the middle of the city and wait for a sign. I knew I had to go there but I didn't have a car. Didn't have a license. I was only thirteen. So I walked all the way, took me all day, and I finally made it to the Falls. I stood there for an hour waiting. Then your dad came walking up. *What the hell are you doing here?* he asked me. I said, *Waiting for a vision.* Then your father said, *All you're going to get here is mugged.* So he drove me over to Denny's, bought me dinner, and then drove me home to the reservation. For a long time I was mad because I thought my dreams had lied to me. But they didn't. Your dad was my vision. *Take care of each other* is what my dreams were saying. *Take care of each other.*"

Victor was quiet for a long time. He searched his mind for memories of his father, found the good ones, found a few bad ones, added it all up, and smiled.

"My father never told me about finding you in Spokane," Victor said.   125

"He said he wouldn't tell anybody. Didn't want me to get in trouble. But he said I had to watch out for you as part of the deal."

"Really?"

"Really. Your father said you would need the help. He was right."

"That's why you came down here with me, isn't it?" Victor asked.

"I came because of your father."                    130

Victor and Thomas climbed into the pickup, drove over to the bank, and claimed the three hundred dollars in the savings account.

Thomas Builds-the-Fire could fly.

Once, he jumped off the roof of the tribal school and flapped his arms like a crazy eagle. And he flew. For a second, he hovered, suspended above all the other Indian boys who were too smart or too scared to jump.

"He's flying," Junior yelled, and Seymour was busy looking for the trick wires or mirrors. But it was real. As real as the dirt when Thomas lost altitude and crashed to the ground.

He broke his arm in two places.                                                    135

"He broke his wing," Victor chanted, and the other Indian boys joined in, made it a tribal song.

"He broke his wing, he broke his wing, he broke his wing," all the Indian boys chanted as they ran off, flapping their wings, wishing they could fly, too. They hated Thomas for his courage, his brief moment as a bird. Everybody has dreams about flying. Thomas flew.

One of his dreams came true for just a second, just enough to make it real.

Victor's father, his ashes, fit in one wooden box with enough left over to fill a cardboard box.

"He always was a big man," Thomas said.                                             140

Victor carried part of his father and Thomas carried the rest out to the pickup. They set him down carefully behind the seats, put a cowboy hat on the wooden box and a Dodgers cap on the cardboard box. That's the way it was supposed to be.

"Ready to head back home?" Victor asked.

"It's going to be a long drive."

"Yeah, take a couple days, maybe."

"We can take turns," Thomas said.                                                   145

"Okay," Victor said, but they didn't take turns. Victor drove for sixteen hours straight north, made it halfway up Nevada toward home before he finally pulled over.

"Hey, Thomas," Victor said. "You got to drive for a while."

"Okay."

Thomas Builds-the-Fire slid behind the wheel and started off down the road. All through Nevada, Thomas and Victor had been amazed at the lack of animal life, at the absence of water, of movement.

"Where is everything?" Victor had asked more than once.                            150

Now when Thomas was finally driving they saw the first animal, maybe the only animal in Nevada. It was a long-eared jackrabbit.

"Look," Victor yelled. "It's alive."

Thomas and Victor were busy congratulating themselves on their discovery when the jackrabbit darted out into the road and under the wheels of the pickup.

"Stop the goddamn car," Victor yelled, and Thomas did stop, backed the pickup to the dead jackrabbit.

"Oh, man, he's dead," Victor said as he looked at the squashed animal. 155

"Really dead."

"The only thing alive in this whole state and we just killed it."

"I don't know," Thomas said. "I think it was suicide."

Victor looked around the desert, sniffed the air, felt the emptiness and loneliness, and nodded his head.

"Yeah," Victor said. "It had to be suicide." 160

"I can't believe this," Thomas said. "You drive for a thousand miles and there ain't even any bugs smashed on the windshield. I drive for ten seconds and kill the only living thing in Nevada."

"Yeah," Victor said. "Maybe I should drive."

"Maybe you should."

Thomas Builds-the-Fire walked through the corridors of the tribal school by himself. Nobody wanted to be anywhere near him because of all those stories. Story after story.

Thomas closed his eyes and this story came to him: "We are all given 165 one thing by which our lives are measured, one determination. Mine are the stories which can change or not change the world. It doesn't matter which as long as I continue to tell the stories. My father, he died on Okinawa in World War II, died fighting for this country, which had tried to kill him for years. My mother, she died giving birth to me, died while I was still inside her. She pushed me out into the world with her last breath. I have no brothers or sisters. I have only my stories which came to me before I even had the words to speak. I learned a thousand stories before I took my first thousand steps. They are all I have. It's all I can do."

Thomas Builds-the-Fire told his stories to all those who would stop and listen. He kept telling them long after people had stopped listening.

Victor and Thomas made it back to the reservation just as the sun was rising. It was the beginning of a new day on earth, but the same old shit on the reservation.

"Good morning," Thomas said.

"Good morning."

The tribe was waking up, ready for work, eating breakfast, reading the 170 newspaper, just like everybody else does. Willene LeBret was out in her garden wearing a bathrobe. She waved when Thomas and Victor drove by.

"Crazy Indians made it," she said to herself and went back to her roses.

Victor stopped the pickup in front of Thomas Builds-the-Fire's HUD house.[4] They both yawned, stretched a little, shook dust from their bodies.

"I'm tired," Victor said.

"Of everything," Thomas added.

They both searched for words to end the journey. Victor needed to 175 thank Thomas for his help, for the money, and make the promise to pay it all back.

---

[4] **HUD house** housing subsidized by the U.S. Department of Housing and Urban Development.

"Don't worry about the money," Thomas said. "It don't make any difference anyhow."

"Probably not, enit?"

"Nope."

Victor knew that Thomas would remain the crazy storyteller who talked to dogs and cars, who listened to the wind and pine trees. Victor knew that he couldn't really be friends with Thomas, even after all that had happened. It was cruel but it was real. As real as the ashes, as Victor's father, sitting behind the seats.

"I know how it is," Thomas said. "I know you ain't going to treat me 180 any better than you did before. I know your friends would give you too much shit about it."

Victor was ashamed of himself. Whatever happened to the tribal ties, the sense of community? The only real thing he shared with anybody was a bottle and broken dreams. He owed Thomas something, anything.

"Listen," Victor said and handed Thomas the cardboard box which contained half of his father. "I want you to have this."

Thomas took the ashes and smiled, closed his eyes, and told this story: "I'm going to travel to Spokane Falls one last time and toss these ashes into the water. And your father will rise like a salmon, leap over the bridge, over me, and find his way home. It will be beautiful. His teeth will shine like silver, like a rainbow. He will rise, Victor, he will rise."

Victor smiled.

"I was planning on doing the same thing with my half," Victor said. 185 "But I didn't imagine my father looking anything like a salmon. I thought it'd be like cleaning the attic or something. Like letting things go after they've stopped having any use."

"Nothing stops, cousin," Thomas said. "Nothing stops."

Thomas Builds-the-Fire got out of the pickup and walked up his driveway. Victor started the pickup and began the drive home.

"Wait," Thomas yelled suddenly from his porch. "I just got to ask one favor."

Victor stopped the pickup, leaned out the window, and shouted back. "What do you want?"

"Just one time when I'm telling a story somewhere, why don't you stop 190 and listen?" Thomas asked.

"Just once?"

"Just once."

Victor waved his arms to let Thomas know that the deal was good. It was a fair trade, and that was all Victor had ever wanted from his whole life. So Victor drove his father's pickup toward home while Thomas went into his house, closed the door behind him, and heard a new story come to him in the silence afterwards.

---

**ETGAR KERET** ▦ **(b. 1967)**

*Etgar Keret was born in Israel, the son of Holocaust survivors. He has worked in television and film, authored comic books and graphic novels, and published six collections of short stories. A master of the condensed form known as the "short-short," he has seen his work become increasingly popular in English translation. His literary influences include science fiction, surrealism, and social satire. About his work he has said, "I think many stories say something that is more complex, ambiguous, and contradictory than just a clear, if coded, message." He currently lives in Tel-Aviv.*

# Creative Writing

The first story Maya wrote was about a world in which people split themselves in two instead of reproducing. In that world, every person could, at any given moment, turn into two beings, each half his/her age. Some chose to do this when they were young; for instance, an eighteen-year-old might split into two nine-year-olds. Others would wait until they'd established themselves professionally and financially and go for it only in middle age. The heroine of Maya's story was splitless. She had reached the age of eighty and, despite all the social pressure, insisted on not splitting. At the end of the story, she died.

It was a good story, except for the ending. There was something depressing about that part, Aviad thought. Depressing and predictable. But in the writing workshop she had signed up for, Maya actually got a lot of compliments on the ending. The instructor, who was supposed to be this well-known writer, even though Aviad had never heard of him, told her that there was something soul-piercing about the banality of the ending, or some other piece of crap. Aviad saw how happy that compliment made Maya. She was very excited when she told him about it. She recited what the writer had said to her the way people recite a verse from the Bible. And Aviad, who had originally tried to suggest a different ending, backpedaled and said that it was all a matter of taste and that he really didn't understand much about it.

It had been her mother's idea that she should go to a creative writing workshop. She'd said that a friend's daughter had attended one and enjoyed it very much. Aviad also thought it would be good for Maya to get out more, to do something with herself. He could always bury himself in work, but since the miscarriage, she never left the house. Whenever he came home he found her in the living room, sitting up straight on the couch. Not reading, not watching TV, not even crying. When Maya hesitated about the course, Aviad knew how to persuade her. "Go once, give it a try," he said, "the way a kid goes to day camp." Later he realized that it had been a little insensitive of him to use a child as an example after what they'd been through two months before. But Maya actually smiled and said that day camp might be just what she needed.

The second story she wrote was about a world in which you could see only the people you loved. The protagonist was a married man in love with his wife. One day, his wife walked right into him in the hallway and the glass he was holding fell and shattered on the floor. A few days later, she sat down on him as he was dozing in an armchair. Both times, she wriggled out of it with an excuse: she'd had something else on her mind; she hadn't been looking when she sat down. But the husband started to suspect that she didn't love him anymore. To test his theory, he decided to do something drastic: he shaved off the left side of his mustache. He came home with half a mustache, clutching a bouquet of anemones. His wife thanked him for the flowers and smiled. He could sense her groping the air as she tried to give him a kiss. Maya called the story "Half a Mustache," and told Aviad that when she had read it aloud in the workshop, some people cried. Aviad said, "Wow," and kissed her on the forehead. That night, they fought about some stupid little thing. She'd forgotten to pass on a message or something like that, and he yelled at her. He was to blame, and in the end he apologized. "I had a hellish day at work," he said, and he stroked her leg, trying to make up for his outburst, "Do you forgive me?" She forgave him.

The workshop instructor had published a novel and a collection of short stories. Neither had been much of a success, but they'd had a few good reviews. At least, that's what the saleswoman at a bookstore near Aviad's office told him. The novel was very thick, 624 pages. Aviad bought the book of short stories. He kept it in his desk and tried to read a little during lunch breaks. Each story in the collection took place in a different country. It was a kind of gimmick. The blurb on the back cover said that the writer had worked for years as a tour guide and had traveled in Cuba and Africa and that his travels had influenced his writing. There was also a small black-and-white photograph of him. In it, he had the kind of smug smile of someone who feels lucky to be who he is. The writer had told Maya, she said to Aviad, that when the workshop was over, he'd send her stories to his editor. And, although she shouldn't get her hopes up, publishers these days were desperate for new talent.

Her third story started out funny. It was about a pregnant woman who gave birth to a cat. The hero of the story was the husband, who suspected that the cat wasn't his. A fat ginger tomcat that slept on the lid of the dumpster right below the window of the couple's bedroom gave the husband a condescending look every time he went downstairs to throw out the garbage. In the end, there was a violent clash between the husband

and the cat. The husband threw a stone at the cat, who countered with bites and scratches. The injured husband, his wife, and the kitten she was breastfeeding went to the clinic for him to get a rabies shot. He was humiliated and in pain, but tried not to cry while they were waiting. The kitten, sensing his suffering, curled itself from its mother's embrace, went over to him, and licked his face tenderly, offering a consoling "Meow."

"Did you hear that?" the mother asked emotionally. "He said 'Daddy.'"

At that point, the husband could no longer hold back his tears. And when Aviad read that passage, he had to try hard not to cry too. Maya said that she'd started writing the story even before she knew she was pregnant again. "Isn't it weird," she asked, "how my brain didn't know yet, but my subconscious did?"

The next Tuesday, when Aviad was supposed to pick her up after the workshop, he arrived half an hour early, parked his car in the lot, and went to find her. Maya was surprised to see him in the classroom, and he insisted that she introduce him to the writer. The writer reeked of body lotion. He shook Aviad's hand limply and told him that if Maya had chosen him for a husband, he must be a very special person.

Three weeks later, Aviad signed up for a beginner's creative writing class. He didn't say anything about it to Maya, and to be on the safe side, he told his secretary that if he had any calls from home, she should say that he was in an important meeting and couldn't be disturbed. The other members of the class were elderly women, who gave him dirty looks. The thin, young instructor wore a headscarf, and the women in the class gossiped about her, saying that she lived in a settlement in the occupied territories and had cancer. She asked everyone to do an exercise in automatic writing. "Write whatever comes into your head," she said. "Don't think, just write." Aviad tried to stop thinking. It was very hard. The old women around him wrote with nervous speed, like students racing to finish an exam before the teacher tells them to put their pens down, and after a few minutes, he began writing too.

The story he wrote was about a fish that was swimming happily along in the sea when a wicked witch turned it into a man. The fish couldn't come to terms with his transformation and decided to chase down the wicked witch and make her turn him back into a fish. Since he was an especially quick and enterprising fish, he managed to get married while he was pursuing her, and even to establish a small company that imported plastic products from the Far East. With the help of the enormous knowledge he had gained as a fish that had crossed the seven seas, the company began to thrive and even went public. Meanwhile, the wicked witch, who was a little tired after all her years of wickedness, decided to find all the people and creatures she'd cast spells on, apologize to them, and restore them to their natural state. At one point, she even went to see the fish she had turned into a man. The fish's secretary asked her to wait until he'd finished a satellite meeting with his partners in Taiwan. At that stage in his life, the fish could hardly remember that he was in fact a fish, and his company now controlled half the world. The witch waited several hours, but when she saw that the meeting wouldn't be ending anytime soon, she climbed onto her broom and flew off. The fish kept doing better and better, until one day, when he was really old, he looked out the window of one of the dozens of huge shoreline buildings he'd purchased in a smart real estate deal, and saw the sea. And suddenly he remembered that he was a fish. A very rich fish who controlled many subsidiary companies that were traded on stock markets around the world, but still a fish. A fish who, for years, had not tasted the salt of the sea.

When the instructor saw that Aviad had put down his pen, she gave him an inquiring look. "I don't have an ending," he whispered apologetically, keeping his voice down so as not to disturb the old ladies who were still writing.

---

**JHUMPA LAHIRI** ▨ **(b. 1967)**

*Born in London to immigrants from Bengal, at the age of three, Lahiri moved to the United States, where her father was a college librarian. After earning degrees at Barnard and Boston University, Lahiri held a two-year fellowship at the Provincetown Arts Center, during which time she tried, with little success, to publish her short fiction. Her first collection of stories, The Interpreter of Maladies, was published in 1999, selling more than 600,000 copies and winning the Pulitzer Prize. Lahiri's fiction appears regularly in The New Yorker, and a new novel, The Lowland, appeared in 2013. Focusing mainly on the experiences of Indian Americans, Lahiri has said, "What drew me to my craft was the desire to force the two worlds I occupied to mingle on the page as I was not brave enough, or mature enough, to allow in life." "A Temporary Matter" describes, with elegant symbolism, a relationship that has run out of future.*

## A Temporary Matter

The notice informed them that it was a temporary matter: for five days their electricity would be cut off for one hour, beginning at 8 P.M. A line had gone down in the last snowstorm, and the repairmen were going to take advantage of the milder evenings to set it right. The work would affect only the houses on their quiet tree-lined street, within walking distance of a row of brick-faced stores and a trolley stop, where Shoba and Shukumar had lived for three years.

"It's good of them to warn us," Shoba conceded after reading the notice aloud, more for her own benefit than for Shukumar's. She let the strap of her leather satchel, plump with files, slip from her shoulders, and left it in the hallway as she walked into the kitchen. She wore a navy-blue poplin raincoat over gray sweatpants and white sneakers, looking, at thirty-three, like the type of woman she'd once claimed she would never resemble.

She'd come from the gym. Her cranberry lipstick was visible only on the outer reaches of her mouth, and her eyeliner had left charcoal patches beneath her lashes. She used to look this way sometimes. Shukumar thought, on mornings after a party or a night at a bar, when she'd been too lazy to wash her face, too eager to collapse into his arms. She dropped a sheaf of mail on the table without a glance. Her eyes were still fixed on the notice in her other hand. "But they should do this sort of thing during the day."

"When I'm here, you mean," Shukumar said. He put a glass lid on a pot of lamb, adjusting it so only the slightest bit of steam could escape. Since January he'd been working at home, trying to complete the final chapters of his dissertation on agrarian revolts in India. "When do the repairs start?"

"It says March 19th. Is today the nineteenth?" Shoba went over to the framed corkboard that hung on the wall by the fridge, bare except for a calendar—a Christmas gift from a friend, even though Shoba and Shukumar hadn't celebrated Christmas last year.

"Today then," Shoba announced. "You have a dentist appointment next Friday, by the way."

Shukumar ran his tongue over the tops of his teeth; he'd forgotten to brush them that morning. He hadn't left the house all day. The more Shoba stayed out, and the more she began putting in extra hours at work and taking on additional projects, the more he wanted to stay in, not even leaving to get the mail, or to buy fruit or wine at the stores by the trolley stop.

Six months ago, in September, Shukumar was at an academic conference in Baltimore when Shoba went into labor, three weeks before her due date. He hadn't wanted to go to the conference, but she had insisted; it was important to make contacts, and he would be entering the Job market next year. She told him that she had his number at the hotel, and a copy of his schedule and flight numbers, and she had arranged with her friend Gillian for a ride to the hospital in the event of an emergency. When the cab had pulled away that morning for the airport, Shoba stood waving goodbye in her robe, with one arm resting on the mound of her belly as if it were a perfectly natural part of her body.

Each time he thought of that moment, the last moment he saw Shoba Pregnant, it was the cab he remembered most, a station wagon, painted red with blue lettering. It was cavernous compared with their own car. Although Shukumar was six feet tall, with hands too big ever to rest comfortably in the pockets of his jeans, he felt dwarfed in the back seat. As the cab sped down Beacon Street, he imagined a day when he and Shoba might need a station wagon of their own. He pictured himself gripping the wheel, as Shoba turned around to hand their children juice boxes. Once, these images of parenthood had troubled Shukumar, adding to his anxiety that he was still a student at thirty-five. But that early-autumn morning, the trees heavy with bronze leaves, he welcomed the image for the first time.

A member of the hotel staff had handed him a stiff square of stationery. It was only a telephone number, but Shukumar knew it was the hospital. When he got back to Boston it was over. The baby had been born dead. Shoba was lying on a bed, asleep, in a private room so small there was barely enough space to stand beside her, in a wing of the hospital they hadn't been to on the tour for expectant parents. Her placenta had weakened and she'd had a cesarean, though not quickly enough. The doctor explained that these things happen. He smiled in the kindest way it was possible to smile at people one knew only professionally. Shoba would be back on her feet in a few weeks. There was nothing to indicate that she would not be able to have children in the future.

Shukumar gathered onion skins in his hands and let them drop into the garbage, on top of the ribbons of fat he'd trimmed from the lamb. He ran the water in the sink, soaking the knife and the cutting board, and rubbed a lemon half along his fingertips to get rid of the garlic smell, a trick he'd learned from Shoba. It was seven-thirty. Through the window he saw the sky, like soft black pitch. Uneven banks of snow still lined the sidewalks, though it was warm enough for people to walk about without hats or gloves. Nearly three feet had fallen in the last storm, and for a week people had to walk in single file, in narrow trenches. For a week, that was Shukumar's excuse for not leaving the house. But now the paths were widening, and water drained steadily into grates in the pavement.

"The lamb won't be done by eight," Shukumar said. "We may have to eat in the dark."

"We can light candles," Shoba said, She unclipped her hair, coiled neatly at her nape during the days, and pried the sneakers from her feet. "I'm going to shower before the lights go," she said, heading for the staircase. "I'll be down."

Shukumar moved her satchel and her sneakers to the side of the fridge. She wasn't this way before. She used to put her coat on a hanger, her sneakers in the closet, and she paid bills as soon as they came. But now she treated the house as if it were a hotel. The fact that the yellow chintz armchair in the living room clashed with the blue-and maroon Turkish carpet no longer bothered her. On the enclosed porch at the back of the house, a crisp white bag still sat on the wicker chaise, filled with lace she had once planned to turn into curtains.

With no lights, they would have to eat together. For months now they'd served themselves from the stove, and he'd take his plate into his study, letting the meal grow cold on his desk before shoving it into his mouth without pause, while Shoba took her plate to the living room and watched game shows, or proofread files with her arsenal of colored pencils at hand.

At some point in the evening she visited him. When he heard her approach he began typing sentences. She would rest her hands on his shoulders and stare with him into the blue glow of the computer screen. "Don't work too hard," she would say after a minute or two, and head off to bed. It was the one time in the day she sought him out, and yet he'd come to dread it. He knew it was something she forced herself to do. She would look around the walls of the room, which they had decorated together last summer with a border of marching ducks and rabbits playing trumpets and drums. By the end of August there was a cherry crib under the window, and a rocking chair with checkered cushions. Shukumar had disassembled it all before bringing Shoba back from the hospital, scraping off the rabbits and ducks with a spatula. For some reason the room did not haunt him the way it haunted Shoba. In January, when he stopped working at his carrel in the library, he set up his desk there deliberately, partly because the room soothed him, and partly because it was a place Shoba avoided.

In the kitchen, Shukumar began to open drawers. He tried to find a candle among the scissors, the eggbeaters and whisks, the mortar and pestle she'd bought in a bazaar in Calcutta and had used to pound garlic cloves and cardamom pods, back when she used to cook. He found a flashlight, but no batteries, and a half-empty box of birthday candles. Shoba had thrown him a surprise birthday party last May. There had been a hundred and twenty people crammed into the house—all the friends and the friends of friends they now systematically avoided. Bottles of Vinho Verde had nested in a bed of ice in the bathtub. Shoba was in her fifth month, drinking ginger ale from a Martini glass. She had made a vanilla cream cake with custard and spun sugar. All night she kept Shukumar's long fingers linked with hers as they walked among the guests at the party.

Since September their only guest had been Shoba's mother. She came from Arizona and stayed with them for two months after Shoba returned from the hospital. She cooked dinner every night, drove herself to the supermarket, washed their clothes, put them away. She was a religious woman. She set up a small shrine, a framed picture of a lavenderfaced goddess and a plate of marigold petals, on the bedside table in the guest room, and prayed twice a day for healthy grandchildren in the future. She was polite to Shukumar without being friendly. She folded his sweaters with an expertise she had learned from her job in a department store. She replaced a missing button on his winter coat and knit him a beige and brown scarf, presenting it to him without the least bit of ceremony, as if he had only dropped it and hadn't noticed. She never talked to him about Shoba; once, when he mentioned the baby's death, she looked up from her knitting and said, "But you weren't even there."

He looked for something to put the birthday candles in and settled on the soil of a potted ivy that normally sat on the windowsill over the sink. Even though the plant was inches from the tap, the soil was so dry that he had to water it first before the candles would stand straight. He pushed aside the things on the kitchen table, the piles of mail, the unread library books. He remembered their first meals there, when they were so thrilled to be married, to be living together at last, that they would just reach for each other foolishly, more eager to make love than to eat. He put down two embroidered placemats, a wedding gift from an uncle in Lucknow, and set out the plates and wine-glasses they usually saved for guests. He put the ivy in the middle, the white-edged, star-shaped leaves girded by ten little candles. He tuned the radio to a jazz station.

"What's all this?" Shoba asked when she came downstairs. Her hair was wrapped in a thick white towel. She undid the towel and draped it over a chair, allowing her hair, damp and dark, to fall across her back. As she walked absently toward the stove she took out a few tangles with her fingers. She wore a clean pair of sweat-pants, a T-shirt, an old flannel robe. Her stomach was flat again, her waist narrow before the flare of her hips, the belt of the robe tied in a floppy knot.

It was nearly eight. Shukumar put some lentils from the night before into the microwave oven, punching the numbers on the timer. "You made rogan josh," Shoba observed, looking through the glass lid at the bright paprika stew.

Shukumar took out a piece of lamb, pinching it quickly between his fingers so as not to scald himself. He prodded a larger piece with a serving spoon to make sure the meat slipped easily from the bone. "It's ready," he announced.

Once she had done all the cooking. Now he combed through her cookbooks every afternoon, following her pencilled-in instructions to use two teaspoons of ground coriander seeds instead of one, or red lentils instead of yellow. Each of the recipes was dated, telling when they had first eaten the dish together. April 2nd, cauliflower with fennel. January 14th, chicken with almonds and sultanas. He had no memory of eating those meals, and yet there they were recorded in her neat proofreader's hand. Shukumar enjoyed cooking now. It was the one thing that made him productive. If it weren't for him, he knew, Shoba would eat a bowl of cereal for her dinner.

The microwave had just beeped when the lights went out, and the music disappeared. "Perfect timing," Shoba said.

"All I could find were birthday candles." He lit up the ivy, keeping the rest of the candles and a book of matches by his plate.

"It doesn't matter," she said, running a finger along the stem of her wineglass. "It looks lovely."

In the dimness, he knew how she sat, a bit forward in her chair, ankles crossed against the lowest rung, left elbow on the table. During his search for the candles, Shukumar had found a bottle of wine in a crate he had thought was empty. Every few minutes he lit a few more birthday candles and drove them into the soil of the pot.

"It's like India," Shoba said, "Sometimes the current disappears for hours at a stretch. I once had to attend an entire rice ceremony in the dark. The baby just cried and cried. It must have been so hot."

Their baby would never have a rice ceremony, Shukumar considered. Shoba had made the guest list, and decided on which of her three brothers she was going to ask to feed the child its first taste of solid food, at six months if it was a boy, seven if it was a girl.

"Are you hot?" he asked her. He pushed the blazing ivy pot to the other end of the table, making it even more difficult for them to see each other. He was suddenly irritated that he couldn't go upstairs and sit in front of the computer.

"No, it's delicious," she said, tapping her plate with her fork. "It really is."

He refilled the wine in her glass. She thanked him.

They weren't like this before. Now he had to struggle to say something that interested her, something that made her look up from her plate, or from her proofreading files. Eventually he had given up trying to amuse her. He learned not to mind the silences.

"I remember during power failures at my grandmother's house, we all had to say something," Shoba continued. He could barely see her face, but from her tone he knew her eyes were narrowed, as if trying to focus on a distant object. It was a habit of hers.

"Like what?"

"I don't know. A little poem. A joke. A fact about the world. For some reason my relatives always wanted me to tell them the names of my friends in America. I don't know why the information was so interesting to them. The last time I saw my aunt, she asked after four girls I went to elementary school with in Tucson. I barely remember them now."

Shukumar hadn't spent as much time in India as Shoba had. His parents, who settled in New Hampshire, used to go back without him. The first time he'd gone as an infant he'd nearly died of amebic dysentery. His father, a nervous type, was afraid to take him again, in case something were to happen, and left him with his aunt and uncle in Concord. As a teenager he preferred sailing camp or scooping ice cream during the summers rather than going to Calcutta. It wasn't until after his father died, in his last year of college, that the country began to interest him, and he studied its history from course books as if it were any other subject. He wished now that he had his own childhood story of India.

"Let's do that," she said suddenly.

"Do what?"

"Say something to each other in the dark."

"Like what? I don't know any jokes."

"No, no jokes." She thought for a minute. "How about telling each other something we've never told before."

"I used to play this game in high school," Shukumar recalled. "When I got drunk."

"You're thinking of Truth or Dare. This is different. O.K., I'll start." She took a sip of wine. "The first time I was alone in your apartment, I looked in your address book to see if you'd written me in. I think we'd known each other two weeks."

"Where was I?"

"You went to answer the telephone in the other room. It was your mother, and I figured it would be a long call. I wanted to know if you'd promoted me from the margins of your newspaper."

"Had I?"

"No. But I didn't give up on you. Now it's your turn."

He couldn't think of anything, but Shoba was waiting for him to speak. She hadn't appeared so determined in months. He thought back to their first meeting, four years earlier at a lecture hall in Cambridge, where a group of Bengali poets were giving a recital. They'd ended up side by side, on folding wooden chairs. Shukumar was soon bored; he was unable to decipher the literary diction, and couldn't join the rest of the audience as they sighed and nodded solemnly after certain phrases. Peering at the newspaper folded in his lap, he studied the temperatures of cities around the world. Ninety-one degrees in Singapore yesterday, fifty-one in Stockholm.

When he turned his head to the left, he saw a woman next to him making a grocery list on the back of a folder, and was startled to find that she was beautiful.

"O.K.," he said, remembering. "The first time we went out to dinner, to the Portuguese place, I forgot to tip the waiter. I went back the next morning, found out his name, left money with the manager."

"You went all the way back to Somerville just to tip a waiter?"

"I took a cab."

"Why did you forget to tip the waiter?"

The birthday candles had run out, but he pictured her face clearly in the dark, the wide tilting eyes, the full grape-toned lips, the fall at age two from her high chair still visible as a comma on her chin. Each day, Shukumar noticed, her beauty, which had once overwhelmed him, seemed to fade. The cosmetics that had seemed superfluous were necessary now— not to improve her but to define her somehow.

"By the end of the meal I had a funny feeling that I might marry you," he said, admitting it to himself as well as to her for the first time. "It must have distracted me."

The next night Shoba came home earlier than usual. There was lamb left over from the evening before, and Shukumar heated it up so that they were able to eat by seven. He'd gone out that day, through the melting snow, and bought a packet of taper candles from the corner store, and batteries to fit the flashlight. He had the candles ready on the countertop, standing in brass holders shaped like lotuses, but they are under the glow of a copper-shaded ceiling lamp that hung over the table.

When they had finished eating, Shukumar was surprised to see that Shoba was stacking her plate on top of his, and then carrying them toward the sink. He had assumed that she would retreat to the living room, behind her barricade of files.

"Don't worry about the dishes," he said, taking them from her hands.

"It seems silly not to," she replied, pouring a drop of detergent onto a sponge. "It's nearly eight o'clock."

His heart quickened. All day Shukumar had looked forward to the lights going out. He thought about what Shoba had said the night before, about looking in his address book. It felt good to remember her as she was then, how bold yet nervous she'd been when they first met, how hopeful. They stood side by side at the sink, their reflections fitting together in the frame of the window. It made him shy, the way he felt the first time they stood before a mirror. He couldn't recall the last time they'd been photographed. They had stopped attending parties, went nowhere together. The film in his camera still contained pictures of Shoba, in the yard, when she was pregnant.

After finishing the dishes, they learned against the counter, drying their hands on either end of a towel. At eight o'clock the house went black. Shukumar lit the wicks of the candles, impressed by their long, steady flames. "Let's sit outside," Shoba said. "I think it's warm still."

They each took a candle and sat down on the steps. It seemed strange to be sitting outside with patches of snow still on the ground. But everyone was out of their houses tonight, the air fresh enough to make people restless. Screen doors opened and closed. A small parade of neighbors passed by with flashlights.

"We're going to the bookstore to browse," a silver-haired man called out. He was walking with his wife, a thin woman in a windbreaker, and holding a dog on a leash. They were the Bradfords, and they had tucked a sympathy card into Shoba and Shukumar's mail-box back in September. "I hear they've got their power."

"They'd better," Shukumar said. "Or you'll be browsing in the dark."

The woman laughed, slipping her arm through the crook of her husband's elbow. "Want to join us?"

"No thanks," Shoba and Shukumar called out together. It surprised Shukumar that his words matched hers.

He wondered what Shoba would tell him in the dark. The worst possibilities had already run through his head. That she'd had an affair. That she didn't respect him for being thirty-five and still a student. That she blamed him for being in Baltimore, the way her mother did. But he knew those things weren't true. She'd been faithful, as had he. She believed in him. It was she who had insisted he go to Baltimore. What didn't they know about each other? He knew she curled her fingers tightly when she slept, that her body twitched during bad dreams. He knew she favored honeydew over cantaloupe. He knew that when they returned from the hospital the first thing she did as she walked into the house was to pick out objects of theirs and toss them into a pile in the hallway; books from the shelves, plants from windowsills, paintings from walls, photos from tables, pots and pans that hung from the hooks over the stove. Shukumar had stepped out of her way, watching as she moved methodically from room to room. When she was satisfied, she stood staring at the pile she'd made, her lips drawn back in such distaste that Shukumar had thought she would spit. Then she'd started to cry.

He began to feel cold as he sat there on the steps. He felt that he needed her to talk first, in order to reciprocate.

"That time when your mother came to visit us," she said finally. "When I said one night that I had to stay late at work, I went out with Gillian and had a Martini."

He looked at her profile, the slender nose, the slightly masculine set of her jaw. He remembered that night well; eating with his mother, tired from teaching two classes back to back, wishing Shoba were there to say more of the right things, because he could come up only with wrong ones. It had been twelve years since his father had died, and his mother had come to spend two weeks with him and Shoba, to honor his memory together. Each night his mother cooked something his father had liked, but she was too upset to eat the dishes herself, and her eyes would well up as Shoba stroked her hand. "It's so touching," Shoba had said to him at the time. Now he saw Shoba with Gillian, in the bar with striped velvet sofas, the one they used to go to after the movies, making sure she got her extra olive, asking Gillian for a cigarette. He imagined her complaining, and Gillian sympathizing about visit from in-laws. It was Gillian who had driven Shoba to the hospital.

"Your turn," she said, stopping his thoughts.

At the end of their street Shukumar heard sounds of a drill and the electricians shouting over it. He looked at the darkened façades of the houses lining the street. Candles glowed in the windows of one. Smoke rose from a chimney.

"I cheated on my Oriental Civilization exam in college," he said. "It was my last semester, my last set of exams. My father had died a few months before. I could see the blue book of the guy next to me. He was an American guy, a maniac. He knew Urdu and Sanskrit. I couldn't remember if the verse we had to identify was an example of a *ghazal* or not. I looked at his answer and copied it down."

It had happened over fifteen years ago. He felt a relief now, having told her.

She turned to him, looking not at his face but at his shoes— old moccasins he wore as if they were slippers, the leather at the back permanently flattened. She took his hand and pressed it. "You didn't have to tell me why you did it," she said, moving closer to him.

They sat together until nine o'clock, when the lights came on. They heard some people across the street clapping from their porch, and televisions being turned on. The Bradfords walked back down the street, eating ice-cream cones, and waving. Shoba and Shukumar waved back. Then they stood up, his hand still in hers, and went inside.

Somehow, without either of them saying anything, it had turned into this. Into an exchange of confessions—the little ways they'd hurt or disappointed each other, and themselves. The following day Shukumar thought for hours about what to say to her. He was torn between admitting that he had once ripped out a photo of a woman in one of the fashion magazines she used to subscribe to and carried it in his books for a week, or saying that he really hadn't lost the sweater-vest she bought him for their third wedding anniversary but had exchanged it at Filene's and that he had got drunk alone in the middle of the day at a hotel bar. For their previous anniversary, Shoba had cooked a tencourse dinner just for him. This gift depressed him. "My wife gave me a sweater-vest for our anniversary," he complained to the bartender, his head heavy with cognac. "What do you expect?" the bartender had replied. "You're married."

As for the picture of the woman, he didn't know why he'd ripped it out. She wasn't as pretty as Shoba. She wore a white sequinned dress, and had a sullen face, and lean, mannish legs. Shoba had been pregnant at the time, her stomach suddenly immense, to the point where Shukumar no longer wanted to touch her. The first time he saw the picture he was lying in bed next to her, watching her as she read. When he noticed the magazine in the recycling pile he found the woman and tore out the page as carefully as he could. For about a week he allowed himself a glimpse each day. He felt an intense desire for the woman, but it was a desire that turned to disgust after a minute or two. It was the closest he'd come to infidelity.

He told Shoba about the sweater on the third night, the picture on the fourth. She said nothing as he spoke. She simply listened, and then she took his hand, pressing it as she had before. On the third night, she told him that once, after a lecture they'd attended, she let him speak to the chairman of his department even though there was a dab of pâté on his chin. She'd been irritated with him, and so she'd let him go on and on, about securing his fellowship for the following semester, without putting a finger to her own chin as a signal. The fourth night, she said that she never liked the one poem he'd ever published, in a literary magazine in Utah. He'd written the poem after meeting Shoba. She added that she found the poem sentimental.

Something happened when the house was dark. They were able to talk to each other again. The third night after supper they'd sat together on the sofa, and once it was dark he began kissing her awkwardly on her forehead and her face. The fourth night they walked carefully upstairs, to bed, feeling together for the final step with their feet before the landing, and making love with a desperation they had forgotten. she wept without sound, and whispered his name, and traced his eyebrows with her finger in the dark. As he made love to her he wondered what he would say to her the next night, and what she would say, the thought of it exciting him. "Hold me," he said. "Hold me in your arms." By the time the lights came back on downstairs, they'd fallen asleep.

The morning of the fifth night Shukumar found another notice from the electric company in the mailbox. The line had been repaired ahead of schedule, it said. He was disappointed. He had planned on making shrimp malai for Shoba, but when he arrived at the store he didn't feel like cooking anymore. It wasn't the same, he thought, knowing that the lights wouldn't go out. In the store the shrimp looked gray and thin. The coconut-milk tin was dusty and overpriced. Still, he bought them, along with a beeswax candle and two bottles of wine.

She came home at seven-thirty. "I suppose this is the end of our game," he said when he saw her reading the notice.

She looked at him. "You can still light candles if you want." She hadn't been to the gym tonight. She wore a suit beneath her raincoat. Her makeup had been retouched.

When she went upstairs to change. Shukumar poured himself some wine and put on a Thelonious Monk record that she liked.

When she came downstairs they ate together. She didn't thank him or compliment him. They simply ate in a darkened room, in the glow of a beeswax candle. They had survived a difficult time. They finished off the shrimp. They finished off the first bottle of wine and moved on to the second. They sat together until the candle had nearly burned away. She shifted in her chair, and Shukumar thought that she was about to say something. But instead she blew out the candle, stood up, turned on the light switch, and sat down again.

"Shouldn't we keep the lights off?" Shukumar asked.

She set her plate aside and clasped her hands on the table. "I want you to see my face when I tell you this," she said gently.

His heart began to pound. The day she told him she was pregnant, she had used the very same words, saying them in the same gentle way, turning off the basketball game he'd been watching on television. He hadn't been prepared then. Now he was.

Only he didn't want her to be pregnant again. He didn't want to have to pretend to be happy.

"I've been looking for an apartment and I've found one," she said, narrowing her eyes on something, it seemed, behind his left shoulder. It was nobody's fault, she continued. They'd been through enough. She needed some time alone. She had money saved up for a security deposit. The apartment was on Beacon Hill, so she could walk to work. She had signed the lease that night before coming home.

She wouldn't look at him, but he stared at her. It was obvious that she'd rehearsed the lines. All this time she'd been looking for an apartment, testing the water pressure, asking a realtor if heat and hot water were included in the rent. It shocked Shukumar, knowing that she had spent these past days preparing for a life without him. He was relieved and yet he was sickened. This was what she'd been trying to tell him for the past four evenings. This was the point of her game.

Now it was his turn to speak. There was something he'd sworn he would never tell her, and for six months he had done his best to block it from his mind. Before the ultrasound she had asked the doctor not to tell her the sex of their child, and Shukumar had agreed. She had wanted it to be a surprise.

Later, those few times they talked about what had happened, she said at least they'd been spared that knowledge. In a way she almost took pride in her decision, for it enabled her to seek refuge in a mystery. He knew that she assumed it was a mystery for him, too. He'd arrived too late from Baltimore—when it was all over and she was lying on the hospital bed. But he hadn't. He'd arrived early enough to see their baby, and to hold him before they cremated him. At first he had recoiled at the suggestion, but the doctor said holding the baby might help him with the process of grieving. Shoba was asleep. The baby had been cleaned off, his bulbous lids shut tight to the world.

"Our baby was a boy," he said. "His skin was more red than brown. He had black hair on his head. He weighed almost five pounds. His fingers were curled shut, just like yours in the night."

Shoba looked at him now, her face contorted with sorrow. He had cheated on a college exam, ripped a picture of a woman out of a magazine. He had returned a sweater and got drunk in the middle of the day instead. These were the things he had told her. He had held his son, who had known life only within her, against his chest in a darkened room in an unknown wing of the hospital. He had held him until a nurse knocked and took him away, and he had promised himself that day that he would never tell Shoba, because he still loved her then, and it was the one thing in her life that she had wanted to be a surprise.

Shukumar stood up and stacked his plate on top of hers. He carried the plates to the sink, but instead of running the tap he looked out the window. Outside, the evening was still warm, and the Bradfords were walking arm in arm. As he watched the couple, the room went dark, and he spun around. Shoba had turned the lights off. She came back to the table and sat down, and after a moment Shukumar joined her. They wept together, for the first time in their lives, for the things they now knew.

—1999

---

**SUSAN PERABO** ■ (b.1969)

*Susan Perabo was born in St. Louis and attended Webster College, where she was the first woman to play on an NCAA men's baseball team, a milestone that is commemorated on a plaque in the Baseball Hall of Fame. Following graduate school at the University of Arkansas, she published her first collection of stories,* Who I Was Supposed to Be, *which was named by the Los Angeles Times as Book of the Year. A novel,* The Broken Places, *appeared in 2001, and her short fiction regularly appears in literary journals. She teaches at Dickinson College in Carlisle, Pennsylvania. "The Payoff," which on the surface is similar to much contemporary young adult fiction, explores the deeper mysteries of adult relationships accidentally discovered by its narrator.*

# The Payoff

When they gave us lumps of clay in art class, I made a pencil holder in the shape of a giraffe, and Louise made an ashtray. She molded and baked it, lopsided and heavy as a brick, as a birthday present for her mom, who smoked Kents vigorously and ground them flat with a callused thumb. So Louise had made this poop-brown ashtray, but she'd left it in the art room cooling outside the kiln and didn't remember it until after school, halfway through softball. When practice ended I yelled to my mom to wait on us and we ran back into the building—the side door was always open until five, so kids with softball and soccer could pee—and thundered down the stairs to the basement where the art room was. We didn't know if it would be unlocked or not, but we thought we'd give it a shot.

Louise reached the door first—it was one of those doors with nine little windows, to give kids nine separate chances at breaking something. No sooner had she put her hand on the knob and her face to the middle pane when she reeled back from the door like someone had grabbed a fistful of her long red hair and *yanked* her back.

"Bullshit," she said, for this was our favorite swear word, and we used it indiscriminately.

"What?" I too stepped to the window and was repelled back a step by what I saw inside: our principal, Dr. Dunn, was standing in the archway of the supply closet with his pants crumpled at his ankles and his hands clawing through the short black hair of Ms. McDaniel, our art teacher, who knelt in front of him with her mouth— well, I'd seen enough. I turned to Louise and we both stared at each other in horror and mute shock for what must have been ten full seconds. Then, at once, we both exploded into riotous laughter and burst into motion away from the scene of the crime, ran full blast down the hall and up the stairs, laughing and gasping for air. By the time we slid into the back seat of my mother's paneled station wagon we had our poker faces set, but the image of what we'd witnessed was so vivid in my mind I couldn't believe my mother couldn't see it herself, reflected with perfect detail in the pools of my eyes.

I had two little brothers, Nick and Sam. Their lives revolved around farting, indian burns, and the time worn torture of repeating everything you said, repeating everything you said. Some day I would enjoy the company of them both, my mother assured me, but until then I would need to exercise tolerance.

"Time for *Grade Your Day*" my father said from behind the curtain of steam that rose from his baked potato. "Anne?"

Though research had not yet proven it, my parents were certain that a well-balanced dinner together and a thorough discussion of the days' events would make us confident and bright children. They didn't know it would actually raise our SAT scores, but they were on the right track.

"B," I said, forking a stalk of asparagus.

"D minus-plus-minus-and-a-half," said Sam. He was six.

"A triple plus!" exclaimed Nick.

My father raised his eyebrows. "Win the lottery?"

"Nuh-uh." Nick grinned. "Two fifth graders got in a fight. They were both named Ben, and one of 'ems tooth got knocked out and flew about fifty feet down the hall."

"How awful," my mother said.

"Did Ben start it?" my father asked, winking at me. Though I was only three years older than Nick, I got to be in on all my father's jokes.

"How 'bout you, kiddo?" he asked me. "News of the day?"

"Mrs. Payne subbed in math."

"Oh no," my mother said. "I thought they'd finally gotten rid of her."

I shrugged. "She was there."

"Mrs. Payne is a pain in the butt," Nick said, and Sam snorted.

"That's original," I said. "Only every single person ever to go to our school for the last hundred years has said that."

"Learn anything?" my father asked, undeterred.

I had learned what a blow job (or bj, as Louise told me on the phone before dinner) looked like. I had learned that men didn't actually need to remove their underpants to have sex.

"I learned how to bunt," I said. "At practice."

"Just hold the bat out there," my father said, pretending his steak knife was a Louisville Slugger and wiggling it over his slab of meat. "Just let the ball hit the bat, right?"

"And keep your fingers out of the way," I added.

"That's the most important part," my mother agreed, for my mother was a dodger from way back. In supermarket aisles, she was always the one scooting her cart around to make room for everybody else.

I was regarded with bemused suspicion in the Hanley home, because when Louise and I were in first grade my parents had voted for Richard Nixon. They'd staked a big red sign in our front yard—

4 More Years!

—which is how the Hanleys even knew about it in the first place. Now, even with a democrat in the White House (a peanut farmer, my father was forever pointing out, with a brother on HeeHaw) Mrs. Hanley still couldn't let it drop.

"There she is again," she would say wryly, smoke puffing from her nostrils. "President of the Young Republicans."

"Mom..." Louise would sigh. "Anne is not—" "... anything," I would finish. "I'm not anything. I swear."

On the mantle, in the place where most people had photos of grinning offspring, Mr. and Mrs. Hanley had framed pictures of John and Bobby Kennedy, looking contemplative and doomed. There was a Spiro Agnew velcro dart board on the refrigerator and a faded bumper sticker slapped crookedly across the oven window which said **50 Americans Died Today In Vietnam.** The Hanleys got at least four different newspapers and apparently felt the need to keep them handy for quick reference; there were waist-high stacks of them in every room of the house except for Louise's bedroom. Mrs. Hanley always sat at the dining room table scouring the articles and smoking her Kents, and when Mr. Hanley came home from work he sat on a tattered lawn chair in the middle of the back yard with his feet soaking in a little yellow tub and read until dark.

My mother called them eccentric; she didn't like all the time I spent there, and she often pumped me to find out if Mrs. Hanley had said anything unusual or confusing, anything that had left me feeling *uneasy*. I never gave a thing away; I'd learned earlier than most that the less your parents knew about the concrete details of your day the better off you were. My father thought the Hanleys were lunatics, but unlike my mother he believed it was important for me to be exposed to lunatics—provided they were harmless—in order to be a well rounded adult.

The day after we saw what we saw in the art room, Louise and I holed up after school in the Hanley's basement. Ever since Louise's sister had left for college we had the basement to ourselves: the paneled walls, the matted shag carpet, the stale air of twenty thousand cigarettes smoked by unhappy members of the generation that directly proceeded ours.

"Ms. McDaniel should watch out," Louise said. She was sucking on a Charms Blow Pop, twirling it back and forth over her tongue. "She could get a disease doing that."

Louise knew things. Her sister Donna was seven years older, a freshman in college and willing to talk. Plus, the Hanleys let Louise see R rated movies and read whatever books she wanted. I'd looked at *Playboy* at her house one time, right at the dining room table. My mother wouldn't even let me read *Seventeen* in checkout lines.

"What kind of disease?" I asked.

"You don't even want to know," Louise said, which was her answer when she herself didn't know. "I wonder if they do that every day."

"I bet they do other things, too," I said, and with no warning whatsoever a vivid picture flashed into my mind of Ms. McDaniel carefully painting Dr. Dunn's penis with the very same blue watercolors we'd used last week on our skyscapes. I blushed at my own fantasy: I hadn't even known I had the capacity to create such an image.

"Dr. Dunn," Louise said thoughtfully, tapping her Blowpop on her top teeth. "Dr. Dickdunn. Dr. Dunn Dick Dunderhead."

"Remember last year," I said, "when he yelled at Melanie Moon when she dropped her Rube Goldberg project in the hallway and spilled all that corn oil?"

She scoffed. "He's such an asshole. We could get him in big trouble, you know. We could turn him in to the school board."

"Would he get fired?"

"Sure he would. Plus his wife would divorce him and his kids would hate him and he'd lose all his friends. And everywhere he went people would make sucking sounds."

She slurped obscenely on her Blowpop and I laughed. On the wall behind her was a torn poster that said "What if they had a war and nobody came?" which I had never understood because if "they" had a war then at the very least "they" would be there so it wasn't really accurate to say that *nobody* came.

"Hey," Louise said. "What about blackmail?"

I frowned. "What about it?"

"We could do blackmail on him. Say we'll turn him in unless he pays up."

"Pays *money?*"

"No, Anne—gum. Of course money. Jeez." She tossed her Blowpop stick in a nearby ashtray.

"How much you think we could ask for?" I said.

"We should start small," she said, her eyes narrowing. "That's how you do it. You get 'em on the hook. You make 'em think it's just one time. Then you start to squeeze a little more, and a little more, and—"

I shook my head. "You're making this up. You don't know bullshit."

"What's to know?" she asked. "It's easy money."

It was hard to look at Ms. McDaniel on Monday. Sitting at our art table— once a victim of the school cafeteria, now dying a slow death of scissor scars and clotted paste—Louise and I smirked at each other and in the general direction of the supply closet, but neither of us managed to look up to the front of the room for several minutes. We entirely missed the instructions for the day's project, so when everyone started climbing out of the table and fil- ing out the door we had no idea why and had to ask around. Turned out we were supposed to go outside and search for nature; this week's project was a spring collage.

Ms. McDaniel oversaw our progress from the front steps of the school, and I found my eyes passing over her again and again. I wondered exactly what it was that Dr. Dunn saw in her that led him down the sinful path to the art room. She was new this year and it showed; she always seemed apprehensive when she talked to us as a group, as if at any moment we might all stand up and start squirting glue at her. She'd loosen up once we'd started working, when she could meander around the room murmuring words of encouragement and gentle direction. She wore short skirts and had bobbed hair just under her ears, like she was a tomboy before she became a teacher. She didn't have much in the way of boobs, hardly more than Louise and me, and we weren't even wearing bras yet.

Louise nudged me. "Check that out," she said. I followed her gaze to the window of the principal's office, which faced the front lawn. Dr. Dunn was standing at the window with his arms crossed over his chest, looking out at us. We could only see him from the waist up and for a moment I imagined he didn't have any pants on, that his penis was dangling just out of view. I shook the thought from my head.

"He's gross," Louise said. "He's practically licking his lips."

"Why do you think he likes her?"

"They always like young ones," Louise said. "Donna said she could pick any man out of a crowd and he'd have sex with her, whether he was married or a hundred years old."

"Not any man," I said, thinking of my father standing among the men in Donna's crowd, my father with his shaggy hair and laugh lines around his mouth. Then I imagined my brothers grown up, tall and bearded but making armpit farts in a frantic attempt to draw Donna's attention.

Louise shrugged. "Check this out," she said, handing me a piece of notebook paper. In wavy, capital letters was written:

> Dear Dr. Dunn,
> It has come to our attention that you are having sexual rela-
> tions with the art teacher Laurie McDaniel. Do not ask how we
> have the information, we just do. Unless you want everyone to
> find out your secret, put twenty dollars in an envelope and leave
> it behind the toilet in the middle stall in the second floor girls
> bathroom. Do this tomorrow (Tuesday) or face the consequences.
> —x and y

"Am I X or Y?" I asked, handing the letter back. "You're Y," Louise said. "How come?" "Because I'm X."

"Y is stupid," I said. "Nobody ever heard of Y. How come we can't both be X?"

"Two X's," she said, rolling her eyes. "Uh-huh. That would look really cool, Anne, really professional."

"No, just one X," I said. "For both of us. Just because we're two people we don't have to be two letters."

"Girls!" Ms. McDaniel shouted. She was standing at the front door waving us in. Her hair was fluttering in the breeze and I recalled how it had moved in waves under Dr. Dunn's thick fingers.

On our way to math after lunch, two more floppy salmon swept along in the river of students, I shrewdly allowed Louise's letter to fall from my fingers and onto the floor outside the main office. The letter was folded and taped closed and said DR DUNN in big block letters we tore from the library copy of *Ranger Rick,* so we assumed the secretary would discover it and simply pass it along to him. I sat in math class imagining him at his giant desk, unfolding the letter, staring at it for a moment, then slowly folding it again. Perhaps after school he'd go down to the art room, wave it in Ms. McDaniel's face.

*They've got us right where they want us*
he'd say, or:
*The jig's up.*
Maybe she would kiss him, poke her tongue between his lips.
*Darling,* she would whisper against his teeth. *What will we do?*
We'll *think of something . . .*
He'd fit his hands over her small breasts, rub them with his thumbs.
"Anne?"

I looked up at Mrs. Payne. She was standing at the blackboard in her hideous orange and white flowered dress, her stomach and breasts an indistinguishable flowery lump. Her grotesque bottom lip trembled slightly, and her words came layered in saliva: "Problem 4?"

I didn't know anything about problem 4. That was problem one. Problem two was that thinking about Dr. Dunn and Ms. McDaniel together had made me feel like I had a bubble expanding in my stomach, emptying me of everything but its own strained vulnerability, filling me up with the most palpable absence I'd ever known. My face was numb below my cheekbones and I felt sad and happy at the same time.

"Problem 4," Mrs. Payne croaked.

A word about Mrs. Payne. My mother (and countless others) had complained to Dr. Dunn about her on several occasions, for Mrs. Payne was prone to catastrophic mood swings of blinding speed. One minute she'd be the sweetest old lady you'd ever known, a cuddle and a peppermint at the ready, and the next she'd turn on you like a viper, call you lazy, stupid, hopeless, slobber insults on you until you cried or (in the now famous case of Chris Brewster) wet your pants. Other times she'd seem positively adrift; at least once in a day she began a sentence with "When Mr. Payne was alive ..." and then would launch into a story that might or might not have anything to do with the subject at hand or even with Mr. Payne himself. For instance, we'd be talking about fractions and suddenly Mrs. Payne would say "When Mr. Payne was alive you could buy a sporty car for five-hundred dollars. I had such a car myself that I drove all the way from Moline, Illinois to Boise, Idaho to visit my dear cousin Edith who was so distraught over a man that the only word she'd spoken for a year was *pecan*."

She'd pause. To remember? To consider? Why *pecan*? And then she'd move on as if no interruption had occurred.

"Fourteen," Louise whispered from behind me. In addition to her numerous other afflictions, Mrs. Payne was also half-deaf, so it was pretty easy to cheat on her.

"Fourteen," I said. My lips were dry and I licked them.

"Fourteen," Mrs. Payne said, as if mulling over the existence of the number itself. "Fourteen. Four-tee-een. Fourteen is correct."

"Space case," Louise said as we gathered our books at the end of class. "Thinking about how to spend the money?"

"Yeah," I said.

The payoff came as two ten dollar bills, perfectly crisp as the ones my grandmother always sent for my birthday. Louise and I hit the bathroom between second and third periods the next morning, when it was packed with primping sixth graders, so that if Dr. Dunn was casing the joint he wouldn't be able to tell who'd actually made the pick-up. It was me who went into the middle stall, me who with trembling fingers opened the envelope, certain it would contain a note which said **Anne Foster you are expelled from school for the rest of your life.** But no—there were the two stiff tens, Andrew Jackson with his sly grin—and I slid the envelope into my backpack and remembered to flush the toilet for cover, even though I hadn't used it, and when I emerged from the stall I gave Louise the sign, which was to brush the side of my nose with my index finger. We had seen this in *The Sting*.

"What're you gonna get?" Louise asked. "Think your mom'll take us to the mall this weekend?"

We were in the Hanley's basement again and I felt like I'd swallowed the twenty dollars—in pennies. My stomach seemed to be sagging to my thighs.

"What's wrong?" Louise asked.

"We're gonna get caught," I said. "We're gonna get caught and my parents are going to kill me."

She rolled her eyes. "They're not going to kill you. What's the worst thing they could do to you, legally?"

"They could be very disappointed," I said. In my mind I could see clearly my parents' Very Disappointed faces, the unique mixture of grief and ire and guilt and pity I was fairly sure the two of them had begun assembling the moment they met, so profound and effective it was.

"Tough life," Louise said. "World's smallest violin, Anne."

I had known for years that Louise envied what she perceived as my perfect life and family. What she didn't know was that sometimes—like today—I envied hers. Whenever I did something I knew was wrong I wished my parents would die in a tragic car accident ASAP, before the truth of my flawed character could be revealed. It was an extreme solution, but the only one I could conceive of. Lucky Louise ... the news of her own flawed character would cause little disruption in the Hanley house. Her mother probably wouldn't even look up from the paper.

"We could get two records each," Louise said. "Or we could save it to spend at Six Flags this summer."

"What if we bought something for Ms. McDaniel?"

She stared at me. "What?"

"I don't know." I dug my hands into the shag carpet. "Just, you know. We could buy her something. You know, with part of it."

She shook her head slowly. "You're a freak, Anne. Do you know that?"

"So?" I said. "You're a freak too."

"But you're a different kind of freak than me," she said thoughtfully. She twisted some hair around her finger. "I come from freaks. But you, like, sprouted up all on your own."

"So?"

"So fine," she said. "I'm just making an observation. What'dya want to buy her, ya freak? Frilly underwear?"

"No," I said, my cheeks warming. "Something cool. Like, drawing pencils or something."

"Drawing pencils," she said flatly. "You've thought about this."

I shrugged.

She gazed at me impatiently, with the look of someone who in two or three years would no longer want to be my friend. We were two weird kids who had leapt from the ship of fools and splashed blindly toward each other, scrambled aboard the same life raft. Perhaps it was only a matter of time before we leapt again and made for separate shores.

She threw me one of the tens. "It's your money," she said.

The next day I ditched recess after lunch and ran with a full heart to the art room. Ms. McDaniel was sitting at her desk nibbling on celery sticks and reading a thick book that bore no title on its cover. I shifted from one foot to the other in the doorway until she noticed me.

"Hello, Anne," she said, sliding the book into a desk drawer. She cocked her head cheerfully in the way of young teachers and enthusiastic babysitters. "What can I do for you?"

"I found these," I said. I approached her desk with the pencils held at arm's length in front of me. "Yesterday my mom needed to go to Art Mart and she gave me five dollars to spend and the thing that I wanted cost three-fifty so I picked these up off the sale table that was right next to the cash register and I thought you might want them."

Exhausted from the lie—I'd practiced it a dozen times that morning in the shower—I dropped the pencils on the desk beside her lunch bag. She looked at them curiously, then at me.

"Well, thank you," she said. "That's quite a story."

"It's what happened," I said emphatically, thinking she was on to my lie, but shortly thereafter realizing she was merely making conversation.

"You're very thoughtful," she said. She brushed a wayward hair from her forehead. "I love working with pencils."

"I know," I said. "One time you said that. In class, I mean. You mentioned that."

"I don't think I realized you had such an interest in art," she said.

"Sure," I said. I looked at her smiling expectantly and I wanted to tell her that she didn't have to do all those things to Dr. Dunn, even if he was the principal. "Art's good," I said. "It's, you know, it's really ... it's amazing."

"What did you get at Art Mart?" she asked.

"Paper," I said.

"Drawing paper?"

"Yes," I said. "White."

"Well, it's very thoughtful of you to think of me," she said again. She wadded up her brown paper bag and turned to throw it in the trash can, and when she did the collar of her shirt shifted so that I could see her bra strap. In a burst of vivid color I imagined Dr. Dunn sinking his teeth into that shoulder, tugging on that bra strap like a dog with a rope, and I felt so dizzy I had to hold onto the desk to keep from falling over.

"Anne?" Ms. McDaniel said, turning back to me. "Honey, are you okay?"

> Dear Dr. Dunn,
> If you want to keep your affair quiet, place forty dollars in the envelope and put it in the appointed place.
>
> The x's
>
> ps Don't you think you're a little old for Ms. McDaniel?

Louise frowned. "What the hell is this?"

We were sitting on the school bus in our usual seat, fourth from the back on the right. This particular bus, for reasons none of us understood, always smelled like tuna salad in the morning and Bit-O-Honey in the afternoon.

"What's wrong with it?" I asked.

She ripped the paper in two and dropped it in my lap. "This is about blackmail," she said. "This is not about you being the pope or something."

"She's nice," I said. The bus went in and out of a pothole and the boys in the back seats whooped. "He's just using her for sex."

"Anne," she said. "You don't know anything about this. You don't have any idea what it's like to be an adult."

"Neither do you," I said, though I was realizing more and more this wasn't really true.

"I'm the letter writer from now on," she said. "We're just gonna stick to blackmail. We're not going to get into stuff we don't know anything about."

We dropped off the note the next morning, with directions that $40 be left in the usual spot by 6$^{th}$ period. Right after lunch, Louise went to the nurses' office and according to another kid who was there with a splinter in his palm—barfed the Thursday Special (Sloppy Joe, Tator Tots) in a steaming pile at Nurse Carol's feet. So Louise got sent home to the loving arms of her mother, and I was left alone to secure the afternoon's payoff.

We had planned poorly; my sixth period class was in the west wing of the building, three halls and a flight of stairs away from the bathroom in question. By the time I reached it the warning bell for seventh period had already rung. A couple girls were drying their hands and rushing out when I bolted myself into the middle stall and reached behind the toilet. Despite my tardiness (the final bell was sounding as I grasped my prize), I remained in the stall and tore open the envelope. Inside was a 3 × 5 note card on which was printed, in tidy black letters:

> Anne, Louise: There is nothing to tell. This foolishness ends right now.

Something that felt like cold water rushed from behind my ears all the way down to my heels. My brain flailed about senselessly for at least ten seconds before lighting upon the first thing it could recognize—I *have to get to social studies*. Hands trembling, I started at the latch, then froze when I heard the door to the hallway whoosh open. Six footsteps on soft soled shoes, then silence.

"Louise?" I whispered hopefully, though I knew full well that Louise was at home safe in bed, which is exactly where I wished I were.

"It's not Louise."

It was Ms. McDaniel. I stood in the stall, my knees quaking, wondering: if I didn't open the door, didn't come out willingly, how long would she stand there? An hour? Overnight? Until school let out for the summer? I imagined my family sitting around the dinner table waiting for me, years passing, my mother's patience waning, my father's smile turning melancholy, my brothers stealing away with their own Ms. McDaniels.

I slid the latch to the side, let the door swing open of its own accord. She was leaning against the wall next to the paper towel dispenser. Her face was all blotchy and her lips were somehow crooked, but she wasn't crying. She looked like she should be in the emergency room.

"Well?" she said.

"Hi," I said.

I was standing there holding the index card; I could have run but it seemed pointless. Suddenly she sprang from the wall and grabbed my wrist, twisted it until the note dropped to the floor. Still gripping my wrist, she leaned over and picked it up, read it once, then read it again. Then she straightened up, loosened her grasp, and regarded me coolly.

"Are you satisfied?" she asked.

I had no idea what she meant. More importantly, I didn't know which answer would get me out the door faster. "Yes," I said, then changed my mind. "I mean no. Yes and no. Not really. Sort of." I bit my lip.

"Some day you'll know what it's like to really love someone," she said. She said it kind of gently, like she was talking to a little kid. "Some day you'll know what it's like to look at a man, his neck and his knees and his warm hands, and know that everything that was missing in your life has come knocking."

"Ms. McDaniel—" I said. I'm not sure what I had it in my mind to say, but it didn't really matter, because she wasn't listening.

"And some day, Anne Foster," she said. "Some day some awful little girl you don't even know will ruin your life for no reason. And when that day comes I want you to think of me."

Louise called that night and my father came to get me. I buried my head in my math book and told him I had to study for a test tomorrow.

When she called again I told him the same thing. He returned to my room a few minutes later.

"Louise says you don't have a test in math tomorrow."

"She wouldn't know," I said. "She had to go home early today."

He leaned in the doorway. "Everything okay?"

I wanted to tell him what had happened in the bathroom. I wanted him to sit on the edge of my bed and explain point for point what had transpired, help me understand whatMs McDaniel had said to me. But I knew, somehow more than I'd ever known anything, that even had I the courage to ask the questions (which I did not) that he would be unable to answer a single one of them. It was a realization that left me cold: the machinations of the human heart were inexplicable, not only to me, but to my parents as well, and thus, apparently, to anyone. Was this what Louise had known all along? I wondered. Was there truly no one in her life from whom she had ever, *ever*, expected a satisfying explanation?

"Everything's fine," I said.

"You're gonna to have to tell me sometime," Louise said from her seat at the desk behind me. We were in math class.

I turned to her, deliberately put my finger to my lips.

"What the hell?" she said. "What happened to you?"

"When Mr. Payne was alive..."Mrs. Payne began.

Mrs. Payne, a pain in the butt, a punch line to the joke of every fifth grader. Yesterday she'd been as flat and clear as a pane of glass. Today I gazed through her sagging breasts and jowls and saw her as a young woman, as young as Ms. McDaniel, a mystery slipping out of her nightgown and into the arms of her beloved.

—1999

---

## JILL PATTERSON

*Leslie Jill Patterson tok her Ph.D at Oklahoma State University. Her prose has appeared in Texas Monthly, Baltimore Review, and the Colorado Review. Her recent awards include the 2013 Everett Southwest Literary Award (judged by Lee K. Abbott), the 2014 Time and Place Prize, and a 2014 Soros Justice Fellowship. She teaches creative writing at Texas Tech University and also writes case narratives for capital murder defense attorneys in the state of Texas. About her own fiction, she has said, "I think that if you're going to tackle a dark subject, you better find a way to incorporate some comic relief, just as when you're writing a comic story, you better find a way to mix it up with a little sobriety. Every story needs balance."*

# The Fires We Can't Control

The oak tree and the cypress
grow not in each other's shadow.

*—Kahlil Gibran, The Prophet*

In the first week of June, after thirty-eight days of drought, in the hottest Colorado summer on record, Durango passes a fire ban forbidding cookouts, trash burns, and cigarette smoking outdoors. The same morning, I read in *Cosmo* that we can heat up our love life if I pen a list of five sizzling moments you've given our marriage. I'm instructed to tuck this gift in your briefcase or lunchbox—white collar or blue, it doesn't matter; this is a surprise all men will enjoy. Your response, *Cosmo* promises, will ignite our bedroom.

Lately, we've suffered a fire ban ourselves, neither of us much interested in matches. And sitting at the kitchen table to write you up, I can't think of anything except the thin varicose vein, the signature of old age, that scrawled up my thigh in the last week. This kind of thought douses the mood, and though my three years at the *Durango Herald* ought to help with writer's block, I manage only one sizzler before I quit the assignment.

I tear the sheet of paper from its pad, fold it into a tidy square, tiptoe into the study where you keep your briefcase, and slip my hand, with its gift, inside the front compartment beside your wallet. I let go of our moment—the afternoon you attempted to climb Mt. Sneffels, missed the summit, but came home grateful to be alive. Funny thing, though: when my hand pulls out of your briefcase, it's holding another letter, postmarked from Naturita, a trailer-trash town on the flip side of the San Juan Range that I've heard *Deliverance* jokes about but never visited.

The envelope is purple. The letter is, too. It begins: *I'm lying in a bubble bath, the suds barely covering my nippels.* Some woman named Lori has beat me to the *Cosmo* punch. Lori misspells *nipples*. She misspells *salon*, too; she's gotten a bikini wax in your honor at the local *saloon*. Or maybe a bikini wax is some flirty mixed drink. Lori's got a husband, her own big sizzler she calls The Monster, and while the other affairs have always found ways to refer to me without writing my name—The Mayhag, Shackles, or simply my initial, E.— Lori calls me The Doll, which sounds complimentary, but by the end of the letter, I see it's a reference to amateur voodoo. Because The Doll holds hostage the life meant for her, Lori has stuck a pin in its thigh. Lori spells *its*, meaning "belonging to," with an apostrophe. I am my thigh.

On Sunday, June 9, an urgent voice crackles over the scanner I listen to when fishing for stories for the *Herald*. It's 2:30 p.m. The voice says, "We have a confirmed wildland fire, Missionary Ridge Road."

A spark—the cause of which won't be determined for weeks—has triggered a blaze in a ditch ten miles northeast of Durango, near the entrance to the Weminuche Wilderness. From US 550, seven miles away, travelers see flames as tall as twenty-story buildings, and a plume of smoke, thirteen thousand feet high, blossoms like an atomic mushroom over the mountains.

Frequently, you brag that I'm the type of woman a man marries because she isn't always yapping, yapping. Sometimes a woman mimes a good marriage because words light fires she can't control. At first, she keeps quiet because accusations might make her husband leave. Later, she stays mute because a conviction means *she* should go.

I don't know why Lori's letter angers me after all the years of evidence—emails, text messages, phone records, Valentine cards, roses to you, gifts wrapped pretty that I find in your closet but never see again, an endless list of recipients. Maybe it's Lori's stupidity that's offensive. If you're going to screw around on me, please do so with a Ph.D. or an attorney. Stupid women don't notice where the nearest Walgreen's is; they don't worry with condoms. They have nipples and write about them in letters. They define *mistress* but can't use the word in a sentence. Which, of course, makes sense: if a man cheats, he gets the job done right. Because this isn't about the long haul. You're not going to take Lori home to your mother.

This time, I don't keep quiet. I find Lori's letter and that very night at dinner, I prop it on my spatula and flip it—not my cheesy chicken and rice—onto your plate. You stare at the envelope. Our son does, too.

Like any five-year-old, Noodle enjoys parties more than he suspects parents of deceit, and so he's almost convinced when you tell him Mommy has given you an early birthday card. His brow wrinkles, and his head cocks to the side: it's the same suspicious look he wears when you swear *Noodle* is a cool nickname, not a ticket to a black eye in the boy's room at school, but something a lanky basketball star earns for having a hook shot that's impossible to guard. He looks around the table and raises his little hands, a spoon in one of them, a fork in the other. "Where's the balloons?" he asks. "The cake?" He thinks maybe I've botched the job. His brown eyes well up. He feels sorry for you because birthdays are supposed to be perfect.

I wipe off his chocolate-milk moustache. "You're too much like me," I say. "Don't be so gullible."

You frown—I'm a horrible mother, he's just a child. Then you promise our son that, while I forgot to bake a cake, we'll have ice cream for dessert.

Later, in our bedroom, you tell me I'm controlling. What was I doing rifling through your briefcase? I've invaded your privacy. I have trust issues.

"Do you hear yourself?" I ask.

"Lori's lonely," you explain. "If you knew her, you'd feel sorry for her."

I hate the fact that you've said her name out loud.

"You wouldn't want me to be ugly to a friend," you say.

I shake my head. "God, no. You should definitely fuck her."

The look on your face—your mouth open but stalled into silence—tells me my language horrifies you. I don't know why. If I wrote *fuck* on a piece of paper, rest assured I could spell it correctly. You sit on the edge of the bed, cross your legs, moderate your voice. Just like our therapist. You tell me husbands and wives fill each other's cups, but they shouldn't drink from the same one. You've started reading poetry recently, instead of *The Wall Street Journal*. Metaphors, like a crowd of new friends, a gang of hoodlums, are starting to influence you. When I look at you sitting there, your hands clasped in your lap, wire-rim reading glasses perched on your nose, I don't recognize who I'm watching.

You say, "I'm an oak. You're a cypress."

I cock my head at you. "Really? That's your excuse? The difference between men and women is wood?"

Live oaks usually survive fire because flames can't reach their lofty crowns. Even if a forest of oak burns, the roots survive and sprout vigorously afterward. And live oaks provide dense cover, prevent a flammable understory, and so they shut out the entry of fire from adjacent wildlands. Cedars and other conifers, on the other hand: they drop needles and pinecones, perfect kindling, and their branches grow scruffy and low to the ground. They're ladders that flames climb, swinging like monkeys from limb to limb into the canopy.

Heat, the mistress of flame, spirits through the forest before the advance of a blaze, warming the air, evaporating moisture, and arousing surrounding fuels. Sometimes she rises from a surface fire like smoke up a chimney. Sometimes she skulks along the ground. Her hand pries inside a nest of oak brush; her tongue flickers in the grass. If you look closely, you might see her, a ripple in the air, a negligee untied. If you aren't watching at all, heat, having gone unchecked, will warm surrounding fuels so rapidly, so intensely, that spontaneous combustion occurs.

The day our house burns, my editor rejects the piece I've written about the Missionary Ridge Fire. "What's with the metaphors?" he asks. "This is a newspaper. We print facts, not poetry." His shirt is wrinkled, sweaty. He looks around the newsroom for someone else he can give this assignment to, but then relinquishes. He squints at me. "You live in Aspen Trails?"

I nod.

He remembers now that our house is in the path of the fire. Maybe he thinks danger has warped my ability to write well. Under duress, I let the facts slump over, the spine of a situation turning limp.

"Go home," he says. "Get the story there. Get it right."

When I arrive, you've packed a suitcase and are stepping onto the front porch. You're not exactly waiting to say good-bye. I've simply caught you as you're sneaking out the door.

Noodle stands beside you, wearing last year's Halloween costume: a yellow slicker and galoshes, a fireman's hat made out of a red plastic mixing bowl. He's getting into the spirit of things. "Daddy gets a vacation, but we have to stay here," he explains. "I've got daycare."

"Don't let Daddy lie to you," I say. "Daycare's been cancelled."

Noodle does a double-take, looking back and forth between us, then pondering your bag and the trunk of your car, the lid propped open. The mixing bowl wobbles on his tiny head.

You glare at me. "This is exactly why—." You don't bother finishing that sentence. "I waited," you say instead, "as long as I could to tell you."

Nevermind that you didn't tell me, that, in fact, you've coached our child to deliver the news. Getting caught, I suppose, might feel like a confession, but it isn't one. And I find it disturbing how dishonesty has snuck into our home, dressed like a small kindness. You would have come clean earlier, but you had my wellbeing in mind.

On Thursday, June 13th, officials give early warning to residents of the Aspen Trails subdivision: the Missionary Ridge Fire is less than three miles away and will approach homes in two to four days. A mere forty-five minutes later, the fire engulfs a dense, unlogged area, erupting with new intensity and exhaling another billow of smoke, this time, one that eclipses the sun. The cycle of heat, wind, and fire spins faster now. Residents report the plunge of dead birds from the sky. Cars flip. A small boat vanishes.

"Some fires generate tornados," an information officer tells reporters.

When the vortex collapses, it spreads a tarp of ash and embers between Aspen Trails and the north end of Lemon Reservoir. Less than fifteen minutes later—and only one hour after officials assured residents the flames wouldn't reach their homes for days— firefighters evacuate Aspen Trails when falling cinders spawn a nearby spot fire that stokes into a full burn.

When Noodle and I abandon our home, three hours on your heels, it rains fire overhead. I douse our son with a hose, the water trickling off his mixing bowl helmet, down his slicker, puddling around his galoshes.

"Maybe we need an umbrella," he says, confused.

Before we leave, I follow instructions. I pile tools from the garage— shovels, buckets, a second hose, a ladder—in our front yard in case firefighters need them. I remove the sheer curtains, so flammable, from the dining room and draw tight the thick fireretardant shades in the bedrooms. I douse the pilot light on the water heater. Though officials tell us to grab essentials—our ATM and credit cards, passports, computer files, photo albums—I leave ours behind. It's a life not even I'm interested in saving.

Around Noodle's mouth and nose, I knot a wet bandanna. His blond bangs are sweaty and matted to his forehead. His eyes are wide now, afraid.

"This year, you'll be a gunslinger for Halloween. You look good in a mask." I shape a finger-pistol at him and fire it.

He nods his head, but I know, under that kerchief, his lips are swelling and the snot from crying drips from his nose like it does when he's frightened.

As we walk out the door, Noodle and I hang white T-shirts, three of them, yours, in the living room window, signaling that everyone inside is safe and gone.

That evening, stowed away in a hotel in Durango, Noodle has settled fine, begging me for quarters to plunk in the old shake-a-bed or in the candy machine outside. I stand on the balcony with our neighbors and watch the bursts of flame, the chug of smoke, on the horizon, a battlefield less than eight miles away. No one asks where you are. I think, maybe, if we stand very still, we might hear the cannon-fire of windows and trees exploding.

In the morning, at the front desk, there's an envelope from you, not purple. It contains $200, cash. The letter says, *Dear E.* It says you never burn bridges.

The Missionary Ridge Fire is a blaze one hundred local firemen cannot smother. In forty days, it scorches nearly 73,000 acres and burns 56 homes and 27 outbuildings. Here's what it takes to stop it: 32 National Guard troops, over 1,100 firefighters, Durango Fire and Rescue Authority, U.S. Forest Service Special Agents, federal fire behavior analysts, the Northern Rockies National Incident Management Team, 99 engines, 8 helicopters, and 5 slurry bombers.

Imagine all those firefighters trekking three to five miles everyday through smoke so thick they can't really breathe or see the sun or another firefighter standing two feet away. Imagine working under conditions that require cumbersome fire-retardant clothes. Imagine a twelve-hour shift humping uphill forty-five pounds of equipment—shovels, axes, bladder bags, drip torches, Pulaskis, flappers. There isn't a training manual that prepares them for such labor.

There isn't any drill that prepares them for the internal battle they fight between duty and self-preservation—which must be any human's natural instinct. Imagine the firefighters herded into an evacuated neighborhood. The streets are blank: no cars, no children jumping rope or tossing a football, no noise of the living, just the eerie swirl of wind—the voice of that siren heat—and the chatter of fire sneaking behind. How odd to ask one group of men and women to risk their lives to save the brick buildings surrendered by others.

In the days after our house burns, Noodle and I rent a furnished apartment downtown near the college. We're surrounded by students wearing T-shirts and baggy shorts. Their bellies and noses are pierced; they carry backpacks and skateboards. One afternoon, I catch Noodle offering a Band-Aid to a co-ed after she crashes her bike in our parking lot. She lets him patch up her knee. He blows on it for good measure, our fiveyear- old to the rescue. Afterward, he smiles, tells her his name is *Noodle*, and asks for her phone number. Maybe he's more like you than I realized. Already, he's transforming limitations into charm. How does he know women find little boys so adorable?

I hear from mutual friends that Lori has left her husband for you. That she chain smokes. That she drinks Vodka and pops pills. That she's losing custody of her kids. If their names are complicated, multisyllabic, she probably can't spell them. One morning, I notice a matching varicose vein squiggling up my other thigh. More voodoo magic, I suppose.

And then, 8 a.m., one Saturday, you're asleep in my living room on the couch as if you haven't been missing for two months, as if you had a key or permission and knew exactly where you were when you stumbled through the door. Your dark hair is tousled; you're missing a shoe. Under the blanket Noodle has given you from his bed, you snore just like you used to. Noodle is eating a bowl of cereal he's poured himself, the milk splattered over the counter, onto the floor, the flakes crumbled beneath his feet.

"Dad's home," he says.

I wake you up, ask what do you think you're doing.

"I was wrong to try and save Lori," you say.

Your take on the situation continues to amaze me. While you recognize the need for contrition, you've failed to grasp the crime.

"You can't save someone who doesn't want to be saved," you add.

I think about our house burned to the foundation, the cement slab black as charcoal. I think how at the precise moment our relationship needed saving, you chose to run off and rescue a stranger. You want me to forgive you now for being a super hero.

Still, I don't throw you out. I shop at Wal-Mart, buying you T-shirts, socks, underwear, jeans, tennis shoes. In the mornings, you wake and put on the same clothes instead of cutting the tags off the new ones. You stay at my apartment, watching TV, calling in sick to work. Noodle slouches on the sofa, too, agreeing to watch game shows and CNN though he'd rather watch cartoons. Occasionally, you lay your head in his lap and take a nap while he pets your hair.

Every afternoon, you visit our old therapist alone. You're losing weight. Sometimes the phone rings but no one speaks when I answer. At night, you weep in our bed.

"Dad's sad cause he misses home," Noodle suggests.

There's no way I'll tell our son you're mourning the loss of another woman, not me, not him. It's never occurred to you that we're lost.

"He feels like a stranger here," Noodle adds. "Right?"

I pull the covers over his shoulders, tuck them tight. "Exactly," I say.

There are before and after photographs of the Missionary Ridge Fire, taken by journalists for the *Herald*. In the early shots, the trees are green, the meadows emerald, the homes pastels, the Animas River cerulean. The later shots look like the photographers used black-and-white film, but they didn't. When speaking of their days in the Weminuche, firefighters tell reporters one of the things they can't forget is the squeal of wood, the highpitched *eee*, just before bark flares then explodes.

In the aftermath, black trees like carcass stick-figures are scattered across the hillsides. It's just the mop-up then. In the field, firemen rake back the soil, gray as ash, to prevent erosion. They search for lingering heat with their bare hands.

Today, late October, the insurance company still holds our funds for the rebuild, and winter looms. Noodle's Halloween costume—a sheriff's getup—hangs, newly pressed and ready for the neighborhood walk that evening, in the kitchen doorsill. Propped open, the ironing board crowds the sink, the fridge; my blouse for work is draped over it. I'm scrambling to get through the day, but last night, first snow dusted Twilight Peak, and more is on the way, so Noodle has already moved on. Over breakfast, he makes plans for six snowmen with Red Wings jerseys and hockey masks, an entire team he'll build in the complex's parking lot. When I open the oven door to slide a sheet of biscuits inside, the flush of heat spins me around, takes me back to that list of sizzlers I started so many months ago, before the fire.

There's still the late afternoon when you failed to top Sneffels. You came home, minutes before your mother and I planned on calling Search and Rescue. It was July, but frigid above the treeline, the snow still thigh-deep, your guide a lunatic who took an abandoned trail instead of the groomed one because a man doesn't truly climb a fourteener if he doesn't slog up it. As I called your mother to let her know you were safe, you pushed me against the dryer, buried your head in my neck, your hand up my skirt. I was still on the phone, giving your parents the details. You whispered, "Sorry." You said, "Hang up the phone." And when I came there in the laundry room, the receiver still in my hand, you cried and said you were so glad to be home.

Then, there's this evening, the last in October, when you've finally stopped claiming post-traumatic stress and have returned to work and worked up an appetite. You beat me home and greet me at the door of our apartment after my long day at the *Herald*. "Noodle is trick-or-treating with the sitter," you say, and step toward me, grab my hand in one of yours, yank my head back by the hair, kiss me hard, then take it to the bedroom. Under the sheets, white and cool, you can't finish. Do you think I don't notice or that I imagine it another kindness, a generous substitute, when you slide south? I think about your tongue, Lori's name said aloud, how many names your mouth has harbored. You haven't spoken mine in years, and right about now the initial *E.* sounds too much like the *i* in *Lori*, which is how the word *wife*, a noun containing both vowels, can confuse a smart woman into feeling like the intruder. And when you can't look me in the eye, there in our bed, I picture the live oak, its roots sprouting after flame, fishing for fresh soil, cool water, and I know already there's yet another woman, maybe someone you found even before you came back to me.

The sitter returns Noodle. He and I divide his candy into daily portions that will last till Christmas. Because he begs, I let him sleep in his sheriff's costume. His slender wrists stretch from the sleeves and his ankles peek from the legs though I bought the getup only two weeks before; another seven days, and it would have been too small. Soon, he'll outgrow sitters, his silly nickname, the willingness to believe anything you and I tell him.

Back in our bedroom, you're already snoring. I climb under the covers and lie beside you, thinking about the day our house caught fire. On our list of sizzling moments, this one falls in the middle: In June, which is not so long ago, I found a suitcase at the front door. Noodle was dressed like the super hero you wish you were. A shower of embers fell from the sky; flames pulsed like drums across the valley floor. And you and I, we stood on the bridge between before and after.

Tonight, while you and Noodle are sleeping, I'll rise from this bed and pack your bags and park them by the front door. In the morning, I'll speak a language even you can understand. I'll say the cypress shelters the smallest ember of anger, the fraction of heat, and when she stands beneath the shadow of another tree, then the only promise she offers is fire.

---

**JONATHAN SAFRAN FOER ▨ (b. 1977)**

*Born in Washington, D.C., Jonathan Safron Foer briefly considered a career in medicine before, encouraged by his college writing teacher, Joyce Carol Oates, becoming a full-time writer. His second novel,* Extremely Loud and Incredibly Close, *which centers on the events of 9/11, was made into an Oscar-nominated film starring Tom Hanks and Sandra Bullock.* Eating Animals *(2009) is a memoir of his on-and-off forays into vegetarianism. He currently lives in Brooklyn. "Here We Aren't, So Quickly" was included in the New Yorker's 2010 special issue featuring fiction writers under forty years old.*

# Here We Aren't, So Quickly

### By Jonathan Safran Foer

I was not good at drawing faces. I was just joking most of the time. I was not decisive in changing rooms or anywhere. I was so late because I was looking for flowers. I was just going through a tunnel whenever my mother called. I was not able to make toast without the radio. I was not able to tell if compliments were back-handed. I was not as tired as I said.

You were not able to ignore furniture imperfections. You were too light to arm the airbag. You were not able to open most jars. You were not sure how you should wear your hair, and so, ten minutes late and halfway down the stairs, you would examine your reflection in a framed picture of dead family. You were not angry, just protecting your dignity.

I was not able to run long distances. You were so kind to my sister when I didn't know how to be kind. I was just trying to remove a stain; I made a bigger stain. You were just asking a simple question. I was almost always at home, but I was not always at home at home. You were not able to cope with a stack of more than three books on my bedside table, or mixed currencies in the change dish, or plastic. I was not afraid of being alone; I just hated it. You were just admiring the progress of someone else's garden. I was so tired of food.

We went to the Atacama. We went to Sarajevo. We went to Tobey Pond every year until we didn't. We braved thirteen inches of snow to attend a lecture in a planetarium. We tried having dinner parties. We tried owning nothing. We left handprints in a moss garden in Kyoto, and got each other off under a towel in Jaffa. We braved my parents' for Thanksgiving and yours for the rest, and how did it happen that we were suddenly at my father's side while he drowned in his own body? I lay beside him on the bed, observed my hand reaching for his brow, said, "Despite everything—" "What everything?" he asked, so I said, "Nothing," or nothing.

I was always destroying my passport in the wash. You were always awful at estimating. You were never willing to think of my habits as charming. I was just insisting that it was already too late to master an instrument or anything. You were never one to mention physical pain.

I couldn't explain the cycles of the moon without pen and paper, or with. You didn't know where e-mails *were*. I wouldn't congratulate a woman until she explicitly said she was pregnant. You spent a few minutes every day secretly regretting your laziness that didn't exist. I should have forgiven you for all that wasn't your fault.

You were terrible in emergencies. You were wonderful in "The Cherry Orchard." I was always never complaining, because confrontation was death to me, and because everything was pretty much always pretty much O.K. with me. You were not able to approach the ocean at night. I didn't know where my voice *was* between my phone and yours. You were never standing by the window at parties, but you were always by the window. I was so paranoid about kind words. I was just not watching the news in the basement. You were just making a heroic effort to make things look easy. I was terrible about acknowledging anyone else's efforts. You were not green-thumbed, but you were not content to be not content. I was always in need of just one good dress shirt, or just one something that I never had. You were too injured by things that happened in the distant past for anything to be effortless in the present. I was always struggling to be natural with my hands. You were never immune to unexpected gifts. I was mostly just joking.

I was not neurotic, just apocalyptic. You were always copying keys and looking up words. I was not afraid of quiet; I just hated it. So my hand was always in my pocket, around a phone I never answered. You were not cheap or handy with tools, just hurt by my distance. I was never indifferent to the children of strangers, just frustrated by my own unrelenting optimism. You were not unsurprised when, that last night in Norfolk, I drove you to Tobey Pond, led you by the hand down the slope of brambles and across the rotting planks to the constellations in the water. Sharing our happiness diminished your happiness. I was not going to dance at our wedding, and you were not going to speak. No part of me was nervous that morning.

When you screamed at no one, I sang to you. When you finally fell asleep, the nurse took him to bathe him, and, still sleeping, you reached out your arms.

He was not a terrible sleeper. I acknowledged to no one my inability to be still with him or anyone. You were not overwhelmed but overtired. I was never afraid of rolling over onto him in my sleep, but I awoke many nights sure that he was underwater on the floor. I loved collapsing things. You loved the tiny socks. You were not depressed, but you were unhappy. Your unhappiness didn't make me defensive; I just hated it. He was never happy unless held. I loved hammering things into walls. You hated having no inner life. I secretly wondered if he was deaf. I hated the gnawing longing that accompanied having everything. We were learning to see each other's blindnesses. I Googled questions that I couldn't ask our doctor or you.

They encouraged us to buy insurance. We had sex to have orgasms. You loved reupholstering. I went to the gym to go somewhere, and looked in the mirror when there was something I was hoping not to see. You hated our bed. He could stand himself up, but not get himself down. They fined us for our neighbor's garbage. We couldn't wait for the beginnings and ends of vacations. I was not able to look at a blueprint and see a renovated kitchen, so I stayed out of it. They came to our door during meals, but I talked to them and gave.

I counted the seconds backward until he fell asleep, and then started counting the seconds backward until he woke up. We took the same walks again and again, and again and again ate at the same easy restaurants. They said he looked like them. I was always watching movie trailers on my computer. You were always wiping surfaces. I was always hearing my father's laugh and never remembering his face. You broke everyone's heart until you suddenly couldn't. He suddenly drew, suddenly spoke, suddenly wrote, suddenly reasoned. One night I couldn't help him with his math. He got married.

We went to London to see a play. We tried putting aside time to do nothing but read, but we did nothing but sleep. We were always never mentioning it, because we didn't know what it was. I did nothing but look for you for twenty-seven years. I didn't even know how electricity worked.

We tried spending more time not together. I was not defensive about your boredom, but my happiness had nothing to do with happiness. I loved it when people who worked for me genuinely liked me. We were always moving furniture and never making eye contact. I hated my inability to visit a foreign city without fantasizing about real estate. And then your father was dead. I often wasn't reading the book that I was holding. You were never not in someone's garden. Our mothers were dying to talk about nothing.

At a certain point you became convinced that you were always reading yesterday's newspaper. At a certain point I stopped agonizing over being understood, and became over-reliant on my car's G.P.S. You couldn't tolerate trace amounts of jelly in the peanut-butter jar. I couldn't tolerate gratuitously boisterous laughter. At a certain point I could stare without pretext or apology. Isn't it funny that if God were to reveal and explain Himself, the majority of the world would necessarily be disappointed? At a certain point you stopped wearing sunscreen.

How can I explain the way I shrugged off nuclear annihilation but mortally feared a small fall? You couldn't tolerate people who couldn't tolerate babies on planes. I couldn't tolerate people who insisted that having a coffee after lunch would keep them up all night. At a certain point I could hear my knees and felt no need to correct other people's grammar. How can I explain why foreign cities came to mean so much to me? At a certain point you stopped agonizing over your ambitiousness, but at a certain point you stopped trying. I couldn't tolerate magicians who did things that someone who actually had magical powers would never do.

We were all doing well. I was still in love with the Olympics. The smaller the matter, the more I allowed your approval to mean to me. They kept producing new things that we didn't need that we needed. I needed your approval more than I needed anything. My sister died at a restaurant. My mother promised anyone who would listen that she was fine. They changed our filters. You wanted to see the northern lights. I wanted to learn a dead language. You were in the garden, not planting, but standing there. You dropped two handfuls of soil.

And here we aren't, so quickly: I'm not twenty-six and you're not sixty. I'm not forty-five or eighty-three, not being hoisted onto the shoulders of anybody wading into any sea. I'm not learning chess, and you're not losing your virginity. You're not stacking pebbles on gravestones; I'm not being stolen from my resting mother's arms. Why didn't you lose your virginity to me? Why didn't we enter the intersection one thousandth of a second sooner, and die instead of die laughing? Everything else happened—why not the things that could have?

I am not unrealistic anymore. You are not unemotional. I am not interested in the news anymore, but I was never interested in the news. What's more,

I am probably ambidextrous. I was probably meant to be effortless. You look like yourself right now. I was so slow to change, but I changed. I was probably a natural tennis player, just like my father used to say over and over.

I changed and changed, and with more time I will change more. I'm not disappointed, just quiet. Not unthinking, just reckless. Not willfully unclear, just trying to say it as it wasn't. The more I remember, the more distant I feel. We reached the middle so quickly. After everything it's like nothing. I have always never been here. What a shame it wasn't easy. What a waste of what? What a joke. But come. No explaining or mending. Be beside me somewhere: on the split stools of this bar, by the edge of this cliff, in the seats of this borrowed car, at the prow of this ship, on the all-forgiving cushions of this threadbare sofa in this one-story copper-crying fixer-upper whose windows we once squinted through for hours before coming to our senses: "What would we even do with such a house?"

# POETRY

# Introduction to Poetry

## An Anecdote: Where Poetry Starts

The room is not particularly grand, a large lecture hall in one of the old buildings on the college campus, and the small group of first-year students whose literature class has been dismissed so that they can attend the poetry reading has taken seats near the back of the room. They have been encouraged to come for several weeks by their instructor, and when she enters, she looks around the room and nods in their direction, smiling.

The seats gradually fill. The crowd is a mixed one—several men and women known by sight as senior faculty members; a scattering of other older visitors, many of them apparently from the community; a large contingent of instructors and graduate students from the English Department sitting in the front rows; and small clusters of undergraduates scattered throughout the room.

One of the students scans the crowd, wondering aloud which is the poet. On the walk to the reading, several fellow class members decided that the poet, a cadaverous gray-haired man wrapped in a black cloak, would recite his poems in a resonant baritone, preferably with a strong breeze tossing his hair. Speculating on how the wind effect might be managed inside a lecture hall made them laugh.

Now the crowd grows quiet as the students' instructor steps to the podium and adjusts the microphone. She makes a few complimentary remarks about the strong turnout and thanks several benefactors for their support of poetry at the university. Then she introduces the guest. Her students know most of this information, for they have studied several of his poems in class that week, but they are still slightly surprised when he rises to polite applause and takes the lectern. The balding middle-age man wearing a golf shirt could be taken for a professor in any campus department, and when he adjusts his glasses and clears his throat, blinking at the audience, there is little about him that would fit anyone's romantic stereotype of a poet.

Surprisingly, he does not begin with a poem. Instead, in a relaxed voice he tells an anecdote about his younger daughter and an overdue science project. When he moves from the background story into reading the poem itself, there is little change in his volume level, and his tone remains conversational. The students find that the poem, which they had discussed in class only a couple of days before, takes on more meaning when its origins are explained by the poet himself. They find themselves listening attentively to his words, even laughing out loud several times. The hour goes by quickly, and at its end their applause, like that of the rest of the audience, is long and sincere.

At the next class meeting, the instructor asks for reactions to the reading. Although some of the class members are slightly critical, faulting the speaker for his informal manner and his failure to maintain eye contact with the room, most of the remarks are positive. The comments that surface most often have to do with how much more meaningful the poems in the textbook become when the poet explains how he came to write them. They now know that one poem is actually spoken in the voice of the poet's dead father and that another is addressed to a friend who was paralyzed in an automobile accident. Although these things could perhaps be inferred from the poems alone, the students are unanimous in their opinion that knowing the details beforehand adds a great deal to the first impression a poem makes. As one student puts it, "It's just that a poem makes a lot more sense when you know who's talking and when and where it's supposed to be taking place."

"It always helps to know where poetry starts," adds one of her classmates.

## Speaker, Listener, and Context

The situation just described is hardly unique. Instructors have long been encouraging, even begging, their students to attend events like this one, and the college poetry reading has become, for many American students, the closest encounter they will have with this complex and often perplexing art form. But what students often find at such readings, sometimes to their amazement, is that poetry need not be intimidating or obscure. Poems that are *performed* provide a gentle reminder that the roots of poetry, like those of all literature, were originally part of the **oral tradition**. In ancient societies, stories and poems were passed down from generation to generation and recited for all members of the tribe, from the wizened elders to the youngest children. For most of its long history, poetry has been a popular art form aimed at audiences (remember that the word *audience* means "hearers"). It is only recently, in the past four or five decades, that its most visible signs of life are to be found on college campuses. Still, it is perhaps worth noting that we are exposed daily to a great deal of poetry in oral form, primarily through the medium of recorded song lyrics. The unique qualities of poetry throughout the ages, that is, its ability to tell stories or summarize complicated emotions in a few well-chosen words, are demonstrated whenever we memorize the lines of a popular song and sing them to ourselves.

Of course, poetry written primarily for the page is usually more demanding than song lyrics. Writers of popular songs aim at a wide commercial audience, and this simple fact of economics, added to the fact that the lyrics are not intended primarily for publication but for being recorded with all the resources of studio technology, tends to make many song lyrics relatively uninteresting when they appear in print. But a poem will exist primarily as a printed text, although its effect may be enhanced greatly through a skillful oral performance in which the poet can also explain the background of the poem, its setting and speaker, and the circumstances under which it was written. In general, these details, so crucial to understanding a poem yet so often only implied when the poem appears in print, are called the **dramatic situation** of a poem. Dramatic situation can be summed up in a question: *Who is speaking to whom under what circumstances?* If the poet fails to provide us with clues or if we are careless in picking up the information that is provided, then we may begin reading with no sense of reference and, thus, may go far astray. Even such words as "on," "upon," or "to" in titles can be crucial to our understanding of dramatic situation, telling us something about an event or object that provided the stimulus for the poem or about the identity of the "you" addressed in the poem.

An illustration may be helpful. Suppose we look at what is unquestionably the most widely known poem ever written by an American. It is a poem that virtually all Americans can recite in part and, in fact, do so by the millions every week. Yet if we were told that this poem is unusual because its best-known section is a long, unanswered question, addressed by the speaker to a nearby companion, about whether or not the object named in the title even exists, then it is likely that most of us would be confused. Before going further, let us look at the poem.

## The Star-Spangled Banner

O say, can you see, by the dawn's early light,
    What so proudly we hailed at the twilight's last gleaming?
Whose broad stripes and bright stars thro' the perilous fight,
    O'er the ramparts we watched, were so gallantly streaming!

And the rockets' red glare, the bombs bursting in air,
  Gave proof through the night that our flag was still there:
O say, does that star-spangled banner yet wave
  O'er the land of the free and the home of the brave?

On the shore, dimly seen thro' the mists of the deep,
  Where the foe's haughty host in dread silence reposes,
What is that which the breeze, o'er the towering steep,
  As it fitfully blows, now conceals, now discloses?
Now it catches the gleam of the morning's first beam,
  In full glory reflected now shines on the stream:
'Tis the star-spangled banner! O long may it wave
  O'er the land of the free and the home of the brave!

And where is that band who so vauntingly swore
  That the havoc of war and the battle's confusion
A home and a country should leave us no more?
  Their blood has washed out their foul footsteps' pollution.
No refuge could save the hireling and slave
  From the terror of flight, or the gloom of the grave:
And the star-spangled banner in triumph doth wave
  O'er the land of the free and the home of the brave!

Oh! thus be it ever, when freemen shall stand
  Between their loved homes and the war's desolation!
Blest with victory and peace, may the heav'n-rescued land
  Praise the Pow'r that hath made and preserved us a nation.
Then conquer we must, when our cause it is just,
  And this be our motto: "In God is our trust."
And the star-spangled banner in triumph shall wave
  O'er the land of the free and the home of the brave!

"Now wait a minute!" you may be complaining. "'The Star-Spangled Banner' is a *song*, not a poem. And what's this *question* business? Don't we always sing it while facing the flag? Besides, it's just a patriotic song. Nobody really worries about what it *means*."

In answer to the first comment, "The Star-Spangled Banner" *was* in fact written as a poem and was set to music only after its composition. Most of us will probably agree that the words are not particularly well-suited to the melody (which was taken, curiously, from a popular British barroom ballad) and the song remains notoriously difficult to sing, even for professional performers. In its original form, "The Star-Spangled Banner" (or "The Defense of Fort McHenry," the title under which it was first published) is an example of **occasional verse**, a poem that is written about or for an important event (or occasion), sometimes private but usually of some public significance. Although poems of this type are not often printed on the front pages of newspapers as they once were, they are still being written. Enough poems appeared after the assassination of President John F. Kennedy in 1963 to fill a book, *Of Poetry and Power*, and the *Challenger* disaster of 1986 stimulated a similar outpouring of occasional poems, one of them by Howard Nemerov, who served as poet laureate of the United States. In 1993, Maya Angelou recited "On the Pulse of Morning" at the first inauguration of President Clinton, and Miller Williams read "Of History and Hope" at the second, in 1997. Since then, Elizabeth Alexander and Richard Sanchez have written inaugural poems. The events of September 11, 2001, stimulated thousands of poems including "The Names" by then-U.S. Poet Laureate Billy Collins. The author of "The Star-Spangled Banner," Francis Scott Key (1779–1843), wrote poetry as an avocation. Yet like many men and women who are not professional writers, Key was so deeply moved by an event that he witnessed that occasional poetry was the only medium through which he could express his feelings.

Now let's go back to our question about dramatic situation, taking it one part at a time: Who is speaking? A technical word that is often used to designate the speaker of a poem is **persona** (plural: **personae**), a word that meant "mask" in ancient Greek. Even though the persona of "The Star-Spangled Banner" never uses the word "I" in the poem, the speaker seems to be Key himself, a fact that can be verified by biographical research. Still, it is probably safer to look at poems carefully to see if they give any evidence that the speaker is someone other than the poet. Poems such as "Ulysses" by Alfred, Lord Tennyson or "Porphyria's Lover" by Robert Browning have titles that identify personae who are, respectively, a character from ancient epic poetry and an unnamed man who is confessing the murder of his lover, Porphyria. In neither case is the persona to be identified with the poet himself. Other poems may be somewhat more problematical. Edgar Allan Poe's famous "The Raven," like many of Poe's short stories, is spoken by a persona who is not to be identified directly with the author, even though he shares many of the same morbid preoccupations of Poe's other characters. Even Sylvia Plath, a poet usually associated with an extremely candid form of autobiographical poetry known as **confessional poetry**, on a radio broadcast identified the persona of her masterpiece "Daddy" as an invented character, "a girl with an Electra complex." Although it now is clear that Plath used many autobiographical details in her poem, readers who try to identify her as a victim of child abuse on its evidence should instead turn to Plath's journals and the many biographies that have been written about her. Sometimes poems have more than one persona, which is the case with Thomas Hardy's "The Ruined Maid" and Robert Frost's "Home Burial," two poems that consist almost entirely of dialogue. In other poems, for instance in many ballads, the voice may simply be a third-person **narrator** such as we might find in a short story or novel. Thus, although it is perhaps true that many poems (including the majority of those included here) are in fact spoken by the poet out of his or her most private feelings, it is not a good idea to leap too quickly to the assumption that the persona of a poem is identical to the poet and shares his or her views. Conclusions about the degree to which a poem is autobiographical can be verified only by research and familiarity with a poet's other works.

To return to our question: Who is speaking to whom? Another useful term is **auditor**, the person or persons spoken to in a poem. Some poems identify no auditor; others clearly do specify an auditor or auditors, in most cases identified by name or by the second-person pronoun "you" (or "thee/thou" in older poetry). Again, the title may give clues: Robert Herrick's "To the Virgins, to Make Much of Time" is addressed to a group of young women; William Cullen Bryant's "To the Fringed Gentian" is addressed to a common New England wildflower. (The figure of speech **apostrophe**—discussed later in this introduction—is used when a nonhuman, inanimate, or abstract thing is directly addressed.) Relatively few poems are addressed directly to the reader, so when we read the opening of William Shakespeare's Sonnet 18 ("Shall I compare thee to a summer's day?"), we should keep in mind that he is not addressing us but another individual, in this case a young male friend who is referred to in many of the sonnets. Claude McKay's sonnet "If We Must Die" begins in this manner:

> If we must die, let it not be like hogs
> Hunted and penned in an inglorious spot,
> While round us bark the mad and hungry dogs,
> Making their mock at our accursed lot.

Later in the poem, McKay identifies his auditors as "Kinsmen." Without outside help, about all we can say with certainty at first glance is that the poet seems to be addressing a group of companions who share his desperate situation; when we learn, possibly through research, that McKay was an African American poet writing in reaction to the Harlem race riots of 1919, the symbolic nature of his exhortation becomes clearer.

Now the final part of the question: Who is speaking to whom *under what circumstances?* First, we might ask if there is a relationship, either implied or stated, between persona and auditor. Obviously many love poems take the form of verbal transactions between two parties and, because relationships have their ups and downs, these shifts of mood are reflected in the poetry. One famous example is Michael Drayton's "Idea: Sonnet 61" ("Since there's no help, come let us kiss and part ..."), which begins with the persona threatening to end the relationship with the auditor but ends with an apparent reconciliation. Such "courtship ritual" poems as John Donne's "The Flea" or Andrew Marvell's "To His Coy Mistress" are witty arguments in favor of the couple's setting aside their hesitations and engaging in sexual relations. An example from poetry about marital love is Matthew Arnold's "Dover Beach," which ends with the plea "Ah, love, let us be true / To one another" as the only hope for stability the persona can find in a world filled with uncertainty and fear. Even an age disparity between persona and auditor can lend meaning to a poem, which is the case with the Herrick poem mentioned earlier or Gerard Manley Hopkins's "Spring and Fall."

Other questions relating to circumstances of the dramatic situation might concern the poem's physical setting (if any), time (of day, year, historical era), even such matters as weather. Thomas Hardy's "Neutral Tones" provides a good example of a poem in which the setting, a gray winter day in a barren outdoor location, symbolically reinforces the persona's memory of the bitter end of a love affair. The shift in setting from the springtime idyll to the "cold hill side" in John Keats's "La Belle Dame sans Merci" cannot be overlooked in discussing the persona's disillusionment. Of course, many poems are explicitly occasional and may even contain an **epigraph** (see Gwendolyn Brooks's "We Real Cool"), a brief explanatory statement or quotation, or a **dedication**, which explains the setting. Sometimes footnotes or even outside research may be necessary. John Milton's "On the Late Massacre in Piedmont" will make little sense to readers if they do not know that the poet is reacting to the massacre of a group of Waldensian Protestants by Roman Catholic soldiers on Easter Sunday, 1655. Milton, an English Puritan, uses the occasion to attack the papacy as a "triple tyrant" and the "Babylonian woe."

To return, then, one final time to "The Star-Spangled Banner," let us apply our question to the poem. We have already determined that Key is the persona. Who is the "you" mentioned four words into the poem? It seems clear that Key is addressing an auditor standing close to him, either a single individual or a group, as he asks the auditor if he can see the flag that they both observed for the last time the previous day at sundown. Key tells us that it is now the first moment of dawn, and that even though the flag could be glimpsed periodically in the "rockets' red glare" of the bombardment throughout the night, it cannot be clearly seen now. It is a crucial question, for if the flag is no longer flying "o'er the ramparts," it will mean that the fort has fallen to the enemy. The tension mounts and moves into the second stanza, where at last, "thro' the mists of the deep," the flag can be discerned, "dimly seen" at first, then clearly as it "catches the gleam" of the full sunlight.

The full story of how Key came to write the poem is fairly well known and supports this reading. The events that the poem describes took place on September 13–14, 1814, during the War of 1812. Key, a lawyer, came aboard a British warship anchored off Baltimore to argue for the release of a client and friend who had been taken hostage by the British. Key won his friend's release, but the British captain, fearing that he might reveal information he had learned on board, kept Key overnight, releasing him and his client in the morning. It was during that night that Key witnessed the bombardment and, with it, the failure of the British to take Baltimore. The final half of the poem celebrates the victory and offers a hopeful prayer that God will continue to smile on America "when our cause . . . is just." One might well argue that Key's phrase "conquer we must" contradicts the spirit of the earlier parts of the poem, but few people have argued that "The Star-Spangled Banner" is a consistently great poem. Still, it is an effective piece of patriotic verse that has a few moments of real drama, expressed in a vivid manner that lets its readers become eyewitnesses to an incident from American history.

## Lyric, Narrative, Dramatic

The starting point for all literary criticism in Western civilization is Aristotle's *Poetics*, a work dating from the fourth century B.C. Although Aristotle's remarks on drama, tragedy in particular, are more complete than his analysis of other types of literature, he does mention three main types of poetry: lyric, epic, and dithyrambic. In doing so, Aristotle outlines for the first time a theory of literature based on **genres**, or separate categories delineated by distinct style, form, and content. This threefold division remains useful today, although in two cases different terminology is employed. The first genre, **lyric poetry**, originally was composed of brief poems that were meant to be sung or chanted to the accompaniment of a lyre. Today we still use the word "lyrics" in a specialized sense when referring to the words of a song, but lyric poetry has become such a large category that it includes virtually all poems that are primarily *about* a subject and contain little narrative content. The subject of a lyric poem may be the poet's emotions, an abstract idea, a satirical insight, or a description of a person or place. The persona in a lyric is usually closely identified with the poet himself or herself, and because we tend to identify the essence of poetry with personal, subjective expression of feelings or ideas, lyric poetry remains the largest genre, with a number of subtypes. Among them are the **epigram**, a short, satirical lyric usually aimed at a specific person; the **elegy**, a lyric on the occasion of a death; and the **ode**, a long lyric in elevated language on a serious theme.

Aristotle's second genre, the epic, has been expanded to include all types of **narrative poetry**, that is, poetry whose main function is to tell a story. Like prose fiction, narrative poems have plots, characters, setting, and point-of-view and may be discussed in roughly the same terms as, say, a short story. The **epic** is a long narrative poem about the exploits of a hero. **Folk epics** like *The Iliad* or *Beowulf* were originally intended for public recitation and existed in oral form for a long period of time before they were transcribed. Little or nothing is known about the authors of folk epics; even Homer, the purported author of the *Iliad* and the *Odyssey*, is primarily a legendary character. **Literary epics**, like Dante's *Inferno* or Henry Wadsworth Longfellow's *The Song of Hiawatha*, differ in that they are the products of known authors who *wrote* their poems for publication. **Ballads** generally are shorter narratives with song-like qualities that often include rhyme and repeated refrains. **Folk ballads**, like folk epics, come from the oral tradition and are anonymously authored; "Bonny Barbara Allan" and "Sir Patrick Spens" are typical examples. **Art** or **literary ballads** are conscious imitations of the ballad style by later poets and are generally somewhat more sophisticated than folk ballads in their techniques. Examples of this popular genre include Keats's "La Belle Dame sans Merci," Robert Burns's "John Barleycorn," and more recently Marilyn Nelson's "The Ballad of Aunt Geneva." **Realistic narratives** of medium length (less than 1000 lines) like Robert Frost's "Home Burial" have been popular since the early nineteenth century and are sometimes discussed as "poetic novels" or "short stories in verse."

There is no exact contemporary analogue for Aristotle's third category, **dithyrambic** poetry. This type of poem, composed to be chanted at religious rituals by a chorus, was the forerunner of tragedy. Today this third type is usually called **dramatic poetry**, because it has perhaps as much in common with the separate genre of drama as with lyric and narrative poetry. In general, the persona in a dramatic poem is an invented character not to be identified with the poet. The poem is presented as a speech or dialogue that might be acted out like a soliloquy or scene from a play. The **dramatic monologue** is a speech for a single character, usually delivered to a silent auditor. Notable examples are Tennyson's "Ulysses," and Browning's "My Last Duchess." A dramatic monologue sometimes implies, in the words of its persona, a distinct setting and interplay between persona and auditor. At the close of "Ulysses," the aged hero urges his "mariners" to listen closely and to observe the ship in the harbor waiting to take them off on a final voyage. Dramatic poetry can also take the form of **dialogue poetry**, in which two personae speak alternately. Examples are Christina Rossetti's "Up-Hill" and Hardy's "The Ruined Maid." A popular type of dialogue poem that originated in the Middle Ages was the **débat**, or mock-debate, in which two characters, usually personified abstractions like the Soul and the Body, argued their respective merits.

Although it is easy enough to find examples of "pure" lyrics, narratives, and dramatic monologues, sometimes the distinction between the three major types may become blurred, even in the same poem. "The Star-Spangled Banner," for example, contains elements of all three genres. The opening stanza, with its vivid re-creation of a question asked at dawn, is closest to dramatic poetry. The second and third stanzas, which tell of the outcome of the battle, are primarily narrative. The final stanza, with its patriotic effusion and religious sentiment, is lyrical. Still, the threefold division is useful in discussing a single author's various ways of dealing with subjects or in comparing examples of one type by separate authors. To cite three poems by the same poet in this collection, we might look at William Blake's "The Tyger," "A Poison Tree," and "The Chimney Sweeper." The first of these is a descriptive lyric, dwelling primarily on the symbolic meaning of the tiger's appearance; the second is a narrative that relates, in the first person and the allegorical manner of a parable, the events leading up to a murder; and the third is a short dramatic monologue spoken by the persona identified in the title.

## The Language of Poetry

One of the most persistent myths about poetry is that its language is artificial, "flowery," and essentially different from the language that people speak every day. Although these beliefs may be true of some poetry, one can easily find numerous examples that demonstrate poetic diction of an entirely different sort. It is impossible to characterize poetic language narrowly, for poetry, which is after all the art of language, covers the widest possible range of linguistic possibilities. For example, here are several passages from different poets, all describing birds:

> Hail to thee, blithe Spirit!
>    Bird thou never wert—
> That from Heaven, or near it,
>    Pourest thy full heart
> In profuse strains of unpremeditated art.
>
> Higher still and higher
>    From the earth thou springest
> Like a cloud of fire;
>    The blue deep thou wingest,
> And singing still dost soar, and soaring ever singest.

Percy Bysshe Shelley, "To a Skylark"

> I caught this morning morning's minion, king-
>    dom of daylight's dauphin, dapple-dawn-drawn Falcon, in his riding
>    Of the rolling level underneath him steady air, and striding
> High there, how he rung upon the rein of a wimpling wing
> In his ecstacy!

Gerard Manley Hopkins, "The Windhover"

> When the lilac-scent was in the air and Fifth-month grass was growing,
> Up this seashore in some briers,
> Two feather'd guests from Alabama, two together,
> And their nest, and four light-green eggs spotted with brown,

And every day the he-bird to and fro near at hand,
And every day the she-bird crouch'd on her nest, silent, with bright eyes,
And every day I, a curious boy, never too close, never disturbing them,
Cautiously peering, absorbing, translating.

*Walt Whitman, "Out of the Cradle Endlessly Rocking"*

At once a voice arose among
   The bleak twigs overhead
In a full-hearted evensong
   Of joy illimited;
An aged thrush, frail, gaunt, and small,
   In blast-beruffled plume,
Had chosen thus to fling his soul
   Upon the growing gloom.

*Thomas Hardy, "The Darkling Thrush"*

There is a singer everyone has heard,
Loud, a mid-summer and a mid-wood bird,
Who makes the solid tree trunks sound again.
He says that leaves are old and that for flowers
Mid-summer is to spring as one to ten.

*Robert Frost, "The Oven Bird"*

The blue booby lives
on the bare rocks
of Galápagos
and fears nothing.
It is a simple life:
they live on fish,
and there are few predators.

*James Tate, "The Blue Booby"*

Of these quotes, only Shelley's, from the early nineteenth century, possesses the stereotypical characteristics of what we mean when we use the term "poetic" in a negative sense. Poetry, like any other art form, follows fashions that change over the years; by Shelley's day, the use of "thee" and "thou" and their related verb forms ("wert" and "wingest") had come full circle from their original use as a familiar form of the second person employed to address intimates and servants to an artificially heightened grammatical form reserved for prayers and poetry. Hopkins's language, from a poem of the 1870s, is artificial in an entirely different way; here the poet's **idiom**, the personal use of words that marks his poetry, is highly individual; indeed, it would be hard to mistake a poem by Hopkins, with its muscular monosyllables and rich texture of sound patterns, with one by any other poet. Whitman's diction should present few difficulties; the only oddity here is the use of "Fifth-month" instead of "May," a linguistic inheritance, perhaps, from the poet's Quaker mother. Of course, one might argue that Whitman's "naturalness" results from his use of free verse, but both Hardy and Frost, who write rhymed, metrical verse, are hardly less natural. When we move to the contemporary period, we can find little difference between the language of many poems and conversational speech, as Tate's lines indicate.

Still, in reading a poem, particularly one from the past, we should be aware of certain problems that may impede our understanding. **Diction** refers to the individual words in a poem and may be classified in several ways. A poem's **level of diction** can range from slang at one extreme to formal usage at the other, although in an age in which most poems use a level of diction that stays in the middle of the scale, ranging from conversational and standard levels, these distinctions are useful only when a poet is being self-consciously formal (perhaps for ironic effect) or going to the opposite extreme to imitate the language of the streets. In past eras, the term **poetic diction** was used to indicate a level of speech somehow refined above ordinary usage and, thus, somehow superior to it. Today the same term would most likely be used as a way of criticizing a poet's language. We should keep in mind that the slang of one era may become the standard usage of another, as is the case with "O.K.," which has become a universal expression. In other cases, a poet may even "invent" an idiom for a poem, the case with Lewis Carroll's famous "Jabberwocky" and Stevie Smith's "Our Bog Is Dood."

A good dictionary is useful in many ways, particularly in dealing with **archaisms** (words that are no longer in common use) and other words that may not be familiar to the reader. Take, for example, the opening lines of Edgar Allan Poe's "To Helen":

> Helen, thy beauty is to me
> > Like those Nicean barks of yore,
> That gently, o'er a perfumed sea,
> > The weary, way-worn wanderer bore
> > To his own native shore.

Several words here may give trouble to the average contemporary reader. First, "o'er," like "ne'er" or similar words like "falt'ring" and "glimm'ring," is simply a contraction; this dropping of a letter, called **syncope**, is done for the sake of maintaining the poem's meter; in the fourth stanza of "The Star-Spangled Banner," the words "Pow'r" and "heav'n" are contracted for the same reason. "Barks of yore" will probably send most of us to the dictionary, for our sense of "bark" as either the outer surface of a tree or the noise that a dog makes does not fit here; likewise, "yore" is unfamiliar, possibly archaic. Looking up the literal sense of a word in a dictionary discloses its **denotation**, or literal meaning. Thus, we find that "barks" are small sailing ships and that "yore" refers to the distant past. Of course, Poe could have said "ships of the past" or a similar phrase, but his word choice was perhaps dictated by **connotation**, the implied meaning or feel that some words have acquired; it may be that even in Poe's day "barks of yore" had a remote quality that somehow evoked ancient Greece in a way that, say, "ancient ships" would not. But what are we to make of "Nicean," a proper adjective that sounds geographical but does not appear in either the dictionary or gazetteer? In this case, we have encountered an example of a **coinage**, or **neologism**, a word made up by the poet. Speculation on the source of "Nicean" has ranged from Nice, in the south of France, to Phoenician, but it is likely that Poe simply coined the word for its exotic sound. Similarly, we might note that the phrase "weary, way-worn wanderer" contains words that seem to have been chosen primarily for their alliterated sounds.

When we put a poem into our own words, we **paraphrase** it, a practice that is often useful when passages are hard to understand. Other than diction, **syntax**, the order of words in a sentence, may also give readers problems. Syntax in poetry, particularly in poems that use rhyme, is likely to be different from that of both speech and prose; if a poet decides to rhyme in a certain pattern, then word order must be modified to fit the formal design, and this may present difficulties to readers in understanding the grammar of a passage. Here is the opening of a familiar piece of American patriotic verse: "My country, 'tis of thee, / Sweet land of liberty, / Of thee I sing." What is the subject of this sentence? Would you be surprised to learn that the grammatical subject is "it" (contained in the contraction "'tis"—"It is of thee, my country, sweet land of liberty, of thee [that] I sing")? The passage from Poe's poem presents few difficulties of this order but does contain one example of **inversion**, words that fall out of their expected order (a related syntactical problem lies in **ellipsis**, words that are consciously omitted by the poet). If we do not allow for this, we are likely to be confused by "the weary, way-worn wanderer bore / To his own native shore." The wanderer bore *what?* A quick mental sentence diagram shows that "wanderer" is the direct object of "bore," not its subject. A good paraphrase should simplify both diction and syntax: "Helen, to me your beauty is like those Nican (?) ships of the ancient past that carried the weary, travel-worn wanderer gently over a perfumed sea to his own native land." In paraphrasing, only the potentially troublesome words and phrases should be substituted, leaving the original language as intact as possible. Paraphrasing is a useful first step toward unfolding a poem's literal sense, but it obviously takes few of a poet's specific nuances of language into account; words like "cool," "cold," "chilly," and "frigid" may denote the same thing, but each has its own connotation. "Poetry," Robert Frost famously remarked, "is what is lost in translation." He might have extended the complaint to include paraphrase as well.

Several other matters relevant to poetic language are worth mentioning. **Etymology**, the study of the sources of words, is a particularly rewarding topic in English because our language has such an unusually rich history—just compare an unabridged French dictionary to its English counterpart. Old English (or Anglo-Saxon), the ancient language of the British Isles, was part of the Germanic family of languages. When the Norman French successfully invaded Britain in 1066, they brought with them their own language, part of the Romance language family (all originally derived from Latin). By the time of Chaucer's death in 1400, these two linguistic traditions had merged into a single language, Middle English, that can be read today, despite its differences in spelling, pronunciation, and vocabulary. We can still, however, distinguish the words that show their Germanic heritage from those of Latinate origin. English is rich in synonyms, and Germanic and Latinate words that "mean" the same thing often have different connotations. "Smart" (from the Old English *smeart*) is not quite the same as "intelligent" (from the Latin *intellegent*). A "mapmaker" is subtly different from a "cartographer"—ask yourself which would have ink on his fingers. Although a poet's preference for words of a certain origin is not always immediately clear, we can readily distinguish the wide gulf that separates a statement like "I live in a house with my folks" from "I occupy a residence with my parents."

A final tension exists in poems between their use of **concrete diction** and **abstract diction**. Concrete words denote that which can be perceived by the senses, and the vividness of a poem's language resides primarily in the way it uses **imagery**, sensory details denoting specific physical experiences. Because sight is the most important of the five senses, **visual imagery** ("a dim light,"; "a dirty rag,"; "a golden daffodil") predominates in poems, but we should also be alert for striking examples of the other types of imagery: **auditory** ("a pounding surf"), **tactile** ("a scratchy beard"), **olfactory** ("the scent of apple blossoms"), and **gustatory** ("the bitter tang of gin"). The use of specific imagery has always been crucial for poetry. Consider, for example, the way Chaucer uses brilliantly chosen concrete details—a nun's coral jewelry, a monk's hood lined with fur, a festering sore on a cook's shin—to bring his pilgrims to life in the prologue to *The Canterbury Tales*. In the early twentieth century, a group of poets led by Americans Ezra Pound and H. D. (Hilda Doolittle) pioneered a poetic movement called **imagism**, in which concrete details predominate in short descriptive poems (see H. D.'s "Sea Rose"). "Go in fear of abstractions," commanded Pound, and his friend William Carlos Williams modified the remark to become a poetic credo: "No ideas but in things."

Still, for most poets, abstract words remain important because they carry the burden of a poem's overall meaning or theme. William Butler Yeats's "Leda and the Swan" provides a good example of how concrete and abstract diction coexist in a poem. In reading this account of the myth in which Zeus, in the form of a swan, rapes and impregnates a human woman and thus sets in action the chain of events that leads to the Trojan War (Leda was the mother of Helen of Troy), we will probably be struck at first by the way that tactile imagery ("a sudden blow," fingers attempting to "push / The feathered glory" away, "A shudder in the loins") is used to describe an act of sexual violation. Even though some abstract words ("terrified," "vague," "glory," "strange") appear in the first eight lines of the poem, they are all linked closely to concrete words like "fingers," "feathered," and "heart." In the last two lines of the poem, Yeats uses three large abstractions—"knowledge," "power," and "indifferent"—to state his theme (or at least ask the crucial rhetorical question about the meaning of the myth). More often than not, one can expect to encounter the largest number of abstract words near the conclusion of poems. Probably the most famous abstract statement in English poetry—John Keats's "'Beauty is truth, truth beauty,' that is all / Ye know on earth, and all ye need to know"—appears in the last two lines of a fifty-line poem that is otherwise filled with lush, sensory details of description.

Two other devices sometimes govern a poet's choice of words. **Onomatopoeia** refers to individual words like "splash" or "thud" whose meanings are closely related to their sounds. Auditory imagery in a poem can often be enhanced by the use of onomatopoeic words. In some cases, however, a whole line can be called onomatopoeic, even if it contains no single word that illustrates the device. Thomas Hardy uses this line to describe the pounding of distant surf: "Where hill-hid tides throb, throe on throe." Here the repetition of similar sounds helps imitate the sound of the ocean. A second device is the **pun**, the use of one word to imply the additional meaning of a similar-sounding word (the formal term is **paranomasia**). Thus, when Anne Bradstreet, in "The Author to Her Book," compares her first book to an illegitimate child, she addresses the book in this manner: "If for thy Father asked, say thou had'st none; / And for thy Mother, she alas is poor, / Which caused her thus to send thee out of door." The closeness of the interjection "alas" to the article and noun "a lass" is hardly coincidental. Poets in Bradstreet's day considered the pun a staple of their repertoire, even in serious poetry, but contemporary poets are more likely to use it primarily for comic effect:

> They have a dozen children; it's their diet,
> For they have bread too often. Please don't try it. (Anonymous)

More often than not, puns like these will elicit a groan from the audience, a response that may be exactly what the poet desires.

## Figurative Language

We use figurative language in everyday speech without thinking of the poetic functions of the same devices. We can always relate experience in a purely literal fashion: "His table manners were deplorable. Mother scolded him severely, and Dad said some angry words to him. He left the table embarrassed and with his feelings hurt." But a more vivid way of saying the same thing might employ language used not in the literal but in the figurative sense. Thus, another version might run, "He made an absolute pig of himself. Mother jumped on his back about it, and Dad scorched his ears. You should have seen him slink off like a scolded puppy." At least four comparisons are made here in an attempt to describe one character's table manners, his mother's scolding, his father's words, and the manner in which the character retreated from the table. In every case, the thing being described, what is called the **tenor** of the figure of speech, is linked with a concrete image or **vehicle**. All of the types of figurative language, what are called **figures of speech**, or **tropes**, involve some kind of comparison, either explicit or implied. Thus, two of the figures in the previous example specifically compare aspects of the character's behavior to animal behavior. The other two imply parental words that were delivered with strong physical force or extreme anger. Some of the most common figures of speech follow:

**Metaphor:**   a direct comparison between two unlike things. Metaphors may take several forms.

> His words were sharp knives.
> The sharp knife of his words cut through the silence.
> He spoke sharp, cutting words with his knife-edged voice.
> His words knifed through the still air.

> *I will speak daggers to her but use none.* (Shakespeare, *Hamlet*)

**Implied metaphor:**   a metaphor in which either the tenor or vehicle is implied, not stated.

> The running back gathered steam and chugged toward the end zone.

Here the player is compared to a steam locomotive without naming it explicitly.

> *While smoke on its chin, that slithering gun*
> *Coiled back from its windowsill* (X. J. Kennedy)

In this passage from a poem about the assassination of President John F. Kennedy, Lee Harvey Oswald's rifle is indirectly compared ("coiled back" and "slithering") to a snake that has struck its victim.

**Simile:**   a comparison using "like," "as," or "than" as a connective device.

> *My love is like a red, red rose* (Robert Burns)

> My love smells as sweet as a rose.
> My love looks fresher than a newly budded rose.

**Conceit:** an extended or far-fetched metaphor, in most cases comparing things that apparently have almost nothing in common.

> *Make me, O Lord, thy spinning wheel complete....* (Edward Taylor)

The poem "Huswifery" draws an analogy between the process of salvation and the manufacture of cloth, ending with the persona attired in "holy robes for glory."

**Petrarchan conceit:** named after the first great master of the sonnet, is a clichéd comparison usually relating to a woman's beauty (see Thomas Campion's "There Is a Garden in Her Face"; Shakespeare's Sonnet 130 parodies this type of trope). The **metaphysical conceit** refers to the extended comparisons favored by such so-called metaphysical poets as John Donne, George Herbert, and Edward Taylor. The conceit in the final three stanzas of Donne's "A Valediction: Forbidding Mourning" compares the poet and his wife with a pair of drafting compasses, hardly an image that most people would choose to celebrate marital fidelity.

**Hyperbole:** an overstatement, a comparison using conscious exaggeration.

> He threw the ball so fast it caught the catcher's mitt on fire.

> *And I will love thee still, my dear,*
> *Till a' the seas gang dry.* (Robert Burns)

**Understatement:** the opposite of hyperbole.

> "I don't think we're in Kansas anymore, Toto." (says Dorothy in *The Wizard of Oz*)

> *The space between, is but an hour,*
> *The frail duration of a flower.* (Philip Freneau)

Freneau is understating a wild honeysuckle's lifespan by saying it is "but an hour." Because, by implication, he is also talking about human life, the understatement is even more pronounced.

> *I watched him; and the sight was not so fair*
> *As one or two that I have seen elsewhere.* (Edwin Arlington Robinson)

In "How Annandale Went Out," the persona is a physician who is about to perform euthanasia on a friend dying in agony. Understatement is often used in conjunction with verbal irony following.

**Allusion:** a metaphor making a direct comparison to a historical or literary event or character, a myth, a biblical reference, and so forth.

> He is a Samson of strength but a Judas of duplicity.

> *He dreamed of Thebes and Camelot,*
> *And Priam's neighbors.* (Edwin Arlington Robinson)

**Metonymy:**   use of a related object to stand for the thing actually being talked about.

It's the only white-collar street in this blue-collar town.

*And O ye high-flown quills that soar the skies,*
*And ever with your prey still catch your praise.* (Anne Bradstreet)

Here, Bradstreet speaks of critics who may be hostile to her work. She identifies them as "quills," referring to their quill pens.

*He stood among a crowd at Dromahair;*
*His heart hung all upon a silken dress.* (William Butler Yeats)

The title character of "The Man Who Dreamed of Faeryland" was interested in the woman *in* the dress, not the dress itself.

**Synecdoche:**   use of a part for the whole, or vice versa (very similar to metonymy).

The crowned heads of Europe were in attendance.

*Before the indifferent beak could let her drop.* (William Butler Yeats)

**Personification:**   giving human characteristics to nonhuman things or to abstractions.

Justice weighs the evidence in her golden scales.
The ocean cursed and spat at us.

*Of all her train, the hands of Spring*
*First plant thee in the watery mould.* (William Cullen Bryant)

Bryant personifies spring by giving it hands with which to plant a yellow violet, which is one of the first wildflowers to appear in the season.

**Apostrophe:**   a variety of personification in which a nonhuman thing, abstraction, or person not physically present is directly addressed as if it could respond.

*Milton! Thou shouldst be living at this hour.* (William Wordsworth)

*Is it, O man, with such discordant noises,*
*    With such accursed instruments as these,*
*Thou drownest Nature's sweet and kindly voices,*
*    And jarrest the celestial harmonies?* (Henry Wadsworth Longfellow)

Longfellow is addressing the human race in general.

**Paradox:**   an apparent contradiction or illogical statement.

I'll never forget old what's-his-name.

*His hand hath made this noble work which Stands,*
*His Glorious Handiwork not made by hands.* (Edward Taylor)

Taylor is describing God's creation of the universe, which He willed into being out of nothingness.

**Oxymoron:**   a short paradox, usually consisting of an adjective and noun with conflicting meanings.

> The touch of her lips was sweet agony.

> *Progress is a comfortable disease* (e. e. cummings)
> *A terrible beauty is born.* (William Butler Yeats)

**Synesthesia:**   a conscious mixing of two types of sensory experience.

> A raw, red wind rushed from the north.

> *Leaves cast in casual potpourris*
> *Whisper their scents from pits and cellar-holes* (Richard Wilbur)

**Transferred epithet:**   not, strictly speaking, a trope, it occurs when an adjective is "transferred" from the word it actually modifies to a nearby word.

> *The plowman homeward plods his weary way.* (Thomas Gray)

In this example, the plowman is weary, not the path ("way") he walks upon.

# Allegory and Symbol

Related to the figurative devices are the various types of symbolism that may occur in poems. In many cases, a poem may seem so simple on the surface that we feel impelled to read deeper meanings into it. Robert Frost's famous lyric "Stopping by Woods on a Snowy Evening" is a classic case in point. There is nothing wrong with searching for larger significance in a poem, but the reader should perhaps be wary of leaping to conclusions about symbolic meanings before fully exhausting the literal sense of a poem. Whatever the case, both allegory and symbolism share the demand that the reader supply abstract or general meanings to the specific concrete details of the poem.

The simplest form that this substitution takes occurs in **allegory**. An allegory is usually a narrative that exists on at least two levels simultaneously, a concrete literal level and a second level of abstract meaning; throughout an allegory, a consistent sequence of parallels exists between the literal and the abstract. Sometimes allegories may imply third or fourth levels of meaning as well, especially in long allegorical poems like Dante's *The Divine Comedy*, which has been interpreted on personal, political, ethical, and Christian levels. The characters and actions in an allegory explicitly signify the abstract level of meaning, and generally this second level of meaning is what the poet primarily intends to convey. For example, Robert Southwell's "The Burning Babe" is filled with fantastic incidents and paradoxical speech that are made clear in the poem's last line: "And straight I callèd unto mind that it was Christmas day." The literal burning babe of the title is the Christ child, who predicts his own future to the amazed watcher. Thus, in interpreting the poem, the reader must substitute theological terms like "redemption" or "original sin" for the literal details it contains.

Two types of prose allegories, the fable and parable, have been universally popular. A fable is a short, nonrealistic narrative that is told to illustrate a universal moral concept. A parable is similar but generally contains realistic characters and events. Thus, Aesop's fable of the tortoise and the hare, instead of telling us something about animal behavior, illustrates the virtue of persistence against seemingly unbeatable competition. Jesus's parable of the Good Samaritan tells the story of a man who is robbed and beaten and eventually rescued by a stranger of another race in order to define the concept of "neighbor" for a questioning lawyer. Poetic allegories like George Herbert's "Redemption" or Christina Rossetti's "Up-Hill" can be read in Christian terms as symbolic accounts of the process of salvation. Robert Burns's witty ballad "John Barleycorn" tells on the literal surface the story of a violent murder, but the astute reader quickly discovers that the underlying meaning involves the poet's native Scotland's legendary talent for distilling and consuming strong drink.

Many poems contain symbolic elements that are somewhat more elusive in meaning than the simple one-for-one equivalences presented by allegory. A **symbol**, then, is any concrete thing or any action in a poem that implies a meaning beyond its literal sense. Many of these things or actions are called **traditional symbols**, that is, symbols that hold roughly the same meanings for members of a given society. Certain flowers, colors, natural objects, and religious emblems possess meanings that we can generally agree on. A white lily and a red rose suggest, respectively, mourning and passion. Few Western cultures would associate a black dress with a festive occasion or a red one with purity and innocence. Dawn and rainbows are traditional natural symbols of hope and new beginnings. It would be unlikely for a poet to mention a cross without expecting readers to think of its Christian symbolism. Other types of symbols can be identified in poems that are otherwise not allegorical. A **private symbol** is one that has acquired certain meanings from a single poet's repeated use of it. William Butler Yeats's use of "gyres" in several poems like "The Second Coming" is explained in some of his prose writings as a symbol for the turning of historical cycles, and his use of the word in his poems obviously goes beyond the literal level. Some visionary poets like Yeats and William Blake devised complicated private symbolic systems, a sort of alternative mythology, and understanding the full import of these symbols becomes primarily the task of critics who have specialized in these poets. Other poets may employ **incidental symbols**, things that are not usually considered symbolic but may be in a particular poem, or symbolic acts, a situation or response that seems of greater than literal import. As noted earlier, one of the most famous poems using these two devices is Robert Frost's "Stopping by Woods on a Snowy Evening." In this poem, some readers see the "lovely, dark and deep" woods as both inviting and threatening and want to view the persona's rejection of their allure ("But I have promises to keep / And miles to go before I sleep") as some sort of life-affirming act. Frost himself was not particularly helpful in guiding his readers, often scoffing at those who had read too much metaphysical portent into such a simple lyric, although in other poems he presents objects such as a fork in the road or an abandoned woodpile in a manner that leads the reader to feel that these obviously possess some larger significance. Many modern poems remain so enigmatic that readers have consistently returned to them seeking new interpretations. Poems like these were to a degree influenced by the Symbolists, a group of French poets of the late nineteenth century, who deliberately wrote poems filled with vague nuances subject to multiple interpretations. Such American attempts at symbolist experiments as Wallace Stevens's "Anecdote of the Jar" or "The Emperor of Ice-Cream" continue to perplex and fascinate readers, particularly those who are versed in recent schools of interpretation that focus on the indeterminacy of a poetic text.

## Tone of Voice

Even the simplest statement is subject to multiple interpretations if it is delivered in several different tones of voice. Consider the shift in emphasis between saying "*I* gave you the money," "I *gave* you the money," and "I gave *you* the money." Even a seemingly innocent compliment like "You look lovely this morning" takes on a different meaning if it is delivered by a woman on New Year's Day to her hungover husband. Still, these variations in **tone**, the speaker's implied attitude toward the words he or she says, depend primarily on vocal inflection. Because a poet only rarely gets the opportunity to elucidate his or her tones in a public performance, it is possible that readers may have difficulties in grasping the tone of a poem printed on the page. Still, many poems establish their tone quite clearly from the outset. The opening of Milton's sonnet "On the Late Massacre in Piedmont" ("Avenge, O Lord, thy slaughtered saints . . .") establishes a tone of righteous anger that is consistent throughout the poem. Thus, in many cases, we can relate the tone of voice in poems to the emotions we employ in our own speech, and we would have to violate quite a few rules of common sense to argue that Milton is being flippant.

**Irony** is the element of tone by which a poet may imply an attitude that is in fact contrary to what his words appear to say. Of course, the simplest form of irony is **sarcasm**, the wounding tone of voice we use to imply exactly the opposite of what we say: "That's really a *great* excuse!" or "What a *wonderful* performance!" For obvious reasons, sarcasm is appropriate primarily to spoken language. It has become almost universal to follow a bit of gentle sarcasm in an e-mail message with a symbolic :) to indicate that the remark is not to be taken "straight." **Verbal irony** is the conscious manipulation of tone by which the poet's actual attitude is the opposite of what he says. In a poem like Thomas Hardy's "The Ruined Maid," it is obvious that one speaker considers the meaning of "ruined" to be somewhat less severe than the other, and the whole poem hinges on this ironic counterpoint of definitions and the different moral and social attitudes they imply. Consider the opening lines of Oliver Wendell Holmes's "Old Ironsides," a piece of propaganda verse that succeeded in raising enough money to save the U.S.S. *Constitution* from the scrapyard: "Ay, tear her tattered ensign down! / Long has it waved on high, / And many an eye has danced to see / That banner in the sky... ." Because Holmes's poetic mission is to *save* the ship, it is obvious that he is speaking ironically in the opening line; he emphatically *does not* want the ship's flag stripped from her, an attitude that is made clear in the third and fourth lines. Verbal irony is also a conspicuous feature of **verse satire**, poetry that exists primarily to mock or ridicule, although often with serious intent. One famous example, in the form of a short satirical piece, or **epigram**, is Sarah N. Cleghorn's "The Golf Links," a poem written before the advent of child labor laws:

> The golf links lie so near the mill
> > That almost every day
> The laboring children can look out
> > And see the men at play.

Here the weight of the verbal irony falls on two words, "laboring" and "play," and the way each is incongruously applied to the wrong group of people.

"The Golf Links," taken as a whole, also represents a second form of irony, **situational irony**, in which the setting of the poem (laboring children watching playing adults) contains a built-in incongruity. One master of ironic situation is Thomas Hardy, who used the title "Satires of Circumstance" in a series of short poems illustrating this sort of irony. Hardy's "Ah, Are You Digging on My Grave?" hinges on this kind of irony, with a ghostly persona asking questions of living speakers who end up offering little comfort to the dead woman. **Dramatic irony**, the third type of irony, occurs when the persona of a poem is less aware of the full import of his or her words than is the reader. William Blake's "The Chimney

Sweeper" (from *Songs of Innocence*) is spoken by a child who does not seem to fully realize how badly he is being exploited by his employer, who has apparently been using the promises of religion as a way of keeping his underage workers in line. A similar statement could be made of the persona of Walter Savage Landor's short dramatic monologue "Mother, I Cannot":

> Mother, I cannot mind my wheel;
>> My fingers ache, my lips are dry:
> Oh! if you felt the pain I feel!
>> But oh, who ever felt as I?
>
> No longer could I doubt him true;
>> All other men may use deceit:
> He always said my eyes were blue,
>> And often swore my lips were sweet.

The young woman who speaks here apparently has not realized (or is deliberately unwilling to admit) that she has been sexually deceived and deserted by a scoundrel; "All other men may use deceit" gives the measure of her tragic naïveté. Dramatic irony, as the term implies, is most often found in dramatic monologues, where the gap between the speaker's perception of the situation and the reader's may be wide indeed.

## Repetition: Sounds and Schemes

Because poetry uses language at its most intense level, we are aware of the weight of individual words and phrases to a degree that is usually lacking when we read prose. Poets have long known that the meanings that they attempt to convey often depend as much on the sound of the words as their meaning. We have already mentioned one sound device, onomatopoeia. Consider how much richer the experience of "the murmuring of innumerable bees" is than a synonymous phrase, "the faint sound of a lot of bees." It has often been said that all art aspires to the condition of music in the way that it affects an audience on some unconscious, visceral level. By carefully exploiting the repetition of sound devices, a poet may attempt to produce some of the same effects that the musical composer does.

Of course, much of this sonic level of poetry is subjective; what strikes one listener as pleasant may overwhelm the ear of another. Still, it is useful to distinguish between a poet's use of **euphony**, a series of pleasant sounds, and **cacophony**, sounds that are deliberately unpleasant. Note the following passages from Alexander Pope's "An Essay on Criticism," a didactic poem that attempts to illustrate many of the devices poets use:

> Soft is the strain when Zephyr gently blows,
> And the smooth stream in smoother numbers flows...

The repetition of the initial consonant sounds is called **alliteration**, and here Pope concentrates on the *s* sound. The vowel sounds are generally long: str*ai*n, bl*ow*s, sm*oo*th, and fl*ow*s. Here the description of the gentle west wind is assisted by the generally pleasing sense of euphony. But Pope, to illustrate the opposite quality, follows this couplet with a second:

> But when loud surges lash the sounding shore,
> The hoarse, rough verse should like the torrent roar.

Now the wind is anything but gentle, and the repetition of the *r* sounds in su*r*ges, sho*r*e, hoa*r*se, *r*ough, ve*r*se, to*rr*ent, and *r*oar forces the reader to speak from the back of the throat, making sounds that are anything but euphonious.

Repetition of sounds has no inherent meaning values (although some linguists may argue that certain sounds do stimulate particular emotions), but this repetition does call attention to itself and can be particularly effective when a poet wishes to emphasize a certain passage. We have already mentioned alliteration. Other sound patterns are **assonance**, the repetition of similar vowel sounds (st*ee*p, *e*v*e*n, rec*ei*ve, v*ea*l), and **consonance,** the repetition of similar consonant sounds (du*ck*, tor*qu*e, stri*k*e, tri*ck*le). It should go without saying that spelling has little to do with any sound pattern; an initial *f* will alliterate with an initial *ph*.

**Rhyme** is the most important sound device, and our pleasure in deftly executed rhymes (consider the possibilities of rhyming "neighbor" with "sabre," as Richard Wilbur does in one of his translations) goes beyond mere sound to include the pleasure we take when an unexpected word is magically made to fit with another. There are several types of rhyme. **Masculine rhyme** occurs between single stressed syllables: *fleece, release, surcease, niece,* and so on. **Feminine rhyme**, also called **double rhyme**, matches two syllables, the first stressed and the second usually unstressed: *stinging, upbringing, flinging.* **Triple rhyme** goes further: *slithering, withering.* **Slant rhyme** (also called **near rhyme** and **off rhyme**) contains hints of sound repetition (sometimes related to assonance and consonance): *chill, dull,* and *sale* are possibilities, although contemporary poets often grant themselves considerable leeway in counting as rhyming words pairs that often have only the slightest similarity. When rhymes fall in a pattern in a poem and are **end rhymes**, occurring at the ends of lines, it is then convenient to assign letters to the sounds and speak of a **rhyme scheme.** Thus, a stanza of four lines ending with *heaven, hell, bell, eleven* would be said to have a rhyme scheme of *abba.* Rhymes may also occasionally be found in the interior of lines, which is called **internal rhyme.** Note how both end and internal rhymes work in the complex stanza that Poe uses in "The Raven."

More complicated patterns of repetition involve more than mere sounds but whole phrases and grammatical units. Ancient rhetoricians, teaching the art of public speaking, identified several of these, and they are also found in poetry. **Parallel structure** is simply the repetition of grammatically similar phrases or clauses: Tennyson's "To strive, to seek, to find, and not to yield." **Anaphora** and **epistrophe** are repeated words or phrases at, respectively, the beginning and end of lines. Walt Whitman uses these schemes extensively, often in the same lines. This passage from "Song of Myself" illustrates both anaphora and epistrophe:

> If they are not yours as much as mine they are nothing, or next to nothing,
> If they are not the riddle and the untying of the riddle they are nothing,
> If they are not just as close as they are distant they are nothing.

**Antithesis** is the matching of parallel units that contain contrasting meanings, such as Whitman's "I am of old and young, of the foolish as much as the wise, / Regardless of others, ever regardful of others, / Maternal as well as paternal, a child as well as a man... ." Although the rhetorical schemes are perhaps more native to the orator, the poet can still make occasional effective use of them. Whitman's poetry was influenced by many sources but by none perhaps so powerfully as the heavily schematic language of the King James Bible.

## Meter and Rhythm

The subject of poetic meter and rhythm can be a difficult one, to say the least, and it is doubtless true that such phrases as *trochaic octameter* or *spondaic substitution* have an intimidating quality. Still, discussions of meter need not be limited to experts, and even beginning readers should be able to apply a few of the metrical principles that are commonly found in poetry written in English.

First, let us distinguish between two terms that are often used synonymously: **poetry** and **verse**. Poetry refers to a whole genre of literature and thus stands with fiction and drama as one of the three major types of writing, whereas verse refers to a mode of writing in lines of a certain length; thus, many poets still retain the old practice of capitalizing the first word of each line to indicate its integrity as a unit of composition. Virtually any piece of writing can be versified (and sometimes rhymed as well). Especially useful are bits of **mnemonic verse**, in which information like the number of days in the months (thirty days hath September ...) or simple spelling rules ("I before E / Except after C ...") is cast in a form that is easy to remember. Although it is not strictly accurate to do so, many writers use verse to denote metrical writing that somehow does not quite measure up to the level of true poetry; phrases like **light verse** or **occasional verse** (lines written for a specific occasion, like a birthday or anniversary) are often used in this manner.

If a writer is unconcerned about the length of individual lines and is governed only by the width of the paper being used, then he or she is not writing verse but **prose**. All verse is metrical writing; prose is not. Surprisingly enough, there is a body of writing called **prose poetry**, which uses language in a poetic manner but avoids any type of meter; Carolyn Forché's "The Colonel" is one example. Perhaps the simplest way to think of **meter** in verse is to think of its synonym **measure** (think of the use of meter in words like odometer or kilometer). Thus, meter refers to the method by which a poet determines line length.

When we talk about meter in poetry, we ordinarily mean that the poet is employing some kind of consistent **prosody** or system of measurement. There are many possible prosodies, depending on what the poet decides to count as the unit of measurement in the line, but only three of these systems are common in English poetry. Perhaps the simplest is **syllabic verse**. In verse of this type, the length of the line is determined by counting the total number of syllables the line contains (Sylvia Plath's "Metaphors," for one example, uses lines of nine syllables, a witty metaphor for the poem's subject, pregnancy). Much French poetry of the past was written in twelve-syllable lines, or **Alexandrines**, and in English a word like **octosyllabic** denotes a line of eight syllables. Because English is a language of strong stresses, most of our poets have favored other prosodic systems, but syllabic poetry has been attempted by many poets, among them Marianne Moore, Richard Wilbur, and Dylan Thomas. Moore, in particular, often wrote in **quantitative syllabics**, that is, stanzas containing the same number of lines with identical numbers of syllables in the corresponding lines of different stanzas. Moore's "The Fish" uses stanzas made of lines of one, three, eight, one, six, and eight syllables, respectively.

More natural to the English language is **accentual** verse, a prosodic system in which only accented or strongly stressed syllables are counted in a line, which can also contain a varying number of unaccented syllables. Much folk poetry, perhaps intended to be recited to the beat of a percussion instrument, retains this stress-based pattern, and the oldest verse in the British tradition, Anglo-Saxon poetry like *Beowulf*, is composed in four-stress lines that were recited to musical accompaniment. Many of the verses we recall from nursery rhymes, children's chanting games ("Red rover, red rover, / Send [any name from one to four syllables can be substituted here—*Bill, Susan, Latisha, Elizabeth*] right over"), and sports cheers ("Two bits, four bits, six bits, a dollar! / All for the [*Owls, Cowboys, Cardinals, Thundering Herd*] stand up and holler!") retain the strong sense of rhythmical pulse that characterizes much accentual verse, a fact we recognize when we clap our hands and move rhythmically to the sound of the words. Indeed, the lyrics to much current rap music are actually composed to a four-stress accentual line, and the stresses or "beats" can be heard plainly when we listen or dance. Gerard Manley Hopkins, attempting to recapture some of the flavor of Anglo-Saxon verse, pioneered a type of accentual prosody that he called **sprung rhythm**, in which he counted only the strong stresses in his lines. Accentual meters still supply possibilities for contemporary poets; indeed, what often appears to be free verse is revealed, on closer inspection, to be a poem written in accentual meter. Richard Wilbur's "The Writer," for example, is written in a stanza containing lines of three, five, and three strong stresses, respectively, but the stresses do not overwhelm the reader's ear.

**Accentual-syllabic verse** is the most important prosodic system in English, dominating our poetry for the five centuries from Chaucer's time down to the early years of the twentieth century. Even though in the past hundred years free verse has become the prevailing style in which poetry is written, accentual-syllabic verse still has many able practitioners. An accentual-syllabic prosody is somewhat more complicated than the two systems we have mentioned because it requires that the poet count both the strongly stressed syllables and the total number of syllables in the line. Because stressed and unstressed syllables alternate fairly regularly in this system, four **metrical feet**, representing the most common patterns, designate the subdivisions of rhythm that make up the line (think of a yardstick divided into three feet). These feet are the **iamb** (or **iambic foot**), one unstressed and one stressed syllable; the **trochee** (or **trochaic foot**), one stressed and one unstressed syllable; the **anapest** (or **anapestic foot**), two unstressed syllables and one stressed syllable; and the **dactyl** (or **dactylic foot**), one stressed and two unstressed syllables. The first two of these, iambic and trochaic, are called **double meters**; the second two, **triple meters**. Iambic and anapestic meters are sometimes called **rising meters** because they "rise" toward the stressed syllable; trochaic and dactylic meters are called **falling meters** for the opposite reason. Simple repetition of words or phrases can give us the sense of how these lines sound in a purely schematic sense. The **breve** (˘) and **ictus** (´) are used to denote unstressed and stressed syllables, respectively.

*Iambic:*

> rĕleáse / rĕleáse / rĕleáse
> tŏ fáll / ĭntó /dĕspáir
> Măríe / dĭscóv /ĕrs cándy

*Trochaic:*

> méltĭng / méltĭng / méltĭng / méltĭng
> Pétĕr / dĭsă /gréed ĕn / tírelў
> clévĕr / wrítĭng / fílled thĕ /páge

*Anapestic:*

> ŭncŏntrólled / ŭn cŏntró lled
> ă rĕtríev / ĕr ăppéared
> ănd ă tér / rĭble thúndĕr

*Dactylic:*

shíveriňg / shíveriňg / shíveriňg / shíveriňg /shíveriňg
térřibľy / íll wǐth thě / sýmptoms ǒf / vírǎl pňeu / moňiǎ
nóte hǒw thě / minǐstěr / whíspeřed ǎt / Émǐľy's / gráve

Because each of these lines contains a certain number of feet, a second specialized term is used to denote how many times a pattern is repeated in a line:

| | |
|---|---|
| one foot | **monometer** |
| two feet | **dimeter** |
| three feet | **trimeter** |
| four feet | **tetrameter** |
| five feet | **pentameter** |
| six feet | **hexameter** |
| seven feet | **heptameter** |
| eight feet | **octameter** |

Thus, in the preceding examples, the first set of lines is iambic trimeter; the second, trochaic tetrameter; the third, anapestic dimeter; and the fourth, dactylic pentameter. The third lines in the iambic and anapestic examples are **hypermetrical**; that is, they contain an extra unstressed syllable or **feminine ending**. Conversely, the third lines in the trochaic and dactylic examples are missing one and two unstressed final syllables, respectively, a common practice called **catalexis**. Although more than thirty combinations of foot type and number per line theoretically are possible, relatively few are ordinarily encountered in poetry. The iambic foot is most common in English, followed by the anapest and the trochee; the dactylic foot is relatively rare. Line lengths tend to be from three to five feet, with anything shorter or longer used only sparingly. Still, there are famous exceptions like Poe's "The Raven," which is composed in trochaic octameters and tetrameters, or Southwell's "The Burning Babe," written in iambic heptameter. Long trochaic and iambic lines sometimes exhibit a kind of rhythmical counterpoint. In the opening line of John Whitworth's "The Examiners," for example, the line of trochaic octameter really has only four strong stresses: "Where the HOUSE is cold and EMPty and the GARden's over-GROWN." Verse like this is called **dipodic** ("double-footed") because two feet (/u|/u) are combined into a single unit (uu/u).

Meter denotes regularity, the "blueprint" for a line from which the poet works. Because iambic pentameter is the most common meter used in English poetry, our subsequent discussion will focus on poems written in it. Most poets quickly learn that a metronomic regularity, five iambic feet marching in lockstep line after line, is not a virtue and quickly becomes predictable. Thus, there are several ways by which poets can add variety to their lines so that the actual **rhythm** of the line, what is actually heard, plays a subtle counterpoint against the regularity of the meter. One way is to vary the placement of the **caesura** (‖) or pause within a line (usually indicated by a mark of punctuation). Another is by mixing **end-stopped lines**, which clearly pause at their conclusion, with **enjambed** lines, which run on into the next line with no pause. The following lines from Tennyson's "Ulysses" illustrate these techniques:

> This is my son, mine own Telemachus,
> To whom I leave the scepter and the isle,
> Well-loved of me, discerning to fulfill
> This labor, by slow prudence to make mild
> A rugged people, and through soft degrees
> Subdue them to the useful and the good.

Lines two and six have no caesurae; the others do, after either the third, fourth, or fifth syllable. Lines one, two, and six are end-stopped; the others are enjambed (or use **enjambment**).

Another technique of varying regularity is **metrical substitution**, where feet of a different type are substituted for what the meter calls for. In iambic meter, trochaic feet are often encountered at the beginnings of lines, or after a caesura. Two other feet, the **pyrrhic** (˘˘) consisting of two unstressed syllables, and the **spondee** (´´), consisting of two stressed syllables, are also commonly substituted. Here are Tennyson's lines with their scansion marked.

> Thís iš / m̆y són, ‖ / miňe ow´n / Telém / ăchús,
> To whóm / Ĭ leáve / the scép / těr aňd / the ísle,
> Wéll-lóved / ŏf m̆e, / ‖ / discérn / iňg tŏ / fŭlfíll
> Thís lá / bŏr, ‖ by / slow´ prú / děnce t̆0 / máke míld
> Ă rúg / ğĕd peó / pl̆e, ‖ aňd / throŭgh sóft / d̆egrées
> Sŭbdúe / thĕm to˘ / the uśe / fŭl aňd / the góod.

Even though these are fairly regular iambic pentameter lines, it should be observed that no single line is without some substitution. Still, the dominant pattern of five iambic feet per line should be apparent (out of thirty total feet, about twenty are iambs); there is even a strong tendency on the reader's part to "promote" the middle syllable of three unstressed syllables ("Subdue / them *to* / the use / ful *and* / the good") to keep the sense of the iambic rhythm.

How far can a poet depart from the pattern without losing contact with the original meter? That is a question that is impossible to answer in general terms. The following scansion will probably strike us at first as a far departure from regular iambic pentameter:

> ´ ‖ ´/ ˘ ‖ ´ / ˜ ‖ ´´ / ˘´ / ˘˘

Yet it is actually the opening line of one of Shakespeare's most often quoted passages, Mark Antony's funeral oration from *Julius Caesar*:

> Fríends, ‖ Ró / măns, ‖ cóun, ‖ tr̆ym̆eň, ‖ ´ / lénd m̆e / y̆our eárs

Poets who have learned to use the full resources of meter do not consider it a restraint; instead, they are able to stretch the pattern to its limits without breaking it. A good analogy might be made between poetry and dance. Beginning dancers watch their feet and count the steps while making them; after considerable practice, the movements become second nature, and a skillful pair of partners can add dips and passes without losing the basic step of the music.

## Free Verse and Open Form

Nothing has been so exhaustively debated in English-language poetry as the exact nature of **free verse**. The simplest definition may be the best: free verse is verse with no consistent metrical pattern. In free verse, line length is a subjective decision made by the poet, and length may be determined by grammatical phrases, the poet's own sense of individual "breath-units," or even by the visual arrangement of lines on the page. Clearly, it is easier to speak of what free verse is not than to explain what it is. Even its practitioners do not seem very happy with the term free verse, which is derived from the French *vers libre*. The extensive use of free verse is a fairly recent phenomenon in the history of poetry. Even though there are many examples of free verse from the past (the Psalms, Ecclesiastes, and the Song of Solomon from the King James Bible), the modern history of free verse begins in 1855 with the publication of Walt Whitman's *Leaves of Grass*. Whitman, influenced by Ralph Waldo Emerson's statement that "it is not meters but meter-making argument that makes a poem," created a unique variety of long-line free verse based on grammatical units—phrases and clauses. Whitman's free verse is so distinctive that he has had few direct imitators, and subsequent poets who have used free verse have written lines that vary widely in syllable count. Good free verse, as T.S. Eliot remarked, still contains some kind of "ghost of meter," and its rhythms can be as terse and clipped as those of Philip Levine or as lushly sensuous as those of Pattiann Rogers. The poet who claims that free verse is somehow easier to write than metrical verse would find many arguments to the contrary. As Eliot said, "No verse is free for the poet who wants to do a good job."

All poems have form, the arrangement of the poem on the page that differentiates it from prose. Sometimes this arrangement indicates that the poet is following a preconceived plan—a metrical pattern, a rhyme scheme, a purely visual design like that of **concrete** or **spatial poetry**, or a scheme like that of **acrostic verse**, in which the first letters of the lines spell a message. An analysis of poetic form notes how the lines are arranged, how long they are, and how they are grouped into blocks or **stanzas**. Further analysis might reveal the existence of types of repetition, rhyme, or the use of a **refrain**, or a repeated line or groups of lines. A large number of the poems composed in the twentieth and twenty-first centuries have been written in **open form**, which simply means that there is no strict pattern of regularity in the elements mentioned earlier; that is, there is no consistent meter and no rhyme scheme. Still, even a famous poem in open form like William Carlos Williams's "The Red Wheelbarrow" can be described in formal terms:

> so much depends
> upon
>
> a red wheel
> barrow
>
> glazed with rain
> water
>
> beside the white
> chickens.

Here we observe that the eight-line poem is divided into **uniform stanzas** of two lines each (or couplets). Line length varies between four and two syllables per line. The odd-numbered lines each contain three words; the even, one. Although there is no apparent use of rhyme or repetition here, many poems in open form contain some rhyme and metrical regularity at their conclusions. Alan Dugan's "Love Song: I and Thou" falls into regular iambic tetrameter in its final lines, and a typical contemporary example of an open form poem, Naomi Shihab Nye's "The Traveling Onion," concludes with a closing rhyme on "career" and "disappear."

**Closed form**, unlike open form, denotes the existence of some kind of regular pattern of meter, stanza, rhyme, or repetition. **Stanza forms** are consistent patterns in the individual units of the poem (stanza means "room" in Italian); **fixed forms** are patterns that encompass a complete poem, for example, a sonnet or a villanelle. **Traditional forms** are patterns that have been used for long periods of time and thus may be associated with certain subjects, themes, or types of poems; the sonnet is one example, for it has been used primarily (but by no means exclusively) for lyric poetry. **Nonce forms** are patterns that originate in an individual poem and have not been widely used by other poets. Of course, it goes without saying that every traditional form was at first a nonce form; the Italian poet (now lost to memory) who first wrote a lyric consisting of fourteen rhymed eleven-syllable lines could not have foreseen that in subsequent centuries poets the world over would produce literally millions of sonnets that are all variations on the original model. Some of the most common stanza and fixed forms are briefly discussed herein.

## Stanza Forms

**Blank verse** is not, strictly speaking, a stanza form because it consists of individual lines of iambic pentameter that do not rhyme. However, long poems in blank verse may be arranged into **verse paragraphs** or stanzas with a varying number of lines. Blank verse originally appeared in English with the Earl of Surrey's translation of the *Aeneid* in the fifteenth century; it has been used extensively for narrative and dramatic purposes since then, particularly in epics like Milton's *Paradise Lost* and in Shakespeare's plays. Also written in stanzas of varying lengths is the **irregular ode**, a poem that employs lines of varying lengths (although usually of a regular rhythm that is iambic or matches one of the other feet) and an irregular rhyme scheme.

Paired rhyming lines *(aabbcc ...)* are called **couplets**, although they are only rarely printed as separate stanzas. **Short couplets** have a meter of iambic tetrameter (and are sometimes called **octosyllabic couplets**). If their rhymes are predominantly feminine and seem chosen for comic effect, they may be called **Hudibrastic couplets** after Samuel Butler's satirical poem *Hudibras* of the late 1600s. **Heroic couplets** have a meter of iambic pentameter and have often been used effectively in satirical poems like Alexander Pope's "mock heroic" poem *The Dunciad* and even in dramatic monologues like Robert Browning's "My Last Duchess," where the rhymes are so effectively buried by enjambment that the poem approximates speech. Two other couplet forms, both rare, are poulter's *measure*, rhyming pairs of alternating lines of iambic hexameter and iambic heptameter, and *fourteeners,* pairs of iambic heptameter (fourteen-syllable) lines that, because a natural caesura usually falls after the fourth foot, closely resemble common meter (a form explained below).

A three-line stanza is called a **tercet**. If it rhymes in an *aaa bbb ...* pattern, it is a **triplet**; sometimes triplets appear in poems written in heroic couplets, especially at the end of sections or where special emphasis is desired. Iambic pentameter tercets rhyming *aba bcb cdc ...* form **terza rima**, a pattern invented by Dante for *The Divine Comedy*.

A four-line stanza is known as a **quatrain**. Alternating lines of tetrameter and trimeter in any foot, rhyming *abcb* or *abab*, make up a **ballad stanza**; if the feet are strictly iambic, then the quatrain is called **common meter**, the form of many popular hymns like "Amazing Grace." **Long meter**, also widely used in hymns, consists of iambic tetrameter lines rhyming *abcb* or *abab*; **short meter** has a similar rhyme scheme but contains first, second, and fourth lines of iambic trimeter and a third line of iambic tetrameter. The ***In Memoriam* stanza**, named after Tennyson's long poetic sequence, is iambic tetra-meter rhyming *abba*. The ***Rubaiyat* stanza**, used by Frost in "Stopping by Woods on a Snowy Evening," is an import from Persia; it consists of lines of either iambic tetrameter or pentameter, rhyming *aaba bbcb*. Lines of iambic pentameter rhyming *abab* are known as an **English quatrain**; lines of the same meter rhyming *abba* make up an **Italian quatrain**. One other unusual quatrain stanza is an import from ancient Greece, the **Sapphic stanza**, named after the poet Sappho. The Sapphic stanza consists of three **hendecasyllabic** (eleven-syllable) lines of this pattern:

´ ˘ / ´ ˘ / ´ ˘ ˘ / ´ ˘ / ´ ˘

and a fourth line called an **Adonic**, which is five syllables long and consists of one dactylic foot and one trochaic foot. The Sapphic stanza is usually unrhymed. The quatrain stanza is also used in another import, the **pantoum**, a poem in which the second and fourth lines of the first stanza become the first and third of the second, and the second and fourth of the second become the first and third of the fourth, and so on. Pantoums may be written in any meter and may or may not employ rhyme.

A five-line stanza is known as a **quintet** and is relatively rare in English poetry. The **sestet**, or six-line stanza, can be found with a number of different meters and rhyme schemes. A seven-line stanza is called a **septet**; one septet stanza form is **rime royal**, seven lines of iambic pentameter rhyming *ababbcc*. An eight-line stanza is called an **octave**; one widely used stanza of this length is **ottava rima**, iambic pentameter lines rhyming *abababcc*. Another octave form is the **Monk's Tale stanza**, named after one of Chaucer's tales. It is iambic pentameter and rhymes *ababbcbc*. The addition of a ninth line, rhyming *c* and having a meter of iambic hexameter, makes a **Spenserian stanza**, named after Edmund Spenser, the poet who invented it for *The Faerie Queene*, a long metrical romance.

## Fixed Forms

**Fixed forms** are combinations of meter, rhyme scheme, and repetition that comprise complete poems. One familiar three-line fixed form is the **haiku**, a Japanese import consisting of lines of five, seven, and five syllables, respectively.

The **clerihew**, named after its inventor, Edward Clerihew Bentley, is a humorous form in which the first line is a person's name; the clerihew has a rhyme scheme of *aa bb*.

Two five-line fixed forms are the **limerick** and the **cinquain**. The common and comic limerick consists of anapestic trimeter in lines one, two, and five, and anapestic dimeter in lines three and four. The rhymes, *aabba*, are usually double rhymes used for comic effect. Robert Conquest, the great historian of the purges of the Soviet Union, is also a celebrated poet and an accomplished author of limericks. Conquest memorably summed up his political conclusions in five lines:

> There was a great Marxist called Lenin
> Who did two or three million men in
>     —That's a lot to have done in
>     —But where he did one in
> That grand Marxist Stalin did ten in.

A cinquain, the invention of American poet Adelaide Crapsey (1878–1914), consists of five unrhymed lines of two, four, six, eight, and two syllables, respectively.

Two other short fixed forms, the triolet and the double-dactyl, have also proven popular. The eight-line triolet, a French form, uses two repeating lines in the pattern *ABaAabAB* (the capital letters represent repeated lines) with all lines having the same meter. The double-dactyl, which also is an eight-line form, was invented by the poets Anthony Hecht and John Hollander. The meter is dactylic dimeter with a rhyme scheme of *abcd efgd*. The other "rules" for the double-dactyl include a nonsense phrase in the first line, a person's name in the second, and a single word in the sixth. Here is an example, Leon Stokesbury's "Room with a View":

> Higgledy-piggledy
> Emily Dickinson
> Looked out her front window
> Struggling for breath—
>
> Suffering slightly from
> Agoraphobia:
> "Think I'll just—stay in and—
> Write about—Death—"

The most important of the fixed forms is the **sonnet**, which consists of fourteen lines of rhymed iambic pentameter. The original form of the sonnet is called the **Italian sonnet** or the **Petrarchan sonnet** after the fourteenth-century poet who popularized it. An Italian sonnet is usually cast in two stanzas, an octave rhyming *abbaabba* and a sestet with a variable rhyme scheme; *cdcdcd, cdecde,* and *cddcee* are some of the possible patterns. A **volta** or "turn," usually a conjunction or conjunctive adverb like "but" or "then," may appear at the beginning of the sestet, signifying a slight change of direction in thought. Many Italian sonnets have a strong logical connection between octave and sestet problem/solution, cause/effect, question/answer and the volta helps to clarify the transition. The **English sonnet**, also known as the **Shakespearean sonnet** after its prime exemplar, was developed in the sixteenth century after the sonnet was imported to England and employs a different rhyme scheme that takes into consideration the relative scarcity of rhymes in English (compared with Italian). The English sonnet has a rhyme scheme of *ababcdcdefefgg* and is usually printed as a single stanza. The pattern of three English quatrains plus a heroic couplet often forces a slightly different organizational scheme on the poet, although many of Shakespeare's sonnets still employ a strong volta at the beginning of the ninth line. Other English sonnets may withhold the turn until the beginning of the closing couplet. A third sonnet type, relatively rare, is the **Spenserian sonnet,** named after Edmund Spenser, author of *Amoretti,* one of the earliest sonnet sequences in English. The Spenserian sonnet rhymes *ababbcbccdcdee.* Many other sonnets have been written over the years that have other rhyme schemes, often hybrids of the Italian and English types. These are usually termed **nonce sonnets.** Shelley's "Ozymandias," with its unusual rhyme scheme of *ababacdcedefef,* is one notable example. In "Ode to the West Wind," Shelley employs a fourteen-line stanza rhyming *aba bcb cdc ded ee,* which has been called a **terza rima sonnet.**

Several other fixed forms, all French imports, have appeared frequently in English poetry. The eight-line **triolet,** usually written in iambic tetrameter, uses two refrains: *ABaAabAB.* The **rondeau** has fifteen lines of iambic tetrameter or pentameter arranged in three stanzas: *aabba aabR aabbaR;* the *R* here stands for the unrhymed refrain, which repeats the first few words of the poem's first line. A maddeningly complex variation is the twenty-five line **rondeau redoublé,** through which Wendy Cope wittily maneuvers in her poem of the same name. The **villanelle** is a nineteen-line poem, usually written in iambic pentameter, employing two refrain lines, $A_1$ and $A_2$, in a pattern of five tercets and a final quatrain: $A_1bA_2$ $abA_1$ $abA_2$ $abA_1$ $abA_2$ $abA_1A_2$. A related form, also nineteen lines long, is the **terzanelle,** which uses several more repeating lines (capitalized here): $A_1BA_2$ $bCB$ $cDC$ $dED$ $eFE$ $f$ $A_1FA_2$. The **ballade** is twenty-eight lines of iambic tetrameter employing a refrain that appears at the end of its three octaves and final quatrain, or **envoy:** *ababbcbC ababbcbC ababbcbC bcbC.* Obviously the rhyming demands of the villanelle, the terzanelle, and the ballade pose serious challenges to English-language poets. A final fixed form is the thirty-nine-line **sestina,** which may be either metrical or in free verse and uses a complicated sequence repeating, in different order, the six words that end the lines of the initial stanza. The sequence for the first six sestets is *123456 615243 364125 532614 451362 246531.* A final tercet uses three words in the interior of the lines and three at the ends in the pattern *(2)5(4)3(6)1.* Many sestinas hinge on the poet's choice of six end words that have multiple meanings and can serve as more than one part of speech.

Two contemporary poets, Billy Collins and Kim Addonizio, have recently created nonce forms. Collins's tongue-in-cheek description of the **paradelle** was taken seriously by many readers, and a whole anthology of poems in the form has been assembled. Addonizio's personalized variation on the sonnet, the **sonnenizio**, has also been imitated by other poets. There are many other less familiar types of stanza forms and fixed forms. Lewis Turco's *The Book of Forms* and Miller Williams's *Patterns of Poetry* are two reference sources that are useful in identifying them.

## Literary History and Poetic Conventions

What a poet attempts to do in any given poem is always governed by the tension that exists between originality and convention, or between the poet's desire, in Ezra Pound's famous phrase, to "make it new," and the various stylistic devices that other poets and readers are familiar with through their understanding of the poetic tradition. If we look at some of the most obscure passages of Pound's *Cantos* (a single page may contain passages in several foreign languages), we may think that the poet has departed about as far from conventional modes of expression as possible, leaving his audience far behind him. Yet it is important to keep two facts in mind. First, this style was not arrived at overnight; Pound's early poetry is relatively traditional and should present little difficulty to most readers. He arrived at the style of the *Cantos* after a twenty-year apprenticeship to the styles of writers as different as Li-Po, Robert Browning, and William Butler Yeats. Second, by the time Pound was writing his mature poetry, the modernist movement was in full flower, forcing the public not only to read poems but also to look at paintings and sculpture and to listen to music in ways that would have been unimaginable only a decade or two earlier. When we talk about the stylistic conventions of any given literary period, we should keep in mind that poets are rarely willing to go much beyond what they have educated their audiences to understand. This mutual sense of agreement is the essence of poetic convention.

One should be wary of making sweeping generalizations about "schools" of poetry or the shared conventions of literary periods. In any era, there is always a significant amount of diversity among individual poets. Further, an anthology of this limited scope, which by its very nature must exclude most long poems, is likely to contribute to a misleading view of literary history and the development of poetry in English. When we read Shakespeare's or Milton's sonnets, we should not forget that their major reputations rest on poetry of a very different sort. The neoclassical era in English poetry, stretching from the late seventeenth century until almost the end of the eighteenth, is poorly represented in this anthology because the satires of John Dryden and Alexander Pope and long philosophical poems like Pope's *An Essay on Man* do not readily lend themselves to being excerpted (an exception is the section on meter from Pope's *An Essay on Criticism*). Edgar Allan Poe once claimed that a long poem is "simply a contradiction in terms," but the continued high reputations of *The Faerie Queene, Paradise*

*Lost, Don Juan,* and even a modern verse-novella like Robinson Jeffers's "The Roan Stallion" demonstrate that Poe's was far from the last word on the subject.

The earliest poems in this volume, all anonymous, represent poetry's links to the oral folk tradition. The American folk songs that children learn to sing in elementary school represent our own inheritance of this rich legacy. The poets of the Tudor (1485–1558) and Elizabethan (1558–1603) eras excelled at lyric poetry; Sir Thomas Wyatt and Henry Howard, Earl of Surrey, had imported the sonnet form from Italy, and the form was perfected during this period. Much of the love poetry of the age is characterized by conventional imagery, so-called Petrarchan conceits, which even a later poet like Thomas Campion employs in "There Is a Garden in Her Face" and which Shakespeare satirizes brilliantly in his Sonnet 130 ("My mistress' eyes are nothing like the sun").

The poetry of the first half of the seventeenth century has several major schools: a smooth lyricism influenced by Ben Jonson that can be traced through the work of Robert Herrick, Edmund Waller, and Richard Lovelace; a serious body of devotional poetry by John Donne, George Herbert, and John Milton; and the metaphysical style, which uses complex extended metaphors or metaphysical conceits—Donne and Herbert are its chief exemplars, followed by the early American poets Anne Bradstreet and Edward Taylor. Shortly after the English Restoration in 1660, a profound period of conservatism began in the arts, and the neoclassical era, lasting through most of the eighteenth century, drew heavily on Greek and Roman models. Poetry written during this period—the age of Jonathan Swift, Alexander Pope, and Thomas Gray—was dominated by one form, the heroic couplet; the genres of epic and satire; and an emphasis on human reason as the poet's chief guide. Never has the private voice been so subordinated to the public as in this period when, as Pope put it, a poet's highest aspiration should be to utter "What oft was thought, but ne'er so well expressed."

The first inklings of the romantic era coincide with the American and French revolutions, and poets of the latter half of the eighteenth century like Robert Burns and William Blake exhibit some of its characteristics. But it was not until the publication of *Lyrical Ballads,* a 1798 book containing the best early work of William Wordsworth and Samuel Taylor Coleridge, that the romantic era can be said to have truly flowered. Wordsworth's famous formulation of a poem as "the spontaneous overflow of powerful feeling recollected in tranquillity" remains one of romanticism's key definitions, with its emphasis on emotion and immediacy and reflection; Wordsworth's own poetry, with its focus on the natural world, was tremendously influential. Most of the English and American poets of the first half of the nineteenth century have ties to romanticism in its various guises, and even a poet as late as Walt Whitman (b. 1819) inherits many of its liberal, democratic attitudes. Poets of the Victorian era (1837–1901), such as Alfred, Lord Tennyson and Robert Browning, continued to explore many of the same themes and genres as their romantic forebears, but certainly much of the optimism of the early years of the century had dissipated by the time poets like Thomas Hardy, A.E. Housman, and William Butler Yeats, with their omnipresent irony and pessimism, arrived on the scene in the century's last decades.

The twentieth century and the beginning of the twenty-first have been ruled by the upheavals that modernism caused in every art form. If anything characterized the first half of the twentieth century, it was its tireless experimentation with the forms of poetry. There is a continuum in English-language poetry from Chaucer through Robert Frost and Edwin Arlington Robinson, but Ezra Pound, T.S. Eliot, William Carlos Williams, and Marianne Moore, to mention only four chief modernists, published poetry that would have totally mystified readers of their grandparents' day, just as Picasso and Matisse produced paintings that represented radical breaks with the visual forms of the past. Although many of the experiments of movements like imagism and surrealism seem not much more than historical curiosities today, they parallel the unusual directions that most of the other arts took during the same period.

For the sake of convenience more than anything else, it has been useful to refer to the era following the end of World War II as the postmodern era. Certainly many of the hard-won modernist gains—open form and increased candor in language and subject matter—have been taken for granted by poets writing in the contemporary period. The confessional poem, a frankly autobiographical narrative that reveals what poets in earlier ages might have striven desperately to conceal, surfaced in the late 1950s in the works of Robert Lowell, W.D. Snodgrass, Sylvia Plath, and Anne Sexton and remains one of the chief postmodern genres. Still, as the selections here will attest, there is considerable variety to be found in the contemporary scene, and it will perhaps be many years before critics have the necessary historical distance to assess the unique characteristics of the present period.

---

**ANONYMOUS**

*Some of the popular ballads and lyrics of England and Scotland, composed for the most part between 1300 and 1500, were first collected in their current forms by Thomas Percy, whose* Reliques of Ancient English Poetry *(1765) helped revive interest in folk poetry. Francis James Child (1825–1896), an American, gathered more than a thousand variant versions of the three hundred-odd core of poems. The romantic poets of the early nineteenth century showed their debt to the folk tradition by writing imitative "art ballads" (see Keats's "La Belle Dame sans Merci" or Burns's "John Barleycorn"), which incorporate many of their stylistic devices.*

## Western Wind

Western wind, when will thou blow,
    The small rain down can rain?
Christ, if my love were in my arms
    And I in my bed again!

—1450?

## Bonny Barbara Allan

It was in and about the Martinmas° time,
    When the green leaves were a falling,
That Sir John Græme, in the West Country,
    Fell in love with Barbara Allan.

He sent his men down through the town,           5
    To the place where she was dwelling.
"O haste and come to my master dear,
    Gin° ye be Barbara Allan."

O hooly,° hooly rose she up,
    To the place where he was lying,           10
And when she drew the curtain by:
    "Young man, I think you're dying."

"O it's I'm sick, and very, very sick,
    And 'tis a'° for Barbara Allan."
"O the better for me ye s'° never be,          15
    Though your heart's blood were a-spilling."

"O dinna° ye mind, young man," said she,
    "When ye was in the tavern a drinking,

1 **Martinmas** November 11   8 **Gin** if   9 **hooly** slowly   14 **a'** all   15 **s'** shall   17 **dinna** do not

That ye made the healths gae° round and round,
    And slighted Barbara Allan?"                                    20

He turned his face unto the wall,
    And death was with him dealing:
"Adieu, adieu, my dear friends all,
    And be kind to Barbara Allan."

And slowly, slowly raise she up,                                   25
    And slowly, slowly left him,
And sighing said she could not stay,
    Since death of life had reft him.

She had not gane° a mile but twa,°
    When she heard the dead-bell ringing,                           30
And every jow° that the dead-bell geid,°
    It cried, "Woe to Barbara Allan!"

"O mother, mother, make my bed!
    O make it saft° and narrow!
Since my love died for me to-day,                                  35
    I'll die for him to-morrow."

                                                              —1500?

## Sir Patrick Spens

The king sits in Dumferling town,
    Drinking the blude-reid° wine:
"O whar will I get guid sailor,
    To sail this ship of mine?"

Up and spak an eldern knicht,°                                     5
    Sat at the king's richt° knee:
"Sir Patrick Spens is the best sailor
    That sails upon the sea."

The king has written a braid° letter,
    And signed it wi' his hand,                                     10
And sent it to Sir Patrick Spens,
    Was walking on the sand.

The first line that Sir Patrick read,
    A loud lauch° lauched he;
The next line that Sir Patrick read,                               15
    The tear blinded his ee.°

"O wha is this has done this deed,
    This ill deed done to me,

19 **gae** go   29 **gane** gone   9 **twa** two   31 **jow** stroke   11 **geid** gave   34 **saft** soft
2 **blude-reid** blood-red   5 **eldern knicht** elderly knight   6 **richt** right   9 **braid** long   14 **lauch** laugh
16 **ee** eye

To send me out this time o' the year,
    To sail upon the sea?                 20

"Mak haste, mak haste, my mirry men all,
    Our guid ship sails the morn."
"O say na sae,° my master dear,
    For I fear a deadly storm.

"Late, late yestre'en° I saw the new moon,      25
    Wi' the auld moon in hir arm,
And I fear, I fear, my dear master,
    That we will come to harm."

O our Scots nobles wer richt laith°
    To weet° their cork-heeled shoon,°       30
But lang or a'° the play were played,
    Their hats they swam aboon.°

O lang, lang may their ladies sit,
    Wi' their fans into their hand,
Or ere they see Sir Patrick Spens          35
    Come sailing to the land.

O lang, lang may the ladies stand,
    Wi' their gold kems° in their hair,
Waiting for their ain dear lords,
    For they'll see them na mair.         40

Half o'er, half o'er to Aberdour
    It's fifty fadom deep,
And there lies guid Sir Patrick Spens
    Wi' the Scots lords at his feet.

                           —1500?

---

### SIR THOMAS WYATT ■ (1503?–1542)

*Sir Thomas Wyatt served Henry VIII as a diplomat in Italy. Wyatt read the love poetry of Petrarch (1304–1374) and is generally credited with having imported both the fashions of these lyrics—hyperbolic "conceits" or metaphorical descriptions of the woman's beauty and the lover's suffering—and their form, the sonnet, to England. "They Flee from Me," an example of one of his original lyrics, displays Wyatt's unique grasp of the rhythms of speech.*

---

**23 na sae** not so   **25 yestre'en** last evening   **29 laith** loath   **30 weet** wet   **shoon** shoes
**31 lang or a'** long before   **32 Their hats they swam aboon** their hats swam above them   **38 kems** combs

# They Flee from Me

They flee from me, that sometime did me seek,
With naked foot stalking in my chamber.
I have seen them gentle, tame and meek,
That now are wild, and do not remember
That sometime they put themself in danger                    5
To take bread at my hand; and now they range,
Busily seeking with a continual change.

Thanke'd be Fortune it hath been otherwise,
Twenty times better; but once in special,
In thin array, after a pleasant guise,°                      10
When her loose gown from her shoulders did fall,
And she me caught in her arms long and small,
And therewith all sweetly did me kiss
And softly said, "Dear heart, how like you this?"
It was no dream, I lay broad waking.                         15
But all is turned, thorough° my gentleness,
Into a strange fashion of forsaking;
And I have leave to go, of her goodness,
And she also to use newfangleness.
But since that I so kindely° am served,                      20
I fain° would know what she hath deserved.

—1557

# Whoso List to Hunt

Whoso list° to hunt, I know where is an hind,°
But as for me, alas, I may no more:
The vain travail hath wearied me so sore.
I am of them that farthest cometh behind;
Yet may I by no means my wearied mind                        5
Draw from the deer: but as she fleeth afore,
Fainting I follow. I leave off therefore,
Since in a net I seek to hold the wind.
Who list her to hunt, I put him out of doubt,
As well as I, may spend his time in vain:                    10
And, graven with diamonds, in letters plain
There is written her fair neck round about:
Noli me tangere,° for Caesar's I am,
And wild for to hold, though I seem tame.

—1557

10 **guise** appearance   16 **thorough** through   20 **kindely** in this manner   21 **fain** gladly
1 **list** desire   2 **hind** doe   3 **Noli me tangere** *Touch me not*; the poem is said to refer to the second wife
of Henry VIII, Anne Boleyn.

---

### EDMUND SPENSER ■ (1552–1599)

*Edmund Spenser was born in London and spent most of his adult life in Ireland, where he held a variety of minor government posts.* The Faerie Queene, *a long allegorical romance about Elizabethan England, was uncompleted at his death. The eighty-odd sonnets that make up the sequence called* Amoretti *are generally thought to detail his courtship of his second wife, Elizabeth Boyle, whom he married in 1594.*

## Amoretti: Sonnet 75

One day I wrote her name upon the strand,
But came the waves and washèd it away:
Agayne I wrote it with a second hand,°
But came the tyde, and made my paynes his pray.
"Vayne man," sayd she, "that doest in vaine assay,°                5
A mortall thing so to immortalize,
For I my selve shall lyke° to this decay
And eek° my name bee wypèd out lykewize."
"Not so," quod° I, "let baser things devize
To dy in dust, but you shall live by fame:                10
My verse your vertues rare shall eternize,
And in the hevens wryte your glorious name.
Where whenas death shall all the world subdew
Our love shall live, and later life renew."

—1595

---

### SIR PHILIP SIDNEY ■ (1554–1586)

*Sir Philip Sidney embodied many of the aspects of the ideal man of the Renaissance; he was a courtier, scholar, patron of the arts, and soldier who died of wounds received at the battle of Zutphen. His sonnet sequence* Astrophel and Stella *appeared in 1591, several years before Spenser's* Amoretti, *and helped precipitate the fashion for sonnets that lasted in England well into the next century.*

---

**3 second hand** second time   **5 assay** attempt   **7 lyke** be similar to   **8 eek** also   **9 quod** said

# Astrophel and Stella: Sonnet 1

*1*

Loving in truth, and fain° in verse my love to show,
That she dear she might take some pleasure of my pain,
Pleasure might cause her read, reading might make her know,
Knowledge might pity win, and pity grace obtain,
I sought fit words to paint the blackest face of woe:                    5
Studying inventions fine, her wits to entertain,
Oft turning others' leaves,° to see if thence would flow
Some fresh and fruitful showers upon my sunburned brain.
But words came halting forth, wanting Invention's stay;
Invention, Nature's child, fled stepdame Study's blows;              10
And others' feet° still seemed but strangers in my way.
Thus, great with child to speak, and helpless in my throes,
Biting my truant pen, beating myself for spite:
"Fool," said my Muse to me, "look in thy heart, and write."

—1582

---

**ROBERT SOUTHWELL** ■ **(1561?–1595)**

*Robert Southwell was a Roman Catholic priest in Elizabeth's Protestant
England, who was executed for his religious beliefs. His devotional poems,
most of them on the subject of spiritual love, were largely written during his
three years in prison. Southwell was declared a saint in the Roman Catholic
Church in 1970.*

# The Burning Babe

As I in hoary winter's night stood shivering in the snow,
Surprised I was with sudden heat which made my heart to glow;
And lifting up a fearful eye to view what fire was near,
A pretty babe all burning bright did in the air appear;
Who, scorchèd with excessive heat, such floods of tears did shed     5
As though his floods should quench his flames which with his tears
     were fed.
"Alas," quoth he, "but newly born in fiery heats I fry,
Yet none approach to warm their hearts or feel my fire but I!
My faultless breast the furnace is, the fuel wounding thorns,
Love is the fire, and sighs the smoke, the ashes shame and scorns; 10
The fuel justice layeth on, and mercy blows the coals,

1 **fain** glad   7 **leaves** pages   11 **feet** metrical feet in poetry

The metal in this furnace wrought are men's defilèd souls,
For which, as now on fire I am to work them to their good,
So will I melt into a bath to wash them in my blood."
With this he vanished out of sight and swiftly shrunk away,     15
And straight I callèd unto mind that it was Christmas day.

—1602

---

**MICHAEL DRAYTON ■ (1563–1631)**

*Michael Drayton, like his contemporary Shakespeare, excelled in several literary genres. He collaborated on plays with Thomas Dekker and wrote long poems on English history, biography, and topography. Drayton labored almost three decades on the sixty-three sonnets in* Idea, *publishing them in their present form in 1619.*

# Idea: Sonnet 61

Since there's no help, come let us kiss and part;
Nay, I have done, you get no more of me,
And I am glad, yea glad with all my heart
That thus so cleanly I myself can free;
Shake hands forever, cancel all our vows,     5
And when we meet at any time again,
Be it not seen in either of our brows
That we one jot of former love retain.
Now at the last gasp of love's latest breath,
When, his pulse failing, passion speechless lies,     10
When faith is kneeling by his bed of death,
And innocence is closing up his eyes,
   Now if thou wouldst, when all have given him over,
   From death to life thou mightst him yet recover.

—1619

---

**WILLIAM SHAKESPEARE ■ (1564–1616)**

*William Shakespeare first printed his sonnets in 1609, during the last years of his active career as a playwright, but they had circulated privately a dozen years before. Given the lack of concrete details about Shakespeare's life outside the theatre, critics have found the sonnets fertile ground for biographical speculation, and the sequence of 154 poems does contain distinct characters—a handsome youth to whom most of the first 126 sonnets are addressed; a "Dark Lady" who figures strongly in the remaining poems; and the poet himself, whose name is the source of many puns in the poems. There is probably no definitive "key" to the sonnets, but there is also little doubt that their place is secure among the monuments of English lyric verse. Shakespeare's other nondramatic poems include narratives; allegories; and songs, of which "When Daisies Pied," the companion pieces from his early comedy* Love's Labour's Lost, *are perhaps the best examples.*

# Sonnet 18

Shall I compare thee to a summer's day?
Thou art more lovely and more temperate:
Rough winds do shake the darling buds of May,
And summer's lease hath all too short a date:
Sometimes too hot the eye of heaven shines,                          5
And often is his gold complexion dimmed;
And every fair from fair° sometimes declines,
By chance or nature's changing course untrimmed;°
But thy eternal summer shall not fade,
Nor lose possession of that fair thou ow'st;°                        10
Nor shall death brag thou wander'st in his shade,
When in eternal lines to time thou grow'st:
So long as men can breathe, or eyes can see,
So long lives this, and this gives life to thee.

—1609

# Sonnet 20

A woman's face, with nature's own hand painted,
Hast thou, the master mistress of my passion—
A woman's gentle heart, but not acquainted
With shifting change, as is false women's fashion;
An eye more bright than theirs, less false in rolling,°               5
Gilding the object whereupon it gazeth;
A man in hue all hues in his controlling,
Which steals men's eyes and women's souls amazeth.
And for a woman wert thou first created,
Till nature as she wrought thee fell a-doting,                       10
And by addition me of thee defeated,
By adding one thing to my purpose nothing.

---

**7 fair from fair** every fair thing from its fairness   **8 untrimmed** stripped   **10 ow'st** ownest
**5 rolling** wandering

But since she pricked thee out for women's pleasure,
Mine be thy love and thy love's use their treasure.

—1609

## Sonnet 29

When, in disgrace with fortune and men's eyes,
I all alone beweep my outcast state,
And trouble deaf heaven with my bootless° cries,
And look upon myself, and curse my fate,
Wishing me like to one more rich in hope,                           5
Featured like him, like him with friends possessed,
Desiring this man's art and that man's scope,
With what I most enjoy contented least;
Yet in these thoughts myself almost despising,
Haply° I think on thee—and then my state,                          10
Like to the lark at break of day arising
From sullen earth, sings hymns at heaven's gate;
For thy sweet love remembered such wealth brings
That then I scorn to change my state with kings.

—1609

## Sonnet 73

That time of year thou mayst in me behold
When yellow leaves, or none, or few, do hang
Upon those boughs which shake against the cold,
Bare ruined choirs, where late the sweet birds sang.
In me thou see'st the twilight of such day                          5
As after sunset fadeth in the west;
Which by and by black night doth take away,
Death's second self, that seals up all in rest.
In me thou see'st the glowing of such fire,
That on the ashes of his youth doth lie,                           10
As the deathbed whereon it must expire,
Consumed with that which it was nourished by.
This thou perceiv'st, which makes thy love more strong,
To love that well which thou must leave ere long.

—1609

3 **bootless** useless   10 **Haply** fortunately

## Sonnet 116

Let me not to the marriage of true minds
Admit impediments. Love is not love
Which alters when it alteration finds,
Or bends with the remover to remove:
Oh, no! it is an ever-fixèd mark,                                    5
That looks on tempests and is never shaken:
It is the star to every wandering bark,°
Whose worth's unknown, although his height be taken.°
Love's not Time's fool, though rosy lips and cheeks
Within his bending sickle's compass° come;                          10
Love alters not with his brief hours and weeks,
But bears it out even to the edge of doom.
If this be error and upon me proved,
I never writ, nor no man ever loved.

—1609

## Sonnet 130

My mistress' eyes are nothing like the sun;
Coral is far more red than her lips' red;
If snow be white, why then her breasts are dun;
If hairs be wires, black wires grow on her head.
I have seen roses damasked,° red and white,                         5
But no such roses see I in her cheeks;
And in some perfumes is there more delight
Than in the breath that from my mistress reeks.
I love to hear her speak, yet well I know
That music hath a far more pleasing sound;                          10
I grant I never saw a goddess go;
My mistress, when she walks, treads on the ground.
And yet, by heaven, I think my love as rare
As any she belied° with false compare.°

—1609

## When Daisies Pied°

*Spring*

When daisies pied and violets blue
    And ladysmocks all silver-white

---

7 **bark** boat   8 **height be taken** elevation be measured   10 **compass** range
5 **damasked** multi-colored   14 **belied** lied about   **compare** comparisons   **Pied** multi-colored

And cuckoobuds of yellow hue
  Do paint the meadows with delight,
The cuckoo then, on every tree,                                    5
Mocks married men;° for thus sings he,
         Cuckoo;
Cuckoo, cuckoo: Oh word of fear,
Unpleasing to a married ear!
When shepherds pipe on oaten straws,                              10
  And merry larks are plowmen's clocks,
When turtles tread,° and rooks, and daws,
And maidens bleach their summer smocks,
The cuckoo then, on every tree,
Mocks married men; for thus sings he,                             15
         Cuckoo;
Cuckoo, cuckoo: Oh word of fear,
Unpleasing to a married ear!

*Winter*
When icicles hang by the wall
And Dick the shepherd blows his nail°                             20
And Tom bears logs into the hall,
  And milk comes frozen home in pail,
When blood is nipped and ways be foul,
Then nightly sings the staring owl,
         Tu-who;                                                  25
Tu-whit, tu-who: a merry note,
While greasy Joan doth keel° the pot.

When all aloud the wind doth blow,
  And coughing drowns the parson's saw,°
And birds sit brooding in the snow,                              30
  And Marian's nose looks red and raw,
When roasted crabs° hiss in the bowl,
Then nightly sings the staring owl,
         Tu-who;
Tu-whit, tu-who: a merry note                                    35
While greasy Joan doth keel the pot.

                                                          —1598

---

**6 Mocks married men** The pun is on the similarity between "cuckoo" and "cuckold."   **12 turtles tread** turtledoves mate   **20 nail** fingernails   **27 keel** stir   **29 saw** saying   **32 crabs** crabapples

---

**THOMAS CAMPION ■ (1567–1620)**

*Thoman Campion was a poet and physician who wrote music and lyrics in a manner that was "chiefly aimed to couple my words and notes lovingly together." The imagery in "There Is a Garden in Her Face" represents a late flowering of the conceits of Petrarchan love poetry, so wittily mocked by Shakespeare in "Sonnet 130."*

# There Is a Garden in Her Face

There is a garden in her face,
Where roses and white lilies grow,
A heavenly paradise is that place,
Wherein all pleasant fruits do flow.
There cherries grow which none may buy          5
Till "Cherry-ripe!" themselves do cry.

Those cherries fairly do enclose
Of orient pearl a double row,
Which when her lovely laughter shows,
They look like rosebuds filled with snow.          10
Yet them nor peer nor prince can buy,
Till "Cherry-ripe!" themselves do cry.

Her eyes like angels watch them still;
Her brows like bended bows do stand,
Threatening with piercing frowns to kill          15
All that attempt with eye or hand
Those sacred cherries to come nigh,
Till "Cherry-ripe!" themselves do cry.

—1617

---

**JOHN DONNE ■ (1572–1631)**

*John Donne was trained in the law for a career in government service, but Donne became the greatest preacher of his day, ending his life as dean of St. Paul's Cathedral in London. Only two of Donne's poems and a handful of his sermons were printed during his life, but both circulated widely in manuscript, and his literary reputation among his contemporaries was considerable. His poetry falls into two distinct periods: the witty love poetry of his youth and the sober religious meditations of his maturity. In both, however, Donne shows remarkable originality in rhythm; diction; and the use of metaphor and conceit, which marks him as the chief poet of what has become commonly known as the metaphysical style.*

# The Flea

Mark but this flea, and mark in this,
How little that which thou deniest me is;
Me it sucked first, and now sucks thee,
And in this flea our two bloods mingled be;
Thou know'st that this cannot be said                    5
A sin, or shame, or loss of maidenhead,
   Yet this enjoys before it woo,
    And pampered swells with one blood made of two,
    And this, alas, is more than we would do.

Oh stay, three lives in one flea spare,                    10
Where we almost, nay more than married are.
This flea is you and I, and this
Our marriage bed and marriage temple is;
Though parents grudge, and you, we are met,
And cloistered in these living walls of jet.°              15
   Though use° make you apt to kill me
    Let not to that, self-murder added be,
    And sacrilege, three sins in killing three.

Cruel and sudden, hast thou since
Purpled thy nail° in blood of innocence?                   20
Wherein could this flea guilty be,
Except in that drop which it sucked from thee?
Yet thou triumph'st, and say'st that thou
Find'st not thy self nor me the weaker now;
   'Tis true; then learn how false fears be:                25
    Just so much honor, when thou yield'st to me,
    Will waste, as this flea's death took life from thee.

—1633

# Holy Sonnet 10

Death, be not proud, though some have callèd thee
Mighty and dreadful, for thou art not so;
For those whom thou think'st thou dost overthrow
Die not, poor Death, nor yet canst thou kill me.
From rest and sleep, which but thy pictures be,            5
Much pleasure; then from thee much more must flow,
And soonest our best men with thee do go,
Rest of their bones, and soul's delivery.

**15 jet** black  **16 use** familiarity, especially in the sexual sense  **20 Purpled thy nail** bloodied your fingernail

Thou'art slave to fate, chance, kings, and desperate men,
And dost with poison, war, and sickness dwell,                    10
And poppy° or charms can make us sleep as well
And better than thy stroke; why swell'st thou then?
One short sleep past, we wake eternally,
And death shall be no more; Death, thou shalt die.

—1633

## Holy Sonnet 14

Batter my heart, three-personed God; for You
As yet but knock, breathe, shine, and seek to mend;
That I may rise, and stand, o'erthrow me, and bend
Your force to break, blow, burn, and make me new.
I, like an usurped town, to another due,                          5
Labor to admit You, but O, to no end;
Reason, Your viceroy in me, me should defend,
But is captived, and proves weak or untrue.
Yet dearly I love You, and would be lovèd fain,°
But am betrothed unto Your enemy.                                 10
Divorce me, untie or break that knot again;
Take me to You, imprison me, for I,
Except You enthrall me, never shall be free,
Nor ever chaste, except You ravish me.

—1633

## A Valediction:° Forbidding Mourning

As virtuous men pass mildly away,
    And whisper to their souls to go,
Whilst some of their sad friends do say
    The breath goes now, and some say, No;

So let us melt, and make no noise,                               5
    No tear-floods, nor sigh-tempests move,
'Twere profanation of our joys
    To tell the laity our love.

Moving of th' earth brings harms and fears,
    Men reckon what it did and meant;                            10
But trepidation of the spheres,°
    Though greater far, is innocent.

**11 poppy** opium
**9 fain** gladly  **Valediction** farewell speech; Donne is addressing his wife before leaving on a diplomatic mission.
**11 trepidation of the spheres** natural trembling of the heavenly spheres, a concept of Ptolemaic astronomy

Dull sublunary° lovers' love,
    (Whose soul is sense) cannot admit
Absence, because it doth remove                15
    Those things which elemented it.

But we by a love so much refined
    That our selves know not what it is,
Inter-assurèd of the mind,
    Care less, eyes, lips, and hands to miss.        20

Our two souls therefore, which are one,
    Though I must go, endure not yet
A breach, but an expansion,
    Like gold to airy thinness beat.

If they be two, they are two so              25
    As stiff twin compasses° are two;
Thy soul, the fixed foot, makes no show
    To move, but doth, if th' other do.

And though it in the center sit,
    Yet when the other far doth roam,        30
It leans and hearkens after it,
    And grows erect, as that comes home.

Such wilt thou be to me, who must
    Like th' other foot, obliquely run;
Thy firmness makes my circle just,°        35
    And makes me end where I begun.

                         —1633

---

## BEN JONSON ■ (1573–1637)

*Ben Jonson was Shakespeare's chief rival on the stage, and their contentious friendship has been the subject of much speculation. Jonson became England's first unofficial poet laureate, receiving a royal stipend from James I, and was a great influence of a group of younger poets who became known as the "Tribe of Ben." His tragedies are little regarded today, and his comedies, while still performed occasionally, have nevertheless failed to hold the stage as brilliantly as Shakespeare's. Still, he was a poet of considerable talents, particularly in short forms. His elegy on Shakespeare contains a famous assessment: "He was not of an age, but for all time!"*

**13 sublunary** under the moon, hence, changeable (a Ptolemaic concept)   **26 stiff twin compasses** drafting compasses   **35 just** complete

# On My First Son

Farewell, thou child of my right hand,° and joy;
My sin was too much hope of thee, loved boy:
Seven years thou'wert lent to me, and I thee pay,
Exacted by thy fate, on the just day.°
Oh, could I lose all father now! for why                          5
Will man lament the state he should envy,
To have so soon 'scaped world's and flesh's rage,
And, if no other misery, yet age?
Rest in soft peace, and asked, say, "Here doth lie
Ben Jonson his best piece of poetry."                            10
For whose sake henceforth all his vows be such
As what he loves may never like too much.

—1616

# Slow, Slow, Fresh Fount

*From Cynthia's Revels°*

Slow, slow, fresh fount, keep time with my salt tears;
Yet slower, yet, O faintly, gentle springs!
List to the heavy part the music bears,
Woe weeps out her division,° when she sings.
    Droop herbs and flowers;                              5
    Fall grief in showers;
Our beauties are not ours. O, I could still,
Like melting snow upon some craggy hill,
    Drop, drop, drop, drop,
Since nature's pride is now a withered daffodil.                  10

—1600

---

### MARY WROTH ■ (1587–1651)

*Mary Wroth was the niece of Sir Philip Sidney and the cousin of Sir Walter Raleigh, both distinguished poets and courtiers. A friend of poet Ben Jonson, who dedicated* The Alchemist *to her, she was prominent in the court of King James I. Her prose romance,* Urania *(1621), stirred controversy because of its similarities to actual people and events. Wroth may have fallen into disfavor at court after the publication of* Urania, *and few facts are known about her later life.*

---

**1 child of my right hand** Benjamin, the child's name, means this in Hebrew.    **4 the just day** Jonson's son died on his seventh birthday.    **Slow, Slow, Fresh Fount: From Cynthia's Revels** spoken in this masque by the nymph Echo about the dead Narcissus
**4 division** part of a song

# In This Strange Labyrinth How Shall I Turn

In this strange labyrinth how shall I turn,
Ways° are on all sides, while the way I miss:
If to the right hand, there in love I burn,
Let me go forward, therein danger is.
If to the left, suspicion hinders bliss:　　　　　　　5
Let me turn back, shame cries I ought return:
Nor faint, though crosses° with my fortunes kiss.
Stand still is harder, although sure to mourn.
Thus let me take the right, or left hand way,
Go forward, or stand still, or back retire:　　　　　10
I must these doubts endure without allay°
Or help, but travail find for my best hire
Yet that which most my troubled sense doth move,
Is to leave all and take the thread of Love°

—1621

---

## ROBERT HERRICK ■ (1591–1674)

*Robert Herrick was the most distinguished member of the "Tribe of Ben." Herrick is grouped with the Cavalier poets, whose graceful lyrics are marked by wit and gentle irony. Surprisingly, Herrick was a minister; his Royalist sympathies during the English Civil War caused him hardship during the Puritan era, but his position in the church was returned to him by Charles II after the Restoration.*

# To the Virgins, to Make Much of Time

Gather ye rosebuds while ye may,
　Old time is still a-flying;
And this same flower that smiles today
　Tomorrow will be dying.

The glorious lamp of heaven, the sun,　　　　　　5
　The higher he's a-getting,
The sooner will his race be run,
　And nearer he's to setting.

That age is best which is the first,
　When youth and blood are warmer;　　　　　　10
But being spent, the worse, and worst
　Times still succeed the former.

2 **Ways** paths　7 **crosses** troubles　11 **allay** alleviation　14 **Love** an allusion to the myth of Theseus, who, with the help of Ariadne, unrolled a thread behind him as he entered the labyrinth of Crete.

Then be not coy, but use your time,
  And, while ye may, go marry;
For, having lost but once your prime,        15
  You may forever tarry.

—1648

---

**GEORGE HERBERT ■ (1593–1633)**

*George Herbert was the great master of the English devotional lyric. Herbert was born into a distinguished family that included his mother, the formidable literary patroness Lady Magdalen Herbert, and his brother, the poet and statesman Edward, Lord Herbert of Cherbury. Like John Donne, with whom he shares the metaphysical label, Herbert early aimed at a political career but turned to the clergy, spending several happy years as rector of Bemerton before his death at age 40. The Temple, which contains most of his poems, was published posthumously in 1633.*

# Easter Wings

Lord, who createdst man in wealth and store,°
  Though foolishly he lost the same,
    Decaying more and more
      Till he became
        Most poor:      5
      With Thee
     O let me rise
   As larks, harmoniously,
  And sing this day Thy victories:
Then shall the fall further the flight in me.    10

My tender age in sorrow did begin;
  And still with sicknesses and shame
    Thou didst so punish sin,
      That I became
        Most thin.     15
      With Thee
     Let me combine,
   And feel this day thy victory;
  For, if I imp my wing on thine,°
Affliction shall advance the flight in me.    20

—1633

**1 store** abundance  **19 imp my wing on thine** to graft feathers from a strong wing onto a weak one, a term from falconry

# The Pulley

When God at first made man,
Having a glass of blessings standing by,
   "Let us," said he, "pour on him all we can.
Let the world's riches, which dispersèd lie,
   Contract into a span."°                5

   So strength first made a way;
Then beauty flowed, then wisdom, honor, pleasure.
   When almost all was out, God made a stay,
Perceiving that, alone of all his treasure,
   Rest in the bottom lay.              10

   "For if I should," said he,
"Bestow this jewel also on my creature,
   He would adore my gifts instead of me,
And rest in Nature, not the God of Nature;
   So both should losers be.          15

   "Yet let him keep the rest,
   But keep them with repining restlessness.
Let him be rich and weary, that at least,
   If goodness lead him not, yet weariness
May toss him to my breast."          20

                             —1633

# Redemption

Having been tenant long to a rich lord,
   Not thriving, I resolvèd to be bold,
   And make a suit° unto him, to afford°
A new small-rented lease, and cancel the old.
In heaven at his manor I him sought;      5
   They told me there that he was lately gone
   About some land, which he had dearly bought
Long since on earth, to take possession.
I straight returned, and knowing his great birth,
   Sought him accordingly in great resorts;    10
   In cities, theaters, gardens, parks, and courts;
At length I heard a ragged noise and mirth
   Of thieves and murderers; there I him espied,°
   Who straight, *Your suit is granted,* said, and died.

                             —1633

**5 span** the distance between thumb tip and the tip of the little finger
**3 make a suit** formally request   **afford** grant (me)   **13 him espied** saw him

---

## EDMUND WALLER ■ (1606–1687)

*Edmund Waller was another Royalist sympathizer who suffered after the English Civil War, during Oliver Cromwell's protectorate. Waller is noted for having pioneered the use of the heroic couplet as a popular verse form. He has been often praised for the smoothness of his rhythms and sound patterns.*

# Song

    Go, lovely rose!
Tell her that wastes her time and me
    That now she knows,
When I resemble° her to thee,
How sweet and fair she seems to be.            5

    Tell her that's young,
And shuns to have her graces spied,
    That hadst thou sprung
In deserts, where no men abide,
Thou must have uncommended died.          10

    Small is the worth
Of beauty from the light retired;
    Bid her come forth,
Suffer herself to be desired,
And not blush so to be admired.          15

    Then die! that she
The common fate of all things rare
    May read in thee;
How small a part of time they share
That are so wondrous sweet and fair!         20

*—1645*

---

## JOHN MILTON ■ (1608–1674)

*John Milton is best known as the author of* Paradise Lost, *the greatest English epic poem. His life included service in the Puritan government of Cromwell, pamphleteering for liberal political causes, and brief imprisonment after the Restoration. Milton suffered from blindness in his later years. He excelled in the sonnet, a form to which he returned throughout his long literary life.*

**4 resemble** compare

# How Soon Hath Time

How soon hath Time, the subtle thief of youth,
    Stol'n on his wing my three and twentieth year!
    My hasting days fly on with full career,
    But my late spring no bud or blossom shew'th.°
Perhaps my semblance might deceive the truth,        5
    That I to manhood am arrived so near,
    And inward ripeness doth much less appear,
    That some more timely-happy spirits endu'th.°
Yet be it less or more, or soon or slow,
    It shall be still in strictest measure even°        10
    To that same lot, however mean or high,
Toward which Time leads me, and the will of Heaven;
    All is, if I have grace to use it so,
    As ever in my great Taskmaster's eye.

*—1645*

# On the Late Massacre in Piedmont°

Avenge, O Lord, thy slaughtered saints, whose bones
    Lie scattered on the Alpine mountains cold,
    Even them who kept thy truth so pure of old
    When all our fathers worshiped stocks and stones,°
Forget not: in thy book record their groans        5
    Who were thy sheep and in their ancient fold
    Slain by the bloody Piedmontese that rolled
    Mother with infant down the rocks. Their moans
The vales redoubled to the hills, and they
    To Heaven. Their martyred blood and ashes sow       10
    O'er all th'Italian fields where still doth sway
The triple tyrant:° that from these may grow
    A hundredfold, who having learnt thy way
    Early may fly the Babylonian woe.°

*—1655*

# When I Consider How My Light Is Spent

When I consider how my light is spent
    Ere half my days, in this dark world and wide,

**4 shew'th** shows  **8 endu'th** endows  **10 even** equal
**Massacre in Piedmont** 1700 Protestants from this North Italian state were massacred by Papal forces on Easter Day, 1655.  **4 stocks and stones** idols  **12 triple tyrant** the Pope  **14 Babylonian woe** Early Protestants often linked ancient Babylon to modern Rome as centers of vice.

And that one talent which is death to hide°
Lodged with me useless, though my soul more bent
To serve therewith my Maker, and present                    5
    My true account, lest he returning chide;
    "Doth God exact day-labor, light denied?"
    I fondly° ask; but Patience to prevent
That murmur, soon replies, "God doth not need
    Either man's work or his own gifts; who best            10
    Bear his mild yoke, they serve him best. His state
Is kingly. Thousands at his bidding speed
And post o'er land and ocean without rest:
They also serve who only stand and wait."

—1673

---

### ANNE BRADSTREET ■ (1612–1672)

*Anne Bradstreet was an American Puritan who was one of the first settlers of the Massachusetts Bay Colony, along with her husband Simon, later governor of the colony.* The Tenth Muse Lately Sprung Up in America, *published abroad by a relative without her knowledge, was the first American book of poetry published in England, and the circumstances of its appearance lie behind the witty tone of "The Author to Her Book."*

# The Author to Her Book

Thou ill-formed offspring of my feeble brain,
Who after birth didst by my side remain,
Till snatched from thence by friends, less wise than true,
Who thee abroad, exposed to public view,
Made thee in rags, halting to th' press° to trudge,           5
Where errors were not lessened (all may judge).
At thy return my blushing was not small,
My rambling brat (in print) should mother call,
I cast thee by as one unfit for light,
Thy visage was so irksome in my sight;                        10
Yet being mine own, at length affection would
Thy blemishes amend, if so I could:
I washed thy face, but more defects I saw,
And rubbing off a spot still made a flaw.
I stretched thy joints to make thee even feet,°               15

3 **talent which is death to hide** See the Parable of the Talents, Matthew 25:14–30.   8 **fondly** foolishly
5 **press** printing press; also a clothes closet or chest   15 **even feet** a pun on metrical feet

Yet still thou run'st more hobbling than is meet;
In better dress to trim thee was my mind,
But nought save homespun cloth i' th' house I find.
In this array 'mongst vulgars° may'st thou roam.
In critic's hands beware thou dost not come,　　　　　　20
And take thy way where yet thou art not known;
If for thy Father asked, say thou had'st none;
And for thy Mother, she alas is poor,
Which caused her thus to send thee out of door.

—1678

## To My Dear and Loving Husband

If ever two were one, then surely we.
If ever man were lov'd by wife, then thee.
If ever wife was happy in a man,
Compare with me, ye women, if you can.
I prize thy love more than whole Mines of gold
Or all the riches that the East doth hold.
My love is such that Rivers cannot quench,
Nor ought but love from thee give recompetence.
Thy love is such I can no way repay.
The heavens reward thee manifold, I pray.
Then while we live, in love let's so persever
That when we live no more, we may live ever.

---

**RICHARD LOVELACE ■ (1618–1658)**

*Richard Lovelace was another Cavalier lyricist who was a staunch supporter
of Charles I, serving as a soldier in Scotland and France. He composed many
of his poems in prison following the English Civil War.*

## To Lucasta, Going to the Wars

Tell me not, sweet, I am unkind
That from the nunnery
Of thy chaste breast and quiet mind,
To war and arms I fly.

True, a new mistress now I chase,　　　　　　5
The first foe in the field;

**19 vulgars** common people, i.e., average readers

And with a stronger faith embrace
A sword, a horse, a shield.

Yet this inconstancy is such
As you too shall adore;                                                      10
I could not love thee, dear, so much,
Loved I not honor more.

—1649

---

### ANDREW MARVELL ■ (1621–1678)

*Andrew Marvell was widely known for the playful sexual wit of this most
famous example of the carpé diem poem in English. Marvell was a learned
Latin scholar who moved in high circles of government under both the
Puritans and Charles II, serving as a member of Parliament for two decades.
Oddly, Marvell was almost completely forgotten as a lyric poet for almost two
hundred years after his death, although today he is considered the last of the
great exemplars of the metaphysical style.*

# To His Coy Mistress

Had we but world enough, and time,
This coyness,° lady, were no crime.
We would sit down, and think which way
To walk, and pass our long love's day.
Thou by the Indian Ganges' side                                              5
Shouldst rubies find; I by the tide
Of Humber° would complain. I would
Love you ten years before the flood,
And you should, if you please, refuse
Till the conversion of the Jews.°                                            10
My vegetable° love should grow
Vaster than empires, and more slow;
An hundred years should go to praise
Thine eyes, and on thy forehead gaze;
Two hundred to adore each breast,                                            15
But thirty thousand to the rest;
An age at least to every part,
And the last age should show your heart.
For, lady, you deserve this state,°
Nor would I love at lower rate.                                              20

2 **coyness** here, artificial sexual reluctance   7 **Humber** an English river near Marvell's home
10 **conversion of the Jews** at the end of time   11 **vegetable** flourishing   19 **state** estate

But at my back I always hear
Time's wingèd chariot hurrying near;
And yonder all before us lie
Deserts of vast eternity.
Thy beauty shall no more be found;                               25
Nor, in thy marble vault, shall sound
My echoing song; then worms shall try°
That long-preserved virginity,
And your quaint° honor turn to dust,
And into ashes all my lust:                                      30
The grave's a fine and private place,
But none, I think, do there embrace.
    Now therefore, while the youthful hue
Sits on thy skin like morning glow,
And while thy willing soul transpires                            35
At every pore with instant fires,
Now let us sport us while we may,
And now, like amorous birds of prey,
Rather at once our time devour
Than languish in his slow-chapped° power.                        40
Let us roll all our strength and all
Our sweetness up into one ball,
And tear our pleasures with rough strife
Thorough the iron gates of life:
Thus, though we cannot make our sun                              45
Stand still, yet we will make him run.

—1681

---

## JOHN DRYDEN ■ (1631–1700)

*John Dryden excelled at long forms—verse dramas like* All for Love, *his version of Shakespeare's* Antony and Cleopatra; *his translation of* Virgil's Aeneid; *political allegories like* Absalom and Achitophel; *and* MacFlecknoe, *the first great English literary satire. Dryden's balance and formal conservatism introduced the neoclassical style to English poetry, a manner that prevailed for a century after his death. He became poet laureate of England in 1668.*

**27 try** test   **29 quaint** too subtle   **40 chapped** jawed

# To the Memory of Mr. Oldham°

Farewell, too little, and too lately known,
Whom I began to think and call my own:
For sure our souls were near allied, and thine
Cast in the same poetic mold with mine.
One common note on either lyre did strike,                               5
And knaves and fools we both abhorred alike.
To the same goal did both our studies drive;
The last set out the soonest did arrive.
Thus Nisus° fell upon the slippery place,
While his young friend performed and won the race.          10
O early ripe! to thy abundant store
What could advancing age have added more?
It might (what nature never gives the young)
Have taught the numbers° of thy native tongue.
But satire needs not those, and wit will shine                  15
Through the harsh cadence of a rugged line:
A noble error, and but seldom made,
When poets are by too much force betrayed.
Thy generous fruits, though gathered ere their prime,
Still showed a quickness, and maturing time                     20
But mellows what we write to the dull sweets of rhyme.
Once more, hail and farewell; farewell, thou young,
But ah too short, Marcellus° of our tongue;
Thy brows with ivy, and with laurels bound
But fate and gloomy night encompass thee around.          25

—1684

---

## JONATHAN SWIFT ■ (1667–1745)

*Jonathan Swift, the author of* Gulliver's Travels, *stands unchallenged as the greatest English prose satirist, but his poetry too is remarkable in the unsparing realism of its best passages. Like many poets of the neoclassical era, Swift adds tension to his poetry by ironically emphasizing parallels between the heroic past and the familiar characters and scenes of contemporary London. A native of Dublin, Swift returned to Ireland in his maturity as dean of St. Patrick's Cathedral.*

---

**John Oldham** (1653–1683) was a poet and a satirist.   **9 Nisus** In Virgil's *Aeneid* he is defeated in a footrace by Euryalus, his friend.   **14 numbers** poetic meters   **23 Marcellus** Roman military leader who died at age twenty

# A Description of a City Shower

Careful observers may foretell the hour
(By sure prognostics)° when to dread a shower:
While rain depends,° the pensive cat gives o'er
Her frolics, and pursues her tail no more.
Returning home at night, you'll find the sink°     5
Strike your offended sense with double stink.
If you be wise, then go not far to dine;
You'll spend in coach hire more than save in wine.
A coming shower your shooting corns presage,
Old achès throb, your hollow tooth will rage.     10
Sauntering in coffeehouse is Dulman° seen;
He damns the climate and complains of spleen.°

    Meanwhile the South, rising with dabbled wings,
A sable cloud athwart the welkin° flings,
That swilled more liquor than it could contain,     15
And, like a drunkard, gives it up again.
Brisk Susan whips her linen from the rope,
While the first drizzling shower is borne aslope:
Such is that sprinkling which some careless quean°
Flirts on you from her mop, but not so clean:     20
You fly, invoke the gods; then turning, stop
To rail; she singing, still whirls on her mop.
Not yet the dust had shunned the unequal strife,
But, aided by the wind, fought still for life,
And wafted with its foe by violent gust,     25
'Twas doubtful which was rain and which was dust.
Ah! where must needy poet seek for aid,
When dust and rain at once his coat invade?
Sole coat, where dust cemented by the rain
Erects the nap, and leaves a mingled stain.     30

    Now in contiguous drops the flood comes down,
Threatening with deluge this devoted° town.
To shops in crowds the daggled° females fly,
Pretend to cheapen° goods, but nothing buy.
The Templar° spruce, while every spout's abroach,°     35
Stays till 'tis fair, yet seems to call a coach.
The tucked-up sempstress walks with hasty strides,

---

**2 prognostics** forecasts   **3 depends** is imminent   **5 sink** sewer   **11 Dulman** i.e., dull man
**12 spleen** mental depression   **14 welkin** sky   **19 quean** ill-mannered woman   **32 devoted**
doomed   **33 daggled** spattered   **34 cheapen** inspect prices of   **35 Templar** law student
**abroach** pouring

While streams run down her oiled umbrella's sides.
Here various kinds, by various fortunes led,
Commence acquaintance underneath a shed.                              40
Triumphant Tories and desponding Whigs°
Forget their feuds, and join to save their wigs.
Boxed in a chair° the beau impatient sits,
While spouts run clattering o'er the roof by fits,
And ever and anon with frightful din                                 45
The leather sounds; he trembles from within.
So when Troy chairmen bore the wooden steed,
Pregnant with Greeks impatient to be freed
(Those bully Greeks, who, as the moderns do,
Instead of paying chairmen, run them through),                       50
Laocoön° struck the outside with his spear,
And each imprisoned hero quaked for fear.
　　　Now from all parts the swelling kennels° flow,
And bear their trophies with them as they go:
Filth of all hues and odors seem to tell                             55
What street they sailed from, by their sight and smell.
They, as each torrent drives with rapid force,
From Smithfield° or St. Pulchre's shape their course,
And in huge confluence joined at Snow Hill ridge,
Fall from the conduit prone to Holborn Bridge.                       60
Sweepings from butchers' stalls, dung, guts, and blood,
Drowned puppies, stinking sprats,° all drenched in mud,
Dead cats, and turnip tops, come tumbling down the flood.

—1710

---

## ALEXANDER POPE ■ (1688–1744)

*Alexander Pope was a tiny man who was afflicted in childhood by a crippling disease. Pope was the dominant poet of eighteenth-century England, particularly excelling as a master of mock-epic satire in "The Rape of the Lock" and "The Dunciad." His translations of* The Iliad *and* The Odyssey *made him famous and financially independent and remained the standard versions of Homer for almost two hundred years. "An Essay on Criticism," a long didactic poem modeled on Horace's* Ars Poetica, *remains the most complete statement of the neoclassical aesthetic.*

---

41 **Tories … Whigs** rival political factions   43 **chair** sedan chair   51 **Laocoön** For his attempt to warn the Trojans, he was crushed by sea serpents sent by Poseidon.   53 **kennels** storm drains   58 **Smithfield** site of London cattle exchange   62 **sprats** small fish

# *From* An Essay on Criticism

But most by numbers judge a poet's song,
And smooth or rough with them is right or wrong.
In the bright Muse though thousand charms conspire,
Her voice is all these tuneful fools admire,
Who haunt Parnassus° but to please their ear,                    5
Not mend their minds; as some to church repair,
Not for the doctrine, but the music there.
These equal syllables alone require,
Though oft the ear the open vowels tire,
While expletives° their feeble aid do join,                      10
And ten low words oft creep in one dull line:
While they ring round the same unvaried chimes,
With sure returns of still expected rhymes;
Where'er you find "the cooling western breeze,"
In the next line, it "whispers through the trees";              15
If crystal streams "with pleasing murmurs creep,"
The reader's threatened (not in vain) with "sleep";
Then, at the last and only couplet fraught
With some unmeaning thing they call a thought,
A needless Alexandrine° ends the song                           20
That, like a wounded snake, drags its slow length along.
Leave such to tune their own dull rhymes, and know
What's roundly smooth or languishingly slow;
And praise the easy vigor of a line
Where Denham's strength and Waller's° sweetness join.            25
True ease in writing comes from art, not chance,
As those move easiest who have learned to dance.
'Tis not enough no harshness gives offense,
The sound must seem an echo to the sense.
Soft is the strain when Zephyr° gently blows,                   30
And the smooth stream in smoother numbers flows;
But when loud surges lash the sounding shore,
The hoarse, rough verse should like the torrent roar.
When Ajax° strives some rock's vast weight to throw,
The line too labors, and the words move slow;                   35
Not so when swift Camilla° scours the plain,
Flies o'er the unbending corn, and skims along the main.
Hear how Timotheus'° varied lays surprise,

5 **Parnassus** mountain of the Muses    10 **expletives** unnecessary filler words (like "do" in this line)
20 **Alexandrine** line of six iambic feet (as in the next line)    25 **Denham's ... Waller's** earlier English
poets praised by Pope    30 **Zephyr** the west wind    34 **Ajax** legendary strong man of the *Iliad*    36
**Camilla** messenger of the goddess Diana    38 **Timotheus** a legendary musician

And bid alternate passions fall and rise!
While at each change the son of Libyan Jove°    40
Now burns with glory, and then melts with love;
Now his fierce eyes with sparkling fury glow,
Now sighs steal out, and tears begin to flow:
Persians and Greeks like turns of nature found
And the world's victor stood subdued by sound!    45
The power of music all our hearts allow,
And what Timotheus was is Dryden now.
  Avoid extremes; and shun the fault of such
Who still are pleased too little or too much.
At every trifle scorn to take offense:    50
That always shows great pride, or little sense.
Those heads, as stomachs, are not sure the best,
Which nauseate all, and nothing can digest.
Yet let not each gay turn thy rapture move;
For fools admire, but men of sense approve:    55
As things seem large which we through mists descry,
Dullness is ever apt to magnify.

               —1711

---

## THOMAS GRAY ■ (1716–1771)

*Thomas Gray possesses a contemporary reputation that rests primarily on a single poem, but it remains one of the most often quoted in the whole English canon, and the quatrain stanza is often called "elegiac" in its honor. Gray lived almost all of his adult life at Cambridge University, where he was a professor of history and languages. He declined the poet laureateship of England in 1757.*

# Elegy Written in a Country Churchyard

The curfew tolls the knell of parting day,
 The lowing herd wind slowly o'er the lea,
The plowman homeward plods his weary way,
 And leaves the world to darkness and to me.

Now fades the glimmering landscape on the sight,    5
 And all the air a solemn stillness holds,
Save where the beetle wheels his droning flight,
 And drowsy tinklings lull the distant folds;

---

**40 son of Libyan Jove** Alexander the Great

Save that from yonder ivy-mantled tower
    The moping owl does to the moon complain 10
Of such, as wandering near her secret bower,
    Molest her ancient solitary reign.

Beneath those rugged elms, that yew tree's shade,
    Where heaves the turf in many a moldering heap,
Each in his narrow cell forever laid, 15
    The rude° forefathers of the hamlet sleep.

The breezy call of incense-breathing morn,
    The swallow twittering from the straw-built shed,
The cock's shrill clarion, or the echoing horn,
    No more shall rouse them from their lowly bed. 20

For them no more the blazing hearth shall burn,
    Or busy housewife ply her evening care;
No children run to lisp their sire's return,
    Or climb his knees the envied kiss to share.

Oft did the harvest to their sickle yield, 25
    Their furrow oft the stubborn glebe° has broke;
How jocund did they drive their team afield!
    How bowed the woods beneath their sturdy stroke!

Let not Ambition mock their useful toil,
    Their homely joys, and destiny obscure; 30
Nor Grandeur hear with a disdainful smile
    The short and simple annals of the poor.

The boast of heraldry, the pomp of power,
    And all that beauty, all that wealth e'er gave,
Awaits alike the inevitable hour. 35
    The paths of glory lead but to the grave.

Nor you, ye proud, impute to these the fault,
    If Memory o'er their tomb no trophies raise,
Where through the long-drawn aisle and fretted° vault
    The pealing anthem swells the note of praise. 40

Can storied urn or animated° bust
    Back to its mansion call the fleeting breath?
Can Honor's voice provoke the silent dust,
    Or Flattery soothe the dull cold ear of Death?

Perhaps in this neglected spot is laid 45
    Some heart once pregnant with celestial fire;

**16 rude** unlearned   **26 glebe** plot of farmland   **39 fretted** carved   **41 animated** lifelike

Hands that the rod of empire might have swayed,
    Or waked to ecstasy the living lyre.

But Knowledge to their eyes her ample page
    Rich with the spoils of time did ne'er unroll;       50
Chill Penury repressed their noble rage,
    And froze the genial current of the soul.

Full many a gem of purest ray serene,
    The dark unfathomed caves of ocean bear:
Full many a flower is born to blush unseen,       55
    And waste its sweetness on the desert air.

Some village Hampden,° that with dauntless breast
    The little tyrant of his field withstood;
Some mute inglorious Milton here may rest,
    Some Cromwell° guiltless of his country's blood.       60

The applause of listening senates to command,
    The threats of pain and ruin to despise,
To scatter plenty o'er a smiling land,
    And read their history in a nation's eyes,

Their lot forbade: nor circumscribed alone       65
    Their growing virtues, but their crimes confined;
Forbade to wade through slaughter to a throne,
    And shut the gates of mercy on mankind,

The struggling pangs of conscious truth to hide,
    To quench the blushes of ingenuous shame,       70
Or heap the shrine of Luxury and Pride
    With incense kindled at the Muse's flame.

Far from the madding° crowd's ignoble strife,
    Their sober wishes never learned to stray;
Along the cool sequestered vale of life       75
    They kept the noiseless tenor of their way.

Yet even these bones from insult to protect
    Some frail memorial still erected nigh,
With uncouth rhymes and shapeless sculpture decked,
    Implores the passing tribute of a sigh.       80

Their name, their years, spelt by the unlettered Muse,
    The place of fame and elegy supply:
And many a holy text around she strews,
    That teach the rustic moralist to die.

**57 Hampden** hero of the English Civil War    **60 Cromwell** Lord Protector of England from 1653 to 1658
**73 madding** frenzied

For who to dumb Forgetfulness a prey,                                85
    This pleasing anxious being e'er resigned,
Left the warm precincts of the cheerful day,
    Nor cast one longing lingering look behind?

On some fond breast the parting soul relies,
    Some pious drops the closing eye requires;          90
Even from the tomb the voice of Nature cries,
    Even in our ashes live their wonted fires.

For thee, who mindful of the unhonored dead
    Dost in these lines their artless tale relate;
If chance, by lonely contemplation led,                              95
    Some kindred spirit shall inquire thy fate,

Haply some hoary°-headed swain° may say,
    "Oft have we seen him at the peep of dawn
Brushing with hasty steps the dews away
    To meet the sun upon the upland lawn.              100

"There at the foot of yonder nodding beech
    That wreathes its old fantastic roots so high,
His listless length at noontide would he stretch,
    And pore upon the brook that babbles by.

"Hard by yon wood, now smiling as in scorn,                          105
    Muttering his wayward fancies he would rove,
Now drooping, woeful wan, like one forlorn,
    Or crazed with care, or crossed in hopeless love.

"One morn I missed him on the customed hill,
    Along the heath and near his favorite tree;         110
Another came; nor yet beside the rill,
    Nor up the lawn, nor at the wood was he;

"The next with dirges due in sad array
    Slow through the churchway path we saw him borne.
Approach and read (for thou canst read) the lay,                     115
    Graved on the stone beneath yon aged thorn."

## The Epitaph

*Here rests his head upon the lap of Earth*
    *A youth to Fortune and to Fame unknown.*
*Fair Science frowned not on his humble birth,*
    *And Melancholy marked him for her own.*              120

**97 hoary** frosty, white   **swain** peasant

*Large was his bounty, and his soul sincere,*
*    Heaven did a recompense as largely send:*
*He gave to Misery all he had, a tear,*
*    He gained from Heaven ('twas all he wished) a friend.*

*No farther seek his merits to disclose,*                 125
*    Or draw his frailties from their dread abode*
*(There they alike in trembling hope repose),*
*    The bosom of his Father and his God.*

—1751

---

### WILLIAM BLAKE ■ (1757–1827)

*William Blake was a poet, painter, engraver, and visionary. Blake does not fit easily into any single category, although his political sympathies link him to the later romantic poets. His first book,* Poetical Sketches, *attracted little attention, but his mature works, starting with* Songs of Innocence *and* Songs of Experience, *combine poetry with his own remarkable illustrations and are unique in English literature. Thought mad by many in his own day, Blake anticipated many future directions of both literature and modern psychology.*

## The Chimney Sweeper

When my mother died I was very young,
And my father sold me while yet my tongue
Could scarcely cry "'weep! 'weep! 'weep! 'weep!"
So your chimneys I sweep & in soot I sleep.

There's little Tom Dacre, who cried when his head          5
That curl'd like a lamb's back, was shav'd, so I said,
"Hush, Tom! never mind it, for when your head's bare,
You know that the soot cannot spoil your white hair."

And so he was quiet, & that very night,
As Tom was a-sleeping, he had such a sight!          10
That thousands of sweepers, Dick, Joe, Ned, & Jack,
Were all of them lock'd up in coffins of black;

And by came an Angel who had a bright key,
And he open'd the coffins & set them all free;
Then down a green plain, leaping, laughing, they run,      15
And wash in a river and shine in the Sun.

Then naked & white, all their bags left behind,
They rise upon clouds, and sport in the wind.

And the Angel told Tom, if he'd be a good boy,
He'd have God for his father, & never want joy.                    20

And so Tom awoke; and we rose in the dark,
And got with our bags & our brushes to work.
Tho' the morning was cold, Tom was happy & warm;
So if all do their duty, they need not fear harm.

—1789

# The Little Black° Boy

My mother bore me in the southern wild,
And I am black, but O! my soul is white;
White as an angel is the English child:
But I am black as if bereav'd of light.

My mother taught me underneath a tree,                            5
And sitting down before the heat of day,
She took me on her lap and kissèd me,
And pointing to the east, began to say:

"Look on the rising sun: there God does live,
And gives his light, and gives his heat away;                     10
And flowers and trees and beasts and men receive
Comfort in morning, joy in the noon day.

"And we are put on earth a little space,
That we may learn to bear the beams of love,
And these black bodies and this sun-burnt face                    15
Is but a cloud, and like a shady grove.

"For when our souls have learn'd the heat to bear,
The cloud will vanish; we shall hear his voice,
Saying: 'Come out from the grove, my love & care,
And round my golden tent like lambs rejoice.'"                    20

Thus did my mother say, and kissèd me;
And thus I say to little English boy:
When I from black and he from white cloud free,
And round the tent of God like lambs we joy,

I'll shade him from the heat till he can bear                     25
To lean in joy upon our father's knee:
And then I'll stand and stroke his silver hair,
And be like him, and he will then love me.

—1789

**Black** probably Indian rather than African

# A Poison Tree

I was angry with my friend:
I told my wrath, my wrath did end.
I was angry with my foe:
I told it not, my wrath did grow.

And I water'd it in fears,                                    5
Night & morning with my tears;
And I sunnèd it with smiles,
And with soft deceitful wiles.

And it grew both day and night,
Till it bore an apple bright;                               10
And my foe beheld it shine,
And he knew that it was mine,

And into my garden stole
When the night had veil'd the pole;
In the morning glad I see                                  15
My foe outstretch'd beneath the tree.

                                                    —1794

# The Tyger

Tyger! Tyger! burning bright
In the forests of the night,
What immortal hand or eye
Could frame thy fearful symmetry?

In what distant deeps or skies                             5
Burnt the fire of thine eyes?
On what wings dare he aspire?
What the hand, dare seize the fire?

And what shoulder, & what art,
Could twist the sinews of thy heart?                      10
And when thy heart began to beat,
What dread hand? & what dread feet?

What the hammer? what the chain?
In what furnace was thy brain?
What the anvil? what dread grasp                          15
Dare its deadly terrors clasp?

When the stars threw down their spears,
And water'd heaven with their tears,

Did he smile his work to see?
Did he who made the Lamb make thee?                          20

Tyger! Tyger! burning bright
In the forests of the night,
What immortal hand or eye,
Dare frame thy fearful symmetry?

—1794

---

### ROBERT BURNS (1759–1796)

*Robert Burns was a Scot known in his day as the "Ploughman Poet" and was
one of the first English poets to put dialect to serious literary purpose. Chiefly
known for his realistic depictions of peasant life, he was also an important
lyric poet who prefigured many of the later concerns of the romantic era.*

# A Red, Red Rose

O my luve's like a red, red rose,
    That's newly sprung in June;
O my luve's like the melodie
    That's sweetly played in tune.

As fair art thou, my bonnie lass,                          5
    So deep in luve am I;
And I will luve thee still, my dear,
    Till a' the seas gang° dry.

Till a' the seas gang dry, my dear,
    And the rocks melt wi' the sun;                         10
O I will luve thee still, my dear,
    While the sands o' life shall run.

And fare thee weel, my only luve,
    And fare thee weel awhile!
And I will come again, my luve                              15
    Though it were ten thousand mile.

—1791

# John Barleycorn

There were three kings into the east,
Three kings both great and high;

8  **gang** go

And they has sworn a solemn oath
John Barleycorn should die.

They took a plough and plough'd him down,                    5
Put clods upon his head;
And they hae sworn a solemn oath
John Barleycorn was dead.

But the cheerful spring came kindly on,
And showers began to fall;                                   10
John Barleycorn got up again,
And sore surprised them all.

The sultry suns of summer came,
And he grew thick and strong;
His head well armed wi' point'd spears,                      15
That no one should him wrong.

The sober autumn enter'd mild,
When he grew wan and pale;
His bending joints and drooping head
Show'd he began to fail.                                     20

His colour sicken'd more and more
He faded into age;
And then his enemies began
To show their deadly rage.

They've ta'en a weapon long and sharp,                       25
And cut him by the knee;
Then tied him fast upon a cart,
Like a rogue for forgery.

They laid him down upon his back,
And cudgell'd him full sore;                                 30
They hung him up before the storm,
And turn'd him o'er and o'er.

They fill'd up a darksome pit
With water to the brim;
They heaved in John Barleycorn,                              35
There let him sink or swim.

They laid him out upon the floor,
To work him further woe;
And still as signs of life appear'd,
They toss'd him to and fro.                                  40

They wasted o'er a scorching flame
The marrow of his bones;

But a miller used him worst of all
He crushed him 'tween two stones.

And they has ta'en his very heart's blood,    45
And drank it round and round,
And still the more and more they drank,
Their joy did more abound.

John Barleycorn was a hero bold,
Of noble enterprise;    50
For if you do but taste his blood,
'Twill make your courage rise.

'Twill make a man forget his woe;
'Twill heighten all his joy;
'Twill make the widow's heart to sing,    55
Though the tear were in her eye.

Then let us toast John Barleycorn,
Each man a glass in hand;
And may his great posterity
Ne'er fail in old Scotland!    60

—1786

---

**WILLIAM WORDSWORTH** ■ **(1770–1850)**

*William Wordsworth is generally considered the first of the English romantics. Lyrical Ballads, the 1798 volume that introduced both his poetry and Samuel Taylor Coleridge's to a wide readership, remains one of the most influential collections of poetry ever published. Wordsworth's preface to the revised edition of 1800 contains the famous romantic formulation of poetry as the "spontaneous overflow of powerful feelings," a theory exemplified in short lyrics like "I Wandered Lonely as a Cloud" and in longer meditative pieces like "Tintern Abbey" (the title by which "Lines" is commonly known). Wordsworth served as poet laureate from 1843 to his death.*

# I Wandered Lonely as a Cloud

I wandered lonely as a cloud
That floats on high o'er vales and hills,
When all at once I saw a crowd,
A host, of golden daffodils;
Beside the lake, beneath the trees,    5
Fluttering and dancing in the breeze.

Continuous as the stars that shine
And twinkle on the milky way,
They stretched in never-ending line
Along the margin of a bay:                                    10
Ten thousand saw I at a glance,
Tossing their heads in sprightly dance.

The waves beside them danced, but they
Outdid the sparkling waves in glee;
A poet could not but be gay,                                  15
In such a jocund company;
I gazed—and gazed—but little thought
What wealth the show to me had brought:

For oft, when on my couch I lie
In vacant or in pensive mood,                                 20
They flash upon that inward eye
Which is the bliss of solitude;
And then my heart with pleasure fills,
And dances with the daffodils.

—1807

# It Is a Beauteous Evening

It is a beauteous evening, calm and free,
The holy time is quiet as a Nun
Breathless with adoration; the broad sun
Is sinking down in its tranquillity;
The gentleness of heaven broods o'er the Sea:                 5
Listen! the mighty Being is awake,
And doth with his eternal motion make
A sound like thunder—everlastingly.
Dear Child! dear Girl!° that walkest with me here,
If thou appear untouched by solemn thought,                   10
Thy nature is not therefore less divine:
Thou liest in Abraham's bosom° all the year,
And worship'st at the Temple's inner shrine,
God being with thee when we know it not.

—1807

**9 Dear Child! dear Girl!** the poet's daughter     **12  Abraham's bosom** where souls rest in Heaven

# Composed a Few Miles above Tintern Abbey, On Revisiting the Banks of the Wye during a Tour. July 13, 1798

Five years have past; five summers, with the length
Of five long winters! and again I hear
These waters, rolling from their mountain-springs
With a soft inland murmur.—Once again
Do I behold these steep and lofty cliffs,
That on a wild secluded scene impress
Thoughts of more deep seclusion; and connect
The landscape with the quiet of the sky.
The day is come when I again repose
Here, under this dark sycamore, and view
These plots of cottage-ground, these orchard-tufts,
Which at this season, with their unripe fruits,
Are clad in one green hue, and lose themselves
'Mid groves and copses. Once again I see
These hedge-rows, hardly hedge-rows, little lines
Of sportive wood run wild: these pastoral farms,
Green to the very door; and wreaths of smoke
Sent up, in silence, from among the trees!
With some uncertain notice, as might seem
Of vagrant dwellers in the houseless woods,
Or of some Hermit's cave, where by his fire
The Hermit sits alone.
                                  These beauteous forms,
Through a long absence, have not been to me
As is a landscape to a blind man's eye:
But oft, in lonely rooms, and 'mid the din
Of towns and cities, I have owed to them,
In hours of weariness, sensations sweet,
Felt in the blood, and felt along the heart;
And passing even into my purer mind
With tranquil restoration:—feelings too
Of unremembered pleasure: such, perhaps,
As have no slight or trivial influence
On that best portion of a good man's life,
His little, nameless, unremembered, acts
Of kindness and of love. Nor less, I trust,
To them I may have owed another gift,
Of aspect more sublime; that blessed mood,
In which the burthen of the mystery,

In which the heavy and the weary weight
Of all this unintelligible world,
Is lightened:—that serene and blessed mood,
In which the affections gently lead us on,—
Until, the breath of this corporeal frame
And even the motion of our human blood
Almost suspended, we are laid asleep
In body, and become a living soul:
While with an eye made quiet by the power
Of harmony, and the deep power of joy,
We see into the life of things.

                             If this
Be but a vain belief, yet, oh! how oft—
In darkness and amid the many shapes
Of joyless daylight; when the fretful stir
Unprofitable, and the fever of the world,
Have hung upon the beatings of my heart—
How oft, in spirit, have I turned to thee,
O sylvan Wye! thou wanderer thro' the woods,
   How often has my spirit turned to thee!

   And now, with gleams of half-extinguished thought,
With many recognitions dim and faint,
And somewhat of a sad perplexity,
The picture of the mind revives again:
While here I stand, not only with the sense
Of present pleasure, but with pleasing thoughts
That in this moment there is life and food
For future years. And so I dare to hope,
Though changed, no doubt, from what I was when first
I came among these hills; when like a roe
I bounded o'er the mountains, by the sides
Of the deep rivers, and the lonely streams,
Wherever nature led: more like a man
Flying from something that he dreads, than one
Who sought the thing he loved. For nature then
(The coarser pleasures of my boyish days
And their glad animal movements all gone by)
To me was all in all.—I cannot paint
What then I was. The sounding cataract
Haunted me like a passion: the tall rock,
The mountain, and the deep and gloomy wood,
Their colours and their forms, were then to me
An appetite; a feeling and a love,

That had no need of a remoter charm,
By thought supplied, not any interest
Unborrowed from the eye.—That time is past,
And all its aching joys are now no more,
And all its dizzy raptures. Not for this
Faint I, nor mourn nor murmur; other gifts
Have followed; for such loss, I would believe,
Abundant recompense. For I have learned
To look on nature, not as in the hour
Of thoughtless youth; but hearing oftentimes
The still sad music of humanity,
Nor harsh nor grating, though of ample power
To chasten and subdue.—And I have felt
A presence that disturbs me with the joy
Of elevated thoughts; a sense sublime
Of something far more deeply interfused,
Whose dwelling is the light of setting suns,
And the round ocean and the living air,
And the blue sky, and in the mind of man:
A motion and a spirit, that impels
All thinking things, all objects of all thought,
And rolls through all things. Therefore am I still
A lover of the meadows and the woods
And mountains; and of all that we behold
From this green earth; of all the mighty world
Of eye, and ear,—both what they half create,
And what perceive; well pleased to recognise
In nature and the language of the sense
The anchor of my purest thoughts, the nurse,
The guide, the guardian of my heart, and soul
Of all my moral being.
              Nor perchance,
If I were not thus taught, should I the more
Suffer my genial spirits to decay:
For thou art with me here upon the banks
Of this fair river; thou my dearest Friend,
My dear, dear Friend; and in thy voice I catch
The language of my former heart, and read
My former pleasures in the shooting lights
Of thy wild eyes. Oh! yet a little while
May I behold in thee what I was once,
My dear, dear Sister! and this prayer I make,
Knowing that Nature never did betray

The heart that loved her; 'tis her privilege,
Through all the years of this our life, to lead
From joy to joy: for she can so inform
The mind that is within us, so impress
With quietness and beauty, and so feed
With lofty thoughts, that neither evil tongues,
Rash judgments, nor the sneers of selfish men,
Nor greetings where no kindness is, nor all
The dreary intercourse of daily life,
Shall e'er prevail against us, or disturb
Our cheerful faith, that all which we behold
Is full of blessings. Therefore let the moon
Shine on thee in thy solitary walk;
And let the misty mountain-winds be free
To blow against thee: and, in after years,
When these wild ecstasies shall be matured
Into a sober pleasure; when thy mind
Shall be a mansion for all lovely forms,
Thy memory be as a dwelling-place
For all sweet sounds and harmonies; oh! then,
If solitude, or fear, or pain, or grief,
Should be thy portion, with what healing thoughts
Of tender joy wilt thou remember me,
And these my exhortations! Nor, perchance—
If I should be where I no more can hear
Thy voice, nor catch from thy wild eyes these gleams
Of past existence—wilt thou then forget
That on the banks of this delightful stream
We stood together; and that I, so long
A worshipper of Nature, hither came
Unwearied in that service: rather say
With warmer love—oh! with far deeper zeal
Of holier love. Nor wilt thou then forget,
That after many wanderings, many years
Of absence, these steep woods and lofty cliffs,
And this green pastoral landscape, were to me
More dear, both for themselves and for thy sake!

—1798

## SAMUEL TAYLOR COLERIDGE (1772–1834)

*Samuel Taylor Coleridge, inspired but erratic, did his best work, like Wordsworth, during the great first decade of their friendship, the period that produced* Lyrical Ballads. *Coleridge's later life is a tragic tale of financial and marital problems, unfinished projects, and a ruinous addiction to opium. A brilliant critic, Coleridge lectured on Shakespeare and other writers and wrote the* Biographia Literaria, *perhaps the greatest literary autobiography ever written.*

# Kubla Khan°

OR A VISION IN A DREAM,°A FRAGMENT

In Xanadu did Kubla Khan
A stately pleasure-dome decree:
Where Alph, the sacred river, ran
Through caverns measureless to man

Down to a sunless sea.                                                    5
So twice five miles of fertile ground
With walls and towers were girdled round:
And there were gardens bright with sinuous rills,
Where blossomed many an incense-bearing tree;
And here were forests ancient as the hills,                   10
Enfolding sunny spots of greenery.

But oh! that deep romantic chasm which slanted
Down the green hill athwart a cedarn cover!
A savage place! as holy and enchanted
As e'er beneath a waning moon was haunted              15
By woman wailing for her demon lover!
And from this chasm, with ceaseless turmoil seething,
As if this earth in fast thick pants were breathing,
A mighty fountain momently was forced:
Amid whose swift half-intermitted burst                        20
Huge fragments vaulted like rebounding hail,
Or chaffy grain beneath the thresher's flail:
And 'mid these dancing rocks at once and ever

**Kubla Khan** ruler of China (1216-1294)   **vision in a dream** Coleridge's own account tells how he took opium for an illness and slept for three hours, during which time he envisioned a complete poem of some 300 lines. When he awoke, he began to write down the details of his dream. "At this moment he was unfortunately called out by a person on business from Porlock, and detained by him above an hour, and on his return to the room found, to his no small surprise and mortification, that though he still retained some vague and dim recollection of the general purport of the vision, yet, with the exception of some eight or ten scattered lines and images on the surface of a stream into which a stone has been cast..." [Coleridge's note].

It flung up momently the sacred river.
Five miles meandering with a mazy motion          25
Through wood and dale the sacred river ran,
Then reached the caverns measureless to man,
And sank in tumult to a lifeless ocean:
And 'mid this tumult Kubla heard from far
Ancestral voices prophesying war!          30

    The shadow of the dome of pleasure
    Floated midway on the waves;
    Where was heard the mingled measure
    From the fountain and the caves.
It was a miracle of rare device,          35
A sunny pleasure-dome with caves of ice!

    A damsel with a dulcimer
    In a vision once I saw:
    It was an Abyssinian maid,
    And on her dulcimer she played,          40
    Singing of Mount Abora.
    Could I revive within me
    Her symphony and song,

    To such a deep delight 'twould win me,
That with music loud and long,          45
I would build that dome in air,
That sunny dome! those caves of ice!
And all who heard should see them there,
And all should cry, Beware! Beware!
His flashing eyes, his floating hair!          50
Weave a circle round him thrice,
And close your eyes with holy dread,
For he on honey-dew hath fed,
And drunk the milk of Paradise.

—1797–98

# Work Without Hope

*Lines Composed 21st February 1825*

All Nature seems at work. Slugs leave their lair—
The bees are stirring—birds are on the wing—
And Winter slumbering in the open air
Wears on his smiling face a dream of Spring!
And I the while, the sole unbusy thing,          5
Nor honey make, nor pair, nor build, nor sing.

Yet well I ken° the banks where amaranths° blow,
Have traced the fount whence streams of nectar flow.
Bloom, O ye amaranths! bloom for whom ye may,
For me ye bloom not! Glide, rich streams, away!                    10
With lips unbrightened, wreathless brow, I stroll:
And would you learn the spells that drowse my soul?
Work without Hope draws° nectar in a sieve,
And Hope without an object cannot live.

—1828

---

## GEORGE GORDON, LORD BYRON ■ (1788–1824)

*George Gordon, Lord Byron attained flamboyant celebrity status, leading
an unconventional lifestyle that contributed to his notoriety. Byron was the
most widely read of all the English romantic poets, but his verse romances
and mock-epic poems like* Don Juan *have not proved as popular in our era.
An English aristocrat who was committed to revolutionary ideals, Byron died
while lending military assistance to the cause of Greek freedom.*

# She Walks in Beauty

She walks in beauty, like the night
    Of cloudless climes and starry skies;
And all that's best of dark and bright
    Meet in her aspect and her eyes:
Thus mellowed to that tender light                    5
    Which heaven to gaudy day denies.

One shade the more, one ray the less,
    Had half impaired the nameless grace
Which waves in every raven tress,
    Or softly lightens o'er her face;                    10
Where thoughts serenely sweet express
    How pure, how dear their dwelling-place.

And on that cheek, and o'er that brow,
    So soft, so calm, yet eloquent,
The smiles that win, the tints that glow,                    15
    But tell of days in goodness spent,
A mind at peace with all below,
    A heart whose love is innocent!

—1815

7 **ken** know  **amaranths** legendary flowers that never fade  13 **draws** dips

## Stanzas

*When A Man Hath No Freedom To Fight For At Home*

When a man hath no freedom to fight for at home,
    Let him combat for that of his neighbors;
Let him think of the glories of Greece and of Rome,
    And get knocked on his head for his labors.

To do good to mankind is the chivalrous plan,          5
    And is always as nobly requited:
Then battle for freedom wherever you can,
    And, if not shot or hanged, you'll get knighted.

—1824

## When We Two Parted

When we two parted
    In silence and tears,
Half broken-hearted
    To sever for years,
Pale grew thy cheek and cold,          5
    Colder thy kiss;
Truly that hour foretold
    Sorrow to this.

The dew of the morning
    Sunk chill on my brow—          10
It felt like the warning
    Of what I feel now.
Thy vows are all broken,
    And light is thy fame;
I hear thy name spoken,          15
    And share in its shame.

They name thee before me,
    A knell to mine ear;
A shudder comes o'er me—
    Why wert thou so dear?          20
They know not I knew thee,
    Who knew thee too well:—
Long, long shall I rue thee,
    Too deeply to tell.

In secret we met—          25
    In silence I grieve
That thy heart could forget,

Thy spirit deceive.
If I should meet thee
After long years,                                                            30
How should I greet thee?—
With silence and tears.

—1813

---

## PERCY BYSSHE SHELLEY ■ (1792–1822)

*Percy Bysshe Shelley, like his friend Byron, has not found as much favor
in recent eras as the other English romantics, although his political liber-
alism anticipates many currents of our own day. Perhaps his unbridled
emotionalism is sometimes too intense for modern readers. His wife, Mary
Wollstonecraft Shelley, will be remembered as the author of the classic horror
novel Frankenstein.*

# Ode to the West Wind

## 1

O wild West Wind, thou breath of Autumn's being,
Thou, from whose unseen presence the leaves dead
Are driven, like ghosts from an enchanter fleeing,
Yellow, and black, and pale, and hectic red,
Pestilence-stricken multitudes: O thou,                                       5
Who chariotest to their dark wintry bed

The wingèd seeds, where they lie cold and low,
Each like a corpse within its grave, until
Thine azure sister of the Spring° shall blow

Her clarion o'er the dreaming earth, and fill                                 10
(Driving sweet buds like flocks to feed in air)
With living hues and odors plain and hill:

Wild Spirit, which art moving everywhere;
Destroyer and preserver; hear, oh, hear!

## 2

Thou on whose stream, mid the steep sky's commotion,                          15
Loose clouds like earth's decaying leaves are shed,
Shook from the tangled boughs of Heaven and Ocean,

**9 azure sister of the Spring** i.e., the South Wind

Angels of rain and lightning: there are spread
On the blue surface of thine aëry surge,
Like the bright hair uplifted from the head                           20

Of some fierce Mænad,° even from the dim verge
Of the horizon to the zenith's height,
The locks of the approaching storm. Thou dirge

Of the dying year, to which this closing night
Will be the dome of a vast sepulcher,                                 25
Vaulted with all thy congregated might

Of vapors, from whose solid atmosphere
Black rain, and fire, and hail will burst: oh, hear!

3

Thou who didst waken from his summer dreams
The blue Mediterranean, where he lay,                                 30
Lulled by the coil of his crystàlline streams,

Beside a pumice isle in Baiae's bay,°
And saw in sleep old palaces and towers
Quivering within the wave's intenser day,

All overgrown with azure moss and flowers                            35
So sweet, the sense faints picturing them! Thou
For whose path the Atlantic's level powers

Cleave themselves into chasms, while far below
The sea-blooms and the oozy woods which wear
The sapless foliage of the ocean, know                               40

Thy voice, and suddenly grow gray with fear,
And tremble and despoil themselves: oh, hear!

4

If I were a dead leaf thou mightest bear;
If I were a swift cloud to fly with thee;
A wave to pant beneath thy power, and share                          45

The impulse of thy strength, only less free
Than thou, O uncontrollable! If even
I were as in my boyhood, and could be

The comrade of thy wanderings over Heaven,
As then, when to outstrip thy skyey speed                            50
Scarce seemed a vision; I would ne'er have striven

21 **Mænad** female worshipper of Bacchus, god of wine   32 **Baiae's bay** near Naples

As thus with thee in prayer in my sore need.
Oh, lift me as a wave, a leaf, a cloud!
I fall upon the thorns of life! I bleed!

A heavy weight of hours has chained and bowed          55
One too like thee: tameless, and swift, and proud.

5

Make me thy lyre, even as the forest is:
What if my leaves are falling like its own!
The tumult of thy mighty harmonies

Will take from both a deep, autumnal tone,              60
Sweet though in sadness. Be thou, Spirit fierce,
My spirit! Be thou me, impetuous one!

Drive my dead thoughts over the universe
Like withered leaves to quicken a new birth!
And, by the incantation of this verse,                 65

Scatter, as from an unextinguished hearth
Ashes and sparks, my words among mankind!
Be through my lips to unawakened earth

The trumpet of a prophecy! O Wind,
If Winter comes, can Spring be far behind?             70

—1820

# Ozymandias°

I met a traveler from an antique land
Who said: Two vast and trunkless legs of stone
Stand in the desert....Near them, on the sand,
Half sunk, a shattered visage lies, whose frown,
And wrinkled lip, and sneer of cold command,            5
Tell that its sculptor well those passions read
Which yet survive, stamped on these lifeless things,
The hand that mocked them, and the heart that fed:
And on the pedestal these words appear:
"My name is Ozymandias, king of kings:                 10
Look on my works, ye Mighty, and despair!"
Nothing beside remains. Round the decay
Of that colossal wreck, boundless and bare
The lone and level sands stretch far away.

—1818

**Ozymandias** Ramses II of Egypt (c. 1250 BC)

**JOHN KEATS ■ (1795–1821)**

*John Keats is now perhaps the most admired of all the major romantics. Certainly his tragic death from tuberculosis in his twenties gives poignancy to thoughts of the doomed young poet writing feverishly in a futile race against time; "Here lies one whose name was writ in water" are the words he chose for his own epitaph. Many of Keats's poems are concerned with glimpses of the eternal, whether a translation of an ancient epic poem or a pristine artifact of a vanished civilization.*

# Bright Star, Would I Were Stedfast as Thou Art°

Bright star, would I were stedfast as thou art—
    Not in lone splendor hung aloft the night,
And watching, with eternal lids apart,
    Like nature's patient, sleepless eremite°,
The moving waters at their priestlike task         5
    Of pure ablution° round earth's human shores,
Or gazing on the new soft-fallen mask
    Of snow upon the mountains and the moors;
No—yet still stedfast, still unchangeable,
    Pillow'd upon my fair love's ripening breast,     10
To feel for ever its soft swell and fall,
    Awake for ever in a sweet unrest,
Still, still to hear her tender-taken breath,
    And so live ever—or else swoon to death°.

                            —1821

# La Belle Dame sans Merci°

O what can ail thee, Knight at arms,
    Alone and palely loitering?
The sedge has withered from the Lake
    And no birds sing!

O what can ail thee, Knight at arms,     5
    So haggard, and so woebegone?

**Bright star, would I were stedfast as thou art** While on a tour of the Lake District in 1818, Keats had said that the austere scenes "refine one's sensual vision into a sort of north star which can never cease to be open lidded and steadfast over the wonders of the great Power." The thought developed into this sonnet, which Keats drafted in 1819, then copied into his volume of Shakespeare's poems at the end of September or the beginning of October 1820, while on his way to Italy, where he died   **4 eremite** Hermit, religious solitary   **6 ablution** warhing, as part of a religious rite   **14 death** in the earlier version: "Half passionless, and so swoon on to death
**La Belle Dame sans Merci** "the beautiful lady without pity"

The squirrel's granary is full
    And the harvest's done.

I see a lily on thy brow
    With anguish moist and fever dew,          10
And on thy cheeks a fading rose
    Fast withereth too.

"I met a Lady in the Meads,
    Full beautiful, a faery's child,
Her hair was long, her foot was light,       15
    And her eyes were wild.

"I made a Garland for her head,
    And bracelets too, and fragrant Zone;°
She looked at me as she did love
    And made sweet moan.          20

"I set her on my pacing steed
    And nothing else saw all day long,
For sidelong would she bend and sing
    A faery's song.

"She found me roots of relish sweet,      25
    And honey wild, and manna dew,
And sure in language strange she said
    'I love thee true.'

"She took me to her elfin grot°
    And there she wept and sighed full sore,   30
And there I shut her wild wild eyes
    With kisses four.

"And there she lullèd me asleep,
    And there I dreamed, Ah Woe betide!
The latest dream I ever dreamt        35
    On the cold hill side.

"I saw pale Kings, and Princes too,
    Pale warriors, death-pale were they all;
They cried, 'La belle Dame sans merci
    Hath thee in thrall!'         40

"I saw their starved lips in the gloam
    With horrid warning gapèd wide,
And I awoke, and found me here
    On the cold hill's side.

**18 Zone** belt   **29 grot** cave

"And this is why I sojourn here                                    45
     Alone and palely loitering;
Though the sedge is withered from the Lake,
     And no birds sing."

                                                              —1819

# Ode on a Grecian Urn 1820

### I

Thou still unravished bride of quietness,
     Thou foster-child of silence and slow time,
Sylvan historian, who canst thus express
     A flowery tale more sweetly than our rhyme:
What leaf-fringed legend haunts about thy shape              5
     Of deities or mortals, or of both,
          In Tempe or the dales of Arcady?
     What men or gods are these? What maidens loth?
What mad pursuit? What struggle to escape?
     What pipes and timbrels? What wild ecstasy?             10

### II

Heard melodies are sweet, but those unheard
     Are sweeter; therefore, ye soft pipes, play on;
Not to the sensual° ear, but, more endeared,
     Pipe to the spirit ditties of no tone:
Fair youth, beneath the trees, thou canst not leave         15
     Thy song, nor ever can those trees be bare;
          Bold Lover, never, never canst thou kiss,
Though winning near the goal—yet, do not grieve;
          She cannot fade, though thou hast not thy bliss,
     For ever wilt thou love, and she be fair!               20

### III

Ah, happy, happy boughs! that cannot shed
     Your leaves, nor ever bid the Spring adieu;
And, happy melodist, unwearièd,
     For ever piping songs for ever new;

**13 sensual** physical

More happy love! more happy, happy love!                    25
    For ever warm and still to be enjoyed,
      For ever panting, and for ever young;
All breathing human passion far above,
    That leaves a heart high-sorrowful and cloyed,
      A burning forehead, and a parching tongue.      30

### IV

Who are these coming to the sacrifice?
    To what green altar, O mysterious priest,
Lead'st thou that heifer lowing at the skies,
    And all her silken flanks with garlands drest?
What little town by river or sea shore,                     35
    Or mountain-built with peaceful citadel,
      Is emptied of this folk, this pious morn?
And, little town, thy streets for evermore
    Will silent be; and not a soul to tell
      Why thou art desolate, can e'er return.         40

### V

O Attic shape! Fair attitude! with brede°
    Of marble men and maidens overwrought,
With forest branches and the trodden weed;
    Thou, silent form, dost tease us out of thought
As doth eternity: Cold Pastoral!                           45
    When old age shall this generation waste,
      Thou shalt remain, in midst of other woe
Than ours, a friend to man, to whom thou say'st,
    Beauty is truth, truth beauty,—that is all
      Ye know on earth, and all ye need to know.

—1820

# On First Looking into Chapman's Homer°

Much have I traveled in the realms of gold,
    And many goodly states and kingdoms seen;
    Round many western islands have I been

**41 brede** ornamental pattern
**Chapman's Homer** translation of the *Iliad* and *Odyssey* by George Chapman (1559–1634)

Which bards in fealty to Apollo° hold.
Oft of one wide expanse had I been told                     5
    That deep-browed Homer ruled as his demesne;
    Yet did I never breathe its pure serene
Till I heard Chapman speak out loud and bold:
Then felt I like some watcher of the skies
    When a new planet swims into his ken;                  10
Or like stout Cortez° when with eagle eyes
    He stared at the Pacific—and all his men
Looked at each other with a wild surmise—
    Silent, upon a peak in Darien.°

—1816

## ELIZABETH BARRETT BROWNING ■ (1806–1861)

*Elizabeth Barrett Browning was already a famous poet when she met her husband-to-be, Robert Browning, who had been corresponding with her on literary matters. She originally published her famous sonnet sequence, written in the first years of her marriage, in the guise of a translation of Portuguese poems, perhaps to mask their personal revelations.*

# Sonnets from the Portuguese, 18

I never gave a lock of hair away
To a man, dearest, except this to thee,
Which now upon my fingers thoughtfully,
I ring out to the full brown length and say
"Take it." My day of youth went yesterday;            5
My hair no longer bounds to my foot's glee,
Nor plant I it from rose or myrtle-tree,
As girls do, any more: it only may
Now shade on two pale cheeks the mark of tears,
Taught drooping from the head that hangs aside        10
Through sorrow's trick. I thought the funeral-shears
Would take this first, but Love is justified,—
Take it thou,—finding pure, from all those years,
The kiss my mother left here when she died.

—1845–46

---

4 **Apollo** here, the god of poetry   11 **Cortez** Balboa was actually the first European to see the Pacific   14 **Darien** in modern-day Panama

# Sonnets from the Portuguese, 43

How do I love thee? Let me count the ways.
I love thee to the depth and breadth and height
My soul can reach, when feeling out of sight
For the ends of Being and ideal Grace.
I love thee to the level of everyday's                               5
Most quiet need, by sun and candle-light.
I love thee freely, as men strive for Right;
I love thee purely, as they turn from Praise.
I love thee with the passion put to use
In my old griefs, and with my childhood's faith.            10
I love thee with a love I seemed to lose
With my lost saints—I love thee with the breath,
Smiles, tears, of all my life!—and, if God choose,
I shall but love thee better after death.

—1845–46

---

**HENRY WADSWORTH LONGFELLOW ■ (1807–1882)**

*Henry Wadsworth Longfellow was by far the most prominent nineteenth-century American poet, and his international fame led to his bust being placed in Westminster Abbey after his death. The long epic poems like* Evangeline *and* Hiawatha *that were immensely popular among contemporary readers are seldom read today, but his shorter poems reveal a level of artistry that few poets have equaled.*

# The Arsenal at Springfield

This is the Arsenal. From floor to ceiling,
   Like a huge organ, rise the burnished arms;
But from their silent pipes no anthem pealing
   Startles the villages with strange alarms.

Ah! what a sound will rise, how wild and dreary,            5
   When the death-angel touches those swift keys!
What loud lament and dismal Miserere°
   Will mingle with their awful symphonies!

---

**7 Miserere** Latin hymn from Psalm 1: "Have mercy on me, Lord."

I hear even now the infinite fierce chorus,
    The cries of agony, the endless groan,           10
Which, through the ages that have gone before us,
    In long reverberations reach our own.

On helm and harness rings the Saxon hammer,
    Through Cimbric° forest roars the Norseman's song,
And loud, amid the universal clamor,           15
    O'er distant deserts sounds the Tartar gong.

I hear the Florentine, who from his palace
    Wheels out his battle-bell with dreadful din,
And Aztec priests upon their teocallis°
    Beat the wild war-drums made of serpent's skin;    20

The tumult of each sacked and burning village;
    The shout that every prayer for mercy drowns;
The soldiers' revels in the midst of pillage;
    The wail of famine in beleaguered towns;

The bursting shell, the gateway wrenched asunder,    25
    The rattling musketry, the clashing blade;
And ever and anon, in tones of thunder
    The diapason° of the cannonade.

Is it, O man, with such discordant noises,
    With such accursed instruments as these,        30
Thou drownest Nature's sweet and kindly voices,
    And jarrest the celestial harmonies?

Were half the power, that fills the world with terror,
    Were half the wealth bestowed on camps and courts,
Given to redeem the human mind from error,    35
    There were no need of arsenals or forts:

The warrior's name would be a name abhorred!
    And every nation, that should lift again
Its hand against a brother, on its forehead
    Would wear forevermore the curse of Cain!    40

Down the dark future, through long generations,
    The echoing sounds grow fainter and then cease;
And like a bell, with solemn, sweet vibrations,
    I hear once more the voice of Christ say, "Peace!"

Peace! and no longer from its brazen portals    45
    The blast of War's great organ shakes the skies!

---

14 **Cimbric** in Denmark   19 **teocallis** temples atop pyramids   28 **diapason** full range of pipe organ

But beautiful as songs of the immortals,
  The holy melodies of love arise.

—1846

# The Cross of Snow

In the long, sleepless watches of the night,
  A gentle face—the face of one long dead—
  Looks at me from the wall, where round its head
  The night-lamp casts a halo of pale light.
Here in this room she died; and soul more white          5
  Never through martyrdom of fire° was led
  To its repose; nor can in books be read
  The legend of a life more benedight.°
There is a mountain in the distant West
  That, sun-defying, in its deep ravines          10
  Displays a cross of snow upon its side.
Such is the cross I wear upon my breast
  These eighteen years, through all the changing scenes
  And seasons, changeless since the day she died.

—1886

---

**EDGAR ALLAN POE** ■ (1809–1849)

*Edgar Allan Poe has survived his own myth as a deranged, drug-crazed genius, despite the wealth of evidence to the contrary that can be gleaned from his brilliant, though erratic, career as a poet, short story writer, critic, and editor. Poe's brand of romanticism seems at odds with that of other American poets of his day and is perhaps more in keeping with the spirit of Coleridge than that of Wordsworth. "The Raven" has been parodied perhaps more than any other American poem, yet it still retains a powerful hold on its audience.*

# The Haunted Palace

In the greenest of our valleys,
  By good angels tenanted,
Once a fair and stately palace—
  Radiant palace—reared its head.

---

**6 martyrdom of fire** Longfellow's second wife, Frances, died as the result of a household fire in 1861.
**8 benedight** blessed

In the monarch Thought's dominion—                                    5
  It stood there!
Never seraph spread a pinion
  Over fabric half so fair!

Banners yellow, glorious, golden,
  On its roof did float and flow,                                     10
(This—all this—was in the olden
  Time long ago,)
And every gentle air that dallied,
  In that sweet day,
Along the ramparts plumed and pallid,                                15
  A wingéd odor went away.

Wanderers in that happy valley,
  Through two luminous windows, saw
Spirits moving musically
  To a lute's well-tunéd law,                                        20
Round about a throne where, sitting,
  Porphyrogene!°
In state his glory well befitting,
  The ruler of the realm was seen.

And all with pearl and ruby glowing                                  25
  Was the fair palace door,
Through which came flowing, flowing, flowing,
  And sparkling evermore,
A troop of Echoes, whose sweet duty
  Was but to sing,                                                   30
In voices of surpassing beauty,
  The wit and wisdom of their king.

But evil things, in robes of sorrow,
  Assailed the monarch's high estate.
(Ah, let us mourn!—for never morrow                                  35
  Shall dawn upon him, desolate!)
And round about his home the glory
  That blushed and bloomed,
Is but a dim-remembered story
  Of the old time entombed.                                         40

and travellers, now, within that valley,
  Through the red-litten windows see
Vast forms that move fantastically
  To a discordant melody,

22 **Porphyrogene** born to the purple, i.e., royal

While, like a ghastly rapid river,                                    45
    Through the pale door
A hideous throng rush out forever,
    And laugh—but smile no more.

—1845

# The Raven

Once upon a midnight dreary, while I pondered, weak and weary,
Over many a quaint and curious volume of forgotten lore—
While I nodded, nearly napping, suddenly there came a tapping,
As of some one gently rapping, rapping at my chamber door.
"'Tis some visitor," I muttered, "tapping at my chamber door—    5
                Only this and nothing more."

Ah, distinctly I remember it was in the bleak December;
And each separate dying ember wrought its ghost upon the floor.
Eagerly I wished the morrow;—vainly I had sought to borrow
From my books surcease of sorrow—sorrow for the lost Lenore—    10
For the rare and radiant maiden whom the angels name Lenore—
              Nameless *here* for evermore.

And the silken, sad, uncertain rustling of each purple curtain
Thrilled me—filled me with fantastic terrors never felt before;
So that now, to still the beating of my heart, I stood repeating    15
"'Tis some visitor entreating entrance at my chamber door;—
Some late visitor entreating entrance at my chamber door;—
            This it is and nothing more."

Presently my soul grew stronger; hesitating then no longer,
"Sir," said I, "or Madam, truly your forgiveness I implore;    20
But the fact is I was napping, and so gently you came rapping,
And so faintly you came tapping, tapping at my chamber door,
That I scarce was sure I heard you"—here I opened wide the door;—
           Darkness there and nothing more.

Deep into that darkness peering, long I stood there wondering,
    fearing,                                    25
Doubting, dreaming dreams no mortal ever dared to dream before;
But the silence was unbroken, and the stillness gave no token,
And the only word there spoken was the whispered word, "Lenore?"
This I whispered, and an echo murmured back the word, "Lenore!"
Merely this and nothing more.                                    30

Back into the chamber turning, all my soul within me burning,
Soon again I heard a tapping somewhat louder than before.
"Surely," said I, "surely that is something at my window lattice;

Let me see, then, what thereat is, and this mystery explore—
Let my heart be still a moment and this mystery explore;—          35
                    'Tis the wind and nothing more!"

Open here I flung the shutter, when, with many a flirt and flutter,
In there stepped a stately Raven of the saintly days of yore;
Not the least obeisance made he; not a minute stopped or stayed he;
But, with mien of lord or lady, perched above my chamber door—   40
Perched upon a bust of Pallas° just above my chamber door—
                  Perched, and sat, and nothing more.

Then this ebony bird beguiling my sad fancy into smiling,
By the grave and stern decorum of the countenance it wore,
"Though thy crest be shorn and shaven, thou," I said, "art sure no
     craven,                                                          45
Ghastly grim and ancient Raven wandering from the Nightly shore—
Tell me what thy lordly name is on the Night's Plutonian° shore!"
                  Quoth the Raven, "Nevermore."

Much I marvelled this ungainly fowl to hear discourse so plainly,
Though its answer little meaning—little relevancy bore;              50
For we cannot help agreeing that no living human being
Ever yet was blessed with seeing bird above his chamber door—
Bird or beast upon the sculptured bust above his chamber door,
                With such name as "Nevermore."

But the Raven, sitting lonely on the placid bust, spoke only         55
That one word, as if his soul in that one word he did outpour.
Nothing farther then he uttered—not a feather then he fluttered—
Till I scarcely more than muttered, "Other friends have flown before—
On the morrow *he* will leave me, as my Hopes have flown before."
            Then the bird said, "Nevermore."         60

Startled at the stillness broken by reply so aptly spoken,
"Doubtless," said I, "what it utters is its only stock and store
Caught from some unhappy master whom unmerciful Disaster
Followed fast and followed faster till his songs one burden bore—
Till the dirges of his Hope that melancholy burden bore             65
             Of 'Never—nevermore.'"

But the Raven still beguiling all my sad fancy into smiling,
Straight I wheeled a cushioned seat in front of bird and bust and door;
Then, upon the velvet sinking, I betook myself to linking
Fancy unto fancy, thinking what this ominous bird of yore—          70
What this grim, ungainly, ghastly, gaunt, and ominous bird of yore
            Meant in croaking "Nevermore."

**41 Pallas** Athena, goddess of wisdom
**47 Plutonian** after Pluto, Roman god of the underworld

This I sat engaged in guessing, but no syllable expressing
To the fowl whose fiery eyes now burned into my bosom's core;
This and more I sat divining, with my head at ease reclining          75
On the cushion's velvet lining that the lamp-light gloated o'er,
But whose velvet-violet lining with the lamp-light gloating o'er,
                              She shall press, ah, nevermore!

Then, methought, the air grew denser, perfumed from an unseen censer
Swung by seraphim whose foot-falls tinkled on the tufted floor.          80
"Wretch," I cried, "thy God hath lent thee—by these angels he hath
    sent thee.
Respite—respite and nepenthe° from thy memories of Lenore;
Quaff, oh quaff this kind nepenthe and forget this lost Lenore!"
                              Quoth the Raven, "Nevermore."

"Prophet!" said I, "thing of evil!—prophet still, if bird or devil!—  85
Whether Tempter sent, or whether tempest tossed thee here ashore,
Desolate yet all undaunted, on this desert land enchanted—
On this home by Horror haunted—tell me truly, I implore—
Is there—*is* there balm in Gilead?—tell me—tell me, I implore!"
                              Quoth the Raven, "Nevermore."          90

"Prophet!" said I, "thing of evil!—prophet still, if bird or devil!
By that Heaven that bends above us—by that God we both adore—
Tell this soul with sorrow laden if, within the distant Aidenn,°
It shall clasp a sainted maiden whom the angels name Lenore—
Clasp a rare and radiant maiden whom the angels name Lenore."          95
                              Quoth the Raven, "Nevermore."

"Be that word our sign of parting, bird or fiend!" I shrieked, upstarting—
"Get thee back into the tempest and the Night's Plutonian shore!
Leave no black plume as a token of that lie thy soul hath spoken!
Leave my loneliness unbroken!—quit the bust above my door!          100
Take thy beak from out my heart, and take thy from off my door!"
                              Quoth the Raven, "Nevermore."

And the Raven, never flitting, still is sitting, *still* is sitting
On the pallid bust of Pallas just above my chamber door;
And his eyes have all the seeming of a demon's that is dreaming, 105
And the lamp-light o'er him streaming throws his shadow on the floor;
And my soul from out that shadow that lies floating on the floor
                              Shall be lifted—nevermore!

                                  —1845

**82 nepenthe** drug causing forgetfulness   **93 Aidenn** Eden

## Sonnet: To Science

Science! true daughter of Old Time thou art!
 Who alterest all things with the peering eyes.
Why preyest thou thus upon the poet's heart,
 Vulture, whose wings are dull realities?
How should he love thee? or how deem thee wise?    5
 Who wouldst not leave him in his wandering
To seek for treasure in the jeweled skies,
 Albeit he soared with an undaunted wing?
Has thou not dragged Diana° from her car?
 And driven the Hamadryad from the wood    10
To seek a shelter in some happier star?
 Hast thou not torn the Naiad from her flood,
The Elfin from the green grass, and from me
 The summer dream beneath the tamarind tree?

              —1829, 1845

---

**ALFRED, LORD TENNYSON** ■ **(1809–1892)**

*Alfred, Lord Tennyson became the most famous English poet with the 1850 pub-
lication of* In Memoriam, *a sequence of poems on the death of his friend A.H.
Hallam. In the same year, he became poet laureate. Modern critical opinion has
focused more favorably on Tennyson's lyrical gifts than on his talents for narrative or drama. T.S. Eliot and W.H. Auden, among other critics, praised Tennyson's
rhythms and sound patterns but had reservations about his depth of intellect,
especially when he took on the role of official apologist for Victorian England.*

## The Lady of Shalott

### Part I

On either side the river lie
Long fields of barley and of rye,
That clothe the wold° and meet the sky;
And through the field the road runs by
 To many-towered Camelot;        5
And up and down the people go,
Gazing where the lilies blow
Round an island there below,

         The island of Shalott.

9 **Diana** Roman goddess, whose chariot was the moon.
3 **wold** plain

Willows whiten, aspens quiver,  10
Little breezes dusk and shiver
Through the wave that runs forever
By the island in the river
      Flowing down to Camelot.

Four gray walls, and four gray towers,  15
Overlook a space of flowers,
And the silent isle embowers
      The Lady of Shalott.

By the margin, willow-veiled,
Slide the heavy barges trailed  20
By slow horses; and unhailed
The shallop° flitteth silken-sailed
      Skimming down to Camelot:
But who hath seen her wave her hand?
Or at the casement seen her stand?  25
Or is she known in all the land,
      The Lady of Shalott?

Only reapers, reaping early
In among the bearded barley,
Hear a song that echoes cheerly  30
From the river winding clearly,
      Down to towered Camelot;
And by the moon the reaper weary,
Piling sheaves in uplands airy,
Listening, whispers, "'Tis the fairy  35
      Lady of Shalott."

## Part II

There she weaves by night and day
A magic web with colors gay.
She has heard a whisper say,
A curse is on her if she stay  40
      To look down to Camelot.
She knows not what the curse may be,
And so she weaveth steadily,
And little other care hath she,
      The Lady of Shalott.  45

And moving through a mirror clear
That hangs before her all the year,

**22 shallop** open boat

Shadows of the world appear.
There she sees the highway near
   Winding down to Camelot;          50
There the river eddy whirls,
And there the surly village-churls,
And the red cloaks of market girls,
   Pass onward from Shalott.

Sometimes a troop of damsels glad,       55
An abbot on an ambling pad,°
Sometimes a curly shepherd-lad,
Or long-haired page in crimson clad,
   Goes by to towered Camelot;
And sometimes through the mirror blue    60
The knights come riding two and two;
She hath no loyal knight and true,
   The Lady of Shalott.

But in her web she still delights
To weave the mirror's magic sights,      65
For often through the silent nights
A funeral, with plumes and lights
   And music, went to Camelot;
Or when the moon was overhead,
Came two young lovers lately wed;     70
"I am half sick of shadows," said
   The Lady of Shalott.

## Part III

A bow-shot from her bower eaves,
He rode between the barley sheaves;
The sun came dazzling through the leaves,   75
And flamed upon the brazen greaves°
   Of bold Sir Lancelot.
A red-cross knight forever kneeled
To a lady in his shield.
That sparkled on the yellow field,     80
   Beside remote Shalott.

The gemmy bridle glittered free,
Like to some branch of stars we see
Hung in the golden Galaxy.
The bridle bells rang merrily     85

**56 pad** horse   **76 greaves** armor for legs

As he rode down to Camelot;
And from his blazoned baldric° slung
A mighty silver bugle hung,
And as he rode his armor rung,
    Beside remote Shalott.           90
All in the blue unclouded weather
Thick-jeweled shone the saddle-leather,
The helmet and the helmet-feather
Burned like one burning flame together
    As he rode down to Camelot;      95
As often through the purple night,
Below the starry clusters bright,
Some bearded meteor, trailing light,
    Moves over still Shalott.

His broad clear brow in sunlight glowed;    100
On burnished hooves his war horse trode;
From underneath his helmet flowed
His coal-black curls as on he rode,
    As he rode down to Camelot.
From the bank and from the river      105
He flashed into the crystal mirror,
"Tirra lirra," by the river
    Sang Sir Lancelot.

She left the web, she left the loom,
She made three paces through the room,    110
She saw the water lily bloom,
She saw the helmet and the plume,
    She looked down to Camelot.
Out flew the web and floated wide;
The mirror cracked from side to side;    115
"The curse is come upon me," cried
    The Lady of Shalott.

## Part IV

In the stormy east wind straining,
The pale yellow woods were waning,
The broad stream in his banks complaining.    120
Heavily the low sky raining
    Over towered Camelot;
Down she came and found a boat

---

**87 baldric** belt to support a sword

Beneath a willow left afloat,
And round about the prow she wrote 125
  *The Lady of Shalott.*
And down the river's dim expanse
Like some bold seer in a trance,
Seeing all his own mischance—
With a glassy countenance 130
  Did she look to Camelot.
And at the closing of the day
She loosed the chain, and down she lay;
The broad stream bore her far away,
  *The Lady of Shalott.* 135

Lying, robed in snowy white
That loosely flew to left and right—
The leaves upon her falling light—
Through the noises of the night
  She floated down to Camelot; 140
And as the boat-head wound along
The willowy hills and fields among,
They heard her singing her last song,
  *The Lady of Shalott.*

Heard a carol, mournful, holy, 145
Chanted loudly, chanted lowly,
Till her blood was frozen slowly,
And her eyes were darkened wholly,
  Turned to towered Camelot.
For ere she reached upon the tide 150
The first house by the waterside,
Singing in her song she died,
  *The Lady of Shalott.*

Under tower and balcony,
By garden wall and gallery, 155
A gleaming shape she floated by,
Dead-pale between the houses high,
  Silent into Camelot.
Out upon the wharfs they came,
Knight and burgher, lord and dame, 160
And round the prow they read her name,
  *The Lady of Shalott.*
Who is this? And what is here?
And in the lighted palace near
Died the sound of royal cheer; 165

And they crossed themselves for fear,
    All the knights at Camelot.
But Lancelot mused a little space;
He said, "She has a lovely face;
God in his mercy lend her grace,          170
    The Lady of Shalott."

—1842

# Tears, Idle Tears

### *from* The Princess

    Tears, idle tears, I know not what they mean,
Tears from the depth of some divine despair
Rise in the heart, and gather to the eyes,
In looking on the happy autumn-fields,
And thinking of the days that are no more.      5

    Fresh as the first beam glittering on a sail,
That brings our friends up from the underworld,
Sad as the last which reddens over one
That sinks with all we love below the verge;
So sad, so fresh, the days that are no more.     10

    Ah, sad and strange as in dark summer dawns
The earliest pipe of half-awakened birds
To dying ears, when unto dying eyes
The casement slowly grows a glimmering square;
So sad, so strange, the days that are no more.    15

    Dear as remembered kisses after death,
And sweet as those by hopeless fancy feigned
On lips that are for others; deep as love,
Deep as first love, and wild with all regret;
O Death in Life, the days that are no more!     20

—1847

# Ulysses°

It little profits that an idle king,
By this still hearth, among these barren crags,
Matched with an aged wife, I mete and dole
Unequal laws unto a savage race,
That hoard, and sleep, and feed, and know not me.    5

---

**Ulysses** Homer's *Odyssey* ends with the return of Odysseus (Ulysses) to his island kingdom, Ithaca. Tennyson's poem takes place some years later.

I cannot rest from travel; I will drink
Life to the lees. All times I have enjoyed
Greatly, have suffered greatly, both with those
That loved me, and alone; on shore, and when
Through scudding drifts the rainy Hyades°                    10
Vexed the dim sea. I am become a name;
For always roaming with a hungry heart
Much have I seen and known—cities of men
And manners, climates, councils, governments,
Myself not least, but honored of them all—                  15
And drunk delight of battle with my peers,
Far on the ringing plains of windy Troy.
I am a part of all that I have met;
Yet all experience is an arch wherethrough
Gleams that untraveled world whose margin fades            20
For ever and for ever when I move.
How dull it is to pause, to make an end,
To rust unburnished, not to shine in use!
As though to breathe were life! Life piled on life
Were all too little, and of one to me                       25
Little remains; but every hour is saved
From that eternal silence, something more,
A bringer of new things; and vile it were
For some three suns to store and hoard myself,
And this gray spirit yearning in desire                     30
To follow knowledge like a sinking star,
Beyond the utmost bound of human thought.
　　　This is my son, mine own Telemachus,
To whom I leave the scepter and the isle,
Well-loved of me, discerning to fulfill                     35
This labor, by slow prudence to make mild
A rugged people, and through soft degrees
Subdue them to the useful and the good.
Most blameless is he, centered in the sphere
Of common duties, decent not to fail                        40
In offices of tenderness, and pay
Meet adoration to my household gods,
When I am gone. He works his work, I mine.
　　　There lies the port; the vessel puffs her sail;
There gloom the dark, broad seas. My mariners,             45
Souls that have toiled, and wrought, and thought with me,
That ever with a frolic welcome took

**10 Hyades** a constellation thought to predict rain

The thunder and the sunshine, and opposed
Free hearts, free foreheads—you and I are old;
Old age hath yet his honor and his toil.                    50
Death closes all; but something ere the end,
Some work of noble note, may yet be done,
Not unbecoming men that strove with gods.
The lights begin to twinkle from the rocks;
The long day wanes; the low moon climbs; the deep          55
Moans round with many voices. Come, my friends,
'Tis not too late to seek a newer world.
Push off, and sitting well in order smite
The sounding furrows; for my purpose holds
To sail beyond the sunset, and the baths                   60
Of all the western stars, until I die.
It may be that the gulfs will wash us down;
It may be we shall touch the Happy Isles,°
And see the great Achilles, whom we knew.
Though much is taken, much abides; and though              65
We are not now that strength which in old days
Moved earth and heaven, that which we are, we are,
One equal temper of heroic hearts,
Made weak by time and fate, but strong in will
To strive, to seek, to find, and not to yield.            70

—1833

---

### ROBERT BROWNING ■ (1812–1889)

*Robert Browning wrote many successful dramatic monologues that are his lasting legacy, for he brings the genre to a level of achievement rarely equaled. Less regarded during his lifetime than his contemporary Tennyson, he has consistently risen in the esteem of modern readers. Often overlooked in his gallery of often grotesque characters are his considerable metrical skills and ability to simulate speech while working in demanding poetic forms.*

## My Last Duchess

FERRARA°

That's my last duchess painted on the wall,
Looking as if she were alive. I call
That piece a wonder, now: Frà Pandolf's° hands

---

**63 Happy Isles** Elysium, the resting place of dead heroes
**Ferrara** The speaker is probably Alfonso II d'Este, Duke of Ferrara (1533–158?)    **3 Frà Pandolf** an imaginary painter

Worked busily a day, and there she stands.
Will't please you sit and look at her? I said                                5
"Frà Pandolf" by design, for never read
Strangers like you that pictured countenance,
The depth and passion of its earnest glance,
But to myself they turned (since none puts by
The curtain I have drawn for you, but I)                                     10
And seemed as they would ask me, if they durst,
How such a glance came there; so, not the first
Are you to turn and ask thus. Sir, 'twas not
Her husband's presence only, called that spot
Of joy into the Duchess' cheek: perhaps                                      15
Frà Pandolf chanced to say "Her mantle laps
Over my lady's wrist too much," or "Paint
Must never hope to reproduce the faint
Half-flush that dies along her throat": such stuff
Was courtesy, she thought, and cause enough                                 20
For calling up that spot of joy. She had
A heart—how shall I say?—too soon made glad,
Too easily impressed; she liked whate'er
She looked on, and her looks went everywhere.
Sir, 'twas all one! My favor at her breast,                                 25
The dropping of the daylight in the West,
The bough of cherries some officious fool
Broke in the orchard for her, the white mule
She rode with round the terrace—all and each
Would draw from her alike the approving speech,                             30
Or blush, at least. She thanked men—good! but thanked
Somehow—I know not how—as if she ranked
My gift of a nine-hundred-years-old name
With anybody's gift. Who'd stoop to blame
This sort of trifling? Even had you skill                                   35
In speech—which I have not—to make your will
Quite clear to such an one, and say, "Just this
Or that in you disgusts me; here you miss,
Or there exceed the mark"—and if she let
Herself be lessoned so, nor plainly set                                     40
Her wits to yours, forsooth, and made excuse,
—E'en then would be some stooping; and I choose
Never to stoop. Oh sir, she smiled, no doubt,
Whene'er I passed her; but who passed without
Much the same smile? This grew; I gave commands;                           45
Then all smiles stopped together. There she stands
As if alive. Will't please you rise? We'll meet

The company below, then. I repeat,
The Count your master's° known munificence
Is ample warrant that no just pretense 50
Of mine for dowry will be disallowed;
Though his fair daughter's self, as I avowed
At starting, is my object. Nay, we'll go
Together down, sir. Notice Neptune, though,
Taming a sea horse, thought a rarity, 55
Which Claus of Innsbruck cast in bronze for me!

—1842

# Porphyria's° Lover

The rain set early in tonight,
    The sullen wind was soon awake,
It tore the elm-tops down for spite,
    And did its worst to vex the lake:
    I listened with heart fit to break. 5
When glided in Porphyria; straight
    She shut the cold out and the storm,
And kneeled and made the cheerless grate
    Blaze up, and all the cottage warm;
    Which done, she rose, and from her form 10
Withdrew the dripping cloak and shawl,
    And laid her soiled gloves by, untied
Her hat and let the damp hair fall,
    And, last, she sat down by my side
    And called me. When no voice replied, 15
She put my arm about her waist,
    And made her smooth white shoulder bare,
And all her yellow hair displaced,
    And, stooping, made my cheek lie there,
    And spread, o'er all, her yellow hair, 20
Murmuring how she loved me—she
    Too weak, for all her heart's endeavor,
To set its struggling passion free
    From pride, and vainer ties dissever,
    And give herself to me forever. 25
But passion sometimes would prevail,
    Nor could tonight's gay feast restrain

**49 Count your master's** The auditor is apparently an envoy sent to arrange a marriage between the Duke of Ferrara and a count's daughter
**Porphyria** name suggesting purple, the color of nobility and royalty

A sudden thought of one so pale
   For love of her, and all in vain:
   So, she was come through wind and rain.          30
Be sure I looked up at her eyes
   Happy and proud; at last I knew
Porphyria worshipped me; surprise
   Made my heart swell, and still it grew
   While I debated what to do.          35
That moment she was mine, mine, fair,
   Perfectly pure and good: I found
A thing to do, and all her hair
   In one long yellow string I wound
   Three times her little throat around,          40
And strangled her. No pain felt she;
   I am quite sure she felt no pain.
As a shut bud that holds a bee,
   I warily oped her lids: again
   Laughed the blue eyes without a stain.          45
And I untightened next the tress
   About her neck; her cheek once more
Blushed bright beneath my burning kiss:
   I propped her head up as before,
   Only, this time my shoulder bore          50
Her head, which droops upon it still:
   The smiling rosy little head
So glad it has its utmost will,
   That all it scorned at once is fled,
   And I, its love, am gained instead!          55
Porphyria's love: she guessed not how
   Her darling one wish would be heard.
And thus we sit together now,
   And all night long we have not stirred,
   And yet God has not said a word!          60

—1842

---

### WALT WHITMAN ■ (1819–1892)

*Walt Whitman pioneered the use of free verse, which established him as one of the forebears of modern poetry, but his subject matter, often dealing with sexual topics, and his unsparing realism were equally controversial in his day. An admirer of Emerson, he adapted many of the ideas of transcendentalism in* Song of Myself, *his first major sequence, and also incorporated many of*

*Emerson's calls for poets to use American subjects and patterns of speech.
Leaves of Grass, which he revised from 1855 until his death, expanded to
include virtually all of his poems, including the graphic poems he wrote while
serving as a volunteer in Civil War army hospitals.*

# A Noiseless Patient Spider

A noiseless patient spider,
I mark'd where on a little promontory it stood isolated,
Mark'd how to explore the vacant vast surrounding,
It launch'd forth filament, filament, filament, out of itself,
Ever unreeling them, ever tirelessly speeding them.                    5
And you O my soul where you stand,
Surrounded, detached, in measureless oceans of space,
Ceaselessly musing, venturing, throwing, seeking the spheres to
      connect them,
Till the bridge you will need be form'd, till the ductile anchor hold,
Till the gossamer thread you fling catch somewhere, O my soul.    10

—1876

# O Captain! My Captain!°

*1*

O Captain! my Captain! our fearful trip is done;
The ship has weather'd every rack, the prize we sought is won;
The port is near, the bells I hear, the people all exulting,
While follow eyes the steady keel, the vessel grim and daring:
      But O heart! heart! heart!                                       5
         O the bleeding drops of red,
            Where on the deck my Captain lies,
               Fallen cold and dead.

*2*

O Captain! my Captain! rise up and hear the bells;
Rise up—for you the flag is flung—for you the bugle trills;           10
For you bouquets and ribbon'd wreaths—for you the shores
      a-crowding;
For you they call, the swaying mass, their eager faces turning;
      Here Captain! dear father!
         This arm beneath your head;
            It is some dream that on the deck,                         15
               You've fallen cold and dead.

**O Captain! My Captain!** This atypical ballad was written after the assassination of Abraham Lincoln
and ironically became Whitman's most popular poem during his lifetime.

*3*

My Captain does not answer, his lips are pale and still;
My father does not feel my arm, he has no pulse nor will;
The ship is anchor'd safe and sound, its voyage closed and done;
From fearful trip, the victor ship, comes in with object won;          20
    Exult, O shores, and ring, O bells!
      But I, with mournful tread,
        Walk the deck my Captain lies,
          Fallen cold and dead.

—1865

# Song of Myself, 6

A child said *What is the grass?* fetching it to me with full hands;
How could I answer the child? I do not know what it is any more than he.

I guess it must be the flag of my disposition, out of hopeful green
    stuff woven.

Or I guess it is the handkerchief of the Lord,
A scented gift and remembrancer designedly dropped,          5
Bearing the owner's name someway in the corners, that we may see
    and remark, and say *Whose?*

Or I guess the grass is itself a child, the produced babe of the vegetation.

Or I guess it is a uniform hieroglyphic,
And it means, Sprouting alike in broad zones and narrow zones,
Growing among black folks as among white,          10
Kanuck,° Tuckahoe,° Congressman, Cuff,° I give them the same,
    I receive them the same.

And now it seems to me the beautiful uncut hair of graves.

Tenderly will I use you curling grass,
It may be you transpire from the breasts of young men,
It may be if I had known them I would have loved them,          15
It may be you are from old people, or from offspring taken soon
    out of their mothers' laps,
And here you are the mothers' laps.
This grass is very dark to be from the white heads of old mothers.
Darker than the colorless beards of old men.
Dark to come from under the faint red roofs of mouths.          20

    O I perceive after all so many uttering tongues,

---

11 **Kanuck** French-Canadian  **Tuckahoe** coastal Virginian  **Cuff** a black slave

And I perceive they do not come from the roofs of mouths for nothing.
I wish I could translate the hints about the dead young men and women,
And the hints about old men and mothers, and the offspring taken
    soon out of their laps.

What do you think has become of the young and old men?     25
And what do you think has become of the women and children?

They are alive and well somewhere,
The smallest sprout shows there is really no death,
And if ever there was it led forward life, and does not wait at the end
    to arrest it.
And ceased the moment life appeared.

All goes onward and outward, nothing collapses.
And to die is different from what anyone supposed, and luckier.

                       —1855

# Song of Myself, 11

Twenty-eight young men bathe by the shore,
Twenty-eight young men and all so friendly;
Twenty-eight years of womanly life and all so lonesome.

She owns the fine house by the rise of the bank,
She hides handsome and richly drest aft the blinds of the window.  5

Which of the young men does she like the best?
Ah the homeliest of them is beautiful to her.

Where are you off to, lady? for I see you,
You splash in the water there, yet stay stock still in your room.

Dancing and laughing along the beach came the twenty-ninth
    bather,                                  10
The rest did not see her, but she saw them and loved them.

The beards of the young men glisten'd with wet, it ran from their long hair,
Little streams pass'd all over their bodies.

An unseen hand also pass'd over their bodies,
It descended trembling from their temples and ribs.        15
The young men float on their backs, their white bellies bulge to the
    sun, they do not ask who seizes fast to them,
They do not know who puffs and declines with pendant and bending
    arch,
They do not think whom they souse with spray.

                       —1855

# When I Heard the Learn'd Astronomer

When I heard the learn'd astronomer,
When the proofs, the figures, were ranged in columns before me,
When I was shown the charts and diagrams, to add, divide, and
    measure them,
When I sitting heard the astronomer where he lectured with much
    applause in the lecture-room,
How soon unaccountable I became tired and sick,          5
Till rising and gliding out I wander'd off by myself,
In the mystical moist night-air, and from time to time,
Look'd up in perfect silence at the stars.

—1865

---

**MATTHEW ARNOLD ■ (1822–1888)**

*Matthew Arnold was the son of the headmaster of Rugby School and himself
served as an inspector of schools during much of his adult life. An influential
essayist as well as a poet, Arnold was unsparing in his criticism of middle-
class "Philistinism." At least part of "Dover Beach" is thought to date from
his honeymoon in 1851.*

# Dover Beach

The sea is calm tonight.
The tide is full, the moon lies fair
Upon the straits; on the French coast the light
Gleams and is gone; the cliffs of England stand,
Glimmering and vast, out in the tranquil bay.          5
Come to the window, sweet is the night-air!
Only, from the long line of spray
Where the sea meets the moon-blanched land,
Listen! you hear the grating roar
Of pebbles which the waves draw back, and fling,          10
At their return, up the high strand,
Begin, and cease, and then again begin,
With tremulous cadence slow, and bring
The eternal note of sadness in.

Sophocles° long ago          15
Heard it on the Aegean, and it brought

---

**15 Sophocles** Athenian tragic poet (496–406 BC)

Into his mind the turbid ebb and flow
Of human misery; we
Find also in the sound a thought,
Hearing it by this distant northern sea.          20

The Sea of Faith
Was once, too, at the full, and round earth's shore
Lay like the folds of a bright girdle° furled.
But now I only hear
Its melancholy, long, withdrawing roar,          25
Retreating, to the breath
Of the night-wind, down the vast edges drear
And naked shingles° of the world.

Ah, love, let us be true
To one another! for the world, which seems          30
To lie before us like a land of dreams,
So various, so beautiful, so new,
Hath really neither joy, nor love, nor light,
Nor certitude, nor peace, nor help for pain;
And we are here as on a darkling plain          35
Swept with confused alarms of struggle and flight,
Where ignorant armies clash by night.

—1867

---

## EMILY DICKINSON ■ (1830–1886)

*Emily Dickinson has been reinvented with each generation, and readers'*
*views of her have ranged between two extremes—one perceiving her as the*
*abnormally shy "Belle of Amherst" making poetry out of her own neuroses*
*and another seeing her as a proto-feminist carving out a world of her own in*
*self-willed isolation. What remains is her brilliant poetry—unique, original,*
*and marked with the stamp of individual talent. Dickinson published only*
*seven poems during her lifetime but left behind hundreds of poems in manu-*
*script at her death. Published by her relatives, they were immediately popu-*
*lar, but it was not until the edition by Thomas Johnson in 1955 that they*
*were read with Dickinson's unusual punctuation and capitalization intact.*

# After Great Pain, a Formal Feeling Comes

After great pain, a formal feeling comes—
The Nerves sit ceremonious, like Tombs—

**23 girdle** sash   **28 shingles** beach pebbles

The stiff Heart questions was it He, that bore,
And Yesterday, or Centuries before? 5

The Feet, mechanical, go round—
Of Ground, or Air, or Ought—

A Wooden way
Regardless grown,
A Quartz contentment, like a stone—

This is the Hour of Lead— 10
Remembered, if outlived,
As Freezing persons, recollect the Snow—
First—Chill—then Stupor—then the letting go—

—1890

# Because I Could Not Stop for Death

Because I could not stop for Death—
He kindly stopped for me—
The Carriage held but just Ourselves—
And Immortality.
We slowly drove—He knew no haste 5
And I had put away
My labor and my leisure too,
For His Civility—

We passed the School, where Children strove
At Recess—in the Ring— 10
We passed the Fields of Gazing Grain—
We passed the Setting Sun—

Or rather—He passed Us—
The Dews drew quivering and chill—
For only Gossamer, my Gown— 15
My Tippet°—only Tulle°—

We paused before a House that seemed
A Swelling of the Ground—
The Roof was scarcely visible—
The Cornice—in the Ground— 20

Since then—'tis Centuries—and yet
Feels shorter than the Day
I first surmised the Horses' Heads
Were toward Eternity—

—1890

16 **Tippet** shawl  **Tulle** net-like fabric

# The Brain Is Wider than the Sky

The Brain—is wider than the Sky—
For—put them side by side—
The one the other will contain
With ease—and You—beside—                                    5

The Brain is deeper than the sea—
For—hold them—Blue to Blue—
The one the other will absorb—
As Sponges—Buckets—do—

The Brain is just the weight of God—                          10
For—Heft them—Pound for Pound—
And they will differ—if they do—
As Syllable from Sound—

                                                            —1896

# A Narrow Fellow in the Grass

A narrow Fellow in the Grass
Occasionally rides—
You may have met Him—did you not
His notice sudden is—

The Grass divides as with a Comb—                             5
A spotted shaft is seen—
And then it closes at your feet
And opens further on—

He likes a Boggy Acre
A Floor to cool for Corn—                                    10
Yet when a Boy, and Barefoot—
I more than once at Noon
Have passed, I thought, a Whip lash
Unbraiding in the Sun
When stooping to secure it                                    15
It wrinkled, and was gone—

Several of Nature's People
I know, and they know me—
I feel for them a transport
Of cordiality—                                                20

But never met this Fellow
Attended, or alone
Without a tighter breathing
And Zero at the Bone—

                                                            —1866

# Some Keep the Sabbath Going to Church

Some keep the Sabbath going to Church—
I keep it, staying at Home—
With a Bobolink for a Chorister—
And an Orchard, for a Dome—

Some keep the Sabbath in Surplice—                                    5
I just wear my Wings—
And instead of tolling the Bell, for Church,
Our little Sexton—sings.

God preaches, a noted Clergyman—
And the sermon is never long,                                          10
So instead of getting to Heaven, at least—
I'm going, all along.

                                                                —1864

# The Soul Selects Her Own Society

The Soul selects her own Society—
Then—shuts the Door—
To her divine Majority—
Present no more—

Unmoved—she notes the Chariots—pausing—                               5
At her low Gate—
Unmoved—an Emperor be kneeling
Upon her Mat—

I've known her—from an ample nation—
Choose One—
Then—close the Valves° of her attention—                              10
Like Stone—

                                                                —1890

# Tell All the Truth, But Tell It Slant

Tell all the Truth but tell it slant—
Success in Circuit lies
Too bright for our infirm Delight
The Truth's superb surprise

As Lightning to the Children eased                                     5
With explanation kind

11 **Valves** sliding doors

The Truth must dazzle gradually
Or every man be blind—

—1868

## Wild Nights—Wild Nights!

Wild Nights—Wild Nights!
Were I with thee
Wild Nights should be
Our luxury!

Futile—the Winds—                                        5
To a Heart in port—
Done with the Compass—
Done with the Chart!

Rowing in Eden—
Ah, the Sea!                                             10
Might I but moor—Tonight—
In Thee!

—1891

---

**CHRISTINA ROSSETTI** ■ (1830–1894)

*Christina Rossetti was the younger sister of Dante Gabriel and William, also distinguished writers, and was the author of numerous devotional poems and prose works. Her collected poems, edited by her brother William, appeared posthumously in 1904.*

## Up-Hill

Does the road wind up-hill all the way?
    Yes, to the very end.
Will the day's journey take the whole long day?
    From morn to night, my friend.

But is there for the night a resting-place?            5
    A roof for when the slow dark hours begin.
May not the darkness hide it from my face?
    You cannot miss that inn.

Shall I meet other wayfarers at night?
    Those who have gone before.                         10

Then must I knock, or call when just in sight?
    They will not keep you waiting at that door.
Shall I find comfort, travel-sore and weak?
    Of labor you shall find the sum.
Will there be beds for me and all who seek?        15
    Yea, beds for all who come.

—1858

---

### THOMAS HARDY ■ (1840–1928)

*Thomas Hardy, after the disappointing response to his novel Jude the Obscure
in 1895, returned to his first love, writing poetry, for the last thirty years of
his long life. The language and life of Hardy's native Wessex inform both his
novels and poems. His subject matter is very much of the nineteenth century,
but his ironic, disillusioned point of view marks him as one of the chief pre-
decessors of modernism.*

# Ah, Are You Digging on My Grave?

"Ah, are you digging on my grave
    My loved one?—planting rue?"°
—"No: yesterday he went to wed
One of the brightest wealth has bred.
'It cannot hurt her now,' he said,        5
    'That I should not be true.'"
"Then who is digging on my grave?
    My nearest dearest kin?"
—"Ah, no; they sit and think, 'What use!
What good will planting flowers produce?        10
No tendance of her mound can loose
    Her spirit from Death's gin.'"°

"But some one digs upon my grave?
    My enemy?—prodding sly?"
—"Nay: when she heard you had passed the Gate    15
That shuts on all flesh soon or late.
She thought you no more worth her hate,
    And cares not where you lie."

"Then who is digging on my grave?
    Say—since I have not guessed!"        20

**2 rue** yellow flower traditionally associated with sadness    **12 gin** grip

—"O it is I, my mistress dear,
Your little dog, who still lives near,
And much I hope my movements here
    Have not disturbed your rest?"
"Ah, yes! *You* dig upon my grave ...           25
    Why flashed it not on me
That one true heart was left behind!
What feeling do we ever find
To equal among human kind
    A dog's fidelity!"              30

"Mistress, I dug upon your grave
    To bury a bone, in case
I should be hungry near this spot
When passing on my daily trot.
I am sorry, but I quite forgot           35
    It was your resting-place."

                    —1914

# Channel Firing

That night your great guns, unawares,
Shook all our coffins as we lay,
And broke the chancel window-squares,
We thought it was the Judgment-day
And sat upright. While drearisome        5
Arose the howl of weakened hounds:
The mouse let fall the alter-crumb,
The worms drew back into the mounds,

The glebe° cow drooled. Till God called, 'No;
It's gunnery practice out at sea        10
Just as before you went below;
The world is as it used to be:

'All nations striving strong to make
Red war yet redder. Mad as hatters
They do no more for Christés sake        15
Than you who are helpless in such matters.

'That this is not the judgment-hour
For some of them's a blessed thing,
For if it were they'd have to scour
Hell's floor for so much threatening....      20

**9 glebe** farmland belonging to a church

'Ha, ha. It will be warmer when
I blow the trumpet (if indeed
I ever do; for you are men,
And rest eternal sorely need).'

So down we lay again. 'I wonder,                          25
Will the world ever saner be,'
Said one, 'than when he sent us under
In our indifferent century!'

And many a skeleton shook his head.
'Instead of preaching forty year,'                        30
My neighbour Parson Thirdly said,
'I wish I had stuck to pipes and beer.'

Again the guns disturbed the hour,
Roaring their readiness to avenge,
As far inland as Stourton Tower,                          35
And Camelot, and starlit Stonehenge.°

                                                    —1914

# Neutral Tones

We stood by a pond that winter day,
And the sun was white, as though chidden of God,
And a few leaves lay on the starving sod;
    —They had fallen from an ash, and were gray.

Your eyes on me were as eyes that rove                     5
Over tedious riddles solved years ago;
And some words played between us to and fro
    On which lost the more by our love.
The smile on your mouth was the deadest thing

Alive enough to have strength to die;                     10
And a grin of bitterness swept thereby
    Like an ominous bird a-wing ...

Since then, keen lessons that love deceives,
And wrings with wrong, have shaped to me
Your face, and the God-curst sun, and a tree,            15
    And a pond edged with grayish leaves.

                                                    —1898

**35–36 Stourton ... Stonehenge** Stourton Tower was built in the late 1700s as a memorial to the Seven
Years War; Camelot was the legendary Castle of King Arthur; Stonehenge dates from prehistoric times.

# The Ruined Maid

"O 'Melia, my dear, this does everything crown!
Who could have supposed I should meet you in Town?
And whence such fair garments, such prosperity?"
"O didn't you know I'd been ruined?" said she.

"You left us in tatters, without shoes or socks,                    5
Tired of digging potatoes, and spudding up docks;°
And now you've gay bracelets and bright feathers three!"
"Yes: that's how we dress when we're ruined," said she.

"At home in the barton° you said 'thee' and 'thou,'
And 'thik oon,' and 'theäs oon,'° and 't'other'; but now          10
Your talking quite fits 'ee for high compa-ny!"
"Some polish is gained with one's ruin," said she.

"Your hands were like paws then, your face blue and bleak
But now I'm bewitched by your delicate cheek,
And your little gloves fit as on any la-dy!"                       15
"We never do work when we're ruined," said she.

"You used to call home-life a hag-ridden dream,
And you'd sigh, and you'd sock; but at present you seem
To know not of megrims° or melancho-ly!"
"True. One's pretty lively when ruined," said she.                20

"I wish I had feathers, a fine sweeping gown,
And a delicate face, and could strut about Town!"
"My dear—a raw country girl, such as you be,
Cannot quite expect that. You ain't ruined," said she.

—1866

---

**GERARD MANLEY HOPKINS** ■ **(1844–1889)**

*Gerard Manley Hopkins was an English Jesuit priest who developed elaborate theories of poetic meter (what he called "sprung rhythm") and language to express his own spiritual ardor. Most of his work was posthumously printed through the efforts of his Oxford friend and later correspondent Robert Bridges, who was poet laureate.*

# God's Grandeur

The world is charged with the grandeur of God.
     It will flame out, like shining from shook foil;°

---

**6 docks** weeds   **9 barton** barnyard   **10 thik oon and theäs oon** dialect: "that one and this one"
**19 megrims** migraines
**2 foil** gold leaf

It gathers to a greatness, like the ooze of oil
Crushed.° Why do men then now not reck his rod?
Generations have trod, have trod, have trod;                                    5
    And all is seared with trade; bleared, smeared with toil;
    And wears man's smudge and shares man's smell: the soil
Is bare now, nor can foot feel, being shod.

And for all this, nature is never spent;
    There lives the dearest freshness deep down things;              10
And though the last lights off the black West went
    Oh, morning, at the brown brink eastward, springs—
Because the Holy Ghost over the bent
    World broods with warm breast and with ah! bright wings.

—1877

# Pied Beauty

Glory be to God for dappled things—
    For skies of couple-color as a brinded° cow;
        For rose-moles all in stipple upon trout that swim;
Fresh-firecoal chestnut-falls;° finches' wings;
    Landscape plotted and pieced—fold, fallow, and plough;         5
        And all trades, their gear and tackle and trim.
All things counter, original, spare, strange;
    Whatever is fickle, freckled (who knows how?)
        With swift, slow; sweet, sour; adazzle, dim;
He fathers-forth whose beauty is past change:                                   10
        Praise him.

—1877

# Spring and Fall

*to a young child*

Márgarét, are you gríeving?
Over Goldengrove unleaving?
Leáves, líke the things of man, you
With your fresh thoughts care for, can you?
Ah! ás the heart grows older                                                    5
It will come to such sights colder
By and by, nor spare a sigh
Though worlds of wanwood leafmeal lie;

---

4 **Crushed** Hopkins is referring to olive oil
2 **brinded** streaked    4 **Fresh-firecoal chestnut-falls** According to the poet, chestnuts have a red color

And yet you will weep and know why.
Now no matter, child, the name:                                10
Sórrow's springs áre the same.
Nor mouth had, no nor mind, expressed
What heart heard of, ghost guessed:
It ís the blight man was born for,
It is Margaret you mourn for.                                  15

—1880

---

## EMMA LAZARUS ■ (1849–1887)

*Emma Lazarus was born in New York City, one of seven children of a wealthy
Jewish American sugar refiner. Her famous sonnet "The New Colossus" was
written in 1883 for an art auction raising money to build a pedestal for the
Statue of Liberty, which had been given to the United States by France. During
Lazarus's short life, she became a powerful spokesperson for the rights of immigrants and called on Jews to claim a homeland in Palestine. Sixteen years after
her death, "The New Colossus" was engraved on a plaque for the statue's base.*

# The New Colossus

Not like the brazen giant of Greek fame,
With conquering limbs astride from land to land;
Here at our sea-washed, sunset gates shall stand
A mighty woman with a torch, whose flame
Is the imprisoned lightning, and her name                      5
Mother of Exiles. From her beacon-hand
Glows world-wide welcome; her mild eyes command
The air-bridged harbor that twin cities frame.
"Keep, ancient lands, your storied pomp!" cries she
With silent lips. "Give me your tired, your poor,              10
Your huddled masses yearning to breathe free,
The wretched refuse of your teeming shore.
Send these, the homeless, tempest-tost to me,
I lift my lamp beside the golden door!"

—1883

---

## A.E. HOUSMAN ■ (1859–1936)

*A.E. Housman was educated in the classics at Oxford and was almost forty
before he began to write verse seriously. His ballad-like poems of Shropshire*

*(an area in which he never actually lived) have proved some of the most pop-
ular lyrics in English, despite their pervasive mood of bittersweet pessimism.*

## Eight O'Clock

He stood, and heard the steeple
    Sprinkle the quarters° on the morning town.
One, two, three, four, to market-place and people
    It tossed them down.

Strapped, noosed, nighing his hour,                5
    He stood and counted them and cursed his luck;
And then the clock collected in the tower
    Its strength, and struck.

—1922

## Loveliest of Trees, the Cherry Now

Loveliest of trees, the cherry now
Is hung with bloom along the bough,
And stands about the woodland ride
Wearing white for Eastertide.

Now, of my threescore years and ten,          5
Twenty will not come again,
And take from seventy springs a score,
It only leaves me fifty more.

And since to look at things in bloom
Fifty springs are little room,               10
About the woodlands I will go
To see the cherry hung with snow.

—1896

## "Terence, This Is Stupid Stuff ..."

"Terence, this is stupid stuff:
You eat your victuals fast enough;
There can't be much amiss, 'tis clear,
To see the rate you drink your beer.
But oh, good Lord, the verse you make,        5
It gives a chap the belly-ache.

**2 quarters** quarter hours

The cow, the old cow, she is dead;
It sleeps well, the hornèd head:
We poor lads, 'tis our turn now
To hear such tunes as killed the cow.          10
Pretty friendship 'tis to rhyme
Your friends to death before their time
Moping melancholy mad:
Come, pipe a tune to dance to, lad."

   Why, if 'tis dancing you would be,          15
There's brisker pipes than poetry.
Say, for what were hop-yards meant,
Or why was Burton built on Trent?°
Oh many a peer of England brews
Livelier liquor than the Muse,          20
And malt does more than Milton can
To justify God's ways to man.
Ale, man, ale's the stuff to drink
For fellows whom it hurts to think:
Look into the pewter pot          25
To see the world as the world's not.
And faith, 'tis pleasant till 'tis past:
The mischief is that 'twill not last.
Oh I have been to Ludlow fair
And left my necktie God knows where,          30
And carried halfway home, or near,
Pints and quarts of Ludlow beer:
Then the world seemed none so bad,
And I myself a sterling lad;
And down in lovely muck I've lain,          35
Happy till I woke again.
Then I saw the morning sky:
Heigho, the tale was all a lie;
The world, it was the old world yet,
I was I, my things were wet,          40
And nothing now remained to do
But begin the game anew.

   Therefore, since the world has still
Much good, but much less good than ill,
And while the sun and moon endure          45
Luck's a chance, but trouble's sure,
I'd face it as a wise man would,

**18 Burton built on Trent** site of breweries

And train for ill and not for good.
'Tis true, the stuff I bring for sale
Is not so brisk a brew as ale:                                          50
Out of a stem that scored the hand
I wrung it in a weary land.
But take it: if the smack is sour,
The better for the embittered hour;
It should do good to heart and head                                     55
When your soul is in my soul's stead;
And I will friend you, if I may,
In the dark and cloudy day.

   There was a king reigned in the East:
There, when kings will sit to feast,                                    60
They get their fill before they think
With poisoned meat and poisoned drink.
He gathered all that springs to birth
From the many-venomed earth;
First a little, thence to more,                                         65
He sampled all her killing store;
And easy, smiling, seasoned sound,
Sate the king when healths went round.
They put arsenic in his meat
And stared aghast to watch him eat;                                     70
They poured strychnine in his cup
And shook to see him drink it up:
They shook, they stared as white's their shirt:
Them it was their poison hurt.
—I tell the tale that I heard told.                                     75
Mithridates,° he died old.

—1896

---

## WILLIAM BUTLER YEATS ■ (1865–1939)

*William Butler Yeats is considered the greatest Irish poet and provides an
important link between the late romantic era and early modernism. His
early poetry, focusing on Irish legend and landscape, is regional in the best
sense of the term, but his later work, with its prophetic tone and symbolist
texture, moves on a larger stage. Yeats lived in London for many years and
was at the center of British literary life. He was awarded the Nobel Prize
in 1923.*

**76 Mithridates** legendary King of Pontus, he protected himself from poisons by taking small doses
regularly

# The Lake Isle of Innisfree

I will arise and go now, and go to Innisfree,
And a small cabin build there, of clay and wattles° made:
Nine bean-rows will I have there, a hive for the honey-bee,
And live alone in the bee-loud glade.

And I shall have some peace there, for peace comes dropping slow,    5
Dropping from the veils of the morning to where the cricket sings;
There midnight's all a glimmer, and noon a purple glow,
And evening full of the linnet's wings.
I will arise and go now, for always night and day
I hear lake water lapping with low sounds by the shore;    10
While I stand on the roadway, or on the pavements gray,
I hear it in the deep heart's core.

—1892

# Leda° and the Swan

A sudden blow: the great wings beating still
Above the staggering girl, her thighs caressed
By the dark webs, her nape caught in his bill,
He holds her helpless breast upon his breast.
How can those terrified vague fingers push    5
The feathered glory from her loosening thighs?
And how can body, laid in that white rush,
But feel the strange heart beating where it lies?
A shudder in the loins engenders there
The broken wall, the burning roof and tower    10
And Agamemnon dead.°
    Being so caught up,
So mastered by the brute blood of the air,
Did she put on his knowledge with his power
Before the indifferent beak could let her drop?

—1923

# Sailing to Byzantium°

*1*

That is no country for old men. The young
In one another's arms, birds in the trees
—Those dying generations—at their song,

2 **Wattles** woven ploes and reeds
**Leda** mortal mother of Helen of Troy and Clytemnestra, wife and assassin of Agamemnon
10–11 **The broken wall ... Agamemnon dead** events that occurred during and after the Trojan War
**Byzantium** Constantinople or Istanbul, capital of the Eastern Roman Empire

The salmon-falls, the mackerel-crowded seas,
Fish, flesh, or fowl, commend all summer long            5
Whatever is begotten, born, and dies.
Caught in that sensual music all neglect
Monuments of unaging intellect.

### 2

An aged man is but a paltry thing,
A tattered coat upon a stick, unless                    10
Soul clap its hands and sing, and louder sing
For every tatter in its mortal dress,
Nor is there singing school but studying
Monuments of its own magnificence;
And therefore I have sailed the seas and come           15
To the holy city of Byzantium.

### 3

O sages standing in God's holy fire
As in the gold mosaic of a wall,
Come from the holy fire, perne in a gyre,°
And be the singing-masters of my soul.                  20
Consume my heart away; sick with desire
And fastened to a dying animal
It knows not what it is; and gather me
Into the artifice of eternity.

### 4

Once out of nature I shall never take                   25
My bodily form from any natural thing,
But such a form as Grecian goldsmiths make
Of hammered gold and gold enamelling
To keep a drowsy Emperor awake;
Or set upon a golden bough to sing                      30
To lords and ladies of Byzantium
Of what is past, or passing, or to come.

—1927

## The Second Coming

Turning and turning in the widening gyre°
The falcon cannot hear the falconer;

19 **perne in a gyre** descend in a spiral; the gyre for Yeats was a private symbol of historical cycles
1 **gyre** see note to "Sailing to Byzantium"

Things fall apart; the center cannot hold;
Mere anarchy is loosed upon the world,
The blood-dimmed tide is loosed, and everywhere          5
The ceremony of innocence is drowned;
The best lack all conviction, while the worst
Are full of passionate intensity.

Surely some revelation is at hand;
Surely the Second Coming is at hand.          10
The Second Coming! Hardly are those words out
When a vast image out of *Spiritus Mundi*°
Troubles my sight: somewhere in the sands of the desert
A shape with lion body and the head of a man,
A gaze blank and pitiless as the sun,          15
Is moving its slow thighs, while all about it
Reel shadows of the indignant desert birds.
The darkness drops again; but now I know
That twenty centuries of stony sleep
Were vexed to nightmare by a rocking cradle,          20
And what rough beast, its hour come round at last,
Slouches towards Bethlehem to be born?

—1921

# The Song of Wandering Aengus°

I went out to the hazel wood,
Because a fire was in my head,
And cut and peeled a hazel wand,
And hooked a berry to a thread;
And when white moths were on the wing,          5
And moth-like stars were flickering out,
I dropped the berry in a stream
And caught a little silver trout.

When I had laid it on the floor
I went to blow the fire aflame,          10
But something rustled on the floor,
And some one called me by my name:
It had become a glimmering girl
With apple blossom in her hair
Who called me by my name and ran          15
And faded through the brightening air.

**12 *Spiritus Mundi*** World-Spirit
**Aengus** Among the Sidhe (native Irish deities), the god of youth, love, beauty, and poetry. Yeats once also called him the "Master of Love." Here, however, he seems mortal.

Though I am old with wandering
Through hollow lands and hilly lands,
I will find out where she has gone,
And kiss her lips and take her hands;                               20
And walk among long dappled grass,
And pluck till time and times are done
The silver apples of the moon,
The golden apples of the sun.

—1899

---

## EDWIN ARLINGTON ROBINSON ■ (1869–1935)

*Edwin Arlington Robinson wrote many poems set in "Tilbury," a re-creation
of his hometown of Gardiner, Maine. These poems continue to present readers with a memorable cast of eccentric characters who somehow manifest
universal human desires. Robinson languished in poverty and obscurity
for many years before his reputation began to flourish as a result of the
interest taken in his work by President Theodore Roosevelt, who obtained
a government job for Robinson and wrote a favorable review of one of his
books.*

# Firelight

Ten years together without yet a cloud,
They seek each other's eyes at intervals
Of gratefulness to firelight and four walls
For love's obliteration of the crowd.
Serenely and perennially endowed                                    5
And bowered as few may be, their joy recalls
No snake, no sword; and over them there falls
The blessing of what neither says aloud.
Wiser for silence, they were not so glad
Were she to read the graven° tale of lines                          10
On the wan face of one somewhere alone;
Nor were they more content could he have had
Her thoughts a moment since of one who shines
Apart, and would be hers if he had known.

—1920

---

**10 graven** engraved

# The Mill

The miller's wife had waited long,
    The tea was cold, the fire was dead;
And there might yet be nothing wrong
    In how he went and what he said:
"There are no millers any more,"                5
    Was all that she had heard him say;
And he had lingered at the door
    So long that it seemed yesterday.

Sick with a fear that had no form
    She knew that she was there at last;      10
And in the mill there was a warm
    And mealy fragrance of the past.
What else there was would only seem
    To say again what he had meant;
And what was hanging from a beam         15
    Would not have heeded where she went.

And if she thought it followed her,
    She may have reasoned in the dark
That one way of the few there were
    Would hide her and would leave no mark:   20
Black water, smooth above the weir
    Like starry velvet in the night,
Though ruffled once, would soon appear
    The same as ever to the sight.

                                —1920

# Richard Cory

Whenever Richard Cory went down town,
We people on the pavement looked at him:
He was a gentleman from sole to crown,
Clean favored, and imperially slim.

And he was always quietly arrayed,         5
And he was always human when he talked;
But still he fluttered pulses when he said,
"Good-morning," and he glittered when he walked.

And he was rich—yes, richer than a king—
And admirably schooled in every grace:     10
In fine, we thought that he was everything
To make us wish that we were in his place.

So on we worked, and waited for the light,
And went without the meat, and cursed the bread;
And Richard Cory, one calm summer night,                    15
Went home and put a bullet through his head.

—1896

---

**STEPHEN CRANE** ■ **(1871–1900)**

*Stephen Crane was the brilliant young journalist who wrote* The Red Badge
of Courage *and was also an unconventional poet whose skeptical epigrams
and fables today seem far ahead of their time. In many ways, he mirrors the
cosmic pessimism of contemporaries like Hardy, Housman, and Robinson, all
of whom were influenced by the currents of determinism that ran so strongly
at the end of the nineteenth century.*

## The Trees in the Garden Rained Flowers

The trees in the garden rained flowers.
Children ran there joyously.
They gathered the flowers
Each to himself.
Now there were some                                         5
Who gathered great heaps—
Having opportunity and skill—
Until, behold, only chance blossoms
Remained for the feeble.
Then a little spindling tutor                               10
Ran importantly to the father, crying:
"Pray, come hither!
See this unjust thing in your garden!"
But when the father had surveyed,
He admonished the tutor:                                    15
"Not so, small sage!
This thing is just.
For, look you,
Are not they who possess the flowers
Stronger, bolder, shrewder                                  20
Than they who have none?
Why should the strong—
The beautiful strong—
Why should they not have the flowers?"

Upon reflection, the tutor bowed to the ground,                25
"My lord," he said,
"The stars are displaced
By this towering wisdom."

—1899

# The Wayfarer

The wayfarer.
Perceiving the pathway to truth,
Was struck with astonishment.
It was thickly grown with weeds.
"Ha," he said,                                                 5
"I see that none has passed here
In a long time."
Later he saw that each weed
Was a singular knife.
"Well," he mumbled at last,                                    10
"Doubtless there are other roads."

—1899

---

**PAUL LAURENCE DUNBAR** ■ (1872–1906)

*Paul Laurence Dunbar, a native of Dayton, Ohio, was one of the first black poets to make a mark in American literature. Many of his dialect poems reflect a sentimentalized view of life in the South, which he did not know directly. However, he was also capable of powerful expressions of racial protest.*

# We Wear the Mask

We wear the mask that grins and lies,
It hides our cheeks and shades our eyes,—
This debt we pay to human guile;
With torn and bleeding hearts we smile,
And mouth with myriad subtleties.                             5
Why should the world be over-wise,
In counting all our tears and sighs?
Nay, let them only see us, while
　　We wear the mask.

We smile, but, O great Christ, our cries                      10
To thee from tortured souls arise.
We sing, but oh the clay is vile

Beneath our feet, and long the mile;
But let the world dream otherwise,
   We wear the mask!               15

                           —1896

---

### ROBERT FROST ■ (1874–1963)

*Robert Frost, during the second half of his long life, was a public figure who attained a popularity unmatched by any American poet of the last century. His reading at the inauguration of John F. Kennedy in 1961 capped an impressive career that included four Pulitzer Prizes. Unattracted by the more exotic aspects of modernism, Frost nevertheless remains a poet who speaks eloquently to contemporary uncertainties about humanity's place in a universe that does not seem to care much for its existence. Although Frost is rarely directly an autobiographical poet ("Home Burial" may reflect the death of Frost's son Elliot at age three), his work always bears the stamp of his powerful personality and identification with the New England landscape.*

## Acquainted with the Night

I have been one acquainted with the night.
I have walked out in rain—and back in rain.
I have outwalked the furthest city light.

I have looked down the saddest city lane.
I have passed by the watchman on his beat        5
And dropped my eyes, unwilling to explain.

I have stood still and stopped the sound of feet
When far away an interrupted cry
Came over houses from another street,

But not to call me back or say good-bye;        10
And further still at an unearthly height
One luminary clock against the sky

Proclaimed the time was neither wrong nor right.
I have been one acquainted with the night.

                           —1928

## After Apple-Picking

My long two-pointed ladder's sticking through a tree
Toward heaven still,
And there's a barrel that I didn't fill
Beside it, and there may be two or three
Apples I didn't pick upon some bough.        5

But I am done with apple-picking now.
Essence of winter sleep is on the night,
The scent of apples: I am drowsing off.
I cannot rub the strangeness from my sight
I got from looking through a pane of glass                           10
I skimmed this morning from the drinking trough
And held against the world of hoary grass.
It melted, and I let it fall and break.
But I was well
Upon my way to sleep before it fell,                                 15
And I could tell
What form my dreaming was about to take.
Magnified apples appear and disappear,
Stem end and blossom end,
And every fleck of russet showing clear.                             20
My instep arch not only keeps the ache,
It keeps the pressure of a ladder-round.
I feel the ladder sway as the boughs bend.
And I keep hearing from the cellar bin
The rumbling sound                                                   25
Of load on load of apples coming in.
For I have had too much
Of apple-picking: I am overtired
Of the great harvest I myself desired.
There were ten thousand thousand fruit to touch,                    30
Cherish in hand, lift down, and not let fall.
For all
That struck the earth,
No matter if not bruised or spiked with stubble,
Went surely to the cider-apple heap                                 35
As of no worth.
One can see what will trouble
This sleep of mine, whatever sleep it is.
Were he not gone,
The woodchuck could say whether it's like his                       40
Long sleep, as I describe its coming on,
Or just some human sleep.

—1914

# Design

I found a dimpled spider, fat and white,
On a white heal-all,° holding up a moth

2 **heal-all** a wildflower, usually blue

Like a white piece of rigid satin cloth—
Assorted characters of death and blight
Mixed ready to begin the morning right,                5
Like the ingredients of a witches' broth—
A snow-drop spider, a flower like a froth,
And dead wings carried like a paper kite.
What had that flower to do with being white,
The wayside blue and innocent heal-all?                10
What brought the kindred spider to that height,
Then steered the white moth thither in the night?
What but design of darkness to appall?—
If design govern in a thing so small.

—1936

## Home Burial

He saw her from the bottom of the stairs
Before she saw him. She was starting down,
Looking back over her shoulder at some fear.
She took a doubtful step and then undid it
To raise herself and look again. He spoke                5
Advancing toward her: "What is it you see
From up there always?—for I want to know."
She turned and sank upon her skirts at that,
And her face changed from terrified to dull.
He said to gain time: "What is it you see?"                10
Mounting until she cowered under him.
"I will find out now—you must tell me, dear."
She, in her place, refused him any help,
With the least stiffening of her neck and silence.
She let him look, sure that he wouldn't see,                15
Blind creature; and awhile he didn't see.
But at last he murmured, "Oh," and again, "Oh."

"What is it—what?" she said.

                              "Just that I see."

"You don't," she challenged. "Tell me what it is."
"The wonder is I didn't see at once.                        20
I never noticed it from here before.
I must be wonted to it—that's the reason.
The little graveyard where my people are!
So small the window frames the whole of it.
Not so much larger than a bedroom, is it?                   25
There are three stones of slate and one of marble,

Broad-shouldered little slabs there in the sunlight
On the sidehill. We haven't to mind *those*.
But I understand: it is not the stones,
But the child's mound—"

                    "Don't, don't, don't, don't," she cried.     30

She withdrew, shrinking from beneath his arm
That rested on the banister, and slid downstairs;
And turned on him with such a daunting look,
He said twice over before he knew himself:
"Can't a man speak of his own child he's lost?"     35

"Not you!—Oh, where's my hat? Oh, I don't need it!
I must get out of here. I must get air.—
I don't know rightly whether any man can."

"Amy! Don't go to someone else this time.
Listen to me. I won't come down the stairs."     40
He sat and fixed his chin between his fists.
"There's something I should like to ask you, dear."
"You don't know how to ask it."

                    "Help me, then."

Her fingers moved the latch for all reply.
"My words are nearly always an offense.     45
I don't know how to speak of anything
So as to please you. But I might be taught,
I should suppose. I can't say I see how.
A man must partly give up being a man
With womenfolk. We could have some arrangement     50
By which I'd bind myself to keep hands off
Anything special you're a-mind to name.
Though I don't like such things 'twixt those that love.
Two that don't love can't live together without them.
But two that do can't live together with them."     55
She moved the latch a little. "Don't—don't go.
Don't carry it to someone else this time.
Tell me about it if it's something human.
Let me into your grief. I'm not so much
Unlike other folks as your standing there     60
Apart would make me out. Give me my chance.
I do think, though, you overdo it a little.
What was it brought you up to think it the thing
To take your mother-loss of a first child
So inconsolably—in the face of love.     65
You'd think his memory might be satisfied—"

"There you go sneering now!"

                    "I'm not, I'm not!

You make me angry. I'll come down to you.
God, what a woman! And it's come to this,
A man can't speak of his own child that's dead."                    70

"You can't because you don't know how to speak.
If you had any feelings, you that dug
With your own hand—how could you?—his little grave;
I saw you from that very window there,
Making the gravel leap and leap in air,                    75
Leap up, like that, like that, and land so lightly
And roll back down the mound beside the hole.
I thought, Who is that man? I didn't know you.
And I crept down the stairs and up the stairs
To look again, and still your spade kept lifting.                    80
Then you came in. I heard your rumbling voice
Out in the kitchen, and I don't know why,
But I went near to see with my own eyes.
You could sit there with the stains on your shoes
Of the fresh earth from your own baby's grave                    85
And talk about your everyday concerns.
You had stood the spade up against the wall
Outside there in the entry, for I saw it."

"I shall laugh the worst laugh I ever laughed.
I'm cursed. God, if I don't believe I'm cursed."                    90

"I can repeat the very words you were saying:
'Three foggy mornings and one rainy day
Will rot the best birch fence a man can build.'
Think of it, talk like that at such a time!
What had how long it takes a birch to rot                    95
To do with what was in the darkened parlor?
You *couldn't* care! The nearest friends can go
With anyone to death, comes so far short
They might as well not try to go at all.
No, from the time when one is sick to death,                    100
One is alone, and he dies more alone.
Friends make pretense of following to the grave,
But before one is in it, their minds are turned
And making the best of their way back to life

And living people, and things they understand.                    105
But the world's evil. I won't have grief so
If I can change it. Oh, I won't, I won't!"

"There, you have said it all and you feel better.
You won't go now. You're crying. Close the door.
The heart's gone out of it: why keep it up?                     110
Amy! There's someone coming down the road!"

"*You*—oh, you think the talk is all. I must go—
Somewhere out of this house. How can I make you—"

"If—you—do!" She was opening the door wider.
"Where do you mean to go? First tell me that.               115
I'll follow and bring you back by force. I *will!*—"

—1914

# The Road Not Taken

Two roads diverged in a yellow wood,
And sorry I could not travel both
And be one traveler, long I stood
And looked down one as far as I could
To where it bent in the undergrowth;                              5

Then took the other, as just as fair,
And having perhaps the better claim,
Because it was grassy and wanted wear;
Though as for that, the passing there
Had worn them really about the same,                           10

And both that morning equally lay
In leaves no step had trodden black.
Oh, I kept the first for another day!
Yet knowing how way leads on to way,
I doubted if I should ever come back.                             15

I shall be telling this with a sigh
Somewhere ages and ages hence:
Two roads diverged in a wood, and I,
I took the one less traveled by,
And that has made all the difference.                            20

—1916

# Stopping by Woods on a Snowy Evening

Whose woods these are I think I know.
His house is in the village though;
He will not see me stopping here
To watch his woods fill up with snow.

My little horse must think it queer                     5
To stop without a farmhouse near
Between the woods and frozen lake
The darkest evening of the year.

He gives his harness bells a shake
To ask if there is some mistake.                       10
The only other sound's the sweep
Of easy wind and downy flake.

The woods are lovely, dark and deep,
But I have promises to keep,
And miles to go before I sleep,                        15
And miles to go before I sleep.

—1923

---

**WALLACE STEVENS ■ (1879–1955)**

*Wallace Stevens was a lawyer specializing in surety bonds and rose to be a vice president of the Hartford Accident and Indemnity Company. His poetry was collected for the first time in* Harmonium *when he was forty-five, and although he published widely during his lifetime, his poetry was only slowly recognized as the work of a major modernist whose original-ity has not been surpassed. Stevens's idea of poetry as a force taking the place of religion has had a profound influence on poets and critics of this century.*

## Anecdote of the Jar

I placed a jar in Tennessee,
And round it was, upon a hill.
It made the slovenly wilderness
Surround that hill.

The wilderness rose up to it,                            5
And sprawled around, no longer wild.
The jar was round upon the ground
And tall and of a port in air.

It took dominion everywhere.
The jar was gray and bare.                              10
It did not give of bird or bush,
Like nothing else in Tennessee.

—1923

# Disillusionment of Ten o'Clock

The houses are haunted
By white night-gowns.
None are green,
Or purple with green rings,
Or green with yellow rings,                                    5
Or yellow with blue rings.
None of them are strange,
With socks of lace
And beaded ceintures.°
People are not going                                           10
To dream of baboons and periwinkles.°
Only, here and there, an old sailor,
Drunk and asleep in his boots,
Catches tigers
In red weather.                                                15

—1923

# The Emperor of Ice-Cream

Call the roller of big cigars,
The muscular one, and bid him whip
In kitchen cups concupiscent° curds.
Let the wenches dawdle in such dress
As they are used to wear, and let the boys             5
Bring flowers in last month's newspapers.
Let be be finale of seem.
The only emperor is the emperor of ice-cream.

Take from the dresser of deal,°
Lacking the three glass knobs, that sheet              10
On which she embroidered fantails° once
And spread it so as to cover her face.
If her horny feet protrude, they come
To show how cold she is, and dumb.
Let the lamp affix its beam.                            15
The only emperor is the emperor of ice-cream.

—1923

# The Snow Man

One must have a mind of winter
To regard the frost and the boughs
Of the pine-trees crusted with snow;

**9 ceintures** sashes   **11 periwinkles** either wildflowers or small mollusks
**3 concupiscent** lustful   **9 deal** cheap wood   **11 fantails** pigeons

And have been cold a long time
To behold the junipers shagged with ice,                                    5
The spruces rough in the distant glitter

Of the January sun; and not to think
Of any misery in the sound of the wind,
In the sound of a few leaves,

Which is the sound of the land                                              10
Full of the same wind
That is blowing in the same bare place

For the listener, who listens in the snow,
And, nothing himself, beholds
Nothing that is not there and the nothing that is.                          15

—1923

# The Worms at Heaven's Gate

Out of the tomb, we bring Badroulbadour,°
Within our bellies, we her chariot.
Here is an eye. And here are, one by one,
The lashes of that eye and its white lid.
Here is the cheek on which that lid declined,                               5
And, finger after finger, here, the hand,
The genius of that cheek. Here are the lips,
The bundle of the body and feet.
Out of the tomb we bring Badroulbadour.                                     10

—1923

---

**WILLIAM CARLOS WILLIAMS ▦ (1883–1963)**

*William Carlos Williams, like his friend Wallace Stevens, followed an uncon-
ventional career for a poet, working until his death as a pediatrician in
Rutherford, New Jersey. Williams is modern poetry's greatest proponent of
the American idiom. His plainspoken poems have been more widely imitated
than those of any other American poet of the twentieth century, perhaps
because he represents a homegrown modernist alternative to the intellectual-
ized Europeanism of Eliot and Ezra Pound (a friend of his from college days).
In his later years, Williams assisted many younger poets, among them Allen
Ginsberg, for whose controversial book Howl he wrote an introduction.*

**1 Badroulbadour** a princess in The Arabian Nights

# The Last Words of My English Grandmother

There were some dirty plates
and a glass of milk
beside her on a small table
near the rank, disheveled bed—

Wrinkled and nearly blind                                5
she lay and snored
rousing with anger in her tones
to cry for food,

Gimme something to eat—
They're starving me—                                     10
I'm all right—I won't go
to the hospital. No, no, no

Give me something to eat!
Let me take you
to the hospital, I said                                  15
and after you are well

you can do as you please.
She smiled, Yes
you do what you please first
then I can do what I please—                             20

Oh, oh, oh! she cried
as the ambulance men lifted
her to the stretcher—
Is this what you call

making me comfortable?                                   25
By now her mind was clear—
Oh you think you're smart
you young people,

she said, but I'll tell you
you don't know anything.                                 30
Then we started.
On the way

We passed a long row
of elms. She looked at them
awhile out of                                            35
the ambulance window and said,

What are all those
fuzzy-looking things out there?
Trees? Well, I'm tired
of them and rolled her head away.                    40

                                                   —1920

## The Red Wheelbarrow

so much depends
upon

a red wheel
barrow

glazed with rain                                    5
water

beside the white
chickens.

                                                   —1923

## Spring and All

By the road to the contagious hospital°
under the surge of the blue
mottled clouds driven from the
northeast—a cold wind. Beyond, the
waste of broad, muddy fields                        5
brown with dried weeds, standing and fallen

patches of standing water
the scattering of tall trees
All along the road the reddish
purplish, forked, upstanding, twiggy                10
stuff of bushes and small trees
with dead, brown leaves under them
leafless vines—

Lifeless in appearance, sluggish
dazed spring approaches—                            15

They enter the new world naked,
cold, uncertain of all
save that they enter. All about them
the cold, familiar wind—

1 **contagious hospital** a hospital for quarantined patients

Now the grass, tomorrow                                          20
the stiff curl of wildcarrot leaf
One by one objects are defined—
It quickens: clarity, outline of leaf

But now the stark dignity of
entrance—Still, the profound change                             25
has come upon them: rooted, they
grip down and begin to awaken

                                                            —1923

---

## EZRA POUND ■ (1885–1972)

*Ezra Pound was the greatest international proponent of modernist poetry. Born in Idaho and reared in Philadelphia, he emigrated to England in 1909, where he befriended Yeats, promoted the early work of Frost, and discovered Eliot. Pound's early promotion of the imagist movement assisted a number of important poetic principles and reputations, including those of H.D. (Hilda Doolittle) and, later, William Carlos Williams. Pound's support of Mussolini during World War II, expressed in controversial radio broadcasts, caused him to be held for more than a decade after the war as a mental patient in the United States, after which he returned to Italy for the final years of his long and controversial life.*

# In a Station of the Metro

The apparition of these faces in the crowd;
Petals on a wet, black bough.

                                                            —1916

# The River-Merchant's Wife: A Letter°

While my hair was still cut straight across my forehead
I played about the front gate, pulling flowers.
You came by on bamboo stilts, playing horse,
You walked about my seat, playing with blue plums.
And we went on living in the village of Chokan:                 5
Two small people, without dislike or suspicion.
At fourteen I married My Lord you.
I never laughed, being bashful.
Lowering my head, I looked at the wall.
Called to, a thousand times, I never looked back.               10

**The River-Merchant's Wife: A Letter** imitation of a poem by Li-Po (AD 701–762)

At fifteen I stopped scowling,
I desired my dust to be mingled with yours
Forever and forever and forever.
Why should I climb the lookout?

At sixteen you departed,                                                   15
You went into far Ku-to-yen, by the river of swirling eddies,
And you have been gone five months.
The monkeys make sorrowful noise overhead.

You dragged your feet when you went out.
By the gate now, the moss is grown, the different mosses,          20
Too deep to clear them away!
The leaves fall early this autumn, in wind.
The paired butterflies are already yellow with August
Over the grass in the West garden;
They hurt me. I grow older.                                                25
If you are coming down through the narrows of the
        river Kiang,
Please let me know beforehand,
And I will come out to meet you
        As far as Cho-Fu-Sa.

                                                                    —1915

---

## H.D. (HILDA DOOLITTLE) ■ (1886–1961)

*H.D. (Hilda Doolittle) was born in Bethlehem, Pennsylvania. Doolittle was a college friend of both Williams and Pound and moved to Europe permanently in 1911. With her husband Richard Aldington, H.D. was an important member of the imagist group promoted by Pound.*

# Pear Tree

Silver dust,
lifted from the earth,
higher than my arms reach,
you have mounted,
O, silver,                                                                 5
higher than my arms reach,
you front us with great mass;

no flower ever opened
so staunch a white leaf,
no flower ever parted silver                                              10
from such rare silver;

O, white pear,
your flower-tufts
thick on the branch
bring summer and ripe fruits                                    15
in their purple hearts.

—1916

## Sea Rose

Rose, harsh rose,
marred and with stint of petals,
meager flower, thin,
sparse of leaf,

more precious                                                  5
than a wet rose
single on a stem—
you are caught in the drift.

Stunted, with small leaf,
you are flung on the sand,                                      10
you are lifted
in the crisp sand
that drives in the wind.
Can the spice-rose
drip such acrid fragrance                                       15
hardened in a leaf?

—1916

---

**SIEGFRIED SASSOON** ■ (1886–1967)

*Siegfried Sassoon was a decorated hero who publicly denounced World War I and became a friend and supporter of other British war poets, including Robert Graves and Wilfred Owen. His sardonic, antiheroic war poems owe much to Thomas Hardy, whom he acknowledged as his chief poetic influence.*

## Dreamers

Soldiers are citizens of death's grey land,
     Drawing no dividend from time's tomorrows.
In the great hour of destiny they stand,
     Each with his feuds, and jealousies, and sorrows.

Soldiers are sworn to action; they must win                    5
    Some flaming, fatal climax with their lives.
Soldiers are dreamers, when the guns begin
    They think of firelit homes, clean beds, and wives.

I see them in foul dug-outs, gnawed by rats,
    And in the ruined trenches, lashed with rain,          10
Dreaming of things they did with balls and bats,
    And mocked by hopeless longing to regain
Bank-holidays, and picture shows, and spats,°
    And going to the office in the train.

—1918

---

### MARIANNE MOORE ■ (1887–1972)

*Marianne Moore called her own work poetry—unconventional and marked with the stamp of a rare personality—because, as she put it, there was no other category for it. For four years, she was editor of the* Dial, *one of the chief modernist periodicals. Moore's wide range of reference, which can leap from the commonplace to the wondrous within a single poem, reflects her unique set of personal interests—which range from exotic natural species to baseball.*

## The Fish

wade
through black jade.
    Of the crow-blue mussel-shells, one
        keeps
        adjusting the ash-heaps;                          5
    opening and shutting itself like
an
injured fan.
    The barnacles which encrust the
        side                                            10
        of the wave, cannot hide
    there for the submerged shafts of the
sun,
split like spun
    glass, move themselves with spotlight swift-        15
        ness
        into the crevices—
    in and out, illuminating

**13 spats** once-fashionable shoe coverings

the
turquoise sea                                        20
    of bodies. The water drives a
        wedge
        of iron through the iron edge
    of the cliff; whereupon the stars,
pink                                                 25
rice-grains, ink-
    bespattered jelly-fish, crabs like
        green
        lilies, and submarine
    toadstools, slide each on the other.     30
All
external
    marks of abuse are present on
        this
        defiant edifice—                   35
    all the physical features of
accident—lack
    of cornice, dynamite grooves, burns,
        and                                40
        hatchet strokes, these things stand
    out on it; the chasm-side is
dead.
Repeated
    evidence has proved that it can      45
        live
        on what can not revive
    its youth. The sea grows old in it.

—1921

## Silence

My father used to say,
"Superior people never make long visits,
have to be shown Longfellow's grave
or the glass flowers at Harvard.
Self-reliant like the cat—                           5
that takes its prey to privacy,
the mouse's limp tail hanging like a shoelace from its mouth—
they sometimes enjoy solitude
and can be robbed of speech
by speech which has delighted them.                  10

The deepest feeling always shows itself in silence;
not in silence, but restraint."
Nor was he insincere in saying, "Make my house your inn."
Inns are not residences.

—1935

---

### T.S. ELIOT ■ (1888–1965)

*T.S. Eliot was the author of* The Waste Land, *one of the most famous and difficult modernist poems, and became an international figure. Born in St. Louis and educated at Harvard, he moved to London in 1914, where he remained for the rest of his life, becoming a British subject in 1927. This chief prophet of modern despair turned to the Church of England in later life and wrote successful dramas on religious themes. As a critic and influential editor, Eliot dominated poetic taste in England and America for more than twenty-five years. He was awarded the Nobel Prize in 1948.*

# The Love Song of J. Alfred Prufrock

*S'io credesse che mia risposta fosse*
*A persona che mai tornasse al mondo,*
*Questa fiamma staria senza più scosse.*
*Ma perciocche giammai di questo fondo*
*Non tornò vivo alcun, s'i'odo il vero,*
*Senza tema d'infamia ti rispondo.*°

Let us go then, you° and I,
When the evening is spread out against the sky
Like a patient etherised upon a table;
Let us go, through certain half-deserted streets,
The muttering retreats                                                       5
Of restless nights in one-night cheap hotels
And sawdust restaurants with oyster-shells:
Streets that follow like a tedious argument
Of insidious intent
To lead you to an overwhelming question...                                  10
Oh, do not ask, "What is it?"
Let us go and make our visit.

In the room the women come and go
Talking of Michelangelo.°

---

*S'io credesse ... rispondo* From Dante's *Inferno* (Canto 27). The speaker is Guido da Montefeltro: "If I thought I spoke to someone who would return to the world, this flame would tremble no longer. But, if what I hear is true, since no one has ever returned alive from this place I can answer you without fear of infamy."   **1 you** Eliot said that the auditor of the poem was a male friend of Prufrock.
**14 Michelangelo** Italian painter and sculptor (1475–1564)

The yellow fog that rubs its back upon the window-panes,                    15
The yellow smoke that rubs its muzzle on the
    window-panes,
Licked its tongue into the corners of the evening,
Lingered upon the pools that stand in drains,
Let fall upon its back the soot that falls from chimneys,
Slipped by the terrace, made a sudden leap,                                 20
And seeing that it was a soft October night,
Curled once about the house, and fell asleep.

And indeed there will be time
For the yellow smoke that slides along the street,

Rubbing its back upon the window-panes;                                    25
There will be time, there will be time
To prepare a face to meet the faces that you meet;
There will be time to murder and create,
And time for all the works and days of hands
That lift and drop a question on your plate:                               30
Time for you and time for me,
And time yet for a hundred indecisions,
And for a hundred visions and revisions,
Before the taking of a toast and tea.
In the room the women come and go                                         35
Talking of Michelangelo.

And indeed there will be time
To wonder, "Do I dare?" and, "Do I dare?"—
Time to turn back and descend the stair,
With a bald spot in the middle of my hair—                                40
(They will say: "How his hair is growing thin!")
My morning coat, my collar mounting firmly to the chin,
My necktie rich and modest, but asserted by a
    simple pin—
(They will say: "But how his arms and legs are thin!")
Do I dare                                                                  45
Disturb the universe?
In a minute there is time
For decisions and revisions which a minute will reverse.

For I have known them all already, known them all:
Have known the evenings, mornings, afternoons,                            50
I have measured out my life with coffee spoons;
I know the voices dying with a dying fall
Beneath the music from a farther room.
    So how should I presume?

And I have known the eyes already, known them all—   55
The eyes that fix you in a formulated phrase,
And when I am formulated, sprawling on a pin,
When I am pinned and wriggling on the wall,
Then how should I begin
To spit out all the butt-ends of my days and ways?   60
    And how should I presume?

And I have known the arms already, known them all—
Arms that are braceleted and white and bare
(But in the lamplight, downed with light brown hair!)
Is it perfume from a dress   65
That makes me so digress?
Arms that lie along a table, or wrap about a shawl.
    And should I then presume?
    And how should I begin?

   . . . . .

Shall I say, I have gone at dusk through narrow streets,   70
And watched the smoke that rises from the pipes
Of lonely men in shirtsleeves, leaning out of windows? . . .

I should have been a pair of ragged claws
Scuttling across the floors of silent seas.

   . . . . .

And the afternoon, the evening, sleeps so peacefully!   75
Smoothed by long fingers,
Asleep . . . tired . . . or it malingers,
Stretched on the floor, here beside you and me.
Should I, after tea and cakes and ices,
Have the strength to force the moment to its crisis?   80
But though I have wept and fasted, wept and prayed,
Though I have seen my head (grown slightly bald) brought in upon a
    platter,
I am no prophet°—and here's no great matter;
I have seen the moment of my greatness flicker,
And I have seen the eternal Footman hold my coat, and snicker,   85
    And in short, I was afraid.

And would it have been worth it, after all,
After the cups, the marmalade, the tea,
Among the porcelain, among some talk of you and me,
Would it have been worth while,   90
To have bitten off the matter with a smile,
To have squeezed the universe into a ball

82–83 **my head ... no prophet** allusion to John the Baptist

To roll it towards some overwhelming question,
To say: "I am Lazarus,° come from the dead,
Come back to tell you all, I shall tell you all"—                    95
If one, settling a pillow by her head,
        Should say: "That is not what I meant at all;
        That is not it, at all."
And would it have been worth it, after all,
Would it have been worth while,                                    100
After the sunsets and the dooryards and the sprinkled streets,
After the novels, after the teacups, after the skirts that trail
        along the floor—
And this, and so much more?—
It is impossible to say just what I mean!
But as if a magic lantern° threw the nerves in patterns
        on a screen:                                              105
Would it have been worth while
If one, settling a pillow or throwing off a shawl,
And turning toward the window, should say:
        "That is not it at all,
        That is not what I meant, at all."                        110
        . . . . .
No! I am not Prince Hamlet, nor was meant to be;
Am an attendant lord, one that will do
To swell a progress, start a scene or two,
Advise the prince; no doubt, an easy tool,
Deferential, glad to be of use,                                    115
Politic, cautious, and meticulous;
Full of high sentence, but a bit obtuse;
At times, indeed, almost ridiculous—
Almost, at times, the Fool.°

I grow old ... I grow old ...                                       120
I shall wear the bottoms of my trousers rolled.

Shall I part my hair behind? Do I dare to eat a peach?
I shall wear white flannel trousers, and walk upon the beach.
I have heard the mermaids singing, each to each.

I do not think that they will sing to me.                          125

I have seen them riding seaward on the waves
Combing the white hair of the waves blown back
When the wind blows the water white and black.

---

**94 Lazarus** raised from the dead in John 11:1–44 or possibly the beggar Lazarus of Luke 16: 19–31
**105 magic lantern** old-fashioned slide projector
**111–119 not Prince Hamlet ... the Fool** The allusion is probably to Polonius, a character in *Hamlet*.

We have lingered in the chambers of the sea
By sea-girls wreathed with seaweed red and brown          130
Till human voices wake us, and we drown.

—1917

---

## EDNA ST. VINCENT MILLAY ■ (1892–1950)

*Raised in the coastal village of Camden, Maine, Edna St. Vincent Millay
was extremely popular in the 1920s, when her sonnets seemed the ultimate
expression of the liberated sexuality of what was then called the New Woman.
Neglected for many years, her poems have recently generated renewed interest, and it seems likely that she will eventually regain her status as one of
the most important female poets of the twentieth century.*

# If I Should Learn, in Some Quite Casual Way

If I should learn, in some quite casual way,
That you were gone, not to return again—
Read from the back-page of a paper, say,
Held by a neighbor in a subway train,
How at the corner of this avenue          5
And such a street (so are the papers filled)
A hurrying man, who happened to be you,
At noon today had happened to be killed—
I should not cry aloud—I could not cry
Aloud, or wring my hands in such a place—          10
I should but watch the station lights rush by
With a more careful interest on my face;
Or raise my eyes and read with greater care
Where to store furs and how to treat the hair.

—1917

# Oh, Oh, You Will Be Sorry for that Word

Oh, oh, you will be sorry for that word!
Give back my book and take my kiss instead.
Was it my enemy or my friend I heard,
"What a big book for such a little head!"
Come, I will show you now my newest hat,          5
And you may watch me purse my mouth and prink!°
Oh, I shall love you still, and all of that.

6 **prink** primp

I never again shall tell you what I think.
I shall be sweet and crafty, soft and sly;
You will not catch me reading any more:          10
I shall be called a wife to pattern by;
And some day when you knock and push the door,
Some sane day, not too bright and not too stormy,
I shall be gone, and you may whistle for me.

—1923

## What Lips My Lips Have Kissed, and Where, and Why

What lips my lips have kissed, and where, and why,
I have forgotten, and what arms have lain
Under my head till morning; but the rain
Is full of ghosts tonight, that tap and sigh
Upon the glass and listen for reply,          5
And in my heart there stirs a quiet pain
For unremembered lads that not again
Will turn to me at midnight with a cry.
Thus in the winter stands the lonely tree,
Nor knows what birds have vanished one by one,          10
Yet knows its boughs more silent than before:
I cannot say what loves have come and gone,
I only know that summer sang in me
A little while, that in me sings no more.

—1923

---

**WILFRED OWEN** ■ **(1893–1918)**

*Wilfred Owen was killed in the trenches only a few days before the armistice that ended World War I. Owen showed more promise than any other English poet of his generation. A decorated officer whose nerves broke down after exposure to battle, he met Siegfried Sassoon at Craiglockhart military hospital. His work was posthumously collected by his friend. A novel by Pat Barker,* Regeneration *(also made into a film), deals with their poetic and personal relationship.*

## Dulce et Decorum Est°

Bent double, like old beggars under sacks,
Knock-kneed, coughing like hags, we cursed through sludge,

**Dulce et Decorum Est (pro patria mori)** from the Roman poet Horace: "It is sweet and proper to die for one's country"

Till on the haunting flares we turned our backs
And towards our distant rest began to trudge.

Men marched asleep. Many had lost their boots                    5
But limped on, blood-shod. All went lame; all blind;
Drunk with fatigue; deaf even to the hoots
Of tired, outstripped Five-Nines° that dropped behind.

Gas! Gas! Quick, boys!—An ecstasy of fumbling
Fitting the clumsy helmets just in time;                         10
But someone still was yelling out and stumbling
And flound'ring like a man in fire or lime . . .
Dim, through the misty panes and thick green light,°
As under a green sea, I saw him drowning.

In all my dreams, before my helpless sight,                      15
He plunges at me, guttering, choking, drowning.
If in some smothering dreams you too could pace
Behind the wagon that we flung him in,
And watch the white eyes writhing in his face,
His hanging face, like a devil's sick of sin;                    20
If you could hear, at every jolt, the blood
Come gargling from the froth-corrupted lungs,
Obscene as cancer, bitter as the cud
Of vile, incurable sores on innocent tongues,—
My friend,° you would not tell with such high zest               25
To children ardent for some desperate glory,
The old Lie: Dulce et decorum est
Pro patria mori.

—1920

---

### E.E. CUMMINGS ■ (1894–1962)

*e.e. cummings was the son of a Harvard professor and Unitarian clergyman.
Edward Estlin Cummings served as a volunteer ambulance driver in France
during World War I. His experimentation with the typographical aspects of
poetry reveals his serious interest in cubist painting, which he studied in
Paris in the 1920s. A brilliant satirist, he also excelled as a writer of lyrical
poems whose unusual appearance and idiosyncratic grammar, spelling, and
punctuation often overshadow their traditional themes.*

---

**8 Five-Nines** German artillery shells (59 mm)    **13 misty panes and thick green light** i.e., through the
gas mask    **25 My friend** The poem was originally addressed to Jessie Pope, a writer of patriotic verse.

# anyone lived in a pretty how town

anyone lived in a pretty how town
(with up so floating many bells down)
spring summer autumn winter
he sang his didn't he danced his did.

Women and men(both little and small)                    5
cared for anyone not at all
they sowed their isn't they reaped their same
sun moon stars rain

children guessed(but only a few
and down they forgot as up they grew                    10
autumn winter spring summer)
that noone loved him more by more

when by now and tree by leaf
she laughed his joy she cried his grief
bird by snow and stir by still                          15
anyone's any was all to her

someones married their everyones
laughed their cryings and did their dance
(sleep wake hope and then) they
said their nevers they slept their dream                20

stars rain sun moon
(and only the snow can begin to explain
how children are apt to forget to remember
with up so floating many bells down)

one day anyone died i guess                             25
(and noone stooped to kiss his face)
busy folk buried them side by side
little by little and was by was

all by all and deep by deep
and more by more they dream their sleep                 30
noone and anyone earth by april
wish by spirit and if by yes.

Women and men (both dong and ding)
summer autumn winter spring
reaped their sowing and went their came                 35
sun moon stars rain

# pity this busy monster, manunkind

pity this busy monster,manunkind,

not. Progress is a comfortable disease:
your victim(death and life safely beyond)

plays with the bigness of his littleness
—electrons° deify one razorblade                              5
into a mountainrange;lenses extend

unwish through curving wherewhen till unwish
returns on its unself.

   A world of made
is not a world of born—pity poor flesh
and trees, poor stars and stones, but never this          10
fine specimen of hypermagical

ultraomnipotence. We doctors know

a hopeless case if—listen: there's a hell
of a good universe next door; let's go

                                 —1944

# plato told

plato told
him: he couldn't
believe it (jesus
told him; he
wouldn't believe                                              5
it) lao

tsze
certainly told
him, and general
(yes

mam)                                                          10
sherman;°

and even
(believe it
Or                                                            15

---

**5 electrons** in an electron microscope
**11 William Tecumseh Sherman** (1820–1891), Union general in the American Civil War. cummings alludes
to his famous statement "War is hell," a sentiment presumably shared by Plato, the Greek philosopher
(427?–347 BC), Jesus, and Lao-tze (c. 604 BC), Chinese philosopher credited as the founder of Taoism.

not) you
told him: i told

him; we told him
(he didn't believe it, no

sir) it took                                    20
a nipponized° bit of
the old sixth

avenue
el; in the top of his head: to tell
him                                             25

—1944

# r-p-o-p-h-e-s-s-a-g-r

                    r-p-o-p-h-e-s-s-a-g-r
              who
a)s w(e loo)k
upnowgath
              PPEGORHRASS                         5
                        eringint(o-
aThe):l
        eA
          !p:
S                              a                  10
        (r
rIvInG              .gRrEaPsPhOs)
                        to
rea(be)rran(com)gi(e)ngly
,grasshopper;                                     15

—1932

---

JEAN TOOMER ■ (1894–1967)

*Jean Toomer was born in Washington, D.C., the grandson of a black man who served as governor of Louisiana during Reconstruction. His book* Cane *(1923) is a mixed collection of prose and verse based on his observations of life in rural Georgia, where he was a schoolteacher. A complete edition of his poetry, most of it unpublished during his life, was assembled more than twenty years after his death.*

---

**21 nipponized** Scrap metal from the Sixth Avenue elevated railway in New York City, torn down in the 1930s, was sold to Japan and turned into armaments used in World War II.

## Georgia Dusk

The sky, lazily disdaining to pursue
   The setting sun, too indolent to hold
   A lengthened tournament for flashing gold,
Passively darkens for night's barbecue,

A feast of moon and men and barking hounds,         5
   An orgy for some genius of the South
   With blood-hot eyes and cane-lipped scented mouth,
Surprised in making folk-songs from soul sounds.

The sawmill blows its whistle, buzz-saws stop,
   And silence breaks the bud of knoll and hill,         10
Soft settling pollen where plowed lands fulfill
Their early promise of a bumper crop.

Smoke from the pyramidal sawdust pile
   Curls up, blue ghosts of trees, tarrying low
   Where only chips and stumps are left to show         15
The solid proof of former domicile.

Meanwhile, the men, with vestiges of pomp,
   Race memories of king and caravan,
   High-priests, an ostrich, and a juju-man,
Go singing through the footpaths of the swamp.         20

Their voices rise ... the pine trees are guitars,
   Strumming, pine-needles fall like sheets of rain ...
   Their voices rise ... the chorus of the cane
Is caroling a vesper to the stars ...

O singers, resinous and soft your songs         25
   Above the sacred whisper of the pines,
   Give virgin lips to cornfield concubines,
Bring dreams of Christ to dusky cane-lipped throngs.

—1923

---

### LOUISE BOGAN ■ (1897–1970)

*Louise Bogan was for many years the poetry editor and resident critic of* The
New Yorker, *and the opinions expressed in her many book reviews have held
up well in the years since her death. In her later years, Bogan suffered from
severe bouts of clinical depression and wrote little poetry, but her relatively
slim output reveals a unique poetic voice.*

# Women

Women have no wilderness in them,
They are provident instead,
Content in the tight hot cell of their hearts
To eat dusty bread.

They do not see cattle cropping red winter grass,                5
They do not hear
Snow water going down under culverts
Shallow and clear.

They wait, when they should turn to journeys,
They stiffen, when they should bend.                             10
They use against themselves that benevolence
To which no man is friend.

They cannot think of so many crops to a field
Or of clean wood cleft by an axe.
Their love is an eager meaninglessness                          15
Too tense, or too lax.

They hear in every whisper that speaks to them
A shout and a cry.
As like as not, when they take life over their door-sills
They should let it go by.                                       20

—1923

---

### LANGSTON HUGHES ■ (1902–1967)

*Langston Hughes was a leading figure in the Harlem Renaissance of the 1920s, and he became the most famous black writer of his day. Phrases from his poems and other writings have become deeply ingrained in the American consciousness. An important experimenter with poetic form, Hughes is credited with incorporating the rhythms of jazz into poetry.*

# Dream Boogie

Good morning, daddy!
Ain't you heard
The boogie-woogie rumble
Of a dream deferred?
Listen closely:                                                 5
You'll hear their feet
Beating out and beating out a—

*You think*
*It's a happy beat?*

Listen to it closely:                                      10
Ain't you heard
something underneath
like a—

*What did I say?*

Sure,                                                      15
I'm happy!
Take it away!

   *Hey, pop!*
   *Re-bop!*
   *Mop!*                                                  20
      *Y-e-a-h!*

—1951

## Theme for English B

The instructor said,

*Go home and write*
*a page tonight.*
*And let that page come out of you—*
*Then, it will be true.*                                   5

I wonder if it's that simple?
I am twenty-two, colored, born in Winston-Salem.
I went to school there, then Durham, then here
to this college on the hill above Harlem.
I am the only colored student in my class.                10
The steps from the hill lead down into Harlem,
through a park, then I cross St. Nicholas,
Eighth Avenue, Seventh, and I come to the Y,
the Harlem Branch Y, where I take the elevator
up to my room, sit down, and write this page:            15
It's not easy to know what is true for you or me
at twenty-two, my age. But I guess I'm what
I feel and see and hear, Harlem, I hear you:
hear you, hear me—we two—you, me, talk on this page.
(I hear New York, too.) Me—who?                           20
Well, I like to eat, sleep, drink, and be in love.
I like to work, read, learn, and understand life.
I like a pipe for a Christmas present,

or records—Bessie, bop, or Bach.
I guess being colored doesn't make me *not* like                                    25
the same things other folks like who are other races.
So will my page be colored that I write?
Being me, it will not be white.
But it will be
a part of you, instructor.                                                           30
You are white—
yet a part of me, as I am a part of you.
That's American.
Sometimes perhaps you don't want to be a part of me.
Nor do I often want to be a part of you.                                             35
But we are, that's true!
As I learn from you,
I guess you learn from me—
although you're older—and white—
and somewhat more free.                                                              40

This is my page for English B.

THEME FOR ENGLISH B. 9 college on the hill above Harlem: Columbia University, where Hughes was briefly a student. (Note, however, that this poem is not autobiographical. The young speaker is a character invented by the middle-aged author.) 24 Bessie: Bessie Smith (1898?–1937) was a popular blues singer often called the "Empress of the Blues."

# The Weary Blues

Droning a drowsy syncopated tune,
Rocking back and forth to a mellow croon,
     I heard a Negro play.
Down on Lenox Avenue the other night
By the pale dull pallor of an old gas light                                          5
     He did a lazy sway. . . .
     He did a lazy sway. . . .
To the tune o' those Weary Blues.
With his ebony hands on each ivory key
He made that poor piano moan with melody.                                            10
     O Blues!
Swaying to and fro on his rickety stool
He played that sad raggy tune like a musical fool.
     Sweet Blues!
Coming from a black man's soul.                                                      15
     O Blues!
In a deep song voice with a melancholy tone

I heard that Negro sing, that old piano moan—
  "Ain't got nobody in all this world,
  Ain't got nobody but ma self.                                20
  I's gwine to quit ma frownin'
  And put ma troubles on the shelf."
Thump, thump, thump, went his foot on the floor.
He played a few chords then he sang some more—
  "I got the Weary Blues                                       25
  And I can't be satisfied.
  Got the Weary Blues
  And can't be satisfied—
  I ain't happy no mo'
  And I wish that I had died."                                 30
And far into the night he crooned that tune.
The stars went out and so did the moon.
The singer stopped playing and went to bed
While the Weary Blues echoed through his head.
He slept like a rock or a man that's dead.                    35

—1926

---

**COUNTEE CULLEN ■ (1903–1946)**

*Countee Cullen, among black writers of the first half of the twentieth century, crafted poetry representing a more conservative style than that of his contemporary, Hughes. Although he wrote a number of lyrics on standard poetic themes, he is best remembered for his eloquent poems on racial subjects.*

# Incident

Once riding in old Baltimore,
  Heart-filled, head-filled with glee,
I saw a Baltimorean
  Keep looking straight at me.

Now I was eight and very small,                                5
  And he was no whit bigger,
And so I smiled, but he poked out
  His tongue, and called me, "Nigger."

I saw the whole of Baltimore
  From May until December;                                     10
Of all the things that happened there
  That's all that I remember.

—1925

# Yet Do I Marvel

I doubt not God is good, well-meaning, kind,
And did He stoop to quibble could tell why
The little buried mole continues blind,
Why flesh that mirrors Him must some day die,
Make plain the reason tortured Tantalus°                        5
Is baited by the fickle fruit, declare
If merely brute caprice dooms Sisyphus°
To struggle up a never-ending stair.
Inscrutable His ways are, and immune
To catechism by a mind too strewn                              10
With petty cares to slightly understand
What awful brain compels His awful hand.
Yet do I marvel at this curious thing:
To make a poet black and bid him sing!

—1925

---

### W.H. AUDEN ■ (1907–1973)

*W.H. Auden was already established as an important younger British poet before he moved to America in 1939 (he later became a U.S. citizen). As a transatlantic link between two literary cultures, Auden was one of the most influential literary figures and cultural spokespersons in the English-speaking world for almost forty years, giving a name to the postwar era when he dubbed it "The Age of Anxiety" in a poem. In his last years, he returned briefly to Oxford, where he occupied the poetry chair.*

# Musée des Beaux Arts°

About suffering they were never wrong,
The Old Masters: how well they understood
Its human position; how it takes place
While someone else is eating or opening a window or just walking
      dully along;
How, when the aged are reverently, passionately waiting          5
For the miraculous birth, there always must be
Children who did not specially want it to happen, skating
On a pond at the edge of the wood:
They never forgot

---

5 **Tantalus** mythological character tortured by unreachable fruit   7 **Sisyphus** figure in myth who endlessly rolls a boulder uphill
**Musée des Beaux Arts** Museum of Fine Arts

That even the dreadful martyrdom must run its course          10
Anyhow in a corner, some untidy spot
Where the dogs go on with their doggy life and the torturer's horse
Scratches its innocent behind on a tree.

In Brueghel's *Icarus,*° for instance: how everything turns away
Quite leisurely from the disaster; the ploughman may          15
Have heard the splash, the forsaken cry,
But for him it was not an important failure; the sun shone
As it had to on the white legs disappearing into the green
Water; and the expensive delicate ship that must have seen
Something amazing, a boy falling out of the sky,          20
Had somewhere to get to and sailed calmly on.

—1938

# The Unknown Citizen

*To JS/07/M/378*
*This Marble Monument Is Erected by the State*

He was found by the Bureau of Statistics to be
One against whom there was no official complaint,
And all the reports on his conduct agree
That, in the modern sense of an old-fashioned word, he was a saint,
For in everything he did he served the Greater Community.          5
Except for the War till the day he retired
He worked in a factory and never got fired,
But satisfied his employers, Fudge Motors Inc.
Yet he wasn't a scab or odd in his views,
For his Union reports that he paid his dues,          10
(Our report on his Union shows it was sound)
And our Social Psychology workers found
That he was popular with his mates and liked a drink.
The Press are convinced that he bought a paper every day
And that his reactions to advertisements were normal
    in every way.          15
Policies taken out in his name prove that he was fully insured,
And his Health-card shows he was once in hospital but left it cured.
Both Producers Research and High-Grade Living declare
He was fully sensible to the advantages of the Installment Plan
And had everything necessary to the Modern Man,          20
A phonograph, a radio, a car and a frigidaire.
Our researchers into Public Opinion are content

---

14 **Brueghel's Icarus** In this painting (c. 1550) the famous event from Greek myth is almost inconspicuous among the other details Auden mentions.

That he held the proper opinions for the time of year;
When there was peace, he was for peace; when there was war, he went.
He was married and added five children to the population,         25
Which our Eugenist says was the right number for a parent of his
    generation,
And our teachers report that he never interfered with their education.
Was he free? Was he happy? The question is absurd:
Had anything been wrong, we should certainly have heard.

—1939

---

**THEODORE ROETHKE ■ (1908–1963)**

*Theodore Roethke was born in Michigan. Roethke was an influential teacher
of poetry at the University of Washington for many years. His father was the
owner of a greenhouse, and Roethke's childhood closeness to nature was an
important influence on his mature poetry. His periodic nervous breakdowns,
the result of bipolar manic-depression, presaged his early death.*

# Dolor°

I have known the inexorable sadness of pencils,
Neat in their boxes, dolor of pad and paper-weight,
All of the misery of manilla folders and mucilage,
Desolation in immaculate public places,
Lonely reception room, lavatory, switchboard,                     5
The unalterable pathos of basin and pitcher,
Ritual of multigraph, paper-clip, comma,
Endless duplication of lives and objects.
And I have seen dust from the walls of institutions,
Finer than flour, alive, more dangerous than silica,°            10
Sift, almost invisible, through long afternoons of tedium,
Dropping a fine film on nails and delicate eyebrows,
Glazing the pale hair, the duplicate grey standard faces.

—1948

# My Papa's Waltz

The whiskey on your breath
Could make a small boy dizzy;
But I hung on like death:
Such waltzing was not easy.

**Dolor** sadness   **10 silica** rock dust, a cause of silicosis, an occupational disease of miners and quarry workers

We romped until the pans                                          5
Slid from the kitchen shelf;
My mother's countenance
Could not unfrown itself.

The hand that held my wrist
Was battered on one knuckle;                                     10
At every step you missed
My right ear scraped a buckle.

You beat time on my head
With a palm caked hard by dirt,
Then waltzed me off to bed                                       15
Still clinging to your shirt.

—1948

# Root Cellar

Nothing would sleep in that cellar, dank as a ditch,
Bulbs broke out of boxes hunting for chinks in the dark,
Shoots dangled and drooped,
Lolling obscenely from mildewed crates,
Hung down long yellow evil necks, like tropical snakes.         5
And what a congress of stinks!—
Roots ripe as old bait,
Pulpy stems, rank, silo-rich,
Leaf-mold, manure, lime, piled against slippery planks.
Nothing would give up life:                                     10
Even the dirt kept breathing a small breath.

—1948

---

### ELIZABETH BISHOP ■ (1911–1979)

*Elizabeth Bishop for most of her life was highly regarded as a "poet's poet,"
winning the Pulitzer Prize for* North and South *in 1956, but in the years since
her death, she has gained a wider readership. She traveled widely and lived in
Brazil for a number of years before returning to the United States to teach at
Harvard during the last years of her life.*

## The Fish

I caught a tremendous fish
and held him beside the boat
half out of water, with my hook

fast in a corner of his mouth.
He didn't fight.                                          5
He hadn't fought at all.
He hung a grunting weight,
battered and venerable
and homely. Here and there
his brown skin hung in strips                            10
like ancient wallpaper,
and its pattern of darker brown
was like wallpaper:
shapes like full-blown roses
stained and lost through age.                            15
He was speckled with barnacles,
fine rosettes of lime,
and infested
with tiny white sea-lice,
and underneath two or three                             20
rags of green weed hung down.
While his gills were breathing in
the terrible oxygen
—the frightening gills,
fresh and crisp with blood,                             25
that can cut so badly—
I thought of the coarse white flesh
packed in like feathers,
the big bones and the little bones,
the dramatic reds and blacks                            30
of his shiny entrails,
and the pink swim-bladder
like a big peony.
I looked into his eyes
which were far larger than mine                          35
but shallower, and yellowed,
the irises backed and packed
with tarnished tinfoil
seen through the lenses
of old scratched isinglass.°                             40
They shifted a little, but not
to return my stare.
—It was more like the tipping
of an object toward the light.

**40 isinglass** semitransparent material made from fish bladders

I admired his sullen face,                                    45
the mechanism of his jaw,
and then I saw
that from his lower lip
—if you could call it a lip—
grim, wet, and weapon-like,                                   50
hung five old pieces of fish-line,
or four and a wire leader
with the swivel still attached,
with all their five big hooks
grown firmly in his mouth.                                    55
A green line, frayed at the end
where he broke it, two heavier lines,
and a fine black thread
still crimped from the strain and snap
when it broke and he got away.                                60
Like medals with their ribbons
frayed and wavering,
a five-haired beard of wisdom
trailing from his aching jaw.
I stared and stared                                           65
and victory filled up
the little rented boat,
from the pool of bilge
where oil had spread a rainbow
around the rusted engine                                      70
to the bailer° rusted orange,
the sun-cracked thwarts,
the oarlocks on their strings,
the gunnels°—until everything
was rainbow, rainbow, rainbow!                                75
And I let the fish go.

                                                        —1946

## One Art

The art of losing isn't hard to master;
so many things seem filled with the intent
to be lost that their loss is no disaster.

Lose something every day. Accept the fluster
of lost door keys, the hour badly spent.                       5
The art of losing isn't hard to master.
Then practice losing farther, losing faster:

71 **bailer** bucket   74 **gunnels** gunwales

places, and names, and where it was you meant
to travel. None of these will bring disaster.

I lost my mother's watch. And look! my last, or                    10
next-to-last, of three loved houses went.
The art of losing isn't hard to master.
I lost two cities, lovely ones. And, vaster,
some realms I owned, two rivers, a continent.
I miss them, but it wasn't a disaster.                             15

—Even losing you (the joking voice, a gesture
I love) I shan't have lied. It's evident
the art of losing's not too hard to master
though it may look like (*Write* it!) like disaster.

—1976

---

**ROBERT HAYDEN** ■ **(1913–1980)**

*Robert Hayden named Countee Cullen as one of the chief early influences on
his poetry. A native of Michigan, he taught for many years at Fisk University
in Nashville and at the University of Michigan. Although many of Hayden's
poems are on African American subjects, he wished to be considered a poet
with strong links to the mainstream English-language tradition.*

## Those Winter Sundays

Sundays too my father got up early
and put his clothes on in the blueblack cold,
then with cracked hands that ached
from labor in the weekday weather made
banked fires blaze. No one ever thanked him.                       5

I'd wake and hear the cold splintering, breaking.
When the rooms were warm, he'd call,
and slowly I would rise and dress,
fearing the chronic angers of that house,

Speaking indifferently to him,                                     10
who had driven out the cold
and polished my good shoes as well.
What did I know, what did I know
of love's austere and lonely offices?°

—1962

**14 offices** daily religious ceremonies

DUDLEY RANDALL ■ (1914—2000)

*Dudley Randall was the founder of Broadside Press, a black-owned publishing firm that eventually attracted important writers like Gwendolyn Brooks and Don L. Lee. For most of his life a resident of Detroit, Randall spent many years working in that city's library system before taking a similar position at the University of Detroit.*

# Ballad of Birmingham

### (On the Bombing of a Church in Birmingham, Alabama, 1963)°

"Mother dear, may I go downtown
Instead of out to play,
And march the streets of Birmingham
In a Freedom March today?"

"No, baby, no, you may not go,                              5
For the dogs are fierce and wild,
And clubs and hoses, guns and jail
Aren't good for a little child."

"But, mother, I won't be alone.
Other children will go with me,                            10
And march the streets of Birmingham
To make our country free."

"No, baby, no, you may not go,
For I fear those guns will fire.
But you may go to church instead                           15
And sing in the children's choir."

She has combed and brushed her night-dark hair,
And bathed rose petal sweet,
And drawn white gloves on her small brown hands,
And white shoes on her feet.                               20

The mother smiled to know her child
Was in the sacred place,
But that smile was the last smile
To come upon her face.

For when she heard the explosion,                          25
Her eyes grew wet and wild.
She raced through the streets of Birmingham
Calling for her child.

---

**Birmingham, Alabama, 1963** during the height of the civil rights movement

She clawed through bits of glass and brick,
Then lifted out a shoe.                                              30
"O, here's the shoe my baby wore,
But, baby, where are you?"

—1969

---

**WILLIAM STAFFORD ■ (1914–1993)**

*William Stafford was one of the most prolific poets of the postwar era. Stafford published in virtually every magazine in the United States. Raised in Kansas as a member of the pacifist Church of the Brethren, Stafford served in a camp for conscientious objectors during World War II. His first book did not appear until he was in his forties, but he published more than thirty collections before his death at age seventy-nine.*

# Traveling Through the Dark

Traveling through the dark I found a deer
dead on the edge of the Wilson River road.
It is usually best to roll them into the canyon:
that road is narrow; to swerve might make more dead.

By glow of the tail-light I stumbled back of the car          5
and stood by the heap, a doe, a recent killing;
she had stiffened already, almost cold.
I dragged her off; she was large in the belly.

My fingers touching her side brought me the reason—
her side was warm; her fawn lay there waiting,             10
alive, still, never to be born.
Beside that mountain road I hesitated.

The car aimed ahead its lowered parking lights;
under the hood purred the steady engine.
I stood in the glare of the warm exhaust turning red;        15
around our group I could hear the wilderness listen.

I thought hard for us all—my only swerving—
then pushed her over the edge into the river.

—1960

---

**DYLAN THOMAS ■ (1914–1953)**

*Dylan Thomas was a legendary performer of his and others' poetry. His popularity in the United States led to several collegiate reading tours, punctuated with outrageous behavior and self-destructive drinking that led to his early death in New York City, the victim of what the autopsy report labeled "insult to the brain." The Wales of his childhood remained a constant source of inspiration for his poetry and for radio dramas like* Under Milk Wood, *which was turned into a film by fellow Welshman Richard Burton and his then-wife, Elizabeth Taylor.*

## Do Not Go Gentle into That Good Night

Do not go gentle into that good night,
Old age should burn and rave at close of day;
Rage, rage against the dying of the light.

Though wise men at their end know dark is right,
Because their words had forked no lightning they          5
Do not go gentle into that good night.

Good men, the last wave by, crying how bright
Their frail deeds might have danced in a green bay,
Rage, rage against the dying of the light.

Wild men who caught and sang the sun in flight,          10
And learn, too late, they grieved it on its way,
Do not go gentle into that good night.

Grave men, near death, who see with blinding sight
Blind eyes could blaze like meteors and be gay,
Rage, rage against the dying of the light.          15

And you, my father, there on the sad height,
Curse, bless, me now with your fierce tears, I pray,
Do not go gentle into that good night.
Rage, rage against the dying of the light.

—1952

---

**WELDON KEES ■ (1914–1955)**

*Weldon Kees was a multitalented poet, painter, jazz musician, and filmmaker who went from the University of Nebraska to New York to California. His reputation, aided by posthumous publication of his stories, criticism, letters, and novels, has grown steadily since his apparent suicide by leaping from the Golden Gate Bridge.*

## For My Daughter

Looking into my daughter's eyes I read
Beneath the innocence of morning flesh

Concealed, hintings of death she does not heed.
Coldest of winds have blown this hair, and mesh
Of seaweed snarled these miniatures of hands;                    5
The night's slow poison, tolerant and bland,
Has moved her blood. Parched years that I have seen
That may be hers appear; foul, lingering
Death in certain war, the slim legs green.
Or, fed on hate, she relishes the sting                         10
Of others' agony; perhaps the cruel
Bride of a syphilitic or a fool.
These speculations sour in the sun.
I have no daughter. I desire none.

—1943

---

**GWENDOLYN BROOKS ■ (1917–2000)**

*Gwendolyn Brooks was the first African American to win a Pulitzer Prize for poetry. Brooks reflected many changes in black culture during her long career, and she wrote about the stages of her own life candidly in* In the Mecca *(1968), her literary autobiography. Brooks was the last poetry consultant of the Library of Congress before that position became poet laureate of the United States. At the end of her life, Brooks was one of the most honored and beloved of American poets.*

## the ballad of chocolate Mabbie

It was Mabbie without° the grammar school gates.
And Mabbie was all of seven.
And Mabbie was cut from a chocolate bar.
And Mabbie thought life was heaven.

The grammar school gates were the pearly gates,            5
For Willie Boone went to school.
When she sat by him in history class
Was only her eyes were cool.

It was Mabbie without the grammar school gates
Waiting for Willie Boone.                                  10
Half hour after the closing bell!
He would surely be coming soon.

Oh, warm is the waiting for joys, my dears!
And it cannot be too long.

1 **without** outside

Oh, pity the little poor chocolate lips                                    15
That carry the bubble of song!

Out came the saucily bold Willie Boone.
It was woe for our Mabbie now.
He wore like a jewel a lemon-hued lynx
With sand-waves loving her brow.                                           20

It was Mabbie alone by the grammar school gates.
Yet chocolate companions had she:
Mabbie on Mabbie with hush in the heart.
Mabbie on Mabbie to be.

                                                                —1945

## the mother

Abortions will not let you forget.
You remember the children you got that you did not get,
The damp small pulps with a little or with no hair,
The singers and workers that never handled the air.
You will never neglect or beat                                            5
them, or silence or buy with a sweet.
You will never wind up the sucking-thumb
Or scuttle off ghosts that come.
You will never leave them, controlling your luscious sigh,
Return for a snack of them, with gobbling mother-eye.                      10

I have heard in the voices of the wind the voices of my dim killed
    children.
I have contracted. I have eased
My dim dears at the breasts they could never suck.
I have said, Sweets, if I sinned, if I seized
Your luck                                                                 15
And your lives from your unfinished reach,
If I stole your births and your names,
Your straight baby tears and your games,
Your stilted or lovely loves, your tumults, your marriages, aches,
    and your deaths,
If I poisoned the beginnings of your breaths,                             20
Believe that even in my deliberateness I was not deliberate.
Though why should I whine,
Whine that the crime was other than mine?—
Since anyhow you are dead.
Or rather, or instead,                                                    25

You were never made.
But that too, I am afraid,
Is faulty: oh, what shall I say, how is the truth to be said?
You were born, you had body, you died.
It is just that you never giggled or planned or cried.                    30
Believe me, I loved you all.
Believe me, I knew you, though faintly, and I loved, I loved you
All.

—1945

# We Real Cool

> *The Pool Players.*
> *Seven at the Golden Shovel.*

We real cool. We
Left school. We

Lurk late. We
Strike straight. We

Sing sin. We                                                          5
Thin gin. We

Jazz June. We
Die soon.

—1960

---

## LAWRENCE FERLINGHETTI ■ (b. 1919)

*Lawrence Ferlinghetti, first owner of a literary landmark, San Francisco's
City Lights Bookstore, has promoted and published the voice of the American
avant-garde since the early 1950s. His own output has been relatively small,
but Ferlinghetti's* A Coney Island of the Mind *remains one of the quintessen-
tial documents of the Beat Generation.*

# A Coney Island of the Mind, #15

Constantly risking absurdity
　　　　　　　and death
　　　whenever he performs
　　　　　　　above the heads
　　　　　　　of his audience                                          5

the poet like an acrobat
climbs on rime
to a high wire of his own making
and balancing on eyebeams
above a sea of faces                    10
paces his way
to the other side of day
performing entrechats
and sleight-of-foot tricks
and other high theatrics                15
and all without mistaking
any thing
for what it may not be
For he's the super realist
who must perforce perceive              20
taut truth
before the taking of each stance or step
in his supposed advance
toward that still higher perch
where Beauty stands and waits           25
with gravity
to start her death-defying leap
And he
a little charleychaplin man
who may or may not catch                30
her fair eternal form
spreadeagled in the empty air
of existence

—1958

---

**MAY SWENSON** ■ (1919—1989)

*May Swenson displayed an inventiveness in poetry that ranges from tradi-tional formalism to many spatial or concrete poems. A careful observer of the natural world, Swenson often attempted to mimic directly the rhythms of the physical universe in her self-labeled "iconographs."*

# How Everything Happens

*(Based on a Study of the Wave)*

```
                                              happen.
                                        to
                                    up
                               stacking
                            is
                        something
When nothing is happening
When it happens
                something
                    pulls
                        back
                            not
                                to
                                 happen.
When                         has happened.
     pulling back        stacking up
                         happens
     has happened                      stacks up.
When it         something          nothing
                    pulls back while
Then nothing is happening
                                    happens.
                                 and
                          forward
                    pushes
               up
            stacks
        something
Then
```

—1967

---

**HOWARD NEMEROV** ■ **(1920–1991)**

*Howard Nemerov served as poet laureate of the United States during 1988 and 1989. A poet of brilliant formal inventiveness, he was also a skilled satirist and observer of the American scene. His sister, Diane Arbus, was a famous photographer. His* Collected Poems *won the Pulitzer Prize in 1978.*

## A Primer of the Daily Round

A peels an apple, while B kneels to God,
C telephones to D, who has a hand
On E's knee, F coughs, G turns up the sod
For H's grave, I do not understand
But J is bringing one clay pigeon down                    5
While K brings down a nightstick on L's head,
And M takes mustard, N drives into town,
O goes to bed with P, and Q drops dead,
R lies to S, but happens to be heard
By T, who tells U not to fire V                           10
For having to give W the word
That X is now deceiving Y with Z,
    Who happens just now to remember A
    Peeling an apple somewhere far away.

—1958

---

**RICHARD WILBUR** ■ **(b. 1921)**

*Richard Wilbur will be remembered by posterity as perhaps the most skillful metricist and exponent of wit that American poetry has produced. His highly polished poetry—against the grain of much contemporary writing—is a monument to his skill and intelligence. Perhaps the most honored of all living American poets, Wilbur served as poet laureate of the United States in 1987. His translations of the verse dramas of Molière and Racine are regularly performed throughout the world.* Collected Poems, 1943–2004 *appeared in 2004.*

## For C.

After the clash of elevator gates
And the long sinking, she emerges where,
A slight thing in the morning's crosstown glare,
She looks up toward the window where he waits,
Then in a fleeting taxi joins the rest                    5
Of the huge traffic bound forever west.

On such grand scale do lovers say good-bye—
Even this other pair whose high romance
Had only the duration of a dance,
And who, now taking leave with stricken eye,              10
See each in each a whole new life forgone.

For them, above the darkling clubhouse lawn,

Bright Perseids flash and crumble; while for these
Who part now on the dock, weighed down by grief
And baggage, yet with something like relief,                    15
It takes three thousand miles of knitting seas
To cancel out their crossing, and unmake
The amorous rough and tumble of their wake.

We are denied, my love, their fine tristesse
And bittersweet regrets, and cannot share                       20
The frequent vistas of their large despair,
Where love and all are swept to nothingness;
Still, there's a certain scope in that long love
Which constant spirits are the keepers of,
And which, though taken to be tame and staid,                   25
Is a wild sostenuto of the heart,
A passion joined to courtesy and art
Which has the quality of something made,
Like a good fiddle, like the rose's scent,
Like a rose window or the firmament.                            30

—2000

# The Writer

In her room at the prow of the house
Where light breaks, and the windows are tossed with linden,
My daughter is writing a story.

I pause in the stairwell, hearing
From her shut door a commotion of typewriter-keys               5
Like a chain hauled over a gunwale.

Young as she is, the stuff
Of her life is a great cargo, and some of it heavy:
I wish her a lucky passage.

But now it is she who pauses,                                   10
As if to reject my thought and its easy figure.
A stillness greatens, in which

The whole house seems to be thinking,
And then she is at it again with a bunched clamor
Of strokes, and again is silent.                                15

I remember the dazed starling
Which was trapped in that very room, two years ago;
How we stole in, lifted a sash

And retreated, not to affright it;
And how for a helpless hour, through the crack of the door,          20
We watched the sleek, wild, dark

And iridescent creature
Batter against the brilliance, drop like a glove
To the hard floor, or the desk-top.

And wait then, humped and bloody,          25
For the wits to try it again; and how our spirits
Rose when, suddenly sure,

It lifted off from a chair-back,
Beating a smooth course for the right window
And clearing the sill of the world.          30

It is always a matter, my darling,
Of life or death, as I had forgotten. I wish
What I wished you before, but harder.

—1976

## Year's End

Now winter downs the dying of the year,
And night is all a settlement of snow;
From the soft street the rooms of houses show
A gathered light, a shapen atmosphere,
Like frozen-over lakes whose ice is thin          5
And still allows some stirring down within.

I've known the wind by water banks to shake
The late leaves down, which frozen where they fell
And held in ice as dancers in a spell
Fluttered all winter long into a lake;          10
Graved on the dark in gestures of descent,
They seemed their own most perfect monument.

There was perfection in the death of ferns
Which laid their fragile cheeks against the stone
A million years. Great mammoths overthrown          15
Composedly have made their long sojourns,
Like palaces of patience, in the gray
And changeless lands of ice. And at Pompeii°

The little dog lay curled and did not rise
But slept the deeper as the ashes rose          20

18 **Pompeii** Roman city destroyed by volcanic eruption in AD 79.

And found the people incomplete, and froze
The random hands, the loose unready eyes
Of men expecting yet another sun
To do the shapely thing they had not done.

These sudden ends of time must give us pause.                    25
We fray into the future, rarely wrought
Save in the tapestries of afterthought.
More time, more time. Barrages of applause
Come muffled from a buried radio.
The New-year bells are wrangling with the snow.                  30

—1950

---

**PHILIP LARKIN** ■ **(1922–1985)**

*Philip Larkin was perhaps the latest British poet to establish a significant body of readers in the United States. The general pessimism of his work is mitigated by a wry sense of irony and brilliant formal control. For many years, he was a librarian at the University of Hull, and he was also a dedicated fan and critic of jazz.*

# Next, Please

Always too eager for the future, we
Pick up bad habits of expectancy.
Something is always approaching; every day
*Till then* we say,

Watching from a bluff the tiny, clear,                            5
Sparkling armada of promises draw near.
How slow they are! And how much time they waste,
Refusing to make haste!

Yet still they leave us holding wretched stalks
Of disappointment, for, though nothing balks                      10
Each big approach, leaning with brasswork prinked,
Each rope distinct,

Flagged, and the figurehead with golden tits
Arching our way, it never anchors; it's
No sooner present than it turns to past.                          15
Right to the last

We think each one will heave to and unload
All good into our lives, all we are owed

For waiting so devoutly and so long.
But we are wrong:                                           20

Only one ship is seeking us, a black-
Sailed unfamiliar, towing at her back
A huge and birdless silence. In her wake
No waters breed or break.

—1951

## This Be the Verse

They fuck you up, your mum and dad.
    They may not mean to, but they do.
They fill you with the faults they had
    And add some extra, just for you.

But they were fucked up in their turn                        5
    By fools in old-style hats and coats,
Who half the time were soppy-stern
    And half at one another's throats.

Man hands on misery to man.
    It deepens like a coastal shelf.                      10
Get out as early as you can,
    And don't have any kids yourself.

—1971

---

**JAMES DICKEY** ■ **(1923–1997)**

*James Dickey became a national celebrity with the success of his novel*
Deliverance *(1970) and the celebrated film version. There was a long*
*background to Dickey's success, with years spent in the advertising busi-*
*ness before he devoted himself fully to writing. Born in Atlanta and edu-*
*cated at Clemson, Vanderbilt, and Rice Universities, Dickey rarely strayed*
*long from the South and taught at the University of South Carolina for*
*more than two decades.*

## The Heaven of Animals

Here they are. The soft eyes open
If they have lived in a wood
It is a wood.

If they have lived on plains
It is grass rolling
Under their feet forever.                                    5

Having no souls, they have come,
Anyway, beyond their knowing.
Their instincts wholly bloom
And they rise.
The soft eyes open.                                          10

To match them, the landscape flowers,
Outdoing, desperately
Outdoing what is required:
The richest wood,
The deepest field.                                           15

For some of these,
It could not be the place
It is, without blood.
These hunt, as they have done,
But with claws and teeth grown perfect,                      20

More deadly than they can believe.
They stalk more silently,
And crouch on the limbs of trees,
And their descent
Upon the bright backs of their prey                          25

May take years
In a sovereign floating of joy.
And those that are hunted
Know this as their life,
Their reward: to walk                                        30

Under such trees in full knowledge
Of what is in glory above them,
And to feel no fear,
But acceptance, compliance.
Fulfilling themselves without pain                           35

At the cycle's center,
They tremble, they walk
Under the tree,
They fall, they are torn,
They rise, they walk again.                                  40

—1962

ALAN DUGAN ■ (1923–2003)

*Alan Dugan received the 1961 Yale Younger Poets Award, leading to the publication of his first collection as he neared forty. His plainspoken poetic voice, often with sardonic overtones, is appropriate for the anti-romantic stance of his most characteristic poems. For many years, Dugan was associated with the Fine Arts Work Center in Provincetown, Massachusetts, on Cape Cod.*

# Love Song: I and Thou

Nothing is plumb, level or square:
　　the studs are bowed, the joists
are shaky by nature, no piece fits
　　any other piece without a gap
or pinch, and bent nails　　　　　　　　　　　　　　5
　　dance all over the surfacing
like maggots. By Christ
　　I am no carpenter. I built
the roof for myself, the walls
　　for myself, the floors　　　　　　　　　　　　　10
for myself, and got
　　hung up in it myself. I
danced with a purple thumb
　　at this house-warming, drunk
with my prime whiskey: rage.　　　　　　　　　　　15
　　Oh I spat rage's nails
into the frame-up of my work:
　　it held. It settled plumb,
level, solid, square and true
　　for that great moment. Then　　　　　　　　　　20
it screamed and went on through,
　　skewing as wrong the other way.
God damned it. This is hell,
　　but I planned it, I sawed it,
I nailed it, and I　　　　　　　　　　　　　　　　25
　　will live in it until it kills me.
I can nail my left palm
　　to the left-hand cross-piece but
I can't do everything myself.
　　I need a hand to nail the right,　　　　　　　　30
a help, a love, a you, a wife.

　　　　　　　　　　　　　　　　　　　　　　　—1961

**ANTHONY HECHT** ■ (1923–2004)

*Anthony Hecht is most often linked with Richard Wilbur as one of the American poets of the postwar era who has most effectively utilized traditional poetic forms. The brilliance of Hecht's technique, however, must be set beside the powerful moral intelligence that informs his poetry.* The Hard Hours, *his second collection, won the Pulitzer Prize in 1968.*

# The Dover Bitch: *A Criticism of Life*

## *for Andrews Wanning*

So there stood Matthew Arnold° and this girl
With the cliffs of England crumbling away behind them,
And he said to her, "Try to be true to me,
And I'll do the same for you, for things are bad
All over, etc., etc."                                               5
Well now, I knew this girl. It's true she had read
Sophocles° in a fairly good translation
And caught that bitter allusion to the sea,
But all the time he was talking she had in mind
The notion of what his whiskers would feel like          10
On the back of her neck. She told me later on
That after a while she got to look out
At the lights across the channel, and really felt sad,
Thinking of all the wine and enormous beds
And blandishments in French and the perfumes.          15
And then she got really angry. To have been brought
All the way down from London, and then be addressed
As a sort of mournful cosmic last resort
Is really tough on a girl, and she was pretty.
Anyway, she watched him pace the room                       20
And finger his watch-chain and seem to sweat a bit,
And then she said one or two unprintable things.
But you mustn't judge her by that. What I mean to say is,
She's really all right. I still see her once in a while
And she always treats me right. We have a drink          25
And I give her a good time, and perhaps it's a year
Before I see her again, but there she is,
Running to fat, but dependable as they come.
And sometimes I bring her a bottle of *Nuit d'Amour.*

—1967

**1 Matthew Arnold** Victorian poet, author of "Dover Beach"    **7 Sophocles** Ancient Greek playwright

# Third Avenue in Sunlight

Third Avenue in sunlight. Nature's error.
Already the bars are filled and John is there.
Beneath a plentiful lady over the mirror°
He tilts his glass in the mild mahogany air.

I think of him when he first got out of college,                5
Serious, thin, unlikely to succeed;
For several months he hung around the Village,
Boldly T-shirted, unfettered but unfreed.

Now he confides to a stranger, "I was first scout,
And kept my glimmers peeled till after dark.                    10
Our outfit had as its sign a bloody knout,
We met behind the museum in Central Park.

Of course, we were kids." But still those savages,
War-painted, a flap of leather at the loins,
File silently against him. Hostages                             15
Are never taken. One summer, in Des Moines,

They entered his hotel room, tomahawks
Flashing like barracuda. He tried to pray.
Three years of treatment. Occasionally he talks
About how he almost didn't get away.                            20

Daily the prowling sunlight whets its knife
Along the sidewalk. We almost never meet.
In the Rembrandt dark he lifts his amber life.
My bar is somewhat further down the street.

—1967

---

### LOUIS SIMPSON ■ (1923 – 2012)

*Louis Simpson was born in Jamaica to a colonial lawyer father and an American mother. Simpson came to the United States in his teens and served in the U.S. Army in World War II. He won the Pulitzer Prize in 1964 for* At the End of the Open Road, *a volume that attempts to reexamine Walt Whitman's nineteenth-century definitions of the American experience. Subsequent collections continued to demonstrate Simpson's unsentimental view of American suburban life.*

**3 lady over the mirror** a painting

# American Classic

It's a classic American scene—
a car stopped off the road
and a man trying to repair it.

The woman who stays in the car
in the classic American scene                    5
stares back at the freeway traffic.

They look surprised, and ashamed
to be so helpless...
let down in the middle of the road!

To think that their car would do this!           10
They look like mountain people
whose son has gone against the law.

But every night they set out food
and the robber goes skulking back to the trees.
That's how it is with the car...                 15

it's theirs, they're stuck with it.
Now they know what it's like to sit
and see the world go whizzing by.

In the fume of carbon monoxide and dust
they are not such good Americans                  20
as they thought they were.

The feeling of being left out
through no fault of your own, is common.
That's why I say, an American classic.

—1980

# My Father in the Night Commanding No

My father in the night commanding No
Has work to do. Smoke issues from his lips;
    He reads in silence.
The frogs are croaking and the street lamps glow.

And then my mother winds the gramophone:        5
The Bride of Lammermoor° begins to shriek—

**6 Bride of Lammermoor** *Lucia di Lammermoor*, opera by Donizetti

Or reads a story
About a prince, a castle, and a dragon.

The moon is glittering above the hill.
I stand before the gateposts of the King—          10
    So runs the story—
Of Thule, at midnight when the mice are still.

And I have been in Thule! It has come true—
The journey and the danger of the world,
    All that there is          15
To bear and to enjoy, endure and do.

Landscapes, seascapes... Where have I been led?
The names of cities—Paris, Venice, Rome—
    Held out their arms.
A feathered god, seductive, went ahead.          20

Here is my house. Under a red rose tree
A child is swinging; another gravely plays.
    They are not surprised
That I am here; they were expecting me.

And yet my father sits and reads in silence,          25
My mother sheds a tear, the moon is still,
    And the dark wind
Is murmuring that nothing ever happens.

Beyond his jurisdiction as I move,
Do I not prove him wrong? And yet, it's true          30
    *They* will not change
There, on the stage of terror and of love.

The actors in that playhouse always sit
In fixed positions—father, mother, child
    With painted eyes.          35
How sad it is to be a little puppet!

Their heads are wooden. And you once pretended
To understand them! Shake them as you will,
    They cannot speak.
Do what you will, the comedy is ended.          40

Father, why did you work? Why did you weep,
Mother? Was the story so important?
    "*Listen!*" the wind
Said to the children, and they fell asleep.

—1963

## VASSAR MILLER ■ (1924–1997)

*Vassar Miller was a lifelong resident of Houston, born with cerebral palsy. Miller published both traditional devotional verse and a large body of autobiographical poetry in open forms.* If I Had Wheels or Love, *her collected poems, appeared in 1990.*

# Subterfuge

I remember my father, slight,
staggering in with his Underwood,°
bearing it in his arms like an awkward bouquet

for his spastic child who sits down
on the floor, one knee on the frame                                      5
of the typewriter, and holding her left wrist

with her right hand, in that precision known
to the crippled, pecks at the keys
with a sparrow's preoccupation.

Falling by chance on rhyme, novel and curious bubble          10
blown with a magic pipe, she tries them over and over,
spellbound by life's clashing in accord or against itself,

pretending pretense and playing at playing,
she does her childhood backward as children do,
her fun a delaying action against what she knows.                15

My father must lose her, his runaway on her treadmill,
will lose the terrible favor that life has done him
as she toils at tomorrow, tensed at her makeshift toy.

—1981

## DONALD JUSTICE ■ (1925–2004)

*Donald Justice published more selectively than most of his contemporaries. His Pulitzer Prize–winning volume of selected poems displays considerable literary sophistication and reveals the poet's familiarity with the traditions of contemporary European and Latin American poetry. As an editor, he was responsible for rescuing the important work of Weldon Kees from obscurity.*

2 **Underwood** popular brand of manual typewriter

## Counting the Mad

This one was put in a jacket,
This one was sent home,
This one was given bread and meat
But would eat none,
And this one cried No No No No                                5
All day long.

This one looked at the window
As though it were a wall,
This one saw things that were not there,
This one things that were,                                   10
And this one cried No No No No
All day long.

This one thought himself a bird,
This one a dog,
And this one thought himself a man,                          15
An ordinary man,
And this one cried No No No No
All day long.

—1960

---

**CAROLYN KIZER ■ (b. 1925)**

*Carolyn Kizer has had a fascinating career that included a year's study in
Taiwan and another year in Pakistan, where she worked for the U.S. State
Department. Her first collection,* The Ungrateful Garden *(1961), demonstrates
an equal facility with formal and free verse, but her subsequent books (including the Pulitzer Prize–winning* Yin *of 1985) have tended more toward the latter. A committed feminist, Kizer anticipated many of today's women's issues
as early as the mid-1950s, just as the poem "The Ungrateful Garden" was
published a decade before "ecology" became a household word.*

## The Ungrateful Garden

Midas watched the golden crust
That formed over his streaming sores,
Hugged his agues, loved his lust,
But damned to hell the out-of-doors

Where blazing motes of sun impaled                           5
The serried° roses, metal-bright.

**6 serried** crowded in rows

"Those famous flowers," Midas wailed,
"Have scorched my retina with light."

This gift, he'd thought, would gild his joys,
Silt up the waters of his grief;                              10
His lawns a wilderness of noise,
The heavy clang of leaf on leaf.

Within, the golden cup is good
To heft, to sip the yellow mead.
Outside, in summer's rage, the rude                           15
Gold thorn has made his fingers bleed.

"I strolled my halls in golden shift,
As ruddy as a lion's meat.
Then I rushed out to share my gift,
And golden stubble cut my feet."                              20

Dazzled with wounds, he limped away
To climb into his golden bed.
Roses, roses can betray.
"Nature is evil," Midas said.

—1961

---

**MAXINE KUMIN** ■ **(b. 1925)**

*Maxine Kumin was born in Philadelphia and educated at Radcliffe. Kumin was
an early literary ally and friend of Anne Sexton, with whom she co authored several children's books. The winner of the 1973 Pulitzer Prize, Kumin has preferred
a rural life raising horses for some years. Her increased interest in the natural
world has paralleled the environmental awareness of many of her readers.*

# Noted in the *New York Times*

## *Lake Buena Vista, Florida, June 16, 1987*

Death claimed the last pure dusky seaside sparrow
today, whose coastal range was narrow,
as narrow as its two-part buzzy song.
From hummocks lost to Cape Canaveral
this mouselike skulker in the matted grass,                    5
a six-inch bird, plain brown, once thousands strong,
sang *toodle-raeee azhee*, ending on a trill
before the air gave way to rocket blasts.

It laid its dull white eggs (brown specked) in small
neat cups of grass on plots of pickleweed,                     10
bulrushes, or salt hay. It dined

on caterpillars, beetles, ticks, the seeds
of sedges. Unremarkable
the life it led with others of its kind.
Tomorrow we can put it on a stamp,                                    15
a first-day cover with Key Largo rat,
Schaus swallowtail, Florida swamp
crocodile, and fading cotton mouse.
How simply symbols replace habitat!
The tower frames of Aerospace                                        20
quiver in the flush of another shot
where, once indigenous, the dusky sparrow
soared trilling twenty feet above its burrow.

—1989

---

**ALLEN GINSBERG** ■ **(1926–1997)**

*Allen Ginsberg became the chief poetic spokesman of the Beat Generation. He was a
force—as poet and celebrity—who continued to outrage and delight four decades
after the appearance of* Howl, *the monumental poem describing how Ginsberg
saw: "the best minds of my generation destroyed by madness." Ginsberg's poems
are cultural documents that provide a key to understanding the radical changes in
American life, particularly among youth, that began in the mid-1950s.*

## A Supermarket in California

What thoughts I have of you tonight, Walt Whitman, for I walked
down the sidestreets under the trees with a headache self-conscious
looking at the full moon.
    In my hungry fatigue, and shopping for images, I went into the
neon fruit supermarket, dreaming of your enumerations!
    What peaches and what penumbras?° Whole families shopping
at night! Aisles full of husbands! Wives in the avocados, babies in the
tomatoes!—and you, García Lorca,° what were you doing down by the
watermelons?
    I saw you, Walt Whitman, childless, lonely old grubber,poking
among the meats in the refrigerator and eyeing the grocery boys.
    I heard you asking questions of each: Who killed the pork chops?
What price bananas? Are you my Angel?                                 5
    I wandered in and out of the brilliant stacks of cans following
you, and followed in my imagination by the store detective.

---

**3 penumbras** shadows   **García Lorca** Federico García Lorca, Spanish poet (1899–1936)

We strode down the open corridors together in our solitary fancy tasting artichokes, possessing every frozen delicacy, and never passing the cashier.

Where are we going, Walt Whitman? The doors close in an hour. Which way does your beard point tonight?

(I touch your book and dream of our odyssey in the super-market and feel absurd.)

Will we walk all night through solitary streets? The trees add shade to shade, lights out in the houses, we'll both be lonely.        10

Will we stroll dreaming of the lost America of love past blue automobiles in driveways, home to our silent cottage?

Ah, dear father, graybeard, lonely old courage-teacher, what America did you have when Charon° quit poling his ferry and you got out on a smoking bank and stood watching the boat disappear on the black waters of Lethe?°

—1956

---

### JAMES MERRILL ■ (1926–1995)

*James Merrill wrote "The Changing Light at Sandover," a long poem that resulted from many years of sessions with a Ouija board. The book became his major work and, among many other things, a remarkable memoir of a long-term gay relationship. Merrill's shorter poems, collected in 2001, reveal meticulous craft and a play of wit unequaled among contemporary American poets.*

## Casual Wear

Your average tourist: Fifty. 2.3
Times married. Dressed, this year, in Ferdi Plinthbower°
Originals. Odds 1 to $9^{10}$
Against her strolling past the Embassy
Today at noon. Your average terrorist:                                    5
Twenty-five. Celibate. No use for trends,
At least in clothing. Mark, though, where it ends.
People have come forth made of colored mist
Unsmiling on one hundred million screens
To tell of his prompt phone call to the station,                          10
"Claiming responsibility"—devastation
Signed with a flourish, like the dead wife's jeans.

—1984

**2 Ferdi Plinthbower** a fictional designer    **12 Charon** ferryman of Hades    **Lethe** river in Hades, means forgetfulness

---

**W.D. SNODGRASS** ■ **(b. 1926)**

*W.D. Snodgrass won the Pulitzer Prize for his first collection,* Heart's Needle *(1959), and is generally considered one of the first important confessional poets. However, in his later career. He turned away from autobiographical subjects, writing, among other poems, a long sequence of dramatic monologues spoken by leading Nazis during the final days of the Hitler regime.*

# Mementos, I

Sorting out letters and piles of my old
    Canceled checks, old clippings, and yellow note cards
That meant something once, I happened to find
    Your picture. *That* picture. I stopped there cold,
Like a man raking piles of dead leaves in his yard       5
    Who has turned up a severed hand.

Still, that first second, I was glad: you stand
    Just as you stood—shy, delicate, slender,
In that long gown of green lace netting and daisies
    That you wore to our first dance. The sight of you stunned    10
Us all. Well, our needs were different, then,
    And our ideals came easy.
Then through the war and those two long years
    Overseas, the Japanese dead in their shacks
Among dishes, dolls, and lost shoes; I carried    15
    This glimpse of you, there, to choke down my fear,
Prove it had been, that it might come back.
    That was before we got married.

—Before we drained out one another's force
    With lies, self-denial, unspoken regret    20
And the sick eyes that blame; before the divorce
    And the treachery. Say it: before we met. Still,
I put back your picture. Someday, in due course,
    I will find that it's still there.

                           —1968

---

**JOHN ASHBERY** ■ **(b. 1927)**

*John Ashbery was born in upstate New York and educated at Harvard University. His first full-length book,* Some Trees, *was chosen by W.H. Auden as winner of the Yale Younger Poets Award in 1956. His enigmatic poems have intrigued readers for so long that much contemporary literary theory seems to have been created expressly for explicating his poems. Impossible to dismiss, Ashbery is now seen as the chief inheritor of the symbolist tradition brought to American locales by Wallace Stevens.* Notes from the Air: Selected Later Poems *appeared in 2007.*

## Paradoxes and Oxymorons

The poem is concerned with language on a very plain level.
Look at it talking to you. You look out a window
Or pretend to fidget. You have it but you don't have it.
You miss it, it misses you. You miss each other.

The poem is sad because it wants to be yours, and cannot.          5
What's a plain level? It is that and other things,
Bringing a system of them into play. Play?
Well, actually, yes, but I consider play to be

A deeper outside thing, a dreamed role-pattern,
As in the division of grace these long August days          10
Without proof. Open-ended. And before you know
It gets lost in the steam and chatter of typewriters.

It has been played once more. I think you exist only
To tease me into doing it, on your level, and then you aren't there
Or have adopted a different attitude. And the poem          15
Has set me softly down beside you. The poem is you.

                                          —1981

---

**W. S.  M E R W I N** ■ **(b. 1927)**

*W.S. Merwin often displays environmental concerns that have motivated much poetry in recent years. Even in earlier work his fears of the results of uncontrolled destruction of the environment are presented allegorically. Born in New York City, he currently resides in Hawaii. He was appointed U.S. poet laureate in 2010.*

## The Last One

Well they'd made up their minds to be everywhere because why not.
Everywhere was theirs because they thought so.
They with two leaves they whom the birds despise.
In the middle of stones they made up their minds.
They started to cut.          5

Well they cut everything because why not.
Everything was theirs because they thought so.

It fell into its shadows and they took both away.
Some to have some for burning.

Well cutting everything they came to the water.                              10
They came to the end of the day there was one left standing.
They would cut it tomorrow they went away.
The night gathered in the last branches.
The shadow of the night gathered in the shadow on the water.
The night and the shadow put on the same head.                               15
And it said Now.

Well in the morning they cut the last one.
Like the others the last one fell into its shadow.
It fell into its shadow on the water.
They took it away its shadow stayed on the water.                            20
Well they shrugged they started trying to get the shadow away.
They cut right to the ground the shadow stayed whole.
They laid boards on it the shadow came out on top.
They shone lights on it the shadow got blacker and clearer.
They exploded the water the shadow rocked.                                   25
They built a huge fire on the roots.
They sent up black smoke between the shadow and the sun.
The new shadow flowed without changing the old one.
They shrugged they went away to get stones.

They came back the shadow was growing.                                       30
They started setting up stones it was growing.
They looked the other way it went on growing.
They decided they would make a stone out of it.
They took stones to the water they poured them into the shadow.
They poured them in they poured them in the stones
        vanished.                                                            35
The shadow was not filled it went on growing.
That was one day.

The next day was just the same it went on growing.
They did all the same things it was just the same.
They decided to take its water from under it.                               40
They took away water they took it away the water went down.
The shadow stayed where it was before.
It went on growing it grew onto the land.
They started to scrape the shadow with machines.
When it touched the machines it stayed on them.                             45
They started to beat the shadow with sticks.
Where it touched the sticks it stayed on them.
They started to beat the shadow with hands.

Where it touched the hands it stayed on them.
That was another day.                                          50

Well the next day started about the same it went on growing.
They pushed lights into the shadow.
Where the shadow got onto them they went out.
They began to stomp on the edge it got their feet.
And when it got their feet they fell down.                    55
It got into eyes the eyes went blind.
The ones that fell down it grew over and they vanished.
The ones that went blind and walked into it vanished.
The ones that could see and stood still
It swallowed their shadows.                                    60
Then it swallowed them too and they vanished.
Well the others ran.
The ones that were left went away to live if it would let them.
They went as far as they could.
The lucky ones with their shadows.                            65

—1969

---

**JAMES WRIGHT ■ (1927–1980)**

*James Wright showed compassion for losers and underdogs of all types, an attitude evident everywhere in his poetry. A native of Martins Ferry, Ohio, he often described lives of quiet desperation in the blue-collar towns of his youth. Like many poets of his generation, Wright wrote formal verse in his early career and shifted to open forms during the 1960s.*

# Autumn Begins in Martins Ferry, Ohio

In the Shreve High football stadium,
I think of Polacks nursing long beers in Tiltonsville,
And gray faces of Negroes in the blast furnace at Benwood,
And the ruptured night watchman of Wheeling Steel,
Dreaming of heroes.                                            5

All the proud fathers are ashamed to go home.
Their women cluck like starved pullets,
Dying for love.

Therefore,
Their sons grow suicidally beautiful                          10
At the beginning of October
And gallop terribly against each other's bodies.

—1963

## Saint Judas

When I went out to kill myself, I caught
A pack of hoodlums beating up a man.
Running to spare his suffering, I forgot
My name, my number, how my day began,
How soldiers milled around the garden stone          5
And sang amusing songs; how all that day
Their javelins measured crowds; how I alone
Bargained the proper coins, and slipped away.

Banished from heaven, I found this victim beaten,
Stripped, kneed, and left to cry. Dropping my rope          10
Aside, I ran, ignored the uniforms:
Then I remembered bread my flesh had eaten,
The kiss that ate my flesh. Flayed without hope,
I held the man for nothing in my arms.

—1959

---

**PHILIP LEVINE ■ (b. 1928)**

*Philip Levine was born in Detroit, Michigan. He is one of many contemporary poets to hold a degree from the University of Iowa Writers' Workshop. The gritty urban landscapes and characters trapped in dead-end industrial jobs that provide Levine subjects for many poems match exactly with his unadorned, informal idiom. As teacher and mentor, Levine has influenced many younger poets.*

## You Can Have It

My brother comes home from work
and climbs the stairs to our room.
I can hear the bed groan and his shoes drop
one by one. You can have it, he says.

The moonlight streams in the window          5
and his unshaven face is whitened
like the face of the moon. He will sleep
long after noon and waken to find me gone.

Thirty years will pass before I remember
that moment when suddenly I knew each man          10
has one brother who dies when he sleeps
and sleeps when he rises to face this life,

and that together they are only one man
sharing a heart that always labors, hands
yellowed and cracked, a mouth that gasps          15
for breath and asks, Am I gonna make it?

All night at the ice plant he had fed
the chute its silvery blocks, and then I
stacked cases of orange soda for the children
of Kentucky, one gray box-car at a time          20

with always two more waiting. We were twenty
for such a short time and always in
the wrong clothes, crusted with dirt
and sweat. I think now we were never twenty.

In 1948 in the city of Detroit, founded          25
by de la Mothe Cadillac for the distant purposes
of Henry Ford, no one wakened or died,
no one walked the streets or stoked a furnace,

for there was no such year, and now
that year has fallen off all the old newspapers,          30
calendars, doctors' appointments, bonds,
wedding certificates, drivers licenses.

The city slept. The snow turned to ice.
The ice to standing pools or rivers
racing in the gutters. Then bright grass rose          35
between the thousands of cracked squares,

and that grass died. I give you back 1948.
I give you all the years from then
to the coming one. Give me back the moon
with its frail light falling across a face.          40

Give me back my young brother, hard
and furious, with wide shoulders and a curse
for God and burning eyes that look upon
all creation and say, You can have it.

—1979

---

**ANNE SEXTON ■ (1928–1974)**

*Anne Sexton lived a tortured life of mental illness and family troubles,
becoming the model of the confessional poet. A housewife with two small
daughters, she began writing poetry as the result of a program on public*

*television, later taking a workshop from Robert Lowell in which Sylvia Plath was a fellow student. For fifteen years until her suicide, she was a vibrant, exciting presence in American poetry. A controversial biography of Sexton by Diane Wood Middlebrook appeared in 1991.*

# Cinderella

You always read about it:
the plumber with twelve children
who wins the Irish Sweepstakes.
From toilets to riches.
That story.                                                                    5

Or the nursemaid,
some luscious sweet from Denmark
who captures the oldest son's heart.
From diapers to Dior.
That story.                                                                   10

Or a milkman who serves the wealthy,
eggs, cream, butter, yogurt, milk,
the white truck like an ambulance
who goes into real estate
and makes a pile.                                                             15
From homogenized to martinis at lunch.

Or the charwoman
who is on the bus when it cracks up
and collects enough from the insurance.
From mops to Bonwit Teller.°                                                  20
That story.

Once
the wife of a rich man was on her deathbed
and she said to her daughter Cinderella:
Be devout. Be good. Then I will smile                                        25
down from heaven in the seam of a cloud.
The man took another wife who had
two daughters, pretty enough
but with hearts like blackjacks.
Cinderella was their maid.                                                   30
She slept on the sooty hearth each night
and walked around looking like Al Jolson.°
Her father brought presents home from town,

20 **Bonwit Teller** an upscale department store    32 **Al Jolson** (1885–1950) American singer and entertainer who often performed in blackface

jewels and gowns for the other women
but the twig of a tree for Cinderella.                    35
She planted that twig on her mother's grave
and it grew to a tree where a white dove sat.
Whenever she wished for anything the dove
would drop it like an egg upon the ground.
The bird is important, my dears, so heed him.            40
Next came the ball, as you all know.
It was a marriage market.
The prince was looking for a wife.
All but Cinderella were preparing
and gussying up for the big event.                       45
Cinderella begged to go too.
Her stepmother threw a dish of lentils
into the cinders and said: Pick them
up in an hour and you shall go.
The white dove brought all his friends;                  50
all the warm wings of the fatherland came,
and picked up the lentils in a jiffy.
No, Cinderella, said the stepmother,
you have no clothes and cannot dance.
That's the way with stepmothers.                         55

Cinderella went to the tree at the grave
and cried forth like a gospel singer:
Mama! Mama! My turtledove,
send me to the prince's ball!
The bird dropped down a golden dress                     60
and delicate little gold slippers.
Rather a large package for a simple bird.
So she went. Which is no surprise.
Her stepmother and sisters didn't
recognize her without her cinder face                    65
and the prince took her hand on the spot
and danced with no other the whole day.

As nightfall came she thought she'd
better get home. The prince walked her home
and she disappeared into the pigeon house                70
and although the prince took an axe and broke
it open she was gone. Back to her cinders.
These events repeated themselves for three days.
However on the third day the prince
covered the palace steps with cobbler's wax              75
And Cinderella's gold shoe stuck upon it.

Now he would find whom the shoe fit
and find his strange dancing girl for keeps.
He went to their house and the two sisters
were delighted because they had lovely feet.                    80
The eldest went into a room to try the slipper on
but her big toe got in the way so she simply
sliced it off and put on the slipper.

The prince rode away with her until the white dove
told him to look at the blood pouring forth.                    85
That is the way with amputations.
They don't just heal up like a wish.
The other sister cut off her heel
but the blood told as blood will.
The prince was getting tired.                                   90
He began to feel like a shoe salesman.
But he gave it one last try.
This time Cinderella fit into the shoe
like a love letter into its envelope.

At the wedding ceremony                                         95
the two sisters came to curry favor
and the white dove pecked their eyes out.
Two hollow spots were left
like soup spoons.

Cinderella and the prince                                       100
lived, they say, happily ever after,
like two dolls in a museum case
never bothered by diapers or dust,
never arguing over the timing of an egg,
never telling the same story twice,                             105
never getting a middle-aged spread,
their darling smiles pasted on for eternity
Regular Bobbsey Twins.°
That story.

—1970

---

**THOM GUNN** ■ **(1929–2004)**

*Thom Gunn was a British expatriate who lived in San Francisco for more than
four decades. Gunn managed to retain his ties to the traditions of British
literature while writing about motorcycle gangs, surfers, gay bars, and drug*

108 **Bobbsey Twins** characters in a series of popular juvenile novels by Laura Lee Hope

*experiences.* The Man with Night Sweats, *his 1992 collection, contains a number of forthright poems on AIDS, of which "Terminal" is one.*

## Terminal

The eight years difference in age seems now
Disparity so wide between the two
That when I see the man who armoured stood
Resistant to all help however good
Now helped through day itself, eased into chairs,                    5
Or else led step by step down the long stairs
With firm and gentle guidance by his friend,
Who loves him, through each effort to descend,
Each wavering, each attempt made to complete
An arc of movement and bring down the feet                    10
As if with that spare strength he used to enjoy,
I think of Oedipus, old, led by a boy.

—1992

---

### X.J. KENNEDY ■ (b. 1929)

*X.J. Kennedy is one the few contemporary American poets who has not been attracted to free verse, preferring to remain what he calls a "dinosaur," one of those poets who continue to write in meter. He is also rare among his contemporaries in his commitment to writing poems with strong ties to song. Kennedy is also the author of* Literature: An Introduction to Fiction, Poetry, and Drama, *perhaps the most widely used college literature text ever written.*

## In a Prominent Bar in Secaucus One Day

*To the tune of "The Old Orange Flute" or the tune of "Sweet Betsy from Pike"*

In a prominent bar in Secaucus one day
Rose a lady in skunk with a topheavy sway,
Raised a knobby red finger—all turned from their beer—
While with eyes bright as snowcrust she sang high and clear:

"Now who of you'd think from an eyeload of me                    5
That I once was a lady as proud as could be?
Oh I'd never sit down by a tumbledown drunk
If it wasn't, my dears, for the high cost of junk.

"All the gents used to swear that the white of my calf
Beat the down of the swan by a length and a half.                    10

In the kerchief of linen I caught to my nose
Ah, there never fell snot, but a little gold rose.

"I had seven gold teeth and a toothpick of gold,
My Virginia cheroot° was a leaf of it rolled
And I'd light it each time with a thousand in cash—    15
Why the bums used to fight if I flicked them an ash.

"Once the toast of the Biltmore, the belle of the Taft,
I would drink bottle beer at the Drake,° never draft,
And dine at the Astor on Salisbury steak
With a clean tablecloth for each bite I did take.    20

"In a car like the Roxy I'd roll to the track,
A steel-guitar trio, a bar in the back,
And the wheels made no noise, they turned over so fast,
Still it took you ten minutes to see me go past.

"When the horses bowed down to me that I might choose,    25
I bet on them all, for I hated to lose.
Now I'm saddled each night for my butter and eggs
And the broken threads race down the backs of my legs.

"Let you hold in mind, girls, that your beauty must pass
Like a lovely white clover that rusts with its grass.    30
Keep your bottoms off barstools and marry you young
Or be left—an old barrel with many a bung.

"For when time takes you out for a spin in his car
You'll be hard-pressed to stop him from going too far
And be left by the roadside, for all your good deeds,    35
Two toadstools for tits and a face full of weeds."

All the house raised a cheer, but the man at the bar
Made a phonecall and up pulled a red patrol car
And she blew us a kiss as they copped her away
From that prominent bar in Secaucus, N.J.    40

—1961

# Little Elegy

*for a child who skipped rope*

Here lies resting, out of breath,
Out of turns, Elizabeth
Whose quicksilver toes not quite
Cleared the whirring edge of night.

14 **cheroot** a thin cigar    17–18 **Biltmore, Taft, Drake** famous hotels

Earth whose circles round us skim                                    5
Till they catch the lightest limb,
Shelter now Elizabeth
And for her sake trip up Death.

—1961

---

### ADRIENNE RICH ■ (1929–2012)

*Adrienne Rich's unusual life journey is unique in American poetry. She won the Yale Younger Poets award for her first book and for years balanced the demands of writing, marriage, and family. In the 1960s she became an outspoken feminist and later came out as a lesbian. She received the National Book Foundation's Medal of Honor in 2006, one of the last of many honors. She published new collections of poems regularly in her final years.*

## Aunt Jennifer's Tigers

Aunt Jennifer's tigers prance across a screen,
Bright topaz denizens of a world of green.
They do not fear the men beneath the tree;
They pace in sleek chivalric certainty.

Aunt Jennifer's fingers fluttering through her wool          5
Find even the ivory needle hard to pull.
The massive weight of Uncle's wedding band
Sits heavily upon Aunt Jennifer's hand.

When Aunt is dead, her terrified hands will lie
Still ringed with ordeals she was mastered by.               10
The tigers in the panel that she made
Will go on prancing, proud and unafraid.

—1950

## Rape

There is a cop who is both prowler and father:
he comes from your block, grew up with your brothers,
had certain ideals.
You hardly know him in his boots and silver badge,
on horseback, one hand touching his gun.                     5

You hardly know him but you have to get to know him:
he has access to machinery that could kill you.
He and his stallion clop like warlords among the trash,
his ideals stand in the air, a frozen cloud
from between his unsmiling lips.                              10

And so, when the time comes, you have to turn to him,
the maniac's sperm still greasing your thighs,
your mind whirling like crazy. You have to confess
to him, you are guilty of the crime
of having been forced.                                        15
And you see his blue eyes, the blue eyes of all the family
whom you used to know, grow narrow and glisten,
his hand types out the details
and he wants them all
but the hysteria in your voice pleases him best.            20

You hardly know him but now he thinks he knows you:
he has taken down your worst moment
on a machine and filed it in a file.
He knows, or thinks he knows, how much you imagined;
he knows, or thinks he knows, what you secretly wanted.    25

He has access to machinery that could get you put away;
and if, in the sickening light of the precinct,
and if, in the sickening light of the precinct,
your details sound like a portrait of your confessor,
will you swallow, will you deny them, will you lie your way home?   30

—1972

---

### GARY SNYDER ■ (b. 1930)

*Gary Snyder was deeply involved in poetic activity in his hometown, San Francisco, when that city became the locus of the Beat Generation in the mid-1950s. Yet Snyder, whose studies in Zen Buddhism and Oriental cultures preceded his acquaintance with Allen Ginsberg and Jack Kerouac, has always exhibited a seriousness of purpose that sets him apart from his peers. His long familiarity with the mountains of the Pacific Northwest dates from his jobs with logging crews during his college days.*

## A Walk

Sunday the only day we don't work:
Mules farting around the meadow,
        Murphy fishing,
The tent flaps in the warm
Early sun: I've eaten breakfast and I'll                     5
        take a walk
To Benson Lake. Packed a lunch,
Goodbye. Hopping on creekbed boulders

Up the rock throat three miles
    Piute Creek—                                                    10
In steep gorge glacier-slick rattlesnake country
Jump, land by a pool, trout skitter,
The clear sky. Deer tracks.
Bad place by a falls, boulders big as houses,
Lunch tied to belt,                                                              15
I stemmed up a crack and almost fell
But rolled out safe on a ledge
    and ambled on.
Quail chicks freeze underfoot, color of stone
Then run cheep! away, hen quail fussing.                                         20
Craggy west end of Benson Lake—after edging
Past dark creek pools on a long white slope—
Lookt down in the ice-black lake
    lined with cliff
From far above: deep shimmering trout.                                           25
A lone duck in a gunsightpass
    steep side hill
Through slide-aspen and talus, to the east end
Down to grass, wading a wide smooth stream
Into camp. At last.                                                              30
    By the rusty three-year-
Ago left-behind cookstove
Of the old trail crew,
Stoppt and swam and ate my lunch.

—1968

---

## MILLER WILLIAMS ■ (b. 1930)

*Miller Williams won the Poets' Prize in 1990 for* Living on the Surface, *a volume of selected poems. A skillful translator of both Giuseppe Belli, a Roman poet of the early nineteenth century, and of Nicanor Parra, a contemporary Chilean, Williams has written many poems about his travels throughout the world yet has retained the relaxed idiom of his native Arkansas. He read a poem at the 1997 presidential inauguration.*

# The Book

I held it in my hands while he told the story.

He had found it in a fallen bunker,
a book for notes with all the pages blank.
He took it to keep for a sketchbook and diary.

He learned years later, when he showed the book                    5
to an old bookbinder, who paled, and stepped back
a long step and told him what he held,
what he had laid the days of his life in.
It's bound, the binder said, in human skin.
I stood turning it over in my hands,                              10
turning it in my head. Human skin.

What child did this skin fit? What man, what woman?
Dragged still full of its flesh from what dream?

Who took it off the meat? Some other one
who stayed alive by knowing how to do this?                       15

I stared at the changing book and a horror grew,
I stared and a horror grew, which was, which is,
how beautiful it was until I knew.

—1989

---

### LINDA PASTAN ■ (b. 1932)

*Linda Pastan served as poet laureate of Maryland, where she has lived and taught for many years. Her first book,* A Perfect Circle of Sun, *appeared in 1971, and a dozen more collections have been published since.*

## Ethics

In ethics class so many years ago
our teacher asked this question every fall:
if there were a fire in a museum
which would you save, a Rembrandt painting
or an old woman who hadn't many                                   5
years left anyhow? Restless on hard chairs
caring little for pictures or old age
we'd opt one year for life, the next for art
and always half-heartedly. Sometimes
the woman borrowed my grandmother's face                         10
leaving her usual kitchen to wander
some drafty, half-imagined museum.
One year, feeling clever, I replied
why not let the woman decide herself?
Linda, the teacher would report, eschews                         15
the burdens of responsibility.
This fall in a real museum I stand

Before a real Rembrandt, old woman,
or nearly so, myself. The colors
within this frame are darker than autumn,                    20
darker even than winter—the browns of earth,
though earth's most radiant elements burn
through the canvas. I know now that woman
and painting and season are almost one                       25
and all beyond saving by children.

—1998

### SYLVIA PLATH ■ (1932–1963)

*Sylvia Plath, whose personal life is often difficult to separate from her poetry,*
*is almost always read as an autobiographical and confessional poet. Brilliant*
*and precocious, she served a long apprenticeship to the tradition of modern*
*poetry before attaining her mature style in the final two years of her life. Only*
*one collection,* The Colossus *(1960), appeared in her lifetime, and her fame*
*has mainly rested on her posthumous books of poetry and the success of her*
*lone novel,* The Bell Jar *(1963). She committed suicide in 1963. Plath has*
*been the subject of a half-dozen biographical studies and a feature film,* Sylvia
*(2003), reflecting the intense interest that readers have in her life and work.*

## Daddy

You do not do, you do not do
Any more, black shoe
In which I have lived like a foot
For thirty years, poor and white,
Barely daring to breathe or Achoo.                           5

Daddy, I have had to kill you.
You died before I had time—
Marble-heavy, a bag full of God,
Ghastly statue with one gray toe
Big as a Frisco seal                                         10

And a head in the freakish Atlantic
Where it pours bean green over blue
In the waters off beautiful Nauset.
I used to pray to recover you.
Ach, du.°                                                    15

15 **Ach, du** "Oh, you"

In the German tongue, in the Polish town
Scraped flat by the roller
Of wars, wars, wars.
But the name of the town is common.
My Polack friend                                         20

Says there are a dozen or two.
So I never could tell where you
Put your foot, your root,
I never could talk to you.
The tongue stuck in my jaw.                               25

It stuck in a barb wire snare.
Ich, ich, ich, ich,°
I could hardly speak.
I thought every German was you.
And the language obscene                                  30

An engine, an engine
Chuffing me off like a Jew.
A Jew to Dachau, Auschwitz, Belsen.°
I began to talk like a Jew.
I think I may well be a Jew.                              35

The snows of the Tyrol, the clear beer of Vienna
Are not very pure or true.
With my gypsy ancestress and my weird luck
And my Taroc pack and my Taroc pack
I may be a bit of a Jew.                                  40

I have always been scared of *you*,
With your Luftwaffe,° your gobbledygoo.
And your neat mustache
And your Aryan eye, bright blue.
Panzer-man, panzer-man, O You—                           45

Not God but a swastika
So black no sky could squeak through.
Every woman adores a Fascist,
The boot in the face, the brute
Brute heart of a brute like you.                          50

You stand at the blackboard, daddy,
In the picture I have of you,
A cleft in your chin instead of your foot
But no less a devil for that, no not
Any less the black man who                                55

**27 Ich, ich, ich, ich** "I, I, I, I"   **33 Dachau, Auschwitz, Belsen** German concentration camps
**42 Luftwaffe** German Air Force

Bit my pretty red heart in two.
I was ten when they buried you.
At twenty I tried to die
And get back, back, back to you.
I thought even the bones would do.          60

But they pulled me out of the sack,
And they stuck me together with glue.
And then I knew what to do.
I made a model of you,
A man in black with a Meinkampf° look          65

And a love of the rack and the screw.
And I said I do, I do.
So daddy, I'm finally through.
The black telephone's off at the root,
The voices just can't worm through.          70

If I've killed one man, I've killed two—
The vampire who said he was you
And drank my blood for a year,
Seven years, if you want to know.
Daddy, you can lie back now.          75

There's a stake in your fat black heart
And the villagers never liked you.
They are dancing and stamping on you.
They always *knew* it was you.
Daddy, daddy, you bastard, I'm through.          80

—1966

# Metaphors

I'm a riddle in nine syllables,
An elephant, a ponderous house,
A melon strolling on two tendrils.
O red fruit, ivory, fine timbers!
This loaf's big with its yeasty rising.          5
Money's new-minted in this fat purse.
I'm a means, a stage, a cow in calf.
I've eaten a bag of green apples,
Boarded the train there's no getting off.

—1960

**65 Meinkampf** title of Hitler's autobiography ("My Struggle")

GERALD BARRAX ■ (b. 1933)

*Gerald Barrax served as the editor of* Obsidian II: Black Literature in Review, *one of the most influential journals of African American writing. The author of five collections of poetry, he taught at North Carolina State University.*

## Strangers Like Us: Pittsburgh, Raleigh, 1945–1985

The sounds our parents heard echoing over
housetops while listening to evening radios
were the uninterrupted cries running and cycling
we sent through the streets and yards, where spring summer
fall we were entrusted to the night, boys                          5
and girls together, to send us home for bath
and bed after the dark had drifted down and eased
contests between pitcher and batter, hider and seeker.

Our own children live imprisoned in light.
They are cycloned into our yards and hearts,                      10
whose gates flutter shut on unfamiliar smiles.
At the rumor of a moon, we call them in
before the monsters who hunt, who hurt, who haunt
us, rise up from our own dim streets.

—1992

MARY OLIVER ■ (b. 1935)

*Mary Oliver was born in Cleveland, Ohio, and educated at Ohio State University and Vassar College. She has served as a visiting professor at a number of universities and at the Fine Arts Work Center in Provincetown, Massachusetts. She has won both the Pulitzer Prize and the National Book Award for her work.*

## The Black Walnut Tree

My mother and I debate:
we could sell
the black walnut tree
to the lumberman,
and pay off the mortgage.                                         5
Likely some storm anyway

will churn down its dark boughs,
smashing the house. We talk
slowly, two women trying
in a difficult time to be wise.                    10
Roots in the cellar drains,
I say, and she replies
that the leaves are getting heavier
every year, and the fruit
harder to gather away.                             15
But something brighter than money
moves in our blood—an edge
sharp and quick as a trowel
that wants us to dig and sow.
So we talk, but we don't do                        20
anything. That night I dream
of my fathers out of Bohemia
filling the blue fields
of fresh and generous Ohio
with leaves and vines and orchards.                25
What my mother and I both know
is that we'd crawl with shame
in the emptiness we'd made
in our own and our fathers' backyard.
So the black walnut tree                           30
swings through another year
of sun and leaping winds,
of leaves and bounding fruit,
and, month after month, the whip-
crack of the mortgage.                             35

—1979

---

**FRED CHAPPELL ■ (b. 1936)**

*Fred Chappell wrote the epic-length poem* Midquest *(1981), and his achievement was recognized when he was awarded the Bollingen Prize in 1985. A four-part poem written over a decade,* Midquest *uses the occasion of the poet's thirty-fifth birthday as a departure for a complex sequence of autobiographical poems that are heavily indebted to Dante for their formal structure. A versatile writer of both poetry and prose, Chappell displays his classical learning brilliantly and in unusual contexts.*

# Narcissus and Echo°

Shall the water not remember *Ember*
my hand's slow gesture, tracing above *of*
its mirror my half-imaginary *airy*
portrait? My only belonging *longing*
is my beauty, which I take *ache*                    5
away and then return as love *of*
teasing playfully the one being *unbeing.*

whose gratitude I treasure *Is your*
moves me. I live apart *heart*
from myself, yet cannot *not*                         10
live apart. In the water's tone, *stone?*
that brilliant silence, a flower *Hour,*
whispers my name with such slight *light,*
moment, it seems filament of air, *fare*
the world become cloudswell. *well.*                  15

—1985

---

**LUCILLE CLIFTON ■ (b. 1936)**

*Lucille Clifton, a native of Depew, New York, was educated at SUNY–Fredonia
and Howard University and taught at several colleges, including American
University in Washington, D.C. About her own work, she commented succinctly,
"I am a Black woman poet, and I sound like one." Clifton won a National Book
Award in 2000.*

# homage to my hips

these hips are big hips
they need space to
move around in.
they don't fit into little
petty places. these hips                              5
are free hips.
they don't like to be held back.
these hips have never been enslaved,
they go where they want to go
they do what they want to do.                         10

---

**Narcissus and Echo** In the myth, the vain Narcissus drowned attempting to embrace his own reflection
in the water. Echo, a nymph who loved him, pined away until only her voice remained.

these hips are mighty hips.
these hips are magic hips.
i have known them
to put a spell on a man and
spin him like a top!                                   15

—1980

## wishes for sons

i wish them cramps.
i wish them a strange town
and the last tampon.
I wish them no 7-11.

i wish them one week early                              5
and wearing a white skirt.
i wish them one week late.

later i wish them hot flashes
and clots like you
wouldn't believe. let the                              10
flashes come when they
meet someone special.
let the clots come
when they want to.

let them think they have accepted                      15
arrogance in the universe,
then bring them to gynecologists
not unlike themselves.

—1991

---

**MARGE PIERCY ■ (b. 1936)**

*Marge Piercy was a political radical during her student days at the University of Michigan. Piercy has continued to be outspoken on political, cultural, and sexual issues. Her phrase "to be of use" has become a key measure by which feminist writers and critics have gauged the meaning of their own life experiences.*

## What's That Smell in the Kitchen?

All over America women are burning dinners.
It's lambchops in Peoria; it's haddock
in Providence; it's steak in Chicago;

tofu delight in Big Sur; red
rice and beans in Dallas.                                        5
All over America women are burning
food they're supposed to bring with calico
smile on platters glittering like wax.
Anger sputters in her brainpan, confined
but spewing out missiles of hot fat.                             10
Carbonized despair presses like a clinker
from a barbecue against the back of her eyes.
If she wants to grill anything, it's
her husband spitted over a slow fire.
If she wants to serve him anything                               15
it's a dead rat with a bomb in its belly
ticking like the heart of an insomniac.
Her life is cooked and digested,
nothing but leftovers in Tupperware.
Look, she says, once I was roast duck                            20
on your platter with parsley but now I am Spam.
Burning dinner is not incompetence but war.

—1982

---

### BETTY ADCOCK ■ (b. 1938)

*Betty Adcock was born in San Augustine, Texas. Adcock has lived for many*
*years in Raleigh, North Carolina, where she is poet-in-residence at Meredith*
*College. Her volume of selected poems,* Intervale, *appeared in 2001.*

## Voyages

We were five girls prowling alleyways behind the houses,
having skipped math class for any and no reason.
Equipped with too many camelhair coats, too many cashmeres,
we were privileged and sure and dumb, isolated
without knowing it, smug in our small crime, playing             5
hooky from Miss Hockaday's Boarding School for young ladies.
Looking for anything that wouldn't be boring
as we defined that, we'd gone off exploring the going-downhill
neighborhoods around our tight Victorian schoolgrounds.
The houses were fronted with concrete porches,                   10
venetian blinds drawn tight against the sun.
Somebody had told us an eccentric lived where one
back fence got strangely high and something stuck over
the top. We didn't care what it was, but we went anyway,

giggling with hope for the freakish: bodies stashed and decaying,   15
a madwoman pulling her hair, maybe a maniac in a cage.
Anything sufficiently awful would have done.

But when we came close enough to look through
the inch of space between two badly placed fenceboards,
we saw only the ordinary, grown grotesque and huge:                 20
somebody was building a sailboat bigger than most city
     backyards,
bigger almost than the house it belonged to,
mast towering high in a brass-and-blue afternoon.
This was in the middle of Dallas, Texas—
the middle of the 1950s, which had us                               25
(though we didn't yet know this) by the throat.
Here was a backyard entirely full of boat,
out of scale, out of the Bible, maybe out of a movie,
all rescue and ornament. It looked to be something between
a galleon and a Viking ship, larger than we could imagine           30
in such a space, with sails and riggings and a face on the prow
(about which we made much but which neither smiled nor frowned).
Gasping, overplaying the scene, we guessed at the kind
of old fool who would give a lifetime to building this thing.
Then one of us asked for a light for a cigarette                    35
and we all knew how easy it would be to swipe
a newspaper, light it, and toss it onto the deck
of that great wooden landlocked ark, watch it go up.

But of course we didn't do it and nobody of course came out
of that house and we of course went back                           40
in time for English and to sneak out of P.E. later
for hamburgers at Mitch's where the blue-collar boys
leaned in their ducktails against the bar.

But before we did that, we stood for a while clumped
and smoking, pushed into silence by palpable obsession             45
where it sat as if it belonged on parched Dallas grass,
a stunned, unfinished restlessness.
And didn't the ground just then, under our penny-
loafers, give the tiniest heave? Didn't we feel how thin
the grass was, like a coat of light paint, like green ice          50
over something unmanageable? How thin the sun
became for a minute, the rest of our future dimming
and wavy and vast, even tomorrow's pop quiz and softball practice—

as if all around us were depths we really could drown in.

—1995

ROBERT PHILLIPS ■ (b. 1938)

*Robert Phillips labored for more than thirty years as a New York advertising executive, a remarkable fact when one considers his many books of poetry, fiction, and criticism and the numerous books he has edited. He currently lives in Houston, where he teaches in the creative writing program at the University of Houston.*

# The Stone Crab: A Love Poem

Joe's serves approximately 1,000 pounds of crab claws each day.
                              —*Florida Gold Coast Leisure Guide*

Delicacy of warm Florida waters,
his body is undesirable. One giant claw
is his claim to fame, and we claim it,

more than once. Meat sweeter than lobster,
less dear than his life, when grown that claw          5
is lifted, broken off at the joint.

Mutilated, the crustacean is thrown back
into the water, back upon his own resources.
One of nature's rarities, he replaces

an entire appendage as you or I                        10
grow a nail. (No one asks how he survives
that crabby sea with just one claw;

two-fisted menaces real as night-
mares, ten-tentacled nights cold
as fright.) In time he grows another,                  15

large, meaty, magnificent as the first.
And one astonished day, *snap!* it too
is twigged off, the cripple dropped
back into treachery. Unlike a twig,
it sprouts again. How many losses                      20
can he endure? Well,

his shell is hard, the sea is wide.
Something vital broken off, he doesn't
nurse the wound; develops something new.

                                          —1994

DABNEY STUART ■ (b. 1938)

*Dabney Stuart has written many poems populated by the supporting cast of the American family romance—parents, wives and ex-wives, and*

*children. A Virginian who taught for many years at Washington and*
*Lee University, Stuart published* Light Years, *a volume of selected poems,*
*in 1995.*

## Discovering My Daughter

Most of your life we have kept our separate places:
After I left your mother you knew an island,
Rented rooms, a slow coastal slide northward
To Boston, and, in summer, another island
Hung at the country's tip. Would you have kept going          5
All the way off the map, an absolute alien?

Sometimes I shiver, being almost forgetful enough
To have let that happen. We've come the longer way
Under such pressure, from one person to
Another. Our trip proves again the world is                          10
Round, a singular island where people may come
Together, as we have, making a singular place.

—1987

---

**MARGARET ATWOOD** ■ **(b. 1939)**

*Margaret Atwood is the leading woman writer of Canada, and she excels at*
*both poetry and prose fiction. Among her many novels,* The Handmaid's
Tale *is perhaps the best known, becoming a best seller in the United*
*States and the subject of a motion picture. Atwood's* Selected Poems
*appeared in 1976.*

## Siren° Song

This is the one song everyone
would like to learn: the song
that is irresistible:

the song that forces men
to leap overboard in squadrons                                            5
even though they see the beached skulls

the song nobody knows
because anyone who has heard it
is dead, and the others can't remember.

**Siren** in Greek myth, one of the women whose irresistible song lured sailors onto the rocks

Shall I tell you the secret                                    10
and if I do, will you get me
out of this bird suit?

I don't enjoy it here
squatting on this island
looking picturesque and mythical                               15

with these two feathery maniacs,
I don't enjoy singing
this trio, fatal and valuable.
I will tell the secret to you,
to you, only to you.                                           20
Come closer. This song

is a cry for help: Help me!
Only you, only you can,
you are unique

at last. Alas                                                  25
it is a boring song
but it works every time.

—1974

---

**STEPHEN DUNN ■ (b. 1939)**

*Stephen Dunn is a graduate of the creative writing program at Syracuse
University. Dunn teaches at The Richard Stockton College of New Jersey in
Pomona, New Jersey. His attempt to blend ordinary experience with larger sig-
nificance is illustrated in the duality of his book titles like* Full of Lust *and* Good
Usage, Work and Love, *and* Between Angels. *Dunn was awarded the Pulitzer
Prize in 2001.*

## The Sacred

After the teacher asked if anyone had
        a sacred place
and the students fidgeted and shrank
in their chairs, the most serious of them all
        said it was his car,                                   5
being in it alone, his tape deck playing

things he'd chosen, and others knew the truth
        had been spoken
and began speaking about their rooms,

their hiding places, but the car kept coming up,                    10
    the car in motion,
music filling it, and sometimes one other person

who understood the bright altar of the dashboard
    and how far away
a car could take him from the need                                  15

to speak, or to answer, the key
    in having a key
and putting it in, and going.

—1989

---

### TED KOOSER ■ (b. 1939)

*Ted Kooser, who lives in Nebraska, writes plainspoken poems about life in America's heartland. Born in Iowa, Kooser studied at Iowa State University and the University of Nebraska. His poetry collections include* Winter Morning Walks: One Hundred Postcards to Jim Harrison, *which was written during Kooser's recovery from cancer surgery and radiation treatment. It received the 2001 Nebraska Book Award for poetry. Kooser is editor and publisher of Windflower Press, a small press specializing in contemporary poetry. A retired vice president of Lincoln Benefit Life, an insurance company, Kooser teaches at the University of Nebraska, Lincoln. In 2004, Kooser was appointed U.S. poet laureate.*

## Abandoned Farmhouse

He was a big man, says the size of his shoes
on a pile of broken dishes by the house;
a tall man too, says the length of the bed
in an upstairs room; and a good, God-fearing man,
says the Bible with a broken back                                   5
on the floor below the window, dusty with sun;
but not a man for farming, say the fields
cluttered with boulders and the leaky barn.

A woman lived with him, says the bedroom wall
papered with lilacs and the kitchen shelves                         10
covered with oilcloth, and they had a child,
says the sandbox made from a tractor tire.
Money was scarce, say the jars of plum preserves
and canned tomatoes sealed in the cellar hole.
And the winters cold, say the rags in the window frames.            15
It was lonely here, says the narrow country road.

Something went wrong, says the empty house
in the weed-choked yard. Stones in the fields
in the cellar say she left in a nervous haste.
And the child? Its toys are strewn in the yard                    20
like branches after a storm—a rubber cow,
a rusty tractor with a broken plow,
a doll in overalls. Something went wrong, they say.

—1980

---

### TOM DISCH ■ (b. 1940–2008)

*Tom Disch was a* science fiction *writer, author of interactive computer fiction, resident critic for magazines as diverse as* Playboy *and* The Nation, *and poet. Disch was possibly the most brilliant satirist in contemporary American poetry.* Yes, Let's, *a collection of his selected poems, appeared in 1989.*

## Ballade of the New God

I have decided I'm divine.
Caligula and Nero knew
A godliness akin to mine,
But they are strictly hitherto.
They're dead, and what can dead gods do?                         5
I'm here and now. I'm dynamite.
I'd worship me if I were you.
A new religion starts tonight!

No booze, no pot, no sex, no swine:
I have decreed them all taboo.                                    10
My words will be your only wine,
The thought of me your honeydew.
All other thoughts you will eschew
And call yourself a Thomasite
And hymn my praise with loud yahoo.                               15
A new religion starts tonight.

But (you might think) that's asinine!
I'm just as much a god as you.
You may have built yourself a shrine
But I won't bend my knee. Who                                     20
Asked you to be my god? I do,
Who am, as god, divinely right.

Now you must join my retinue:
A new religion starts tonight.

All that I have said is true.                                        25
I'm god and you're my acolyte.
Surrender's bliss: I envy you.
A new religion starts tonight.

—1995

---

**FLORENCE CASSEN MAYERS** ■ **(b. 1940)**

*Florence Cassen Mayers is a widely published poet and children's author.
Her "ABC" books include children's guides to baseball and to the National
Basketball Association.*

## All-American Sestina

One nation, indivisible
two-car garage
three strikes you're out
four-minute mile
five-cent cigar                                                     5
six-string guitar

six-pack Bud
one-day sale
five-year warranty
two-way street                                                      10
fourscore and seven years ago
three cheers

three-star restaurant
sixty-
four-dollar question                                               15
one-night stand
two-pound lobster
five-star general

five-course meal
three sheets to the wind                                            20
two bits
six-shooter
one-armed bandit
four-poster

four-wheel drive                                                    25
five-and-dime

hole in one
three-alarm fire
sweet sixteen
two-wheeler                                                   30

two-tone Chevy
four rms, hi flr, w/vu
six-footer
high five
three-ring circus                                            35
one-room schoolhouse

two thumbs up, five-karat diamond
Fourth of July, three-piece suit
six feet under, one-horse town

—1996

---

**PATTIANN ROGERS ■ (b. 1940)**

*Pattiann Rogers is the foremost naturalist among contemporary American poets. Her poems resound with the rich names of unfamiliar species of plants and animals, most of which she seems to know on intimate terms.* Song of the World Becoming: New and Collected Poems 1981–2001 *was published in 2001.*

# Foreplay

When it first begins, as you might expect,
the lips and thin folds are closed, the pouting
layers pressed, lapped lightly,
almost languidly, against one another
in a sealed bud.                                             5

However, with certain prolonged
and random strokings of care
along each binding line, with soft
intrusions traced beneath each pursed
gathering and edge, with inquiring                           10
intensities of gesture—as the sun
swinging slowly from winter back

to spring, touches briefly,
between moments of moon and masking
clouds, certain stunning points                              15
and inner nubs of earth—so
with such ministrations, a slight

swelling, a quiver of reaching,
a tendency toward space,
might be noticed to commence.                              20

Then with dampness from the dark,
with moisture from the falling
night of morning, from hidden places
within the hills, each seal begins
to loosen, each recalcitrant clasp                         25
sinks away into itself, and every tucked
grasp, every silk tack willingly relents,
releases, gives way, proclaims a turning,
declares a revolution, assumes,
in plain sight, a surging position                         30
that offers, an audacious offering
that beseeches, every petal parted wide.

Remember the spiraling, blue
valerian, remember the violet, sucking
larkspur, the laurel and rosebay                           35
and pea cockle flung backwards, remember
the fragrant, funnelling lily, the lifted
honeysuckle, the sweet, open pucker
of the ground ivy blossom?

Now even the darkest crease possessed,                     40
the most guarded, pulsing, least drop
of pearl bead, moon grain trembling
deep within is fully revealed, fully exposed
to any penetrating wind or shaking fur
or mad hunger or searing, plunging surprise               45
the wild descending sky in delirium
has to offer.

                                        —1994

---

### BILLY COLLINS ■ (b. 1941)

*Billy Collins was born in New York City and continues to teach there. One of the few contemporary poets to reach a wide popular audience, Collins has been an enthusiastic performer, commentator on National Public Radio, and advocate for poetry. Beginning in 2001, he served two years as U.S. poet laureate, establishing the online anthology "Poetry 180," a website that presents a poem for every day in the school year.* Sailing Alone Around the Room: New and Selected Poems *was published in 2001.*

# The Lanyard

The other day I was ricocheting slowly
off the blue walls of this room,
moving as if underwater from typewriter to piano,
from bookshelf to an envelope lying on the floor,
when I found myself in the L section of the dictionary
where my eyes fell upon the word lanyard.

No cookie nibbled by a French novelist
could send one into the past more suddenly—
a past where I sat at a workbench at a camp
by a deep Adirondack lake
learning how to braid long thin plastic strips
into a lanyard, a gift for my mother.

I had never seen anyone use a lanyard
or wear one, if that's what you did with them,
but that did not keep me from crossing
strand over strand again and again
until I had made a boxy
red and white lanyard for my mother.

She gave me life and milk from her breasts,
and I gave her a lanyard.
She nursed me in many a sick room,
lifted spoons of medicine to my lips,
laid cold face-cloths on my forehead,
and then led me out into the airy light

and taught me to walk and swim,
and I, in turn, presented her with a lanyard.
Here are thousands of meals, she said,
and here is clothing and a good education.
And here is your lanyard, I replied,
which I made with a little help from a counselor.
Here is a breathing body and a beating heart,
strong legs, bones and teeth,
and two dear eyes to read the world, she whispered,
and here, I said, is the lanyard I made at camp.
And here, I wish to say to her now,
is a smaller gift—not the worn truth

that you can never repay your mother,
but the rueful admission that when she took
the two-tone lanyard from my hand,

I was as sure as a boy could be
that this useless, worthless thing I wove
out of boredom would be enough to make us even.

---

**GIBBONS RUARK** ■ **(b. 1941)**

*Gibbons Ruark is a native of North Carolina. Ruark is the author of five col-
lections of poetry.* Passing Through Customs, *a volume of new and selected
poems, appeared in 1999. He recently retired from teaching at the University
of Delaware.*

# The Visitor

Holding the arm of his helper, the blind
Piano tuner comes to our piano.
He hesitates at first, but once he finds
The keyboard, his hands glide over the slow
Keys, ringing changes finer than the eye                          5
Can see. The dusty wires he touches, row
On row, quiver like bowstrings as he
Twists them one notch tighter. He runs his
Finger along a wire, touches the dry
Rust to his tongue, breaks into a pure bliss                     10
And tells us, "One year more of damp weather
Would have done you in, but I've saved it this
Time. Would one of you play now, please? I hear
It better at a distance." My wife plays
*Stardust.* The blind man stands and smiles in her               15
Direction, then disappears into the blaze
Of new October. Now the afternoon,
The long afternoon that blurs in a haze
Of music ... Chopin nocturnes, *Clair de Lune,*
All the old familiar, unfamiliar                                 20
Music-lesson pieces, *Papa Haydn's
Dead and gone, gently down the stream...* Hours later,
After the latest car has doused its beams,
Has cooled down and stopped its ticking, I hear
Our cat, with the grace of animals free                          25
To move in darkness, strike one key only,
And a single lucid drop of water stars my dream.

—1971

GLADYS CARDIFF ■ (b. 1942)

*Gladys Cardiff is a member of the Cherokee nation. "Combing" is taken from her first collection,* To Frighten a Storm, *which was originally published in 1976.*

# Combing

Bending, I bow my head
And lay my hand upon
Her hair, combing, and think
How women do this for
Each other. My daughter's hair                    5
Curls against the comb,
Wet and fragrant—orange
Parings. Her face, downcast,
Is quiet for one so young.

I take her place. Beneath                          10
My mother's hands I feel
The braids drawn up tight
As a piano wire and singing,
Vinegar-rinsed. Sitting
Before the oven I hear                             15
The orange coils tick
The early hour before school.

She combed her grandmother
Mathilda's hair using
A comb made out of bone.                           20
Mathilda rocked her oak wood
Chair, her face downcast,
Intent on tearing rags
In strips to braid a cotton
Rug from bits of orange                            25
and brown. A simple act,
Preparing hair. Something
Women do for each other,
Plaiting the generations.

—1976

CHARLES MARTIN ■ (b. 1942)

*Charles Martin is a lifelong resident of New York City. Martin has taught for many years at Queensborough College. "E.S.L." appeared as a prefatory poem to Martin's sequence "Passages from Friday," an ironic retelling of the Robinson Crusoe story from his servant's point of view. A respected classicist, Martin has translated Ovid and Catullus.*

# E.S.L.°

<pre>
        My frowning students carve
        Me monsters out of prose:
This one—a gargoyle—thumbs its contemptuous nose
At how, in English, subject must agree
With verb—for any such agreement shows              5
        Too great a willingness to serve,
                A docility

        Which wiry Miss Choi
        Finds un-American.
She steals a hard look at me. I wink. Her grin       10
Is my reward. *In his will, our peace, our Pass:*
Gargoyle erased, subject and verb now in
        Agreement, reach object, enjoy
                Temporary truce.

        Tonight my students must                     15
        *Agree or disagree:*
America is still a land of opportunity.
The answer is always, uniformly, *Yes*—even though
*"It has no doubt that here were to much free,"*
        As Miss Torrico will insist.                 20
                She and I both know

        That Language binds us fast,
        And those of us without
Are bound and gagged by those within. Each fledgling
Polyglot must shake old habits: tapping her sneakered feet, 25
Miss Choi exorcises incensed ancestors, flout-
        ing the ghosts of her Chinese past.
                Writhing in the seat

        Next to Miss Choi, Mister
        Fedakis, in anguish                          30
Labors to express himself in a tongue which
Proves *Linear B* to me, when I attempt to read it
Later. They're here for English as a Second Language,
        Which I'm teaching this semester.
                God knows they need it,               35
</pre>

**E.S.L.** English as a Second Language

And so, thank God, do they.
    The night's made easier
By our agreement: I am here to help deliver
Them into the good life they write me papers about.
English is pre-requisite for that endeavor,          40
    Explored in their nightly essays
        Boldly setting out
    To reconnoiter the fair
    New World they would enter:
Suburban Paradise, the endless shopping center      45
Where one may browse for hours before one chooses
Some new necessity—gold-flecked magenta
    Wallpaper to re-do the spare
        Bath no one uses,

    Or a machine which can,          50
    In seven seconds, crush
A newborn calf into such seamless mush
As a *mousse* might be made of—or our true sublime:
The gleaming counters where frosted cosmeticians brush
    Decades from the allotted span,      55
        Abrogating Time

    As the spring tide brushes
    A single sinister
Footprint from the otherwise unwrinkled shore
Of America the Blank. In absolute confusion      60
Poor Mister Fedakis rumbles with despair
    And puts the finishing smutches
        To his conclusion

    While Miss Choi erases:
    One more gargoyle routed.      65
Their pure, erroneous lines yield an illuminated
Map of the new found land. We will never arrive there,
Since it exists only in what we say about it,
    As all the rest of my class is
        Bound to discover.      70

        —1987

---

### SHARON OLDS ■ (b. 1942)

*Sharon Olds displays a candor in dealing with the intimacies of family romance covering three generations that has made her one of the chief*

*contemporary heirs to the confessional tradition. A powerful and dramatic*
*reader, she is much in demand on the lecture circuit. Born in San Francisco,*
*she currently resides in New York City.*

# The One Girl at the Boys Party

When I take my girl to the swimming party
I set her down among the boys. They tower and
bristle, she stands there smooth and sleek,
her math scores unfolding in the air around her.
They will strip to their suits, her body hard and       5
indivisible as a prime number,
they'll plunge into the deep end, she'll subtract
her height from ten feet, divide it into
hundreds of gallons of water, the numbers
bouncing in her mind like molecules of chlorine       10
in the bright blue pool. When they climb out,
her ponytail will hang its pencil lead
down her back, her narrow silk suit
with hamburgers and french fries printed on it
will glisten in the brilliant air, and they will       15
see her sweet face, solemn and
sealed, a factor of one, and she will
see their eyes, two each,
their legs, two each, and the curves of their sexes,
one each, and in her head she'll be doing her       20
wild multiplying, as the drops
sparkle and fall to the power of a thousand from her body.

—1983

---

**ALFRED CORN** ■ **(b. 1943)**

*Alfred Corn was born in south Georgia and educated at Emory University and*
*Columbia University, majoring in French. A widely traveled poet and critic,*
*he has taught at many universities here and abroad and has also published*
*a study of English prosody,* The Poem's Heartbeat. *He has been a leading*
*spokesperson for gay perspectives in literature and the arts.*

## Upbringing

"Yes, ma'am," "No, sir!" Parents' blandest questions
Took for granted a standard honorific

When I answered. Lazy omission of which
Triggered on the spot a sharp "Yes, *who*?"
Till ma'ams or sirs—but properly intoned—
Were reinstated in the heart and mind
Of a Southern boy who had been well brought up.

A civil tongue. And basic training, too,
In table manners, being seen and not
Heard, respect for elders and for members
Of the female sex, referred to always as *ladies*
Once they were no longer girls. (A *woman*
Was someone who cleaned, invariably black,
Who said "please" and "thank you" every chance she got.)

How a gentleman behaved was dinned in
His ears from day one, an ideal as crucial
As soldiering in the army of the saints.
Yet ladies were a holier, a frailer
Vessel, deserving, therefore, special treatment.
*Her parcels, you carry. What she drops, pick up.*
*Open the door, and let her enter first.*

Into Heaven, too, it still seems plausible.
Do we ever trash a brain washed clean so early?
"The first shall be the last, and the last, first,"
Gates of Paradox inform the hopeful
Who knocks.... I give that upbringing this much:
"Let others pass before you" didn't mean
"Just freeze, and let them push on by themselves."

---

## DIANE LOCKWARD ■ (b. 1943)

*Diane Lockward is a former high school English teacher who now works as a poet-in-the-schools for both the New Jersey State Council on the Arts and the Geraldine R. Dodge Foundation. She has received numerous awards for her poetry, which has appeared in many literary journals, but her first full-length collection,* Eve's Red Dress, *did not appear until 2003. "My Husband Discovers Poetry" has been read by Garrison Keillor several times on National Public Radio's* The Writer's Almanac. *Lockward has commented that "My Husband Discovers Poetry" is, in fact, her husband's favorite poem.*

# My Husband Discovers Poetry

Because my husband would not read my poems,
I wrote one about how I did not love him.
In lines of strict iambic pentameter,
I detailed his coldness, his lack of humor.
It felt good to do this.                                                        5

Stanza by stanza, I grew bolder and bolder.
Towards the end, struck by inspiration,
I wrote about my old boyfriend,
a boy I had not loved enough to marry
but who could make me laugh and laugh.                          10
I wrote about a night years after we parted
when my husband's coldness drove me from the house
and back to my old boyfriend.
I even included the name of a seedy motel
well-known for hosting quickies.                                        15
I have a talent for verisimilitude.

In sensuous images, I described
how my boyfriend and I stripped off our clothes,
got into bed, and kissed and kissed,
then spent half the night telling jokes,                              20
many of them about my husband.
I left the ending deliberately ambiguous,
then hid the poem away
in an old trunk in the basement.

You know how this story ends,                                            25
how my husband one day loses something,
goes into the basement,
and rummages through the old trunk,
how he uncovers the hidden poem
and sits down to read it.                                                      30

But do you hear the strange sounds
that floated up the stairs that day,
the sounds of an animal, its paw caught
in one of those traps with teeth of steel?
Do you see the wounded creature                                        35
at the bottom of the stairs,
his shoulders hunched over and shaking,
fist in his mouth and choking back sobs?
It was my husband paying tribute to my art.

—2003

**ELLEN BRYANT VOIGT ■ (b. 1943)**

*Ellen Bryant Voigt is a native of Virginia. Voigt was trained as a concert pia-nist before earning her creative writing degree from the University of Iowa. She has taught poetry at a number of colleges in New England and the South.*

# Daughter

There is one grief worse than any other.

When your small feverish throat clogged, and quit,
I knelt beside the chair on the green rug
and shook you and shook you,
but the only sound was mine shouting you back,                    5
the delicate curls at your temples,
the blue wool blanket,
your face blue,
your jaw clamped against remedy—

how could I put a knife to that white neck?                         10
With you in my lap,
my hands fluttering like flags,
I bend instead over your dead weight
to administer a kiss so urgent, so ruthless,
pumping breath into your stilled body,                             15
counting out the rhythm for how long until
the second birth, the second cry
oh Jesus that sudden noisy musical inhalation
that leaves me stunned
by your survival.                                                   20

—1983

**CRAIG RAINE ■ (b. 1944)**

*Craig Raine early in his career displayed a comic surrealism that was responsible for so many imitations that critic James Fenton dubbed him the founder of the "Martian School" of contemporary poetry. Born in Bishop Auckland, England, and educated at Oxford, Raine is publisher of the literary magazine* Arete.

# A Martian Sends a Postcard Home

Caxtons° are mechanical birds with many wings
and some are treasured for their markings—

**1 Caxtons** i.e., books after William Caxton (1422–1491), first English printer

they cause the eyes to melt
or the body to shriek without pain.

I have never seen one fly, but                                    5
sometimes they perch on the hand.

Mist is when the sky is tired of flight
and rests its soft machine on ground:

then the world is dim and bookish
like engravings under tissue paper.                              10

Rain is when the earth is television.
It has the property of making colours darker.

Model T is a room with the lock inside—
a key is turned to free the world

for movement, so quick there is a film                          15
to watch for anything missed.
But time is tied to the wrist
or kept in a box, ticking with impatience.

In homes, a haunted apparatus sleeps,
that snores when you pick it up.                                 20

If the ghost cries, they carry it
to their lips and soothe it to sleep

with sounds. And yet, they wake it up
deliberately, by tickling with a finger.

Only the young are allowed to suffer                            25
openly. Adults go to a punishment room

with water but nothing to eat.
They lock the door and suffer the noises
alone. No one is exempt
and everyone's pain has a different smell.                      30

At night, when all the colours die,
they hide in pairs

and read about themselves—
in colour, with their eyelids shut.

—1978

---

**ENID SHOMER** ■ **(b. 1944)**

*Enid Shomer grew up in Washington, D.C., and lived for a number of years
in Florida. Her first collection,* Stalking the Florida Panther *(1987), explored*

*both the Jewish traditions of her childhood and her adult attachment to her
adopted state.*

## Women Bathing at Bergen-Belsen°

### April 24, 1945

Twelve hours after the Allies arrive
there is hot water, soap. Two women bathe
in a makeshift, open-air shower while nearby
fifteen thousand are flung naked into mass graves
by captured SS guards. Clearly legs and arms                    5
are the natural handles of a corpse. The bathers,
taken late in the war, still have flesh
on their bones, still have breasts. Though nudity was
a death sentence here, they have undressed,
oblivious to the soldiers and the cameras.                      10
The corpses push through the limed earth like upended
headstones. The bathers scrub their feet, bending
in beautiful curves, mapping the contours
of the body, that kingdom to which they've returned.

—1987

---

### WENDY COPE ■ (b. 1945)

*Wendy Cope says, "I hardly ever tire of love or rhyme. / That's why I'm poor
and have a rotten time." Her first collection,* Making Cocoa for Kingsley Amis
*(1986), was a best seller in England. Whether reducing T.S. Eliot's modern-
ist classic "The Waste Land" to a set of five limericks or chronicling the life
and loves of Jason Strugnell, her feckless poetic alter-ego, Cope remains one
of the wisest and wittiest poets writing today: "I dislike the term 'light verse'
because it is used as a way of dismissing poets who allow humor into their
work. I believe that a humorous poem can also be 'serious'; deeply felt and
saying something that matters."*

## Rondeau Redoublé

There are so many kinds of awful men—
One can't avoid them all. She often said
She'd never make the same mistake again:
She always made a new mistake instead.

**Bergen-Belsen** German concentration camp in WWII

The chinless type who made her feel ill-bred;    5
The practised charmer, less than charming when
He talked about the wife and kids and fled—
There are so many kinds of awful men.

The half-crazed hippy, deeply into Zen,
Whose cryptic homilies she came to dread;    10
The fervent youth who worshipped Tony Benn°—
'One can't avoid them all,' she often said.

The ageing banker, rich and overfed,
who held forth on the dollar and the yen—
Though there were many more mistakes ahead,    15
She'd never make the same mista ke again.

The budding poet, scribbling in his den
Odes not to her but to his pussy, Fred;
The drunk who fell asleep at nine or ten—
She always made a new mistake instead.    20

And so the gambler was at least unwed
And didn't preach or sneer or wield a pen
Or hoard his wealth or take the Scotch to bed.
She'd lived and learned and lived and learned but then
There are so many kinds.    25

—1986

---

### KAY RYAN ■ (b. 1945)

*Kay Ryan has taught for many years in California. She published her first collection at the age of thirty-eight in 1983, and her poems have appeared in four subsequent books and numerous appearances in* Poetry *and* The New Yorker. *Ryan has often been compared to Emily Dickinson and Marianne Moore for her attention to details from the natural world and for her gentle, often witty moralizing. She is a former U.S. poet laureate.*

## Bestiary

A bestiary catalogs
bests. The mediocres
both higher and lower
are suppressed in favor
of the singularly savage    5

---

**11 Tony Benn** British politician of the 1960s

or clever, the spectacularly
pincered, the archest
of the arch deceivers
who press their advantage
without quarter even after                 10
they've won as of course they would.
*Best* is not to be confused with *good*—
a different creature altogether,
and treated of in the goodiary—
a text alas lost now for centuries.           15

—1996

---

**LEON STOKESBURY** ■ **(b. 1945)**

*Leon Stokesbury, as an undergraduate at Lamar State College of Technology (now Lamar University), published a poem in* The New Yorker. *The author of three collections of poetry, including* Autumn Rhythm: New and Selected Poems, *Stokesbury has also edited anthologies of contemporary Southern poetry and the poetry of World War II.*

# The Day Kennedy Died

Suppose that on the day Kennedy died
you had a vision. But this was no inner movie
with a discernible plot or anything like it.
Not even very visual when you get down
to admitting what actually occurred.            5
About two-thirds of the way through 4th period
Senior Civics, fifteen minutes before
the longed-for lunchtime, suppose you stood up
for no good reason—no reason at all really—
and announced, as you never had before,         10
to the class in general and to yourself
as well, "Something. Something is happening.
I see. Something coming. I can see. I ..."
And that was all. You stood there: blank.
The class roared. Even Phyllis Hoffpaur, girl     15
most worshipped by you from afar that year,
turned a vaguely pastel shade of red
and smiled, and Richard Head, your best friend,
Dick Head to the chosen few, pulled you down

to your desk whispering, "Jesus, man! Jesus                    20
Christ!" Then you went numb. You did not know
for sure what had occurred. But less than one hour
later, when Stella (despised) Vandenburg, teacher
of twelfth grade English, came sashaying
into the auditorium, informing, left and right,            25
as many digesting members of the student body
as she could of what she had just heard,
several students began to glance at you,
remembering what you'd said. A few pointed,
whispering to their confederates, and on that             30
disturbing day they slinked away in the halls.
Even Dick Head did not know what to say.

In 5th period Advanced Math, Principal
Crawford played the radio over the intercom
and the school dropped deeper into history.               35
For the rest of that day, everyone slinked away—
except for the one moment Phyllis Hoffpaur
stared hard, the look on her face asking,
assuming you would know, "Will it be ok?"
And you did not know. No one knew.                        40
Everyone staggered back to their houses
that evening aimless and lost, not knowing,
certainly sensing something had been
changed forever. *Silsbee High forever!*
*That is our claim! Never, no never!*                     45
*Will we lose our fame!* you often sang.
But this was to be the class of 1964,
afraid of the future at last, who would select,
as the class song, Terry Stafford's *Suspicion.*
And this was November—even in Texas                       50
the month of failings, month of sorrows—
from which there was no turning.
It would be a slow two-months slide until
the manic beginnings of the British Invasion,
three months before Clay's ascension to the throne,      55
but all you saw walking home that afternoon
were the gangs of gray leaves clotting the curbs
and culverts, the odors of winter forever
in the air: cold, damp, bleak, dead, dull:
dragging you toward the solstice like a tide.             60

                                                        —2004

---

### JOHN WHITWORTH ■ (b. 1945)

*John Whitworth was born in Nasik, India, the son of a civil servant, and grew up in Edinburgh. After graduating from Merton College, Oxford, he taught English as a foreign language for some years before becoming a full-time writer. The author of numerous collections of verse, including the children's book* The Complete Poetical Works of Phoebe Flood, *he lives in Canterbury.*

## Little

*My daughters' work at 'Footprints'. a respite home for disabled children, supplied the material for this poem.*

When Archie died the Year was dying too.
Late loitering leaves were drifting to the ground,
A time when dying has a lot to do,
And does it with a dry, susurrant sound.

Some say when Archie died it was not much-
A boy who did not walk or talk. But he
Did love to smile and laugh and look and touch.
He did do that. He did it constantly.

So small, so weak, so fragile, yet when Death,
That most ingenious and practised thief,
Unlocked the house and stooped and stopped the breath,
He left a strong sufficiency of grief.

Now is a winter and a summer since,
And now the days of dying come again-
A year since Archie died, our Little Prince,
A year of rain and sun, and sun and rain.

---

### MARILYN NELSON ■ (b. 1946)

*Marilyn Nelson is the author of* The Homeplace, *a sequence of poems on family history.* The Homeplace *is remarkable for its sensitive exploration of the mixed white and black bloodlines in the poet's family history.* Carver: A Life in Poems, *a poetic biography of George Washington Carver, appeared in 2001 and won a National Book Award.* A Wreath for Emmett Till, *a sonnet sequence about a famous hate crime in 1995 Mississippi, appeared in 2005. Both of these books are for young readers.*

# The Ballad of Aunt Geneva

Geneva was the wild one.
Geneva was a tart.
Geneva met a blue-eyed boy
and gave away her heart.

Geneva ran a roadhouse.                                5
Geneva wasn't sent
to college like the others:
Pomp's pride her punishment.

She cooked out on the river,
watching the shore slide by,                           10
her lips pursed into hardness,
her deep-set brown eyes dry.

They say she killed a woman
over a good black man
by braining the jealous heifer                         15
with an iron frying pan.

They say, when she was eighty,
she got up late at night
and sneaked her old, white lover in
to make love, and to fight.                            20

First, they heard the tell-tale
singing of the springs,
then Geneva's voice rang out:
*I need to buy some things,*

*So next time, bring more money.*                      25
*And bring more moxie, too.*
*I ain't got no time to waste*
*on limp white mens like you.*

*Oh yeah? Well, Mister White Man,*
*it sure might be stone-white,*                        30
*but my thing's white as it is.*
*And you know damn well I'm right.*

*Now listen: take your heart pills*
*and pay the doctor mind.*
*If you up and die on me,*                             35
*I'll whip your white behind.*

They tiptoed through the parlor
on heavy, time-slowed feet.

She watched him, from her front door,
walk down the dawnlit street.                                    40

Geneva was the wild one.
Geneva was a tart.
Geneva met a blue-eyed boy
and gave away her heart.

—1990

---

JIM HALL ■ (b. 1947)

*Jim Hall is one of the most brilliantly inventive comic poets in recent years.*
*He has also written a successful series of crime novels set in his native south*
*Florida, beginning with* Under Cover of Daylight *in 1987.*

# Maybe Dats Your Pwoblem Too

All my pwoblems,
who knows, maybe evwybody's pwoblems
is due to da fact, due to da awful twuth
dat I am SPIDERMAN.
I know, I know. All da dumb jokes:                               5
No flies on you, ha ha,
and da ones about what do I do wit all
doze extwa legs in bed. Well, dat's funny yeah.
But you twy being
SPIDERMAN for a month or two. Go ahead.                          10

You get doze cwazy calls fwom da
Gubbener askin you to twap some booglar who's
only twying to wip off color T.V. sets.
Now, what do I cawre about T.V. sets?
But I pull on da suit, da stinkin suit,                          15
wit da sucker cups on da fingers,
and get my wopes and wittle bundle of
equipment and den I go flying like cwazy
acwoss da town fwom woof top to woof top.
Till der he is. Some poor dumb color T.V. slob                   20
and I fall on him and we westle a widdle
until I get him all woped. So big deal.

You tink when you SPIDERMAN
der's sometin big going to happen to you.
Well, I tell you what. It don't happen dat way.                  25

Nuttin happens. Gubbener calls, I go.
Bwing him to powice, Gubbener calls again,
like dat over and over.
I tink I twy sometin diffunt. I tink I twy
sometin excitin like wacing cawrs. Sometin to make    30
my heart beat at a difwent wate.
But den you just can't quit being sometin like
SPIDERMAN.
You SPIDERMAN for life. Fowever. I can't even
buin my suit. It won't buin. It's fwame wesistent.    35
So maybe dat's youwr pwoblem too, who knows.
Maybe dat's da whole pwoblem wif evwytin.
Nobody can buin der suits, dey all fwame wesistent.
Who knows?

—1980

---

### YUSEF KOMUNYAKAA ■ (b. 1947)

*Yusef Komunyakaa is a native of Bogulusa, Louisiana. Komunyakaa has written memorably on a wide range of subjects, including jazz and his service during the Vietnam War.* Neon Vernacular: New and Selected Poems *(1993) won the Pulitzer Prize in 1994, and* Pleasure Dome: New and Collected Poems *appeared in 2001.*

## Facing It

My black face fades,
hiding inside the black granite.
I said I wouldn't,
dammit: No tears.
I'm stone. I'm flesh.    5
My clouded reflection eyes me
like a bird of prey, the profile of night
slanted against morning. I turn
this way—the stone lets me go.
I turn this way—I'm inside    10
the Vietnam Veterans Memorial
again, depending on the light
to make a difference.
I go down the 58,022 names,
half-expecting to find    15
my own in letters like smoke.

I touch the name Andrew Johnson;
I see the booby trap's white flash.
Names shimmer on a woman's blouse
but when she walks away                                    20
the names stay on the wall.
Brushstrokes flash, a red bird's
wings cutting across my stare.
The sky. A plane in the sky.
A white vet's image floats                                 25
closer to me, then his pale eyes
look through mine. I'm a window.
He's lost his right arm
inside the stone. In the black mirror
a woman's trying to erase names:                           30
No, she's brushing a boy's hair.

—1988

---

**TIMOTHY STEELE** ■ **(b. 1948)**

*Timothy Steele has written a successful scholarly study of the rise of free verse,*
*Missing Measures, and is perhaps the most skillful craftsman of the contempo-*
*rary New Formalist poets. Born in Vermont, he has lived for a number of years*
*in Los Angeles, where he teaches at California State University, Los Angeles.*

# Sapphics° Against Anger

Angered, may I be near a glass of water;
May my first impulse be to think of Silence,
Its deities (who are they? do, in fact, they
        Exist? etc.).

May I recall what Aristotle says of                        5
The subject: to give vent to rage is not to
Release it but to be increasingly prone
        To its incursions.

May I imagine being in the Inferno,
Hearing it asked: "Virgilio mio,° who's                    10
That sulking with Achilles there?" and hearing
        Virgil say: "Dante,

**Sapphics** stanza form named after Sappho (c. 650 BC)
**10 Virgilio mio** Dante is addressing Virgil, his guide through hell.

That fellow, at the slightest provocation,
Slammed phone receivers down, and waved his
    arms like
A madman. What Attila did to Europe,       15
      What Genghis Khan did

To Asia, that poor dope did to his marriage."
May I, that is, put learning to good purpose,
Mindful that melancholy is a sin, though
      Stylish at present.       20

Better than rage is the post-dinner quiet,
The sink's warm turbulence, the streaming platters,
The suds rehearsing down the drain in spirals
    In the last rinsing.

For what is, after all, the good life save that      25
Conducted thoughtfully, and what is passion
If not the holiest of powers, sustaining
      Only if mastered.

—1986

---

**JAMES FENTON** ◼ **(b. 1949)**

*James Fenton was born in Lincoln, England, and educated at Oxford. Fenton has worked extensively as a book and drama critic. A brilliant satirical poet, he has also written lyrics for Les Misérables, the musical version of Victor Hugo's novel, and has served as a journalist in Asia.*

# God, a Poem

A nasty surprise in a sandwich,
A drawing-pin caught in your sock,
The limpest of shakes from a hand which
You'd thought would be firm as a rock,

A serious mistake in a nightie,      5
A grave disappointment all around
Is all that you'll get from th'Almighty.
Is all that you'll get underground.

Oh, he *said:* 'If you lay off the crumpet°
I'll see you alright in the end.      10
Just hang on until the last trumpet.

**9 crumpet** vulgar British slang for women

Have faith in me, chum—I'm your friend.'

But if you remind him, he'll tell you:
'I'm sorry, I must have been pissed°—
Though your name rings a sort of a bell. You                    15
Should have guessed that I do not exist.

'I didn't exist at Creation,
I didn't exist at the Flood.
And I won't be around for Salvation
To sort out the sheep from the cud—                             20

'Or whatever the phrase is. The fact is
In soteriological° terms
I'm a crude existential malpractice
And you are a diet of worms.

'You're a nasty surprise in a sandwich.                         25
You're a drawing-pin caught in my sock.
You're the limpest of shakes from a hand which
I'd have thought would be firm as a rock,

'You're a serious mistake in a nightie,
You're a grave disappointment all round—                       30
That's all that you are,' says th'Almighty,
'And that's all that you'll be underground.'

—1983

---

### SARAH CORTEZ ■ (b. 1950)

*Sarah Cortez grew up in Houston, Texas, and holds degrees in psychology and religion, classical studies, and accounting. She also serves as Visiting Scholar at the University of Houston's Center for Mexican American Studies. She has served as a deputy constable in Harris County, Texas.*

## Tu Negrito

She's got to bail me out,
he says into the phone outside the holding cell.
She's going there tomorrow anyway for Mikey.
Tell her she's got to do this for me.

He says into the phone outside the holding cell,                5
Make sure she listens. Make her feel guilty, man.

**14 pissed** drunk   **22 soteriological** relation to salvation

Tell her she's got to do this for me.
She can have all my money, man.

Make sure she listens. Make her feel guilty, man.
Tell her she didn't bail me out the other times.                  10
She can have all my money, man.
She always bails out Mikey.

Tell her she didn't bail me out the other times.
I don't got no one else to call, cousin.
She always bails out Mikey.                                       15
Make sure you write all this down, cousin.

I don't got no one else to call, cousin.
I really need her now.
Make sure you write this all down, cousin.
Page her. Put in code 333. That's me.                             20

I really need her now.
Write down "Mommie." Change it from "Mom."
Page her. Put in code 333. That's me.
Write down *Tu Negrito.* Tell her I love her.

Write down "Mommie." Change it from
    "Mom."                                                        25
I'm her littlest. Remind her.
Write down *Tu Negrito.*
Tell her I love her. She's got to bail me out.

—2000

---

**CAROLYN FORCHÉ** ■ (b. 1950)

*Carolyn Forché won the Yale Younger Poets Award for her first collection,*
*Gathering the Tribes (1975).* The Country Between Us, *Forché's second col-*
*lection, contains poems and prose-poems based on the poet's experiences in*
*the war-torn country of El Salvador in the early 1980s.*

# The Colonel

What you have heard is true. I was in his house.° His wife carried a tray
of coffee and sugar. His daughter filed her nails, his son went out for
the night. There were daily papers, pet dogs, a pistol on the cushion
beside him. The moon swung bare on its black cord over the house. On the

**his house** in El Salvador

television was a cop show. It was in English. Broken bottles were embedded in the walls around the house to scoop the kneecaps from a man's legs or cut his hands to lace. On the windows there were gratings like those in liquor stores. We had dinner, rack of lamb, good wine, a gold bell was on the table for calling the maid. The maid brought green mangoes, salt, a type of bread. I was asked how I enjoyed the country. There was a brief commercial in Spanish. His wife took everything away. There was some talk then of how difficult it had become to govern. The parrot said hello on the terrace. The colonel told it to shut up, and pushed himself from the table. My friend said to me with his eyes: say nothing. The colonel returned with a sack used to bring groceries home. He spilled many human ears on the table. They were like dried peach halves. There is no other way to say this. He took one of them in his hands, shook it in our faces, dropped it into a water glass. It came alive there. I am tired of fooling around he said. As for the rights of anyone, tell your people they can go fuck themselves. He swept the ears to the floor with his arm and held the last of his wine in the air. Something for your poetry, no? he said. Some of the ears on the floor caught this scrap of his voice. Some of the ears on the floor were pressed to the ground.

—1978

---

**DANA GIOIA** ■ (b. 1950)

*Dana Gioia grew up in the suburbs of Los Angeles. He took a graduate degree in English from Harvard but made a successful career in business before devoting his full time to writing. The editor of several textbooks and anthologies, he is also an influential critic whose essay "Can Poetry Matter?" stimulated much discussion when it appeared in* The Atlantic. *Gioia became chairman of the National Endowment for the Arts in 2002, serving until 2009.*

# Planting a Sequoia

All afternoon my brothers and I have worked in the orchard,
Digging this hole, laying you into it, carefully packing the soil.
Rain blackened the horizon, but cold winds kept it over the Pacific,
And the sky above us stayed the dull gray
Of an old year coming to an end.                                        5

In Sicily a father plants a tree to celebrate his first son's birth—
An olive or a fig tree—a sign that the earth has one more life
    to bear.
I would have done the same, proudly laying new stock into my
    father's orchard,

A green sapling rising among the twisted apple boughs,
A promise of new fruit in other autumns.                                    10

But today we kneel in the cold planting you, our native giant,
Defying the practical custom of our fathers,
Wrapping in your roots a lock of hair, a piece of an infant's
    birth cord,
All that remains above earth of a first-born son,
A few stray atoms brought back to the elements.                             15

We will give you what we can—our labor and our soil,
Water drawn from the earth when the skies fail,
Nights scented with the ocean fog, days softened by the circuit of bees.
We plant you in the corner of the grove, bathed in western light,
A slender shoot against the sunset.                                         20

And when our family is no more, all of his unborn brothers dead,
Every niece and nephew scattered, the house torn down,
His mother's beauty ashes in the air,
I want you to stand among strangers, all young and ephemeral to you,
Silently keeping the secret of your birth.                                  25

—1991

---

**RODNEY JONES** ■ **(b. 1950)**

*Rodney Jones was born in Alabama and received important national attention when Transparent Gestures won the Poets' Prize in 1990. Like many younger southern poets, he often deals with the difficult legacy of racism and the adjustments that a new era have forced on both whites and blacks.*

# Winter Retreat: Homage to Martin Luther King, Jr.

There is a hotel in Baltimore where we came together,
we black and white educated and educators,
for a week of conferences, for important counsel
sanctioned by the DOE° and the Carter administration,
to make certain difficult inquiries, to collate notes                      5
on the instruction of the disabled, the deprived,
the poor, who do not score well on entrance tests,

**4 DOE** Department of Education

who, failing school, must go with mop and pail
skittering across the slick floors of cafeterias,
or climb dewy girders to balance high above cities,                    10
or, jobless, line up in the bone cold. We felt
substantive burdens lighter if we stated it right.
Very delicately, we spoke in turn. We walked
together beside the still waters of behaviorism.
Armed with graphs and charts, with new strategies                      15
to devise objectives and determine accountability,
we empathetic black and white shone in seminar rooms.
We enunciated every word clearly and without accent.
We moved very carefully in the valley of the shadow
of the darkest agreement error. We did not digress.                    20
We ascended the trunk of that loftiest cypress
of Latin grammar the priests could never
successfully graft onto the rough green chestnut
of the English language. We extended ourselves
with that sinuous motion of the tongue that is half                    25
pain and almost eloquence. We black and white
politely reprioritized the parameters of our agenda
to impact equitably on the Seminole and the Eskimo.
We praised diversity and involvement, the sacrifices
of fathers and mothers. We praised the next white                      30
Gwendolyn Brooks° and the next black Robert Burns.°
We deep made friends. In that hotel we glistened
over the *pommes au gratin*° and the *poitrine de veau*.°
The morsels of lamb flamed near where we talked.
The waiters bowed and disappeared among the ferns.                     35
And there is a bar there, there is a large pool.
Beyond the tables of the drinkers and raconteurs,
beyond the hot tub brimming with Lebanese tourists
and the women in expensive bathing suits doing laps,
if you dive down four feet, swim out far enough,                       40
and emerge on the other side, it is sixteen degrees.
It is sudden and very beautiful and colder
than thought, though the air frightens you at first,
not because it is cold, but because it is visible,
almost palpable, in the fog that rises from difference.                45
While I stood there in the cheek-numbing snow,
all Baltimore was turning blue. And what I remember
of that week of talks is nothing the record shows,
but the revelation outside, which was the city

---

**31 Gwendolyn Brooks** African-American poet (1917–2000)   **Robert Burns** Scottish poet
(1759–1796)   **33 pommes au gratin** potatoes baked with cheese   **poitrine de veau** brisket of veal

many came to out of the fields, then the thought          50
that we had wanted to make the world kinder,
but, in speaking proudly, we had failed a vision.

—1989

---

## TIMOTHY MURPHY ■ (b. 1951)

*Timothy Murphy, a former student of Robert Penn Warren at Yale, returned
to his native North Dakota to make a career as a venture capitalist in the
agricultural field. Unpublished until his mid-forties, Murphy has brought several collections to print during the past last decade and is a regular contributor of verse to Gray's Sporting Journal.*

# Case Notes

## for Dr. Richard Kolotkin
### March 7, 2002

Raped at an early age
by older altar boy.
"Damned by the Church to Hell,
never to sire a son,
perhaps man's greatest joy,"          5
said father in a rage.
Patient was twenty-one.
Handled it pretty well.

### March 14, 2002

Curiously, have learned
patient was Eagle Scout.          10
Outraged that Scouts have spurned
each camper who is "out."
Questioned if taunts endured
are buried? "No, immured."

### March 21, 2002
Immersed in verse and drink          15
when he was just sixteen,
turned to drugs at Yale.
Patient began to sink,
to fear he was a "queen,"

a "queer" condemned to fail                                        20
or detox in a jail.

### April 1, 2002

Into a straight town
he brought a sober lover.
"Worked smarter, drank harder
to stock an empty larder,"                                         25
wrote poetry, the cover
for grief he cannot drown.

### April 9, 2002

Uneasy with late father,
feared for by his mother,
lover, and younger brother.                                        30
Various neuroses,
but no severe psychosis.
Precarious prognosis.

—2004

---

**ANDREW HUDGINS** ■ (b. 1951)

*Andrew Hudgins, reared in Montgomery, Alabama, has demonstrated his poetic skills in a wide variety of poems, including a book-length sequence of dramatic monologues,* After the Lost War, *in the voice of Sidney Lanier, the greatest Southern poet of the late nineteenth century.*

# Air View of an Industrial Scene

There is a train at the ramp, unloading people
who stumble from the cars and toward the gate.
The building's shadows tilt across the ground
and from each shadow juts a longer one
and from that shadow crawls a shadow of smoke                      5
black as just-plowed earth. Inside the gate
is a small garden and someone on his knees.
Perhaps he's fingering the yellow blooms
to see which ones have set and will soon wither,
clinging to a green tomato as it swells.                           10
The people hold back, but are forced to the open gate,
and when they enter they will see the garden

and some, gardeners themselves, will yearn
to fall to their knees there, untangling vines,
plucking at weeds, cooling their hands in damp earth.   15
They're going to die soon, a matter of minutes.
Even from our height, we see in the photograph
the shadow of the plane stamped dark and large
on Birkenau,° one black wing shading the garden.
We can't tell which are guards, which prisoners.   20
We're watchers. But if we had bombs we'd drop them.

—1985

---

**JUDITH ORTIZ COFER ■ (b. 1952)**

*Judith Ortiz Cofer was born in Puerto Rico, the daughter of a member of the
United States Navy, and came to the United States at the age of four, when
her father was posted to the Brooklyn Navy Yard. After college, she studied at
Oxford and began her teaching career in the United States. A skilled writer of
fiction and autobiography, she published* The Year of Our Revolution: New
and Selected Stories and Poems *in 1998.*

# The Latin Deli: An Ars Poetica

Presiding over a formica counter,
plastic Mother and Child magnetized
to the top of an ancient register,
the heady mix of smells from the open bins
of dried codfish, the green plantains   5
hanging in stalks like votive offerings,
she is the Patroness of Exiles,
a woman of no-age who was never pretty,
who spends her days selling canned memories
while listening to the Puerto Ricans complain   10
that it would be cheaper to fly to San Juan
than to buy a pound of Bustelo coffee here,
and to Cubans perfecting their speech
of a "glorious return" to Havana—where no one
has been allowed to die and nothing to change until then,   15
to Mexicans who pass through, talking lyrically
of *dólares* to be made in El Norte—
                    all wanting the comfort
of spoken Spanish, to gaze upon the family portrait
of her plain wide face, her ample bosom   20

19 **Birkenau** German concentration camp in World War II

resting on her plump arms, her look of maternal interest
as they speak to her and each other
of their dreams and their disillusions—
how she smiles understanding,
when they walk down the narrow aisles of her store                    25
reading the labels of packages aloud, as if
they were the names of lost lovers: *Suspiros*,
*Merengues*, the stale candy of everyone's childhood.
                                        She spends her days
slicing *jamón y queso* and wrapping it in wax paper                   30
tied with string: plain ham and cheese
that would cost less at the A&P, but it would not satisfy
the hunger of the fragile old man lost in the folds
of his winter coat, who brings her lists of items
that he reads to her like poetry, or the others,                      35
whose needs she must divine, conjuring up products
from places that now exist only in their hearts—
closed ports she must trade with.

                                                        —1995

---

### RITA DOVE ■ (b. 1952)

*Rita Dove won the Pulitzer Prize in 1987 for* Thomas and Beulah, *a sequence
of poems about her grandparents' lives in Ohio. She is one of the most important voices of contemporary African American poetry and served as poet
laureate of the United States from 1993 to 1995. She is also a competitive
ballroom dancer.*

## American Smooth

We were dancing—it must have
been a foxtrot or a waltz,
something romantic but
requiring restraint,
rise and fall, precise                                                5
execution as we moved
into the next song without
stopping, two chests heaving
above a seven-league
stride—such perfect agony                                             10
one learns to smile through,
ecstatic mimicry

being the sine qua non°
of American Smooth.
And because I was distracted                          15
by the effort of
keeping my frame
(the leftward lean, head turned
just enough to gaze out
past your ear and always                              20
smiling, smiling),
I didn't notice
how still you'd become until
we had done it
(for two measures?                                    25
four?)—achieved flight,
that swift and serene
magnificence, before the earth
remembered who we were
and brought us down.                                  30

—2004

---

**MARK JARMAN** ■ **(b. 1952)**

*Mark Jarman was born in Kentucky and has lived in California and Tennessee,
where he currently teaches at Vanderbilt University. With Robert McDowell, he
edited* The Reaper, *a magazine specializing in narrative poetry.*

## After Disappointment

To lie in your child's bed when she is gone
Is calming as anything I know. To fall
Asleep, her books arranged above your head,
Is to admit that you have never been
So tired, so enchanted by the spell                    5
Of your grown body. To feel small instead
Of blocking out the light, to feel alone,
Not knowing what you should or shouldn't feel,
Is to find out, no matter what you've said
About the cramped escapes and obstacles                10
You plan and face and have to call the world,
That there remain these places, occupied
By children, yours if lucky, like the girl
Who finds you here and lies down by your side.

—1997

13 **sine qua non** an essential part (Latin)

JULIE KANE ■ (b. 1952)

*Julie Kane was born and raised in New Jersey and studied creative writing with Anne Sexton. For many years a resident of Louisiana, she has a Ph.D. from Louisiana State University and currently teaches at Northwestern State University in Natchitoches, Louisiana. Rhythm & Booze (2003) was selected for the National Poetry Series by Maxine Kumin. Skilled in such difficult forms as the villanelle (the subject of her dissertation), Kane currently serves as poet laureate of her adopted state.*

# Alan Doll Rap

When I was ten
I wanted a Ken
to marry Barbie
I was into patriarchy
for plastic dolls                                                    5
eleven inches tall
cuz the sixties hadn't yet
happened at all
Those demonstrations
assassinations                                                     10
conflagrations across the nation
still nothin but a speck in the imagination
Yeah, Ken was the man
but my mama had the cash
and the boy doll she bought me                        15
was ersatz
"Alan" was his name
from the discount store
He cost a dollar ninety-nine
Ken was two dollars more                                   20
Alan's hair was felt
stuck on with cheap glue
like the top of a pool table
scuffed up by cues
and it fell out in patches                                     25
when he was brand new
Ken's hair was plastic
molded in waves
coated with paint
no Ken bad-hair days                                          30

Well they wore the same size
and they wore the same clothes
but Ken was a player
and Alan was a boze
Barbie looked around                                    35
at all the other Barbies
drivin up in Dream Cars
at the Ken-and-Barbie party
and knew life had dealt her
a jack, not a king                                      40
knew if Alan bought her
an engagement ring
it wouldn't scratch glass
bet your ass
no class                                                45
made of cubic zirconia
or cubic Plexiglas
Kens would move Barbies
out of their townhouses
into their dreamhouses                                  50
Pepto-Bismol pink
from the rugs to the sink
wrap her in mink
but Alan was a bum
Our doll was not dumb                                   55
She knew a fronter from a chum
Take off that tuxedo
Alan would torpedo
for the Barcalounger
Bye-bye libido                                          60
Hello VCR
No job, no car
Drinkin up her home bar
Stinkin up her boudoir with his cigar
Shrinkin up the line of cash                            65
on her MasterCard
Till she'd be pleading:
"Where's that giant *hand*
used to make him *stand*,
used to make him *walk*?"                               70

—2004

**NAOMI SHIHAB NYE** ■ (b. 1952)

*Naomi Shihab Nye, a dedicated world traveler and humanitarian, has read her poetry in Bangladesh and the Middle East. Many of her poems are informed by her Palestinian ancestry, and she has translated contemporary Arabic poetry.*

# The Traveling Onion

It is believed that the onion originally came from India. In Egypt it was an object of worship—why I haven't been able to find out. From Egypt the onion entered Greece and on to Italy, thence into all of Europe.

*—Better Living Cookbook*

When I think how far the onion has traveled
just to enter my stew today, I could kneel and praise
all small forgotten miracles,
crackly paper peeling on the drainboard,
pearly layers in smooth agreement,                                    5
the way knife enters onion, straight
and onion falls apart on the chopping block,
a history revealed.

And I would never scold the onion
for causing tears.                                                    10
It is right that tears fall
for something small and forgotten.
How at meal, we sit to eat,
commenting on texture of meat or herbal aroma
but never on the translucence of onion,                               15
now limp, now divided,
or its traditionally honorable career:
For the sake of others,
disappear.

*—1986*

**ALBERTO RÍOS** ■ (b. 1952)

*Alberto Ríos was born in Nogales, Arizona, the son of a Mexican American father and an English-born mother. He won the Walt Whitman Award of the Academy of American Poets for his first book,* Whispering to Fool the Wind *(1982). He has also written a collection of short stories,* The Iguana Killer: Twelve Stories of the Heart, *which won the Western States Book Award.*

# The Purpose of Altar Boys

Tonio told me at catechism
the big part of the eye
admits good, and the little
black part is for seeing
evil—his mother told him            5
who was a widow and so
an authority on such things.
That's why at night
the black part gets bigger.
That's why kids can't go out        10
at night, and at night
girls take off their clothes
and walk around their
bedrooms or jump on their
beds or wear only sandals        15
and stand in their windows.
I was the altar boy
who knew about these things,
whose mission on some Sundays
was to remind people of        20
the night before as they
knelt for Holy Communion.
To keep Christ from falling
I held the metal plate under chins,
while on the thick        25
red carpet of the altar
I dragged my feet
and waited for the precise
moment: plate to chin
I delivered without expression        30
the Holy Electric Shock,
the kind that produces
a really large swallowing
and makes people think.
I thought of it as justice.        35
But on other Sundays the fire
in my eyes was different,
my mission somehow changed.
I would hold the metal plate
a little too hard        40
against those certain same
nervous chins, and I

I would look
with authority down
the tops of white dresses.                                                45

—1982

---

**JULIA ALVAREZ** ■ (b. 1953)

*Julia Alvarez published her first collection,* Homecoming, *in 1984. It contained
both free verse and "33," a sequence of 33 sonnets on the occasion of the poet's
thirty-third birthday. She has gained acclaim for* In the Time of the Butterflies,
*a work of fiction, and* The Other Side/El Otro Lado, *a collection of poems.*

# Bilingual Sestina

Some things I have to say aren't getting said
in this snowy, blond, blue-eyed, gum-chewing English:
dawn's early light sifting through *persianas*° closed
the night before by dark-skinned girls whose words
evoke *cama,*°*aposento,*°*sueños*° in *nombres*°                         5
from that first world I can't translate from Spanish.

Gladys, Rosario, Altagracia—the sounds of Spanish
wash over me like warm island waters as I say
your soothing names: a child again learning the *nombres*
of things you point to in the world before English                        10
turned *sol,*°*sierra,*°*cielo,*°*luna*° to vocabulary words—
*sun, earth, sky, moon.* Language closed

like the touch-sensitive *morivivi*° whose leaves closed
when we kids poked them, astonished. Even Spanish
failed us back then when we saw how frail a word is                       15
when faced with the thing it names. How saying
its name won't always summon up in Spanish or English
the full blown genie from the bottled *nombre.*

Gladys, I summon you back by saying your *nombre.*
Open up again the house of slatted windows closed                         20
since childhood, where *palabras*° left behind for English
stand dusty and awkward in neglected Spanish.
*Rosario,* muse of *el patio,*° sing in me and through me say
that world again, begin first with those first words

---

3 **persianas** venetian blinds   5 **cama** bed   **aposento** apartment   **sueños** dreams   **nombres** names
11 **sol** sun   **sierra** mountain   **cielo** sky   **luna** moon   13 **morivivi** a type of Caribbean bush
21 **palabras** words   23 **el patio** outdoor terrace

you put in my mouth as you pointed to the world—                25
not Adam, not God, but a country girl numbering
the stars, the blades of grass, warming the sun by saying,
*¡Qué calor!*° as you opened up the morning closed
inside the night until you sang in Spanish,
*Estas son las mañanitas,*° and listening in bed, no English      30

yet in my head to confuse me with translations, no English
doubling the world with synonyms, no dizzying array
    of words
—the world was simple and intact in Spanish—
*luna, sol, casa,*°*luz, flor,*° as if the *nombres*
were the outer skin of things, as if words were so close        35
one left a mist of breath on things by saying
their names, an intimacy I now yearn for in English—
words so close to what I mean that I almost hear
    my Spanish
heart beating, beating inside what I say *en inglés.*°

—1995

---

**HARRYETTE MULLEN** ■ **(b. 1953)**

*Harryette Mullen says, "I intend the poem to be meaningful: to allow, or sug-
gest, to open up, or insinuate possible meanings, even in those places where
the poem drifts between intentional utterance and improvisational word-
play." Born in Florence, Alabama, Mullen grew up in Fort Worth, Texas, and
holds degrees from the University of Texas and the University of California,
Santa Cruz. She currently teaches African American literature and creative
writing at the University of California, Los Angeles.*

# Dim Lady°

My honeybunch's peepers are nothing like neon. Today's special at Red Lobster
is redder than her kisser. If Liquid Paper is white, her racks are institutional
beige. If her mop were Slinkys, dishwater Slinkys would grow on her noggin.
I have seen tablecloths in Shakey's Pizza Parlors, red and white, but no such
picnic colors do I see in her mug. And in some minty-fresh mouthwashes
there is more sweetness than in the garlic breeze my main squeeze wheezes.
I love to hear her rap, yet I'm aware that Muzak has a hipper beat. I don't

28 **Qué calor** What heat!   30 **Estas son las mañanitas** These are birthday songs   34 **casa** house
**flor** flower   39 **en inglés** in English
**Dim Lady** See Shakespeare's *Sonnet* 130

know any Marilyn Monroes. My ball and chain is plain from head to toe. And yet, by gosh, my scrumptious Twinkie has as much sex appeal for me as any lanky model or platinum movie idol who's hyped beyond belief.

—2003

### KIM ADDONIZIO ■ (b. 1954)

*Kim Addonizio is the author of four books of poetry and a book of short stories. Born in Washington, D.C., Addonizio earned a B.A. and an M.A. from San Francisco State University and has worked as a waitress, tennis instructor, Kelly Girl, attendant for the disabled, and auto parts store bookkeeper. She currently teaches private writing workshops in the San Francisco Bay area. Addonizio's poems achieve a delicate balance between the confessional and the universal and manage to be simultaneously lyrical and gritty.*

# Sonnenizio° on a Line from Drayton°

Since there's no help, come let us kiss and part;
or kiss anyway, let's start with that, with the kissing part,
because it's better than the parting part, isn't it—
we're good at kissing, we like how that part goes:
we part our lips, our mouths get near and nearer,                   5
then we're close, my breasts, your chest, our bodies partway
to making love, so we might as well, part of me thinks—
the wrong part, I know, the bad part, but still
let's pretend we're at that party where we met
and scandalized everyone, remember that part? Hold me         10
like that again, unbutton my shirt, part of you
wants to I can tell, I'm touching that part and it says
*yes,* the ardent partisan, let it win you over,
it's hopeless, come, we'll kiss and part forever.

—2004

### DAVID MASON ■ (b. 1954)

*David Mason is best known for the title poem of* The Country I Remember, *a long narrative about the life of a Civil War veteran and his daughter. The*

**Sonnenizio** The sonnenizio was originated in Florence in the thirteenth century by Vanni Fucci as an irreverent form whose subject was usually the impossibility of everlasting love. Dante retaliated by putting Fucci into the seventh chasm of the *Inferno* as a thief. Originally composed in hendecasyllabics, the sonnenizio gradually moved away from metrical constraints and began to tackle a wider variety of subject matter. The sonnenizio is 14 lines long. It opens with a line from someone else's sonnet, repeats a word from that line in each succeeding line of the poem, and closes with a rhymed couplet. [Addonizio's note]  **Drayton** Michael Drayton (1563–1631) see *Idea: Sonnet 61* *poem has been performed in a theatrical version. Mason edited, with Mark Jarman,* Rebel Angels, *an anthology of contemporary poetry written in traditional forms. A new verse-novel,* Ludlow *(2007), concerns a 1914 coal-miners' strike in Colorado.*

# Fog Horns

The loneliest days,
damp and indistinct,
sea and land a haze.

And purple fog horns
blossomed over tides —                                    5
bruises being born

in silence, so slow,
so out there, around,
above and below.

In such hurts of sound                                    10
the known world became
neither flat nor round.

The steaming tea pot
was all we fathomed
of *is* and *is not.*                                     15

The hours were hallways
with doors at the ends
opened into days

fading into night
and the scattering                                        20
particles of light.

Nothing was done then.
Nothing was ever
done. Then it was done.

—2004

---

**MARY JO SALTER** ■ (b. 1954)

*Mary Jo Salter has lived in Japan, Italy, and Iceland. A student of Elizabeth Bishop at Harvard, Salter brings to her art a devotion to the poet's craft that mirrors that of her mentor. She has published six collections of poetry and* The Moon Comes Home, *a children's book.*

# Welcome to Hiroshima

is what you first see, stepping off the train:
a billboard brought to you in living English
by Toshiba Electric. While a channel
silent in the TV of the brain

projects those flickering re-runs of a cloud                    5
that brims its risen columnful like beer
and, spilling over, hangs its foamy head,
you feel a thirst for history: what year

it started to be safe to breathe the air,
and when to drink the blood and scum afloat                     10
on the Ohta River. But no, the water's clear,
they pour it for your morning cup of tea

in one of the countless sunny coffee shops
whose plastic dioramas advertise
mutations of cuisine behind the glass:                          15
a pancake sandwich; a pizza someone tops

with a maraschino cherry. Passing by
the Peace Park's floral hypocenter (where
how bravely, or with what mistaken cheer,
humanity erased its own erasure),                               20

you enter the memorial museum
and through more glass are served, as on a dish
of blistered grass, three mannequins. Like gloves
a mother clips to coatsleeves, strings of flesh

hang from their fingertips; or as if tied                       25
to recall a duty for us, *Reverence*
*the dead whose mourners too shall soon be dead,*
but all commemoration's swallowed up

in questions of bad taste, how re-created
horror mocks the grim original,                                 30
and thinking at last *They should have left it all*
you stop. This is the wristwatch of a child.

Jammed on the moment's impact, resolute
to communicate some message, although mute,
it gestures with its hands at eight-fifteen                     35
and eight-fifteen and eight-fifteen again

while tables of statistics on the wall
update the news by calling on a roll

of tape, death gummed on death, and in the case
adjacent, an exhibit under glass                    40

is glass itself: a shard the bomb slammed in
a woman's arm at eight-fifteen, but some
three decades on—as if to make it plain
hope's only as renewable as pain,

and as if all the unsung                             45
debasements of the past may one day come
rising to the surface once again—
worked its filthy way out like a tongue.

                                        —1985

---

**GINGER ANDREWS** ■ **(b. 1956)**

*Ginger Andrews won the 1999 Nicholas Roerich Poetry Prize for her first
book,* An Honest Answer, *which explores the difficulties of working-class
life in a northwestern lumber town. Born in North Bend, Oregon, she cleans
houses for a living and is a janitor and Sunday school teacher. Her poems
have been featured many times on National Public Radio's "The Writer's
Almanac."*

# Primping in the Rearview Mirror

after a solid ten-minute bout of tears,
hoping that the Safeway man who stocks the shelves
and talked to you once for thirty minutes about
        specialty jams,
won't ask if you're all right, or tell you you look like shit
and then have to apologize as he remembers that you don't    5
like cuss words and you don't date ex-prison guards
because you're married. The truth is you're afraid
this blue-eyed charismatic sexist hunk of a reject just might
trigger another round of tears, that you'll lean into him
right in front of the eggs and milk, crying like a baby,      10
your face buried in his chest just below the two opened
buttons of his tight white knit shirt, his big cold hands
pressed to the small of your back, pulling you closer
to whisper that everything will be all right.

                                        —2002

---

**AMY GERSTLER ■ (b. 1956)**

*A resident of Los Angeles, Gerstler has published six collections of poetry since 1986. Her seventh,* Animal Planet, *appeared in 2010. A prolific writer of art criticism and book reviews, Gerstler has also collaborated with visual artists. She has taught writing at a number of universities, including Bennington, her graduate alma mater.*

# Advice from a Caterpillar

Chew your way into a new world.
Munch leaves. Molt. Rest. Molt
again. Self-reinvention is *everything*.
Spin many nests. Cultivate stinging
bristles. Don't get sentimental
about your discarded skins. Grow
quickly. Develop a yen for nettles.
Alternate crumpling and climbing. Rely
on your antennae. Sequester poisons
in your body for use at a later date.
When threatened, emit foul odors
in self-defense. Behave cryptically
to confuse predators: change colors, spit,
or feign death. If all else fails, taste terrible.

—2008

---

**REBECCA FOUST ■ (b. 1957)**

*Born in Altoona, Pennsylvania, and educated at Smith College, Foust worked for some years as an attorney, leaving law for motherhood and full-time writing. Her chapbook of poems about raising her autistic son,* Dark Card, *appeared in 2008, the winner of a competition sponsored by Texas Review Press; the next year a second brief collection,* Mom's Canoe, *won the same prize. Her first full-length book,* All That Gorgeous Pitiless Song, *was published in 2010. She lives in Marin County, California.*

# Family Story

Mom talked about how when the x-ray
they used in those day before the ultrasound
confirmed she was pregnant the second time

with twins, she buttoned up her best
going-out dress, wondering what are those dark spots,
adjusted her hat and left. Weeks later it occurred to her
they were tears, wept for the long year behind
the long years ahead of diapers, glass bottles,
nights without sleep, no help with wailing kids
but from wailing kids. She wept
like she lived; when tears dripped and bloomed
on the gray wool of her dress, she looked up
at the changing room ceiling, expecting to find rain.

—2009

---

## DENISE DUHAMEL ■ (b. 1961)

*Duhamel was born in Rhode Island and educated at Emerson College and
Sarah Lawrence College. A feminist known for her humor, she once wrote
a satirical sequence of poems about the Barbie Doll. She currently teaches
at Florida International University and edited the 2013 edition of* The Best
American Poetry.

# My Strip Club

In my strip club
the girls crawl on stage
wearing overalls
and turtlenecks
then slowly pull on
gloves, ski masks,
and hiking boots.
As the music slows,
they lick the pole
and for a tantalizing second
their tongues stick
because it's so cold.
They zip up parkas
and tie tight bows
under their hoods.
A big spender
can take one of my girls
into a back room
where he can clamp
on her snowshoes.

---

### CATHERINE TUFARIELLO ■ (b. 1963)

*Catherine Tufariello grew up in upstate New York and holds a Ph.D. from Cornell University. Her first full-length collection,* Keeping My Name, *appeared in 2004. A translator of the sonnets of Petrarch, she has taught at Valparaiso University.*

# Useful Advice

You're 37? Don't you think that maybe
It's time you settled down and had a baby?

No wine? You're pregnant, aren't you? I knew it!

Hey, are you sure you two know how to do it?
All Dennis has to do is look at me                                               5
And I'm knocked up.
                          Some things aren't meant to be.
It's sad, but try to see this as God's will.
I've heard that sometimes when you take the Pill—
A friend of mine got pregnant when she stopped                    10
Working so hard.
                          Why don't you two adopt?
You'll have one of your own then, like my niece.
At work I heard about this herb from Greece—
My sister swears by dong quai. Want to try it?                        15
Forget the high-tech stuff. Just change your diet.
It's true! Too much caffeine can make you sterile.
Yoga is good for that. My cousin Carol—
They have these ceremonies in Peru—
You mind my asking, is it him or you?                                    20
Have you tried acupuncture? Meditation?
It's in your head. Relax! Take a vacation
And have some fun. You think too much. Stop trying.
Did I say something wrong? Why are you crying?

—2004

---

### NATASHA TRETHEWEY ■ (b. 1966)

*Pulitzer Prize winner Natasha Trethewey grew up on the Gulf Coast, the child of an interracial marriage (her father is poet Eric Trethewey). Her first collection,* Domestic Work, *appeared in 2000, and her second,* Bellocq's Ophelia *(2002), focused on the life of a mixed-race prostitute in Storyville, New*

*Orleans's notorious red-light district. She won the Pulitzer Prize in 2007 and was appointed U.S. Poet Laureate in 2012.*

# Domestic Work, 1937

All week she's cleaned
someone else's house,
stared down her own face
in the shine of copper-
bottomed pots, polished                                    5
wood, toilets she'd pull
the lid to—that look saying

*Let's make a change, girl.*

But Sunday mornings are hers—
church clothes starched                                   10
and hanging, a record spinning
on the console, the whole house
dancing. She raises the shades,
washes the rooms in light,
buckets of water, Octagon soap.                           15

*Cleanliness is next to godliness...*

Windows and doors flung wide,
curtains two-stepping
forward and back, neck bones
bumping in the pot, a choir                                20
of clothes clapping on the line.

*Nearer my God to Thee...*

She beats time on the rugs,
blows dust from the broom
like dandelion spores, each one                            25
a wish for something better.

—2000

---

**CRAIG ARNOLD** ■ **(1967–2009)**

*Craig Arnold's first book of poetry,* Shells, *was selected by W.S. Merwin for the Yale Series of Younger Poets, and his second,* Made Flesh, *was published in 2008. Arnold won numerous awards and fellowships during his brief career, including a National Endowment for the Arts grant. He was in Japan on a*

*U.S.–Japan Friendship Commission Creative Artists' Exchange grant, research-
ing on the island of Kuchinoerabushima for his most recent project, a book
of lyric essays focused on the trope of the volcano, when he disappeared,
presumably the victim of a hiking accident. Despite extensive searches and
worldwide concern, his body was never found.*

# The Singers

They are threatening to leave us the nimble-throated singers
    the little murderers with the quick pulses
They perch at the ends of bare branches their tails
    are ragged and pitiful the long green
feathers are fallen out They go on eating and eating
    last autumn's yellow melia berries
They do not care that you approach cold corpses
    rot in the grass in the reeds
The gray-shouldered crows hobble about the wren
    barely a mouthful cocks her pert tail
and threatens to slaughter the white-footed cat in the bushes
    They do not understand that they are dying

They are threatening to leave us how quickly we forget
    the way they taught us how to play our voices
opening soul to weightlessness like the Spartan poet
    singing under the burden of his old bones
to the chorus girls with their honey songs and their holy voices
    how he wished he could scoot like a kingfisher
lightly over the flower of the waves who boasted
    *I know the tunes of every bird but I Alcman*
*found my words and song in the tongue of the strident partridge*
    Where will we find songs when the sleek-headed
mallards are gone who chase each other around the pond
    the reluctant duck and the lovesick drake
The way she turns her head to the side to scold him
    *whack whack whack whack whack the way her boyfriend*
chases off his rival and then swims back reeb reeb
    with feeble reassurances the way
he sits on top of her the way she flaps her wings
    to keep above water the way they look
pleased with themselves wagging their tails smoothing
    each feather back in its right place

They are threatening to leave but you may still catch them
    saying goodbye stealthed in the cedar and cypress
at dawn in the dark clarity between sleep and waking
    A run of five notes on a black flute

another and another buried deep in the mix
    how many melodies can the air hold
And what they sing so lovely and so meaningless
    may urge itself upon you with the ache
of something just beyond the point of being remembered
    the trace of a brave thought in the face of sadness

—2008

---

**ALLISON JOSEPH ■ (b. 1967)**

*Allison Joseph was born in London, the child of immigrants from Jamaica and Grenada. When she was a child, her parents relocated to New York, where she attended the Bronx High School of Science. Following graduation from Kenyon College and the University of Indiana, she began college teaching and is now a member of the creative writing faculty at Southern Illinois University. She is currently readying for publication a sequence of sonnets about her father, who died in 1997.*

## The Athlete

would like to be my friend,
but between volleyball tryouts
and broad-jump practice,
there's just no time to chat,
no time to hang out at lunch,                                    5
blushing and gossiping over boys.
Hell, there isn't anything boys
can do that she can't—she'll
throw a ball just as hard,
run gutsy miles on the track                                     10
to match their distances,
ski cross-country or downhill,
topping their speed and endurance.
I admire her toughness, her
out-of-my-way attitude, her                                      15
assignments in on time, grades
better than mine even though I'm
only on one committee. She even
works after school, selling shoes
at Lady Footlocker to weekend jocks,                             20
slinky aerobics babes. And they have
no idea how fast that girl can move,
long legs trained to respond

to whatever command her brain
issues, whatever demand                                    25
she puts on her muscles.
Once she asked if I'd like
to run track, hoping to pull me
into her world, make me as swift
as she. And I had to laugh at that,                        30
at her ability to see an athlete
when all I could see was a scrawny girl
with fallen arches. I told her no,
but thanks, glad that she saw something
to work with when she looked                               35
at me, something to mold, shape.

—1998

---

**BRIAN TURNER** ■ (b. 1967)

*After completing a degree in creative writing at the University of Oregon,
Brian Turner served seven years in the U.S. Army, including service in Bosnia-
Herzegovina and a year in Iraq. His book about his military experiences,* Here,
Bullet, *was named an "Editor's Choice" by the* New York Times *and was the
2007 recipient of the Poets' Prize.*

# Here, Bullet

If a body is what you want,
then here is bone and gristle and flesh.
Here is the clavicle-snapped wish,
the aorta's opened valves, the leap
thought makes at the synaptic gap.                         5
Here is the adrenaline rush you crave,
that inexorable flight, that insane puncture
into heat and blood. And I dare you to finish
what you've started. Because here, Bullet,
here is where I complete the word you bring                10
hissing through the air, here is where I moan
the barrel's cold esophagus, triggering
my tongue's explosives for the rifling I have
inside of me, each twist of the round
spun deeper, because here, Bullet,                         15
here is where the world ends, every time.

—2005

### SUJI KWOCK KIM ■ (b. 1968)

*Suzi Kwock Kim received the 2002 Walt Whitman Award, for* Notes *from* the Divided Country, *an exploration of the Japanese occupation of Korea and of the Korean War and its aftermath. Kim's family emigrated to Poughkeepsie, New York, in the 1970s. She studied at Yale; the Iowa Writers' Workshop; Seoul National University, where she was a Fulbright Scholar; and Stanford University, where she was a Stegner Fellow. She lives in San Francisco and New York.*

# Occupation

The soldiers
are hard at work
building a house.
They hammer
bodies into the earth                                   5
like nails,
they paint the walls
with blood.
Inside the doors
stay shut, locked                                       10
as eyes of stone.
Inside the stairs
feel slippery,
all flights go down.
There is no floor:                                      15
only a roof,
where ash is falling—
dark snow,
human snow,
thickly, mutely                                         20
falling.
Come, they say.
This house will
last forever.
You must occupy it.                                     25
And you, and you—
And you, and you—
Come, they say.
There is room
for everyone.                                           30

—2003

**A.E. STALLINGS** ■ (b. 1968)

*Alicia is the author of* Archaic Smile, *chosen for the 1999 Richard Wilbur Award. Written exclusively in received forms, the book is noteworthy for the vigor and humor with which Stallings rewrites classical myths. Raised in Decatur, Georgia, Stallings studied at the University of Georgia and Oxford University. She composed the Latin lyrics for the opening music of the Paramount film* The Sum of All Fears *and has done a verse translation of Lucretius'* De Rerum Natura. *She lives in Athens, Greece, with her husband, John Psaropoulos, editor of the* Athens News.

# First Love: A Quiz

He came up to me:

    a. in his souped-up Camaro

    b. to talk to my skinny best friend

    c. and bumped my glass of wine so I wore the ferrous stain on my sleeve

    d. from the ground, in a lead chariot drawn by a team of stallions black as crude oil and breathing sulfur; at his heart, he sported a tiny golden arrow

He offered me:

    a. a ride

    b. dinner and a movie, with a wink at the cliché

    c. an excuse not to go back alone to the apartment with its sink of dirty knives

    d. a narcissus with a hundred dazzling petals that breathed a sweetness as cloying as decay

I went with him because:

    a. even his friends told me to beware

    b. I had nothing to lose except my virginity

    c. he placed his hand in the small of my back and I felt the tread of honeybees

    d. he was my uncle, the one who lived in the half-finished basement, and he took me by the hair

The place he took me to:

    a. was dark as my shut eyes

    b. and where I ate bitter seed and became ripe

    c. and from which my mother would never take me wholly back, though she wept and walked the earth and made the bearded ears of barley wither on their stalks and the blasted flowers drop from their sepals

    d. is called by some men hell and others love

    e. all of the above

—2006

**KEVIN PRUFER** ■ **(b. 1969)**

*A native of Cleveland, Prufer has published five collections of poetry since 1998 and has also edited five anthologies. On his own work, he has said, "I continue to believe that almost every good poem has buried in it somewhere the seed of narrative. Sometimes the narrative isn't directly stated in the poem, but is implied by the speaker's urgent need to say the poem." He currently teaches at the University of Houston.*

# The Villain and his Helicopter: Possible Movie Rental Versions

In the simple, VHS version
the blasted helicopter
falls into the sea
and disappears just before
the credits scroll
the picture away. On DVD
a commotion in the pod
is visible, the rotors
scurling up smoke, the helicopter
tilting dangerously into
the sea. In the Digit-L Letterbox
Limited Release, the villain presses
his white face to the glass
and groans, the helicopter's
rotors grinding and coughing
smoke. In the Director's Cut
you can hear the sound his fingers make
against the glass, like little
suction cups. In D-Lux
Dolby Stereo, the engine
dies in slow motion, every
gear grinding away,
the villain mouthing these words:
*tell my wife ... my son...*
In the Premier Unrated DVD
you can just discern a flashback
to the villain's past, his mother
singing him to sleep.
In the Wide-Screen, Criterion Edition
a single tear streaks his flushed cheek
as the helicopter smiles,
like any good machine,
into the senseless, reflecting sea.

ROB GRIFFITH ■ (b. 1970)

*Rob Griffith teaches at the University of Evansville and is the co-founder and -editor (with Paul Bone) of* Measure, *a journal dedicated to metrical poetry. Originally from Memphis, he studied writing at the University of Arkansas. Along with his writing and editing, Griffith also directs a summer writing program at Harlaxton College in England.*

# In the Kitchen

It's a minor juggling act—in one hand
a chicken breast as ice-slick as any stone
beside a winter stream; in the other,
a fistful of fresh carrots for the soup;
and on the counter, a cutting board, knife,
and pot. As if preparing for the toss
or measuring their weights, I raise one hand
and then the other. What to drop or hold?

And here's where all the metaphor kicks in,
where I can't help but chain this simple still-life
to something more profound. I place the chicken
on a plate then chop the carrots, thinking
of all I hold against the stream of time:
love, friends, career—even the present itself.
It's all too much for hands and a heart that grieves.

Then you burst in, smiling and smelling of rain,
and your umbrella sheds perfect stars
all over the kitchen. Decisions disappear
like steam above the soup, and light reflects
from every pot and every darkened window.

ERNEST HILBERT ■ (b. 1970)

*Ernest Hilbert was born in Philadelphia and educated at Rutgers University and Oxford. With founding editor Garrick Davis, he helped to establish* Contemporary Poetry Review *as one of the most comprehensive online journals of literary criticism. He has been credited as one of several contemporary poets who had led a revitalization of the sonnet. He works as an antiquarian book dealer in his hometown.*

# Domestic Situation

Maybe you've heard about this. Maybe not.
A man came home and chucked his girlfriend's cat
In the wood chipper. This really happened.
Dinner wasn't ready on time. A lot
Of other little things went wrong. He spat                    5
On her father, who came out when he learned
About it. He also broke her pinky,
Stole her checks, and got her sister pregnant.
But she stood by him, stood strong, through it all,
Because she loved him. She loved him, you see.                10
She actually said that, and then she went
And married him. She felt some unique call.
Don't try to understand what another
Person means by love. Don't even bother.

—2009

---

**ALEXANDER LONG** ■ **(b. 1972)**

*Alexander Long grew up in Pennsylvania and currently teaches at John Jay College in New York City. He also plays bass in a band, Redhead Betty Takeout. About "Flash Forward with The Amistad before Us in the Distance," he notes that the poem was rejected at first by many magazines but is now the one poem that he is most often asked to read and comment on, especially in classes with high school students.*

# Flash Forward with *The Amistad* Before Us in the Distance

"Next," the cashier says. I step up, tissues,
Coffee, ask for Marlboro Lights. "Shit,"
The guy behind me says, "I was here first."
He wasn't. I watched him saunter in, cool,
Decked out in colors I've barely dreamed of.
"Yo, dawg," he says, "I take two blunts and twenty
Scratch offs," and pushes me a side, gently,
Almost. In this moment, I believe him:
He was here first. The cashier rings it up:
"$8.36." "Yo, for what? That's a good deal,"
And he laugh-coughs, looks at me, lays down a ten.
"Not you," the cashier says. "Him."

The present

Has descended upon us again. Some-
One has been displaced again. This is no
Morality play, no history lesson.
This is a day like all the rest, but one
I feel more quickly than the rest. This is
The day that happens over and over
From now on.
                             I lay my ten next to his,
Look away. That's as close as we'll ever be,
I fear. I, too, have rage. He takes my ten
And leaves his for the cashier. I get my change
And stuff in a bag. "So that's how it is,"
The guy, now beside me, says. "Even now,
This day and age, a man can't even get
What he ask for? Nothing don't ever change...."
I guess he went rightly on. The doors whooshed
Before me, and I walked home. I walked home.

---

### CHELSEA RATHBURN ■ (b. 1975)

*Chelsea Rathburn lives in Atlanta with her husband, poet Jim May, working as a free-lance editor and consultant. Her first book,* The Shifting Line, *was the winner of the 2005 Richard Wilbur Award. About the poems in her 2013 collection,* A Raft of Grief, *she says, "As a poet, I am most interested in exploring relationships: the relationships between people, between the self and the world, between the self and the self, but also the relationships between memory and fact, and between form and content."*

# What Was Left

The headboard to the guest room bed,
its mattress gone, the buckled frame
still joined to one unyielding bolt.
Three pairs of wrinkled dress pants
wadded at the bottom of the hamper,
six black t-shirts, an IBM
circa nineteen-eighty-six.
A snorkel, mask, and fins, white socks,
loose change, a broken film projector,
the television. Restaurant matchbooks,
tax records and old license plates,
boxes and bags of photographs—
Venice, Vienna, Cadaqués—

the way that we once lived, the notes
and valentines sporting *forever*
and *always*, a jar of sauerkraut.

---

### EMILY MOORE (b. 1977)

*Emily Moore teaches English at Stuyvesant High School in New York. Her poetry has been published in* Ploughshares, The Paris Review, *and* The New Yorker, *where "Auld Lang Syne" originally appeared. She also performs with a three-woman band, Ménage à Twang.*

## Auld Lang Syne

Here's to the rock star with the crooked teeth,
the cellist, banker, mezzo bearing gifts,
the teacher with the flask inside her jeans—
those girls who made us sweat and lick our lips.

To the *jeune fille* who broke my heart in France,                5
the tramp who warmed your lap and licked your ear,
the one who bought me shots at 2 A.M.
that night I tied your pink tie at the bar.

Who smoked. Who locked you out. Who kissed my eyes
then pulled my hair and left me for a boy.                10
The girl who bit my upper, inner thigh.
My raspy laugh when I first heard your voice

toasting through broken kisses sloppy drunk:
*To women! To abundance! To enough!*

—2008

---

### CAKI WILKINSON ▪ (b. 1980)

*Caki Wilkinson attended Rhodes College, The Johns Hopkins University, and the University of Cincinnati, where she earned a Ph. D. She has recently returned to Rhodes to teach. She was the winner of the* Atlantic Monthly *Student Writing Contest, and her first collection,* Circles Where the Head Should Be *was the recipient of the Vassar Miller Poetry Prize. She is also an avid basketball player.*

## Itinerant

He's driving, one hand down an Arby's sack,
and—Jesus Bleeping Christ—we're nowhere close,

sentenced to Kansas. Kansas: home of wheat,
the nation's largest prairie dog, and plains
that lend some credence to the pancake-world
hypothesis. I need to pee. Again.
You stick two people in an F-150
for three days, lugging pets and plants and far
more baggage than they're willing to admit,
their separate self-reflection starts to breed
apotheosis or abomination—
and usually the latter: we're both pissed.
Who died and made you king? I say. He says,
Sometimes your big mouth bites you in the ass,
and then he pegs me with a chicken finger—
not *at* me, *near* me, he'll maintain for weeks
after the incident, but either way,
it whips my left ear, hard, a deep-fried dart,
before it's sucked into the floorboard vortex,
that point of no return between our seats.

# DRAMA

# Introduction to Drama

## The Play's the Thing

The theater, located in the heart of a rejuvenated downtown business district, is a relic of the silent movie era that has been restored to something approaching its former glory. Although only a few members of tonight's audience can actually remember it in its prime, the expertise of the organist seated at the antique Wurlitzer instills a sense of false nostalgia in the crowd, now settling by twos and threes into red, plush-covered seats and looking around in search of familiar faces. Just as the setting is somewhat out of the ordinary, so is this group. Unlike movie audiences, they are for the most part older and less casually dressed. There are few small children present, and even the teenagers seem to be on their best behavior. Oddly, no one is eating popcorn or noisily drawing on a soda straw. A mood of seriousness and anticipation hovers over the theater, and those who have lived in the town long enough can spot the spouse or partner of one of the principal actors nervously folding a program or checking a watch.

As the organ magically descends into the recesses of the orchestra pit, the lights dim, a hush falls over the crowd, and the curtain creakily rises. There is a general murmur of approval at the ingenuity and many hours of hard work that have transformed empty space into a remarkable semblance of an upper-class drawing room in the early 1900s. Dressed as a domestic servant, a young woman, known to the audience from her frequent appearances in local television commercials, enters and begins to dust a table. She hums softly to herself. A tall young man, in everyday life a junior partner in a local law firm, wanders in carrying a tennis racket. The maid turns, sees him, and catches her breath, startled. "Why Mr. Fenton!" she exclaims. ...

And the world begins.

The full experience of drama—whether at an amateur production like the little theater performance described here or at a huge Broadway playhouse—is much more complex than that of any other form of literature. The word **drama** itself comes from a Greek word meaning "a thing that is done," and the roots of both **theater** and **audience** call to mind the acts of seeing and hearing, respectively. Like other communal public activities—religious services, sporting events, meetings of political or fraternal organizations—drama has evolved, over many centuries, its own set of customs, rituals, and rules. The exact shape of these characteristics—**dramatic conventions**—may differ from country to country or from period to period, but they all have one aim in common, namely to define and govern an art form whose essence is to be found in public performances of written texts. No other form of literature shares this primary goal. Before we can discuss drama purely as literature, we should first ponder some aspects of its unique status as "a thing that is done."

It is worth noting that dramatists are also called playwrights. Note the spelling—a "wright" is a maker, as old family names like Cartwright or Boatwright attest. If a play is in fact *made* rather than written, then a playwright is similar to an architect who has designed a unique building. The concept may be his or hers, but the construction project requires the contributions of many other hands before the sparkling steel and glass tower alters the city's skyline. In the case of a new play, money will have to be raised by a producer, a director chosen, a cast found, a crew assembled, a set designed and built, and many hours of rehearsal completed before the curtain can be raised for the first time. Along the way, modifications to the original play may become necessary, and it is possible that the author will listen to advice from the actors, director, or stage manager and incorporate their opinions into any revisions. Professional theater is, after all, a branch of show business, and no play will survive its premiere for long if it does not attract paying crowds. The dramatists we read and study so reverently today managed to reach large popular audiences in their time. Even ancient Greek playwrights like Sophocles and Euripides must have stood by surreptitiously "counting the house" as the open-air seats slowly filled, and Shakespeare prospered as part-owner of the Globe Theatre to the extent that he was able to retire to his hometown at the ripe old age of forty-seven.

Set beside this rich communal experience, the solitary act of reading a play seems a poor substitute, contrary to the play's very nature (only a small category known as **closet drama** comprises plays intended to be read instead of acted). Yet dramatists like Shakespeare and Ibsen are counted among the giants of world literature, and their works are annually read by far more people than actually see their plays performed. In reading a play, we are forced to pay close attention to such matters as **set description,** particularly with a playwright like Ibsen, who lavishes great attention on the design of his set; references to **properties** or "props" that will figure in the action of the play; physical description of characters and costumes; **stage directions** indicating the movements and gestures made by actors in scenes; and any other **stage business,** that is, action without dialogue. Many modern dramatists are very scrupulous in detailing these matters; writers of earlier periods, however, provided little or no instruction. Reading Sophocles or Shakespeare, we are forced to concentrate on the characters' words to envision how actions and other characters were originally conceived. Reading aloud, alone or in a group, or following along in the text while listening to or watching an audio or video performance is particularly recommended for verse plays such as *Antigone* or *Twelfth Night*. Also, versions of many of the plays contained in this book are currently available on DVD or Blu-Ra. While viewing a film is an experience of a different kind from seeing a live performance, film versions obviously provide a convenient insight into the ways in which great actors have interpreted their roles.

# Origins of Drama

No consensus exists about the exact date of the birth of drama, but according to most authorities, it originated in Greece more than 2500 years ago, an outgrowth of rites of worship of the god Dionysus, who was associated with male fertility, agriculture (especially the cultivation of vineyards), and seasonal renewal. In these Dionysian festivals, a group of fifty citizens of Athens, known as a **chorus,** outfitted and trained by a leader, or *choragos,* would perform hymns of praise to the god, known as **dithyrambic poetry.** The celebration concluded with the ritual sacrifice of a goat, or *tragos.* The two main genres of drama originally took their names from these rituals; comedy comes from *kômos,* the Greek word for a festivity. These primitive revels were invariably accompanied with a union of the sexes ( *gamos* in Greek, a word that survives in English words like "monogamy") celebrating fertility and continuance of the race, an ancient custom still symbolically observed in the "fade-out kiss" that concludes most comedies. Tragedy, on the other hand, literally means "song of the goat," taking its name from the animal that was killed on the altar *(thymele),* cooked, and shared by the celebrants with their god.

Around 600 B.C., certain refinements took place. In the middle of the sixth century B.C., an official springtime festival, known as the Greater or City Dionysia, was established in Athens, and prizes for the best dithyrambic poems were first awarded. At about the same time, a special *orchestra,* or "dancing place," was constructed, a circular area surrounding the altar, and permanent seats, or a *theatron* ("seeing place"), arranged in a semicircle around the orchestra were added. At the back of the orchestra, the façade of a temple (the *skene*) and a raised "porch" in front of it (the **proskenion,** in later theaters the **proscenium**) served as a backdrop, usually representing the palace of the ruler; walls extending to either side of the *skene,* the *parodoi,* served to conceal backstage activity from the audience. A wheeled platform, or *eccyclema,* could be pushed through the door of the *skene* to reveal the tragic consequences of a play's climax (there was no onstage "action" in Greek tragedy). Behind the *skene,* a crane-like device called a *mechane* (or *deus ex machina*) could be used to lower a god from the heavens or represent a spectacular effect like the flying chariot drawn by dragons at the conclusion of Euripides' *Medea.*

In 535 B.C., a writer named Thespis won the annual competition with a startling innovation. Thespis separated one member of the chorus (called a *hypocrites,* or "actor") and had him engage in **dialogue,** spoken lines representing conversation, with the remaining members. If we define drama primarily as a story related through live action and recited dialogue, then Thespis may rightly be called the father of drama, and his name endures in "thespian," a synonym for actor.

The century after Thespis, from 500–400 B.C., saw many refinements in the way tragedies were performed and is considered the golden age of Greek drama. In this century, the careers of the three great tragic playwrights—Aeschylus (525–456 B.C.), Sophocles (496?–406 B.C.), and Euripides (c. 480–406 B.C.)—and the greatest comic playwright, Aristophanes (450?–385? B.C.) overlapped. It is no coincidence that in this remarkable period, Athens, under the leadership of the general Pericles (495–429 B.C.), reached the height of its wealth, influence, and cultural development and was home to the philosophers Socrates (470–399

B.C.) and Plato (c. 427–347 B.C.). Aristotle (384–322 B.C.), the third of the great Athenian philosophers, was also a literary critic who wrote the first extended analysis of drama.

# Aristotle on Tragedy

The earliest work of literary criticism in Western civilization is Aristotle's *Poetics,* an attempt to define and classify the different literary **genres** that use rhythm, language, and harmony. Aristotle identifies four genres—epic poetry, dithyrambic poetry, comedy, and tragedy—which have in common their attempts at imitation, or *mimesis,* of various types of human activity.

Aristotle comments most fully on tragedy, and his definition of the genre demands close examination:

> A tragedy, then, is the imitation of an action that is serious and also, as having magnitude, complete in itself; in language with pleasurable accessories, each kind brought in separately in the parts of the work; in a dramatic, not in a narrative form; with incidents arousing pity and fear, wherewith to accomplish its catharsis of such emotions.

First we should note that the imitation here is of *action.* Later in the passage, when Aristotle differentiates between narrative and dramatic forms of literature, it is clear that he is referring to tragedy as a type of literature written primarily for public performance. Furthermore, tragedy must be serious and must have magnitude. By this, Aristotle implies that issues of life and death must be involved and that these issues must be of public import. In many Greek tragedies, the fate of the *polis,* or city, of which the chorus is the voice, is bound up with the actions taken by the main character in the play. Despite their rudimentary form of democracy, the people of Athens would have been perplexed by a tragedy with an ordinary citizen at its center; magnitude in tragedy demands that only the affairs of persons of high rank are of sufficient importance for tragedy. Aristotle further requires that this imitated action possess a sense of completeness. At no point does he say that a tragedy has to end with a death or even in a state of unhappiness; he does require, however, that the audience sense that after the last words are spoken, no further story cries out to be told.

The next part of the passage may confuse the modern reader. By "language with pleasurable accessories," Aristotle means the poetic devices of rhythm and, in the choral parts of the tragedy, music and dance as well. Reading the choral passages in a Greek tragedy, we are likely to forget that these passages were intended to be chanted or sung ("chorus" and "choir" share the same root) and danced as well ("choreography" comes from this root as well).

The rest of Aristotle's definition dwells on the emotional effects of tragedy on the audience. Pity and fear are to be evoked—pity because we must care for the characters and to some extent empathize with them, fear because we come to realize that the fate they endure involves acts—of which murder and incest are only two—that civilized men and women most abhor. Finally, Aristotle's word **catharsis** has proved controversial over the centuries. The word literally means "a purging," but readers have debated whether Aristotle is referring to a release of harmful emotions or a transformation of them. In either case, the implication is that viewing a tragedy has a beneficial effect on an audience, perhaps because the viewers' deepest fears are brought to light in a make-believe setting. How many of us, at the end of some particularly wrenching film, have turned to a companion and said, "Thank god, it was only a movie"? The sacrificial animal from whom tragedy took its name was, after all, only a stand-in whose blood was offered to the gods as a substitute for a human subject. The protagonist of a tragedy remains, in many ways, a "scapegoat" on whose head we project our own unconscious terrors.

Aristotle identifies six elements of a tragedy, and these elements are still useful in analyzing not only tragedies but other types of plays as well. In order of importance, they are **plot, characterization, theme, diction, melody,** and **spectacle.** Despite the fact that the *Poetics* is more than two thousand years old, Aristotle's elements still provide a useful way of understanding how plays work.

## *Plot*

Aristotle considers plot the chief element of a play, and it is easy to see this when we consider that in discussing a film with a friend, we usually give a brief summary, or **synopsis,** of the plot, stopping just short of "giving it away" by telling how the story concludes. Aristotle defines plot as "the combination of incidents, or things done in the story," and goes on to give the famous formulation that a plot "is that which has a beginning, middle, and end." Aristotle notes that the best plots are selective in their use of material and have an internal coherence and logic. Two opposite terms that Aristotle introduced are still in use, although with slightly different meanings. By a **unified plot**, we generally mean one that takes place in roughly a twenty-four-hour period; in a short play with a unified plot like Susan Glaspell's *Trifles,* the action is continuous. By **episodic plot**, we mean one that spreads its action out over a longer period of time. A play that has a unified plot, a single setting, and no subplots is said to observe the **three unities,** which critics in some eras have virtually insisted on as ironclad rules. Although most plots are chronological, playwrights in the past half-century have experimented, sometimes radically, with such straightforward progression through time. Arthur Miller's *Death of a Salesman* effectively blends **flashbacks** to past events with his action, and David Ives's *Sure Thing* plays havoc with chronology, allowing his protagonist to "replay" his previous scenes until he has learned the way to the "sure thing" of the title.

Two other important elements of most successful plots that Aristotle mentions are **reversal** (*peripeteia* in Greek, also known as **peripety**), and **recognition** (*anagnorisis* in Greek, also known as **discovery**). By reversal, he means a change "from one state of things within the play to its opposite." Aristotle cites one example from *Oedipus the King,* the tragedy he focuses on, "the Messenger, who, coming to gladden Oedipus and to remove his fears as to his mother, reveals the secret of his birth"; but an earlier reversal in the same play occurs when Jocasta, attempting to alleviate Oedipus's fears of prophecies, inadvertently mentions the "place where three roads meet" where Oedipus killed a man he took to be a stranger. Most plays have more than a single reversal; each episode or act builds on the main character's hopes that his or her problems will be solved, only to dash those expectations as the play proceeds. Recognition, the second term, is perhaps more properly an element of characterization because it involves a character's "change from ignorance to knowledge." If the events of the plot have not served to illuminate the character about his or her failings, then the audience is likely to feel that the story has lacked depth. The kind of self-knowledge that tragedies provide is invariably accompanied by suffering and won at great emotional cost. In comedy, on the other hand, reversals may bring relief to the characters, and recognition may bring about the happy conclusion of the play.

A typical plot may be broken down into several components. First comes the **exposition**, which provides the audience with essential information—who, what, when, where—that it needs to know before the play can continue. A novelist or short story writer can present information directly with some sort of variation on the "Once upon a time" opening. But dramatists have particular problems with exposition because facts must be presented in the form of dialogue and action. Greek dramatists used the first two parts of a tragedy, relying on the audience's familiarity with the myths being retold, to set up the initial situation of the play. Other types of drama use a single character to provide expository material. Medieval morality plays often use a "heavenly messenger" to deliver the opening speech, and some of Shakespeare's plays employ a single character named "Chorus" who speaks an introductory prologue and "sets the scene" for later portions of the plays as well. In *The Glass Menagerie,* Tom Wingfield fulfills this role in an unusual manner, telling the audience at the beginning, "I am the narrator of the play, and also a character in it." Occasionally, we even encounter the least elegant solution to the problem of dramatic exposition, employing minor characters whose sole function is to provide background information in the play's opening scene. Countless drawing-room comedies have raised the curtain on a pair of servants in the midst of a gossipy conversation that catches the audience up on the doings of the family members who comprise the rest of the cast.

The second part of a plot is called the **complication,** the interjection of some circumstance or event that shakes up the stable situation that has existed before the play's opening and begins the **rising action** of the play, during which the audience's tension and expectations become tightly intertwined and involved with the characters and the events they experience. Complication in a play may be both external and internal. A plague, a threatened invasion, or a conclusion of a war are typical examples of external complication, outside events that affect the characters' lives. Many other plays rely primarily on an internal complication, a single character's failure in business or love that comes from a weakness in his or her personality. Often the complication is heightened by **conflict** between two characters whom events have forced into collision with each other. Whatever the case, the complication of the plot usually introduces a problem that the characters cannot avoid. The rising action, which constitutes the body of the play, usually contains a number of moments of **crisis,** when solutions crop up momentarily but quickly disappear. These critical moments in the scenes may take the form of the kinds of reversals discussed earlier, and the audience's emotional involvement in the plot generally hinges on the characters' rising and falling hopes.

The central moment of crisis in the play is the **climax,** or the moment of greatest tension, which initiates the **falling action** of the plot. Perhaps "moments" of greatest tension would be a more exact phrase, for skillful playwrights know how to wring as much tension as possible from the audience. In the best plots, everything in earlier parts of the play has pointed to this scene. In tragedy, the climax is traditionally accompanied with physical action and violence—a duel, a suicide, a murder—and the play's highest pitch of emotion.

The final part of a plot is the **dénouement,** or **resolution.** The French word literally refers to the untying of a knot, and we might compare the emotional effects of climax and dénouement to a piece of cloth twisted tighter and tighter as the play progresses and then untwisted as the action winds down. The dénouement returns the play and its characters to a stable situation, although not the same one that existed at the beginning of the play, and gives some indication of what the future holds for them. A dénouement may be either closed or open. A **closed dénouement** ties up everything neatly and explains all unanswered questions the audience might have; an **open dénouement** leaves a few tantalizing loose ends.

Several other plot terms should also be noted. Aristotle mentions, not altogether favorably, plots with "double issues." The most common word for this is **subplot,** a less important story involving minor characters that may mirror the main plot of the play. Some plays may even have more than one subplot. Occasionally, a playwright finds it necessary to drop hints about coming events in the plot, perhaps to keep the audience from complaining that certain incidents have happened "out of the blue." This is called **foreshadowing.** If a climactic incident that helps resolve the plot has not been adequately prepared for, the playwright may be accused of having resorted to a *deus ex machina* ending, which takes its name from the *mechane* that once literally lowered a god or goddess into the midst of the dramatic proceedings. An ending of this sort, like that of an old western movie in which the cavalry arrives out of nowhere just as the wagon train is about to be annihilated, is rarely satisfactory.

Finally, the difference between **suspense** and **dramatic irony** should be addressed. Both of these devices generate tension in the audience, although through opposite means—suspense when the audience does not know what is about to happen; dramatic irony, paradoxically, when it does. Much of our pleasure in reading a new play lies in speculating about what will happen next, but in Greek tragedy, the original audience would be fully familiar with the basic outlines of the mythic story before the action even began. Thus, dramatic irony occurs at moments when the audience is more knowledgeable about events than the on-stage characters are. In some plays, our foreknowledge of certain events is so strong that we may want to cry out a warning to the characters.

## Characterization

The Greek word *agon* means "debate" and refers to the central issue or conflict of a play. From *agon* we derive two words commonly used to denote the chief characters in a play: **protagonist,** literally the "first speaker," and **antagonist,** one who speaks against him. Often the word *hero* is used as a synonym for protagonist, but we should be careful in its application; indeed, in many modern plays, it may be more appropriate to speak of the protagonist as an **anti-hero** because she or he may possess few, if any, of the traditional attributes of a hero. Similarly, the word *villain* brings to mind a black-mustached, sneering character in a top hat and opera cloak from an old-fashioned **melodrama** (a play whose complications are solved happily at the last minute by the "triumph of good over evil") and usually has little application to the complex characters one encounters in a serious play.

Aristotle, in his discussion of characterization, stresses the complexity that marks the personages in the greatest plays. Nothing grows tiresome more quickly than a perfectly virtuous man or woman at the center of a play, and nothing is more offensive to the audience than seeing absolute innocence despoiled. Although Aristotle stresses that a successful protagonist must be better than ordinary men and women, he also insists that the protagonist be somewhat less than perfect:

> There remains, then, the intermediate kind of personage, a man not preeminently virtuous and just, whose misfortune, however, is brought upon him not by vice and depravity but by some error of judgment.

Aristotle's word for this error is **hamartia,** which is commonly translated as "tragic flaw" but might more properly be termed a "great error." Whether he means some innate flaw, like a psychological defect, or simply a great mistake is open to question, but writers of tragedies have traditionally created deeply flawed protagonists. In ordinary circumstances, the protagonist's strength of character may allow him to prosper, but under the pressure of events he may crack when one small chink in his armor widens and leaves him vulnerable. A typical flaw in tragedies is **hubris,** arrogance or excessive pride, which leads the protagonist into errors that might have been avoided if he or she had listened to the advice of others. Although he does not use the term himself, Aristotle touches on the concept of **poetic justice,** the audience's sense that virtue and vice have been fairly dealt with in the play and that the protagonist's punishment is to some degree deserved.

We should bear in mind that the greatest burden of characterization in drama falls on the actor or actress who undertakes a role. No matter how well written a part is, in the hands of an incompetent or inappropriate performer, the character will not be credible. Vocal inflection, gesture, and even the strategic use of silence are the stock in trade of actors, for it is up to them to convince us that we are involved in the sufferings and joys of real human beings. No two actors will play the same part in the same manner. We are lucky to have two excellent film versions of Shakespeare's *Henry the Fifth* available. Comparing the cool elegance of Laurence Olivier with the rough and ready exuberance of Kenneth Branagh is a wonderful short course in the equal validity of two radically different approaches to the same role.

In reading, there are several points to keep in mind about main characters. Physical description, while it may be minimal at best, is worth paying close attention to. Sometimes an author will give a character a name that is an indicator of his or her personality and a device called a **characternym.**

**Character motivation** is another point of characterization to ponder. Why do characters act in a certain manner? What do they hope to gain from their actions? In some cases, these motives are clear enough and may be discussed openly by the characters. In other plays, motivation is more elusive, as the playwright deliberately mystifies the audience by presenting characters who perhaps are not fully aware of the reasons for their compulsions. Modern dramatists, influenced by advances in psychology, have often refused to reduce characters' actions to simple equations of cause and effect.

Two conventions that the playwright may employ in revealing motivation are **soliloquy** and **aside.** A soliloquy is a speech made by a single character on stage alone. Hamlet's soliloquies, among them some of the most famous passages in all drama, show us the process of his mind as he toys with various plans of revenge but delays putting them into action. The aside is a brief remark (traditionally delivered to the side of a raised hand) that an actor makes directly to the audience and that the other characters on stage cannot hear. Occasionally, an aside reveals a reason for a character's behavior in a scene. Neither of these devices is as widely used in today's theater as in earlier periods, but they remain part of the dramatist's collection of techniques.

Minor characters are also of great importance in a successful play, and there are several different traditional types. A **foil,** a minor character with whom a major character sharply contrasts, is used primarily as a sounding board for ideas. A **confidant** is a trusted friend or servant to whom a major character speaks frankly and openly; confidants fulfill in some respects one role that the chorus plays in Greek tragedy. **Stock characters** are stereotypes that are useful for advancing the plot and fleshing out the scenes, particularly in comedies. Hundreds of plays have employed pairs of innocent young lovers, sharp-tongued servants, and meddling mothers-in-law as part of their casts. **Allegorical characters** in morality plays like *Everyman* are clearly labeled by their names and, for the most part, are personifications of human attributes (Beauty, Good Deeds) or of theological concepts (Confession). **Comic relief** in a tragedy may be provided by minor characters like Shakespeare's fools or clowns.

## Theme

Aristotle has relatively little to say about the theme of a play, simply noting, "Thought of the personages is shown in everything to be effected by their language." Because he focuses to such a large degree on the emotional side of tragedy—its stimulation of pity and fear—he seems to give less importance to the role of drama as a serious forum for the discussion of ideas, referring his readers to another of his works, *The Art of Rhetoric,* where these matters have greater prominence. Nevertheless, **theme,** the central idea or ideas that a play discusses, is important in Greek tragedy and in the subsequent history of the theater. The trilogies of early playwrights were thematically unified around an *aition,* a Greek word for the origin of a custom, just as a typical elementary school Thanksgiving pageant portrays how the holiday traditions were first established in the Plymouth Colony.

Some dramas are explicitly **didactic** in their intent, existing with the specific aim of instructing the audience in ethical, religious, or political areas. A **morality play,** a popular type of drama in the late Middle Ages, is essentially a sermon on sin and redemption rendered in dramatic terms. More subtle in its didacticism is the **problem play** of the late nineteenth century, popularized by Ibsen, which uses the theater as a forum for the serious debate of social issues like industrial pollution or women's rights. The **drama of ideas** of playwrights like George Bernard Shaw does not merely present social problems; it goes further, actually advancing programs of reform. In the United States during the Great Depression of the 1930s, Broadway theaters featured a great deal of **social drama,** in which radical social and political programs were openly propagandized. In the ensuing decades, the theater has remained a popular site for examining issues of race, class, and gender.

Keep in mind, however, that plays are not primarily religious or political forums. If we are not entertained and moved by a play's language, action, and plot, then it is unlikely that we will respond to its message. The author who has to resort to long sermons from a *raisonneur,* the French word for a character who serves primarily as the voice of reason (i.e., the mouthpiece for the playwright's opinions), is not likely to hold the audience's sympathy or attention for long. The best plays are complex enough that they cannot be reduced to simple "thesis statements" that sum up their meaning in a few words.

## Diction

Aristotle was also the author of the first important manual of public speaking, *The Art of Rhetoric,* so it should come as no surprise that he devotes considerable attention in the *Poetics* to the precise words, either alone or in combinations, that playwrights use. Instead of "diction," we would probably speak today of a playwright's "style" or discuss his or her handling of various levels of idiom in the dialogue. Much of what Aristotle has to say about parts of speech and the sounds of words in Greek is of little interest to us; of chief importance is his emphasis on clarity and originality in the choice of words. For Aristotle, the language of tragedy should be "poetic" in the best sense, somehow elevated above the level of ordinary speech but not so ornate that it loses the power to communicate feelings and ideas to an audience. Realism in speech is largely a matter of illusion, and close inspection of the actual lines of modern drama-tists like Miller and Williams reveals a discrepancy between the carefully chosen words that characters speak in plays, often making up lengthy **monologues,** and the halting, often inarticulate ("Ya know what I mean?") manner in which we express ourselves in everyday life. The language of the theater has always been an artificial one. The idiom of plays, whether by Shakespeare or by August Wilson, *imitates* the language of life; it does not duplicate it.

Ancient Greek is a language with a relatively small vocabulary and, even in transla-tion, we encounter a great deal of repetition of key words. *Polis,* the Greek word for city, appears many times in Sophocles' *Antigone,* stressing the communal fate that the pro-tagonist and the chorus, representing the citizens, share. Shakespeare's use of the full resources of the English language has been the standard against which all subsequent writers in the language can measure themselves. Shakespeare's language presents some special difficulties to the modern reader. His vocabulary is essentially the same as ours, but many words have changed in meaning or become obsolete over the past four hundred years. Shakespeare is also a master of different **levels of diction.** In the space of a few lines, he can range from self-consciously flowery heights ("If after every tempest come such calms, / May the winds blow till they have waken'd death! / And let the labouring bark climb hills of seas / Olympus-high and duck again as low / As hell's to heaven!" exults Othello on being reunited with his bride in Cyprus) to the slangy level of the streets—he is a master of the off-color joke and the sarcastic put-down. We should remember that Shakespeare's poetic drama lavishly uses figurative language; his lines abound with simi-les, metaphors, personifications, and hyperboles, all characteristic devices of the language of poetry. Shakespeare's theater had little in the way of scenery and no "special effects," so a passage from *Hamlet* like "But, look, the morn, in russet mantle clad / Walks o'er the dew of yon high eastward hill" is not merely pretty or picturesque; it has the dramatic function of helping the audience visualize the welcome end of a long, fearful night.

It is true that playwrights since the middle of the nineteenth century have striven for more fidelity to reality, more verisimilitude, in the language their characters use, but even realistic dramatists often rise to rhetorical peaks that have little relationship to the way people actually speak. Both Ibsen and Williams began their careers as poets and, surprisingly, the first draft of Miller's "realistic" tragedy *Death of a Salesman* was largely written in verse.

## Melody

Greek tragedy was accompanied by music. None of this music survives, and we cannot be certain how it was integrated into the drama. Certainly the choral parts of the play were sung and danced, and it is likely that even the dialogue involved highly rhythmical chanting, especially in passages employing **stichomythia,** rapid alternation of single lines between two actors, a device often encountered during moments of high dramatic tension. In the original language, the different poetic rhythms used in Greek tragedy are still evident, although these are for the most part lost in English translation. At any rate it is apparent that the skillful manipulation of a variety of **poetic meters,** combinations of line lengths and rhythms, for different types of scenes was an important part of the tragic poet's repertoire.

Both tragedies and comedies have been written in verse throughout the ages, often employing rhyme as well as rhythm. *Antigone* is written in a variety of poetic meters, some of which are appropriate for dialogue between actors and others for the choral odes. Shakespeare's *Othello* is composed, like all of his plays, largely in **blank verse,** that is, unrhymed lines of iambic pentameter (lines of ten syllables, alternating unstressed and stressed syllables). He also uses rhymed couplets, particularly for emphasis at the close of scenes; songs (there are three in *Othello*); and even prose passages, especially when dealing with comic or "low" characters. A study of Shakespeare's versification is beyond the scope of this discussion, but suffice it to say that a trained actor must be aware of the rhythmical patterns that Shakespeare utilized if she or he is to deliver the lines with anything approaching accuracy.

Of course, not only verse drama has rhythm. The last sentences of Tennessee Williams's prose drama *The Glass Menagerie* can be easily recast as blank verse that would not have embarrassed Shakespeare himself:

> *Then all at once my sister touches my shoulder.*
> *I turn around and look into her eyes ...*
> *Oh, Laura, Laura, I tried to leave you behind me,*
> *but I am more faithful than I intended to be!*
> *I reach for a cigarette, I cross the street,*
> *I run into the movies or a bar,*
> *I buy a drink, I speak to the nearest stranger—*
> *anything that can blow your candles out!*
> *—for nowadays the world is lit by lightning!*
> *Blow your candles out, Laura—and so good-bye ...*

The ancient verse heritage of tragedy lingers on in the modern theater and has proved resistant to even the prosaic rhythms of what Williams calls a "world lit by lightning."

## *Spectacle*

Spectacle (sometimes called *mise en scène,* French for "putting on stage") is the last of Aristotle's elements of tragedy and, in his view, the least important. By spectacle, we mean the purely visual dimension of a play; in ancient Greece, this meant costumes, a few props, and effects carried out by the use of the *mechane.* Costumes in Greek tragedy were simple but impressive. The tragic mask, or **persona,** and a high-heeled boot *(cothurnus)* were apparently designed to give characters a larger-than-life appearance. Historians also speculate that the mask might have additionally served as a crude megaphone to amplify the actors' voices, a necessary feature when we consider that the open-air theater in Athens could seat more than 10,000 spectators.

Other elements of set decoration were kept to a minimum, although playwrights occasionally employed a few well-chosen spectacular effects like the triumphant entrance of the victorious king in Aeschylus's *Agamemnon.* Elizabethan drama likewise relied little on spectacular stage effects. Shakespeare's plays call for few props, and little attempt was made at historical accuracy in costumes, with a noble patron's cast-off clothing dressing Caesar one week, Othello the next.

Advances in technology since Shakespeare's day have obviously facilitated more elaborate effects in what we now call **staging** than patrons of earlier centuries could have envisioned. In the nineteenth century, first gas and then electric lighting not only made effects like sunrises possible but also, through the use of different combinations of color, added atmosphere to certain scenes. By Ibsen's day, realistic **box sets** were designed to resemble, in the smallest details, interiors of houses and apartments with an invisible "fourth wall" nearest the audience. Modern theater has experimented in all directions with set design, from the bare stage to barely suggested walls and furnishings, from revolving stages to scenes that "break the plane" by involving the audience in the drama. Tennessee Williams's *The Glass Menagerie* employs music, complicated lighting and sound effects, and semitransparent **scrims** onto which images are projected, all to enhance the play's dream-like atmosphere. The most impressive uses of spectacle in today's Broadway productions may represent anything from the catacombs beneath the Paris Opera House to thirty-foot-high street barricades manned by soldiers firing muskets. Modern technology can create virtually any sort of stage illusion; the only limitations in today's professional theater are imagination and budget.

Before we leave our preliminary discussion, one further element should be mentioned—**setting.** Particular locales—Thebes, Corinth, and Mycenæ—are the sites of different tragedies, and each city has its own history; in the case of Thebes, this history involves a family curse that touches the members of three generations. But for the most part, specific locales in the greatest plays are less important than the universal currents that are touched. If we are interested in the particular features of Norwegian civic government in the late nineteenth century, we would perhaps do better going to history texts than to Ibsen's *An Enemy of the People.*

Still, every play implies a larger sense of setting, a sense of history that is called the **enveloping action.** The "southern belle" youth of Amanda Wingfield, in Williams's *The Glass Menagerie,* is a fading dream as anachronistic as the "gentlemen callers" she still envisions knocking on her daughter's door. Even though a play from the past may still speak eloquently today, it also provides a "time capsule" whose contents tell us how people lived and what they most valued during the period when the play was written and first performed.

# Brief History and Description of Dramatic Conventions

## Greek Tragedy

By the time of Sophocles, tragedy had evolved into an art form with a complex set of conventions. Each playwright would submit a **tetralogy,** or set of four plays, to the yearly competition. The first three plays, or **trilogy,** would be tragedies, perhaps unified like those of Aeschylus's *Oresteia,* which deals with Agamemnon's tragic homecoming from the Trojan War. The fourth, called a **satyr-play,** was comic, with a chorus of goatmen engaging in bawdy revels that, oddly, mocked the serious content of the preceding tragedies. Only one complete trilogy, the *Oresteia* by Aeschylus, and one satyr-play, *The Cyclops* by Euripides, have survived. Three plays by Sophocles derived from the myths surrounding Oedipus and his family—*Oedipus the King, Oedipus at Colonus,* and *Antigone*—are still performed and read, but they were written at separate times and accompanied by other tragedies that are now lost. As tragedy developed during this period, it seems clear that playwrights thought increasingly of individual plays as complete in themselves; *Antigone* does not leave the audience with the feeling that there is more to be told, even though Creon is still alive at the end of the play.

Each tragedy was composed according to a prescribed formula, as ritualized as the order of worship in a contemporary church service. The tragedy begins with a **prologue *(prologos)*,** "that which is said first." The prologue is an introductory scene that tells the audience important information about the play's setting, characters, and events immediately preceding the opening of the drama. The second part of the tragedy is called the ***parodos,*** the first appearance of the chorus in the play. As the members of the chorus enter the orchestra, they dance and sing more generally of the situation in which the city finds itself. Choral parts in some translations are divided into sections called **strophes** and **antistrophes,** indicating choral movements to left and right, respectively. The body of the play is made up of two types of alternating scenes. The first, an **episode *(episodos)*** is a passage of dialogue between two or more actors or between the actors and the chorus. Each of these "acts" of the tragedy is separated from the rest by a choral **ode *(stasimon;* pl. *stasima)*** during which the chorus is alone on the orchestra, commenting, as the voice of public opinion, about the course of action being taken by the main characters. Typically, there are four pairs of episodes and odes in the play. The final scene of the play is called the ***exodos.*** During this part, the climax occurs out of sight of the audience, and a vivid description of this usually violent scene is sometimes delivered by a messenger or other witness. After the messenger's speech, the main character reappears and the resolution of his or her fate is determined. In some plays, a wheeled platform called an ***eccyclema*** was used to move this fatal tableau into view of the spectators. A tragedy concludes with the exit of the main characters, sometimes leaving the chorus to deliver a brief speech or **epilogue,** a final summing up of the play's meaning.

Although we may at first find such complicated rituals bizarre, we should keep in mind that dramatic conventions are primarily customary and artificial and have little to do with "reality" as we usually experience it. The role of the chorus (set by the time of Sophocles at fifteen members) may seem puzzling to modern readers, but in many ways, the conventions of Greek tragedy are no stranger than those of contemporary musical comedy, in which a pair of lovers bursts into a duet and dance in the middle of a stroll in the park, soon to be joined by a host of other cast members. What is most remarkable about the history of drama is not how much these conventions have changed but how remarkably similar they have remained for more than twenty-five centuries.

## Medieval Drama

Drama flourished during Greek and Roman times, but after the fall of the Roman Empire (A.D. 476), it declined during four centuries of eclipse and was kept alive throughout Europe only by wandering troupes of actors performing various types of **folk drama.** The "Punch and Judy" puppet show, still popular in parts of Europe, is a late survivor of this tradition, as are the ancient slapstick routines of circus clowns. Even though drama was officially discouraged by the Church for a long period, when it did reemerge, it was as an outgrowth of the Roman Catholic mass, in the form of **liturgical drama.** Around the ninth century, short passages of sung dialogue between the priest and choir, called **tropes,** were added on special holidays to commemorate the event. These tropes grew more elaborate over the years until full-fledged religious pageants were being performed in front of the altar. In 1210, Pope Innocent III, wishing to restore the dignity of the services, banned such performances from the interior of the church. Moving them outside, first to the church porch and later entirely off church property, provided greater opportunity for inventiveness in action and staging.

In the fourteenth and fifteenth centuries, much of the work of putting on plays passed to the guilds, organizations of skilled artisans, and their productions became part of city-wide festivals in many continental and British cities. Several types of plays evolved. **Mystery plays** were derived from holy scripture. **Passion plays** (some of which survive unchanged today) focused on the crucifixion of Christ. **Miracle plays** dramatized the lives of the saints. The last and most complex, **morality plays,** were dramatized sermons with allegorical characters (e.g., Everyman, Death, Good Deeds) representing various generalized aspects of human life.

## Elizabethan Drama

Although the older morality plays were still performed throughout the sixteenth century, during the time of Queen Elizabeth I (b. 1533, reigned 1558–1603) a new type of drama, typical in many ways of other innovative types of literature developed during the Renaissance, began to be produced professionally by companies of actors not affiliated with any religious institutions. This **secular drama,** beginning in short pieces called **interludes** that may have been designed for entertainment during banquets or other public celebrations, eventually evolved into full-length tragedies and comedies designed for performance in large outdoor theaters like Shakespeare's famous Globe.

A full history of this fertile period would take many pages, but a few of its dramatic conventions are worth noting. We have already mentioned blank verse, the poetic line perfected by Shakespeare's contemporary Christopher Marlowe (1564–1593). Shakespeare wrote tragedies, comedies, and historical dramas with equal success, all characterized by passages that remain the greatest examples of poetic expression in English.

The raised platform stage in an Elizabethan theater used little or no scenery, with the author's descriptive talents setting the scene and indicating lighting and weather. The stage itself had two supporting columns, which might be used to represent trees or hiding places; a raised area at the rear, which could represent a balcony or upper story of a house; a small curtained alcove at its base; and a trap door, which could serve as a grave or hiding place. In contrast to the relatively bare stage, costumes were elaborate and acting was highly stylized. Female roles were played by young boys, and the same actor might play several different minor roles in the same play. The Oscar-winning film *Shakespeare in Love* reveals a great amount of information about Elizabethan staging.

A few more brief words about Shakespeare's plays are in order. First, drama in Shakespeare's time was intended for performance, with publication being of only secondary importance. The text of many of Shakespeare's plays were published in cheap editions called **quartos** that were full of misprints and often contained different versions of the same play. Any play by Shakespeare contains words and passages that different editors have trouble agreeing on. Second, originality, in the sense that we value it, meant little to a playwright in a time before copyright laws; virtually every one of Shakespeare's plays is derived from an earlier source—Greek myth, history, another play or, in the case of Twelfth Night, a contemporary prose tale of questionable literary merit. The true test of Shakespeare's genius rests in his ability to transform these raw materials into art. Finally, we should keep in mind that Shakespeare's plays were designed to appeal to a wide audience—educated aristocrats and illiterate "groundlings" filled the theater—and this fact may account for the great diversity of tones and levels of language in the plays. Purists of later eras may have been dismayed by some of Shakespeare's wheezy clowns and bad puns, but for us the mixture of "high" and "low" elements gives his plays their remarkable texture.

## The Comic Genres

Shakespeare's ability to move easily between "high" and "low," between tragic and comic, should be a reminder that comedy has developed along lines parallel to tragedy and has never been wholly separate from it. Most of Aristotle's remarks on comedy are lost, but he does make the observation that comedy differs from tragedy in that comedy depicts men and women as worse than they are, whereas tragedy generally stresses their best qualities. During the great age of Greek tragedy, comedies were regularly performed at Athenian festivals. The greatest of the early comic playwrights was Aristophanes (450?–385? B.C.). The plays of Aristophanes are classified as **Old Comedy** and share many of the same structural elements as tragedy. Old Comedy was always satirical and usually obscene; in *Lysistrata*, written during the devastating Athenian wars with Sparta, the men of both sides are brought to their knees by the women of the two cities, who engage in a sex strike until the men relent. Features of Old Comedy included the use of two semi-choruses (in *Lysistrata,* old men and old women); an *agon,* an extended debate between the protagonist and an authority figure; and a *parabasis,* an ode sung by the chorus at an intermission in the action that reveals the author's own views on the play's subject. **New Comedy,** which evolved in the century after Aristophanes, tended to observe more traditional moral values and stressed romance. The New Comedy of Greece greatly influenced the writings of Roman playwrights like Plautus (254–184 B.C.) and Terence (190–159 B.C.). Plautus's *Pseudolus* (combined with elements from two of his other comedies) still finds favor in its modern musical adaptation *A Funny Thing Happened on the Way to the Forum.*

Like other forms of drama, comedy virtually vanished during the early Middle Ages. Its spirit was kept alive primarily by roving companies of actors who staged improvisational dramas in the squares of towns throughout Europe. The popularity of these plays is evidenced by certain elements in the religious dramas of the same period; the *Second Shepherd's Play* (c. 1450) involves a sheep-rustler with three shepherds in an uproarious parody of the Nativity that still evokes laughter today. Even a serious play such as *Everyman* contains satirical elements in the involved excuses that gods and other characters contrive for not accompanying the protagonist on his journey with Death.

On the continent, a highly stylized form of improvisational drama appeared in sixteenth-century Italy, apparently an evolution from earlier types of folk drama. ***Commedia dell'arte*** involved a cast of masked stock characters (the miserly old man, the young wife, the ardent seducer) in situations involving mistaken identity and cuckoldry. *Commedia dell'arte,* because it is an improvisational form, does not survive, but its popularity influenced the direction that comedy would take in the following century. The great French comic playwright Molière (1622–1673) incorporated many of its elements into his own plays, which combine elements of **farce,** a type of comedy that hinges on broadly drawn characters and embarrassing situations usually involving sexual misconduct, with serious social satire. Comedy such as Molière's, which exposes the hypocrisy and pretensions of people in social situations, is called **comedy of manners;** as Molière put it, the main purpose of his plays was "the correction of mankind's vices."

Other types of comedy have also been popular in different eras. Shakespeare's comedies begin with the farcical complications of *The Comedy of Errors,* progress through romantic **pastoral** comedies such as *As You Like It,* which present an idealized view of rural life, and end with the philosophical comedies of his final period, of which *The Tempest* is the greatest example. His contemporary Ben Jonson (1572–1637) favored a type known as **comedy of humours,** a type of comedy of manners in which the conduct of the characters is determined by their underlying dominant trait (the four humours were thought to be bodily fluids whose proportions determined personality). English plays of the late seventeenth and early eighteenth centuries tended to combine the hard-edged satire of comedy of manners with varying amounts of sentimental romance. A play of this type, usually hinging on matters of inheritance and marriage, is known as a **drawing-room comedy,** and its popularity, peaking in the mid-nineteenth century, endures today.

Modern comedy in English can be said to begin with Oscar Wilde (1854–1900) and George Bernard Shaw (1856–1950). Wilde's brilliant wit and skillful incorporation of paradoxical

**epigrams,** witty sayings that have made him one of the most quoted authors of the nineteenth century, have rarely been equaled. Shaw, who began his career as a drama critic, admired both Wilde and Ibsen and succeeded in combining the best elements of the comedy of manners and the problem play in his works. *Major Barbara* (1905), a typical **comedy of ideas,** frames serious discussion of war, religion, and poverty with a search for an heir to a millionaire's fortune and a suitable husband for one of his daughters. Most subsequent writers of comedy, from Neil Simon to Wendy Wasserstein, reveal their indebtedness to Wilde and Shaw.

One striking development of comedy in recent times lies in its deliberate harshness. So-called **black humor,** an extreme type of satire in which barriers of taste are assaulted and pain seems the constant companion of laughter, has characterized much of the work of playwrights like Samuel Beckett (1906–1989), Eugene Ionesco (1912–1994), and Edward Albee (b. 1928).

## Realistic Drama, the Modern Stage, and Beyond

Realism is a term that is loosely employed as a synonym for "true to life," but in literary history, it denotes a style of writing that developed in the mid-nineteenth century, first in the novels of such masters as Charles Dickens, Gustave Flaubert, and Leo Tolstoy, and later in the dramas of Ibsen and Anton Chekhov. Many of the aspects of dramatic realism have to do with staging and acting. The box set, with its invisible "fourth wall" facing the audience, could, with the added subtleties of artificial lighting, successfully mimic the interior of a typical middle-class home. Realistic prose drama dropped devices like the soliloquy in favor of more natural methods of acting such as that championed by Konstantin Stanislavsky (1863–1938), the Russian director who worked closely with Chekhov (1860–1904) to perfect a process whereby actors learned to identify with their characters' psychological problems from "inside out." This "method" acting often tries, as is the case in Chekhov's plays and, later, in those of Williams and Miller, to develop a play's **subtext,** the crucial issue in the play that no one can bear to address directly. Stanislavsky's theories have influenced several generations of actors and have become standard throughout the world of the theater. Ibsen's plays, which in fact ushered in the modern era of the theater, are often called **problem plays** because they deal with serious, even controversial or taboo, issues in society. Shaw said that Ibsen's great originality as a playwright lay in his ability to shock the members of the audience into thinking about their own lives. As the barriers of censorship have fallen over the years, the capacity of the theater to shock has perhaps been diminished, but writers still find it a forum admirably suited for debating the controversial issues which divide society.

American and world drama in the twentieth and the present centuries has gone far beyond realism to experiment with the dream-like atmosphere of **expressionism** (which may employs distorted sets to mirror the troubled, perhaps even unbalanced, psyches of the play's characters) or **theater of the absurd,** which depicts a world, like that of Samuel Beckett's *Waiting for Godot* or the early plays of Edward Albee, without meaning in which everything seems ridiculous. Nevertheless, realism is still the dominant style of today's theater, even if our definition of it has to be modified to take into account plays as diverse as *The Glass Menagerie, The Piano Lesson,* and *The God of Carnage.*

---

### S O P H O C L E S ▪ (496?–406 B.C.)

*Sophocles lived in Athens in the age of Pericles, during the city's greatest period of culture, power, and influence. Sophocles distinguished himself as an athlete, a musician, a military advisor, a politician, and, most important, a dramatist. At sixteen, he was chosen to lead a chorus in reciting a poem on the Greek naval victory over the Persians at Salamis, and he won his first prizes as a playwright before he was thirty. Although both Aeschylus, his senior, and Euripides, his younger rival, have their champions, Sophocles, whose career spanned so long a period that he competed against both of them, is generally considered to be the most important Greek writer of tragedies; his thirty victories in the City Dionysia surpass the combined totals of his two great colleagues. Of his 123 plays, only seven survive intact, including three plays relating to Oedipus and his children, Oedipus the King, Antigone, and Oedipus at Colonus, which was produced after Sophocles' death by his grandson. He is generally credited with expanding the technical possibilities of drama by introducing a third actor in certain scenes (Aeschylus used only two) and by both reducing the number of lines given to the chorus and increasing its integration into his plays. Sophocles was intimately involved in both civic and military affairs, twice serving as a chief advisor to Pericles, and his sense of duty to the polis (Greek for "city") is apparent in many of his plays. Sophocles' importance can be judged by the many references that Aristotle makes to his works in his discussion of tragedy in the Poetics.*

# Antigone

## Dramatis Personae

**ANTIGONE**: daughter of Oedipus.
**ISMENE**: daughter of Oedipus, sister of Antigone
**CREON**: king of Thebes
**EURYDICE**: wife of Creon
**HAEMON**: son of Creon and Euridice, engaged to Antigone.
**TEIRESIAS**: an old blind prophet
**BOY**: a young lad guiding Teiresias
**GUARD**: a soldier serving Creon.
**MESSENGER CHORUS**: Theban Elders
**ATTENDANTS**

*[In Thebes, directly in front of the royal palace, which stands in the background, its main doors facing the audience. Enter Antigone leading Ismene away from the palace]*

**ANTIGONE:**   Now, dear Ismene, my own blood sister,
do you have any sense of all the troubles
Zeus keeps bringing on the two of us,
as long as we're alive? All that misery
which stems from Oedipus? There's no suffering,
no shame, no ruin—not one dishonour—
which I have not seen in all the troubles

you and I go through. What's this they're saying now,
something our general has had proclaimed
throughout the city? Do you know of it?      10
Have you heard? Or have you just missed the news?
Dishonours which better fit our enemies
are now being piled up on the ones we love.      [10]

**ISMENE:**    I've had no word at all, Antigone,
nothing good or bad about our family,
not since we two lost both our brothers,
killed on the same day by a double blow.
And since the Argive army, just last night,
has gone away, I don't know any more
if I've been lucky or face total ruin.      20

**ANTIGONE:**    I know that. That's why I brought you here,
outside the gates, so only you can hear.

**ISMENE:**    What is it? The way you look makes it seem      [20]
you're thinking of some dark and gloomy news.

**ANTIGONE:**    Look—what's Creon doing with our two brothers?
He's honouring one with a full funeral
and treating the other one disgracefully!
Eteocles, they say, has had his burial
according to our customary rites,
to win him honour with the dead below.      30
But as for Polyneices, who perished
so miserably, an order has gone out
throughout the city—that's what people say.
He's to have no funeral or lament,
but to be left unburied and unwept,
a sweet treasure for the birds to look at,
for them to feed on to their heart's content.      [30]
That's what people say the noble Creon
has announced to you and me—I mean to me—
and now he's coming to proclaim the fact,      40
to state it clearly to those who have not heard.
For Creon this matter's really serious.
Anyone who acts against the order
will be stoned to death before the city.
Now you know, and you'll quickly demonstrate
whether you are nobly born, or else
a girl unworthy of her splendid ancestors.

**ISMENE:**    Oh my poor sister, if that's what's happening,
what can I say that would be any help
to ease the situation or resolve it?      50    [40]

**ANTIGONE:**    Think whether you will work with me in this
and act together.

**ISMENE:**   In what kind of work?
　　What do you mean?
**ANTIGONE:**   Will you help these hands
　　take up Polyneices' corpse and bury it?
**ISMENE:**   What? You're going to bury Polyneices,
　　when that's been made a crime for all in Thebes?
**ANTIGONE:**   Yes. I'll do my duty to my brother—
　　and yours as well, if you're not prepared to.
　　I won't be caught betraying him.
**ISMENE:**   You're too rash.
　　Has Creon not expressly banned that act?                    60
**ANTIGONE:**   Yes. But he's no right to keep me from what's mine.
**ISMENE:**   O dear. Think, Antigone. Consider
　　how our father died, hated and disgraced,                   [50]
　　when those mistakes which his own search revealed
　　forced him to turn his hand against himself
　　and stab out both his eyes. Then that woman,
　　his mother and his wife—her double role—
　　destroyed her own life in a twisted noose.
　　Then there's our own two brothers, both butchered
　　in a single day—that ill-fated pair                         70
　　with their own hands slaughtered one another
　　and brought about their common doom.
　　Now, the two of us are left here quite alone.
　　Think how we'll die far worse than all the rest,
　　if we defy the law and move against                         [60]
　　the king's decree, against his royal power.
　　We must remember that by birth we're women,
　　and, as such, we shouldn't fight with men.
　　Since those who rule are much more powerful,
　　we must obey in this and in events                          80
　　which bring us even harsher agonies.
　　So I'll ask those underground for pardon—
　　since I'm being compelled, I will obey
　　those in control. That's what I'm forced to do.
　　It makes no sense to try to do too much.
**ANTIGONE:**   I wouldn't urge you to. No. Not even
　　if you were keen to act. Doing this with you
　　would bring me no joy. So be what you want.                 [70]
　　I'll still bury him. It would be fine to die
　　while doing that. I'll lie there with him,                  90
　　with a man I love, pure and innocent,
　　for all my crime. My honours for the dead
　　must last much longer than for those up here.
　　I'll lie down there forever. As for you,

well, if you wish, you can show contempt
for those laws the gods all hold in honour.
**ISMENE:**   I'm not disrespecting them. But I can't act
against the state. That's not in my nature.
**ANTIGONE:**   Let that be your excuse. I'm going now                    [80]
to make a burial mound for my dear brother.                    100
**ISMENE:**   Oh poor Antigone, I'm so afraid for you.
**ANTIGONE:**   Don't fear for me. Set your own fate in order.
**ISMENE:**   Make sure you don't reveal to anyone
what you intend. Keep it closely hidden.
I'll do the same.
**ANTIGONE:**   No, no. Announce the fact—
if you don't let everybody know,
I'll despise your silence even more.
**ISMENE:**   Your heart is hot to do cold deeds.
**ANTIGONE:**   But I know
I'll please the ones I'm duty bound to please.
**ISMENE:**   Yes, if you can. But you're after something          110   [90]
which you're incapable of carrying out.
**ANTIGONE:**   Well, when my strength is gone, then I'll give up.
**ISMENE:**   A vain attempt should not be made at all.
**ANTIGONE:**   I'll hate you if you're going to talk that way.
And you'll rightly earn the loathing of the dead.
So leave me and my foolishness alone—
we'll get through this fearful thing. I won't suffer
anything as bad as a disgraceful death.
**ISMENE:**   All right then, go, if that's what you think right.
But remember this—even though your mission            120
makes no sense, your friends do truly love you.

*[Exit Antigone away from the palace. Ismene watches her go and then
returns slowly into the palace. Enter the Chorus of Theban elders]*

**CHORUS:**   O ray of sunlight,                                        [100]
most beautiful that ever shone
on Thebes, city of the seven gates,
you've appeared at last,
you glowing eye of golden day,
moving above the streams of Dirce,°
driving into headlong flight
the white-shield warrior from Argos,
who marched here fully armed,                                130
now forced back by your sharper power.
**CHORUS LEADER:**   Against our land he marched,                     [110]
sent here by the warring claims

°**Dirce:** one of the rivers beside Thebes.

of Polyneices, with piercing screams,
an eagle flying above our land,
covered wings as white as snow,
and hordes of warriors in arms,
helmets topped with horsehair crests.

CHORUS:  Standing above our homes, '
he ranged around our seven gates,                    140
with threats to swallow us
and spears thirsting to kill.
Before his jaws had had their fill                   [120]
and gorged themselves on Theban blood,
before Hephaistos'° pine-torch flames
had seized our towers, our fortress crown,°
he went back, driven in retreat.
Behind him rings the din of war—
his enemy, the Theban dragon-snake,
too difficult for him to overcome.                   150

CHORUS LEADER:    Zeus hates an arrogant boasting tongue.
Seeing them march here in a mighty stream,
in all their clanging golden pride,                  [130]
he hurled his fire and struck the man,
up there, on our battlements, as he began
to scream aloud his victory.

CHORUS:  The man swung down, torch still in hand,
and smashed into unyielding earth—
the one who not so long ago attacked,
who launched his furious, enraged assault,           160
to blast us, breathing raging storms.
But things turned out not as he'd hoped.
Great war god Ares assisted us—
he smashed them down and doomed them all             [140]
to a very different fate.

CHORUS LEADER:    Seven captains at seven gates
matched against seven equal warriors
paid Zeus their full bronze tribute,
the god who turns the battle tide,
all but that pair of wretched men,                   170
born of one father and one mother, too—
who set their conquering spears against each other
and then both shared a common death.
CHORUS:    Now victory with her glorious name
has come, bringing joy to well-armed Thebes.
The battle's done—let's strive now to forget        [150]

°**Hephaistos:** god of fire.

with songs and dancing all night long,
with Bacchus leading us to make Thebes shake.

*[The palace doors are thrown open and guards appear at the doors]*

**CHORUS LEADER:**   But here comes Creon, new king of our land,
son of Menoikeos. Thanks to the gods,                              180
who've brought about our new good fortune.
What plan of action does he have in mind?
What's made him hold this special meeting,                         [160]
with elders summoned by a general call?

*[Enter Creon from the palace. He addresses the assembled elders]*

**CREON:**   Men, after much tossing of our ship of state,
the gods have safely set things right again.
Of all the citizens I've summoned you,
because I know how well you showed respect
for the eternal power of the throne,
first with Laius and again with Oedipus,                           190
once he restored our city.° When he died,
you stood by his children, firm in loyalty.
Now his sons have perished in a single day,
killing each other with their own two hands,
a double slaughter, stained with brother's blood.                 [170]
And so I have the throne, all royal power,
for I'm the one most closely linked by blood
to those who have been killed. It's impossible
to really know a man, to know his soul,
his mind and will, before one witnesses                            200
his skill in governing and making laws.
For me, a man who rules the entire state
and does not take the best advice there is,
but through fear keeps his mouth forever shut,                     [180]
such a man is the very worst of men—
and always will be. And a man who thinks
more highly of a friend than of his country,
well, he means nothing to me. Let Zeus know,
the god who always watches everything,
I would not stay silent if I saw disaster                          210
moving here against the citizens,
a threat to their security. For anyone
who acts against the state, its enemy,
I'd never make my friend. For I know well
our country is a ship which keeps us safe,
and only when it sails its proper course                           [190]

°**Laius:** king of Thebes and father of Oedipus. Oedipus killed him (not knowing who he was) and
became the next king of Thebes by saving the city from the devastation of the Sphinx.

do we make friends. These are the principles
I'll use in order to protect our state.
That's why I've announced to all citizens
my orders for the sons of Oedipus—                    220
Eteocles, who perished in the fight
to save our city, the best and bravest
of our spearmen, will have his burial,
with all those purifying rituals
which accompany the noblest corpses,
as they move below. As for his brother—
that Polyneices, who returned from exile,
eager to wipe out in all-consuming fire          [200]
his ancestral city and its native gods,
keen to seize upon his family's blood                 230
and lead men into slavery—for him,
the proclamation in the state declares
he'll have no burial mound, no funeral rites,
and no lament. He'll be left unburied,
his body there for birds and dogs to eat,
a clear reminder of his shameful fate.
That's my decision. For I'll never act
to respect an evil man with honours
in preference to a man who's acted well.
Anyone who's well disposed towards our state,        240
alive or dead, that man I will respect.              [210]
**CHORUS LEADER:**   Son of Menoikeos, if that's your will
for this city's friends and enemies,
it seems to me you now control all laws
concerning those who've died and us as well—
the ones who are still living.
**CREON:**   See to it then,
and act as guardians of what's been proclaimed.
**CHORUS:**   Give that task to younger men to deal with.
**CREON:**   There are men assigned to oversee the corpse.
**CHORUS LEADER:**   Then what remains that you would have us do?   250
**CREON:**   Don't yield to those who contravene my orders.
**CHORUS LEADER:**
No one is such a fool that he loves death.           [220]
**CREON:**   Yes, that will be his full reward, indeed.
And yet men have often been destroyed
because they hoped to profit in some way.
{{dir}}}[Enter a guard, coming towards the palace]
**GUARD:**   My lord, I can't say I've come out of breath
by running here, making my feet move fast.
Many times I stopped to think things over—
and then I'd turn around, retrace my steps.

My mind was saying many things to me,          260
"You fool, why go to where you know for sure
your punishment awaits?"—"And now, poor man,
why are you hesitating yet again?
If Creon finds this out from someone else,          [230]
how will you escape being hurt?" Such matters
kept my mind preoccupied. And so I went,
slowly and reluctantly, and thus made
a short road turn into a lengthy one.
But then the view that I should come to you
won out. If what I have to say is nothing,          270
I'll say it nonetheless. For I've come here
clinging to the hope that I'll not suffer
anything that's not part of my destiny.
**CREON:**  What's happening that's made you so upset?
**GUARD:**  I want to tell you first about myself.
    I did not do it. And I didn't see
    the one who did. So it would be unjust
    if I should come to grief.          [240]
**CREON:**  You hedge so much.
    Clearly you have news of something ominous.
**GUARD:**  Yes. Strange things that make me pause a lot.      280
**CREON:**  Why not say it and then go—just leave.
**GUARD:**  All right, I'll tell you. It's about the corpse.
    Someone has buried it and disappeared,
    after spreading thirsty dust onto the flesh
    and undertaking all appropriate rites.
**CREON:**  What are you saying? What man would dare this?
**GUARD:**  I don't know. There was no sign of digging,
    no marks of any pick axe or a mattock.      [250]
    The ground was dry and hard and very smooth,
    without a wheel track. Whoever did it      290
    left no trace. When the first man on day watch
    revealed it to us, we were all amazed.
    The corpse was hidden, but not in a tomb.
    It was lightly covered up with dirt,
    as if someone wanted to avert a curse.
    There was no trace of a wild animal
    or dogs who'd come to rip the corpse apart.
    Then the words flew round among us all,
    with every guard accusing someone else.      [260]
    We were about to fight, to come to blows—      300
    no one was there to put a stop to it.
    Every one of us was responsible,
    but none of us was clearly in the wrong.
    In our defence we pleaded ignorance.

Then we each stated we were quite prepared
to pick up red-hot iron, walk through flames,
or swear by all the gods that we'd not done it,
we'd no idea how the act was planned,
or how it had been carried out. At last,
when all our searching had proved useless,                     310
one man spoke up, and his words forced us all
to drop our faces to the ground in fear.                      [270]
We couldn't see things working out for us,
whether we agreed or disagreed with him.
He said we must report this act to you—
we must not hide it. And his view prevailed.
I was the unlucky man who won the prize,
the luck of the draw. That's why I'm now here,
not of my own free will or by your choice.
I know that—for no one likes a messenger                      320
who comes bearing unwelcome news with him.
**CHORUS LEADER:**   My lord, I've been wondering for some time now—
could this act not be something from the gods?
**CREON:**   Stop now—before what you're about to say           [280]
enrages me completely and reveals
that you're not only old but stupid, too.
No one can tolerate what you've just said,
when you claim gods might care about this corpse.
Would they pay extraordinary honours
and bury as a man who'd served them well                      330
someone who came to burn their offerings,
their pillared temples, to torch their lands
and scatter all its laws? Or do you see
gods paying respect to evil men? No, no.
For quite a while some people in the town
have secretly been muttering against me.                      [290]
They don't agree with what I have decreed.
They shake their heads and have not kept their necks
under my yoke, as they are duty bound to do
if they were men who are content with me.                     340
I well know that these guards were led astray—
such men urged them to carry out this act
for money. To foster evil actions,
to make them commonplace among all men,
nothing is as powerful as money.
It destroys cities, driving men from home.
Money trains and twists the minds in worthy men,
so they then undertake disgraceful acts.
Money teaches men to live as scoundrels,                      [300]

familiar with every profane enterprise.                    350
But those who carry out such acts for cash
sooner or later see how for their crimes
they pay the penalty. For if great Zeus
still has my respect, then understand this—
I swear to you on oath—unless you find
the one whose hands really buried him,
unless you bring him here before my eyes,
then death for you will never be enough.
No, not before you're hung up still alive
and you confess to this gross, violent act.        360
That way you'll understand in future days,              [310]
when there's a profit to be gained from theft,
you'll learn that it's not good to be in love
with every kind of monetary gain.
You'll know more men are ruined than are saved
when they earn profits from dishonest schemes.
**GUARD:**   Do I have your permission to speak now,
or do I just turn around and go away?
**CREON:**   But I find your voice so irritating—
don't you realize that?
**GUARD:**   Where does it hurt?                    370
Is it in your ears or in your mind?
**CREON:**   Why try to question where I feel my pain?
**GUARD:**   The man who did it—he upsets your mind.
I offend your ears.
**CREON:**   My, my, it's clear to see
it's natural for you to chatter on.                     [320]
**GUARD:**   Perhaps. But I never did this.
**CREON:**   This and more—
you sold your life for silver.
**GUARD:**   How strange and sad
when the one who sorts this out gets it all wrong.
**CREON:**   Well, enjoy your sophisticated views.
But if you don't reveal to me who did this,        380
you'll just confirm how much your treasonous gains
have made you suffer.

*[Exit Creon back into the palace. The doors close behind him]*

**GUARD:**   Well, I hope he's found.
That would be best. But whether caught or not—
and that's something sheer chance will bring about—
you won't see me coming here again.
This time, against all hope and expectation,        [330]
I'm still unhurt. I owe the gods great thanks.

*[Exit the Guard away from the palace]*

**CHORUS:**   There are many strange and wonderful things,
        but nothing more strangely wonderful than man.
        He moves across the white-capped ocean seas          390
        blasted by winter storms, carving his way
        under the surging waves engulfing him.
        With his teams of horses he wears down
        the unwearied and immortal earth,
        the oldest of the gods, harassing her,
        as year by year his ploughs move back and forth.          [340]
        He snares the light-winged flocks of birds,
        herds of wild beasts, creatures from deep seas,
        trapped in the fine mesh of his hunting nets.
        O resourceful man, whose skill can overcome          400
        ferocious beasts roaming mountain heights.          [350]
        He curbs the rough-haired horses with his bit
        and tames the inexhaustible mountain bulls,
        setting their savage necks beneath his yoke.
        He's taught himself speech and wind-swift thought,
        trained his feelings for communal civic life,
        learning to escape the icy shafts of frost,
        volleys of pelting rain in winter storms,
        the harsh life lived under the open sky.
        That's man—so resourceful in all he does.          410 [360]
        There's no event his skill cannot confront—
        other than death—that alone he cannot shun,
        although for many baffling sicknesses
        he has discovered his own remedies.
        The qualities of his inventive skills
        bring arts beyond his dreams and lead him on,
        sometimes to evil and sometimes to good.
        If he treats his country's laws with due respect
        and honours justice by swearing on the gods,
        he wins high honours in his city.          420
        But when he grows bold and turns to evil,          [370]
        then he has no city. A man like that—
        let him not share my home or know my mind.

*[Enter the Guard, bringing Antigone with him. She is not resisting]*

**CHORUS LEADER:**   What this? I fear some omen from the gods.
        I can't deny what I see here so clearly—
        that young girl there—it's Antigone.
        Oh you poor girl, daughter of Oedipus,
        child of a such a father, so unfortunate,
        what's going on? Surely they've not brought you here
        because you've disobeyed the royal laws,          430
        because they've caught you acting foolishly?          [380]

**GUARD:**   This here's the one who carried out the act.
We caught her as she was burying the corpse.
Where's Creon?

*[The palace doors open. Enter Creon with attendants]*

**CHORUS LEADER:**   He's coming from the house—
and just in time.
**CREON:**   Why have I come "just in time"?
What's happening? What is it?
**GUARD:**   My lord,
human beings should never take an oath
there's something they'll not do—for later thoughts
contradict what they first meant. I'd have sworn                    [390]
I'd not soon venture here again. Back then,                 440
the threats you made brought me a lot of grief.
But there's no joy as great as what we pray for
against all hope. And so I have come back,
breaking that oath I swore. I bring this girl,
captured while she was honouring the grave.
This time we did not draw lots. No. This time
I was the lucky man, not someone else.
And now, my lord, take her for questioning.
Convict her. Do as you wish. As for me,
by rights I'm free and clear of all this trouble. 450           [400]
**CREON:**   This girl here—how did you catch her? And where?
**GUARD:**   She was burying that man. Now you know
all there is to know.
**CREON:**   Do you understand
just what you're saying? Are your words the truth?
**GUARD:**   We saw this girl giving that dead man's corpse
full burial rites—an act you'd made illegal.
Is what I say simple and clear enough?
**CREON:**   How did you see her, catch her in the act?
**GUARD:**   It happened this way. When we got there,
after hearing those awful threats from you,                 460
we swept off all the dust covering the corpse,
so the damp body was completely bare.                        [410]
Then we sat down on rising ground up wind,
to escape the body's putrid rotting stench.
We traded insults just to stay awake,
in case someone was careless on the job.
That's how we spent the time right up 'til noon,
when the sun's bright circle in the sky
had moved half way and it was burning hot.
Then suddenly a swirling windstorm came,                     470

whipping clouds of dust up from the ground,
filling the plain—some heaven-sent trouble.
In that level place the dirt storm damaged
all the forest growth, and the air around                                      [420]
was filled with dust for miles. We shut our mouths
and just endured this scourge sent from the gods.
A long time passed. The storm came to an end.
That's when we saw the girl. She was shrieking—
a distressing painful cry, just like a bird
who's seen an empty nest, its fledglings gone.                    480
That's how she was when she saw the naked corpse.
She screamed out a lament, and then she swore,
calling evil curses down upon the ones
who'd done this. Then right away her hands
threw on the thirsty dust. She lifted up
a finely made bronze jug and then three times                      [430]
poured out her tributes to the dead.
When we saw that, we rushed up right away
and grabbed her. She was not afraid at all.
We charged her with her previous offence                          490
as well as this one. She just kept standing there,
denying nothing. That made me happy—
though it was painful, too. For it's a joy
escaping troubles which affect oneself,
but painful to bring evil on one's friends.
But all that is of less concern to me
than my own safety.                                                              [440]
**CREON:**    You there—you with your face
bent down towards the ground, what do you say?
Do you deny you did this or admit it?
**ANTIGONE:**    I admit I did it. I won't deny that.          500
CREON:    *[to the Guard]*
You're dismissed—go where you want. You're free—
no serious charges made against you.

*[Exit the Guard. Creon turns to interrogate Antigone]*

Tell me briefly—not in some lengthy speech—
were you aware there was a proclamation
forbidding what you did?
**ANTIGONE:**    I'd heard of it.
How could I not? It was public knowledge.
**CREON:**    And yet you dared to break those very laws?
**ANTIGONE:**    Yes. Zeus did not announce those laws to me.          [450]
And Justice living with the gods below
sent no such laws for men. I did not think                          510
anything which you proclaimed strong enough

to let a mortal override the gods
and their unwritten and unchanging laws.
They're not just for today or yesterday,
but exist forever, and no one knows
where they first appeared. So I did not mean
to let a fear of any human will
lead to my punishment among the gods.
I know all too well I'm going to die—                          [460]
how could I not?—it makes no difference          520
what you decree. And if I have to die
before my time, well, I count that a gain.
When someone has to live the way I do,
surrounded by so many evil things,
how can she fail to find a benefit
in death? And so for me meeting this fate
won't bring any pain. But if I'd allowed
my own mother's dead son to just lie there,
an unburied corpse, then I'd feel distress.
What's going on here does not hurt me at all.          530
If you think what I'm doing now is stupid,
perhaps I'm being charged with foolishness          [470]
by someone who's a fool.
**CHORUS LEADER:**   It's clear enough
the spirit in this girl is passionate—
her father was the same. She has no sense
of compromise in times of trouble.
**CREON:**   *[to the Chorus Leader]*
But you should know the most obdurate wills
are those most prone to break. The strongest iron
tempered in the fire to make it really hard—
that's the kind you see most often shatter.          540
I'm well aware the most tempestuous horses
are tamed by one small bit. Pride has no place
in anyone who is his neighbour's slave.
This girl here was already very insolent          [480]
in contravening laws we had proclaimed.
Here she again displays her proud contempt—
having done the act, she now boasts of it.
She laughs at what she's done. Well, in this case,
if she gets her way and goes unpunished,
then she's the man here, not me. No. She may be          550
my sister's child, closer to me by blood
than anyone belonging to my house
who worships Zeus Herkeios° in my home,

°**Zeus Herkeios:** Zeus of the Courtyard, a patron god of worship within the home.

but she'll not escape my harshest punishment—
her sister, too, whom I accuse as well.
She had an equal part in all their plans                                    [490]
to do this burial. Go summon her here.
I saw her just now inside the palace,
her mind out of control, some kind of fit.

*[Exit attendants into the palace to fetch Ismene]*

When people hatch their mischief in the dark                         560
their minds often convict them in advance,
betraying their treachery. How I despise
a person caught committing evil acts
who then desires to glorify the crime.

**ANTIGONE:**   Take me and kill me—what more do you want?

**CREON:**   Me? Nothing. With that I have everything.

**ANTIGONE:**   Then why delay? There's nothing in your words
that I enjoy—may that always be the case!                              [500]
And what I say displeases you as much.
But where could I gain greater glory                                        570
than setting my own brother in his grave?
All those here would confirm this pleases them
if their lips weren't sealed by fear—being king,
which offers all sorts of various benefits,
means you can talk and act just as you wish.

**CREON:**   In all of Thebes, you're the only one
who looks at things that way.

**ANTIGONE:**   They share my views,
but they keep their mouths shut just for you.

**CREON:**   These views of yours—so different from the rest—
don't they bring you any sense of shame?                          580 [510]

**ANTIGONE:**   No—there's nothing shameful in honouring
my mother's children.

**CREON:**   You had a brother
killed fighting for the other side.

**ANTIGONE:**   Yes—from the same mother and father, too.

**CREON:**   Why then give tributes which insult his name?

**ANTIGONE:**   But his dead corpse won't back up what you say.

**CREON:**   Yes, he will, if you give equal honours
to a wicked man.

**ANTIGONE:**   But the one who died
was not some slave—it was his own brother.

**CREON:**   Who was destroying this country—the other one          590
went to his death defending it.

**ANTIGONE:**   That may be,
but Hades° still desires equal rites for both.

°**Hades:** god of the underworld, lord of the dead.

**CREON:**   A good man does not wish what we give him          [520]
    to be the same an evil man receives.
**ANTIGONE:**   Who knows? In the world below perhaps
    such actions are no crime.
**CREON:**   An enemy
    can never be a friend, not even in death.
**ANTIGONE:**   But my nature is to love. I cannot hate.
**CREON:**   Then go down to the dead. If you must love,
    love them. No woman's going to govern me—          600
    no, no—not while I'm still alive.

*[Enter two attendants from the house bringing Ismene to Creon]*

**CHORUS LEADER:**   Ismene's coming. There—right by the door.
    She's crying. How she must love her sister!
    From her forehead a cloud casts its shadow
    down across her darkly flushing face—
    and drops its rain onto her lovely cheeks.          [530]
**CREON:**   You there—you snake lurking in my house,
    sucking out my life's blood so secretly.
    I'd no idea I was nurturing two pests,
    who aimed to rise against my throne. Come here.          610
    Tell me this—do you admit you played your part
    in this burial, or will you swear an oath
    you had no knowledge of it?
**ISMENE:**   I did it—
    I admit it, and she'll back me up.
    So I bear the guilt as well.
**ANTIGONE:**   No, no—
    justice will not allow you to say that.
    You didn't want to. I didn't work with you.
**ISMENE:**   But now you're in trouble, I'm not ashamed          [540]
    of suffering, too, as your companion.
**ANTIGONE:**   Hades and the dead can say who did it—          620
    I don't love a friend whose love is only words.
**ISMENE:**   You're my sister. Don't dishonour me.
    Let me respect the dead and die with you.
**ANTIGONE:**   Don't try to share my death or make a claim
    to actions which you did not do. I'll die—
    and that will be enough.
**ISMENE:**   But if you're gone,
    what is there in life for me to love?
**ANTIGONE:**   Ask Creon. He's the one you care about.
**ISMENE:**   Why hurt me like this? It doesn't help you.          [550]
**ANTIGONE:**   If I am mocking you, it pains me, too.          630

ISMENE:   Even now is there some way I can help?

ANTIGONE:   Save yourself. I won't envy your escape.

ISMENE:   I feel so wretched leaving you to die.

ANTIGONE:   But you chose life—it was my choice to die.

ISMENE:   But not before I'd said those words just now.

ANTIGONE:   Some people may approve of how you think—
        others will believe my judgment's good.

ISMENE:   But the mistake's the same for both of us.

ANTIGONE:   Be brave. You're alive. But my spirit died
        some time ago so I might help the dead                    640 [560]

CREON:   I'd say one of these girls has just revealed
        how mad she is—the other's been that way
        since she was born.

ISMENE:   My lord, whatever good sense
        people have by birth no longer stays with them
        once their lives go wrong—it abandons them.

CREON:   In your case, that's true, once you made your choice
        to act in evil ways with wicked people.

ISMENE:   How could I live alone, without her here?

CREON:   Don't speak of her being here. Her life is over.

ISMENE:   You're going to kill your own son's bride?            650

CREON:   Why not? There are other fields for him to plough.

ISMENE:   No one will make him a more loving wife
        than she will.

CREON:   I have no desire my son
        should have an evil wife.

ANTIGONE:   Dearest Haemon,                                       [570]
        how your father wrongs you.

CREON:   I've had enough of this—
        you and your marriage.

ISMENE:   You really want that?
        You're going to take her from him?

CREON:   No, not me.
        Hades is the one who'll stop the marriage.

CHORUS LEADER:   So she must die—that seems decided on.

CREON:   Yes—for you and me the matter's closed.               660

{{dir}}}[Creon turns to address his attendants]

        No more delay. You slaves, take them inside.
        From this point on they must act like women
        and have no liberty to wander off.
        Even bold men run when they see Hades                     [580]
        coming close to them to snatch their lives.

[The attendants take Antigone and Ismene into the palace, leaving
Creon and the Chorus on stage]

**CHORUS:**   Those who live without tasting evil
    have happy lives—for when the gods
    shake a house to its foundations,
    then inevitable disasters strike,
    falling upon whole families,               670
    just as a surging ocean swell
    running before cruel Thracian winds
    across the dark trench of the sea
    churns up the deep black sand           [590]
    and crashes headlong on the cliffs,
    which scream in pain against the wind.
    I see this house's age-old sorrows,
    the house of Labdakos'° children,
    sorrows falling on the sorrows of the dead,
    one generation bringing no relief        680
    to generations after it—some god
    strikes at them—on and on without an end.
    For now the light which has been shining
    over the last roots of Oedipus' house     [600]
    is being cut down with a bloody knife
    belonging to the gods below—
    for foolish talk and frenzy in the soul.
    Oh Zeus, what human trespasses
    can check your power? Even Sleep,
    who casts his nets on everything,      690
    cannot master that—nor can the months,
    the tireless months the gods control.
    A sovereign who cannot grow old,
    you hold Olympus° as your own,
    in all its glittering magnificence.      [610]
    From now on into all future time,
    as in the past, your law holds firm.
    It never enters lives of human beings
    in its full force without disaster.
    Hope ranging far and wide brings comfort   700
    to many men—but then hope can deceive,
    delusions born of volatile desire.
    It comes upon the man who's ignorant
    until his foot is seared in burning fire.
    Someone's wisdom has revealed to us    [620]
    this famous saying—sometimes the gods
    lure a man's mind forward to disaster,
    and he thinks evil's something good.

°**Labdakos:** father of Laius and hence grandfather of Oedipus and great-grandfather of Antigone and Ismene.
°**Olympus:** a mountain in northern Greece where, according to tradition, the major gods live.

But then he lives only the briefest time
free of catastrophe.

*[The palace doors open]*

**CHORUS LEADER:**   Here comes Haemon,                    710
    your only living son. Is he grieving
    the fate of Antigone, his bride,
    bitter that his marriage hopes are gone?              [630]
**CREON:**   We'll soon find out—more accurately
    than any prophet here could indicate.

*[Enter Haemon from the palace]*

My son, have you heard the sentence that's been passed
upon your bride? And have you now come here
angry at your father? Or are you loyal to me,
on my side no matter what I do?
**HAEMON:**   Father, I'm yours. For me your judgments        720
    and the ways you act on them are good—
    I shall follow them. I'll not consider
    any marriage a greater benefit
    than your fine leadership.
**CREON:**   Indeed, my son,
    that's how your heart should always be resolved,
    to stand behind your father's judgment                [640]
    on every issue. That's what men pray for—
    obedient children growing up at home
    who will pay back their father's enemies,
    evil to them for evil done to him,                    730
    while honouring his friends as much as he does.
    A man who fathers useless children—
    what can one say of him except he's bred
    troubles for himself, and much to laugh at
    for those who fight against him? So, my son,
    don't ever throw good sense aside for pleasure,
    for some woman's sake. You understand
    how such embraces can turn freezing cold             [650]
    when an evil woman shares your life at home.
    What greater wound is there than a false friend?      740
    So spit this girl out—she's your enemy.
    Let her marry someone else in Hades.
    Since I caught her clearly disobeying,
    the only culprit in the entire city,
    I won't perjure myself before the state.
    No—I'll kill her. And so let her appeal
    to Zeus, the god of blood relationships.

If I foster any lack of full respect
in my own family, I surely do the same
with those who are not linked to me by blood.    750 [660]
The man who acts well with his household
will be found a just man in the city.°
I'd trust such a man to govern wisely
or to be content with someone ruling him.
And in the thick of battle at his post    [670]
he'll stand firm beside his fellow soldier,
a loyal, brave man. But anyone who's proud
and violates our laws or thinks he'll tell
our leaders what to do, a man like that
wins no praise from me. No. We must obey    760
whatever man the city puts in charge,
no matter what the issue—great or small,
just or unjust. For there's no greater evil
than a lack of leadership. That destroys
whole cities, turns households into ruins,
and in war makes soldiers break and run away.
When men succeed, what keeps their lives secure
in almost every case is their obedience.
That's why they must support those in control,
and never let some woman beat us down.    770
If we must fall from power, let that come
at some man's hand—at least, we won't be called
inferior to any woman.    [680]

**CHORUS LEADER:**    Unless we're being deceived by our old age,
    what you've just said seems reasonable to us.

**HAEMON:**    Father, the gods instill good sense in men—
    the greatest of all the things which we possess.
    I could not find your words somehow not right—
    I hope that's something I never learn to do.
    But other words might be good, as well.    780
    Because of who you are, you can't perceive
    all the things men say or do—or their complaints.
    Your gaze makes citizens afraid—they can't    [690]
    say anything you would not like to hear.
    But in the darkness I can hear them talk—
    the city is upset about the girl.
    They say of all women here she's least deserves
    the worst of deaths for her most glorious act.
    When in the slaughter her own brother died,
    she did not just leave him there unburied,    790
    to be ripped apart by carrion dogs or birds.

Surely she deserves some golden honour?
That's the dark secret rumour people speak.                    [700]
For me, father, nothing is more valuable
than your well being. For any children,
what could be a greater honour to them
than their father's thriving reputation?
A father feels the same about his sons.
So don't let your mind dwell on just one thought,
that what you say is right and nothing else.                   800
A man who thinks that only he is wise,
that he can speak and think like no one else,
when such men are exposed, then all can see
their emptiness inside. For any man,                           [710]
even if he's wise, there's nothing shameful
in learning many things, staying flexible.
You notice how in winter floods the trees
which bend before the storm preserve their twigs.
The ones who stand against it are destroyed,
root and branch. In the same way, those sailors               810
who keep their sails stretched tight, never easing off,
make their ship capsize—and from that point on
sail with their rowing benches all submerged.
So end your anger. Permit yourself to change.
For if I, as a younger man, may state
my views, I'd say it would be for the best                    [720]
if men by nature understood all things—
if not, and that is usually the case,
when men speak well, it good to learn from them.

**CHORUS LEADER:**   My lord, if what he's said is relevant,     820
it seems appropriate to learn from him,
and you too, Haemon, listen to the king.
The things which you both said were excellent.

**CREON:**   And men my age—are we then going to school
to learn what's wise from men as young as him?

**HAEMON:**   There's nothing wrong in that. And if I'm young,
don't think about my age—look at what I do.

CREON:   And what you do—does that include this,         [730]
honouring those who act against our laws?

**HAEMON:**   I would not encourage anyone                       830
to show respect to evil men.

**CREON:**   And her—
is she not suffering from the same disease?

**HAEMON:**   The people here in Thebes all say the same—
they deny she is.

**CREON:**   So the city now
will instruct me how I am to govern?
**HAEMON:**   Now you're talking like someone far too young.
Don't you see that?
**CREON:**   Am I to rule this land
at someone else's whim or by myself?
**HAEMON:**   A city which belongs to just one man
is no true city.
**CREON:**   According to our laws,                            840
does not the ruler own the city?
**HAEMON:**   By yourself you'd make an excellent king
but in a desert.
CREON:   It seems as if this boy                              [740]
is fighting on the woman's side.
**HAEMON:**   That's true—
if you're the woman. I'm concerned for you.
**CREON:**   You're the worst there is—you set your judgment up
against your father.
**HAEMON:**   No, not when I see
you making a mistake and being unjust.
**CREON:**   Is it a mistake to honour my own rule?
**HAEMON:**   You're not honouring that by trampling on          850
the gods' prerogatives.
**CREON:**   You foul creature—
you're worse than any woman.
**HAEMON:**   You'll not catch me
giving way to some disgrace.
**CREON:**   But your words
all speak on her behalf.
**HAEMON:**   And yours and mine—
and for the gods below.
**CREON:**   You woman's slave—
don't try to win me over.
**HAEMON:**   What do you want—
to speak and never hear someone reply?°
CREON:   You'll never marry her while she's alive.             [750]
**HAEMON:**   Then she'll die—and in her death kill someone else.
**CREON:**   Are you so insolent you threaten me?                860
**HAEMON:**   Where's the threat in challenging a bad decree?
**CREON:**   You'll regret parading what you think like this—
you—a person with an empty brain!
**HAEMON:**   If you were not my father, I might say
you were not thinking straight.
**CREON:**   Would you, indeed?
Well, then, by Olympus, I'll have you know

you'll be sorry for demeaning me
with all these insults.

*[Creon turns to his attendants]*

Go bring her out—                                                    [760]
that hateful creature, so she can die right here,
with him present, before her bridegroom's eyes.                      870
HAEMON:   No. Don't ever hope for that. She'll not die
with me just standing there. And as for you—
your eyes will never see my face again.
So let your rage charge on among your friends
who want to stand by you in this.

*[Exit Haemon, running back into the palace]*

CHORUS LEADER:   My lord, Haemon left in such a hurry.
He's angry—in a young man at his age
the mind turns bitter when he's feeling hurt.
CREON:   Let him dream up or carry out great deeds
beyond the power of man, he'll not save these girls—                 880
their fate is sealed.
CHORUS LEADER:   Are you going to kill them both?                    [770]
CREON:   No—not the one whose hands are clean. You're right.
CHORUS LEADER:   How do you plan to kill Antigone?
CREON:   I'll take her on a path no people use,
and hide her in a cavern in the rocks,
while still alive. I'll set out provisions,
as much as piety requires, to make sure
the city is not totally corrupted.°
Then she can speak her prayers to Hades,
the only god she worships, for success                               890
avoiding death—or else, at least, she'll learn,
although too late, how it's a waste of time
to work to honour those whom Hades holds.                            [780]
CHORUS:   O Eros°, the conqueror in every fight,
Eros, who squanders all men's wealth,
who sleeps at night on girls' soft cheeks,
and roams across the ocean seas
and through the shepherd's hut—
no immortal god escapes from you,
nor any man, who lives but for a day.                                900
And the one whom you possess goes mad.                               [790]
Even in good men you twist their minds,

---

°**corrupted**: the killing of a family member could bring on divine punishment in the form of a pollution involving the entire city (as in the case of Oedipus). Creon is, one assumes, taking refuge in the notion that he will not be executing Antigone directly.   °**Eros**: the god of erotic sexual passion.

perverting them to their own ruin.
You provoke these men to family strife.
The bride's desire seen glittering in her eyes—
that conquers everything, its power
enthroned beside eternal laws, for there
the goddess Aphrodite° works her will,                    [800]
whose ways are irresistible.

*[Antigone enters from the palace with attendants who are taking her away to her execution]*

**CHORAL LEADER:**   When I look at her I forget my place.       910
I lose restraint and can't hold back my tears—
Antigone going to her bridal room
where all are laid to rest in death.
**ANTIGONE:**   Look at me, my native citizens,
as I go on my final journey,
as I gaze upon the sunlight one last time,
which I'll never see again—for Hades,
who brings all people to their final sleep,
leads me on, while I'm still living,                       [810]
down to the shores of Acheron.°                           920
I've not yet had my bridal chant,
nor has any wedding song been sung—
for my marriage is to Acheron.
**CHORUS:**   Surely you carry fame with you and praise,
as you move to the deep home of the dead.
You were not stricken by lethal disease
or paid your wages with a sword.                          [820]
No. You were in charge of your own fate.
So of all living human beings, you alone
make your way down to Hades still alive.                  930
**ANTIGONE:**   I've heard about a guest of ours,
daughter of Tantalus, from Phrygia—
she went to an excruciating death
in Sipylus, right on the mountain peak.
The stone there, just like clinging ivy,
wore her down, and now, so people say,
the snow and rain never leave her there,                  [830]
as she laments. Below her weeping eyes
her neck is wet with tears. God brings me
to a final rest which most resembles hers.                940
**CHORUS:**   But Niobe was a goddess, born divine—
and we are human beings, a race which dies.
But still, it's a fine thing for a woman,

°**Aphrodite:** goddess of sexual desire.    °**Acheron:** one of the major rivers of the underworld.

once she's dead, to have it said she shared,
in life and death, the fate of demi-gods.°
**ANTIGONE:**    Oh, you are mocking me! Why me—
by our fathers' gods—why do you all,
my own city and the richest men of Thebes,
insult me now right to my face,
without waiting for my death?                                    950
Well at least I have Dirce's springs,
the holy grounds of Thebes,
a city full of splendid chariots,
to witness how no friends lament for me
as I move on—you see the laws
which lead me to my rock-bound prison,
a tomb made just for me. Alas!
In my wretchedness I have no home,                              [850]
not with human beings or corpses,
not with the living or the dead.                                 960
CHORUS:    You pushed your daring to the limit, my child,
and tripped against Justice's high altar—
perhaps your agonies are paying back
some compensation for your father.°
**ANTIGONE:**    Now there you touch on my most painful thought—
my father's destiny—always on my mind,
along with that whole fate which sticks to us,                   [860]
the splendid house of Labdakos—the curse
arising from a mother's marriage bed,
when she had sex with her own son, my father.                    970
From what kind of parents was I born,
their wretched daughter? I go to them,
unmarried and accursed, an outcast.
Alas, too, for my brother Polyneices,
who made a fatal marriage and then died—                         [870]
and with that death killed me while still alive.°
**CHORUS:**    To be piously devout shows reverence,
but powerful men, who in their persons
incorporate authority, cannot bear
anyone to break their rules. Hence, you die                      980
because of your own selfish will.
**ANTIGONE:**    Without lament, without a friend,
and with no marriage song, I'm being led

---

°The last two speeches refer to Niobe, daughter of Tantalus (a son of Zeus). Niobe had seven sons and daughters and boasted that she had more children than the goddess Leto. As punishment Artemis and Apollo, Leto's two children, destroyed all Niobe's children. Niobe turned to stone in grief and was reportedly visible on Mount Sipylus (in Asia Minor). The Chorus' claim that Niobe was a goddess or semi-divine is very odd here, since her story is almost always a tale of human presumption and divine punishment for human arrogance.    °**father:** The Chorus here is offering the traditional suggestion that present afflictions can arise from a family curse originating in previous generations.    °**still alive:** Polyneices married the daughter of Adrastus, an action which enabled him to acquire the army to attack Thebes.

in this miserable state, along my final road.
So wretched that I no longer have the right                    [880]
to look upon the sun, that sacred eye.
But my fate prompts no tears, and no friend mourns.

**CREON:**   Don't you know that no one faced with death
would ever stop the singing and the groans,
if that would help? Take her and shut her up,                    990
as I have ordered, in her tomb's embrace.
And get it done as quickly as you can.
Then leave her there alone, all by herself—
she can sort out whether she wants suicide
or remains alive, buried in a place like that.
As far as she's concerned, we bear no guilt.
But she's lost her place living here with us.°                    [890]

**ANTIGONE:**   Oh my tomb and bridal chamber—
my eternal hollow dwelling place,
where I go to join my people. Most of them                    1000
have perished—Persephone° has welcomed them
among the dead. I'm the last one, dying here
the most evil death by far, as I move down
before the time allotted for my life is done.
But I go nourishing the vital hope
my father will be pleased to see me come,
and you, too, my mother, will welcome me,
as well as you, my own dear brother.
When you died, with my own hands I washed you.                    [900]
I arranged your corpse and at the grave mound                    1010
poured out libations. But now, Polyneices,
this is my reward for covering your corpse.°
However, for wise people I was right
to honour you. I'd never have done it
for children of my own, not as their mother,
nor for a dead husband lying in decay—
no, not in defiance of the citizens.
What law do I appeal to, claiming this?
If my husband died, there'd be another one,
and if I were to lose a child of mine                    1020
I'd have another with some other man.                    [910]
But since my father and my mother, too,

°**here with us**: Creon's logic seems to suggest that because he is not executing Antigone directly and is leaving her a choice between committing suicide and slowly starving to death in the cave, he has no moral responsibility for what happens.   °**Persephone** is the wife of Hades and thus goddess of the underworld.   °**In these lines** Antigone seems to be talking about both her brothers, first claiming she washed and dressed the body of Eteocles and then covered Polyneices. However, the pronoun references in the Greek are confusing. Lines 904 to 920 in the Greek text have prompted a great deal of critical debate, since they seem incompatible with Antigone's earlier motivation and do not make much sense in context (in addition most of them appear closely derived from Herodotus 3.119). Hence, some editors insist that the lines (or most of them) be removed. Brown provides a useful short summary of the arguments and some editorial options (199-200).

are hidden away in Hades' house,
I'll never have another living brother.
That was the law I used to honour you.
But Creon thought that I was in the wrong
and acting recklessly for you, my brother.
Now he seizes me by force and leads me here—
no wedding and no bridal song, no share
in married life or raising children. 1030
Instead I go in sorrow to my grave,
without my friends, to die while still alive. [920]
What holy justice have I violated?
In my wretchedness, why should I still look
up to the gods? Which one can I invoke
to bring me help, when for my reverence
they charge me with impiety? Well, then,
if this is something fine among the gods,
I'll come to recognize that I've done wrong.
But if these people here are being unjust 1040
may they endure no greater punishment
than the injustices they're doing to me.

**CHORUS LEADER:** The same storm blasts continue to attack
the mind in this young girl. [930]

**CREON:** Then those escorting her
will be sorry they're so slow.

**ANTIGONE:** Alas, then,
those words mean death is very near at hand.

**CREON:** I won't encourage you or cheer you up,
by saying the sentence won't be carried out.

**ANTIGONE:** O city of my fathers
in this land of Thebes— 1050
and my ancestral gods,
I am being led away.
No more delaying for me.
Look on me, you lords of Thebes, [940]
the last survivor of your royal house,
see what I have to undergo,
the kind of men who do this to me,
for paying reverence to true piety.

*[Antigone is led away under escort]*

**CHORUS:** In her brass-bound room fair Danae° as well
endured her separation from the heaven's light, 1060

°**Danae:** daughter of Acrisus, King of Argos. Because of a prophecy that he would be killed by a son
born to Danae, Acrisus imprisoned her. But Zeus made love to her in the form of a golden shower, and
she gave birth to Perseus, who, once grown, killed Acrisus accidentally.

a prisoner hidden in a chamber like a tomb,
although she, too, came from a noble line.
And she, my child, had in her care
the liquid streaming golden seed of Zeus.                    [950]
But the power of fate is full of mystery.
There's no evading it, no, not with wealth,
or war, or walls, or black sea-beaten ships.
And the hot-tempered child of Dryas,
king of the Edonians, was put in prison,
closed up in the rocks by Dionysus,                   1070
for his angry mocking of the god.°
There the dreadful flower of his rage                        [960]
slowly withered, and he came to know
the god who in his frenzy he had mocked
with his own tongue. For he had tried
to hold in check women in that frenzy
inspired by the god, the Bacchanalian fire.
More than that—he'd made the Muses angry,
challenging the gods who love the flute.°
Beside the black rocks where the twin seas meet,     1080
by Thracian Salmydessos at the Bosphorus,°
close to the place where Ares dwells,                        [970]
the war god witnessed the unholy wounds
which blinded the two sons of Phineus,
inflicted by his savage wife—the sightless holes
cried out for someone to avenge those blows
made with her sharpened comb in blood-stained hands.°
In their misery they wept, lamenting
their wretched suffering, sons of a mother
whose marriage had gone wrong. And yet,              1090  [980]
she was an offspring of an ancient family,
the race of Erechtheus, raised far away,
in caves surrounded by her father's winds,
Boreas' child, a girl who raced with horses
across steep hills—child of the gods.
But she, too, my child, suffered much
from the immortal Fates.°

*[Enter Teiresias, led by a young boy]*

°**mocking of the god**: a reference to Lycurgus son of Dryas, a Thracian king. He attacked the god
Dionysus and was punished with blinding or with being torn apart.   °**flute**: the anger of the Muses
at a Thracian who boasted of his flute playing is not normally a part of the Lycurgus story but refers
to another Thracian, Thamyras.   °**dark rocks ... Bosphorus**: the dark rocks were a famous hazard to
shipping. They moved together to smash any ship moving between them. The Bosphorus is the strait
between the Black Sea and the Propontis (near the Hellespont).   °**blood-stained hands**: this verse
and the next refer to the Thracian king Phineas, whose second wife blinded her two step sons (from
Phineas' first wife Cleopatra) by stabbing out their eyes.   °**immortal Fates**: Cleopatra was the granddaughter of Erechtheus, king of Athens. Boreas, father of Erechtheus, was god of the North Wind.

**TEIRESIAS:**    Lords of Thebes, we two have walked a common path,
one person's vision serving both of us.
The blind require a guide to find their way.                          1100    [990]
**CREON:**    What news do you have, old Teiresias?
**TEIRESIAS:**    I'll tell you—and you obey the prophet.
**CREON:**    I've not rejected your advice before.
**TEIRESIAS:**    That's the reason why you've steered the city
on its proper course.
**CREON:**    From my experience
I can confirm the help you give.
**TEIRESIAS:**    Then know this—
your luck is once more on fate's razor edge.
**CREON:**    What? What you've just said makes me nervous.
**TEIRESIAS:**    know—once you hear the tokens of my art.
As I was sitting in my ancient place                                  1110
receiving omens from the flights of birds
who all come there where I can hear them,                                      [1000]
I note among those birds an unknown cry—
evil, unintelligible, angry screaming.
I knew that they were tearing at each other
with murderous claws. The noisy wings
revealed that all too well. I was afraid.
So right away up on the blazing altar
I set up burnt offerings. But Hephaestus
failed to shine out from the sacrifice—                               1120
dark slime poured out onto the embers,
oozing from the thighs, which smoked and spat,
bile was sprayed high up into the air,                                         [1010]
and the melting thighs lost all the fat
which they'd been wrapped in. The rites had failed—
there was no prophecy revealed in them.
I learned that from this boy, who is my guide,
as I guide other men.° Our state is sick—
your policies have done this. In the city
our altars and our hearths have been defiled,                         1130
all of them, with rotting flesh brought there
by birds and dogs from Oedipus' son,
who lies there miserably dead. The gods
no longer will accept our sacrifice,
our prayers, our thigh bones burned in fire.                                  [1020]
No bird will shriek out a clear sign to us,
for they have gorged themselves on fat and blood
from a man who's dead. Consider this, my son.
All men make mistakes—that's not uncommon.

°**other men:** Teiresias' offering failed to catch fire. His interpretation is that it has been rejected by the gods, a very unfavourable omen.

But when they do, they're no longer foolish                    1140
or subject to bad luck if they try to fix
the evil into which they've fallen,
once they give up their intransigence.
Men who put their stubbornness on show
invite accusations of stupidity.
Make concessions to the dead—don't ever stab
a man who's just been killed. What's the glory
in killing a dead person one more time?                    [1030]
I've been concerned for you. It's good advice.
Learning can be pleasant when a man speaks well,              1150
especially when he seeks your benefit.

**CREON:**    Old man, you're all like archers shooting at me—
For you all I've now become your target—
even prophets have been aiming at me.
I've long been bought and sold as merchandise
among that tribe. Well, go make your profits.
If it's what you want, then trade with Sardis
for their golden-silver alloy—or for gold
from India, but you'll never hide that corpse
in any grave. Even if Zeus' eagles                    1160 [1040]
should choose to seize his festering body
and take it up, right to the throne of Zeus,
not even then would I, in trembling fear
of some defilement, permit that corpse
a burial. For I know well that no man
has the power to pollute the gods.
But, old Teiresias, among human beings
the wisest suffer a disgraceful fall
when, to promote themselves, they use fine words
to spread around abusive insults.                    1170

**TEIRESIAS:**    Alas, does any man know or think about …

CREON:    *[interrupting]*
Think what? What sort of pithy common thought
are you about to utter?

TEIRESIAS    *[ignoring the interruption]*
… how good advice
is valuable—worth more than all possessions.                    [1050]

**CREON:**    I think that's true, as much as foolishness
is what harms us most.

**TEIRESIAS:**    Yet that's the sickness
now infecting you.

**CREON:**    I have no desire
to denigrate a prophet when I speak.

**TEIRESIAS:**    But that's what you are doing, when you claim
my oracles are false.

CREON:   The tribe of prophets—                                    1180
   all of them—are fond of money

TEIRESIAS:   And kings?
   Their tribe loves to benefit dishonestly.

CREON:   You know you're speaking of the man who rules you.

TEIRESIAS:   I know—thanks to me you saved the city
   and now are in control.°

CREON:   You're a wise prophet,
   but you love doing wrong.

TEIRESIAS:   You'll force me
   to speak of secrets locked inside my heart.                    [1060]

CREON:   Do it—just don't speak to benefit yourself.

TEIRESIAS:   I don't think that I'll be doing that—
   not as far as you're concerned.

   CREON:   You can be sure                                       1190
   you won't change my mind to make yourself more rich.

TEIRESIAS:   Then understand this well—you will not see
   the sun race through its cycle many times
   before you lose a child of your own loins,
   a corpse in payment for these corpses.
   You've thrown down to those below someone
   from up above—in your arrogance
   you've moved a living soul into a grave,
   leaving here a body owned by gods below—                        [1070]
   unburied, dispossessed, unsanctified.                         1200
   That's no concern of yours or gods above.
   In this you violate the ones below.
   And so destroying avengers wait for you,
   Furies of Hades and the gods, who'll see
   you caught up in this very wickedness.
   Now see if I speak as someone who's been bribed.
   It won't be long before in your own house
   the men and women all cry out in sorrow,
   and cities rise in hate against you—all those                   [1080]
   whose mangled soldiers have had burial rites                  1210
   from dogs, wild animals, or flying birds
   who carry the unholy stench back home,
   to every city hearth.° Like an archer,
   I shoot these arrows now into your heart
   because you have provoked me. I'm angry—
   so my aim is good. You'll not escape their pain.

°**in control**: This is the second reference to the fact that at some point earlier Teiresias has given important political help to Creon. It is not at all clear what this refers to.   °Teiresias here is apparently accusing Creon of refusing burial to the dead allied soldiers Polyneices brought with him from other cities. There is no mention of this anywhere else in the play, although the detail is present in other versions of the story.

Boy, lead us home so he can vent his rage
on younger men and keep a quieter tongue
and a more temperate mind than he has now.                [1090]

*[Exit Teiresias, led by the young boy]*

**CHORUS LEADER:**   My lord, my lord, such dreadful prophecies—   1220
and now he's gone. Since my hair changed colour
from black to white, I know here in the city
he's never uttered a false prophecy.
**CREON:**   I know that, too—and it disturbs my mind.
It's dreadful to give way, but to resist
and let destruction hammer down my spirit—
that's a fearful option, too.
**CHORUS LEADER:**   Son of Menoikeos,
you need to listen to some good advice.
**CREON:**   Tell me what to do. Speak up. I'll do it.
**CHORUS LEADER:**   Go and release the girl from her rock tomb.   1230 [1100]
Then prepare a grave for that unburied corpse.
**CREON:**   This is your advice? You think I should concede?
**CHORUS LEADER:**   Yes, my lord, as fast as possible.
Swift footed injuries sent from the gods
hack down those who act imprudently.
**CREON:**   Alas—it's difficult. But I'll give up.
I'll not do what I'd set my heart upon.
It's not right to fight against necessity.
**CHORUS LEADER:**   Go now and get this done. Don't give the work
to other men to do.
CREON:   I'll go just as I am.                        1240
Come, you servants, each and every one of you.
Come on. Bring axes with you. Go there quickly—
up to the higher ground. I've changed my mind.       [1110]
Since I'm the one who tied her up, I'll go
and set her free myself. Now I'm afraid.
Until one dies the best thing well may be
to follow our established laws.

*[Creon and his attendants hurry off stage]*

**CHORUS:**   Oh you with many names,
you glory of that Theban bride,
and child of thundering Zeus,                         1250
you who cherish famous Italy,
and rule the welcoming valley lands
of Eleusianian Deo—                                  [1120]
O Bacchus—you who dwell
in the bacchants' mother city Thebes,
beside Ismenus' flowing streams,
on land sown with the teeth

of that fierce dragon.°
Above the double mountain peaks,
the torches flashing through the murky smoke                    1260
have seen you where Corcyian nymphs
move on as they worship you
by the Kastalian stream.                                        [1130]
And from the ivy-covered slopes
of Nysa's hills, from the green shore
so rich in vines, you come to us,
visiting our Theban ways,
while deathless voices all cry out
in honour of your name, "Evoe."°
You honour Thebes, our city,                                    1270
above all others, you and your mother
blasted by that lightning strike.°
And now when all our people here                                [1140]
are captive to a foul disease,
on your healing feet you come
across the moaning strait
or over the Parnassian hill.
You who lead the dance,
among the fire-breathing stars,
who guard the voices in the night,                              1280
child born of Zeus, oh my lord,                                 [1150]
appear with your attendant Thyiads,
who dance in frenzy all night long,
for you their patron, Iacchus.°

*[Enter a Messenger]*

**MESSENGER:**    All you here who live beside the home
of Amphion° and Cadmus—in human life
there's no set place which I would praise or blame.
The lucky and unlucky rise or fall
by chance day after day—and how these things
are fixed for men no one can prophesy.                          1290 [1160]
For Creon, in my view, was once a man
we all looked up to. For he saved the state,
this land of Cadmus, from its enemies.
He took control and reigned as its sole king—
and prospered with the birth of noble children.
Now all is gone. For when a man has lost

---

°**fierce dragon:** In these lines the Chorus celebrates Dionysus, the god born in Thebes to Semele, daughter of King Cadmus. The bacchants are those who worship Dionysus. Eleusis, a region on the coast near Athens, was famous for the its Eleusinian Mysteries, a secret ritual of worship. Deo is a reference to the goddess Demeter, who was worshipped at Eleusis. The Theban race sprang up from dragon's teeth sown in a field by Cadmus, founder of the city.    °**Evoe:** a cry of celebration made by worshippers of Bacchus.    °**lightning strike:** Semele, Dionysus human mother, was destroyed by Zeus lightning bolt, because of the jealousy of Hera, Zeus' wife.    °**Iacchus:** Thyiads are worshippers of Dionysus, Iacchus a divinity associated with Dionysus.    °**Amphion:** legendary king of Thebes, husband of Niobe.

what gives him pleasure, I don't include him
among the living—he's a breathing corpse.
Pile up a massive fortune in your home,
if that's what you want—live like a king.          1300
If there's no pleasure in it, I'd not give
to any man a vapour's shadow for it,                [1170]
not compared to human joy.
**CHORUS LEADER:**   Have you come with news of some fresh trouble
in our house of kings?
**MESSENGER:**   They're dead—
and those alive bear the responsibility
for those who've died.
**CHORUS LEADER:**   Who did the killing?
Who's lying dead? Tell us.
**MESSENGER:**   Haemon has been killed.
No stranger shed his blood.
**CHORUS LEADER:**   At his father's hand?
Or did he kill himself?
**MESSENGER:**   By his own hand—
angry at his father for the murder.                1310
**CHORUS LEADER:**   Teiresias, how your words have proven true!
**MESSENGER:**   That's how things stand. Consider what comes next.
CHORUS LEADER:   I see Creon's wife, poor Eurydice—        [1180]
she's coming from the house—either by chance,
or else she's heard there's news about her son.

*[Enter Eurydice from the palace with some attendants]*

**EURYDICE:**   Citizens of Thebes, I heard you talking,
as I was walking out, going off to pray,
to ask for help from goddess Pallas.
While I was unfastening the gate,
I heard someone speaking of bad news               1320
about my family. I was terrified.
I collapsed, fainting back into the arms
of my attendants. So tell the news again—          [1190]
I'll listen. I'm no stranger to misfortune.
**MESSENGER:**   Dear lady, I'll speak of what I saw,
omitting not one detail of the truth.
Why should I ease your mind with a report
which turns out later to be incorrect?
The truth is always best. I went to the plain,
accompanying your husband as his guide.            1330
Polyneices' corpse, still unlamented,
was lying there, the greatest distance off,
torn apart by dogs. We prayed to Pluto
and to Hecate, goddess of the road,

for their good will and to restrain their rage.                    [1200]
We gave the corpse a ritual wash, and burned
what was left of it on fresh-cut branches.
We piled up a high tomb of his native earth.
Then we moved to the young girl's rocky cave,
the hollow cavern of that bride of death.                          1340
From far away one man heard a voice
coming from the chamber where we'd put her
without a funeral—a piercing cry.
He went to tell our master Creon,
who, as he approached the place, heard the sound,
an unintelligible scream of sorrow.
He groaned and then spoke out these bitter words,                  [1210]
"Has misery made me a prophet now?
And am I travelling along a road
that takes me to the worst of all disasters?                       1350
I've just heard the voice of my own son.
You servants, go ahead—get up there fast.
Remove the stones piled in the entrance way,
then stand beside the tomb and look in there
to see if that was Haemon's voice I heard,
or if the gods have been deceiving me."
Following what our desperate master asked,
we looked. In the furthest corner of the tomb                      [1220]
we saw Antigone hanging by the neck,
held up in a noose—fine woven linen.                               1360
Haemon had his arms around her waist—
he was embracing her and crying out
in sorrow for the loss of his own bride,
now among the dead, his father's work,
and for his horrifying marriage bed.
Creon saw him, let out a fearful groan,
then went inside and called out anxiously,
"You unhappy boy, what have you done?
What are you thinking? Have you lost your mind?
Come out, my child—I'm begging you—please come."                  1370
But the boy just stared at him with savage eyes,                   [1230]
spat in his face and, without saying a word,
drew his two-edged sword. Creon moved away,
so the boy's blow failed to strike his father.
Angry at himself, the ill-fated lad
right then and there leaned into his own sword,
driving half the blade between his ribs.
While still conscious he embraced the girl
in his weak arms, and, as he breathed his last,
he coughed up streams of blood on her fair cheek.                  1380

Now he lies there, corpse on corpse, his marriage                    [1240]
has been fulfilled in chambers of the dead.
The unfortunate boy has shown all men
how, of all the evils which afflict mankind,
the most disastrous one is thoughtlessness.

*[Eurydice turns and slowly returns into the palace]*

**CHORUS LEADER:**   What do you make of that? The queen's gone back.
She left without a word, good or bad.
**MESSENGER:**   I'm surprised myself. It's about her son—
she heard that terrible report. I hope
she's gone because she doesn't think it right                    1390
to mourn for him in public. In the home,
surrounded by her servants, she'll arrange
a period of mourning for the house.
She's discreet and has experience—
she won't make mistakes.                                          [1250]
**CHORUS LEADER:**   I'm not sure of that.
to me her staying silent was extreme—
it seems to point to something ominous,
just like a vain excess of grief.
**MESSENGER:**   I'll go in.
We'll find out if she's hiding something secret,
deep within her passionate heart. You're right—                  1400
excessive silence can be dangerous.

*[The Messenger goes up the stairs into the palace. Enter Creon from the
side, with attendants. Creon is holding the body of Haemon]*

**CHORUS LEADER:**   Here comes the king in person—carrying
in his arms, if it's right to speak of this,
a clear reminder that this evil comes
not from some stranger, but his own mistakes.                    [1260]
**CREON:**   Aaiii—mistakes made by a foolish mind,
cruel mistakes that bring on death.
You see us here, all in one family—
the killer and the killed.
Oh the profanity of what I planned.                              1410
Alas, my son, you died so young—
a death before your time.
Aaiii ... aaiii ... you're dead ... gone—
not your own foolishness but mine.
**CHORUS LEADER:**   Alas, it seems you've learned to see what's right—
but far too late. &nb sp;                                        [1270]
**CREON:**   Aaiiii ... I've learned it in my pain.
Some god clutching a great weight struck my head,
then hurled me onto paths in wilderness,

throwing down and casting underfoot
what brought me joy.                                          1420
So sad ... so sad ...
the wretched agony of human life.

*[The Messenger reappears from the palace]*

**MESSENGER:**  My lord, you come like one who stores up evil,
what you hold in your arms and what you'll see
before too long inside the house.                          [1280]
**CREON:**  What's that?
Is there something still more evil than all this?
**MESSENGER:**  Your wife is dead—blood mother of that corpse—
slaughtered with a sword—her wounds are very new,
poor lady.
**CREON:**  Aaiiii ... . a gathering place for death ...
no sacrifice can bring this to an end.                     1430
Why are you destroying me? You there—
you bringer of this dreadful news, this agony,
what are you saying now? Aaiii ...
You kill a man then kill him once again.
What are you saying, boy? What news?
A slaughter heaped on slaughter—                           [1290]
my wife, alas ... she's dead?
**MESSENGER**  *[opening the palace doors, revealing the body of Eurydice]*
Look here. No longer is she concealed inside.
**CREON:**  Alas, how miserable I feel—to look upon
this second horror. What remains for me,
what's fate still got in store? I've just held            1440
my own son in my arms, and now I see
right here in front of me another corpse.
Alas for this suffering mother.                           [1300]
Alas, my son.
**MESSENGER:**  Stabbed with a sharp sword at the altar,
she let her darkening eyesight fail,
once she had cried out in sorrow
for the glorious fate of Megareos,°
who died some time ago, and then again
for Haemon, and then, with her last breath,               1450
she called out evil things against you,
the killer of your sons.
**CREON:**  Aaaii ... My fear now makes me tremble.
Why won't someone now strike out at me,
pierce my heart with a double bladed sword?
How miserable I am ... aaiii ...                          [1310]
how full of misery and pain ...
**MESSENGER:**  By this woman who lies dead you stand charged
with the deaths of both your sons.

**CREON:**   What about her?
How did she die so violently?
MESSENGER: She killed herself,                                    1460
with her own hands she stabbed her belly,
once she heard her son's unhappy fate.
**CREON:**   Alas for me ... the guilt for all of this is mine—
it can never be removed from me or passed
to any other mortal man. I, and I alone ...
I murdered you ... I speak the truth.
Servants—hurry and lead me off,                                  [1320]
get me away from here, for now
what I am in life is nothing.
CHORUS LEADER   What you advise is good—if good can come   1470
with all these evils. When we face such things
the less we say the better.
**CREON:**   Let that day come, oh let it come,
the fairest of all destinies for me,
the one which brings on my last day.                             [1330]
Oh, let it come, so that I never see
another dawn.
**CHORUS LEADER:**   That's something for the times ahead.
Now we need to deal with what confronts us here.
What's yet to come is the concern of those                       1480
whose task it is to deal with it.
**CREON:**   In that prayer
I included everything I most desire.
**CHORUS:**   Pray for nothing.
There's no release for mortal human beings,
not from events which destiny has set.
**CREON:**   Then take this foolish man away from here.
I killed you, my son, without intending to,                      [1340]
and you, as well, my wife. How useless I am now.
I don't know where to look or find support.
Everything I touch goes wrong, and on my head
fate climbs up with its overwhelming load.                       1490

*[The Attendants help Creon move up the stairs into the palace, taking
Haemon's body with them]*

**CHORUS:**   The most important part of true success
is wisdom—not to act impiously
    towards the gods, for boasts of arrogant men                 [1350]
bring on great blows of punishment—
so in old age men can discover wisdom.

°**Megareos:** Haemon's brother, who, we are to understand on the basis of this reference, died nobly
some time before the play begins. It is not clear how Creon might have been responsible for his death.
In another version of the story, Creon has a son Menoeceos, who kills himself in order to save the city.

---

### WILLIAM SHAKESPEARE ■ (1564–1616)

*William Shakespeare, the supreme writer of English, was born, baptized, and buried in the market town of Stratford-on-Avon, eighty miles from London. Son of a glove maker and merchant who was high bailiff (or mayor) of the town, he probably attended grammar school and learned to read Latin authors in the original. At eighteen, he married Anne Hathaway, twenty-six, by whom he had three children, including twins. By 1592, he had become well known and envied as an actor and playwright in London. From 1594 until he retired, he belonged to the same theatrical company, the Lord Chamberlain's Men (later renamed the King's Men in honor of their patron, James I), for whom he wrote thirty-six plays—some of them, such as* Hamlet *and* King Lear, *profound reworkings of old plays. As an actor, Shakespeare is believed to have played supporting roles, such as Hamlet's father's ghost. The company prospered, moved into the Globe Theatre in 1599, and in 1608 bought the fashionable Blackfriars as well; Shakespeare owned an interest in both theaters. When plagues shut down the theaters from 1592 to 1594, Shakespeare turned to story poems; his great sonnets (published only in 1609) probably also date from the 1590s. Plays were regarded as entertainments of little literary merit, and Shakespeare did not bother to supervise their publication. After* The Tempest *(1611), the last play entirely from his hand, he retired to Stratford, where since 1597 he had owned the second largest house in town.*

# Twelfth Night; or, What You Will

[*Dramatis Personae*
ORSINO, *Duke (sometimes called Count) of Illyria*
VALENTINE, *gentleman attending on Orsino*
CURIO, *gentleman attending on Orsino*
VIOLA, *a shipwrecked lady, later disguised as Cesario*
SEBASTIAN, *twin brother of Viola*
ANTONIO, *a sea captain, friend to Sebastian*
CAPTAIN *of the shipwrecked vessel*
OLIVIA, *a rich countess of Illyria*
MARIA, *gentlewoman in Olivia's household*
SIR TOBY BELCH, *Olivia's uncle*
SIR ANDREW AGUECHEEK, *a companion of Sir Toby*
MALVOLIO, *steward of Olivia's household*
FABIAN, *a member of Olivia's household*
FESTE, *a clown, also called FOOL, Olivia's jester*

A PRIEST
FIRST OFFICER
SECOND OFFICER

*Lords, Sailors, Musicians, and other Attendants*
　　　　　　　SCENE: *Illyria°*]

## 1.1

　　*Enter Orsino Duke of Illyria, Curio, and other lords [with musicians].*
**ORSINO:**　If music be the food of love, play on;
　　Give me excess of it, that surfeiting,
　　The appetite may sicken and so die.
　　That strain again! It had a dying fall;°
　　Oh, it came o'er my ear like the sweet sound　　　　　　　5
　　That breathes upon a bank of violets,
　　Stealing and giving odor. Enough, no more.
　　'Tis not so sweet now as it was before.
　　O spirit of love, how quick and fresh° art thou,
　　That, notwithstanding thy capacity　　　　　　　10
　　Receiveth as the sea, naught enters there,
　　Of what validity° and pitch° soe'er,
　　But falls into abatement° and low price
　　Even in a minute! So full of shapes° is fancy°
　　That it alone is high fantastical.°　　　　　　　15
**CURIO:**　Will you go hunt, my lord?
**ORSINO:**　　　　　　　　What, Curio?
**CURIO:**　　　　　　　　　　　The hart.
**ORSINO:**　Why, so I do, the noblest that I have.°
　　Oh, when mine eyes did see Olivia first,
　　Methought she purged the air of pestilence.
　　That instant was I turned into a hart,　　　　　　　20
　　And my desires, like fell° and cruel hounds,
　　E'er since pursue me.°
　　　　*Enter Valentine.*
　　　　　　　　　　How now, what news from her?
**VALENTINE:**　So please my lord, I might not be admitted,
　　But from her handmaid do return this answer;

SCENE *Illyria* Nominally on the east coast of the Adriatic Sea, but with a suggestion also of "illusion" and "delirium." **4 fall** cadence **9 quick and fresh** keen and hungry **12 validity** value. **pitch** superiority. (Literally, the highest point of a falcon's flight.) **13 abatement** depreciation. (The lover's brain entertains innumerable fantasies but soon tires of them all.) **14 shapes** imagined forms. **fancy** love **15 it ... fantastical** it surpasses everything else in imaginative power. **17 the noblest ... have** i.e., my noblest part, my heart. (Punning on *hart.*) **21 fell** fierce **22 pursue me** (Alludes to the story in Ovid of Actaeon, who, having seen Diana bathing, was transformed into a stag and killed by his own hounds.)

The element° itself, till seven years' heat,°                           25
Shall not behold her face at ample view;
But like a cloistress° she will veilèd walk,
And water once a day her chamber round
With eye-offending brine—all this to season°
A brother's dead love,° which she would keep fresh       30
And lasting in her sad remembrance.

**ORSINO:**    Oh, she that hath a heart of that fine frame°
To pay this debt of love but to a brother,
How will she love, when the rich golden shaft°
Hath killed the flock of all affections else°                           35
That live in her; when liver, brain, and heart,
These sovereign thrones, are all supplied, and filled
Her sweet perfections, with one self king!°
Away before me to sweet beds of flowers.
Love-thoughts lie rich when canopied with bowers.       40

*Exeunt.*

## 1.2

*Enter Viola, a Captain, and sailors.*

**VIOLA:**    What country, friends, is this?
**CAPTAIN:**    This is Illyria, lady.
**VIOLA:**    And what should I do in Illyria?
My brother he is in Elysium.°
Perchance he is not drowned. What think you, sailors?       5
**CAPTAIN:**    It is perchance that you yourself were saved.
**VIOLA:**    Oh, my poor brother! And so perchance may he be.
**CAPTAIN:**    True, madam, and to comfort you with chance,°
Assure yourself, after our ship did split,
When you and those poor number saved with you             10
Hung on our driving° boat, I saw your brother,
Most provident in peril, bind himself,
Courage and hope both teaching him the practice,
To a strong mast that lived° upon the sea;
Where, like Arion° on the dolphin's back,                           15

25 **element** sky.    **seven years' heat** seven summers    27 **cloistress** nun secluded in a religious
community    29 **season** keep fresh. (Playing on the idea of the salt in her tears.)    30 **A brother's
dead love** her love for her dead brother and the memory of his love for her    32 **frame** construction    34 **golden shaft** Cupid's golden-tipped arrow, causing love. (His lead-tipped arrow causes
aversion.)    35 **affections else** other feelings    36–8 **when ... king** i.e., when passion, thought, and
feeling all sit in majesty in their proper thrones (liver, brain, and heart), and her sweet perfections are
brought to completion by her union with a single lord and husband.
4 **Elysium** classical abode of the blessed dead.    6–7 **perchance ... perchance** Perhaps ... by mere
chance    8 **chance** i.e., what one may hope that chance will bring about    11 **driving** drifting, driven
by the seas    14 **lived** i.e., kept afloat    15 **Arion** a Greek poet who so charmed the dolphins with his
lyre that they saved him when he leaped into the sea to escape murderous sailors

I saw him hold acquaintance with the waves
So long as I could see.

**VIOLA:**   For saying so, there's gold. [*She gives money.*]
Mine own escape unfoldeth to my hope,
Whereto thy speech serves for authority,   20
The like of him.° Know'st thou this country?

**CAPTAIN:**   Ay, madam, well, for I was bred and born
Not three hours' travel from this very place.

**VIOLA:**   Who governs here?

**CAPTAIN:**   A noble duke, in nature as in name.   25

**VIOLA:**   What is his name?

**CAPTAIN:**   Orsino.

**VIOLA:**   Orsino! I have heard my father name him.
He was a bachelor then.

**CAPTAIN:**   And so is now, or was so very late;°   30
For but a month ago I went from hence,
And then 'twas fresh in murmur°—as, you know,
What great ones do the less° will prattle of—
That he did seek the love of fair Olivia.

**VIOLA:**   What's she?   35

**CAPTAIN:**   A virtuous maid, the daughter of a count
That died some twelvemonth since, then leaving her
In the protection of his son, her brother,
Who shortly also died; for whose dear love,
They say, she hath abjured the sight
And company of men.   40

**VIOLA:**   Oh, that I served that lady,
And might not be delivered° to the world
Till I had made mine own occasion mellow,°
What my estate° is!

**CAPTAIN:**   That were hard to compass,°
Because she will admit no kind of suit,   45
No, not° the Duke's.

**VIOLA:**   There is a fair behavior in thee, Captain,
And though that° nature with a beauteous wall
Doth oft close in pollution, yet of thee
I will believe thou hast a mind that suits   50
With this thy fair and outward character.°
I prithee, and I'll pay thee bounteously,
Conceal me what I am, and be my aid

---

**19-21 unfoldeth ... him** offers a hopeful example that he may have escaped similarly, to which hope
your speech provides support.   **30 late** lately.   **32 murmur** rumor   **33 less** social inferiors
**42 delivered** revealed, made known. (With suggestion of "born.")   **43 Till ... mellow** until the time
is ripe for my purpose   **44 estate** social rank.   **compass** encompass, bring about   **46 not** not even
**48 though that** though   **51 character** face or features as indicating moral qualities.

For such disguise as haply shall become
The form of my intent.° I'll serve this duke.                              55
Thou shalt present me as an eunuch° to him.
It may be worth thy pains, for I can sing
And speak to him in many sorts of music
That will allow° me very worth his service.
What else may hap, to time I will commit;                                  60
Only shape thou thy silence to my wit.°

**CAPTAIN:**    Be you his eunuch, and your mute° I'll be;
When my tongue blabs, then let mine eyes not see.

**VIOLA:**    I thank thee. Lead me on.                *Exeunt.*

## 1.3

*Enter Sir Toby [Belch] and Maria.*

**SIR TOBY:**    What a plague means my niece to take the death of
her brother thus? I am sure care's an enemy to life.

**MARIA:**    By my troth, Sir Toby, you must come in earlier o'nights.
Your cousin,° my lady, takes great exceptions to your ill hours.

**SIR TOBY:**    Why, let her except before excepted.°                      5

**MARIA:**    Ay, but you must confine yourself within the modest°
limits of order.

**SIR TOBY:**    Confine? I'll confine myself no finer° than I am.
These clothes are good enough to drink in, and so be these
boots too. An° they be not, let them hang them-selves in their
own straps.                                                               10

**MARIA:**    That quaffing and drinking will undo you. I heard my lady
talk of it yesterday, and of a foolish knight that you brought in
one night here to be her wooer.

**SIR TOBY:**    Who, Sir Andrew Aguecheek?

**MARIA:**    Ay, he.                                                      15

**SIR TOBY:**    He's as tall° a man as any's in Illyria.

**MARIA:**    What's that to th' purpose?

**SIR TOBY:**    Why, he has three thousand ducats° a year.

**MARIA:**    Ay, but he'll have but a year in all these ducats.° He's a
very fool and a prodigal.                                                 20

---

54–5 **as haply … intent** as may suit the nature of my purpose.    56 **eunuch** castrato, high-voiced
singer    59 **allow** prove    61 **wit** plan, invention.    62 **mute** silent attendant. (Sometimes used of
nonspeaking actors.)
4 **cousin** kinswoman    5 **let … excepted** i.e., let her take exception to my conduct all she wants;
I don't care. (Plays on the legal phrase *exceptis excipiendis,* "with the exceptions before named.")
6 **modest** moderate    8 **I'll … finer** (1) I'll constrain myself no more rigorously (2) I'll dress myself no more finely    10 **An** If    16 **tall** brave. (But Maria pretends to take the word in the common
sense.)    18 **ducats** coins worth about four or five shillings    19 **he'll … ducats** he'll spend all his
money within a year.

**SIR TOBY:** Fie, that you'll say so! He plays o'th' viol-de-gamboys,° and speaks three or four languages word for word without book,° and hath all the good gifts of nature.

**MARIA:** He hath indeed, almost natural,° for, besides that he's a fool, he's a great quarreler, and but that he hath the gift° of a coward to allay the gust° he hath in quarreling, 'tis thought among the prudent he would quickly have the gift of a grave.  25

**SIR TOBY:** By this hand, they are scoundrels and substractors° that say so of him. Who are they?

**MARIA:** They that add, moreover, he's drunk nightly in your company.  30

**SIR TOBY:** With drinking healths to my niece. I'll drink to her as long as there is a passage in my throat and drink in Illyria. He's a coward and a coistrel° that will not drink to my niece till his brains turn o'th' toe like a parish top.° What, wench? *Castiliano vulgo!*° For here comes Sir Andrew Agueface.°  35

[*Enter Sir Andrew [Aguecheek].*]

**SIR ANDREW:** Sir Toby Belch! How now, Sir Toby Belch?

**SIR TOBY:** Sweet Sir Andrew!

**SIR ANDREW:** [*to Maria*] Bless you, fair shrew.°

**MARIA:** And you too, sir.

**SIR TOBY:** Accost,° Sir Andrew, accost.  40

**SIR ANDREW:** What's that?

**SIR TOBY:** My niece's chambermaid.°

**SIR ANDREW:** Good Mistress Accost, I desire better acquaintance.

**MARIA:** My name is Mary, sir.

**SIR ANDREW:** Good Mistress Mary Accost—  45

**SIR TOBY:** You mistake, knight. "Accost" is front° her, board° her, woo her, assail her.

**SIR ANDREW:** By my troth, I would not undertake° her in this company. Is that the meaning of "accost"?  50

**MARIA:** Fare you well, gentlemen. [*Going.*]

**SIR TOBY:** An thou let part° so, Sir Andrew, would thou mightst never draw sword again.

---

**21 viol-de-gamboys** viola da gamba, leg-viol, bass viol  **22–3 without book** by heart  **24 natural** (With a play on the sense "born idiot.")  **25 gift** natural ability. (But shifted to mean "present" in line 33.)  **26 allay the gust** moderate the taste  **28 substractors** detractors  **33 coistrel** horse-groom, base fellow  **34 parish top** a large top provided by the parish to be spun by whipping, apparently for exercise.  **35 Castiliano vulgo!** (Of uncertain meaning. Possibly Sir Toby is saying "Speak of the devil!" Castiliano is the name adopted by a devil in Haughton's *Grim the Collier of Croydon*.)  **35 Agueface** (Like *Aguecheek,* this name betokens the thin, pale countenance of one suffering from an ague or fever.)  **38 shrew** i.e., diminutive creature. (But with probably unintended suggestion of shrewishness.)  **40 Accost** Go alongside (a nautical term), i.e., greet her, address her  **42 chambermaid** lady-in-waiting (a gentlewoman, not one who would do menial tasks).  **46 front** confront, come alongside.  **46 board** greet, approach (as though preparing to board in a naval encounter)  **48 undertake** have to do with. (Here with unintended sexual suggestion, to which Maria mirthfully replies with her jokes about *dry jests, barren,* and *buttery-bar.*)  **51 An ... part** If you let her leave

**SIR ANDREW:**   An you part so, mistress, I would I might never draw
sword again. Fair lady, do you think you have fools in hand?°    55
**MARIA:**   Sir, I have not you by the hand.
**SIR ANDREW:**   Marry,° but you shall have, and here's my hand.

*[He gives her his hand.]*

**MARIA:**   Now, sir, thought is free.° I pray you, bring your hand to
th' buttery-bar,° and let it drink.
**SIR ANDREW:**   Wherefore, sweetheart? What's your metaphor?    60
**MARIA:**   It's dry,° sir.
**SIR ANDREW:**   Why, I think so. I am not such an ass but I can keep
my hand dry.° But what's your jest?
**MARIA:**   A dry jest, sir.
**SIR ANDREW:**   Are you full of them?    65
**MARIA:**   Ay, sir, I have them at my fingers' ends.° Marry, now I let
go your hand, I am barren.°

*[She lets go his hand.] Exit Maria.*

**SIR TOBY:**   Oh, knight, thou lack'st a cup of canary!° When did I
see thee so put down?
**SIR ANDREW:**   Never in your life, I think, unless you see canary
put me down.° Methinks sometimes I have no more wit than a
Christian or an ordinary man has. But I am a great eater of beef,    70
and I believe that does harm to my wit.
**SIR TOBY:**   No question.
**SIR ANDREW:**   An I thought that, I'd forswear it. I'll ride home
tomorrow, Sir Toby.    75
**SIR TOBY:**   *Pourquoi,*° my dear knight?
**SIR ANDREW:**   What is "*pourquoi*"? Do or not do? I would I had
bestowed that time in the tongues° that I have in fencing,
dancing, and bearbaiting.° Oh, had I but followed the arts!°
**SIR TOBY:**   Then hadst thou had an excellent head of hair.    80
**SIR ANDREW:**   Why, would that have mended° my hair?

---

**54–5 have ... hand** i.e., have to deal with fools. (But Maria puns on the literal sense.)   **57 Marry**
i.e., Indeed. (Originally, "By the Virgin Mary.")   **58 thought is free** i.e., I may think what I like.
(Proverbial; replying to *do you think ... in hand,* above.)   **59 buttery-bar** ledge on top of the half-
door to the buttery or the wine cellar. (Maria's language is sexually suggestive, though Sir Andrew
seems oblivious to that.)   **61 dry** thirsty; also dried up, a sign of age and sexual debility   **63 dry** (1)
ironic (2) dull, barren. (Referring to Sir Andrew.)   **66 at my fingers' ends** (1) at the ready (2) by the
hand.   **66 barren** i.e., empty of jests and of Sir Andrew's hand.   **68 thou ... canary** i.e., you look as
if you need a drink. (*Canary* is a sweet wine from the Canary Islands.)   **71 put me down** (1) baffle my
wits (2) lay me out flat.   **76 *Pourquoi*** Why   **78 tongues** languages. (Sir Toby then puns on "tongs,"
curling irons.)   **79 bearbaiting** the sport of setting dogs on a chained bear.   **the arts** the liberal
arts, learning. (But Sir Toby plays on the phrase as meaning "artifice," the antithesis of *nature.*)
**81 mended** improved

**SIR TOBY:**   Past question, for thou see'st it will not curl by nature.

**SIR ANDREW:**   But it becomes me well enough, does't not?

**SIR TOBY:**   Excellent. It hangs like flax on a distaff;° and I hope to see a huswife take thee between her legs and spin it off.°   85

**SIR ANDREW:**   Faith, I'll home tomorrow, Sir Toby. Your niece will not be seen, or if she be, it's four to one she'll none of me. The Count° himself here hard° by woos her.

**SIR TOBY:**   She'll none o'th' Count. She'll not match above her degree,° neither in estate,° years, nor wit; I have heard her   90 swear't. Tut, there's life in't,° man.

**SIR ANDREW:**   I'll stay a month longer. I am a fellow o'th' strangest mind i'th' world; I delight in masques and revels sometimes altogether.

**SIR TOBY:**   Art thou good at these kickshawses,° knight?   95

**SIR ANDREW:**   As any man in Illyria, whatsoever he be, under the degree of my betters,° and yet I will not compare with an old man.°

**SIR TOBY:**   What is thy excellence in a galliard,° knight?

**SIR ANDREW:**   Faith, I can cut a caper.°

**SIR TOBY:**   And I can cut the mutton to't.   100

**SIR ANDREW:**   And I think I have the back-trick° simply as strong as any man in Illyria.

**SIR TOBY:**   Wherefore are these things hid? Wherefore have these gifts a curtain before 'em? Are they like to take dust, like Mistress Mall's picture?° Why dost thou not go to church in a   105 galliard° and come home in a coranto?° My very walk should be a jig; I would not so much as make water but in a sink-a-pace.° What dost thou mean? Is it a world to hide virtues° in? I did think, by the excellent constitution of thy leg, it was formed under the star of a galliard.°   110

**SIR ANDREW:**   Ay, 'tis strong, and it does indifferent well° in a dun-colored stock.° Shall we set about some revels?

**SIR TOBY:**   What shall we do else? Were we not born under Taurus?°

---

**84 distaff** a staff for holding the flax, tow, or wool in spinning   **85 spin it off** i.e., (1) treat your flaxen hair as though it were flax on a distaff to be spun (2) cause you to lose hair as a result of venereal disease (3) make you ejaculate. (*Huswife* suggests "hussy," "whore.")   **88 Count** i.e., Duke Orsino, sometimes referred to as Count.   **hard** near   **90 degree** social position.   **estate** fortune, social position   **91 there's life in't** i.e., while there's life there's hope   **95 kickshawses** delicacies, fancy trifles. (From the French, *quelque chose*.)   **96–7 under ... betters** excepting those who are above me   **97–8 old man** i.e., one experienced through age.   **98 galliard** lively dance in triple time   **99 cut a caper** make a lively leap. (But Sir Toby puns on the *caper* used to make a sauce served with mutton. *Mutton*, in turn, suggests "whore.")   **101 back-trick** backward step in the galliard. (With sexual innuendo; the back was associated with sexual vigor.)   **104 like to take** likely to collect   **105 Mistress Mall's picture** i.e., perhaps the portrait of some woman protected from light and dust, as many pictures were, by curtains. (*Mall* is a diminutive of *Mary*.)   **106 coranto** lively running dance.   **107–8 sink-a-pace** dance like the galliard. (French *cinquepace*. *Sink* also suggests a cesspool into which one might urinate.)   **108 virtues** talents   **110 under ... galliard** i.e., under a star favorable to dancing. **111 indifferent well** well enough. (Said complacently.)   **112 dun-colored stock** mouse-colored stocking.   **114 Taurus** zodiacal sign. (Sir Andrew is mistaken, since Leo governed sides and hearts in medical astrology. Taurus governed legs and thighs, or, more commonly, neck and throat.)

**SIR ANDREW:**  Taurus? That's sides and heart.                    115
**SIR TOBY:**  No, sir, it is legs and thighs. Let me see thee caper. [*Sir Andrew capers.*] Ha, higher! Ha, ha, excel-lent!                    *Exeunt.*

## 1.4

*Enter Valentine, and Viola in man's attire.*

**VALENTINE:**  If the Duke continue these favors towards you, Cesario, you are like° to be much advanced. He hath known you but three days, and already you are no stranger.
**VIOLA:**  You either fear his humor° or my negligence, that you call in question the continuance of his love. Is he inconstant, sir, in his favors?
**VALENTINE:**  No, believe me.                    5

*Enter Duke [Orsino], Curio, and attendants.*

**VIOLA:**  I thank you. Here comes the Count.
**ORSINO:**  Who saw Cesario, ho?
**VIOLA:**  On your attendance,° my lord, here.
**ORSINO:**  Stand you awhile aloof.° [*The others stand aside.*] Cesario,
Thou know'st no less but all. I have unclasped                    10
To thee the book even of my secret soul.
Therefore, good youth, address thy gait° unto her;
Be not denied access, stand at her doors,
And tell them,° there thy fixèd foot shall grow
Till thou have audience.
**VIOLA:**  Sure, my noble lord,                    15
If she be so abandoned to her sorrow
As it is spoke, she never will admit me.
**ORSINO:**  Be clamorous and leap all civil bounds°
Rather than make unprofited return.
**VIOLA:**  Say I do speak with her, my lord, what then?                    20
**ORSINO:**  Oh, then unfold the passion of my love;
Surprise° her with discourse of my dear° faith.
It shall become° thee well to act my woes;
She will attend it better in thy youth
Than in a nuncio's° of more grave aspect.                    25
**VIOLA:**  I think not so, my lord.
**ORSINO:**  Dear lad, believe it;
For they shall yet belie thy happy years

2 **like** likely  3 **humor** changeableness  8 **On your attendance** Ready to do you service  9 **aloof** aside.  12 **address thy gait** go  14 **them** i.e., Olivia's servants  18 **civil bounds** bounds of civility  22 **Surprise** Take by storm. (A military term.)  **dear** heartfelt  23 **become** suit  25 **nuncio's** messenger's

That say thou art a man. Diana's lip
Is not more smooth and rubious;° thy small pipe°          30
Is as the maiden's organ, shrill and sound,°
And all is semblative° a woman's part.
I know thy constellation° is right apt
For this affair.—Some four or five attend him.
All, if you will, for I myself am best          35
When least in company.—Prosper well in this,
And thou shalt live as freely as thy lord,
To call his fortunes thine.

**VIOLA:**   I'll do my best
To woo your lady. [*Aside*] Yet a barful strife!°          40
Whoe'er I woo, myself would be his wife.          *Exeunt.*

## 1.5

*Enter Maria and Clown [Feste].*

**MARIA:**   Nay, either tell me where thou hast been, or I will not
open my lips so wide as a bristle may enter in way of thy excuse.
My lady will hang thee for thy absence.

**FESTE:**   Let her hang me. He that is well hanged in this world needs
to fear no colors.°          5

**MARIA:**   Make that good.°

**FESTE:**   He shall see none to fear.°

**MARIA:**   A good Lenten° answer. I can tell thee where that saying
was born, of "I fear no colors."

**FESTE:**   Where, good Mistress Mary?

**MARIA:**   In the wars,° and that may you be bold to say in your
foolery.°          10

**FESTE:**   Well, God give them wisdom that have it; and those that
are fools, let them use their talents.°

**MARIA:**   Yet you will be hanged for being so long absent; or to be
turned away,° is not that as good as a hanging to you?

**FESTE:**   Many a good hanging° prevents a bad marriage; and for°
turning away, let summer bear it out.°          15

---

30 **rubious** ruby red.   **pipe** voice, throat   31 **shrill and sound** high and clear, uncracked   32 **semblative** resembling, like   33 **constellation** i.e., nature as determined by your horoscope   40 **barful strife** endeavor full of impediments.   5 **fear no colors** i.e., fear no foe, fear nothing. (With pun on *colors*, worldly deceptions, and "collars," halters or nooses.)   6 **Make that good** Explain that.   7 **He ... fear** i.e., The hanged man will be dead and unable to see anything.   8 **Lenten** meager, scanty (like Lenten fare), and morbid   9 **In the wars** (Where *colors* would mean "military standards, enemy flags"—the literal meaning of the proverb.)   9–10 **that ... foolery** that's an answer you may be bold to use in your fool's conundrums. (*Colors* here refer to military banners and insignia used to align rows of fighting men in battle.)   11 **talents** abilities. (Also alluding to the parable of the talents, Matthew 25:14–29, and to "talons," claws.)   13 **turned away** dismissed. (Possibly also meaning "turned off," "hanged.")   14 **good hanging** (With possible bawdy pun on "being well hung.")   14 **for** as for.   15 **let ... out** i.e., let mild weather make dismissal endurable.

**MARIA:**  You are resolute, then?

**FESTE:**  Not so, neither, but I am resolved on two points.°

**MARIA:**  That if one break, the other will hold; or if both break, your gaskins° fall.

**FESTE:**  Apt, in good faith, very apt. Well, go thy way. If Sir Toby would leave drinking, thou wert as witty a piece of Eve's flesh      20
as any in Illyria.°

**MARIA:**  Peace, you rogue, no more o' that. Here comes my lady. Make your excuse wisely, you were best.°      [*Exit.*]

*Enter Lady Olivia with Malvolio, [and attendants].*

**FESTE:**  [*aside*] Wit, an't° be thy will, put me into good fooling! Those wits that think they have thee do very oft prove fools, and I that am sure I lack thee may pass for a wise man. For      25
what says Quinapalus?° "Better a witty fool than a foolish wit."—God bless thee, lady!

**OLIVIA:**  [*to attendants*] Take the fool away.

**FESTE:**  Do you not hear, fellows? Take away the lady.

**OLIVIA:**  Go to,° you're a dry° fool. I'll no more of you. Besides, you grow dishonest.      30

**FESTE:**  Two faults, madonna,° that drink and good counsel will amend. For give the dry fool drink, then is the fool not dry. Bid the dishonest man mend himself; if he mend, he is no longer dishonest; if he cannot, let the botcher° mend him. Anything that's mended is but patched;° virtue that trans-      35
gresses is but patched with sin, and sin that amends is but patched with virtue. If that this simple syllogism will serve, so;° if it will not, what remedy? As there is no true cuckold but calamity, so beauty's a flower.° The lady bade take away the fool; therefore I say again, take her away.

**OLIVIA:**  Sir, I bade them take away you.      40

**FESTE:**  Misprision° in the highest degree! Lady, *cucullus non facit monachum;*° that's as much to say as I wear not motley° in my brain. Good madonna, give me leave to prove you a fool.

**OLIVIA:**  Can you do it?

**FESTE:**  Dexteriously, good madonna.

---

17 **points** (Maria plays on the meaning "laces used to hold up hose or breeches.")  18 **gaskins** wide breeches  20 **thou ... Illyria** (Feste may be hinting ironically that Maria would be a suitable mate for Sir Toby.)  22 **you were best** it would be best for you.  23 **an't** if it  26 **Quinapalus** (Feste's invented authority.)  29 **Go to** (An expression of annoyance or expostulation.)  **dry** dull  31 **madonna** my lady  34 **botcher** mender of old clothes and shoes. (Playing on two senses of *mend:* "reform" and "repair.")  34–5 **Anything ... patched** i.e., Life is patched or parti-colored like the Fool's garment, a mix of good and bad  37 **so** well and good  38–9 **As ... flower** (Nonsense, yet with a suggestion that Olivia has wedded calamity but should not be faithful to it, for the natural course is to seize the moment of youth and beauty before we lose it.)  41 **Misprision** Mistake, misunderstanding. (A legal term meaning a wrongful action or misdemeanor.)  41–2 *cucullus ... monachum* the cowl does not make the monk  42 **motley** the many-colored garment of jesters

**OLIVIA:**  Make your proof.                                                                    45

**FESTE:**  I must catechize you for it, madonna. Good my mouse of virtue,° answer me.

**OLIVIA:**  Well, sir, for want of other idleness,° I'll bide° your proof.

**FESTE:**  Good madonna, why mourn'st thou?

**OLIVIA:**  Good fool, for my brother's death.

**FESTE:**  I think his soul is in hell, madonna.                                                 50

**OLIVIA:**  I know his soul is in heaven, fool.

**FESTE:**  The more fool, madonna, to mourn for your brother's soul, being in heaven.—Take away the fool, gentlemen.

**OLIVIA:**  What think you of this fool, Malvolio? Doth he not mend?°

**MALVOLIO:**  Yes, and shall do till the pangs of death shake him.         55
Infirmity, that decays the wise, doth ever make the better fool.

**FESTE:**  God send you, sir, a speedy infirmity for the better increasing your folly! Sir Toby will be sworn that I am no fox, but he will not pass° his word for two pence that you are no fool.

**OLIVIA:**  How say you to that, Malvolio?                                                       60

**MALVOLIO:**  I marvel Your Ladyship takes delight in such a barren rascal. I saw him put down the other day with° an ordinary fool that has no more brain than a stone. Look you now, he's out of his guard° already. Unless you laugh and minister occasion° to him, he is gagged. I protest° I take these wise men      65
that crow° so at these set° kind of fools no better than the fools' zanies.°

**OLIVIA:**  Oh, you are sick of self-love, Malvolio, and taste with a distempered° appetite. To be generous,° guiltless, and of free° disposition is to take those things for bird-bolts° that you          70
deem cannon bullets. There is no slander in an allowed° fool, though he do nothing but rail; nor no railing in a known discreet man, though he do nothing but reprove.°

**FESTE:**  Now Mercury endue thee with leasing,° for thou speak'st well of fools!

*Enter Maria.*

**MARIA:**  Madam, there is at the gate a young gentleman much desires to speak with you.

---

**46–47 Good ... virtue** My good, virtuous mouse. (A term of endearment.)   **48 idleness** pastime.   **bide** endure   **54 mend** i.e., improve, grow more amusing. (But Malvolio uses the word to mean "grow more like a fool.")   **59 pass** give   **62 with** by   **64 out of his guard** defenseless, unprovided with a witty answer   **64–65 minister occasion** provide opportunity (for his fooling)   **65 protest** avow, declare.   **67 crow** laugh stridently   **set** artificial, stereotyped.   **zanies** assistants, aping attendants.   **68 distempered** diseased.   **generous** noble-minded.   **free** magnanimous   **69 bird-bolts** blunt arrows for shooting small birds   **70 allowed** licensed (to speak freely)

**70–72 There ... reprove** Both a licensed fool and a man known for discretion can criticize freely without being accused of slander in the first instance or railing in the second. (In rebuking Malvolio here, Olivia implies that he is not behaving like a "known discreet man.")   **73 Now ... leasing** i.e., May Mercury, the god of deception, make you a skillful liar

**OLIVIA:**  From the Count Orsino, is it?                                         75

**MARIA:**  I know not, madam. 'Tis a fair young man, and well attended.

**OLIVIA:**  Who of my people hold him in delay?

**MARIA:**  Sir Toby, madam,° your kinsman.

**OLIVIA:**  Fetch him off, I pray you. He speaks nothing but madman.°
Fie on him!   [*Exit Maria.*]
Go you, Malvolio. If it be a suit from the Count, I am            80
sick or not at home; what you will, to dismiss it.

> *Exit Malvolio.* Now you see, sir, how your fooling grows
> old,° and people dislike it.

**FESTE:**  Thou hast spoke for us, madonna, as if thy eldest son
should be a fool; whose skull Jove cram with brains, for—here
he comes—

> *Enter Sir Toby.*

one of thy kin has a most weak *pia mater.*°

**OLIVIA:**  By mine honor, half drunk.—What is he at the gate, cousin?°

**SIR TOBY:**  A gentleman.                                                        85

**OLIVIA:**  A gentleman? What gentleman?

**SIR TOBY:**  'Tis a gentleman here—[*He belches.*] A plague o' these
pickle-herring! [*To Feste*] How now, sot?°

**FESTE:**  Good Sir Toby.

**OLIVIA:**  Cousin,° cousin, how have you come so early by this
lethargy?

**SIR TOBY:**  Lechery? I defy lechery. There's one at the gate.          90

**OLIVIA:**  Ay, marry, what is he?

**SIR TOBY:**  Let him be the devil an he will, I care not. Give me
faith,° say I. Well, it's all one.°   *Exit.*

**OLIVIA:**  What's a drunken man like, Fool?                              95

**FESTE:**  Like a drowned man, a fool, and a madman. One draft
above heat° makes him a fool, the second mads him, and a third
drowns him.

**OLIVIA:**  Go thou and seek the crowner,° and let him sit o' my
coz;° for he's in the third degree of drink, he's drowned. Go,
look after him.                                                            100

**FESTE:**  He is but mad yet, madonna; and the fool shall look to the
madman.   [*Exit.*]

> *Enter Malvolio.*

**MALVOLIO**  Madam, yond young fellow swears he will speak with
you. I told him you were sick; he takes on him to understand

**78 Madam   79 madman** i.e., the words of madness.   **81 old** stale   **83 pia mater** i.e., brain.
(Actually the soft membrane enclosing the brain.)   **87 sot** (1) fool (2) drunkard.   **89 Cousin** Kinsman.
(Here, uncle.)   **92–93 Give me faith** i.e., to resist the devil.   **93 it's all one** it doesn't matter.   **96–
97 draft above heat** helping of drink raising his temperature above normal bodily warmth.   **98
crowner** coroner   **98–99 sit o' my coz** hold an inquest on my kinsman (Sir Toby)

so much, and therefore comes to speak with you. I told him you
were asleep; he seems to have a foreknowledge of that too, and    105
therefore comes to speak with you. What is to be said to him,
lady? He's fortified against any denial.

**OLIVIA:**  Tell him he shall not speak with me.

**MALVOLIO:**  He's been told so; and he says he'll stand at your door
like a sheriff's post,° and be the supporter° to a bench, but he'll
speak with you.

**OLIVIA:**  What kind o' man is he?    110

**MALVOLIO:**  Why, of mankind.

**OLIVIA:**  What manner of man?

**MALVOLIO:**  Of very ill manner. He'll speak with you, will you or no.

**OLIVIA:**  Of what personage and years is he?

**MALVOLIO:**  Not yet old enough for a man, nor young enough for
a boy; as a squash° is before 'tis a peascod,° or a codling° when
'tis almost an apple. 'Tis with him in standing water° between
boy and man. He is very well-favored,° and he speaks very
shrewishly.° One would think his mother's milk were scarce out
of him.

**OLIVIA:**  Let him approach. Call in my gentlewoman.    120

**MALVOLIO:**  Gentlewoman, my lady calls.    *Exit.*

    *Enter Maria.*

**OLIVIA:**  Give me my veil. Come, throw it o'er my face.
We'll once more hear Orsino's embassy.    [*Olivia veils.*]

    *Enter Viola.*

**VIOLA:**  The honorable lady of the house, which is she?

**OLIVIA:**  Speak to me; I shall answer for her. Your will?

**VIOLA:**  Most radiant, exquisite, and unmatchable beauty—I pray    125
you, tell me if this be the lady of the house, for I never saw her.
I would be loath to castaway my speech; for besides that it is
excellently well penned, I have taken great pains to con° it.
Good beauties, let me sustain no scorn; I am very comptible,°
even to the least sinister° usage.

**OLIVIA:**  Whence came you, sir?    130

**VIOLA:**  I can say little more than I have studied, and that question's out of my part. Good gentle one, give me modest° assurance if you be the lady of the house, that I may proceed in my speech.

**OLIVIA:**  Are you a comedian?°

**108 sheriff's post** post before the sheriff's door to mark a residence of authority, often elaborately
carved and decorated.  **supporter** prop  **116 squash** unripe pea pod.  **peascod** ripe pea pod. (The
image suggests that the boy's testicles have not yet dropped.)  **codling** unripe apple  **117 in standing water** at the turn of the tide  **118 well-favored** good-looking.  **119 shrewishly** sharply.
**127 con** memorize  **128 comptible** susceptible, sensitive  **129 least sinister** slightest discourteous
**132 modest** reasonable  **134 comedian** actor.

**VIOLA:** No, my profound heart;° and yet, by the very fangs of     135
malice, I swear I am not that I play.° Are you the lady of the
house?

**OLIVIA:** If I do not usurp myself,° I am.

**VIOLA:** Most certain, if you are she, you do usurp your-self;° for
what is yours to bestow is not yours to reserve. But this is from°
my commission. I will on with my speech in your praise, and
then show you the heart of my message.

**OLIVIA:** Come to what is important in't. I forgive you° the praise.     140

**VIOLA:** Alas, I took great pains to study it, and 'tis poetical.

**OLIVIA:** It is the more like to be feigned. I pray you, keep it in.
I heard you were saucy at my gates, and allowed your approach
rather to wonder at you than to hear you. If you be not mad,°
begone; if you have reason,° be brief. 'Tis not that time of
moon° with me to make one° in so skipping a dialogue.

**MARIA:** Will you hoist sail, sir? Here lies your way.     145

**VIOLA:** No, good swabber,° I am to hull° here a little longer.—
Some mollification for° your giant,° sweet lady. Tell me your
mind; I am a messenger.

**OLIVIA:** Sure you have some hideous matter to deliver, when the
courtesy° of it is so fearful. Speak your office.°

**VIOLA:** It alone concerns your ear. I bring no overture° of war, no     150
taxation of homage.° I hold the olive° in my hand; my words are
as full of peace as matter.

**OLIVIA:** Yet you began rudely.° What are you? What would you?

**VIOLA:** The rudeness that hath appeared in me have I learned
from my entertainment.° What I am and what I would are as
secret as maidenhead°—to your ears, divinity;° to any other's,     155
profanation.

**OLIVIA:** [*to the others*] Give us the place here alone. We will hear
this divinity. [*Exeunt Maria and attendants.*]
Now, sir, what is your text?

**VIOLA:** Most sweet lady—

**OLIVIA:** A comfortable° doctrine, and much may be said of it.
Where lies your text?     160

135 **my profound heart** my most wise lady; or, in all sincerity   135–6 **by ... I play** (Viola hints
at her true identity, which malice itself might not detect.)   137 **do ... myself** am not an impostor   138 **usurp yourself** i.e., misappropriate yourself, by withholding yourself from love and marriage   139 **from** outside of   140 **forgive you** excuse you from repeating   143 **not mad** i.e., not
altogether mad   144 **reason** sanity. **moon** (The moon was thought to affect lunatics according to its
changing phases.) **make one** take part.   146 **swabber** one in charge of washing the decks. (A nautical retort to *hoist sail.*) **hull** lie with sails furled   147 **Some ... for** i.e., Please mollify, pacify.
**giant** i.e., the diminutive Maria who, like many giants in medieval romances, is guarding the lady
149 **courtesy** i.e., complimentary, "poetical" introduction. (Or Olivia may refer to Cesario's importunate
manner at her gate, as reported by Malvolio.) **office** commission, business.   150 **overture** declaration.
(Literally, opening.)   151 **taxation of homage** demand for tribute. **olive** olive-branch (signifying
peace)   153 **Yet ... rudely** i.e., Yet you were saucy at my gates.   154 **entertainment** reception.
155 **maidenhead** virginity   155 **divinity** sacred discourse   159 **comfortable** comforting

**VIOLA:** In Orsino's bosom.

**OLIVIA:** In his bosom? In what chapter of his bosom?

**VIOLA:** To answer by the method,° in the first of his heart.

**OLIVIA:** Oh, I have read it. It is heresy. Have you no more to say?

**VIOLA:** Good madam, let me see your face. 165

**OLIVIA:** Have you any commission from your lord to negotiate with my face? You are now out of° your text. But we will draw the curtain and show you the picture. [*Unveiling.*] Look you, sir, such a one I was this present.° Is't not well done?

**VIOLA:** Excellently done, if God did all. 170

**OLIVIA:** 'Tis in grain,° sir; 'twill endure wind and weather.

**VIOLA:** 'Tis beauty truly blent,° whose red and white
Nature's own sweet and cunning° hand laid on.
Lady, you are the cruel'st she alive
If you will lead these graces to the grave 175
And leave the world no copy.°

**OLIVIA:** Oh, sir, I will not be so hard hearted. I will give out divers schedules° of my beauty. It shall be inventoried, and every particle and utensil° labeled° to my will: as, item, two lips, indifferent° red; item, two gray eyes, with lids to them; 180 item, one neck, one chin, and so forth. Were you sent hither to praise° me?

**VIOLA:** I see you what you are: you are too proud.
But, if° you were the devil, you are fair.
My lord and master loves you. Oh, such love
Could be but recompensed, though you were crowned 185
The nonpareil of beauty!°

**OLIVIA:** How does he love me?

**VIOLA:** With adorations, fertile° tears,
With groans that thunder love, with sighs of fire.

**OLIVIA:** Your lord does know my mind; I cannot love him. 190
Yet I suppose him virtuous, know him noble,
Of great estate, of fresh and stainless youth,
In voices well divulged,° free,° learned, and valiant,
And in dimension and the shape of nature°
A gracious° person. But yet I cannot love him. 195
He might have took his answer long ago.

---

163 **To ... method** i.e., To continue the metaphor of delivering a sermon, begun with *divinity* and *what is your text* and continued in *doctrine, heresy,* etc.   167 **out of** straying from   169 **such ... present** this is a recent portrait of me. (Since it was customary to hang curtains in front of pictures, Olivia in unveiling speaks as if she were displaying a picture of herself.)   171 **in grain** fast dyed   172 **blent** blended   173 **cunning** skillful   176 **copy** i.e., a child. (But Olivia uses the word to mean "transcript.")   178 **schedules** inventories   179 **utensil** article, item.   **labeled** added as a codicil   180 **indifferent** somewhat   181 **praise** (With pun on "appraise.")   183 **if** even if   184–6 **Oh ... beauty!** i.e., Even if you were the most beautiful woman alive, that beauty could do no more than repay my master's love for you!   188 **fertile** copious   193 **In ... divulged** well spoken of.   **free** generous   194 **in ... nature** in his physical form   195 **gracious** graceful, attractive

**VIOLA:**   If I did love you in my master's flame,°
With such a suff'ring, such a deadly° life,
In your denial I would find no sense;
I would not understand it.                                                 200
**OLIVIA:**   Why, what would you?
**VIOLA:**   Make me a willow cabin° at your gate
And call upon my soul° within the house;
Write loyal cantons° of contemnèd° love
And sing them loud even in the dead of night;                             205
Hallow° your name to the reverberate hills,
And make the babbling gossip of the air°
Cry out "Olivia!" Oh, you should not rest
Between the elements of air° and earth
But you should pity me!                                                    210
**OLIVIA:**   You might do much.
What is your parentage?
**VIOLA:**   Above my fortunes, yet my state° is well:
I am a gentleman.
**OLIVIA:**   Get you to your lord.                                        215
I cannot love him. Let him send no more—
Unless, perchance, you come to me again
To tell me how he takes it. Fare you well.
I thank you for your pains. Spend this for me.

*[She offers a purse.]*

**VIOLA:**   I am no fee'd post,° lady. Keep your purse.                   220
My master, not myself, lacks recompense.
Love make his heart of flint that you shall love,°
And let your fervor, like my master's, be
Placed in contempt! Farewell, fair cruelty.   *Exit.*
**OLIVIA:**   "What is your parentage?"                                    225
"Above my fortunes, yet my state is well:
I am a gentleman." I'll be sworn thou art!
Thy tongue, thy face, thy limbs, actions, and spirit
Do give thee fivefold blazon.° Not too fast! Soft,° soft!
Unless the master were the man.° How now?                                 230
Even so quickly may one catch the plague?
Methinks I feel this youth's perfections
With an invisible and subtle stealth

---

197 **flame** passion   198 **deadly** deathlike   202 **willow cabin** shelter, hut. (Willow was a symbol of
unrequited love.)   203 **my soul** i.e., Olivia   204 **cantons** songs.   **contemnèd** rejected   206 **Hallow**
(1) halloo (2) bless   207 **babbling ... air** echo   209 **Between ... air** i.e., anywhere   213 **state** social
standing   220 **fee'd post** messenger to be tipped   223 **Love ... love** May Cupid make the heart of the
man you love as hard as flint   229 **blazon** heraldic description.   **Soft** Wait a minute   230 **Unless ...**
**man** i.e., Unless Cesario and Orsino changed places.

To creep in at mine eyes. Well, let it be.—
What ho, Malvolio! 235

*Enter Malvolio.*

**MALVOLIO:**  Here, madam, at your service.
**OLIVIA:**  Run after that same peevish messenger,
The County's° man. He left this ring behind him,

*[giving a ring]*

Would I or not.° Tell him I'll none of it. 240
Desire him not to flatter with° his lord,
Nor hold him up with hopes; I am not for him.
If that the youth will come this way tomorrow,
I'll give him reasons for't. Hie thee,° Malvolio.
**MALVOLIO:**  Madam, I will. *Exit.*
**OLIVIA:**  I do I know not what, and fear to find 245
Mine eye too great a flatterer for my mind.°
Fate, show thy force. Ourselves we do not owe.°
What is decreed must be; and be this so.   *[Exit.]*

## 2.1

*Enter Antonio and Sebastian.*

**ANTONIO:**  Will you stay no longer? Nor will you not° that I go
with you?
**SEBASTIAN:**  By your patience,° no. My stars shine darkly over me.
The malignancy° of my fate might perhaps distemper° yours;
therefore I shall crave of you your leave that I may bear my evils
alone. It were a bad recompense for your love to lay any of them
on you. 5
**ANTONIO:**  Let me yet know of you whither you are bound.
**SEBASTIAN:**  No, sooth,° sir; my determinate° voyage is mere extravagancy.° But I perceive in you so excellent a touch of modesty that you will not extort from me what I am willing° to
keep in; therefore it charges me in manners° the rather to 10
express° myself. You must know of me then, Antonio, my
name is Sebastian, which I called Roderigo. My father was that
Sebastian of Messaline° whom I know you have heard of. He

---

239 **County's** Count's, i.e., Duke's   240 **Would I or not** whether I wanted it or not.   241 **flatter
with** encourage   243 **Hie thee** Hasten   246 **Mine ... mind** i.e., that my eyes (through which love
enters the soul) have deceived my reason.   247 **owe** own, control.
1 **Nor will you not** Do you not wish   2 **patience** leave   3 **malignancy** malevolence (of the stars; also
in a medical sense)   **distemper** infect   7 **sooth** truly.   **determinate** intended, determined upon
8 **extravagancy** aimless wandering.   9 **am willing ... in** wish to keep secret   10 **it ... manners** it is
incumbent upon me in all courtesy   11 **express** reveal   13 **Messaline** possibly Messina, or, more likely,
Massila (the modern Marseilles). In Plautus's *Menaechmi*, Massilians and Illyrians are mentioned together.

left behind him myself and a sister, both born in an hour.° If
the heavens had been pleased, would we had so ended! But you,      15
sir, altered that, for some hour° before you took me from the
breach of the sea° was my sister drowned.

**ANTONIO:** Alas the day!

**SEBASTIAN:** A lady, sir, though it was said she much resembled
me, was yet of many accounted beautiful. But though I could      20
not with such estimable wonder° over-far believe that, yet
thus far I will boldly publish° her: she bore a mind that envy°
could not but call fair. She is drowned already, sir, with salt
water, though I seem to drown her remembrance again with
more.

**ANTONIO:** Pardon me, sir, your bad entertainment.°      25

**SEBASTIAN:** O good Antonio, forgive me your trouble.°

**ANTONIO:** If you will not murder° me for my love, let me be your
servant.

**SEBASTIAN:** If you will not undo what you have done, that is, kill
him whom you have recovered,° desire it not. Fare ye well at
once. My bosom is full of kindness,° and I am yet so near the      30
manners of my mother° that upon the least occasion more mine
eyes will tell tales of me. I am bound to the Count Orsino's court.
Farewell. *Exit.*

**ANTONIO:** The gentleness of all the gods go with thee!
I have many enemies in Orsino's court,      35
Else would I very shortly see thee there.
But come what may, I do adore thee so
That danger shall seem sport, and I will go.   *Exit.*

## 2.2

*Enter Viola and Malvolio, at several° doors.*

**MALVOLIO:** Were not you ev'n now with the Countess Olivia?

**VIOLA:** Even now, sir. On a moderate pace I have since arrived but hither.

**MALVOLIO:** She returns this ring to you, sir. You might have
saved me my pains, to have taken° it away yourself. She adds,
moreover, that you should put your lord into a desperate° as-      5
surance she will none of him. And one thing more: that you
be never so hardy to come° again in his affairs, unless it be to
report your lord's taking of this. Receive it so.

14 **in an hour** in the same hour.   16 **some hour** about an hour   17 **breach of the sea** surf
21 **estimable wonder** admiring judgment   22 **publish** proclaim   22 **envy** even malice   25 **Pardon ...
entertainment** i.e., I'm sorry I cannot offer you better hospitality and comfort.   26 **your trouble** the
trouble I put you to.   27 **murder ... love** i.e., cause me to die from lacking your love   29 **recovered**
rescued, restored   30 **kindness** emotion, affection   31 **manners of my mother** i.e., womanly inclination to weep   0.1 *several* different   4 **to have taken** by taking   5 **desperate** without hope
7 **so hardy to come** so bold as to come

**VIOLA:**    She took the ring of me. I'll none of it.°

**MALVOLIO:**    Come, sir, you peevishly threw it to her, and her will is it
should be so returned. [*He throws down the ring.*] If it be worth
stooping for, there it lies, in your eye;° if not, be it his that finds it.
*Exit.*

**VIOLA:**    [*picking up the ring*]
I left no ring with her. What means this lady?
Fortune forbid my outside have not charmed° her!                    15
She made good view of me, indeed so much
That sure methought her eyes had lost her tongue,°
For she did speak in starts, distractedly.
She loves me, sure! The cunning of her passion
Invites me in° this churlish messenger.                              20
None of my lord's ring? Why, he sent her none.
I am the man.° If it be so—as 'tis—
Poor lady, she were better love a dream.
Disguise, I see, thou art a wickedness
Wherein the pregnant enemy° does much.                              25
How easy is it for the proper false°
In women's waxen° hearts to set their forms!°
Alas, our frailty is the cause, not we,
For such as we are made of, such we be.°
How will this fadge?° My master loves her dearly,                   30
And I, poor monster,° fond° as much on him;
And she, mistaken, seems to dote on me.
What will become of this? As I am man,
My state is desperate for my master's love;
As I am woman—now, alas the day!—                                   35
What thriftless° sighs shall poor Olivia breathe!
O Time, thou must untangle this, not I;
It is too hard a knot for me t'untie.    [*Exit.*]

## 2.3

*Enter Sir Toby and Sir Andrew.*

**SIR TOBY:**    Approach, Sir Andrew. Not to be abed after midnight is
to be up betimes;° and *diluculo surgere,*° thou know'st—

---

**9 She ... it** (Viola tells a quick and friendly lie to shield Olivia.)    **12 in your eye** in plain sight    **15
charmed** enchanted    **17 her eyes ... tongue** i.e., the sight of me had deprived her of speech    **20 in**
in the person of    **22 the man** the man of her choice.    **25 the pregnant enemy** the resourceful enemy
(either Satan or Cupid)    **26 the proper false** deceptively handsome men    **27 waxen** i.e., malleable,
impressionable.    **set their forms** stamp their images (as of a seal).    **28–9 our ... be** i.e., the fault
lies not in us as individuals, but in the frailty of female nature    **30 fadge** turn out    **31 monster** i.e.,
being both man and woman.    **fond** dote    **36 thriftless** unprofitable
**2 betimes** early.    *diluculo surgere* (*saluberrimum est*) to rise early is most healthful. (A sentence
from Lilly's *Latin Grammar.*)

**SIR ANDREW:** Nay, by my troth, I know not, but I know to be up late is to be up late.

**SIR TOBY:** A false conclusion. I hate it as an unfilled can.° To be 5
up after midnight and to go to bed then, is early; so that to go
to bed after midnight is to go to bed betimes. Does not our lives
consist of the four elements?°

**SIR ANDREW:** Faith, so they say, but I think it rather consists of
eating and drinking. 10

**SIR TOBY:** Thou'rt a scholar; let us therefore eat and drink.—
Marian, I say, a stoup° of wine!

*Enter Clown [Feste].*

**SIR ANDREW:** Here comes the Fool, i'faith.

**FESTE:** How now, my hearts! Did you never see the picture of
"we three"°?

**SIR TOBY:** Welcome, ass. Now let's have a catch.° 15

**SIR ANDREW:** By my troth, the Fool has an excellent breast.° I
had rather than forty shillings I had such a leg,° and so sweet
a breath to sing, as the Fool has. In sooth, thou wast in very
gracious fooling last night, when thou spok'st of Pigrogromitus,
of the Vapians passing the equinoctial of Queubus.° 'Twas very 20
good, i'faith. I sent thee sixpence for thy leman.° Hadst it?

**FESTE:** I did impeticos thy gratillity;° for Malvolio's nose is no
whipstock.° My lady has a white hand,° and the Myrmidons°
are no bottle-ale houses.°

**SIR ANDREW:** Excellent! Why, this is the best fooling, when all is
done. Now, a song. 25

**SIR TOBY:** Come on, there is sixpence for you. [*He gives money.*]
Let's have a song.

**SIR ANDREW:** There's a testril° of me too. [*He gives money.*] If one
knight give a—

**FESTE:** Would you have a love song, or a song of good life?

**SIR TOBY:** A love song, a love song. 30

**SIR ANDREW:** Ay, ay, I care not for good life.°

**FESTE:** (*sings*)

---

5 **can** tankard   8 **four elements** i.e., fire, air, water, and earth, the elements that were thought to
make up all matter.   12 **stoup** drinking vessel   13–4 **picture of "we three"** picture of two fools or
asses inscribed "we three," the spectator being the third   15 **catch** round.   16 **breast** voice.
17 **leg** (for dancing)   19–20 **Pigrogromitus … Queubus** (Feste's mock erudition.)   21 **leman** sweetheart.   22 **impeticos thy gratillity** (Suggests "impetticoat, or pocket up, thy gratuity.")   22–3 **is no
whipstock** is no whip-handle. (More nonsense, but perhaps suggesting that Malvolio's nose for smelling
out faults does not give him the right to punish, so that he need not be feared.)   23 **has a white hand**
i.e., is lady-like. (But Feste's speech may be mere nonsense.)   **Myrmidons** followers of Achilles.
23–4 **bottle-ale houses** (Used contemptuously of taverns because they sold low-class drink.)   27 **testril**
tester, a coin worth sixpence   31 **good life** virtuous living. (Or perhaps Feste means simply "life's
pleasures," but is misunderstood by Sir Andrew to mean "virtuous living.")

O mistress mine, where are you roaming?
Oh, stay and hear, your true love 's coming,
That can sing both high and low.　　　　　　　　　　　35
Trip no further, pretty sweeting;
Journeys end in lovers' meeting,
Every wise man's son doth know.

**SIR ANDREW:**　Excellent good, i'faith.

**SIR TOBY:**　Good, good.　　　　　　　　　　　　　　40

**FESTE:**　[*sings*]

What is love? 'Tis not hereafter;
Present mirth hath present laughter;
What's to come is still° unsure.
In delay there lies no plenty.
Then come kiss me, sweet and twenty;°　　　　　45
Youth's a stuff will not endure.

**SIR ANDREW:**　A mellifluous voice, as I am true knight.

**SIR TOBY:**　A contagious° breath.

**SIR ANDREW:**　Very sweet and contagious, i'faith.　　50

**SIR TOBY:**　To hear by the nose, it is dulcet in contagion.° But shall
we make the welkin dance° indeed? Shall we rouse the night
owl in a catch that will draw three souls° out of one weaver?°
Shall we do that?

**SIR ANDREW:**　An you love me, let's do't. I am dog at° a catch.°　　55

**FESTE:**　By'r Lady,° sir, and some dogs will catch well.

**SIR ANDREW:**　Most certain. Let our catch be "Thou knave."°

**FESTE:**　"Hold thy peace, thou knave," knight? I shall be constrained
in't to call thee knave, knight.°

**SIR ANDREW:**　'Tis not the first time I have constrained one to　　60
call me knave. Begin, Fool. It begins, "Hold thy peace."

**FESTE:**　I shall never begin if I hold my peace.

**SIR ANDREW:**　Good, i'faith. Come, begin.　*Catch sung.*

　　　　*Enter Maria.*

**MARIA:**　What a caterwauling do you keep° here! If my lady have
not called up her steward Malvolio and bid him turn you out of
doors, never trust me.　　　　　　　　　　　　　65

---

**43 still** always　**45 sweet and twenty** i.e., sweet and twenty times sweet, or twenty years old
**49 contagious** infectiously delightful　**51 To ... contagion** i.e., If we were to describe hearing in
olfactory terms, we could say it is sweet in stench.　**52 make ... dance** i.e., drink till the sky seems
to turn around　**53 draw three souls** (Refers to the threefold nature of the soul—vegetal, sensible,
and intellectual—or to the three singers of the three-part catch; or, just a comic exaggeration.)
**54 weaver** (Weavers were often associated with psalm singing.)　**55 dog at** very clever at. (But Feste
uses the word literally.)　**catch** round. (But Feste uses it to mean "seize.")　**56 By 'r Lady** (An oath,
originally, "by the Virgin Mary.")　**57 "Thou knave"** (This popular round is arranged so that the three
singers repeatedly accost one another with "Thou knave.")　**58–9 "Hold ... knight** ("Knight and
knave" is a common antithesis, like "rich and poor.")　**63 keep** keep up

**SIR TOBY:**  My lady's a Cataian,° we are politicians,° Malvolio's a Peg-o'-Ramsey,° and [*he sings*] "Three merry men be we."° Am not I consanguineous?° Am I not of her blood? Tillyvally!° Lady!° [*He sings.*] "There dwelt a man in Babylon, lady, lady."°

**FESTE:**  Beshrew° me, the knight's in admirable fooling.     70

**SIR ANDREW:**  Ay, he does well enough if he be disposed, and so do I too. He does it with a better grace, but I do it more natural.°

**SIR TOBY:**  [*sings*]
   "O' the twelfth day of December"°—

**MARIA:**  For the love o' God, peace!

*Enter Malvolio.*

**MALVOLIO:**  My masters, are you mad? Or what are you? Have     75
you no wit,° manners, nor honesty° but to gabble like tinkers at this time of night? Do ye make an ale-house of my lady's house, that ye squeak out your coziers'° catches without any mitigation or remorse° of voice? Is there no respect of place, persons, nor time in you?

**SIR TOBY:**  We did keep time, sir, in our catches. Sneck up!°     80

**MALVOLIO:**  Sir Toby, I must be round° with you. My lady bade me tell you that though she harbors you as her kinsman, she's nothing allied to your disorders. If you can separate yourself and your misdemeanors, you are welcome to the house; if not, an it would please you to take leave of her, she is very willing to bid you farewell.     85

**SIR TOBY:**  [*sings*]
   "Farewell, dear heart, since I must needs be gone."°

**MARIA:**  Nay, good Sir Toby.

**FESTE:**  [*sings*]
   "His eyes do show his days are almost done."

**MALVOLIO:**  Is't even so?

**SIR TOBY:**  [*sings*]
   "But I will never die."     90

**FESTE:**  "Sir Toby, there you lie."

**MALVOLIO:**  This is much credit to you.

**SIR TOBY:**  [*sings*]
   "Shall I bid him go?"

---

66 **Cataian** Cathayan, i.e., Chinese, a trickster or inscrutable; or, just nonsense. **politicians** schemers, intriguers   67 **Peg-o'-Ramsey** character in a popular song. (Used here contemptuously.)   **"Three ... we"** (A snatch of an old song.)   68 **consanguineous** i.e., a blood relative of Olivia.   **Tillyvally!** Nonsense, fiddle-faddle!   69 **"There ... lady"** (The first line of a ballad, "The Constancy of Susanna," together with the refrain, "Lady, lady.")   70 **Beshrew** i.e., The devil take. (A mild curse.)   73 **natural** naturally. (But unconsciously suggesting idiocy.)   74 **"O' ... December"** (Possibly part of a ballad about the Battle of Musselburgh Field, or Toby's error for the "twelfth day of Christmas," i.e., Twelfth Night.)   76 **wit** common sense.   **honesty** decency   78 **coziers'** cobblers'   79 **mitigation or remorse** i.e., considerate lowering   80 **Sneck up!** Go hang!   81 **round** blunt   86 **"Farewell ... gone"** (From the ballad "*Cory*don's Farewell to Phyllis.")

**FESTE:** [*sings*]
  "What an if you do?"
**SIR TOBY:** [*sings*]
  "Shall I bid him go, and spare not?"                                              95
**FESTE:** [*sings*]
  "Oh, no, no, no, no, you dare not."
**SIR TOBY:** Out o' tune,° sir? Ye lie. Art any more than a steward?
  Dost thou think, because thou art virtuous, there shall be no
  more cakes and ale?
**FESTE:** Yes, by Saint Anne,° and ginger° shall be hot i'th' mouth,
  too.                                                                               100
**SIR TOBY:** Thou'rt i'the right.—Go, sir, rub your chain with
  crumbs.°—A stoup of wine, Maria!
**MALVOLIO:** Mistress Mary, if you prized my lady's favor at any-
  thing more than contempt, you would not give means° for this
  uncivil rule.° She shall know of it, by this hand.     *Exit.*
**MARIA:** Go shake your ears.°                                                     105
**SIR ANDREW:** 'Twere as good a deed as to drink when a man's
  a-hungry to challenge him the field° and then to break promise
  with him and make a fool of him.
**SIR TOBY:** Do't, knight. I'll write thee a challenge, or I'll deliver thy
  indignation to him by word of mouth.
**MARIA:** Sweet Sir Toby, be patient for tonight. Since the youth of     110
  the Count's was today with my lady, she is much out of quiet.
  For° Monsieur Malvolio, let me alone with him. If I do not gull°
  him into a nayword° and make him° a common recreation,° do
  not think I have wit enough to lie straight in my bed. I know I
  can do it.
**SIR TOBY:** Possess° us, possess us. Tell us something of him.          115
**MARIA:** Marry, sir, sometimes he is a kind of Puritan.°
**SIR ANDREW:** Oh, if I thought that, I'd beat him like a dog.
**SIR TOBY:** What, for being a Puritan? Thy exquisite reason, dear
  knight?
**SIR ANDREW:** I have no exquisite reason for't, but I have reason
  good enough.

---

97 **Out o' tune** (Perhaps a quibbling reply—"We did too keep time in our tune"—to Malvolio's accusation
of having no respect for place or time, line 91. Often emended to *Out o' time,* easily misread in secretary
hand.)   99 **Saint Anne** mother of the Virgin Mary. (Her cult was derided in the Reformation, much as
Puritan reformers also derided the tradition of *cakes and ale* at church feasts.)   **ginger** (Commonly used
to spice ale.)   101–2 **rub ... crumbs** i.e., scour or polish your steward's chain; attend to your own business and remember your station.   104 **give means** i.e., supply drink.   **rule** conduct.   105 **your ears** i.e.,
your ass's ears.   107 **the field** i.e., to a duel   112 **For** As for.   **let ... him** leave him to me.   113 **gull**
trick.   **nayword** byword. (His name will be synonymous with "dupe.")   113–4 **recreation** sport
115 **Possess** Inform   116 **puritan** (Maria's point is that Malvolio is sometimes a *kind* of Puritan, insofar as
he is precise about moral conduct and censorious of others for immoral conduct, but that he is nothing consistently except a time-server. He is not, then, simply a satirical type of the Puritan sect. The extent of the
resemblance is left unstated.)

**MARIA:** The devil a Puritan that he is, or anything constantly,° 120
but a time-pleaser;° an affectioned° ass, that cons state without book° and utters it by great swaths;° the best persuaded° of
himself, so crammed, as he thinks, with excellencies, that it is
his grounds of faith° that all that look on him love him; and on
that vice in him will my revenge find notable cause to work.

**SIR TOBY:** What wilt thou do? 125

**MARIA:** I will drop in his way some obscure epistles° of love,
wherein by the color of his beard, the shape of his leg, the
manner of his gait, the expressure° of his eye, forehead, and
complexion, he shall find himself most feelingly personated.° I
can write very like my lady your niece; on a forgotten matter°
we can hardly make distinction of our hands.° 130

**SIR TOBY:** Excellent! I smell a device.

**SIR ANDREW:** I have't in my nose too.

**SIR TOBY:** He shall think, by the letters that thou wilt drop, that
they come from my niece, and that she's in love with him.

**MARIA:** My purpose is indeed a horse of that color.

**SIR ANDREW:** And your horse now would make him an ass. 135

**MARIA:** Ass,° I doubt not.

**SIR ANDREW:** Oh, 'twill be admirable!

**MARIA:** Sport royal, I warrant you. I know my physic° will work
with him. I will plant you two, and let the Fool make a third,
where he shall find the letter. Observe his construction° of it. 140
For this night, to bed, and dream on the event.° Farewell.
*Exit.*

**SIR TOBY:** Good night, Penthesilea.°

**SIR ANDREW:** Before me,° she's a good wench.

**SIR TOBY:** She's a beagle° true-bred and one that adores me.
What o' that? 145

**SIR ANDREW:** I was adored once, too.

**SIR TOBY:** Let's to bed, knight. Thou hadst need send for more money.

**SIR ANDREW:** If I cannot recover° your niece, I am a foul way out.°

**SIR TOBY:** Send for money, knight. If thou hast her not i'th' end,
call me cut.°

**SIR ANDREW:** If I do not, never trust me, take it how you will. 150

---

120 **constantly** consistently   121 **time-pleaser** time-server, sycophant.   **affectioned** affected   122–3 **cons ... book** learns by heart the phrases and mannerisms of the great   123 **by
great swaths** in great sweeps, like rows of mown grain.   **the best persuaded** having the best opinion   124 **grounds of faith** creed, belief   126 **some obscure epistles** an ambiguously worded letter   127 **expressure** expression   128 **personated** represented.   129 **on a forgotten matter** when
we've forgotten which of us wrote something or what it was about   130 **hands** handwriting.
136 **Ass, I** (With a pun on "as I.")   138 **physic** medicine   140 **construction** interpretation
141 **event** outcome.   142 **Penthesilea** Queen of the Amazons. (Another ironical allusion to Maria's
diminutive stature.)   143 **Before me** i.e., On my soul. (A mild oath.)   144 **beagle** a small, intelligent hunting dog   148 **recover** win.   **foul way out** i.e., miserably out of pocket. (Literally, out of
my way and in the mire.)   149 **cut** A proverbial term of abuse: literally, a horse with a docked tail;
also, a gelding, or the female genital organ.

**SIR TOBY:**   Come, come, I'll go burn some sack.° 'Tis too late to go
to bed now. Come, knight; come, knight.

*Exeunt.*°

## 2.4

*Enter Duke [Orsino], Viola, Curio, and others.*

**ORSINO:**   Give me some music. Now, good morrow,° friends.
Now, good Cesario, but° that piece of song,
That old and antique° song we heard last night.
Methought it did relieve my passion much,
More than light airs and recollected terms°                          5
Of these most brisk and giddy-pacèd times.
Come, but one verse.
**CURIO:**   He is not here, so please Your Lordship, that should sing it.
**ORSINO:**   Who was it?
**CURIO:**   Feste the jester, my lord, a fool that the Lady Olivia's father    10
took much delight in. He is about the house.
**ORSINO:**   Seek him out, and play the tune the while.

*[Exit Curio.] Music plays.*

[*To Viola*] Come hither, boy. If ever thou shalt love,
In the sweet pangs of it remember me;
For such as I am, all true lovers are,                                15
Unstaid and skittish in all motions else°
Save in the constant image of the creature
That is beloved. How dost thou like this tune?
**VIOLA:**   It gives a very echo to the seat°
Where Love is throned.                                               20
**ORSINO:**   Thou dost speak masterly.
My life upon't, young though thou art, thine eye
Hath stayed upon some favor° that it loves.
Hath it not, boy?
**VIOLA:**   A little, by your favor.°                               25
**ORSINO:**   What kind of woman is't?
**VIOLA:**   Of your complexion.
**ORSINO:**   She is not worth thee, then. What years, i'faith?
**VIOLA:**   About your years, my lord.
**ORSINO:**   Too old, by heaven. Let still° the woman take           30

---

151 **burn some sack** warm some Spanish wine.   157.1 *Exeunt* (Feste may have left earlier; he says
nothing after line 117 and is perhaps referred to without his being present at 172–3.)
1 **morrow** morning   2 **but** i.e., I ask only   3 **antique** old, quaint, fantastic   5 **recollected terms**
studied and artificial expressions   16 **all motions else** all other thoughts and emotions   19 **the seat**
i.e., the heart   23 **stayed ... favor** rested upon some face   25 **by your favor** if you please. (But also
hinting at "like you in feature.")   30 **still** always

An elder than herself. So wears she° to him;
So sways she level° in her husband's heart.
For, boy, however we do praise ourselves,
Our fancies are more giddy and unfirm,
More longing, wavering, sooner lost and worn,°                        35
Than women's are.

**VIOLA:**    I think it well, my lord.

**ORSINO:**    Then let thy love be younger than thyself,
Or thy affection cannot hold the bent;°
For women are as roses, whose fair flower                              40
Being once displayed,° doth fall that very hour.

**VIOLA:**    And so they are. Alas that they are so,
To die even when° they to perfection grow!

*Enter Curio and Clown [Feste].*

**ORSINO:**    Oh, fellow, come, the song we had last night.
Mark it, Cesario, it is old and plain;                                 45
The spinsters° and the knitters in the sun,
And the free° maids that weave their thread with bones,°
Do use° to chant it. It is silly sooth,°
And dallies with° the innocence of love,
Like the old age.°                                                     50

**FESTE:**    Are you ready, sir?

**ORSINO:**    Ay, prithee, sing.    *Music.*

*The Song.*

**FESTE:**    [*sings*]
Come away,° come away, death,
And in sad cypress° let me be laid.                                    55
Fly away, fly away, breath;
I am slain by a fair cruel maid.
My shroud of white, stuck all with yew,°
Oh, prepare it!
My part of death, no one so true                                      60
Did share it.°
Not a flower, not a flower sweet
On my black coffin let there be strown;°
Not a friend, not a friend greet

---

**31 wears she** she adapts herself    **32 sways she level** she keeps a perfect equipoise and steady affection    **35 worn** exhausted. (Sometimes emended to *won*.)    **39 hold the bent** hold steady, keep the intensity (like the tension of a bow)    **41 displayed** full blown    **43 even when** just as    **46 spinsters** spinners    **47 free** carefree, innocent.    **bones** bobbins on which bone-lace was made    **48 Do use** are accustomed.    **silly sooth** simple truth    **49 dallies with** dwells lovingly on, sports with    **50 Like ... age** as in the good old times.    **54 Come away** Come hither    **55 cypress** i.e., a coffin of cypress wood, or bier strewn with sprigs of cypress    **58 yew** yew sprigs. (Emblematic of mourning, like cypress.)    **60–1 My ... it** No one died for love so true to love as I.    **63 strown** strewn

My poor corpse, where my bones shall be thrown.                           65
A thousand thousand sighs to save,
Lay me, oh, where
Sad true lover never find my grave,
To weep there!

**ORSINO:**  [*offering money*] There's for thy pains.                     70
**FESTE:**  No pains, sir. I take pleasure in singing, sir.
**ORSINO:**  I'll pay thy pleasure then.
**FESTE:**  Truly, sir, and pleasure will be paid, one time or another.°
**ORSINO:**  Give me now leave to leave° thee.
**FESTE:**  Now, the melancholy god° protect thee, and the tailor
make thy doublet° of changeable taffeta,° for thy mind is a
very opal.° I would have men of such constancy put to sea,
that their business might be everything and their intent
everywhere,° for that's it that always makes a good voyage of
nothing.° Farewell.                                          *Exit.*   80
**ORSINO:**  Let all the rest give place.°

[*Curio and attendants withdraw.*]

Once more, Cesario,
Get thee to yond same sovereign cruelty.
Tell her, my love, more noble than the world,
Prizes not quantity of dirty lands;
The parts° that fortune hath bestowed upon her,                           85
Tell her, I hold as giddily as fortune;°
But 'tis that miracle and queen of gems°
That nature pranks° her in attracts° my soul.
**VIOLA:**  But if she cannot love you, sir?
**ORSINO:**  I cannot be so answered.                                      90
**VIOLA:**  Sooth,° but you must.
Say that some lady—as perhaps there is—
Hath for your love as great a pang of heart
As you have for Olivia. You cannot love her;
You tell her so. Must she not then be answered?°                          95
**ORSINO:**  There is no woman's sides
Can bide° the beating of so strong a passion

---

**73 pleasure ... another** sooner or later one must pay for indulgence.   **74 leave to leave** permission
to take leave of, dismiss   **75 the melancholy god** i.e., Saturn, whose planet was thought to control
the melancholy temperament   **76 doublet** close-fitting jacket.   **changeable taffeta** a silk so woven
of various-colored threads that its color shifts with changing perspective   **77 opal** an iridescent
precious stone that changes color when seen from various angles or in different lights.   **78–9 that ...
everywhere** i.e., so that in the changeableness of the sea their inconstancy could always be exer-
cised   **79–80 for ... nothing** because that's the quality that is satisfied with an aimless voyage.
**81 give place** withdraw.   **85 parts** attributes such as wealth or rank   **86 I ... fortune** I esteem
as carelessly as I do fortune, that fickle goddess   **87 that miracle ... gems** i.e., her beauty
**88 pranks** adorns.   **attracts** that attracts   **91 Sooth** In truth   **95 be answered** be satisfied with
your answer.   **97 bide** withstand

As love doth give my heart; no woman's heart
So big, to hold° so much. They lack retention.°
Alas, their love may be called appetite,                              100
No motion° of the liver, but the palate,°
That suffer surfeit, cloyment,° and revolt;°
But mine is all as hungry as the sea,
And can digest as much. Make no compare°
Between that love a woman can bear me                        105
And that I owe° Olivia.

**VIOLA:** Ay, but I know—

**ORSINO:** What dost thou know?

**VIOLA:** Too well what love women to men may owe.
In faith, they are as true of heart as we.                         110
My father had a daughter loved a man
As it might be, perhaps, were I a woman,
I should Your Lordship.

**ORSINO:** And what's her history?                                 115

**VIOLA:** A blank, my lord. She never told her love,
But let concealment, like a worm i'th' bud,
Feed on her damask° cheek. She pined in thought,
And with a green and yellow° melancholy;
She sat like Patience on a monument,°                           120
Smiling at grief. Was not this love indeed?
We men may say more, swear more, but indeed
Our shows° are more than will;° for still° we prove
Much in our vows, but little in our love.

**ORSINO:** But died thy sister of her love, my boy?       125

**VIOLA:** I am all the daughters of my father's house,
And all the brothers too—and yet I know not.
Sir, shall I to this lady?

**ORSINO:** Ay, that's the theme.
To her in haste; give her this jewel. [*He gives a jewel.*] Say    130
My love can give no place, bide no denay.°

*Exeunt [separately].*

## 2.5

*Enter Sir Toby, Sir Andrew, and Fabian.*

**SIR TOBY:** Come thy ways,° Signor Fabian.

---

**99 to hold** as to contain.   **retention** constancy, the power of retaining.   **101 motion** impulse.   **liver ... palate** (Real love is a passion of the liver, whereas fancy, light love, is born in the eye and nourished in the palate.)   **102 cloyment** satiety.   **revolt** revulsion   **104 compare** comparison   **106 owe** have for   **118 damask** pink and white like the damask rose   **119 green and yellow** pale and sallow   **120 on a monument** carved in statuary on a tomb   **124 shows** displays of passion.   **more than will** greater than our determination.   **still** always   **131 can ... denay** cannot yield or endure denial.   **1 Come thy ways** Come along

**FABIAN:**   Nay, I'll come. If I lose a scruple° of this sport, let me be
boiled° to death with melancholy.

**SIR TOBY:**   Wouldst thou not be glad to have the niggardly rascally
sheep-biter° come by some notable shame?

**FABIAN:**   I would exult, man. You know he brought me out o'favor   5
with my lady about a bearbaiting° here.

**SIR TOBY:**   To anger him we'll have the bear again, and we will fool
him black and blue.° Shall we not, Sir Andrew?

**SIR ANDREW:**   An° we do not, it is pity of our lives.°   10

*Enter Maria [with a letter].*

**SIR TOBY:**   Here comes the little villain.°—How now, my metal°
of India!

**MARIA:**   Get ye all three into the boxtree.° Malvolio's coming
down this walk. He has been yonder i' the sun practicing behavior to his own shadow this half hour. Observe him, for the
love of mockery, for I know this letter will make a contempla-   15
tive° idiot of him. Close,° in the name of jesting! [*The others
hide.*] Lie thou there [*throwing down a letter*]; for here comes
the trout that must be caught with tickling.°       *Exit.*

*Enter Malvolio.*

**MALVOLIO:**   'Tis but fortune; all is fortune. Maria once told me
she° did affect° me; and I have heard herself come thus near,   20
that should she fancy,° it should be one of my complexion.
Besides, she uses me with a more exalted respect than anyone
else that follows° her. What should I think on't?

**SIR TOBY:**   Here's an overweening rogue!

**FABIAN:**   Oh, peace! Contemplation makes a rare° turkey-cock of
him. How he jets° under his advanced° plumes!   25

**SIR ANDREW:**   'Slight,° I could so beat the rogue!

**SIR TOBY:**   Peace, I say.

**MALVOLIO:**   To be Count Malvolio.

**SIR TOBY:**   Ah, rogue!

**SIR ANDREW:**   Pistol him, pistol him.   30

**SIR TOBY:**   Peace, peace!

---

**2 a scruple** the least bit   **3 boiled** (With a pun on "biled"; black bile was the "humor" of melancholy
and was thought to be a cold humor.)   **5 sheep-biter** a dog that bites sheep, i.e., a scoundrel
**7 bearbaiting** (A special target of Puritan disapproval.)   **9 fool ... blue** mock him until he is figura-
tively black and blue.   **10 An** If.   **pity of our lives** a pity we should live.   **11 villain** (Here, a term of
endearment.)   **metal** gold, i.e., priceless one   **12 boxtree** an evergreen shrub.   **15–6 contemplative**
i.e., from his musings.   **16 Close** i.e., Keep close, stay hidden   **18 tickling** (1) stroking gently about
the gills—an actual method of fishing (2) deception.   **20 she** Olivia.   **affect** have fondness for
**21 fancy** fall in love   **23 follows** serves   **25 rare** extraordinary   **26 jets** struts.   **advanced**
prominent   **27 'Slight** By His (God's) light

**MALVOLIO:** There is example° for't. The lady of the Strachy° married the yeoman of the wardrobe.

**SIR ANDREW:** Fie on him, Jezebel!°

**FABIAN:** Oh, peace! Now he's deeply in. Look how imagination blows° him.

**MALVOLIO:** Having been three months married to her, sitting in my state°—    35

**SIR TOBY:** Oh, for a stone-bow,° to hit him in the eye!

**MALVOLIO:** Calling my officers about me, in my branched° velvet gown; having come from a daybed,° where I have left Olivia sleeping—

**SIR TOBY:** Fire and brimstone!

**FABIAN:** Oh, peace, peace!    40

**MALVOLIO:** And then to have the humor of state;° and after a demure travel of regard,° telling them I know my place as I would they should do theirs, to ask for my kinsman Toby.°

**SIR TOBY:** Bolts and shackles!

**FABIAN:** Oh, peace, peace, peace! Now, now.    45

**MALVOLIO:** Seven of my people, with an obedient start, make out for him. I frown the while, and perchance wind up my watch, or play with my°—some rich jewel. Toby approaches; curtsies° there to me—

**SIR TOBY:** Shall this fellow live?

**FABIAN:** Though our silence be drawn from us with cars,° yet peace.    50

**MALVOLIO:** I extend my hand to him thus, quenching my familiar° smile with an austere regard of control°—

**SIR TOBY:** And does not Toby take° you a blow o' the lips then?

**MALVOLIO:** Saying, "Cousin Toby, my fortunes having cast me on your niece give me this prerogative of speech—"    55

**SIR TOBY:** What, what?

**MALVOLIO:** "You must amend your drunkenness."

**SIR TOBY:** Out, scab!°

**FABIAN:** Nay, patience, or we break the sinews of° our plot.

**MALVOLIO:** "Besides, you waste the treasure of your time with a foolish knight—"    60

---

32 **example** precedent.  **lady of the Strachy** (Apparently a lady who had married below her station; no certain identification.)  33 **Jezebel** the proud queen of Ahab, King of Israel.  34 **blows** puffs up  35 **state** chair of state  36 **stone-bow** crossbow that shoots stones  37 **branched** adorned with a figured pattern suggesting branched leaves or flowers.  38 **daybed** sofa, couch  41 **have ... state** adopt the imperious manner of authority  42 **demure ... regard** grave survey of the company  43 **Toby** (Malvolio omits the title *Sir*.)  48 **play with my** (Malvolio perhaps means his steward's chain but checks himself in time; as "Count Malvolio," he would not be wearing it. A bawdy meaning of playing with himself is also suggested.)  **curtsies** bows  50 **with cars** with chariots, i.e., pulling apart by force  51 **familiar** (1) customary (2) friendly.  52 **regard of control** look of authority  53 **take** deliver  58 **scab** scurvy fellow.  59 **break ... of** hamstring, disable

**SIR ANDREW:** That's me, I warrant you.

**MALVOLIO:** "One Sir Andrew."

**SIR ANDREW:** I knew 'twas I, for many do call me fool.

**MALVOLIO:** What employment° have we here?

[*Taking up the letter.*]

**FABIAN:** Now is the woodcock° near the gin.° 65

**SIR TOBY:** Oh, peace, and the spirit of humors° intimate reading aloud to him!

**MALVOLIO:** By my life, this is my lady's hand. These be her very c's, her u's, and her t's;° and thus makes she her great° P's. It is in contempt of° question her hand.

**SIR ANDREW:** Her c's, her u's, and her t's. Why that? 70

**MALVOLIO:** [*reads*] "To the unknown beloved, this, and my good wishes."—Her very phrases! By your leave, wax.° Soft!° And the impressure° her Lucrece,° with which she uses° to seal. 'Tis my lady. To whom should this be? [*He opens the letter.*]

**FABIAN:** This wins him, liver° and all. 75

**MALVOLIO:** [*reads*]
"Jove knows I love,
But who?
Lips, do not move;
No man must know." 80
"No man must know." What follows? The numbers altered!°
"No man must know." If this should be thee, Malvolio?

**SIR TOBY:** Marry, hang thee, brock!°

**MALVOLIO:** [*reads*]
"I may command where I adore, 85
But silence, like a Lucrece knife,
With bloodless stroke my heart doth gore;
M.O.A.I. doth sway my life."

**FABIAN:** A fustian° riddle!

**SIR TOBY:** Excellent wench, say I. 90

**MALVOLIO:** "M.O.A.I. doth sway my life." Nay, but first, let me see, let me see, let me see.

**FABIAN:** What° dish o' poison has she dressed° him!

**SIR TOBY:** And with what wing° the staniel° checks at it!°

---

**64 employment** business  **65 woodcock** (A bird proverbial for its stupidity.)  **gin** snare.  **66 humors** whim, caprice  **68 c's ... t's** i.e., *cut*, slang for the female pudenda.  **great** (1) uppercase (2) copious. (*P* suggests "pee.")  **69 in contempt of** beyond  **72 By ... wax** (Addressed to the seal on the letter.)  **Soft** Softly, not so fast.  **73 impressure** device imprinted on the seal.  **Lucrece** Lucretia, chaste matron who, ravished by Tarquin, committed suicide  **uses** is accustomed  **75 liver** i.e., the seat of passion  **81 The numbers altered!** More verses, in a different meter!  **83 brock** badger. (Used contemptuously.)  **89 fustian** bombastic, ridiculously pompous  **92 What** What a.  **dressed** prepared for  **93 wing** speed.  **staniel** kestrel, a sparrow hawk. (The word is used contemptuously because of the uselessness of the staniel for falconry.)  **checks at it** turns to fly at it.

**MALVOLIO:** "I may command where I adore." Why, she may command me; I serve her, she is my lady. Why, this is evident to any formal capacity.° There is no obstruction in this. And    95
the end—what should that alphabetical position° portend? If I could make that resemble something in me! Softly! "M.O.A.I."—

**SIR TOBY:** Oh, ay,° make up° that. He is now at a cold scent.

**FABIAN:** Sowter° will cry upon't for all this, though it be as rank as a fox.

**MALVOLIO:** "M"—Malvolio. "M"! Why, that begins my name!    100

**FABIAN:** Did not I say he would work it out? The cur is excellent at faults.°

**MALVOLIO:** "M"—But then there is no consonancy in the sequel that suffers under probation:° "A" should follow, but "O" does.

**FABIAN:** And "O" shall end,° I hope.

**SIR TOBY:** Ay, or I'll cudgel him, and make him cry "Oh!"    105

**MALVOLIO:** And then "I" comes behind.

**FABIAN:** Ay, an you had any eye° behind you, you might see more detraction at your heels° than fortunes before you.

**MALVOLIO:** "M.O.A.I." This simulation° is not as the former. And yet, to crush this a little, it would bow to me, for every one of    110
these letters are in my name. Soft! Here follows prose.
[*He reads.*] "If this fall into thy hand, revolve.° In my stars° I am above thee, but be not afraid of greatness. Some are born great, some achieve greatness, and some have greatness thrust upon 'em. Thy Fates open their hands;° let thy blood and spirit embrace them; and, to inure° thyself to what thou    115
art like° to be, cast° thy humble slough° and appear fresh. Be opposite° with a kinsman, surly with servants. Let thy tongue tang° arguments of state;° put thyself into the trick of singularity.° She thus advises thee that sighs for thee.    120
Remember who commended thy yellow stockings, and wished to see thee ever cross-gartered.° I say, remember. Go to,° thou art made, if thou desir'st to be so. If not, let me see

---

**95 formal capacity** normal understanding.   **96 position** arrangement   **97 Oh, ay** (Playing on *O.I.* of *M.O.A.I.*)   **make up** work out   **98–9 Sowter ... fox** The hound Sowter (literally, "Cobbler") will bay triumphantly at picking up this false scent, even though the smell is as rank as a fox. ("M.O.A.I." is a false lead that reeks.)   **101 at faults** i.e., at maneuvering his way past breaks in the line of scent—in this case, on a false trail.   **102–3 no consonancy ... probation** no pattern in the following letters that stands up under examination. (In fact, the letters "M.O.A.I." represent the first, last, second, and next to last letters of Malvolio's name.)   **104 "O" shall end** (1) "O" ends Malvolio's name (2) *omega* ends the Greek alphabet and is thus a symbol for the ending of the world, *alpha* to *omega* (3) Malvolio's cry of pain will end the matter, as Sir Toby suggests in the next line.   **107 eye** (punning on the "I" of "Oh, ay" and "M.O.A.I.")   **108 detraction ... heels** defamation pursuing you   **109 simulation** disguise, puzzle   **112 revolve** consider.   **stars** fortune   **115 open their hands** offer their bounty   **116 inure** accustom.   **117 like** likely.   **cast** cast off.   **slough** skin of a snake; hence, former demeanor of humbleness.   **118 opposite** contradictory   **119 tang** sound loud with.   **state** politics, statecraft.   **trick of singularity** eccentricity of manner.   **121 cross-gartered** wearing garters above and below the knee so as to cross behind it.   **122 Go to** (An expression of remonstrance.)

thee a steward still, the fellow of servants, and not worthy to
touch Fortune's fingers. Farewell. She that would alter      125
services° with thee, The Fortunate-Unhappy."

Daylight and champaign° discovers° not more! This is open. I will
be proud, I will read politic° authors, I will baffle° Sir Toby,
I will wash off gross° acquaintance, I will be point-devise°
the very man. I do not now fool myself, to let° imagination      130
jade me;° for every reason excites to this,° that my lady loves me.
She did commend my yellow stockings of late, she did praise
my leg being cross-gartered; and in this° she manifests
herself to my love, and with a kind of injunction drives me to
these habits° of her liking. I thank my stars, I am happy.° I will      135
be strange, stout,° in yellow stockings and cross-gartered, even
with the swiftness of putting on. Jove and my stars be praised!
Here is yet a post-script. [*He reads.*] "Thou canst not choose but
know who I am. If thou entertain'st° my love, let it appear in
thy smiling; thy smiles become thee well. Therefore in my      140
presence still° smile, dear my sweet, I prithee." Jove, I thank
thee. I will smile; I will do everything that thou wilt have me.

                                                        *Exit.*

      [*Sir Toby, Sir Andrew, and Fabian come from hiding.*]

**FABIAN:**  I will not give my part of this sport for a pension of
thousands to be paid from the Sophy.°
**SIR TOBY:**  I could marry this wench for this device.
**SIR ANDREW:**  So could I too.      145
**SIR TOBY:**  And ask no other dowry with her but such another jest.

      *Enter Maria.*

**SIR ANDREW:**  Nor I neither.
**FABIAN:**  Here comes my noble gull-catcher.°
**SIR TOBY:**  Wilt thou set thy foot o' my neck?
**SIR ANDREW:**  Or o' mine either?      150
**SIR TOBY:**  Shall I play° my freedom at tray-trip,° and become thy
bond slave?
**SIR ANDREW:**  I'faith, or I either?
**SIR TOBY:**  Why, thou hast put him in such a dream that when the
image of it leaves him he must run mad.      155

**125–26 alter services** i.e., exchange place of mistress and servant   **127 champaign** open country.   **discovers** discloses   **128 politic** dealing with state affairs.   **baffle** deride, degrade. (A technical
chivalric term used to describe the disgrace of a perjured knight.)   **129 gross** base.   **point-devise**
correct to the letter   **130 to let** by letting.   **130–1 jade me** trick me, make me look ridiculous
(as an unruly horse might do).   **131 excites to this** prompts this conclusion   **133 this** this letter   **135 these habits** this attire   **happy** fortunate.   **136 strange, stout** aloof, haughty   **139 thou
entertain'st** you accept   **141 still** continually   **143 Sophy** Shah of Persia.   **148 gull-catcher** tricker
of *gulls* or dupes.   **151 play** gamble.   **tray-trip** a game of dice, success in which depended on throwing a three (*tray*)

**MARIA:** Nay, but say true, does it work upon him?

**SIR TOBY:** Like aqua vitae° with a midwife.

**MARIA:** If you will then see the fruits of the sport, mark his first
approach before my lady. He will come to her in yellow stockings, and 'tis a color she abhors, and cross-gartered, a fashion      160
she detests; and he will smile upon her, which will now be so
unsuitable to her disposition, being addicted to a melancholy as
she is, that it cannot but turn him into a notable contempt.° If
you will see it, follow me.

**SIR TOBY:** To the gates of Tartar,° thou most excellent devil of wit!      165

**SIR ANDREW:** I'll make one° too. *Exeunt.*

### 3.1

*Enter Viola, and Clown [Feste, playing his pipe and tabor].*

**VIOLA:** Save° thee, friend, and thy music. Dost thou live by°
thy tabor?°

**FESTE:** No, sir, I live by the church.

**VIOLA:** Art thou a churchman?

**FESTE:** No such matter, sir. I do live by the church, for I do live at
my house, and my house doth stand by the church.      5

**VIOLA:** So thou mayst say the king lies by° a beggar if a beggar
dwell near him, or the church stands by thy tabor if thy tabor
stand by° the church.

**FESTE:** You have said,° sir. To see this age! A sentence° is but a
cheveril° glove to a good wit. How quickly the wrong side may
be turned outward!      10

**VIOLA:** Nay, that's certain. They that dally nicely° with words may
quickly make them wanton.°

**FESTE:** I would therefore my sister had had no name, sir.

**VIOLA:** Why, man?

**FESTE:** Why, sir, her name's a word, and to dally with that word      15
might make my sister wanton. But indeed, words are very rascals
since bonds disgraced them.°

**VIOLA:** Thy reason, man?

**FESTE:** Troth, sir, I can yield you none without words, and words
are grown so false I am loath to prove reason with them.

---

157 **aqua vitae** brandy or other distilled liquor    163 **notable contempt** notorious object of contempt.    165 **Tartar** Tartarus, the infernal regions    166 **make one** i.e., tag along
1 **Save** God save.    **live by** earn your living with. (But Feste uses the phrase to mean "dwell near.")
2 **tabor** small drum.    6 **lies by** (1) lies sexually with (2) dwells near    7–8 **stands by … stand by**
(1) is maintained by (2) is placed near    9 **You have said** You've expressed your opinion.    **sentence**
maxim, judgment, opinion    10 **cheveril** kidskin    11 **dally nicely** (1) play subtly (2) toy amo-
rously    12 **wanton** (1) equivocal (2) licentious, unchaste. (Feste then "dallies" with the word in its
sexual sense; see line 20.)    17 **since … them** i.e., since bonds have been needed to make sworn statements good. (Words cannot be relied on since not even contractual promises are reliable.)

**VIOLA:**  I warrant thou art a merry fellow and car'st for nothing.°    20

**FESTE:**  Not so, sir, I do care for something; but in my conscience, sir, I do not care for you. If that be to care for nothing, sir, I would it would make you invisible.°

**VIOLA:**  Art not thou the Lady Olivia's fool?

**FESTE:**  No indeed, sir. The Lady Olivia has no folly. She will keep no fool, sir, till she be married, and fools are as like husbands    25 as pilchers° are to herrings—the husband's the bigger.° I am indeed not her fool but her corrupter of words.

**VIOLA:**  I saw thee late° at the Count Orsino's.

**FESTE:**  Foolery, sir, does walk about the orb° like the sun; it shines everywhere. I would be sorry, sir, but the fool should be    30 as oft with your master as with my mistress.° I think I saw Your Wisdom° there.

**VIOLA:**  Nay, an thou pass upon me,° I'll no more with thee. Hold, there's expenses for thee.

[*She gives a coin.*]

**FESTE:**  Now Jove, in his next commodity° of hair, send thee a beard!

**VIOLA:**  By my troth, I'll tell thee, I am almost sick for one°— [*aside*] though I would not have it grow on my chin.—Is thy    35 lady within?

**FESTE:**  Would not a pair of these have bred, sir?

**VIOLA:**  Yes, being kept together and put to use.°

**FESTE:**  I would play Lord Pandarus° of Phrygia, sir, to bring a Cressida to this Troilus.

**VIOLA:**  I understand you, sir. 'Tis well begged.

[*She gives another coin.*]

**FESTE:**  The matter, I hope, is not great, sir, begging but a beggar; Cressida was a beggar.° My lady is within, sir. I will conster° to    40 them whence you come. Who you are and what you would are out of my welkin°—I might say "element,"° but the word is overworn.  *Exit.*

---

**20 car'st for nothing** are without any worries. (But Feste puns on *care for* in lines 29–30 in the sense of "like.")   **23 invisible** i.e., nothing; absent.   **26 pilchers** pilchards, fish resembling herring but smaller  **the bigger** (1) the larger (2) the bigger fool.   **28 late** recently   **29 orb** earth   **30–1 I would ... mistress** (1) I should be sorry not to visit Orsino's house often (2) It would be a shame if folly were no less common there than in Olivia's household.   **31 Your Wisdom** i.e., you. (A title of mock courtesy.)   **32 an ... me** if you fence (verbally) with me, pass judgment on me   **33 commodity** supply   **34 sick for one** (1) eager to have a beard (2) in love with a bearded man   **37 put to use** put out at interest.   **38 Pandarus** the go-between in the love story of Troilus and Cressida; uncle to Cressida   **40–1 begging ... was a beggar** (A reference to Henryson's *Testament of Cresseid* in which Cressida became a leper and a beggar. Feste desires another coin to be the mate of the one he has, just as Cressida, the beggar, was mate to Troilus.)   **41 conster** construe, explain   **43 welkin** sky.   **element** (The word can be synonymous with *welkin*, but the common phrase *out of my element* means "beyond my scope.")

**VIOLA:**   This fellow is wise enough to play the fool,
And to do that well craves a kind of wit. 45
He must observe their mood on whom he jests,
The quality° of persons, and the time,
Not, like the haggard,° check at every feather
That comes before his eye.° This is a practice°
As full of labor as a wise man's art; 50
For folly that he wisely shows is fit,
But wise men, folly-fall'n, quite taint their wit.°

*Enter Sir Toby and [Sir] Andrew.*

**SIR TOBY:**   Save you, gentleman.
**VIOLA:**   And you, sir.
**SIR ANDREW:**   *Dieu vous garde, monsieur.°* 55
**VIOLA:**   *Et vous aussi; votre serviteur.°*
**SIR ANDREW:**   I hope, sir, you are, and I am yours.
**SIR TOBY:**   Will you encounter° the house? My niece is desirous you
should enter, if your trade° be to her.
**VIOLA:**   I am bound° to your niece, sir; I mean, she is the list° of 60
my voyage.
**SIR TOBY:**   Taste° your legs, sir. Put them to motion.
**VIOLA:**   My legs do better understand° me, sir, than I understand
what you mean by bidding me taste my legs.
**SIR TOBY:**   I mean, to go, sir, to enter.
**VIOLA:**   I will answer you with gait and entrance.°—But we are 65
prevented.°

*Enter Olivia and gentlewoman [Maria].*

Most excellent accomplished lady, the heavens rain odors on you!
**SIR ANDREW:**   [*to Sir Toby*] That youth's a rare courtier. "Rain
odors"—well.
**VIOLA:**   [*to Olivia*] My matter hath no voice,° lady, but to your own
most pregnant and vouchsafed° ear.
**SIR ANDREW:**   [*to Sir Toby*] "Odors," "pregnant," and "vouchsafed." 70
I'll get 'em all three all ready.°
**OLIVIA:**   Let the garden door be shut, and leave me to my hearing.
[*Exeunt Sir Toby, Sir Andrew, and Maria.*] Give me your hand, sir.

**47 quality** character, rank   **48 haggard** untrained adult hawk, hence unmanageable   **48–9 check ... eye** strike at every bird it sees, i.e., dart from subject to subject.   **49 practice** exercise of skill **51–2 For ... wit** for the folly he judiciously displays is appropriate and clever, whereas when wise men fall into folly they utterly infect their own intelligence.   **55 *Dieu ... monsieur*** God keep you, sir.   **56 *Et ... serviteur*** And you, too; (I am) your servant. (Sir Andrew is not quite up to a reply in French.)   **58 encounter** (High-sounding word to express "approach.")   **59 trade** business. (Suggesting also a commercial venture.)   **60 I am bound** (1) I am on a journey. (Continuing Sir Toby's metaphor in *trade*.) (2) I am confined, obligated.   **list** limit, destination   **61 Taste** Try   **62 understand** stand under, support   **65 gait and entrance** going and entering. (With a pun on *gate*:[1] stride [2] entryway.)   **prevented** anticipated.   **68 hath no voice** cannot be uttered   **69 pregnant and vouchsafed** receptive and attentive   **70 all ready** committed to memory for future use.

**VIOLA:** My duty, madam, and most humble service.

**OLIVIA:** What is your name?

**VIOLA:** Cesario is your servant's name, fair princess. 75

**OLIVIA:** My servant, sir? 'Twas never merry world
Since lowly feigning was called compliment.°
You're servant to the Count Orsino, youth.

**VIOLA:** And he is yours,° and his° must needs be yours;
Your servant's servant is your servant, madam. 80

**OLIVIA:** For° him, I think not on him. For his thoughts,
Would they were blanks,° rather than filled with me!

**VIOLA:** Madam, I come to whet your gentle thoughts
On his behalf.

**OLIVIA:** Oh, by your leave,° I pray you. 85
I bade you never speak again of him.
But, would you undertake another suit,
I had rather hear you to solicit that
Than music from the spheres.°

**VIOLA:** Dear lady— 90

**OLIVIA:** Give me leave, beseech you. I did send,
After the last enchantment you did here,
A ring in chase of you; so did I abuse°
Myself, my servant, and, I fear me, you.
Under your hard construction° must I sit, 95
To force that° on you in a shameful cunning
Which you knew none of yours. What might you think?
Have you not set mine honor at the stake°
And baited° it with all th' unmuzzled thoughts
That tyrannous heart can think? To one of your receiving° 100
Enough is shown; a cypress, not a bosom,
Hides my heart.° So, let me hear you speak.

**VIOLA:** I pity you.

**OLIVIA:** That's a degree to love.

**VIOLA:** No, not a grece;° for 'tis a vulgar proof° 105
That very oft we pity enemies.

**OLIVIA:** Why then, methinks 'tis time to smile° again.

---

75–6 **'Twas ... compliment** Things have never been the same since affected humility (like calling oneself another's servant) began to be mistaken for courtesy. 79 **is yours** is your servant. **his** those belonging to him 81 **For** As for 82 **blanks** blank coins ready to be stamped or empty sheets of paper 85 **by your leave** i.e., allow me to interrupt 89 **music from the spheres** (The heavenly bodies were thought to be fixed in hollow concentric spheres that revolved one about the other, producing a harmony too exquisite to be heard by human ears.) 93 **abuse** wrong, mislead 95 **hard construction** harsh interpretation 96 **To force** that for forcing the ring 98 **at the stake** (The figure is from bearbaiting.) 99 **baited** harassed. (Literally, set the unmuzzled dogs on to bite the bear.) 100 **receiving** capacity, intelligence 101–2 **a cypress ... heart** i.e., I have shown my heart to you, veiled only with thin, gauzelike cypress cloth rather than the opaque flesh of my bosom. 105 **grece** step. (Synonymous with *degree* in the preceding line.) **vulgar proof** common experience 107 **smile** i.e., cast off love's melancholy

Oh, world, how apt the poor are to be proud!°
If one should be a prey, how much the better
To fall before the lion than the wolf!° *Clock strikes.*          110
The clock upbraids me with the waste of time.
Be not afraid, good youth, I will not have you;
And yet, when wit and youth is come to harvest
Your wife is like° to reap a proper° man.
There lies your way, due west.                                    115

**VIOLA:**   Then westward ho!°
Grace and good disposition attend Your Ladyship.°
You'll nothing, madam, to my lord by me?

**OLIVIA:**   Stay.
I prithee, tell me what thou think'st of me.                      120

**VIOLA:**   That you do think you are not what you are.°

**OLIVIA:**   If I think so, I think the same of you.°

**VIOLA:**   Then think you right. I am not what I am.

**OLIVIA:**   I would you were as I would have you be!

**VIOLA:**   Would it be better, madam, than I am?                 125
I wish it might, for now I am your fool.°

**OLIVIA:**   [*aside*]
Oh, what a deal of scorn looks beautiful
In the contempt and anger of his lip!
A murderous guilt shows not itself more soon                      130
Than love that would seem hid; love's night is noon.°—
Cesario, by the roses of the spring,
By maidhood, honor, truth, and everything,
I love thee so that, maugre° all thy pride,
Nor° wit nor reason can my passion hide.                          135
Do not extort thy reasons from this clause,
For that I woo, thou therefore hast no cause.°
But rather reason thus with reason fetter°
Love sought is good, but given unsought is better.

**VIOLA:**   By innocence I swear, and by my youth,               140
I have one heart, one bosom, and one truth,
And that no woman has, nor never none
Shall mistress be of it save I alone.

108 **how ... proud!** how ready the unfortunate and rejected (like myself) are to find something to be proud of in their distress! Or, how apt are persons of comparatively low social station like yourself to show pride in rejecting love!   110 **To fall ... wolf!** i.e., to fall before a noble adversary rather than to a person like you who attacks me thus!   114 **like** likely.   **proper** handsome, worthy   116 **westward ho** (The cry of Thames watermen to attract westward-bound passengers.)   117 **Grace ... Ladyship** May you enjoy God's blessing and a happy frame of mind.   120–1 **That ... are** i.e., That you think you are in love with a man, and you are mistaken.   122 **If ... you** (Olivia may interpret Viola's cryptic statement as suggesting that Olivia "does not know herself," i.e., is distracted with passion; she may also hint at her suspicion that "Cesario" is higher born than he admits.)   126 **fool** butt.   131 **love's ... noon** i.e., love, despite its attempt to be secret, reveals itself as plain as day.   134 **maugre** in spite of   135 **Nor** neither   136–7 **Do ... cause** Do not rationalize your indifference along these lines, that because I am the wooer you have no cause to reciprocate.   138 **But ... fetter** But instead control your reasoning with the following reason

And so adieu, good madam. Nevermore
Will I my master's tears to you deplore.°                        145

**OLIVIA:**  Yet come again, for thou perhaps mayst move
That heart, which now abhors, to like his love.

       *Exeunt [separately].*

## 3.2

       *Enter Sir Toby, Sir Andrew, and Fabian.*

**SIR ANDREW:**  No, faith, I'll not stay a jot longer.

**SIR TOBY:**  Thy reason, dear venom,° give thy reason.

**FABIAN:**  You must needs yield your reason, Sir Andrew.

**SIR ANDREW:**  Marry, I saw your niece do more favors to the
Count's servingman than ever she bestowed upon me. I saw't      5
i' th' orchard.°

**SIR TOBY:**  Did she see thee the while, old boy? Tell me that.

**SIR ANDREW:**  As plain as I see you now.

**FABIAN:**  This was a great argument° of love in her toward you.

**SIR ANDREW:**  'Slight,° will you make an ass o' me?

**FABIAN:**  I will prove it° legitimate, sir, upon the oaths° of judg-    10
ment and reason.

**SIR TOBY:**  And they have been grand-jurymen since before Noah
was a sailor.

**FABIAN:**  She did show favor to the youth in your sight only to
exasperate you, to awake your dormouse° valor, to put fire in
your heart and brimstone in your liver. You should then have       15
accosted her, and with some excellent jests, fire-new from the
mint,° you should have banged° the youth into dumbness. This
was looked for at your hand, and this was balked.° The double
gilt° of this opportunity you let time wash off, and you are now
sailed into the north of my lady's opinion,° where you will hang    20
like an icicle on a Dutchman's beard° unless you do redeem it by
some laudable attempt either of valor or policy.°

**SIR ANDREW:**  An't be any way, it must be with valor, for policy I
hate. I had as lief be a Brownist° as a politician.°

**SIR TOBY:**  Why, then, build me thy fortunes upon the basis of valor.    25
Challenge me° the Count's youth to fight with him; hurt him in

---

**145 deplore** beweep.  **2 venom** i.e., person filled with venomous anger  **6 orchard** garden.
**8 argument** proof  **9 'Slight** By his (God's) light  **10 it** my contention.  **oaths** i.e., testimony
under oath  **14 dormouse** i.e., sleepy and timid  **16–7 fire-new ... mint** newly coined  **17 banged**
struck  **18 balked** missed, neglected.  **19 double gilt** thick layer of gold, i.e., rare worth  **20 into
... opinion** i.e., out of the warmth and sunshine of Olivia's favor  **21 icicle ... beard** (Alludes to the
arctic voyage of William Barents in 1596–1597.)  **22 policy** stratagem.  **24 Brownist** (An early name
of the Congregationalists, from the name of the founder, Robert Browne.)  **politician** intriguer. (Sir
Andrew misinterprets Fabian's more neutral use of *policy,* "clever stratagem.")  **25–6 build me ...
Challenge me** build ... Challenge. ("Me" is idiomatic.)

eleven places. My niece shall take note of it; and assure thyself, there is no love-broker° in the world can more prevail in man's commendation with woman than report of valor.

**FABIAN:**   There is no way but this, Sir Andrew.                                    30

**SIR ANDREW:**   Will either of you bear me a challenge to him?

**SIR TOBY:**   Go, write it in a martial hand. Be curst° and brief; it is no matter how witty, so it be eloquent and full of invention. Taunt him with the license of ink.° If thou "thou"-est° him some thrice, it shall not be amiss; and as many lies° as will lie    35 in thy sheet of paper, although the sheet were big enough for the bed of Ware° in England, set 'em down. Go, about it. Let there be gall° enough in thy ink, though thou write with a goose pen,° no matter. About it.

**SIR ANDREW:**   Where shall I find you?                                             40

**SIR TOBY:**   We'll call thee° at the cubiculo.° Go.

          *Exit Sir Andrew.*

**FABIAN:**   This is a dear manikin° to you, Sir Toby.

**SIR TOBY:**   I have been dear° to him, lad, some two thousand strong or so.

**FABIAN:**   We shall have a rare° letter from him; but you'll not deliver't?                                                                         45

**SIR TOBY:**   Never trust me, then; and by all means stir on the youth to an answer. I think oxen and wainropes° cannot hale° them together. For° Andrew, if he were opened and you find so much blood in his liver° as will clog the foot of a flea, I'll eat the rest of th' anatomy.°                                                                 50

**FABIAN:**   And his opposite,° the youth, bears in his visage no great presage of cruelty.

          *Enter Maria.*

**SIR TOBY:**   Look where the youngest wren of nine° comes.

**MARIA:**   If you desire the spleen,° and will laugh your-selves into stitches, follow me. Yond gull Malvolio is turned heathen, a    55 very renegado;° for there is no Christian that means to be saved by believing rightly can ever believe such impossible passages of grossness.° He's in yellow stockings.

---

28 **love-broker** agent between lovers   32 **curst** fierce   34 **with … ink** i.e., with all the unfettered eloquence at your disposal as a writer.   **"thou"-est** ("Thou" was used only between friends or to inferiors.)   35 **lies** charges of lying   37 **bed of Ware** a famous bedstead capable of holding twelve persons, about eleven feet square, said to have been at the Stag Inn in Ware, Hertfordshire   38 **gall** (1) bitterness, rancor (2) a growth found on certain oaks, used as an ingredient of ink   39 **goose pen** (1) goose quill (2) foolish style   41 **call thee** call for you.   **cubiculo** little chamber, bedchamber.   42 **manikin** puppet   43 **dear** expensive. (Playing on *dear*, "fond," in the previous speech.)   45 **rare** extraordinary   47 **wainropes** wagon ropes.   **hale** haul.   48 **For** As for   49 **liver** (A pale and bloodless liver was a sign of cowardice.)   50 **th' anatomy** the cadaver.   51 **opposite** adversary   53 **youngest … nine** the last hatched and smallest of a nest of wrens   54 **the spleen** a laughing fit. (The spleen was thought to be the seat of immoderate laughter.)   56 **renegado** renegade, deserter of his religion   57–8 **impossible … grossness** gross impossibilities (i.e., in the letter).

**SIR TOBY:**   And cross-gartered?

**MARIA:**   Most villainously,° like a pedant° that keeps a school i' th'   60
church. I have dogged him like his murderer. He does obey
every point of the letter that I dropped to betray him. He does
smile his face into more lines than is in the new map with the
augmentation of the Indies.° You have not seen such a thing
as 'tis. I can hardly forbear hurling things at him. I know my   65
lady will strike him. If she do, he'll smile and take't for a great favor.

**SIR TOBY:**   Come, bring us, bring us where he is.

*Exeunt omnes.*

## 3.3

*Enter Sebastian and Antonio.*

**SEBASTIAN:**   I would not by my will have troubled you,
But since you make your pleasure of your pains,
I will no further chide you.

**ANTONIO:**   I could not stay behind you. My desire,
More sharp than filèd steel, did spur me forth,   5
And not all° love to see you—though so much°
As might have drawn one to a longer voyage—
But jealousy° what might befall your travel,
Being skilless in° these parts, which to a stranger,
Unguided and unfriended, often prove   10
Rough and unhospitable. My willing love,
The rather° by these arguments of fear,
Set forth in your pursuit.

**SEBASTIAN:**   My kind Antonio,
I can no other answer make but thanks,   15
And thanks; and ever oft good turns°
Are shuffled off° with such uncurrent° pay.
But were my worth,° as is my conscience,° firm,
You should find better dealing.° What's to do?
Shall we go see the relics° of this town?   20

**ANTONIO:**   Tomorrow, sir. Best first go see your lodging.

**SEBASTIAN:**   I am not weary, and 'tis long to night.
I pray you, let us satisfy our eyes

---

**60 villainously** i.e., abominably.   **pedant** schoolmaster   **63–4 the new ... Indies** (Probably a reference to a map made by Emmeric Mollineux in 1599–1600 to be printed in Hakluyt's *Voyages*, showing more of the East indies, including Japan, than had ever been mapped before.)
**6 all** only, merely.   **so much** i.e., that was great enough   **8 jealousy** anxiety   **9 skilless in** unacquainted with   **12 The rather** made all the more willing   **16 And ... turns** (This probably corrupt line is usually made to read, "And thanks and ever thanks; and oft good turns.")   **17 shuffled off** turned aside.   **uncurrent** worthless (such as mere thanks)   **18 worth** wealth.   **conscience** i.e., moral inclination to assist   **19 dealing** treatment, payment.   **20 relics** antiquities

With the memorials and the things of fame
That do renown° this city.                                          25
**ANTONIO**   Would you'd pardon me.
I do not without danger walk these streets.
Once in a sea fight 'gainst the Count his° galleys
I did some service, of such note indeed
That were I ta'en here it would scarce be answered.°      30
**SEBASTIAN**   Belike° you slew great number of his people?
**ANTONIO**   Th' offense is not of such a bloody nature,
Albeit the quality of the time and quarrel
Might well have given us bloody argument.°
It might have since been answered° in repaying          35
What we took from them, which for traffic's° sake
Most of our city did. Only myself stood out,
For which, if I be lapsèd° in this place,
I shall pay dear.
**SEBASTIAN**   Do not then walk too open.                       40
**ANTONIO**   It doth not fit me. Hold, sir, here's my purse.

            [*He gives his purse.*]

In the south suburbs, at the Elephant,°
Is best to lodge. I will bespeak our diet,°
Whiles you beguile the time and feed your knowledge
With viewing of the town. There shall you have° me.      45
**SEBASTIAN**   Why I your purse?
**ANTONIO**   Haply° your eye shall light upon some toy°
You have desire to purchase; and your store°
I think is not for idle markets,° sir.
**SEBASTIAN**   I'll be your purse-bearer and leave you       50
For an hour.
**ANTONIO**   To th' Elephant.
**SEBASTIAN**   I do remember.

            *Exeunt* [*separately*].

### 3.4

*Enter Olivia and Maria.*

**OLIVIA**   [*aside*]
I have sent after him; he says he'll come.°
How shall I feast him? What bestow of° him?

25 **renown** make famous   28 **Count his** Count's, i.e., Duke's   30 **it … answered** I'd be hard put to
offer a defense.   31 **Belike** Perhaps   34 **bloody argument** cause for bloodshed.   35 **answered** com-
pensated   36 **traffic's** trade's   38 **lapsèd** caught off guard, surprised   42 **Elephant** the name of an
inn   43 **bespeak our diet** order our food   45 **have** find   47 **Haply** Perhaps.  **toy** trifle   48 **store**
store of money   49 **is not … markets** cannot afford luxuries   1 **he … come** i.e., suppose he says
he'll come.   2 **of** on

For youth is bought more oft than begged or borrowed.
I speak too loud.—
Where's Malvolio? He is sad and civil,°                 5
And suits well for a servant with my fortunes.
Where is Malvolio?

**MARIA**   He's coming, madam, but in very strange manner. He is,
sure, possessed,° madam.

**OLIVIA**   Why, what's the matter? Does he rave?           10

**MARIA**   No, madam, he does nothing but smile. Your Ladyship were
best to have some guard about you if he come, for sure the man
is tainted in's° wits.

**OLIVIA**   Go call him hither. [*Maria summons Malvolio.*] I am as mad as he,
If sad and merry madness equal be.°           15

      *Enter Malvolio, [cross-gartered and in yellow stockings].*

How now, Malvolio?

**MALVOLIO**   Sweet lady, ho, ho!

**OLIVIA**   Smil'st thou? I sent for thee upon a sad° occasion.

**MALVOLIO**   Sad, lady? I could be sad.° This does make some obstruction in the blood, this cross-gartering, but what of that? If     20
it please the eye of one, it is with me as the very true sonnet°
is, "Please one and please all."°

**OLIVIA**   Why, how dost thou, man? What is the matter with thee?

**MALVOLIO**   Not black° in my mind, though yellow in my legs. It°
did come to his° hands, and commands shall be executed. I
think we do know the sweet roman hand.°           25

**OLIVIA**   Wilt thou go to bed,° Malvolio?

**MALVOLIO**   To bed! "Ay, sweetheart, and I'll come to thee."°

**OLIVIA**   God comfort thee! Why dost thou smile so and kiss thy
hand so oft?

**MARIA**   How do you, Malvolio?

**MALVOLIO**   At your request? Yes, nightingales answer daws.°     30

**MARIA**   Why appear you with this ridiculous boldness before my lady?

**MALVOLIO**   "Be not afraid of greatness." 'Twas well writ.

**OLIVIA**   What mean'st thou by that, Malvolio?

**MALVOLIO**   "Some are born great—"

**OLIVIA**   Ha?           35

**MALVOLIO**   "Some achieve greatness—"

---

**5 sad and civil** sober and decorous   **9 possessed** (1) possessed with an evil spirit (2) mad   **13 in's** in his
**15 If ... equal be** i.e., if love melancholy and smiling madness are essentially alike. (Love melancholy was
regarded as a kind of madness.)   **18 sad** serious   **19 sad** (1) serious (2) melancholy.   **21 sonnet** song,
ballad   **22 "Please ... all"** "To please one special person is as good as to please everybody." (The refrain of
a ballad.)   **23 black** i.e., melancholic. **It** i.e., The letter.   **24 his** Malvolio's   **25 roman hand** fashionable italic or Italian style of handwriting rather than English "secretary" handwriting.   **26 go to bed** i.e.,
try to sleep off your mental distress. (But Malvolio misinterprets as a sexual invitation.)   **27 "Ay ... thee"**
(Malvolio quotes from a popular song of the day.)   **30 nightingales answer daws** i.e. (to Maria), do you
suppose a fine fellow like me would answer a lowly creature (a *daw*, a "jackdaw") like you?

**OLIVIA** What say'st thou?

**MALVOLIO** "And some have greatness thrust upon them."

**OLIVIA** Heaven restore thee!

**MALVOLIO** "Remember who commended thy yellow stockings—"     40

**OLIVIA** Thy yellow stockings?

**MALVOLIO** "And wished to see thee cross-gartered."

**OLIVIA** Cross-gartered?

**MALVOLIO** "Go to, thou art made, if thou desir'st to be so—"

**OLIVIA** Am I made?     45

**MALVOLIO** "If not, let me see thee a servant still."

**OLIVIA** Why, this is very midsummer madness.°

   *Enter Servant.*

**SERVANT** Madam, the young gentleman of the Count Orsino's is returned. I could hardly entreat him back. He attends Your Ladyship's pleasure.

**OLIVIA** I'll come to him. [*Exit Servant.*]     50
Good Maria, let this fellow be looked to. Where's my cousin Toby? Let some of my people have a special care of him. I would not have him miscarry° for the half of my dowry.

   *Exeunt [Olivia and Maria, different ways].*

**MALVOLIO** Oho, do you come near° me now? No worse man than Sir Toby to look to me! This concurs directly with the let-     55
ter. She sends him on purpose that I may appear stubborn to him, for she incites me to that in the letter. "Cast thy humble slough," says she; "be opposite with a kinsman, surly with servants; let thy tongue tang with arguments of state; put thyself into the trick of singularity." And consequently° sets down the     60
manner how: as, a sad° face, a reverend carriage, a slow tongue, in the habit of some sir of note,° and so forth. I have limed° her, but it is Jove's doing, and Jove make me thankful! And when she went away now, "Let this fellow be looked to." "Fellow!"° Not "Malvolio," nor after my degree,° but "fellow."     65
Why, everything adheres together, that no dram° of a scruple, no scruple° of a scruple, no obstacle, no incredulous° or unsafe° circumstance—what can be said?—nothing that can be can come between me and the full prospect of my hopes. Well, Jove, not I, is the doer of this, and he is to be thanked.     70

   *Enter [Sir] Toby, Fabian, and Maria.*

47 **midsummer madness** (A proverbial phrase; the midsummer moon was supposed to cause madness.)
52 **miscarry** come to harm   53 **come near** understand, appreciate   60 **consequently** thereafter
61 **sad** serious   62 **habit ... note** attire suited to a man of distinction   63 **limed** caught like a bird with birdlime (a sticky substance spread on branches)   65 **Fellow** (Malvolio takes the basic meaning, "companion.")   65 **after my degree** according to my position   66 **dram** (Literally, one-eighth of a fluid ounce.)
67 **scruple** (Literally, one-third of a dram.)   **incredulous** incredible   67–8 **unsafe** uncertain, unreliable

**SIR TOBY**  Which way is he, in the name of sanctity? If all the devils
of hell be drawn in little,° and Legion° himself possessed him,
yet I'll speak to him.

**FABIAN**  Here he is, here he is.—How is't with you, sir? How is't
with you, man?

**MALVOLIO**  Go off. I discard you. Let me enjoy my private.° Go off.      75

**MARIA**  Lo, how hollow the fiend speaks within him! Did not I tell
you? Sir Toby, my lady prays you to have a care of him.

**MALVOLIO**  Aha, does she so?

**SIR TOBY**  Go to, go to! Peace, peace, we must deal gently with
him. Let me alone.°—How do you, Malvolio? How is't with you?      80
What, man, defy° the devil! Consider, he's an enemy to mankind.

**MALVOLIO**  Do you know what you say?

**MARIA**  La you,° an you speak ill of the devil, how he takes it at
heart! Pray God he be not bewitched!

**FABIAN**  Carry his water° to th' wise woman.°      85

**MARIA**  Marry, and it shall be done tomorrow morning, if I live. My
lady would not lose him for more than I'll say.

**MALVOLIO**  How now, mistress?

**MARIA**  Oh, Lord!

**SIR TOBY**  Prithee, hold thy peace; this is not the way. Do you not      90
see you move° him? Let me alone with him.

**FABIAN**  No way but gentleness, gently, gently. The fiend is rough,
and will not be roughly used.

**SIR TOBY**  Why, how now, my bawcock!° How dost thou, chuck?°

**MALVOLIO**  Sir!      95

**SIR TOBY**  Ay, biddy,° come with me. What, man, 'tis not for grav-
ity° to play at cherry-pit° with Satan. Hang him, foul collier!°

**MARIA**  Get him to say his prayers, good Sir Toby, get him to pray.

**MALVOLIO**  My prayers, minx?

**MARIA**  No, I warrant you, he will not hear of godliness.      100

**MALVOLIO**  Go hang yourselves all! You are idle,° shallow things;
I am not of your element.° You shall know more° hereafter.

*Exit.*

**SIR TOBY**  Is't possible?

**FABIAN**  If this were played upon a stage, now, I could condemn
it as an improbable fiction.      105

**SIR TOBY**  His very genius° hath taken the infection of the device, man.

**72 drawn in little** (1) portrayed in miniature (2) gathered into a small space.   **Legion** an unclean spirit.
("My name is Legion, for we are many," Mark 5:9.)   **75 private** privacy.   **80 Let me alone** Leave him
to me.   **81 defy** renounce   **83 La you** Look you   **85 water** urine (for medical analysis).   **wise woman**
sorceress.   **91 move** upset, excite   **94 bawcock** fine fellow. (From the French *beau-coq*.)   **95 chuck**
(A form of "chick," term of endearment.)   **96 biddy** chicken   **96–7 for gravity** suitable for a man of your
dignity.   **97 cherry-pit** a children's game consisting of throwing cherry stones into a little hole.   **collier**
i.e., Satan. (Literally, a coal vendor.)   **101 idle** foolish   **102 element** sphere.   **know more** i.e., hear about
this   **106 genius** i.e., soul, spirit

**MARIA**  Nay, pursue him now, lest the device take air and taint.°

**FABIAN**  Why, we shall make him mad indeed.

**MARIA**  The house will be the quieter.

**SIR TOBY**  Come, we'll have him in a dark room and bound.° My  110
niece is already in the belief that he's mad. We may carry° it
thus for our pleasure and his penance till our very pastime, tired
out of breath, prompt us to have mercy on him, at which time
we will bring the device to the bar° and crown thee for a finder
of madmen.° But see, but see!  115

*Enter Sir Andrew [with a letter].*

**FABIAN**  More matter for a May morning.°

**SIR ANDREW**  Here's the challenge. Read it. I warrant there's
vinegar and pepper in't.

**FABIAN**  Is't so saucy?°

**SIR ANDREW**  Ay, is't, I warrant him.° Do but read.  120

**SIR TOBY**  Give me. [*He reads.*] "Youth, whatsoever thou art, thou
art but a scurvy fellow."

**FABIAN**  Good, and valiant.

**SIR TOBY**  [*reads*] "Wonder not, nor admire° not in thy mind, why
I do call thee so, for I will show thee no reason for't."

**FABIAN**  A good note,° that keeps you from the blow of the law.  125

**SIR TOBY**  [*reads*] "Thou com'st to the Lady Olivia, and in my sight
she uses thee kindly. But thou liest in thy throat; that is not the
matter I challenge thee for."

**FABIAN**  Very brief, and to exceeding good sense—less.

**SIR TOBY**  [*reads*] "I will waylay thee going home, where if it be  130
thy chance to kill me—"

**FABIAN**  Good.

**SIR TOBY**  [*reads*] "Thou kill'st me like a rogue and a villain."

**FABIAN**  Still you keep o' th' windy° side of the law. Good.

**SIR TOBY**  [*reads*] "Fare thee well, and God have mercy upon one of  135
our souls! He may have mercy upon mine, but my hope is better,° and so look to thyself. Thy friend, as thou usest him, and
thy sworn enemy, Andrew Aguecheek."If this letter move° him
not, his legs cannot. I'll give't him.

**MARIA**  You may have very fit occasion for't. He is now in some  140
commerce° with my lady, and will by and by depart.

---

107 **take ... taint** become exposed to air (i.e., become known) and thus spoil.   110 **have ... bound**
(The standard treatment for insanity at this time.)   111 **carry** manage   114 **bar** i.e., bar of judgment
115 **finder of madmen** member of a jury changed with "finding" if the accused is insane.   116 **matter ...
morning** sport for Mayday plays or games.   119 **saucy** (1) spicy (2) insolent.   120 **him** it.   123 **admire**
marvel   125 **note** observation, remark   134 **windy** windward, i.e., safe, where one is less likely to be
driven onto legal rocks and shoals   136–7 **my hope is better** (Sir Andrew's comically inept way of saying
he hopes to be the survivor; instead, he seems to say, "May I be damned.")   139 **move** (1) stir up (2) set in
motion   141 **commerce** transaction

**SIR TOBY**  Go, Sir Andrew. Scout me° for him at the corner of the
orchard like a bum-baily.° So soon as ever thou see'st him, draw,
and as thou draw'st, swear horrible;° for it comes to pass oft
that a terrible oath, with a swaggering accent sharply twanged        145
off, gives manhood more approbation° than ever proof° itself
would have earned him. Away!

**SIR ANDREW**  Nay, let me alone for swearing.°  *Exit.*

**SIR TOBY**  Now will not I deliver his letter, for the behavior of
the young gentleman gives him out to be of good capacity            150
and breeding; his employment between his lord and my niece
confirms no less. Therefore this letter, being so excellently ignorant, will breed no terror in the youth. He will find it comes
from a clodpoll.° But, sir, I will deliver his challenge by word of
mouth, set upon Aguecheek a notable report of valor, and drive       155
the gentleman—as I know his youth will aptly receive it°—into
a most hideous opinion of his rage, skill, fury, and impetuosity.
This will so fright them both that they will kill one another by
the look, like cockatrices.°

*Enter Olivia and Viola.*

**FABIAN**  Here he comes with your niece. Give them way° till he     160
take leave, and presently° after him.

**SIR TOBY**  I will meditate the while upon some horrid° message for
a challenge.

*[Exeunt Sir Toby, Fabian, and Maria.]*

**OLIVIA**  I have said too much unto a heart of stone
And laid° mine honor too unchary on't.°                             165
There's something in me that reproves my fault,
But such a headstrong potent fault it is
That it but mocks reproof.

**VIOLA**  With the same havior that your passion bears
Goes on my master's griefs.°                                        170

**OLIVIA**  *[giving a locket]*
Here, wear this jewel for me. 'Tis my picture.
Refuse it not; it hath no tongue to vex you.
And I beseech you come again tomorrow.
What shall you ask of me that I'll deny,                            175
That honor, saved, may upon asking give?°

---

142 **Scout me** Keep watch   143 **bum-baily** minor sheriff's officer employed in making arrests.   144 **hor-**
**rible** horribly   146 **approbation** reputation (for courage).   147 **proof** performance   148 **let ... swearing**
don't worry about my ability in swearing.   154 **clodpoll** blockhead.   156–7 **his ... it** his inexperience will
make him all the more ready to believe it   159 **cockatrices** basilisks, fabulous serpents reputed to be able
to kill by a mere look.   160 **Give them way** Stay out of their way   161 **presently** immediately   162 **hor-**
**rid** terrifying. (Literally, "bristling.")   165 **laid** hazarded.   **unchary on't** recklessly on it.   169–70 **With**
**... griefs** i.e., Orsino's sufferings in love are as reckless and uncontrollable as your feelings.
176 **That ... give?** that can be granted without compromising my honor?

**VIOLA**  Nothing but this: your true love for my master.

**OLIVIA**  How with mine honor may I give him that
Which I have given to you?

**VIOLA**  I will acquit you.°                                                                180

**OLIVIA**  Well, come again tomorrow. Fare thee well.
A fiend like thee might bear my soul to hell.°  [*Exit.*]

*Enter [Sir] Toby and Fabian.*

**SIR TOBY**  Gentleman, God save thee.

**VIOLA**  And you, sir.

**SIR TOBY**  That defense thou hast, be take thee to't.° Of what        185
nature the wrongs are thou hast done him, I know not, but thy
intercepter,° full of despite,° bloody as the hunter,° attends
thee at the orchard end. Dismount thy tuck,° be yare° in thy
preparation, for thy assailant is quick, skillful, and deadly.

**VIOLA**  You mistake sir. I am sure no man hath any quarrel to° me.     190
My remembrance is very free and clear from any image of offense
done to any man.

**SIR TOBY**  You'll find it otherwise, I assure you. Therefore, if you
hold your life at any price, be take you to your guard, for your
opposite° hath in him what° youth, strength, skill, and wrath        195
can furnish man withal.°

**VIOLA**  I pray you, sir, what is he?

**SIR TOBY**  He is knight, dubbed with unhatched° rapier and on
carpet consideration,° but he is a devil in private brawl. Souls and
bodies hath he divorced three, and his incensement at this moment is so implacable that satisfaction can be none but by pangs    200
of death and sepulchre. Hob, nob° is his word;° give't or take't.

**VIOLA**  I will return again into the house and desire some conduct°
of the lady. I am no fighter. I have heard of some kind of men
that put quarrels purposely on others, to taste° their valor.
Belike° this is a man of that quirk.°                                          205

**SIR TOBY**  Sir, no. His indignation derives itself out of a very com-
petent° injury; therefore, get you on and give him his desire.
Back you shall not to the house unless you undertake that with
me which with as much safety you might answer him. Therefore,

---

180 **acquit you** release you of your promise.    181 **A fiend ... hell** i.e., You are my torment. (*Like
thee* means "in your likeness.")    185 **That ... to't** Get ready to deploy whatever skill you have in fencing.    187 **intercepter** he who lies in wait.    **despite** defiance, ill will.    **bloody as the hunter** bloodthirsty as a hunting dog    188 **Dismount thy tuck** Draw your rapier.    **yare** ready, nimble    190 **to**
with    195 **opposite** opponent.    **what** whatsoever.    196 **withal** with.    197 **unhatched** unhacked,
unused in battle    198 **carpet consideration** (A carpet knight was one whose title was obtained, not in
battle, but through connections at court.)    201 **Hob, nob** Have or have not, i.e., give it or take it, kill
or be killed.    **word** motto    202–3 **conduct** safe-conduct, escort    204 **taste** test, prove    205 **Belike**
Probably.    **quirk** peculiar humor.    207 **competent** sufficient

on, or strip your sword stark naked;° for meddle° you must, 210
that's certain, or for swear to wear iron° about you.

**VIOLA**  This is as uncivil as strange. I beseech you, do me this courteous office as to know of° the knight what my offense to him
is. It is something of my negligence, nothing of my purpose.°

**SIR TOBY**  I will do so.—Signor Fabian, stay you by this gentleman 215
till my return.  *Exit [Sir] Toby.*

**VIOLA**  Pray you, sir, do you know of this matter?

**FABIAN**  I know the knight is incensed against you, even to a mortal arbitrament,° but nothing of the circumstance more.

**VIOLA**  I beseech you, what manner of man is he? 220

**FABIAN**  Nothing of that wonderful promise, to read him by his
form,° as you are like° to find him in the proof of his valor. He
is, indeed, sir, the most skillful, bloody, and fatal opposite that
you could possibly have found in any part of Illyria. Will you°
walk towards him, I will make your peace with him if I can. 225

**VIOLA**  I shall be much bound to you for't. I am one that had rather
go with° Sir Priest° than Sir Knight. I care not who knows so
much of my mettle.  *Exeunt.*

*Enter [Sir] Toby and [Sir] Andrew.*

**SIR TOBY**  Why, man, he's a very devil; I have not seen such a
firago.° I had a pass° with him, rapier, scabbard, and all, and 230
he gives me the stuck-in° with such a mortal motion that it is
inevitable; and on the answer,° he pays you as surely as your
feet hits the ground they step on. They say he has been fencer
to° the Sophy.

**SIR ANDREW**  Pox on't, I'll not meddle with him.

**SIR TOBY**  Ay, but he will not now be pacified. Fabian can scarce 235
hold him yonder.

**SIR ANDREW**  Plague on't, an I thought he had been valiant and
so cunning in fence, I'd have seen him damned ere I'd have
challenged him. Let him let the matter slip and I'll give him my
horse, gray Capilet.°

**SIR TOBY**  I'll make the motion.° Stand here, make a good show
on't. This shall end without the perdition of souls.° [*Aside, as* 240
*he crosses to meet Fabian*] Marry, I'll ride your horse as well as
I ride you.

*Enter Fabian and Viola.*

---

210 **strip ... naked** draw your sword from its sheath.  **meddle** engage (in conflict)  211 **forswear ... iron**
give up your right to wear a sword  213 **know of** inquire from  214 **It is ... purpose** It is the result of some
oversight, not anything I intended.  219 **mortal arbitrament** trial to the death  221–2 **read ... form** judge
him by his appearance  222 **like** likely  224 **Will you** If you will  227 **go with** associate with.  **Sir Priest**
(*Sir* was a courtesy title for priests.)  230 **firago** virago.  **pass** bout  231 **stuck-in** stoccado, a thrust in
fencing  232 **answer** return hit  233 **to** in the service of  238 **Capilet** i.e., "little horse." (From "capel," a
nag.)  239 **motion** offer.  240 **perdition of souls** i.e., loss of lives.

[*Aside to Fabian*] I have his horse to take up° the quarrel. I
have persuaded him the youth's a devil.

**FABIAN** He is as horribly conceited of him,° and pants and looks
pale as if a bear were at his heels.                                    245

**SIR TOBY** [*to Viola*] There's no remedy, sir, he will fight with you
for's oath's sake. Marry, he hath better be thought him of his
quarrel, and he finds that now scarce to be worth talking of.
Therefore draw, for the supportance° of his vow; he protests he
will not hurt you.

**VIOLA** [*aside*] Pray God defend me! A little thing would make me    250
tell them how much I lack of a man.°

**FABIAN** Give ground, if you see him furious.

**SIR TOBY** [*crossing to Sir Andrew*] Come, Sir Andrew, there's no remedy. The gentleman will, for his honor's sake, have one bout with
you. He cannot by the *duello*° avoid it. But he has promised me, as  255
he is a gentleman and a soldier, he will not hurt you. Come on, to't.

**SIR ANDREW** Pray God he keep his oath!

*Enter Antonio.*

**VIOLA** [*to Fabian*] I do assure you, 'tis against my will.

[*They draw.*]

**ANTONIO** [*drawing, to Sir Andrew*]
Put up your sword. If this young gentleman
Have done offense, I take the fault on me;                              260
If you offend him, I for him defy you.

**SIR TOBY** You, sir? Why, what are you?

**ANTONIO** One, sir, that for his love dares yet do more
Than you have heard him brag to you he will.

**SIR TOBY** [*drawing*]                                                265
Nay, if you be an undertaker,° I am for you.°

*Enter Officers.*

**FABIAN** Oh, good Sir Toby, hold! Here come the officers.

**SIR TOBY** [*to Antonio*] I'll be with you anon.

**VIOLA** [*to Sir Andrew*] Pray, sir, put your sword up, if you please.

**SIR ANDREW** Marry, will I, sir; and for that° I promised you, I'll be   270
as good as my word. He° will bear you easily, and reins well.

**FIRST OFFICER** This is the man. Do thy office.

**SECOND OFFICER** Antonio, I arrest thee at the suit

---

242 **take up** settle, make up  244 **He ... him** i.e., Cesario has as horrible a conception of Sir
Andrew  249 **supportance** upholding  250–1 **A little ... man** (With bawdy suggestion of the
penis.)  255 ***duello*** dueling code  266 **undertaker** one who takes upon himself a task or business;
here, a challenger.  **for you** ready for you.  270 **for that** as for what  271 **He** i.e., The horse

Of Count Orsino.
**ANTONIO**   You do mistake me, sir.                                              275
**FIRST OFFICER**   No, sir, no jot. I know your favor° well,
  Though now you have no sea-cap on your head.—
  Take him away. He knows I know him well.
**ANTONIO**   I must obey. [*To Viola*] This comes with seeking you.
  But there's no remedy; I shall answer it.°                                      280
  What will you do, now my necessity
  Makes me to ask you for my purse? It grieves me
  Much more for what I cannot do for you
  Than what befalls myself. You stand amazed,
  But be of comfort.                                                              285
**SECOND OFFICER**   Come, sir, away.
**ANTONIO**   [*to Viola*]
  I must entreat of you some of that money.
**VIOLA**   What money, sir?
  For the fair kindness you have showed me here,                                  290
  And part° being prompted by your present trouble,
  Out of my lean and low ability
  I'll lend you something. My having° is not much;
  I'll make division of my present° with you.
  Hold, there's half my coffer.° [*She offers money.*]                           295
**ANTONIO**   Will you deny me now?
  Is't possible that my deserts to you
  Can lack persuasion?° Do not tempt° my misery,
  Lest that it make me so unsound° a man
  As to upbraid you with those kindnesses                                         300
  That I have done for you.
**VIOLA**   I know of none,
  Nor know I you by voice or any feature.
  I hate ingratitude more in a man
  Than lying, vainness,° babbling drunkenness,                                    305
  Or any taint of vice whose strong corruption
  Inhabits our frail blood.
**ANTONIO**   Oh, heavens themselves!
**SECOND OFFICER**   Come, sir, I pray you, go.
**ANTONIO**   Let me speak a little. This youth that you see here                  310
  I snatched one half out of the jaws of death,
  Relieved him with such sanctity of love,°
  And to his image,° which methought did promise

---

**276 favor** face   **280 answer it** stand trial and make reparation for it.   **291 part** partly   **293 having** wealth
**294 present** present store   **295 coffer** purse. (Literally, strongbox.)   **297–8 deserts … persuasion** claims on
you can fail to persuade you to help me.   **298 tempt** try too severely   **299 unsound** morally weak, lacking in
self-control   **305 vainness** vaingloriousness   **312 such … love** i.e., such veneration as is due to a sacred relic
**313 image** what he appeared to be. (Playing on the idea of a religious icon to be venerated.)

Most venerable worth,° did I devotion.

**FIRST OFFICER**   What's that to us? The time goes by. Away!                    315

**ANTONIO**   But, oh, how vile an idol proves this god!

Thou hast, Sebastian, done good feature shame.°

In nature there's no blemish but the mind;

None can be called deformed but the unkind.°

Virtue is beauty, but the beauteous evil°                                      320

Are empty trunks° o'erflourished° by the devil.

**FIRST OFFICER**   The man grows mad. Away with him! Come,

come, sir.

**ANTONIO**   Lead me on.    *Exit [with Officers].*

**VIOLA**   *[aside]*

Methinks his words do from such passion fly

That he believes himself. So do not I.°                                        325

Prove true, imagination, oh, prove true,

That I, dear brother, be now ta'en for you!

**SIR TOBY**   Come hither, knight. Come hither, Fabian.

We'll whisper o'er a couplet or two of most sage saws.°

*[They gather apart from Viola.]*

**VIOLA**   He named Sebastian. I my brother know                               330

Yet living in my glass;° even such and so

In favor° was my brother, and he went

Still° in this fashion, color, ornament,

For him I imitate. Oh, if it prove,°

Tempests are kind, and salt waves fresh in love!                              335

*[Exit.]*

**SIR TOBY**   A very dishonest° paltry boy, and more a coward than a

hare. His dishonesty° appears in leaving his friend here in ne-

cessity and denying° him; and for his cowardship, ask Fabian.

**FABIAN**   A coward, a most devout coward, religious in it.°

**SIR ANDREW**   'Slid,° I'll after him again and beat him.                     340

**SIR TOBY**   Do, cuff him soundly, but never draw thy sword.

**SIR ANDREW**   An I do not—   *[Exit.]*

**FABIAN**   Come, let's see the event.°

**SIR TOBY**   I dare lay° any money 'twill be nothing yet.°

*Exeunt.*

314 **venerable worth** worthiness of being venerated   317 **Thou ... shame** i.e., You have shamed physical beauty by showing that it does not always reflect inner beauty.   319 **unkind** ungrateful, unnatural.
320 **beauteous evil** those who are outwardly beautiful but evil within   321 **trunks** (1) chests (2) bodies.   **o'erflourished** (1) covered with ornamental carvings (2) made outwardly beautiful   325 **So ... I** i.e., I do not believe myself (in the hope that has arisen in me).   329 **We'll ... saws** i.e., Let's converse privately. (*Saws* are sayings.)   330–1 **I ... glass** i.e., I know that my brother's likeness lives in me   332 **favor** appearance   333 **Still** always   334 **prove** prove true   336 **dishonest** dishonorable   337 **dishonesty** dishonor   338 **denying** refusing to acknowledge   339 **religious in it** making a religion of cowardice.
340 **'Slid** By his (God's) eyelid   343 **event** outcome.   344 **lay** wager.   **yet** nevertheless, after all.

## 4.1

*Enter Sebastian and Clown [Feste].*

**FESTE**　Will you make me believe that I am not sent for you?

**SEBASTIAN**　Go to, go to, thou art a foolish fellow. Let me be clear of thee.

**FESTE**　Well held out,° i' faith! No, I do not know you, nor I am not sent to you by my lady to bid you come speak with her, nor your name is not Master Cesario, nor this is not my nose, neither. Nothing that is so is so.

**SEBASTIAN**　I prithee, vent° thy folly somewhere else. Thou know'st not me. 　5

**FESTE**　Vent my folly! He has heard that word of° some great man, and now applies it to a fool. Vent my folly! I am afraid this great lubber,° the world, will prove a cockney.° I prithee now, ungird thy strangeness° and tell me what I shall vent to my lady. Shall I vent to her that thou art coming?

**SEBASTIAN**　I prithee, foolish Greek,° depart from me. There's money for thee. [*He gives money.*] If you tarry longer, I shall 　10 give worse payment.

**FESTE**　By my troth, thou hast an open° hand. These wise men that give fools money get themselves a good report°—after fourteen years' purchase.°

*Enter [Sir] Andrew, [Sir] Toby, and Fabian.* 　15

**SIR ANDREW**　Now, sir, have I met you again? There's for you! [*He strikes Sebastian.*]

**SEBASTIAN**　Why, there's for thee, and there, and there!

[*He beats Sir Andrew with the hilt of his dagger.*]

Are all the people mad?

**SIR TOBY**　Hold, sir, or I'll throw your dagger o'er the house. 　20

**FESTE**　This will I tell my lady straight.° I would not be in some of your coats° for two pence.　[*Exit.*]

---

**3 held out** kept up　**6 vent** (1) utter (2) void, excrete, get rid of　**7 of** from, suited to the diction of; or, with reference to　**9 lubber** lout.　**cockney** effeminate or foppish fellow. (Feste comically despairs of finding common sense anywhere if people start using affected phrases like those Sebastian uses.)　**10 ungird thy strangeness** put off your affectation of being a stranger. (Feste apes the kind of high-flown speech he has just deplored.)　**12 Greek** (1) one who speaks gibberish (as in "It's all Greek to me") (2) buffoon (as in "merry Greek")　**14 open** generous. (With money or with blows.)　**15 report** reputation.　**15–6 after ... purchase** i.e., at great cost and after long delays. (Land was ordinarily valued at the price of twelve years' rental; the Fool adds two years to this figure.)　**20 straight** at once.　**20–21 in ... coats** i.e., in your shoes

**SIR TOBY**    Come on, sir, hold!    [*He grips Sebastian.*]

**SIR ANDREW**    Nay, let him alone. I'll go another way to work with
him. I'll have an action of battery° against him, if there be any law
in Illyria. Though I struck him first, yet it's no matter for that.

**SEBASTIAN**    Let go thy hand!                                                    25

**SIR TOBY**    Come, sir, I will not let you go. Come, my young soldier,
put up your iron. You are well fleshed.° Come on.

**SEBASTIAN**    I will be free from thee. [*He breaks free and draws his
sword.*] What wouldst thou now?
    If thou dar'st tempt° me further, draw thy sword.                30

**SIR TOBY**    What, what? Nay, then I must have an ounce or two of
this malapert° blood from you.    [*He draws.*]

    *Enter Olivia.*

**OLIVIA**    Hold, Toby! On thy life I charge thee, hold!

**SIR TOBY**    Madam—

**OLIVIA**    Will it be ever thus? Ungracious wretch,                   35
    Fit for the mountains and the barbarous caves,
    Where manners ne'er were preached! Out of my sight!—
    Be not offended, dear Cesario.—
    Rudesby,° begone!

    [*Exeunt Sir Toby, Sir Andrew, and Fabian.*]

    I prithee, gentle friend,                                                      40
    Let thy fair wisdom, not thy passion, sway
    In this uncivil and unjust extent°
    Against thy peace. Go with me to my house,
    And hear thou there how many fruitless pranks
    This ruffian hath botched up,° that thou thereby                45
    Mayst smile at this. Thou shalt not choose but go.°
    Do not deny.° Beshrew° his soul for me!°
    He started one poor heart of mine, in thee.°

**SEBASTIAN**    [*aside*]
    What relish is in this?° How runs the stream?                     50
    Or° I am mad, or else this is a dream.
    Let fancy still my sense in Let he steep;°
    If it be thus to dream, still let me sleep!

**OLIVIA**    Nay, come, I prithee. Would thou'dst be ruled by me!

**SEBASTIAN**    Madam, I will.                                                   55

**OLIVIA**    Oh, say so, and so be!    *Exeunt.*

---

**23 action of battery** lawsuit for physical assault    **27 fleshed** initiated into battle.    **30 tempt** make trial
of    **32 malapert** saucy, impudent    **39 Rudesby** Ruffian    **42 extent** attack    **45 botched up** clumsily
contrived    **46 Thou ... go** I insist on your going with me.    **47 deny** refuse.    **Beshrew** Curse. (A mild
oath.)    **for me** for my part.    **48 He ... thee** i.e., He alarmed that part of my heart which lies in your
bosom. (To *start* is also to drive an animal such as a *hart* [*heart*] from its cover.)    **50 What ... this?** i.e.,
What am I to make of this? (*Relish* means "taste.")    **51 Or** Either    **52 Let ... steep** i.e., Let this fantasy
continue to steep my senses in forgetfulness. (*Lethe* is the river of forgetfulness in the underworld.)

## 4.2

*Enter Maria [carrying a gown and a false beard], and Clown [Feste].*

**MARIA**   Nay, I prithee, put on this gown and this beard; make him
believe thou art Sir° Topas° the curate. Do it quickly. I'll call Sir
Toby the whilst.° [*Exit.*]

**FESTE**   Well, I'll put it on, and I will dissemble° myself in't, and I
would I were the first that ever dissembled in such a gown. [*He
disguises himself in gown and beard.*] I am not tall enough to become the function° well, nor lean° enough to be thought a good
student;° but to be said an honest man and a good housekeeper
goes as fairly as to say a careful man and a great scholar.° The
competitors° enter.

      *Enter [Sir] Toby [and Maria].*

**SIR TOBY**   Jove bless thee, Master Parson.                                           10
**FESTE**   *Bonos dies,*° Sir Toby. For, as the old hermit of Prague,°
that never saw pen and ink, very wittily said to a niece of King
Gorboduc,° "That that is, is"; so I, being Master Parson, am
Master Parson; for what is "that" but "that," and "is" but "is"?
**SIR TOBY**   To him, Sir Topas.                                                        15
**FESTE**   What, ho, I say! Peace in this prison!

      [*He approaches the door behind which Malvolio is
      confined.*]

**SIR TOBY**   The knave counterfeits well; a good knave.
**MALVOLIO**   (*within*) Who calls there?
**FESTE**   Sir Topas the curate, who comes to visit Malvolio the lunatic.
**MALVOLIO**   Sir Topas, Sir Topas, good Sir Topas, go to my lady—           20
**FESTE**   Out, hyperbolical° fiend!° How vexest thou this man!
Talkest thou nothing but of ladies?
**SIR TOBY**   Well said, Master Parson.
**MALVOLIO**   Sir Topas, never was man thus wronged. Good Sir
Topas, do not think I am mad. They have laid me here in           25
hideous darkness.
**FESTE**   Fie, thou dishonest Satan! I call thee by the most modest°
terms, for I am one of those gentle ones that will use the devil
himself with courtesy. Say'st thou that house° is dark?

2 **Sir** (An honorific title for priests.)   **Topas** (A name perhaps derived from Chaucer's comic knight in the
"Rime of Sir Thopas" or from a similar character in Lyly's *Endymion.* Topaz, a semiprecious stone, was believed to be a cure for lunacy.)   3 **the whilst** in the meantime.   4 **dissemble** disguise. (With a play on
"feign.")   7 **become the function** adorn the priestly office   **lean** (Scholars were proverbially sparing of
diet.)   8 **student** scholar (in divinity)   **8–9 to be ... scholar** to be accounted honest and hospitable is as
good as being known as a painstaking scholar. (Feste suggests that honesty and charity are found as often
in ordinary men as in clerics.)   9 **competitors** associates, partners (in this plot)   11 ***Bonos dies*** Good
day.   **hermit of Prague** (Probably another invented authority.)   **12–3 King Gorboduc** a legendary king of
ancient Britain, protagonist in the English tragedy *Gorboduc* (1562)   21 **hyperbolical** vehement, boisterous.
**fiend** i.e., the devil supposedly possessing Malvolio.   27 **modest** moderate   29 **house** i.e., room

**MALVOLIO**    As hell, Sir Topas.

**FESTE**    Why, it hath bay windows transparent as barricadoes,°    30
and the clerestories° toward the south north are as lustrous as
ebony; and yet complainest thou of obstruction?

**MALVOLIO**    I am not mad, Sir Topas. I say to you this house is dark.

**FESTE**    Madman, thou errest. I say there is no darkness but ignorance, in which thou art more puzzled than the Egyptians in    35
their fog.°

**MALVOLIO**    I say this house is as dark as ignorance, though ignorance were as dark as hell; and I say there was never man thus
abused. I am no more mad than you are. Make the trial of it in
any constant question.°

**FESTE**    What is the opinion of Pythagoras concerning wildfowl?°    40

**MALVOLIO**    That the soul of our grandam might haply° inhabit a bird.

**FESTE**    What think'st thou of his opinion?

**MALVOLIO**    I think nobly of the soul, and no way approve his opinion.

**FESTE**    Fare thee well. Remain thou still in darkness. Thou shalt
hold th' opinion of Pythagoras ere I will allow of thy wits,° and    45
fear to kill a woodcock° lest thou dispossess the soul of thy
grandam. Fare thee well.

[*He moves away from Malvolio's prison.*]

**MALVOLIO**    Sir Topas, Sir Topas!

**SIR TOBY**    My most exquisite Sir Topas!

**FESTE**    Nay, I am for all waters.°    50

**MARIA**    Thou mightst have done this without thy beard and gown.
He sees thee not.

**SIR TOBY**    To him in thine own voice, and bring me word how thou
find'st him.—I would we were well rid of this knavery. If he may
be conveniently delivered,° I would he were, for I am now so far    55
in offense with my niece that I cannot pursue with any safety
this sport to the upshot.° Come by and by to my chamber.

*Exit* [*with Maria*].

**FESTE**    [*singing as he approaches Malvolio's prison*]
"Hey, Robin, jolly Robin,
Tell me how thy lady does."°    60

**MALVOLIO**    Fool!

---

30 **barricadoes** barricades. (Which are opaque. Feste speaks comically in impossible paradoxes, but Malvolio
seems not to notice.)    31 **clerestories** windows in an upper wall    35 **Egyptians ... fog** (Alluding to the
darkness brought upon Egypt by Moses; see Exodus 10:21–3.)    39 **constant question** problem that requires
consecutive reasoning.    40 **Pythagoras ... wildfowl** (An opening for the discussion of transmigration of
souls, a doctrine held by Pythagoras.)    41 **haply** perhaps    45 **allow of thy wits** certify your sanity.
46 **woodcock** (A proverbially stupid bird, easily caught.)    50 **Nay ... waters** i.e., Indeed, I can turn my
hand to anything.    55 **delivered** i.e., delivered from prison    57 **upshot** conclusion.    59–60 **"Hey, Robin
... does"** (Another fragment of an old song, a version of which is attributed to Sir Thomas Wyatt.)

**FESTE**  "My lady is unkind, pardie."°

**MALVOLIO**  Fool!

**FESTE**  "Alas, why is she so?"

**MALVOLIO**  Fool, I say!  65

**FESTE**  "She loves another—" Who calls, ha?

**MALVOLIO**  Good Fool, as ever thou wilt deserve well at my hand, help me to a candle, and pen, ink, and paper. As I am a gentleman, I will live to be thankful to thee for't.

**FESTE**  Master Malvolio?  70

**MALVOLIO**  Ay, good Fool.

**FESTE**  Alas, sir, how fell you besides° your five wits?°

**MALVOLIO**  Fool, there was never man so notoriously abused.° I am as well in my wits, Fool, as thou art.

**FESTE**  But° as well? Then you are mad indeed, if you be no better  75
in your wits than a fool.

**MALVOLIO**  They have here propertied me,° keep me in darkness, send ministers to me—asses—and do all they can to face me out of my wits.°

**FESTE**  Advise you° what you say. The minister is here. [*He speaks as Sir Topas.*] Malvolio, Malvolio, thy wits the heavens restore! Endeavor thyself to sleep, and leave thy vain bibble-babble.  80

**MALVOLIO**  Sir Topas!

**FESTE**  [*in Sir Topas's voice*] Maintain no words with him, good fellow. [*In his own voice*] Who, I, sir? Not I, sir. God b'wi'you, good Sir Topas. [*In Sir Topas's voice*] Marry, amen. [*In his own voice*] I will, sir, I will.

**MALVOLIO**  Fool! Fool! Fool, I say!  85

**FESTE**  Alas, sir, be patient. What say you, sir? I am shent° for speaking to you.

**MALVOLIO**  Good Fool, help me to some light and some paper. I tell thee I am as well in my wits as any man in Illyria.

**FESTE**  Welladay° that you were, sir!

**MALVOLIO**  By this hand, I am. Good Fool, some ink, paper, and  90
light; and convey what I will set down to my lady. It shall advantage thee more than ever the bearing of letter did.

**FESTE**  I will help you to't. But tell me true, are you not mad indeed, or do you but counterfeit?

**MALVOLIO**  Believe me, I am not. I tell thee true.  95

**FESTE**  Nay, I'll ne'er believe a madman till I see his brains. I will fetch you light and paper and ink.

---

**62 pardie** i.e., by God, certainly.   **72 besides** out of.   **five wits** The intellectual faculties, usually listed as common wit, imagination, fantasy, judgment, and memory.   **73 notoriously abused** egregiously ill treated.   **75 But** Only   **76 propertied me** i.e., treated me as property and thrown me into the lumberroom   **77 face ... wits** brazenly represent me as having lost my wits.   **78 Advise you** Take care.   **86 shent** scolded, rebuked   **89 Welladay** Alas, would that

**MALVOLIO**  Fool, I'll requite it in the highest degree. I prithee, begone.

**FESTE**  [*sings*]

  I am gone, sir,             100
  And anon, sir,
  I'll be with you again,
  In a trice,
  Like to the old Vice,°
  Your need to sustain;           105
  Who, with dagger of lath,°
  In his rage and his wrath,
  Cries, "Aha!" to the devil;
  Like a mad lad,
  "Pare thy nails,° dad?          110
  Adieu, goodman° devil!" *Exit.*

## 4.3

    *Enter Sebastian [with a pearl].*

**SEBASTIAN**  This is the air; that is the glorious sun;
  This pearl she gave me, I do feel't and see't;
  And though 'tis wonder that enwraps me thus,
  Yet 'tis not madness. Where's Antonio, then?
  I could not find him at the Elephant;     5
  Yet there he was,° and there I found this credit,°
  That he did range the town to seek me out.
  His counsel now might do me golden service;
  For though my soul disputes well with my sense°
  That this may be some error, but no madness,   10
  Yet doth this accident° and flood of fortune
  So far exceed all instance,° all discourse,°
  That I am ready to distrust mine eyes
  And wrangle with my reason that persuades me
  To any other trust° but that I am mad,     15
  Or else the lady's mad. Yet if 'twere so,
  She could not sway° her house, command her followers,
  Take and give back affairs and their dispatch°
  With such a smooth, discreet, and stable bearing

---

**104 Vice** comic tempter of the "old" morality plays **106 dagger of lath** comic weapon of the Vice in at least some morality plays **110 Pare thy nails** (This may allude to the belief that evil spirits could use nail parings to get control of their victims; cf. Dromio of Syracuse in *The Comedy of Errors*, 4.3.69, "Some devils ask but the parings of one's nail," and the Boy's characterization of Pistol in *Henry V*, 4.4.72–3, as "this roaring devil i'th' old play, that everyone may pare his nails with a wooden dagger.") **111 goodman** title for a person of substance but not of gentle birth. (This line could be Feste's farewell to Malvolio and his "devil.") **6 was** was previously. **credit** report **9 my soul ... sense** i.e., both my rational faculties and my physical senses come to the conclusion **11 accident** unexpected event **12 instance** precedent. **discourse** reason **15 trust** belief **17 sway** rule **18 Take ... dispatch** receive reports on matters of household business and see to their execution

As I perceive she does. There's something in't                          20
That is deceivable.° But here the lady comes.

*Enter Olivia and Priest.*

**OLIVIA**   Blame not this haste of mine. If you mean well,
Now go with me and with this holy man
Into the chantry by.° There, before him,
And underneath that consecrated roof,                                   25
Plight me the full assurance of your faith,
That my most jealous° and too doubtful° soul
May live at peace. He shall conceal it
Whiles° you are willing it shall come to note,°
What time° we will our celebration° keep                                30
According to my birth.° What do you say?
**SEBASTIAN**   I'll follow this good man, and go with you,
And having sworn truth, ever will be true.
**OLIVIA**   Then lead the way, good father, and heavens so shine
That they may fairly note° this act of mine!   *Exeunt.*                 35

## 5.1

*Enter Clown [Feste] and Fabian.*

**FABIAN**   Now, as thou lov'st me, let me see his letter.
**FESTE**   Good Master Fabian, grant me another request.
**FABIAN**   Anything.
**FESTE**   Do not desire to see this letter.
**FABIAN**   This is to give a dog and in recompense desire my dog again.°   5

*Enter Duke [Orsino], Viola, Curio, and lords.*

**ORSINO**   Belong you to the Lady Olivia, friends?
**FESTE**   Ay, sir, we are some of her trappings.°
**ORSINO**   I know thee well. How dost thou, my good fellow?
**FESTE**   Truly, sir, the better for° my foes and the worse for my friends.
**ORSINO**   Just the contrary—the better for thy friends.            10
**FESTE**   No, sir, the worse.
**ORSINO**   How can that be?
**FESTE**   Marry, sir, they praise me, and make an ass of me.° Now my
foes tell me plainly I am an ass, so that by my foes, sir, I profit
in the knowledge of myself, and by my friends I am abused;° so

**21 deceivable** deceptive.   **24 chantry by** private endowed chapel nearby (where mass would be said for
the souls of the dead, including Olivia's brother).   **27 jealous** anxious, mistrustful.   **doubtful** full of
doubts   **29 Whiles** until.   **come to note** become known   **30 What time** at which time.   **our celebration**
i.e., the actual marriage. (What they are about to perform is a binding betrothal.)   **31 birth** social position.   **35 fairly note** look upon with favor
**5 This … again** (Apparently a reference to a well-known reply of Dr. Bulleyn when Queen Elizabeth asked
for his dog and promised a gift of his choosing in return; he asked to have his dog back.)   **7 trappings** ornaments, decorations.   **9 for** because of   **13 make an ass of me** i.e., flatter me into foolishly thinking well
of myself.   **15 abused** flatteringly deceived

that, conclusions to be as kisses, if your four negatives make     15
your two affirmatives,° why then the worse for my friends and
the better for my foes.

**ORSINO**  Why, this is excellent.

**FESTE**  By my troth, sir, no, though° it please you to be one of my
friends.°

**ORSINO**  Thou shalt not be the worse for me. There's gold.     20

[*He gives a coin.*]

**FESTE**  But° that it would be double-dealing,° sir, I would you
could make it another.

**ORSINO**  Oh, you give me ill counsel.

**FESTE**  Put your grace in your pocket,° sir, for this once, and let
your flesh and blood obey it.°     25

**ORSINO**  Well, I will be so much a sinner to be° a double-dealer.
There's another. [*He gives another coin.*]

**FESTE**  *Primo, secundo, tertio,*° is a good play,° and the old saying is, the third pays for all.° The triplex,° sir, is a good tripping measure; or the bells of Saint Bennet,° sir, may put you in
mind—one, two, three.     30

**ORSINO**  You can fool no more money out of me at this throw.° If
you will let your lady know I am here to speak with her, and
bring her along with you, it may awake my bounty further.

**FESTE**  Marry, sir, lullaby to your bounty till I come again. I go, sir,
but I would not have you to think that my desire of having is     35
the sin of covetousness. But as you say, sir, let your bounty take
a nap. I will awake it anon.    *Exit.*

*Enter Antonio and Officers.*

**VIOLA**  Here comes the man, sir, that did rescue me.

**ORSINO**  That face of his I do remember well,
Yet when I saw it last it was besmeared     40
As black as Vulcan° in the smoke of war.
A baubling° vessel was he captain of,
For° shallow draft° and bulk unprizable,°
With which such scatheful° grapple did he make

---

**15–6 conclusions … affirmatives** i.e., as when a young lady, asked for a kiss, says "no, no" really meaning "yes"; or, as in grammar, two negatives make an affirmative   **18 though** even though   **19 friends** i.e., those who, according to Feste's syllogism, flatter him.   **21 But** Except for the fact.   **double-dealing** (1) giving twice (2) deceit, duplicity   **24 Put … pocket** (1) Pay no attention to your honor, put it away (2) Reach in your pocket or purse and show your customary grace or munificence. (*Your Grace* is also the formal way of address-ing a duke.)   **25 it** i.e., my "ill counsel."   **26 to be** as to be   **27 Primo … tertio** Latin ordinals: first, second, third.   **play** (Perhaps a mathematical game or game of dice.)   **28 the third … all** the third time is lucky. (Proverbial.)   **triplex** triple time in music   **29 Saint Bennet** church of St. Benedict   **32 throw** (1) time (2) throw of the dice.   **41 Vulcan** Roman god of fire and smith to the other gods; his face was blackened by the fire   **42 baubling** insignificant, trifling   **43 For** because of.   **draft** depth of water a ship draws.   **unprizable** of value too slight to be estimated, not worth taking as a "prize"   **44 scatheful** destructive

With the most noble bottom° of our fleet                45
That very envy° and the tongue of loss°
Cried fame and honor on him. What's the matter?
**FIRST OFFICER**   Orsino, this is that Antonio
That took the *Phoenix* and her freight from Candy,°
And this is he that did the *Tiger* board                50
When your young nephew Titus lost his leg.
Here in the streets, desperate of shame and state,°
In private brabble° did we apprehend him.
**VIOLA**   He did me kindness, sir, drew on my side,
But in conclusion put strange speech upon me.°          55
I know not what 'twas but distraction.°
**ORSINO**   Notable° pirate, thou saltwater thief,
What foolish boldness brought thee to their mercies
Whom thou in terms so bloody and so dear°
Hast made thine enemies?                                60
**ANTONIO**   Orsino, noble sir,
Be pleased that I° shake off these names you give me.
Antonio never yet was thief or pirate,
Though, I confess, on base and ground° enough
Orsino's enemy. A witchcraft drew me hither.            65
That most ingrateful boy there by your side
From the rude sea's enraged and foamy mouth
Did I redeem; a wreck° past hope he was.
His life I gave him, and did thereto add
My love, without retention° or restraint,              70
All his in dedication.° For his sake
Did I expose myself—pure° for his love—
Into° the danger of this adverse° town,
Drew to defend him when he was beset;
Where being apprehended, his false cunning,            75
Not meaning to partake with me in danger,
Taught him to face me out of his acquaintance°
And grew a twenty years' removèd thing
While one would wink;° denied me mine own purse,
Which I had recommended° to his use                    80
Not half an hour before.

45 **bottom** ship   46 **very envy** i.e., even those who had most reason to hate him, his enemies.   **loss** i.e., the losers   49 **from Candy** on her return from Candia, or Crete   52 **desperate ... state** recklessly disregarding the disgrace and danger to himself   53 **brabble** brawl   55 **put ... me** spoke to me strangely.   56 **but distraction** unless (it was) madness.   57 **Notable** Notorious   59 **in terms ... dear** in so bloodthirsty and costly a manner   62 **Be pleased that I** Allow me to   64 **base and ground** solid grounds   68 **wreck** shipwrecked person   70 **retention** reservation   71 **All ... dedication** devoted wholly to him.   72 **pure** entirely, purely   73 **Into** unto.   **adverse** hostile   77 **face ... acquaintance** brazenly deny he knew me   78–9 **grew ... wink** in the twinkling of an eye acted as though we had been estranged for twenty years   80 **recommended** consigned

**VIOLA**  How can this be?

**ORSINO**  When came he to this town?

**ANTONIO**  Today, my lord; and for three months before,
No interim, not a minute's vacancy,                                85
Both day and night did we keep company.

*Enter Olivia and attendants.*

**ORSINO**  Here comes the Countess. Now heaven walks on earth.
But for° thee, fellow—fellow, thy words are madness.
Three months this youth hath tended upon me;
But more of that anon.—Take him aside.                           90

**OLIVIA**  [*to Orsino*]
What would my lord—but that he may not have°—
Wherein Olivia may seem serviceable?—
Cesario, you do not keep promise with me.

**VIOLA**  Madam?                                                 95

**ORSINO**  Gracious Olivia—

**OLIVIA**  What do you say, Cesario?—Good my lord°—

**VIOLA**  My lord would speak. My duty hushes me.

**OLIVIA**  If it be aught to the old tune, my lord,
It is as fat and fulsome° to mine ear                            100
As howling after music.

**ORSINO**  Still so cruel?

**OLIVIA**  Still so constant, lord.

**ORSINO**  What, to perverseness? You uncivil lady,
To whose ingrate and unauspicious° altars                        105
My soul the faithfull'st off'rings have breathed out
That e'er devotion tendered! What shall I do?

**OLIVIA**  Even what it please my lord that shall become° him.

**ORSINO**  Why should I not, had I the heart to do it,
Like to th' Egyptian thief° at point of death                    110
Kill what I love?—a savage jealousy
That sometime savors nobly.° But hear me this
Since you to nonregardance° cast my faith,
And that° I partly know the instrument
That screws° me from my true place in your favor,                115
Live you the marble-breasted tyrant still.
But this your minion,° whom I know you love,

---

**88 for** as for   **91 but ... have** except that which he may not have—i.e., my love   **97 Good my lord** (Olivia urges Orsino to listen to Cesario.)   **100 fat and fulsome** gross and offensive   **105 ingrate and unauspicious** thankless and unpropitious   **108 become** suit   **110 th' Egyptian thief** (An allusion to the story of Theagenes and Chariclea in the *Ethiopica*, a Greek romance by Heliodorus. The robber chief, Thyamis of Memphis, having captured Chariclea and fallen in love with her, is attacked by a larger band of robbers; threatened with death, he attempts to slay her first.)   **112 savors nobly** is not without nobility.
**113 nonregardance** neglect   **114 that** since   **115 screws** pries, forces   **117 minion** darling, favorite

And whom, by heaven I swear, I tender° dearly,
Him will I tear out of that cruel eye
Where he sits crownèd in his master's spite.°—                    120
Come, boy, with me. My thoughts are ripe in mischief.
I'll sacrifice the lamb that I do love,
To spite a raven's heart within a dove.°   [*Going.*]

**VIOLA**   And I, most jocund, apt,° and willingly,
To do you rest,° a thousand deaths would die.                    125

    [*Going.*]

**OLIVIA**   Where goes Cesario?

**VIOLA**   After him I love
More than I love these eyes, more than my life,
More by all mores° than e'er I shall love wife.
If I do feign, you witnesses above                                130
Punish my life for tainting of my love!°

**OLIVIA**   Ay me, detested!° How am I beguiled!

**VIOLA**   Who does beguile you? Who does do you wrong?

**OLIVIA**   Hast thou forgot thyself? Is it so long?
Call forth the holy father.   [*Exit an attendant.*]

**ORSINO**   [*to Viola*]   Come, away!                          135

**OLIVIA**   Whither, my lord?—Cesario, husband, stay.

**ORSINO**   Husband?

**OLIVIA**   Ay, husband. Can he that deny?

**ORSINO**   [*to Viola*]
Her husband, sirrah?°                                            140

**VIOLA**   No, my lord, not I.

**OLIVIA**   Alas, it is the baseness of thy fear
That makes thee strangle thy propriety.°
Fear not, Cesario, take thy fortunes up;
Be that° thou know'st thou art, and then thou art             145
As great as that thou fear'st.°

    *Enter Priest.*

Oh, welcome, father!
Father, I charge thee by thy reverence
Here to unfold—though lately we intended
To keep in darkness what occasion° now                           150
Reveals before 'tis ripe—what thou dost know
Hath newly passed between this youth and me.

---

**118 tender** regard   **119–20 Him … spite** I will tear Cesario away from Olivia, in whose cruel eye he sits like a king to spite me, his true master.   **122–3 I'll … dove** i.e., I'll kill Cesario, whom I love, to revenge myself on this seemingly gracious but black-hearted lady.   **124 apt** readily   **125 do you rest** give you ease **129 by all mores** by all such comparisons   **131 Punish … love!** punish me with death for being disloyal to the love I feel!   **132 detested** hated and denounced by another.   **140 sirrah** (The normal way of addressing an inferior.)   **143 strangle thy propriety** i.e., deny what is properly yours, disavow your marriage to me.   **145 that** that which   **146 as that thou fear'st** as him you fear, i.e., Orsino.   **150 occasion** necessity

**PRIEST**   A contract of eternal bond of love,
    Confirmed by mutual joinder° of your hands,
    Attested by the holy close° of lips,            155
    Strengthened by interchangement of your rings,
    And all the ceremony of this compact
    Sealed in my function,° by my testimony;
    Since when, my watch hath told me, toward my grave
    I have traveled but two hours.          160
**ORSINO**   [to Viola]
    Oh, thou dissembling cub! What wilt thou be
    When time hath sowed a grizzle° on thy case?°
    Or will not else thy craft so quickly grow
    That thine own trip° shall be thine overthrow?
    Farewell, and take her, but direct thy feet    165
    Where thou and I henceforth may never meet.
**VIOLA**   My Lord, I do protest—
**OLIVIA**   Oh, do not swear!
    Hold little faith, though thou hast too much fear.°

    *Enter Sir Andrew.*

**SIR ANDREW**   For the love of God, a surgeon! Send one presently°
    to Sir Toby.    170
**OLIVIA**   What's the matter?
**SIR ANDREW**   He's broke° my head across, and has given
    Sir Toby a bloody coxcomb° too. For the love of God, your help!
    I had rather than forty pound I were at home.
**OLIVIA**   Who has done this, Sir Andrew?    175
**SIR ANDREW**   The Count's gentleman, one Cesario. We took him for
    a coward, but he's the very devil incardinate.°
**ORSINO**   My gentleman, Cesario?
**SIR ANDREW**   'Od's lifelings,° here he is!—You broke my head
    for nothing, and that that I did I was set on to do't by Sir
    Toby.    180
**VIOLA**   Why do you speak to me? I never hurt you.
    You drew your sword upon me without cause,
    But I bespake you fair,° and hurt you not.    185
**SIR ANDREW**   If a bloody coxcomb be a hurt, you have hurt me. I
    think you set nothing by° a bloody cox-comb.

    *Enter [Sir] Toby and Clown [Feste].*

**154 joinder** joining   **155 close** meeting   **158 Sealed ... function** ratified through my carrying out of my priestly office   **162 grizzle** scattering of gray hair.   **case** skin.   **164 trip** wrestling trick used to throw an opponent. (You'll get overclever and trip yourself up.)   **169 Hold ... fear** Keep to your oath as well as you can, even if you are frightened by Orsino's threats.   **170 presently** immediately   **173 broke** broken the skin, cut   **174 coxcomb** fool's cap resembling the crest of a cock; here, head   **178 incardinate** (For "incarnate.")   **180 'Od's lifelings** By God's little lives   **185 bespake you fair** addressed you courteously   **187 set nothing by** regard as insignificant

Here comes Sir Toby, halting.° You shall hear more. But if he
had not been in drink, he would have tickled you othergates°
than he did.

**ORSINO**   How now, gentleman? How is't with you?   190

**SIR TOBY**   That's all one.° He's hurt me, and there's th'end on't.°—
Sot,° didst see Dick surgeon, sot?

**FESTE**   Oh, he's drunk, Sir Toby, an hour agone;° his eyes were set°
at eight i'th' morning.

**SIR TOBY**   Then he's a rogue, and a passy measures pavane.° I hate   195
a drunken rogue.

**OLIVIA**   Away with him! Who hath made this havoc with them?

**SIR ANDREW**   I'll help you, Sir Toby, because we'll be dressed°
together.

**SIR TOBY**   Will you help? An ass-head and a coxcomb and a knave,   200
a thin-faced knave, a gull!

**OLIVIA**   Get him to bed, and let his hurt be looked to.
                    [*Exeunt Feste, Fabian, Sir Toby, and Sir Andrew.*]

*Enter Sebastian.*

**SEBASTIAN**   I am sorry, madam, I have hurt your kinsman;
But, had it been the brother of my blood,°
I must have done no less with wit and safety.°—   205
You throw a strange regard upon me,° and by that
I do perceive it hath offended you.
Pardon me, sweet one, even for the vows
We made each other but so late ago.

**ORSINO**   One face, one voice, one habit,° and two persons,   210
A natural perspective,° that is and is not!

**SEBASTIAN**   Antonio, O my dear Antonio!
How have the hours racked° and tortured me
Since I have lost thee!

**ANTONIO**   Sebastian are you?   215

**SEBASTIAN**   Fear'st thou that,° Antonio?

**ANTONIO**   How have you made division of yourself?
An apple cleft in two is not more twin
Than these two creatures. Which is Sebastian?

**OLIVIA**   Most wonderful!   220

**SEBASTIAN**   [*seeing Viola*]
Do I stand there? I never had a brother;

**188 halting** limping.   **189 othergates** otherwise   **191 That's all one** It doesn't matter; never
mind.   **191–2 there's ... on't** that's all there is to it.   **192 Sot** (1) Fool (2) Drunkard   **193 agone**
ago   **194 set** fixed or closed   **195 passy measures pavane** passe-measure pavane, a slow-moving, stately
dance. (Suggesting Sir Toby's impatience to have his wounds dressed.)   **198 be dressed** have our wounds
surgically dressed   **204 the brother ... blood** my own brother   **205 with wit and safety** with intelligent
concern for my own safety.   **206 You ... me** You look strangely at me   **210 habit** dress   **211 A natural
perspective** an optical device or illusion created in this instance by nature   **213 racked** tortured
**216 Fear'st thou that** Do you doubt that

Nor can there be that deity in my nature
Of here and everywhere.° I had a sister,
Whom the blind° waves and surges have devoured.
Of charity,° what kin are you to me?                                225
What countryman? What name? What parentage?

**VIOLA**   Of Messaline. Sebastian was my father.
Such a Sebastian was my brother, too.
So went he suited° to his watery tomb.
If spirits can assume both form and suit,°                         230
You come to fright us.

**SEBASTIAN**   A spirit I am indeed,
But am in that dimension grossly clad°
Which from the womb I did participate.°
Were you a woman, as the rest goes even,°                          235
I should my tears let fall upon your cheek
And say, "Thrice welcome, drownèd Viola!"

**VIOLA**   My father had a mole upon his brow.

**SEBASTIAN**   And so had mine.

**VIOLA**   And died that day when Viola from her birth            240
Had numbered thirteen years.

**SEBASTIAN**   Oh, that record° is lively in my soul!
He finishèd indeed his mortal act
That day that made my sister thirteen years.

**VIOLA**   If nothing lets° to make us happy both                245
But this my masculine usurped attire,
Do not embrace me till each circumstance
Of place, time, fortune, do cohere and jump°
That I am Viola—which to confirm
I'll bring you to a captain in this town                           250
Where lie my maiden weeds,° by whose gentle help
I was preserved to serve this noble count.
All the occurrence of my fortune since
Hath been between this lady and this lord.

**SEBASTIAN**   [to Olivia]
So comes it, lady, you have been mistook.                          255
But nature to her bias drew in that.°
You would have been contracted to a maid,°
Nor are you therein, by my life, deceived.
You are betrothed both to a maid and man.

---

223 **here and everywhere** omnipresence.   224 **blind** heedless, indiscriminate   225 **Of charity** (Tell me) in kindness   229 **suited** dressed; clad in human form   230 **form and suit** physical appearance and dress   233 **in ... clad** clothed in that fleshly shape   234 **participate** possess in common with all humanity.   235 **as ... even** since everything else agrees   242 **record** recollection   245 **lets** hinders   248 **jump** coincide, fit exactly   251 **weeds** clothes   256 **nature ... that** nature followed her bent in that. (The metaphor is from the game of bowls.)   257 **a maid** i.e., a virgin man

**ORSINO**  [*to Olivia*]
    Be not amazed; right noble is his blood.          260
    If this be so, as yet the glass° seems true,
    I shall have share in this most happy wreck.°
    [*To Viola*] Boy, thou hast said to me a thousand times
    Thou never shouldst love woman like to me.°
**VIOLA**    And all those sayings will I over swear,°        265
    And all those swearings keep as true in soul
    As doth that orbèd continent the fire°
    That severs day from night.
**ORSINO**    Give me thy hand,
    And let me see thee in thy woman's weeds.       270
**VIOLA**    The captain that did bring me first on shore
    Hath my maid's garments. He upon some action°
    Is now in durance,° at Malvolio's suit,
    A gentleman and follower of my lady's.
**OLIVIA**    He shall enlarge° him. Fetch Malvolio hither.    275
    And yet, alas, now I remember me,
    They say, poor gentleman, he's much distract.

       *Enter Clown* [*Feste*] *with a letter, and Fabian.*

    A most extracting° frenzy of mine own
    From my remembrance clearly banished his.°
    How does he, sirrah?            280
**FESTE**    Truly, madam, he holds Beelzebub at the stave's end° as
    well as a man in his case may do. He's here writ a letter to you;
    I should have given't you today morning. But as a madman's
    epistles are no gospels,° so it skills° not much when they are
    delivered.°
**OLIVIA**    Open't and read it.           285
**FESTE**    Look then to be well edified when the fool delivers° the
    madman. [*He reads loudly.*] "By the Lord, madam—"
**OLIVIA**    How now, art thou mad?
**FESTE**    No, madam, I do but read madness. An Your Ladyship will
    have it as it ought to be, you must allow *vox.*°    290
**OLIVIA**    Prithee, read i'thy right wits.
**FESTE**    So I do, madonna; but to read his right wits° is to read thus.
    Therefore perpend,° my princess, and give ear.

---

**261 the glass** i.e., the *natural perspective* of line 216   **262 wreck** shipwreck, accident.   **264 like to me**
as well as you love me.   **265 over swear** swear again   **267 As … fire** i.e., as the sphere of the sun keeps
the fire   **272 action** legal charge   **273 in durance** imprisoned   **275 enlarge** release   **278 extracting** i.e.,
that obsessed me and drew all thoughts except of Cesario from my mind   **279 his** i.e., his madness.
**281 holds … end** i.e., keeps the devil at a safe distance. (The metaphor is of fighting with quarterstaffs
or long poles.)   **283–4 a madman's … gospels** i.e., there is no truth in a madman's letters. (An allusion
to readings in the church service of selected passages from the epistles and the gospels.)   **284 skills** matters.   **delivered** (1) delivered to their recipient (2) read aloud.   **286 delivers** speaks the words of
**290 vox** voice, i.e., an appropriately loud voice.   **292 to read … wits** to express his true state of mind
**293 perpend** consider, attend. (A deliberately lofty word.)

**OLIVIA**    [*to Fabian*] Read it you, sirrah.

**FABIAN**    (*reads*) "By the Lord, madam, you wrong me, and the    295
world shall know it. Though you have put me in to darkness and
given your drunken cousin rule over me, yet have I the benefit
of my senses as well as Your Ladyship. I have your own letter
that induced me to the semblance I put on, with the which°
I doubt not but to do myself much right or you much shame.    300
Think of me as you please. I leave my duty a little unthought of,
and speak out of my injury.° The madly used Malvolio."

**OLIVIA**    Did he write this?

**FESTE**    Ay, madam.    305

**ORSINO**    This savors not much of distraction.

**OLIVIA**    See him delivered,° Fabian. Bring him hither.

[*Exit Fabian.*]

My lord, so please you, these things further thought on,°
To think me as well a sister as a wife,°
One day shall crown th' alliance on't,° so please you,    310
Here at my house and at my proper° cost.

**ORSINO**    Madam, I am most apt° t'embrace your offer.
[*To Viola*] Your master quits° you; and for your service done him,
So much against the mettle° of your sex,
So far beneath your soft and tender breeding,    315
And since you called me master for so long,
Here is my hand. You shall from this time be
Your master's mistress.

**OLIVIA**    A sister! You are she.

Enter [*Fabian, with*] Malvolio.

**ORSINO**    Is this the madman?    320

**OLIVIA**    Ay, my lord, this same.
How now, Malvolio?

**MALVOLIO**    Madam, you have done me wrong,
Notorious wrong.

**OLIVIA**    Have I, Malvolio? No.    325

**MALVOLIO**    [*showing a letter*]
Lady, you have. Pray you, peruse that letter.
You must not now deny it is your hand.
Write from it,° if you can, in hand or phrase,
Or say 'tis not your seal, not your invention.°    330
You can say none of this. Well, grant it then,

299–300 **the which** i.e., the letter    301–2 **I leave ... injury** I leave unsaid the expressions of duty with which I would normally conclude, and convey instead my sense of having been wronged.    307 **delivered** released    308 **so ... on** if you are pleased on further consideration of all that has happened    309 **To ... wife** to regard me as favorably as a sister-in-law as you had hoped to regard me as a wife    310 **crown ... on't** i.e., serve as occasion for two marriages confirming our new relationships    311 **proper** own    312 **apt** ready    313 **quits** releases    314 **mettle** natural disposition    329 **from it** differently    330 **invention** composition.

And tell me, in the modesty of honor,°
Why you have given me such clear lights° of favor,
Bade me come smiling and cross-gartered to you,
To put on yellow stockings, and to frown                    335
Upon Sir Toby and the lighter° people?
And, acting this in an obedient hope,°
Why have you suffered me to be imprisoned,
Kept in a dark house, visited by the priest,°
And made the most notorious geck° and gull               340
That e'er invention played on?° Tell me why?

**OLIVIA**  Alas, Malvolio, this is not my writing,
Though, I confess, much like the character;°
But out of° question 'tis Maria's hand.
And now I do bethink me, it was she                          345
First told me thou wast mad; then cam'st° in smiling,
And in such forms which here were presupposed°
Upon thee in the letter. Prithee, be content.
This practice° hath most shrewdly passed° upon thee;
But when we know the grounds and authors of it,          350
Thou shalt be both the plaintiff and the judge
Of thine own cause.

**FABIAN**                  Good madam, hear me speak,
And let no quarrel nor no brawl to come°
Taint the condition° of this present hour,                    355
Which I have wondered at. In hope it shall not,
Most freely I confess, myself and Toby
Set this device against Malvolio here,
Upon° some stubborn and uncourteous parts°
We had conceived against him.° Maria writ                  360
The letter at Sir Toby's great importance,°
In recompense whereof he hath married her.
How with a sportful malice it was followed°
May rather pluck on° laughter than revenge,
If that° the injuries be justly weighed                         365
That have on both sides passed.

**OLIVIA**  [*to Malvolio*]
Alas, poor fool, how have they baffled° thee!

**FESTE**  Why, "Some are born great, some achieve greatness, and
    some have greatness thrown upon them." I was one, sir, in this

---

**332 in ... honor** in the name of all that is decent and honorable  **333 clear lights** evident signs
**336 lighter** lesser  **337 acting ... hope** when I acted thus out of obedience to you and in hope of your
favor  **339 priest** i.e., Feste  **340 geck** dupe  **341 invention played on** contrivance sported with.
**343 the character** my handwriting  **344 out of** beyond  **346 cam'st** you came  **347 presupposed** specified beforehand  **349 practice** plot.  **shrewdly passed** mischievously been perpetrated  **354 to come**
in the future  **355 condition** (happy) nature  **359 Upon** on account of.  **parts** qualities, deeds  **360
conceived against him** seen and resented in him.  **361 importance** importunity  **363 followed** carried
out  **364 pluck on** induce  **365 If that** if  **367 baffled** disgraced, quelled

interlude,° one Sir Topas, sir, but that's all one.° "By the Lord,    370
fool, I am not mad." But do you remember? "Madam, why laugh
you at such a barren rascal? An you smile not, he's gagged." And
thus the whirligig° of time brings in his revenges.

**MALVOLIO**  I'll be revenged on the whole pack of you!    375

    *[Exit.]*

**OLIVIA**  He hath been most notoriously abused.
**ORSINO**  Pursue him, and entreat him to a peace.
He hath not told us of the captain yet.
When that is known, and golden time convents,°
A solemn combination shall be made    380
Of our dear souls. Meantime, sweet sister,
We will not part from hence. Cesario, come—
For so you shall be, while you are a man;
But when in other habits° you are seen,
Orsino's mistress and his fancy's° queen.    385

    *Exeunt [all, except Feste].*

**FESTE**  *(sings)*
When that I was and a little° tiny boy,
  With hey, ho, the wind and the rain,
A foolish thing was but a toy,°
  For the rain it raineth every day.
But when I came to man's estate,    390
  With hey, ho, the wind and the rain,
'Gainst knaves and thieves men shut their gate,
  For the rain it raineth every day.
But when I came, alas, to wive,
  With hey, ho, the wind and the rain,    395
By swaggering could I never thrive,
  For the rain it raineth every day.
But when I came unto my beds,°
  With hey, ho, the wind and the rain,
With tosspots° still had drunken heads,    400
  For the rain it raineth every day.
A great while ago the world begun,
  With hey, ho, the wind and the rain,
But that's all one, our play is done,
  And we'll strive to please you every day.    405

    *[Exit.]*

**370 interlude** little play.  **that's all one** no matter for that.  **373 whirligig** spinning top  **379 convents** (1) summons, calls together (2) suits  **384 habits** attire  **385 fancy's** love's  **386 and a little** a little  **388 toy** trifle  **398 unto my beds** i.e., (1) drunk to bed, or, perhaps, (2) in the evening of life  **400 tosspots** drunkards

# The Tragedy of Othello, The Moor of Venice

Edited by David Bevington

## Characters

Othello, *the Moor*
Brabantio [*a senator*], *father to Desdemona*
Cassio, *an honorable lieutenant* [*to Othello*]
Iago [*Othello's ancient*], *a villain*
Roderigo, *a gulled gentleman*
Duke of Venice
Senators [*of Venice*]
Montano, *governor of Cyprus*
Gentlemen of Cyprus
Lodovico and Gratiano [*kinsmen to Brabantio*], *two noble Venetians*
Sailors
Clown
Desdemona [*daughter to Brabantio and*], *wife to Othello*
Emilia, *wife to Iago*
Bianca, *a courtesan* [*and mistress to Cassio*]
A Messenger
A Herald
A Musician
Servants, Attendants, Officers, Senators, Musicians, Gentlemen]

[Scene: *Venice; a seaport in Cyprus*]

## Act I

**Scene I. Venice. A street**

*Enter Roderigo and Iago.*

**RODERIGO:**   Tush, never tell me!° I take it much unkindly
That thou, Iago, who hast had my purse
As if the strings were thine, shouldst know of this.°
**IAGO:**   'Sblood,° but you'll not hear me.
If ever I did dream of such a matter,                                            5
Abhor me.
**RODERIGO:**   Thou toldst me thou didst hold him in thy hate.
**IAGO:**   Despise me
If I do not. Three great ones of the city,
In personal suit to make me his lieutenant,                                      10
Off-capped to him;° and by the faith of man,

---

**1 never tell me** (An expression of incredulity, like "tell me another one.")   **3 this** i.e., Desdemona's
elopement   **4 'Sblood** by His (Christ's) blood   **11 him** i.e., Othello

I know my price, I am worth no worse a place.
But he, as loving his own pride and purposes,
Evades them with a bombast circumstance°
Horribly stuffed with epithets of war,°                                    15
And, in conclusion,
Nonsuits° my mediators. For, "Certes,"° says he,
"I have already chose my officer."
And what was he?
Forsooth, a great arithmetician,°                                          20
One Michael Cassio, a Florentine,
A fellow almost damned in a fair wife,°
That never set a squadron in the field
Nor the division of a battle° knows
More than a spinster°—unless the bookish theoric,°                         25
Wherein the togaed° consuls° can propose°
As masterly as he. Mere prattle without practice
Is all his soldiership. But he, sir, had th' election;
And I, of whom his° eyes had seen the proof
At Rhodes, at Cyprus, and on other grounds                                 30
Christened° and heathen, must be beeled and calmed°
By debitor and creditor.° This countercaster,°
He, in good time,° must his lieutenant be,
And I—God bless the mark!°—his Moorship's ancient.°
RODERIGO: By heaven, I rather would have been his hangman.°                35
IAGO: Why, there's no remedy. 'Tis the curse of service;
Preferment° goes by letter and affection,°
And not by old gradation,° where each second
Stood heir to th' first. Now, sir, be judge yourself
Whether I in any just term° am affined°                                    40
To love the Moor.
RODERIGO: I would not follow him then.
IAGO: O sir, content you.°
I follow him to serve my turn upon him.
We cannot all be masters, nor all masters                                 45

14 **bombast circumstance** wordy evasion. (Bombast is cotton padding.)  15 **epithets of war** military expressions  17 **Nonsuits** rejects the petition of.  **Certes** certainly  20 **arithmetician** i.e., a man whose military knowledge is merely theoretical, based on books of tactics  22 **A ... wife** (Cassio does not seem to be married, but his counterpart in Shakespeare's source does have a woman in his house. See also Act IV, Scene i, line 127.)  24 **division of a battle** disposition of a military unit  25 **a spinster** i.e., a housewife, one whose regular occupation is spinning.  **theoric** theory  26 **togaed** wearing the toga.  **consuls** counselors, senators.  **propose** discuss  29 **his** i.e., Othello's  31 **Christened** Christian.  **beeled and calmed** left to leeward without wind, becalmed. (A sailing metaphor.)  32 **debitor and creditor** (A name for a system of bookkeeping, here used as a contemptuous nickname for Cassio.)  **countercaster** i.e., bookkeeper, one who tallies with *counters*, or "metal disks." (Said contemptuously.)  33 **in good time** opportunely, i.e., forsooth  34 **God bless the mark** (Perhaps originally a formula to ward off evil; here an expression of impatience.)  **ancient** standard-bearer, ensign  35 **his hangman** the executioner of him  37 **Preferment** promotion.  **letter and affection** personal influence and favoritism  38 **old gradation** step-by-step seniority, the traditional way  40 **term** respect  **affined** bound  43 **content you** don't you worry about that

Cannot be truly° followed. You shall mark
Many a duteous and knee-crooking knave
That, doting on his own obsequious bondage,
Wears out his time, much like his master's ass,
For naught but provender, and when he's old, cashiered.°          50
Whip me° such honest knaves. Others there are
Who, trimmed in forms and visages of duty,°
Keep yet their hearts attending on themselves,
And, throwing but shows of service on their lords,
Do well thrive by them, and when they have lined their coats,°     55
Do themselves homage.° These fellows have some soul,
And such a one do I profess myself. For, sir,
It is as sure as you are Roderigo,
Were I the Moor I would not be Iago.°
In following him, I follow but myself—                              60
Heaven is my judge, not I for love and duty,
But seeming so for my peculiar° end.
For when my outward action doth demonstrate
The native° act and figure° of my heart
In compliment extern,° 'tis not long after                          65
But I will wear my heart upon my sleeve
For daws° to peck at. I am not what I am.°
**RODERIGO:**   What a full° fortune does the thick-lips° owe°
If he can carry 't thus!°
**IAGO:**                   Call up her father.
Rouse him, make after him, poison his delight,                      70
Proclaim him in the streets; incense her kinsmen,
And, though he in a fertile climate dwell,
Plague him with flies.° Though that his joy be joy,°
Yet throw such changes of vexation° on 't
As it may° lose some color.°                                        75
**RODERIGO:**   Here is her father's house. I'll call aloud.
**IAGO:**   Do, with like timorous° accent and dire yell
As when, by night and negligence,° the fire
Is spied in populous cities.

---

46 **truly** faithfully   50 **cashiered** dismissed from service   51 **Whip me** whip, as far as I'm concerned
52 **trimmed ... duty** dressed up in the mere form and show of dutifulness   55 **lined their coats** i.e.,
stuffed their purses   56 **Do themselves homage** i.e., attend to self-interest solely   59 **Were ... Iago**
i.e., if I were able to assume command, I certainly would not choose to remain a subordinate, or, I
would keep a suspicious eye on a flattering subordinate   62 **peculiar** particular, personal
64 **native** innate.   **figure** shape, intent   65 **compliment extern** outward show. (Conforming in this
case to the inner workings and intention of the heart.)   67 **daws** small crowlike birds, proverbially
stupid and avaricious.   **I am not what I am** i.e., I am not one who wears his heart on his sleeve
68 **full** swelling.   **thick-lips** (Elizabethans often applied the term "Moor" to Negroes.)   **owe** own
69 **carry 't thus** carry this off   72–73 **though ... flies** though he seems prosperous and happy now,
vex him with misery   73 **Though ... be joy** although he seems fortunate and happy. (Repeats the idea
of line 72.)   74 **changes of vexation** vexing changes   75 **As it may** that may cause it to.   **some
color** some of its fresh gloss   77 **timorous** frightening   78 **and negligence** i.e., by negligence

**RODERIGO:**   What ho, Brabantio! Signor Brabantio, ho!                          80
**IAGO:**   Awake! What ho, Brabantio! Thieves, thieves, thieves!
  Look to your house, your daughter, and your bags!
  Thieves, thieves!

  *Brabantio [enters] above [at a window].°*

**BRABANTIO:**   What is the reason of this terrible summons?
  What is the matter° there?                                                      85
**RODERIGO:**   Signor, is all your family within?
**IAGO:**   Are your doors locked?
**BRABANTIO:**                    Why, wherefore ask you this?
**IAGO:**   Zounds,° sir, you're robbed. For shame, put on your gown!
  Your heart is burst; you have lost half your soul.
  Even now, now, very now, an old black ram                                       90
  Is tupping° your white ewe. Arise, arise!
  Awake the snorting° citizens with the bell,
  Or else the devil° will make a grandsire of you.
  Arise, I say!
**BRABANTIO:**   What, have you lost your wits?
**RODERIGO:**   Most reverend signor, do you know my voice?                        95
**BRABANTIO:**   Not I. What are you?
**RODERIGO:**   My name is Roderigo.
**BRABANTIO:**   The worser welcome.
  I have charged thee not to haunt about my doors.
  In honest plainness thou hast heard me say                                      100
  My daughter is not for thee; and now, in madness,
  Being full of supper and distempering° drafts,
  Upon malicious bravery° dost thou come
  To start° my quiet.
**RODERIGO:**   Sir, sir, sir—
**BRABANTIO:**                    But thou must needs be sure                      105
  My spirits and my place° have in their power
  To make this bitter to thee.
**RODERIGO:**                    Patience, good sir.
**BRABANTIO:**   What tell'st thou me of robbing? This is Venice;
  My house is not a grange.°
**RODERIGO:**                    Most grave Brabantio,
  In simple° and pure soul I come to you.                                         110
**IAGO:**   Zounds, sir, you are one of those that will not serve God if
  the devil bid you. Because we come to do you service and you

83 [s.d.] at a window (This stage direction, from the Quarto, probably calls for an appearance on the gallery above and rearstage.)   85 the matter your business   88 Zounds by His (Christ's) wounds   91 tupping covering, copulating with. (Said of sheep.)   92 snorting snoring   93 the devil (The devil was conventionally pictured as black.)   102 distempering intoxicating   103 Upon malicious bravery with hostile intent to defy me   104 start startle, disrupt   106 My spirits and my place my temperament and my authority of office.   have in have it in   109 grange isolated country house   110 simple sincere

think we are ruffians, you'll have your daughter covered with a
Barbary° horse; you'll have your nephews° neigh to you; you'll
have coursers° for cousins° and jennets° for germans.°  115

**BRABANTIO:**  What profane wretch art thou?

**IAGO:**  I am one, sir, that comes to tell you your daughter and the
Moor are now making the beast with two backs.

**BRABANTIO:**  Thou art a villain.

**IAGO:**                      You are—a senator.°

**BRABANTIO:**  This thou shalt answer.° I know thee, Roderigo.

**RODERIGO:**  Sir, I will answer anything. But I beseech you,  120
If't be your pleasure and most wise° consent—
As partly I find it is—that your fair daughter,
At this odd-even° and dull watch o' the night,
Transported with° no worse nor better guard
But with a knave° of common hire, a gondolier,  125
To the gross clasps of a lascivious Moor—
If this be known to you and your allowance°
We then have done you bold and saucy° wrongs.
But if you know not this, my manners tell me
We have your wrong rebuke. Do not believe  130
That, from° the sense of all civility,°
I thus would play and trifle with your reverence.°
Your daughter, if you have not given her leave,
I say again, hath made a gross revolt,
Tying her duty, beauty, wit,° and fortunes  135
In an extravagant° and wheeling° stranger°
Of here and everywhere. Straight° satisfy yourself.
If she be in her chamber or your house,
Let loose on me the justice of the state
For thus deluding you.  140

**BRABANTIO:**  Strike on the tinder,° ho!
Give me a taper! Call up all my people!
This accident° is not unlike my dream.
Belief of it oppresses me already.
Light, I say, light!                    *Exit [above]*.

**IAGO:**  Farewell, for I must leave you.  145
It seems not meet° nor wholesome to my place°

114 **Barbary** from northern Africa (and hence associated with Othello).  **nephews** i.e., grandsons
115 **coursers** powerful horses.  **cousins** kinsmen.  **jennets** small Spanish horses.  **germans** near relatives  118 **a senator** (Said with mock politeness, as though the word itself were an insult.)  119 **answer**
be held accountable for  121 **wise** well-informed  123 **odd-even** between one day and the next, i.e.,
about midnight  124 **with** by  125 **But with a knave** than by a low fellow, a servant  127 **allowance**
permission  128 **saucy** insolent  131 **from** contrary to.  **civility** good manners, decency  132 **your**
**reverence** the respect due to you  135 **wit** intelligence  136 **extravagant** expatriate, wandering far
from home.  **wheeling** roving about, vagabond.  **stranger** foreigner  137 **Straight** straightway
141 **tinder** charred linen ignited by a spark from flint and steel, used to light torches or tapers (lines
142, 167)  143 **accident** occurrence, event  146 **meet** fitting.  **place** position (as ensign)

To be producted°—as, if I stay, I shall—
Against the Moor. For I do know the state,
However this may gall° him with some check,°
Cannot with safety cast° him, for he's embarked°                    150
With such loud reason° to the Cyprus wars,
Which even now stands in act,° that, for their souls,°
Another of his fathom° they have none
To lead their business; in which regard,°
Though I do hate him as I do hell pains,                            155
Yet for necessity of present life°
I must show out a flag and sign of love,
Which is indeed but sign. That you shall surely find him,
Lead to the Sagittary° the raisèd search,°
And there will I be with him. So farewell.                         160

                                                          [*Exit.*]

*Enter [below] Brabantio [in his nightgown°] with servants and*
*torches.*

**BRABANTIO:**   It is too true an evil. Gone she is;
And what's to come of my despisèd time°
Is naught but bitterness. Now, Roderigo,
Where didst thou see her?—O unhappy girl!—
With the Moor, sayst thou?—Who would be a father!—                 165
How didst thou know 'twas she?—O, she deceives me
Past thought!—What said she to you?—Get more tapers.
Raise all my kindred.—Are they married, think you?
**RODERIGO:**   Truly, I think they are.
**BRABANTIO:**   O heaven! How got she out? O treason of the blood!  170
Fathers, from hence trust not your daughters' minds
By what you see them act. Is there not charms°
By which the property° of youth and maidhood
May be abused?° Have you not read, Roderigo,
Of some such thing?
**RODERIGO:**   Yes, sir, I have indeed.                             175
**BRABANTIO:**   Call up my brother.—O, would you had had her!—
Some one way, some another.—Do you know
Where we may apprehend her and the Moor?
**RODERIGO:**   I think I can discover° him, if you please

---

147 **producted** produced (as a witness)   149 **gall** rub; oppress.   **check** rebuke   150 **cast** dismiss.
**embarked** engaged   151 **loud reason** unanimous shout of confirmation (in the Senate)   152 **stands
in act** are going on.   **for their souls** to save themselves   153 **fathom** i.e., ability, depth of experience
154 **in which regard** out of regard for which   156 **life** livelihood   159 **Sagittary** (An inn or house where
Othello and Desdemona are staying, named for its sign of Sagittarius, or Centaur.)   **raisèd search** search
party roused out of sleep   160 **[s.d.] nightgown** dressing gown. (This costuming is specified in the Quarto
text.)   162 **time** i.e., remainder of life   172 **charms** spells   173 **property** special quality, nature
174 **abused** deceived   179 **discover** reveal, uncover

To get good guard and go along with me.                                                    180
**BRABANTIO:**   Pray you, lead on. At every house I'll call;
I may command° at most.—Get weapons, ho!
And raise some special officers of night.—
On, good Roderigo. I will deserve° your pains.

*[Exeunt.]*

**Scene II. Venice. Another street, before Othello's lodgings**

*Enter Othello, Iago, attendants with torches.*

**IAGO:**   Though in the trade of war I have slain men,
Yet do I hold it very stuff° o' the conscience
To do no contrived° murder. I lack iniquity
Sometimes to do me service. Nine or ten times
I had thought t' have yerked° him° here under the ribs.       5
**OTHELLO:**   'Tis better as it is.
**IAGO:**                            Nay, but he prated,
And spoke such scurvy and provoking terms
Against your honor
That, with the little godliness I have,
I did full hard forbear him.° But, I pray you, sir,           10
Are you fast married? Be assured of this,
That the magnifico° is much beloved,
And hath in his effect° a voice potential°
As double as the Duke's. He will divorce you,
Or put upon you what restraint or grievance                   15
The law, with all his might to enforce it on,
Will give him cable.°
**OTHELLO:**               Let him do his spite.
My services which I have done the seigniory°
Shall out-tongue his complaints. 'Tis yet to know°—
Which, when I know that boasting is an honor,                 20
I shall promulgate—I fetch my life and being
From men of royal siege,° and my demerits°
May speak unbonneted° to as proud a fortune
As this that I have reached. For know, Iago,
But that I love the gentle Desdemona,                         25
I would not my unhousèd° free condition

---

**182 command** demand assistance   **184 deserve** show gratitude for
**2 very stuff** essence, basic material (continuing the metaphor of *trade* from line 1)   **3 contrived**
premeditated   **5 yerked** stabbed.   **him** i.e., Roderigo   **10 I ... him** I restrained myself with great
difficulty from assaulting him   **12 magnifico** Venetian grandee, i.e., Brabantio   **13 in his effect** at
his command.   **potential** powerful   **17 cable** i.e., scope   **18 seigniory** Venetian government   **19
yet to know** not yet widely known   **22 siege** i.e., rank. (Literally, a seat used by a person of distinction.)   **demerits** deserts   **23 unbonneted** without removing the hat, i.e., on equal terms (? Or "with
hat off," "in all due modesty.")   **26 unhousèd** unconfined, undomesticated

Put into circumscription and confine°
For the sea's worth.° But look, what lights come yond?

*Enter Cassio [and certain officers°] with torches.*

**IAGO:**    Those are the raisèd father and his friends.
You were best go in.
**OTHELLO:**                    Not I. I must be found.                    30
My parts, my title, and my perfect soul°
Shall manifest me rightly. Is it they?
**IAGO:**    By Janus,° I think no.
**OTHELLO:**    The servants of the Duke? And my lieutenant?
The goodness of the night upon you, friends!                    35
What is the news?
**CASSIO:**                    The Duke does greet you, General,
And he requires your haste-post-haste appearance
Even on the instant.
**OTHELLO:**                    What is the matter,° think you?
**CASSIO:**    Something from Cyprus, as I may divine.°
It is a business of some heat.° The galleys                    40
Have sent a dozen sequent° messengers
This very night at one another's heels,
And many of the consuls,° raised and met,
Are at the Duke's already. You have been hotly called for;
When, being not at your lodging to be found,                    45
The Senate hath sent about° three several° quests
To search you out.
**OTHELLO:**                    'Tis well I am found by you.
I will but spend a word here in the house
And go with you.                                        [*Exit.*]
**CASSIO:**                    Ancient, what makes° he here?
**IAGO:**    Faith, he tonight hath boarded° a land carrack.°                    50
If it prove lawful prize,° he's made forever.
**CASSIO:**    I do not understand.
**IAGO:**                    He's married.
**CASSIO:**                    To who?

[*Enter Othello.*]

**IAGO:**    Marry,° to—Come, Captain, will you go?
**OTHELLO:**    Have with you.°

27 **circumscription and confine** restriction and confinement    28 **the sea's worth** all the riches at
the bottom of the sea.    **[s.d.] officers** (The Quarto text calls for "Cassio with lights, officers with
torches.")    31 **My ... soul** my natural gifts, my position or reputation, and my unflawed conscience
33 **Janus** Roman two-faced god of beginnings    38 **matter** business    39 **divine** guess    40 **heat** urgency    41 **sequent** successive    43 **consuls** senators    46 **about** all over the city.    **several** separate
49 **makes** does    50 **boarded** gone aboard and seized as an act of piracy (with sexual suggestion).
**carrack** large merchant ship    51 **prize** booty    53 **Marry** (An oath, originally "by the Virgin Mary";
here used with wordplay on *married.*)    54 **Have with you** i.e., let's go

**CASSIO:** Here comes another troop to seek for you. 55

[*Enter Brabantio, Roderigo, with officers and torches.°*]

**IAGO:** It is Brabantio. General, be advised.°
He comes to bad intent.
**OTHELLO:** Holla! Stand there!
**RODERIGO:** Signor, it is the Moor.
**BRABANTIO:** Down with him, thief!

[*They draw on both sides.*]

**IAGO:** You, Roderigo! Come, sir, I am for you.
**OTHELLO:** Keep up° your bright swords, for the dew will rust them. 60
  Good signor, you shall more command with years
  Than with your weapons.
**BRABANTIO:** O thou foul thief, where hast thou stowed my
    daughter?
  Damned as thou art, thou hast enchanted her!
  For I'll refer me° to all things of sense,° 65
  If she in chains of magic were not bound
  Whether a maid so tender, fair, and happy,
  So opposite to marriage that she shunned
  The wealthy curlèd darlings of our nation,
  Would ever have, t' incur a general mock, 70
  Run from her guardage° to the sooty bosom
  Of such a thing as thou—to fear, not to delight.
  Judge me the world if 'tis not gross in sense°
  That thou hast practiced on her with foul charms,
  Abused her delicate youth with drugs or minerals° 75
  That weakens motion.° I'll have 't disputed on;°
  'Tis probable and palpable to thinking.
  I therefore apprehend and do attach° thee
  For an abuser of the world, a practicer
  Of arts inhibited° and out of warrant.°— 80
  Lay hold upon him! If he do resist,
  Subdue him at his peril.
**OTHELLO:** Hold your hands,
  Both you of my inclining° and the rest.
  Were it my cue to fight, I should have known it
  Without a prompter.—Whither will you that I go 85

55 **[s.d.] officers and torches** (The Quarto text calls for "others with lights and weapons.") 56 **be advised** be on your guard 60 **Keep up** keep in the sheath 65 **refer me** submit my case. **things of sense** commonsense understandings, or, creatures possessing common sense 71 **her guardage** my guardianship of her 73 **gross in sense** obvious 75 **minerals** i.e., poisons 76 **weakens motion** impair the vital faculties. **disputed on** argued in court by professional counsel, debated by experts 78 **attach** arrest 80 **arts inhibited** prohibited arts, black magic. **out of warrant** illegal 83 **inclining** following, party

To answer this your charge?

**BRABANTIO:**   To prison, till fit time
Of law and course of direct session°
Call thee to answer.

**OTHELLO:**                 What if I do obey?
How may the Duke be therewith satisfied,                                     90
Whose messengers are here about my side
Upon some present business of the state
To bring me to him?

**OFFICER:**                       'Tis true, most worthy signor.
The Duke's in council, and your noble self,
I am sure, is sent for.

**BRABANTIO:**                  How? The Duke in council?          95
In this time of the night? Bring him away.°
Mine's not an idle° cause. The Duke himself,
Or any of my brothers of the state,
Cannot but feel this wrong as 'twere their own;
For if such actions may have passage free,°                                  100
Bondslaves and pagans shall our statesmen be.

[*Exeunt.*]

### Scene III. Venice. A council chamber

*Enter Duke [and] Senators [and sit at a table, with lights], and
Officers.° [The Duke and Senators are reading dispatches.]*

**DUKE:**   There is no composition° in these news
That gives them credit.

**FIRST SENATOR:**   Indeed, they are disproportioned.°
My letters say a hundred and seven galleys.

**DUKE:**   And mine, a hundred forty.

**SECOND SENATOR:**                       And mine, two hundred.          5
But though they jump° not on a just° account—
As in these cases, where the aim° reports
'Tis oft with difference—yet do they all confirm
A Turkish fleet, and bearing up to Cyprus.

**DUKE:**   Nay, it is possible enough to judgment.                          10
I do not so secure me in the error
But the main article I do approve°
In fearful sense.

**88 course of direct session** regular or specially convened legal proceedings   **96 away** right along
**97 idle** trifling   **100 have passage free** are allowed to go unchecked   **[s.d.] Enter ... Officers**
(The Quarto text calls for the Duke and senators to "sit at a table with lights and attendants.")
**1 composition** consistency   **3 disproportioned** inconsistent   **6 jump** agree.   **just** exact   **7 the aim**
conjecture   **11–12 I do not ... approve** I do not take such (false) comfort in the discrepancies that
I fail to perceive the main point, i.e., that the Turkish fleet is threatening

**SAILOR** *[within]:*   What ho, what ho, what ho!

[*Enter Sailor.*]

**OFFICER:**   A messenger from the galleys.

**DUKE:**   Now, what's the business?                                              15

**SAILOR:**   The Turkish preparation° makes for Rhodes.
So was I bid report here to the state
By Signor Angelo.

**DUKE:**   How say you by° this change?

**FIRST SENATOR:**                                      This cannot be
By no assay° of reason. 'Tis a pageant°                                          20
To keep us in false gaze.° When we consider
Th' importancy of Cyprus to the Turk,
And let ourselves again but understand
That, as it more concerns the Turk than Rhodes,
So may he with more facile question bear it,°                                    25
For that° it stands not in such warlike brace,
But altogether lacks th' abilities°
That Rhodes is dressed in°—if we make thought of this,
We must not think the Turk is so unskillful°
To leave that latest° which concerns him first,                                 30
Neglecting an attempt of ease and gain
To wake° and wage° a danger profitless.

**DUKE:**   Nay, in all confidence, he's not for Rhodes.

**OFFICER:**   Here is more news.

[*Enter a Messenger.*]

**MESSENGER:**   The Ottomites, reverend and gracious,                          35
Steering with due course toward the isle of Rhodes,
Have there injointed them° with an after° fleet.

**FIRST SENATOR:**   Ay, so I thought. How many, as you guess?

**MESSENGER:**   Of thirty sail; and now they do restem
Their backward course,° bearing with frank appearance°                         40
Their purposes toward Cyprus. Signor Montano,
Your trusty and most valiant servitor,°
With his free duty° recommends° you thus,
And prays you to believe him.

**DUKE:**                            'Tis certain then for Cyprus.              45
Marcus Luccicos, is not he in town?

---

16 **preparation** fleet prepared for battle   19 **by** about   20 **assay** test.   **pageant** mere show   21 **in false gaze** looking the wrong way   25 **So may ... it** so also he (the Turk) can more easily capture it (Cyprus)   26 **For that** since.   **brace** state of defense   27 **abilities** means of self-defense   28 **dressed in** equipped with   29 **unskillful** deficient in judgment   30 **latest** last   32 **wake** stir up.   **wage** risk   37 **injointed them** joined themselves.   **after** second, following   39–40 **restem ... course** retrace their original course   40 **frank appearance** undisguised intent   42 **servitor** officer under your command   43 **free duty** freely given and loyal service.   **recommends** commends himself and reports to

**FIRST SENATOR:**   He's now in Florence.

**DUKE:**   Write from us to him, post-post-haste. Dispatch.

**FIRST SENATOR:**   Here comes Brabantio and the valiant Moor.

[*Enter Brabantio, Othello, Cassio, Iago, Roderigo, and officers.*]

**DUKE:**   Valiant Othello, we must straight° employ you          50
Against the general enemy° Ottoman.
[*To Brabantio.*] I did not see you; welcome, gentle° signor.
We lacked your counsel and your help tonight.

**BRABANTIO:**   So did I yours. Good Your Grace, pardon me;
Neither my place° nor aught I heard of business          55
Hath raised me from my bed, nor doth the general care
Take hold on me, for my particular° grief
Is of so floodgate° and o'erbearing nature
That it engluts° and swallows other sorrows
And it is still itself.°

**DUKE:**                            Why, what's the matter?          60

**BRABANTIO:**   My daughter! O, my daughter!

**DUKE AND SENATORS:**                      Dead?

**BRABANTIO:**                                 Ay, to me.
She is abused,° stol'n from me, and corrupted
By spells and medicines bought of mountebanks;
For nature so preposterously to err,
Being not deficient,° blind, or lame of sense,°          65
Sans° witchcraft could not.

**DUKE:**   Whoe'er he be that in this foul proceeding
Hath thus beguiled your daughter of herself,
And you of her, the bloody book of law
You shall yourself read in the bitter letter          70
After your own sense°—yea, though our proper° son
Stood in your action.°

**BRABANTIO:**                      Humbly I thank Your Grace.
Here is the man, this Moor, whom now it seems
Your special mandate for the state affairs
Hath hither brought.

**ALL:**                      We are very sorry for 't.          75

**DUKE** [*To Othello*]:   What, in your own part, can you say to this?

**BRABANTIO:**   Nothing, but this is so.

**OTHELLO:**   Most potent, grave, and reverend signors,

---

**50 ... straight** straightway.   **51 general enemy** universal enemy to all Christendom   **52 gentle** noble
**55 place** official position   **57 particular** personal   **58 floodgate** i.e., overwhelming (as when flood-
gates are opened)   **59 engluts** engulfs   **60 is still itself** remains undiminished   **62 abused** deceived
**65 deficient** defective.   **fame of sense** deficient in sensory perception   **66 Sans** without   **71 After
... sense** according to your own interpretation.   **our proper** my own   **72 Stood ... action** were under
your accusation

My very noble and approved° good masters:
That I have ta'en away this old man's daughter,                          80
It is most true; true, I have married her.
The very head and front° of my offending
Hath this extent, no more. Rude° am I in my speech,
And little blessed with the soft phrase of peace;
For since these arms of mine had seven years' pith,°                     85
Till now some nine moons wasted,° they have used
Their dearest° action in the tented field;
And little of this great world can I speak
More than pertains to feats of broils and battle,
And therefore little shall I grace my cause                             90
In speaking for myself. Yet, by your gracious patience,
I will a round° unvarnished tale deliver
Of my whole course of love—what drugs, what charms,
What conjuration, and what mighty magic,
For such proceeding I am charged withal,°                               95
I won his daughter.
**BRABANTIO:**          A maiden never bold;
Of spirit so still and quiet that her motion
Blushed at herself;° and she, in spite of nature,
Of years,° of country, credit,° everything,
To fall in love with what she feared to look on!                        100
It is a judgment maimed and most imperfect
That will confess° perfection so could err
Against all rules of nature, and must be driven
To find out practices° of cunning hell
Why this should be. I therefore vouch° again                            105
That with some mixtures powerful o'er the blood,°
Or with some dram conjured to this effect,°
He wrought upon her.
**DUKE:**                   To vouch this is no proof,
Without more wider° and more overt test°
Than these thin habits° and poor likelihoods°                           110
Of modern seeming° do prefer° against him.
**FIRST SENATOR:**   But Othello, speak.
Did you by indirect and forcèd courses°

**79 approved** proved, esteemed   **82 head and front** height and breadth, entire extent   **83 Rude** unpolished
**85 since ... pith** i.e., since I was seven. **pith** strength, vigor   **86 Till ... wasted** until some nine months
ago (since when Othello has evidently not been on active duty, but in Venice); alternately, Othello may
be revealing his age in saying that his life is nine-twelfths over (making him in his early 50s).
**87 dearest** most valuable   **92 round** plain   **95 withal** with   **97–98 her ... herself** i.e., she blushed
easily at herself. (*Motion* can suggest the impulse of the soul or of the emotions, or physical movement.)
**99 years** i.e., difference in age.   **credit** virtuous reputation   **102 confess** concede (that)   **104 practices** plots   **105 vouch** assert   **106 blood** passions   **107 dram ... effect** dose made by magical spells
to have this effect   **109 more wider** fuller.   **test** testimony   **110 habits** garments, i.e., appearances.
**poor likelihoods** weak inferences   **111 modern seeming** commonplace assumption.   **prefer** bring forth
**113 forcèd courses** means used against her will

Subdue and poison this young maid's affections?
Or came it by request and such fair question°    115
As soul to soul affordeth?

**OTHELLO:**                 I do beseech you,
Send for the lady to the Sagittary
And let her speak of me before her father.
If you do find me foul in her report,
The trust, the office I do hold of you    120
Not only take away, but let your sentence
Even fall upon my life.

**DUKE:**                 Fetch Desdemona hither.

**OTHELLO:**    Ancient, conduct them. You best know the place.

                *[Exeunt Iago and attendants.]*

And, till she come, as truly as to heaven
I do confess the vices of my blood,°    125
So justly° to your grave ears I'll present
How I did thrive in this fair lady's love,
And she in mine.

**DUKE:**    Say it, Othello.

**OTHELLO:**    Her father loved me, oft invited me,    130
Still° questioned me the story of my life
From year to year—the battles, sieges, fortunes
That I have passed.
I ran it through, even from my boyish days
To th' very moment that he bade me tell it,    135
Wherein I spoke of most disastrous chances,
Of moving accidents° by flood and field,
Of hairbreadth scapes i' th' imminent deadly breach,°
Of being taken by the insolent foe
And sold to slavery, of my redemption thence,    140
And portance° in my travels' history,
Wherein of antres° vast and deserts idle,°
Rough quarries,° rocks, and hills whose heads touch heaven,
It was my hint° to speak—such was my process—
And of the Cannibals that each other eat,    145
The Anthropophagi,° and men whose heads
Do grow beneath their shoulders. These things to hear
Would Desdemona seriously incline;
But still the house affairs would draw her thence,

115 **question** conversation    125 **blood** passions, human nature    126 **justly** truthfully, accurately    131 **Still** continually    137 **moving accidents** stirring happenings    138 **imminent ... breach** death-threatening gaps made in a fortification    141 **portance** conduct    142 **antres** caverns.    **idle** barren, desolate    143 **Rough quarries** rugged rock formations    144 **hint** occasion, opportunity    146 **Anthropophagi** man-eaters. (A term from Pliny's *Natural History*.)

Which ever as she could with haste dispatch 150
She'd come again, and with a greedy ear
Devour up my discourse. Which I, observing,
Took once a pliant° hour, and found good means
To draw from her a prayer of earnest heart
That I would all my pilgrimage dilate,° 155
Whereof by parcels° she had something heard,
But not intentively.° I did consent,
And often did beguile her of her tears,
When I did speak of some distressful stroke
That my youth suffered. My story being done, 160
She gave me for my pains a world of sighs.
She swore, in faith, 'twas strange, 'twas passing° strange,
'Twas pitiful, 'twas wondrous pitiful.
She wished she had not heard it, yet she wished
That heaven had made her° such a man. She thanked me, 165
And bade me, if I had a friend that loved her,
I should but teach him how to tell my story,
And that would woo her. Upon this hint° I spake.
She loved me for the dangers I had passed,
And I loved her that she did pity them. 170
This only is the witchcraft I have used.
Here comes the lady. Let her witness it.

[*Enter Desdemona, Iago, [and] attendants.*]

**DUKE:** I think this tale would win my daughter too.
Good Brabantio,
Take up this mangled matter at the best.° 175
Men do their broken weapons rather use
Than their bare hands.
**BRABANTIO:**     I pray you, hear her speak.
If she confess that she was half the wooer,
Destruction on my head if my bad blame
Light on the man!—Come hither, gentle mistress. 180
Do you perceive in all this noble company
Where most you owe obedience?
**DESDEMONA:**     My noble Father,
I do perceive here a divided duty.
To you I am bound for life and education;°
My life and education both do learn° me 185

---

153 **pliant** well-suiting  155 **dilate** relate in detail  156 **by parcels** piecemeal  157 **intentively** with full attention, continuously  162 **passing** exceedingly  165 **made her** created her to be  168 **hint** opportunity. (Othello does not mean that she was dropping hints.)  175 **Take … best** make the best of a bad bargain  184 **education** upbringing  185 **learn** teach

How to respect you. You are the lord of duty;°
I am hitherto your daughter. But here's my husband,
And so much duty as my mother showed
To you, preferring you before her father,
So much I challenge° that I may profess                                    190
Due to the Moor my lord.

**BRABANTIO:**    God be with you! I have done.
Please it Your Grace, on to the state affairs.
I had rather to adopt a child than get° it.
Come hither, Moor.                                                         195

[*He joins the hands of Othello and Desdemona.*]

I here do give thee that with all my heart°
Which, but thou hast already, with all my heart°
I would keep from thee.—For your sake,° jewel,
I am glad at soul I have no other child,
For thy escape° would teach me tyranny,                                    200
To hang clogs° on them.—I have done, my lord.

**DUKE:**    Let me speak like yourself,° and lay a sentence°
Which, as a grece° or step, may help these lovers
Into your favor.
When remedies° are past, the griefs are ended                              205
By seeing the worst, which late on hopes depended.°
To mourn a mischief° that is past and gone
Is the next° way to draw new mischief on.
What° cannot be preserved when fortune takes,
Patience her injury a mockery makes.°                                      210
The robbed that smiles steals something from the thief;
He robs himself that spends a bootless grief.°

**BRABANTIO:**    So let the Turk of Cyprus us beguile,
We lose it not, so long as we can smile.
He bears the sentence well that nothing bears                              215
But the free comfort which from thence he hears,
But he bears both the sentence and the sorrow
That, to pay grief, must of poor patience borrow.°
These sentences, to sugar or to gall,

---

186 **of duty** to whom duty is due   190 **challenge** claim   194 **get** beget   196 **with all my heart**
wherein my whole affection has been engaged   197 **with all my heart** willingly, gladly   198 **For your
sake** on your account   200 **escape** elopement   201 **clogs** (Literally, blocks of wood fastened to the legs
of criminals or convicts to inhibit escape.)   202 **like yourself** i.e., as you would, in your proper temper.   **lay a sentence** apply a maxim   203 **grece** step   205 **remedies** hopes of remedy   206 **which ...
depended** which griefs were sustained until recently by hopeful anticipation   207 **mischief** misfortune,
injury   208 **next** nearest   209 **What** whatever   210 **Patience ... makes** patience laughs at the injury
inflicted by fortune (and thus eases the pain)   212 **spends a bootless grief** indulges in unavailing
grief   215–218 **He bears ... borrow** a person well bears out your maxim who can enjoy its platitudinous
comfort, free of all genuine sorrow, but anyone whose grief bankrupts his poor patience is left with your
saying and his sorrow, too. (*Bears the sentence* also plays on the meaning, "receives judicial sentence.")

Being strong on both sides, are equivocal.°          220
But words are words. I never yet did hear
That the bruised heart was piercèd through the ear.°
I humbly beseech you, proceed to th' affairs of state.

**DUKE:** The Turk with a most mighty preparation makes for Cyprus.
Othello, the fortitude° of the place is best known to you; and   225
though we have there a substitute° of most allowed° sufficiency,
yet opinion, a sovereign mistress of effects, throws a more safer
voice on you.° You must therefore be content to slubber° the
gloss of your new fortunes with this more stubborn° and boisterous expedition.

**OTHELLO:** The tyrant custom, most grave senators,         230
Hath made the flinty and steel couch of war
My thrice-driven° bed of down. I do agnize°
A natural and prompt alacrity
I find in hardness,° and do undertake
These present wars against the Ottomites.          235
Most humbly therefore bending to your state,°
I crave fit disposition for my wife,
Due reference of place and exhibition,°
With such accommodation° and besort°
As levels° with her breeding.°            240

**DUKE:** Why, at her father's.

**BRABANTIO:**              I will not have it so.

**OTHELLO:** Nor I.

**DESDEMONA:** Nor I. I would not there reside,
To put my father in impatient thoughts
By being in his eye. Most gracious Duke,
To my unfolding° lend your prosperous° ear,        245
And let me find a charter° in your voice,
T' assist my simpleness.

**DUKE:** What would you, Desdemona?

**DESDEMONA:** That I did love the Moor to live with him,
My downright violence and storm of fortunes°       250
May trumpet to the world. My heart's subdued
Even to the very quality of my lord.°

---

**219–220 These ... equivocal** these fine maxims are equivocal, either sweet or bitter in their application
**222 piercèd ... ear** i.e., surgically lanced and cured by mere words of advice    **225 fortitude** strength
**226 substitute** deputy. **allowed** acknowledged    **226–227 opinion ... on you** general opinion, an
important determiner of affairs, chooses you as the best man    **228 slubber** soil, sully. **stubborn**
harsh, rough    **232 thrice-driven** thrice sifted, winnowed. **agnize** know in myself, acknowledge
**234 hardness** hardship    **236 bending ... state** bowing or kneeling to your authority    **238 reference
... exhibition** provision of appropriate place to live and allowance of money    **239 accommodation**
suitable provision. **besort** attendance    **240 levels** equals, suits. **breeding** social position, upbringing    **245 unfolding** explanation, proposal. **prosperous** propitious    **246 charter** privilege, autho-
rization    **250 My ... fortunes** my plain and total breach of social custom, taking my future by storm
and disrupting my whole life    **251–252 My heart's ... lord** my heart is brought wholly into accord
with Othello's virtues; I love him for his virtues

I saw Othello's visage in his mind,
And to his honors and his valiant parts°
Did I my soul and fortunes consecrate.                          255
So that, dear lords, if I be left behind
A moth° of peace, and he go to the war,
The rites° for why I love him are bereft me,
And I a heavy interim shall support
By his dear° absence. Let me go with him.                      260
**OTHELLO:**   Let her have your voice.°
Vouch with me, heaven, I therefor beg it not
To please the palate of my appetite,
Nor to comply with heat°—the young affects°
In me defunct—and proper° satisfaction,                        265
But to be free° and bounteous to her mind.
And heaven defend° your good souls that you think°
I will your serious and great business scant
When she is with me. No, when light-winged toys
Of feathered Cupid seel° with wanton dullness                  270
My speculative and officed instruments,°
That° my disports° corrupt and taint° my business,
Let huswives make a skillet of my helm,
And all indign° and base adversities
Make head° against my estimation!°                             275
**DUKE:**   Be it as you shall privately determine,
Either for her stay or going. Th' affair cries haste,
And speed must answer it.
**A SENATOR:**                 You must away tonight.
**DESDEMONA:**   Tonight, my lord?
**DUKE:**                        This night.
**OTHELLO:**                         With all my heart.
**DUKE:**   At nine i' the morning here we'll meet again.       280
Othello, leave some officer behind,
And he shall our commission bring to you,
With such things else of quality and respect°
As doth import° you.
**OTHELLO:**           So please Your Grace, my ancient;
A man he is of honesty and trust.                              285

---

**254 parts** qualities   **257 moth** i.e., one who consumes merely   **258 rites** rites of love (with a suggestion, too, of "rights," sharing)   **260 dear** (1) heartfelt (2) costly   **261 voice** consent   **264 heat** sexual passion.   **young affects** passions of youth, desires   **265 proper** personal   **266 free** generous   **267 defend** forbid.   **think** should think   **270 seel** i.e., make blind (as in falconry, by sewing up the eyes of the hawk during training)   **271 speculative ... instruments** eyes and other faculties used in the performance of duty   **272 That** so that.   **disports** sexual pastimes.   **taint** impair   **274 indign** unworthy, shameful   **275 Make head** raise an army.   **estimation** reputation   **283 of quality and respect** of importance and relevance   **284 import** concern

To his conveyance I assign my wife,
With what else needful Your Good Grace shall think
To be sent after me.

**DUKE:**                    Let it be so.
Good night to everyone. [*To Brabantio.*] And, noble signor,
If virtue no delighted° beauty lack,                                        290
Your son-in-law is far more fair than black.

**FIRST SENATOR:**   Adieu, brave Moor. Use Desdemona well.

**BRABANTIO:**   Look to her, Moor, if thou hast eyes to see.
She has deceived her father, and may thee.

[*Exeunt* [*Duke, Brabantio, Cassio, Senators, and officers*].]

**OTHELLO:**   My life upon her faith! Honest Iago,                         295
My Desdemona must I leave to thee.
I prithee, let thy wife attend on her,
And bring them after in the best advantage.°
Come, Desdemona. I have but an hour
Of love, of worldly matters and direction,°                                300
To spend with thee. We must obey the time.°

*Exit* [*with Desdemona*].

**RODERIGO:**   Iago—

**IAGO:**   What sayst thou, noble heart?

**RODERIGO:**   What will I do, think'st thou?

**IAGO:**   Why, go to bed and sleep.                                        305

**RODERIGO:**   I will incontinently° drown myself.

**IAGO:**   If thou dost, I shall never love thee after. Why, thou silly
gentleman?

**RODERIGO:**   It is silliness to live when to live is torment; and then
have we a prescription° to die when death is our physician.

**IAGO:**   O villainous!° I have looked upon the world for four times
times seven years, and, since I could distinguish betwixt a ben-         310
efit and an injury, I never found man that knew how to love
himself. Ere I would say I would drown myself for the love of a
guinea hen,° I would change my humanity with a baboon.

**RODERIGO:**   What should I do? I confess it is my shame to be so
fond,° but it is not in my virtue° to amend it.                            315

**IAGO:**   Virtue? A fig!° 'Tis in ourselves that we are thus or thus.
Our bodies are our gardens, to the which our wills are gardeners;
so that if we will plant nettles or sow lettuce, set hyssop° and

290 **delighted** capable of delighting   298 **in … advantage** at the most favorable opportunity   300 **direction** instructions   301 **the time** the urgency of the present crisis   306 **incontinently** immediately, without self-restraint   308–309 **prescription** (1) right based on long-established custom (2) doctor's prescription   310 **villainous** i.e., what perfect nonsense   313 **guinea hen** (A slang term for a prostitute.)   314 **fond** infatuated   315 **virtue** strength, nature   316 **fig** (To give a fig is to thrust the thumb between the first and second fingers in a vulgar and insulting gesture.)   318 **hyssop** an herb of the mint family

weed up thyme, supply it with one gender° of herbs or distract
it with° many, either to have it sterile with idleness° or ma-
nured with industry—why, the power and corrigible authority°
of this lies in our wills. If the beam° of our lives had not one
scale of reason to poise° another of sensuality, the blood° and          320
baseness of our natures would conduct us to most preposterous
conclusions. But we have reason to cool our raging motions,°
our carnal stings, our unbitted° lusts, whereof I take this that
you call love to be a sect or scion.°                                    325

**RODERIGO:**   It cannot be.

**IAGO:**   It is merely a lust of the blood and a permission of the will.
Come, be a man. Drown thyself? Drown cats and blind puppies.
I have professed me thy friend, and I confess me knit to thy deserving with cables of perdurable° toughness. I could never better stead° thee than now. Put money in thy purse. Follow thou
the wars; defeat thy favor° with an usurped° beard. I say, put          330
money in thy purse. It cannot be long that Desdemona should
continue her love to the Moor—put money in thy purse—nor he
his to her. It was a violent commencement in her, and thou shalt
see an answerable sequestration°—put but money in thy purse.
These Moors are changeable in their wills°—fill thy purse with        335
money. The food that to him now is as luscious as locusts° shall
be to him shortly as bitter as coloquintida.° She must change
for youth; when she is sated with his body, she will find the
error of her choice. She must have change, she must. Therefore
put money in thy purse. If thou wilt needs damn thyself, do it
a more delicate way than drowning. Make° all the money thou        340
canst. If sanctimony° and a frail vow betwixt an erring° barbar-
ian and a supersubtle Venetian be not too hard for my wits and
all the tribe of hell, thou shalt enjoy her. Therefore make money.
A pox of drowning thyself! It is clean out of the way.° Seek thou
rather to be hanged in compassing° thy joy than to be drowned
and go without her.

**RODERIGO:**   Wilt thou be fast° to my hopes if I depend on the issue?°     345

**IAGO:**   Thou art sure of me. Go, make money. I have told thee often,
and I retell thee again and again, I hate the Moor. My cause is

---

**319 gender** kind.   **distract it with** divide it among.   **320 idleness** want of cultivation.   **corrigible
authority** power to correct   **321 beam** balance.   **322 poise** counterbalance.   **blood** natural passions   **324 motions** appetites.   **unbitted** unbridled, uncontrolled   **325 sect or scion** cutting or
offshoot   **329 perdurable** very durable   **330 stead** assist   **331 defeat thy favor** disguise your
face.   **usurped** (The suggestion is that Roderigo is not man enough to have a beard of his own.)
**334–335 an answerable sequestration** a corresponding separation or estrangement   **336 wills** carnal
appetites   **337 locusts** fruit of the carob tree (see Matthew 3:4), or perhaps honeysuckle.   **coloquintida**
colocynth or bitter apple, a purgative   **341 Make** raise, collect.   **sanctimony** sacred ceremony
**342 erring** wandering, vagabond, unsteady   **344 clean ... way** entirely unsuitable as a course of
action.   **compassing** encompassing, embracing   **346 fast** true.   **issue** (successful) outcome

hearted;° thine hath no less reason. Let us be conjunctive° in
our revenge against him. If thou canst cuckold him, thou dost
thyself a pleasure, me a sport. There are many events in the
womb of time which will be delivered. Traverse,° go, provide thy
money. We will have more of this tomorrow. Adieu.                    350

**RODERIGO:** Where shall we meet i' the morning?

**IAGO:** At my lodging.

**RODERIGO:** I'll be with thee betimes.° [*He starts to leave.*]     355

**IAGO:** Go to, farewell.—Do you hear, Roderigo?

**RODERIGO:** What say you?

**IAGO:** No more of drowning, do you hear?

**RODERIGO:** I am changed.

**IAGO:** Go to, farewell. Put money enough in your purse.           360

**RODERIGO:** I'll sell all my land.                        *Exit.*

**IAGO:** Thus do I ever make my fool my purse;
    For I mine own gained knowledge should profane
    If I would time expend with such a snipe°
    But for my sport and profit. I hate the Moor;                365
    And it is thought abroad° that twixt my sheets
    He's done my office.° I know not if 't be true;
    But I, for mere suspicion in that kind,
    Will do as if for surety.° He holds me well;°
    The better shall my purpose work on him.                     370
    Cassio's a proper° man. Let me see now:
    To get his place and to plume up° my will
    In double knavery—How, how?—Let's see:
    After some time, to abuse° Othello's ear
    That he° is too familiar with his wife.                       375
    He hath a person and a smooth dispose°
    To be suspected, framed to make women false.
    The Moor is of a free° and open° nature,
    That thinks men honest that but seem to be so,
    And will as tenderly° be led by the nose                      380
    As asses are.
    I have 't. It is engendered. Hell and night
    Must bring this monstrous birth to the world's light.

*[Exit.]*

---

348 **hearted** fixed in the heart, heartfelt   349 **conjunctive** united   351 **Traverse** (A military
marching term.)   355 **betimes** early   364 **snipe** woodcock, i.e., fool   366 **it is thought abroad** it
is rumored   367 **my office** i.e., my sexual function as husband   369 **do ... surety** act as if on
certain knowledge.   **holds me well** regards me favorably   371 **proper** handsome   372 **plume up**
put a feather in the cap of, i.e., glorify, gratify   374 **abuse** deceive   375 **he** i.e., Cassio   376 **dispose**
disposition   378 **free** frank, generous.   **open** unsuspicious   380 **tenderly** readily

## Act II

Scene I. A seaport in Cyprus. An open place near the quay

*Enter Montano and two Gentlemen*

**MONTANO:**   What from the cape can you discern at sea?
**FIRST GENTLEMAN:**   Nothing at all. It is a high-wrought flood.°
    I cannot, twixt the heaven and the main,°
    Descry a sail.
**MONTANO:**   Methinks the wind hath spoke aloud at land;                    5
    A fuller blast ne'er shook our battlements.
    If it hath ruffianed° so upon the sea,
    What ribs of oak, when mountains° melt on them,
    Can hold the mortise?° What shall we hear of this?
**SECOND GENTLEMAN:**   A segregation° of the Turkish fleet.                    10
    For do but stand upon the foaming shore,
    The chidden° billow seems to pelt the clouds;
    The wind-shaked surge, with high and monstrous mane,°
    Seems to cast water on the burning Bear°
    And quench the guards of th' ever-fixèd pole.                    15
    I never did like molestation° view
    On the enchafèd° flood.
**MONTANO:**   If that° the Turkish fleet
    Be not ensheltered and embayed,° they are drowned;
    It is impossible to bear it out.°                    20

*Enter a [Third] Gentleman.*

**THIRD GENTLEMAN:**   News, lads! Our wars are done.
    The desperate tempest hath so banged the Turks
    That their designment° halts.° A noble ship of Venice
    Hath seen a grievous wreck° and sufferance°
    On most part of their fleet.                    25
**MONTANO:**   How? Is this true?
**THIRD GENTLEMAN:**   The ship is here put in,
    A Veronesa;° Michael Cassio,
    Lieutenant to the warlike Moor Othello,
    Is come on shore; the Moor himself at sea,                    30

---

**2 high-wrought flood** very agitated sea   **3 main** ocean (also at line 41)   **7 ruffianed** raged   **8 mountains** i.e., of water   **9 hold the mortise** hold their joints together. (A *mortise* is the socket hollowed out in fitting timbers.)   **10 segregation** dispersal   **12 chidden** i.e., rebuked, repelled (by the shore), and thus shot into the air   **13 monstrous mane** (The surf is like the mane of a wild beast.)   **14 the burning Bear** i.e., the constellation Ursa Minor or the Little Bear, which includes the polestar (and hence regarded as the guards of th' *ever-fixèd pole* in the next line; sometimes the term *guards* is applied to the two "pointers" of the Big Bear or Dipper, which may be intended here.)   **16 like molestation** comparable disturbance   **17 enchafèd** angry   **18 If that** if   **19 embayed** sheltered by a bay   **20 bear it out** survive, weather the storm   **23 designment** design, enterprise.   **halts** is lame   **24 wreck** shipwreck.   **sufferance** damage, disaster   **28 Veronesa** i.e., fitted out in Verona for Venetian service, or possibly *Verennessa* (the Folio spelling), i.e., *verrìnessa*, a cutter (from *verrinare*, "to cut through")

And is in full commission here for Cyprus.

**MONTANO:**   I am glad on 't. 'Tis a worthy governor.

**THIRD GENTLEMAN:**   But this same Cassio, though he speak of comfort

Touching the Turkish loss, yet he looks sadly°

And prays the Moor be safe, for they were parted          35

With foul and violent tempest.

**MONTANO:**                                       Pray heaven he be,

For I have served him, and the man commands

Like a full° soldier. Let's to the seaside, ho!

As well to see the vessel that's come in

As to throw out our eyes for brave Othello,                    40

Even till we make the main and th' aerial blue°

An indistinct regard.°

**THIRD GENTLEMAN:**   Come, let's do so,

For every minute is expectancy°

Of more arrivance.°

[*Enter Cassio.*]

**CASSIO:**   Thanks, you the valiant of this warlike isle,      45

That so approve° the Moor! O, let the heavens

Give him defense against the elements,

For I have lost him on a dangerous sea.

**MONTANO:**   Is he well shipped?

**CASSIO:**   His bark is stoutly timbered, and his pilot      50

Of very expert and approved allowance;°

Therefore my hopes, not surfeited to death,°

Stand in bold cure.°

[*A cry*] *within:* "A sail, a sail, a sail!"

**CASSIO:**   What noise?

**A GENTLEMAN:**   The town is empty. On the brow o' the sea°   55

Stand ranks of people, and they cry "A sail!"

**CASSIO:**   My hopes do shape him for° the governor.

[*A shot within.*]

**SECOND GENTLEMAN:**   They do discharge their shot of courtesy;°

Our friends at least.

**CASSIO:**                       I pray you, sir, go forth,

And give us truth who 'tis that is arrived.                        60

**SECOND GENTLEMAN:**   I shall.                                       *Exit.*

---

**34 sadly** gravely   **38 full** perfect   **41 the main … blue** the sea and the sky   **42 An indistinct regard** indistinguishable in our view   **43 is expectancy** gives expectation   **44 arrivance** arrival **46 approve** admire, honor   **51 approved allowance** tested reputation   **52 surfeited to death** i.e., overextended, worn thin through repeated application or delayed fulfillment   **53 in bold cure** in strong hopes of fulfillment   **55 brow o' the sea** cliff-edge   **57 My … for** I hope it is   **58 discharge … courtesy** fire a salute in token of respect and courtesy

**MONTANO:**   But, good Lieutenant, is your general wived?

**CASSIO:**   Most fortunately. He hath achieved a maid

That paragons° description and wild fame,°

One that excels the quirks° of blazoning° pens,               65

And in th' essential vesture of creation

Does tire the enginer.°

[*Enter [Second] Gentleman.*°]

How now? Who has put in?°

**SECOND GENTLEMAN:**   'Tis one Iago, ancient to the General.

**CASSIO:**   He's had most favorable and happy speed.

Tempests themselves, high seas, and howling winds,               70

The guttered° rocks and congregated sands—

Traitors ensteeped° to clog the guiltless keel—

As° having sense of beauty, do omit°

Their mortal° natures, letting go safely by

The divine Desdemona.

**MONTANO:**                    What is she?               75

**CASSIO:**   She that I spake of, our great captain's captain,

Left in the conduct of the bold Iago,

Whose footing° here anticipates our thoughts

A sennight's° speed. Great Jove, Othello guard,

And swell his sail with thine own powerful breath,               80

That he may bless this bay with his tall° ship,

Make love's quick pants in Desdemona's arms,

Give renewed fire to our extincted spirits,

And bring all Cyprus comfort!

[*Enter Desdemona, Iago, Roderigo, and Emilia.*]

                    O, behold,

The riches of the ship is come on shore!               85

You men of Cyprus, let her have your knees.

[*The gentlemen make curtsy to Desdemona.*]

Hail to thee, lady! And the grace of heaven

Before, behind thee, and on every hand

Enwheel thee round!

**DESDEMONA:**          I thank you, valiant Cassio.

What tidings can you tell me of my lord?               90

---

**64 paragons** surpasses.  **wild fame** extravagant report   **65 quirks** witty conceits.  **blazoning**
setting forth as though in heraldic language   **66–67 in … enginer** in her real, God-given, beauty,
(she) defeats any attempt to praise her.  **enginer** engineer, i.e., poet, one who devises.  **[s.d.]**
**Second Gentleman** (So identified in the Quarto text here and in lines 58, 61, 68, and 96; the Folio
calls him a gentleman.)   **67 put in** i.e., to harbor   **71 guttered** jagged, trenched   **72 ensteeped**
lying under water   **73 As** as if.  **omit** forbear to exercise   **74 mortal** deadly   **78 footing** landing
**79 sennight's** week's   **81 tall** splendid, gallant

**CASSIO:**   He is not yet arrived, nor know I aught
　　But that he's well and will be shortly here.
**DESDEMONA:**   O, but I fear—How lost you company?
**CASSIO:**   The great contention of the sea and skies
　　Parted our fellowship.

　　　　　　　(*Within*) "*A sail, a sail!*" [*A shot.*]
　　　　　　　But hark. A sail!　　　　　　　　　　　　　95
**SECOND GENTLEMAN:**   They give their greeting to the citadel.
　　This likewise is a friend.
**CASSIO:**　　　　　　　　　See for the news.

　　　　　　　[*Exit Second Gentleman.*]

　　Good Ancient, you are welcome. [*Kissing Emilia.*] Welcome, mistress.
　　Let it not gall your patience, good Iago,
　　That I extend° my manners; 'tis my breeding°　　　　100
　　That gives me this bold show of courtesy.
**IAGO:**   Sir, would she give you so much of her lips
　　As of her tongue she oft bestows on me,
　　You would have enough.
**DESDEMONA:**   Alas, she has no speech!°　　　　　　105
**IAGO:**   In faith, too much.
　　I find it still,° when I have list° to sleep.
　　Marry, before your ladyship, I grant,
　　She puts her tongue a little in her heart
　　And chides with thinking.°
**EMILIA:**　　　　　　　　　You have little cause to say so.　　110
**IAGO:**   Come on, come on. You are pictures out of doors,°
　　Bells° in your parlors, wildcats in your kitchens,°
　　Saints° in your injuries, devils being offended,
　　Players° in your huswifery,° and huswives° in your beds.
**DESDEMONA:**   O, fie upon thee, slanderer!　　　　　　115
**IAGO:**   Nay, it is true, or else I am a Turk.°
　　You rise to play, and go to bed to work.
**EMILIA:**   You shall not write my praise.
**IAGO:**　　　　　　　　　No, let me not.
**DESDEMONA:**   What wouldst write of me, if thou shouldst praise me?
**IAGO:**   O gentle lady, do not put me to 't,　　　　　　120
　　For I am nothing if not critical.°
**DESDEMONA:**   Come on, essay.°—There's one gone to the harbor?

---

**100 extend** give scope to.　**breeding** training in the niceties of etiquette　**105 she has no speech**
i.e., she's not a chatterbox, as you allege　**107 still** always.　**list** desire　**110 with thinking** i.e.,
in her thoughts only　**111 pictures out of doors** i.e., silent and well-behaved in public　**112 Bells**
i.e., jangling, noisy, and brazen.　**in your kitchens** i.e., in domestic affairs. (Ladies would not do the
cooking.)　**113 Saints** martyrs　**114 Players** idlers, triflers, or deceivers.　**huswifery** housekeeping.　**huswives** hussies (i.e., women are "busy" in bed, or unduly thrifty in dispensing sexual favors)
**116 a Turk** an infidel, not to be believed　**121 critical** censorious　**122 essay** try

**IAGO:**   Ay, madam.

**DESDEMONA:**   I am not merry, but I do beguile

    The thing I am° by seeming otherwise.                                              125

    Come, how wouldst thou praise me?

**IAGO:**   I am about it, but indeed my invention

    Comes from my pate as birdlime° does from frieze°—

    It plucks out brains and all. But my Muse labors,°

    And thus she is delivered:                                                                    130

    If she be fair and wise, fairness and wit,

    The one's for use, the other useth it.°

**DESDEMONA:**   Well praised! How if she be black° and witty?

**IAGO:**   If she be black, and thereto have a wit,

    She'll find a white° that shall her blackness fit.°                            135

**DESDEMONA:**   Worse and worse.

**EMILIA:**                                                   How if fair and foolish?

**IAGO:**   She never yet was foolish that was fair,

    For even her folly° helped her to an heir.°

**DESDEMONA:**   These are old fond° paradoxes to make fools laugh i'

    th' alehouse.

    What miserable praise hast thou for her that's foul and foolish?     140

**IAGO:**   There's none so foul° and foolish thereunto,°

    But does foul° pranks which fair and wise ones do.

**DESDEMONA:**   O heavy ignorance! Thou praisest the worst best. But

    what praise couldst thou bestow on a deserving woman indeed,

    one that, in the authority of her merit, did justly put on the

    vouch° of very malice itself?                                                           145

**IAGO:**   She that was ever fair, and never proud,

    Had tongue at will, and yet was never loud,

    Never lacked gold and yet went never gay,°

    Fled from her wish, and yet said, "Now I may,"°

    She that being angered, her revenge being nigh,                           150

    Bade her wrong stay° and her displeasure fly,

    She that in wisdom never was so frail

    To change the cod's head for the salmon's tail,°

    She that could think and ne'er disclose her mind,

    See suitors following and not look behind,                                     155

    She was a wight, if ever such wight were—

---

125 **The thing I am** i.e., my anxious self   128 **birdlime** sticky substance used to catch small birds.
**frieze** coarse woolen cloth   129 **labors** (1) exerts herself (2) prepares to deliver a child (with a following
pun on *delivered* in line 130)   132 **The one's ... it** i.e., her cleverness will make use of her beauty
133 **black** dark-complexioned, brunette   135 **a white** a fair person (with word-play on "wight," a person)
**fit** (with sexual suggestion of mating)   138 **folly** (with added meaning of "lechery, wantonness")   **to an
heir** i.e., to bear a child   139 **fond** foolish   141 **foul** ugly.   **thereunto** in addition   142 **foul** sluttish
145 **put ... vouch** compel the approval   148 **gay** extravagantly clothed   149 **Fled ... may** avoided
temptation where the choice was hers   151 **Bade ... stay** i.e., resolved to put up with her injury patiently
153 **To ... tail** i.e., to exchange a lackluster husband for a sexy lover (?) (**Cod's head** is slang for "penis,"
and tail, for "pudendum.")

**DESDEMONA:** To do what?

**IAGO:** To suckle fools° and chronicle small beer.°

**DESDEMONA:** O most lame and impotent conclusion! Do not learn
of him, Emilia, though he be thy husband. How say you, Cassio?     160
Is he not a most profane° and liberal° counselor?

**CASSIO:** He speaks home,° madam. You may relish° him more in°
the soldier than in the scholar.

[*Cassio and Desdemona stand together, conversing intimately.*]

**IAGO** [*aside*]: He takes her by the palm. Ay, well said,° whisper.
With as little a web as this will I ensnare as great a fly as Cassio.     165
Ay, smile upon her, do; I will gyve° thee in thine own courtship.° You say true;° 'tis so, indeed. If such tricks as these strip
you out of your lieutenantry, it had been better you had not
kissed your three fingers so oft, which now again you are most
apt to play the sir° in. Very good; well kissed! An excellent
courtesy! 'Tis so, indeed. Yet again your fingers to your lips?
Would they were clyster pipes° for your sake! [*Trumpet within.*]     170
The Moor! I know his trumpet.

**CASSIO:** 'Tis truly so.

**DESDEMONA:** Let's meet him and receive him.

**CASSIO:** Lo, where he comes!

[*Enter Othello and attendants.*]

**OTHELLO:** O my fair warrior!

**DESDEMONA:**                    My dear Othello!     175

**OTHELLO:** It gives me wonder great as my content
To see you here before me. O my soul's joy,
If after every tempest come such calms,
May the winds blow till they have wakened death,
And let the laboring bark climb hills of seas     180
Olympus-high, and duck again as low
As hell's from heaven! If it were now to die,
'Twere now to be most happy, for I fear
My soul hath her content so absolute
That not another comfort like to this     185
Succeeds in unknown fate.°

**DESDEMONA:**                    The heavens forbid
But that our loves and comforts should increase
Even as our days do grow!

---

158 **suckle fools** breastfeed babies   **chronicle small beer** i.e., keep petty household accounts; keep
track of trivial matters   161 **profane** irreverent, ribald   **liberal** licentious free-spoken   162 **home**
right to the target (a term from fencing)   **relish** appreciate   **in** in the character of   164 **well said** well
done   166 **gyve** fetter, shackle.   **courtship** courtesy, show of courtly manners.   **You say true** i.e.,
that's right, go ahead   169 **the sir** i.e., the fine gentleman   170 **clyster pipes** tubes used for enemas
and douches   186 **Succeeds ... fate** i.e., can follow in the unknown future

**OTHELLO:**   Amen to that, sweet powers!
I cannot speak enough of this content.                                    190
It stops me here; it is too much of joy.
And this, and this, the greatest discords be

[*They kiss.*]°

That e'er our hearts shall make!
**IAGO** [*aside*]:   O, you are well tuned now!
But I'll set down° the pegs that make this music,                         195
As honest as I am.°
**OTHELLO:**   Come, let us to the castle.
News, friends! Our wars are done, the Turks are drowned.
How does my old acquaintance of this isle?—
Honey, you shall be well desired° in Cyprus;                              200
I have found great love amongst them. O my sweet,
I prattle out of fashion,° and I dote
In mine own comforts.—I prithee, good Iago,
Go to the bay and disembark my coffers.°
Bring thou the master° to the citadel;                                    205
He is a good one, and his worthiness
Does challenge° much respect.—Come, Desdemona.—
Once more, well met at Cyprus!

> [*Exeunt Othello and Desdemona* [*and all
> but Iago and Roderigo*].]

**IAGO** [*to an attendant*]:   Do thou meet me presently at the harbor.
[*To Roderigo.*] Come hither. If thou be'st valiant—as, they say,
base men° being in love have then a nobility in their natures     210
more than is native to them—list° me. The Lieutenant tonight
watches on the court of guard.° First, I must tell thee this:
Desdemona is directly in love with him.
**RODERIGO:**   With him? Why, 'tis not possible.
**IAGO:**   Lay thy finger thus,° and let thy soul be instructed. Mark     215
me with what violence she first loved the Moor, but° for bragging and telling her fantastical lies. To love him still for prat-
ing? Let not thy discreet heart think it. Her eye must be fed;
and what delight shall she have to look on the devil? When the
blood is made dull with the act of sport,° there should be, again
to inflame it and to give satiety a fresh appetite, loveliness in

---

192 **[s.d.] They kiss** (The direction is from the Quarto.)   195 **set down** loosen (and hence untune
the instrument)   196 **As ... I am** for all my supposed honesty   200 **desired** welcomed   202 **out of
fashion** irrelevantly, incoherently (?)   204 **coffers** chests, baggage   205 **master** ship's captain
207 **challenge** lay claim to, deserve   210 **base men** even lowly born men   211 **list** listen to
212 **court of guard** guardhouse. (Cassio is in charge of the watch.)   215 **thus** i.e., on your lips
216 **but** only   219 **the act of sport** sex

favor,° sympathy° in years, manners,and beauties—all which    220
the Moor is defective in. Now, for want of these required conveniences,° her delicate tenderness will find itself abused,° begin
to heave the gorge,° disrelish and abhor the Moor. Very nature°
will instruct her in it and compel her to some second choice.
Now, sir, this granted—as it is a most pregnant° and unforced
position—who stands so eminent in the degree of° this fortune    225
as Cassio does? A knave very voluble,° no further conscionable°
than in putting on the mere form of civil and humane° seeming
for the better compassing of his salt° and most hidden loose
affection.° Why, none, why, none. A slipper° and subtle knave,
a finder out of occasions, that has an eye can stamp° and coun-    230
terfeit advantages,° though true advantage never present itself;
a devilish knave. Besides, the knave is handsome, young, and
hath all those requisites in him that folly° and green° minds
look after. A pestilent complete knave, and the woman hath
found him° already.

**RODERIGO:** I cannot believe that in her. She's full of most blessed
condition.°    235

**IAGO:** Blessed fig's end!° The wine she drinks is made of grapes.
If she had been blessed, she would never have loved the Moor.
Blessed pudding!° Didst thou not see her paddle with the palm
of his hand? Didst not mark that?

**RODERIGO:** Yes, that I did; but that was but courtesy.

**IAGO:** Lechery, by this hand. An index° and obscure° prologue to    240
the history of lust and foul thoughts. They met so near with their
lips that their breaths embraced together. Villainous thoughts,
Roderigo! When these mutualities° so marshal the way, hard
at hand° comes the master and main exercise, th' incorporate°
conclusion. Pish! But, sir, be you ruled by me. I have brought
you from Venice. Watch you° tonight; for the command, I'll lay 't    245
upon you.° Cassio knows you not. I'll not be far from you. Do
you find some occasion to anger Cassio, either by speaking too
loud, or tainting° his discipline, or from what other course you
please, which the time shall more favorably minister.°

---

**220 favor** appearance. **sympathy** correspondence, similarity   **222 required conveniences** things
conducive to sexual compatibility   **223 abused** cheated, revolted.   **heave the gorge** experience
nausea   **224 Very nature** her very instincts   **225 pregnant** evident, cogent   **226 in ... of** as next
in line for   **227 voluble** facile, glib.   **conscionable** conscientious, conscience-bound   **228 hu-
mane** polite, courteous.   **salt** licentious   **229 affection** passion.   **slipper** slippery   **230 an eye
can stamp** an eye that can coin, create   **231 advantages** favorable opportunities   **233 folly** wantonness.   **green** immature   **234 found him** sized him up, perceived his intent   **235 condition**
disposition   **236 fig's end** (See Act I, Scene iii, line 316 for the vulgar gesture of the fig.)
**237 pudding** sausage   **240 index** table of contents.   **obscure** (i.e., the *lust and foul thoughts* in line
241 are secret, hidden from view)   **243 mutualities** exchanges, intimacies.   **hard at hand** closely
following   **244 incorporate** carnal   **245 Watch you** stand watch   **245–246 for the command ... you**
I'll arrange for you to be appointed, given orders   **247 tainting** disparaging   **249 minister** provide

**RODERIGO:**   Well.                                                                                   250

**IAGO:**   Sir, he's rash and very sudden in choler,° and haply° may
strike at you. Provoke him that he may, for even out of that will
I cause these of Cyprus to mutiny,° whose qualification° shall
come into no true taste° again but by the displanting of Cassio.
So shall you have a shorter journey to your desires by the means
I shall then have to prefer° them, and the impediment most      255
profitably removed, without the which there were no expectation of our prosperity.

**RODERIGO:**   I will do this, if you can bring it to any opportunity.

**IAGO:**   I warrant° thee. Meet me by and by° at the citadel. I must
fetch his necessaries ashore. Farewell.                                          260

**RODERIGO:**   Adieu. [*Exit.*]

**IAGO:**   That Cassio loves her, I do well believe 't;
That she loves him, 'tis apt° and of great credit.°
The Moor, howbeit that I endure him not,
Is of a constant, loving, noble nature,                                           265
And I dare think he'll prove to Desdemona
A most dear husband. Now, I do love her too,
Not out of absolute lust—though peradventure
I stand accountant° for as great a sin—
But partly led to diet° my revenge                                               270
For that I do suspect the lusty Moor
Hath leaped into my seat, the thought whereof
Doth, like a poisonous mineral, gnaw my innards;
And nothing can or shall content my soul
Till I am evened with him, wife for wife,                                         275
Or failing so, yet that I put the Moor
At least into a jealousy so strong
That judgment cannot cure. Which thing to do,
If this poor trash of Venice, whom I trace°
For° his quick hunting, stand the putting on,°                                   280
I'll have our Michael Cassio on the hip,°
Abuse° him to the Moor in the rank garb—°
For I fear Cassio with my nightcap° too—
Make the Moor thank me, love me, and reward me
For making him egregiously an ass                                                285
And practicing upon° his peace and quiet

251 **choler** wrath   **haply** perhaps   253 **mutiny** riot.   **qualification** appeasement.   **true taste** i.e.,
acceptable state   255 **prefer** advance   259 **warrant** assure.   **by and by** immediately   263 **apt**
probable.   **credit** credibility   269 **accountant** accountable   270 **diet** feed   279 **trace** i.e., train, or
follow (?), or perhaps *trash*, a hunting term, meaning to put weights on a hunting dog in order to slow
him down   280 **For** to make more eager.   **stand ... on** respond properly when I incite him to quarrel
281 **on the hip** at my mercy, where I can throw him. (A wrestling term.)   282 **Abuse** slander.   **rank
garb** coarse manner, gross fashion   283 **with my nightcap** i.e., as a rival in my bed, as one who gives
me cuckold's horns   286 **practicing upon** plotting against

Even to madness. 'Tis here, but yet confused.
Knavery's plain face is never seen till used.

[*Exit.*]

## Scene II. Cyprus. A street

*Enter Othello's Herald with a proclamation.*

**HERALD:** It is Othello's pleasure, our noble and valiant general,
that, upon certain tidings now arrived, importing the mere per-
dition° of the Turkish fleet, every man put himself into triumph:° some to dance, some to make bonfires, each man to
what sport and revels his addiction° leads him. For, besides
these beneficial news, it is the celebration of his nuptial. So
much was his pleasure should be proclaimed. All offices° are
open, and there is full liberty of feasting from this present hour
of five till the bell have told eleven. Heaven bless the isle of
Cyprus and our noble general Othello!

[*Exit.*]

## Scene III. Cyprus. The Citadel

*Enter Othello, Desdemona, Cassio, and attendants.*

**OTHELLO:** Good Michael, look you to the guard tonight.
Let's teach ourselves that honorable stop°
Not to outsport° discretion.
**CASSIO:** Iago hath direction what to do,
But notwithstanding, with my personal eye          5
Will I look to 't.
**OTHELLO:**          Iago is most honest.
Michael, good night. Tomorrow with your earliest°
Let me have speech with you. [*To Desdemona.*]
Come, my dear love,
The purchase made, the fruits are to ensue;
That profit's yet to come 'tween me and you.°—          10
Good night.

[*Exit [Othello, with Desdemona and attendants].*]

[*Enter Iago.*]

**CASSIO:** Welcome, Iago. We must to the watch.

---

2 **mere perdition** complete destruction   3 **triumph** public celebration   4 **addiction** inclination
6 **offices** rooms where food and drink are kept   2 **stop** restraint   3 **outsport** celebrate beyond the
bounds of   7 **with your earliest** at your earliest convenience   9–10 **The purchase ... you** i.e.,
though married, we haven't yet consummated our love

**IAGO:**  Not this hour,° Lieutenant; 'tis not yet ten o' the clock. Our
general cast° us thus early for the love of his Desdemona; who°
let us not therefore blame. He hath not yet made wanton the
night with her, and she is sport for Jove.                                    15

**CASSIO:**  She's a most exquisite lady.

**IAGO:**  And, I'll warrant her, full of game.

**CASSIO:**  Indeed, she's a most fresh and delicate creature.

**IAGO:**  What an eye she has! Methinks it sounds a parley° to
provocation.

**CASSIO:**  An inviting eye, and yet methinks right modest.                   20

**IAGO:**  And when she speaks, is it not an alarum° to love?

**CASSIO:**  She is indeed perfection.

**IAGO:**  Well, happiness to their sheets! Come, Lieutenant, I have a
stoup° of wine, and here without° are a brace° of Cyprus gallants
that would fain have a measure° to the health of black Othello.               25

**CASSIO:**  Not tonight, good Iago. I have very poor and unhappy
brains for drinking. I could well wish courtesy would invent
some other custom of entertainment.

**IAGO:**  O, they are our friends. But one cup! I'll drink for you.°

**CASSIO:**  I have drunk but one cup tonight, and that was craftily          30
qualified° too, and behold what innovation° it makes here.° I
am unfortunate in the infirmity and dare not task my weakness
with any more.

**IAGO:**  What, man? 'Tis a night of revels. The gallants desire it.

**CASSIO:**  Where are they?

**IAGO:**  Here at the door. I pray you, call them in.

**CASSIO:**  I'll do 't, but it dislikes me.°                    *Exit.*    35

**IAGO:**  If I can fasten but one cup upon him,
With that which he hath drunk tonight already,
He'll be as full of quarrel and offense°
As my young mistress' dog. Now, my sick fool Roderigo,
Whom love hath turned almost the wrong side out,                             40
To Desdemona hath tonight caroused°
Potations pottle-deep;° and he's to watch.°
Three lads of Cyprus—noble swelling° spirits,
That hold their honors in a wary distance,°
The very elements° of this warlike isle—                                     45

13 **Not this hour** not for an hour yet.  **cast** dismissed   14 **who** i.e., Othello   19 **sounds a parley**
calls for a conference, issues an invitation   21 **alarum** signal calling men to arms (continuing the
military metaphor of *parley,* line 19)   23 **stoup** measure of liquor, two quarts   24 **without** outside.  **brace** pair   24–25 **fain have a measure** gladly drink a toast   28 **for you** in your place. (Iago
will do the steady drinking to keep the gallants company while Cassio has only one cup.)   29 **quali-
fied** diluted   30 **innovation** disturbance, insurrection.  **here** i.e., in my head   35 **it dislikes me**
i.e., I'm reluctant   38 **offense** readiness to take offense   41 **caroused** drunk off   42 **pottle-deep** to
the bottom of the tankard.  **watch** stand watch   43 **swelling** proud   44 **hold … distance** i.e., are
extremely sensitive of their honor   45 **very elements** typical sort

Have I tonight flustered with flowing cups,
And they watch° too. Now, 'mongst this flock of drunkards
Am I to put our Cassio in some action
That may offend the isle.—But here they come.

[*Enter Cassio, Montano, and gentlemen; [servants following with wine].*]

If consequence do but approve my dream,°                    50
My boat sails freely both with wind and stream.°
**CASSIO:**  'Fore God, they have given me a rouse° already.
**MONTANO:**  Good faith, a little one; not past a pint, as I am a
soldier.
**IAGO:**  Some wine, ho! [*He sings.*]
    "And let me the cannikin° clink, clink,                 55
    And let me the cannikin clink.
    A soldier's a man,
    O, man's life's but a span;°
    Why, then, let a soldier drink."
Some wine, boys!                                            60
**CASSIO:**  'Fore God, an excellent song.
**IAGO:**  I learned it in England, where indeed they are most potent
in potting.° Your Dane, your German, and your swag-bellied
Hollander—drink, ho!—are nothing to your English.
**CASSIO:**  Is your Englishman so exquisite in his drinking?        65
**IAGO:**  Why, he drinks you,° with facility, your Dane° dead drunk;
he sweats not° to overthrow your Almain;° he gives your
Hollander a vomit ere the next pottle can be filled.
**CASSIO:**  To the health of our general!
**MONTANO:**  I am for it, Lieutenant, and I'll do you justice.°      70
**IAGO:**  O sweet England! [*He sings.*]

    "King Stephen was and—a worthy peer,
      His breeches cost him but a crown;
    He held them sixpence all too dear,
      With that he called the tailor lown.°                 75
    He was a wight of high renown,
      And thou art but of low degree.
    'Tis pride° that pulls the country down;
      Then take thy auld° cloak about thee."

Some wine, ho!                                              80

47 **watch** are members of the guard   50 **If ... dream** if subsequent events will only substantiate my
scheme   51 **stream** current   52 **rouse** full draft of liquor   55 **cannikin** small drinking vessel   58 **span**
brief span of time. (Compare Psalm 39:6 as rendered in the 1928 *Book of Common Prayer:* "Thou hast made
my days as it were a span long.")   62 **potting** drinking   66 **drinks you** drinks.   **your Dane** your typical Dane.   **sweats not** i.e., need not exert himself   67 **Almain** German   70 **I'll ... justice** i.e., I'll drink
as much as you   75 **lown** lout, rascal   78 **pride** i.e., extravagance in dress   79 **auld** old

**CASSIO:**  'Fore God, this is a more exquisite song than the other.

**IAGO:**  Will you hear 't again?

**CASSIO:**  No, for I hold him to be unworthy of his place that does
those things. Well, God's above all; and there be souls must be
saved, and there be souls must not be saved.                               85

**IAGO:**  It's true, good Lieutenant.

**CASSIO:**  For mine own part—no offense to the General, nor any
man of quality°—I hope to be saved.

**IAGO:**  And so do I too, Lieutenant.

**CASSIO:**  Ay, but, by your leave, not before me; the lieutenant is
to be saved before the ancient. Let's have no more of this; let's      90
to our affairs.—God forgive us our sins!—Gentlemen, let's look
to our business. Do not think, gentlemen, I am drunk. This is
my ancient; this is my right hand, and this is my left. I am not
drunk now. I can stand well enough, and speak well enough.

**GENTLEMEN:**  Excellent well.                                              95

**CASSIO:**  Why, very well then; you must not think then that I am dr
unk.                                                          *Exit.*

**MONTANO:**  To th' platform, masters. Come, let's set the watch.°

[*Exeunt Gentlemen.*]

**IAGO:**  You see this fellow that is gone before.
He's a soldier fit to stand by Caesar
And give direction; and do but see his vice.                           100
'Tis to his virtue a just equinox,°
The one as long as th' other. 'Tis pity of him.
I fear the trust Othello puts him in,
On some odd time of his infirmity,
Will shake this island.

**MONTANO:**                    But is he often thus?                        105

**IAGO:**  'Tis evermore the prologue to his sleep.
He'll watch the horologe a double set,°
If drink rock not his cradle.

**MONTANO:**  It were well
The General were put in mind of it.
Perhaps he sees it not, or his good nature                              110
Prizes the virtue that appears in Cassio
And looks not on his evils. Is not this true?

[*Enter Roderigo.*]

**IAGO**  [aside to him]:  How now, Roderigo?
I prayyou, after the Lieutenant; go.            [*Exit Roderigo.*]

88 **quality** rank   97 **set the watch** mount the guard   101 **just equinox** exact counterpart.
(*Equinox* is a day on which daylight and nighttime hours are equal.)   107 **watch ... set** stay awake
twice around the clock or *horologe*

**MONTANO:** And 'tis great pity that the noble Moor     115
  Should hazard such a place as his own second
  With° one of an engraffed° infirmity.
  It were an honest action to say so
  To the Moor.
**IAGO:**         Not I, for this fair island.
  I do love Cassio well and would do much     120
  To cure him of this evil.       *[Cry within: "Help! Help!"]*
              But, hark! What noise?

*[Enter Cassio, pursuing° Roderigo.]*

**CASSIO:**   Zounds, you rogue! You rascal!
**MONTANO:**   What's the matter, Lieutenant?
**CASSIO:**   A knave teach me my duty? I'll beat the knave into a
  twiggen° bottle.
**RODERIGO:**   Beat me?     125
**CASSIO:**   Dost thou prate, rogue? *[He strikes Roderigo.]*
**MONTANO:**   Nay, good Lieutenant. *[Restraining him.]* I pray you,
  sir, hold your hand.
**CASSIO:**   Let me go, sir, or I'll knock you o'er the mazard.°
**MONTANO:**   Come, come, you're drunk.
**CASSIO:**   Drunk?                   *[They fight.]*   130
**IAGO**  *[aside to Roderigo]:*Away, I say. Go out and cry a mutiny.°
                      *[Exit Roderigo.]*
  Nay, good Lieutenant—God's will, gentlemen—
  Help, ho!—Lieutenant—sir—Montano—sir—
  Help, masters!°—Here's a goodly watch indeed!

*[A bell rings.]°*

  Who's that which rings the bell?—Diablo,° ho!     135
  The town will rise.° God's will, Lieutenant, hold!
  You'll be ashamed forever.

*Enter Othello and attendants [with weapons].*

**OTHELLO:**   What is the matter here?
**MONTANO:**                 Zounds, I bleed still.
  I am hurt to th' death. He dies! *[He thrusts at Cassio.]*
**OTHELLO:**                Hold, for your lives!
**IAGO:**   Hold, ho! Lieutenant—sir—Montano—gentlemen—   140
  Have you forgot all sense of place and duty?
  Hold! The General speaks to you. Hold, for shame!

---

**116–117 hazard … With** risk giving such an important position as his second in command to
**117 engraffed** engraffed, inveterate   **121 [s.d.] pursuing** (The Quarto text reads, "driving in.")
**124 twiggen** wicker-covered. (Cassio vows to assail Roderigo until his skin resembles wickerwork
or until he has driven Roderigo through the holes in a wickerwork.)   **128 mazard** i.e., head
(literally, a drinking vessel)   **131 mutiny** riot   **134 masters** sirs   **[s.d.] A bell rings** (This direction is from the Quarto, as are *Exit Roderigo* at line 114, *They fight* at line 130, and *with weapons* at
line 137.)   **135 Diablo** the devil   **136 rise** grow riotous

**OTHELLO:**   Why, how now, ho! From whence ariseth this?
Are we turned Turks, and to ourselves do that
Which heaven hath forbid the Ottomites?°                                    145
For Christian shame, put by this barbarous brawl!
He that stirs next to carve for° his own rage
Holds his soul light;° he dies upon his motion.°
Silence that dreadful bell. It frights the isle
From her propriety.° What is the matter, masters?                          150
Honest Iago, that looks dead with grieving,
Speak. Who began this? On thy love, I charge thee.

**IAGO:**   I do not know. Friends all but now, even now,
In quarter° and in terms° like bride and groom
Devesting them° for bed; and then, but now—                                155
As if some planet had unwitted men—
Swords out, and tilting one at others' breasts
In opposition bloody. I cannot speak°
Any beginning to this peevish odds;°
And would in action glorious I had lost                                     160
Those legs that brought me to a part of it!

**OTHELLO:**   How comes it, Michael, you are thus forgot?°

**CASSIO:**   I pray you, pardon me. I cannot speak.

**OTHELLO:**   Worthy Montano, you were wont be° civil;
The gravity and stillness° of your youth                                    165
The world hath noted, and your name is great
In mouths of wisest censure.° What's the matter
That you unlace° your reputation thus
And spend your rich opinion° for the name
Of a night-brawler? Give me answer to it.                                   170

**MONTANO:**   Worthy Othello, I am hurt to danger.
Your officer, Iago, can inform you—
While I spare speech, which something° now offends° me—
Of all that I do know; nor know I aught
By me that's said or done amiss this night,                                 175
Unless self-charity be sometimes a vice,
And to defend ourselves it be a sin
When violence assails us.

**OTHELLO:**                     Now, by heaven,
My blood° begins my safer guides° to rule,

---

**144–145 to ourselves ... Ottomites** inflict on ourselves the harm that heaven has prevented the Turks from doing (by destroying their fleet)   **147 carve for** i.e., indulge, satisfy with his sword   **148 Holds ... light** i.e., places little value on his life   **upon his motion** if he moves   **150 propriety** proper state or condition   **154 In quarter** in friendly conduct, within bounds.   **in terms** on good terms   **155 Devesting them** undressing themselves   **158 speak** explain   **159 peevish odds** childish quarrel   **162 are thus forgot** have forgotten yourself thus   **164 wont be** accustomed to be   **165 stillness** sobriety   **167 censure** judgment   **168 unlace** undo, lay open (as one might loose the strings of a purse containing reputation)   **169 opinion** reputation   **173 something** somewhat   **offends** pains   **179 blood** passion (of anger)   **guides** i.e., reason

And passion, having my best judgment collied,°                    180
Essays° to lead the way. Zounds, if I stir,
Or do but lift this arm, the best of you
Shall sink in my rebuke. Give me to know
How this foul rout° began, who set it on;
And he that is approved in° this offense,                         185
Though he had twinned with me, both at a birth,
Shall lose me. What? In a town of° war
Yet wild, the people's hearts brim full of fear,
To manage° private and domestic quarrel?
In night, and on the court and guard of safety?°                 190
'Tis monstrous. Iago, who began 't?
**MONTANO** [*to Iago*]:   If partially affined,° or leagued in office,°
Thou dost deliver more or less than truth,
Thou art no soldier.
**IAGO:**                    Touch me not so near.
I had rather have this tongue cut from my mouth                   195
Than it should do offense to Michael Cassio;
Yet, I persuade myself, to speak the truth
Shall nothing wrong him. Thus it is, General.
Montano and myself being in speech,
There comes a fellow crying out for help,                         200
And Cassio following him with determined sword
To execute° upon him. Sir, this gentleman

[*indicating Montano*]

Steps in to Cassio and entreats his pause.°
Myself the crying fellow did pursue,
Lest by his clamor—as it so fell out—                            205
The town might fall in fright. He, swift of foot,
Outran my purpose, and I returned, the rather°
For that I heard the clink and fall of swords
And Cassio high in oath, which till tonight
I ne'er might say before. When I came back—                      210
For this was brief—I found them close together
At blow and thrust, even as again they were
When you yourself did part them.
More of this matter cannot I report.
But men are men; the best sometimes forget.°                     215
Though Cassio did some little wrong to him,

---

**180 collied** darkened   **181 Essays** undertakes   **184 rout** riot   **185 approved in** found guilty of
**187 town of** town garrisoned for   **189 manage** undertake   **190 on … safety** at the main guardhouse or
headquarters and on watch   **192 partially affined** made partial by some personal relationship
**leagued in office** in league as fellow officers   **202 execute** give effect to (his anger)   **203 his pause**
him to stop   **207 rather** sooner   **215 forget** forget themselves

As men in rage strike those that wish them best,°
Yet surely Cassio, I believe, received
From him that fled some strange indignity,
Which patience could not pass.°

**OTHELLO:**  I know, Iago,                                          220
Thy honesty and love doth mince this matter,
Making it light to Cassio. Cassio, I love thee,
But nevermore be officer of mine.

[*Enter Desdemona, attended.*]

Look if my gentle love be not raised up.
I'll make thee an example.                                          225

**DESDEMONA:**  What is the matter, dear?

**OTHELLO:**  All's well now, sweeting;
Come away to bed. [*To Montano.*] Sir, for your hurts,
Myself will be your surgeon.°—Lead him off.

[*Montano is led off.*]

Iago, look with care about the town
And silence those whom this vile brawl distracted.                  230
Come, Desdemona. 'Tis the soldiers' life
To have their balmy slumbers waked with strife.

*Exit* [*with all but Iago and Cassio*].

**IAGO:**  What, are you hurt, Lieutenant?

**CASSIO:**  Ay, past all surgery.

**IAGO:**  Marry, God forbid!                                       235

**CASSIO:**  Reputation, reputation, reputation! O, I have lost my
reputation! I have lost the immortal part of myself, and what
remains is bestial. My reputation, Iago, my reputation!

**IAGO:**  As I am an honest man, I thought you had received some
bodily wound; there is more sense in that than in reputation.       240
Reputation is an idle and most false imposition,° oft got without merit and lost without deserving. You have lost no reputation at all, unless you repute yourself such a loser. What, man,
there are more ways to recover° the General again. You are but
now cast in his mood°—a punishment more in policy° than in
malice, even so as one would beat his offenseless dog to affright
an imperious lion.° Sue° to him again and he's yours.              245

**CASSIO:**  I will rather sue to be despised than to deceive so good
a commander with so slight,° so drunken, and so indiscreet an

**217 those ... best** i.e., even those who are well disposed   **220 pass** pass over, overlook   **228 be your**
**surgeon** i.e., make sure you receive medical attention   **241 false imposition** thing artificially imposed and
of no real value   **243 recover** regain favor with   **244 cast in his mood** dismissed in a moment of anger.
**in policy** done for expediency's sake and as a public gesture   **245 would ... lion** i.e., would make an
example of a minor offender in order to deter more important and dangerous offenders   **246 Sue** petition

officer. Drunk? And speak parrot?° And squabble? Swagger? Swear? And discourse fustian with one's own shadow? O thou invisible spirit of wine, if thou hast no name to be known by, let us call thee devil!                                                                      250

**IAGO:**  What was he that you followed with your sword? What had he done to you?

**CASSIO:**  I know not.

**IAGO:**  Is 't possible?

**CASSIO:**  I remember a mass of things, but nothing distinctly; a      255
quarrel, but nothing wherefore.° O God, that men should put an enemy in their mouths to steal away their brains! That we should, with joy, pleasance, revel, and applause° transform ourselves into beasts!

**IAGO:**  Why, but you are now well enough. How came you thus recovered?

**CASSIO:**  It hath pleased the devil drunkenness to give place to the devil wrath. One unperfectness shows me another, to make me frankly despise myself.                                                           260

**IAGO:**  Come, you are too severe a moraler.° As the time, the place, and the condition of this country stands, I could heartily wish this had not befallen; but since it is as it is, mend it for your own good.

**CASSIO:**  I will ask him for my place again; he shall tell me I am      265
a drunkard. Had I as many mouths as Hydra,° such an answer would stop them all. To be now a sensible man, by and by a fool, and presently a beast! O, strange! Every inordinate cup is unblessed, and the ingredient is a devil.

**IAGO:**  Come, come, good wine is a good familiar creature, if it be well used. Exclaim no more against it. And, good Lieutenant, I       270
think you think I love you

**CASSIO:**  I have well approved° it, sir. I drunk!

**IAGO:**  You or any man living may be drunk at a time,° man. I'll tell you what you shall do. Our general's wife is now the general—I may say so in this respect, for that° he hath devoted and given      275
up himself to the contemplation, mark, and denotement° of her parts° and graces. Confess yourself freely to her; importune her help to put you in your place again. She is of so free,° so kind, so apt, so blessed a disposition, she holds it a vice in her goodness not to do more than she is requested. This broken joint

---

**248 slight** worthless   **248–249 speak parrot** talk nonsense, rant   **256 wherefore** why   **258 applause** desire for applause   **262 moraler** moralizer   **266 Hydra** the Lernaean Hydra, a monster with many heads and the ability to grow two heads when one was cut off, slain by Hercules as the second of his twelve labors   **272 approved** proved   **273 at a time** at one time or another   **274–275 in ... that** in view of this fact, that   **275–276 mark, and denotement** (Both words mean "observation.")   **276 parts** qualities   **277 free** generous

between you and her husband entreat her to splinter;° and, my
fortunes against any lay° worth naming, this crack of your love          280
shall grow stronger than it was before.

**CASSIO:**  You advise me well.

**IAGO:**  I protest,° in the sincerity of love and honest kindness.

**CASSIO:**  I think it freely;° and betimes in the morning I will beseech the virtuous Desdemona to undertake for me. I am desper-          285
ate of my fortunes if they check° me here.

**IAGO:**  You are in the right. Good night, Lieutenant. I must to the
watch.

**CASSIO:**  Good night, honest Iago.

                                          [*Exit Cassio.*]

**IAGO:**  And what's he then that says I play the villain,
When this advice is free° I give, and honest,                          290
Probal° to thinking, and indeed the course
To win the Moor again? For 'tis most easy
Th' inclining° Desdemona to subdue°
In any honest suit; she's framed as fruitful°
As the free elements.° And then for her                                295
To win the Moor—were 't to renounce his baptism,
All seals and symbols of redeemèd sin—
His soul is so enfettered to her love
That she may make, unmake, do what she list,
Even as her appetite° shall play the god                               300
With his weak function.° How am I then a villain,
To counsel Cassio to this parallel° course
Directly to his good? Divinity of hell!°
When devils will the blackest sins put on,°
They do suggest° at first with heavenly shows,                         305
As I do now. For whiles this honest fool
Plies Desdemona to repair his fortune,
And she for him pleads strongly to the Moor,
I'll pour this pestilence into his ear,
That she repeals him° for her body's lust;                             310
And by how much she strives to do him good,
She shall undo her credit with the Moor.
So will I turn her virtue into pitch,°

---

**280 splinter** bind with splints  **lay** stake, wager  **283 protest** insist, declare  **284 freely** unreserv-
edly  **286 check** repulse  **290 free** (1) free from guile (2) freely given  **291 Probal** probable, reasonable  **293 inclining** favorably disposed.  **subdue** persuade  **294 framed as fruitful** created as
generous  **295 free elements** i.e., earth, air, fire, and water, unrestrained and spontaneous  **300 her
appetite** her desire, or, perhaps, his desire for her  **301 function** exercise of faculties (weakened by his
fondness for her)  **302 parallel** corresponding to these facts and to his best interests  **303 Divinity
of hell** inverted theology of hell (which seduces the soul to its damnation)  **304 put on** further, in-
stigate  **305 suggest** tempt  **310 repeals him** attempts to get him restored  **313 pitch** i.e., (1) foul
blackness (2) a snaring substance

And out of her own goodness make the net
That shall enmesh them all.

[*Enter Roderigo.*]

How now, Roderigo?                                    315

**RODERIGO:**   I do follow here in the chase, not like a hound that
hunts, but one that fills up the cry.° My money is almost spent;
I have been tonight exceedingly well cudgeled; and I think the
issue will be I shall have so much° experience for my pains, and
so, with no money at all and a little more wit, return again to
Venice.                                                    320

**IAGO:**   How poor are they that have not patience!
What wound did ever heal but by degrees?
Thou know'st we work by wit, and not by witchcraft,
And wit depends on dilatory time.
Does 't not go well? Cassio hath beaten thee,          325
And thou, by that small hurt, hast cashiered° Cassio.
Though other things grow fair against the sun,
Yet fruits that blossom first will first be ripe.°
Content thyself awhile. By the Mass, 'tis morning!
Pleasure and action make the hours seem short.        330
Retire thee; go where thou art billeted.
Away, I say! Thou shalt know more hereafter.
Nay, get thee gone.                       [*Exit Roderigo.*]
                    Two things are to be done.
My wife must move° for Cassio to her mistress;
I'll set her on;                                          335
Myself the while to draw the Moor apart
And bring him jump° when he may Cassio find
Soliciting his wife. Ay, that's the way.
Dull not device° by coldness    and delay.                       *Exit.*

## Act III

### Scene I. Before the chamber of Othello and Desdemona

*Enter Cassio [and] Musicians.*

**CASSIO:**   Masters, play here—I will content your pains°—
Something that's brief, and bid "Good morrow, General."

[*They play.*]

[*Enter*] *Clown.*

---

**317 fills up the cry** merely takes part as one of the pack   **318 so much** just so much and no more
**326 cashiered** dismissed from service   **327–328 Though ... ripe** i.e., plans that are well-prepared and
set expeditiously in motion will soonest ripen into success   **334 move** plead   **337 jump** precisely
**339 device** plot   **coldness** lack of zeal
**1 content your pains** reward your efforts

**CLOWN:**   Why, masters, have your instruments been in Naples, that
they speak i' the nose° thus?

**A MUSICIAN:**   How, sir, how?                                                            5

**CLOWN:**   Are these, I pray you, wind instruments?

**A MUSICIAN:**   Ay, marry, are they, sir.

**CLOWN:**   O, thereby hangs a tail.

**A MUSICIAN:**   Whereby hangs a tale, sir?

**CLOWN:**   Marry, sir, by many a wind instrument° that I know.    10
But, masters, here's money for you. [*He gives money.*] And the
General so likes your music that he desires you, for love's sake,°
to make no more noise with it.

**A MUSICIAN:**   Well, sir, we will not.

**CLOWN:**   If you have any music that may not° be heard, to 't again;
but, as they say, to hear music the General does not greatly care.    15

**A MUSICIAN:**   We have none such, sir.

**CLOWN:**   Then put up your pipes in your bag, for I'll away.° Go,
vanish into air, away!                                   [*Exeunt Musicians.*]

**CASSIO:**   Dost thou hear, mine honest friend?

**CLOWN:**   No, I hear not your honest friend; I hear you.                20

**CASSIO:**   Prithee, keep up° thy quillets.° There's a poor piece of
gold for thee. [*He gives money*.] If the gentle-woman that attends the General's wife be stirring, tell her there's one Cassio
entreats her a little favor of speech.° Wilt thou do this?

**CLOWN:**   She is stirring, sir. If she will stir° hither, I shall seem° to
notify unto her.                                                                   25

**CASSIO:**   Do, good my friend.                             [*Exit Clown.*]

[*Enter Iago.*]

In happy time,° Iago.

**IAGO:**   You have not been abed, then?

**CASSIO:**   Why, no. The day had broke
Before we parted. I have made bold, Iago,
To send in to your wife. My suit to her                                    30
Is that she will to virtuous Desdemona
Procure me some access.

**IAGO:**   I'll send her to you presently;
And I'll devise a means to draw the Moor
Out of the way, that your converse and business                       35
May be more free.

3–4 **speak i' the nose** (1) sound nasal (2) sound like one whose nose has been attacked by syphilis. (Naples
was popularly supposed to have a high incidence of venereal disease.)   10 **wind instrument** (With a joke
on flatulence. The *tail*, line 8, that hangs nearby the *wind instrument* suggests the penis.)   12 **for love's
sake** (1) out of friendship and affection (2) for the sake of lovemaking in Othello's marriage   14 **may not**
cannot   17 **I'll away** (Possibly a misprint, or a snatch of song?)   21 **keep up** do not bring out, do not
use.   **quillets** quibbles, puns   23 **a little … speech** the favor of a brief talk   25 **stir** bestir herself (with a
play on *stirring*, "rousing herself from rest")   **seem** deem it good, think fit   26 **In happy time** i.e., well-met

**CASSIO:** I humbly thank you for 't.                              *Exit [Iago].*

                                        I never knew

A Florentine° more kind and honest.

*Enter Emilia.*

**EMILIA:** Good morrow, good Lieutenant. I am sorry

For your displeasure;° but all will sure be well.                       40

The General and his wife are talking of it,

And she speaks for you stoutly.° The Moor replies

That he you hurt is of great fame° in Cyprus

And great affinity,° and that in wholesome wisdom

He might not but refuse you; but he protests° he loves you          45

And needs no other suitor but his likings

To take the safest occasion by the front°

To bring you in again.

**CASSIO:**                              Yet I beseech you,

If you think fit, or that it may be done,

Give me advantage of some brief discourse                           50

With Desdemona alone.

**EMILIA:**                              Pray you, come in.

I will bestow you where you shall have time

To speak your bosom° freely.

**CASSIO:** I am much bound to you.                       *[Exeunt.]*

**Scene II. The Citadel**

*Enter Othello, Iago, and Gentlemen.*

**OTHELLO** [*giving letterss*]:These letters give, Iago, to the pilot.

And by him do my duties° to the Senate.

That done, I will be walking on the works;°

Repair° there to me.

**IAGO:** Well, my good lord, I'll do 't.

**OTHELLO:** This fortification, gentlemen, shall we see 't?          5

**GENTLEMEN:** We'll wait upon° your lordship.          *[Exeunt.]*

**Scene III. The garden of the Citadel**

*Enter Desdemona, Cassio, and Emilia.*

**DESDEMONA:** Be thou assured, good Cassio, I will do

All my abilities in thy behalf.

---

**38 Florentine** i.e., even a fellow Florentine. (Iago is a Venetian; Cassio is a Florentine.)   **40 displea-sure** fall from favor   **42 stoutly** spiritedly   **43 fame** reputation, importance   **44 affinity** kindred, family connection   **45 protests** insists   **47 occasion … front** opportunity by the forelock   **53 bosom** inmost thoughts
**2 do my duties** convey my respects   **3 works** breastworks, fortifications   **4 Repair** return, come
**6 wait upon** attend

**EMILIA:**    Good madam, do. I warrant it grieves my husband
    As if the cause were his.

**DESDEMONA:**    O, that's an honest fellow. Do not doubt, Cassio,      5
    But I will have my lord and you again
    As friendly as you were.

**CASSIO:**               Bounteous madam,
    Whatever shall become of Michael Cassio,
    He's never anything but your true servant.

**DESDEMONA:**    I know 't. I thank you. You do love my lord;      10
    You have known him long, and be you well assured
    He shall in strangeness° stand no farther off
    Than in a politic° distance.

**CASSIO:**               Ay, but, lady,
    That policy may either last so long,
    Or feed upon such nice and waterish diet,°      15
    Or breed itself so out of circumstance,°
    That, I being absent and my place supplied,°
    My general will forget my love and service.

**DESDEMONA:**    Do not doubt° that. Before Emilia here
    I give thee warrant° of thy place. Assure thee,      20
    If I do vow a friendship I'll perform it
    To the last article. My lord shall never rest.
    I'll watch him tame° and talk him out of patience;°
    His bed shall seem a school, his board° a shrift;°
    I'll intermingle everything he does      25
    With Cassio's suit. Therefore be merry, Cassio,
    For thy solicitor° shall rather die
    Than give thy cause away.°

*Enter Othello and Iago [at a distance].*

**EMILIA:**    Madam, here comes my lord.

**CASSIO:**    Madam, I'll take my leave.      30

**DESDEMONA:**    Why, stay, and hear me speak.

**CASSIO:**    Madam, not now. I am very ill at ease,
    Unfit for mine own purposes.

**DESDEMONA:**    Well, do your discretion.°      *[Exit Cassio.]*

**IAGO:**    Ha? I like not that.      35

**OTHELLO:**    What dost thou say?

**IAGO:**    Nothing, my lord; or if—I know not what.

---

**12 strangeness** aloofness   **13 politic** required by wise policy   **15 Or ... diet** or sustain itself at
length upon such trivial and meager technicalities   **16 breed ... circumstance** continually renew itself
so out of chance events, or yield so few chances for my being pardoned   **17 supplied** filled by another
person   **19 doubt** fear   **20 warrant** guarantee   **23 watch him tame** tame him by keeping him from
sleeping (a term from falconry)   **out of patience** past his endurance   **24 board** dining table.   **shrift**
confessional   **27 solicitor** advocate   **28 away** up   **34 do your discretion** act according to your own
discretion

**OTHELLO:**  Was not that Cassio parted from my wife?

**IAGO:**  Cassio, my lord? No, sure, I cannot think it,
That he would steal away so guiltylike,                              40
Seeing you coming.

**OTHELLO:**  I do believe 'twas he.

**DESDEMONA:**  How now, my lord?
I have been talking with a suitor here,
A man that languishes in your displeasure.                          45

**OTHELLO:**  Who is 't you mean?

**DESDEMONA:**  Why, your lieutenant, Cassio. Good my lord,
If I have any grace or power to move you,
His present reconciliation take;°
For if he be not one that truly loves you,                          50
That errs in ignorance and not in cunning,°
I have no judgment in an honest face.
I prithee, call him back.

**OTHELLO:**  Went he hence now?

**DESDEMONA:**  Yes, faith, so humbled                               55
That he hath left part of his grief with me
To suffer with him. Good love, call him back.

**OTHELLO:**  Not now, sweet Desdemon. Some other time.

**DESDEMONA:**  But shall 't be shortly?

**OTHELLO:**  The sooner, sweet, for you.                            60

**DESDEMONA:**  Shall 't be tonight at supper?

**OTHELLO:**  No, not tonight.

**DESDEMONA:**  Tomorrow dinner,° then?

**OTHELLO:**  I shall not dine at home.
I meet the captains at the citadel.                                 65

**DESDEMONA:**  Why, then, tomorrow night, or Tuesday morn,
On Tuesday noon, or night, on Wednesday morn.
I prithee, name the time, but let it not
Exceed three days. In faith, he's penitent;
And yet his trespass, in our common reason°—                       70
Save that, they say, the wars must make example
Out of her best°—is not almost° a fault
T' incur a private check.° When shall he come?
Tell me, Othello. I wonder in my soul
What you would ask me that I should deny,                           75
Or stand so mammering on.° What? Michael Cassio,

---

49 **His ... take** let him be reconciled to you right away   51 **in cunning** wittingly   63 **dinner** (The
noontime meal.)   70 **common reason** everyday judgments   71–72 **Save ... best** were it not that, as
the saying goes, military discipline requires making an example of the very best men. (*Her* refers to
wars as a singular concept.)   72 **not almost** scarcely   73 **private check** even a private reprimand
76 **mammering on** wavering about

That came a-wooing with you, and so many a time,
When I have spoke of you dispraisingly,
Hath ta'en your part—to have so much to do
To bring him in!° By 'r Lady, I could do much—                80
**OTHELLO:**   Prithee, no more. Let him come when he will;
I will deny thee nothing.
**DESDEMONA:**   Why, this is not a boon.
'Tis as I should entreat you wear your gloves,
Or feed on nourishing dishes, or keep you warm,              85
Or sue to you to do a peculiar° profit
To your own person. Nay, when I have a suit
Wherein I mean to touch° your love indeed,
It shall be full of poise° and difficult weight,
And fearful to be granted.                                   90
**OTHELLO:**   I will deny thee nothing.
Whereon,° I do beseech thee, grant me this,
To leave me but a little to myself.
**DESDEMONA:**   Shall I deny you? No. Farewell, my lord.
**OTHELLO:**   Farewell, my Desdemona. I'll come to thee straight.°   95
**DESDEMONA:**   Emilia, come.—Be as your fancies° teach you;
Whate'er you be, I am obedient.                *Exit [with Emilia].*
**OTHELLO:**   Excellent wretch!° Perdition catch my soul
But I do love thee! And when I love thee not,
Chaos is come again.°                                        100
**IAGO:**   My noble lord—
**OTHELLO:**   What dost thou say, Iago?
**IAGO:**   Did Michael Cassio, when you wooed my lady,
Know of your love?
**OTHELLO:**   He did, from first to last. Why dost thou ask?     105
**IAGO:**   But for a satisfaction of my thought;
No further harm.
**OTHELLO:**          Why of thy thought, Iago?
**IAGO:**   I did not think he had been acquainted with her.
**OTHELLO:**   O, yes, and went between us very oft.
**IAGO:**   Indeed?                                             110
**OTHELLO:**   Indeed? Ay, indeed. Discern'st thou aught in that?
Is he not honest?
**IAGO:**   Honest, my lord?
**OTHELLO:**   Honest. Ay, honest.

---

**80 bring him in** restore him to favor   **86 peculiar** particular, personal   **88 touch** test   **89 poise** weight, heaviness; or equipoise, delicate balance involving hard choice   **92 Whereon** in return for which   **95 straight** straightway   **96 fancies** inclinations   **98 wretch** (A term of affectionate endearment.)   **99–100 And ... again** i.e., my love for you will last forever, until the end of time when chaos will return. (But with an unconscious, ironic suggestion that, if anything should induce Othello to cease loving Desdemona, the result would be chaos.)

**IAGO:**  My lord, for aught I know. 115

**OTHELLO:**  What dost thou think?

**IAGO:**  Think, my lord?

**OTHELLO:**  "Think, my lord?" By heaven, thou echo'st me,
As if there were some monster in thy thought
Too hideous to be shown. Thou dost mean something. 120
I heard thee say even now, thou lik'st not that,
When Cassio left my wife. What didst not like?
And when I told thee he was of my counsel°
In my whole course of wooing, thou criedst "Indeed?"
And didst contract and purse° thy brow together 125
As if thou then hadst shut up in thy brain
Some horrible conceit.° If thou dost love me,
Show me thy thought.

**IAGO:**  My lord, you know I love you.

**OTHELLO:**  I think thou dost; 130
And, for° I know thou'rt full of love and honesty,
And weigh'st thy words before thou giv'st them breath,
Therefore these stops° of thine fright me the more;
For such things in a false disloyal knave
Are tricks of custom,° but in a man that's just 135
They're close dilations,° working from the heart
That passion cannot rule.°

**IAGO:**                              For° Michael Cassio,
I dare be sworn I think that he is honest.

**OTHELLO:**  I think so too.

**IAGO:**                          Men should be what they seem;
Or those that be not, would they might seem none!° 140

**OTHELLO:**  Certain, men should be what they seem.

**IAGO:**  Why, then, I think Cassio's an honest man.

**OTHELLO:**  Nay, yet there's more in this.
I prithee, speak to me as to thy thinkings,
As thou dost ruminate, and give thy worst of thoughts 145
The worst of words.

**IAGO:**                          Good my lord, pardon me.
Though I am bound to every act of duty,
I am not bound to that° all slaves are free to.°
Utter my thoughts? Why, say they are vile and false,
As where's the palace whereinto foul things 150

123 **of my counsel** in my confidence   125 **purse** knit   127 **conceit** fancy   131 **for** because
133 **stops** pauses   135 **of custom** customary   136 **close dilations** secret or involuntary expressions
or delays   137 **That passion cannot rule** i.e., that are too passionately strong to be restrained
(referring to the workings), or ... that cannot rule its own passions (referring to the heart).   137 **For**
as for   140 **none** i.e., not to be men, or not seem to be honest   148 **that** that which.   **free to** free
with respect to

Sometimes intrude not? Who has that breast so pure
But some uncleanly apprehensions
Keep leets and law days,° and in sessions sit
With° meditations lawful?°

**OTHELLO:**    Thou dost conspire against thy friend,° Iago,                 155
If thou but think'st him wronged and mak'st his ear
A stranger to thy thoughts.

**IAGO:**                              I do beseech you,
Though I perchance am vicious° in my guess—
As I confess it is my nature's plague
To spy into abuses, and oft my jealousy°                 160
Shapes faults that are not—that your wisdom then,°
From one° that so imperfectly conceits,°
Would take no notice, nor build yourself a trouble
Out of his scattering° and unsure observance.
It were not for your quiet nor your good,                 165
Nor for my manhood, honesty, and wisdom,
To let you know my thoughts.

**OTHELLO:**                              What dost thou mean?

**IAGO:**   Good name in man and woman, dear my lord,
Is the immediate° jewel of their souls.
Who steals my purse steals trash; 'tis something, nothing;                 170
'Twas mine, 'tis his, and has been slave to thousands;
But he that filches from me my good name
Robs me of that which not enriches him
And makes me poor indeed.

**OTHELLO:**   By heaven, I'll know thy thoughts.                 175

**IAGO:**   You cannot, if° my heart were in your hand,
Nor shall not, whilst 'tis in my custody.

**OTHELLO:**   Ha?

**IAGO:**   O, beware, my lord, of jealousy.
It is the green-eyed monster which doth mock
The meat it feeds on.° That cuckold lives in bliss                 180
Who, certain of his fate, loves not his wronger;°
But O, what damnèd minutes tells° he o'er
Who dotes, yet doubts, suspects, yet fondly loves!

**OTHELLO:**   O misery!

---

**153 Keep leets and law days** i.e., hold court, set up their authority in one's heart. (*Leets* are a kind of manor court; *law days* are the days courts sit in session, or those sessions.)   **154 With** along with.
**lawful** innocent   **155 thy friend** i.e., Othello   **158 vicious** wrong   **160 jealousy** suspicious nature
**161 then** on that account   **162 one** i.e., myself, iago.   **conceits** judges, conjectures   **164 scattering**
random   **169 immediate** essential, most precious   **176 if** even if   **179–180 doth mock ... on** mocks
and torments the heart of its victim, the man who suffers jealousy   **181 his wronger** i.e., his faithless wife.
(The unsuspecting cuckold is spared the misery of loving his wife only to discover she is cheating on him.)
**182 tells** counts

IAGO:   Poor and content is rich, and rich enough,°                    185
　　　But riches fineless° is as poor as winter
　　　To him that ever fears he shall be poor.
　　　Good God, the souls of all my tribe defend
　　　From jealousy!

OTHELLO:   Why, why is this?                                          190
　　　Think'st thou I'd make a life of jealousy,
　　　To follow still the changes of the moon
　　　With fresh suspicions?° No! To be once in doubt
　　　Is once° to be resolved.° Exchange me for a goat
　　　When I shall turn the business of my soul                       195
　　　To such exsufflicate and blown° surmises
　　　Matching thy inference.° 'Tis not to make me jealous
　　　To say my wife is fair, feeds well, loves company,
　　　Is free of speech, sings, plays, and dances well;
　　　Where virtue is, these are more virtuous.                       200
　　　Nor from mine own weak merits will I draw
　　　The smallest fear or doubt of her revolt,°
　　　For she had eyes, and chose me. No, Iago,
　　　I'll see before I doubt; when I doubt, prove;
　　　And on the proof, there is no more but this—                    205
　　　Away at once with love or jealousy.

IAGO:   I am glad of this, for now I shall have reason
　　　To show the love and duty that I bear you
　　　With franker spirit. Therefore, as I am bound,
　　　Receive it from me. I speak not yet of proof.                   210
　　　Look to your wife; observe her well with Cassio.
　　　Wear your eyes thus, not° jealous nor secure.°
　　　I would not have your free and noble nature,
　　　Out of self-bounty,° be abused.° Look to 't.
　　　I know our country disposition well;                            215
　　　In Venice they do let God see the pranks
　　　They dare not show their husbands; their best conscience
　　　Is not to leave 't undone, but keep 't unknown.

OTHELLO:   Dost thou say so?

IAGO:   She did deceive her father, marrying you;                     220
　　　And when she seemed to shake and fear your looks,
　　　She loved them most.

---

185 **Poor ... enough** to be content with what little one has is the greatest wealth of all. (Proverbial.)
186 **fineless** boundless   192–193 **To follow ... suspicions** to be constantly imagining new causes for suspicion, changing incessantly like the moon   194 **once** once and for all.   **resolved** free of doubt, having settled the matter   196 **exsufflicate and blown** inflated and blown up, rumored about, or, spat out and flyblown, hence, loathsome, disgusting   197 **inference** description or allegation   202 **doubt ... revolt** fear of her unfaithfulness   212 **not** neither.   **secure** free from uncertainty   214 **self-bounty** inherent or natural goodness and generosity.   **abused** deceived

**OTHELLO:**              And so she did.

**IAGO:**                              Why, go to,° then!
She that, so young, could give out such a seeming,°
To seel° her father's eyes up close as oak,°
He thought 'twas witchcraft! But I am much to blame.                    225
I humbly do beseech you of your pardon
For too much loving you.

**OTHELLO:**   I am bound° to thee forever.

**IAGO:**   I see this hath a little dashed your spirits.

**OTHELLO:**   Not a jot, not a jot.

**IAGO:**                              I' faith, I fear it has.                    230
I hope you will consider what is spoke
Comes from my love. But I do see you're moved.
I am to pray you not to strain my speech
To grosser issues° nor to larger reach°
Than to suspicion.                    235

**OTHELLO:**   I will not.

**IAGO:**   Should you do so, my lord,
My speech should fall into such vile success°
Which my thoughts aimed not. Cassio's my worthy friend.
My lord, I see you're moved.

**OTHELLO:**                              No, not much moved.                    240
I do not think but Desdemona's honest.°

**IAGO:**   Long live she so! And long live you to think so!

**OTHELLO:**   And yet, how nature erring from itself—

**IAGO:**   Ay, there's the point! As—to be bold with you—
Not to affect° many proposèd matches                    245
Of her own clime, complexion, and degree,°
Whereto we see in all things nature tends—
Foh! One may smell in such a will° most rank,
Foul disproportion,° thoughts unnatural.
But pardon me. I do not in position°                    250
Distinctly speak of her, though I may fear
Her will, recoiling° to her better° judgment,
May fall to match you with her country forms°
And happily repent.°

**OTHELLO:**                              Farewell, farewell!
If more thou dost perceive, let me know more.                    255

---

222 **go to** (An expression of impatience.)   223 **seeming** false appearance   224 **seel** blind (a term
from falconry)   **oak** (A close-grained wood.)   228 **bound** indebted (but perhaps with ironic sense of
"tied")   234 **issues** significances.   **reach** meaning, scope   238 **success** effect, result   241 **honest**
chaste   245 **affect** prefer, desire   246 **clime ... degree** country, color, and social position
248 **will** sensuality, appetite   249 **disproportion** abnormality   250 **position** argument, proposition
252 **recoiling** reverting.   **better** i.e., more natural and reconsidered   253 **fall ... forms** undertake
to compare you with Venetian norms of handsomeness

Set on thy wife to observe. Leave me, Iago.

**IAGO** [*going*]:　My lord, I take my leave.

**OTHELLO:**　Why did I marry? This honest creature doubtless
　　Sees and knows more, much more, than he unfolds.

**IAGO** [*returning*]:　My Lord, I would I might entreat your honor　　260
　　To scan° this thing no farther. Leave it to time.
　　Although 'tis fit that Cassio have his place—
　　For, sure, he fills it up with great ability—
　　Yet, if you please to hold him off awhile,
　　You shall by that perceive him and his means.°　　265
　　Note if your lady strain his entertainment°
　　With any strong or vehement importunity;
　　Much will be seen in that. In the meantime,
　　Let me be thought too busy° in my fears—
　　As worthy cause I have to fear I am—　　270
　　And hold her free,° I do beseech your honor.

**OTHELLO:**　Fear not my government.°

**IAGO:**　I once more take my leave.　　　　　　　　[*Exit.*]

**OTHELLO:**　This fellow's of exceeding honesty,
　　And knows all qualities,° with a learnèd spirit,　　275
　　Of human dealings. If I do prove her haggard,°
　　Though that her jesses° were my dear heartstrings,
　　I'd whistle her off and let her down the wind°
　　To prey at fortune.° Haply, for° I am black
　　And have not those soft parts of conversation°　　280
　　That chamberers° have, or for I am declined
　　Into the vale of years—yet that's not much—
　　She's gone. I am abused,° and my relief
　　Must be to loathe her. O curse of marriage,
　　That we can call these delicate creatures ours　　285
　　And not their appetites! I had rather be a toad
　　And live upon the vapor of a dungeon
　　Than keep a corner in the thing I love
　　For others' uses. Yet, 'tis the plague of great ones;
　　Prerogatived° are they less than the base.°　　290

---

**254 happily repent** haply repent her marriage　**261 scan** scrutinize　**265 his means** the method
he uses (to regain his post)　**266 strain his entertainment** urge his reinstatement　**269 busy** in-
terfering　**271 hold her free** regard her as innocent　**272 government** self-control, conduct　**275
qualities** natures, types　**276 haggard** wild (like a wild female hawk)　**277 jesses** straps fastened
around the legs of a trained hawk　**278 I'd ... wind** i.e., I'd let her go forever. (To release a hawk
downwind was to invite it not to return.)　**279 prey at fortune** fend for herself in the wild.　**Haply,
for** perhaps because　**280 soft ... conversation** pleasing graces of social behavior　**281 chamber-
ers** gallants　**283 abused** deceived　**290 Prerogatived** privileged (to have honest wives).　**the base**
ordinary citizens. (Socially prominent men are especially prone to the unavoidable destiny of being
cuckolded and to the public shame that goes with it.)

'Tis destiny unshunnable, like death.
Even then this forkèd° plague is fated to us
When we do quicken.° Look where she comes.

[*Enter Desdemona and Emilia.*]

If she be false, O, then heaven mocks itself!
I'll not believe 't.

**DESDEMONA:**  How now, my dear Othello?                                    295
Your dinner, and the generous° islanders
By you invited, do attend° your presence.

**OTHELLO:**   I am to blame.

**DESDEMONA:**                    Why do you speak so faintly?
Are you not well?

**OTHELLO:**   I have a pain upon my forehead here.                          300

**DESDEMONA:**   Faith, that's with watching.° 'Twill away again.

[*She offers her handkerchief.* ]

Let me but bind it hard, within this hour
It will be well.

**OTHELLO:**        Your napkin° is too little.
Let it alone.° Come, I'll go in with you.

[*He puts the handkerchief from him, and it drops.*]

**DESDEMONA:**   I am very sorry that you are not well.                       305

                                             *Exit* [*with Othello*].

**EMILIA**   [*picking up the handkerchief*]:I am glad I have found this
    napkin.
This was her first remembrance from the Moor.
My wayward° husband hath a hundred times
Wooed me to steal it, but she so loves the token—
For he conjured her she should ever keep it—                                 310
That she reserves it evermore about her
To kiss and talk to. I'll have the work ta'en out,°
And give 't Iago. What he will do with it
Heaven knows, not I;
I nothing but to please his fantasy.°                                        315

[*Enter Iago.*]

**IAGO:**   How now? What do you here alone?

**EMILIA:**   Do not you chide. I have a thing for you.

---

**292 forkèd** (An allusion to the horns of the cuckold.)   **293 quicken** receive life. (Quicken may also mean
to swarm with maggots as the body festers, as in Act IV, Scene ii, line 69, in which case lines 292–293 suggest that *even then*, in death, we are cuckolded by *forkèd* worms.)   **296 generous** noble   **297 attend**
await   **301 watching** too little sleep   **303 napkin** handkerchief   **304 Let it alone** i.e., never mind
**308 wayward** capricious   **312 work ta'en out** design of the embroidery copied   **315 fantasy** whim

**IAGO:** You have a thing for me? It is a common thing°—
**EMILIA:** Ha?
**IAGO:** To have a foolish wife.                                                            320
**EMILIA:** O, is that all? What will you give me now
  For that same handkerchief?
**IAGO:** What handkerchief?
**EMILIA:** What handkerchief?
  Why, that the Moor first gave to Desdemona;                                    325
  That which so often you did bid me steal.
**IAGO:** Hast stolen it from her?
**EMILIA:** No, faith. She let it drop by negligence,
  And to th' advantage° I, being here, took 't up.
  Look, here 'tis.
**IAGO:**                          A good wench! Give it me.                             330
**EMILIA:** What will you do with 't, that you have been so earnest
  To have me filch it?
**IAGO** [*snatching it*]:Why, what is that to you?
**EMILIA:** If it be not for some purpose of import,
  Give 't me again. Poor lady, she'll run mad
  When she shall lack° it.
**IAGO:**                                        Be not acknown on't.°                335
  I have use for it. Go, leave me.                        [*Exit Emilia.*]
  I will in Cassio's lodging lose° this napkin
  And let him find it. Trifles light as air
  Are to the jealous confirmations strong
  As proofs of Holy Writ. This may do something.                             340
  The Moor already changes with my poison.
  Dangerous conceits° are in their natures poisons,
  Which at the first are scarce found to distaste,°
  But with a little act° upon the blood
  Burn like the mines of sulfur.

  [*Enter Othello.*]

                              I did say so.                                                      345
  Look where he comes! Not poppy nor mandragora°
  Nor all the drowsy syrups of the world
  Shall ever medicine thee to that sweet sleep
  Which thou owedst° yesterday.
**OTHELLO:**                              Ha, ha, false to me?
**IAGO:** Why, how now, General? No more of that.                           350

---

**318 common thing** (With bawdy suggestion; *common* suggests coarseness and availability to all comers, and *thing* is a slang term for the pudendum.)   **329 to th' advantage** taking the opportunity
**335 lack** miss.   **Be … on't** do not confess knowledge of it   **337 lose** (The Folio spelling, *loose*, is a normal spelling for "lose," but it may also contain the idea of "let go," "release.")   **342 conceits** fancies, ideas   **343 distaste** be distasteful   **344 act** action, working   **346 mandragora** an opiate made of the mandrake root   **349 thou owedst** you did own

**OTHELLO:** Avaunt! Begone! Thou hast set me on the rack.
 I swear 'tis better to be much abused
 Than but to know 't a little.
**IAGO:** How now, my lord?
**OTHELLO:** What sense had I of her stolen hours of lust?
 I saw 't not, thought it not, it harmed not me.                    355
 I slept the next night well, fed well, was free° and merry;
 I found not Cassio's kisses on her lips.
 He that is robbed, not wanting° what is stolen,
 Let him not know 't and he's not robbed at all.
**IAGO:** I am sorry to hear this.                                   360
**OTHELLO:** I had been happy if the general camp,
 Pioners° and all, had tasted her sweet body,
 So° I had nothing known. O, now, forever
 Farewell the tranquil mind! Farewell content!
 Farewell the plumèd troops and the big° wars                        365
 That makes ambition virtue! O, farewell!
 Farewell the neighing steed and the shrill trump,
 The spirit-stirring drum, th' ear-piercing fife,
 The royal banner, and all quality,°
 Pride,° pomp, and circumstance° of glorious war!                    370
 And O, you mortal engines,° whose rude throats
 Th' immortal Jove's dread clamors° counterfeit,
 Farewell! Othello's occupation's gone.
**IAGO:** Is 't possible, my lord?
**OTHELLO:** Villain, be sure thou prove my love a whore!            375
 Be sure of it. Give me the ocular proof,
 Or, by the worth of mine eternal soul,
 Thou hadst been better have been born a dog
 Than answer my waked wrath!
**IAGO:**                                Is 't come to this?
**OTHELLO:** Make me to see 't, or at the least so prove it          380
 That the probation° bear no hinge nor loop
 To hang a doubt on, or woe upon thy life!
**IAGO:** My noble lord—
**OTHELLO:** If thou dost slander her and torture me,
 Never pray more; abandon all remorse;°                              385
 On horror's head horrors accumulate;°
 Do deeds to make heaven weep, all earth amazed;°
 For nothing canst thou to damnation add
 Greater than that.

**356 free** carefree  **358 wanting** missing  **362 Pioners** diggers of mines, the lowest grade of soldiers
**363 So** provided  **365 big** stately  **369 quality** character, essential nature  **370 Pride** rich display.
**circumstance** pageantry  **371 mortal engines** i.e., cannon. (*Mortal* means "deadly.")  **372 Jove's
dread clamors** i.e., thunder  **381 probation** proof  **385 remorse** pity, penitent hope for salvation
**386 horrors accumulate** add still more horrors  **387 amazed** confounded with horror

**IAGO:**                    O grace! O heaven forgive me!
  Are you a man? Have you a soul or sense?                    390
  God b' wi' you; take mine office. O wretched fool,°
  That lov'st to make thine honesty a vice!°
  O monstrous world! Take note, take note, O world,
  To be direct and honest is not safe.
  I thank you for this profit,° and from hence°                    395
  I'll love no friend, sith° love breeds such offense.°
**OTHELLO:**    Nay, stay. Thou shouldst be° honest.
**IAGO:**    I should be wise, for honesty's a fool
  And loses that° it works for.
**OTHELLO:**                    By the world,
  I think my wife be honest and think she is not;                    400
  I think that thou art just and think thou art not.
  I'll have some proof. My name, that was as fresh
  As Dian's° visage, is now begrimed and black
  As mine own face. If there be cords, or knives,
  Poison, or fire, or suffocating streams,                    405
  I'll not endure it. Would I were satisfied!
**IAGO:**    I see, sir, you are eaten up with passion.
  I do repent me that I put it to you.
  You would be satisfied?
**OTHELLO:**                    Would? Nay, and I will.
**IAGO:**    And may; but how? How satisfied, my lord?                    410
  Would you, the supervisor,° grossly gape on?
  Behold her topped?
**OTHELLO:**                    Death and damnation! O!
**IAGO:**    It were a tedious difficulty, I think,
  To bring them to that prospect. Damn them then,°
  If ever mortal eyes do see them bolster°                    415
  More° than their own.° What then? How then?
  What shall I say? Where's satisfaction?
  It is impossible you should see this,
  Were they as prime° as goats, as hot as monkeys,
  As salt° as wolves in pride,° and fools as gross                    420
  As ignorance made drunk. But yet I say,
  If imputation and strong circumstances°
  Which lead directly to the door of truth
  Will give you satisfaction, you might have 't.

**391 O wretched fool** (Iago addresses himself as a fool for having carried honesty too far.)   **392 vice** failing, something overdone   **395 profit** profitable instruction.   **hence** henceforth   **396 sith** since. **offense** i.e., harm to the one who offers help and friendship   **397 Thou shouldst be** it appears that you are. (But Iago replies in the sense of "ought to be.")   **399 that** what   **403 Dian** Diana, goddess of the moon and of chastity   **411 supervisor** onlooker   **414 Damn them then** i.e., they would have to be really incorrigible   **415 bolster** go to bed together, share a bolster   **416 More** other.   **own** own eyes   **419 prime** lustful   **420 salt** wanton, sensual.   **pride** heat   **422 imputation ... circumstances** strong circumstantial evidence

**OTHELLO:**   Give me a living reason she's disloyal.                    425
**IAGO:**   I do not like the office.
   But sith° I am entered in this cause so far,
   Pricked° to 't by foolish honesty and love,
   I will go on. I lay with Cassio lately,
   And being troubled with a raging tooth                               430
   I could not sleep. There are a kind of men
   So loose of soul that in their sleeps will mutter
   Their affairs. One of this kind is Cassio.
   In sleep I heard him say, "Sweet Desdemona,
   Let us be wary, let us hide our loves!"                              435
   And then, sir, would he grip and wring my hand,
   Cry "O sweet creature!", then kiss me hard,
   As if he plucked up kisses by the roots
   That grew upon my lips; then laid his leg
   Over my thigh, and sighed, and kissed, and then                     440
   Cried, "Cursèd fate that gave thee to the Moor!"
**OTHELLO:**   O monstrous! Monstrous!
**IAGO:**                                    Nay, this was but his dream.
**OTHELLO:**   But this denoted a foregone conclusion.°
   'Tis a shrewd doubt,° though it be but a dream.
**IAGO:**   And this may help to thicken other proofs                    445
   That do demonstrate thinly.
**OTHELLO:**                           I'll tear her all to pieces.
**IAGO:**   Nay, but be wise. Yet we see nothing done;
   She may be honest yet. Tell me but this:
   Have you not sometimes seen a handkerchief
   Spotted with strawberries° in your wife's hand?                     450
**OTHELLO:**   I gave her such a one. 'Twas my first gift.
**IAGO:**   I know not that; but such a handkerchief—
   I am sure it was your wife's—did I today
   See Cassio wipe his beard with.
**OTHELLO:**                           If it be that—
**IAGO:**   If it be that, or any that was hers,                        455
   It speaks against her with the other proofs.
**OTHELLO:**   O, that the slave° had forty thousand lives!
   One is too poor, too weak for my revenge.
   Now do I see 'tis true. Look here, Iago,
   All my fond° love thus do I blow to heaven.                         460
   'Tis gone.

---

427 **sith** since   428 **Pricked** spurred   443 **foregone conclusion** concluded experience or action
444 **shrewd doubt** suspicious circumstance   450 **Spotted with strawberries** embroidered with a
strawberry pattern   457 **the slave** i.e., Cassio   460 **fond** foolish (but also suggesting "affectionate")

Arise, black vengeance, from the hollow hell!
Yield up, O love, thy crown and hearted° throne
To tyrannous hate! Swell, bosom, with thy freight°,
For 'tis of aspics'° tongues! 465

**IAGO:** Yet be content.°

**OTHELLO:** O, blood, blood, blood!

**IAGO:** Patience, I say. Your mind perhaps may change.

**OTHELLO:** Never, Iago. Like to the Pontic Sea,°
Whose icy current and compulsive course 470
Ne'er feels retiring ebb, but keeps due on
To the Propontic° and the Hellespont,°
Even so my bloody thoughts with violent pace
Shall ne'er look back, ne'er ebb to humble love,
I that a capable° and wide revenge 475
Swallow them up. Now, by yond marble° heaven,
[*Kneeling*] In the due reverence of a sacred vow
I here engage my words.

**IAGO:** Do not rise yet.
[*He kneels.*]° Witness, you ever-burning lights above,
You elements that clip° us round about, 480
Witness that here Iago doth give up
The execution° of his wit,° hands, heart,
To wronged Othello's service. Let him command,
And to obey shall be in me remorse,°
What bloody business ever.° [*They rise.*]

**OTHELLO:** I greet thy love, 485
Not with vain thanks, but with acceptance bounteous,
And will upon the instant put thee to 't.°
Within these three days let me hear thee say
That Cassio's not alive.

**IAGO:** My friend is dead;
'Tis done at your request. But let her live. 490

**OTHELLO:** Damn her, lewd minx!° O, damn her, damn her!
Come, go with me apart. I will withdraw
To furnish me with some swift means of death
For the fair devil. Now art thou my lieutenant.

**IAGO:** I am your own forever. [*Exeunt.*] 495

---

**463 hearted** fixed in the heart  **464 freight** burden  **465 aspics'** venomous serpents'  **466 content** calm  **469 Pontic Sea** Black Sea  **472 Propontic** Sea of Marmara, between the Black Sea and the Aegean.  **Hellespont** Dardanelles, straits where the Sea of Marmara joins with the Aegean  **475 capable** ample, comprehensive  **476 marble** i.e., gleaming like marble and unrelenting  **479 [s.d.] He kneels** (In the Quarto text, Iago kneels here after Othello has knelt at line 477.)  **480 clip** encompass  **482 execution** exercise, action.  **wit** mind  **484 remorse** pity (for Othello's wrongs)  **485 ever** soever  **487 to 't** to the proof  **491 minx** wanton

### Scene IV. Before the Citadel

*Enter Desdemona, Emilia, and Clown.*

**DESDEMONA:** Do you know, sirrah,° where Lieutenant Cassio lies?°
**CLOWN:** I dare not say he lies anywhere.
**DESDEMONA:** Why, man?
**CLOWN:** He's a soldier, and for me to say a soldier lies, 'tis stabbing.
**DESDEMONA:** Go to. Where lodges he?                                                5
**CLOWN:** To tell you where he lodges is to tell you where I lie.
**DESDEMONA:** Can anything be made of this?
**CLOWN:** I know not where he lodges, and for me to devise a lodg-
ing and say he lies here, or he lies there, were to lie in mine own
throat.°
**DESDEMONA:** Can you inquire him out, and be edified by report?        10
**CLOWN:** I will catechize the world for him; that is, make ques-
tions, and by them answer.
**DESDEMONA:** Seek him, bid him come hither. Tell him I have
moved° my lord on his behalf and hope all will be well.
**CLOWN:** To do this is within the compass of man's wit, and
therefore I will attempt the doing it.                                          15

*[Exit Clown.]*

**DESDEMONA:** Where should I lose that handkerchief, Emilia?
**EMILIA:** I know not, madam.
**DESDEMONA:** Believe me, I had rather have lost my purse
Full of crusadoes;° and but my noble Moor                                      20
Is true of mind and made of no such baseness
As jealous creatures are, it were enough
To put him to ill thinking.
**EMILIA:**                              Is he not jealous?
**DESDEMONA:** Who, he? I think the sun where he was born
Drew all such humors° from him.
**EMILIA:**                              Look where he comes.                      25

*[Enter Othello.]*

**DESDEMONA:** I will not leave him now till Cassio
Be called to him.—How is 't with you, my lord?
**OTHELLO:** Well, my good lady. *[Aside.]* O, hardness to dissemble!—
How do you, Desdemona?
**DESDEMONA:**                        Well, my good lord.
**OTHELLO:** Give me your hand. *[She gives her hand.]* This hand is
moist, my lady.

---

**1 sirrah** (A form of address to an inferior.) **lies** lodges. (But the Clown makes the obvious pun.)
**9 lie ... throat** (1) lie egregiously and deliberately (2) use the windpipe to speak a lie   **13 moved**
petitioned   **20 crusadoes** Portuguese gold coins   **25 humors** (Refers to the four bodily fluids
thought to determine temperament.)

**DESDEMONA:** It yet hath felt no age nor known no sorrow.

**OTHELLO:** This argues° fruitfulness° and liberal° heart.   30
Hot, hot, and moist. This hand of yours requires
A sequester° from liberty, fasting and prayer,
Much castigation,° exercise devout;°   35
For here's a young and sweating devil here
That commonly rebels. 'Tis a good hand,
A frank° one.

**DESDEMONA:**                     You may indeed say so,
For 'twas that hand that gave away my heart.

**OTHELLO:** A liberal hand. The hearts of old gave hands,°   40
But our new heraldry is hands, not hearts.°

**DESDEMONA:** I cannot speak of this. Come now, your promise.

**OTHELLO:** What promise, chuck?°

**DESDEMONA:** I have sent to bid Cassio come speak with you.

**OTHELLO:** I have a salt and sorry rheum° offends me;   45
Lend me thy handkerchief.

**DESDEMONA:** Here, my lord. [*She offers a handkerchief.*]

**OTHELLO:** That which I gave you.

**DESDEMONA:**                     I have it not about me.

**OTHELLO:** Not?

**DESDEMONA:** No, faith, my lord.   50

**OTHELLO:** That's a fault. That handkerchief
Did an Egyptian to my mother give.
She was a charmer,° and could almost read
The thoughts of people. She told her, while she kept it
'Twould make her amiable° and subdue my father   55
Entirely to her love, but if she lost it
Or made a gift of it, my father's eye
Should hold her loathèd and his spirits should hunt
After new fancies.° She, dying, gave it me,
And bid me, when my fate would have me wived,   60
To give it her.° I did so; and take heed on 't;
Make it a darling like your precious eye.
To lose 't or give 't away were such perdition°
As nothing else could match.

**DESDEMONA:**                     Is 't possible?

**OTHELLO:** 'Tis true. There's magic in the web° of it.   65

---

**32 argues** gives evidence of. **fruitfulness** generosity, amorousness, and fecundity. **liberal** generous and sexually free   **34 sequester** separation, sequestration   **35 castigation** corrective discipline. **exercise devout** i.e., prayer, religious meditation, etc.   **38 frank** generous, open (with sexual suggestion)   **40 The hearts ... hands** i.e., in former times, people would give their hearts when they gave their hands to something   **41 But ... hearts** i.e., in our decadent times, the joining of hands is no longer a badge to signify the giving of hearts   **43 chuck** (A term of endearment.)   **45 salt ... rheum** distressful head cold or watering of the eyes   **53 charmer** sorceress   **55 amiable** desirable   **59 fancies** loves   **61 her** i.e., to my wife   **63 perdition** loss   **65 web** fabric, weaving

A sibyl, that had numbered in the world
The sun to course two hundred compasses,°
In her prophetic fury° sewed the work;°
The worms were hallowed that did breed the silk,
And it was dyed in mummy° which the skillful                          70
Conserved of° maidens' hearts.

**DESDEMONA:**                    I' faith! Is 't true?

**OTHELLO:**   Most veritable. Therefore look to 't well.

**DESDEMONA:**   Then would to God that I had never seen 't!

**OTHELLO:**   Ha? Wherefore?

**DESDEMONA:**   Why do you speak so startingly and rash?°           75

**OTHELLO:**   Is 't lost? Is 't gone? Speak, is 't out o' the way?°

**DESDEMONA:**   Heaven bless us!

**OTHELLO:**   Say you?

**DESDEMONA:**   It is not lost; but what an if° it were?

**OTHELLO:**   How?                                                  80

**DESDEMONA:**   I say it is not lost.

**OTHELLO:**                        Fetch 't, let me see 't.

**DESDEMONA:**   Why, so I can, sir, but I will not now.
This is a trick to put me from my suit.
Pray you, let Cassio be received again.

**OTHELLO:**   Fetch me the handkerchief! My mind misgives.         85

**DESDEMONA:**   Come, come,
You'll never meet a more sufficient° man.

**OTHELLO:**   The handkerchief!

**DESDEMONA:**                    I pray, talk° me of Cassio.

**OTHELLO:**   The handkerchief!

**DESDEMONA:**                        A man that all his time°
Hath founded his good fortunes on your love,                          90
Shared dangers with you—

**OTHELLO:**   The handkerchief!

**DESDEMONA:**   I' faith, you are to blame.

**OTHELLO:**   Zounds!                           [*Exit Othello.*]

**EMILIA:**   Is not this man jealous?                                95

**DESDEMONA:**   I ne'er saw this before.
Sure, there's some wonder in this handkerchief.
I am most unhappy in the loss of it.

**EMILIA:**   'Tis not a year or two shows us a man.°

**67 compasses** annual circlings. (The *sibyl*, or prophetess, was two-hundred years old.)   **68 prophetic fury** frenzy of prophetic inspiration.   **work** embroidered pattern   **70 mummy** medicinal or magical preparation drained from mummified bodies   **71 Conserved of** prepared or preserved out of   **75 startingly and rash** disjointedly and impetuously excitedly   **76 out o' the way** lost, misplaced   **79 an if** if   **87 sufficient** able, complete   **88 talk** talk to   **89 all his time** throughout his career   **99 'Tis ... man** i.e., you can't really know a man even in a year or two of experience (?), or, real men come along seldom (?)

They are all but stomachs, and we all but° food;                    100
They eat us hungerly,° and when they are full
They belch us.

[*Enter Iago and Cassio.*]

                  Look you, Cassio and my husband.

**IAGO** [*to Cassio*]:   There is no other way; 'tis she must do 't.
    And, lo, the happiness!° Go and importune her.
**DESDEMONA:**   How now, good Cassio? What's the news with you?      105
**CASSIO:**   Madam, my former suit. I do beseech you
    That by your virtuous° means I may again
    Exist and be a member of his love
    Whom I, with all the office° of my heart,
    Entirely honor. I would not be delayed.                          110
    If my offense be of such mortal° kind
    That nor my service past, nor° present sorrows,
    Nor purposed merit in futurity
    Can ransom me into his love again,
    But to know so must be my benefit;°                             115
    So shall I clothe me in a forced content,
    And shut myself up in° some other course,
    To fortune's alms.°
**DESDEMONA:**         Alas, thrice-gentle Cassio,
    My advocation° is not now in tune.
    My lord is not my lord; nor should I know him,                   120
    Were he in favor° as in humor° altered.
    So help me every spirit sanctified
    As I have spoken for you all my best
    And stood within the blank° of his displeasure
    For my free speech! You must awhile be patient.                  125
    What I can do I will, and more I will
    Than for myself I dare. Let that suffice you.
**IAGO:**   Is my lord angry?
**EMILIA:**              He went hence but now,
    And certainly in strange unquietness.
**IAGO:**   Can he be angry? I have seen the cannon                     130
    When it hath blown his ranks into the air,
    And like the devil from his very arm
    Puffed his own brother—and is he angry?

---

**100 but** nothing but   **101 hungerly** hungrily   **104 the happiness** in happy time, fortunately met
**107 virtuous** efficacious   **109 office** loyal service   **111 mortal** fatal   **112 nor ... nor** neither ...
nor   **115 But ... benefit** merely to know that my case is hopeless will have to content me (and will be
better than uncertainty)   **117 shut ... in** confine myself to   **118 To fortune's alms** throwing myself
on the mercy of fortune   **119 advocation** advocacy   **121 favor** appearance.  **humor** mood
**124 within the blank** within point-blank range. (The *blank* is the center of the target.)

Something of moment° then. I will go meet him.
There's matter in 't indeed, if he be angry.                                    135
**DESDEMONA:**   I prithee, do so.                          *Exit [Iago].*
                                      Something, sure, of state,°
Either from Venice, or some unhatched practice°
Made demonstrable here in Cyprus to him,
Hath puddled° his clear spirit; and in such cases
Men's natures wrangle with inferior things,                                     140
Though great ones are their object. 'Tis even so;
For let our finger ache, and it indues°
Our other, healthful members even to a sense
Of pain. Nay, we must think men are not gods,
Nor of them look for such observancy°                                           145
As fits the bridal.° Beshrew me° much, Emilia,
I was, unhandsome° warrior as I am,
Arraigning his unkindness with° my soul;
But now I find I had suborned the witness,°
And he's indicted falsely.
**EMILIA:**                           Pray heaven it be                          150
State matters, as you think, and no conception
Nor no jealous toy° concerning you.
**DESDEMONA:**   Alas the day! I never gave him cause.
**EMILIA:**   But jealous souls will not be answered so;
They are not ever jealous for the cause,                                        155
But jealous for° they're jealous. It is a monster
Begot upon itself,° born on itself.
**DESDEMONA:**   Heaven keep that monster from Othello's mind!
**EMILIA:**   Lady, amen.
**DESDEMONA:**   I will go seek him. Cassio, walk hereabout.                     160
If I do find him fit, I'll move your suit
And seek to effect it to my uttermost.
**CASSIO:**   I humbly thank your ladyship.

                              *Exit [Desdemona with Emilia].*

[*Enter Bianca.*]

**BIANCA:**   Save° you, friend Cassio!
**CASSIO:**                           What make° you from home?
How is 't with you, my most fair Bianca?                                        165
I' faith, sweet love, I was coming to your house.

---

**134 of moment** of immediate importance, momentous   **136 of state** concerning state affairs   **137 unhatched practice** as yet unexecuted or undiscovered plot   **139 puddled** muddied   **142 indues** brings to
the same condition   **145 observancy** attentiveness   **146 bridal** wedding (when a bridegroom is newly attentive to his bride).   **Beshrew me** (A mild oath.)   **147 unhandsome** insufficient, unskillful   **148 with**
before the bar of   **149 suborned the witness** induced the witness to give false testimony   **152 toy** fancy
**156 for** because   **157 Begot upon itself** generated solely from itself   **164 Save** God save.   **make** do

**BIANCA:**   And I was going to your lodging, Cassio.
  What, keep a week away? Seven days and nights?
  Eightscore-eight° hours? And lovers' absent hours
  More tedious than the dial° eightscore times?                            170
  O weary reckoning!
**CASSIO:**                    Pardon me, Bianca.
  I have this while with leaden thoughts been pressed;
  But I shall, in a more continuate° time,
  Strike off this score° of absence. Sweet Bianca,

[*giving her Desdemona's handkerchief*]

  Take me this work out.°
**BIANCA:**                    O Cassio, whence came this?                   175
  This is some token from a newer friend.°
  To the felt absence now I feel a cause.
  Is 't come to this? Well, well.
**CASSIO:**                            Go to, woman!
  Throw your vile guesses in the devil's teeth,
  From whence you have them. You are jealous now           180
  That this is from some mistress, some remembrance.
  No, by my faith, Bianca.
**BIANCA:**                    Why, whose is it?
**CASSIO:**   I know not, neither. I found it in my chamber.
  I like the work well. Ere it be demanded°—
  As like° enough it will—I would have it copied.              185
  Take it and do 't, and leave me for this time.
**BIANCA:**   Leave you? Wherefore?
**CASSIO:**   I do attend here on the General,
  And think it no addition,° nor my wish,
  To have him see me womaned.                                 190
**BIANCA:**   Why, I pray you?
**CASSIO:**   Not that I love you not.
**BIANCA:**   But that you do not love me.
  I pray you, bring° me on the way a little,
  And say if I shall see you soon at night.                      195
**CASSIO:**   'Tis but a little way that I can bring you,
  For I attend here; but I'll see you soon.
**BIANCA:**   'Tis very good. I must be circumstanced.°

                                                    [*Exeunt omnes.*]

---

**169 Eightscore-eight** one hundred sixty-eight, the number of hours in a week   **170 the dial** a complete revolution of the clock   **173 continuate** uninterrupted   **174 Strike ... score** settle this account   **175 Take ... out** copy this embroidery for me   **176 friend** mistress   **184 demanded** inquired for   **185 like** likely   **189 addition** i.e., addition to my reputation   **194 bring** accompany   **198 be circumstanced** be governed by circumstance, yield to your conditions

## *Act IV*

### Scene I. Before the Citadel

*Enter Othello and Iago.*

**IAGO:**  Will you think so?

**OTHELLO:**                    Think so, Iago?

**IAGO:**                                    What,
To kiss in private?

**OTHELLO:**            An unauthorized kiss!

**IAGO:**  Or to be naked with her friend in bed
An hour or more, not meaning any harm?

**OTHELLO:**  Naked in bed, Iago, and not mean harm?                    5
It is hypocrisy against the devil.
They that mean virtuously and yet do so,
The devil their virtue tempts, and they tempt heaven.

**IAGO:**  If they do nothing, 'tis a venial° slip.
But if I give my wife a handkerchief—                                    10

**OTHELLO:**  What then?

**IAGO:**  Why then, 'tis hers, my lord, and being hers,
She may, I think, bestow 't on any man.

**OTHELLO:**  She is protectress of her honor too.
May she give that?                                                        15

**IAGO:**  Her honor is an essence that's not seen;
They have it° very oft that have it not.
But, for the handkerchief—

**OTHELLO:**  By heaven, I would most gladly have forgot it.
Thou saidst—O, it comes o'er my memory                                   20
As doth the raven o'er the infectious house,°
Boding to all—he had my handkerchief.

**IAGO:**  Ay, what of that?

**OTHELLO:**                That's not so good now.

**IAGO:**                                    What
If I had said I had seen him do you wrong?
Or heard him say—as knaves be such abroad,°                               25
Who having, by their own importunate suit,
Or voluntary dotage° of some mistress,
Convincèd or supplied° them, cannot choose
But they must blab—

**OTHELLO:**                Hath he said anything?

**IAGO:**  He hath, my lord; but, be you well assured,                    30
No more than he'll unswear.

---

9 **venial** pardonable   17 **They have it** i.e., they enjoy a reputation for it   21 **raven ... house**
(Allusion to the belief that the raven hovered over a house of sickness or infection, such as one visited
by the plague.)   25 **abroad** around about   27 **voluntary dotage** willing infatuation   28 **Convincèd**
**or supplied** seduced or sexually gratified

**OTHELLO:**                    What hath he said?

**IAGO:**  Faith, that he did—I know not what he did.

**OTHELLO:**  What? What?

**IAGO:**  Lie—

**OTHELLO:**  With her?

**IAGO:**            With her, on her; what you will.

**OTHELLO:**  Lie with her? Lie on her? We say "lie on her" when
they belie° her. Lie with her? Zounds, that's fulsome.°—          35
Handkerchief—confessions—handkerchief!—To confess and be
hanged for his labor—first to be hanged and then to confess.°—
I tremble at it. Nature would not invest herself in such shadow-
ing passion without some instruction.° It is not words° that
shakes me thus. Pish! Noses, ears, and lips.—Is 't possible?—
Confess—handkerchief!—O devil!                                    40

[*Falls in a trance.*]

**IAGO:**  Work on,
My medicine, work! Thus credulous fools are caught,
And many worthy and chaste dames even thus,
All guiltless, meet reproach.—What, ho! My lord!                  45
My lord, I say! Othello!

*Enter Cassio.*

                          How now, Cassio?

**CASSIO:**  What's the matter?

**IAGO:**  My lord is fall'n into an epilepsy.
This is his second fit. He had one yesterday.

**CASSIO:**  Rub him about the temples.

**IAGO:**                              No, forbear.                 50
The lethargy° must have his° quiet course.
If not, he foams at mouth, and by and by
Breaks out to savage madness. Look, he stirs.
Do you withdraw yourself a little while.
He will recover straight. When he is gone,                        55
I would on great occasion° speak with you.

                                    [*Exit Cassio.*]

How is it, General? Have you not hurt your head?

**OTHELLO:**  Dost thou mock me?°

---

**35 belie** slander  **36 fulsome** foul  **37–38 first ... to confess** (Othello reverses the proverbial *confess*
and be *hanged*; Cassio is to be given no time to confess before he dies.)  **38–39 Nature ... instruction**
i.e., without some foundation in fact, nature would not have dressed herself in such an overwhelming
passion that comes over me now and fills my mind with images, or in such a lifelike fantasy as Cassio
had in his dream of lying with Desdemona  **39 words** mere words  **51 lethargy** coma.  **his** its
**56 on great occasion** on a matter of great importance  **58 mock me** (Othello takes Iago's question
about hurting his head to be a mocking reference to the cuckold's horns.)

**IAGO:**                                    I mock you not, by heaven.
Would you would bear your fortune like a man!

**OTHELLO:**   A hornèd man's a monster and a beast.                          60

**IAGO:**   There's many a beast then in a populous city,
And many a civil° monster.

**OTHELLO:**   Did he confess it?

**IAGO:**   Good sir, be a man.
Think every bearded fellow that's but yoked°                              65
May draw with you.° There's millions now alive
That nightly lie in those unproper° beds
Which they dare swear peculiar.° Your case is better.°
O, 'tis the spite of hell, the fiend's arch-mock,
To lip° a wanton in a secure° couch                                      70
And to suppose her chaste! No, let me know,
And knowing what I am,° I know what she shall be.°

**OTHELLO:**   O, thou art wise. 'Tis certain.

**IAGO:**   Stand you awhile apart;
Confine yourself but in a patient list.°                                  75
Whilst you were here o'erwhelmèd with your grief—
A passion most unsuiting such a man—
Cassio came hither. I shifted him away,°
And laid good 'scuse upon your ecstasy,°
Bade him anon return and here speak with me,                             80
The which he promised. Do but encave° yourself
And mark the fleers,° the gibes, and notable° scorns
That dwell in every region of his face;
For I will make him tell the tale anew,
Where, how, how oft, how long ago, and when                              85
He hath and is again to cope° your wife.
I say, but mark his gesture. Marry, patience!
Or I shall say you're all-in-all in spleen,°
And nothing of a man.

**OTHELLO:**                              Dost thou hear, Iago?
I will be found most cunning in my patience;                             90
But—dost thou hear?—most bloody.

**IAGO:**                              That's not amiss;
But yet keep time° in all. Will you withdraw?

[*Othello stands apart.*]

**62 civil** i.e., dwelling in a city   **65 yoked** (1) married (2) put into the yoke of infamy and cuckoldry
**66 draw with you** pull as you do, like oxen who are yoked, i.e., share your fate as cuckold   **67 unproper**
not exclusively their own   **68 peculiar** private, their own.   **better** i.e., because you know the truth
**70 lip** kiss.   **secure** free from suspicion   **72 what I am** i.e., a cuckold.   **she shall be** will happen to
her   **75 in … list** within the bounds of patience   **78 shifted him away** used a dodge to get rid of
him   **79 ecstasy** trance   **81 encave** conceal   **82 fleers** sneers.   **notable** obvious   **86 cope** encounter with, have sex with   **88 all-in-all in spleen** utterly governed by passionate impulses   **92 keep
time** keep yourself steady (as in music)

Now will I question Cassio of Bianca,
A huswife° that by selling her desires
Buys herself bread and clothes. It is a creature                    95
That dotes on Cassio—as 'tis the strumpet's plague
To beguile many and be beguiled by one.
He, when he hears of her, cannot restrain°
From the excess of laughter. Here he comes.

[*Enter Cassio.*]

As he shall smile, Othello shall go mad;                            100
And his unbookish° jealousy must conster°
Poor Cassio's smiles, gestures, and light behaviors
Quite in the wrong.—How do you now, Lieutenant?
**CASSIO:**   The worser that you give me the addition°
Whose want° even kills me.                                          105
**IAGO:**   Ply Desdemona well and you are sure on 't.
[*Speaking lower.*] Now, if this suit lay in Bianca's power,
How quickly should you speed!
**CASSIO** [*laughing*]:   Alas, poor caitiff!°
**OTHELLO** [*aside*]:   Look how he laughs already!                110
**IAGO:**   I never knew a woman love man so.
**CASSIO:**   Alas, poor rogue! I think, i' faith, she loves me.
**OTHELLO:**   Now he denies it faintly, and laughs it out.
**IAGO:**   Do you hear, Cassio?
**OTHELLO:**                          Now he importunes him
To tell it o'er. Go to!° Well said,° well said.                    115
**IAGO:**   She gives it out that you shall marry her.
Do you intend it?
**CASSIO:**   Ha, ha, ha!
**OTHELLO:**   Do you triumph, Roman?° Do you triumph?
**CASSIO:**   I marry her? What? A customer?° Prithee, bear some char-
ity to my wit;° do not think it so unwholesome. Ha, ha, ha!

**OTHELLO:**   So, so, so, so! They laugh that win.°
**IAGO:**   Faith, the cry° goes that you shall marry her.
**CASSIO:**   Prithee, say true.
**IAGO:**   I am a very villain else.°                              125
**OTHELLO:**   Have you scored me?° Well.

---

94 **huswife** hussy   98 **restrain** refrain   101 **unbookish** uninstructed.   **conster** construe   104 **addition**
title   105 **Whose want** the lack of which   109 **caitiff** wretch   115 **Go to** (An expression of remonstrance.)   **Well said** well done   119 **Roman** (The Romans were noted for their *triumphs* or triumphal
processions.)   120 **customer** i.e., prostitute.   **bear ... wit** be more charitable to my judgment
122 **They ... win** i.e., they that laugh last laugh best   123 **cry** rumor   125 **I ... else** call me a complete
rogue if I'm not telling the truth   126 **scored me** scored off me, beaten me, made up my reckoning,
branded me

**CASSIO:**   This is the monkey's own giving out. She is persuaded I
will marry her out of her own love and flattery,° not out of my
promise.

**OTHELLO:**   Iago beckons me.° Now he begins the story.

**CASSIO:**   She was here even now; she haunts me in every place. I     130
was the other day talking on the seabank° with certain
Venetians, and thither comes the bauble,° and, by this hand,°
she falls me thus about my neck—

[*He embraces Iago.*]

**OTHELLO:**   Crying, "O dear Cassio!" as it were; his gesture
imports it.

**CASSIO:**   So hangs and lolls and weep upon me, so shakes and pulls
me. Ha, ha, ha!

**OTHELLO:**   Now he tells how she plucked him to my chamber. O,     135
I see that nose of yours, but not that dog I shall throw it to.°

**CASSIO:**   Well, I must leave her company.

**IAGO:**   Before me,° look where she comes.

*Enter Bianca [with Othello's handkerchief].*

**CASSIO:**   'Tis such another fitchew!° Marry, a perfumed one.—What
do you mean by this haunting of me?

**BIANCA:**   Let the devil and his dam° haunt you! What did you     140
mean by that same handkerchief you gave me even now? I was
a fine fool to take it. I must take out the work? A likely piece
of work,° that you should find it in your chamber and know not
who left it there! This is some minx's token, and I must take
out the work? There; give it your hobbyhorse.° [*She gives him*     145
*the handkerchief.*] Wheresoever you had it, I'll take out no work
on 't.

**CASSIO:**   How now, my sweet Bianca? How now? How now?

**OTHELLO:**   By heaven, that should be° my handkerchief!

**BIANCA:**   If you'll come to supper tonight, you may; if you will not,
come when you are next prepared for.°     150

[*Exit.*]

**IAGO:**   After her, after her.

**CASSIO:**   Faith, I must. She'll rail in the streets else.

**IAGO:**   Will you sup there?

**CASSIO:**   Faith, I intend so.

---

128 **flattery** self-flattery, self-deception   129 **beckons** signals   131 **seabank** seashore   132 **bauble**
plaything   **by this hand** I make my vow   136 **not ... to** (Othello imagines himself cutting off Cassio's
nose and throwing it to a dog.)   138 **Before** me i.e., on my soul   139 **'Tis ... fitchew** what a polecat
she is! Just like all the others. (Polecats were often compared with prostitutes because of their rank
smell and presumed lechery.)   141 **dam** mother   143 **A likely ... work** a fine story   145 **hobby-**
**horse** harlot   148 **should be** must be   149–150 **when ... for** when I'm ready for you (i.e., never)

**IAGO:**　Well, I may chance to see you, for I would very fain speak
　　with you.　　　　　　　　　　　　　　　　　　　　　　　155

**CASSIO:**　Prithee, come. Will you?

**IAGO:**　Go to.° Say no more.

　　　　　　　　　　　　　　　　　　　　　[*Exit Cassio.*]

**OTHELLO**　[*advancing*]:How shall I murder him, Iago?

**IAGO:**　Did you perceive how he laughed at his vice?

**OTHELLO:**　O, Iago!　　　　　　　　　　　　　　　　160

**IAGO:**　And did you see the handkerchief?

**OTHELLO:**　Was that mine?

**IAGO:**　Yours, by this hand. And to see how he prizes the foolish
　　woman your wife! She gave it him, and he hath given it his
　　whore.

**OTHELLO:**　I would have him nine years a-killing. A fine woman! A
　　fair woman! A sweet woman!　　　　　　　　　　165

**IAGO:**　Nay, you must forget that.

**OTHELLO:**　Ay, let her rot and perish, and be damned tonight, for
　　she shall not live. No, my heart is turned to stone; I strike it,
　　and it hurts my hand. O, the world hath not a sweeter creature!
　　She might lie by an emperor's side and command him tasks.　　170

**IAGO:**　Nay, that's not your way.°

**OTHELLO:**　Hang her! I do but say what she is. So delicate with her
　　needle! An admirable musician! O, she will sing the savage-ness
　　out of a bear. Of so high and plenteous wit and invention!°　　175

**IAGO:**　She's the worse for all this.

**OTHELLO:**　O, a thousand, a thousand times! And then, of so gentle
　　a condition!°

**IAGO:**　Ay, too gentle.°

**OTHELLO:**　Nay, that's certain. But yet the pity of it, Iago! O, Iago,
　　the pity of it, Iago!　　　　　　　　　　　　　180

**IAGO:**　If you are so fond° over her iniquity, give her patent° to of-
　　fend, for if it touch not you it comes near nobody.

**OTHELLO:**　I will chop her into messes.° Cuckold me?

**IAGO:**　O, 'tis foul in her.

**OTHELLO:**　With mine officer?　　　　　　　　　　185

**IAGO:**　That's fouler.

**OTHELLO:**　Get me some poison, Iago, this night. I'll not ex-postulate
　　with her, lest her body and beauty unprovide° my mind again.
　　This night, Iago.

---

**157 Go to** (an expression of remonstrance)　**172 your way** i.e., the way you should think of her
**175 invention** imagination　**177 gentle a condition** well-born and well-bred　**178 gentle** generous,
yielding (to other men)　**181 fond** foolish.　**patent** license　**183 messes** portions of meat, i.e., bits
**188 unprovide** weaken, render unfit

**IAGO:**  Do it not with poison. Strangle her in her bed, even the bed
she hath contaminated.                                                          190

**OTHELLO:**  Good, good! The justice of it pleases. Very good.

**IAGO:**  And for Cassio, let me be his undertaker.° You shall hear
more by midnight.

**OTHELLO:**  Excellent good. [*A trumpet within.*] What trumpet is
that same?

**IAGO:**  I warrant, something from Venice.

[*Enter Lodovico, Desdemona, and attendants.*]

'Tis Lodovico. This comes from the Duke.                                        195
See, your wife's with him.

**LODOVICO:**  God save you, worthy General!

**OTHELLO:**                                With all my heart,° sir.

**LODOVICO** [*giving him a letter*]:  The Duke and the senators of
Venice greet you.

**OTHELLO:**  I kiss the instrument of their pleasures.

[*He opens the letter, and reads.*]

**DESDEMONA:**  And what's the news, good cousin Lodovico?                       200

**IAGO:**  I am very glad to see you, signor.
Welcome to Cyprus.

**LODOVICO:**  I thank you. How does Lieutenant Cassio?

**IAGO:**  Lives, sir.

**DESDEMONA:**  Cousin, there's fall'n between him and my lord                   205
An unkind° breach; but you shall make all well.

**OTHELLO:**  Are you sure of that?

**DESDEMONA:**  My lord?

**OTHELLO** [*reads*]:  "This fail you not to do, as you will—"

**LODOVICO:**  He did not call; he's busy in the paper.                          210
Is there division twixt my lord and Cassio?

**DESDEMONA:**  A most unhappy one. I would do much
T' atone° them, for the love I bear to Cassio.

**OTHELLO:**  Fire and brimstone!

**DESDEMONA:**  My lord?                                                         215

**OTHELLO:**  Are you wise?

**DESDEMONA:**  What, is he angry?

**LODOVICO:**                                Maybe the letter moved him;
For, as I think, they do command him home,
Deputing Cassio in his government.°

**DESDEMONA:**  By my troth, I am glad on 't.°                                   220

---

**192 be his undertaker** undertake to dispatch him   **197 With all my heart** i.e., I thank you most heartily
**206 unkind** unnatural, contrary to their natures; hurtful   **213 atone** reconcile   **219 government**
office   **220 on 't** of it

**OTHELLO:**  Indeed?

**DESDEMONA:**  My lord?

**OTHELLO:**  I am glad to see you mad.°

**DESDEMONA:**  Why, sweet Othello—

**OTHELLO** [*striking her*]:  Devil!    225

**DESDEMONA:**  I have not deserved this.

**LODOVICO:**  My lord, this would not be believed in Venice,
Though I should swear I saw 't. 'Tis very much.°
Make her amends; she weeps.

**OTHELLO:**                    O devil, devil!
If that the earth could teem° with woman's tears,    230
Each drop she falls would prove a crocodile.°
Out of my sight!

**DESDEMONA:**  I will not stay to offend you. [*Going.*]

**LODOVICO:**  Truly, an obedient lady.
I do beseech your lordship, call her back.

**OTHELLO:**  Mistress!    235

**DESDEMONA** [*returning*]:  My lord?

**OTHELLO:**  What would you with her, sir?°

**LODOVICO:**  Who, I, my lord?

**OTHELLO:**  Ay, you did wish that I would make her turn.
Sir, she can turn, and turn, and yet go on    240
And turn again; and she can weep, sir, weep;
And she's obedient,° as you say, obedient,
Very obedient.—Proceed you in your tears.—
Concerning this, sir—O well-painted passion!°—
I am commanded home.—Get you away;    245
I'll send for you anon.—Sir, I obey the mandate
And will return to Venice.—Hence, avaunt!

                         [*Exit Desdemona.*]

Cassio shall have my place. And, sir, tonight
I do entreat that we may sup together.
You are welcome, sir, to Cyprus.—Goats and monkeys!°    [*Exit.*]    250

**LODOVICO:**  Is this the noble Moor whom our full Senate
Call all in all sufficient? Is this the nature
Whom passion could not shake? Whose solid virtue
The shot of accident nor dart of chance
Could neither graze nor pierce?

---

**223 I am ... mad** i.e., I am glad to see that you are insane enough to rejoice in Cassio's promotion
(? Othello bitterly plays on Desdemona's *I am glad.*)    **228 very much** too much, outrageous
**230 teem** breed, be impregnated    **231 falls ... crocodile** (Crocodiles were supposed to weep hypocriti-
cal tears for their victims.)    **237 What ... sir** (Othello implies that Desdemona is pliant and will do a
*turn*, lines 239–241, for any man.)    **242 obedient** (with much the same sexual connotation as *turn* in
lines 239–241)    **244 passion** i.e., grief    **250 Goats and monkeys** (See Act III, Scene iii, line 419.)

**IAGO:**                              He is much changed.                    255
**LODOVICO:**   Are his wits safe? Is he not light of brain?
**IAGO:**   He's that he is. I may not breathe my censure
   What he might be. If what he might he is not,
   I would to heaven he were!°
**LODOVICO:**                      What, strike his wife?
**IAGO:**   Faith, that was not so well; yet would I knew        260
   That stroke would prove the worst!
**LODOVICO:**                      Is it his use?°
   Or did the letters work upon his blood°
   And new-create his fault?
**IAGO:**                      Alas, alas!
   It is not honesty in me to speak
   What I have seen and known. You shall observe him,   265
   And his own courses will denote° him so
   That I may save my speech. Do but go after,
   And mark how he continues.
**LODOVICO:**   I am sorry that I am deceived in him.        *Exeunt.*

### Scene II. The Citadel

*Enter Othello and Emilia.*

**OTHELLO:**   You have seen nothing then?
**EMILIA:**   Nor ever heard, nor ever did suspect.
**OTHELLO:**   Yes, you have seen Cassio and she together.
**EMILIA:**   But then I saw no harm, and then I heard
   Each syllable that breath made up between them.        5
**OTHELLO:**   What, did they never whisper?
**EMILIA:**   Never, my lord.
**OTHELLO:**   Nor send you out o' the way?
**EMILIA:**   Never.
**OTHELLO:**   To fetch her fan, her gloves, her mask, nor nothing?    10
**EMILIA:**   Never, my lord.
**OTHELLO:**   That's strange.
**EMILIA:**   I durst, my lord, to wager she is honest,
   Lay down my soul at stake.° If you think other,
   Remove your thought; it doth abuse your bosom.°        15
   If any wretch have put this in your head,
   Let heaven requite it with the serpent's curse!°

---

257–259 **I may ... were** i.e., I dare not venture an opinion as to whether he's of unsound mind, as you suggest, but, if he isn't, then it might be better to wish he were in fact insane, since only that could excuse his wild behavior   261 **use** custom   262 **blood** passions   266 **courses will denote** actions will reveal   14 **at stake** as the wager   15 **abuse your bosom** deceive you   17 **the serpent's curse** the curse pronounced by God on the serpent for deceiving Eve, just as some man has done to Othello and Desdemona. (See Genesis 3:14.)

For if she be not honest, chaste, and true,
There's no man happy; the purest of their wives
Is foul as slander.

**OTHELLO:**          Bid her come hither. Go.                    20

[*Exit Emilia.*]

She says enough; yet she's a simple bawd
That cannot say as much.° This° is a subtle whore,
A closet lock and key° of villainous secrets.
And yet she'll kneel and pray; I have seen her do 't.

[*Enter Desdemona and Emilia.*]

**DESDEMONA:**   My lord, what is your will?                    25
**OTHELLO:**   Pray you, chuck, come hither.
**DESDEMONA:**   What is your pleasure?
**OTHELLO:**                              Let me see your eyes.
   Look in my face.
**DESDEMONA:**          What horrible fancy's this?
**OTHELLO** [*to Emilia*]:   Some of your function,° mistress.
   Leave procreants° alone and shut the door;                    30
   Cough or cry "hem" if anybody come.
   Your mystery, your mystery!° Nay, dispatch.

[*Exit Emilia.*]

**DESDEMONA** [*kneeling*]:   Upon my knees, what doth your speech
   import?
I understand a fury in your words,
But not the words.                    35
**OTHELLO:**   Why, what art thou?
**DESDEMONA:**                              Your wife, my lord, your true
   And loyal wife.
**OTHELLO:**          Come, swear it, damn thyself,
   Lest, being like one of heaven,° the devils themselves
   Should fear to seize thee. Therefore be double damned:
   Swear thou art honest.
**DESDEMONA:**          Heaven doth truly know it.                    40
**OTHELLO:**   Heaven truly knows that thou art false as hell.
**DESDEMONA:**   To whom, my lord? With whom? How am I false?
**OTHELLO** [*weeping*]:   Ah, Desdemon! Away, away, away!
**DESDEMONA:**   Alas the heavy day! Why do you weep?

---

**21-22 she's ... much** i.e., any procuress or go-between who couldn't make up as plausible a story
as Emilia's would have to be pretty stupid   **22 This** i.e., Desdemona   **23 closet lock and key** i.e.,
concealer   **29 Some ... function** i.e., practice your chosen profession, that of bawd (by guarding the
door)   **30 procreants** mating couples   **32 mystery** trade, occupation   **38 being ... heaven** looking
like an angel

Am I the motive° of these tears, my lord?                              45
If haply you my father do suspect
An instrument of this your calling back,
Lay not your blame on me. If you have lost him,
I have lost him too.

**OTHELLO:**                    Had it pleased heaven
To try me with affliction, had they° rained                            50
All kinds of sores and shames on my bare head,
Steeped me in poverty to the very lips,
Given to captivity me and my utmost hopes,
I should have found in some place of my soul
A drop of patience. But, alas, to make me                              55
A fixèd figure for the time of scorn°
To point his° slow and moving finger° at!
Yet could I bear that too, well, very well.
But there where I have garnered° up my heart,
Where either I must live or bear no life,                              60
The fountain° from the which my current runs
Or else dries up—to be discarded thence!
Or keep it as a cistern° for foul toads
To knot° and gender° in! Turn thy complexion there,°
Patience, thou young and rose-lipped cherubin—                        65
Ay, there look grim as hell!°

**DESDEMONA:**   I hope my noble lord esteems me honest.°
**OTHELLO:**   O, ay, as summer flies are in the shambles,°
That quicken° even with blowing.° O thou weed,
Who art so lovely fair and smell'st so sweet                          70
That the sense aches at thee, would thou hadst ne'er been born!

**DESDEMONA:**   Alas, what ignorant° sin have I committed?
**OTHELLO:**   Was this fair paper, this most goodly book,
Made to write "whore" upon? What committed?
Committed? O thou public commoner!°                                    75
I should make very forges of my cheeks,
That would to cinders burn up modesty,
Did I but speak thy deeds. What committed?
Heaven stops the nose at it and the moon winks;°

45 **motive** cause   50 **they** i.e., heavenly powers   56 **time of scorn** i.e., scornful world   57 **his** its.   **slow and moving finger** i.e., hour hand of the clock, moving so slowly it seems hardly to move at all. (Othello envisages himself as being eternally pointed at by the scornful world as the numbers on a clock are pointed at by the hour hand.)   59 **garnered** stored   61 **fountain** spring   63 **cistern** cesspool   64 **knot** couple.   **gender** engender.   **Turn ... there** change your color, grow pale, at such a sight   65–66 **Patience ... hell** (Even Patience, that rose-lipped cherub, will look grim and pale at this spectacle.)   67 **honest** chaste   68 **shambles** slaughterhouse   69 **quicken** come to life.   **with blowing** i.e., with the puffing up of something rotten in which maggots are breeding   72 **ignorant sin** sin in ignorance   75 **commoner** prostitute   79 **winks** closes her eyes. (The moon symbolizes chastity.)

The bawdy° wind, that kisses all it meets,  80
Is hushed within the hollow mine° of earth
And will not hear 't. What committed?
Impudent strumpet!
**DESDEMONA:**          By heaven, you do me wrong.
**OTHELLO:**  Are not you a strumpet?
**DESDEMONA:**  No, as I am a Christian.  85
If to preserve this vessel° for my lord
From any other foul unlawful touch
Be not to be a strumpet, I am none.
**OTHELLO:**  What, not a whore?
**DESDEMONA:**  No, as I shall be saved.  90
**OTHELLO:**  Is 't possible?
**DESDEMONA:**  O, heaven forgive us!
**OTHELLO:**                    I cry you mercy,° then.
I took you for that cunning whore of Venice
That married with Othello. [*Calling out.*] You, mistress,
That have the office opposite to Saint Peter  95
And keep the gate of hell!

[*Enter Emilia.*]
                    You, you, ay, you!
We have done our course.° There's money for your pains.
    [*He gives money.*]
I pray you, turn the key and keep our counsel.     [*Exit.*]
**EMILIA:**  Alas, what does this gentleman conceive?°
How do you, madam? How do you, my good lady?  100
**DESDEMONA:**  Faith, half asleep.°
**EMILIA:**  Good madam, what's the matter with my lord?
**DESDEMONA:**  With who?
**EMILIA:**  Why, with my lord, madam.
**DESDEMONA:**  Who is thy lord?
**EMILIA:**                    He that is yours, sweet lady.  105
**DESDEMONA:**  I have none. Do not talk to me, Emilia.
I cannot weep, nor answers have I none
But what should go by water.° Prithee, tonight
Lay on my bed my wedding sheets, remember;
And call thy husband hither.  110
**EMILIA:**  Here's a change indeed!     [*Exit.*]
**DESDEMONA:**  'Tis meet I should be used so, very meet.°
How have I been behaved, that he might stick°

80 **bawdy** kissing one and all  81 **mine** cave (where the winds were thought to dwell)  86 **vessel** body  92 **cry you mercy** beg your pardon  97 **course** business (with an indecent suggestion of "trick," turn at sex)  99 **conceive** suppose, think  101 **half asleep** i.e., dazed  108 **go by water** be expressed by tears  112 **meet** fitting  113 **stick** attach

The small'st opinion° on my least misuse?°

[*Enter Iago and Emilia.*]

**IAGO:**   What is your pleasure, madam? How is 't with you?          115
**DESDEMONA:**   I cannot tell. Those that do teach young babes
　　Do it with gentle means and easy tasks.
　　He might have chid me so, for, in good faith,
　　I am a child to chiding.
**IAGO:**   What is the matter, lady?          120
**EMILIA:**   Alas, Iago, my lord hath so bewhored her,
　　Thrown such despite and heavy terms upon her,
　　That true hearts cannot bear it.
**DESDEMONA:**   Am I that name, Iago?
**IAGO:**   What name, fair lady?          125
**DESDEMONA:**   Such as she said my lord did say I was.
**EMILIA:**   He called her whore. A beggar in his drink
　　Could not have laid such terms upon his callet.°
**IAGO:**   Why did he so?
**DESDEMONA** [*weeping*]:   I do not know. I am sure I am none
　　such.          130
**IAGO:**   Do not weep, do not weep. Alas the day!
**EMILIA:**   Hath she forsook so many noble matches,
　　Her father and her country and her friends,
　　To be called whore? Would it not make one weep?
**DESDEMONA:**   It is my wretched fortune.
**IAGO:**                               Beshrew° him for 't!          135
　　How comes this trick° upon him?
**DESDEMONA:**                               Nay, heaven doth know.
**EMILIA:**   I will be hanged if some eternal° villain,
　　Some busy and insinuating° rogue,
　　Some cogging,° cozening° slave, to get some office,
　　Have not devised this slander. I will be hanged else.          140
**IAGO:**   Fie, there is no such man. It is impossible.
**DESDEMONA:**   If any such there be, heaven pardon him!
**EMILIA:**   A halter° pardon him! And hell gnaw his bones!
　　Why should he call her whore? Who keeps her company?
　　What place? What time? What form?° What likelihood?          145
　　The Moor's abused by some most villainous knave,
　　Some base notorious knave, some scurvy fellow.
　　O heaven, that° such companions° thou'dst unfold,°

---

114 **opinion** censure. **least misuse** slightest misconduct   128 **callet** whore   135 **Beshrew** curse
136 **trick** strange behavior, delusion   137 **eternal** inveterate   138 **insinuating** ingratiating, fawn-
ing, wheedling   139 **cogging** cheating.   **cozening** defrauding   143 **halter** hangman's noose
145 **form** appearance, circumstance   148 **that** would that   **companions** fellows   **unfold** expose

And put in every honest hand a whip
To lash the rascals naked through the world                       150
Even from the east to th' west!

**IAGO:**                                 Speak within door.°

**EMILIA:**   O, fie upon them! Some such squire° he was
That turned your wit the seamy side without°
And made you to suspect me with the Moor.

**IAGO:**   You are a fool. Go to.°

**DESDEMONA:**                           Alas, Iago,                       155
What shall I do to win my lord again?
Good friend, go to him; for, by this light of heaven,
I know not how I lost him. Here I kneel. [*She kneels.*]
If e'er my will did trespass 'gainst his love,
Either in discourse° of thought or actual deed,                  160
Or that° mine eyes, mine ears, or any sense
Delighted them° in any other form;
Or that I do not yet,° and ever did,
And ever will—though he do shake me off
To beggarly divorcement—love him dearly,                         165
Comfort forswear° me! Unkindness may do much,
And his unkindness may defeat° my life,
But never taint my love. I cannot say "whore."
It does abhor° me now I speak the word;
To do the act that might the addition° earn                      170
Not the world's mass of vanity° could make me.

  [*She rises.*]

**IAGO:**   I pray you, be content. 'Tis but his humor.°
The business of the state does him offense,
And he does chide with you.

**DESDEMONA:**   If 'twere no other—                              175

**IAGO:**   It is but so, I warrant. [*Trumpets within.*]
Hark, how these instruments summon you to supper!
The messengers of Venice stays the meat.°
Go in, and weep not. All things shall be well.

                    [*Exeunt Desdemona and Emilia.*]

  [*Enter Roderigo.*]

How now, Roderigo?                                                180

**RODERIGO:**   I do not find that thou deal'st justly with me.

---

151 **within door** i.e., not so loud   152 **squire** fellow   153 **seamy side without** wrong side out
155 **Go to** i.e., that's enough   160 **discourse of thought** process of thinking   161 **that** if (also in line
163)   162 **Delighted them** took delight   163 **yet** still   166 **Comfort forswear** may heavenly comfort
forsake   167 **defeat** destroy   169 **abhor** (1) fill me with abhorrence (2) make me whorelike   170 **addition** title   171 **vanity** showy splendor   172 **humor** mood   178 **stays the meat** are waiting to dine

**IAGO:**    What in the contrary?

**RODERIGO:**    Every day thou daff'st me° with some device,° Iago, and rather, as it seems to me now, keep'st from me all conveniency° than suppliest me with the least advantage° of hope.    185
I will indeed no longer endure it, nor am I yet persuaded to put up° in peace what already I have foolishly suffered.

**IAGO:**    Will you hear me, Roderigo?

**RODERIGO:**    Faith, I have heard too much, for your words and performances are no kin together.

**IAGO:**    You charge me most unjustly.    190

**RODERIGO:**    With naught but truth. I have wasted myself out of my means. The jewels you have had from me to deliver° Desdemona would half have corrupted a votarist.° You have told me she hath received them and returned me expectations and comforts of sudden respect° and acquaintance, but I find none.    195

**IAGO:**    Well, go to, very well.

**RODERIGO:**    "Very well"! "Go to"! I cannot go to,° man, nor 'tis not very well. By this hand, I think it is scurvy, and begin to find myself fopped° in it.

**IAGO:**    Very well.

**RODERIGO:**    I tell you 'tis not very well.° I will make myself known    200
to Desdemona. If she will return me my jewels, I will give over my suit and repent my unlawful solicitation; if not, assure yourself I will seek satisfaction° of you.

**IAGO:**    You have said now?°

**RODERIGO:**    Ay, and said nothing but what I protest intendment° of doing.

**IAGO:**    Why, now I see there's mettle in thee, and even from this    205
instant do build on thee a better opinion than ever before. Give me thy hand, Roderigo. Thou hast taken against me a most just exception; but yet I protest I have dealt most directly in thy affair.

**RODERIGO:**    It hath not appeared.

**IAGO:**    I grant indeed it hath not appeared, and your suspicion is    210
not without wit and judgment. But, Roderigo, if thou hast that in thee indeed which I have greater reason to believe now than ever—I mean purpose, courage, and valor—this night show it.
If thou the next night following enjoy not Desdemona, take me from this world with treachery and devise engines for° my life.    215

**183 thou daff'st me** you put me off.  **device** excuse, trick  **184 conveniency** advantage, opportunity  **185 advantage** increase  **186 put up** submit to, tolerate  **192 deliver** deliver to  **193 votarist** nun  **194 sudden respect** immediate consideration  **197 I cannot go to** (Roderigo changes Iago's go to, an expression urging patience, to *I cannot go to,* "I have no opportunity for success in wooing.")  **198 fopped** fooled, duped  **200 not very well** (Roderigo changes Iago's *very well,* "all right, then," to *not very well,* "not at all good.")  **202 satisfaction** repayment. (The term normally means settling of accounts in a duel.)  **203 You ... now** have you finished?  **204 intendment** intention  **214 engines for** plots against

**RODERIGO:** Well, what is it? Is it within reason and compass?

**IAGO:** Sir, there is especial commission come from Venice to depute Cassio in Othello's place.

**RODERIGO:** Is that true? Why, then Othello and Desdemona return again to Venice.                                                                               220

**IAGO:** O, no; he goes into Mauritania and takes away with him the fair Desdemona, unless his abode be lingered here by some accident; wherein none can be so determinate° as the removing of Cassio.

**RODERIGO:** How do you mean, removing of him?

**IAGO:** Why, by making him uncapable of Othello's place—knocking        225
out his brains.

**RODERIGO:** And that you would have me to do?

**IAGO:** Ay, if you dare do yourself a profit and a right. He sups to-night with a harlotry,° and thither will I go to him. He knows not yet of his honorable fortune. If you will watch his going thence, which I will fashion to fall out° between twelve and        230
one, you may take him at your pleasure. I will be near to second your attempt, and he shall fall between us. Come, stand not amazed at it, but go along with me. I will show you such a ne-cessity in his death that you shall think yourself bound to put it on him. It is now high° suppertime, and the night grows to waste.° About it.                                                                                   235

**RODERIGO:** I will hear further reason for this.

**IAGO:** And you shall be satisfied.                                       [*Exeunt.*]

### Scene III. The Citadel

*Enter Othello, Lodovico, Desdemona, Emilia, and attendants.*

**LODOVICO:** I do beseech you, sir, trouble yourself no further.

**OTHELLO:** O, pardon me; 'twill do me good to walk.

**LODOVICO:** Madam, good night. I humbly thank your ladyship.

**DESDEMONA:** Your honor is most welcome.

**OTHELLO:**                                               Will you walk, sir?
O, Desdemona!                                                                       5

**DESDEMONA:** My lord?

**OTHELLO:** Get you to bed on th' instant.
I will be returned forthwith. Dismiss your attendant there. Look 't be done.

**DESDEMONA:** I will, my lord.                                             10

*Exit [Othello, with Lodovico and attendants].*

223 **determinate** conclusive   229 **harlotry** slut   230 **fall out** occur   234 **high** fully   235 **grows to waste** wastes away

**EMILIA:**   How goes it now? He looks gentler than he did.

**DESDEMONA:**   He says he will return incontinent,°
And hath commanded me to go to bed,
And bid me to dismiss you.

**EMILIA:**   Dismiss me?                                                                    15

**DESDEMONA:**   It was his bidding. Therefore, good Emilia,
Give me my nightly wearing, and adieu.
We must not now displease him.

**EMILIA:**   I would you had never seen him!

**DESDEMONA:**   So would not I. My love doth so approve him          20
That even his stubbornness,° his checks,° his frowns—
Prithee, unpin me—have grace and favor in them.

[*Emilia prepares Desdemona for bed.*]

**EMILIA:**   I have laid those sheets you bade me on the bed.

**DESDEMONA:**   All's one.° Good faith, how foolish are our minds!
If I do die before thee, prithee shroud me                                      25
In one of these same sheets.

**EMILIA:**                                    Come, come, you talk.°

**DESDEMONA:**   My mother had a maid called Barbary.
She was in love, and he she loved proved mad°
And did forsake her. She had a song of "Willow."
An old thing 'twas, but it expressed her fortune,                          30
And she died singing it. That song tonight
Will not go from my mind; I have much to do
But to go hang° my head all at one side
And sing it like poor Barbary. Prithee, dispatch.

**EMILIA:**   Shall I go fetch your nightgown?°                                   35

**DESDEMONA:**   No, unpin me here.
This Lodovico is a proper° man.

**EMILIA:**   A very handsome man.

**DESDEMONA:**   He speaks well.

**EMILIA:**   I know a lady in Venice would have walked barefoot to    40
Palestine for a touch of his nether lip.

**DESDEMONA**   [*singing*]:
"The poor soul sat sighing by a sycamore tree,
Sing all a green willow;°
Her hand on her bosom, her head on her knee,
Sing willow, willow, willow.                                                          45
The fresh streams ran by her and murmured her moans;
Sing willow, willow, willow;

12 **incontinent** immediately   21 **stubbornness** roughness   **checks** rebukes   24 **All's one** all right.
It doesn't really matter   26 **talk** i.e., prattle   28 **mad** wild, i.e., faithless   32–33 **I ... hang** I can
scarcely keep myself from hanging   35 **nightgown** dressing gown   37 **proper** handsome   43 **willow**
(A conventional emblem of disappointed love.)

Her salt tears fell from her, and softened the stones—"
Lay by these.
   [*Singing.*] "Sing willow, willow, willow—"      50
Prithee, hie thee.° He'll come anon.°
[*Singing.*] "Sing all a green willow must be my garland.
Let nobody blame him; his scorn I approve—"
Nay, that's not next.—Hark! Who is 't that knocks?

**EMILIA:**  It's the wind.

**DESDEMONA**   [*singing*]:
   "I called my love false love; but what said he then?      55
   Sing willow, willow, willow;
   If I court more women, you'll couch with more men."
So, get thee gone. Good night. Mine eyes do itch;
Doth that bode weeping?

**EMILIA:**                             'Tis neither here nor there.      60

**DESDEMONA:**  I have heard it said so. O, these men, these men!
Dost thou in conscience think—tell me, Emilia—
That there be women do abuse° their husbands
In such gross kind?

**EMILIA:**               There be some such, no question.

**DESDEMONA:**  Wouldst thou do such a deed for all the world?      65

**EMILIA:**  Why, would not you?

**DESDEMONA:**                     No, by this heavenly light!

**EMILIA:**  Nor I neither by this heavenly light;
I might do 't as well i' the dark.

**DESDEMONA:**  Wouldst thou do such a deed for all the world?

**EMILIA:**  The world's a huge thing. It is a great price      70
For a small vice.

**DESDEMONA:**  Good troth, I think thou wouldst not.

**EMILIA:**  By my troth, I think I should, and undo 't when I had
done. Marry, I would not do such a thing for a joint ring,° nor for
measures of lawn,° nor for gowns, petticoats, nor caps, nor any
petty exhibition.° But for all the whole world! Uds° pity, who      75
would not make her husband a cuckold to make him a monarch?
I should venture purgatory for 't.

**DESDEMONA:**  Beshrew me if I would do such a wrong
For the whole world.

**EMILIA:**  Why, the wrong is but a wrong i' the world, and having
the world for your labor, 'tis a wrong in your own world, and you
might quickly make it right.      80

**DESDEMONA:**  I do not think there is any such woman.

---

**51 hie thee** hurry.   **anon** right away   **63 abuse** deceive   **74 joint ring** a ring made in separate
halves.   **lawn** fine linen   **75 exhibition** gift   **76 Uds** God's

**EMILIA:**   Yes, a dozen, and as many

To th' vantage° as would store° the world they played° for.                85

But I do think it is their husbands' faults

If wives do fall. Say that they slack their duties°

And pour our treasures into foreign laps,°

Or else break out in peevish jealousies,

Throwing restraint upon us? Or say they strike us,°                90

Or scant our former having in despite?°

Why, we have galls,° and though we have some grace,

Yet have we some revenge. Let husbands know

Their wives have sense° like them. They see, and smell,

And have their palates both for sweet and sour,                95

As husbands have. What is it that they do

When they change us for others? Is it sport?°

I think it is. And doth affection° breed it?

I think it doth. Is 't frailty that thus errs?

It is so, too. And have not we affections,                100

Desires for sport, and frailty, as men have?

Then let them use us well; else let them know,

The ills we do, their ills instruct us so.

**DESDEMONA:**   Good night, good night. God me such uses° send

Not to pick bad from bad, but by bad mend!°                105

[*Exeunt.*]

## Act V

**Scene I. A Street in Cyprus**

*Enter Iago and Roderigo.*

**IAGO:**   Here stand behind this bulk.° Straight will he come.

Wear thy good rapier bare,° and put it home.

Quick, quick! Fear nothing. I'll be at thy elbow.

It makes us or it mars us. Think on that,

And fix most firm thy resolution.                5

**RODERIGO:**   Be near at hand. I may miscarry in 't.

**IAGO:**   Here, at thy hand. Be bold, and take thy stand.

[*Iago stands aside. Roderigo conceals himself.*]

**85 To th' vantage** in addition, to boot   **store** populate   **played** (1) gambled (2) sported sexually
**87 duties** marital duties   **88 pour … laps** i.e., are unfaithful, give what is rightfully ours (semen) to
other women   **90 Throwing … us** i.e., jealously restricting our freedom to see other men   **91 scant
… despite** reduce our allowance to spite us   **92 have galls** i.e., are capable of resenting injury and
insult   **94 sense** physical sense   **97 sport** sexual pastime   **98 affection** passion   **104 uses** habit,
practice   **105 Not … mend** i.e., not to learn bad conduct from others' badness (as Emilia has suggested women learn from men), but to mend my ways by perceiving what badness is, making spiritual
benefit out of evil and adversity
**1 bulk** framework projecting from the front of a shop   **2 bare** unsheathed

**RODERIGO:** I have no great devotion to the deed;
And yet he hath given me satisfying reasons.
'Tis but a man gone. Forth, my sword! He dies.                    10

[*He draws.*]

**IAGO:** I have rubbed this young quat° almost to the sense,°
And he grows angry. Now, whether he kill Cassio
Or Cassio him, or each do kill the other,
Every way makes my gain. Live Roderigo,°
He calls me to a restitution large                               15
Of gold and jewels that I bobbed° from him
As gifts to Desdemona.
It must not be. If Cassio do remain,
He hath a daily beauty in his life
That makes me ugly; and besides, the Moor                        20
May unfold° me to him; there stand I in much peril.
No, he must die. Be 't so. I hear him coming.

[*Enter Cassio.*]

**RODERIGO**[*coming forth*]: I know his gait, 'tis he.—Villain, thou diest!

[*He attacks Cassio.*]

**CASSIO:** That thrust had been mine enemy indeed,
But that my coat° is better than thou know'st.                   25
I will make proof° of thine.

[*He draws, and wounds Roderigo.*]

**RODERIGO:**                          O, I am slain! [*He falls.*]

[*Iago, from behind, wounds Cassio in the leg, and exits.*]

**CASSIO:** I am maimed forever. Help, ho! Murder! Murder!

[*Enter Othello.*]

**OTHELLO:** The voice of Cassio! Iago keeps his word.
**RODERIGO:** O, villain that I am!
**OTHELLO:** It is even so.                                      30
**CASSIO:** O, help, ho! Light! A surgeon!
**OTHELLO:** 'Tis he. O brave Iago, honest and just,
That hast such noble sense of thy friend's wrong!
Thou teachest me. Minion,° your dear lies dead,
And your unblest fate hies.° Strumpet, I come.                   35
Forth of° my heart those charms, thine eyes, are blotted;
Thy bed, lust-stained, shall with lust's blood be spotted.

[*Exit Othello.*]

11 **quat** pimple, pustule.  **to the sense** to the quick  14 **Live Roderigo** if Roderigo lives  16 **bobbed** swindled  21 **unfold** expose  25 **coat** (Possibly a garment of mail under the outer clothing, or simply a tougher coat than Roderigo expected.)  26 **proof** a test  34 **Minion** hussy (i.e., Desdemona)  35 **hies** hastens on  36 **Forth of** from out

[*Enter Lodovico and Gratiano.*]

**CASSIO:**  What ho! No watch? No passage?° Murder! Murder!

**GRATIANO:**  'Tis some mischance. The voice is very direful.

**CASSIO:**  O, help!                                                                        40

**LODOVICO:**  Hark!

**RODERIGO:**  O wretched villain!

**LODOVICO:**  Two or three groan.'Tis heavy° night;
These may be counterfeits. Let's think 't unsafe
To come in to° the cry without more help.                                45

[*They remain near the entrance.*]

**RODERIGO:**  Nobody come? Then shall I bleed to death.

*Enter Iago* [*in his shirtsleeves, with a light*].

**LODOVICO:**  Hark!

**GRATIANO:**  Here's one comes in his shirt, with light and weapons.

**IAGO:**  Who's there? Whose noise is this that cries on° murder?

**LODOVICO:**  We do not know.

**IAGO:**                            Did not you hear a cry?                    50

**CASSIO:**  Here, here! For heaven's sake, help me!

**IAGO:**                                          What's the matter?

[*He moves toward Cassio.*]

**GRATIANO** [*to Lodovico*]:  This is Othello's ancient, as I take it.

**LODOVICO** [*to Gratiano*]:  The same indeed, a very valiant fellow.

**IAGO** [*to Cassio*]:  What° are you here that cry so grievously?

**CASSIO:**  Iago? O, I am spoiled,° undone by villains!                    55
Give me some help.

**IAGO:**  O me, Lieutenant! What villains have done this?

**CASSIO:**  I think that one of them is hereabout,
And cannot make° away.

**IAGO:**                            O treacherous villains!

[*To Lodovico and Gratiano.*]

What are you there? Come in, and give some help. [*They advance.*]  60

**RODERIGO:**  O, help me there!

**CASSIO:**  That's one of them.

**IAGO:**                            O murderous slave! O villain!

[*He stabs Roderigo.*]

**RODERIGO:**  O damned Iago! O inhuman dog!

**IAGO:**  Kill men i' the dark?—Where be these bloody thieves?—

---

38 **passage** people passing by   43 **heavy** thick, dark   45 **come in to** approach   49 **cries on** cries
out   54 **What** who (also at lines 60 and 66)   55 **spoiled** ruined, done for   59 **make** get

How silent is this town!—Ho! Murder, murder!—    65
[*To Lodovico and Gratiano.*] What may you be? Are you of good
   or evil?
**LODOVICO:**  As you shall prove us, praise° us.
**IAGO:**  Signor Lodovico?
**LODOVICO:**  He, sir.
**IAGO:**  I cry you mercy.° Here's Cassio hurt by villains.    70
**GRATIANO:**  Cassio?
**IAGO:**  How is 't, brother?
**CASSIO:**  My leg is cut in two.
**IAGO:**  Marry, heaven forbid!
   Light, gentlemen! I'll bind it with my shirt.    75

[*He hands them the light, and tends to Cassio's wound.*]

[*Enter Bianca.*]

**BIANCA:**  What is the matter, ho? Who is 't that cried?
**IAGO:**  Who is 't that cried?
**BIANCA:**                 O my dear Cassio!
   My sweet Cassio! O Cassio, Cassio, Cassio!
**IAGO:**  O notable strumpet! Cassio, may you suspect
   Who they should be that have thus mangled you?    80
**CASSIO:**  No.
**GRATIANO:**  I am sorry to find you thus. I have been to seek you.
**IAGO:**  Lend me a garter. [*He applies a tourniquet.*] So.—O, for a chair,°
   To bear him easily hence!
**BIANCA:**  Alas, he faints! O Cassio, Cassio, Cassio!    85
**IAGO:**  Gentlemen all, I do suspect this trash
   To be a party in this injury.—
   Patience awhile, good Cassio.—Come, come;
   Lend me a light. [*He shines the light on Roderigo.*] Know we this
      face or no?
   Alas, my friend and my dear countryman    90
   Roderigo! No.—Yes, sure.—O heaven! Roderigo!
**GRATIANO:**  What, of Venice?
**IAGO:**  Even he, sir. Did you know him?
**GRATIANO:**  Know him? Ay.
**IAGO:**  Signor Gratiano? I cry your gentle° pardon.    95
   These bloody accidents° must excuse my manners
   That so neglected you.
**GRATIANO:**  I am glad to see you.
**IAGO:**  How do you, Cassio? O, a chair, a chair!
**GRATIANO:**  Roderigo!

**67 praise** appraise  **70 I cry you mercy** I beg your pardon  **83 chair** litter  **95 gentle** noble
**96 accidents** sudden events

**IAGO:**   He, he, 'tis he. [*A litter is brought in.*] O, that's well said;° 
the chair.                                                                          100
Some good man bear him carefully from hence;
I'll fetch the General's surgeon. [*To Bianca.*] For you, mistress,
Save you your labor.°—He that lies slain here, Cassio,
Was my dear friend. What malice° was between you?

**CASSIO:**   None in the world, nor do I know the man.                             105

**IAGO** [*to Bianca*]:   What, look you pale?—O, bear him out o' th' air.°

[*Cassio and Roderigo are borne off.*]

Stay you,° good gentlemen.—Look you pale, mistress?—
Do you perceive the gastness° of her eye?—
Nay, if you stare,° we shall hear more anon.—
Behold her well; I pray you, look upon her.                                        110
Do you see, gentlemen? Nay, guiltiness
Will speak, though tongues were out of use.

[*Enter Emilia.*]

**EMILIA:**   'Las, what's the matter? What's the matter, husband?

**IAGO:**   Cassio hath here been set on in the dark
By Roderigo and fellows that are scaped.                                           115
He's almost slain, and Roderigo dead.

**EMILIA:**   Alas, good gentleman! Alas, good Cassio!

**IAGO:**   This is the fruits of whoring. Prithee, Emilia,
Go know° of Cassio where he supped tonight.
[*To Bianca.*] What, do you shake at that?                                          120

**BIANCA:**   He supped at my house, but I therefore shake not.

**IAGO:**   O, did he so? I charge you go with me.

**EMILIA:**   O, fie upon thee, strumpet!

**BIANCA:**   I am no strumpet, but of life as honest°
As you that thus abuse me.                                                          125

**EMILIA:**   As I? Faugh! Fie upon thee!

**IAGO:**   Kind gentlemen, let's go see poor Cassio dressed.°—
Come, mistress, you must tell's another tale.
Emilia, run you to the citadel
And tell my lord and lady what hath happed.—                                       130
Will you go on afore? [*Aside.*] This is the night
That either makes me or fordoes° me quite.                    *Exeunt.*

**100 well said** well done   **103 Save ... labor** i.e., never you mind tending Cassio   **104 malice** enmity   **106 bear ... air** (Fresh air was thought to be dangerous for a wound.)   **107 Stay you** (Lodovico and Gratiano are evidently about to leave.)   **108 gastness** terror   **109 stare** (Iago pretends to interpret Bianca's wild looks as an involuntary confession of guilt.)   **119 know** learn   **124 honest** chaste   **127 Cassio dressed** Cassio's wounds dressed   **132 fordoes** undoes, ruins   **[s.d.] in her bed** (Either the curtains are drawn back to reveal the bed in a recessed area backstage, or the bed is "thrust out" onstage as the scene begins.)

**Scene II. A bedchamber in the Citadel**

*Enter Othello [with a light], and Desdemona in her bed.*°

**OTHELLO:** It is the cause,° it is the cause, my soul.
Let me not name it to you, you chaste stars!
It is the cause. Yet I'll not shed her blood,
Nor scar that whiter skin of hers than snow,
And smooth as monumental° alabaster.                                    5
Yet she must die, else she'll betray more men.
Put out the light, and then put out the light.°
If I quench thee, thou flaming minister,°
I can again thy former light restore,
Should I repent me;° but once put out thy light,                        10
Thou cunning'st pattern° of excelling nature,
I know not where is that Promethean heat°
That can thy light relume.° When I have plucked thy rose,
I cannot give it vital growth again;
It needs must wither. I'll smell thee on the tree.                      15

[*He kisses her.*]

O balmy breath, that dost almost persuade
Justice to break her sword! One more, one more.
Be thus when thou art dead, and I will kill thee,
And love thee after. One more, and that's the last.

[*He kisses her.*]

So sweet was ne'er so fatal. I must weep,                               20
But they are cruel° tears. This sorrow's heavenly;
It strikes where it doth love.° She wakes.
**DESDEMONA:** Who's there? Othello?
**OTHELLO:** Ay, Desdemona.
**DESDEMONA:** Will you come to bed, my lord?                            25
**OTHELLO:** Have you prayed tonight, Desdemon?
**DESDEMONA:** Ay, my lord.
**OTHELLO:** If you bethink yourself of any crime°
Unreconciled as yet to heaven and grace,
Solicit° for it straight.°                                              30
**DESDEMONA:** Alack, my lord, what may you mean by that?

---

**1 cause** i.e., cause of justice, the offense itself, which Othello must correct as an agent of justice
**5 monumental** i.e., used in making tombs and funeral monuments  **7 the light ... light** the torch or
lamp ... Desdemona's life  **8 flaming minister** torch or lamp that serves me  **10 repent me** change
my mind  **11 Thou ... pattern** you skillfully wrought perfect example  **12 Promethean heat** divine
fire (alluding to the theft of fire from heaven by Prometheus)  **13 relume** rekindle  **21 cruel** unrelenting  **22 It ... love** (Compare Hebrews 12:6: "For whom the Lord loveth he chasteneth.")
**28 crime** sin  **30 Solicit** petition, pray.  **straight** immediately

**OTHELLO:**  Well, do it, and be brief. I will walk by.

I would not kill thy unprepared spirit.

No, heaven forfend!° I would not kill thy soul.

**DESDEMONA:**  Talk you of killing?

**OTHELLO:**                      Ay, I do.

**DESDEMONA:**                              Then heaven          35

Have mercy on me!

**OTHELLO:**  Amen, with all my heart!

**DESDEMONA:**  If you say so, I hope you will not kill me.

**OTHELLO:**  Humh!

**DESDEMONA:**  And yet I fear you; for you're fatal then

When your eyes roll so. Why I should fear I know not,          40

Since guiltiness I know not; but yet I feel I fear.

**OTHELLO:**  Think on thy sins.

**DESDEMONA:**                      They are loves I bear to you.°

**OTHELLO:**  Ay, and for that thou diest.

**DESDEMONA:**  That death's unnatural that kills for loving.

Alas, why gnaw you so your nether lip?          45

Some bloody passion shakes your very frame.

These are portents; but yet I hope, I hope,

They do not point on° me.

**OTHELLO:**  Peace, and be still!

**DESDEMONA:**  I will so. What's the matter?          50

**OTHELLO:**  That handkerchief which I so loved and gave thee

Thou gav'st to Cassio.

**DESDEMONA:**                  No, by my life and soul!

Send for the man and ask him.

**OTHELLO:**  Sweet soul, take heed, take heed of perjury.

Thou art on thy deathbed.          55

**DESDEMONA:**  Ay, but not yet to die.

**OTHELLO:**                              Yes, presently.°

Therefore confess thee freely of thy sin;

For to deny each article with oath

Cannot remove nor choke the strong conception°

That I do groan withal.° Thou art to die.          60

**DESDEMONA:**  Then Lord have mercy on me!

**OTHELLO:**                              I say, amen.

**DESDEMONA:**  And have you mercy too! I never did

Offend° you in my life; never loved Cassio

But with such general warranty° of heaven

---

**34 forfend** forbid   **42 They are ... you** i.e., if I sinned, it was in loving you more than my father or
more than God   **48 point on** point at, predict what is to happen to   **56 presently** immediately
**59 conception** (1) belief in your guilt (2) plan in my mind   **60 groan withal** (1) groan at in sorrow
(2) as in giving birth   **63 Offend** wrong   **64 warranty** sanction

As I might love. I never gave him token.                                          65
**OTHELLO:**   By heaven, I saw my handkerchief in 's hand.
   O perjured woman! Thou dost stone° my heart,
   And makes me call what I intend to do
   A murder, which I thought a sacrifice.
   I saw the handkerchief.
**DESDEMONA:**                 He found it, then.                              70
   I never gave it him. Send for him hither;
   Let him confess a truth.
**OTHELLO:**                 He hath confessed.
**DESDEMONA:**   What, my lord?
**OTHELLO:**   That he hath used thee.
**DESDEMONA:**                 How? Unlawfully?
**OTHELLO:**                                 Ay.
**DESDEMONA:**   He will not say so.
**OTHELLO:**                 No, his mouth is stopped;                         75
   Honest Iago hath ta'en order° for 't.
**DESDEMONA:**   O, my fear interprets. What, is he dead?
**OTHELLO:**   Had all his hairs been lives, my great revenge
   Had stomach for them all.
**DESDEMONA:**   Alas, he is betrayed and I undone! [*She weeps.*]           80
**OTHELLO:**   Out, strumpet! Weep'st thou for him to my face?
**DESDEMONA:**   O, banish me, my lord, but kill me not!
**OTHELLO:**   Down, strumpet!
**DESDEMONA:**   Kill me tomorrow; let me live tonight!
**OTHELLO:**   Nay, if you strive—                                            85
**DESDEMONA:**   But half an hour!
**OTHELLO:**                 Being done,° there is no pause.
**DESDEMONA:**   But while I say one prayer!
**OTHELLO:**                                 It is too late.

   [*Smothers her.*]

**EMILIA** [*at the door*]:   My lord, my lord! What, ho! My lord, my lord!
**OTHELLO:**   What noise is this? Not dead? Not yet quite dead?
   I that am cruel am yet merciful;                                              90
   I would not have thee linger in thy pain.

   [*He dispatches her.*]

                              So, so.

**EMILIA** [*within*]:   What, ho! My lord, my lord!
**OTHELLO:**                                 Who's there?
**EMILIA** [*within*]:   O, good my lord, I would speak a word with you!

**67 stone** turn to stone, harden   **76 ta'en order** taken measures   **86 Being done** i.e., since justice has
begun its relentless course

**OTHELLO:**   Yes, 'tis Emilia.—By and by.—She's dead.
'Tis like° she comes to speak of Cassio's death.—                                       95
The noise was here.° Ha! No more moving?
Still as the grave. Shall she come in? Were 't good?—
I think she stirs again. No. What's best to do?
If she come in, she'll sure speak to my wife.
My wife! My wife! What wife? I have no wife.                                          100
O, insupportable! O heavy hour!
Methinks it should be now a huge eclipse
Of sun and moon, and that th' affrighted globe
Should yawn° at alteration.°
**EMILIA** [*within*]:                         I do beseech you
That I may speak with you, O, good my lord!                                           105
**OTHELLO:**   I had forgot thee. O, come in, Emilia.—
Soft,° by and by. Let me the curtains draw.—

[*He closes the bed-curtains and opens the door.*]

Where art thou?

[*Enter Emilia.*]

                          What's the matter with thee now?
**EMILIA:**   O, my good lord, yonder's foul murders done!
**OTHELLO:**   What, now?                                                             110
**EMILIA:**   But now, my lord.
**OTHELLO:**   It is the very error° of the moon;
She comes more nearer earth than she was wont,
And makes men mad.
**EMILIA:**   Cassio, my lord, hath killed a young Venetian                           115
Called Roderigo.
**OTHELLO:**   Roderigo killed?
And Cassio killed?
**EMILIA:**   No, Cassio is not killed.
**OTHELLO:**   Not Cassio killed? Then murder's out of tune,
And sweet revenge grows harsh.
**DESDEMONA:**   O, falsely, falsely murdered!                                        120
**EMILIA:**   O Lord, what cry is that?
**OTHELLO:**   That? What?
**EMILIA:**   Out° and alas, that was my lady's voice.

[*She opens the bed-curtains.*]

---

**95 like** likely that   **96 here** (The Folio's *high* is possible, suggesting that the commotion of the attack on Cassio was loud.)   **104 yawn** gape in amazement, i.e., move in an earthquake. (According to Pliny, earthquakes often happen during eclipses.)   **at alteration** at these cataclysmic events in nature, well-suited to express the horror of Desdemona's death   **107 Soft** wait a minute   **112 error** aberration, irregularity   **123 Out** (A cry of dismay, intensifying *alas.*)

Help, help, ho, help! O lady, speak again!
Sweet Desdemona! O sweet mistress, speak!                            125
**DESDEMONA:**   A guiltless death I die.
**EMILIA:**   O, who hath done this deed?
**DESDEMONA:**   Nobody; I myself. Farewell.
Commend me to my kind lord. O, farewell!              [*She dies.*]
**OTHELLO:**   Why, how should she be murdered?
**EMILIA:**                                          Alas, who knows?    130
**OTHELLO:**   You heard her say herself it was not I.
**EMILIA:**   She said so. I must needs report the truth.
**OTHELLO:**   She's like a liar gone to burning hell!
'Twas I that killed her.
**EMILIA:**                       O, the more angel she,
And you the blacker devil!                                           135
**OTHELLO:**   She turned to folly,° and she was a whore.
**EMILIA:**   Thou dost belie° her, and thou art a devil.
**OTHELLO:**   She was false as water.
**EMILIA:**                           Thou art rash as fire to say
That she was false. O, she was heavenly true!                       140
**OTHELLO:**   Cassio did top her. Ask thy husband else.°
O, I were damned beneath all depth in hell
But that I did proceed upon just grounds
To this extremity. Thy husband knew it all.
**EMILIA:**   My husband?                                             145
**OTHELLO:**   Thy husband.
**EMILIA:**   That she was false to wedlock?
**OTHELLO:**   Ay, with Cassio. Nay, had she been true,
If heaven would make me such another world
Of one entire and perfect chrysolite,°                              150
I'd not have sold her for it.
**EMILIA:**   My husband?
**OTHELLO:**   Ay, 'twas he that told me on her first.
An honest man he is, and hates the slime
That sticks on filthy deeds.                                        155
**EMILIA:**   My husband?
**OTHELLO:**   What needs this iterance,° woman? I say thy husband.
**EMILIA:**   O mistress, villainy hath made mocks with° love!
My husband say she was false?
**OTHELLO:**                           He, woman;
I say thy husband. Dost understand the word?                        160
My friend, thy husband, honest, honest Iago.

---

136 **folly** i.e., wantonness, fleshly sin   137 **belie** slander   141 **else** i.e., if you don't believe me
150 **chrysolite** precious topaz   157 **iterance** iteration, repetition   158 **made mocks with** derided, made sport of

**EMILIA:**  If he say so, may his pernicious soul
    Rot half a grain a day! He lies to th' heart.
    She was too fond of her most filthy bargain.
**OTHELLO:**  Ha?                                    [*He draws.*]        165
**EMILIA:**  Do thy worst!
    This deed of thine is no more worthy heaven
    Than thou wast worthy her.
**OTHELLO:**                      Peace, you were best.°
**EMILIA:**  Thou hast not half that power to do me harm
    As I have to be hurt.° O gull!° O dolt!                    170
    As ignorant as dirt! Thou hast done a deed—
    I care not for thy sword; I'll make thee known,
    Though I lost twenty lives.—Help! Help, ho, help!
    The Moor hath killed my mistress! Murder, murder!

[*Enter Montano, Gratiano, and Iago.*]

**MONTANO:**  What is the matter? How now, General?            175
**EMILIA:**  O, are you come, Iago? You have done well,
    That men must lay their murders on your neck.
**GRATIANO:**  What is the matter?
**EMILIA** [*to Iago*]:  Disprove this villain, if thou be'st a man.
    He says thou toldst him that his wife was false.        180
    I know thou didst not; thou'rt not such a villain.
    Speak, for my heart is full.
**IAGO:**  I told him what I thought, and told no more
    Than what he found himself was apt° and true.
**EMILIA:**  But did you ever tell him she was false?        185
**IAGO:**  I did.
**EMILIA:**  You told a lie, an odious, damnèd lie!
    Upon my soul, a lie, a wicked lie.
    She false with Cassio? Did you say with Cassio?
**IAGO:**  With Cassio, mistress. Go to, charm° your tongue.    190
**EMILIA:**  I will not charm my tongue; I am bound to speak.
    My mistress here lies murdered in her bed—
**ALL:**  O heavens forfend!
**EMILIA:**  And your reports have set the murder on.
**OTHELLO:**  Nay, stare not, masters. It is true indeed.    195
**GRATIANO:**  'Tis a strange truth.
**MONTANO:**  O monstrous act!
**EMILIA:**                      Villainy, villainy, villainy!
    I think upon 't—I think I smell 't! O villainy!

---

**168 you were best** it would be best for you    **170 to be hurt** i.e., to endure hurt.    **gull** dupe    **184**
**apt** plausible    **190 charm** keep silent (as though by a magic spell)

I thought so then°—I'll kill myself for grief—
O villainy, villainy!                                                       200
**IAGO:**   What, are you mad? I charge you, get you home.
**EMILIA:**   Good gentlemen, let me have leave to speak.
'Tis proper I obey him, but not now.
Perchance, Iago, I will ne'er go home.
**OTHELLO:** O! O! O!          [*Othello falls on the bed.*°]
**EMILIA:**               Nay, lay thee down and roar,                       205
For thou hast killed the sweetest innocent
That e'er did lift up eye.°
**OTHELLO** [*rising*]:          O, she was foul!
I scarce did know you, uncle. There lies your niece,
Whose breath indeed these hands have newly stopped.
I know this act shows° horrible and grim.                                   210
**GRATIANO:**   Poor Desdemona! I am glad thy father's dead.
Thy match was mortal to him, and pure grief
Shore his old thread° in twain. Did he live now,
This sight would make him do a desperate turn,°
Yea, curse his better angel from his side,                                  215
And fall to reprobance.°
**OTHELLO:**   'Tis pitiful. But yet Iago knows
That she with Cassio hath the act of shame
A thousand times committed. Cassio confessed it;
And she did gratify° his amorous works                                      220
With that recognizance° and pledge of love
Which I first gave her. I saw it in his hand;
It was a handkerchief, an antique token
My father gave my mother.
**EMILIA:**   O God! O heavenly God!                                        225
**IAGO:**   Zounds, hold your peace.
**EMILIA:**                     'Twill out, 'twill out! I peace?
No, I will speak as liberal as the north.°
Let heaven and men and devils, let them all,
All, all, cry shame against me, yet I'll speak.
**IAGO:**   Be wise, and get you home.
**EMILIA:**                     I will not.

[*Iago threatens Emilia.*]

**GRATIANO:**                         Fie                                   230
Your sword upon a woman?

---

**199 then** (Perhaps at Act III, Scene iii, lines 331–332 and Act IV, Scene ii, lines 137–154.)
**205 [s.d.] Othello ... bed** (This direction is from the Quarto, as also *He kisses her* at line 19 and *She dies* at line 129.)   **207 lift up eye** i.e., lift her eyes to heaven   **210 shows** looks   **213 Shore ... thread** sheared the thread of his old age (as Atropos, one of the three Fates, was thought to do)   **214 turn** deed   **216 reprobance** damnation, i.e., suicide   **220 gratify** reward   **221 recognizance** token   **227 liberal as the north** freely as the north wind (blows)

**EMILIA:**   O thou dull Moor! That handkerchief thou speak'st of
I found by fortune and did give my husband;
For often, with a solemn earnestness,
More than indeed belonged° to such a trifle,                                    235
He begged of me to steal 't.
**IAGO:**                                Villainous whore!
**EMILIA:**   She give it Cassio? No, alas! I found it,
And I did give 't my husband.
**IAGO:**                                Filth, thou liest!
**EMILIA:**   By heaven, I do not, I do not, gentlemen.
O murderous coxcomb!° What should such a fool                                   240
Do with so good a wife?
**OTHELLO:**   Are there no stones° in heaven
But what serves for the thunder?—Precious° villain!

[*He runs at Iago; Montano disarms Othello. Iago, from behind,
stabs Emilia.*°]

**GRATIANO:**   The woman falls! Sure he hath killed his wife.
**EMILIA:**   Ay, ay. O, lay me by my mistress' side.                           245

Exit [*Iago.*]

**GRATIANO:**   He's gone, but his wife's killed.
**MONTANO:**   'Tis a notorious villain. Take you this weapon,
Which I have here recovered from the Moor.
Come, guard the door without. Let him not pass,
But kill him rather. I'll after that same villain,                             250
For 'tis a damnèd slave.

Exit [*with all but Othello and Emilia, who has been laid by
Desdemona's side*].

**OTHELLO:**   I am not valiant neither,
But every puny whipster° gets my sword.
But why should honor° outlive honesty?°
Let it go all.
**EMILIA:**      What did thy song bode, lady?                                  255
Hark, canst thou hear me? I will play the swan,
And die in music. [*She sings.*] "Willow, willow, willow."
Moor, she was chaste. She loved thee, cruel Moor.
So come my soul to bliss as I speak true.

---

235 **belonged** was appropriate   240 **coxcomb** fool. (Addressed to Othello.)   242 **stones** bolts, such
as those used for thunderbolts   243 **Precious** i.e., arrant, utter.   **[s.d.] He ... Emilia** (The Quarto
text reads, "The Moor runs at Iago. Iago kills his wife." The Quarto also specifies the exit of Iago at line
245 and the death of Emilia at line 260.)   253 **whipster** contemptible fellow (one who is always ready
to whip out his sword)   254 **honor** i.e., the bravery for which one enjoys a soldier's reputation.
**honesty** true integrity

So speaking as I think, alas, I die.          [*She dies.*]          260

**OTHELLO:**   I have another weapon in this chamber;
It was a sword of Spain, the ice-brook's temper°—
O, here it is. [*He finds a sword.*] Uncle, I must come forth.

**GRATIANO** [*within*]:   If thou attempt it, it will cost thee dear.
Thou hast no weapon, and perforce must suffer.          265

**OTHELLO:**   Look in upon me then and speak with me,
Or, naked° as I am, I will assault thee.

[*Enter Gratiano.*]

**GRATIANO:**   What is the matter?

**OTHELLO:**                          Behold, I have a weapon;
A better never did itself sustain
Upon a soldier's thigh. I have seen the day          270
That, with this little arm and this good sword,
I have made my way through more impediments
Than twenty times your stop.° But O, vain boast!
Who can control his fate? 'Tis not so now.
Be not afraid, though you do see me weaponed;          275
Here is my journey's end, here is my butt°
And very seamark° of my utmost sail.

[*Gratiano steps back.*]
Do you go back dismayed? 'Tis a lost° fear;
Man but a rush° against Othello's breast
And he retires. Where should Othello go?          280

[*He turns to Desdemona.*]

Now, how dost thou look now? O ill-starred wench!
Pale as thy smock! When we shall meet at compt,°
This look of thine will hurl my soul from heaven,
And fiends will snatch at it. Cold, cold, my girl?
Even like thy chastity. O cursèd, cursèd slave!°          285
Whip me, ye devils,
From the possession of this heavenly sight!
Blow me about in winds! Roast me in sulfur!
Wash me in steep-down gulfs of liquid fire!
O Desdemon! Dead, Desdemon! Dead! O! O!          290

*Enter Lodovico, Cassio* [*carried in a litter*°]*, Montano, and Iago*
[*prisoner*]*, with officers.*

---

**262 the ice-brook's temper** tempered in ice-cold water   **267 naked** unarmed   **273 stop** power (to stop)   **276 butt** goal, limit (an archery term)   **277 seamark** beacon (marking his destination or limit)   **278 lost** wasted, unneeded   **279 Man ... rush** wield no more than a reed   **282 compt** account, judgment day   **285 slave** i.e., Othello himself   **290 [s.d.] in a litter** (The Quarto specifies that Cassio is "in a chair.")

**LODOVICO:**   Where is this rash and most unfortunate man?

**OTHELLO:**   That's he that was Othello. Here I am.

**LODOVICO:**   Where is that viper? Bring the villain forth.

[*Iago is led forward.*]

**OTHELLO:**   I look down towards his feet;° but that's a fable.

If that thou be'st a devil, I cannot kill thee.                                   295

[*He wounds Iago.*]

**LODOVICO:**   Wrench his sword from him.

[*Othello is disarmed.*]

**IAGO:**                                       I bleed, sir, but not killed.

**OTHELLO:**   I am not sorry neither. I'd have thee live,

For in my sense° 'tis happiness to die.

**LODOVICO:**   O thou Othello, that was once so good,

Fall'n in the practice° of a cursèd slave,°                                       300

What shall be said to thee?

**OTHELLO:**                         Why, anything.

An honorable murderer, if you will,

For naught I did in hate, but all in honor.

**LODOVICO:**   This wretch hath part confessed his villainy.

Did you and he consent° in Cassio's death?                                       305

**OTHELLO:**   Ay.

**CASSIO:**   Dear General, I never gave you cause.

**OTHELLO:**   I do believe it, and I ask your pardon.

Will you, I pray, demand that demi-devil

Why he hath thus ensnared my soul and body?                                       310

**IAGO:**   Demand me nothing. What you know, you know.

From this time forth I never will speak word.

**LODOVICO:**   What, not to pray?

**GRATIANO:**   Torments° will ope your lips.

**OTHELLO:**   Well, thou dost best.                                       315

**LODOVICO:**   Sir, you shall understand what hath befall'n,

Which, as I think, you know not. Here is a letter

Found in the pocket of the slain Roderigo;

And here another. [*He produces letters.*] The one of them

imports

The death of Cassio, to be undertook                                       320

By Roderigo.

---

**294 towards his feet** i.e., to see if they are cloven, as the devil's are fabled to be   **298 in my sense**
to one who feels as I do   **300 in the practice** through the plotting, into the snare.   **slave** villain
**305 consent** agree   **314 Torments** torture   **322 gross** monstrous

**OTHELLO:**   O villain!

**CASSIO:**                    Most heathenish and most gross!°

**LODOVICO** [*showing another paper*]:   Now here's another
   discontented° paper
   Found in his pocket too. And this, it seems,
   Roderigo meant t' have sent this damnèd villain;                    325
   But that belike° Iago in the interim
   Came in and satisfied him.°

**OTHELLO:**   O thou pernicious caitiff!—
   How came you, Cassio, by that handkerchief
   That was my wife's?

**CASSIO:**                    I found it in my chamber;                    330
   And he himself confessed but even now
   That there he dropped it for a special purpose
   Which wrought to his desire.°

**OTHELLO:**                    O fool, fool, fool!

**CASSIO:**   There is besides in Roderigo's letter
   How he upbraids Iago, that he made him                    335
   Brave° me upon the watch, whereon it came°
   That I was cast;° and even but now he spake,
   After long seeming dead, Iago hurt him,
   Iago set him on.

**LODOVICO** [*to Othello*]:   You must forsake this room and go                    340
   with us.
   Your power and your command is taken off,°
   And Cassio rules in Cyprus. For this slave,
   If there be any cunning cruelty
   That can torment him much and hold him long,°
   It shall be his. You shall close prisoner rest°                    345
   Till that the nature of your fault be known
   To the Venetian state.—Come, bring away.

**OTHELLO:**   Soft you;° a word or two before you go.
   I have done the state some service, and they know 't.
   No more of that. I pray you, in your letters,                    350
   When you shall these unlucky° deeds relate,
   Speak of me as I am; nothing extenuate,
   Nor set down aught in malice. Then must you speak
   Of one that loved not wisely but too well;

---

**323 discontented** full of discontent   **326 belike** most likely   **327 Came ... him** interposed and gave him satisfactory explanation   **333 wrought ... desire** worked out as he wished, fitted in with his plan   **336 Brave** defy.   **whereon it came** whereof it came about   **337 cast** dismissed   **341 taken off** taken away   **344 hold him long** keep him alive a long time (during his torture)   **345 rest** remain   **348 Soft you** one moment   **351 unlucky** unfortunate

Of one not easily jealous but, being wrought,° 355
Perplexed° in the extreme; of one whose hand,
Like the base Indian,° threw a pearl away
Richer than all his tribe; of one whose subdued° eyes,
Albeit unusèd to the melting mood,
Drops tears as fast as the Arabian trees 360
Their medicinable gum.° Set you down this;
And say besides that in Aleppo once,
Where a malignant and a turbaned Turk
Beat a Venetian and traduced the state,
I took by th' throat the circumcisèd dog 365
And smote him, thus.                    [*He stabs himself.*°]

**LODOVICO:**   O bloody period!°

**GRATIANO:**   All that is spoke is marred.

**OTHELLO:**   I kissed thee ere I killed thee. No way but this,
Killing myself, to die upon a kiss. 370

[*He kisses Desdemona and*] *dies.*

**CASSIO:**   This did I fear, but thought he had no weapon;
For he was great of heart.

**LODOVICO** [*to Iago*]:       O Spartan dog,°
More fell° than anguish, hunger, or the sea!
Look on the tragic loading of this bed.
This is thy work. The object poisons sight; 375
Let it be hid.° Gratiano, keep° the house,

[*The bed curtains are drawn*]

And seize upon° the fortunes of the Moor,
For they succeed on° you. [*To Cassio.*] To you, Lord Governor,
Remains the censure° of this hellish villain,
The time, the place, the torture. O, enforce it! 380
Myself will straight aboard, and to the state
This heavy act with heavy heart relate.                    *Exeunt.*

—*1604?*

355 **wrought** worked upon, worked into a frenzy   356 **Perplexed** distraught   357 **Indian** (This reading from the Quarto pictures an ignorant savage who cannot recognize the value of a precious jewel. The Folio reading, *Iudean* or *Judean*, i.e., infidel or disbeliever, may refer to Herod, who slew Mariamne in a fit of jealousy, or to Judas Iscariot, the betrayer of Christ.)   358 **subdued** i.e., overcome by grief   361 **gum** i.e., myrrh   366 **[s.d.] He stabs himself** (This direction is in the Quarto text.)   367 **period** termination, conclusion   372 **Spartan dog** (Spartan dogs were noted for their savagery and silence.)   373 **fell** cruel   376 **Let it be hid** i.e., draw the bed curtains. (No stage direction specifies that the dead are to be carried offstage at the end of the play.)   **keep** remain in   377 **seize upon** take legal possession of   378 **succeed on** pass as though by inheritance to   379 **censure** sentencing

## HENRIK IBSEN ▥ (1828–1906)

*Henrik Ibsen, universally acknowledged as the first of the great modern play-wrights, was born in Skien, a small town in Norway, the son of a merchant who went bankrupt during Ibsen's childhood. Ibsen first trained for a medical career but drifted into the theater, gaining, like Shakespeare and Molière, important dramatic training through a decade's service as a stage manager and director. Ibsen was unsuccessful in establishing a theater in Oslo, and he spent almost thirty years living and writing in Germany and Italy. The fame he won through early poetic dramas like* Peer Gynt *(1867), which is considered the supreme exploration of the Norwegian national character, was overshadowed by the realistic prose plays he began writing, starting with* Pillars of Society *(1877).* A Doll's House *(1879) and* Ghosts *(1881), which deal, respectively, with a woman's struggle for independence and self-respect and with the taboo subject of venereal disease, made Ibsen an internationally famous, if controversial, figure. In fact, Ibsen wrote* An Enemy of the People *as a response to the public outcry over* Ghosts, *whose subject was considered so controversial that it could not be performed in London until 1891, and then for only a single performance in a private subscription theater. Although Ibsen's type of realism, displayed in "problem plays" such as these and later psychological dramas like* The Wild Duck *(1885) and* Hedda Gabler *(1890), has become so fully assimilated into our literary heritage that now it is difficult to think of him as an innovator, his marriage of the tightly constructed plots of the conventional "well-made play" to serious discussion of social issues was one of the most significant developments in the history of drama. His most influential advocate in English-speaking countries was George Bernard Shaw, whose* The Quintessence of Ibsenism *(1891) is one of the earliest and most influential studies of Ibsen's dramatic methods and ideas.*

# A Doll's House

by Henrik Ibsen 1879
translated by William Archer; revised and edited by Sarah Sjodin

Characters
Torvald Helmer.
Nora, his wife.
Doctor Rank.
Mrs. Linden.°
Nils Krogstad.
The Helmers' three children.
Anna,°(2) their nanny.
A maid (ellen).
Doorman.

The action passes in Helmer's house (a flat) in Christiania.

## Act One

A room, comfortably and tastefully, but not expensively, furnished. In the back, on the right, a door leads to the hall; on the left another door leads to HELMER's study. Between the two doors a pianoforte. In the middle of the left wall a door, and nearer the front a window. Near the window a round table with armchairs and a small sofa. In the right wall, somewhat to the back, a door, and against the same wall, further forward, a porcelain stove; in front of it a couple of arm chairs and a rocking chair. Between the stove and the side door a small table. Engravings on the walls. A whatnot with china and bric-a-brac. A small bookcase filled with handsomely bound books. Carpet. A fire in the stove. It is a winter day.

A bell rings in the hall outside. Presently the outer door of the flat is heard to open. Then NORA enters, humming gaily. She is in outdoor dress, and carries several packages, which she lays on the right-hand table. She leaves the door into the hall open, and a doorman is seen outside, carrying a Christmas tree and a basket, which he gives to the MAID who has opened the door.

**NORA:**  Hide the Christmas tree carefully, Ellen; the children must not see it before this evening, when it's lighted up.

[*To the doorman, taking out her purse.*] *How much?*

**DOORMAN:**  Seventy-five cents.

**NORA:**  There is a dollar. No, keep the change.

[*The DOORMAN thanks her and goes. NORA shuts the door. She continues smiling in quiet glee as she takes off her outdoor things. Taking from her pocket a bag of macaroons, she eats one or two. Then she goes on tip-toe to her husband's door and listens.*]

**NORA:**  Yes; he is at home.

[*She begins humming again, crossing to the table on the right.*]

**HELMER:**  [*In his room.*]  Is that my lark twittering there?

**NORA:**  [*Busy opening some of her packages.*] Yes, it is.

**HELMER:**  Is it the squirrel frisking around?

**NORA:**  Yes!

**HELMER:**  When did the squirrel get home?

**NORA:**  Just now. [*Hides the bag of macaroons in her pocket and wipes her mouth.*] Come here, Torvald, and see what I've been buying.

**HELMER:**  Don't interrupt me. [*A little later he opens the door and looks in, pen in hand.*] Buying, did you say? What! All that? Has my little spendthrift been making the money fly again?

**NORA:**  Why, Torvald, surely we can afford to launch out a little now. It's the first Christmas we haven't had to pinch.

**HELMER:**  Come, come; we can't afford to squander money.

**NORA:**  Oh yes, Torvald, do let us squander a little, now—just the least little bit! You know you'll soon be earning heaps of money.

**HELMER:**  Yes, from New Year's Day. But there's a whole quarter before my first salary is due.

**NORA:**  Never mind; we can borrow in the meantime.

**HELMER:**  Nora! [*He goes up to her and takes her playfully by the ear.*] Still my little featherbrain! Supposing I borrowed a thousand crowns today, and you squander them during Christmas week, and then on New Year's Eve a tile blew off the roof and knocked my brains out-

**NORA:**  [*Laying her hand on his mouth.*] Hush! How can you talk so horridly?

**HELMER:**  But supposing it were to happen—what then?

**NORA:**  If anything so dreadful happened, it would be all the same to me whether I was in debt or not.

**HELMER:**  But what about the creditors?

**NORA:**  They! Who cares for them? They're only strangers.

**HELMER:**  Nora, Nora! What a woman you are! But seriously, Nora, you know my principles on these points. No debts! No borrowing! Home life ceases to be free and beautiful as soon as it is founded on borrowing and debt. We two have held out bravely till now, and we are not going to give in at the last.

**NORA:**  [*Going to the fireplace.*] Very well— as you please, Torvald.

**HELMER:**  [*Following her.*] Come come; my little lark mustn't droop her wings like that. What? Is my squirrel in the sulks? [*Takes out his wallet.*] Nora, what do you think I have here?

**NORA:**  [*Turning round quickly.*] Money!

**HELMER:**  There! [*Gives her some money.*] Of course I know all sorts of things are wanted at Christmas.

**NORA:**  [*Counting.*] Ten, twenty, thirty, forty. Oh, thank you, thank you, Torvald! This will go a long way.

**HELMER:**  I should hope so.

**NORA:**  Yes, indeed; a long way! But come here, and let me show you all I've been buying. And so cheap! Look, here's a new suit for Ivar, and a little sword. Here are a horse and a trumpet for Bob. And here are a doll and a cradle for Emmy. They're only common; but they're good enough for her to pull to pieces. And dress-stuffs and kerchiefs for the servants. I ought to have got something better for old Anna.

**HELMER:**  And what's in that other package?

**NORA:**  [*Crying out.*] No, Torvald, you're not to see that until this evening.

**HELMER:**  Oh! Ah! But now tell me, you little spendthrift, have you thought of anything for yourself?

**NORA:**  For myself! Oh, I don't want anything.

**HELMER:**  Nonsense! Just tell me something sensible you would like to have.

**NORA:**    No, really I don't know of anything—Well, listen, Torvald—

**HELMER:**    Well?

**NORA:**    [*Playing with his coat buttons, without looking him in the face.*] If you really want to give me something, you might, you know—you might—

**HELMER:**    Well? Out with it!

**NORA:**    [*Quickly.*] You might give me money, Torvald. Only just what you think you can spare; then I can buy something with it later on.

**HELMER:**    But, Nora—

**NORA:**    Oh, please do, dear Torvald, please do! I should hang the money in lovely gilt paper on the Christmas tree. Wouldn't that be fun?

**HELMER:**    What do they call the birds that are always making the money fly?

**NORA:**    Yes, I know—spendthrifts, of course. But please do as I ask you, Torvald. Then I shall have time to think what I want most. Isn't that very sensible, now?

**HELMER:**    [*Smiling.*] Certainly; that is to say, if you really kept the money I gave you, and really spent it on something for yourself. But it all goes in housekeeping, and for all manner of useless things, and then I have to pay up again.

**NORA:**    But, Torvald—

**HELMER:**    Can you deny it, Nora dear? [*He puts his arm round her.*] It's a sweet little lark, but it gets through a lot of money. No one would believe how much it costs a man to keep such a little bird as you.

**NORA:**    For shame! How can you say so? Why, I save as much as I can.

**HELMER:**    [*Laughing.*] Very true—as much as you can—but that's precisely nothing.

**NORA:**    [*Hums and smiles with covert glee.*] H'm! If you only knew, Torvald, what expenses we larks and squirrels have.

**HELMER:**    You're a strange little being! Just like your father—always on the lookout for all the money you can lay your hands on; but the moment you have it, it seems to slip through your fingers; you never know what becomes of it. Well, one must take you as you are. It's in the blood. Yes, Nora, that sort of thing's hereditary.

**NORA:**    I wish I had inherited many of papa's qualities.

**HELMER:**    And I don't wish you anything but just what you are—my own, sweet little songbird. But I say—it strikes me you look so—so—what shall I call it?—so suspicious today—

**NORA:**    Do I?

**HELMER:**    You do, indeed. Look me full in the face.

**NORA:**    [*Looking at him.*] Well?

**HELMER:**    [*Threatening with his finger.*] Hasn't the little Sweet tooth been playing pranks today?

**NORA:**    No; how can you think such a thing!

**HELMER:**    Didn't she just look in at the confectioner's?

**NORA:**  No, Torvald; really—

**HELMER:**  Not to sip a little jelly?

**NORA:**  No; certainly not.

**HELMER:**  Hasn't she even nibbled a macaroon or two?

**NORA:**  No, Torvald, indeed, indeed!

**HELMER:**  Well, well, well; of course I'm only joking.

**NORA:**  [*Goes to the table on the right.*] I shouldn't think of doing what you disapprove of.

**HELMER:**  No, I'm sure of that; and, besides, you've given me your word— [*Going towards her.*] Well, keep your little Christmas secrets to yourself, Nora darling. The Christmas tree will bring them all to light, I daresay.

**NORA:**  Have you remembered to invite Doctor Rank?

**HELMER:**  No. But it's not necessary; he'll come as a matter of course. Besides, I'll ask him when he looks in today. I've ordered some capital wine. Nora, you can't think how I look forward to this evening.

**NORA:**  Me too. How the children will enjoy themselves, Torvald!

**HELMER:**  Ah, it's glorious to feel that one has an assured position and ample means. Isn't it delightful to think of?

**NORA:**  Oh, it's wonderful!

**HELMER:**  Do you remember last Christmas? For three whole weeks beforehand you shut yourself up every evening till long past midnight to make flowers for the Christmas tree, and all sorts of other marvels that were to have astonished us. I was never so bored in my life.

**NORA:**  I didn't bore myself at all.

**HELMER:**  [*Smiling.*] But it came to little enough in the end, Nora.

**NORA:**  Oh, you're going to tease me about that again? How could I help the cat getting in and pulling it all to pieces?

**HELMER:**  To be sure you couldn't, my poor little Nora. You did your best to give us all pleasure, and that's the main point. But, all the same, it's a good thing the hard times are over.

**NORA:**  Oh, isn't it wonderful?

**HELMER:**  Now I needn't sit here boring myself all alone; and you needn't tire your blessed eyes and your delicate little fingers—

**NORA:**  [*Clapping her hands.*] No, I needn't, need I, Torvald? Oh, how wonderful it is to think of? [*Takes his arm.*] And now I'll tell you how I think we should manage, Torvald. As soon as Christmas is over— [*The hall-door bell rings.*] Oh, there's a ring! [*Arranging the room.*] Someone's here. How tiresome!

**HELMER:**  I'm "not at home" to visitors; remember that.

**ELLEN:**  [*In the doorway.*] A lady to see you, ma'am.

**NORA:**  Show her in.

**ELLEN:**  [*To HELMER.*] And the doctor has just come, sir.

**HELMER:**  Has he gone into my study?

**ELLEN:**  Yes, sir.

[*HELMER goes into his study. ELLEN ushers in MRS. LINDEN, in travelling clothes, and goes out, closing the door.*]

**MRS. LINDEN:**    [*Embarrassed and hesitating.*] How are you, Nora?

**NORA:**    [*Doubtfully.*] How are you?

**MRS. LINDEN:**    I see you don't recognize me!

**NORA:**    No, I don't think—oh yes!—I believe—[*Suddenly brightening.*] What, Christina! Is it really you?

**MRS. LINDEN:**    Yes; it's really me!

**NORA:**    Christina! And to think I didn't know you! But how could I—[*More softly.*] You've changed; Christina!

**MRS. LINDEN:**    Yes, no doubt. In nine or ten years-

**NORA:**    Has it really been so long since we met? Yes, it has. Oh, the last eight years have been a happy time, I tell you. And now you've come to town? All that long journey in mid-winter! How brave of you!

**MRS. LINDEN:**    I arrived by this morning's steamer.

**NORA:**    To have a merry Christmas, of course. Oh, how delightful! Yes, we'll have a merry Christmas. Do take your things off. Aren't you frozen? [*Helping her.*] There; now we'll sit cozily by the fire. No, you take the arm chair; I'll sit in this rocking chair. [*Seizes her hands.*] Yes, now I can see the dear old face again. It was only at the first glance—But you're a little paler, Christina—and perhaps a little thinner.

**MRS. LINDEN:**    And much, much older, Nora.

**NORA:**    Yes, perhaps a little older—not much—ever so little. [*She suddenly checks herself; seriously.*] Oh, what a thoughtless wretch I am! Here I sit chattering on, and—Dear, dear Christina, can you forgive me!

**MRS. LINDEN:**    What do you mean, Nora?

**NORA:**    [*Softly.*] Poor Christina! I forgot: you are a widow.

**MRS. LINDEN:**    Yes; my husband died three years ago.

**NORA:**    I know, I know; I saw it in the papers. Oh, believe me, Christina, I did mean to write you; but I kept putting it off, and something always got in the way.

**MRS. LINDEN:**    I can quite understand that, Nora dear.

**NORA:**    No, Christina; it was horrid of me. Oh, you poor darling! how much you must've gone through!—And he left you nothing?

**MRS. LINDEN:**    Nothing.

**NORA:**    And no children?

**MRS. LINDEN:**    None.

**NORA:**    Nothing, nothing at all?

**MRS. LINDEN:**    Not even a sorrow or a longing to dwell upon.

**NORA:**    [*Looking at her incredulously.*] My dear Christina, how's that possible?

**MRS. LINDEN:**    [*Smiling sadly and stroking her hair.*] Oh, it happens so sometimes, Nora.

**NORA:**  So utterly alone! How dreadful that must be! I have three of the loveliest children. I can't show them to you just now; they're out with their nanny. But now you must tell me everything.

**MRS. LINDEN:**  No, no; I want you to tell me-

**NORA:**  No, you must begin; I won't be egotistical today. Today I'll think only of you. Oh! but I must tell you one thing—perhaps you've heard of our great stroke of fortune?

**MRS. LINDEN:**  No. What is it?

**NORA:**  Only think! my husband's been made manager of the Joint Stock Bank.

**MRS. LINDEN:**  Your husband! Oh, how fortunate!

**NORA:**  Yes; isn't it? A lawyer's position is so uncertain, you see, especially when he won't touch any business that's the least bit shady, as of course Torvald never would; and there I quite agree with him. Oh! you can imagine how glad we are. He's to enter his new position at the New Year, and then he'll have a large salary, and percentages. In future we'll be able to live quite differently—just as we please, in fact. Oh, Christina, I feel so lighthearted and happy! It's delightful to have lots of money, and no need to worry about things, isn't it?

**MRS. LINDEN:**  Yes; at any rate it must be delightful to have what you need.

**NORA:**  No, not only what you need, but heaps of money—heaps!

**MRS. LINDEN:**  [*Smiling.*] Nora, Nora, haven't you learnt reason yet? In our school days you were a shocking little spendthrift.

**NORA:**  [*Quietly smiling.*] Yes; that's what Torvald says I am still. [*Holding up her forefinger.*] But "Nora, Nora" isn't so silly as you all think. Oh! I haven't had the chance to be much of a spendthrift. We've both had to work.

**MRS. LINDEN:**  You too?

**NORA:**  Yes, light fancy work: crochet, and embroidery, and things of that sort; [*Carelessly*] and other work too. You know, of course, that Torvald left the Government service when we were married. He had little chance of promotion, and of course he required to make more money. But in the first year after our marriage he overworked himself terribly. He had to undertake all sorts of extra work, you know, and to slave early and late. He couldn't stand it, and fell dangerously ill. Then the doctors declared he must go to the South.

**MRS. LINDEN:**  You spent a whole year in Italy, didn't you?

**NORA:**  Yes, we did. It wasn't easy to manage, I can tell you. It was just after Ivar's birth. But of course we had to go. Oh, it was a wonderful, delicious journey! And it saved Torvald's life. But it cost a frightful lot of money, Christina.

**MRS. LINDEN:**  So I should think.

**NORA:**  Twelve hundred dollars! Four thousand eight hundred crowns! °
Isn't that a lot of money?

**MRS. LINDEN:** How lucky you had the money to spend!

**NORA:** We got it from father, you must know.

**MRS. LINDEN:** Ah, I see. He died just about that time, didn't he?

**NORA:** Yes, Christina, just then. And only think! I couldn't go and nurse him! I was expecting little Ivar's birth daily; and then I had my poor sick Torvald to attend to. Dear, kind old father! I never saw him again, Christina. Oh! that's the hardest thing I've had to bear since my marriage.

**MRS. LINDEN:** I know how fond you were of him. But then you went to Italy?

**NORA:** Yes; you see, we had the money, and the doctors said we must lose no time. We started a month later.

**MRS. LINDEN:** And your husband came back completely cured.

**NORA:** Sound as a bell.

**MRS. LINDEN:** But—the doctor?

**NORA:** What do you mean?

**MRS. LINDEN:** I thought as I came in your servant announced the doctor-

**NORA:** Oh, yes; Doctor Rank. But he doesn't come professionally. He's our best friend, and never lets a day pass without stopping by. No, Torvald hasn't had an hour's illness since that time. And the children are so healthy and well, and so am I. [*Jumps up and claps her hands.*] Oh, Christina, Christina, what a wonderful thing it is to live and to be happy!—Oh, but it's really too horrid of me! Here am I talking about nothing but my own concerns. [*Seats herself upon a footstool close to CHRISTINA, and lays her arms on her friend's lap.*] Oh. don't be angry with me!

Now tell me, is it really true that you didn't love your husband? What made you marry him, then?

**MRS. LINDEN:** My mother was still alive, you see, bedridden and helpless; and then I had my two younger brothers to think of. I didn't think it'd be right for me to refuse him.

**NORA:** Perhaps it wouldn't have been. I suppose he was rich then?

**MRS. LINDEN:** Very well off, I believe. But his business was uncertain. It fell to pieces at his death, and there was nothing left.

**NORA:** And then?

**MRS. LINDEN:** Then I had to fight my way by keeping a shop, a little school, anything I could turn my hand to. The last three years have been one long struggle for me. But now it's over, Nora. My poor mother no longer needs me; she's at rest. And the boys are in business, and can look after themselves.

**NORA:** How free your life must feel!

**MRS. LINDEN:** No, Nora; only inexpressibly empty. No one to live for! [*Stands up restlessly.*] That's why I couldn't bear to stay any longer in that out-of-the-way corner. Here it must be easier to find something to take one up—to occupy one's thoughts. If I could only get some settled employment—some office work.

**NORA:** But, Christina, that's such drudgery, and you look worn out already. It'd be ever so much better for you to go to some spa and rest.

**MRS. LINDEN:** [*Going to the window.*] I have no father to give me the money, Nora.

**NORA:** [*Rising.*] Oh, don't be vexed with me.

**MRS. LINDEN:** [*Going to her.*] My dear Nora, don't you be vexed with me. The worst of a position like mine is that it makes one so bitter. You have no one to work for, yet you have to be always on the strain. You must live; and so you become selfish. When I heard of the happy change in your fortunes—can you believe it?—I was glad for my own sake more than for yours.

**NORA:** How do you mean? Ah, I see! You think Torvald can perhaps do something for you.

**MRS. LINDEN:** Yes; I thought so.

**NORA:** And so he will, Christina. Just you leave it all to me. I'll lead up to it beautifully!—I'll think of some delightful plan to put him in a good mood! Oh, I'd so love to help you.

**MRS. LINDEN:** How good of you, Nora, to stand by me so warmly! Doubly good in you, who knows so little of the troubles and burdens of life.

**NORA:** I? I know so little of-?

**MRS. LINDEN:** [*Smiling.*] Oh, well—a little fancy-work, and so forth.— You're a child, Nora.

**NORA:** [*Tosses her head and paces the room.*] Oh, come, you mustn't be so patronizing!

**MRS. LINDEN:** No?

**NORA:** You're like the rest. You all think I'm fit for nothing really serious-

**MRS. LINDEN:** Well, well-

**NORA:** You think I've had no troubles in this weary world.

**MRS. LINDEN:** My dear Nora, you've just told me all your troubles.

**NORA:** Pooh—those trifles! [*Softly.*] I haven't told you the great thing.

**MRS. LINDEN:** The great thing? What do you mean?

**NORA:** I know you look down upon me, Christina; but you've no right to. You're proud of having worked so hard and so long for your mother.

**MRS. LINDEN:** I'm sure I don't look down upon any one; but it's true I'm both proud and glad when I remember that I was able to keep my mother's last days free from care.

**NORA:** And you're proud to think of what you've done for your brothers, too.

**MRS. LINDEN:** Have I not the right to be?

**NORA:** Yes indeed. But now let me tell you, Christina—I, too, have something to be proud and glad of.

**MRS. LINDEN:** I don't doubt it. But what do you mean?

**NORA:** Hush! Not so loud. Only think, if Torvald were to hear! He mustn't— not for worlds! No one must know about it, Christina—no one but you.

MRS LINDEN:   Why, what can it be?

**NORA:**   Come over here. [*Draws her down beside her on the sofa.*] Yes, Christina—I, too, have something to be proud and glad of. I saved Torvald's life.

**MRS. LINDEN:**   Saved his life? How?

**NORA:**   I told you about our going to Italy. Torvald would have died but for that.

**MRS. LINDEN:**   Well—and your father gave you the money.

**NORA:**   [*Smiling.*] Yes, so Torvald and everyone believes; but—

**MRS. LINDEN:**   But-?

**NORA:**   Papa didn't give us one penny. It was I that found the money.

**MRS. LINDEN:**   You? All that money?

**NORA:**   Twelve hundred dollars. What do you say to that?

**MRS. LINDEN:**   My dear Nora, how'd you manage it? Did you win it in the lottery?

**NORA:**   [*Contemptuously.*] In the lottery? Pooh! Anyone could have done that!

**MRS. LINDEN:**   Then where'd you get it from?

**NORA:**   [*Hums and smiles mysteriously.*] H'm; tra-la-la-la!

**MRS. LINDEN:**   Of course you couldn't borrow it.

**NORA:**   No? Why not?

**MRS. LINDEN:**   Why, a wife can't borrow without her husband's consent.

**NORA:**   [*Tossing her head.*] Oh! when the wife has some idea of business, and knows how to set about things-

**MRS. LINDEN:**   But, Nora, I don't understand-

**NORA:**   Well, you needn't. I never said I borrowed the money. There are many ways I may've got it. [*Throws herself back on the sofa.*] I may've got it from some admirer. When one is so—attractive as I am-

**MRS. LINDEN:**   You're too silly, Nora.

**NORA:**   Now I'm sure you're dying of curiosity, Christina-

**MRS. LINDEN:**   Listen to me, Nora dear: haven't you been a little rash?

**NORA:**   [*Sitting upright again.*] It's rash to save one's husband's life?

**MRS. LINDEN:**   I think it was rash of you, without his knowledge-

**NORA:**   But it would've been fatal for him to know! Can't you understand that? He wasn't even to suspect how ill he was. The doctors came to me privately and told me his life was in danger—that nothing could save him but a winter in the South. Do you think I didn't try diplomacy first? I told him how I longed to have a trip abroad, like other young wives; I wept and prayed; I said he should think of my condition, and not to thwart me; and then I hinted that he could borrow the money. But then, Christina, he got almost angry. He said I was frivolous, and that it was his duty as a husband not to yield to my whims and fancies—so he called them. Very well, thought I, but saved you must be; and then I found the way to do it.

**MRS. LINDEN:** And did your husband never learn from your father that the money was not from him?

**NORA:** No; never. Papa died at that very time. I meant to have told him all about it, and begged him to say nothing. But he was so ill—unhappily, it wasn't necessary.

**MRS. LINDEN:** And you've never confessed to your husband?

**NORA:** Good heavens! What can you be thinking of of? Tell him when he has such a loathing of debt And besides—how painful and humiliating it would be for Torvald, with his manly self-respect, to know that he owed anything to me! It would utterly upset the relation between us; our beautiful, happy home would never again be what it is.

**MRS. LINDEN:** You'll never tell him?

**NORA:** [*Thoughtfully, half-smiling.*] Yes, some time perhaps—many, many years hence, when I'm—not so pretty. You mustn't laugh at me! Of course I mean when Torvald's not so much in love with me as he is now; when it doesn't amuse him any longer to see me dancing about, and dressing up and acting. Then it might be well to have something in reserve. [*Breaking off.*] Nonsense! nonsense! That time'll never come. Now, what do you say to my grand secret, Christina? Am I fit for nothing now? You may believe it's cost me a lot of anxiety. It's been no joke to meet my engagements punctually. You must know, Christina, that in business there are things called installments, and quarterly interest, that are terribly hard to provide for. So I've had to pinch a little here and there, wherever I could. I couldn't save much out of the housekeeping, for of course Torvald had to live well. And I couldn't let the children go about badly dressed; all I got for them, I spent on them, the blessed darlings!

**MRS. LINDEN:** Poor Nora! So it had to come out of your own pocket money.

**NORA:** Yes, of course. After all, the whole thing was my doing. When Torvald gave me money for clothes, and so on, I never spent more than half of it; I always bought the simplest and cheapest things. It's a mercy that everything suits me so well—Torvald never had any suspicions. But it was often very hard, Christina dear. For it's nice to be beautifully dressed—now, isn't it?

**MRS. LINDEN:** Indeed it is.

**NORA:** Well, and besides that, I made money in other ways. Last winter I was so lucky—I got a heap of copying to do. I shut myself up every evening and wrote far into the night. Oh, sometimes I was so tired, so tired. And yet it was splendid to work in that way and earn money. I almost felt as if I was a man.

**MRS. LINDEN:** Then how much've you been able to pay off?

**NORA:** Well, I can't precisely say. It's difficult to keep that sort of business clear. I only know that I've paid everything I could scrape together. Sometimes I really didn't know where to turn. [*Smiles.*] Then I used to sit here and pretend that a rich old gentleman was in love with me—

**MRS. LINDEN:**   What! gentleman?

**NORA:**   Oh, nobody!—that he was dead now, and that when his will was opened, there stood in large letters: "Pay over at once everything of which I die possessed to that charming person, Mrs. Nora Helmer."

**MRS. LINDEN:**   But, my dear Nora—what gentleman do you mean?

**NORA:**   Oh dear, can't you understand? There wasn't any old gentleman: it's only what I used to dream and dream when I was at my wits' end for money. But it doesn't matter now—the tiresome old creature may stay where he is for me. I care nothing for him or his will; for now my troubles are over. [*Springing up.*] Oh, Christina, how glorious it is to think of! Free from all anxiety! Free, quite free. To be able to play and romp about with the children; to have things tasteful and pretty in the house, exactly as Torvald likes it! And then the spring'll soon be here, with the great blue sky. Perhaps then we'll have a little holiday. Perhaps I'll see the sea again. Oh, what a wonderful thing it is to live and to be happy!

[*The hall-door bell rings.*]

**MRS. LINDEN:**   [*Rising.*] There's a ring. Perhaps I'd better go.

**NORA:**   No; do stay. No one'll come here. It's sure to be someone for Torvald.

**ELLEN:**   [*In the doorway.*] If you please, ma'am, there's a gentleman to speak to Mr. Helmer.

**NORA:**   Who's the gentleman?

**KROGSTAD:**   [*In the doorway.*] It's I, Mrs. Helmer.

[*MRS. LINDEN starts and turns away to the window.*]

**NORA:**   [*Goes a step towards him, anxiously, speaking low.*] You? What is it? What do you want with my husband?

**KROGSTAD:**   Bank business—in a way. I hold a small post in the Joint Stock Bank, and your husband's to be our new chief, I hear.

**NORA:**   Then it's-?

**KROGSTAD:**   Only tiresome business, Mrs. Helmer; nothing more.

**NORA:**   Then will you please go to his study.

[*KROGSTAD goes. She bows indifferently while she closes the door into the hall. Then she goes to the stove and looks to the fire.*]

**MRS. LINDEN:**   Nora—who was that man?

**NORA:**   A Mr. Krogstad—a lawyer.

**MRS. LINDEN:**   Then it's really he?

**NORA:**   Do you know him?

**MRS. LINDEN:**   I used to know him—many years ago. He was in a lawyer's office in our town.

**NORA:**   Yes, so he was.

**MRS. LINDEN:**   How he's changed!

**NORA:**   I believe his marriage was unhappy.

**MRS. LINDEN:**   And he's a widower now?

**NORA:**   With a lot of children. There! Now it'll burn up. [*She closes the stove, and pushes the rocking chair a little aside.*]

**MRS. LINDEN:**   His business is not of the most creditable, they say?

**NORA:**   Isn't it? I daresay not. I don't know. But don't let us think of business—it's so tiresome.

[*DR. RANK comes out of HELMER'S room.*]

**RANK:**   [*Still in the doorway.*] No, no; I'm in your way. I'll go and have a chat with your wife. [*Shuts the door and sees MRS. LINDEN.*] Oh, I beg your pardon. I'm in the way here too.

**NORA:**   No, not in the least. [*Introduces them.*] Doctor Rank—Mrs. Linden.

**RANK:**   Oh, indeed; I've often heard Mrs. Linden's name; I think I passed you on the stairs as I came up.

**MRS. LINDEN:**   Yes; I go so very slowly. Stairs try me so much.

**RANK:**   Ah—you're not very strong?

**MRS. LINDEN:**   Only overworked.

**RANK:**   Nothing more? Then no doubt you've come to town to find rest in a round of dissipation?

**MRS. LINDEN:**   I've come to look for employment.

**RANK:**   Is that an approved remedy for overwork?

**MRS. LINDEN:**   One must live, Doctor Rank.

**RANK:**   Yes, that seems to be the general opinion.

**NORA:**   Come, Doctor Rank—you want to live yourself.

**RANK:**   To be sure I do. However wretched I may be, I want to drag on as long as possible. All my patients, too, have the same mania. And it's the same with people whose complaint is moral. At this very moment Helmer's talking to just such a moral incurable-

**MRS. LINDEN:**   [*Softly.*] Ah!

**NORA:**   Whom do you mean?

**RANK:**   Oh, a fellow named Krogstad, a man you know nothing about— corrupt to the very core of his character. But even he began by announcing, as a matter of vast importance, that he must live.

**NORA:**   Indeed? And what did he want with Torvald?

**RANK:**   I haven't an idea; I only gathered that it's some bank business.

**NORA:**   I didn't know that Krog—that this Mr. Krogstad had anything to do with the Bank?

**RANK:**   Yes. He's got some sort of place there. [*To MRS. LINDEN.*] I don't know whether in your part of the country, you've people who go grubbing and sniffing around in search of moral rottenness—and then, when they have found a "case," don't rest till they have got their man into some good position, where they can keep a watch upon him. Men with a clean bill of health they leave out in the cold.

**MRS. LINDEN:**   Well, I suppose the—delicate characters require most care.

**RANK:**   [*Shrugs his shoulders.*] There we have it! It's that notion that makes society a hospital.

[*NORA, deep in her own thoughts, breaks into half-stifled laughter and claps her hands.*]

**RANK:**   Why do you laugh at that? Have you any idea what "society" is?

**NORA:**   What do I care for your tiresome society? I was laughing at something else—something excessively amusing. Tell me, Doctor Rank, are all the employees at the Bank dependent on Torvald now?

**RANK:**   Is that what strikes you as excessively amusing?

**NORA:**   [*Smiles and hums.*] Never mind, never mind! [*Walks about the room.*] Yes, it is funny to think that we—that Torvald has such power over so many people. [*Takes the bag from her pocket.*] Doctor Rank, will you have a macaroon?

**RANK:**   What!—macaroons! I thought they were contraband here.

**NORA:**   Yes; but Christina brought me these.

**MRS. LINDEN:**   What! I-?

**NORA:**   Oh, well! Don't be frightened. You couldn't possibly know that Torvald had forbidden them. The fact is, he's afraid of me spoiling my teeth. But, oh bother, just for once!—That's for you, Doctor Rank! [*Puts a macaroon into his mouth.*] And you too, Christina. And I'll have one while we're about it—only a tiny one, or at most two. [*Walks about again.*] Oh dear, I am happy! There's only one thing in the world I really want.

**RANK:**   Well; what's that?

**NORA:**   There's something I'd so like to say—in Torvald's hearing.

**RANK:**   Then why don't you say it?

**NORA:**   Because I daren't, it's so ugly.

**MRS. LINDEN:**   Ugly!

**RANK:**   In that case you'd better not. But to us you might—What is it you'd so like to say in Helmer's hearing?

**NORA:**   I should so love to say "Damn it all!"

**RANK:**   Are you out of your mind?

**MRS. LINDEN:**   Good gracious, Nora—!

**RANK:**   Say it—there he is!

**NORA:**   [*Hides the macaroons.*] Hush—sh—sh!

[*HELMER comes out of his room, hat in hand, with his overcoat on his arm.*]

**NORA:**   [*Going to him.*] Well, Torvald dear, you've got rid of him?

**HELMER:**   Yes; he's just gone.

**NORA:**   Let me introduce you—this is Christina, who's come to town—

**HELMER:**   Christina? Pardon me, I don't know—

**NORA:**   Mrs. Linden, Torvald dear—Christina Linden.

**HELMER:**   [*To MRS. LINDEN.*] Indeed! A school-friend of my wife's, no doubt?

**MRS. LINDEN:** Yes; we knew each other as girls.

**NORA:** And only think! She's taken this long journey on purpose to speak to you.

**HELMER:** To speak to me!

**MRS. LINDEN:** Well, not quite—

**NORA:** You see, Christina is tremendously clever at office-work, and she's so anxious to work under a first-rate man of business in order to learn still more—

**HELMER:** [*To MRS. LINDEN.*] Very sensible indeed.

**NORA:** And when she heard you were appointed manager—it was telegraphed, you know—she started off at once, and—Torvald, dear, for my sake, you must do something for Christina. Now can't you?

**HELMER:** It's not impossible. I presume Mrs. Linden is a widow?

**MRS. LINDEN:** Yes.

**HELMER:** And you've already had some experience of business?

**MRS. LINDEN:** A good deal.

**HELMER:** Well, then, it's very likely I may be able to find a place for you.

**NORA:** [*Clapping her hands.*] There now! There now!

**HELMER:** You've come at a fortunate moment, Mrs. Linden.

**MRS. LINDEN:** Oh, how can I thank you?

**HELMER:** [*Smiling.*] There is no occasion. [*Puts on his overcoat.*] But for the present you must excuse me—

**RANK:** Wait; I'm going with you. [*Fetches his fur coat from the hall and warms it at the fire.*]

**NORA:** Don't be long, Torvald dear.

**HELMER:** Only an hour; not more.

**NORA:** Are you going too, Christina?

**MRS. LINDEN:** [*Putting on her walking things.*] Yes; I must set about looking for lodgings.

**HELMER:** Then perhaps we can go together?

**NORA:** [*Helping her.*] What a pity we haven't a spare room for you; but it's impossible—

**MRS. LINDEN:** I shouldn't think of troubling you. Goodbye, dear Nora, and thank you for all your kindness.

**NORA:** Goodbye for the present. Of course you'll come back this evening. And you, too, Doctor Rank. What! If you're well enough? Of course you'll be well enough. Only wrap up warmly. [*They go out, talking, into the hall. Outside on the stairs are heard children's voices.*] There they are! There they are! [*She runs to the outer door and opens it. The nanny, ANNA, enters the hall with the children.*] Come in! Come in! [*Stoops down and kisses the children.*] Oh, my sweet darlings! Do you see them, Christina? Aren't they lovely?

**RANK:** Don't let us stand here chattering in the draught.

**HELMER:** Come, Mrs. Linden; only mothers can stand such a temperature.

[*DR. RANK, HELMER, and MRS. LINDEN go down the stairs; ANNA enters the room with the children; NORA also, shutting the door.*]

**NORA:**  How fresh and bright you look! And what red cheeks you've got! Like apples and roses. [*The children chatter to her during what follows.*] Have you had great fun? That's splendid! Oh, really! You've been giving Emmy and Bob a ride on your sledge!—both at once, only think, Why, you're quite a man, Ivar. Oh, give her to me a little, Anna. My sweet little dolly! [*Takes the smallest from the nanny and dances with her.*] Yes, yes; mother'll dance with Bob too. What! Did you've a game of snowballs? Oh, I wish I'd been there. No; leave them, Anna; I'll take their things off. Oh, yes, let me do it; it's such fun. Go to the nursery; you look frozen. You'll find some hot coffee on the stove.

[*The NANNY goes into the room on the left. NORA takes off the children's things and throws them down anywhere, while the children talk all together.*]

Really! A big dog ran after you? But he didn't bite you? No; dogs don't bite dear little dolly children. Don't peep into those packages, Ivar. What is it? Wouldn't you like to know? Take care—it'll bite! What? Can we have a game? What'll we play at? Hide-and-seek? Yes, let's play hide-and-seek. Bob'll hide first. Am I to? Yes, let me hide first.

[*She and the children play, with laughter and shouting, in the room and the adjacent one to the right. At last NORA hides under the table; the children come rushing in, look for her, but cannot find her, hear her half-choked laughter, rush to the table, lift up the cover and see her. Loud shouts. She creeps out, as though to frighten them. Fresh shouts. Meanwhile there has been a knock at the door leading into the hall. No one has heard it. Now the door is half opened and KROGSTAD appears. He waits a little; the game is renewed.*]

**KROGSTAD:**  I beg your pardon, Mrs. Helmer—

**NORA:**  [*With a suppressed cry, turns round and half jumps up.*] Ah! What do you want?

**KROGSTAD:**  Excuse me; the outer door was ajar—somebody must've forgotten to shut it—

**NORA:**  [*Standing up.*] My husband is not at home, Mr. Krogstad.

**KROGSTAD:**  I know it.

**NORA:**  Then what do you want here?

**KROGSTAD:**  To say a few words to you.

**NORA:**  To me? [*To the children, softly.*] Go in to Anna. What? No, the strange man won't hurt mamma. When he's gone we'll go on playing. [*She leads the children into the left-hand room, and shuts the door behind them. Uneasy, in suspense.*] It is to me you wish to speak?

**KROGSTAD:**   Yes, to you.

**NORA:**   Today? But it's not the first yet—

**KROGSTAD:**   No, today is Christmas Eve. It will depend upon yourself whether you have a merry Christmas.

**NORA:**   What do you want? I'm not ready today—

**KROGSTAD:**   Never mind that just now. I've come about another matter. You've a minute to spare?

**NORA:**   Oh, yes, I suppose so; although—

**KROGSTAD:**   Good. I was sitting in the restaurant opposite, and I saw your husband go down the street—

**NORA:**   Well?

**KROGSTAD:**   —with a lady.

**NORA:**   What then?

**KROGSTAD:**   May I ask if the lady was a Mrs. Linden?

**NORA:**   Yes.

**KROGSTAD:**   Who's just come to town?

**NORA:**   Yes. Today.

**KROGSTAD:**   I believe she's an intimate friend of yours.

**NORA:**   Certainly. But I don't understand—

**KROGSTAD:**   I used to know her too.

**NORA:**   I know you did.

**KROGSTAD:**   Ah! You know all about it. I thought as much. Now, frankly, is Mrs. Linden to have a place in the Bank?

**NORA:**   How dare you catechize me in this way, Mr. Krogstad—you, a subordinate of my husband's? But since you ask, you'll know. Yes, Mrs. Linden is to be employed. And it's I who recommended her, Mr. Krogstad. Now you know.

**KROGSTAD:**   Then my guess was right.

**NORA:**   [*Walking up and down.*] You see one has a wee bit of influence, after all. It doesn't follow because one's only a woman—When people are in a subordinate position, Mr. Krogstad, they ought really to be careful how they offend anybody who—h'm—

**KROGSTAD:**   —who has influence?

**NORA:**   Exactly.

**KROGSTAD:**   [*Taking another tone.*] Mrs. Helmer, you'll have the kindness to employ your influence on my behalf?

**NORA:**   What? How do you mean?

**KROGSTAD:**   Will you be so good as to see that I retain my subordinate position in the Bank?

**NORA:**   What do you mean? Who wants to take it from you?

**KROGSTAD:**   Oh, you needn't pretend ignorance. I can very well understand that it can't be pleasant for your friend to meet me; and I can also understand now for whose sake I'm to be hounded out.

**NORA:**   But I assure you—

**KROGSTAD:**   Come come now, once for all: there's time yet, and I advise you to use your influence to prevent it.

**NORA:**   But, Mr. Krogstad, I've no influence—absolutely none.

**KROGSTAD:**   None? I thought you said a moment ago—

**NORA:**   Of course not in that sense. I! How can you imagine that I'd have any such influence over my husband?

**KROGSTAD:**   Oh, I know your husband from our college days. I don't think he's any more inflexible than other husbands.

**NORA:**   If you talk disrespectfully of my husband, I must request you to leave the house.

**KROGSTAD:**   You're bold, madam.

**NORA:**   I'm afraid of you no longer. When New Year's Day's over, I'll soon be out of the whole business.

**KROGSTAD:**   [*Controlling himself.*] Listen to me, Mrs. Helmer. If need be, I'll fight as though for my life to keep my little place in the Bank.

**NORA:**   Yes, so it seems.

**KROGSTAD:**   It's not only for the salary: that's what I care least about. It's something else—Well, I had better make a clean breast of it. Of course you know, like everyone else, that some years ago I—got into trouble.

**NORA:**   I think I've heard something of the sort.

**KROGSTAD:**   The matter never came into court; but from that moment all paths were barred to me. Then I took up the business you know about. I had to turn my hand to something; and I don't think I've been one of the worst. But now I must get clear of it all. My sons are growing up; for their sake I must try to recover my character as well as I can. This place in the Bank was the first step; and now your husband wants to kick me off the ladder, back into the mire.

**NORA:**   But I assure you, Mr. Krogstad, I haven't the least power to help you.

**KROGSTAD:**   That's because you haven't the will; but I can compel you.

**NORA:**   You won't tell my husband that I owe you money?

**KROGSTAD:**   H'm; suppose I did?

**NORA:**   It'd be shameful of you. [*With tears in her voice.*] The secret that's my joy and my pride—that he'd learn it in such an ugly, coarse way—and from you. It'd involve me in all sorts of unpleasantness—

**KROGSTAD:**   Only unpleasantness?

**NORA:**   [*Hotly.*] But just do it. It's you that'll come off worst, for then my husband'll see what a bad man you are, and then you certainly won't keep your place.

**KROGSTAD:**   I asked whether it's only domestic unpleasantness you feared?

**NORA:**   If my husband knows about it, he'll of course pay you off at once, and then we'll have nothing more to do with you.

**KROGSTAD:**   [*Coming a pace nearer.*] Listen, Mrs. Helmer: either your memory is defective, or you don't know much about business. I must make the position a little clearer to you.

**NORA:** How so?

**KROGSTAD:** When your husband was ill, you came to me to borrow twelve hundred dollars.

**NORA:** I knew of nobody else.

**KROGSTAD:** I promised to find you the money—

**NORA:** And you did find it.

**KROGSTAD:** I promised to find you the money, on certain conditions. You were so much taken up at the time about your husband's illness, and so eager to have the financing for your journey, that you probably didn't give much thought to the details. Allow me to remind you of them. I promised to find you the amount in exchange for a note of hand, which I drew up.

**NORA:** Yes, and I signed it.

**KROGSTAD:** Quite right. But then I added a few lines, making your father security for the debt. Your father was to sign this.

**NORA:** Was to—? He did sign it!

**KROGSTAD:** I'd left the date blank. That's to say, your father was himself to date his signature. Do you recollect that?

**NORA:** Yes, I believe—

**KROGSTAD:** Then I gave you the paper to send to your father, by post. Isn't that so?

**NORA:** Yes.

**KROGSTAD:** And of course you did so at once; for within five or six days you brought me back the document with your father's signature; and I handed you the money.

**NORA:** Well? Haven't I made my payments punctually?

**KROGSTAD:** Fairly—yes. But to return to the point: You were in great trouble at the time, Mrs. Helmer.

**NORA:** I was indeed!

**KROGSTAD:** Your father was very ill, I believe?

**NORA:** He was on his death-bed.

**KROGSTAD:** And died soon after?

**NORA:** Yes.

**KROGSTAD:** Tell me, Mrs. Helmer: do you happen to recollect the day of his death? The day of the month, I mean?

**NORA:** Father died on the 29th of September.

**KROGSTAD:** Quite correct. I've made inquiries. And here comes in the remarkable point—[*Produces a paper.*] which I can't explain.

**NORA:** What remarkable point? I don't know—

**KROGSTAD:** The remarkable point, madam, that your father signed this paper three days after his death!

**NORA:** What! I don't understand—

**KROGSTAD:** Your father died on the 29th of September. But look here: He's dated his signature October 2nd! Isn't that remarkable, Mrs. Helmer?

[*NORA is silent.*] Can you explain it? [*NORA continues silent.*] It's note-worthy, too, that the words "October 2nd" and the year aren't in your father's handwriting, but in one which I believe I know. Well, this may be explained; your father may've forgotten to date his signature, and somebody may've added the date at random, before the fact of your father's death was known. There is nothing wrong in that.
Everything depends on the signature. Of course it's genuine, Mrs. Helmer? It's really your father himself who wrote his name here?

**NORA:** [*After a short silence, throws her head back and looks defiantly at him.*] No, it wasn't. I wrote father's name.

**KROGSTAD:** Ah!—You're aware, madam, that that's a dangerous admission?

**NORA:** How so? You'll soon get your money.

**KROGSTAD:** May I ask you one more question? Why didn't you send the paper to your father?

**NORA:** It was impossible. Father was ill. If I'd asked him for his signature, I'd've had to tell him why I wanted the money; but he was so ill I really couldn't tell him that my husband's life was in danger. It was impossible.

**KROGSTAD:** Then it would've been better to've given up your tour.

**NORA:** No, I couldn't do that; my husband's life depended on that journey. I couldn't give it up.

**KROGSTAD:** And did it never occur to you that you were playing me false?

**NORA:** That's nothing to me. I didn't care in the least about you. I couldn't endure you for all the cruel difficulties you made, although you knew how ill my husband was.

**KROGSTAD:** Mrs. Helmer, you evidently do not realize what you've been guilty of. But I can assure you it's nothing more and nothing worse that made me an outcast from society.

**NORA:** You! You want me to believe that you did a brave thing to save your wife's life?

**KROGSTAD:** The law takes no account of motives.

**NORA:** Then it must be a very bad law.

**KROGSTAD:** Bad or not, if I produce this document in court, you'll be condemned according to law.

**NORA:** I don't believe that. Do you mean to tell me that a daughter has no right to spare her dying father trouble and anxiety?—that a wife has no right to save her husband's life? I don't know much about the law, but I'm sure you'll find, somewhere or another, that that's allowed. And you don't know that—you, a lawyer! You must be a bad one, Mr. Krogstad.

**KROGSTAD:** Possibly. But business—such business as ours—I do understand. You believe that? Very well; now do as you please. But this I'll tell you, that if I'm flung into the gutter a second time, you'll keep me company.

[*Bows and goes out through hall.*]

**NORA:**  [*Stands a while thinking, then tosses her head.*] Oh nonsense! He wants to frighten me. I'm not so foolish as that. [*Begins folding the children's clothes. Pauses.*] But—? No, it's impossible! Why, I did it for love!

**CHILDREN:**  [*At the door, left.*] Mamma, the strange man's gone now.

**NORA:**  Yes, yes, I know. But don't tell anyone about the strange man. Do you hear? Not even papa!

**CHILDREN:**  No, mamma; and now you'll play with us again?

**NORA:**  No, no; not now.

**CHILDREN:**  Oh, do, mamma; you know you promised.

**NORA:**  Yes, but I can't just now. Run to the nursery; I've so much to do. Run along,—run along, and be good, my darlings! [*She pushes them gently into the inner room, and closes the door behind them. Sits on the sofa, embroiders a few stitches, but soon pauses.*] No! [*Throws down the work, rises, goes to the hall door and calls out.*] Ellen, bring in the Christmas tree! [*Goes to table, left, and opens the drawer, again pauses.*] No, it's quite impossible!

**ELLEN:**  [*With Christmas tree.*] Where should I stand it, ma'am?

**NORA:**  There, in the middle of the room.

**ELLEN:**  Should I bring in anything else?

**NORA:**  No, thank you, I have all I want.

[*ELLEN, having put down the tree, goes out.*]

**NORA:**  [*Busy dressing the tree.*] There must be a candle here—and flowers there.—That horrible man! Nonsense, nonsense! there's nothing to be afraid of. The Christmas tree'll be beautiful. I'll do everything to please you, Torvald; I'll sing and dance,—

[*Enter HELMER by the hall door, with a bundle of documents.*]

**NORA:**  Oh! You're back already?

**HELMER:**  Yes. Has anybody been here?

**NORA:**  No.

**HELMER:**  That's odd. I saw Krogstad come out of the house.

**NORA:**  Did you? Oh, yes, by-the-bye, he was here for a minute.

**HELMER:**  Nora, I can see by your manner that he's been begging you to put in a good word for him.

**NORA:**  Yes.

**HELMER:**  And you're to do it as if of your own accord? You were to say nothing to me of his having been here. Didn't he suggest that too?

**NORA:**  Yes, Torvald; but—

**HELMER:**  Nora, Nora! And you'd condescend to that! To speak to such a man, to make him a promise! And then to tell me an untruth about it!

**NORA:**  An untruth!

**HELMER:**  Didn't you say that nobody had been here? [*Threatens with his finger.*] My little bird must never do that again! A song-bird must sing clear and true; no false notes. [*Puts his arm round her.*] That's so, isn't it? Yes, I was sure of it. [*Lets her go.*] And now we'll say no more about it. [*Sits down before the fire.*] Oh, how cozy and quiet it is here! [*Glances into his documents.*]

**NORA:**  [*Busy with the tree, after a short silence.*] Torvald!

**HELMER:**  Yes.

**NORA:**  I'm looking forward so much to the Stenborgs' fancy ball the day after tomorrow.

**HELMER:**  And I'm anxious to see what surprise you have in store for me.

**NORA:**  Oh, it's too tiresome!

**HELMER:**  What?

**NORA:**  I can't think of anything good. Everything seems so foolish and meaningless.

**HELMER:**  Has little Nora made that discovery?

**NORA:**  [*Behind his chair, with her arms on the back.*] Are you very busy, Torvald?

**HELMER:**  Well—

**NORA:**  What papers are those?

**HELMER:**  Bank business.

**NORA:**  Already!

**HELMER:**  I've got the retiring manager to let me make some necessary changes in the staff and the organization. I can do this during Christmas week. I want to have everything straight by the New Year.

**NORA:**  Then that's why that poor Krogstad—

**HELMER:**  H'm.

**NORA:**  [*Still leaning over the chair back and slowly stroking his hair.*] If you hadn't been so very busy, I should've asked you a great, great favour, Torvald.

**HELMER:**  What can it be? Out with it.

**NORA:**  Nobody has such perfect taste as you; and I'd so love to look well at the fancy ball. Torvald, dear, couldn't you take me in hand, and settle what I'm to be, and arrange my costume for me?

**HELMER:**  Aha! So my wilful little woman is at a loss, and making signals of distress.

**NORA:**  Yes, please, Torvald. I can't get on without your help.

**HELMER:**  Well, well, I'll think it over, and we'll soon hit upon something.

**NORA:**  Oh, how good of you! [*Goes to the tree again; pause.*] How well the red flowers show.—Tell me, was it anything so very dreadful this Krogstad got into trouble about?

**HELMER:**  Forgery, that's all. Don't you know what that means?

**NORA:**  Mayn't he've been driven to it by need?

**HELMER:** Yes; or, like so many others, he may've done it in pure heedlessness. I am not so cold hearted as to condemn a man absolutely for a single fault.

**NORA:** No, surely not, Torvald!

**HELMER:** Many a man can retrieve his character, if he owns his crime and takes the punishment.

**NORA:** Punishment—?

**HELMER:** But Krogstad didn't do that. He evaded the law by means of tricks and subterfuges; and that's what has morally ruined him.

**NORA:** Do you think that—?

**HELMER:** Just think how a man with a thing of that sort on his conscience must be always lying and canting and shamming. Think of the mask he must wear even towards those who stand nearest him—towards his own wife and children. The effect on the children—that's the most terrible part of it, Nora.

**NORA:** Why?

**HELMER:** Because in such an atmosphere of lies home life is poisoned and contaminated in every fiber. Every breath the children draw contains some germ of evil.

**NORA:** [*Closer behind him.*] Are you sure of that?

**HELMER:** As a lawyer, my dear, I've seen it often enough. Nearly all cases of early corruption may be traced to lying mothers.

**NORA:** Why—mothers?

**HELMER:** It generally comes from the mother's side; but of course the father's influence may act in the same way. Every lawyer knows it too well. And here's this Krogstad been poisoning his own children for years past by a life of lies and hypocrisy—that's why I call him morally ruined. [*Holds out both hands to her.*] So my sweet little Nora must promise not to plead his cause. Shake hands upon it. Come, come, what's this? Give me your hand. That's right. Then it's a bargain. I assure you it would've been impossible for me to work with him. It gives me a positive sense of physical discomfort to come in contact with such people.

[*NORA draws her hand away, and moves to the other side of the Christmas tree.*]

**NORA:** How warm it is here. And I've so much to do.

**HELMER:** [*Rises and gathers up his papers.*] Yes, and I must try to get some of these papers looked through before dinner. And I'll think over your costume too. Perhaps I may even find something to hang in gilt paper on the Christmas tree—. [*Lays his hand on her head.*] My precious little song-bird!

[*He goes into his room and shuts the door.*]

**NORA:** [*Softly, after a pause.*] It can't be. It's impossible. It must be impossible!

**ANNA:** [*At the door, left.*] The little ones are begging so prettily to come to mamma.

**NORA:** No, no, no; don't let them come to me! Keep them with you, Anna.

**ANNA:** Very well, ma'am. [*Shuts the door.*]

**NORA:** [*Pale with terror.*] Corrupt my children!—Poison my home! [*Short pause. She throws back her head.*] It's not true! It can never, never be true!

## Act Two

The same room. In the corner, beside the piano, stands the Christmas tree, stripped, and with the candles burnt out. NORA's outdoor things lie on the sofa. NORA, alone, is walking about restlessly. At last she stops by the sofa, and takes up her cloak.

**NORA:** [*Dropping the cloak.*] There's somebody coming! [*Goes to the hall door and listens.*] Nobody; of course nobody'll come today, Christmas day; or tomorrow either. But perhaps—[*Opens the door and looks out.*]—No, nothing in the letter box; quite empty. [*Comes forward.*] Stuff and nonsense! Of course he won't really do anything. Such a thing couldn't happen. It's impossible! Why, I've three little children.

[*ANNA enters from the left, with a large cardboard box.*]

**ANNA:** I've found the box with the fancy dress at last.

**NORA:** Thanks; put it down on the table.

**ANNA:** [*Does so.*] But I'm afraid it's very much out of order.

**NORA:** Oh, I wish I could tear it into a hundred thousand pieces!

**ANNA:** Oh, no. It can easily be put to rights—just a little patience.

**NORA:** I'll go and get Mrs. Linden to help me.

**ANNA:** Going out again? In such weather as this! You'll catch cold, ma'am, and be ill.

**NORA:** Worse things might happen.—What're the children doing?

**ANNA:** They're playing with their Christmas presents, poor little dears; but—

**NORA:** Do they often ask for me?

**ANNA:** You see they've been so used to having their mamma with them.

**NORA:** Yes; but, Anna, I can't have them with me so much in future.

**ANNA:** Well, little children get used to anything.

**NORA:** Do you think they do? Do you believe they'd forget their mother if she went quite away?

**ANNA:** Gracious me! Quite away?

**NORA:** Tell me, Anna—I've so often wondered about it—how'd you bring yourself to give your child up to strangers?

**ANNA:** I had to when I came to nurse my little Miss Nora.

**NORA:** But how'd you make up your mind about it?

**ANNA:** When I had the chance of such a good place? A poor girl who's been in trouble must take what comes. That wicked man did nothing for me.

**NORA:** But your daughter must've forgotten you.

**ANNA:**  Oh, no, ma'am, she hasn't. She wrote to me both when she was confirmed and when she was married.

**NORA:**  [*Embracing her.*] Dear old Anna—you were a good mother to me when I was little.

**ANNA:**  My poor little Nora had no mother but me.

**NORA:**  And if my little ones had nobody else, I'm sure you would—Nonsense, nonsense! [*Opens the box.*] Go in to the children. Now I must—You'll see how lovely I'll be tomorrow.

**ANNA:**  I'm sure there'll be no one at the ball so lovely as my Miss Nora.

[*She goes into the room on the left.*]

**NORA:**  [*Takes the costume out of the box, but soon throws it down again.*] Oh, if I dared go out. If only nobody would come. If only nothing would happen here in the meantime. Rubbish; nobody's coming. Only not to think. What a delicious muff! Beautiful gloves, beautiful gloves! To forget—to forget! One, two, three, four, five, six—[*With a scream.*] Ah, there they come. [*Goes towards the door, then stands irresolute.*]

**MRS. LINDEN**  enters from the hall, where she has taken off her things.

**NORA:**  Oh, it's you, Christina. There's nobody else there? I'm so glad you've come.

**MRS. LINDEN:**  I hear you called at my lodgings.

**NORA:**  Yes, I was just passing. There's something you must help me with. Let's sit here on the sofa. Tomorrow evening there's to be a fancy ball at Consul Stenborg's upstairs, and Torvald wants me to appear as a Neapolitan fisher-girl, and dance the tarantella; I learned it at Capri.

**MRS. LINDEN:**  I see—quite a performance.

**NORA:**  Yes, Torvald wishes it. Look, this is the costume; Torvald had it made for me in Italy. But now it's all so torn, I don't know—

**MRS. LINDEN:**  Oh, we'll soon set that right. It's only the trimming that's come loose here and there. Have you a needle and thread? Ah, here's the very thing.

**NORA:**  Oh, how kind of you.

**MRS. LINDEN:**  [*Sewing.*] So you're to be in costume tomorrow, Nora? I'll tell you what—I'll come in for a moment to see you in all your glory. But I've quite forgotten to thank you for the pleasant evening yesterday.

**NORA:**  [*Rises and walks across the room.*] Oh, yesterday, it didn't seem so pleasant as usual.—You should've come to town a little sooner, Christina.—Torvald has certainly the art of making home bright and beautiful.

**MRS. LINDEN:**  You too, I'd think, or you wouldn't be your father's daughter. But tell me—is Doctor Rank always so depressed as he was last evening?

**NORA:**  No, yesterday it was particularly noticeable. You see, he suffers from a dreadful illness. He has spinal consumption, poor fellow. They say his father was a horrible man, who kept mistresses and all sorts of things—so the son's been sickly from his childhood, you understand.

**MRS. LINDEN:** [*Lets her sewing fall into her lap.*] Why, my darling Nora, how do you come to know such things?

**NORA:** [*Moving about the room.*] Oh, when one has three children, one sometimes has visits from women who are half—half doctors—and they talk of one thing and another.

**MRS. LINDEN:** [*Goes on sewing; a short pause.*] Does Doctor Rank come here every day?

**NORA:** Every day of his life. He's been Torvald's most intimate friend from boyhood, and he's a good friend of mine too. Doctor Rank is quite one of the family.

**MRS. LINDEN:** But tell me—is he quite sincere? I mean, isn't he rather given to flattering people?

**NORA:** No, quite the contrary. Why should you think so?

**MRS. LINDEN:** When you introduced us yesterday he said he'd often heard my name; but I noticed afterwards that your husband had no notion who I was. How could Doctor Rank—?

**NORA:** He's quite right, Christina. You see, Torvald loves me so indescribably, he wants to have me all to himself, as he says. When we were first married he was almost jealous if I even mentioned any of my old friends at home; so naturally I gave up doing it. But I often talk of the old times to Doctor Rank, for he likes to hear about them.

**MRS. LINDEN:** Listen to me, Nora! You're still a child in many ways. I'm older than you, and have had more experience. I'll tell you something? You should to get clear of all this with Dr. Rank.

**NORA:** Get clear of what?

**MRS. LINDEN:** The whole affair, I'd say. You're talking yesterday of a rich admirer who was to find you money—

**NORA:** Yes, one who never existed, worse luck. What then?

**MRS. LINDEN:** Has Doctor Rank money?

**NORA:** Yes, he has.

**MRS. LINDEN:** And nobody to provide for?

**NORA:** Nobody. But—?

**MRS. LINDEN:** And he comes here every day?

**NORA:** Yes, I told you so.

**MRS. LINDEN:** I should've thought he would've had better taste.

**NORA:** I don't understand you a bit.

**MRS. LINDEN:** Don't pretend, Nora. Do you suppose I can't guess who lent you the twelve hundred dollars?

**NORA:** Are you out of your senses? How can you think such a thing? A friend who comes here every day! Why, the position would be unbearable!

**MRS. LINDEN:** Then it really isn't him?

**NORA:** No, I assure you. It never for a moment occurred to me—Besides, at that time he'd nothing to lend; he came into his property afterwards.

**MRS. LINDEN:** Well, I believe that's lucky for you, Nora dear.

**NORA:** No, really, it'd never've struck me to ask Dr. Rank—And yet, I'm certain that if I did—

**MRS. LINDEN:** But of course you never would.

**NORA:** Of course not. It's inconceivable that it'd ever be necessary. But I'm quite sure that if I spoke to Doctor Rank—

**MRS. LINDEN:** Behind your husband's back?

**NORA:** I must get clear of the other thing; that's behind his back too. I must get clear of that.

**MRS. LINDEN:** Yes, yes, I told you so yesterday; but—

**NORA:** [*Walking up and down.*] A man can manage these things much better than a woman.

**MRS. LINDEN:** One's own husband, yes.

**NORA:** Nonsense. [*Stands still.*] When everything's paid, one gets back the paper.

**MRS. LINDEN:** Of course.

**NORA:** And can tear it into a hundred thousand pieces, and burn it up, the nasty, filthy thing!

**MRS. LINDEN:** [*Looks at her fixedly, lays down her work, and rises slowly.*] Nora, you're hiding something from me.

**NORA:** Can you see it in my face?

**MRS. LINDEN:** Something's happened since yesterday morning. Nora, what is it?

**NORA:** [*Going towards her.*] Christina—! [*Listens.*] Hush! There's Torvald coming home. Do you mind going into the nursery for the present? Torvald can't bear to see dressmaking going on. Get Anna to help you.

**MRS. LINDEN:** [*Gathers some of the things together.*] Very well; but I won't go away until you have told me all about it.

[*She goes out to the left, as HELMER enters from the hall.*]

**NORA:** [*Runs to meet him.*] Oh, how I've been longing for you to come, Torvald dear!

**HELMER:** Was that the dressmaker—?

**NORA:** No, Christina. She's helping me with my costume. You'll see how nice I'll look.

**HELMER:** Yes, wasn't that a happy thought of mine?

**NORA:** Splendid! But isn't it good of me, too, to've given in to you about the tarantella?

**HELMER:** [*Takes her under the chin.*] Good of you! To give in to your own husband? Well, well, you little madcap, I know you don't mean it. But I won't disturb you. I daresay you want to be "trying on."

**NORA:** And you're going to work, I suppose?

**HELMER:** Yes. [*Shows her a bundle of papers.*] Look here. I've just come from the Bank—

[*Goes towards his room.*]

**NORA:**   Torvald.

**HELMER:**   [*Stopping.*] Yes?

**NORA:**   If your little squirrel were to beg you for something so prettily—

**HELMER:**   Well?

**NORA:**   Would you do it?

**HELMER:**   I must know first what it is.

**NORA:**   The squirrel would skip about and play all sorts of tricks if You'd only be nice and kind.

**HELMER:**   Come, then, out with it.

**NORA:**   Your lark would twitter from morning till night—

**HELMER:**   Oh, that she does in any case.

**NORA:**   I'll be an elf and dance in the moonlight for you, Torvald.

**HELMER:**   Nora—you can't mean what you were hinting at this morning?

**NORA:**   [*Coming nearer.*] Yes, Torvald, I beg and implore you!

**HELMER:**   Have you really the courage to begin that again?

**NORA:**   Yes, yes; for my sake, you must let Krogstad keep his place in the Bank.

**HELMER:**   My dear Nora, it's his place I intend for Mrs. Linden.

**NORA:**   Yes, that's so good of you. But instead of Krogstad, you could dismiss some other clerk.

**HELMER:**   Why, this is incredible obstinacy! Because you've thoughtlessly promised to put in a word for him, I am to—!

**NORA:**   It's not that, Torvald. It's for your own sake. This man writes for the most scurrilous newspapers; you said so yourself. He can do you no end of harm. I'm so terribly afraid of him—

**HELMER:**   Ah, I understand; it's old recollections that're frightening you.

**NORA:**   What do you mean?

**HELMER:**   Of course you're thinking of your father.

**NORA:**   Yes—yes, of course. Only think of the shameful slanders wicked people used to write about father. I believe they'd have got him dismissed if you hadn't been sent to look into the thing, and been kind to him, and helped him.

**HELMER:**   My little Nora, between your father and me there's all the difference in the world. Your father was not altogether unimpeachable. I am; and I hope to remain so.

**NORA:**   Oh, no one knows what wicked men may hit upon. We could live so quietly and happily now, in our cozy, peaceful home, you and I and the children, Torvald! That's why I beg and implore you—

**HELMER:**   And it's just by pleading his cause that you make it impossible for me to keep him. It's already known at the Bank that I intend to dismiss Krogstad. If it were now reported that the new manager let himself be turned round his wife's little finger—

**NORA:**   What then?

**HELMER:** Oh, nothing, so long as a wilful woman can have her way! I'm to make myself a laughing-stock to the whole staff, and set people saying that I'm open to all sorts of outside influence? Take my word for it, I'd soon feel the consequences. And besides there's one thing that makes Krogstad impossible for me to work with—

**NORA:** What thing?

**HELMER:** I could perhaps have overlooked his moral failings at a pinch—

**NORA:** Yes, couldn't you, Torvald?

**HELMER:** And I hear he is good at his work. But the fact is, he was a college chum of mine—there was one of those cash friendships between us that one so often repents of later. I may as well confess it at once—he calls me by my Christian name; and he's tactless enough to do it even when others are present. He delights in putting on airs of familiarity—Torvald here, Torvald there! I assure you it's most painful to me. He'd make my position at the Bank perfectly unendurable.

**NORA:** Torvald, surely you're not serious?

**HELMER:** No? Why not?

**NORA:** That's such a petty reason.

**HELMER:** What! Petty! Do you consider me petty!

**NORA:** No, on the contrary, Torvald dear; and that's just why—

**HELMER:** Never mind; you call my motives petty; then I must be petty too. Petty! Very well!—Now we'll put an end to this, once for all. [*Goes to the door into the hall and calls.*] Ellen!

**NORA:** What do you want?

**HELMER:** [*Searching among his papers.*] To settle the thing. [*ELLEN enters.*] Here; take this letter; give it to a messenger. See that he takes it at once. The address is on it. Here's the money.

**ELLEN:** Very well, sir.

[*Goes with the letter.*]

**HELMER:** [*Putting his papers together.*] There, Madam Obstinacy.

**NORA:** [*Breathless.*] Torvald—what's in the letter?

**HELMER:** Krogstad's dismissal.

**NORA:** Call it back again, Torvald! There's still time. Oh, Torvald, call it back again! For my sake, for your own, for the children's sake! Do you hear, Torvald? Do it! You don't know what that letter may bring upon us all.

**HELMER:** Too late.

**NORA:** Yes, too late.

**HELMER:** My dear Nora, I forgive your anxiety, though it's anything but flattering to me. Why'd you suppose that I'd be afraid of a wretched scribbler's spite? But I forgive you all the same, for it's a proof of your great love for me. [*Takes her in his arms.*] That's as it should be, my own dear Nora. Let what will happen—when it comes to the pinch, I'll have strength and courage enough. You'll see: my shoulders are broad enough to bear the whole burden.

**NORA:**  [*Terror-struck.*] What do you mean by that?

**HELMER:**  The whole burden, I say—

**NORA:**  [*With decision.*] That you'll never, never do!

**HELMER:**  Very well; then we'll share it, Nora, as man and wife. That's how it should be. [*Petting her.*] Are you satisfied now? Come, come, come, don't look like a scared dove. It's all nothing—foolish fancies.—Now you should play the tarantella through and practice with the tambourine. I'll sit in my inner room and shut both doors, so that I'll hear nothing. as much noise as you please. [*Turns round in doorway.*] And when Rank comes, just tell him where I'm to be found.

[*He nods to her, and goes with his papers into his room, closing the door.*]

**NORA:**  [*Bewildered with terror, stands as though rooted to the ground, and whispers.*] He'd do it. Yes, he'd do it. He'd do it, in spite of all the world.—No, never that, never, never! Anything rather than that! Oh, for some way of escape! What'll I do—! [*Hall bell rings.*] Doctor Rank—!— Anything, anything, rather than—!

[*NORA draws her hands over her face, pulls herself together, goes to the door and opens it. RANK stands outside hanging up his fur coat. During what follows it begins to grow dark.*]

**NORA:**  Good afternoon, Doctor Rank, I knew you by your ring. But you mustn't go to Torvald now. I believe he's busy.

**RANK:**  And you?

[*Enters and closes the door.*]

**NORA:**  Oh, you know very well, I've always time for you.

**RANK:**  Thank you. I'll avail myself of your kindness as long as I can.

**NORA:**  What do you mean? As long as you can?

**RANK:**  Yes. Does that frighten you?

**NORA:**  I think it's an odd expression. Do you expect anything to happen?

**RANK:**  Something I've long been prepared for; but I didn't think it'd come so soon.

**NORA:**  [*Catching at his arm.*] What've you discovered? Doctor Rank, you must tell me!

**RANK:**  [*Sitting down by the stove.*] I'm running downhill. There's no help for it.

**NORA:**  [*Draws a long breath of relief.*] It's you—?

**RANK:**  Who else should it be?—Why lie to one's self? I'm the most wretched of all my patients, Mrs. Helmer. In these last days I've been auditing my life-account—bankrupt! Perhaps before a month is over, I'll lie rotting in the churchyard.

**NORA:**   Oh! What an ugly way to talk.

**RANK:**   The thing itself is so confoundedly ugly, you see. But the worst of it is, so many other ugly things have to be gone through first. There's only one last investigation to be made, and when that's over I'll know pretty certainly when the breakup will begin. There's one thing I want to say to you: Helmer's delicate nature shrinks so from all that's horrible: I'll not have him in my sickroom—

**NORA:**   But, Doctor Rank—

**RANK:**   I won't have him, I say—not on any account! I'll lock my door against him.—As soon as I'm quite certain of the worst, I'll send you my business card with a black cross on it; and then you'll know that the final horror's begun.

**NORA:**   Why, you're perfectly unreasonable today; and I did so want you to be in a really good humor.

**RANK:**   With death staring me in the face?—And to suffer thus for another's sin! Where's the justice of it? And in one way or another you can trace in every family some such inexorable retribution—

**NORA:**   [*Stopping her ears.*] Nonsense, nonsense! Now cheer up!

**RANK:**   Well, after all, the whole thing's only worth laughing at. My poor innocent spine must do penance for my father's wild oats.

**NORA:**   [*At table, left.*] I suppose he was too fond of asparagus and Strasbourg pate, wasn't he?

**RANK:**   Yes; and truffles.

**NORA:**   Yes, truffles, to be sure. And oysters, I believe?

**RANK:**   Yes, oysters; oysters, of course.

**NORA:**   And then all the port and champagne! It's sad that all these good things should attack the spine.

**RANK:**   Especially when the luckless spine attacked never had any good of them.

**NORA:**   Ah, yes, that's the worst of it.

**RANK:**   [*Looks at her searchingly.*] H'm—

**NORA:**   [*A moment later.*] Why'd you smile?

**RANK:**   No; it's you that laughed.

**NORA:**   No; it's you that smiled, Doctor Rank.

**RANK:**   [*Standing up.*] I see you're deeper than I thought.

**NORA:**   I'm in such a crazy mood today.

**RANK:**   So it seems.

**NORA:**   [*With her hands on his shoulders.*] Dear, dear Doctor Rank, death shall not take you away from Torvald and me.

**RANK:**   Oh, you'll easily get over the loss. The absent are soon forgotten.

**NORA:**   [*Looks at him anxiously.*] Do you think so?

**RANK:**   People make fresh ties, and then—

**NORA:**    Who make fresh ties?

**RANK:**    You and Helmer will,—when I'm gone. You yourself are taking time by the forelock, it seems to me. What's that Mrs. Linden doing here yesterday?

**NORA:**    Oh!—you're surely not jealous of poor Christina?

**RANK:**    Yes, I am. She'll be my successor in this house. When I'm out of the way, this woman will perhaps—

**NORA:**    Hush! Not so loud! She's in there.

**RANK:**    Today as well? You see!

**NORA:**    Only to put my costume in order—dear me, how unreasonable you are! [*Sits on sofa.*] Now do be good, Doctor Rank! Tomorrow you'll see how beautifully I'll dance; and then you may fancy that I'm doing it all to please you—and of course Torvald as well. [*Takes various things out of box.*] Doctor Rank, sit down here, and I'll show you something.

**RANK:**    [*Sitting.*] What is it?

**NORA:**    Look here. Look!

**RANK:**    Silk stockings.

**NORA:**    Flesh colored. Aren't they lovely? It's so dark here now; but tomorrow—No, no, no; you must only look at the feet. Oh, well, I suppose you may look at the rest too.

**RANK:**    H'm—

**NORA:**    What're you looking so critical about? Do you think they won't fit me?

**RANK:**    I can't possibly give any competent opinion on that point.

**NORA:**    [*Looking at him a moment.*] For shame! [*Hits him lightly on the ear with the stockings.*] Take that.

[*Rolls them up again.*]

**RANK:**    And what other wonders am I to see?

**NORA:**    You won't see anything more; for you don't behave nicely.

[*She hums a little and searches among the things.*]

**RANK:**    [*After a short silence.*] When I sit here gossiping with you, I can't imagine—I simply cannot conceive—what would've become of me if I'd never entered this house.

**NORA:**    [*Smiling.*] Yes, I think you do feel at home with us.

**RANK:**    [*More softly—looking straight before him.*] And now to have to leave it all—

**NORA:**    Nonsense. You won't leave us.

**RANK:**    [*In the same tone.*] And not to be able to leave behind the slightest token of gratitude; scarcely even a passing regret—nothing but an empty place, that can be filled by the first comer.

**NORA:**    And if I were to ask you for—? No—

**RANK:**    For what?

**NORA:**    For a great proof of your friendship.

**RANK:**   Yes—yes?

**NORA:**   I mean—for a very, very great service—

**RANK:**   Would you really, for once, make me so happy?

**NORA:**   Oh, you don't know what it is.

**RANK:**   Then tell me.

**NORA:**   No, I really can't, Doctor Rank. It's far, far too much—not only a service, but help and advice besides—

**RANK:**   So much the better. I can't think what you can mean. But go on. Don't you trust me?

**NORA:**   As I trust no one else. I know you're my best and truest friend. So I'll tell you. Well then, Doctor Rank, there's something you must help me to prevent. You know how deeply, how wonderfully Torvald loves me; he wouldn't hesitate a moment to give his very life for my sake.

**RANK:**   [*Bending towards her.*] Nora—do you think he's the only one who—?

**NORA:**   [*With a slight start.*] Who—?

**RANK:**   Who'd gladly give his life for you?

**NORA:**   [*Sadly.*] Oh!

**RANK:**   I've sworn that you'll know it before I—go. I'll never find a better opportunity.—Yes, Nora, now I've told you; and now you know that you can trust me as you can no one else.

**NORA:**   [*Standing up; simply and calmly.*] Let me pass, please.

**RANK:**   [*Makes way for her, but remains sitting.*] Nora—

**NORA:**   [*In the doorway.*] Ellen, bring the lamp. [*Crosses to the stove.*] Oh dear, Doctor Rank, that's too bad of you.

**RANK:**   [*Rising.*] That I've loved you as deeply as—anyone else? That's too bad of me?

**NORA:**   No, but that you'd have told me so. It was so unnecessary—

**RANK:**   What do you mean? Did you know—?

[*ELLEN enters with the lamp; sets it on the table and goes out again.*]

**RANK:**   Nora—Mrs. Helmer—I ask you, did you know?

**NORA:**   Oh, how can I tell what I knew or didn't know? I really can't say— How could you be so clumsy, Doctor Rank? It was all so nice!

**RANK:**   Well, at any rate, you know now that I'm at your service, body and soul. And now, go on.

**NORA:**   [*Looking at him.*] Go on—now?

**RANK:**   I beg you to tell me what you want.

**NORA:**   I can tell you nothing now.

**RANK:**   Yes, yes! You mustn't punish me in that way. Let me do for you whatever a man can.

**NORA:**   You can do nothing for me now.—Besides, I really want no help. You'll see it was only my fancy. Yes, it must be so. Of course! [*Sits in the rocking-chair, looks at him and smiles.*] You are a nice person, Doctor Rank! Aren't you ashamed of yourself, now that the lamp's on the table?

**RANK:**  No; not exactly. But perhaps I should go—for ever.

**NORA:**  No, indeed you mustn't. Of course you must come and go as you've always done. You know very well that Torvald can't do without you.

**RANK:**  Yes, but you?

**NORA:**  Oh, you know I always like to have you here.

**RANK:**  That's just what led me astray. You're a riddle to me. It's often seemed to me as if you liked being with me almost as much as being with Helmer.

**NORA:**  Yes; don't you see? There're people one loves, and others one likes to talk to.

**RANK:**  Yes—there's something in that.

**NORA:**  When I was a girl, of course I loved papa best. But it always delighted me to steal into the servants' room. In the first place they never lectured me, and in the second it was such fun to hear them talk.

**RANK:**  Ah, I see; then it's their place I've taken?

**NORA:**  [*Jumps up and hurries towards him.*] Oh, my dear Doctor Rank, I don't mean that. But you understand, with Torvald it's the same as with papa—

[*ELLEN enters from the hall.*]

**ELLEN:**  Please, ma'am—

[*Whispers to NORA, and gives her a card.*]

**NORA:**  [*Glancing at card.*] Ah!

[*Puts it in her pocket.*]

**RANK:**  Anything wrong?

**NORA:**  No, no, not in the least. It's only—it's my new costume—

**RANK:**  Your costume! Why, it's there.

**NORA:**  Oh, that one, yes. But this is another that—I've ordered it— Torvald mustn't know—

**RANK:**  Aha! So that's the great secret.

**NORA:**  Yes, of course. Please go to him; he's in the inner room. Do keep him while I—

**RANK:**  Don't be alarmed; he won't escape.

[*RANK goes into HELMER's room.*]

**NORA:**  [*To ELLEN.*] Is he waiting in the kitchen?

**ELLEN:**  Yes, he came up the back stair—

**NORA:**  Didn't you tell him I was engaged?

**ELLEN:**  Yes, but it's no use.

**NORA:**  He won't go away?

**ELLEN:**  No, ma'am, not until he has spoken to you.

**NORA:**  Then let him come in; but quietly. And, Ellen—say nothing about it; it's a surprise for my husband.

**ELLEN:**   Oh, yes, ma'am, I understand.

[*She goes out.*]

**NORA:**   It's coming! The dreadful thing's coming, after all. No, no, no, it can never be; it will not!

[*She goes to* HELMER'S *door and slips the bolt.* ELLEN *opens the hall door for* KROGSTAD, *and shuts it after him. He wears a travelling-coat, high boots, and a fur cap.*]

**NORA:**   [*Goes towards him.*] Speak softly; my husband's at home.

**KROGSTAD:**   All right. That's nothing to me.

**NORA:**   What do you want?

**KROGSTAD:**   A little information.

**NORA:**   Be quick, then. What is it?

**KROGSTAD:**   You know I've got my dismissal.

**NORA:**   I couldn't prevent it, Mr. Krogstad. I fought for you to the last, but it's of no use.

**KROGSTAD:**   Does your husband care for you so little? He knows what I can bring upon you, and yet he dares—

**NORA:**   How could you think I'd tell him?

**KROGSTAD:**   Well, as a matter of fact, I didn't think it. It wasn't like my friend Torvald Helmer to show so much courage—

**NORA:**   Mr. Krogstad, be good enough to speak respectfully of my husband.

**KROGSTAD:**   Certainly, with all due respect. But since you're so anxious to keep the matter secret, I suppose you're a little clearer than yesterday as to what you've done.

**NORA:**   Clearer than you'd ever make me.

**KROGSTAD:**   Yes, such a bad lawyer as I—

**NORA:**   What is it you want?

**KROGSTAD:**   Only to see how you're getting on, Mrs. Helmer. I've been thinking about you all day. Even a mere broker, a gutter-journalist, a— in short, a creature like me—has a little bit of what people call feeling.

**NORA:**   Then show it; think of my little children.

**KROGSTAD:**   Did you and your husband think of mine? But enough of that. I only wanted to tell you that you needn't take this matter too seriously. I'll not lodge any information, for the present.

**NORA:**   No, surely not. I knew you wouldn't.

**KROGSTAD:**   The whole thing can be settled quite amicably. Nobody need know. It can remain among us three.

**NORA:**   My husband must never know.

**KROGSTAD:**   How can you prevent it? Can you pay off the balance?

**NORA:**   No, not at once.

**KROGSTAD:**   Or have you any means of raising the money in the next few days?

**NORA:**  None—that I'll make use of.

**KROGSTAD:.**   And if you had, it wouldn't help you now. If you offered me ever so much money down, you shouldn't get back your I.O.U.

**NORA:**  Tell me what you want to do with it.

**KROGSTAD:**  I only want to keep it—to have it in my possession. No outsider shall hear anything of it. So, if you've any desperate scheme in your head—

**NORA:**  What if I have?

**KROGSTAD:**  If you'd think of leaving your husband and children—

**NORA:**  What if I do?

**KROGSTAD:**  Or if you'd think of—something worse—

**NORA:**  How'd you know that?

**KROGSTAD:**  Put all that out of your head.

**NORA:**  How'd you know what I had in my mind?

**KROGSTAD:**  Most of us think of that at first. I thought of it, too; but I hadn't the courage—

**NORA:**  [*Tonelessly.*] Nor I.

**KROGSTAD:**  [*Relieved.*] No, one hasn't. You haven't the courage either, have you?

**NORA:**  I haven't, I haven't.

**KROGSTAD:**  Besides, it would be very foolish.—Just one domestic storm, and it's all over. I've a letter in my pocket for your husband—

**NORA:**  Telling him everything?

**KROGSTAD:**  Sparing you as much as possible.

**NORA:**  [*Quickly.*] He must never read that letter. Tear it up. I'll manage to get the money somehow—

**KROGSTAD:**  Pardon me, Mrs. Helmer, but I believe I told you—

**NORA:**  Oh, I'm not talking about the money I owe you. Tell me how much you demand from my husband—I'll get it.

**KROGSTAD:**  I demand no money from your husband.

**NORA:**  What do you demand then?

**KROGSTAD:**  I'll tell you. I want to regain my footing in the world. I want to rise; and your husband will help me do it. For the last eighteen months my record has been spotless; I've been in bitter need all the time; but I was content to fight my way up, step by step. Now, I've been thrust down again, and I'll not be satisfied with merely being reinstated as a matter of grace. I want to rise, I tell you. I must get into the Bank again, in a higher position than before. Your husband will create a place on purpose for me—.

**NORA:**  He'll never do that!

**KROGSTAD:**  He'll do it; I know him—he won't dare to show fight! And when he and I are together there, you'll soon see! Before a year is out I'll be the manager's right hand. It won't be Torvald Helmer, but Nils Krogstad, that manages the Joint Stock Bank.

**NORA:**  That'll never be.

**KROGSTAD:**  Perhaps you will—?

**NORA:**  Now I've the courage for it.

**KROGSTAD:**  Oh, you don't frighten me! A sensitive, petted creature like you—

**NORA:**  You'll see, you'll see!

**KROGSTAD:**  Under the ice, perhaps? Down into the cold, black water? And next spring to come up again, ugly, hairless, unrecognizable—

**NORA:**  You can't terrify me.

**KROGSTAD:**  Nor you me. People don't do that sort of thing, Mrs. Helmer. And, after all, what'd be the use of it? I've your husband in my pocket, all the same.

**NORA:**  Afterwards? When I am no longer—?

**KROGSTAD:**  You forget, your reputation remains in my hands! [*NORA stands speechless and looks at him.*] Well, how you're prepared. Do nothing foolish. As soon as Helmer has received my letter, I expect to hear from him. And remember that it's your husband himself who has forced me back again into such paths. That I'll never forgive him. Good-bye, Mrs. Helmer.

[*Goes out through the hall. NORA hurries to the door, opens it a little, and listens.*]

**NORA:**  He's going. He's not putting the letter into the box. No, no, it would be impossible! [*Opens the door further and further.*] What's that. He's standing still; not going downstairs. He's changed his mind? He's—?

[*A letter falls into the box.*]

**KROGSTAD'S**  footsteps are heard gradually receding down the stair.

**NORA**  utters a suppressed shriek, and rushes forward towards the coffee table; pause.] In the letter-box! [*Slips shrinking up to the hall door.*] There it lies.—Torvald, Torvald—now we're lost!

**MRS. LINDEN**  enters from the left with the costume.

**MRS. LINDEN:**  There, I think it's all right now. We'll just try it on?

**NORA:**  [*Hoarsely and softly.*] Christina, come here.

**MRS. LINDEN:**  [*Throws down the dress on the sofa.*] What's the matter? You look quite distracted.

**NORA:**  Come here. Do you see that letter? There, see—through the glass of the mailbox.

**MRS. LINDEN:**  Yes, yes, I see it.

**NORA:**  That letter's from Krogstad—

**MRS. LINDEN:**  Nora—it's Krogstad who lent you the money?

**NORA:**  Yes; and now Torvald'll know everything.

**MRS. LINDEN:**  Believe me, Nora, it's the best thing for both of you.

**NORA:**  You don't know all yet. I've forged a name—

**MRS. LINDEN:**  Good heavens!

**NORA:**  Now, listen to me, Christina; you'll bear me witness—

**MRS. LINDEN:**  How "witness"? What am I to—?

**NORA:**  If I go out of my mind—it might easily happen—

**MRS. LINDEN:**  Nora!

**NORA:**  Or if anything else should happen to me—so that I couldn't be here—!

**MRS. LINDEN:**  Nora, Nora, you're quite beside yourself!

**NORA:**  In case anyone wanted to take it all upon himself—the whole blame—you understand—

**MRS. LINDEN:**  Yes, yes; but how can you think—?

**NORA:**  You'll bear witness that it's not true, Christina. I'm not out of my mind at all; I know quite well what I'm saying; and I tell you nobody else knew anything about it; I did the whole thing, I myself. Remember that.

**MRS. LINDEN:**  I'll remember. But I don't understand what you mean—

**NORA:**  Oh, how should you? It's the miracle coming to pass.

**MRS. LINDEN:**  The miracle?

**NORA:**  Yes, the miracle. But it's so terrible, Christina; it mustn't happen for all the world.

**MRS. LINDEN:**  I'll go straight to Krogstad and talk to him.

**NORA:**  Don't; he'll do you some harm.

**MRS. LINDEN:**  Once he would've done anything for me.

**NORA:**  He?

**MRS. LINDEN:**  Where does he live?

**NORA:**  Oh, how can I tell—? Yes—[*Feels in her pocket.*] Here's his card. But the letter, the letter—!

**HELMER:**  [Knocking outside.] Nora!

**NORA:**  [*Shrieks in terror.*] Oh, what is it? What do you want?

**HELMER:**  Well, well, don't be frightened. We're not coming in; you've bolted the door. Are you trying on your dress?

**NORA:**  Yes, yes, I'm trying it on. It suits me so well, Torvald.

**MRS. LINDEN:**  [*Who has read the card.*] Why, he lives close by here.

**NORA:**  Yes, but it's no use now. We're lost. The letter's there in the box.

**MRS. LINDEN:**  And your husband has the key?

**NORA:**  Always.

**MRS. LINDEN:**  Krogstad must demand his letter back, unread. He must find some pretext—

**NORA:**  But this is the very time when Torvald generally—

**MRS. LINDEN:**  Prevent him. Keep him occupied. I'll come back as quickly as I can.

[*She goes out hastily by the hall door.*]

**NORA:**  [*Opens HELMER'S door and peeps in.*] Torvald!

**HELMER:**  Well, may one come into one's own room again at last? Come, Rank, we'll have a look—[In the doorway.] But how's this?

**NORA:** What, Torvald dear?

**HELMER:** Rank led me to expect a grand transformation.

**RANK:** [*In the doorway.*] So I understood. I suppose I was mistaken.

**NORA:** No, no one'll see me in my glory till tomorrow evening.

**HELMER:** Why, Nora dear, you look so tired. Have you been practicing too hard?

**NORA:** No, I haven't practiced at all yet.

**HELMER:** But you'll have to—

**NORA:** Oh yes, I must, I must! But, Torvald, I can't get on at all without your help. I've forgotten everything.

**HELMER:** Oh, we'll soon freshen it up again.

**NORA:** Yes, do help me, Torvald. You must promise me—Oh, I'm so nervous about it. Before so many people—This evening you must give yourself up entirely to me. You mustn't do a stroke of work; you mustn't even touch a pen. Do promise, Torvald dear!

**HELMER:** I promise. All this evening I'll be your slave. Little helpless thing—! But, by-the-bye, I must just—

[*Going to hall door.*]

**NORA:** What do you want there?

**HELMER:** Only to see if there are any letters.

**NORA:** No, no, don't do that, Torvald.

**HELMER:** Why not?

**NORA:** Torvald, I beg you not to. There are none there.

**HELMER:** Let me just see.

[*Is going.*]

[*NORA, at the piano, plays the first bars of the tarantella.*]

**HELMER:** [*At the door, stops.*] Aha!

**NORA:** I can't dance tomorrow if I don't rehearse with you first.

**HELMER:** [*Going to her.*] Are you really so nervous, dear Nora?

**NORA:** Yes, dreadfully! Let me rehearse at once. We've time before dinner. Oh, do sit down and play for me, Torvald dear; direct me and put me right, as you used to do.

**HELMER:** With all the pleasure in life, since you wish it. [*Sits at piano.*]

[*NORA snatches the tambourine out of the box, and hurriedly drapes herself in a long parti-colored shawl; then, with a bound, stands in the middle of the floor.*]

**NORA:** Now play for me! Now I'll dance!

[*HELMER plays and NORA dances. RANK stands at the piano behind HELMER and looks on.*]

**HELMER:** [*Playing.*] Slower! Slower!

**NORA:**  Can't do it slower!

**HELMER:**  Not so violently, Nora!

**NORA:**  I must! I must!

**HELMER:**  [*Stops.*] No, no, Nora—that'll never do.

**NORA:**  [*Laughs and swings her tambourine.*] Didn't I tell you so!

**RANK:**  Let me play for her.

**HELMER:**  [*Rising.*] Yes, do—then I can direct her better.

[*RANK sits down to the piano and plays; NORA dances more and more wildly. HELMER stands by the stove and addresses frequent corrections to her; she seems not to hear. Her hair breaks loose, and falls over her shoulders. She does not notice it, but goes on dancing. MRS. LINDEN enters and stands spellbound in the doorway.*]

**MRS. LINDEN:**  Ah—!

**NORA:**  [*Dancing.*] We're having such fun here, Christina!

**HELMER:**  Why, Nora dear, you're dancing as if it were a matter of life and death.

**NORA:**  So it is.

**HELMER:**  Rank, stop! This is the merest madness. Stop, I say!

[*RANK stops playing, and NORA comes to a sudden standstill.*]

**HELMER:**  [*Going towards her.*] I couldn't have believed it. You've positively forgotten all I taught you.

**NORA:**  [*Throws the tambourine away.*] You see for yourself.

**HELMER:**  You really do want teaching.

**NORA:**  Yes, you see how much I need it. You must practice with me up to the last moment. Will you promise me, Torvald?

**HELMER:**  Certainly, certainly.

**NORA:**  Neither today nor tomorrow must you think of anything but me. You mustn't open a single letter—mustn't look at the mailbox.

**HELMER:**  Ah, you're still afraid of that man—

**NORA:**  Oh yes, yes, I am.

**HELMER:**  Nora, I can see it in your face—there's a letter from him in the box.

**NORA:**  I don't know, I believe so. But you're not to read anything now; nothing ugly must come between us until all is over.

**RANK:**  [*Softly, to HELMER.*] You mustn't contradict her.

**HELMER:**  [*Putting his arm around her.*] The child will have her own way. But tomorrow night, when the dance is over—

**NORA:**  Then you'll be free.

[*ELLEN appears in the doorway, right.*]

**ELLEN:**  Dinner's on the table, ma'am.

**NORA:**  We'll have some champagne, Ellen.

**ELLEN:**  Yes, ma'am.

[*Goes out.*]

**HELMER:** Dear me! Quite a banquet.

**NORA:** Yes, and we'll keep it up till morning. [*Calling out.*] And macaroons, Ellen—plenty—just this once.

**HELMER:** [*Seizing her hand.*] Come, come, don't let us have this wild excitement! Be my own little lark again.

**NORA:** Oh yes, I will. But now go into the dining room; and you too, Doctor Rank. Christina, you must help me to do up my hair.

**RANK:** [*Softly, as they go.*] There's nothing in the wind? Nothing—I mean—?

**HELMER:** Oh no, nothing of the kind. It's merely this babyish anxiety I was telling you about.

[*They go out to the right.*]

**NORA:** Well?

**MRS. LINDEN:** He's gone out of town.

**NORA:** I saw it in your face.

**MRS. LINDEN:** He comes back tomorrow evening. I left a note for him.

**NORA:** You shouldn't have done that. Things must take their course. After all, there's something glorious in waiting for the miracle.

**MRS. LINDEN:** What is it you're waiting for?

**NORA:** Oh, you can't understand. Go to them in the dining room; I'll come in a moment.

[*MRS. LINDEN goes into the dining room. NORA stands for a moment as though collecting her thoughts; then looks at her watch.*]

**NORA:** Seven hours till midnight. Then twenty-four hours till the next midnight. Then the tarantella will be over. Twenty-four and seven? Thirty-one hours to live.

[*HELMER appears at the door, right.*]

**HELMER:** What's become of my little lark?

**NORA:** [*Runs to him with open arms.*] Here she is!

## Act Three

*The same room. The table, with the chairs around it, in the middle. A lighted lamp on the table. The door to the hall stands open. Dance music is heard from the floor above.*

[*MRS. LINDEN sits by the table and absently turns the pages of a book. She tries to read, but seems unable to fix her attention; she frequently listens and looks anxiously towards the hall door.*]

**MRS. LINDEN.** [*Looks at her watch.*] Not here yet; and the time is nearly up. If only he hasn't—[*Listens again.*] Ah, there he is. [*She goes into the hall and cautiously opens the outer door; soft footsteps are heard on the stairs; she whispers.*] Come in; there's no one here.

**KROGSTAD.**  [*In the doorway.*] I found a note from you at my house. What does it mean?

**MRS. LINDEN.**  I must speak to you.

**KROGSTAD.**  Indeed? And in this house?

**MRS. LINDEN.**  I couldn't see you at my rooms. They've no separate entrance. Come in; we're quite alone. The servants are asleep, and the Helmers are at the ball upstairs.

**KROGSTAD.**  [*Coming into the room.*] Ah! So the Helmers are dancing this evening? Really?

**MRS. LINDEN.**  Yes. Why not?

**KROGSTAD.**  Quite right. Why not?

**MRS. LINDEN.**  And now let us talk a little.

**KROGSTAD.**  Have we two anything to say to each other?

**MRS. LINDEN.**  A great deal.

**KROGSTAD.**  I shouldn't have thought so.

**MRS. LINDEN.**  Because you've never really understood me.

**KROGSTAD.**  What's there to understand? The most natural thing in the world—a heartless woman throws a man over when a better match offers.

**MRS. LINDEN.**  Do you really think me so heartless? Do you think I broke with you lightly?

**KROGSTAD.**  Didn't you?

**MRS. LINDEN.**  Do you really think so?

**KROGSTAD.**  If not, why'd you write me that letter?

**MRS. LINDEN.**  Wasn't it best? Since I'd to break with you, wasn't it right that I'd try to put an end to all that you felt for me?

**KROGSTAD.**  [*Clenching his hands together.*] So that's it? And all this—for the sake of money!

**MRS. LINDEN.**  You shouldn't forget that I had a helpless mother and two little brothers. We couldn't wait for you, Nils, as your prospects then stood.

**KROGSTAD.**  Perhaps not; but you'd no right to cast me off for the sake of others, whoever the others might be.

**MRS. LINDEN.**  I don't know. I've often asked myself whether I had the right.

**KROGSTAD.**  [*More softly.*] When I'd lost you, I seemed to have no firm ground left under my feet. Look at me now. I'm a shipwrecked man clinging to a spar.

**MRS. LINDEN.**  Rescue may be at hand.

**KROGSTAD.**  It was at hand; but then you came and stood in the way.

**MRS. LINDEN.**  Without my knowledge, Nils. I didn't know till today that it was you I was to replace in the Bank.

**KROGSTAD.**  Well, I take your word for it. But now that you do know, do you mean to give way?

**MRS. LINDEN.**   No, for that'd not help you in the least.

**KROGSTAD.**   Oh, help, help—! I'd do it whether or no.

**MRS. LINDEN.**   I've learned prudence. Life and bitter necessity have schooled me.

**KROGSTAD.**   And life's taught me not to trust fine speeches.

**MRS. LINDEN.**   Then life has taught you a very sensible thing. But deeds you will trust?

**KROGSTAD.**   What do you mean?

**MRS. LINDEN.**   You said you were a shipwrecked man, clinging to a spar.

**KROGSTAD.**   I've good reason to say so.

**MRS. LINDEN.**   I too am shipwrecked, and clinging to a spar. I've no one to mourn for, no one to care for.

**KROGSTAD.**   You made your own choice.

**MRS. LINDEN.**   No choice was left me.

**KROGSTAD.**   Well, what then?

**MRS. LINDEN.**   Nils, how if we two shipwrecked people could join hands?

**KROGSTAD.**   What!

**MRS. LINDEN.**   Two on a raft have a better chance than if each clings to a separate spar.

**KROGSTAD.**   Christina!

**MRS. LINDEN.**   What do you think brought me to town?

**KROGSTAD.**   Had you any thought of me?

**MRS. LINDEN.**   I must have work or I can't bear to live. All my life, as long as I can remember, I've worked; work's been my one great joy. Now I stand quite alone in the world, aimless and forlorn. There's no happiness in working for one's self. Nils, give me somebody and something to work for.

**KROGSTAD.**   I can't believe in all this. It's simply a woman's romantic craving for self-sacrifice.

**MRS. LINDEN.**   Have you ever found me romantic?

**KROGSTAD.**   Would you really—? Tell me: do you know all my past?

**MRS. LINDEN.**   Yes.

**KROGSTAD.**   And do you know what people say of me?

**MRS. LINDEN.**   Didn't you say just now that with me you could've been another man?

**KROGSTAD.**   I'm sure of it.

**MRS. LINDEN.**   Is it too late?

**KROGSTAD.**   Christina, do you know what you're doing? Yes, you do; I see it in your face. Have you the courage then—?

**MRS. LINDEN.**   I need someone to be a mother to, and your children need a mother. You need me, and I—I need you. Nils, I believe in your better self. With you I fear nothing.

**KROGSTAD.**   [*Seizing her hands.*] Thank you—thank you, Christina. Now I'll make others see me as you do.—Ah, I forgot—

**MRS. LINDEN.**    [*Listening.*] Hush! The tarantella! Go! go!

**KROGSTAD.**    Why? What is it?

**MRS. LINDEN.**    Don't you hear the dancing upstairs? As soon as that is over they'll be here.

**KROGSTAD.**    Oh yes, I'll go. Nothing will come of this, after all. Of course, you don't know the step I've taken against the Helmers.

**MRS. LINDEN.**    Yes, Nils, I do know.

**KROGSTAD.**    And yet you've the courage to—?

**MRS. LINDEN.**    I know to what lengths despair can drive a man.

**KROGSTAD.**    Oh, if I could only undo it!

**MRS. LINDEN.**    You could. Your letter's still in the box.

**KROGSTAD.**    Are you sure?

**MRS. LINDEN.**    Yes; but—

**KROGSTAD.**    [*Looking to her searchingly.*] Is that what it all means? You want to save your friend at any price. Say it out—is that your idea?

**MRS. LINDEN.**    Nils, a woman who's once sold herself for the sake of others, doesn't do so again.

**KROGSTAD.**    I'll demand my letter back again.

**MRS. LINDEN.**    No, no.

**KROGSTAD.**    Yes, of course. I'll wait till Helmer comes; I'll tell him to give it back to me—that it's only about my dismissal—that I don't want it read—

**MRS. LINDEN.**    No, Nils, you mustn't recall the letter.

**KROGSTAD.**    But tell me, wasn't that just why you got me to come here?

**MRS. LINDEN.**    Yes, in my first alarm. But a day has passed since then, and in that day I've seen incredible things in this house. Helmer must know everything; there must be an end to this unhappy secret. These two must come to a full understanding. They must've done with all these shifts and subterfuges.

**KROGSTAD.**    Very well, if you like to risk it. But one thing I can do, and at once—

**MRS. LINDEN.**    [*Listening.*] Make haste! Go, go! The dance is over; we're not safe another moment.

**KROGSTAD.**    I'll wait for you in the street.

**MRS. LINDEN.**    Yes, do; you must see me home.

**KROGSTAD.**    I never was so happy in all my life!

KROGSTAD goes out by the outer door. The door between the room and the hall remains open.

**MRS. LINDEN:**    [*Arranging the room and getting her outdoor things together.*] What a change! What a change! To have someone to work for, to live for; a home to make happy! Well, it'll not be my fault if I fail.—I wish they'd come.—[*Listens.*] Ah, here they are! I must get my things on.

[*Takes bonnet and cloak. HELMER'S and NORA'S voices are heard outside, a key's turned in the lock, and HELMER drags NORA almost by force into the hall. She wears the Italian costume with a large black shawl over it. He's in evening dress and wears a black domino, open.*]

**NORA:** [*Struggling with him in the doorway.*] No, no, no! I won't go in! I want to go upstairs again; I don't want to leave so early!

**HELMER:** But, my dearest girl—!

**NORA:** Oh, please, please, Torvald, I beseech you—only one hour more!

**HELMER:** Not one minute more, Nora dear; you know what we agreed. Come, come in; you're catching cold here.

[*He leads her gently into the room in spite of her resistance.*]

**MRS. LINDEN:** Good evening.

**NORA:** Christina!

**HELMER:** What, Mrs. Linden! You're so late?

**MRS. LINDEN:** Yes, I should apologize. I did so want to see Nora in her costume.

**NORA:** You've been sitting here waiting for me?

**MRS. LINDEN:** Yes; unfortunately I came too late. You'd gone upstairs already, and I felt I couldn't go away without seeing you.

**HELMER:** [*Taking Nora's shawl off.*] Well then, just look at her! I assure you she's worth it. isn't she lovely, Mrs. Linden?

**MRS. LINDEN:** Yes, I must say—

**HELMER:** Isn't she exquisite? Every one said so. But she's dreadfully obstinate, dear little creature. What's to be done with her? Just think, I'd almost to force her away.

**NORA:** Oh, Torvald, you'll be sorry some day that you didn't let me stay, if only for one half hour more.

**HELMER:** There! You hear her, Mrs. Linden? She dances her tarantella with wild applause, and well she deserved it, I must say—though there was, perhaps, a little too much nature in her rendering of the idea—more than was, strictly speaking, artistic. But never mind—the point is, she made a great success, a tremendous success. Was I to let her remain after that—to weaken the impression? Not if I know it. I took my sweet little Capri girl—my capricious little Capri girl, I might say—under my arm; a rapid turn round the room, a curtsey to all sides, and—as they say in novels—the lovely apparition vanished! An exit should always be effective, Mrs. Linden; but I can't get Nora to see it. By Jove! it's warm here. [*Throws his domino on a chair and opens the door to his room.*] What! No light there? Oh, of course. Excuse me—

[*Goes in and lights candle.*]

**NORA:** [*Whispers breathlessly.*] Well?

**MRS. LINDEN:** [*Softly.*] I've spoken to him.

**NORA:** And—?

**MRS. LINDEN:**   Nora—you must tell your husband everything—

**NORA:**   [*Tonelessly.*] I knew it!

**MRS. LINDEN:**   You've nothing to fear from Krogstad; but you must speak out.

**NORA:**   I'll not speak!

**MRS. LINDEN:**   Then the letter will.

**NORA:**   Thank you, Christina. Now I know what I have to do. Hush—!

**HELMER:**   [*Coming back.*] Well, Mrs. Linden, you've admired her?

**MRS. LINDEN:**   Yes; and now I must say goodnight.

**HELMER:**   What, already? Does this knitting belong to you?

**MRS. LINDEN:**   [*Takes it.*] Yes, thanks; I was nearly forgetting it.

**HELMER:**   Then you do knit?

**MRS. LINDEN:**   Yes.

**HELMER:**   Do you know, you should embroider instead?

**MRS. LINDEN:**   Indeed! Why?

**HELMER:**   Because it's so much prettier. Look now! You hold the embroidery in the left hand, so, and then work the needle with the right hand, in a long, graceful curve—don't you?

**MRS. LINDEN:**   Yes, I suppose so.

**HELMER:**   But knitting is always ugly. Just look—your arms close to your sides, and the needles going up and down—there's something Chinese about it.—They really gave us splendid champagne tonight.

**MRS. LINDEN:**   Well, goodnight, Nora, and don't be obstinate any more.

**HELMER:**   Well said, Mrs. Linden!

**MRS. LINDEN:**   Goodnight, Mr. Helmer.

**HELMER:**   [*Accompanying her to the door.*] Goodnight, goodnight; I hope you get safely home. I'd be glad to—but you've such a short way to go. Goodnight, goodnight. [*She goes; HELMER shuts the door after her and comes forward again.*] At last we've got rid of her: she's a terrible bore.

**NORA:**   Aren't you very tired, Torvald?

**HELMER:**   No, not in the least.

**NORA:**   Nor sleepy?

**HELMER:**   Not a bit. I feel particularly lively. But you? You do look tired and sleepy.

**NORA:**   Yes, very tired. I'll soon sleep now.

**HELMER:**   There, you see. I was right after all not to let you stay longer.

**NORA:**   Oh, everything you do is right.

**HELMER:**   [*Kissing her forehead.*] Now my lark's speaking like a reasonable being. Did you notice how jolly Rank was this evening?

**NORA:**   Indeed? Was he? I'd no chance of speaking to him.

**HELMER:**   Nor I, much; but, I haven't seen him in such good spirits for a long time. [*Looks at NORA a little, then comes nearer her.*] It's splendid to be back in our own home, to be quite alone together!—Oh, you enchanting creature!

**NORA:**  Don't look at me in that way, Torvald.

**HELMER:**  I'm not to look at my dearest treasure?—at all the loveliness that's mine, mine only, wholly and entirely mine?

**NORA:**  [*Goes to the other side of the table.*] You mustn't say these things to me this evening.

**HELMER:**  [*Following.*] I see you've the tarantella still in your blood—and that makes you all the more enticing. Listen! the other people are going now. [*More softly.*] Nora—soon the whole house'll be still.

**NORA:**  Yes, I hope so.

**HELMER:**  Yes, don't you, Nora darling? When we're among strangers, do you know why I speak so little to you, and keep so far away, and only steal a glance at you now and then—do you know why I do it? Because I'm fancying that we love each other in secret, that I'm secretly engaged to you, and that no one dreams that there's anything between us.

**NORA:**  Yes, yes, yes. I know all your thoughts are with me.

**HELMER:**  And then, when the time comes to go, and I put the shawl about your smooth, soft shoulders, and this glorious neck of yours, I imagine you're my bride, that our marriage is just over, that I'm bringing you for the first time to my home—that I'm alone with you for the first time—quite alone with you, in your trembling loveliness! All this evening I've been longing for you, and you only. When I watched you swaying and whirling in the tarantella—my blood boiled—I'd endure it no longer; and that's why I made you come home with me so early—

**NORA:**  Go now, Torvald! Go away from me. I won't have all this.

**HELMER:**  What do you mean? Ah, I see you're teasing me, little Nora! Won't—won't! Am I not your husband—?

[*A knock at the outer door.*]

**NORA:**  [*Starts.*] Did you hear—?

**HELMER:**  [*Going towards the hall.*] Who's there?

**RANK:**  [*Outside.*] It's I; may I come in for a moment?

**HELMER:**  [*In a low tone, annoyed.*] Oh, what can he want just now? [*Aloud.*] Wait a moment. [*Opens door.*] Come, it's nice of you to look in.

**RANK:**  I thought I heard your voice, and that put it into my head. [*Looks round.*] Ah, this dear old place! How cozy you two are here!

**HELMER:**  You seemed to find it pleasant enough upstairs, too.

**RANK:**  Exceedingly. Why not? Why shouldn't one take one's share of everything in this world? All one can, at least, and as long as one can. The wine was splendid—

**HELMER:**  Especially the champagne.

**RANK:**  Did you notice it? It's incredible the quantity I contrived to get down.

**NORA:**  Torvald drank plenty of champagne, too.

**RANK:**  Did he?

**NORA:**  Yes, and it always puts him in such spirits.

**RANK:**  Well, why shouldn't one have a jolly evening after a well spent day?

**HELMER:**  Well spent! Well, I haven't much to boast of in that respect.

**RANK:**  [*Slapping him on the shoulder.*] But I have, don't you see?

**NORA:**  I suppose you've been engaged in a scientific investigation, Doctor Rank?

**RANK:**  Quite right.

**HELMER:**  Bless me! Little Nora talking about scientific investigations!

**NORA:**  Am I to congratulate you on the result?

**RANK:**  By all means.

**NORA:**  It was good then?

**RANK:**  The best possible, both for doctor and patient—certainty.

**NORA:**  [*Quickly and searchingly.*] Certainty?

**RANK:**  Absolute certainty. Wasn't I right to enjoy myself after that?

**NORA:**  Yes, quite right, Doctor Rank.

**HELMER:**  And so say I, provided you don't have to pay for it tomorrow.

**RANK:**  Well, in this life nothing's to be had for nothing.

**NORA:**  Doctor Rank—I'm sure you're very fond of masquerades?

**RANK:**  Yes, when there're plenty of amusing disguises—

**NORA:**  Tell me, what'll we two be at our next masquerade?

**HELMER:**  Little featherbrain! Thinking of your next already!

**RANK:**  We two? I'll tell you. You must go as a good fairy.

**HELMER:**  Ah, but what costume would indicate that?

**RANK:**  She's simply to wear her everyday dress.

**HELMER:**  Capital! But don't you know what you'll be yourself?

**RANK:**  Yes, my dear friend, I'm perfectly clear upon that point.

**HELMER:**  Well?

**RANK:**  At the next masquerade I'll be invisible.

**HELMER:**  What a comical idea!

**RANK:**  There's a big black hat—haven't you heard of the invisible hat? It comes down all over you, and then no one can see you.

**HELMER:**  [*With a suppressed smile.*] No, you're right there.

**RANK:**  But I'm quite forgetting what I came for. Helmer, give me a cigar— one of the dark Havanas.

**HELMER:**  With the greatest pleasure.

[*Hands cigar-case.*]

**RANK:**  [*Takes one and cuts the end off.*] Thank you.

**NORA:**  [*Striking a wax match.*] Let me give you a light.

**RANK:**  A thousand thanks.

[*She holds the match. He lights his cigar at it.*]

**RANK:**  And now, goodbye!

**HELMER.**  Goodbye, goodbye, my dear fellow.

**NORA:**   Sleep well, Doctor Rank.

**RANK:**   Thanks for the wish.

**NORA:**   Wish me the same.

**RANK:**   You? Very well, since you ask me—Sleep well. And thanks for the light.

[*He nods to them both and goes out.*]

**HELMER:**   [*In an undertone.*] He's been drinking a good deal.

**NORA:**   [*Absently.*] I daresay. [*HELMER takes his bunch of keys from his pocket and goes into the hall.*] Torvald, what're you doing there?

**HELMER:**   I must empty the mailbox; it's quite full; there'll be no room for the newspapers tomorrow morning.

**NORA:**   You're going to work tonight?

**HELMER:**   You know very well I'm not.—Why, how's this? Some one's been at the lock.

**NORA:**   The lock—?

**HELMER:**   I'm sure of it. What does it mean? I can't think that the servants—? Here's a broken hair-pin. Nora, it's one of yours.

**NORA:**   [*Quickly.*] It must've been the children—

**HELMER:**   Then you must break them of such tricks.—There! At last I've got it open. [*Takes contents out and calls into the kitchen.*] Ellen!—Ellen, just put the hall door lamp out.

[*He returns with letters in his hand, and shuts the inner door.*]

**HELMER:**   Just see how they've accumulated. [*Turning them over.*] Why, what's this?

**NORA:**   [*At the window.*] The letter! Oh no, no, Torvald!

**HELMER:**   Two business cards—from Rank.

**NORA:**   From Doctor Rank?

**HELMER:**   [*Looking at them.*] Doctor Rank. They're on the top. He must've just put them in.

**NORA:**   Is there anything on them?

**HELMER:**   There's a black cross over the name. Look at it. What an unpleasant idea! It looks just as if he were announcing his own death.

**NORA:**   So he is.

**HELMER:**   What! Do you know anything? Has he told you anything?

**NORA:**   Yes. These cards mean that he's taken his last leave of us. He's going to shut himself up and die.

**HELMER:**   Poor fellow! Of course I knew we couldn't hope to keep him long. But so soon—! And to go and creep into his lair like a wounded animal—

**NORA:**   When we must go, it's best to go silently. Don't you think so, Torvald?

**HELMER:**   [*Walking up and down.*] He'd so grown into our lives, I can't realize that he's gone. He and his sufferings and his loneliness formed a sort of cloudy background to the sunshine of our happiness.—Well, perhaps it's best as it is—at any rate for him. [*Stands still.*] And perhaps for us too, Nora. Now we two are thrown entirely upon each other. [*Takes her in his arms.*] My darling wife! I feel as if I could never hold you close enough. Do you know, Nora, I often wish some danger might threaten you, that I might risk body and soul, and everything, everything, for your dear sake.

**NORA:** [*Tears herself from him and says firmly.*] Now you'll read your letters, Torvald.

**HELMER:** No, no; not tonight. I want to be with you, my sweet wife.

**NORA:** With the thought of your dying friend—?

**HELMER:** You're right. This has shaken us both. Unloveliness has come between us—thoughts of death and decay. We must seek to cast them off. Till then—we'll remain apart.

**NORA:** [*Her arms round his neck.*] Torvald! Goodnight! goodnight!

**HELMER:** [*Kissing her forehead.*] Goodnight, my little songbird. Sleep well, Nora. Now I'll go and read my letters.

[*He goes with the letters in his hand into his room and shuts the door.*]

**NORA:** [*With wild eyes, gropes about her, seizes HELMER'S domino, throws it round her, and whispers quickly, hoarsely, and brokenly.*] Never to see him again. Never, never, never. [*Throws her shawl over her head.*] Never to see the children again. Never, never.—Oh that black, icy water! Oh that bottomless—! If it were only over! Now he has it; he's reading it. Oh, no, no, no, not yet. Torvald, good-bye-! Good-bye, my little ones—!

[*She's rushing out by the hall; at the same moment HELMER flings his door open, and stands there with an open letter in his hand.*]

**HELMER:** Nora!

**NORA:** [*Shrieks.*] Ah—!

**HELMER:** What's this? Do you know what's in this letter?

**NORA:** Yes, I know. Let me go! Let me pass!

**HELMER:** [*Holds her back.*] Where do you want to go?

**NORA:** [*Tries to break away from him.*] You'll not save me, Torvald.

**HELMER:** [*Falling back.*] True! Is what he writes true? No, no, it's impossible that this can be true.

**NORA:** It's true. I've loved you beyond all else in the world.

**HELMER:** Pshaw—no silly evasions!

**NORA:** [*A step nearer him.*] Torvald—!

**HELMER:** Wretched woman—what've you done!

**NORA:** Let me go—you'll not save me! You'll not take my guilt upon yourself!

**HELMER:** I don't want any melodramatic airs. [*Locks the outer door.*] Here you'll stay and give an account of yourself. Do you understand what you've done? Answer! Do you understand it?

**NORA:**  [*Looks at him fixedly, and says with a stiffening expression.*] Yes; now I begin fully to understand it.

**HELMER:**  [*Walking up and down.*] Oh! what an awful awakening! During all these eight years—she who was my pride and my joy—a hypocrite, a liar—worse, worse—a criminal. Oh, the unfathomable hideousness of it all! Ugh! Ugh!

[*NORA says nothing, and continues to look fixedly at him.*]

**HELMER:**  I should've known how it'd be. I should've foreseen it. All your father's want of principle—be silent!—all your father's want of principle you've inherited—no religion, no morality, no sense of duty. How I'm punished for screening him! I did it for your sake; and you reward me like this.

**NORA:**  Yes—like this.

**HELMER:**  You've des*T*royed my whole happiness. You've ruined my future. Oh, it's frightful to think of! I'm in the power of a scoundrel; he can do whatever he pleases with me, demand whatever he chooses; he can domineer over me as much as he likes, and I must submit. And all this disaster and ruin is brought upon me by an unprincipled woman!

**NORA:**  When I'm out of the world, you'll be free.

**HELMER:**  Oh, no fine phrases. Your father, too, was always ready with them. What good would it do me, if you were "out of the world," as you say? No good whatever! He can publish the story all the same; I might even be suspected of collusion. People'll think I was at the bottom of it all and egged you on. And for all this I've you to thank—you whom I've done nothing but pet and spoil during our whole married life. Do you understand now what you've done to me?

**NORA:**  [*With cold calmness.*] Yes.

**HELMER:**  The thing is so incredible, I can't grasp it. But we must come to an understanding. Take that shawl off. Take it off, I say! I must try to pacify him in one way or another—the matter must be hushed up, cost what it may.—As for you and me, we must make no outward change in our way of life—no outward change, you understand. Of course, you'll continue to live here. But the children can't be left in your care. I dare not trust them to you.—Oh, to have to say this to one I've loved so tenderly—whom I still-! But that must be a thing of the past. Henceforward there can be no question of happiness, but merely of saving the ruins, the shreds, the show—[*A ring; HELMER starts.*] What's that? So late! Can it be the worst? Can he-? Hide yourself, Nora; say you're ill.

[*NORA stands motionless. HELMER goes to the door and opens it.*]

**ELLEN:**  [*Half dressed, in the hall.*] Here's a letter for you, ma'am.

**HELMER:**  Give it to me. [*Seizes the letter and shuts the door.*] Yes, from him. You'll not have it. I'll read it.

**NORA:**  Read it?

**HELMER:**  [*By the lamp.*] I've hardly the courage to. We may both be lost, both you and I. Ah! I must know. [*Hastily tears the letter open; reads a few lines, looks at an enclosure; with a cry of joy.*] Nora!

[*Nora looks inquiringly at him.*]

**HELMER:**  Nora!—Oh! I must read it again.—Yes, yes, it's so. I'm saved! Nora, I'm saved!

**NORA:**  And I?

**HELMER:**  You too, of course; we're both saved, both of us. Look here—he sends you back your promissory note. He writes that he regrets and apologizes, that a happy turn in his life—Oh, what matter what he writes. We're saved, Nora! No one can harm you. Oh, Nora, Nora—; but first to get rid of this hateful thing. I'll just see—[*Glances at the I.O.U.*] No, I'll not look at it; the whole thing'll be nothing but a dream to me. [*Tears the I.O.U. and both letters in pieces. Throws them into the fire and watches them burn.*] There! it's gone!—He said that ever since Christmas Eve—Oh, Nora, they must've been three terrible days for you! Nora, I've fought a hard fight for the last three days.

**HELMER:**  And in your agony you saw no other outlet but—No; we won't think of that horror. We'll only rejoice and repeat—it's over, all over! Don't you hear, Nora? You don't seem able to grasp it. Yes, it's over. What's this set look on your face? Oh, my poor Nora, I understand; you can't believe that I've forgiven you. But I have, Nora; I swear it. I've forgiven everything. I know that what you did was all for love of me.

**NORA:**  That's true.

**HELMER:**  You loved me as a wife should love her husband. It was only the means that, in your inexperience, you misjudged. But do you think I love you the less because you can't do without guidance? No, no. Only lean on me; I will counsel you, and guide you. I'd be no true man if this very womanly helplessness didn't make you doubly dear in my eyes. You mustn't dwell upon the hard things I said in my first moment of terror, when the world seemed to be tumbling about my ears. I've forgiven you, Nora—I swear I've forgiven you.

**NORA:**  I thank you for your forgiveness.

[*Goes out, to the right.*]

**HELMER:**  No, stay—! [*Looking through the doorway.*] What're you going to do?

**NORA:**  [*Inside.*] To take off my masquerade dress.

**HELMER:**  [*In the doorway.*] Yes, do, dear. Try to calm down, and recover your balance, my scared little songbird. You may rest secure. I've broad wings to shield you. [*Walking up and down near the door.*] Oh, how lovely—how cozy our home is, Nora! Here you're safe; here I can shelter you like a hunted dove whom I've saved from the claws of the hawk. I'll soon bring your poor beating heart to rest; believe me, Nora, very soon.

Tomorrow all this'll seem quite different—everything'll be as before. I'll not need to tell you again that I forgive you; you'll feel for yourself that it's true. How could you think I'd find it in my heart to drive you away, or even so much as to reproach you? Oh, you don't know a true man's heart, Nora.: There's something indescribably sweet and soothing to a man in having forgiven his wife—honestly forgiven her, from the bottom of his heart. She becomes his property in a double sense. She's as though born again; she's become, so to speak, at once his wife and his child. That's what you'll henceforth be to me, my bewildered, helpless darling. Don't be troubled about anything, Nora; only open your heart to me, and I'll be both will and conscience to you. [*NORA enters in everyday dress.*] Why, what's this? Not gone to bed You've changed your dress?

**NORA:** Yes, Torvald; now I've changed my dress.

**HELMER:** But why now, so late—?

**NORA:** I'll not sleep tonight.

**HELMER:** But, Nora dear—

**NORA:** [*Looking at her watch.*] It's not so late yet. Sit down, Torvald; you and I have much to say to each other.

[*She sits at one side of the table.*]

**HELMER:** Nora—what does this mean? Your cold, set face—

**NORA:** Sit down. It'll take some time. I've much to talk over with you.

[*HELMER sits at the other side of the table.*]

**HELMER:** You alarm me, Nora. I don't understand you.

**NORA:** No, that's just it. You don't understand me; and I've never understood you—till tonight. No, don't interrupt. Only listen to what I say.—We must come to a final settlement, Torvald.

**HELMER:** How do you mean?

**NORA:** [*After a short silence.*] Does not one thing strike you as we sit here?

**HELMER:** What should strike me?

**NORA:** We've been married eight years. Doesn't it strike you that this is the first time we two, you and I, man and wife, have talked together seriously?

**HELMER:** Seriously! What do you call seriously?

**NORA:** During eight whole years, and more—ever since the day we first met—we've never exchanged one serious word about serious things.

**HELMER:** Was I always to trouble you with the cares you couldn't help me to bear?

**NORA:** I'm not talking of cares. I say that we've never yet set ourselves seriously to get to the bottom of anything.

**HELMER:** Why, my dearest Nora, what've you to do with serious things?

**NORA:**   There we have it! You've never understood me.—I've had great injustice done me, Torvald; first by father, and then by you.

**HELMER:**   What! By your father and me?—By us, who've loved you more than all the world?

**NORA:**   [*Shaking her head.*] You've never loved me. You only thought it amusing to be in love with me.

**HELMER:**   Why, Nora, what a thing to say!

**NORA:**   Yes, it's so, Torvald. While I was at home with father, he used to tell me all his opinions, and I held the same opinions. If I'd others I said nothing about them, because he wouldn't have liked it. He used to call me his doll child, and played with me as I played with my dolls. Then I came to live in your house—

**HELMER:**   What an expression to use about our marriage!

**NORA:**   [*Undisturbed.*] I mean I passed from father's hands into yours. You arranged everything according to your taste; and I got the same tastes as you; or I pretended to—I don't know which—both ways, perhaps; sometimes one and sometimes the other. When I look back on it now, I seem to have been living here like a beggar, from hand to mouth. I lived by performing tricks for you, Torvald. But you'd have it so. You and father have done me a great wrong. It's your fault that my life has come to nothing.

**HELMER:**   Why, Nora, how unreasonable and ungrateful you are! Haven't you been happy here?

**NORA:**   No, never. I thought I was; but I never was.

**HELMER:**   Not—not happy!

**NORA:**   No; only merry. And you've always been so kind to me. But our house's been nothing but a playroom. Here I've been your doll wife, just as at home I used to be papa's doll child. And the children, in their turn, have been my dolls. I thought it fun when you played with me, just as the children did when I played with them. That's been our marriage, Torvald.

**HELMER:**   There's some truth in what you say, exaggerated and overstrained though it be. But from now on it'll be different. Playtime's over; now comes the time for education.

**NORA:**   Whose education? Mine, or the children's?

**HELMER:**   Both, my dear Nora.

**NORA:**   Oh, Torvald, you're not the man to teach me to be a fit wife for you.

**HELMER:**   And you can say that?

**NORA:**   And I—how have I prepared myself to educate the children?

**HELMER:**   Nora!

**NORA:**   Didn't you say yourself, a few minutes ago, you dared not trust them to me?

**HELMER:**   In the excitement of the moment! Why'd you dwell upon that?

**NORA:** No—you were perfectly right. That problem's beyond me. There's another to be solved first—I must try to educate myself. You're not the man to help me in that. I must set about it alone. And that's why I'm leaving you.

**HELMER:** [*Jumping up.*] What—do you mean to say—?

**NORA:** I must stand quite alone if I'm ever to know myself and my surroundings; so I can't stay with you.

**HELMER:** Nora! Nora!

**NORA:** I'm going at once. I daresay Christina'll take me in for tonight—

**HELMER:** You're mad! I'll not allow it! I forbid it!

**NORA:** It's of no use your forbidding me anything now. I'll take with me what belongs to me. From you I'll accept nothing, either now or afterwards.

**HELMER:** What madness this is!

**NORA:** Tomorrow I'll go home—I mean to what was my home. It'll be easier for me to find some opening there.

**HELMER:** Oh, in your blind inexperience—

**NORA:** I must try to gain experience, Torvald.

**HELMER:** To forsake your home, your husband, and your children! And you don't consider what the world'll say.

**NORA:** I can pay no heed to that. I only know that I must do it.

**HELMER:** This is monstrous! Can you forsake your holiest duties in this way?

**NORA:** What do you consider my holiest duties?

**HELMER:** Do I need to tell you that? Your duties to your husband and your children.

**NORA:** I've other duties equally sacred.

**HELMER:** Impossible! What duties do you mean?

**NORA:** My duties towards myself.

**HELMER:** Before all else you are a wife and a mother.

**NORA:** That I no longer believe. I believe that before all else I'm a human being, just as much as you are—or at least that I should try to become one. I know that most people agree with you, Torvald, and that they say so in books. But from now on I can't be satisfied with what most people say, and what's in books. I must think things out for myself, and try to get clear about them.

**HELMER:** You're not clear about your place in your own home? You've not an infallible guide in questions like these? You've not religion?

**NORA:** Oh, Torvald, I don't really know what religion is.

**HELMER:** What do you mean?

**NORA:** I know nothing but what Pastor Hansen told me when I was confirmed. He explained that religion was this and that. When I get away from all this and stand alone, I'll look into that matter too. I'll see whether what he taught me is right, or, at any rate, whether it's right for me.

**HELMER:** Oh, this is unheard of! And from so young a woman! But if religion cannot keep you right, let me appeal to your conscience—for I suppose you've some moral feeling? Or, answer me: perhaps you have none?

**NORA:** Well, Torvald, it's not easy to say. I really don't know—I'm all at sea about these things. I only know that I think quite differently from you about them. I hear, too, that the laws are different from what I thought: but I can't believe that they can be right. It appears that a woman has no right to spare her dying father, or to save her husband's life! I don't believe that.

**HELMER:** You talk like a child. You don't understand the society in which you live.

**NORA:** No, I don't. But now I'll try to learn. I must make up my mind which is right—society or I.

**HELMER:** Nora, you're ill; you're feverish; I almost think you're out of your senses.

**NORA:** I've never felt so much clearness and certainty as tonight.

**HELMER:** You're clear and certain enough to forsake husband and children?

**NORA:** Yes, I am.

**HELMER:** Then there's only one explanation possible.

**NORA:** What's that?

**HELMER:** You no longer love me.

**NORA:** No; that's just it.

**HELMER:** Nora!—Can you say so!

**NORA:** Oh, I'm so sorry, Torvald; for you've always been so kind to me. But I can't help it. I don't love you anymore.

**HELMER:** [*Mastering himself with difficulty*.] Are you clear and certain on this point too?

**NORA:** Yes, quite. That's why I won't stay here any longer.

**HELMER:** And can you also make clear to me how I have forfeited your love?

**NORA:** Yes, I can. It was this evening, when the miracle didn't happen; for then I saw you aren't the man I had imagined.

**HELMER:** Explain yourself more clearly; I don't understand

**NORA:** I've waited so patiently all these eight years. for of course I saw clearly enough that miracles don't happen every day. When this crushing blow threatened me, I said to myself so confidently, "Now comes the miracle!" When Krogstad's letter lay in the box, it never for a moment occurred to me that you'd think of submitting to that man's conditions. I was convinced that you'd say to him, "Make it known to all the world"; and that then—

**HELMER:** Well? When I'd given my own wife's name up to disgrace and shame—?

**NORA:** Then I firmly believed that you'd come forward, take everything upon yourself, and say, "I'm the guilty one."

**HELMER:** Nora—!

**NORA:** You mean I'd never have accepted such a sacrifice? No, certainly not. But what would my assertions have been worth in opposition to yours?—That's the miracle that I hoped for and dreaded. And it was to hinder that that I wanted to die.

**HELMER:** I'd gladly work for you day and night, Nora—bear sorrow and want for your sake. But no man sacrifices his honor, even for one he loves.

**NORA:** Millions of women have done so.

**HELMER:** Oh, you think and talk like a silly child.

**NORA:** Very likely. But you neither think nor talk like the man I can share my life with. When your terror was over—not for what threatened me, but for yourself—when there's nothing more to fear—then it seemed to you as though nothing had happened. I was your lark again, your doll, just as before—whom you'd take twice as much care of in future, because she's so weak and fragile. [*Stands up.*] Torvald—in that moment it burst upon me that I'd been living here these eight years with a strange man, and had borne him three children.—Oh, I can't bear to think of it! I could tear myself to pieces!

**HELMER:** [*Sadly.*] I see it, I see it; an abyss has opened between us.—But, Nora, can it never be filled up?

**NORA:** As I now am, I'm no wife for you.

**HELMER:** I've strength to become another man.

**NORA:** Perhaps—when your doll's taken away from you.

**HELMER:** To part—to part from you! No, Nora, no; I can't grasp the thought.

**NORA:** [*Going into room on the right.*] The more reason for the thing to happen.

[*She comes back with outdoor things and a small travelling bag, which she places on a chair.*]

**HELMER:** Nora, Nora, not now! Wait till tomorrow.

**NORA:** [*Putting on cloak.*] I can't spend the night in a strange man's house.

**HELMER:** But can't we live here, as brother and sister—?

**NORA:** [*Fastening her hat.*] You know very well that wouldn't last long. [*Puts on the shawl.*] Goodbye, Torvald. No. I won't go to the children. I know they're in better hands than mine. As I now am, I can be nothing to them.

**HELMER:** But some time, Nora—some time—?

**NORA:** How can I tell? I've no idea what'll become of me.

**HELMER:** But you're my wife, now and always!

**NORA:** Listen, Torvald—when a wife leaves her husband's house, as I'm doing, I've heard that in the eyes of the law he's free from all duties towards her. At any rate, I release you from all duties. You mustn't feel yourself bound, any more than I will. There must be perfect freedom on both sides. There, I give you back your ring. Give me mine.

**HELMER:**  That too?

**NORA:**  That too.

**HELMER:**  Here it is.

**NORA:**  Very well. Now it's all over. I lay the keys here. The servants know about everything in the house—better than I do. Tomorrow, when I've started, Christina'll come to pack up the things I brought with me from home. I'll have them sent after me.

**HELMER:**  All over! all over! Nora, will you never think of me again?

**NORA:**  Oh, I'll often think of you, and the children, and this house.

**HELMER:**  May I write to you, Nora?

**NORA:**  No—never. You mustn't.

**HELMER:**  But I must send you—

**NORA:.**  Nothing, nothing.

**HELMER:**  I must help you if you need it.

**NORA:**  No, I say. I take nothing from strangers.

**HELMER:**  Nora—can I never be more than a stranger to you?

**NORA:**  [*Taking her travelling bag.*] Oh, Torvald, then the miracle of miracles would have to happen—

**HELMER:**  What's the miracle of miracles?

**NORA:**  Both of us would have to change so that—Oh, Torvald, I no longer believe in miracles.

**HELMER:.**  But I'll believe. Tell me! We must so change that—?

**NORA:.**  That communion between us will be a marriage. Goodbye.

[*She goes out by the hall door.*]

**HELMER:**  [*Sinks into a chair by the door with his face in his hands.*] Nora! Nora! [*He looks round and rises.*] Empty. She's gone. [*A hope springs up in him.*] Ah! The miracle of miracles—?!

[*From below is heard the reverberation of a heavy door closing.*]

---

### SUSAN GLASPELL ▪ [1882–1948]

*Susan Glaspell was born in Iowa and educated at Drake University. Glaspell was one of the founders, with her husband George Cram Cook, of the Provincetown Players. This company, founded in the Cape Cod resort village, was committed to producing experimental drama, an alternative to the standard fare playing in Broadway theaters. Eventually, it was relocated to New York. Along with Glaspell, Eugene O'Neill, America's only Nobel Prize–winning dramatist, wrote plays for this group. Trained as a journalist and the author of short stories and* novels, Glaspell wrote *Trifles* (1916), her first play, shortly after the founding of the Players, basing her plot on an Iowa murder case she had covered. The one-act play, with both Glaspell and her husband in the cast, premiered during the Players' second season and also exists in a short-story version. Glaspell won the Pulitzer Prize for Drama in 1930 for *Alison's House*, basing the title character on poet Emily Dickinson. A socialist and feminist, Glaspell lived in Provincetown in her last years, writing *The Road to the Temple*, a memoir of her husband's life, and novels.

# Trifles

## Characters

> George Henderson, *County Attorney*
> Mrs. Peters
> Henry Peters, *Sheriff*
> Lewis Hale, *a neighbor*
> Mrs. Hale

*The kitchen in the now abandoned farmhouse of John Wright, a gloomy kitchen, and left without having been put in order—unwashed pans under the sink, a loaf of bread outside the breadbox, a dish towel on the table—other signs of incompleted work. At the rear the outer door opens, and the Sheriff comes in, followed by the County Attorney and Hale. The Sheriff and Hale are men in middle life, the County Attorney is a young man; all are much bundled up and go at once to the stove. They are followed by the two women—the Sheriff's Wife first; she is a slight wiry woman, a thin nervous face. Mrs. Hale is larger and would ordinarily be called more comfortable looking, but she is disturbed now and looks fearfully about as she enters. The women have come in slowly and stand close together near the door.*

**COUNTY ATTORNEY** [*rubbing his hands*]:   This feels good. Come up to the fire, ladies.

**MRS. PETERS** [*after taking a step forward*]:   I'm not—cold.

**SHERIFF** [*unbuttoning his overcoat and stepping away from the stove as if to the beginning of official business*]:   Now, Mr. Hale, before we move things about, you explain to Mr. Henderson just what you saw when you came here yesterday morning.

**COUNTY ATTORNEY:**   By the way, has anything been moved? Are things just as you left them yesterday?

**SHERIFF** [*looking about*]:   It's just the same. When it dropped below zero last night, I thought I'd better send Frank out this morning to make a fire for us—no use getting pneumonia with a big case on; but I told him not to touch anything except the stove—and you know Frank.

**COUNTY ATTORNEY:**   Somebody should have been left here yesterday.

**SHERIFF:**   Oh—yesterday. When I had to send Frank to Morris Center for that man who went crazy—I want you to know I had my hands full yesterday. I knew you could get back from Omaha by today, and as long as I went over everything here myself—

**COUNTY ATTORNEY:**   Well, Mr. Hale, tell just what happened when you came here yesterday morning.

**HALE:**   Harry and I had started to town with a load of potatoes. We came along the road from my place; and as I got here, I said, "I'm going to see if I can't get John Wright to go in with me on a party telephone." I spoke to Wright about it once before, and he put me off, saying folks talked too much anyway, and all he asked was peace and quiet—I guess you know about how much he talked himself; but I thought maybe if I went to the house and talked about it before his wife, though I said to Harry that I didn't know as what his wife wanted made much difference to John—

**COUNTY ATTORNEY:**   Let's talk about that later, Mr. Hale. I do want to talk about that, but tell now just what happened when you got to the house.

**HALE:**   I didn't hear or see anything; I knocked at the door, and still it was all quiet inside. I knew they must be up, it was past eight o'clock. So I knocked again, and I thought I heard somebody say, "Come in." I wasn't sure, I'm not sure yet, but I opened the door—this door [*indicating the door by which the two women are still standing*], and there in that rocker—[*pointing to it*] sat Mrs. Wright. [*They all look at the rocker.*]

**COUNTY ATTORNEY:**   What—was she doing?

**HALE:**   She was rockin' back and forth. She had her apron in her hand and was kind of—pleating it.

**COUNTY ATTORNEY:**   And how did she—look?

**HALE:**   Well, she looked queer.

**COUNTY ATTORNEY:**   How do you mean—queer?

**HALE:**   Well, as if she didn't know what she was going to do next. And kind of done up.

**COUNTY ATTORNEY:**   How did she seem to feel about your coming?

**HALE:**   Why, I don't think she minded—one way or other. She didn't pay much attention. I said, "How do, Mrs. Wright, it's cold, ain't it?" And she said, "Is it?"—and went on kind of pleating at her apron. Well, I was surprised; she didn't ask me to come up to the stove, or to set down, but just sat there, not even looking at me, so I said, "I want to see John." And then she—laughed. I guess you would call it a laugh. I thought of Harry and the team outside, so I said a little sharp: "Can't I see John?" "No," she says, kind o' dull like. "Ain't he home?" says I. "Yes," says she, "he's home." "Then why can't I see him?" I asked her, out of patience. "'Cause he's dead," says she. *"Dead?"* says I. She just nodded her head, not getting a bit excited, but rockin' back and forth.

"Why—where is he?" says I, not knowing what to say. She just pointed upstairs—like that [*himself pointing to the room above*]. I got up, with the idea of going up there. I walked from there to here—then I says, "Why, what did he die of?" "He died of a rope around his neck," says she, and just went on pleatin' at her apron. Well, I went out and called Harry. I thought I might—need help. We went upstairs, and there he was lyin'—

**COUNTY ATTORNEY:** I think I'd rather have you go into that upstairs, where you can point it all out. Just go on now with the rest of the story.

**HALE:** Well, my first thought was to get that rope off. I looked ... [*Stops, his face twitches.*] ... but Harry, he went up to him, and he said, "No, he's dead all right, and we'd better not touch anything." So we went back downstairs. She was still sitting that same way. "Has anybody been notified?" I asked. "No," says she, unconcerned. "Who did this, Mrs. Wright?" said Harry. He said it businesslike—and she stopped pleatin' of her apron. "I don't know," she says. "You don't *know?*" says Harry. "No," says she, "Weren't you sleepin' in the bed with him?" says Harry. "Yes," says she, "but I was on the inside." "Somebody slipped a rope round his neck and strangled him, and you didn't wake up?" says Harry. "I didn't wake up," she said after him. We must 'a looked as if we didn't see how that could be, for after a minute she said, "I sleep sound." Harry was going to ask her more questions, but I said maybe we ought to let her tell her story first to the coroner, or the sheriff, so Harry went fast as he could to Rivers' place, where there's a telephone.

**COUNTY ATTORNEY:** And what did Mrs. Wright do when she knew that you had gone for the coroner?

**HALE:** She moved from that chair to this over here ... [*Pointing to a small chair in the corner.*] ... and just sat there with her hands held together and looking down. I got a feeling that I ought to make some conversation, so I said I had come in to see if John wanted to put in a telephone, and at that she started to laugh, and then she stopped and looked at me—scared. [*The County Attorney, who has had his notebook out, makes a note.*] I dunno, maybe it wasn't scared. I wouldn't like to say it was. Soon Harry got back, and then Dr. Lloyd came, and you, Mr. Peters, and so I guess that's all I know that you don't.

**COUNTY ATTORNEY** [*looking around*]: I guess we'll go upstairs first—and then out to the barn and around there. [*To the Sheriff.*] You're convinced that there was nothing important here—nothing that would point to any motive?

**SHERIFF:** Nothing here but kitchen things.

[*The County Attorney, after again looking around the kitchen, opens the door of a cupboard closet. He gets up on a chair and looks on a shelf. Pulls his hand away, sticky.*]

**COUNTY ATTORNEY:** Here's a nice mess.

*[The women draw nearer.]*

**MRS. PETERS** [*to the other woman*]: Oh, her fruit; it did freeze. [*To the Lawyer.*] She worried about that when it turned so cold. She said the fir'd go out and her jars would break.

**SHERIFF:** Well, can you beat the women! Held for murder and worryin' about her preserves.

**COUNTY ATTORNEY:** I guess before we're through she may have something more serious than preserves to worry about.

**HALE:** Well, women are used to worrying over trifles.

*The two women move a little closer together.*

**COUNTY ATTORNEY** [*with the gallantry of a young politician*]: And yet, for all their worries, what would we do without the ladies? [*The women do not unbend. He goes to the sink, takes a dipperful of water from the pail and, pouring it into a basin, washes his hands. Starts to wipe them on the roller towel, turns it for a cleaner place.*] Dirty towels! [*Kicks his foot against the pans under the sink.*] Not much of a housekeeper, would you say, ladies?

**MRS. HALE** [*stiffly*]: There's a great deal of work to be done on a farm.

**COUNTY ATTORNEY:** To be sure. And yet ... [*With a little bow to her.*] ... I know there are some Dickson county farmhouses which do not have such roller towels. [*He gives it a pull to expose its full length again.*]

**MRS. HALE:** Those towels get dirty awful quick. Men's hands aren't always as clean as they might be.

**COUNTY ATTORNEY:** Ah, loyal to your sex, I see. But you and Mrs. Wright were neighbors. I suppose you were friends, too.

**MRS. HALE** [*shaking her head*]: I've not seen much of her of late years. I've not been in this house—it's more than a year.

**COUNTY ATTORNEY:** And why was that? You didn't like her?

**MRS. HALE:** I liked her all well enough. Farmers' wives have their hands full, Mr. Henderson. And then—

**COUNTY ATTORNEY:** Yes—?

**MRS. HALE** [*looking about*]: It never seemed a very cheerful place.

**COUNTY ATTORNEY:** No—it's not cheerful. I shouldn't say she had the homemaking instinct.

**MRS. HALE:** Well, I don't know as Wright had, either.

**COUNTY ATTORNEY:** You mean that they didn't get on very well?

**MRS. HALE:** No, I don't mean anything. But I don't think a place'd be any cheerfuler for John Wright's being in it.

**COUNTY ATTORNEY:** I'd like to talk more of that a little later. I want to get the lay of things upstairs now. [*He goes to the left, where three steps lead to a stair door.*]

**SHERIFF:** I suppose anything Mrs. Peters does'll be all right. She was to take in some clothes for her, you know, and a few little things. We left in such a hurry yesterday.

**COUNTY ATTORNEY:** Yes, but I would like to see what you take, Mrs. Peters, and keep an eye out for anything that might be of use to us.

**MRS. PETERS:** Yes, Mr. Henderson.

[*The women listen to the men's steps on the stairs, then look about the kitchen.*]

**MRS. HALE:** I'd hate to have men coming into my kitchen, snooping around and criticizing. [*She arranges the pans under the sink which the Lawyer had shoved out of place.*]

**MRS. PETERS:** Of course it's no more than their duty.

**MRS. HALE:** Duty's all right, but I guess that deputy sheriff that came out to make the fire might have got a little of this on. [*Gives the roller towel a pull.*] Wish I'd thought of that sooner. Seems mean to talk about her for not having things slicked up when she had to come away in such a hurry.

**MRS. PETERS** [*who has gone to a small table in the left rear corner of the room, and lifted one end of a towel that covers a pan*]: She had bread set. [*Stands still.*]

**MRS. HALE** [*eyes fixed on a loaf of bread beside the breadbox, which is on a low shelf at the other side of the room. Moves slowly toward it*]: She was going to put this in there. [*Picks up loaf, then abruptly drops it. In a manner of returning to familiar things.*] It's a shame about her fruit. I wonder if it's all gone. [*Gets up on the chair and looks.*] I think there's some here that's all right, Mrs. Peters. Yes—here; [*Holding it toward the window.*] this is cherries, too. [*Looking again.*] I declare I believe that's the only one. [*Gets down, bottle in her hand. Goes to the sink and wipes it off on the outside.*] She'll feel awful bad after all her hard work in the hot weather. I remember the afternoon I put up my cherries last summer. [*She puts the bottle on the big kitchen table, center of the room, front table. With a sigh, is about to sit down in the rocking chair. Before she is seated realizes what chair it is; with a slow look at it, steps back. The chair, which she has touched, rocks back and forth.*]

**MRS. PETERS:** Well, I must get those things from the front room closet. [*She goes to the door at the right, but after looking into the other room steps back.*] You coming with me, Mrs. Hale? You could help me carry them. [*They go into the other room; reappear, Mrs. Peters carrying a dress and skirt, Mrs. Hale following with a pair of shoes.*]

**MRS. PETERS:** My, it's cold in there. [*She puts the cloth on the big table, and hurries to the stove.*]

**MRS. HALE** [*examining the skirt*]: Wright was close. I think maybe that's why she kept so much to herself. She didn't even belong to the Ladies'

Aid. I suppose she felt she couldn't do her part, and then you don't enjoy things when you feel shabby. She used to wear pretty clothes and be lively, when she was Minnie Foster, one of the town girls singing in the choir. But that—oh, that was thirty years ago. This all you was to take in?

**MRS. PETERS:**   She said she wanted an apron. Funny thing to want, for there isn't much to get you dirty in jail, goodness knows. But I suppose just to make her feel more natural. She said they was in the top drawer in this cupboard. Yes, here. And then her little shawl that always hung behind the door. [*Opens stair door and looks.*] Yes, here it is. [*Quickly shuts door leading upstairs.*]

**MRS. HALE** [*abruptly moving toward her*]:   Mrs. Peters?

**MRS. PETERS:**   Yes, Mrs. Hale?

**MRS. HALE:**   Do you think she did it?

**MRS. PETERS** [*in a frightened voice*]:   Oh, I don't know.

**MRS. HALE:**   Well, I don't think she did. Asking for an apron and her little shawl. Worrying about her fruit.

**MRS. PETERS** [*starts to speak, glances up, where footsteps are heard in the room above. In a low voice*]:   Mr. Peters says it looks bad for her. Mr. Henderson is awful sarcastic in speech, and he'll make fun of her sayin' she didn't wake up.

**MRS. HALE:**   Well, I guess John Wright didn't wake when they was slipping that rope under his neck.

**MRS. PETERS:**   No, it's strange. It must have been done awful crafty and still. They say it was such a—funny way to kill a man, rigging it all up like that.

**MRS. HALE:**   That's just what Mr. Hale said. There was a gun in the house. He says that's what he can't understand.

**MRS. PETERS:**   Mr. Henderson said coming out that what was needed for the case was a motive; something to show anger, or—sudden feeling.

**MRS. HALE** [*who is standing by the table*]:   Well, I don't see any signs of anger around here. [*She puts her hand on the dish towel which lies on the table, stands looking down at the table, one half of which is clean, the other half messy.*] It's wiped here. [*Makes a move as if to finish work, then turns and looks at loaf of bread outside the breadbox. Drops towel. In that voice of coming back to familiar things.*] Wonder how they are finding things upstairs? I hope she had it a little more red-up there. You know, it seems kind of *sneaking*. Locking her up in town and then coming out here and trying to get her own house to turn against her!

**MRS. PETERS:**   But, Mrs. Hale, the law is the law.

**MRS. HALE:**   I s'pose 'tis. [*Unbuttoning her coat.*] Better loosen up your things, Mrs. Peters. You won't feel them when you go out.

[*Mrs. Peters takes off her fur tippet, goes to hang it on a hook at the back of room, stands looking at the under part of the small corner table.*]

**MRS. PETERS:** She was piecing a quilt. [*She brings the large sewing basket, and they look at the bright pieces.*]

**MRS. HALE:** It's log cabin pattern. Pretty, isn't it? I wonder if she was goin' to quilt or just knot it?

[*Footsteps have been heard coming down the stairs. The Sheriff enters, followed by Hale and the County Attorney.*]

**SHERIFF:** They wonder if she was going to quilt it or just knot it. [*The men laugh, the women look abashed.*]

**COUNTY ATTORNEY** [*rubbing his hands over the stove*]: Frank's fire didn't do much up there, did it? Well, let's go out to the barn and get that cleared up.

[*The men go outside.*]

**MRS. HALE** [*resentfully*]: I don't know as there's anything so strange, our takin' up our time with little things while we're waiting for them to get the evidence. [*She sits down at the big table, smoothing out a block with decision.*] I don't see as it's anything to laugh about.

**MRS. PETERS** [*apologetically*]: Of course they've got awful important things on their minds. [*Pulls up a chair and joins Mrs. Hale at the table.*]

**MRS. HALE** [*examining another block*]: Mrs. Peters, look at this one. Here, this is the one she was working on, and look at the sewing! All the rest of it has been so nice and even. And look at this! It's all over the place! Why, it looks as if she didn't know what she was about! [*After she has said this, they look at each other, then started to glance back at the door. After an instant Mrs. Hale has pulled at a knot and ripped the sewing.*]

**MRS. PETERS:** Oh, what are you doing, Mrs. Hale?

**MRS. HALE** [*mildly*]: Just pulling out a stitch or two that's not sewed very good. [*Threading a needle.*] Bad sewing always made me fidgety.

**MRS. PETERS** [*nervously*]: I don't think we ought to touch things.

**MRS. HALE:** I'll just finish up this end. [*Suddenly stopping and leaning forward.*] Mrs. Peters?

**MRS. PETERS:** Yes, Mrs. Hale?

**MRS. HALE:** What do you suppose she was so nervous about?

**MRS. PETERS:** Oh—I don't know. I don't know as she was nervous. I sometimes sew awful queer when I'm just tired. [*Mrs. Hale starts to say something, looks at Mrs. Peters, then goes on sewing.*] Well, I must get these things wrapped up. They may be through sooner than we think. [*Putting apron and other things together.*] I wonder where I can find a piece of paper, and string.

**MRS. HALE:** In that cupboard, maybe.

**MRS. PETERS** [*looking in cupboard*]: Why, here's a birdcage. [*Holds it up.*] Did she have a bird, Mrs. Hale?

MRS. HALE:  Why, I don't know whether she did or not—I've not been here for so long. There was a man around last year selling canaries cheap, but I don't know as she took one; maybe she did. She used to sing real pretty herself.

MRS. PETERS [glancing around]:  Seems funny to think of a bird here. But she must have had one, or why should she have a cage? I wonder what happened to it?

MRS. HALE:  I s'pose maybe the cat got it.

MRS. PETERS:  No, she didn't have a cat. She's got that feeling some people have about cats—being afraid of them. My cat got in her room, and she was real upset and asked me to take it out.

MRS. HALE:  My sister Bessie was like that. Queer, ain't it?

MRS. PETERS [examining the cage]:  Why, look at this door. It's broke. One hinge is pulled apart.

MRS. HALE [looking, too]:  Looks as if someone must have been rough with it.

MRS. PETERS:  Why, yes. [She brings the cage forward and puts it on the table.]

MRS. HALE:  I wish if they're going to find any evidence they'd be about it. I don't like this place.

MRS. PETERS:  But I'm awful glad you came with me, Mrs. Hale. It would be lonesome for me sitting here alone.

MRS. HALE:  It would, wouldn't it? [Dropping her sewing.] But I tell you what I do wish, Mrs. Peters. I wish I had come over sometimes when she was here. I—[Looking around the room.]—wish I had.

MRS. PETERS:  But of course you were awful busy, Mrs. Hale—your house and your children.

MRS. HALE:  I could've come. I stayed away because it weren't cheerful—and that's why I ought to have come. I—I've never liked this place. Maybe because it's down in a hollow, and you don't see the road. I dunno what it is, but it's a lonesome place and always was. I wish I had come over to see Minnie Foster sometimes. I can see now—[Shakes her head.]

MRS. PETERS:  Well, you mustn't reproach yourself, Mrs. Hale. Somehow we just don't see how it is with other folks until—something comes up.

MRS. HALE:  Not having children makes less work—but it makes a quiet house, and Wright out to work all day, and no company when he did come in. Did you know John Wright, Mrs. Peters?

MRS. PETERS:  Not to know him; I've seen him in town. They say he was a good man.

MRS. HALE:  Yes—good; he didn't drink, and kept his word as well as most, I guess, and paid his debts. But he was a hard man, Mrs. Peters. Just to pass the time of day with him. [Shivers.] Like a raw wind that gets to the bone. [Pauses, her eye falling on the cage.] I should think she would 'a wanted a bird. But what do you suppose went with it?

**MRS. PETERS:**   I don't know, unless it got sick and died. [*She reaches over and swings the broken door, swings it again; both women watch it.*]

**MRS. HALE:**   You weren't raised round here, were you? [*Mrs. Peters shakes her head.*] You didn't know—her?

**MRS. PETERS:**   Not till they brought her yesterday.

**MRS. HALE:**   She—come to think of it, she was kind of like a bird herself—real sweet and pretty, but kind of timid and—fluttery. How—she—did—change. [*Silence; then as if struck by a happy thought and relieved to get back to everyday things.*] Tell you what, Mrs. Peters, why don't you take the quilt in with you? It might take up her mind.

**MRS. PETERS:**   Why, I think that's a real nice idea, Mrs. Hale. There couldn't possibly be any objection to it, could there? Now, just what would I take? I wonder if her patches are in here—and her things. [*They look in the sewing basket.*]

**MRS. HALE:**   Here's some red. I expect this has got sewing things in it [*Brings out a fancy box.*] What a pretty box. Looks like something somebody would give you. Maybe her scissors are in here. [*Opens box. Suddenly puts her hand to her nose.*] Why—[*Mrs. Peters bends nearer, then turns her face away.*] There's something wrapped up in this piece of silk.

**MRS. PETERS:**   Why, this isn't her scissors.

**MRS. HALE** [*lifting the silk*]:   Oh, Mrs. Peters—it's—[*Mrs. Peters bends closer.*]

**MRS. PETERS:**   It's the bird.

**MRS. HALE** [*jumping up*]:   But, Mrs. Peters—look at it. Its neck! Look at its neck! It's all—other side *to.*

**MRS. PETERS:**   Somebody—wrung—its neck.

[*Their eyes meet. A look of growing comprehension of horror. Steps are heard outside. Mrs. Hale slips box under quilt pieces, and sinks into her chair. Enter Sheriff and County Attorney. Mrs. Peters rises.*]

**COUNTY ATTORNEY** [*as one turning from serious things to little pleasantries*]:   Well, ladies, have you decided whether she was going to quilt it or knot it?

**MRS. PETERS:**   We think she was going to—knot it.

**COUNTY ATTORNEY:**   Well, that's interesting, I'm sure. [*Seeing the birdcage.*] Has the bird flown?

**MRS. HALE** [*putting more quilt pieces over the box*]:   We think the—cat got it.

**COUNTY ATTORNEY** [*preoccupied*]:   Is there a cat?

[*Mrs. Hale glances in a quick covert way at Mrs. Peters.*]

**MRS. PETERS:**   Well, not now. They're superstitious, you know. They leave.

**COUNTY ATTORNEY** [*to Sheriff Peters, continuing an interrupted conversation*]:   No sign at all of anyone having come from the outside. Their own rope. Now let's go up again and go over it piece by piece. [*They start upstairs.*] It would have to have been someone who knew just the—

[*Mrs. Peters sits down. The two women sit there not looking at one another, but as if peering into something and at the same time holding back. When they talk now, it is the manner of feeling their way over strange ground, as if afraid of what they are saying, but as if they cannot help saying it.*]

MRS. HALE:   She liked the bird. She was going to bury it in that pretty box.

MRS. PETERS [*in a whisper*]:   When I was a girl—my kitten—there was a boy took a hatchet, and before my eyes—and before I could get there—[*Covers her face an instant.*] If they hadn't held me back, I would have—[*Catches herself, looks upstairs where steps are heard, falters weakly.*]—hurt him.

MRS. HALE [*with a slow look around her*]:   I wonder how it would seem never to have had any children around. [*Pause.*] No, Wright wouldn't like the bird—a thing that sang. She used to sing. He killed that, too.

MRS. PETERS [*moving uneasily*]:   We don't know who killed the bird.

MRS. HALE:   I knew John Wright.

MRS. PETERS:   It was an awful thing was done in this house that night, Mrs. Hale. Killing a man while he slept, slipping a rope around his neck that choked the life out of him.

MRS. HALE:   His neck. Choked the life out of him.

[*Her hand goes out and rests on the birdcage.*]

MRS. PETERS [*with a rising voice*]:   We don't know who killed him. We don't *know*.

MRS. HALE [*her own feeling not interrupted*]:   If there'd been years and years of nothing, then a bird to sing to you, it would be awful—still, after the bird was still.

MRS. PETERS [*something within her speaking*]:   I know what stillness is. When we homesteaded in Dakota, and my first baby died—after he was two years old, and me with no other then—

MRS. HALE [*moving*]:   How soon do you suppose they'll be through, looking for evidence?

MRS. PETERS:   I know what stillness is. [*Pulling herself back.*] The law has got to punish crime, Mrs. Hale.

MRS. HALE [*not as if answering that*]:   I wish you'd seen Minnie Foster when she wore a white dress with blue ribbons and stood up there in the choir and sang. [*A look around the room.*] Oh, I *wish* I'd come over here once in a while! That was a crime! That was a crime! Who's going to punish that?

**MRS. PETERS** [*looking upstairs*]:  We mustn't—take on.

**MRS. HALE:**  I might have known she needed help! I know how things can be—for women. I tell you, it's queer, Mrs. Peters. We live close together and we live far apart. We all go through the same things—it's all just a different kind of the same thing. [*Brushes her eyes, noticing the bottle of fruit, reaches out for it.*] If I was you, I wouldn't tell her her fruit was gone. Tell her it *ain't*. Tell her it's all right. Take this in to prove it to her. She—she may never know whether it was broke or not.

**MRS. PETERS** [*takes the bottle, looks about for something to wrap it in; takes petticoat from the clothes brought from the other room, very nervously begins winding this around the bottle. In a false voice*]:  My, it's a good thing the men couldn't hear us. Wouldn't they just laugh! Getting all stirred up over a little thing like a—dead canary. As if that could have anything to do with—with—wouldn't they *laugh*!

[*The men are heard coming downstairs.*]

**MRS. HALE** [*under her breath*]:  Maybe they would—maybe they wouldn't.

**COUNTY ATTORNEY:**  No, Peters, it's all perfectly clear except a reason for doing it. But you know juries when it comes to women. If there was some definite thing. Something to show—something to make a story about—a thing that would connect up with this strange way of doing it.

[*The women's eyes meet for an instant. Enter Hale from outer door.*]

**HALE:**  Well, I've got the team around. Pretty cold out there.

**COUNTY ATTORNEY:**  I'm going to stay here awhile by myself. [*To the Sheriff.*] You can send Frank out for me, can't you? I want to go over everything. I'm not satisfied that we can't do better.

**SHERIFF:**  Do you want to see what Mrs. Peters is going to take in?

[*The Lawyer goes to the table, picks up the apron, laughs.*]

**COUNTY ATTORNEY:**  Oh I guess they're not very dangerous things the ladies have picked up. [*Moves a few things about, disturbing the quilt pieces which cover the box. Steps back.*] No, Mrs. Peters doesn't need supervising. For that matter, a sheriff's wife is married to the law. Ever think of it that way, Mrs. Peters?

**MRS. PETERS:**  Not—just that way.

**SHERIFF** [*chuckling*]:  Married to the law. [*Moves toward the other room.*] I just want you to come in here a minute, George. We ought to take a look at these windows.

**COUNTY ATTORNEY** [*scoffingly*]:  Oh, windows!

**SHERIFF:**  We'll be right out, Mr. Hale.

[*Hale goes outside. The Sheriff follows the County Attorney into the other room. Then Mrs. Hale rises, hands tight together, looking intensely at Mrs. Peters, whose eyes take a slow turn, finally meeting, Mrs. Hale's.*

*A moment Mrs. Hale holds her, then her own eyes point the way to where the box is concealed. Suddenly Mrs. Peters throws back quilt pieces and tries to put the box in the bag she is wearing. It is too big. She opens box, starts to take the bird out, cannot touch it, goes to pieces, stands there helpless. Sound of a knob turning in the other room. Mrs. Hale snatches the box and puts it in the pocket of her big coat. Enter County Attorney and Sheriff.*]

**COUNTY ATTORNEY** [*facetiously*]:    Well, Henry, at least we found out that she was not going to quilt it. She was going to—what is it you call it, ladies?

**MRS. HALE** [*her hand against her pocket*]:    We call it—knot it, Mr. Henderson.    Curtain

*—1917*

---

## AUGUST WILSON ■ (1945–2005)

*August Wilson, whose birth name was Frederick August Kittel, was born in Pittsburgh's predominantly African American Hill District, the setting of many of his plays. The child of a mixed-race marriage, he grew up fatherless and credits his real education in life and, incidentally, in language to the older men in his neighborhood, whose distinctive voices echo memorably in his plays. A school dropout at fifteen after a teacher unjustly accused him of plagiarism, he joined in the Black Power movement of the 1960s, eventually founding the Black Horizon on the Hill, an African American theater company. Wilson admits to having had little confidence in his own ability to write dialogue during his early career, and his first publications were poems. A move to St. Paul, Minnesota, led to work with the Minneapolis Playwrights' Center. After his return to Pittsburgh, he wrote* Jitney *and* Fullerton Street, *which were staged by regional theaters. His career hit full stride with the successful debut of* Ma Rainey's Black Bottom *(1984), which was first produced at the Yale Repertory Theater and later moved to Broadway.* Joe Turner's Come and Gone *(1986) was his next success, and* Fences *(1987) and* The Piano Lesson *(1990) both won Pulitzer Prizes and other major awards, establishing Wilson as the most prominent African American dramatist. In most of Wilson's plays, a historical theme is prominent, as Wilson attempts to piece together the circumstances that led African Americans to northern cities, depicting how they remain united and sometimes divided by a common cultural heritage that transcends even the ties of friendship and family. But to these social concerns, Wilson brings a long training in the theater and a poet's love of language. As he said to an interviewer in 1991, "[Poetry] is the bedrock of my playwriting.... The idea of metaphor is a very large idea in my plays and* something that I find lacking in most contemporary plays. I think I write the kinds of plays that I do because I have twenty-six years of writing poetry underneath all of that." Two Trains Running *(1992),* Seven Guitars *(1995),* and King Hedley II *(2001) were among his late works.*

# Fences

*For Lloyd Richards, Who Adds to Whatever He Touches*
> When the sins of our fathers visit us
> We do not have to play host.
> We can banish them with forgiveness
> As God, in His Largeness and Laws.

> *—AUGUST WILSON*

## LIST OF CHARACTERS

*Troy Maxson*
*Jim Bono, Troy's* friend
*Rose, Troy's* wife
*Lyons, Troy's* oldest son by previous marriage
*Gabriel, Troy's* brother
*Cory, Troy* and Rose's son
*Raynell, Troy's* daughter

SETTING. *The setting is the yard which fronts the only entrance to the Maxson household, an ancient two-story brick house set back off a small alley in a big-city neighborhood. The entrance to the house is gained by two or three steps leading to a wooden porch badly in need of paint.*

*A relatively recent addition to the house and running its full width, the porch lacks congruence. It is a sturdy porch with a flat roof. One or two chairs of dubious value sit at one end where the kitchen window opens onto the porch. An old-fashioned icebox stands silent guard at the opposite end.*

*The yard is a small dirt yard, partially fenced, except for the last scene, with a wooden saw horse, a pile of lumber, and other fence-building equipment set off to the side. Opposite is a tree from which hangs a ball made of rags. A baseball bat leans against the tree. Two oil drums serve as garbage receptacles and sit near the house at right to complete the setting.*

THE PLAY. *Near the turn of the century, the destitute of Europe sprang on the city with tenacious claws and an honest and solid dream. The city devoured them. They swelled its belly until it burst into a thousand furnaces and sewing machines, a thousand butcher shops and bakers' ovens, a thousand churches and hospitals and funeral parlors and moneylenders. The city* grew. *It nourished itself and offered each man a partnership limited only by his talent, his guile, and his willingness and capacity for hard work. For the immigrants of Europe, a dream dared and won true.*

*The descendants of African slaves were offered no such welcome or participation. They came from places called the Carolinas and the Virginias, Georgia, Alabama, Mississippi, and Tennessee. They came strong, eager, searching. The city rejected them and they fled and settled along the riverbanks and under bridges in shallow, ramshackle houses made of sticks and tarpaper. They collected rags and wood. They sold the use of their muscles and their bodies. They cleaned houses and washed clothes, they shined shoes, and in quiet desperation and vengeful pride, they stole, and lived in pursuit of their own dream. That they could breathe free, finally, and stand to meet life with the force of dignity and whatever eloquence the heart could call upon.*

*By 1957, the hard-won victories of the European immigrants had solidified the industrial might of America. War had been confronted and won with new energies that used loyalty and patriotism as its fuel. Life was rich, full, and flourishing. The Milwaukee Braves won the World Series, and the hot winds of change that would make the sixties a turbulent, racing, dangerous, and provocative decade had not yet begun to blow full.*

# ACT I

## SCENE I

*It is 1957. Troy and Bono enter the yard, engaged in conversation. Troy is fifty-three years old, a large man with thick, heavy hands; it is this largeness that he strives to fill out and make an accommodation with. Together with his blackness, his largeness informs his sensibilities and the choices he has made in his life.*

*Of the two men, Bono is obviously the follower. His commitment to their friendship of thirty-odd years is rooted in his admiration of Troy's honesty, capacity for hard work, and his strength, which Bono seeks to emulate.*

*It is Friday night, payday, and the one night of the week the two men engage in a ritual of talk and drink. Troy is usually the most talkative and at times he can be crude and almost vulgar, though he is capable of rising to profound heights of expression. The men carry lunch buckets and wear or carry burlap aprons and are dressed in clothes suitable to their jobs as garbage collectors.*

**BONO:**   *Troy, you ought to stop that lying!*
**TROY:**   I ain't lying! The nigger had a watermelon this big. (*He indicates with his hands.*) Talking about…"What watermelon, Mr. Rand?" I liked to fell out! "What watermelon, Mr. Rand?"…And it sitting there big as life.
**BONO:**   What did Mr. Rand say?

**TROY:**   Ain't said nothing. Figure if the nigger too dumb to know he carrying a watermelon, he wasn't gonna get much sense out of him. Trying to hide that great big old watermelon under his coat. Afraid to let the white man see him carry it home.

**BONO:**   I'm like you...I ain't got no time for them kind of people.

**TROY:**   Now what he look like getting mad cause he see the man from the union talking to Mr. Rand?

**BONO:**   He come to me talking about..."Maxson gonna get us fired." I told him to get away from me with that. He walked away from me calling you a troublemaker. What Mr. Rand say?

**TROY:**   Ain't said nothing. He told me to go down the Commissioner's office next Friday. They called me down there to see them.

**BONO:**   Well, as long as you got your complaint filed, they can't fire you. That's what one of them white fellows tell me.

**TROY:**   I ain't worried about them firing me. They gonna fire me cause I asked a question? That's all I did. I went to Mr. Rand and asked him, "Why? Why you got the white mens driving and the colored lifting?" Told him, "what's the matter, don't I count? You think only white fellows got sense enough to drive a truck. That ain't no paper job! Hell, anybody can drive a truck. How come you got all whites driving and the colored lifting?" He told me "take it to the union." Well, hell, that's what I done! Now they wanna come up with this pack of lies.

**BONO:**   I told Brownie if the man come and ask him any questions...just tell the truth! It ain't nothing but something they done trumped up on you cause you filed a complaint on them.

**TROY:**   Brownie don't understand nothing. All I want them to do is change the job description. Give everybody a chance to drive the truck. Brownie can't see that. He ain't got that much sense.

**BONO:**   How you figure he be making out with that gal be up at Taylors' all the time...that Alberta gal?

**TROY:**   Same as you and me. Getting just as much as we is. Which is to say nothing.

**BONO:**   It is, huh? I figure you doing a little better than me...and I ain't saying what I'm doing.

**TROY:**   Aw, nigger, look here...I know you. If you had got anywhere near that gal, twenty minutes later you be looking to tell somebody. And the first one you gonna tell...that you gonna want to brag to...is gonna be me.

**BONO:**   I ain't saying that. I see where you be eyeing her.

**TROY:**   I eye all the women. I don't miss nothing. Don't never let nobody tell you *Troy* Maxson don't eye the women.

**BONO:**   You been doing more than eyeing her. You done bought her a drink or two.

**TROY:**  Hell yeah, I bought her a drink! What that mean? I bought you one, too. What that mean cause I buy her a drink? I'm just being polite.

**BONO:**  It's alright to buy her one drink. That's what you call being polite. But when you wanna be buying two or three... that's what you call eyeing her.

**TROY:**  Look here, as long as you known me... you ever known me to chase after women?

**BONO:**  Hell yeah! Long as I done known you. You forgetting I knew you when.

**TROY:**  Naw, I'm talking about since I been married to Rose?

**BONO:**  Oh, not since you been married to Rose. Now, that's the truth, there. I can say that.

**TROY:**  Alright then! Case closed.

**BONO:**  I see you be walking up around Alberta's house. You supposed to be at Taylors' and you be walking up around there.

**TROY:**  What you watching where I'm walking for? I ain't watching after you.

**BONO:**  I seen you walking around there more than once.

**TROY:**  Hell, you liable to see me walking anywhere! That don't mean nothing cause you see me walking around there.

**BONO:**  Where she come from anyway? She just kinda showed up one day.

**TROY:**  Tallahassee. You can look at her and tell she one of them Florida gals. They got some big healthy women down there. Grow them right up out the ground. Got a little bit of Indian in her. Most of them niggers down in Florida got some Indian in them.

**BONO:**  I don't know about that Indian part. But she damn sure big and healthy. Woman wear some big stockings. Got them great big old legs and hips as wide as the Mississippi River.

**TROY:**  Legs don't mean nothing. You don't do nothing but push them out of the way. But them hips cushion the ride!

**BONO:**  *Troy,* you ain't got no sense.

**TROY:**  It's the truth! Like you riding on Goodyears!

*(Rose enters from the house. She is ten years younger than Troy, her devotion to him stems from her recognition of the possibilities of her life without him: a succession of abusive men and their babies, a life of partying and running the streets, the Church, or aloneness with its attendant pain and frustration. She recognizes Troy's spirit as a fine and illuminating one and she either ignores or forgives his faults, only some of which she recognizes. Though she doesn't drink, her presence is an integral part of the Friday night rituals. She alternates between the porch and the kitchen, where supper preparations are under way.)*

**ROSE:**  What you all out here getting into?

**TROY:**  What you worried about what we getting into for? This is men talk, woman.

**ROSE:**  What I care what you all talking about? Bono, you gonna stay for supper?

**BONO:**  No, I thank you, Rose. But Lucille say she cooking up a pot of pigfeet.

**TROY:**  Pigfeet! Hell, I'm going home with you! Might even stay the night if you got some pigfeet. You got something in there to top them pig-feet, Rose?

**ROSE:**  I'm cooking up some chicken. I got some chicken and collard greens.

**TROY:**  Well, go on back in the house and let me and Bono finish what we was talking about. This is men talk. I got some talk for you later. You know what kind of talk I mean. You go on and powder it up.

**ROSE:**  *Troy* Maxson, don't you start that now!

**TROY** (*puts his arm around her*):  Aw, woman... come here. Look here, Bono...when I met this woman... I got out that place, say, "Hitch up my pony, saddle up my mare... there's a woman out there for me some-where. I looked here. Looked there. Saw Rose and latched on to her." I latched on to her and told her—I'm gonna tell you the truth—I told her, "Baby, I don't wanna marry, I just wanna be your man." Rose told me...tell him what you told me, Rose.

**ROSE:**  I told him if he wasn't the marrying kind, then move out the way so the marrying kind could find me.

**TROY:**  That's what she told me. "Nigger, you in my way. You blocking the view! Move out the way so I can find me a husband." I thought it over two or three days. Come back—

**ROSE:**  Ain't no two or three days nothing. You was back the same night.

**TROY:**  Come back, told her..."Okay, baby... but I'm gonna buy me a banty rooster and put him out there in the backyard... and when he see a stranger come, he'll flap his wings and crow..." Look here, Bono, I could watch the front door by myself... it was that back door I was worried about.

**ROSE:**  *Troy*, you ought not talk like that. *Troy* ain't doing nothing but telling a lie.

**TROY:**  Only thing is... when we first got married... forget the rooster... we ain't had no yard!

**BONO:**  I hear you tell it. Me and Lucille was staying down there on Logan Street. Had two rooms with the outhouse in the back. I ain't mind the outhouse none. But when that goddamn wind blow through there in the winter...that's what I'm talking about! To this day I wonder why in the hell I ever stayed down there for six long years. But see, I didn't know I could do no better. I thought only white folks had inside toilets and things.

**ROSE:**    There's a lot of people don't know they can do no better than they doing now. That's just something you got to learn. A lot of folks still shop at Bella's.

**TROY:**    Ain't nothing wrong with shopping at Bella's. She got fresh food.

**ROSE:**    I ain't said nothing about if she got fresh food. I'm talking about what she charge. She charge ten cents more than the A&P.

**TROY:**    The A&P ain't never done nothing for me. I spends my money where I'm treated right. I go down to Bella, say, "I need a loaf of bread, I'll pay you Friday." She give it to me. What sense that make when I got money to go and spend it somewhere else and ignore the person who done right by me? That ain't in the Bible.

**ROSE:**    We ain't talking about what's in the Bible. What sense it make to shop there when she overcharge?

**TROY:**    You shop where you want to. I'll do my shopping where the people been good to me.

**ROSE:**    Well, I don't think it's right for her to overcharge. That's all I was saying.

**BONO:**    Look here... I got to get on. Lucille going be raising all kind of hell.

**TROY:**    Where you going, nigger? We ain't finished this pint. Come here, finish this pint.

**BONO:**    Well, hell, I am... if you ever turn the bottle loose.

**TROY** (*hands him the bottle*):    The only thing I say about the A&P is I'm glad *Cory* got that job down there. Help him take care of his school clothes and things. Gabe done moved out and things getting tight around here. He got that job... He can start to look out for himself.

**ROSE:**    *Cory* done went and got recruited by a college football team.

**TROY:**    I told that boy about that football stuff. The white man ain't gonna let him get nowhere with that football. I told him when he first come to me with it. Now you come telling me he done went and got more tied up in it. He ought to go and get recruited in how to fix cars or something where he can make a living.

**ROSE:**    He ain't talking about making no living playing football. It's just something the boys in school do. They gonna send a recruiter by to talk to you. He'll tell you he ain't talking about making no living playing football. It's a honor to be recruited.

**TROY:**    It ain't gonna get him nowhere. Bono'll tell you that.

**BONO:**    If he be like you in the sports... he's gonna be alright. Ain't but two men ever played baseball as good as you. That's Babe Ruth and Josh Gibson.° Them's the only two men ever hit more home runs than you.

**TROY:**    What it ever get me? Ain't got a pot to piss in or a window to throw it out of.

---

*Josh Gibson:* legendary catcher in the Negro Leagues whose batting average and home-run totals far outstripped Major League records; he died of a stroke at age 35 in January 1947, three months before Jackie Robinson's debut with the Brooklyn Dodgers.

**ROSE:**   Times have changed since you was playing baseball, *Troy*. That was before the war. Times have changed a lot since then.

**TROY:**   How in hell they done changed?

**ROSE:**   They got lots of colored boys playing ball now. Baseball and football.

**BONO:**   You right about that, Rose. Times have changed, *Troy*. You just come along too early.

**TROY:**   There ought not never have been no time called too early! Now you take that fellow...what's that fellow they had playing right field for the Yankees back then? You know who I'm talking about, Bono. Used to play right field for the Yankees.

**ROSE:**   Selkirk?°

**TROY:**   Selkirk! That's it! Man batting .269, understand? .269. What kind of sense that make? I was hitting .432 with thirty-seven home runs! Man batting .269 and playing right field for the Yankees! I saw Josh Gibson's daughter yesterday. She walking around with raggedy shoes on her feet. Now I bet you Selkirk's daughter ain't walking around with raggedy shoes on her feet! I bet you that!

**ROSE:**   They got a lot of colored baseball players now. Jackie Robinson° was the first. Folks had to wait for Jackie Robinson.

**TROY:**   I done seen a hundred niggers play baseball better than Jackie Robinson. Hell, I know some teams Jackie Robinson couldn't even make! What you talking about Jackie Robinson. Jackie Robinson wasn't nobody. I'm talking about if you could play ball then they ought to have let you play. Don't care what color you were. Come telling me I come along too early. If you could play... then they ought to have let you play.

*(Troy takes a long drink from the bottle.)*

**ROSE:**   You gonna drink yourself to death. You don't need to be drinking like that.

**TROY:**   Death ain't nothing. I done seen him. Done wrassled with him. You can't tell me nothing about death. Death ain't nothing but a fastball on the outside corner. And you know what I'll do to that! Lookee here, Bono... am I lying? You get one of them fastballs, about waist high, over the outside corner of the plate where you can get the meat of the bat on it... and good god! You can kiss it goodbye. Now, am I lying?

**BONO:**   Naw, you telling the truth there. I seen you do it.

**TROY:**   If I'm lying... that 450 feet worth of lying! *(Pause.)* That's all death is to me. A fastball on the outside corner.

**ROSE:**   I don't know why you want to get on talking about death.

**TROY:**   Ain't nothing wrong with talking about death. That's part of life. Everybody gonna die. You gonna die, I'm gonna die. Bono's gonna die. Hell, we all gonna die.

*Selkirk:* Andy Selkirk, Yankee outfielder who hit .269 in 118 games in 1940. *Jackie Robinson:* the first African American to play in major league baseball, joined the Brooklyn Dodgers in 1947.

**ROSE:**  But you ain't got to talk about it. I don't like to talk about it.

**TROY:**  You the one brought it up. Me and Bono was talking about baseball... you tell me I'm gonna drink myself to death. Ain't that right, Bono? You know I don't drink this but one night out of the week. That's Friday night. I'm gonna drink just enough to where I can handle it. Then I cuts it loose. I leave it alone. So don't you worry about me drinking myself to death. 'Cause I ain't worried about Death. I done seen him. I done wrestled with him.

Look here, Bono... I looked up one day and Death was marching straight at me. Like Soldiers on Parade! The Army of Death was marching straight at me. The middle of July, 1941. It got real cold just like it be winter. It seem like Death himself reached out and touched me on the shoulder. He touch me just like I touch you. I got cold as ice and Death standing there grinning at me.

**ROSE:**  *Troy*, why don't you hush that talk.

**TROY:**  I say...what you want, Mr. Death? You be wanting me? You done brought your army to be getting me? I looked him dead in the eye. I wasn't fearing nothing. I was ready to tangle. Just like I'm ready to tangle now. The Bible say be ever vigilant. That's why I don't get but so drunk. I got to keep watch.

**ROSE:**  *Troy* was right down there in Mercy Hospital. You remember he had pneumonia? Laying there with a fever talking plumb out of his head.

**TROY:**  Death standing there staring at me... carrying that sickle in his hand. Finally he say, "You want bound over for another year?" See, just like that..."You want bound over for another year?" I told him, "Bound over hell! Let's settle this now!"

It seem like he kinda fell back when I said that, and all the cold went out of me. I reached down and grabbed that sickle and threw it just as far as I could throw it... and me and him commenced to wrestling.

We wrestled for three days and three nights. I can't say where I found the strength from. Everytime it seemed like he was gonna get the best of me, I'd reach way down deep inside myself and find the strength to do him one better.

**ROSE:**  Every time *Troy* tell that story he find different ways to tell it. Different things to make up about it.

**TROY:**  I ain't making up nothing. I'm telling you the facts of what happened. I wrestled with Death for three days and three nights and I'm standing here to tell you about it. (*Pause.*) Alright. At the end of the third night we done weakened each other to where we can't hardly move. Death stood up, throwed on his robe... had him a white robe with a hood on it. He threwed on that robe and went off to look for his sickle. Say, "I'll be back." Just like that. "I'll be back." I told him, say, "Yeah, but... you gonna have to find me!" I wasn't no fool. I wasn't going looking for him. Death ain't nothing to play with. And I know he's gonna get me. I know I got to join his army... his camp followers. But as long as I keep my strength and see him coming... as long as I keep up my vigilance...he's gonna have to fight to get me. I ain't going easy.

**BONO:**  Well, look here, since you got to keep up your vigilance... let me have the bottle.

**TROY:**  Aw hell, I shouldn't have told you that part. I should have left out that part.

**ROSE:**  *Troy* be talking that stuff and half the time don't even know what he be talking about.

**TROY:**  Bono know me better than that.

**BONO:**  That's right. I know you. I know you got some Uncle Remus in your blood. You got more stories than the devil got sinners.

**TROY:**  Aw hell, I done seen him too! Done talked with the devil.

**ROSE:**  *Troy*, don't nobody wanna be hearing all that stuff.

*(Lyons enters the yard from the street. Thirty-four years old, Troy's son by a previous marriage, he sports a neatly trimmed goatee, sport coat, white shirt, tieless and buttoned at the collar. Though he fancies himself a musician, he is more caught up in the ritu-als and "idea" of being a musician than in the actual practice of the music. He has come to borrow money from Troy, and while he knows he will be successful, he is uncertain as to what extent his lifestyle will be held up to scrutiny and ridicule.)*

**LYONS:**  Hey, Pop.

**TROY:**  What you come "Hey, Popping" me for?

**LYONS:**  How you doing, Rose? *(He kisses her.)* Mr. Bono. How you doing?

**BONO:**  Hey, Lyons... how you been?

**TROY:**  He must have been doing alright. I ain't seen him around here last week.

**ROSE:**  *Troy*, leave your boy alone. He come by to see you and you wanna start all that nonsense.

**TROY:**  I ain't bothering Lyons. *(Offers him the bottle.)* Here... get you a drink. We got an understanding. I know why he come by to see me and he know I know.

**LYONS:**  Come on, Pop... I just stopped by to say hi... see how you was doing.

**TROY:**  You ain't stopped by yesterday.

**ROSE:**  You gonna stay for supper, Lyons? I got some chicken cooking in the oven.

**LYONS:**  No, Rose...thanks. I was just in the neighborhood and thought I'd stop by for a minute.

**TROY:**  You was in the neighborhood alright, nigger. You telling the truth there. You was in the neighborhood cause it's my payday.

**LYONS:**  Well, hell, since you mentioned it... let me have ten dollars.

**TROY:**  I'll be damned! I'll die and go to hell and play blackjack with the devil before I give you ten dollars.

**BONO:**  That's what I wanna know about... that devil you done seen.

**LYONS:**   What... Pop done seen the devil? You too much, Pops.

**TROY:**   Yeah, I done seen him. Talked to him too!

**ROSE:**   You ain't seen no devil. I done told you that man ain't had nothing to do with the devil. Anything you can't understand, you want to call it the devil.

**TROY:**   Look here, Bono... I went down to see Hertzberger about some furniture. Got three rooms for two-ninety-eight. That what it say on the radio. "Three rooms... two-ninety-eight." Even made up a little song about it. Go down there... man tell me I can't get no credit. I'm working every day and can't get no credit. What to do? I got an empty house with some raggedy furniture in it. *Cory* ain't got no bed. He's sleeping on a pile of rags on the floor. Working every day and can't get no credit. Come back here—Rose'll tell you—madder than hell. Sit down...try to figure what I'm gonna do. Come a knock on the door. Ain't been living here but three days. Who know I'm here? Open the door... devil standing there bigger than life. White fellow... got on good clothes and everything. Standing there with a clipboard in his hand. I ain't had to say nothing. First words come out of his mouth was... "I understand you need some furniture and can't get no credit." I liked to fell over. He say "I'll give you all the credit you want, but you got to pay the interest on it." I told him, "Give me three rooms worth and charge whatever you want." Next day a truck pulled up here and two men unloaded them three rooms. Man what drove the truck give me a book. Say send ten dollars, first of every month to the address in the book and every thing will be alright. Say if I miss a payment the devil was coming back and it'll be hell to pay. That was fifteen years ago. To this day... the first of the month I send my ten dollars, Rose'll tell you.

**ROSE:**   *Troy* lying.

**TROY:**   I ain't never seen that man since. Now you tell me who else that could have been but the devil? I ain't sold my soul or nothing like that, you understand. Naw, I wouldn't have truck with the devil about nothing like that. I got my furniture and pays my ten dollars the first of the month just like clockwork.

**BONO:**   How long you say you been paying this ten dollars a month?

**TROY:**   Fifteen years!

**BONO:**   Hell, ain't you finished paying for it yet? How much the man done charged you?

**TROY:**   Aw hell, I done paid for it. I done paid for it ten times over! The fact is I'm scared to stop paying it.

**ROSE:**   *Troy* lying. We got that furniture from Mr. Glickman. He ain't paying no ten dollars a month to nobody.

**TROY:**   Aw hell, woman. Bono know I ain't that big a fool.

**LYONS:**   I was just getting ready to say...I know where there's a bridge for sale.

**TROY:** Look here, I'll tell you this... it don't matter to me if he was the devil. It don't matter if the devil give credit. Somebody has got to give it.

**ROSE:** It ought to matter. You going around talking about having truck with the devil... God's the one you gonna have to answer to. He's the one gonna be at the Judgment.

**LYONS:** Yeah, well, look here, Pop... Let me have that ten dollars. I'll give it back to you. Bonnie got a job working at the hospital.

**TROY:** What I tell you, Bono? The only time I see this nigger is when he wants something. That's the only time I see him.

**LYONS:** Come on, Pop, Mr. Bono don't want to hear all that. Let me have the ten dollars. I told you Bonnie working.

**TROY:** What that mean to me? "Bonnie working." I don't care if she working. Go ask her for the ten dollars if she working. Talking about "Bonnie working." Why ain't you working?

**LYONS:** Aw, Pop, you know I can't find no decent job. Where am I gonna get a job at? You know I can't get no job.

**TROY:** I told you I know some people down there. I can get you on the rubbish if you want to work. I told you that the last time you came by here asking me for something.

**LYONS:** Naw, Pop... thanks. That ain't for me. I don't wanna be carrying nobody's rubbish. I don't wanna be punching nobody's time clock.

**TROY:** What's the matter, you too good to carry people's rubbish? Where you think that ten dollars you talking about come from? I'm just supposed to haul people's rubbish and give my money to you cause you too lazy to work. You too lazy to work and wanna know why you ain't got what I got.

**ROSE:** What hospital Bonnie working at? Mercy?

**LYONS:** She's down at Passavant working in the laundry.

**TROY:** I ain't got nothing as it is. I give you that ten dollars and I got to eat beans the rest of the week. Naw... you ain't getting no ten dollars here.

**LYONS:** You ain't got to be eating no beans. I don't know why you wanna say that.

**TROY:** I ain't got no extra money. Gabe done moved over to Miss Pearl's paying her the rent and things done got tight around here. I can't afford to be giving you every payday.

**LYONS:** I ain't asked you to give me nothing. I asked you to loan me ten dollars. I know you got ten dollars.

**TROY:** Yeah, I got it. You know why I got it? Cause I don't throw my money away out there in the streets. You living the fast life... wanna be a musician... running around in them clubs and things... then, you learn to take care of yourself. You ain't gonna find me going and asking nobody for nothing. I done spent too many years without.

**LYONS:**  You and me is two different people, Pop.

**TROY:**  I done learned my mistake and learned to do what's right by it. You still trying to get something for nothing. Life don't owe you nothing. You owe it to yourself. Ask Bono. He'll tell you I'm right.

**LYONS:**  You got your way of dealing with the world... I got mine. The only thing that matters to me is the music.

**TROY:**  Yeah, I can see that! It don't matter how you gonna eat... where your next dollar is coming from. You telling the truth there.

**LYONS:**  I know I got to eat. But I got to live too. I need something that gonna help me to get out of the bed in the morning. Make me feel like I belong in the world. I don't bother nobody. I just stay with my music cause that's the only way I can find to live in the world. Otherwise there ain't no telling what I might do. Now I don't come criticizing you and how you live. I just come by to ask you for ten dollars. I don't wanna hear all that about how I live.

**TROY:**  Boy, your mama did a hell of a job raising you.

**LYONS:**  You can't change me, Pop. I'm thirty-four years old. If you wanted to change me, you should have been there when I was growing up. I come by to see you... ask for ten dollars and you want to talk about how I was raised. You don't know nothing about how I was raised.

**ROSE:**  Let the boy have ten dollars, *Troy*.

*Troy (to Lyons):*  What the hell you looking at me for? I ain't got no ten dollars. You know what I do with my money. (*To Rose.*) Give him ten dollars if you want him to have it.

**ROSE:**  I will. Just as soon as you turn it loose.

*Troy (handing Rose the money):*  There it is. Seventy-six dollars and forty-two cents. You see this, Bono? Now, I ain't gonna get but six of that back.

**ROSE:**  You ought to stop telling that lie. Here, Lyons. (*She hands him the money.*)

**LYONS:**  Thanks, Rose. Look... I got to run... I'll see you later.

**TROY:**  Wait a minute. You gonna say, "thanks, Rose" and ain't gonna look to see where she got that ten dollars from? See how they do me, Bono?

**LYONS:**  I know she got it from you, Pop. Thanks. I'll give it back to you.

**TROY:**  There he go telling another lie. Time I see that ten dollars... he'll be owing me thirty more.

**LYONS:**  See you, Mr. Bono.

**BONO:**  Take care, Lyons!

**LYONS:**  Thanks, Pop. I'll see you again.

*(Lyons exits the yard.)*

**TROY:**  I don't know why he don't go and get him a decent job and take care of that woman he got.

**BONO:**  He'll be alright, *Troy*. The boy is still young.

**TROY:** The *boy* is thirty-four years old.

**ROSE:** Let's not get off into all that.

**BONO:** Look here... I got to be going. I got to be getting on. Lucille gonna be waiting.

*Troy (puts his arm around* ROSE): See this woman, Bono? I love this woman. I love this woman so much it hurts. I love her so much... I done run out of ways of loving her. So I got to go back to basics. Don't you come by my house Monday morning talking about time to go to work... 'cause I'm still gonna be stroking!

**ROSE:** *Troy!* Stop it now!

**BONO:** I ain't paying him no mind, Rose. That ain't nothing but gin-talk. Go on, *Troy*. I'll see you Monday.

**TROY:** Don't you come by my house, nigger! I done told you what I'm gonna be doing.

*(The lights go down to black.)*

## SCENE II

*The lights come up on Rose hanging up clothes. She hums and sings softly to herself. It is the following morning.*

**ROSE** (*sings*):

Jesus, be a fence all around me every day

Jesus, I want you to protect me as I travel on my way.

Jesus, be a fence all around me every day.

*(Troy enters from the house.)*

Jesus, I want you to protect me

As I travel on my way.

*(To Troy.)* 'Morning. You ready for breakfast? I can fix it soon as I finish hanging up these clothes.

**TROY:** I got the coffee on. That'll be alright. I'll just drink some of that this morning.

**ROSE:** That 651 hit yesterday. That's the second time this month. Miss Pearl hit for a dollar... seem like those that need the least always get lucky. Poor folks can't get nothing.

**TROY:** Them numbers don't know nobody. I don't know why you fool with them. You and Lyons both.

**ROSE:** It's something to do.

**TROY:** You ain't doing nothing but throwing your money away.

**ROSE:** *Troy*, you know I don't play foolishly. I just play a nickel here and a nickel there.

**TROY:** That's two nickels you done thrown away.

**ROSE:** Now I hit sometimes... that makes up for it. It always comes in handy when I do hit. I don't hear you complaining then.

**TROY:**    I ain't complaining now. I just say it's foolish. Trying to guess out of six hundred ways which way the number gonna come. If I had all the money niggers, these Negroes, throw away on numbers for one week—just one week—I'd be a rich man.

**ROSE:**    Well, you wishing and calling it foolish ain't gonna stop folks from playing numbers. That's one thing for sure. Besides ... some good things come from playing numbers. Look where Pope done bought him that restaurant off of numbers.

**TROY:**    I can't stand niggers like that. Man ain't had two dimes to rub together. He walking around with his shoes all run over bumming money for cigarettes. Alright. Got lucky there and hit the numbers ...

**ROSE:**    *Troy,* I know all about it.

**TROY:**    Had good sense, I'll say that for him. He ain't throwed his money away. I seen niggers hit the numbers and go through two thousand dollars in four days. Man bought him that restaurant down there ... fixed it up real nice .... and then didn't want nobody to come in it! A Negro go in there and can't get no kind of service. I seen a white fellow come in there and order a bowl of stew. Pope picked all the meat out of the pot for him. Man ain't had nothing but a bowl of meat! Negro come behind him and ain't got nothing but the potatoes and carrots. Talking about what numbers do for people, you picked a wrong example. Ain't done nothing but make a worser fool out of him than he was before.

**ROSE:**    *Troy,* you ought to stop worrying about what happened at work yesterday.

**TROY:**    I ain't worried. Just told me to be down there at the Commissioner's office on Friday. Everybody think they gonna fire me. I ain't worried about them firing me. You ain't got to worry about that. (*Pause.*) Where's *Cory? Cory* in the house? (*Calls.*) *Cory?*

**ROSE:**    He gone out.

**TROY:**    Out, huh? He gone out 'cause he know I want him to help me with this fence. I know how he is. That boy scared of work.

(*Gabriel enters. He comes halfway down the alley and, hearing Troy's voice, stops.*)

*Troy (continues):*    He ain't done a lick of work in his life.

**ROSE:**    He had to go to football practice. Coach wanted them to get in a little extra practice before the season start.

**TROY:**    I got his practice ... running out of here before he get his chores done.

**ROSE:**    *Troy,* what is wrong with you this morning? Don't nothing set right with you. Go on back in there and go to bed ... get up on the other side.

**TROY:**    Why something got to be wrong with me? I ain't said nothing wrong with me.

**ROSE:**    You got something to say about everything. First it's the numbers ... then it's the way the man runs his restaurant ... then you done got on

*Cory.* What's it gonna be next? Take a look up there and see if the weather suits you…or is it gonna be how you gonna put up the fence with the clothes hanging in the yard?

**TROY:**   You hit the nail on the head then.

**ROSE:**   I know you like I know the back of my hand. Go on in there and get you some coffee…see if that straighten you up. 'Cause you ain't right this morning.

*(Troy starts into the house and sees Gabriel. Gabriel starts singing. Troy's brother, he is seven years younger than Troy. Injured in World War II, he has a metal plate in his head. He carries an old trumpet tied around his waist and believes with every fiber of his being that he is the Archangel Gabriel. He carries a chipped basket with an assortment of discarded fruits and vegetables he has picked up in the Strip District and which he attempts to sell.)*

*Gabriel* (*singing*):

> Yes, ma'am, I got plums
> You ask me how I sell them
> Oh ten cents apiece
> Three for a quarter
> Come and buy now
> 'Cause I'm here today
> And tomorrow I'll be gone

*(Gabriel enters.)*

Hey, Rose!

**ROSE:**   How you doing, Gabe?

**GABRIEL:**   There's *Troy*…Hey, *Troy*!

**TROY:**   Hey, Gabe.

*(Exit into kitchen.)*

*Rose* (*to Gabriel*):   What you got there?

**GABRIEL:**   You know what I got, Rose. I got fruits and vegetables.

*Rose* (*looking in basket*):   Where's all these plums you talking about?

**GABRIEL:**   I ain't got no plums today, Rose. I was just singing that. Have some tomorrow. Put me in a big order for plums. Have enough plums tomorrow for St. Peter and everybody.

*(Troy reenters from kitchen, crosses to steps.)*

*(To Rose.) Troy's* mad at me.

**TROY:**   I ain't mad at you. What I got to be mad at you about? You ain't done nothing to me.

**GABRIEL:**   I just moved over to Miss Pearl's to keep out from in your way. I ain't mean no harm by it.

**TROY:**   Who said anything about that? I ain't said anything about that.

**GABRIEL:**   You ain't mad at me, is you?

**TROY:** Naw... I ain't mad at you, Gabe. If I was mad at you I'd tell you about it.

**GABRIEL:** Got me two rooms. In the basement. Got my own door too. Wanna see my key? (*He holds up a key.*) That's my own key! Ain't nobody else got a key like that. That's my key! My two rooms!

**TROY:** Well, that's good, Gabe. You got your own key... that's good.

**ROSE:** You hungry, Gabe? I was just fixing to cook *Troy* his breakfast.

**GABRIEL:** I'll take some biscuits. You got some biscuits? Did you know when I was in heaven... every morning me and St. Peter would sit down by the gate and eat some big fat biscuits? Oh, yeah! We had us a good time. We'd sit there and eat us them biscuits and then St. Peter would go off to sleep and tell me to wake him up when it's time to open the gates for the judgment.

**ROSE:** Well, come on... I'll make up a batch of biscuits.

(*Rose exits into the house.*)

**GABRIEL:** *Troy*... St. Peter got your name in the book. I seen it. It say... *Troy* Maxson. I say... I know him! He got the same name like what I got. That's my brother!

**TROY:** How many times you gonna tell me that, Gabe?

**GABRIEL:** Ain't got my name in the book. Don't have to have my name. I done died and went to heaven. He got your name though. One morning St. Peter was looking at his book... marking it up for the judgment... and he let me see your name. Got it in there under M. Got Rose's name... I ain't seen it like I seen yours... but I know it's in there. He got a great big book. Got everybody's name what was ever been born. That's what he told me. But I seen your name. Seen it with my own eyes.

**TROY:** Go on in the house there. Rose going to fix you something to eat.

**GABRIEL:** Oh, I ain't hungry. I done had breakfast with Aunt Jemimah. She come by and cooked me up a whole mess of flapjacks. Remember how we used to eat them flapjacks?

**TROY:** Go on in the house and get you something to eat now.

**GABRIEL:** I got to sell my plums. I done sold some tomatoes. Got me two quarters. Wanna see? (*He shows Troy his quarters.*) I'm gonna save them and buy me a new horn so St. Peter can hear me when it's time to open the gates. (*Gabriel stops suddenly. Listens.*) Hear that? That's the hellhounds. I got to chase them out of here. Go on get out of here! Get out!

(*Gabriel exits singing.*)

> Better get ready for the judgment
> Better get ready for the judgment
> My Lord is coming down

(*Rose enters from the house.*)

**TROY:**   He gone off somewhere.

*Gabriel (offstage):*

        Better get ready for the judgment

        Better get ready for the judgment morning

        Better get ready for the judgment

        My God is coming down

**ROSE:**   He ain't eating right. Miss Pearl say she can't get him to eat nothing.

**TROY:**   What you want me to do about it, Rose? I done did everything I can for the man. I can't make him get well. Man got half his head blown away... what you expect?

**ROSE:**   Seem like something ought to be done to help him.

**TROY:**   Man don't bother nobody. He just mixed up from that metal plate he got in his head. Ain't no sense for him to go back into the hospital.

**ROSE:**   Least he be eating right. They can help him take care of himself.

**TROY:**   Don't nobody wanna be locked up, Rose. What you wanna lock him up for? Man go over there and fight the war... messin' around with them Japs, get half his head blown off... and they give him a lousy three thousand dollars. And I had to swoop down on that.

**ROSE:**   Is you fixing to go into that again?

**TROY:**   That's the only way I got a roof over my head... cause of that metal plate.

**ROSE:**   Ain't no sense you blaming yourself for nothing. Gabe wasn't in no condition to manage that money. You done what was right by him. Can't nobody say you ain't done what was right by him. Look how long you took care of him... till he wanted to have his own place and moved over there with Miss Pearl.

**TROY:**   That ain't what I'm saying, woman! I'm just stating the facts. If my brother didn't have that metal plate in his head... I wouldn't have a pot to piss in or a window to throw it out of. And I'm fifty-three years old. Now see if you can understand that!

*(Troy gets up from the porch and starts to exit the yard.)*

**ROSE:**   Where you going off to? You been running out of here every Saturday for weeks. I thought you was gonna work on this fence?

**TROY:**   I'm gonna walk down to Taylors'. Listen to the ball game. I'll be back in a bit. I'll work on it when I get back.

*(He exits the yard. The lights go to black.)*

## SCENE III

*The lights come up on the yard. It is four hours later. Rose is taking down the clothes from the line. Cory enters carrying his football equipment.*

**ROSE:**   Your daddy like to had a fit with you running out of here this morning without doing your chores.

**CORY:**   I told you I had to go to practice.

**ROSE:**    He say you were supposed to help him with this fence.

**CORY:**    He been saying that the last four or five Saturdays, and then he don't never do nothing, but go down to Taylors'. Did you tell him about the recruiter?

**ROSE:**    Yeah, I told him.

**CORY:**    What he say?

**ROSE:**    He ain't said nothing too much. You get in there and get started on your chores before he gets back. Go on and scrub down them steps before he gets back here hollering and carrying on.

**CORY:**    I'm hungry. What you got to eat, Mama?

**ROSE:**    Go on and get started on your chores. I got some meat loaf in there. Go on and make you a sandwich... and don't leave no mess in there.

*(Cory exits into the house. Rose continues to take down the clothes. Troy enters the yard and sneaks up and grabs her from behind.)*

*Troy!* Go on, now. You liked to scared me to death. What was the score of the game? Lucille had me on the phone and I couldn't keep up with it.

**TROY:**    What I care about the game? Come here, woman. *(He tries to kiss her.)*

**ROSE:**    I thought you went down Taylors' to listen to the game. Go on, *Troy!* You supposed to be putting up this fence.

*Troy (attempting to kiss her again):*    I'll put it up when I finish with what is at hand.

**ROSE:**    Go on, *Troy.* I ain't studying you.

*Troy (chasing after her):*    I'm studying you... fixing to do my homework!

**ROSE:**    *Troy,* you better leave me alone.

**TROY:**    Where's *Cory?* That boy brought his butt home yet?

**ROSE:**    He's in the house doing his chores.

*Troy (calling):*    Cory! Get your butt out here, boy!

*(Rose exits into the house with the laundry. Troy goes over to the pile of wood, picks up a board, and starts sawing. Cory enters from the house.)*

**TROY:**    You just now coming in here from leaving this morning?

**CORY:**    Yeah, I had to go to football practice.

**TROY:**    Yeah, what?

**CORY:**    Yes sir.

**TROY:**    I ain't but two seconds off you noway. The garbage sitting in there overflowing... you ain't done none of your chores... and you come in here talking about "Yeah."

**CORY:**    I was just getting ready to do my chores now, Pop...

**TROY:**    Your first chore is to help me with this fence on Saturday. Everything else come after that. Now get that saw and cut them boards.

*(Cory takes the saw and begins cutting the boards. Troy continues working. There is a long pause.)*

**CORY:** Hey, Pop... why don't you buy a TV?

**TROY:** What I want with a TV? What I want one of them for?

**CORY:** Everybody got one. Earl, Ba Bra... Jesse!

**TROY:** I ain't asked you who had one. I say what I want with one?

**CORY:** So you can watch it. They got lots of things on TV. Baseball games and everything. We could watch the World Series.

**TROY:** Yeah... and how much this TV cost?

**CORY:** I don't know. They got them on sale for around two hundred dollars.

**TROY:** Two hundred dollars, huh?

**CORY:** That ain't that much, Pop.

**TROY:** Naw, it's just two hundred dollars. See that roof you got over your head at night? Let me tell you something about that roof. It's been over ten years since that roof was last tarred. See now... the snow come this winter and sit up there on that roof like it is... and it's gonna seep inside. It's just gonna be a little bit... ain't gonna hardly notice it. Then the next thing you know, it's gonna be leaking all over the house. Then the wood rot from all that water and you gonna need a whole new roof. Now, how much you think it cost to get that roof tarred?

**CORY:** I don't know.

**TROY:** Two hundred and sixty-four dollars... cash money. While you thinking about a TV, I got to be thinking about the roof... and whatever else go wrong here. Now if you had two hundred dollars, what would you do... fix the roof or buy a TV?

**CORY:** I'd buy a TV. Then when the roof started to leak... when it needed fixing... I'd fix it.

**TROY:** Where you gonna get the money from? You done spent it for a TV. You gonna sit up and watch the water run all over your brand new TV.

**CORY:** Aw, Pop. You got money. I know you do.

**TROY:** Where I got it at, huh?

**CORY:** You got it in the bank.

**TROY:** You wanna see my bankbook? You wanna see that seventy-three dollars and twenty-two cents I got sitting up in there?

**CORY:** You ain't got to pay for it all at one time. You can put a down payment on it and carry it on home with you.

**TROY:** Not me. I ain't gonna owe nobody nothing if I can help it. Miss a payment and they come and snatch it right out of your house. Then what you got? Now, soon as I get two hundred dollars clear, then I'll buy a TV. Right now, as soon as I get two hundred and sixty-four dollars, I'm gonna have this roof tarred.

**CORY:** Aw... Pop!

**TROY:** You go on and get you two hundred dollars and buy one if ya want it. I got better things to do with my money.

**CORY:** I can't get no two hundred dollars. I ain't never seen two hundred dollars.

**TROY:** I'll tell you what… you get you a hundred dollars and I'll put the other hundred with it.

**CORY:** Alright, I'm gonna show you.

**TROY:** You gonna show me how you can cut them boards right now.

*(Cory begins to cut the boards. There is a long pause.)*

**CORY:** The Pirates won today. That makes five in a row.

**TROY:** I ain't thinking about the Pirates. Got an all-white team. Got that boy…that Puerto Rican boy…Clemente.° Don't even half-play him. That boy could be something if they give him a chance. Play him one day and sit him on the bench the next.

**CORY:** He gets a lot of chances to play.

**TROY:** I'm talking about playing regular. Playing every day so you can get your timing. That's what I'm talking about.

**CORY:** They got some white guys on the team that don't play every day. You can't play everybody at the same time.

**TROY:** If they got a white fellow sitting on the bench… you can bet your last dollar he can't play! The colored guy got to be twice as good before he get on the team. That's why I don't want you to get all tied up in them sports. Man on the team and what it get him? They got colored on the team and don't use them. Same as not having them. All them teams the same.

**CORY:** The Braves got Hank Aaron and Wes Covington. Hank Aaron hit two home runs today. That makes forty-three.

**TROY:** Hank Aaron ain't nobody. That's what you supposed to do. That's how you supposed to play the game. Ain't nothing to it. It's just a matter of timing… getting the right follow-through. Hell, I can hit forty-three home runs right now!

**CORY:** Not off no major-league pitching, you couldn't.

**TROY:** We had better pitching in the Negro leagues. I hit seven home runs off of Satchel Paige.° You can't get no better than that!

**CORY:** Sandy Koufax.° He's leading the league in strikeouts.

**TROY:** I ain't thinking of no Sandy Koufax.

**CORY:** You got Warren Spahn° and Lew Burdette.° I bet you couldn't hit no home runs off of Warren Spahn.

**TROY:** I'm through with it now. You go on and cut them boards. *(Pause.)* Your mama tell me you done got recruited by a college football team? Is that right?

*Clemente:* Hall of Fame outfielder Roberto Clemente, a dark-skinned Puerto Rican, played 17 seasons with the Pittsburgh Pirates. *Satchel Paige . . . Sandy Koufax . . . Warren Spahn . . . Lew Burdette:* The great Satchel Paige pitched many years in the Negro Leagues; beginning in 1948, when he was in his forties and long past his prime, he appeared in nearly 200 games in the American League. Star pitchers Sandy Koufax of the Dodgers and Warren Spahn and Lew Burdette of the Braves were all white.

**CORY:**　Yeah. Coach Zellman say the recruiter gonna be coming by to talk to you. Get you to sign the permission papers.

**TROY:**　I thought you supposed to be working down there at the A&P. Ain't you suppose to be working down there after school?

**CORY:**　Mr. Stawicki say he gonna hold my job for me until after the football season. Say starting next week I can work weekends.

**TROY:**　I thought we had an understanding about this football stuff? You suppose to keep up with your chores and hold that job down at the A&P. Ain't been around here all day on a Saturday. Ain't none of your chores done... and now you telling me you done quit your job.

**CORY:**　I'm going to be working weekends.

**TROY:**　You damn right you are! And ain't no need for nobody coming around here to talk to me about signing nothing.

**CORY:**　Hey, Pop... you can't do that. He's coming all the way from North Carolina.

**TROY:**　I don't care where he coming from. The white man ain't gonna let you get nowhere with that football noway. You go on and get your book-learning so you can work yourself up in that A&P or learn how to fix cars or build houses or something, get you a trade. That way you have something can't nobody take away from you. You go on and learn how to put your hands to some good use. Besides hauling people's garbage.

**CORY:**　I get good grades, Pop. That's why the recruiter wants to talk with you. You got to keep up your grades to get recruited. This way I'll be going to college. I'll get a chance...

**TROY:**　First you gonna get your butt down there to the A&P and get your job back.

**CORY:**　Mr. Stawicki done already hired somebody else 'cause I told him I was playing football.

**TROY:**　You a bigger fool than I thought... to let somebody take away your job so you can play some football. Where you gonna get your money to take out your girlfriend and whatnot? What kind of foolishness is that to let somebody take away your job?

**CORY:**　I'm still gonna be working weekends.

**TROY:**　Naw... naw. You getting your butt out of here and finding you another job.

**CORY:**　Come on, Pop! I got to practice. I can't work after school and play football too. The team needs me. That's what Coach Zellman say...

**TROY:**　I don't care what nobody else say. I'm the boss... you understand? I'm the boss around here. I do the only saying what counts.

**CORY:**　Come on, Pop!

**TROY:**　I asked you... did you understand?

**CORY:**　Yeah...

**TROY:**　What?!

**CORY:**　Yes sir.

**TROY:** You go on down there to that A&P and see if you can get your job back. If you can't do both... then you quit the football team. You've got to take the crookeds with the straights.

**CORY:** Yes sir. (*Pause.*) Can I ask you a question?

**TROY:** What the hell you wanna ask me? Mr. Stawicki the one you got the questions for.

**CORY:** How come you ain't never liked me?

**TROY:** Liked you? Who the hell say I got to like you? What law is there say I got to like you? Wanna stand up in my face and ask a damn fool-ass question like that. Talking about liking somebody. Come here, boy, when I talk to you.

(*Cory comes over to where Troy is working. He stands slouched over and Troy shoves him on his shoulder.*)

Straighten up, goddammit! I asked you a question... what law is there say I got to like you?

**CORY:** None.

**TROY:** Well, alright then! Don't you eat every day? (*Pause.*) Answer me when I talk to you! Don't you eat every day?

**CORY:** Yeah.

**TROY:** Nigger, as long as you in my house, you put that sir on the end of it when you talk to me.

**CORY:** Yes... sir.

**TROY:** You eat every day.

**CORY:** Yes sir!

**TROY:** Got a roof over your head.

**CORY:** Yes sir!

**TROY:** Got clothes on your back.

**CORY:** Yes sir.

**TROY:** Why you think that is?

**CORY:** Cause of you.

**TROY:** Aw, hell I know it's cause of me... but why do you think that is?

**CORY** (*hesitant*): 'Cause you like me.

**TROY:** Like you? I go out of here every morning... bust my butt... putting up with them crackers every day... cause I like you? You about the biggest fool I ever saw. (*Pause.*) It's my job. It's my responsibility! You understand that? A man got to take care of his family. You live in my house... sleep you behind on my bedclothes... fill you belly up with my food... cause you my son. You my flesh and blood. Not cause I like you! Cause it's my duty to take care of you. I owe a responsibility to you! Let's get this straight right here... before it go along any further... I ain't got to like you. Mr. Rand don't give me my money come payday cause he likes me. He gives me cause he owe me. I done give you everything I had to give you. I gave you your life! Me and your mama worked that out between us. And liking your black ass wasn't part of the bargain. Don't you try and go through life worrying about if somebody like you or not. You best be making sure they doing right by you. You understand what I'm saying, boy?

**CORY:** Yes sir.

**TROY:** Then get the hell out of my face, and get on down to that A&P.

*(Rose has been standing behind the screen door for much of the scene. She enters as Cory exits.)*

**ROSE:** Why don't you let the boy go ahead and play football, *Troy*? Ain't no harm in that. He's just trying to be like you with the sports.

**TROY:** I don't want him to be like me! I want him to move as far away from my life as he can get. You the only decent thing that ever happened to me. I wish him that. But I don't wish him a thing else from my life. I decided seventeen years ago that boy wasn't getting involved in no sports. Not after what they did to me in the sports.

**ROSE:** *Troy*, why don't you admit you was too old to play in the major leagues? For once... why don't you admit that?

**TROY:** What do you mean too old? Don't come telling me I was too old. I just wasn't the right color. Hell, I'm fifty-three years old and can do better than Selkirk's . 269 right now!

**ROSE:** How's was you gonna play ball when you were over forty? Sometimes I can't get no sense out of you.

**TROY:** I got good sense, woman. I got sense enough not to let my boy get hurt over playing no sports. You been mothering that boy too much. Worried about if people like him.

**ROSE:** Everything that boy do... he do for you. He wants you to say "Good job, son." That's all.

**TROY:** Rose, I ain't got time for that. He's alive. He's healthy. He's got to make his own way. I made mine. Ain't nobody gonna hold his hand when he get out there in that world.

**ROSE:** Times have changed from when you was young, *Troy*. People change. The world's changing around you and you can't even see it.

**TROY** (*slow, methodical*): Woman... I do the best I can do. I come in here every Friday. I carry a sack of potatoes and a bucket of lard. You all line up at the door with your hands out. I give you the lint from my pockets. I give you my sweat and my blood. I ain't got no tears. I done spent them. We go upstairs in that room at night... and I fall down on you and try to blast a hole into forever. I get up Monday morning... find my lunch on the table. I go out. Make my way. Find my strength to carry me through to the next Friday. (*Pause.*) That's all I got, Rose. That's all I got to give. I can't give nothing else.

*(Troy exits into the house. The lights go down to black.)*

## SCENE IV

*It is Friday. Two weeks later. Cory starts out of the house with his football equipment. The phone rings.*

**CORY** (*calling*):    I got it! (*He answers the phone and stands in the screen door talking.*) Hello? Hey, Jesse. Naw...I was just getting ready to leave now.

**ROSE** (*calling*):    *Cory!*

**CORY:**    I told you, man, them spikes is all tore up. You can use them if you want, but they ain't no good. Earl got some spikes.

**ROSE** (*calling*):    *Cory!*

*Cory* (*calling to Rose*):    Mam? I'm talking to Jesse. (*Into phone.*) When she say that? (*Pause.*) Aw, you lying, man. I'm gonna tell her you said that.

**ROSE** (*calling*):    *Cory, don't you go nowhere!*

**CORY:**    I got to go to the game, Ma! (*Into the phone.*) Yeah, hey, look, I'll talk to you later. Yeah, I'll meet you over Earl's house. Later. Bye, Ma.

*(Cory exits the house and starts out the yard.)*

**ROSE:**    Cory, where you going off to? You got that stuff all pulled out and thrown all over your room.

*Cory* (*in the yard*):    I was looking for my spikes. Jesse wanted to borrow my spikes.

**ROSE:**    Get up there and get that cleaned up before your daddy get back in here.

**CORY:**    I got to go to the game! I'll clean it up when I get back.

*(Cory exits.)*

**ROSE:**    That's all he need to do is see that room all messed up.

*(Rose exits into the house. Troy and Bono enter the yard. Troy is dressed in clothes other than his work clothes.)*

**BONO:**    He told him the same thing he told you. Take it to the union.

**TROY:**    Brownie ain't got that much sense. Man wasn't thinking about nothing. He wait until I confront them on it...then he wanna come crying seniority. (*Calls.*) Hey, Rose!

**BONO:**    I wish I could have seen Mr. Rand's face when he told you.

**TROY:**    He couldn't get it out of his mouth! Liked to bit his tongue! When they called me down there to the Commissioner's office...he thought they was gonna fire me. Like everybody else.

**BONO:**    I didn't think they was gonna fire you. I thought they was gonna put you on the warning paper.

**TROY:**    Hey, Rose! (*To Bono.*) Yeah, Mr. Rand like to bit his tongue.

*(Troy breaks the seal on the bottle, takes a drink, and hands it to Bono.)*

**BONO:**    I see you run right down to Taylors' and told that Alberta gal.

**TROY** (*calling*):   Hey, Rose! (*To Bono.*) I told everybody. Hey, Rose! I went down there to cash my check.

**ROSE** (*entering from the house*):   Hush all that hollering, man! I know you out here. What they say down there at the Commissioner's office?

**TROY:**   You supposed to come when I call you, woman. Bono'll tell you that. (*To Bono.*) Don't Lucille come when you call her?

**ROSE:**   Man, hush your mouth. I ain't no dog... talk about "come when you call me."

**TROY** (*puts his arm around Rose*):   You hear this, Bono? I had me an old dog used to get uppity like that. You say, "C'mere, Blue!"... and he just lay there and look at you. End up getting a stick and chasing him away trying to make him come.

**ROSE:**   I ain't studying you and your dog. I remember you used to sing that old song.

**TROY** (*he sings*):
>    Hear it ring! Hear it ring!
>    I had a dog his name was Blue.

**ROSE:**   Don't nobody wanna hear you sing that old song.

**TROY** (*sings*):   You know Blue was mighty true.

**ROSE:**   Used to have *Cory* running around here singing that song.

**BONO:**   Hell, I remember that song myself.

**TROY** (*sings*):
>    You know Blue was a good old dog.
>    Blue treed a possum in a hollow log.

That was my daddy's song. My daddy made up that song.

**ROSE:**   I don't care who made it up. Don't nobody wanna hear you sing it.

**TROY** (*makes a song like calling a dog*):   Come here, woman.

**ROSE:**   You come in here carrying on, I reckon they ain't fired you. What they say down there at the Commissioner's office?

**TROY:**   Look here, Rose... Mr. Rand called me into his office today when I got back from talking to them people down there... it come from up top... he called me in and told me they was making me a driver.

**ROSE:**   *Troy*, you kidding!

**TROY:**   No I ain't. Ask Bono.

**ROSE:**   Well, that's great, *Troy*. Now you don't have to hassle them people no more.

*(Lyons enters from the street.)*

**TROY:**   Aw hell, I wasn't looking to see you today. I thought you was in jail. Got it all over the front page of the *Courier* about them raiding Sefus's place... where you be hanging out with all them thugs.

**LYONS:**   Hey, Pop... that ain't got nothing to do with me. I don't go down there gambling. I go down there to sit in with the band. I ain't got nothing to do with the gambling part. They got some good music down there.

**TROY:**  They got some rogues... is what they got.

**LYONS:**  How you been, Mr. Bono? Hi, Rose.

**BONO:**  I see where you playing down at the Crawford Grill tonight.

**ROSE:**  How come you ain't brought Bonnie like I told you? You should have brought Bon nie with you, she ain't been over in a month of Sundays.

**LYONS:**  I was just in the neighborhood... thought I'd stop by.

**TROY:**  Here he come...

**BONO:**  Your daddy got a promotion on the rubbish. He's gonna be the first colored driver. Ain't got to do nothing but sit up there and read the paper like them white fellows.

**LYONS:**  Hey, Pop... if you knew how to read you'd be alright.

**BONO:**  Naw... naw... you mean if the nigger knew how to *drive* he'd be alright. Been fighting with them people about driving and ain't even got a license. Mr. Rand know you ain't got no driver's license?

**TROY:**  Driving ain't nothing. All you do is point the truck where you want it to go. Driving ain't nothing.

**BONO:**  Do Mr. Rand know you ain't got no driver's license? That's what I'm talking about. I ain't asked if driving was easy. I asked if Mr. Rand know you ain't got no driver's license.

**TROY:**  He ain't got to know. The man ain't got to know my business. Time he find out, I have two or three driver's licenses.

**LYONS** (*going into his pocket*):  Say, look here, Pop...

**TROY:**  I knew it was coming. Didn't I tell you, Bono? I know what kind of "Look here, Pop" that was. The nigger fixing to ask me for some money. It's Friday night. It's my payday. All them rogues down there on the avenue... the ones that ain't in jail... and Lyons is hopping in his shoes to get down there with them.

**LYONS:**  See, Pop... if you give somebody else a chance to talk sometime, you'd see that I was fixing to pay you back your ten dollars like I told you. Here... I told you I'd pay you when Bonnie got paid.

**TROY:**  Naw... you go ahead and keep that ten dollars. Put it in the bank. The next time you feel like you wanna come by here and ask me for something... you go on down there and get that.

**LYONS:**  Here's your ten dollars, Pop. I told you I don't want you to give me nothing. I just wanted to borrow ten dollars.

**TROY:**  Naw... you go on and keep that for the next time you want to ask me.

**LYONS:**  Come on, Pop... here go your ten dollars.

**ROSE:**  Why don't you go on and let the boy pay you back, *Troy?*

**LYONS:**  Here you go, Rose. If you don't take it I'm gonna have to hear about it for the next six months. (*He hands her the money.*)

**ROSE:**  You can hand yours over here too, *Troy.*

**TROY:**  You see this, Bono. You see how they do me.

**BONO:**  Yeah, Lucille do me the same way.

(*Gabriel is heard singing offstage. He enters.*)

**GABRIEL:** Better get ready for the Judgment! Better get ready for... Hey!... Hey!... There's *Troy's* boy!

**LYONS:** How are you doing, Uncle Gabe?

**GABRIEL:** Lyons... The King of the Jungle! Rose... hey, Rose. Got a flower for you. (*He takes a rose from his pocket.*) Picked it myself. That's the same rose like you is!

**ROSE:** That's right nice of you, Gabe.

**LYONS:** What you been doing, Uncle Gabe?

**GABRIEL:** Oh, I been chasing hellhounds and waiting on the time to tell St. Peter to open the gates.

**LYONS:** You been chasing hellhounds, huh? Well... you doing the right thing, Uncle Gabe. Somebody got to chase them.

**GABRIEL:** Oh, yeah... I know it. The devil's strong. The devil ain't no pushover. Hellhounds snipping at everybody's heels. But I got my trumpet waiting on the judgment time.

**LYONS:** Waiting on the Battle of Armageddon, huh?

**GABRIEL:** Ain't gonna be too much of a battle when God get to waving that Judgment sword. But the people's gonna have a hell of a time trying to get into heaven if them gates ain't open.

*Lyons (putting his arm around Gabriel):* You hear this, Pop. Uncle Gabe, you alright!

*Gabriel (laughing with Lyons):* Lyons! King of the Jungle.

**ROSE:** You gonna stay for supper, Gabe? Want me to fix you a plate?

**GABRIEL:** I'll take a sandwich, Rose. Don't want no plate. Just wanna eat with my hands. I'll take a sandwich.

**ROSE:** How about you, Lyons? You staying? Got some short ribs cooking.

**LYONS:** Naw, I won't eat nothing till after we finished playing. (*Pause.*) You ought to come down and listen to me play, Pop.

**TROY:** I don't like that Chinese music. All that noise.

**ROSE:** Go on in the house and wash up, Gabe... I'll fix you a sandwich.

*Gabriel (to Lyons, as he exits):* Troy's mad at me.

**LYONS:** What you mad at Uncle Gabe for, Pop?

**ROSE:** He thinks *Troy's* mad at him cause he moved over to Miss Pearl's.

**TROY:** I ain't mad at the man. He can live where he want to live at.

**LYONS:** What he move over there for? Miss Pearl don't like nobody.

**ROSE:** She don't mind him none. She treats him real nice. She just don't allow all that singing.

**TROY:** She don't mind that rent he be paying... that's what she don't mind.

**ROSE:** *Troy,* I ain't going through that with you no more. He's over there cause he want to have his own place. He can come and go as he please.

**TROY:** Hell, he could come and go as he please here. I wasn't stopping him. I ain't put no rules on him.

**ROSE:** It ain't the same thing, *Troy.* And you know it.

*(Gabriel comes to the door.)*

Now, that's the last I wanna hear about that. I don't wanna hear nothing else about Gabe and Miss Pearl. And next week...

**GABRIEL:**  I'm ready for my sandwich, Rose.

**ROSE:**  And next week ... when that recruiter come from that school ... I want you to sign that paper and go on and let *Cory* play football. Then that'll be the last I have to hear about that.

**TROY** (*to Rose as she exits into the house*):  I ain't thinking about *Cory* nothing.

**LYONS:**  What ... *Cory* got recruited? What school he going to?

**TROY:**  That boy walking around here smelling his piss ... thinking he's grown. Thinking he's gonna do what he want, irrespective of what I say. Look here, Bono ... I left the Commissioner's office and went down to the A&P ... that boy ain't working down there. He lying to me. Telling me he got his job back ... telling me he working weekends ... telling me he working after school ... Mr. Stawicki tell me he ain't working down there at all!

**LYONS:**  *Cory* just growing up. He's just busting at the seams trying to fill out your shoes.

**TROY:**  I don't care what he's doing. When he get to the point where he wanna disobey me ... then it's time for him to move on. Bono'll tell you that. I bet he ain't never disobeyed his daddy without paying the consequences.

**BONO:**  I ain't never had a chance. My daddy came on through ... but I ain't never knew him to see him ... or what he had on his mind or where he went. Just moving on through. Searching out the New Land. That's what the old folks used to call it. See a fellow moving around from place to place ... woman to woman ... called it searching out the New Land. I can't say if he ever found it. I come along, didn't want no kids. Didn't know if I was gonna be in one place long enough to fix on them right as their daddy. I figured I was going searching too. As it turned out I been hooked up with Lucille near about as long as your daddy been with Rose. Going on sixteen years.

**TROY:**  Sometimes I wish I hadn't known my daddy. He ain't cared nothing about no kids. A kid to him wasn't nothing. All he wanted was for you to learn how to walk so he could start you to working. When it come time for eating ... he ate first. If there was anything left over, that's what you got. Man would sit down and eat two chickens and give you the wing.

**LYONS:**  You ought to stop that, Pop. Everybody feed their kids. No matter how hard times is ... everybody care about their kids. Make sure they have something to eat.

**TROY:**  The only thing my daddy cared about was getting them bales of cotton in to Mr. Lubin. That's the only thing that mattered to him. Sometimes I used to wonder why he was living. Wonder why the devil hadn't come and got him. "Get them bales of cotton in to Mr. Lubin" and find out he owe him money ...

**LYONS:** He should have just went on and left when he saw he couldn't get nowhere. That's what I would have done.

**TROY:** How he gonna leave with eleven kids? And where he gonna go? He ain't knew how to do nothing but farm. No, he was trapped and I think he knew it. But I'll say this for him ... he felt a responsibility toward us. Maybe he ain't treated us the way I felt he should have ... but without that responsibility he could have walked off and left us ... made his own way.

**BONO:** A lot of them did. Back in those days what you talking about ... they walk out their front door and just take on down one road or another and keep on walking.

**LYONS:** There you go! That's what I'm talking about.

**BONO:** Just keep on walking till you come to something else. Ain't you never heard of nobody having the walking blues? Well, that's what you call it when you just take off like that.

**TROY:** My daddy ain't had them walking blues! What you talking about? He stayed right there with his family. But he was just as evil as he could be. My mama couldn't stand him. Couldn't stand that evilness. She run off when I was about eight. She sneaked off one night after he had gone to sleep. Told me she was coming back for me. I ain't never seen her no more. All his women run off and left him. He wasn't good for nobody.

When my turn come to head out, I was fourteen and got to sniffing around Joe Canewell's daughter. Had us an old mule we called Greyboy. My daddy sent me out to do some plowing and I tied up Greyboy and went to fooling around with Joe Canewell's daughter. We done found us a nice little spot, got real cozy with each other. She about thirteen and we done figured we was grown anyway ... so we down there enjoying ourselves ... ain't thinking about nothing. We didn't know Greyboy had got loose and wandered back to the house and my daddy was looking for me. We down there by the creek enjoying ourselves when my daddy come up on us. Surprised us. He had them leather straps off the mule and commenced to whupping me like there was no tomorrow. I jumped up, mad and embarrassed. I was scared of my daddy. When he commenced to whupping on me ... quite naturally I run to get out of the way. (*Pause.*) Now I thought he was mad cause I ain't done my work. But I see where he was chasing me off so he could have the gal for himself. When I see what the matter of it was, I lost all fear of my daddy. Right there is where I become a man ... at fourteen years of age. (*Pause.*) Now it was my turn to run him off. I picked up them same reins that he had used on me. I picked up them reins and commenced to whupping on him. The gal jumped up and run off ... and when my daddy turned to face me, I could see why the devil had never come to get him ... cause he was the devil himself. I don't know what happened. When I woke up, I was laying right there by the creek, and Blue ... this old dog we had ... was licking my face. I thought I was blind. I couldn't see nothing. Both my eyes were swollen shut. I layed there and cried. I didn't know what I was gonna do. The only thing I knew was the time had come for me to leave my daddy's house. And right there the world suddenly got big. And it was a long time before I could cut it down to where I could handle it.

Part of that cutting down was when I got to the place where I could feel him kicking in my blood and knew that the only thing that separated us was the matter of a few years.

*(Gabriel enters from the house with a sandwich.)*

**LYONS:**   What you got there, Uncle Gabe?

**GABRIEL:**   Got me a ham sandwich. Rose gave me a ham sandwich.

**TROY:**   I don't know what happened to him. I done lost touch with every-body except *Gabriel.* But I hope he's dead. I hope he found some peace.

**LYONS:**   That's a heavy story, Pop. I didn't know you left home when you was fourteen.

**TROY:**   And didn't know nothing. The only part of the world I knew was the forty-two acres of Mr. Lubin's land. That's all I knew about life.

**LYONS:**   Fourteen's kinda young to be out on your own. *(Phone rings.)* I don't even think I was ready to be out on my own at fourteen. I don't know what I would have done.

**TROY:**   I got up from the creek and walked on down to Mobile. I was through with farming. Figured I could do better in the city. So I walked the two hundred miles to Mobile.

**LYONS:**   Wait a minute ... you ain't walked no two hundred miles, Pop. Ain't nobody gonna walk no two hundred miles. You talking about some walking there.

**BONO:**   That's the only way you got anywhere back in them days.

**LYONS:**   Shhh. Damn if I wouldn't have hitched a ride with somebody!

**TROY:**   Who you gonna hitch it with? They ain't had no cars and things like they got now. We talking about 1918.

**ROSE** *(entering)*:   What you all out here getting into?

*Troy (to Rose):*   I'm telling Lyons how good he got it. He don't know noth-ing about this I'm talking.

**ROSE:**   Lyons, that was Bonnie on the phone. She say you supposed to pick her up.

**LYONS:**   Yeah, okay, Rose.

**TROY:**   I walked on down to Mobile and hitched up with some of them fellows that was heading this way. Got up here and found out ... not only couldn't you get a job ... you couldn't find no place to live. I thought I was in freedom. Shhh. Colored folks living down there on the riverbanks in whatever kind of shelter they could find for themselves. Right down there under the Brady Street Bridge. Living in shacks made of sticks and tarpaper. Messed around there and went from bad to worse. Started stealing. First it was food. Then I figured, hell, if I steal money I can buy me some food. Buy me some shoes too! One thing led to another. Met your mama. I was young and anxious to be a man. Met your mama and had you. What I do that for? Now I got to worry about feeding you and her. Got to steal three times as much. Went out one day looking for somebody to rob ... that's what I was, a robber. I'll tell you the truth. I'm ashamed of it today. But it's the truth. Went to rob this fellow ... pulled out my knife ... and he pulled out a gun. Shot me in the chest. It felt just like somebody had taken a hot branding iron and laid it on me. When he shot me I jumped at him with my knife. They told me I killed him and they put me in the penitentiary and locked me up for fifteen years. That's where I met Bono. That's where I learned how to play baseball. Got out that place and your mama had taken you and went on to make life without me. Fifteen years was a long time for her to wait. But that fifteen years cured me of that robbing stuff. Rose'll tell you. She asked me when I met her if I had gotten all that foolishness out of my system. And I told her, "Baby, it's you and baseball all what count with me." You hear me, Bono? I meant it too. She say, "Which one comes first?" I told her, "Baby, ain't no doubt it's baseball ... but you stick and get old with me and we'll both outlive this baseball." Am I right, Rose? And it's true.

**ROSE:** Man, hush your mouth. You ain't said no such thing. Talking about, "Baby you know you'll always be number one with me." That's what you was talking.

**TROY:** You hear that, Bono. That's why I love her.

**BONO:** Rose'll keep you straight. You get off the track, she'll straighten you up.

**ROSE:** Lyons, you better get on up and get Bonnie. She waiting on you.

**LYONS** (*gets up to go*)**:** Hey, Pop, why don't you come on down to the Grill and hear me play?

**TROY:** I ain't going down there. I'm too old to be sitting around in them clubs.

**BONO:** You got to be good to play down at the Grill.

**LYONS:** Come on, Pop ...

**TROY:** I got to get up in the morning.

**LYONS:** You ain't got to stay long.

**TROY:** Naw, I'm gonna get my supper and go on to bed.

**LYONS:** Well, I got to go. I'll see you again.

**TROY:** Don't you come around my house on my payday.

**ROSE:**  Pick up the phone and let somebody know you coming. And bring Bonnie with you. You know I'm always glad to see her.

**LYONS:**  Yeah, I'll do that, Rose. You take care now. See you, Pop. See you, Mr. Bono. See you, Uncle Gabe.

**GABRIEL:**  Lyons! King of the Jungle!

*(Lyons exits.)*

**TROY:**  Is supper ready, woman? Me and you got some business to take care of. I'm gonna tear it up too.

**ROSE:**  *Troy,* I done told you now!

**TROY** (*puts his arm around Bono*):  Aw hell, woman ... this is Bono. Bono like family. I done known this nigger since ... how long I done know you?

**BONO:**  It's been a long time.

**TROY:**  I done know this nigger since Skippy was a pup. Me and him done been through some times.

**BONO:**  You sure right about that.

**TROY:**  Hell, I done know him longer than I known you. And we still standing shoulder to shoulder. Hey, look here, Bono ... a man can't ask for no more than that. (*Drinks to him.*) I love you, nigger.

**BONO:**  Hell, I love you too ... but I got to get home see my woman. You got yours in hand. I got to go get mine.

*(Bono starts to exit as Cory enters the yard, dressed in his football uniform. He gives Troy a hard, uncompromising look.)*

**CORY:**  What you do that for, Pop?

*(He throws his helmet down in the direction of Troy.)*

**ROSE:**  What's the matter? *Cory* ... what's the matter?

**CORY:**  Papa done went up to the school and told Coach Zellman I can't play football no more. Wouldn't even let me play the game. Told him to tell the recruiter not to come.

**ROSE:**  *Troy* ...

**TROY:**  What you *Troying* me for. Yeah, I did it. And the boy know why I did it.

**CORY:**  Why you wanna do that to me? That was the one chance I had.

**ROSE:**  Ain't nothing wrong with *Cory* playing football, *Troy.*

**TROY:**  The boy lied to me. I told the nigger if he wanna play football ... to keep up his chores and hold down that job at the A&P. That was the conditions. Stopped down there to see Mr. Stawicki ...

**CORY:**  I can't work after school during the football season, Pop! I tried to tell you that Mr. Stawicki's holding my job for me. You don't never want to listen to nobody. And then you wanna go and do this to me!

**TROY:**  I ain't done nothing to you. You done it to yourself.

**CORY:** Just cause you didn't have a chance! You just scared I'm gonna be better than you, that's all.

**TROY:** Come here.

**ROSE:** *Troy ...*

*(Cory reluctantly crosses over to Troy.)*

**TROY:** Alright! See. You done made a mistake.

**CORY:** I didn't even do nothing!

**TROY:** I'm gonna tell you what your mistake was. See ... you swung at the ball and didn't hit it. That's strike one. See, you in the batter's box now. You swung and you missed. That's strike one. Don't you strike out!

*(Lights fade to black.)*

# ACT II

## SCENE I

*The following morning. Cory is at the tree hitting the ball with the bat. He tries to mimic Troy, but his swing is awkward, less sure. Rose enters from the house.*

**ROSE:** *Cory,* I want you to help me with this cupboard.

**CORY:** I ain't quitting the team. I don't care what Poppa say.

**ROSE:** I'll talk to him when he gets back. He had to go see about your Uncle Gabe. The police done arrested him. Say he was disturbing the peace. He'll be back directly. Come on in here and help me clean out the top of this cupboard.

*(Cory exits into the house. Rose sees Troy and Bono coming down the alley.)*

*Troy ...* what they say down there?

**TROY:** Ain't said nothing. I give them fifty dollars and they let him go. I'll talk to you about it. Where's *Cory?*

**ROSE:** He's in there helping me clean out these cupboards.

**TROY:** Tell him to get his butt out here.

*(Troy and Bono go over to the pile of wood. Bono picks up the saw and begins sawing.)*

**TROY** *(to Bono)*: All they want is the money. That makes six or seven times I done went down there and got him. See me coming they stick out their *hands.*

**BONO:** Yeah. I know what you mean. That's all they care about ... that money. They don't care about what's right. *(Pause.)* Nigger, why you got to go and get some hard wood? You ain't doing nothing but building a little old fence. Get you some soft pine wood. That's all you need.

**TROY:** I know what I'm doing. This is outside wood. You put pine wood inside the house. Pine wood is inside wood. This here is outside wood. Now you tell me where the fence is gonna be?

**BONO:** You don't need this wood. You can put it up with pine wood and it'll stand as long as you gonna be here looking at it.

**TROY:** How you know how long I'm gonna be here, nigger? Hell, I might just live forever. Live longer than old man Horsely.

**BONO:** That's what Magee used to say.

**TROY:** Magee's a damn fool. Now you tell me who you ever heard of gonna pull their own teeth with a pair of rusty pliers.

**BONO:** The old folks ... my granddaddy used to pull his teeth with pliers. They ain't had no dentists for the colored folks back then.

**TROY:** Get clean pliers! You understand? Clean pliers! Sterilize them! Besides we ain't living back then. All Magee had to do was walk over to Doc Goldblum's.

**BONO:** I see where you and that Tallahassee gal ... that Alberta ... I see where you all done got tight.

**TROY:** What you mean "got tight"?

**BONO:** I see where you be laughing and joking with her all the time.

**TROY:** I laughs and jokes with all of them, Bono. You know me.

**BONO:** That ain't the kind of laughing and joking I'm talking about.

*(Cory enters from the house.)*

**CORY:** How you doing, Mr. Bono?

**TROY:** *Cory?* Get that saw from Bono and cut some wood. He talking about the wood's too hard to cut. Stand back there, Jim, and let that young boy show you how it's done.

**BONO:** He's sure welcome to it.

*(Cory takes the saw and begins to cut the wood.)*

Whew-e-e! Look at that. Big old strong boy. Look like Joe Louis. Hell, must be getting old the way I'm watching that boy whip through that wood.

**CORY:** I don't see why Mama want a fence around the yard noways.

**TROY:** Damn if I know either. What the hell she keeping out with it? She ain't got nothing nobody want.

**BONO:** Some people build fences to keep people out ... and other people build fences to keep people in. Rose wants to hold on to you all. She loves you.

**TROY:** Hell, nigger, I don't need nobody to tell me my wife loves me. *Cory* ... go on in the house and see if you can find that other saw.

**CORY:** Where's it at?

**TROY:** I said find it! Look for it till you find it!

*(Cory exits into the house.)*

What's that supposed to mean? Wanna keep us in?

**BONO:**   *Troy* … I done known you seem like damn near my whole life. You and Rose both. I done know both of you all for a long time. I remember when you met Rose. When you was hitting them baseball out the park. A lot of them old gals was after you then. You had the pick of the litter. When you picked Rose, I was happy for you. That was the first time I knew you had any sense. I said … My man *Troy* knows what he's doing … I'm gonna follow this nigger … he might take me somewhere. I been following you too. I done learned a whole heap of things about life watching you. I done learned how to tell where the shit lies. How to tell it from the alfalfa. You done learned me a lot of things. You showed me how to not make the same mistakes … to take life as it comes along and keep putting one foot in front of the other. (*Pause.*) Rose a good woman, *Troy*.

**TROY:**   Hell, nigger, I know she a good woman. I been married to her for eighteen years. What you got on your mind, Bono?

**BONO:**   I just say she a good woman. Just like I say anything. I ain't got to have nothing on my mind.

**TROY:**   You just gonna say she a good woman and leave it hanging out there like that? Why you telling me she a good woman?

**BONO:**   She loves you, *Troy*. Rose loves you.

**TROY:**   You saying I don't measure up. That's what you trying to say. I don't measure up cause I'm seeing this other gal. I know what you trying to say.

**BONO:**   I know what Rose means to you, *Troy*. I'm just trying to say I don't want to see you mess up.

**TROY:**   Yeah, I appreciate that, Bono. If you was messing around on Lucille I'd be telling you the same thing.

**BONO:**   Well, that's all I got to say. I just say that because I love you both.

**TROY:**   Hell, you know me … I wasn't out there looking for nothing. You can't find a better woman than Rose. I know that. But seems like this woman just stuck onto me where I can't shake her loose. I done wrestled with it, tried to throw her off me … but she just stuck on tighter. Now she's stuck on for good.

**BONO:**   You's in control … that's what you tell me all the time. You responsible for what you do.

**TROY:**   I ain't ducking the responsibility of it. As long as it sets right in my heart … then I'm okay. Cause that's all I listen to. It'll tell me right from wrong every time. And I ain't talking about doing Rose no bad turn. I love Rose. She done carried me a long ways and I love and respect her for that.

**BONO:**   I know you do. That's why I don't want to see you hurt her. But what you gonna do when she find out? What you got then? If you try and juggle both of them … sooner or later you gonna drop one of them. That's common sense.

**TROY:** Yeah, I hear what you saying, Bono. I been trying to figure a way to work it out.

**BONO:** Work it out right, *Troy*. I don't want to be getting all up between you and Rose's business ... but work it so it come out right.

**TROY:** Aw hell, I get all up between you and Lucille's business. When you gonna get that woman that refrigerator she been wanting? Don't tell me you ain't got no money now. I know who your banker is. Mellon° don't need that money bad as Lucille want that refrigerator. I'll tell you that.

**BONO:** Tell you what I'll do ... when you finish building this fence for Rose ... I'll buy Lucille that refrigerator.

**TROY:** You done stuck your foot in your mouth now!

*(Troy grabs up a board and begins to saw. Bono starts to walk out the yard.)*

Hey, nigger ... where you going?

**BONO:** I'm going home. I know you don't expect me to help you now. I'm protecting my money. I wanna see you put that fence up by yourself. That's what I want to see. You'll be here another six months without me.

**TROY:** Nigger, you ain't right.

**BONO:** When it comes to my money ... I'm right as fireworks on the Fourth of July.

**TROY:** Alright, we gonna see now. You better get out your bankbook.

*(Bono exits, and Troy continues to work. Rose enters from the house.)*

**ROSE:** What they say down there? What's happening with Gabe?

**TROY:** I went down there and got him out. Cost me fifty dollars. Say he was disturbing the peace. Judge set up a hearing for him in three weeks. Say to show cause why he shouldn't be re-committed.

**ROSE:** What was he doing that cause them to arrest him?

**TROY:** Some kids was teasing him and he run them off home. Say he was howling and carrying on. Some folks seen him and called the police. That's all it was.

**ROSE:** Well, what's you say? What'd you tell the judge?

**TROY:** Told him I'd look after him. It didn't make no sense to recommit the man. He stuck out his big greasy palm and told me to give him fifty dollars and take him on home.

**ROSE:** Where's he at now? Where'd he go off to?

**TROY:** He's gone on about his business. He don't need nobody to hold his hand.

**ROSE:** Well, I don't know. Seem like that would be the best place for him if they did put him into the hospital. I know what you're gonna say. But that's what I think would be best.

**TROY:** The man done had his life ruined fighting for what? And they wanna take and lock him up. Let him be free. He don't bother nobody.

---

*Mellon:* banker and industrialist Andrew Mellon (1855–1937), U.S. Treasury Secretary 1921–32, was active in philanthropic enterprises, especially in his native Pittsburgh.

**ROSE:**   Well, everybody got their own way of looking at it I guess. Come on and get your lunch. I got a bowl of lima beans and some cornbread in the oven. Come on get something to eat. Ain't no sense you fretting over Gabe.

*(Rose turns to go into the house.)*

**TROY:**   Rose ... got something to tell you.
**ROSE:**   Well, come on ... wait till I get this food on the table.
**TROY:**   Rose!

*(She stops and turns around.)*

I don't know how to say this. *(Pause.)* I can't explain it none. It just sort of grows on you till it gets out of hand. It starts out like a little bush ... and the next thing you know it's a whole forest.
**ROSE:**   *Troy* ... what is you talking about?
**TROY:**   I'm talking, woman, let me talk. I'm trying to find a way to tell you ... I'm gonna be a daddy. I'm gonna be somebody's daddy.
**ROSE:**   *Troy* ... you're not telling me this? You're gonna be ... what?
**TROY:**   Rose ... now ... see ...
**ROSE:**   You telling me you gonna be somebody's daddy? You telling your *wife* this?

*(Gabriel enters from the street. He carries a rose in his hand.)*

**GABRIEL:**   Hey, *Troy*! Hey, Rose!
**ROSE:**   I have to wait eighteen years to hear something like this.
**GABRIEL:**   Hey, Rose ... I got a flower for you. *(He hands it to her.)* That's a rose. Same rose like you is.
**ROSE:**   Thanks, Gabe.
**GABRIEL:**   *Troy*, you ain't mad at me is you? Them bad mens come and put me away. You ain't mad at me is you?
**TROY:**   Naw, Gabe, I ain't mad at you.
**ROSE:**   Eighteen years and you wanna come with this.
*Gabriel (takes a quarter out of his pocket)*:   See what I got? Got a brand new quarter.
**TROY:**   Rose ... it's just ...
**ROSE:**   Ain't nothing you can say, *Troy*. Ain't no way of explaining that.
**GABRIEL:**   Fellow that give me this quarter had a whole mess of them. I'm gonna keep this quarter till it stop shining.
**ROSE:**   Gabe, go on in the house there. I got some watermelon in the Frigidaire. Go on and get you a piece.
**GABRIEL:**   Say, Rose ... you know I was chasing hellhounds and them bad mens come and get me and take me away. *Troy* helped me. He come down there and told them they better let me go before he beat them up. Yeah, he did!

**ROSE:** You go on and get you a piece of watermelon, Gabe. Them bad mens is gone now.

**GABRIEL:** Okay, Rose ... gonna get me some watermelon. The kind with the stripes on it.

*(Gabriel exits into the house.)*

**ROSE:** Why, *Troy*? Why? After all these years to come dragging this in to me now. It don't make no sense at your age. I could have expected this ten or fifteen years ago, but not now.

**TROY:** Age ain't got nothing to do with it, Rose.

**ROSE:** I done tried to be everything a wife should be. Everything a wife could be. Been married eighteen years and I got to live to see the day you tell me you been seeing another woman and done fathered a child by her. And you know I ain't never wanted no half nothing in my family. My whole family is half. Everybody got different fathers and mothers ... my two sisters and my brother. Can't hardly tell who's who. Can't never sit down and talk about Papa and Mama. It's your papa and your mama and my papa and my mama ...

**TROY:** Rose ... stop it now.

**ROSE:** I ain't never wanted that for none of my children. And now you wanna drag your behind in here and tell me something like this.

**TROY:** You ought to know. It's time for you to know.

**ROSE:** Well, I don't want to know, goddamn it!

**TROY:** I can't just make it go away. It's done now. I can't wish the circumstance of the thing away.

**ROSE:** And you don't want to either. Maybe you want to wish me and my boy away. Maybe that's what you want? Well, you can't wish us away. I've got eighteen years of my life invested in you. You ought to have stayed upstairs in my bed where you belong.

**TROY:** Rose ... now listen to me ... we can get a handle on this thing. We can talk this out ... come to an understanding.

**ROSE:** All of a sudden it's "we." Where was "we" at when you was down there rolling around with some godforsaken woman? "We" should have come to an understanding before you started making a damn fool of yourself. You're a day late and a dollar short when it comes to an understanding with me.

**TROY:** It's just ... She gives me a different idea ... a different understanding about myself. I can step out of this house and get away from the pressures and problems ... be a different man. I ain't got to wonder how I'm gonna pay the bills or get the roof fixed. I can just be a part of myself that I ain't never been.

**ROSE:** What I want to know ... is do you plan to continue seeing her. That's all you can say to me.

**TROY:** I can sit up in her house and laugh. Do you understand what I'm saying. I can laugh out loud ... and it feels good. It reaches all the way down to the bottom of my shoes. (*Pause.*) Rose, I can't give that up.

**ROSE:** Maybe you ought to go on and stay down there with her ... if she's a better woman than me.

**TROY:** It ain't about nobody being a better woman or nothing. Rose, you ain't the blame. A man couldn't ask for no woman to be a better wife than you've been. I'm responsible for it. I done locked myself into a pattern trying to take care of you all that I forgot about myself.

**ROSE:** What the hell was I there for? That was my job, not somebody else's.

**TROY:** Rose, I done tried all my life to live decent ... to live a clean ... hard ... useful life. I tried to be a good husband to you. In every way I knew how. Maybe I come into the world backwards, I don't know. But ... you born with two strikes on you before you come to the plate. You got to guard it closely ... always looking for the curve-ball on the inside corner. You can't afford to let none get past you. You can't afford a call strike. If you going down ... you going down swinging. Everything lined up against you. What you gonna do. I fooled them, Rose. I bunted. When I found you and *Cory* and a halfway decent job ... I was safe. Couldn't nothing touch me. I wasn't gonna strike out no more. I wasn't going back to the penitentiary. I wasn't gonna lay in the streets with a bottle of wine. I was safe. I had me a family. A job. I wasn't gonna get that last strike. I was on first looking for one of them boys to knock me in. To get me home.

**ROSE:** You should have stayed in my bed, *Troy.*

**TROY:** Then when I saw that gal ... she firmed up my backbone. And I got to thinking that if I tried ... I just might be able to steal second. Do you understand after eighteen years I wanted to steal second.

**ROSE:** You should have held me tight. You should have grabbed me and held on.

**TROY:** I stood on first base for eighteen years and I thought ... well, goddamn it ... go on for it!

**ROSE:** We're not talking about baseball! We're talking about you going off to lay in bed with another woman ... and then bring it home to me. That's what we're talking about. We ain't talking about no baseball.

**TROY:** Rose, you're not listening to me. I'm trying the best I can to explain it to you. It's not easy for me to admit that I been standing in the same place for eighteen years.

**ROSE:** I been standing with you! I been right here with you, *Troy.* I got a life too. I gave eighteen years of my life to stand in the same spot with you. Don't you think I ever wanted other things? Don't you think I had dreams and hopes? What about my life? What about me. Don't you think it ever crossed my mind to want to know other men? That I wanted to lay up somewhere and forget about my responsibilities? That I wanted someone to make me laugh so I could feel good? You not the only one who's got wants and needs. But I held on to you, *Troy*. I took all my feelings, my wants and needs, my dreams ... and I buried them inside you. I planted a seed and watched and prayed over it. I planted myself inside you and waited to bloom. And it didn't take me no eighteen years to find out the soil was hard and rocky and it wasn't never gonna bloom.

But I held on to you, *Troy*. I held you tighter. You was my husband. I owed you everything I had. Every part of me I could find to give you. And upstairs in that room ... with the darkness falling in on me ... I gave everything I had to try and erase the doubt that you wasn't the finest man in the world. And wherever you was going ... I wanted to be there with you. Cause you was my husband. Cause that's the only way I was gonna survive as your wife. You always talking about what you give ... and what you don't have to give. But you take too. You take ... and don't even know nobody's giving!

*(Rose turns to exit into the house; Troy grabs her arm.)*

**TROY:**  You say I take and don't give!

**ROSE:**  *Troy!* You're hurting me!

**TROY:**  You say I take and don't give.

**ROSE:**  *Troy* ... you're hurting my arm! Let go!

**TROY:**  I done give you everything I got. Don't you tell that lie on me.

**ROSE:**  *Troy!*

**TROY:**  Don't you tell that lie on me!

*(Cory enters from the house.)*

**CORY:**  Mama!

**ROSE:**  *Troy.* You're hurting me.

**TROY:**  Don't you tell me about no taking and giving.

*(Cory comes up behind Troy and grabs him. Troy, surprised, is thrown off balance just as Cory throws a glancing blow that catches him on the chest and knocks him down. Troy is stunned, as is Cory.)*

**ROSE:**  *Troy. Troy. No!*

*(Troy gets to his feet and starts at Cory.)*

*Troy* ... no. Please! *Troy!*

*(Rose pulls on Troy to hold him back. Troy stops himself.)*

*Troy (to Cory):*  Alright. That's strike two. You stay away from around me, boy. Don't you strike out. You living with a full count. Don't you strike out.

*(Troy exits out the yard as the lights go down.)*

## SCENE II

*It is six months later, early afternoon. Troy enters from the house and starts to exit the yard. Rose enters from the house.*

**ROSE:**  *Troy*, I want to talk to you.

**TROY:**  All of a sudden, after all this time, you want to talk to me, huh? You ain't wanted to talk to me for months. You ain't wanted to talk to me last night. You ain't wanted no part of me then. What you wanna talk to me about now?

**ROSE:**  Tomorrow's Friday.

**TROY:**  I know what day tomorrow is. You think I don't know tomorrow's Friday? My whole life I ain't done nothing but look to see Friday coming and you got to tell me it's Friday.

**ROSE:**  I want to know if you're coming home.

**TROY:**  I always come home, Rose. You know that. There ain't never been a night I ain't come home.

**ROSE:**  That ain't what I mean ... and you know it. I want to know if you're coming straight home after work.

**TROY:**  I figure I'd cash my check ... hang out at Taylors' with the boys ... maybe play a game of checkers ...

**ROSE:**  *Troy*, I can't live like this. I won't live like this. You livin' on borrowed time with me. It's been going on six months now you ain't been coming home.

**TROY:**  I be here every night. Every night of the year. That's 365 days.

**ROSE:**  I want you to come home tomorrow after work.

**TROY:**  Rose ... I don't mess up my pay. You know that now. I take my pay and I give it to you. I don't have no money but what you give me back. I just want to have a little time to myself ... a little time to enjoy life.

**ROSE:**  What about me? When's my time to enjoy life?

**TROY:**  I don't know what to tell you, Rose. I'm doing the best I can.

**ROSE:**  You ain't been home from work but time enough to change your clothes and run out ... and you wanna call that the best you can do?

**TROY:**  I'm going over to the hospital to see Alberta. She went into the hospital this afternoon. Look like she might have the baby early. I won't be gone long.

**ROSE:**  Well, you ought to know. They went over to Miss Pearl's and got Gabe today. She said you told them to go ahead and lock him up.

**TROY:**  I ain't said no such thing. Whoever told you that is telling a lie. Pearl ain't doing nothing but telling a big fat lie.

**ROSE:**  She ain't had to tell me. I read it on the papers.

**TROY:**  I ain't told them nothing of the kind.

**ROSE:**  I saw it right there on the papers.

**TROY:**  What it say, huh?

**ROSE:**  It said you told them to take him.

**TROY:**   Then they screwed that up, just the way they screw up everything. I ain't worried about what they got on the paper.

**ROSE:**   Say the government send part of his check to the hospital and the other part to you.

**TROY:**   I ain't got nothing to do with that if that's the way it works. I ain't made up the rules about how it work.

**ROSE:**   You did Gabe just like you did *Cory*. You wouldn't sign the paper for *Cory* ... but you signed for Gabe. You signed that paper.

*(The telephone is heard ringing inside the house.)*

**TROY:**   I told you I ain't signed nothing, woman! The only thing I signed was the release form. Hell, I can't read, I don't know what they had on that paper! I ain't signed nothing about sending Gabe away.

**ROSE:**   I said send him to the hospital ... you said let him be free ... now you done went down there and signed him to the hospital for half his money. You went back on yourself, *Troy*. You gonna have to answer for that.

**TROY:**   See now ... you been over there talking to Miss Pearl. She done got mad cause she ain't getting Gabe's rent money. That's all it is. She's liable to say anything.

**ROSE:**   *Troy*, I seen where you signed the paper.

**TROY:**   You ain't seen nothing I signed. What she doing got papers on my brother anyway? Miss Pearl telling a big fat lie. And I'm gonna tell her about it too! You ain't seen nothing I signed. Say ... you ain't seen nothing I signed.

*(Rose exits into the house to answer the telephone. Presently she returns.)*

**ROSE:**   *Troy* ... that was the hospital. Alberta had the baby.

**TROY:**   What she have? What is it?

**ROSE:**   It's a girl.

**TROY:**   I better get on down to the hospital to see her.

**ROSE:**   *Troy* ...

**TROY:**   Rose ... I got to go see her now. That's only right ... what's the matter ... the baby's alright, ain't it?

**ROSE:**   Alberta died having the baby.

**TROY:**   Died ... you say she's dead? Alberta's dead?

**ROSE:**   They said they done all they could. They couldn't do nothing for her.

**TROY:**   The baby? How's the baby?

**ROSE:**   They say it's healthy. I wonder who's gonna bury her.

**TROY:**   She had family, Rose. She wasn't living in the world by herself.

**ROSE:**   I know she wasn't living in the world by herself.

**TROY:**   Next thing you gonna want to know if she had any insurance.

**ROSE:**   *Troy*, you ain't got to talk like that.

**TROY:**  That's the first thing that jumped out your mouth. "Who's gonna bury her?" Like I'm fixing to take on that task for myself.

**ROSE:**  I am your wife. Don't push me away.

**TROY:**  I ain't pushing nobody away. Just give me some space. That's all. Just give me some room to breathe.

*(Rose exits into the house. Troy walks about the yard.)*

**TROY** (*with a quiet rage that threatens to consume him*):  Alright ... Mr. Death. See now ... I'm gonna tell you what I'm gonna do. I'm gonna take and build me a fence around this yard. See? I'm gonna build me a fence around what belongs to me. And then I want you to stay on the other side. See? You stay over there until you're ready for me. Then you come on. Bring your army. Bring your sickle. Bring your wrestling clothes. I ain't gonna fall down on my vigilance this time.

You ain't gonna sneak up on me no more. When you ready for me ... when the top of your list say *Troy* Maxson ... that's when you come around here. You come up and knock on the front door. Ain't nobody else got nothing to do with this. This is between you and me. Man to man. You stay on the other side of that fence until you ready for me. Then you come up and knock on the front door. Anytime you want. I'll be ready for you.

*(The lights go down to black.)*

## SCENE III

*The lights come up on the porch. It is late evening three days later. Rose sits listening to the ball game waiting for Troy. The final out of the game is made and Rose switches off the radio. Troy enters the yard carrying an infant wrapped in blankets. He stands back from the house and calls.*

*Rose enters and stands on the porch. There is a long, awkward silence, the weight of which grows heavier with each passing second.*

**TROY:**  Rose ... I'm standing here with my daughter in my arms. She ain't but a wee bittie little old thing. She don't know nothing about grown-ups' business. She innocent ... and she ain't got no mama.

**ROSE:**  What you telling me for, *Troy*?

*(She turns and exits into the house.)*

**TROY:**  Well ... I guess we'll just sit out here on the porch.

*(He sits down on the porch. There is an awkward indelicateness about the way he handles the baby. His largeness engulfs and seems to swallow it. He speaks loud enough for Rose to hear.)*

A man's got to do what's right for him. I ain't sorry for nothing I done. It felt right in my heart. (*To the baby.*) What you smiling at? Your daddy's a big man. Got these great big old hands. But sometimes he's scared. And right now your daddy's scared cause we sitting out here and ain't got no home. Oh, I been homeless before. I ain't had no little baby with me. But I been homeless. You just be out on the road by your lonesome and you see one of them trains coming and you just kinda go like this …

*(He sings as a lullaby.)*

> Please, Mr. Engineer let a man ride the line
> Please, Mr. Engineer let a man ride the line
> I ain't got no ticket please let me ride the blinds

*(Rose enters from the house. Troy, hearing her steps behind him, stands and faces her.)*

She's my daughter, Rose. My own flesh and blood. I can't deny her no more than I can deny them boys. *(Pause.)* You and them boys is my family. You and them and this child is all I got in the world. So I guess what I'm saying is … I'd appreciate it if you'd help me take care of her.

**ROSE:**  Okay, *Troy* … you're right. I'll take care of your baby for you … cause … like you say … she's innocent … and you can't visit the sins of the father upon the child. A motherless child has got a hard time. *(She takes the baby from him.)* From right now … this child got a mother. But you a womanless man.

*(Rose turns and exits into the house with the baby. Lights go down to black.)*

## SCENE IV

*It is two months later. Lyons enters the street. He knocks on the door and calls.*

**LYONS:**  Hey, Rose! *(Pause.)* Rose!

**ROSE** *(from inside the house)*:  Stop that yelling. You gonna wake up Raynell. I just got her to sleep.

**LYONS:**  I just stopped by to pay Papa this twenty dollars I owe him. Where's Papa at?

**ROSE:**  He should be here in a minute. I'm getting ready to go down to the church. Sit down and wait on him.

**LYONS:**  I got to go pick up Bonnie over her mother's house.

**ROSE:**  Well, sit it down there on the table. He'll get it.

**LYONS** *(enters the house and sets the money on the table)*:  Tell Papa I said thanks. I'll see you again.

**ROSE:**  Alright, Lyons. We'll see you.

*(Lyons starts to exit as Cory enters.)*

**CORY:**  Hey, Lyons.

**LYONS:**  What's happening, *Cory*? Say man, I'm sorry I missed your graduation. You know I had a gig and couldn't get away. Otherwise, I would
have been there, man. So what you doing?

**CORY:**  I'm trying to find a job.

**LYONS:**  Yeah I know how that go, man. It's rough out here. Jobs are scarce.

**CORY:**  Yeah, I know.

**LYONS:**  Look here, I got to run. Talk to Papa ... he know some people.
He'll be able to help get you a job. Talk to him ... see what he say.

**CORY:**  Yeah ... alright, Lyons.

**LYONS:**  You take care. I'll talk to you soon. We'll find some time to talk.

*(Lyons exits the yard. Cory wanders over to the tree, picks up the
bat, and assumes a batting stance. He studies an imaginary pitcher
and swings. Dissatisfied with the result, he tries again. Troy enters.
They eye each other for a beat. Cory puts the bat down and exits
the yard. Troy starts into the house as Rose exits with Raynell. She
is carrying a cake.)*

**TROY:**  I'm coming in and everybody's going out.

**ROSE:**  I'm taking this cake down to the church for the bake sale. Lyons
was by to see you. He stopped by to pay you your twenty dollars. It's
laying in there on the table.

*Troy (going into his pocket):*  Well ... here go this money.

**ROSE:**  Put it in there on the table, *Troy*. I'll get it.

**TROY:**  What time you coming back?

**ROSE:**  Ain't no use in you studying me. It don't matter what time I come
back.

**TROY:**  I just asked you a question, woman. What's the matter ... can't I
ask you a question?

**ROSE:**  *Troy*, I don't want to go into it. Your dinner's in there on the stove.
All you got to do is heat it up. And don't you be eating the rest of them
cakes in there. I'm coming back for them. We having a bake sale at the
church tomorrow.

*(Rose exits the yard. Troy sits down on the steps, takes a pint bottle
from his pocket, opens it and drinks. He begins to sing.)*

**TROY:**  Hear it ring! Hear it ring!
Had an old dog his name was Blue
You know Blue was mighty true
You know Blue was a good old dog
Blue trees a possum in a hollow log
You know from that he was a good old dog

*(Bono enters the yard.)*

**BONO:**  Hey, *Troy*.

**TROY:**  Hey, what's happening, Bono?

**BONO:**   I just thought I'd stop by to see you.

**TROY:**   What you stop by and see me for? You ain't stopped by in a month of Sundays. Hell, I must owe you money or something.

**BONO:**   Since you got your promotion I can't keep up with you. Used to see you every day. Now I don't even know what route you working.

**TROY:**   They keep switching me around. Got me out in Greentree now ... hauling white folks' garbage.

**BONO:**   Greentree, huh? You lucky, at least you ain't got to be lifting them barrels. Damn if they ain't getting heavier. I'm gonna put in my two years and call it quits.

**TROY:**   I'm thinking about retiring myself.

**BONO:**   You got it easy. You can *drive* for another five years.

**TROY:**   It ain't the same, Bono. It ain't like working the back of the truck. Ain't got nobody to talk to ... feel like you working by yourself. Naw, I'm thinking about retiring. How's Lucille?

**BONO:**   She alright. Her arthritis get to acting up on her sometime. Saw Rose on my way in. She going down to the church, huh?

**TROY:**   Yeah, she took up going down there. All them preachers looking for somebody to fatten their pockets. (*Pause.*) Got some gin here.

**BONO:**   Naw, thanks. I just stopped by to say hello.

**TROY:**   Hell, nigger ... you can take a drink. I ain't never known you to say no to a drink. You ain't got to work tomorrow.

**BONO:**   I just stopped by. I'm fixing to go over to Skinner's. We got us a domino game going over his house every Friday.

**TROY:**   Nigger, you can't play no dominoes. I used to whup you four games out of five.

**BONO:**   Well, that learned me. I'm getting better.

**TROY:**   Yeah? Well, that's alright.

**BONO:**   Look here ... I got to be getting on. Stop by sometime, huh?

**TROY:**   Yeah, I'll do that, Bono. Lucille told Rose you bought her a new refrigerator.

**BONO:**   Yeah, Rose told Lucille you had finally built your fence ... so I figured we'd call it even.

**TROY:**   I knew you would.

**BONO:**   Yeah ... okay. I'll be talking to you.

**TROY:**   Yeah, take care, Bono. Good to see you. I'm gonna stop over.

**BONO:**   Yeah. Okay, *Troy.*

(*Bono exits. Troy drinks from the bottle.*)

**TROY:**

> Old Blue died and I dug his grave
> Let him down with a golden chain
> Every night when I hear old Blue bark
> I know Blue treed a possum in Noah's Ark.
> Hear it ring! Hear it ring!

*(Cory enters the yard. They eye each other for a beat. Troy is sitting in the middle of the steps. Cory walks over.)*

**CORY:**   I got to get by.

**TROY:**   Say what? What's you say?

**CORY:**   You in my way. I got to get by.

**TROY:**   You got to get by where? This is my house. Bought and paid for. In full. Took me fifteen years. And if you wanna go in my house and I'm sitting on the steps ... you say excuse me. Like your mama taught you.

**CORY:**   Come on, Pop ... I got to get by.

*(Cory starts to maneuver his way past Troy. Troy grabs his leg and shoves him back.)*

**TROY:**   You just gonna walk over top of me?

**CORY:**   I live here too!

**TROY** *(advancing toward him)*:   You just gonna walk over top of me in my own house?

**CORY:**   I ain't scared of you.

**TROY:**   I ain't asked if you was scared of me. I asked you if you was fixing to walk over top of me in my own house? That's the question. You ain't gonna say excuse me? You just gonna walk over top of me?

**CORY:**   If you wanna put it like that.

**TROY:**   How else am I gonna put it?

**CORY:**   I was walking by you to go into the house cause you sitting on the steps drunk, singing to yourself. You can put it like that.

**TROY:**   Without saying excuse me???

*(Cory doesn't respond.)*

I asked you a question. Without saying excuse me???

**CORY:**   I ain't got to say excuse me to you. You don't count around here no more.

**TROY:**   Oh, I see ... I don't count around here no more. You ain't got to say excuse me to your daddy. All of a sudden you done got so grown that your daddy don't count around here no more ... Around here in his own house and yard that he done paid for with the sweat of his brow. You done got so grown to where you gonna take over. You gonna take over my house. Is that right? You gonna wear my pants. You gonna go in there and stretch out on my bed. You ain't got to say excuse me cause I don't count around here no more. Is that right?

**CORY:**   That's right. You always talking this dumb stuff. Now, why don't you just get out my way?

**TROY:**   I guess you got someplace to sleep and something to put in your belly. You got that, huh? You got that? That's what you need. You got that, huh?

**CORY:**   You don't know what I got. You ain't got to worry about what I got.

**TROY:**  You right! You one hundred percent right! I done spent the last seventeen years worrying about what you got. Now it's your turn, see? I'll tell you what to do. You grown ... we done established that. You a man. Now, let's see you act like one. Turn your behind around and walk out this yard. And when you get out there in the alley ... you can forget about this house. See? Cause this is my house. You go on and be a man and get your own house. You can forget about this. Cause this is mine. You go on and get yours cause I'm through with doing for you.

**CORY:**  You talking about what you did for me ... what'd you ever give me?

**TROY:**  Them feet and bones! That pumping heart, nigger! I give you more than anybody else is ever gonna give you.

**CORY:**  You ain't never gave me nothing! You ain't never done nothing but hold me back. Afraid I was gonna be better than you. All you ever did was try and make me scared of you. I used to tremble every time you called my name. Every time I heard your footsteps in the house. Wondering all the time ... what's Papa gonna say if I do this? ... What's he gonna say if I do that? ... What's Papa gonna say if I turn on the radio? And Mama, too ... she tries ... but she's scared of you.

**TROY:**  You leave your mama out of this. She ain't got nothing to do with this.

**CORY:**  I don't know how she stand you ... after what you did to her.

**TROY:**  I told you to leave your mama out of this!

*(He advances toward Cory.)*

**CORY:**  What you gonna do ... give me a whupping? You can't whup me no more. You're too old. You just an old man.

*Troy (shoves him on his shoulder):*  Nigger! That's what you are. You just another nigger on the street to me!

**CORY:**  You crazy! You know that?

**TROY:**  Go on now! You got the devil in you. Get on away from me!

**CORY:**  You just a crazy old man ... talking about I got the devil in me.

**TROY:**  Yeah, I'm crazy! If you don't get on the other side of that yard ... I'm gonna show you how crazy I am! Go on ... get the hell out of my yard.

**CORY:**  It ain't your yard. You took Uncle Gabe's money he got from the army to buy this house and then you put him out.

**TROY** *(advances on Cory):*  Get your black ass out of my yard!

*(Troy's advance backs Cory up against the tree. Cory grabs up the bat.)*

**CORY:**  I ain't going nowhere! Come on ... put me out! I ain't scared of you.

**TROY:**  That's my bat!

**CORY:**  Come on!

**TROY:**  Put my bat down!

**CORY:**  Come on, put me out.

*(Cory swings at Troy, who backs across the yard.)*

What's the matter? You so bad ... put me out!

*(Troy advances toward Cory.)*

**CORY** *(backing up)*:   Come on! Come on!
**TROY:**   You're gonna have to use it! You wanna draw that bat back on me ... you're gonna have to use it.
**CORY:**   Come on! ... Come on!

*(Cory swings the bat at Troy a second time. He misses. Troy continues to advance toward him.)*

**TROY:**   You're gonna have to kill me! You wanna draw that bat back on me. You're gonna have to kill me.

*(Cory, backed up against the tree, can go no farther. Troy taunts him. He sticks out his head and offers him a target.)*

Come on! Come on!

*(Cory is unable to swing the bat. Troy grabs it.)*

**TROY:**   Then I'll show you.

*(Cory and Troy struggle over the bat. The struggle is fierce and fully engaged. Troy ultimately is the stronger, and takes the bat from Cory and stands over him ready to swing. He stops himself.)*

Go on and get away from around my house.

*(Cory, stung by his defeat, picks himself up, walks slowly out of the yard and up the alley.)*

**CORY:**   Tell Mama I'll be back for my things.
**TROY:**   They'll be on the other side of that fence.

*(Cory exits.)*

**TROY:**   I can't taste nothing. Helluljah! I can't taste nothing no more. *(Troy assumes a batting posture and begins to taunt Death, the fastball on the outside corner.)* Come on! It's between you and me now! Come on! Anytime you want! Come on! I be ready for you ... but I ain't gonna be easy.

*(The lights go down on the scene.)*

## SCENE V

*The time is 1965. The lights come up in the yard. It is the morning of Troy's funeral. A funeral plaque with a light hangs beside the door. There is a small garden plot off to the side. There is noise and activity in the house as Rose, Lyons, and Bono have gathered. The door opens and Raynell, seven years old, enters dressed in a flannel nightgown. She crosses to the garden and pokes around with a stick. Rose calls from the house.*

**ROSE:**   Raynell!

**RAYNELL:**   Mam?

**ROSE:**   What you doing out there?

**RAYNELL:**   Nothing.

*(Rose comes to the door.)*

**ROSE:**   Girl, get in here and get dressed. What you doing?

**RAYNELL:**   Seeing if my garden growed.

**ROSE:**   I told you it ain't gonna grow overnight. You got to wait.

**RAYNELL:**   It don't look like it never gonna grow. Dag!

**ROSE:**   I told you a watched pot never boils. Get in here and get dressed.

**RAYNELL:**   This ain't even no pot, Mama.

**ROSE:**   You just have to give it a chance. It'll grow. Now you come on and
do what I told you. We got to be getting ready. This ain't no morning to
be playing around. You hear me?

**RAYNELL:**   Yes, Mam.

*(Rose exits into the house. Raynell continues to poke at her garden
with a stick. Cory enters. He is dressed in a Marine corporal's uniform, and carries a duffelbag. His posture is that of a military man,
and his speech has a clipped sternness.)*

**CORY** *(to Raynell)***:**   Hi. *(Pause.)* I bet your name is Raynell.

**RAYNELL:**   Uh huh.

**CORY:**   Is your mama home?

*(Raynell runs up on the porch and calls through the screen door.)*

**RAYNELL:**   Mama ... there's some man out here. Mama?

*(Rose comes to the door.)*

**ROSE:**   *Cory?* Lord have mercy! Look here, you all!

*(Rose and Cory embrace in a tearful reunion as Bono and Lyons
enter from the house dressed in funeral clothes.)*

**BONO:**   Aw, looka here ...

**ROSE:**   Done got all grown up!

**CORY:**   Don't cry, Mama. What you crying about?

**ROSE:**   I'm just so glad you made it.

**CORY:**   Hey Lyons. How you doing, Mr. Bono.

*(Lyons goes to embrace Cory.)*

**LYONS:**   Look at you, man. Look at you. Don't he look good, Rose. Got
them Corporal stripes.

**ROSE:**   What took you so long?

**CORY:**   You know how the Marines are, Mama. They got to get all their
paperwork straight before they let you do anything.

**ROSE:** Well, I'm sure glad you made it. They let Lyons come. Your Uncle Gabe's still in the hospital. They don't know if they gonna let him out or not. I just talked to them a little while ago.

**LYONS:** A Corporal in the United States Marines.

**BONO:** Your daddy knew you had it in you. He used to tell me all the time.

**LYONS:** Don't he look good, Mr. Bono?

**BONO:** Yeah, he remind me of *Troy* when I first met him. (*Pause.*) Say, Rose, Lucille's down at the church with the choir. I'm gonna go down and get the pallbearers lined up. I'll be back to get you all.

**ROSE:** Thanks, Jim.

**CORY:** See you, Mr. Bono.

**LYONS** (*with his arm around Raynell*)**:** *Cory* ... look at Raynell. Ain't she precious?

She gonna break a whole lot of hearts.

**ROSE:** Raynell, come and say hello to your brother. This is your brother, *Cory*. You remember *Cory*.

**RAYNELL:** No, Mam.

**CORY:** She don't remember me, Mama.

**ROSE:** Well, we talk about you. She heard us talk about you. (*To Raynell.*) This is your brother, *Cory*. Come on and say hello.

**RAYNELL:** Hi.

**CORY:** Hi. So you're Raynell. Mama told me a lot about you.

**ROSE:** You all come on into the house and let me fix you some breakfast. Keep up your strength.

**CORY:** I ain't hungry, Mama.

**LYONS:** You can fix me something, Rose. I'll be in there in a minute.

**ROSE:** *Cory*, you sure you don't want nothing? I know they ain't feeding you right.

**CORY:** No, Mama ... thanks. I don't feel like eating. I'll get something later.

**ROSE:** Raynell ... get on upstairs and get that dress on like I told you.

(*Rose and Raynell exit into the house.*)

**LYONS:** So ... I hear you thinking about getting married.

**CORY:** Yeah, I done found the right one, Lyons. It's about time.

**LYONS:** Me and Bonnie been split up about four years now. About the time Papa retired. I guess she just got tired of all them changes I was putting her through. (*Pause.*) I always knew you was gonna make something out yourself. Your head was always in the right direction. So ... you gonna stay in ... make it a career ... put in your twenty years?

**CORY:** I don't know. I got six already, I think that's enough.

**LYONS:** Stick with Uncle Sam and retire early. Ain't nothing out here. I guess Rose told you what happened with me. They got me down the workhouse. I thought I was being slick cashing other people's checks.

**CORY:** How much time you doing?

**LYONS:** They give me three years. I got that beat now. I ain't got but nine more months. It ain't so bad. You learn to deal with it like anything else. You got to take the crookeds with the straights. That's what Papa used to say. He used to say that when he struck out. I seen him strike out three times in a row … and the next time up he hit the ball over the grandstand. Right out there in Homestead Field. He wasn't satisfied hitting in the seats … he want to hit it over everything! After the game he had two hundred people standing around waiting to shake his hand. You got to take the crookeds with the straights. Yeah, Papa was something else.

**CORY:** You still playing?

**LYONS:** *Cory* … you know I'm gonna do that. There's some fellows down there we got us a band … we gonna try and stay together when we get out … but yeah, I'm still playing. It still helps me to get out of bed in the morning. As long as it do that I'm gonna be right there playing and trying to make some sense out of it.

**ROSE** (*calling*): Lyons, I got these eggs in the pan.

**LYONS:** Let me go on and get these eggs, man. Get ready to go bury Papa. (*Pause.*) How you doing? You doing alright?

(*Cory nods. Lyons touches him on the shoulder and they share a moment of silent grief. Lyons exits into the house. Cory wanders about the yard. Raynell enters.*)

**RAYNELL:** Hi.

**CORY:** Hi.

**RAYNELL:** Did you used to sleep in my room?

**CORY:** Yeah … that used to be my room.

**RAYNELL:** That's what Papa call it. "Cory's room." It got your football in the closet.

(*Rose comes to the door.*)

**ROSE:** Raynell, get in there and get them good shoes on.

**RAYNELL:** Mama, can't I wear these? Them other one hurt my feet.

**ROSE:** Well, they just gonna have to hurt your feet for a while. You ain't said they hurt your feet when you went down to the store and got them.

**RAYNELL:** They didn't hurt then. My feet done got bigger.

**ROSE:** Don't you give me no backtalk now. You get in there and get them shoes on.

(*Raynell exits into the house.*)

Ain't too much changed. He still got that piece of rag tied to that tree. He was out here swinging that bat. I was just ready to go back in the house. He swung that bat and then he just fell over. Seem like he swung it and stood there with this grin on his face … and then he just fell over. They carried him on down to the hospital, but I knew there wasn't no need ... why don't you come on in the house?

**CORY:** Mama ... I got something to tell you. I don't know how to tell you this ... but I've got to tell you ... I'm not going to Papa's funeral.

**ROSE:** Boy, hush your mouth. That's your daddy you talking about. I don't want hear that kind of talk this morning. I done raised you to come to this? You standing there all healthy and grown talking about you ain't going to your daddy's funeral?

**CORY:** Mama ... listen ...

**ROSE:** I don't want to hear it, *Cory*. You just get that thought out of your head.

**CORY:** I can't drag Papa with me everywhere I go. I've got to say no to him. One time in my life I've got to say no.

**ROSE:** Don't nobody have to listen to nothing like that. I know you and your daddy ain't seen eye to eye, but I ain't got to listen to that kind of talk this morning. Whatever was between you and your daddy ... the time has come to put it aside. Just take it and set it over there on the shelf and forget about it. Disrespecting your daddy ain't gonna make you a man, *Cory*. You got to find a way to come to that on your own. Not going to your daddy's funeral ain't gonna make you a man.

**CORY:** The whole time I was growing up ... living in his house ... Papa was like a shadow that followed you everywhere. It weighed on you and sunk into your flesh. It would wrap around you and lay there until you couldn't tell which one was you anymore. That shadow digging in your flesh. Trying to crawl in. Trying to live through you. Everywhere I looked, *Troy* Maxson was staring back at me ... hiding under the bed ... in the closet. I'm just saying I've got to find a way to get rid of that shadow, Mama.

**ROSE:** You just like him. You got him in you good.

**CORY:** Don't tell me that, Mama.

**ROSE:** You *Troy* Maxson all over again.

**CORY:** I don't want to be *Troy* Maxson. I want to be me.

**ROSE:** You can't be nobody but who you are, *Cory*. That shadow wasn't nothing but you growing into yourself. You either got to grow into it or cut it down to fit you. But that's all you got to make life with. That's all you got to measure yourself against that world out there. Your daddy wanted you to be everything he wasn't ... and at the same time he tried to make you into everything he was. I don't know if he was right or wrong ... but I do know he meant to do more good than he meant to do harm. He wasn't always right. Sometimes when he touched he bruised. And sometimes when he took me in his arms he cut.

When I first met your daddy I thought ... Here is a man I can lay down with and make a baby. That's the first thing I thought when I seen him. I was thirty years old and had done seen my share of men.

But when he walked up to me and said, "I can dance a waltz that'll make you dizzy," I thought, Rose Lee, here is a man that you can open yourself up to and be filled to bursting. Here is a man that can fill all them empty spaces you been tipping around the edges of. One of them empty spaces was being somebody's mother.

I married your daddy and settled down to cooking his supper and keeping clean sheets on the bed. When your daddy walked through the house he was so big he filled it up. That was my first mistake. Not to make him leave some room for me. For my part in the matter. But at that time I wanted that. I wanted a house that I could sing in. And that's what your daddy gave me. I didn't know to keep up his strength I had to give up little pieces of mine. I did that. I took on his life as mine and mixed up the pieces so that you couldn't hardly tell which was which anymore. It was my choice. It was my life and I didn't have to live it like that. But that's what life offered me in the way of being a woman and I took it. I grabbed hold of it with both hands.

By the time Raynell came into the house, me and your daddy had done lost touch with one another. I didn't want to make my blessing off of nobody's misfortune ... but I took on to Raynell like she was all them babies I had wanted and never had.

*(The phone rings.)*

Like I'd been blessed to relive a part of my life. And if the Lord see fit to keep up my strength ... I'm gonna do her just like your daddy did you ... I'm gonna give her the best of what's in me.

**RAYNELL** *(entering, still with her old shoes)*: Mama ... Reverend Tolliver on the phone.

*(Rose exits into the house.)*

**RAYNELL:** Hi.

**CORY:** Hi.

**RAYNELL:** You in the Army or the Marines?

**CORY:** Marines.

**RAYNELL:** Papa said it was the Army. Did you know Blue?

**CORY:** Blue? Who's Blue?

**RAYNELL:** Papa's dog what he sing about all the time.

**CORY** *(singing):*

Hear it ring! Hear it ring!
I had a dog his name was Blue
You know Blue was mighty true
You know Blue was a good old dog
Blue treed a possum in a hollow log
You know from that he was a good old dog.
Hear it ring! Hear it ring!

*(Raynell joins in singing.)*

**CORY AND RAYNELL:**

>Blue treed a possum out on a limb
>Blue looked at me and I looked at him
>Grabbed that possum and put him in a sack
>Blue stayed there till I came back
>Old Blue's feets was big and round
>Never allowed a possum to touch the ground.
>Old Blue died and I dug his grave
>I dug his grave with a silver spade
>Let him down with a golden chain
>And every night I call his name
>Go on Blue, you good dog you
>Go on Blue, you good dog you.

**RAYNELL:**

>Blue laid down and died like a man
>Blue laid down and died ...

**BOTH:**

>Blue laid down and died like a man
>Now he's treeing possums in the Promised Land
>I'm gonna tell you this to let you know
>Blue's gone where the good dogs go
>When I hear old Blue bark
>When I hear old Blue bark
>Blue treed a possum in Noah's Ark
>Blue treed a possum in Noah's Ark.

*(Rose comes to the screen door.)*

**ROSE:** *Cory,* we gonna be ready to go in a minute.

**CORY** *(to Raynell)*: You go on in the house and change them shoes like Mama told you so we can go to Papa's funeral.

**RAYNELL:** Okay, I'll be back.

*(Raynell exits into the house. Cory gets up and crosses over to the tree. Rose stands in the screen door watching him. Gabriel enters from the alley.)*

*Gabriel (calling):* Hey, Rose!

**ROSE:** Gabe?

**GABRIEL:** I'm here, Rose. Hey, Rose, I'm here!

*(Rose enters from the house.)*

**ROSE:** Lord ... Look here, Lyons!

**LYONS:** See, I told you, Rose ... I told you they'd let him come.

**CORY:** How you doing, Uncle Gabe?

**LYONS:** How you doing, Uncle Gabe?

**GABRIEL:** Hey, Rose. It's time. It's time to tell St. Peter to open the gates. *Troy,* you ready? You ready, *Troy.* I'm gonna tell St. Peter to open the gates. You get ready now.

*(Gabriel, with great fanfare, braces himself to blow. The trumpet is without a mouthpiece. He puts the end of it into his mouth and blows with great force, like a man who has been waiting some twenty-odd years for this single moment. No sound comes out of the trumpet. He braces himself and blows again with the same result. A third time he blows. There is a weight of impossible description that falls away and leaves him bare and exposed to a frightful realization. It is a trauma that a sane and normal mind would be unable to withstand. He begins to dance. A slow, strange dance, eerie and life-giving. A dance of atavistic signature and ritual. Lyons attempts to embrace him. Gabriel pushes Lyons away. He begins to howl in what is an attempt at song, or perhaps a song turning back into itself in an attempt at speech. He finishes his dance and the gates of heaven stand open as wide as God's closet.)*

That's the way that go!

---

## DAVID IVES ■ (b. 1950)

*David Ives grew up on Chicago's South Side, the son of working-class parents, and wrote his first play at the age of nine: "But then I realized you had to have a copy of the script for each person in the play, so that was the end of it." Impressed by theatrical productions he saw in his teens, Ives entered Northwestern University and after graduation attended Yale Drama School. After several attempts to become a "serious writer," he decided to "aspire to silliness on a daily basis" and began creating the short comic plays on which his reputation rests. An evening of six one-act comedies,* All in the Timing, *had a successful off-Broadway production in 1994, running more than two years. In 1996, it was the most performed contemporary play in the nation, and* Sure Thing, *its signature piece, remains popular, especially with student drama groups. A second collection of one acts,* Mere Mortals, *had a successful run at Primary Stages in 1997, and a third collection,* Lives of Saints, *was produced in 1999. A number of his collections—including* All in the Timing *(1995),* Time Flies *(2001), and* Polish Joke and Other Plays *(2004)—have been published. Ives's comedic skills range from a hilarious parody of David Mamet's plays (presented at an event honoring Mamet) to his witty revision of a legendary character in the full-length* Don Juan in Chicago *(1995). His short plays, in many cases, hinge on brilliant theatrical conceits; in* Mayflies, *a boy mayfly and girl mayfly must meet, court, and consummate their relationship before their one day of adult life ends.* Sure Thing, *a piece that plays witty tricks with time, resembles a scene in the Bill Murray film* Groundhog Day, *the script of which was written some years after Ives's play. Among many other activities, Ives has written the books for concert versions of a number of classic American musicals. In an article titled "Why I Shouldn't Write Plays," Ives notes, among other reasons, "All reviews should carry a Surgeon General's warning. The good ones turn your head, the bad ones break your heart."*

# Sure Thing

## *Characters*

Betty
Bill

***Scene:*** *A café.*

*Betty, a woman in her late twenties, is reading at a café table. An empty chair is opposite her. Bill, same age, enters.*

**BILL:**   Excuse me. Is this chair taken?

**BETTY:**   Excuse me?

**BILL:**   Is this taken?

**BETTY:**   Yes it is.

**BILL:**   Oh. Sorry.

**BETTY:**   Sure thing.

> *A bell rings softly.*

**BILL:**   Excuse me. Is this chair taken?

**BETTY:**   Excuse me?

**BILL:**   Is this taken?

**BETTY:**   No, but I'm expecting somebody in a minute.

**BILL:**   Oh. Thanks anyway.

**BETTY:**   Sure thing.

> *A bell rings softly.*

**BILL:**   Excuse me. Is this chair taken?

**BETTY:**   No, but I'm expecting somebody very shortly.

**BILL:**   Would you mind if I sit here till he or she or it comes?

**BETTY** [*glances at her watch*]:   They do seem to be pretty late....

**BILL:**   You never know who you might be turning down.

**BETTY:**   Sorry. Nice try, though.

**BILL:**   Sure thing.

> *Bell.*

Is this seat taken?

**BETTY:**   No it's not.

**BILL:**   Would you mind if I sit here?

**BETTY:**   Yes I would.

**BILL:**   Oh.

> *Bell.*

Is this chair taken?

**BETTY:** No it's not.

**BILL:** Would you mind if I sit here?

**BETTY:** No. Go ahead.

**BILL:** Thanks. [*He sits. She continues reading.*] Everyplace else seems to be taken.

**BETTY:** Mm-hm.

**BILL:** Great place.

**BETTY:** Mm-hm.

**BILL:** What's the book?

**BETTY:** I just wanted to read in quiet, if you don't mind.

**BILL:** No. Sure thing.

    *Bell.*

**BILL:** Everyplace else seems to be taken.

**BETTY:** Mm-hm.

**BILL:** Great place for reading.

**BETTY:** Yes, I like it.

**BILL:** What's the book?

**BETTY:** *The Sound and the Fury.*

**BILL:** Oh. Hemingway.

    *Bell.*

    What's the book?

**BETTY:** *The Sound and the Fury.*

**BILL:** Oh. Faulkner.

**BETTY:** Have you read it?

**BILL:** Not ... actually. I've sure read *about* it, though. It's supposed to be great.

**BETTY:** It is great.

**BILL:** I hear it's great. [*Small pause.*] Waiter?

    *Bell.*

    What's the book?

**BETTY:** *The Sound and the Fury.*

**BILL:** Oh. Faulkner.

**BETTY:** Have you read it?

**BILL:** I'm a Mets fan, myself.

    *Bell.*

**BETTY:** Have you read it?

**BILL:** Yeah, I read it in college.

**BETTY:** Where was college?

**BILL:** I went to Oral Roberts University.

    *Bell.*

**BETTY:**  Where was college?

**BILL:**  I was lying. I never really went to college. I just like to party.

*Bell.*

**BETTY:**  Where was college?

**BILL:**  Harvard.

**BETTY:**  Do you like Faulkner?

**BILL:**  I love Faulkner. I spent a whole winter reading him once.

**BETTY:**  I've just started.

**BILL:**  I was so excited after ten pages that I went out and bought everything else he wrote. One of the greatest reading experiences of my life. I mean, all that incredible psychological understanding. Page after page of gorgeous prose. His profound grasp of the mystery of time and human existence. The smells of the earth ... What do you think?

**BETTY:**  I think it's pretty boring.

*Bell.*

**BILL:**  What's the book?

BETTY:  *The Sound and the Fury.*

**BILL:**  Oh! Faulkner!

**BETTY:**  Do you like Faulkner?

**BILL:**  I love Faulkner.

**BETTY:**  He's incredible.

**BILL:**  I spent a whole winter reading him once.

**BETTY:**  I was so excited after ten pages that I went out and bought everything else he wrote.

**BILL:**  All that incredible psychological understanding.

**BETTY:**  And the prose is so gorgeous.

**BILL:**  And the way he's grasped the mystery of time—

**BETTY:**  —and human existence. I can't believe I've waited this long to read him.

**BILL:**  You never know. You might not have liked him before.

**BETTY:**  That's true.

**BILL:**  You might not have been ready for him. You have to hit these things at the right moment or it's no good.

**BETTY:**  That's happened to me.

**BILL:**  It's all in the timing. [*Small pause.*] My name's Bill, by the way.

**BETTY:**  I'm Betty.

**BILL:**  Hi.

**BETTY:**  Hi. [*Small pause.*]

**BILL:**  Yes I thought reading Faulkner was ... a great experience.

**BETTY:**  Yes. [*Small pause.*]

**BILL:**  *The Sound and the Fury* ... [*Another small pause.*]

**BETTY:**   Well. Onwards and upwards. [*She goes back to her book.*]
**BILL:**   Waiter—?

*Bell.*

You have to hit these things at the right moment or it's no good.
**BETTY:**   That's happened to me.
**BILL:**   It's all in the timing. My name's Bill, by the way.
**BETTY:**   I'm Betty.
**BILL:**   Hi.
**BETTY:**   Hi.
**BILL:**   Do you come in here a lot?
**BETTY:**   Actually I'm just in town for two days from Pakistan.
**BILL:**   Oh. Pakistan.

*Bell.*

My name's Bill, by the way.
**BETTY:**   I'm Betty.
**BILL:**   Hi.
**BETTY:**   Hi.
**BILL:**   Do you come in here a lot?
**BETTY:**   Every once in a while. Do you?
**BILL:**   Not so much anymore. Not as much as I used to. Before my nervous
breakdown.

*Bell.*

Do you come in here a lot?
**BETTY:**   Why are you asking?
**BILL:**   Just interested.
**BETTY:**   Are you really interested, or do you just want to pick me up?
**BILL:**   No, I'm really interested.
**BETTY:**   Why would you be interested in whether I come in here a lot?
**BILL:**   I'm just … getting acquainted.
**BETTY:**   Maybe you're only interested for the sake of making small talk
long enough to ask me back to your place to listen to some music, or
because you've just rented this great tape for your VCR, or because
you've got some terrific unknown Django Reinhardt record, only all
you really want to do is fuck—which you won't do very well—after
which you'll go into the bathroom and pee very loudly, then pad into
the kitchen and get yourself a beer from the refrigerator without
asking me whether I'd like anything, and then you'll proceed to lie
back down beside me and confess that you've got a girlfriend named
Stephanie who's away at medical school in Belgium for a year, and
that you've been involved with her—*off and on*—in what you'll call a
very "intricate" relationship, for the past *seven YEARS*. None of which
*interests* me, mister!

**BILL:** Okay.

*Bell.*

Do you come in here a lot?

**BETTY:** Every other day, I think.

**BILL:** I come in here quite a lot and I don't remember seeing you.

**BETTY:** I guess we must be on different schedules.

**BILL:** Missed connections.

**BETTY:** Yes. Different time zones.

**BILL:** Amazing how you can live right next door to somebody in this town and never even know it.

**BETTY:** I know.

**BILL:** City life.

**BETTY:** It's crazy.

**BILL:** We probably pass each other in the street every day. Right in front of this place, probably.

**BETTY:** Yep.

**BILL** [*looks around*]: Well the waiters here sure seem to be in some different time zone. I can't seem to locate one anywhere.... Waiter! [*He looks back.*] So what do you—[*He sees that she's gone back to her book.*]

**BETTY:** I beg pardon?

**BILL:** Nothing. Sorry.

*Bell.*

**BETTY:** I guess we must be on different schedules.

**BILL:** Missed connections.

**BETTY:** Yes. Different time zones.

**BILL:** Amazing how you can live right next door to somebody in this town and never even know it.

**BETTY:** I know.

**BILL:** City life.

**BETTY:** It's crazy.

**BILL:** You weren't waiting for somebody when I came in, were you?

**BETTY:** Actually I was.

**BILL:** Oh. Boyfriend?

**BETTY:** Sort of.

**BILL:** What's a sort-of boyfriend?

**BETTY:** My husband.

**BILL:** Ah-ha.

*Bell.*

You weren't waiting for somebody when I came in, were you?

**BETTY:** Actually I was.

**BILL:** Oh. Boyfriend?

**BETTY:** Sort of.

**BILL:**   What's a sort-of boyfriend?
**BETTY:**   We were meeting here to break up.
**BILL:**   Mm-hm ...

*Bell.*

What's a sort-of boyfriend?
**BETTY:**   My lover. Here she comes right now!

*Bell.*

**BILL:**   You weren't waiting for somebody when I came in, were you?
**BETTY:**   No, just reading.
**BILL:**   Sort of a sad occupation for a Friday night, isn't it? Reading here, all by yourself?
**BETTY:**   Do you think so?
**BILL:**   Well sure. I mean, what's a good-looking woman like you doing out alone on a Friday night?
**BETTY:**   Trying to keep away from lines like that.
**BILL:**   No, listen—

*Bell.*

You weren't waiting for somebody when I came in, were you?
**BETTY:**   No, just reading.
**BILL:**   Sort of a sad occupation for a Friday night, isn't it? Reading here all by yourself?
**BETTY:**   I guess it is, in a way.
**BILL:**   What's a good-looking woman like you doing out alone on a Friday night anyway? No offense, but ...
**BETTY:**   I'm out alone on a Friday night for the first time in a very long time.
**BILL:**   Oh.
**BETTY:**   You see, I just recently ended a relationship.
**BILL:**   Oh.
**BETTY:**   Of rather long standing.
**BILL:**   I'm sorry. [*Small pause.*] Well listen, since reading by yourself *is* such a sad occupation for a Friday night, would you like to go elsewhere?
**BETTY:**   No ...
**BILL:**   Do something else?
**BETTY:**   No thanks.
**BILL:**   I was headed out to the movies in a while anyway.
**BETTY:**   I don't think so.
**BILL:**   Big chance to let Faulkner catch his breath. All those long sentences get him pretty tired.
**BETTY:**   Thanks anyway.
**BILL:**   Okay.

**BETTY:** I appreciate the invitation.

**BILL:** Sure thing.

*Bell.*

You weren't waiting for somebody when I came in, were you?

**BETTY:** No, just reading.

**BILL:** Sort of a sad occupation for a Friday night, isn't it? Reading here all by yourself?

**BETTY:** I guess I was trying to think of it as existentially romantic. You know—cappuccino, great literature, rainy night ...

**BILL:** That only works in Paris. We *could* hop the late plane to Paris. Get on a Concorde. Find a café ...

**BETTY:** I'm a little short on plane fare tonight.

**BILL:** Darn it, so am I.

**BETTY:** To tell you the truth, I was headed to the movies after I finished this section. Would you like to come along? Since you can't locate a waiter?

**BILL:** That's a very nice offer, but ...

**BETTY:** Uh-huh. Girlfriend?

**BILL:** Two, actually. One of them's pregnant, and Stephanie—

*Bell.*

**BETTY:** Girlfriend?

**BILL:** No, I don't have a girlfriend. Not if you mean the castrating bitch I dumped last night.

*Bell.*

**BETTY:** Girlfriend?

**BILL:** Sort of. Sort of.

**BETTY:** What's a sort-of girlfriend?

**BILL:** My mother.

*Bell.*

I just ended a relationship, actually.

**BETTY:** Oh.

**BILL:** Of rather long standing.

**BETTY:** I'm sorry to hear it.

**BILL:** This is my first night out alone in a long time. I feel a little bit at sea, to tell you the truth.

**BETTY:** So you didn't stop to talk because you're a Moonie, or you have some weird political affiliation—?

**BILL:** Nope. Straight-down-the-ticket Republican.

*Bell.*

Straight-down-the-ticket Democrat.

*Bell.*

Can I tell you something about politics?

*Bell.*

I like to think of myself as a citizen of the universe.

*Bell.*

I'm unaffiliated.

**BETTY:**   That's a relief. So am I.

**BILL:**   I vote my beliefs.

**BETTY:**   Labels are not important.

**BILL:**   Labels are not important, exactly. Take me, for example. I mean, what does it matter if I had a two-point at—

*Bell.*

three-point at—

*Bell.*

four-point at college? Or if I did come from Pittsburgh—

*Bell.*

Cleveland—

*Bell.*

Westchester County?

**BETTY:**   Sure.

**BILL:**   I believe that a man is what he is.

*Bell.*

A person is what he is.

*Bell.*

A person is ... what they are.

**BETTY:**   I think so too.

**BILL:**   So what if I admire Trotsky?

*Bell.*

So what if I once had a total-body liposuction?

*Bell.*

So what if I don't have a penis?

*Bell.*

So what if I spent a year in the Peace Corps? I was acting on my convictions.

**BETTY:**   Sure.

**BILL:**  You just can't hang a sign on a person.
**BETTY:**  Absolutely. I'll bet you're a Scorpio.

*Many bells ring.*

Listen, I was headed to the movies after I finished this section. Would you like to come along?
**BILL:**  That sounds like fun. What's playing?
**BETTY:**  A couple of the really early Woody Allen movies.
**BILL:**  Oh.
**BETTY:**  You don't like Woody Allen?
**BILL:**  Sure. I like Woody Allen.
**BETTY:**  But you're not crazy about Woody Allen.
**BILL:**  Those early ones kind of get on my nerves.
**BETTY:**  Uh-huh.

*Bell.*

**BILL:**  Y'know I was headed to the—
**BETTY** [*simultaneously*]:  I was thinking about—
**BILL:**  I'm sorry.
**BETTY:**  No, go ahead.
**BILL:**  I was going to say that I was headed to the movies in a little while, and ...
**BETTY:**  So was I.
**BILL:**  The Woody Allen festival?
**BETTY:**  Just up the street.
**BILL:**  Do you like the early ones?
**BETTY:**  I think anybody who doesn't ought to be run off the planet.
**BILL:**  How many times have you seen *Bananas?*
**BETTY:**  Eight times.
**BILL:**  Twelve. So are you still interested? [*Long pause.*]
**BETTY:**  Do you like Entenmann's crumb cake ... ?
**BILL:**  Last night I went out at two in the morning to get one. Did you have an Etch-a-Sketch as a child?
**BETTY:**  Yes! And do you like Brussels sprouts? [*Pause.*]
**BILL:**  No, I think they're disgusting.
**BETTY:**  They *are* disgusting!
**BILL:**  Do you still believe in marriage in spite of current sentiments against it?
**BETTY:**  Yes.
**BILL:**  And children?
**BETTY:**  Three of them.
**BILL:**  Two girls and a boy.
**BETTY:**  Harvard, Vassar, and Brown.
**BILL:**  And will you love me?

**BETTY:**   Yes.
**BILL:**   And cherish me forever?
**BETTY:**   Yes.
**BILL:**   Do you still want to go to the movies?
**BETTY:**   Sure thing.
**BILL AND BETTY**   [*together*]:   Waiter!

Blackout

—1988

---

**MILCHA SANCHEZ-SCOTT** ▪ **(b. 1953)**

*Milcha Sanchez-Scott was born in Bali of Indonesian and Colombian parents. She attended school in England and moved to California in her teens. Following college at the University of San Diego, she had her first plays produced in the early 1980s. The* Cuban Swimmer, *first performed in 1984, displays elements of the "magic realism" practiced in fiction by Colombian Nobel Prize–winner Gabriel García Márquez. Her most successful full-length play is* Roosters *(1987), which was made into a 1995 film starring Edward James Olmos.*

# The Cuban Swimmer

## Characters

Margarita Suárez, *the swimmer*
Eduardo Suárez, *her father, the coach*
Simón Suárez, *her brother*
Aída Suárez, *the mother*
Abuela, *her grandmother*
Voice of Mel Munson
Voice of Mary Beth White
Voice of Radio Operator

**Scene:**   *The Pacific Ocean between San Pedro and Catalina Island.*
*Time:*   *Summer.*
*Live conga drums can be used to punctuate the action of the play.*

## Scene I

*Pacific Ocean. Midday. On the horizon, in perspective, a small boat enters upstage left, crosses to upstage right, and exits. Pause. Lower on the horizon, the same boat, in larger perspective, enters upstage right, crosses and exits upstage left. Blackout.*

## Scene II

*Pacific Ocean. Midday. The swimmer, Margarita Suárez, is swimming. On the boat following behind her are her father, Eduardo Suárez, holding a megaphone, and Simón, her brother, sitting on top of the cabin with his shirt off, punk sunglasses on, binoculars hanging on his chest.*

**EDUARDO:**  [*Leaning forward, shouting in time to Margarita's swimming.*] *Uno, dos, uno, dos. Y uno, dos* ... keep your shoulders parallel to the water.

**SIMÓN:**  I'm gonna take these glasses off and look straight into the sun.

**EDUARDO:**  [*Through megaphone.*] *Muy bien, muy bien* ... but punch those arms in, baby.

**SIMÓN:**  [*Looking directly at the sun through binoculars.*] Come on, come on, zap me. Show me something. [*He looks behind at the shoreline and ahead at the sea.*] Stop! Stop, *Papi!* Stop!

*Aída Suárez and Abuela, the swimmer's mother and grandmother, enter running from the back of the boat.*

**AÍDA AND ABUELA:**  *Qué? Qué es?*

**AÍDA:**  *Es un* shark?

**EDUARDO:**  Eh?

**ABUELA:**  *Que es un* shark *dicen?*

*Eduardo blows whistle. Margarita looks up at the boat.*

**SIMÓN:**  No, *Papi*, no shark, no shark. We've reached the halfway mark.

**ABUELA:**  [*Looking into the water.*] *A dónde está?*

**AÍDA:**  It's not in the water.

**ABUELA:**  Oh, no? Oh, no?

**AÍDA:**  No! *A poco* do you think they're gonna have signs in the water to say you are halfway to Santa Catalina? No. It's done very scientific. *A ver, hijo,* explain it to your grandma.

**SIMÓN:**  Well, you see, Abuela—[*He points behind.*] There's San Pedro. [*He points ahead.*] And there's Santa Catalina. Looks halfway to me.

*Abuela shakes her head and is looking back and forth, trying to make the decision, when suddenly the sound of a helicopter is heard.*

**ABUELA:**  [*Looking up.*] Virgencita de la Caridad del Cobre. *Qué es eso?*

*Sound of helicopter gets closer. Margarita looks up.*

**MARGARITA:**  *Papi, Papi!*

*A small commotion on the boat, with Everybody pointing at the helicopter above. Shadows of the helicopter fall on the boat. Simón looks up at it through binoculars.*

Papi—*qué es?* What is it?

**EDUARDO:** [*Through megaphone.*] Uh ... uh ... uh, *un momentico ... mi hija.* ... Your *papi*'s got everything under control, understand? Uh ... you just keep stroking. And stay ... uh ... close to the boat.

**SIMÓN:** Wow, *Papi!* We're on TV, man! Holy Christ, we're all over the fucking U.S.A.! It's Mel Munson and Mary Beth White!

**AÍDA:** *Por Dios!* Simón, don't swear. And put on your shirt.

*Aída fluffs her hair, puts on her sunglasses and waves to the helicopter. Simón leans over the side of the boat and yells to Margarita.*

**SIMÓN:** Yo, Margo! You're on TV, man.

**EDUARDO:** Leave your sister alone. Turn on the radio.

**MARGARITA:** *Papi! Qué está pasando?*

**ABUELA:** *Que es la televisión dicen?* [*She shakes her head.*] *Porque como yo no puedo ver nada sin mis espejuelos.*

*Abuela rummages through the boat, looking for her glasses. Voices of Mel Munson and Mary Beth White are heard over the boat's radio.*

**MEL'S VOICE:** As we take a closer look at the gallant crew of *La Havana* ... and there ... yes, there she is ... the little Cuban swimmer from Long Beach, California, nineteen-year-old Margarita Suárez. The unknown swimmer is our Cinderella entry ... a bundle of tenacity, battling her way through the choppy, murky waters of the cold Pacific to reach the Island of Romance ... Santa Catalina ... where should she be the first to arrive, two thousand dollars and a gold cup will be waiting for her.

**AÍDA:** Doesn't even cover our expenses.

**ABUELA:** *Qué dice?*

**EDUARDO:** Shhhh!

**MARY BETH'S VOICE:** This is really a family effort, Mel, and—

**MEL'S VOICE:** Indeed it is. Her trainer, her coach, her mentor, is her father, Eduardo Suárez. Not a swimmer himself, it says here, Mr. Suárez is head usher of the Holy Name Society and the owner-operator of Suárez Treasures of the Sea and Salvage Yard. I guess it's one of those places—

**MARY BETH'S VOICE:** If I might interject a fact here, Mel, assisting in this swim is Mrs. Suárez, who is a former Miss Cuba.

**MEL'S VOICE:** And a beautiful woman in her own right. Let's try and get a closer look.

*Helicopter sound gets louder. Margarita, frightened, looks up again.*

**MARGARITA:** *Papi!*

**EDUARDO:** [*Through megaphone.*] *Mi hija,* don't get nervous ... it's the press. I'm handling it.

**AÍDA:** I see how you're handling it.

**EDUARDO:** [*Through megaphone.*] Do you hear? Everything is under control. Get back into your rhythm. Keep your elbows high and kick and kick and kick and kick ...

**ABUELA**  [*Finds her glasses and puts them on.*]:    *Ay sí, es la televisión ...* [*She points to helicopter.*] *Qué lindo mira ...* [*She fluffs her hair, gives a big wave.*] *Aló América! Viva mi Margarita, viva todo los Cubanos en los Estados Unidos!*

**AÍDA:**  *Ay por Dios,* Cecilia, the man didn't come all this way in his helicopter to look at you jumping up and down, making a fool of yourself.

**ABUELA:**  I don't care. I'm proud.

**AÍDA:**  He can't understand you anyway.

**ABUELA:**  *Viva ...* [*She stops.*] Simón, *cómo se dice viva?*

**SIMÓN:**  Hurray.

**ABUELA:**  Hurray for *mi Margarita y* for all the Cubans living *en* the United States, *y un abrazo ...* Simón, *abrazo ...*

**SIMÓN:**  A big hug.

**ABUELA:**  *Sí,* a big hug to all my friends in Miami, Long Beach, Union City, except for my son Carlos, who lives in New York in sin! He lives ... [*She crosses herself.*] in Brooklyn with a Puerto Rican woman in sin! *No decente ...*

**SIMÓN:**  Decent.

**ABUELA:**  Carlos, *no decente.* This family, *decente.*

**AÍDA:**  Cecilia, *por Dios.*

**MEL'S VOICE:**  Look at that enthusiasm. The whole family has turned out to cheer little Margarita on to victory! I hope they won't be too disappointed.

**MARY BETH'S VOICE:**  She seems to be making good time, Mel.

**MEL'S VOICE:**  Yes, it takes all kinds to make a race. And it's a testimonial to the all-encompassing fairness ... the greatness of this, the Wrigley Invitational Women's Swim to Catalina, where among all the professionals there is still room for the amateurs ... like these, the simple people we see below us on the ragtag *La Havana,* taking their long-shot chance to victory. *Vaya con Dios!*

*Helicopter sound fading as family, including Margarita, watch silently. Static as Simón turns radio off. Eduardo walks to bow of boat, looks out on the horizon.*

**EDUARDO:**  [*To himself.*] Amateurs.

**AÍDA:**  Eduardo, that person insulted us. Did you hear, Eduardo? That he called us a simple people in a ragtag boat? Did you hear ...?

**ABUELA**  [*Clenching her fist at departing helicopter.*]:    *Mal-Rayo los parta!*

**SIMÓN:**  [*Same gesture.*] Asshole!

*Aída follows Eduardo as he goes to side of boat and stares at Margarita.*

**AÍDA:**  This person comes in his helicopter to insult your wife, your family, your daughter ...

**MARGARITA** [*POPS HER HEAD OUT OF THE WATER.*]:    *Papi?*

**AÍDA:**  Do you hear me, Eduardo? I am not simple.

**ABUELA:**  *Sí.*

**AÍDA:**  I am complicated.

**ABUELA:**  *Sí, demasiada complicada.*

**AÍDA:**  Me and my family are not so simple.

**SIMÓN:**  Mom, the guy's an asshole.

**ABUELA**  [*Shaking her fist at helicopter.*]:  Asshole!

**AÍDA:**  If my daughter was simple, she would not be in that water swimming.

**MARGARITA:**  Simple? *Papi* ...?

**AÍDA:**  *Ahora,* Eduardo, this is what I want you to do. When we get to Santa Catalina, I want you to call the TV station and demand an apology.

**EDUARDO:**  *Cállete mujer! Aquí mando yo.* I will decide what is to be done.

**MARGARITA:**  *Papi,* tell me what's going on.

**EDUARDO:**  Do you understand what I am saying to you, Aída?

**SIMÓN**  [*Leaning over side of boat, to Margarita.*]:  Yo Margo! You know that Mel Munson guy on TV? He called you a simple amateur and said you didn't have a chance.

**ABUELA**  [*Leaning directly behind Simón.*]:  *Mi hija, insultó a la familia. Desgraciado!*

**AÍDA**  [*Leaning in behind Abuela.*]:  He called us peasants! And your father is not doing anything about it. He just knows how to yell at me.

**EDUARDO**  [*Through megaphone.*]:  Shut up! All of you! Do you want to break her concentration? Is that what you are after? Eh?

*Abuela, Aída, and Simón shrink back. Eduardo paces before them.*

Swimming is rhythm and concentration. You win a race *aquí.* [*Pointing to his head.*] Now ... [*To Simón.*] you, take care of the boat, Aída y Mama ... do something. Anything. Something practical. *Abuela and Aída get on knees and pray in Spanish.*

*Hija,* give it everything, eh? ... *por la familia. Uno ... dos....* You must win.

*Simón goes into cabin. The prayers continue as lights change to indicate bright sunlight, later in the afternoon.*

## Scene III

*Tableau for a couple of beats. Eduardo on bow with timer in one hand as he counts strokes per minute. Simón is in the cabin steering, wearing his sunglasses, baseball cap on backward. Abuela and Aída are at the side of the boat, heads down, hands folded, still muttering prayers in Spanish.*

**AÍDA AND ABUELA:**  [*Crossing themselves.*] *En el nombre del Padre, del Hijo y del Espíritu Santo amén.*

**EDUARDO:**  [*Through megaphone.*] You're stroking seventy-two!

**SIMÓN:**  [*Singing.*] Mama's stroking, Mama's stroking seventy-two....

**EDUARDO:** [*Through megaphone.*] You comfortable with it?

**SIMÓN:** [*Singing.*] Seventy-two, seventy-two, seventy-two for you.

**AÍDA:** [*Looking at the heavens.*] Ay, Eduardo, *ven acá*, we should be grateful that *Nuestro Señor* gave us such a beautiful day.

**ABUELA:** [*Crosses herself.*] *Sí, gracias a Dios.*

**EDUARDO:** She's stroking seventy-two, with no problem [*He throws a kiss to the sky.*] It's a beautiful day to win.

**AÍDA:** *Qué hermoso!* So clear and bright. Not a cloud in the sky. *Mira! Mira!* Even rainbows on the water ... a sign from God.

**SIMÓN:** [*Singing.*] Rainbows on the water ... you in my arms ...

**ABUELA AND EDUARDO:** [*Looking the wrong way.*] *Dónde?*

**AÍDA:** [*Pointing toward Margarita.*] There, dancing in front of margarita, leading her on ...

**EDUARDO:** Rainbows on ... *Ay coño!* It's an oil slick! You ... you ... [*To Simón.*] Stop the boat. [*Runs to bow, yelling.*] Margarita! Margarita!

*On the next stroke, Margarita comes up all covered in black oil.*

**MARGARITA:** *Papi! Papi ... !*

*Everybody goes to the side and stares at Margarita, who stares back. Eduardo freezes.*

**AÍDA:** *Apúrate*, Eduardo, move ... what's wrong with you ... *no me oíste*, get my daughter out of the water.

**EDUARDO:** [*Softly.*] We can't touch her. If we touch her, she's disqualified.

**AÍDA:** But I'm her mother.

**EDUARDO:** Not even by her own mother. Especially by her own mother.... You always want the rules to be different for you, you always want to be the exception. [*To Simón.*] And you ... you didn't see it, eh? You were playing again?

**SIMÓN:** *Papi,* I was watching ...

**AÍDA:** [*Interrupting.*] *Pues,* do something Eduardo. You are the big coach, the monitor.

**SIMÓN:** Mentor! Mentor!

**EDUARDO:** How can a person think around you? [*He walks off to bow, puts head in hands.*]

**ABUELA:** [*Looking over side.*] *Mira como todos los* little birds are dead. [*She crosses herself.*]

**AÍDA:** Their little wings are glued to their sides.

**SIMÓN:** Christ, this is like the La Brea tar pits.

**AÍDA:** They can't move their little wings.

**ABUELA:** *Esa niña tiene que moverse.*

**SIMÓN:** Yeah, Margo, you gotta move, man.

*Abuela and Simón gesture for Margarita to move. Aída gestures for her to swim.*

**ABUELA:**    *Anda niña, muévete.*

**AÍDA:**    Swim, *hija,* swim or the *aceite* will stick to your wings.

**MARGARITA:**    *Papi?*

**ABUELA:**    [*Taking megaphone.*] Your *papi* say "move it!"

*Margarita with difficulty starts moving.*

**ABUELA, AÍDA AND SIMÓN**    [*Laboriously counting.*]:    *Uno, dos ... uno, dos ... anda ... uno, dos.*

**EDUARDO:**    [*Running to take megaphone from Abuela.*] *Uno, dos ...*

*Simón races into cabin and starts the engine. Abuela, Aída and Eduardo count together.*

**SIMÓN:**    [*Looking ahead.*] *Papi,* it's over there!

**EDUARDO:**    Eh?

**SIMÓN:**    [*Pointing ahead and to the right.*] It's getting clearer over there.

**EDUARDO:**    [*Through megaphone.*] Now pay attention to me. Go to the right.

*Simón, Abuela, Aída and Eduardo all lean over side. They point ahead and to the right, except Abuela, who points to the left.*

**FAMILY:**    [*Shouting together.*] *Para yá! Para yá!*

*Lights go down on boat. A special light on Margarita, swimming through the oil, and on Abuela, watching her.*

**ABUELA:**    *Sangre de mi sangre,* you will be another to save us. En Bolondron, where your great-grandmother Luz Suárez was born, they say one day it rained blood. All the people, they run into their houses. They cry, they pray, *pero* your great-grandmother Luz she had cojones like a man. She run outside. She look straight at the sky. She shake her fist. And she say to the evil one, "*Mira* ... [*Beating her chest.*] *coño, Diablo, aquí estoy si me quieres.*" And she open her mouth, and she drunk the blood.

*Blackout.*

## Scene IV

*Lights up on boat. Aída and Eduardo are on deck watching Margarita swim. We hear the gentle, rhythmic lap, lap, lap of the water, then the sound of inhaling and exhaling as Margarita's breathing becomes louder. Then Margarita's heartbeat is heard, with the lapping of the water and the breathing under it. These sounds continue beneath the dialogue to the end of the scene.*

**AÍDA:**    *Dios mío.* Look how she moves through the water....

**EDUARDO:**    You see, it's very simple. It is a matter of concentration.

**AÍDA:**    The first time I put her in water she came to life, she grew before my eyes. She moved, she smiled, she loved it more than me. She didn't want my breast any longer. She wanted the water.

**EDUARDO:**  And of course, the rhythm. The rhythm takes away the pain and helps the concentration.

*Pause. Aída and Eduardo watch Margarita.*

**AÍDA:**  Is that my child or a seal....

**EDUARDO:**  Ah, a seal, the reason for that is that she's keeping her arms very close to her body. She cups her hands, and then she reaches and digs, reaches and digs.

**AÍDA:**  To think that a daughter of mine....

**EDUARDO:**  It's the training, the hours in the water. I used to tie weights around her little wrists and ankles.

**AÍDA:**  A spirit, an ocean spirit, must have entered my body when I was carrying her.

**EDUARDO:**  [*To Margarita.*] Your stroke is slowing down.

*Pause. We hear Margarita's heartbeat with the breathing under, faster now.*

**AÍDA:**  Eduardo, that night, the night on the boat...

**EDUARDO:**  Ah, the night on the boat again ... the moon was ...

**AÍDA:**  The moon was full. We were coming to America.... *Qué romantico.*

*Heartbeat and breathing continue.*

**EDUARDO:**  We were cold, afraid, with no money, and on top of everything, you were hysterical, yelling at me, tearing at me with your nails. [*Opens his shirt, points to the base of his neck.*] Look, I still bear the scars ... telling me that I didn't know what I was doing ... saying that we were going to die....

**AÍDA:**  You took me, you stole me from my home ... you didn't give me a chance to prepare. You just said we have to go now, now! Now, you said. You didn't let me take anything. I left everything behind.... I left everything behind.

**EDUARDO:**  Saying that I wasn't good enough, that your father didn't raise you so that I could drown you in the sea.

**AÍDA:**  You didn't let me say even a good-bye. You took me, you stole me, you tore me from my home.

**EDUARDO:**  I took you so we could be married.

**AÍDA:**  That was in Miami. But that night on the boat, Eduardo.... We were not married, that night on the boat.

**EDUARDO:**  *No pasó nada!* Once and for all get it out of your head, it was cold, you hated me, and we were afraid....

AÍDA:  *Mentiroso!*

**EDUARDO:**  A man can't do it when he is afraid.

**AÍDA:**  Liar! You did it very well.

**EDUARDO:**  I did?

**AÍDA:** *Sí.* Gentle. You were so gentle and then strong … my passion for you so deep. Standing next to you … I would ache … looking at your hands I would forget to breathe, you were irresistible.

**EDUARDO:** I was?

**AÍDA:** You took me into your arms, you touched my face with your finger-tips … you kissed my eyes … *la esquina de la boca y …*

**EDUARDO:** *Sí, Sí,* and then …

**AÍDA:** I look at your face on top of mine, and I see the lights of Havana in your eyes. That's when you seduced me.

**EDUARDO:** Shhh, they're gonna hear you.

*Lights go down. Special on Aída.*

**AÍDA:** That was the night. A woman doesn't forget those things … and later that night was the dream … the dream of a big country with fields of fertile land and big, giant things growing. And there by a green, slimy pond I found a giant pea pod and when I opened it, it was full of little, tiny baby frogs.

*Aída crosses herself as she watches Margarita. We hear louder breathing and heartbeat.*

**MARGARITA:** Santa Teresa. Little Flower of God, pray for me. San Martín de Porres, pray for me. Santa Rosa de Lima, *Virgencita de la Caridad del Cobre,* pray for me.… Mother pray for me.

## Scene V

*Loud howling of wind is heard, as lights change to indicate unstable weather, fog, and mist. Family on deck, braced and huddled against the wind. Simón is at the helm.*

**AÍDA:** *Ay Dios mío, qué viento.*

**EDUARDO:** [*Through megaphone.*] Don't drift out … that wind is pushing you out. [*To Simón.*] You! Slow down. Can't you see your sister is drift-ing out?

**SIMÓN:** It's the wind, *Papi.*

**AÍDA:** Baby, don't go so far.…

**ABUELA:** [*To heaven.*] *Ay Gran Poder de Dios, quita este maldito viento.*

**SIMÓN:** Margo! Margo! Stay close to the boat.

**EDUARDO:** Dig in. Dig in hard . .…Reach down from your guts and dig in.

**ABUELA:** [*To heaven.*] *Ay Virgen de la Caridad del Cobre, por lo más tú quieres a pararla.*

**AÍDA:** [*Putting her hand out, reaching for Margarita.*] Baby, don't go far.

*Abuela crosses herself. Action freezes. Lights get dimmer, special on Margarita. She keeps swimming, stops, starts again, stops, then, finally exhausted, stops altogether. The boat stops moving.*

**EDUARDO:** What's going on here? Why are we stopping?

**SIMÓN:** *Papi,* she's not moving! Yo Margo!

*The family all run to the side.*

**EDUARDO:** *Hija!* ... *Hijita!* You're tired, eh?

**AÍDA:** *Por supuesto* she's tired. I like to see you get in the water, waving your arms and legs from San Pedro to Santa Catalina. A person isn't a machine, a person has to rest.

**SIMÓN:** Yo, Mama! Cool out, it ain't fucking brain surgery.

**EDUARDO:** [*To Simón.*] Shut up, you. [*Louder to Margarita.*] I guess your mother's right for once, huh? ... I guess you had to stop, eh? ... Give your brother, the idiot ... a chance to catch up with you.

**SIMÓN:** [*Clowning like Mortimer Snerd.*] Dum dee dum dee dum ooops, ah shucks ...

**EDUARDO:** I don't think he's Cuban.

**SIMÓN:** [*Like Ricky Ricardo.*] *Oye,* Lucy! I'm home! Ba ba lu!

**EDUARDO:** [*Joins in clowning, grabbing Simón in a headlock.*] What am I gonna do with this idiot, eh? I don't understand this idiot. He's not like us, Margarita. [*Laughing.*] You think if we put him into your bathing suit with a cap on his head ... [*He laughs hysterically.*] You think any-one would know ... huh? Do you think anyone would know? [*Laughs.*]

**SIMÓN:** [*Vamping.*] *Ay, mi amor.* Anybody looking for tits would know.

*Eduardo slaps Simón across the face, knocking him down. Aída runs to Simón's aid. Abuela holds Eduardo back.*

**MARGARITA:** *Mía culpa! Mía culpa!*

**ABUELA:** *Qué dices hija?*

**MARGARITA:** *Papi,* it's my fault, it's all my fault.... I'm so cold, I can't move.... I put my face in the water ... and I hear them whispering ... laughing at me....

**AÍDA:** Who is laughing at you?

**MARGARITA:** The fish are all biting me ... they hate me ... they whis-per about me. She can't swim, they say. She can't glide. She has no grace.... Yellowtails, bonita, tuna, man-o'-war, snub-nose sharks, *los baracudas* ... they all hate me ... only the dolphins care ... and some-times I hear the whales crying ... she is lost, she is dead. I'm so numb, I can't feel. *Papi! Papi!* Am I dead?

**EDUARDO:** *Vamos,* baby, punch those arms in. Come on ... do you hear me?

**MARGARITA:** *Papi* ... *Papi* ... forgive me....

*All is silent on the boat. Eduardo drops his megaphone, his head bent down in dejection. Abuela, Aída, Simón, all leaning over the side of the boat. Simón slowly walks away.*

**AÍDA:** *Mi hija, qué tienes?*

**SIMÓN:** Oh, Christ, don't make her say it. Please don't make her say it.

**ABUELA:** Say what? *Qué cosa?*

**SIMÓN:** She wants to quit, can't you see she's had enough?

**ABUELA:** *Mira, para eso. Esta niña* is turning blue.

**AÍDA:** *Oyeme, mi hija.* Do you want to come out of the water?

**MARGARITA:** *Papi?*

**SIMÓN:** [*To Eduardo.*] She won't come out until *you* tell her.

**AÍDA:** Eduardo ... answer your daughter.

**EDUARDO:** *Le dije* to concentrate ... concentrate on your rhythm. Then the rhythm would carry her ... ay, it's a beautiful thing, Aída. It's like yoga, like meditation, the mind over matter ... the mind controlling the body ... that's how the great things in the world have been done. I wish you ... I wish my wife could understand.

**MARGARITA:** *Papi?*

**SIMÓN:** [*To Margarita.*] Forget him.

**AÍDA:** [*Imploring.*] Eduardo, *por favor.*

**EDUARDO:** [*Walking in circles.*] Why didn't you let her concentrate? Don't you understand, the concentration, the rhythm is everything. But no, you wouldn't listen. [*Screaming to the ocean.*] Goddamn Cubans, why, God, why do you make us go everywhere with our families? [*He goes to back of boat.*]

**AÍDA:** [*Opening her arms.*] *Mi hija, ven,* come to *Mami.* [*Rocking.*] Your *mami* knows.

*Abuela has taken the training bottle, puts it in a net. She and Simón lower it to Margarita.*

**SIMÓN:** Take this. Drink it. [*As Margarita drinks, Abuela crosses herself.*]

**ABUELA:** *Sangre de mi sangre.*

*Music comes up softly. Margarita drinks, gives the bottle back, stretches out her arms, as if on a cross. Floats on her back. She begins a graceful backstroke. Lights fade on boat as special lights come up on Margarita. She stops. Slowly turns over and starts to swim, gradually picking up speed. Suddenly as if in pain she stops, tries again, then stops in pain again. She becomes disoriented and falls to the bottom of the sea. Special on Margarita at the bottom of the sea.*

**MARGARITA:** *Ya no puedo* ... I can't.... A person isn't a machine ... *es mi culpa* ... Father forgive me ... *Papi! Papi!* One, two. *Uno, dos.* [*Pause.*] *Papi! A dónde estás?* [*Pause.*] One, two, one, two. *Papi! Ay, Papi!* Where are you ...? Don't leave me.... Why don't you answer me? [*Pause. She starts to swim, slowly.*] *Uno, dos, uno, dos.* Dig in, dig in. [*Stops swimming.*] *Por favor, Papi!* [*Starts to swim again.*] One, two, one, two. Kick from your hip, kick from your hip. [*Stops swimming. Starts to cry.*] Oh

God, please.... [*Pause.*] Hail Mary, full of grace ... dig in, dig in ... the Lord is with thee.... [*She swims to the rhythm of her Hail Mary.*] Hail Mary, full of grace ... dig in, dig in ... the Lord is with thee ... dig in, dig in.... Blessed art thou among women.... *Mami*, it hurts. You let go of my hand. I'm lost.... And blessed is the fruit of thy womb, now and at the hour of our death. Amen. I don't want to die, I don't want to die.

*Margarita is still swimming. Blackout. She is gone.*

## Scene VI

*Lights up on boat, we hear radio static. There is a heavy mist. On deck we see only black outline of Abuela with shawl over her head. We hear the voices of Eduardo, Aída, and Radio Operator.*

**EDUARDO'S VOICE:** *La Havana!* Coming from San Pedro. Over.

**RADIO OPERATOR'S VOICE:** Right, DT6-6, you say you've lost a swimmer.

**AÍDA'S VOICE:** Our child, our only daughter ... listen to me. Her name is Margarita Inez Suárez, she is wearing a black one-piece bathing suit cut high in the legs with a white racing stripe down the sides, a white bathing cap with goggles and her whole body covered with a ... with a ...

**EDUARDO'S VOICE:** With lanolin and paraffin.

**AÍDA'S VOICE:** *Sí ... con lanolin and paraffin.*

*More radio static. Special on Simón, on the edge of the boat.*

**SIMÓN:** Margo! Yo Margo! [*Pause.*] Man don't do this. [*Pause.*] Come on.... Come on.... [*Pause.*] God, why does everything have to be so hard? [*Pause.*] Stupid. You know you're not supposed to die for this. Stupid. It's his dream and he can't even swim. [*Pause.*] Punch those arms in. Come home. Come home. I'm your little brother. Don't forget what Mama said. You're not supposed to leave me behind. *Vamos*, Margarita, take your little brother, hold his hand tight when you cross the street. He's so little. [*Pause.*] Oh Christ, give us a sign.... I know! I know! Margo, I'll send you a message ... like mental telepathy. I'll hold my breath, close my eyes, and I'll bring you home. [*He takes a deep breath; a few beats.*] This time I'll beep ... I'll send out sonar signals like a dolphin. [*He imitates dolphin sounds.*]

*The sound of real dolphins takes over from Simón, then fades into sound of Abuela saying the Hail Mary in Spanish, as full lights come up slowly.*

## Scene VII

*Eduardo coming out of cabin, sobbing, Aída holding him. Simón anxiously scanning the horizon. Abuela looking calmly ahead.*

**EDUARDO:**  Es mi culpa, sí, es mi culpa. [He hits his chest.]

**AÍDA:**  *Ya, ya viejo.* ... it was my sin ... I left my home.

**EDUARDO:**  Forgive me, forgive me. I've lost our daughter, our sister, our granddaughter, *mi carne, mi sangre, mis ilusiones.* [*To heaven.*] *Dios mío,* take me ... take me, I say ... Goddammit, take me!

**SIMÓN:**  I'm going in.

**AÍDA AND EDUARDO:**  No!

**EDUARDO** [*Grabbing and holding Simón, speaking to heaven*]:  God, take me, not my children. They are my dreams, my illusions ... and not this one, this one is my mystery ... he has my secret dreams. In him are the parts of me I cannot see.

*Eduardo embraces Simón. Radio static becomes louder.*

**AÍDA:**  I ... I think I see her.

**SIMÓN:**  No, it's just a seal.

**ABUELA** [*Looking out with binoculars.*]:  *Mi nietacita, dónde estás?* [*She feels her heart.*] I don't feel the knife in my heart ... my little fish is not lost.

*Radio crackles with static. As lights dim on boat, Voices of Mel and Mary Beth are heard over the radio.*

**MEL'S VOICE:**  Tragedy has marred the face of the Wrigley Invitational Women's Race to Catalina. The Cuban swimmer, little Margarita Suárez, has reportedly been lost at sea. Coast Guard and divers are looking for her as we speak. Yet in spite of this tragedy the race must go on because ...

**MARY BETH'S VOICE:**  [*Interrupting loudly.*] Mel!

**MEL'S VOICE:**  [*Startled.*] What!

**MARY BETH'S VOICE:**  Ah ... excuse me, Mel ... we have a winner. We've just received word from Catalina that one of the swimmers is just fifty yards from the breakers ... it's, oh, it's ... Margarita Suárez!

*Special on family in cabin listening to radio.*

**MEL'S VOICE:**  What? I thought she died!

*Special on Margarita, taking off bathing cap, trophy in hand, walking on the water.*

**MARY BETH'S VOICE:**  Ahh ... unless ... unless this is a tragic ... No ... there she is, Mel. Margarita Suárez! The only one in the race wearing a black bathing suit cut high in the legs with a racing stripe down the side.

*Family cheering, embracing.*

**SIMÓN:**  [*Screaming.*]Way to go, Margo!

**MEL'S VOICE:**  This is indeed a miracle! It's a resurrection! Margarita Suárez, with a flotilla of boats to meet her, is now walking on the waters, through the breakers … onto the beach, with crowds of people cheering her on. What a jubilation! This is a miracle!

*Sound of crowds cheering. Lights and cheering sounds fade.*

*Blackout.*

*—1984*

# Writing About Literature

## First Considerations

You are in your first college-level literature class, and you have probably already completed a composition course in which you used different organizational schemes—example and illustration, comparison and contrast, cause and effect—in writing five-hundred-word essays that were drawn largely from your own personal experiences. When your first effort was returned by your instructor with a bewildering array of correction symbols and a grade that was lower than any you had ever received for your writing, you were at first discouraged. But then you noticed your classmates also shaking their heads in dismay, and you realized that there were certain skills that you would have to learn if you were ever going to get out of English Composition I. You corrected your spelling errors; matched your instructor's grading symbols to those in your handbook; revised mistakes in usage, punctuation, and grammar; and polished your first draft and handed it in again. This time, when it was returned, you were pleased to find fewer correction marks and a couple of encouraging bits of praise in your margins. If you weren't exactly assured that you had permanently mastered every fine point of composition, at least you now had some hope that, with practice, hard work, and careful application of the skills you were learning, your writing would improve and the improvement would be rewarded.

Everyone has been there. Even your instructor was once a student in a first-year writing class, and very few instructors are candid enough to have preserved their own early writing efforts to display to their students. But the problem is no longer your instructor's. She has survived the process to acquire an advanced degree, and her job now is teaching you the writing skills that she has acquired. You have some confidence in your own ability, but you also have begun to suspect that writing about literature is quite a bit more demanding than writing about your own life. An introduction to literature course places equal weight on your demonstrated skills as a writer and on your ability to go beyond what you have discussed in the classroom to formulate critical responses to the works that you have read. You may have written thesis papers and completed research projects that you were assigned in high school, but you still do not feel entirely confident about your ability to write about literature. You enjoy reading stories, poems, and plays, but you may find expressing your thoughts about their meaning or their literary merit intimidating. With these thoughts in mind, here are a few general strategies that may help you write successful critical papers.

## Topic into Thesis

Writing assignments differ greatly, and your instructions may range from general (**Discuss the roles of three minor characters in any of the plays we have read**) to very specific (**Contrast, in not less than five hundred words, the major differences in the plot, characterization, and setting between Joyce Carol Oates's short story "Where Are You Going, Where Have You Been?" and Joyce Chopra's** *Smooth Talk,* **the 1985 film version of the story**). In some cases, especially in essay-type examinations, your instructor may give the whole class the same topic; in others, you may be allowed considerable freedom in selecting one. Length requirements may range from a single paragraph to the standard five-hundred-word theme (in some cases, written during a single class period) to a full-scale research paper of three or four times that length. The assignment will probably ask you to support your assertions with quotes from the story, poem, or play, or it may require that you add further supporting evidence from secondary critical sources. There is no way to predict the precise kinds of papers you may have to write in a literature course; however, there are a few simple guidelines to remember that may help you make the prewriting process easier.

Consider a typical assignment for an essay on poetry: **Discuss any three poems in our textbook that share a similar theme.** Although this is a topic that allows you some latitude in selecting the poems you wish to write about, paradoxically it is just this type of assignment that may cause you the most distress. Why is this so? Simply because there are more than three hundred poems in this book, and it is usually impossible for the typical class to cover more than a fraction of that number in the time allotted during the semester to the study of poetry. Before despairing, however, consider the different ways the topic could be limited. Instead of "three poems," you might narrow the field by selecting a more specific group, for example, "three ballads," "three war poems," or "three poems by contemporary African American poets." Suppose you settle on a group that is limited yet still allows some selection. Choosing "three sonnets by Shakespeare" would allow you to pick from a total of six sonnets included here. In the same way, the second half of the assignment, to find three sonnets with a similar theme, can be limited in various ways. After reading the sonnets, you might observe that #18, #20, and #30 deal with friendship; after further consideration, you might decide that #116, because it deals with a "marriage of true minds," is also about a type of friendship. Reading the same group of sonnets a second time, you might be struck by how #18, #73, and #130 deal with physical beauty and its loss. Or, a third time, you might notice that #29, #30, and #73 all possess a depressed tone that sometimes verges on self-pity. After weighing your options and deciding which three sonnets you feel most comfortable discussing, you might formulate a thesis sentence: "In three of his sonnets, Shakespeare stresses that ideal love should be based on more than mere physical beauty." Always keep in mind that the process of choosing, limiting, and developing a topic and thesis sentence should follow the same steps that you practiced in earlier composition courses. As an aid to locating stories, poems, and plays that share similarities, you will find at the end of this book an appendix that groups works thematically.

What is next? A certain amount of informal preparation is always useful: "brainstorming" by taking notes on random ideas and refining those ideas further through discussing them with your peers and instructor. Many composition and introduction to literature courses now include group discussion and peer review of rough drafts as part of the writing process. Even if your class does not use formal group discussion as part of its prewriting activities, there is still nothing to prevent you from talking over your ideas with your classmates or scheduling a conference with your instructor. The conference, especially, is a good idea, as it allows you to get a clearer sense of what is expected from you. In many cases, after a conference with your instructor, you may discover that you could have limited your topic even further or that you could have selected other more pertinent examples to support your thesis.

## Explication, Analysis, Reviewing

In general, writing assignments on literature fall into three broad categories: explication, analysis, and reviewing. Explication, which literally means "an unfolding" and is also known as "close reading," is a painstaking analysis of the details of a piece of writing. Because of its extremely limited focus—only on the specific words that the author uses—explication is a consistent favorite for writing assignments on individual poems. In such assignments, the writer attempts to discuss every possible nuance of meaning that a poet has employed. The most useful aid to explication is the dictionary; a full-scale assignment of this type may even involve using the multivolume *Oxford English Dictionary* to demonstrate how a word in a poem may have once possessed a meaning different from what it presently has or to support your contention that a phrase may have several possible meanings. Explication assignments are also possible in writing about fiction and drama. You might be expected to focus closely on a single short passage from a story, for example, explicating the passages describing Arnold Friend in Joyce Carol Oates's "Where Are You Going, Where Have You Been?"; or you might be limited to one scene from a play, being asked to discuss how Othello's speeches in act 1, scene 3 reveal both his strengths of character and the weaknesses that will prove his undoing. There are many useful critical sources to support assignments of this type, and some of them are mentioned later in the section on research methods.

Analysis uses the same general techniques of explication, that is, the use of specific details from the text to support your statements. But where explication attempts to exhaust the widest possible range of meanings, analysis is more selective in its focus, requiring that you examine how a single element—a theme, a technique, a structural device—functions in a single work or in a related group of works. Instead of being assigned to explicate Thomas Gray's "Elegy Written in a Country Churchyard" (a formidable task given its length), you might be asked to analyze only the poet's use of various figures of speech or to examine his imagery or to focus exclusively on the structure of the verse form. Analysis assignments often take the form of comparison-contrast essays (**Compare and contrast the sacrifices and motivations for them of the female protagonists of "Mother Savage" and "Where Are You Going, Where Have You Been?"**) or essays that combine definition with example-illustration (**Define the ballad and discuss ballads written by three poets born since 1900, showing their links to the tradition of this type of poem**). In the case of these examples, general reference books such as William Harmon and C. Hugh Holman's *A Handbook to Literature* or the exhaustive *The New Princeton Encyclopedia of Poetry and Poetics* will help you establish your definitions and an overall context for your examples.

The third category, reviewing, is less common in introductory literature courses. A review is a firsthand reaction to a performance or a publication and combines literary analysis with the techniques of journalism. A review of a play or film would evaluate the theatrical elements—acting, direction, sets, and so on—of the performance. Reviews are largely descriptive reporting, but they also should provide evaluation and recommendation. Many of the stories and plays in this volume have been filmed, and you could be asked to discuss how one of them has been adapted for a different medium. Even a local production of a play that you are reading in class is a possibility, and you might find yourself jotting down notes on how the outgoing young woman who sits beside you in a chemistry lab has transformed herself into the role of Williams's Laura. It is even possible that you might find yourself reviewing a public reading given by a poet or fiction writer whose works you first encountered in this book, and you may find yourself commenting on the distance between the image that the writer projects in the poems or stories and his or her actual "stage presence" as a performer. On the purely literary side, book reviews of new collections of stories and poems regularly appear in periodicals such as the *Hudson Review* or the literary sections of major newspapers (the *New York Times Book Review*, published as a separate section of the Sunday *Times*, is the most comprehensive of these), and it is simple enough to find many excellent models should you be assigned to write a paper of this type.

One last word of warning: Note that there are no primarily biographical essays about authors listed as possible writing assignments. Research assignments may ask you to discuss how the particular circumstances of a writer's life may have influenced his or her works, but for the most part biographical information should reside in the background, not the foreground, of literary analysis. An explication of a single poem that begins "Richard Wilbur was born in 1921 in New York City ..." gives the erroneous impression that you are writing about the poet's life instead of about his work. Try to find a more direct (and original) way of opening your paper.

## Critical Approaches

Although most instructors of introduction to literature classes stress a formalist approach (or "close reading") to literary works, other instructors may lecture from a distinct critical perspective and ask their students to employ these techniques in their writing. You might be encouraged to apply a certain kind of critical strategy—feminist criticism or a type of historical approach—to the works you have studied. An instructor might stress that you should emphasize the socioeconomic situation and concerns of a fiction writer and her or his characters. Or you may be asked to explore how female poets employ visual images that differ from those used by males. Appendix B, Literature: Thematic and Critical Approaches, provides suggestions about how works may be grouped together for analysis using various critical methods. Here you will find some brief notes on six of the most often used areas of literary criticism and some advice on how to use the thematic listings to find stories, poems, and plays that might best profit from analysis that employs a specific critical approach. Applying complicated critical theories to individual works is a demanding assignment, and frequent instructor–student conferences may not just be helpful, they may be essential.

## Style and Content

Style is the major stumbling block that many students find in writing an effective piece of literary analysis. Aware perhaps that their vocabularies and sentence structures are less sophisticated than those found in the primary and secondary materials being discussed, they sometimes try to overcompensate by adopting, usually without much success, the language of professional critics. This practice can result in garbled sentences and jargon-filled writing. It is much better to write simple, direct sentences, avoiding slang and contractions and using only words with which you are familiar.

Writing in a style with which you are comfortable allows you to make clear transitions between your own writing and the sources that you are citing for supporting evidence. In introducing a quote from a critic, use a phrase such as "As so-and-so notes in his essay on …" to guide the reader from your own style into one that is very different. Never include a statement from a critical work that you do not understand yourself, and do not hesitate to go on for a sentence or two after a supporting quote to explain it in your own words. Remember that literary criticism has its own technical vocabulary and that many of these literary terms are discussed elsewhere in this book. Accepted literary terminology should be used instead of homemade substitutes. Thus, to talk about the "highpoint of the story line" instead of "the climax of the plot" or the "style of the rhythm and rhyme" instead of "the formal strategies of the poem" is to invite an unfavorable response.

As far as the content of your paper is concerned, try to avoid eccentric personal responses for which you can find no critical support. This rule holds for all types of literature but is especially true if you are writing about poetry. Because poetry compresses language and detail, you may have to fill in more than a few blank spaces to make sense of a poem. Good poems often *suggest* information instead of explicitly stating it; the shorter the poem, the more that may be suggested. If you do not begin by determining a poem's dramatic situation—the basic *who, what, where,* and *when* of a poem—you will not have established the basis on which your subsequent remarks must be anchored. It is possible for a student to go far astray on a poem as simple as A.E. Housman's "Eight o'Clock" because he or she failed to notice the poem's most important detail, that the only character in it has a *noose* around his neck.

In writing about other genres, you may have a brilliant intuition that Emily Grierson's servant Tobe is the real murderer of Homer Barron in Faulkner's "A Rose for Emily," but you may encounter difficulty in finding support for these conclusions either in the text or in the work of critics. Also, unless you are specifically asked to take a biographical approach, don't try to make close connections between an author's work and the events of his or her life; literature and autobiography are not identical. Some perfectly decent people (poets Robert Browning and Ai are two examples) have relished creating characters who are masterpieces of madness or evil, and some perfectly awful people have created beautiful works of literature. It may be the professional biographer's job to judge literary merit on the basis of what he or she perceives as the moral virtues or lack thereof of a writer, but unless you are specifically asked to take a biographical approach, you should probably limit your remarks to the text that you are analyzing.

# Writing about Fiction

As mentioned earlier, an explication assignment on a single short story demands close attention to detail because it focuses on the subtleties of a writer's language. "Close reading" means exactly what it sounds like: you should carefully weigh every word in the passage you are explicating. Typically, an explication assignment might ask you to look carefully at a key section of a short story, explaining how it contains some element on which the whole story hinges and without which it could not succeed. Suppose, for example, that you are asked to explicate the opening paragraph of Cheever's "Reunion" and are explicitly requested to explain what the paragraph conveys beyond obvious expository information. After poring over the paragraph several times, you might decide that it contains ample foreshadowing of the disastrous events that are about to occur. In particular, you might cite such tell-tale phrases as "his secretary wrote to say" or "my mother divorced him" as Cheever's way of dropping hints about the father's unstable personality. Then you might go on to mention Charlie's forebodings of his own "doom," all leading up to the aroma of prelunch cocktails that Charlie notices when he and his father embrace. Any explication demands that you quote extensively from the text, explaining why certain choices of words and details are important and speculating about why the writer made these choices.

Student Michelle Ortiz decided to examine the significance of the colors used in Alice Walker's "Everyday Use."

> Walker establishes the color contrasts carefully. The opening paragraph describes the clean-swept "hard clay" of the front yard, which the mother says "is like an extended living room." She describes how she wears "flannel nightgowns to bed and overalls during the day." Maggie, the stay-at-home daughter, wears a "pink skirt and red blouse," colors that perhaps relate to the house fire years ago that scarred her. The items in the house that Dee wants to take away are drably colored, an old wooden bench and a wooden churn top. The handmade quilts, which become the chief bone of contention between the mother and Maggie and the acquisitive Dee are made from scraps of old clothing. The colors that Walker mentions are "one teeny faded blue piece" from an ancestor's Civil War uniform and some "lavender ones" from one of her great-grandmother's dresses. Contrasting with the bright colors ("yellows and

oranges") of the flamboyant Dee's outfit ("so loud it *hurts* my eyes," the mother says), the colors associated with the family home are muted and soft, suggesting things that have faded from years of "everyday use."

A typical analysis assignment in short fiction might ask you to explain what a "rites of passage" story is and demonstrate that "Reunion" has most of the characteristics of the type. Here you might want to first define the initiation story, using your lecture notes, general literary reference books, and your familiarity with other stories from popular sources like fairy tales or motion pictures. After demonstrating that this type of story is indeed well established and having described its chief characteristics, you might then focus on such matters in "Reunion" as Charlie's age, his naive expectations, his disillusioning experience, and his eventual "passage" out of his father's life at the end of the story. A slightly more complicated analysis assignment might involve comparison and contrast. Generally, comparison seeks out common ground between two subjects, whereas contrast finds differences; most papers of this type will do both, first pointing out the similarities before going on to demonstrate how each story represents a variation on the theme. Comparison-contrast essays may examine a single story, analyzing two characters' approaches to a similar situation, or even a single character's "before and after" view of another character or event. Or these essays may compare and contrast two or more works that have common threads. If you are examining a single author in depth, you might be required to locate other stories that deal with similar themes. Because Cheever writes extensively about alcoholism, family tensions, and divorce, you might choose several of his stories that reflect the same basic themes as "Reunion." Even more demanding might be a topic asking you to find stories (or even poems or plays) by other authors to compare or contrast. Among the stories in this book, there are several examples of initiation stories and others that deal with tensions between parents and children. Assignments in comparative analysis require careful selection and planning, and it is essential to find significant examples of both similarities and differences to support your thesis.

# Writing about Poetry

Because explication of a poem involves careful close reading on a line-by-line basis, an assignment of this type will usually deal with a relatively short poem or a passage from a longer one. Some poems yield most of their meaning on a single reading; others, however, may contain complexities and nuances that deserve a careful inspection of how the poet utilizes all of the resources at his or her command. A typical explication examines both form and content. Because assignments in analysis usually involve many of the same techniques as explication, we will look at explication more closely. Poetry explications usually require much more familiarity with the technical details of poems than do those about fiction and drama, so here is a checklist of questions that you might ask before explicating a poem. Student Marc Potter's answers apply to a poem from this book, Edwin Arlington Robinson's sonnet "Firelight."

*Form*

1. How many lines does the poem contain? How are they arranged into stanzas? Is either the whole poem or the stanza an example of a traditional poetic form?

   "Firelight" is an Italian sonnet. It is divided into two stanzas, an octave and sestet, and there is a shift, or what is known in sonnets as a "turn" or *volta*, at the beginning of line nine, though here there is no single word that signals the shift.

2. Is there anything worth noting in the visual arrangement of the poem—indentation, spacing, and so on? Are capitalization and punctuation unusual?

   Capitalization and punctuation are standard in the poem, and Robinson follows the traditional practice of capitalizing the first word of each line.

3. What meter, if any, is the poem written in? Does the poet use any notable examples of substitution in the meter? Are the lines primarily end-stopped or enjambed?

   The meter is regular iambic pentameter ("Hĕr thóughts/ ă mó / mĕnt sińce / ŏf ońe / w̆ho shínes") with occasional substitutions of trochees ("Wísĕr / fŏr sĭ / lĕnce") and spondees ("théir jóy / rĕcálls / Nó snáke, / nó swórd"). Enjambment, found at the ends of lines two, five, six, seven, nine, ten, twelve, and thirteen, has the effect of masking the regular meter and rhymes and enforcing a conversational tone, an effect that is assisted by the caesurae in lines six, seven, nine, and (most importantly) fourteen. The caesura in this last line calls attention to "Apart," which ironically contrasts with the poem's opening phrase: "Ten years together."

4. What is the rhyme scheme, if any, of the poem? What types of rhyme are used?

   The rhyme scheme of this poem is abbaabba cdecde. Robinson uses exact masculine rhyme, with the rhyming sounds falling on single stressed syllables; the only possible exception is "intervals," where the meter forces a secondary stress on the third syllable.

5. Are significant sound patterns evident? Is there any repetition of whole lines, phrases, or words?

   Alliteration is present in "*f*irelight" and "*f*our" in line three and "*w*an" and "*o*ne" in line eleven, and there are several instances of assonance ("W*i*ser for s*i*lence"; "end*owe*d / And b*owe*red") and consonance ("*S*erene*ly* and *p*erennia*lly* end*owe*d"; the *w*an face of *o*ne somewhere a*lo*ne"). However, these sound patterns do not call excessive attention to themselves and depart from the poem's relaxed, conversational sound. "Firelight" contains no prominent use of repetition, with the possible exception of the pronoun "they" and its variant forms "their" and "them" and the related use of the third-person singular pronouns "he" and "she" in the last five lines of the poem. This pronoun usage, confusing at first glance, indirectly carries the poem's theme of the separateness of the couple's thoughts. The only notable instance of parallel phrasing occurs in line seven with "No snake, no sword."

## Content

1. To what genre (lyric, narrative, dramatic) does the poem belong? Does it contain elements of more than one genre?

   "Firelight" is a short narrative poem. Even though it has little plot in the conventional sense, it contains two characters in a specific setting who perform actions that give the reader insight into the true nature of their relationship. The sonnet form has traditionally been used for lyrical poetry.

2. Who is the persona of the poem? Is there an auditor? If so, who? What is the relationship between persona and auditor? Does the poem have a specific setting? If so, where and when is it taking place? Is there any action that has taken place before the poem opens? What actions take place during the poem?

   The persona here is a third-person omniscient narrator such as might be encountered in a short story; the narrator has the ability to read "Her thoughts a moment since" and directly comments that the couple is "Wiser for silence." The unnamed characters in the poem are a man and woman who have been married for ten years. The poem is set in their home, apparently in a comfortable room with a fireplace where they are spending a quiet evening together. Neither character speaks during the poem; the only action is their looking at "each other's eyes at intervals / Of gratefulness." Much of the poem's ironic meaning hinges on the couple's silence: "what neither says aloud."

3. Does the poem contain any difficulties with grammar or syntax? What individual words or phrases are striking because of their denotation or connotation?

   The syntax of "Firelight" is straightforward and contains no inversions or ellipses. The poem's sentence structure is deceptively simple. The first four lines make up a single sentence with one main clause; the second four lines also make up a single sentence, this time with two main clauses; the final six lines also make up a single sentence, broken into two equal parts by the semicolon, and consisting of both main and dependent clauses. The vocabulary of "Firelight" is not unusual, though "obliteration" (literally an *erasure*) seems at first a curious choice to describe the effects of love. One should note the allusion to the book of Genesis that is implied by "bowered," "snake," and "sword" in the octave and the rather complicated use of the subjunctive "were" in lines nine, ten, and twelve. Again, this slight alteration in grammar bears indirectly on the theme of the poem. "Yet" in the first line provides an interesting touch since it injects a slight negative note into the picture of marital bliss.

4. Does the poem use any figures of speech? If so, how do they add to the overall meaning? Is the action of the poem to be taken literally, symbolically, or both ways?

   "Firelight" uses several figures of speech. "Cloud" is a commonly employed metaphor for "foreboding." "Firelight" and "four walls" are a metonymy and synecdoche, respectively, for the couple's comfortable home. The allusion to the "snake" and "sword" make the reader think of the unhappy ending of the Garden of Eden story. It is significant that Robinson repeats "no" when referring to what the couple's "joy recalls." "Wiser for silence" is a slight paradox. "The graven tale of lines / on the wan face" is an implied metaphor which compares the lines on a person's face to the written ("graven" means *engraved* and also sounds like a word with several negative connotations: *grave*) story of her life. To say that a person "shines" instead of "excels" is another familiar metaphor. "Firelight" is to be understood primarily on the literal level. The characters are symbolic only in that the man and woman are perhaps representative of many married couples, who outwardly express happiness yet inwardly carry regrets and fantasies from past relationships.

5. Is the title of the poem appropriate? What are its subject, tone of voice, and theme? Is the theme stated or implied?

"Firelight" is a good title since it carries both the connotation of domestic tranquility and a hint of danger. "To bring to the light" means to reveal the truth, and the narrator in this poem does this. Robinson's attitude toward the couple is ironic. On the surface they seem to be the picture of ideal happiness, but Robinson reveals that this happiness has been purchased, in the man's case, at the expense of an earlier lover and, in the woman's, by settling for someone who has achieved less than another man for whom she apparently had unrequited love. Robinson's ironic view of marital stability is summed up in the phrase "Wiser for silence." Several themes are implied: the difference between surface appearance and deeper insight; the cynical idea that in love ignorance of what one's partner is thinking may be the key to bliss; the sense that individual happiness is not without its costs. All of these are possible ways to state Robinson's bittersweet theme.

Your instructor may ask you to employ specific strategies in your explication and may require a certain type of organization for the paper. In writing the body of the explication, you will probably proceed through the poem from beginning to end, summarizing and paraphrasing some lines and quoting others fully when you feel an explanation is required. It should be stressed that there are many ways, in theory, to approach a poem and that no two explications of the same poem will agree in every detail.

A writing assignment in analysis might examine the way a single element—dramatic situation, meter, form, imagery, one or more figures of speech, theme—functions in poetry. An analysis would probably require that you write about two or more poems, using the organizational patterns of comparison-contrast or definition/example-illustration. Such an assignment might examine two or more related poems by the same poet, or it might inspect the way that several poets have used a poetic device or theme. Comparison-contrast essays might explore both similarities and differences found in two poems. Definition–illustration papers usually begin with a general discussion of the topic, say, a popular theme such as the *carpe diem* motif, and then go on to illustrate how it may be found in several different poems. Assignments in analysis often lead to longer papers that may require the use of secondary sources. These two paragraphs from Jennifer Haughton's research paper on A.

D. Hope's uses of various quatrain forms in his poetry include parenthetical citations both to the poem and to works by two critics, Paul Fussell and Robert Darling, who have made comments relevant to her argument.

> Another poem in which Hope uses quatrains contrary to convention is "Imperial Adam," which is written in elegiac stanzas (*Selected* 44). Traditionally, the elegiac stanza was often (though not always) employed to lament someone's death; however, it became so associated with this function over time that modern poets may now use it for irony (Fussell 135). Hope said he intended the poem "Imperial Adam" to be a satire of the profane image of Eve (thus the use of the elegiac stanza), yet at least one critic believes that he did his job too well and ended up perpetuating Eve's wicked image (Darling 44). The extent to which "Imperial Adam" succeeds as a satire depends on whether its content or its form becomes dominant in the poem.
>
> The first two stanzas maintain a fairly regular iambic meter and show a "puzzled" Adam discovering the loss of his rib. By the fourth quatrain, Eve has been introduced, and a double spondaic substitution ("dark hairs winked crisp") in the last line spotlights a part of Eve's anatomy that will spark the fall. Instead of eating a forbidden apple, the taboo of this poem centers on sex: "She promised on the turf of Paradise / Delicious pulp of the forbidden fruit" (18-19). In the absence of a literal serpent in the poem tempting Adam and Eve, the origin of evil becomes the question.

## Writing About Drama

A review of a play is an evaluation of an actual performance and will focus less on the text of the play itself (especially if it is a well-known one) than on the actors' performances, the overall direction of the production, and the elements of staging. Because reviews are, first, news stories, basic information about the time and place of production should be given at the beginning of the review. A short summary of the play's plot might follow, and subsequent paragraphs will evaluate the performers and the production. Remember that a review is chiefly a *recommendation*, either positive or negative, to readers. Films of most of the plays in this book are available on videotape, and you also might be asked to review one of these versions, paying attention to the ways in which directors have "opened up" the action by utilizing the complex technical resources of motion pictures. Excellent examples of drama and film reviews can be found in almost any major newspaper or in the pages of popular magazines such as *Time* or *The New Yorker*.

Explication assignments, such as, the examples from fiction and poetry given earlier, will probably require that you pay close attention to a selected passage, giving a detailed account of all the fine shadings of language in a scene or perhaps a single speech. Because Shakespeare's poetry is often full of figurative language that may not be fully understood until it has been subjected to explication, close reading of one of the monologues or soliloquies in *Twelfth Night* would be a likely choice for this type of writing assignment. For a short writing assignment in a Shakespeare class, Brandon Frank chose to explicate one speech from *Othello*, the title character's defense of himself to the Venetian senate against charges brought by his new bride Desdemona's father, Brabantio, that Othello has used witchcraft to seduce his daughter. Here are his remarks on the opening of Othello's speech in act 1, scene 3:

> Othello is a subtle and intelligent man. He realizes that the charges against him are serious, and he also knows that the Duke and other members of the senate are inclined to trust Brabantio, one of their own to whom the Duke has just said, "Welcome gentle signior, / We lacked your counsel and your help tonight" (1.3.50-51). Othello counters, first, by deferring to the "most potent, grave, and reverend signiors" whom he calls his "very noble and approved good masters" (1.3.76-77). Next, he freely admits to one part of Brabantio's charge, that he and Desdemona have married:
>
> > That I have ta'en away this old man's daughter,
> > It is most true—true, I have married her.
> > The very head and front of my offending
> > Hath this extent, no more. (1.3.78-81)
>
> Having at least partially defused Brabantio's charges by showing respect to the senate which will decide his fate and by stating that has in fact wed Desdemona, he makes a humble reference to how, because he has spent most of his life "in the tented field" (1.3.85) and then proceeds to the heart of his defense, in which he will "a round unvarnished tale deliver / Of my whole course of love" (1.3.90-91). He will inform the senate that it was the power of love, not "what drugs, what charms, / What conjuration and mighty magic" (1.3.91-92), that brought him and Desdemona together.

Analysis assignments typically hinge on only one of the elements of the play like plot or characterization, or on a concept set forth by a critic. For example, you might be asked to explain Aristotle's statements about reversal and recognition and then apply his terminology to a modern play such as *The Piano Lesson*. Here you would attempt to locate relevant passages from the play to support Aristotle's contentions about the importance of these reversals in the best plots. Or you might be asked to provide a summary of his comments about the tragic hero and then apply this definition to a character like Othello. Again, comparison and contrast schemes are useful. You might be asked to contrast two or more characters in a single play (Antigone versus her sister Ismene in terms of women's role in society) or to compare characters in two different plays as undeserving victims of fate. In an extended essay on Tennessee Williams's play *Cat on a Hot Tin Roof*, Beverly Williams examines attitudes toward God and religion that are revealed by the characters. Here is her paragraph on the family patriarch, Big Daddy :

> For Big Daddy Pollitt, God does not exist in any religious order, and he tells Brick, "Church!—it bores the bejesus out of me but I go!" (1155). Instead, his God has two manifestations, money and his youngest son Brick. To Big Daddy, money means power and freedom from want, but there are some wants that money cannot buy, no matter how much a man acquires. Though he states his worth at "Close on ten million

in cash an' blue-chip stocks" (1143), Big Daddy knows that "a man can't buy back his life with it when his life has been spent" (1143), and it cannot buy "life everlasting." No one can escape mortality. In *The Broken World of Tennessee Williams*, Esther Merle Jackson states it best, "Big Daddy has believed in the power of money. He speaks of its failure as a god" (142).

# The Process of Research: The Library and the Internet

Research is a time-consuming and sometimes frustrating process, but a  few general principles may help you to streamline it. First, bear in mind that about 90% of the time you spend on assembling research materials will take place in one section of the library, the reference room, and that a large amount of information about where to find certain materials and the critical materials themselves are now available on electronic databases. If you rush off to consult a book on the fifthfloor shelves every time you locate a mention of something that is potentially useful to you, you may gain more expertise in operating an elevator than in conducting effective research. Thus, use the reference room to assemble the "shopping list" of items you will have to find in other parts of the library. Also, remember that the online indexes and sources have greatly enhanced the mechanics of research. It may be frustrating to learn that an article you spotted in a musty index and found, after a long search, in a bound volume of a journal that could have been downloaded and printed out in seconds from an online database.

Most contemporary students have literally grown up writing with computers and are familiar with the Internet. Still, a few words about the use of the Internet for online research may be helpful. In recent years, the Internet has facilitated the chores of research, and many online databases, reference works, and periodicals may be quickly located using search engines including Yahoo! (www.yahoo.com) and Google (www.google.com). The Internet also holds a wealth of information in the form of individual Web sites devoted to authors. Many of these Web sites are run by universities or private organizations. Students should be aware, however, that Web sites vary widely in quality. Some are legitimate sources displaying sound scholarship; others are little more than "fan pages" that may contain erroneous or misleading information. Online information, like any other kind of research material, should be carefully evaluated before it is used.

Careful documentation of your sources is essential; if you use any material other than what is termed "common knowledge" you must cite it in your paper. Common knowledge includes biographical information, an author's publications, prizes and awards received, and other information that can be found in more than one reference book. Anything else— direct quotes or material you have put in your own words by paraphrasing—requires both a parenthetical citation in the body of your paper and an entry on your works cited pages.

The first step in successful research is very simple: read the assigned text before looking for secondary sources. After you have read the story, poem, or play that you have been assigned, you may have already begun to formulate a workable thesis sentence. If you have done this before beginning your research, you will eliminate any number of missteps and repetitions. Next, perform a subject search for books that will be useful to you. If, for example, you are writing on one of Keats's odes, a subject search may reveal one or more books devoted solely to this single type of poem. Computerized library databases are set up in different configurations, but many of them allow multiple "keyword" searches; a search command like KEATS AND ODE might automatically cross-reference all journal articles that mention both subjects. If you are unfamiliar with your terminology and do not know, for example, how an ode differs from other kinds of poems, you should consult a reference book containing a discussion of literary terms. After you have located books and reference sources that will be of use, check the journals that publish literary criticism. The standard index for these is the *MLA International Bibliography*, which is available both in bound volumes and in an online version, and many items listed after a search may exist in full-text electronic versions. A reference librarian also may direct you to other indexes such as the *Literary Criticism Index* and the *Essay and General Literature Index*. It is a good idea to check indexes like these early in your research. No single college library carries all of the journals listed in the *MLA International Bibliography*, and you may discover that getting a reprint through interlibrary services can take a week or more.

Once you have located and assembled your sources, you can decide which of them will be most valuable to you. Again, if you have already formulated your thesis and perhaps completed a tentative outline as well, you can move more swiftly. Two blessed additions to almost every library are the copying machine and the network printer, which remove the tedious chore of taking notes by hand on $3 \times 5$ cards. Note cards may still be useful if you want to try different arrangements of your material, but most students have happily discarded them as relics of the distant past.

It is impossible to guess what research materials will be available in any given library, but most college libraries contain many different kinds of indexes and reference books for literary research. If you are writing about a living writer, particularly recommended are three popular reference sets published by Gale Research: *Dictionary of Literary Biography* (*DLB*), *Contemporary Authors* (*CA*), and *Contemporary Literary Criticism* (*CLC*). Both of these two last reference works are also available in editions that cover the nineteenth and twentieth centuries. These will provide you both with useful overviews of careers and with generous samples of criticism about the authors. *DLB* and *CA* articles also contain extensive bibliographies of other relevant sources; *CLC* contains reprints of book reviews and relevant passages from critical works. Similar to these reference works are those in the *Critical Survey* series from Magill Publishers, multivolume sets that focus on short and long fiction, poetry, drama, and film. Another reliable source of information on individual writers can be found in several series of critical books published by Twayne Publishers, which can be located in a subject search.

For locating explications, several indexes are available, including *Poetry Explication: A Checklist of Interpretations since 1925 of British and American Poems Past and Present* and *The Explicator Cyclopedia*, which reprints explications originally appearing in the periodical of the same name. *Poetry Criticism* and *Short Story Criticism* are multivolume reference works that reprint excerpts from critical essays and books. There are several popular indexes of book reviews; one of these, the annual *Book Review Digest*, reprints brief passages from the most representative reviews. Two reference sources providing, respectively, examples of professional drama and film reviews are *The New York Times Theater Reviews, 1920–1970* (and subsequent volumes) and *The New York Times Film Reviews*. Popular magazines containing book, drama, and film reviews (and occasionally poetry reviews as well) include *Time*, *Newsweek*, and *The New Yorker*, and these reviews are indexed in the *Readers' Guide to Periodical Literature*, more recent volumes of which are available online. Also, yearbooks such as *Theatre World* or the *Dictionary of Literary Biography Yearbook* provide a wealth of information about the literary activities of a given year.

# Plagiarism: Proper Quotation and Citation of Sources

First, a warning about plagiarism. Few students knowingly plagiarize, and those who do are usually not successful at it. An instructor who has read four or five weak papers from a student is likely to be suspicious if the same student suddenly begins to sound like an officer of the Modern Language Association, writing, with no citations, about "paradigms" or "*différance*" in the "*texte*." A definition of "common knowledge," the kind of information that does not require a citation, is given above. Otherwise, any *opinion* about a writer and his or her work must be followed by a citation indicating its source. If the opinion is directly quoted, paraphrased, or even summarized in passing you should still include a citation. Doing less than this is to commit an act of plagiarism, for which the penalties are usually severe. Internet materials, which are so easily cut and pasted into a manuscript, provide an easy temptation but are immediately noticeable, and there has been much media scrutiny in recent years about the widespread "epidemic" of Internet plagiarism. Nothing is easier to spot in a paper than an uncited "lift" from a source; in most cases the vocabulary and sentence structure will be radically different from the rest of the paper, and a simple text search with Google will probably reveal its source. Particularly bothersome are the numerous Web sites offering "free" research papers; a quick perusal of some of these papers indicates that even at a free price they are significantly overpriced. Additionally, many educational institutions have subscribed to "plagiarism-detection" software services that maintain huge, searchable files of research papers that have seen more than one user.

You should always support the general statements you make about a story, poem, or play by quoting directly from the text or, if required, by using secondary sources for additional critical opinion. The *MLA Handbook for Writers of Research Papers*, 7th ed., which you will find in the reference section of almost any library, contains standard formats for bibliographies and manuscripts; indeed, most of the writing handbooks used in college composition courses follow MLA style guidelines. Purdue University maintains a useful online source on MLA style at http://owl.english.purdue.edu/owl/resource/747/01/. However, if you have doubts or if you have not been directed to use a certain format, ask your instructor which one he or she prefers.

The type of parenthetical citation used in MLA-style format to indicate the source of quotations is simple to learn and dispenses with such tedious and repetitive chores as footnotes and endnotes. In using parenthetical citations, remember that your goal is to direct your reader from the quoted passage in the paper to the corresponding entry on your works cited pages and from there, if necessary, to the book or periodical from which the quote was taken. A good parenthetical citation gives only the *minimal* information needed to accomplish this task. Here are a few typical examples from student papers on fiction, poetry, and drama. The first discusses Cheever's "Reunion":

> Cheever moves very quickly to indicate that the "Reunion" may well be memorable but will not be happy. As soon as father and son enter the first restaurant and are seated, Charlie's father begins to act strangely: "We sat down, and my father hailed the waiter in a loud voice. '*Kellner!*' he shouted. '*Garçon! Cameriere! You!*' His boisterousness in the empty restaurant seemed out of place" (518).

Here you should note a couple of conventions of writing about fiction and literature in general. One is that the present tense is used in speaking of the events of the story; in general, use the present tense throughout your critical writing except when you are giving biographical or historical information. Second, note the use of single and double quotation marks. Double quotes from the story are changed to single quotes here, as they appear within the writer's own quotation marks. The parenthetical citation lists only a page number, for earlier in this paper the writer has mentioned Cheever by name and the context makes it clear that the quotation comes from the story. Only one work by Cheever appears among the works cited entries. If several works by Cheever had been listed there, the parenthetical citation would clarify which one was being referred to by adding a shortened form of the book's title: (Stories 518). The reader finds the following entry among the sources:

Cheever, John. *The Stories of John Cheever*. New York: Knopf, 1978. Print

Similarly, quotes and paraphrases from secondary critical sources should follow the same rules of common sense:

> Cheever's daughter Susan, in her candid memoir of her father, observes that the author's alcoholism followed an increasingly destructive pattern:
>
> > Long before I was even aware that he was alcoholic, there were bottles hidden all over the house, and even outside in the privet hedge and the garden shed. Drink was his crucible, his personal hell. As early as the 1950s...he spent a lot of energy trying not to drink before 4 p.m., and then before noon, and then before 10 a.m., and then before breakfast. (43)
>
> But she goes on to observe that Cheever's drinking had not yet affected his skills as a writer.

This quotation is longer than four lines, so it is indented one inch. Indented quotes of this type do not require quotation marks. Also note how ellipses are used to omit extraneous information. Because the author of the quotation is identified, only the page number is included in the parenthetical citation. The reader knows where to look among the sources:

Cheever, Susan. *Home Before Dark*. Boston: Houghton, 1984. Print

Notice that a paraphrase of the same passage requires the citation as well:

> Cheever's daughter Susan, in her candid memoir of her father, observes that the author's alcoholism followed an increasingly destructive pattern. She notes that as a child she found bottles hidden in the house, in outbuildings, and even in the hedge. She recalls that he spent a great deal of energy simply trying not to drink before a certain hour, at first before 4 p.m. but eventually before breakfast (43).

To simplify parenthetical citations, it is recommended that quotes from secondary sources be introduced, whenever possible, in a manner that identifies the author so that only the page number of the quote is needed inside of the parentheses.

Slightly different conventions govern quotations from poetry. Here are a few examples from papers on Edwin Arlington Robinson's poetry:

> Robinson's insights into character are never sharper than in "Miniver Cheevy," a portrait of a town drunk who loves "the days of old / When swords were bright and steeds were prancing" and dreams incongruously "of Thebes and Camelot, / And Priam's neighbors" (5–6, 11–12).

Pay attention to how only parts of numbered lines are quoted here to support the sentence and how the parts fit smoothly into the writer's sentence structure. In general, ellipses (...) are not necessary at the beginning or end of these quotes because it is clear that they are quoted fragmentarily; they should, however, be used if something is omitted from the middle of a quote ("the days of old / When...steeds were prancing"). The virgule or slash (/) is used to indicate line breaks; a double slash (//) indicates stanza breaks. Quotes of up to three lines should be treated in this manner. If a quote is longer than three lines it should be indented one inch (with no quotation marks) and printed as it appears in the original poem:

> Robinson opens one of his most effective and pitiless character sketches with an unsparing portrait of failure and bitterness:
>
>> Miniver Cheevy, child of scorn,
>>> Grew lean while he assailed the seasons;
>> He wept that he was ever born,
>>> And he had reasons. (1–4)

As in the example from the Cheever story, the parenthetical citation here lists only a page number because only one work by Robinson appears in the bibliography. If you are dealing with a classic poem that can be found in many editions (an ode by Keats or a Shakespeare sonnet, for example) the *MLA Handbook* recommends using line numbers instead of page numbers inside the parentheses. This practice also should be followed if you have included a copy of the poem that you are explicating with the paper.

Quoting from a play follows similar procedures. These papers discuss Shakespeare's tragedy *Othello:*

> In a disarming display of modesty before the Venetian senators, Othello states that his military background has not prepared him to act as an eloquent spokesman in his own defense, readily admitting that "little shall I grace my cause / In speaking for myself" (1.3.90–91).

Classic poetic dramas such as *Othello* may be cited by act, scene, and line numbers instead of by page numbers. The reader knows that Shakespeare is the author, so the citation here will simply direct him or her to the edition of Shakespeare listed in the works cited pages at the end of the paper. Also note that verse dramas should be quoted in the same manner as poems; quotations of more than three lines should be indented one inch. In this paper, a scene involving dialogue is quoted:

In the climactic scene of *Othello*, Shakespeare's practice of fragmenting his blank verse lines into two or more parts emphasizes the violence that is about to occur:

> **OTHELLO:**          He hath confessed.
> **DESDEMONA:**  What, my lord?
> **OTHELLO:**   That he hath used thee.
> **DESDEMONA:**          How? Unlawfully?
> **OTHELLO:**          Ay.
> **DESDEMONA:**   He will not say so. (5.2.73–75)

If you are quoting from a prose drama, you would cite a page number from the edition of the play that you used:

> In *A Doll's House* Ibsen wants to demonstrate immediately that Nora and Helmer share almost childlike attitudes toward each other. "Is that my little lark twittering out there?" is Helmer's initial line in the play (43).

Remember that common sense is the best test to apply to any parenthetical citation. Have you given the reader enough information in the citation to locate the source from which the quote was taken?

## Sample Works Cited Entries

Here are formats for some of the most commonly used types of materials used in literary research. More detailed examples may be found in the *MLA Handbook for Writers of Research Papers*, 7th ed.

### Book by a Single Author

Finch, Annie. *The Ghost of Meter: Culture and Prosody in American Free Verse*. Ann Arbor: U of Michigan P, 1993. Print.

Ives, David. *All in the Timing: Fourteen Plays*. New York: Vintage, 1995. Print.

Reynolds, Clay. *Ars Poetica*. Lubbock: Texas Tech UP, 2003. Print.

Sanderson, Jim. *Semi-Private Rooms*. Youngstown: Pig Iron, 1994. Print.

Wilbur, Richard. *Collected Poems 1943–2004*. New York: Harcourt, 2004. Print.

### Book with Author and Editor

Robinson, Edwin Arlington. *Edwin Arlington Robinson's Letters to Edith Brower*. Ed. Richard Cary. Cambridge: Harvard UP, 1968. Print.

### Casebook or Edited Collection of Critical Essays

Dean, Leonard Fellows, ed. *A Casebook on Othello*. New York: Crowell, 1961. Print.

Snyder, Susan, ed. *Othello: Critical Essays*. New York: Garland, 1988. Print.

### Individual Selection from a Casebook or Edited Collection

Urbanski, Marie Mitchell Oleson. "Existential Allegory: Joyce Carol Oates's 'Where Are You Going, Where Have You Been?'" *"Where Are You Going, Where Have You Been?": Joyce Carol Oates.* Ed. Elaine Showalter. New Brunswick: Rutgers UP, 1994. 75–79. Print.

Woodring, Carl R. "Once More The Windhover." *Gerard Manley Hopkins: The Windhover.* Ed. John Pick. Columbus: Merrill, 1969. 52–56. Print.

### Story, Poem, or Play Reprinted in Anthology or Textbook

Cheever, John. "The Swimmer." *The Longman Anthology of Short Fiction: Stories and Authors in Context.* Ed. Dana Gioia and R. S. Gwynn. New York: Longman, 2001. 390–99. Print.

Hansberry, Lorraine. *A Raisin in the Sun. Black Theater: A Twentieth-Century Collection of the Work of Its Best Playwrights.* Ed. Lindsay Patterson. New York: Dodd, 1971. 221–76. Print.

Robinson, Edwin Arlington. "Richard Cory." *Literature: An Introduction to Poetry, Fiction, and Drama.* 11th ed. Ed. X. J. Kennedy and Dana Gioia. New York: Longman, 2010. 792. Print.

### Article in Reference Book

Johnson, Richard A. "Auden, W. H." *Academic American Encyclopedia (Electronic Edition).* 2002 ed. Danbury: Grolier, 2002. CD-ROM.

"Othello." *The Oxford Companion to English Literature.* Ed. Margaret Drabble. 5th ed. New York: Oxford UP, 1985. Print.

Seymour-Smith, Martin. "Cheever, John." *Who's Who in Twentieth Century Literature.* New York: McGraw, 1976. Print.

### Article, Book Review, Story, or Poem in Scholarly Journal

Berry, Edward. "Othello's Alienation." *Studies in English Literature, 1500-1900* 30 (1990): 315–33. Print.

Horgan, Paul. "To Meet Mr. Eliot: Three Glimpses." *American Scholar* 60 (1991): 407–13. Web. 22 Feb. 2011.

McDonald, Walter. "Sandstorms." *Negative Capability* 3.4 (1983): 93. Print.

Read, Arthur M., II. "Robinson's 'The Man Against the Sky.'" *Explicator* 26 (1968): 49. Print.

### Article, Book Review, Story, or Poem in Magazine

Becker, Alida. Rev. of *Morning, Noon, and Night*, by Sidney Sheldon. *New York Times Book Review* 15 Oct. 1995: 20. Print.

Iyer, Pico. "Magic Carpet Ride." Rev. of *The English Patient*, by Michael Ondattje. *Time* 2 Nov. 1992: 71. *Time Man of the Year.* Compact. 1993. CD-ROM.

Jones, Rodney. "TV." *Atlantic Monthly* Jan. 1993: 52. Web. 29 Mar. 2011.

Spires, Elizabeth. "One Life, One Art: Elizabeth Bishop in Her Letters." Rev. of *One Art: Letters*, by Elizabeth Bishop. *New Criterion* May 1994: 18–23. Web. 30 Jan. 2011.

### Interview

Cheever, John. Interview. "John Cheever: The Art of Fiction LXII." By Annette Grant. *Paris Review* 17 (1976): 39–66. Print.

### Review of Play Production

Brantley, Ben. "Big Daddy's Ego Defies Death and His Family." *New York Times.* 3 Nov. 2003: E1. Web. 13 Feb. 2011.

### Film, Video, or Audio Recording

Harjo, Joy, and Poetic Justice. *The Woman Who Fell from the Sky*. Norton, 1994. Audiocassette.
*Pygmalion*. Dir. Anthony Asquith and Leslie Howard. Perf. Leslie Howard and Wendy Hiller.
    Paschal, 1938. DVD.

### Online: Article or Review

Wasserstein, Wendy. "A Place They'd Never Been: The Theater." *Theater Development Fund*. 7
    June 2000. Web. 6 Mar. 2011.

### Online: Author or Critical Web Site

"August Wilson." *Literature Online*. Rev. 12 May. 2001. Web. 15 Mar. 2011.
"A Page for Edwin." 5 Feb. 1998. Web. 20 Feb. 2011.

### Online: Play Production Web Site

"Death of a Salesman." 15 Nov. 2000. Web. 12 Jan. 2011.

### Online: Reference Work

"Sophocles." *Britannica Online*. Web. 15 Feb. 2011.

# Final Considerations

Finally, some basic matters of common sense are worth pondering. Consider the first
impression that the paper that you are about to turn in will make on your instructor. He
or she may teach as many as five composition classes and, with an average classroom load
of thirty students writing six to eight essays per class, may have to read, mark, and grade
something approaching a half-million words of student writing in a single semester. No
instructor, with the clock ticking past midnight and the coffee growing cold, likes trying
to read an essay in scrawled handwriting, with pieces of its torn edges, hastily ripped from
a spiral notebook, drifting to the carpet. If your instructor does allow handwritten work,
try to present a copy that can be read without extensive training in cryptographic analysis; in other words, make sure your writing is legible. But don't go to the opposite extreme
and present a masterpiece of computer wizardry, complete with multiple sizes, shapes, and
colors of fonts. In a word, plain vanilla is always the safest flavor to choose. Handwritten
work, if allowed, should be done on one side of standard-ruled notebook paper, leaving
generous margins on both the right-hand side and the bottom of the pages. In most cases,
it will be required that your work be computer-generated. Your final copy should be dou-
ble-spaced, using a printer set at high resolution. Choose a standard typewriter-style font
(Times Roman 12 pt is the most widely used), and do not expect a faint, smeared copy to
receive as much attention as a readable manuscript printed on good-quality paper. Do not
put your paper in any kind of folder or binder unless you are specifically asked to do so.
You may have been given specific instructions about title pages and page numbering, so be
sure to follow them. If you are required to submit your work electronically, make sure that
your attachment is in the prescribed word-processing format.

It should go without saying that you should proofread your final draft carefully, paying particular attention to some of the special problems in writing mechanics (punctuation

and verb tenses are two of the most common) that arise in critical papers. And, please, remember two things about the computer. One is that a paper that has not been spell-checked is absolute proof of lack of diligence. The other is that even the most sophisticated spell-checker cannot distinguish between "there" and "their" or "it's" and "its." Errors in proper nouns such as the names of authors or publishers also must be checked manually. Writing assignments are graded both for content and for their demonstration that the writer knows the basics of composition. A spelling error on the title page is not the best introduction to the body of your paper, and even the most original insights into a literary work will not receive due credit if the rules of standard English are consistently ignored.

Effective writing requires a long process involving topic selection, assembly of support, organization, rough drafts, and final adjustments. By the time you have finished printing out your final draft you may feel that not only have you exhausted the topic, it has exhausted *you*. Still, the most important element that you can bring to any assignment is the simplest one: *care*. May your efforts be rewarded!

# Thematic Approaches to Literature

Because it is possible to classify the stories, poems, and plays in the anthology in many different ways, the following listings are not exhaustive. They should, however, provide suggestions for reading and writing about works from the same genre or about works from different genres that share thematic similarities. Works are listed by genre, and works in each genre are listed in chronological order. Consult the *Index of Authors, Titles, and First Lines of Poems* for their page numbers in the text.

Following the thematic listings is a brief discussion of several key critical approaches and their applications to the thematic groups.

## Aging (See also Carpe Diem Poetry)

**Stories**

Ballard, "The autobiography of J.G.B."
Faulkner, "A Rose for Emily"
García Márquez, "A Very Old Man with Enormous Wings"

**Poems**

Wordsworth, "Composed a Few Miles Above Tintern Abbey, On Revising the Banks of the Wye During a Tour. July 13, 1798"
Cummings, "Anyone Lived in a Pretty How Town"

Shakespeare, "Sonnet 73"
Milton, "How Soon Hath Time"
Tennyson, "Ulysses"
Wordsworth, "Lines: Composed, a Few Miles Above Tintern Abbey, On Revisiting the banks of the Wye During a Tour July 13, 1798"
Williams, "The Last Words of My English Grandmother"
Eliot, "The Love Song of J. Alfred Prufrock"
Millay, "What Lips My Lips Have Kissed, and Where, and Why"
Kennedy, "In a Prominent Bar in Secaucus One Day"
Pastan, "Ethics"

## Plays

Shakespeare, "The Tragedy of Othello, The Moor of Venice"

## Allegorical and Symbolic Works

### Stories

Keret, "Creative Writing"
Patterson, "The Fires We Can't Control"
Hawthorne, "Young Goodman Brown"
Ballard, "The Autobiography of J.G. B."
Jackson, "The Lottery"
García Márquez, "A Very Old Man with Enormous Wings"
Oates, "Where Are You Going, Where Have You Been?"

### Poems

Prufer, "The Villain and His Helicopter: Possible Movie Rental Versions"
Southwell, "The Burning Babe"
Herbert, "Redemption"
Burns, "John Barleycorn"
Poe, "The Haunted Palace"
Tennyson, "The Lady of Shalott"
Keats, "Ode on a Grecian Urn"
Dickinson, "Because I Could Not Stop for Death"
Rossetti, "Up-Hill"
Crane, "The Trees in the Garden Rained Flowers"
Crane, "The Wayfarer"
Frost, "The Road Not Taken"
Stevens, "Anecdote of the Jar"
Stevens, "The Emperor of Ice-Cream"
Stevens, "The Snow Man"
Larkin, "Next, Please"
Kizer, "The Ungrateful Garden"
Merwin, "The Last One"

## Animals

### Stories

Ballard, "The Autobipgraphy of J.G.B."
Jewett, "A White Heron"

### Poems

Blake, "The Tyger"
Dickinson, "A Narrow Fellow in the Grass"
Moore, "The Fish"
cummings, "r-p-o-p-h-e-s-s-a-g-r"
Bishop, "The Fish"
Stafford, "Traveling Through the Dark"
Dickey, "The Heaven of Animals"

### Plays

Glaspell, *Trifles*

## Art

### Poems

Prufer, "The Villain and His Helicopter: Possible Movie Rental Versions"
Collins, "The Lanyard"
Spenser, "Amoretti: Sonnet 75"
Shakespeare, "Sonnet 18"
Shelley, "Ozymandias"
Yeats, "Sailing to Byzantium"
Stevens, "Anecdote of the Jar"
Auden, "Musée des Beaux Arts"
Keats, "Ode on a Grecian Urn"

## *Ballads and Narrative Poetry

### Poems

Long, "Flash Forward with *The Amistad* Before Us in the Distance"
Anonymous, "Bonny Barbara Allan"
Anonymous, "Sir Patrick Spens"
Burns, "John Barleycorn"
Keats, "La Belle Dame sans Merci"
Poe, "The Haunted Palace"
Tennyson, "The Lady of Shalott"

Randall, "Ballad of Birmingham"
Fairchild, "Body and Soul"
Stokesbury, "The Day Kennedy Died"
Nelson, "The Ballad of Aunt Geneva"

## Carpe Diem

### Poems

Griffith, "In the Kitchen"
Herrick, "To the Virgins, to Make Much
    of Time"
Waller, "Song"
Marvell, "To His Coy Mistress"
Housman, "Loveliest of Trees, the
    Cherry Now"
Stevens, "The Emperor of Ice-Cream"

## Childhood and Adolescence (Initiation)

### Stories

Jewett, "A White Heron"
Joyce, "Araby"
Wright, "The Man Who Was Almost
    a Man"
Cheever, "Reunion"
Ellison, "A Party Down at the Square"
Tan, "Two Kinds"
Moody, "Boys"
Updike, "A & P"
Yamamoto, "Seventeen Syllables"
Oates, "Where Are You Going, Where
    Have You Been?"
Perabo, "The Payoff"

### Poems

Wordsworth, "Lines: Composed a Few
    Miles Above Tintern Abbey, On
    Revisiting the Banks of the Wye
    During a Tour. July 13, 1798"
Corn, "Upbringing"
Collins, "The Lanyard"
Blake, "The Chimney Sweeper"

Blake, "The Little Black Boy"
Kennedy, "Little Elegy"
Dunn, "The Sacred"
Olds, "The One Girl at the Boys Party"
Kane, "Alan Doll Rap"
Rios, "The Purpose of Altar Boys"
Stallings. "First Love: A Quiz"
Cummings, "Anyone Lived in a Pretty
    How Town"

### Plays

Sanchez-Scott, *The Cuban Swimmer*

### Poems

Duhamel, "My Strip Club"
Prufer, "The Villian and His
    Helicopter: Possible Movie
    Rental Versions"

## Conceit and Extended Metaphor (Poetry)

### Poems

Dunamel, "My Strip Club"
Prufer, The Villain and His
    Helicopter: Possible Movie
    Rental Versions
Donne, "Holy Sonnet 14"
Donne, "A Valediction: Forbidding
    Mourning"
Herbert, "Easter Wings"
Herbert, "The Pulley"
Bradstreet, "The Author to Her Book"
Longfellow, "The Arsenal at
    Springfield"
Poe, "The Haunted Palace"
Dugan, "Love Song: I and Thou"
Plath, "Metaphors"
Chappell, "Narcissus and Echo"
Phillips, "The Stone Crab:
    A Love Poem"
Gerstler, "Advice from a
    Caterpillar"

## Conceit Petrarchan (Poetry)

Shakespeare, "Sonnet 130"
Campion, "There Is a Garden in Her Face"
Mullen, "Dim Lady"

## Death (See also Elegy)

### Stories

Ballard, "The Autobiography of J.G.B."
Poe, "The Cask of Amontillado"
Faulkner, "A Rose for Emily"
Hurston, "Sweat"
Ellison, "A Party Down at the Square"
Jackson, "The Lottery"
Achebe, "Dead Men's Path"
Erdrich, "The Red Convertible"

### Poems

Cummings, "Anyone Lived in a Pretty
    How Town"
Whitworth, "Little"
Donne, "Holy Sonnet 10"
Keats, "Bright Stars, Would I Were
    Stedfast as Thou Art"
Longfellow, "The Cross of Snow"
Dickinson, "After Great Pain, a Formal
    Feeling Comes"
Dickinson, "Because I Could Not Stop
    for Death"
Hardy, "Ah, Are You Digging on My Grave?"
Housman, "Eight O'Clock"
Frost, "Home Burial"
Stevens, "The Emperor of Ice-Cream,"
Stevens, "The Worms at Heaven's Gate"
Williams, "The Last Words of My English
    Grandmother"
Thomas, "Do Not Go Gentle into That
    Good Night"
Brooks, "We Real Cool"
Larkin, "Next, Please"
Gunn, "Terminal"
Kennedy, "Little Elegy"

## Plays

Shakespeare, "Othello"
Sophocles, *Antigone*
Glaspell, *Trifles*

## Dramatic Dialogues

### Poems

Hardy, "Ah, Are You Digging on My
    Grave?"
Hardy, "The Ruined Maid"
Frost, "Home Burial"
Randall, "Ballad of Birmingham"
Chappell, "Narcissus and Echo"

## Dramatic Monologues

### Stories

Poe, "The Cask of Amontillado"
Moody, "Boys"

### Poems

Huges, "Themes for English B"
Blake, "The Chimney Sweeper"
Blake, "The Little Black Boy"
Blake, "A Poison Tree"
Tennyson, "Ulysses"
Browning, "My Last Duchess"
Browning, "Porphyria's Lover"
Pound, "The River-Merchant's Wife:
    A Letter"
Eliot, "The Love Song of J. Alfred
    Prufrock"
Brooks, "The Mother"
Brooks, "We Real Cool"
Wright, "Saint Judas"
Kennedy, "In a Prominent Bar in
    Secaucus One Day"
Atwood, "Siren Song"
Hall, "Maybe Dats Your
    Problem Too"
Cortez, *"Tu Negrito"*
Gertstler, "Advice from a
    Caterpillar"

## Duty

### Stories

Updike, "A & P"
Jewett, "A White Heron"
Maupassant, "The Necklace"

### Poems

Anonymous, "Sir Patrick Spens"
Lovelace, "To Lucasta, Going to
the Wars"

### Plays

Shakespeare, "Twelfth Night"
Sophocles, "Antigone"
Shakespeare, "Othello"

## Elegy

### Poems

Jonson, "On My First Son"
Dryden, "To the Memory of
Mr. Oldham"
Gray, "Elegy Written in a Country
Churchyard"
Longfellow, "The Cross of Snow"
Millay, "If I Should Learn, in Some
Quite Casual Way"
Whitworth, "Little"
Gunn, "Terminal"
Gioia, "Planting a Sequoia"

## Ethnic/Racial Identity and
Racism

### Stories

Wright, "The Man Who Was Almost a Man"
Ellison, "A Party Down at the Square"
Yamamoto, "Seventeen Syllables"
Tan, "Two Kinds"
Walker, "Everyday Use"
Erdrich, "The Red Convertible"
Alexie, "This Is What It Means to Say
Phoenix, Arizona"

### Poems

Long, "Flash Forward with
The Amistad Before Us in the
Distance"
Blake, "The Little Black Boy"
Lazarus, "The New Colossus"
Dunbar, "We Wear the Mask"
Toomer, "Georgia Dusk"
Hughes, "Dream Boogie"
Hughes, "Theme for English B"
Hughes, "The Weary Blues"
Cullen, "Incident"
Cullen, "Yet Do I Marvel"
Randall, "Ballad of Birmingham"
Nelson, "The Ballad of Aunt Geneva"
Jones, "Winter Retreat: Homage to
Martin Luther King, Jr."
Cofer, "The Latin Deli: An Ars
Poetica"
Trethewey, "Domestic Work, 1937"
Kim, "Occupation"

### Plays

Wilson, "Fences"
Shakespeare, "Othello"
Sanchez-Scott, *The Cuban Swimmer*

## Fate

### Stories

Jackson, "The Lottery"
Ballard, "The Autobiography of J.G.B."

### Poems

Yeats, "Leda and the Swan"
Frost, "Design"
Auden, "The Unknown Citizen"
Randall, "Ballad of Birmingham"
Kooser, "Abandoned Farmhouse"

### Plays

Sophocles, "Antigone"
Ives, *Sure Thing*

# History

### Stories

Hawthorne, "Young Goodman Brown"
Faulkner, "A Rose for Emily"
Ellison, "A Party Down at the Square"
Jackson, "The Lottery"
Achebe, "Dead Men's Path"
Walker, "Everyday Use"

### Poems

Milton, "On the Late Massacre in
Piedmont"
Gray, "Elegy Written in a Country
Churchyard"
Keats, "Ode on a Grecian Urn"
Long, "Flash Forward with *The Amistad*
Before Us in the Distance"
Shelley, "Ozymandias"
Yeats, "The Second Coming"
Wilbur, "Year's End"
Merrill, "Casual Wear"
Stokesbury, "The Day Kennedy Died"
Forché, "The Colonel"

### Plays

Shakespeare, "Othello"
Wilson, "Fences"
Sophocles, *Antigone*

# Holocaust

### Poems

Williams, "The Book"
Plath, "Daddy"
Shomer, "Women Bathing at
Bergen-Belsen"
Hudgins, "Air View of an Industrial Scene"

# Humanity

### Stories

Hawthorne, "Young Goodman Brown"
O'Brien, "The Things They Carried"
Moody, "Boys"

Long, "Flash Forward with *The Amistad*
Before Us in the Distance"
Updike, "A & P"

### Poems

Keats, "Ode on a Grecian Urn 1820"
Long, "Flash Forward with *The Amistad*
Before Us in the Distance"
Crane, "The Trees in the Garden Rained
Flowers"
Stafford, "Traveling Through the Dark"
Nemerov, "A Primer of the Daily Round"
Justice, "Counting the Mad"
Ginsberg, "A Supermarket in California"
Wright, "Saint Judas"
Kooser, "Abandoned Farmhouse"
Mayers, "All-American Sestina"
Steele, "Sapphics Against Anger"
Nye, "The Traveling Onion"

### Plays

Shakespeare, "Twelfth Night"

# Language

### Stories

Hurston, "Sweat"
Atwood, "Happy Endings"

### Poems

cummings, "r-p-o-p-h-e-s-s-a-g-r"
Cummings, "Anyone Lived in a Pretty
How Town"
Corn, "Upbringing"
Martin, "E.S.L."
Raine, "A Martian Sends a Postcard Home"
Alvarez, "Bilingual Sestina"
Mullen, "Dim Lady"

# Love

### Stories

Hemingway, "Hills Like Write Elephants"
Joyce, "Araby"
O'Conner, "Good Country People"

Atwood, "Happy Endings"
Perabo, "The Payoff"

**Poems**

Collins, "The Lanyard"
Wilkinson, "Itinerant"
Shakespeare, "Sonnet 29"
Shakespeare, "Sonnet 116"
Wroth, "In This Strange Labyrinth How
 Shall I Turn"
Burns, "A Red, Red Rose"
Browning, "Sonnets from the
 Portuguese, 18"
Browning, "Sonnets from the
 Portuguese, 43"
Dugan, "Love Song; I and Thou"
Addonizio, "Sonnenizio on a Line from
 Drayton"
Stallings, "First Love: A Quiz"

**Plays**

Shakespeare, *Twelfth Night*
Ives, *Sure Thing*

## Love: Loss of

**Stories**

Hawthorne, "Young Goodman
 Brown"
Foer, "Here We Aren't, So Quickly"
Faulkner, "A Rose for Emily"

**Poems**

Rathburn, "What Was Left"
Wilkinson, "Itinerant"
Anonymous, "Western Wind"
Wyatt, "They Flee from Me"
Wyatt, "Whoso List to Hunt"
Byron, "When We Two Parted"
Keats, "La Belle Dame sans Merci"
Poe, "The Raven"
Hardy, "Neutral Tones"
Millay, "What Lips My Lips Have Kissed,
 and Where, and Why"

Bishop, "One Art"
Snodgrass, "Mementos, I"
Phillips, "The Stone Crab: A Love Poem"
Moore, "Auld Lang Syne"
Hilbert, "Domestic Situation"

**Plays**

Shakespeare, "Othello"
Ibsen, "A Doll's House"

## Love: Marital Relationships

**Stories**

Keret, "Creative Writing"
Patterson, "The Fires We Can't Control"
Hawthorne, "Young Goodman
 Brown"
Maupassant, "The Necklace"
Foer, "Here We Aren't, So Quickly"
Hurston, "Sweat"
Atwood, "Happy Endings"
Mason, "Shiloh"

**Poems**

Griffith, "In the Kitchen"
Rathburn, "What Was Left"
Shakespeare, "Sonnet 116"
Donne, "A Valediction: Forbidding
 Mourning"
Longfellow, "The Cross of Snow"
Browning, "My Last Duchess"
Arnold, "Dover Beach"
Robinson, "Firelight"
Frost, "Home Burial"
Pound, "The River-Merchant's Wife:
 A Letter"
Wilbur, "For C."
Dugan, "Love Song: I and Thou"
Rich, "Aunt Jennifer's Tigers"
Piercy, "What's That Smell in the Kitchen"
Lockward, "My Husband Discovers
 Poetry"
Dove, "American Smooth"
Hilbert, "Domestic Situation"

Bradstreet, "To My Dear and Loving Husband"
Cummings, "Anyone Lived in a Pretty How Town"

## Plays

Shakespeare, "Othello"
Ibsen, "A Doll's House"

## Myth

### Stories

Jackson, "The Lottery"
García Márquez, "A Very Old Man with Enormous Wings"

### Poems

Tennyson, "The Lady of Shalott"
Yeats, "Leda and the Swan"
Eliot, "The Love Song of J. Alfred Prufrock"
Auden, "Musée des Beaux Arts"
Merwin, "The Last One"
Chappell, "Narcissus and Echo"
Atwood, "Siren Song"
Stallings, "First Love: A Quiz"

### Plays

Sophocles, *Antigone*

## Nature and God

### Stories

Jewett, "A White Heron"

### Poems

Keats, "Ode on a Grecian Urn 1820"
Wordsworth, "It Is a Beauteous Evening"
Wordsworth, "Lines: Composed a Few Miles Above Tintern Abbey, On Revisiting the Banks of the Wye During a Tour. July 13, 1798."
Whitman, "A Noiseless Patient Spider"
Whitman, "Song of Myself, 6"

Whitman, "When I Heard the Learn'd Astronomer"
Dickinson, "A Narrow Fellow in the Grass"
Dickinson, "Some Keep the Sabbath Going to Church"
Hopkins, "God's Grandeur"
Frost, "Design"
Stevens, "The Snow Man"

## Nature: Descriptive Poetry

Wordsworth, "Lines: Composed a Few Miles Above Tintern Abbey, On Revisitng the Banks of the Wye During a Tour. July 13, 1798
Swift, "A Description of a City Shower"
Wordsworth, "I Wandered Lonely as a Cloud"
Hopkins, "Pied Beauty"
Frost, "Stopping by Woods on a Snowy Evening"
H. D., "Pear Tree"
H. D., "Sea Rose"
Toomer, "Georgia Dusk"
Roethke, "Root Cellar"
Swenson, "How Everything Happens"
Wilbur, "Year's End"
Snyder, "A Walk"
Mason, "Fog Horns"
Gerstler, "Advice from a Caterpillar"

## Nature: The Environment

### Stories

Patterson, "The Fires We Can't Control"
Jewett, "A White Heron"
Ballard, "The Autobiography of J.G.B."

### Poems

Hopkins, "God's Grandeur"
Jeffers, "The Purse-Seine"
cummings, "pity this busy monster, manunkind"
Bishop, "The Fish"

Stafford, "Traveling Through the Dark"
Kizer, "The Ungrateful Garden"
Kumin, "Noted in the *New York Times*"
Merwin, "The Last One"
Oliver, "The Black Walnut Tree"
Arnold, "The Singers"

## Nature: Seasons of the Year

**Poems**

Cummings, "Anyone Lived in a Pretty How Town"
Whitworth, "Little"
Shakespeare, "When Daisies Pied (Spring and Winter)"
Shelley, "Ode to the West Wind"
Hopkins, "Spring and Fall: To a Young Child"
Housman, "Loveliest of Trees, the Cherry Now"
Williams, "Spring and All"
Wilbur, "Year's End"
Wright, "Autumn Begins in Martins Ferry, Ohio"

## Parents and Children

**Stories**

Patterson, "The Fires We Can't Control"
O'Conner, "Good Country People"
Tan, "Two Kinds"
Moody, "Boys"
Faulkner, "A Rose for Emily"
Cheever, "Reunion"
Yamamoto, "Seventeen Syllables"
Oates, "Where Are You Going, Where Have You Been?"
Walker, "Everyday Use"
Alexie, "This Is What It Means to Say Phoenix, Arizona"
Perabo, "The Payoff"

**Poems**

Collins, "The Lanyard"
Corn, "Upbringing"

Whitworth, "Little"
Moore, "Silence"
Roethke, "My Papa's Waltz"
Hayden, "Those Winter Sundays"
Thomas, "Do Not Go Gentle into That Good Night"
Kees, "For My Daughter"
Brooks, "the mother"
Wilbur, "The Writer"
Larkin, "This Be the Verse"
Simpson, "My Father in the Night Commanding No"
Plath, "Daddy"
Stuart, "Discovering My Daughter"
Voigt, "Daughter"
Cortez, *"Tu Negrito"*
Foust, "Family Story"

**Plays**

Sophoeles, *Antigone*

## Physical and Emotional Problems

**Stories**

Keret, "Creative Writing"
Carver, "Cathedral"

**Poems**

Milton, "When I Consider How My Light Is Spent"
Hecht, "Third Avenue in Sunlight"
Miller, "Subterfuge"
Ruark, "The Visitor"
Murphy, "Case Notes"

## Poetry

**Story**

Yamamoto, "Seventeen Syllables"

**Poems**

Bradstreet, "The Author to Her Book"
Pope, "From *An Essay on Criticism*"

Keats, "On First Looking into Chapman's Homer"

Dickinson, "The Brain Is Wider Than the Sky"

Dickinson, "Tell All the Truth but Tell It Slant"

Housman, "'Terence, This Is Stupid Stuff ...'"

Hecht, "The Dover Bitch"

Ashbery, "Paradoxes and Oxymorons"

Lockward, "My Husband Discovers Poetry"

Mullen, "Dim Lady"

## Poetry: Inspiration

### Poems

Sidney, "Astrophel and Stella: Sonnet 1"

Coleridge, "Kubla Khan"

Hopkins, "Pied Beauty"

Wilbur, "The Writer"

Duhamel, "My Strip Club"

Prufer, "The Villian and His Helicopter: Possible Movie Rental Versions"

Wordsworth, "Lines: Composed a Few Miles Above Tintern Abbey on Revisiting the Banks of the Wye During a Tour. July 13, 1798"

## Political and Social Themes

### Stories

Ballard, "The Autobiography of J.G.B."

Achebe, "Dead Men's Path"

Erdrich, "The Red Convertible"

Updike, "A & P"

### Poems

Long, "Flash Forward with the Amistad Before Us in the Distance"

Milton, "On the Late Massacre in Piedmont"

Blake, "The Chimney Sweeper"

Whitman, "O Captain! My Captain!"

Lazarus, "The New Colossus"

Housman, "Eight O'Clock"

Robinson, "The Mill"

Auden, "The Unknown Citizen"

Roethke, "Dolor"

Brooks, "the mother"

Simpson, "American Classic"

Merrill, "Casual Wear"

Cortez, *Tu Negrito*

Forché, "The Colonel"

Song, "Stamp Collecting"

### Plays

Sophocles, *Antigone*

Shakespeare, "Othello"

## Satire and Humor

### Stories

Walker, "Everyday Use"

O'Conner, "Good Country People"

### Poems

Byron, "Stanzas"

Swift, "A Description of a City Shower"

Hardy, "The Ruined Maid"

Stevens, "Disillusionment of Ten O'Clock"

cummings, "plato told"

Auden, "The Unknown Citizen"

Martin, "E.S.L."

Fenton, "God, a Poem"

Kane, "Alan Doll Rap"

Collins, "The Lanyard"

Duhamel, "My Strip Club"

Prufer, "The Villain and His Helicopter Possible Movie Rental Versions"

### Plays

Shakespeare, Twelfth Night

## Sexual Themes (See also Carpe Diem)

### Stories

Foer, "Here We Aren't, So Quickly"
Keret, "Creative Writing"
Updike, "A & P"
Hemingway, "Hills Like White Elephants"
Faulkner, "A Rose for Emily"
O'Conner, "Good Country People"
Oates, "Where Are You Going, Where Have You Been?"
Parabo, "The Payoff"

### Poems

Rathburn, "What Was Left"
Moore, "Auld Lang Syne"
Wyatt, "Whoso List to Hunt"
Shakespeare, "Sonnet 20"
Donne, "The Flea,"
Duhamel, "My Strip Club"
Marvell, "To His Coy Mistress"
Whitman, "Song of Myself, 11"
Hardy, "The Ruined Maid"
Eliot, "The Love Song of J. Alfred Prufrock"
Hecht, "The Dover Bitch"
Rich, "Rape"
Rogers, "Foreplay"
Ríos, "The Purpose of Altar Boys"
Addonizio, "First Poem for You"
Moore, "Auld Lang Syne"

### Plays

Shakespeare, "Twelfth Night"
Shakespeare, "Othello"
Ives, *Sure Thing*

## Solitude

### Stories

Hemingway, "Young Goodman Brown"
Ballard, "The autobiography of J.G.B."
Jewett, "A White Heron"
Faulkner, "A Rose for Emily"

### Poems

Dickinson, "The Soul Selects Her Own Society"
Yeats, "The Lake Isle of Innisfree"
Frost, "Acquainted with the Night"
Frost, "Home Burial"

### Plays

Glaspell, *Trifles*

## Sports and Games

### Poems

Wright, "Autumn Begins in Martins Ferry, Ohio"
Dove, "American Smooth"
Joseph, "The Athlete"

### Play

Wilson, "Fences"
Sanchez-Scott, *The Cuban Swimmer*

## Suicide

### Stories

Erdrich, "The Red Convertible"

### Poems

Anonymous, "Bonny Barbara Allan"
Tennyson, "The Lady of Shalott"
Robinson, "The Mill"
Robinson, "Richard Cory"
Wright, "Saint Judas"

### Plays

Sophocles, "Antigone"

## War

### Poems

Byron, "Stanzas"
Longfellow, "The Arsenal at Springfield"
Hardy, "Channel Firing,"
Sassoon, "Dreamers"
Owen, "Dulce et Decorum Est"
cummings, "plato told"

Snodgrass, "Mementos, I"
Komunyakaa, "Facing It"
Salter, "Welcome to Hiroshima"
Turner, "Here, Bullet"
Kim, "Occupation"

### Plays

Shakespeare, "Othello"

## Women's Issues

### Stories

Gilman, "The Yellow Wallpaper"
Maupassant, "The Necklace"
Hurston, "Sweat"
Hemingway, "Hills Like White Elephants"
Yamamoto, "Seventeen Syllables"
Oates, "Where Are You Going, Where Have You Been?"
Atwood, "Happy Endings"
Mason, "Shiloh"
Walker, "Everyday Use"
Foer, "Here We Aren't, So Quickly"

### Poems

Duhamel, "My Strip Club"
Griffith, "In the Kitchen"
Whitman, "Song of Myself, 11"
Dickinson, "Wild Nights—Wild Nights"
Millay, "Oh, Oh, You Will Be Sorry for That Word"

Bogan, "Women"
Sexton, "Cinderella"
Wilkinson, "Intinerant"
Rathburn, "What Was Left"
Rich, "Aunt Jennifer's Tigers"
Rich, "Rape"
Plath, "Daddy"
Plath, "Metaphors"
Clifton, "homage to my hips"
Clifton, "wishes for sons"
Piercy, "What's That Smell in the Kitchen"
Atwood, "Siren Song"
Cardiff, "Combing"
Olds, "The One Girl at the Boys Party"
Lockward, "My Husband Discovers Poetry"
Cope, "Rondeau Redoublé"
Kane, "Alan Doll Rap"
Andrews, "Primping in the Rearview Mirror"
Foust, "Family Story"
Tufariello, "Useful Advice"
Stallings, "First Love: A Quiz"
Moore, "Auld Lang Syne"

### Plays

Sophocles, "Antigone"
Glaspell, *Trifles*
Ibsen, "A Doll's House"

# acknowledgments

## Fiction

Inc. Reprinted by permission of John Hawkins & Associates, Inc.

"Happy Endings" From GOOD BONES and SIMPLE MURDERS, by Margaret Atwood, published by Nan A. Talese Books/The Knopf Doubleday Publishing Group, a division of Random House LLC, 1994. Copyright © 1983, 1992, 1994 by O.W. Toad Ltd. Used with permission of the author.

"Shiloh" by Bobbie Ann Mason from SHILOH AND OTHER STORIES. Reproduced by permission of ICM PARTNERS, INC. Copyright © 1982 by Bobbie Ann Mason.

"Everyday Use" from IN LOVE & TROUBLE: Stories of Black Women by Alice Walker. Copyright © 1973, and renewed 2001 by Alice Walker. Reprinted by permission of Houghton Mifflin Harcourt Publishing Company. All rights reserved.

"Two Kinds", from THE JOY LUCK CLUB by Amy Tan, copyright © 1989 by Amy Tan. Used by permission of G.P. Putnam's Sons, a division of Penguin Group (USA) LLC.

"The Red Convertible" from the book LOVE MEDICINE, new and expanded version by Louise Erdrich. Copyright © 1984, 1993 by Louise Erdrich. Reprinted by permission of Henry Holt and Company, LLC.

"Boys" by rick Moody from DEMONOLOGY. Copyright © 2001 by Rick Moody. Used by permission of Little, Brown and Company. All rights reserved.

"This is What It Means to Say Phoenix, Arizona" from The Lone Ranger and Tonto Fistfight in Heaven, copyright © 1993, 2005 by Sherman Alexie. Used by permission of Grove/Atlantic, Inc. Any third party use of this material, outside of this publication, is prohibited.

"Creative Writing" from SUDDENLY A KNOCK ON THE DOOR by Etgar Keret. Translation copyright © 2010 by Miriam Shlesinger, Sondra Silverston and Nathan Englander. Reprinted by permission of Farrar, Straus and Giroux, LLC.

"A Temporary Matter" from INTERPRETER OF MALADIES by Jhumpa Lahiri. Copyright © 1999 by Jhumpa Lahiri. Reprinted by permission of Houghton Mifflin Harcourt Publishing Company. All rights reserved. First appeared in the New Yorker, April 1998.

"The Payoff" by Susan Perabo. Reprinted with the permission of Simon & Schuster Publishing Group from the forthcoming book TEN STORIES by Susan Perabo to be published in 2015.

# Poetry

"After great pain a formal feeling comes". Reprinted by permission of the publishers and the Trustees of Amherst College from THE POEMS OF EMILY DICKINSON, Thomas H. Johnson, ed., Cambridge, Mass.: The Belknap Press of Harvard University Press, Copyright © 1951, 1955, 1979, 1983 by the President and Fellows of Harvard College.

"Tell all the truth but tell it slant". Reprinted by permission of the publishers and the Trustees of Amherst College from THE POEMS OF EMILY DICKINSON, Thomas H. Johnson, ed., Cambridge, Mass.: The Belknap Press of Harvard University Press, Copyright © 1951, 1955, 1979, 1983 by the President and Fellows of Harvard College.

"Leda and the Swan" by W. B. Yeats from THE COLLECTED WORKS OF W. B. YEATS, VOLUME I: THE POEMS. Reprinted with the permission of Scribner Publishing Group from THE COLLECTED WORKS OF W. B. YEATS, VOLUME I: THE POEMS, REVISED by W. B. Yeats, edited by Richard J. Finneran. Copyright © 1928 by The Macmillan Company, renewed 1956 by Georgie Yeats. All rights reserved.

"Sailing to Byzantium" by W. B. Yeats from THE COLLECTED WORKS OF W. B. YEATS, VOLUME I: THE POEMS. Reprinted with the permission of Scribner Publishing Group from THE COLLECTED WORKS OF W. B. YEATS, VOLUME I: THE POEMS, REVISED by W. B. Yeats, edited by Richard J. Finneran. Copyright © 1928 by The Macmillan Company, renewed 1956 by Georgie Yeats. All rights reserved.

"Acquainted With the Night", "The Road Not Taken", and "Stopping by Woods on a Snowy Evening" from the book THE POETRY OF ROBERT FROST edited by Edward Connery Lathem. Copyright © 1916, 1923, 1928, 1930, 1939, 1969 by Henry Holt and Company, LLC. Copyright © 1936, 1944, 1951, 1956, 1958 by Robert Frost. Copyright © 1964, 1967 by Lesley Frost Ballantine. Reprinted by permission of Henry Holt and Company, LLC.

"After Apple-Picking", "Design", and "Home Burial" from the book THE POETRY OF ROBERT FROST edited by Edward Connery Lathem. Copyright © 1916, 1923, 1928, 1930, 1939, 1969 by Henry Holt and Company, LLC. Copyright © 1936, 1944, 1951, 1956, 1958 by Robert Frost. Copyright © 1964, 1967 by Lesley Frost Ballantine. Reprinted by permission of Henry Holt and Company, LLC.

© Alexander Nemerov. Courtesy of Estate of Howard Nemerov.

"For C" from MAYFLIES: NEW POEMS AND TRANSLATIONS by Richard Wilbur. Copyright © 2000 by Richard Wilbur. Reprinted by permission of Houghton Mifflin Harcourt Publishing Company. All rights reserved.

"The Writer" from THE MIND-READER by Richard Wilbur. Copyright © 1971, renewed 1999 by Richard Wilbur. Reprinted by permission of Houghton Mifflin Harcourt Publishing Company. All rights reserved.

"Years-End" from CEREMONY AND OTHER POEMS by Richard Wilbur. Copyright 1949 by Richard Wilbur. Copyright © Renewed 1977 by Richard Wilbur. Reprinted by permission of Houghton Mifflin Harcourt Publishing Company. All rights reserved.

Next, Please by Philip Larkin from THE LESS DECEIVED. Copyright by Marvell Press (Australia).

"This Be The Verse" from THE COMPLETE POEMS by Philip Larkin, edited by Archie Burnett. Copyright © 2012 by The Estate of Philip Larkin. Introduction copyright © 2012 by Archie Burnett. Reprinted by permission of Farrar, Straus and Giroux, LLC.

"The Heaven of Animals," from POEMS 1957–1967 © 1967 by James Dickey. Reprinted by permission of Wesleyan University Press.

Alan Dugan, "Love Song: I and Thou" from POEMS SEVEN: NEW AND COMPLETE POETRY. Copyright © 2001 by Alan Dugan. Reprinted with the permission of The Permissions Company, Inc., on behalf of Seven Stories Press, www.sevenstories.com.

"The Dover Bitch" from COLLECTED EARLIER POEMS by Anthony Hecht, copyright © 1990 by Anthony E. Hecht. Used by permission of Alfred A. Knopf, an imprint of the Knopf Doubleday Publishing Group, a division of Random House LLC. All rights reserved. Any third party use of this material, outside of this publication, is prohibited. Interested parties must apply directly to Random House LLC for permission.

"Third Avenue in Sunlight" from COLLECTED EARLIER POEMS by Anthony Hecht, copyright © 1990 by Anthony E. Hecht. Used by permission of Alfred A. Knopf, an imprint of the Knopf Doubleday Publishing Group, a division of Random House LLC. All rights reserved. Any third party use of this material, outside of this publication, is prohibited. Interested parties must apply directly to Random House LLC for permission.

Louis Simpson, "American Classic" from THE OWNER OF THE HOUSE: NEW COLLECTED POEMS 1940–2001. Copyright © 2001 by Louis Simpson. Reprinted with the permission of The Permissions Company, Inc., on behalf of BOA Editions, Ltd., www.boaeditions.org.

"My Father in The Night Commanding No," from AT THE END OF THE OPEN ROAD © 1963 by Louis Simpson. Used by permission of Wesleyan University Press.

Subterfuge by Vassar Miller from IF I HAD WHEELS OR LOVE: COLLECTED POEMS. Copyright by Southern Methodist University - Hamon Arts Library.

"Counting the Mad" from COLLECTED POEMS by Donald Justice, copyright © 2004 by Donald Justice. Used by permission of Alfred A. Knopf, an imprint of the Knopf Doubleday Publishing Group, a division of Random House LLC. All rights reserved. Any third party use of this material, outside of this publication, is prohibited. Interested parties must apply directly to Random House LLC for permission.

Carolyn Kizer, "The Ungrateful Garden" from Cool, Calm and Collected: Poems 1960–2000. Copyright © 2001 by Carolyn Kizer. Reprinted with the permission of The Permissions Company, Inc. on behalf of Copper Canyon Press, www.coppercanyonpress.org.

Maxine Kumin, "Noted in the New York Times," copyright © 1989 by Maxine W. Kumin. Reprinted with permisson of author.

All pages from "A SUPERMARKET IN CALIFORNIA" FROM COLLECTED POEMS 1947–1980 by ALLEN GINSBERG. Copyright © 1955 by Allen Ginsberg. Used by permission of HarperCollins Publishers.

"Casual Wear" from SELECTED POEMS 1946–1985 by James Merrill, copyright © 1992 by James Merrill. Used by permission of Alfred A. Knopf, an imprint of the Knopf Doubleday Publishing Group, a division of Random House LLC. All rights reserved. Any third party use of this material, outside of this publication, is prohibited. Interested parties must apply directly to Random House LLC for permission.

Mementos, I by W D Snodgrass from SELECTED POEMS 1957–1987. Copyright by Kathleen Snodgrass.

"Paradoxes and Oxymorons" by John Ashbery from SHADOW TRAIN. Copyright © 1980, 1981 by John Ashbery. Used by permission of Georges Borchardt, Inc., for the author.

"The Last One" by W.S. Merwin from MIGRATION. Copyright © 2005 by W.S. Merwin for "For the Anniversary of my Death" currently collected in MIGRATION, used by permission of The Wylie Agency LLC. No changes shall be made to the Work without the written consent of W. S. Merwin or W. S. Merwin's representative. No further use of this material in extended distribution, other media, or future editions shall be made without the express written consent of The Wylie Agency. All rights not expressly granted herein are hereby reserved and retained by W. S. Merwin.

"Autumn Begins in Martin's Ferry, Ohio" from COLLECTED POEMS © 1971 by James Wright. Reprinted with permission of Wesleyan University Press.

"Saint Judas" from COLLECTED POEMS © 1971 by James Wright. Reprinted by permission of Wesleyan University Press.

"You Can Have It" from NEW SELECTED POEMS by Philip Levine, copyright © 1984, 1991 by Philip Levine. Used by permission of Alfred A. Knopf, an imprint of the Knopf Doubleday Publishing Group, a division of Random House LLC. All rights reserved. Any third party use of this material, outside of this publication, is prohibited. Interested parties must apply directly to Random House LLC for permission.

"Cinderella" from TRANSFORMATIONS by Anne Sexton. Copyright © 1971by Anne Sexton, renewed 1999 by Linda G. Sexton. Reprinted by permission of Houghton Mifflin Harcourt Publishing Company. All rights reserved.

"Terminal" from COLLECTED POEMS by Thom Gunn. Copyright © 1994 by Thom Gunn. Reprinted by permission of Farrar, Straus and Giroux, LLC.

"Terminal" by Thom Gunn from COLLECTED POEMS. Used by permission of Faber and Faber Ltd. https://rms.pearson.com/Images/WebDataGrid/ig_checkbox_on.gif

Kennedy, X. J. "In a Prominent Bar in Secaucus One Day." In a Prominent Bar in Secaucus: New and Selected Poems, 1955-2007. pp. 11-12. © 2007 X. J. Kennedy. Reprinted with permission of Johns Hopkins University Press.

Kennedy, X. J. "Little Elegy." In a Prominent Bar in Secaucus: New and Selected Poems, 1955-2007. pp. 20. © 2007 X. J. Kennedy. Reprinted with permission of Johns Hopkins University Press.

"Aunt Jennifer's Tigers". Copyright © 2002, 1951 by Adrienne Rich. Copyright © 1973 by W. W. Norton & Company, Inc., from THE FACT OF A DOOR FRAME: SELECTED POEMS 1950-2001 by Adrienne Rich. Used by permission of W. W. Norton & Company, Inc.

"Rape". Copyright © 2002 by Adrienne Rich. Copyright © 1973 by W. W. Norton & Company, Inc., from THE FACT OF A DOOR FRAME: SELECTED POEMS 1950-2001 by Adrienne Rich. Used by permission of W. W. Norton & Company, Inc.

By Gary Snyder, from THE BACK COUNTRY, Copyright © 1968 by Gary Snyder. Reprinted by permission of New Directions Publishing Corp.

"The Book" from LIVING ON THE SURFACE by Miller Williams. Copyright by Miller Williams. Reproduced by permission of Louisiana State University Press.

"Ethics". Copyright © 1981 by Linda Pastan, from CARNIVAL EVENING: NEW AND SELECTED POEMS 1968-1998 by Linda Pastan. Used by permission of W. W. Norton & Company, Inc.

"Daddy" from ARIEL: POEMS by SYLVIA PLATH. Copyright © 1961, 1962, 1963, 1964, 1965, 1966 by Ted Hughes. Used by permission of HarperCollins Publishers.

"Daddy" by Sylvia Plath from COLLECTED POEMS. Used by permission of Faber and Faber Ltd.

All lines from "METAPHORS" FROM CROSSING THE WATER by SYLVIA PLATH. Copyright © 1960 by Ted Hughes. Used by permission of HarperCollins Publishers.

"Metaphors" by Sylvia Plath from COLLECTED POEMS. Used by permission of Faber and Faber Ltd.

"Strangers Like Us: Pittsburgh, Raleigh" from FROM A PERSON SITTING IN DARKNESS by Gerald Barrax. Copyright by Gerald Barrax. Reproduced by permission of Louisiana State University Press.

"The Black Walnut Tree" from TWELVE MOONS by Mary Oliver. Copyright © 1972, 1973, 1974, 1976, 1977, 1978, 1979 by Mary Oliver. By permission of Little, Brown and Company. All rights reserved.

"Narcissus and Echo" from Source by Fred Chapell. Copyright by Fred Chapell. Reproduced with permission of Louisiana StateUniversity Press.

"homage to my hips" by Lucille Clifton. First published in "two-headed woman". Copyright © 1980 by Lucille Clifton. Now appears in THE COLLECTED POEMS OF LUCILLE CLIFTON 1965-2010 by Lucille Clifton, published by BOA Editions. Used by permission of Curtis Brown, Ltd.

Lucille Clifton, "wishes for sons" from COLLECTED POEMS OF LUCILLE CLIFTON. Copyright © 1987,

1991, 1996, 2004 by Lucille Clifton. Reprinted with the permission of The Permissions Company, Inc., on behalf of BOA Editions, Ltd., www.boaeditions.org.

"What's that smell in the kitchen?" from CIRCLES ON THE WATER by Marge Piercy, copyright © 1982 by Middlemarsh, Inc. Used by permission of Alfred A. Knopf, an imprint of the Knopf Doubleday Publishing Group, a division of Random House LLC. All rights reserved. Any third party use of this material, outside of this publication, is prohibited. Interested parties must apply directly to Random House LLC for permission.

"Voyages" from THE DIFFICULT WHEEL by Betty Adcock. Copyright by Betty Adcock. Reproduced by permission of Louisiana State University Press.

Phillips, Robert. "The Stone Crab: A Love Poem." Breakdown Lane. pp. 32. © 1994 Robert Phillips. Reprinted with permission of Johns Hopkins University Press.

"Discovering My Daughter" from LIGHT YEARS: NEW AND SELECTED POEMS by Dabney Stuart. Copyright by Dabney Stuart. Reproduced with permission of Louisiana State University Press.

"Siren Song" from SELECTED POEMS1965–1975 by Margaret Atwood. Reprinted by permission of Hougton Mifflin Harcourt Publishing Company. All rights reserved.

"The Sacred", from BETWEEN ANGELS by Stephen Dunn. Copyright © 1989 by Stephen Dunn. Used by permission of W. W. Norton & Company, Inc.

"Abandoned Farmhouse" from SURE SIGNS: NEW AND SELECTED POEMS, by Ted Kooser, © 1980. Reprinted by permission of the University of Pittsburg Press.

Ballade of the New God by Tom Disch from THE DARK HORSE. Copyright by Writers' Representatives LLC.

All-American Sestina by Florence Cassen Mayers from The Atlantic Monthly, 1997. Copyright by The Atlantic Monthly Company.

Foreplay by Pattiann Rogers from SONG OF THE WORLD BECOMING: NEW AND COLLECTED POEMS, 1981–2001. Copyright by Milkweed Editions.

"The Lanyard" from THE TROUBLE WITH POETRY: AND OTHER POEMS by Billy Collins, copyright © 2005 by Billy Collins. Used by permission of Random House, an imprint and division of Random House LLC. All rights reserved. Any third party use of this material, outside of this publication, is prohibited. Interested parties must apply directly to Random House LLC for permission.

"The Visitor" from PASSING THROUGH CUSTOMS by Gibbons Ruark. Copyright by Gibbons Ruark. Reproduced by permission of Louisiana State University Press.

Combing by Gladys Cardiff from TO FRIGHTEN A STORM. Copyright by Gladys Cardiff.

From "E.S.L." from STARTING FROM SLEEP by Charles Martin. Copyright © 2002 by Charles Martin. Published in 2002 by The Overlook Press, Peter Mayer Publishers, Inc. New York, NY. www.overlookpress.com. All rights reserved.

"The One Girl at the Boys' Party" from THE DEAD & THE LIVING by Sharon Olds, copyright © 1987 by Sharon Olds. Used by permission of Alfred A. Knopf, an imprint of the Knopf Doubleday Publishing Group, a division of Random House LLC. All rights reserved. Any third party use of this material, outside of this publication, is prohibited. Interested parties must apply directly to Random House LLC for permission.

"Upbringing" by Alfred Corn in TABLES. Copyright © Alfred Corn. Reprinted by permission of Alfred Corn.

My Husband Discovers Poetry by Diane Lockwood from EVE'S RED DRESS. Copyright by Wind Publications.

"Daughter", from THE FORCES OF PLENTY by Ellen Bryant Voigt. Copyright © 1983 by Ellen Bryant Voigt. Used by permission of W. W. Norton & Company, Inc.

"A Martian Sends a Postcard Home" by Craig Raine from A MARTIAN SENDS A POSTCARD HOME. Copyright © 1979 by Craig Raine. Used by permission of Oxford University Press (US).

Copyright 1985 by Enid Shomer. Printed in her book STALKING THE FLORIDA PANTHER (The Word Works, Washington, D.C., 1987)

"Rondeau Redouble" by Wendy Cope from MAKING COCOA FOR KINGSLEY AMIS. Published by Faber and Faber Ltd. Used by permission of United Agents on behalf of Wendy Cope.

"Bestiary" from Elephant Rocks, copyright © 1996 by Kay Ryan. Used by permission of Grove/Atlantic, Inc. Any third party use of this material, outside of this publication, is prohibited.

Leon Stokesbury's "The Day Kennedy Died" originally appeared in Crazyhorse 65.

"Little" by John Whitworth from GIRLIE GANGS. Copyright © 2012 by John Whitworth. Used by permission of Enitharmon Press.

"The Ballad of Aunt Geneva" from THE HOMEPLACE by Marilyn Nelson. Copyright by Marilyn Nelson. Reproduced with permission of Louisiana State University Press.

Jim Hall, "Maybe Dats Your Pwoblem Too" from The Mating Reflex. Copyright © 1980 by Jim Hall. Reprinted with the permission of The Permissions Company, Inc., on behalf of Carnegie Mellon University Press, www.cmu.edu/universitypress.

"Facing It" from PLEASURE DOME: NEW AND COLLECTED POEMS © 2001 by Yusef Komunyakaa. Reprinted by permission of Wesleyan University Press.

"Timothy Steele, "Sapphics Against Anger" from Sapphics and Uncertainties: Poems 1970–1986. Copyright © 1986, 1995 by Timothy Steele. Reprinted with the permission of The Permissions Company, Inc., on behalf of the University of Arkansas Press, www.uapress.com."

1986. Copyright © 1986, 1995 by Timothy Steele. Reprinted with the permission of The Permissions Company, Inc., on behalf of the University of Arkansas Press, www.uapress.com.

"Tu Negrito" is reprinted with permission from the publisher of HOW TO UNDRESS A COP by Sarah Cortez (Copyright © 2000 Arte Publico Press - University of Houston)

All text [prose poem] from "THE COLONEL" FROM THE COUNTRY BETWEEN US by CAROLYN FORCHE. Copyright © 1981 by Carolyn Forche. Originally appeared in WOMEN'S INTERNATIONAL RESOURCE EXCHANGE. Used by permission of HarperCollins Publishers.

Dana Gioia, "Planting a Sequoia" from THE GODS OF WINTER. Copyright © 1991 by Dana Gioia. Reprinted with permission of The Permissions Company, Inc., on behalf of Graywolf Press, Minneapolis, Minnesota, www.graywolfpress.org.

"Winter Retreat: Homage to Martin Luther King, Jr." from TRANSPARENT GESTURES by Rodney Jones. Copyright © 1989 by Rodney Jones. Reprinted by permission of Houghton Mifflin Harcourt Publishing Company. All rights reserved.

Case Notes by Timothy Murphy from The Hudson Review, Vol LVI, No. 4, 2004. Copyright by Hudson Review.

"Air View of an Industrial Scene" from SAINTS AND STRANGERS by Andrew Hudgins. Copyright © 1985 by Andrew Hudgins. Reprinted by permission of Houghton Mifflin Harcourt Publishing Company. All rights reserved.

"The Latin Deli" is reprinted with permission from the publisher of THE LATIN DELI by Judith Ortiz Cofer (Copyright © 1988 Arte Publico Press - University of Houston)

"American Smooth" from AMERICAN SMOOTH by Rita Dove, W. W. Norton & Company, New York, NY. Copyright © 2004 by Rita Dove. Reprinted by permission of author.

"After Disappointment" from QUESTIONS FOR ECCLESIASTES by Mark Jarman. Copyright © Mark Jarman. Reprinted by permission of Storyline Press.

"Alan Doll Rap" by Julie Kane from ALAN DOLL RAP. Copyright © Julie Kane. Reprinted with permission of Julie Kane.

"The Traveling Onion" from YELLOW GLOVE by Naomi Shihab Nye. Copyright © Naomi Shihab Nye. REprinted by permission of author.

"The Purpose of Altar Boys" from WHISPERING TO FOOL THE WIND by Alberto Rios. Copyright © by Alberto Rios. Reprinted by permission of the author.

"Bilingual Sestina" by Julai Alvarez from THE OTHER SIDE/EL OTRO LADO. Copyright © 1995 by Julia Alvarez. Published by Plume/Penguin, a division of Penguin Group (USA). Originally published in The George Washington Review. By permission of Susan Bergholz Literary Services, New York, NY and Lamy, NM. All rights reserved.

"Dim Lady" from SLEEPING WITH THE DICTIONARY by Harryette Mullen. Copyright © Harryette Mullen. Reprinted with permission from University of California Press.

"Sonnenizio on a Line from Drayton", from WHAT IS THIS THING CALLED LOVE: POEMS by Kim Addonizio. Copyright © 2004 by Kim Addonizio. Used by permission of W. W. Norton & Company, Inc.

David Mason, "Fog Horns". First published in POETRY SEPTEMBER 2004. By permission of author.

"Welcome to Hiroshima" from HENRY PURCELL IN JAPAN by Mary Jo Salter, copyright © 1984 by Mary Jo Salter. Used by permission of Alfred A. Knopf, an imprint of the Knopf Doubleday Publishing Group, a division of Random House LLC. All rights reserved. Any third party use of this material, outside of this publication, is prohibited. Interested parties must apply directly to Random House LLC for permission.

Primping in the Rearview Mirror by Ginger Andrews from The Hudson Review, Vol. LV, No. 2 (Summer), 2002. Copyright by Hudson Review.

"Advice from a Caterpillar", from DEAREST CREATURE by Amy Gerstler, copyright © 2009 by Amy Gerstler. Used by permission of Penguin, a division of Penguin Group (USA) LLC.

"Family Story" appeared in Rebecca Faust's Mom's Canoe, Texas Review Press, 2009.

"My Strip Club" from Blowout, by Denise Duhamel, © 2013. Reprinted by permission of the University of Pittsburgh Press.

Useful Advice by Catherine Tufariello. Copyright by Tar River Poetry.

"The Singers" by Craig Arnold. Copyright © 2007. Reprinted by permission of Rebecca Lindenberg.

"The Athlete," from WORLDLY PLEASURES, by Allison Joseph Copyright © 2003 WordTech Communications, Cincinnati, Ohio, USA.

Brian Turner, "Here, Bullet" from HERE, BULLET. Copyright © 2005 by Brian Turner. Used by permission of The Permissions Company, Inc., on behalf of Alice James Books, www.alicejames-books.org.

"Occupation" from NOTES FROM THE DIVIDED COUNTRY: POEMS by Suji Kwock Kim. Copyright by Suji Kwock Kim. Reproduced by permission of Louisiana State University Press.

"First Love: A Quiz" from Hapax:Poems. Copyright © 2006 by A.E. Stallings. Published 2006 by Tri Quarterly Books/Northwestern University Press. All rights reserved.

Kevin Prufer, "The Villain and His Helicopter: Possible Movie Rental Versions" from IN A BEAUTIFUL COUNTRY. Copyright © 2011 by Kevin Prufer. Reprinted with the permission of The Permissions Company, Inc., on behalf of behalf of Four Way Books, www.fourwaybooks.com.

""In The Kitchen"" from The Moon from Every Window, by Rob Griffith Copyright © 2011 WordTech Communications, Cincinnati, Ohio, USA."

"Domestic Situation" by Ernest Hilbert from SIXTY SONNETS. Copyright © Ernest Hilbert. Reprinted with permission of Red Hen Press.

Alexander Long, "Flash Forward with The Amistad Before Us in the Distance" from STILL LIFE. Copyright © 2011 by Alexander Long. Reprinted with the permission of The Permissions Company, Inc., on behalf of behalf of White Pine Press, www.whitepine.org.

Copyright © 2013 Chelsea Rathburn A RAFT OF GRIEF. Reprinted by permission of Autumn House Press.

"Auld Lang Syne" by Emily Moore in THE NEW YORKER. Copyright © Emily Moore. Reprinted with permission of Emily Moore.

"Itinerant" from CIRCLES WHERE THE HEAD SHOULD BE POEMS by Caki Wilkinson. Copyright © Caki Wilkinson. Reprinted by permission of Caki Wilkinson.

# Drama

"Antigone" by Sophocles, translated by Ian Johnston. Copyright © 2005 by Ian Johnston. Used with permission by Richer Resources Publications, LLC.

Henrik Ibsen. A DOLL'S HOUSE.

"Sure Thing" from ALL IN THE TIMING: FOURTEEN PLAYS by David Ives, copyright © 1989,1990,1992 by David Ives. Used by permission of Vintage Books, an imprint of the Knopf Doubleday Publishing Group, a division of Random House LLC. All rights reserved. Any third party use of this material, outside of this publication, is prohibited. Interested parties must apply directly to Random House LLC for permission.

"The Cuban Swimmer" by Milcha Sanchez-Scott. Copyright © 1984, 1988 by Milcha Sanchez-Scott. Published by Dramatists Play Service. Used by permission of William Morris Endeavor Entertainment, LLC.

FENCES by August Wilson, copyright © 1986 by August Wilson. Dutton Signet, a division of Penguin Group (USA) Inc.

# index of authors, titles, and first line of poems

Note: Authors' names appear in boldface type. Titles of short stories appear in double quotation marks and italics. Titles of poems appear in double quotation marks. Titles of plays appear in italics.

# index of critical terms